CW01499199

INTRODUCTION 1

THE BUILDINGS OF SCOTLAND

FOUNDING EDITORS:
NIKOLAUS PEVSNER & COLIN MCWILLIAM

ABERDEENSHIRE: SOUTH
AND
ABERDEEN

JOSEPH SHARPLES
DAVID W. WALKER
AND
MATTHEW WOODWORTH

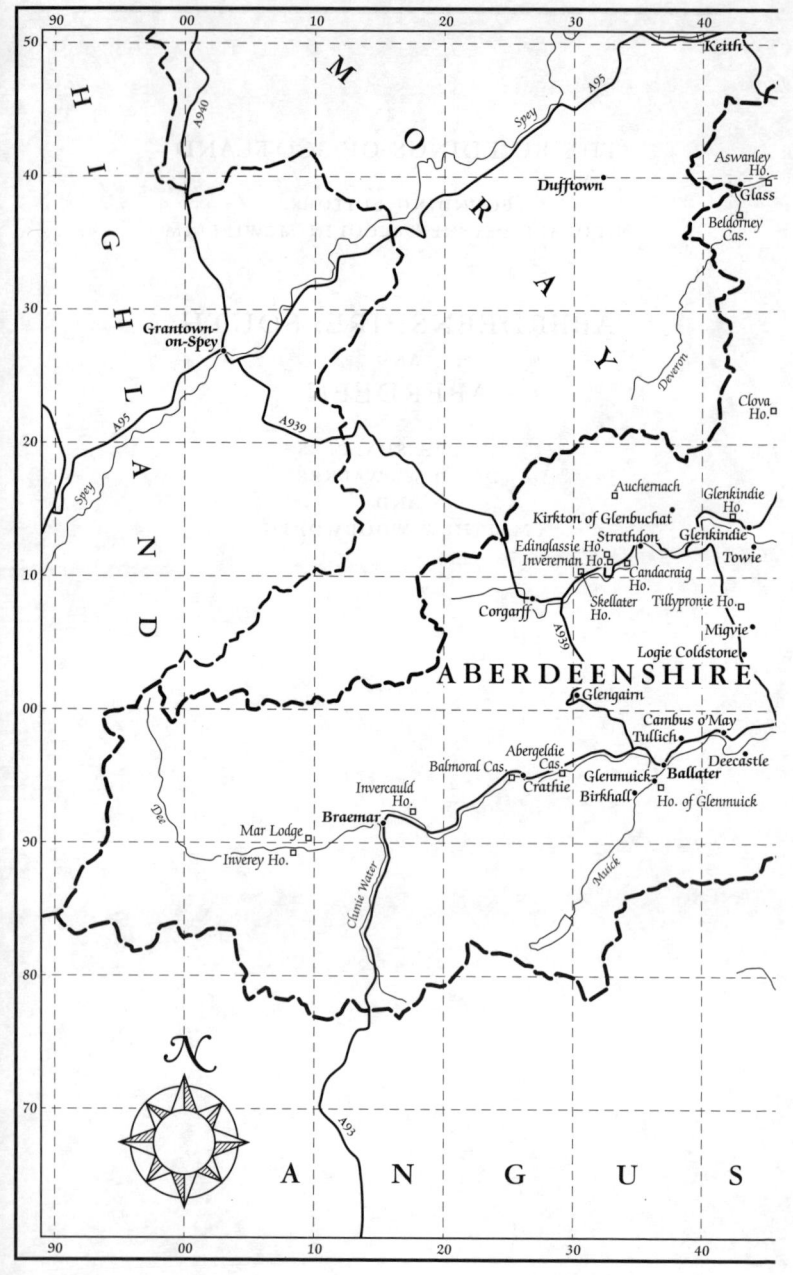

PEVSNER ARCHITECTURAL GUIDES

The Buildings of Scotland was founded by
Sir Nikolaus Pevsner (1902–83) and
Colin McWilliam (1928–89) as a companion series
to *The Buildings of England*. Between 1978 and
2001 it was published by Penguin Books.

For a considerable period the National Trust for Scotland carried
the financial responsibility for management and finance of the
research programme needed to sustain the first editions of guides
in the *Buildings of Scotland* series. Between 1991 and 2012 that
role was taken over by the Buildings of Scotland Trust, sponsored by Historic Scotland (on behalf of Scottish Ministers), the
National Trust for Scotland and the Royal Commission on the
Ancient and Historical Monuments of Scotland. During its lifetime the Trust received the support of many individuals, charitable trusts and foundations, companies and local authorities.
Without that support it would not have been possible to look
forward to the completion of the series. Since 2012 funding has
been administered through The Paul Mellon Centre for Studies
in British Art.

For this volume very special thanks are due to

THE LEVERHULME TRUST
and
THE UNIVERSITY OF ABERDEEN
(College of Arts & Social Sciences and Development Trust)

and the following donors

Aberbrothock Skea Trust, the Earl of Aboyne, John A. Akroyd,
Astor of Hever Trust, The Binks Trust, Chivas Brothers,
William Cowie, Diageo, Friends of Aberdeen University
Library, Ann Harper, Richard Marsh, Paul Mellon Trust,
Pernod Ricard, Portrack Charitable Trust, the Earl of
Southesk, Stichting Teuntje Anna, William and Dorothy
Newlands and two anonymous donors who believe in the
significance of Scotland's built heritage

and

The Paul Mellon Centre for Studies in British Art
for a grant towards the cost of illustrations.

Aberdeenshire: South and Aberdeen

BY

JOSEPH SHARPLES
DAVID W. WALKER
AND
MATTHEW WOODWORTH

WITH CONTRIBUTIONS FROM

RICHARD FAWCETT
JANE GEDDES
ANDREW A. MCMILLAN
GORDON NOBLE
and
CHARLES O'BRIEN

THE BUILDINGS OF SCOTLAND

YALE UNIVERSITY PRESS
NEW HAVEN AND LONDON

YALE UNIVERSITY PRESS
NEW HAVEN AND LONDON

302 Temple Street, New Haven CT 06511
47 Bedford Square, London WC1B 3DP
www.pevsner.co.uk
www.yalebooks.co.uk
www.yalebooks.com

Published by Yale University Press 2015
2 4 6 8 10 9 7 5 3 1

ISBN 978 0 300 21555 7

Printed in China
through World Print
Set in Monotype Plantin

IN MEMORY OF
CHARLES MCKEAN
IAN SHEPHERD
AND
WILLIAM DOUGLAS SIMPSON

ACCESS TO BUILDINGS

Many of the buildings described in this book are public places, and in some obvious cases their interiors (at least the public sections of them) can be seen without formality. But it must be emphasized that the mention of buildings or lands does not imply any rights of public access to them, or the existence of any arrangements for visiting them.

Some churches are open within regular hours, and it is usually possible to see the interiors of others by arrangement with the minister or church officer. Particulars of admission to Ancient Monuments and other buildings in the care of Scottish Ministers (free to the Friends of Historic Scotland) are available from Historic Scotland, Longmore House, Salisbury Place, Edinburgh EH9 ISH or its website, www.historic-scotland.gov.uk. Details of access to properties of the National Trust for Scotland are available from the Trust's head office at Hermiston Quay, 5 Cultins Road, Edinburgh, EH11 4DF or via its website, www.nts.org.uk. Admission is free to members, on whose subscriptions and donation's the Trust's work depends.

Scotland's Gardens Scheme, 42a Castle Street, Edinburgh EH2 3BN, provides a list of gardens open to visitors, also available on the National Gardens Scheme website, www.gardensofscotland.org. Scotland's Churches Scheme, Dunedin, Holehouse Road, Eaglesham, Glasgow G76 0JF, has a searchable database (www.sacredscotland.org.uk) of churches in Scotland including details of opening arrangements and publishes a series of regional guides. *Hudson's Historic Houses, Castles and Gardens Open to the Public*, published annually, includes many private houses open to visitors.

Local Tourist Offices can advise the visitor on what properties in each area are open to the public and will usually give helpful directions as to how to get to them.

LIST OF TEXT FIGURES AND MAPS

Every effort has been made to contact or trace all copyright holders. The publishers would be glad to make good any errors or omissions brought to our attention in future editions.

We are grateful to the Society of Antiquaries of Scotland for permission to reproduce the following: Brass rubbing of monument to Dr Liddel; Plans of Arbuthnott House, Balbithan House, Beldorney Castle, Castle Fraser, Huntly Castle, Kildrummy Castle, Midmar Castle, Monymusk House, Sir George Skene's House.

ABERDEENSHIRE: SOUTH

MAPS

ACKNOWLEDGEMENTS FOR ILLUSTRATIONS

Royal
Commission on the
Ancient and
Historical
Monuments of
Scotland

The plates are indexed in the indexes of names and places, and references to them are given by numbers in the margin of the text.

Photographs are the copyright of RCAHMS with the exception of the following:

© Aberdeen Art Gallery & Museums: 80, 81
Alice Foster, Park House Archives: 65
Andor Gomme, courtesy of David M. Walker: 36
Blairs Museum: 108
Bruce Mann, Aberdeenshire Council Archaeology Service
 © ACAS: 14
© Castle Forbes: 66
© Cathy MacIver: 9
Charles O'Brien: 41, 75
Claire Herbert, Aberdeenshire Council Archaeology Service
 © Aberdeenshire Council: 4
© Country Life: 56, 58, 69, 72
© Crown Copyright Reproduced Courtesy of Historic
 Scotland: 43, 44, 100
© Crown Copyright: RCAHMS: 2, 8, 10, 11, 12, 13, 16, 17, 18,
 19, 20, 22, 24, 25, 26, 28, 30, 31, 32, 34, 37, 38, 39, 46, 50,
 51, 54, 57, 62, 64, 78, 79, 82, 83, 84, 85, 87, 88, 89, 90, 91,
 92, 93, 94, 95, 96, 97, 98, 99, 100, 101, 103, 104, 106, 107,
 109, 112, 113, 114, 115, 117, 119, 120, 121, 122, 123, 127
© David Porter: 77
David W. Walker: 29, 33, 42, 49, 60, 63, 73, 76, 86, 124
Courtesy of George Hart: 102
Glenbuchat Heritage: 27
Graeme Davidson: 5, 35
Jane Geddes / University of Aberdeen: 21, 23, 40
Jeremy Dixon Edward Jones: 125
Jim Henderson / Crooktree.com: 1
© John Lord: 118
Joseph Sharples: 59, 111
© Keith Arbuthnott: 61
Matthew Woodworth: 68, 70, 73, 105
© National Trust for Scotland: 45, 47, 48, 52, 53, 55, 74
Radharc Images / Alamy: 6
© Robert Gordon University: 126
Simon Price / Alamy: 3

MAP REFERENCES

The numbers printed in italic type in the margin against the place names in the gazetteer indicate the position of the place in question on the area map (pages ii–iii), which are divided into sections by the 10-kilometre reference lines of the National Grid. The reference given here omits the two initial letters (formerly numbers), which in a full grid reference refer to the 100-kilometre squares into which the county is divided. The first two numbers indicate the western boundary, and the last two the southern boundary, of the 10-kilometre square in which the place is situated. For example, Abergeldie Castle reference 2090 will be found in the 10-kilometre square bounded by grid lines 20 (on the *west*) and 30, and 90 (on the *south*) and 00; Whiterashes, reference 8020 in the square bounded by grid lines 80 (on the *west*) and 90, and 20 (on the *south*) and 30.

EDITOR'S FOREWORD

This is the second of two volumes to be published covering the North-East of Scotland. The extent of the area covered is that of the historic counties of Aberdeenshire, Kincardineshire, Banffshire and Morayshire which were abolished in 1975 and replaced by the Grampian Region. This was itself succeeded in 1996 by Aberdeen City Council, Aberdeenshire Council and Moray Council and it is the boundaries of the areas administered by these authorities that are observed by the *Buildings of Scotland* guides. The whole of the City of Aberdeen is described in this volume but it has been necessary to divide the gazetteer for Aberdeenshire between this volume and its companion guide to *Aberdeenshire: North and Moray*. The division follows the boundary between Aberdeenshire Council's committee districts of Banff, Buchan and Formartine (in the north) and Mar, Garioch and Kincardine & Mearns (in the south). Readers should note that all places in the county of Kincardineshire before 1975 are described in this volume and are indicated by [K] next to the relevant gazetteer heading.

FOREWORD

The completion of this volume, and its companion which covers *Aberdeenshire: North & Moray*, represents six years' work, and it simply would not have been possible but for the initiative shown by Professor Jane Geddes, of the University of Aberdeen, Ian Riches, Secretary of the Buildings of Scotland Trust in Edinburgh, and Charles O'Brien, Series Editor of the Pevsner Architectural Guides at Yale University Press. They conceived the project in the first place and then showed astonishing persistence in securing the necessary funding from the Leverhulme Trust and other charitable bodies in the face of some extremely difficult circumstances. Our heartfelt thanks go out to them, and also – among many other colleagues – to Professor Margaret Ross, Head of the College of Arts & Social Sciences, and to Graeme Benvie, of the Development Trust at Aberdeen University.

The area covered by this volume is large and architecturally rich and so the work of compiling the gazetteer has been shared. Joseph Sharples has written the entries for the buildings of the City of Aberdeen and Stonehaven. The entries for Aberdeenshire within its historic (pre-1975) boundaries were written by David W. Walker, except for the parishes of Drumoak and Aboyne & Glentanar which were written by Charles O'Brien, and Crathie & Braemar and Glenmuick, Tullich & Glengairn – including the burgh of Ballater – which were written by Jane Geddes. The description of Balmoral Castle is by David Walker and that of its policies by Jane Geddes. The entries for former Kincardineshire were mostly written by Matthew Woodworth but buildings in the parishes of Banchory-Devenick and Banchory-Ternan – including the burgh of Banchory – are by Charles O'Brien and those in Strachan, Durris, Maryculter and Glenbervie are by David Walker. Daniel MacCannell kindly provided the entry on Glassel House. We are particularly grateful to our specialist contributors, who have written sections of the Introduction: Andrew McMillan, lately of the British Geological Survey, for geology and building stones, Dr Gordon Noble, of the University of Aberdeen, for the archaeological record and selected gazetteer entries denoted (GN) in the text, and Professor Richard Fawcett of St Andrews University for medieval ecclesiastical buildings and his entries on the major medieval churches. The remainder of the Introduction is by David W. Walker and Charles O'Brien.

In writing about the architecture of this part of the country, we have relied on the Lists of Buildings of Architectural & Historic Significance, which were first published by the Historic Buildings Branch of the Scottish Development Department during the late 1960s. Although amended since, the original Lists for historic (pre-1975) Aberdeenshire including the City of Aberdeen were mostly compiled by David M. Walker, now Emeritus Professor at St Andrews University, and those for Kincardineshire by the late William Murray Jack. The present Lists, together with the Inventory of Gardens and Designed Landscapes, have been made available online by Historic Scotland (*Historic-scotland.gov.uk*). We have also drawn on the scholarship of the Royal Commission on the Ancient & Historical Monuments of Scotland, both through its CANMORE database (Canmore.rcahms.gov.uk) and – whenever we were in Edinburgh and opportunity allowed – at its library and offices in Bernard Terrace. A particularly special debt is owed to the late John Gifford, who as Head of the Buildings of Scotland Research Unit compiled the Series' own reference files for North-East Scotland, as he did for nearly all of the country, somehow finding time to write six volumes of the Series himself, and to contribute to two others. The Buildings of Scotland files contain extracts from a very wide variety of sources, a great many of which fall into the 'difficult' or 'obscure' categories: charters from the Register of the Great Seal (in medieval Latin); Heritors' Records; c18 newspapers such as the *Caledonian Mercury* and *Edinburgh Evening Courant*; c19 periodicals – including not just the four main architectural journals, the *Architect*, the *British Architect*, the *Builder* and the *Building News*, but more specialist publications (*e.g.* the *Scottish Guardian*); and, from more recent times, short-run publications by local historians which but for John's diligence might otherwise have been lost to us. So often these sources have helped us to discover an architect, fine-tune a date or occasionally answer the still more basic questions of what existed where and when. With the completion of our Project these files will be deposited with the Royal Commission for more general public reference.

For information on individual buildings we could not have managed without the two magisterial surveys by David MacGibbon and Thomas Ross on *The Castellated & Domestic Architecture of Scotland* (5 vols, 1887–92) and *The Ecclesiastical Architecture of Scotland* (3 vols, 1896–7) or the forensic examination and detailed recording of many individual buildings by Dr William Douglas Simpson, sometime lecturer and librarian at the University of Aberdeen, and Harry Gordon Slade, several of whose articles were published in the *Proceedings of the Society of Antiquaries of Scotland* (available online on the Archaeology Data Service website *http://archaeologydataservice.ac.uk/archives/view/psas/*). Information in respect of particular architects, engineers and builders and their works has been derived from: Sir Howard Colvin's *Biographical Dictionary of British Architects 1600–1840*, (4th edn, 2008); the *Biographical Dictionary of Civil Engineers 1500–1830* (A.W. Skempton et al., eds, 2002) and *Biographical Dictionary of Civil Engineers 1830–90* (P. S. M. Cross-Rudkin et al., eds, 2008); and the on-line *Dictionary of Scottish Architects 1840–1980* (*www.scottisharchitects.org*), for which Professor David

Walker, as Founder-Editor, wrote almost all the major entries for individuals in practice before the Second World War. Other more general sources of information have included the *Statistical Accounts* and Groome's *Gazetteer of Scotland*, the various editions of the Ordnance Survey, and local newspapers of the C19 and early C20, particularly the *Aberdeen Journal*, the *Aberdeen Free Press*, the *Dundee Advertiser* and the *Dundee Courier*, which have helped to fill many gaps in information in the sources above. These too are available online via British Newspaper Archive (*www.britishnewspaperarchive.co.uk*).

We have all been indebted to the guides produced by the Royal Incorporation of Architects in Scotland under the editorship of the late Charles McKean: *Aberdeen* by W. A. Brogden (1998); *Deeside & The Mearns* by Jane Geddes (2001) and *Aberdeenshire: Donside & Strathbogie* by Ian Shepherd (2006). It was Ian, as Principal Archaeologist at Aberdeenshire Council, who first agreed to write the Buildings of Scotland volumes for the North-East before ill-health prevented his further progress. It is to his memory and to that of Charles McKean that this volume is dedicated.

We have particularly valued Aberdeenshire's wider heritage of historical publishing, as well as its collections of manuscripts, photographs, drawings and plans, and by extension the libraries and archives that look after them. We are most grateful to the library staff of Aberdeen University (particularly the Special Collections & Local Studies Centre – Michelle Gait, June Ellner, Mary Sabiston, Jan Smith and Paul Logie), Robert Gordon University and the Scott Sutherland School of Architecture; to Aberdeen City & Shire Archives, and also to the Central Library in Aberdeen and the Public Library in Stonehaven.

Our editor at Yale University Press, Charles O'Brien, read our typescript in its entirety to ensure that it conformed to the expectations of a Buildings of Scotland volume and made countless useful suggestions along the way. In addition, much of the script was read by Professor David Walker, by Professor Peter Davidson of the University of Aberdeen, and by Norman Marr, late of Aberdeen City Council. But we should also like to thank a great many individuals who provided us with detailed specialist help in respect of particular sites or subjects, or supported us in other ways: Thomas Addyman (Balnacraig, Castle Fraser, Craigievar, Leith Hall and St Bride's Church, Leochel-Cushnie); Jim Argo; Gary Atkinson; Dr William Brogden; Jennifer Brown; John Coyne (Tilquhillie); Dr David Bertie; David Coleman (Tillypronie, *per* Philip Astor); Dr Christopher Croly (Aberdeen Tolbooth); Jane Cromar; Tom and Linda Cross (Culter House); Neil Curtis; A. C. Stuart Donald (episcopal churches); Dr Penelope Dransart (Fetternear); Professor David Dumville; Shona Elliott; Alexander Forbes; Ian Forbes (Blairs College); Dr Shannon Fraser (Castle Fraser, Craigievar, Crathes Castle, Drum Castle, Leith Hall); Claire Gapper (plasterwork); Ian Gow (Castle Fraser, Crathes Castle, Leith Hall); Simon Green (Balmoral Castle); George Greig; Penelope Hartley (Robert Gordon's College); Lorraine

Hesketh-Campbell (House of Monymusk); Canon Jeffrey Hopewell (stained glass); Marc Johnson; Michael Kerney (stained glass); Zyg Krukowski; Scott Leiper; Duncan A. MacGregor; Dr Aonghus MacKechnie (Mergie House); Dr Jennifer Melville; Mary Miers; Iain Morrison (Crathes Castle); Steve Murray; Peter and Dawn Nicholson; the Very Rev. Dr Emsley Nimmo (St Margaret, Gallowgate, Aberdeen); Allan Paterson (Aberdeen Environmental Education Centre); David and Julia Paton (Grandhome House); Paul Pillath; Canon Dr Isaac Poobalan (St John's Episcopal Church, Aberdeen); Simon Power (MacRobert Estates); Maria Robertson (Society of Advocates in Aberdeen); Alison Robertson (Scottish Stained Glass Symposium & Trust); Michael Shippobottom (Ogston's Building, Gallowgate, Aberdeen); the Rev. Douglas Somerset (Alford Place Church, Aberdeen); Professor Jane Stevenson; Richard Swinscoe; Philip Taylor; Dr Dimitrios Theodossopoulos (Wardhouse); Dr Christopher Wakeling (Unitarian Church, Aberdeen); Simon Welfare (Alastrean House); W. Stewart Wilson (Banchory); and Atholl Wing for his unpublished M.A. thesis on Old Aberdeen High Street. We would also like to thank the many building owners and custodians who made us feel so welcome as we travelled throughout North-East Scotland.

The completed text has been painstakingly copy-edited by Dr Hester Higton. Martin Brown has graced us with his area map, town plans and building plans. Clare Sorensen has acted as our liaison with the Royal Commission, which provided the majority of the photographs: some derived from their existing collections, but others were taken by Zoë Ballantine and Steve Wallace especially for us. Charlotte Chapman undertook proofreading, Judith Wardman the indexing.

Finally we would like to thank Catherine Bankhurst and Phoebe Lowndes, our Production Editors, and Elizabeth O'Rafferty, our Picture Editor at Yale, for putting up with our vagaries as authors and astonishing us once again by turning our typescripts into the book which you are now holding.

Errors are inevitable so this foreword must end with the traditional invitation for corrections to be sent to the publisher.

Joseph Sharples, David W. Walker and Matthew Woodworth
March 2015

NORTH-EAST SCOTLAND

INTRODUCTION

The North-East is like a country in itself: it is quite distinct from other parts of Scotland. The present-day counties of Aberdeenshire and Moray have expanded to embrace two other historic counties, Banffshire and Kincardineshire, which in the minds of local people retain a strong sense of separate identity.

Aberdeen lies relatively near the SE corner of this great land mass, between the river mouths of the Don and the Dee. Banff, the former county town of Banffshire, and Elgin, the capital of Moray, were both founded on the northern coast. That the town of Kincardine ceased to exist, with Stonehaven now the provincial capital, and that almost all the other important towns are ports with large harbours reflects the primary importance not just of fishing but of communication, the exchange of trade and culture, in the world of Northern Europe, centred and dependent on the sea.

But beyond its coast the North-East is chiefly comprised of a deep hinterland, some of it very sparse but much of it verdant and even luscious. It is separated and sheltered from the rest of Scotland by the Grampian and Cairngorm Mountains, but the hinterland itself is a low-lying, undulating country with only a few landmark peaks, among them Tap O'Noth, Bennachie, the Bin Hill of Cullen, Clachnaben and Mormond. Cutting through the landscape are the rivers Bervie, Esk, Dee, Don, Ythan, Ugie, Deveron, Spey, Lossie and Findhorn, each with its tributary burns and waters.

The names are Pictish or – progressively, from the C9 – Gaelic: when those languages were spoken here, the hills and rivers were lines of defence and communication and sacred places. Change comes gradually to the North-East. The Old Order suffered a seismic shock after the collapse of the Jacobite Rising of 1745, but unravelled only so far as it needed to; and afterwards the Improvers drained, cleared and enclosed the low ground, dotted it with farmhouses and steadings, planted shelterbelts and, in doing so, within a surprisingly propitious climate created the best agricultural land anywhere in Scotland. Their roads and bridges fall naturally into the folds of that land, interrupted by occasional villages, and the low horizons often result in skies which dazzle travellers with their vastness: sometimes brilliant pale blues reflected off the sea which bathe the countryside in gentle colours, at other times magnificent dark grey cloudscapes which harden those colours into very sharp focus. In such a land as this life, death and the divine seem close.

The North-East faces challenges from the modern world, both of change and neglect. It preserves and expresses its identity through its deep-rooted, vibrant culture – the Doric language both spoken and sung, instrumental music and dance, the narrative folklore of ferm-toun and fisher-toun, a sense of history intuitively understood: it is at heart a rural community which honours traditional values. That culture finds its most tangible, everyday form in the places described in this book, churches, castles and country houses, towns and villages, isolated mills, farm steadings and bothies, and monoliths and carved stones set into the landscape. The authors extend their thanks to previous historians of the North-East, as well as to all those who helped them on their travels, who proved to be – in the words of the *Statistical Accounts* – 'sober, industrious and hospitable to strangers'.

LANDSCAPE, GEOLOGY AND BUILDING STONES
BY ANDREW A. MCMILLAN

The expansive LANDSCAPE of Aberdeenshire and Moray is one of many contrasts. In the south-west of the district, the Cairngorm massif, a dissected granite plateau, generally lies over 1,000 m. above sea level. Notable summits include Cairn Toul (1,291 m.), Braeriach (1,296 m.), Ben Macdui (1,309 m.) and Cairn Gorm (1,245 m.); with the exception of Ben Nevis these are the highest mountains in Britain. Eastwards, and south of Deeside, are Lochnagar (1,155 m.), Mount Keen (939 m.) and the lower rounded hills of the Mounth. The elevation of the land decreases eastwards and northwards towards the undulating coastal agricultural lowlands of Moray, Buchan, Aberdeen and Strathmore. In Buchan and Moray the lowlands are characterized by a series of ancient plateau surfaces eroded across a wide variety of rock types. Overlooked on its south-western margin by the tor-capped hill of Bennachie (528 m.), a granite landmark steeped in local folklore, the rolling Buchan plateau lies between 60 and 150 m. above sea level. Punctuating the Buchan landscape are small hills composed of the most resistant rock types, for example the quartzite of Mormond Hill (234 m.) between Fraserburgh and Peterhead and the Hill of Dudwick (174 m.), NE of Ellon. In Moray, Ben Rinnes (840 m.), a granite hill SW of Dufftown, dominates the scenery of the fertile countryside of the Speyside whisky industry. The rivers Findhorn, Lossie, Spey and Deveron all flow northwards to the Moray Firth by the coastal settlements of Findhorn, Lossiemouth, Garmouth and Banff respectively. The principal easterly flowing rivers of Aberdeenshire are the Dee, rising within the heart of the Cairngorms, and the much shorter Don, which meet the North Sea in the city of Aberdeen, while the lowlands of Buchan are drained by the River Ythan through Ellon and the River Ugie at Peterhead.

The lowland plateau landscape has been moulded by successive Quaternary ice sheets which moved broadly eastwards along the Moray Firth from a centre of ice accumulation in the northern Highlands, and north-eastwards across the district from the Cairngorms. The tip of Buchan and the E coast has been impinged

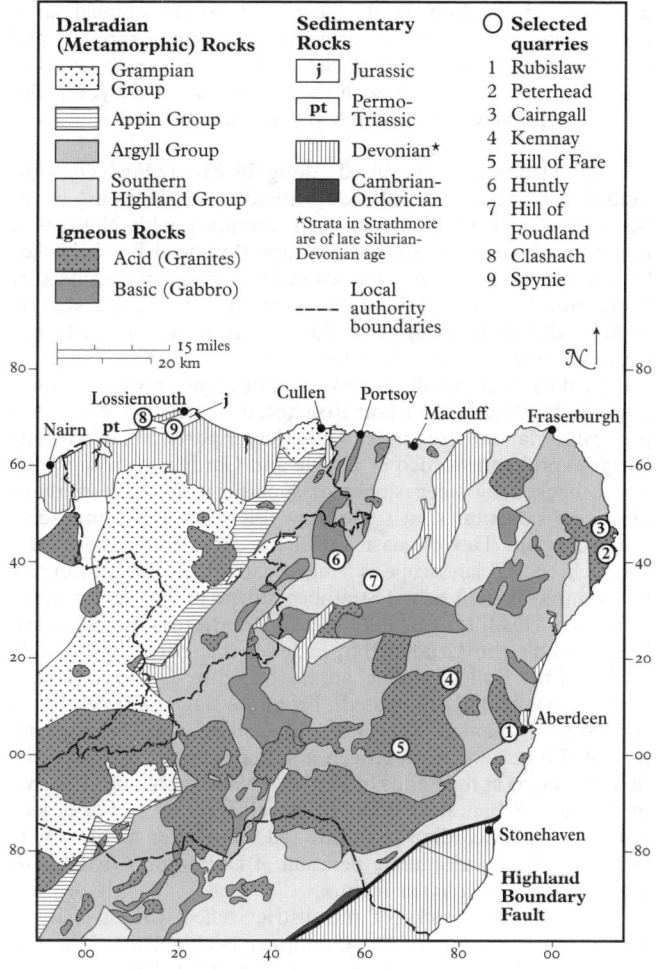

Geological map of Aberdeenshire and Moray

by ice of Scandinavian origin locally diverting Scottish ice south-eastwards. The form of today's landscape can be attributed to pre-glacial, glacial and post-glacial erosion of a wide variety of sedimentary, igneous and metamorphic rock types. From Troup Head above Gardenstown on the N coast the Buchan Plateau is crossed by a broad, undulating south-westward trending ridge developed on both slates and Old Red Sandstone lithologies. From the rugged Moray coast between Banff and Portknockie a similar series of broad south-westward trending ridges, developed on steeply dipping quartzite at elevations between 220 and 310 m. above sea level, extend westwards towards the N-flowing River Spey, where they merge into a dissected plateau, between 180 and 265 m. above sea level, developed across a range of lithologies. The ice sheets also left a succession of superficial deposits, ranging from boulder clay (till) to glaciofluvial sands and gravels (in the form of terraced and moundy spreads) and glaciolacustrine clays. Late glacial coastal and marine deposits, evidence for former sea level higher than that of today, are also present, especially between Cullen and Banff, at Crovie and N of Peterhead.

Coastal landscapes are varied. Along the Moray Firth coast the sand dunes of the Culbin Forest, extending to the mouth of the River Findhorn, mark the western boundary with Nairnshire. Eastwards from Findhorn and Kinloss, Burghead Bay is backed by low-lying dunes. A rocky coastline extends from Burghead to Lossiemouth. E of the River Lossie, the dune-dominated scenery of Spey Bay ends abruptly at Buckie. From thereon eastwards a predominantly rocky coastline extending to Fraserburgh is occupied by many small settlements. The largest towns – Cullen, Portsoy, Banff, Macduff and Rosehearty – are built where less precipitous land offered potential for larger ports. Isolated fishing villages and hamlets such as Crovie and Gardenstown sit within coves, backed by steep slopes of superficial deposits overlying Devonian sandstones: in some ways this scenery is reminiscent of parts of the Devon coast. On the E coast, N of Peterhead a subdued coastal landscape is fringed with extensive sand dunes, for example by the Loch of Strathbeg, inland of the rocky outcrop of Rattray Head, N of St Fergus. S of Peterhead a granite coast-line, extending to Cruden Bay, includes the spectacular natural arches of the Bullers of Buchan, described by Dr Johnson as 'a rock perpendicularly tubulated'. From the Bay of Cruden to the appropriately named Rockend S of Collieston rocky outcrops prevail. From here to Aberdeen a softer coastline is backed by sand dunes, as at the Sands of Forvie, a National Nature Reserve, by the River Ythan, near Ellon. Rocky cliffs return S of Aberdeen to fringe the Kincardine coast through Stonehaven all the way to St Cyrus, the conglomerate pedestal of Dunnottar Castle being a particularly spectacular feature.

The underlying rocks of the district reflect the diversity of origin and age range of the Grampian Highlands. Of the two major boundaries that define the Grampian Highlands, the Great Glen and the Highland Boundary Faults, only the latter is present within the district. Here, it spectacularly defines the Highland edge along the N side of Strathmore and makes its appearance in the coastal cliffs N of Stonehaven. The oldest rocks of the district belong to the DALRADIAN SUPERGROUP, the term 'Dalradian' being introduced by Sir Archibald Geikie in 1891 for the varied assemblage of metamorphic rocks lying E of the Great Glen. Many of these rock types were employed locally as sources of rubble stone but were generally not used more widely, either because of their tendency to split too much or because of their intractability.

In the main, the original rocks of the Dalradian Supergroup were of sedimentary origin, formed between about 730 and 470 million years ago (Ma) (Late Neoproterozoic to Early Ordovician). The Dalradian Basin developed on the edge of a continental mass known as Laurentia as it broke away from the supercontinent of Rodinia and drifted off, opening up the Iapetus Ocean. After reaching its maximum width in the Early Ordovician (490 Ma) the ocean began to close. Evidence of the resultant collision of a volcanic arc system with the Laurentian margin can be traced from North America through Ireland and Scotland. In Scotland the collision (resulting in the 'Grampian Event') started around 470 Ma ago, during the Ordovician, and as it progressed the volcanic arc became buried under the leading edge of the continent and the Dalradian succession was progressively deformed and metamorphosed. In most of the Grampian Highlands the early deformation resulted in major, flat-lying recumbent folds, in which, on a regional scale, beds on the lower limb are overturned. However, in the North-East the deformation was less intense and the strata remained right way up. This area is known as the 'Buchan Block', bounded to the W and S by two shear zones, the Portsoy–Duchray Hill Lineament and the Deeside Lineament respectively. This area is also notable for relatively high heat flow during metamorphism, accompanied by the intrusion of gabbroic and granitic suites.

The Dalradian sequence is subdivided into five Groups. From oldest to youngest, rocks of the Grampian, Appin, Argyll and Southern Highland groups underlie much of Aberdeenshire and Moray. The Trossachs Group is confined to the Highland Boundary Fault zone. The surface geographical distribution of the Dalradian rocks is controlled by the geological structure of the district, and locally they are concealed by younger strata. Across much of the Grampians the orientation of major fold axes is NE–SW. In contrast, Buchan is dominated by broad, open upright folds, synclines and anticlines, with axes trending N and NNE. Notable structures include the Turriff Syncline and Buchan Anticline. The GRAMPIAN GROUP crops out in the coastal zone W of Cullen, where it is represented by the Cullen Quartzite (e.g. Bow Fiddle Rock). Inland, between Rothes and the N side of the Cairngorm Granite, the Grampian Group consists of interbedded quartzites and metamorphosed micaceous sandstones. APPIN GROUP rocks, also cropping out from the coast at Cullen but extending south-westwards, consist of thinly bedded successions of metamorphosed sandstones, with quartzites, metamorphosed mudstones (now represented by mica-schists) and several important limestones. The group includes the Findlater Flags, once a source of roofing material much used in Tomintoul, which crop out near Keith. The ARGYLL GROUP, which underlies much of eastern Buchan and southern Aberdeenshire including Donside and Deeside, comprises a mixed succession beginning with mainly quartzite and passing up into metasandstone and schist. The group includes some thin lava successions in the Tomintoul area, and, between Tomintoul and the Banffshire coast, numerous limestones including the Portsoy Limestone and Boyne Limestone. The limestones were exploited for agricultural purposes and roadstone and in the C19 were used in the walls of many houses in Banffshire. The SOUTHERN HIGHLAND GROUP forms much of the coastal outcrop between Banff and Fraserburgh and extends southwards under Buchan to Maud, New Deer and Turriff. Schists and locally coarse metasandstone predominate. The group also includes MacDuff Slate Formation, which in the C19 yielded a good resource of dark purple-grey slate for roofing from quarries lying SE of Huntly at Hill of Kirkney, Corskie, Hill of Foudland and Hill of Tillymorgan. Along the Highland Boundary Fault, metamorphosed sandstones, limestones and black mudstones of the Trossachs Group (Cambrian to Ordovician) mark the end of Dalradian sedimentation.

Cutting through the Dalradian sequence are numerous bodies of igneous and meta-igneous plutonic rocks which were emplaced prior to, and during and following, the 'Grampian Event'. These, generally coarsely crystalline rocks, range from acid (silica-rich) varieties such as granite to basic (silica-poor) varieties such as gabbro. Generally the older intrusions, intruded during the waning stages of deformation, exhibit a mineral foliation which is absent in the post-deformation younger rocks.

The Aberdeenshire GRANITES are famed for their exploitation, most notably in Donside where John Fyfe began his industry in the mid C19, in Deeside and in Buchan. Early uses are medieval rubble constructions and unworked granite, in the form of boulders gathered from the fields and rivers, may be seen in numerous places including the castles of Crathes, Drum, Midmar and Fraser. The earliest known use in mortar-built masonry is the late C12 tower of Monymusk church. But the working of granite was not well understood until much later and the early buildings of Old Aberdeen and King's College employed softer, more easily worked, imported sandstone. Only from the C18 do Aberdeen's buildings use granite ashlar from its numerous quarries for houses, public buildings, bridges, docks, lighthouses and monumental work.

Many of the granites were capable of taking a beautiful polish. The principal quarries supplied a range of grey granites, their colour and texture dependent on the proportion of the minerals quartz, feldspar (orthoclase and plagioclase) and mica (muscovite and biotite). Rubislaw (opened *c.* 1741; quarry workers were wont to say that 'Nearly half o'Aiberdeen has come oot o'

Rubislaw'), Sclattie, Dyce and Tillyfourie produced a greyish-blue variety; Kemnay and Toms Forest worked silver-grey granite for building and monumental purposes (best seen in Marischal College, Aberdeen); Persley and Cairncry produced finer, light grey granite; and Dancing Cairns yielded light grey-blue granite (as in the façade and gateway, of 1830, in front of the E and W churches of St Nicholas). The silver-grey of Invergelder, Deeside (not unlike Kemnay but with a tinge of brown), was used for Balmoral Castle and building on the royal estates.

Coloured granites owe their hue to the presence of coloured feldspars, notably to small quantities of iron oxides in the ortho-clase crystals. The salmon pink of Corrennie, near Kemnay, was much used for polished work and Aberdeen Art Gallery is a fine example. Other coloured granites include, in Buchan, the reddish-brown Peterhead granite, not only used for the building of Peterhead and Fraserburgh but also worldwide for monumental and heavy engineering work. Blue-grey granite from Cairngall, N of Peterhead, was in great demand for major engineering works (e.g. the foundations of the Bell Rock Lighthouse, the foundations of Old London Bridge and the pier walls of the Houses of Parliament). Elsewhere, in the S, formerly Kincardineshire, dark grey granite was worked at Cove and Nigg. The Hill of Fare quarries, N of Banchory, yielded a fine dark red granite (finer than Peterhead or Corrennie). In Banffshire, smaller bodies of granite were worked for building, including the distinctively foliated Keith Granite seen in many local buildings.

Generally hard and compact basic and meta-basic plutonic igneous rocks, colloquially referred to as 'whinstone', are present in several masses including those of Belhelvie, Insch, Kennethmont, Boganclogh, Huntly and Morven-Cabrach. A principal constituent rock type in many of these plutons is GABBRO, a coarsely crystalline black igneous rock. Capable of being roughly worked, squared blocks of gabbro were used as local building stone in various parts of Aberdeenshire. Huntly Castle is a fine example, where the C17 reconstructed main wall is of Huntly Gabbro with the heraldic doorway in Old Red Sandstone. At Kennethmont, cottages display the typical use of basic igneous rocks with squared blocks and courses made up with snecks of gabbro, and door and window surrounds in pink sandstone. Ultramafic rocks including red and green serpentinite, were worked at Portsoy from the early C18 for ornamental and decorative purposes, and exported by sea to Europe (e.g. for use in the Palace of Versailles).

The principal building stone of the North-East is SANDSTONE. Several small basins or outliers, including those at Tomintoul, Rhynie, Cabrach, Turriff and Aberdeen, are considered to be remnants of a once more extensive development of the Lower Old Red Sandstone (Lower Devonian), and several of these outcrops are important as former sources of stone. These basins represent irregular sedimentary infills on the southern margin of the Orcadian Basin. At Tomintoul and Cabrach basal breccias are overlain by conglomerates and red and grey sandstones. The

Rhynie Outlier, a succession of conglomerates, sandstones and mudstones, is internationally recognized for the occurrence near the top of the sequence of the Rhynie Chert (formed as siliceous sinter by hot springs during contemporary volcanic activity), which contains exquisitely preserved fossils of early land plants. In the Turriff Basin, Lower Devonian sediments of the Crovie Group are, in the main, sandstones and conglomerates formed on river flood plains and alluvial fans. Well exposed at Crovie, New Aberdour and Gardenstown, the strata rest unconformably on the Macduff Slate Formation and are in turn unconformably overlain by conglomerates of the Findon Group (Middle Devonian), which notably contains the grey and red mudstones of the Gamrie Fish Bed, a correlative of the Achanarras Fish Bed in Caithness. Local red sandstone has been used for many of Turriff's buildings and for many of the coastal villages. Conglomerates of the Inverness Sandstone Group (Middle Devonian) are seen E and SE of Elgin, where they are overlain by red-brown and purple-brown flaggy sandstones of the Fochabers Sandstone Formation. NW of Elgin these are succeeded by brownish-grey, yellow and red sandstones of the Alves and Rosebrae Beds (Upper Devonian). Quarries at Rosebrae, Alves and Pluscarden once yielded good building sandstone.

S of the Highland Boundary Fault, the northern extension of Strathmore is underlain by a thick sequence (several kilometres) of late Silurian to early Devonian fluviatile sediments, mainly sandstones and conglomerates with interbedded andesite lava flows. They belong to six groups, named, from oldest to youngest, the Stonehaven, Dunnottar, Crawton, Arbuthnott, Garvock and Strathmore groups. The older part of this succession is well exposed in coastal sections between St Cyrus and Stonehaven. Local red-brown sandstones supplied much building stone, as can be seen in Stonehaven and Inverbervie. Inland, local coarse-grained brown sandstones of the Strathmore Group were used in many villages, for example Fettercairn.

Mesozoic (Permian and Triassic) sedimentary rocks which developed within the mainly offshore Moray Firth Basin extend onto the land and are preserved in a coastal strip between Lossiemouth and Burghead. The Upper Permian to Lower Triassic Cutties Hillock and Hopeman Sandstones comprise yellow to buff to white aeolian sandstones with large-scale dune bedding and sparse fluviatile deposits. The strata are notable for having yielded a reptilian fossil fauna, fine examples of which may be seen in the excellent geological exhibitions of the Elgin Museum. The overlying fluviatile sandstones and conglomerates of the Burghead Beds are succeeded by the Upper Triassic Lossiemouth Sandstone, of aeolian origin. Many of these sandstones have been worked for building, particularly in Forres and Elgin. Notable quarries include Cutties Hillock, Knock of Alves, Burghead, Greenbrae, Clashach, Newton, Lossiemouth and Spynie. Of these, only Clashach, worked by Moray Stone Cutters, continues in full production to supply both local and national building projects.

Jurassic rocks (mainly calcareous mudstones and sandstones) of the Moray Firth Basin crop out just S of Lossiemouth. Rocks of Cretaceous age do not crop out in the district although there is indirect evidence that, during this period, parts of Buchan were inundated by the sea. Relict gravel deposits of possible Neogene age, containing flint pebbles and boulders, are present at Fyvie and on the Moss of Cruden, W of Peterhead. At Den of Boddam flints were mined in prehistoric times.

CLAYS suitable for BRICK AND TILE-MAKING are widely distributed within the Quaternary deposits of North-East Scotland. Nearly twenty sites were exploited, mainly along the coast of Moray and Aberdeenshire over the last 200 years. Both boulder clay (till) and glaciolacustrine clays have been used. The most recent brick production congregated between Peterhead and Aberdeen, where reddish-brown laminated clays were worked for brickmaking until the mid 1980s at the Cruden Bay Brick and Tile Works at Errolston and Tipperty (N). Numerous SAND AND GRAVEL pits have exploited the moundy and flat-topped glacio-fluvial deposits of the district, principally for concrete products and also for mortaring and plastering sand. The best resources flank the valleys of the major rivers and lie on the coastal lowlands between Forres and Elgin.

PREHISTORIC, ROMAN AND EARLY MEDIEVAL ABERDEENSHIRE AND MORAY
BY GORDON NOBLE

The diverse landscapes of North-East Scotland, stretching from the coastal plains of the eastern lowlands to the eastern Grampian Mountains and the southern Cairngorms, supported substantial settlement in prehistoric and early medieval Scotland. The earliest settlers were the hunter-gatherers of the MESOLITHIC, who colonized the early landscapes of Scotland after the end of the last Ice Age. Settlement during the Mesolithic in Scotland (*c.* 9000–4000 B.C.) stretches back to at least the ninth millennium B.C. (over 10,000 years ago), a few thousand years after the end of the Ice Age. Such settlement in North-East Scotland is represented primarily by scatters of stone tools found in modern ploughed fields and along the coasts and rivers – the residues of a hunting–gathering–fishing lifestyle. Excavated sites can reveal tantalizing traces of settlement in the form of pits and post-holes, while coastal sites are often represented by significant accumulations of shells, traces of shell middens where Mesolithic people gathered the bounty of the coast and the sea. These sites are only fragments of lives that may have been relatively mobile, following the herds of wild animals and occupying the ever-changing riverine landscapes and coasts of the North-East. After the ice this would have been a relatively barren landscape, but by the end of the Mesolithic period in the late fifth millennium B.C., the

North-East would have been cloaked by a thick woodland dominated by oak.

Mesolithic sites in the North-East are concentrated along the banks of the Rivers Dee, Don and Ythan and their tributaries, and these rivers would have formed the main routes through the wooded landscape. Traces of the Mesolithic can be found from Aberdeen, where excavations on the medieval parts of the city have uncovered prehistoric layers containing Mesolithic flints, to upland landscapes at the foot of the Grampians. Little remains, however, in the landscape to identify these sites – those most intensively studied are along the Dee in South Aberdeenshire and consist of extensive scatters of stone tools. A site at Nethermills, Banchory, was excavated in the 1980s and more than 20,000 stone tools were found, along with possible traces of Mesolithic timber dwellings. Slightly upriver at Warren Field, Crathes, giant pits dug from the eighth millennium onwards have been found: these may have been animal traps or may have had more ritualized roles in prehistoric life.

A significant transformation occurred in the landscapes of North-East Scotland in the centuries after 4000 B.C. At this time the fringes of Western Europe, including Scotland, came into contact with new ways of life associated with communities that practised the agricultural routines of crop-growing and animal husbandry. This period of prehistory is known as the NEOLITHIC or New Stone Age. In Scotland, as in the rest of Britain and Ireland, the era lasted for over 1,500 years (c. 4000–2500 B.C.). The Neolithic is generally recognized as the period when domesticated animals and crops such as cattle, sheep and barley, and new technologies such as pottery and stone axes to clear woodland for crops and animal-grazing were introduced. The Neolithic was not merely about the spread of new types of animals and technologies, however; archaeological finds also document the spread of new ideas about life, death and the world around.

Many Neolithic sites and artefacts lie buried and are discovered only through excavation, but the most visible remains of the period in the Scottish landscape are monuments for burial and ceremony. In the earlier Neolithic period (4000–3300 B.C.) large stone-built cairns were constructed. Few of these have been excavated in North-East Scotland, but they comprise massive mounds of earth or stone known as LONG BARROWS or LONG CAIRNS. The construction of these monuments was connected with the disposal, display and curation of the remains of the dead, but may also have marked land and territory among the early agricultural societies of the North-East. Elsewhere in Scotland at this time chambered cairns were built to hold multiple human bodies – perhaps as family or lineage monuments. In the North-East, less is known about the long mounds or cairns, but they may have covered the remains of fewer individuals – perhaps important members of the community or individuals who represented the collective ancestral dead. The only well-excavated example in the North-East was dug at Dalladies, Fettercairn, excavated in advance of its destruction through quarrying. The mound was around 70 m. long, stood to a height of over 2 m. and dated to around 3700 B.C. The turf-built mound was found to cover a timber setting defined by a split tree trunk and a stone-built chamber. Inside the stone chamber a fragment of human skull and a flint knife were found. The other long mounds of the North-East, such as that which survives at Capo Plantation, Fettercairn, close to Dalladies, are likely to cover similar mortuary structures and burial deposits.

Settlements belonging to the Neolithic period in North-East Scotland are harder to identify than some of the monumental structures. At present we have only a very basic understanding of the settlement patterns and economy of this era. Investigations of prehistoric life more generally are hampered by the acidic nature of soils in Scotland, which is detrimental to the survival of bone and organic material. In the Neolithic the emphasis may have been on herding cattle with cereal farming probably undertaken as part of small-scale garden agriculture. The period has long been assumed to be accompanied by a sedentary lifestyle, yet in North-East Scotland and in much of lowland Scotland generally we only have sporadic occurrences of what could be interpreted as Neolithic domestic structures. It has been suggested by some archaeologists that Neolithic people may have retained a large degree of settlement mobility, despite the uptake of agriculture. In this respect, there may have been a continuation of some of the lifestyles and settlement practices that occurred in the Mesolithic period. However, two Neolithic structures that had at least some role in domestic life are worth mentioning here – the 'TIMBER HALLS' discovered at Crathes and Balbridie on the S side of the Dee. These were monumental buildings over 20 m. long, constructed with large oak timbers, radiocarbon-dated to the period c. 3800–3600 B.C. Neither building had

Crathes, Warren Field timber hall reconstruction.
Reconstruction by Hilary Murray, drawing by Jay Dunbar

surviving floor surfaces, but traces of cereals including naked barley and emmer wheat were recovered from the hall at Crathes, along with fragments of Neolithic pottery vessels and stone tools. Over 20,000 carbonized cereal grains were found at Balbridie. There has been great debate about the role of these structures in Neolithic life – were they the houses of extended families of early Neolithic incomers to the area or were they more specialized and perhaps ritualized structures for communal gatherings? Unfortunately the evidence is ambiguous at present, but these structures reveal rare insights into the nature of Neolithic life in the North-East of Scotland. Settlement more generally is harder to identify and consists of very rare timber buildings of more modest proportions and pits and post-holes of more ephemeral (or less well-preserved) settlements. Aberdeenshire also preserves a unique insight into the more mundane aspects of life in the later Neolithic. The flint-working site at Den of Boddam (N) is Scotland's only flint mine and only major inland source of flint in northern Britain. The flint dug out of the gravel deposits would have been an invaluable resource in earlier prehistory that could be traded and used to make stone tools. The outlines of some of the hundreds of pits dug can still be seen at the site today.

Around the middle of the third millennium B.C. (c. 2400 B.C.) there was a transformation of Stone Age society to societies that increasingly adopted new metalworking technologies along with traditions and practices that found their ultimate origin in Continental Europe. Recently, the term 'CHALCOLITHIC' has been used to describe the period from the C25 to the C22 B.C., describing a transitional period between the Late Neolithic and the BRONZE AGE. The Chalcolithic (c. 2450–2150 B.C.) is characterized by the appearance of new cultural practices and novel objects, including the first metal objects, new traditions of pottery (finely decorated Beakers) and new burial practices. The changes that characterize the centuries around the beginning of the second half of the third millennium B.C. are most obvious in funerary traditions with the increased visibility of burial – predominately inhumation in stone cist graves, with grave goods much more common than in Neolithic burial traditions. Some Bronze Age graves were covered by monumental earthen barrows or ROUND CAIRNS, as survive in the incongruous setting of a C20 housing development at Bieldside (Aberdeen). The burials of the Chalcolithic and Bronze Age can include grave goods such as Beaker pots, archery equipment (arrowheads, belt rings and wristguards) and, more rarely, modest metal objects such as copper knives or gold objects. North-East Scotland swiftly adopted the new practices associated with metalworking and from the end of the third millennium this area was an important region in the spread of full bronze-working traditions from the C22 B.C. onwards across Britain and Ireland. Many of the stone moulds for early bronze metalworking are concentrated in this area despite the fact that the materials for bronze itself came from Ireland (copper) and South-West England (tin).

New traditions of megalithic and monumental architecture emerged in the later Neolithic and Early Bronze Age and include some of North-East Scotland's most famous monuments – the RECUMBENT STONE CIRCLES, a distinctive type of stone circle found exclusively in this part of Scotland and defined by a ring of standing stones with a massive recumbent stone on the S flanked by two tall standing stones. These circles enclosed central cairns which covered pyres used for cremating the dead. The dating for this tradition of architecture is still loose, but the presence of Beaker pottery at a number of these monuments implies that at least some were in use in the Chalcolithic/Early Bronze Age and their construction may have been closely linked to the importance of this area in the new era of metal and Beakers. Southern Aberdeenshire has some of the finest examples of recumbent stone circles, including those at Easter Aquhorthies, Sunhoney and Midmar Kirk, which are easily accessible. The   8 most extensively excavated site is that at Tomnaverie near Tarland, which has been the subject of detailed investigation and reconstruction. The excavations at Tomnaverie showed that the first episode of activity on the hill was the use of the hilltop for pyres: cremated bone, ashes and burnt soil survived as a low mound under the later central cairn. Over these pyres a polygonal cairn was constructed and the hill-slope was revetted and a low platform of stones built to support the cairn. A secondary phase of construction involved encircling the cairn with thirteen standing stones and a recumbent measuring over 3 m. in length, arranged in a circle 17 m. in diameter. The stones were graded in height towards the SW, emphasizing the recumbent setting. Sherds of Beaker pottery were found beneath the outer platform at the foot of the kerb of the central cairn. Radiocarbon-dating suggests construction in the C26–C25 B.C. Most of the original complement of stones survive and the circle has been sensitively restored.

A number of other forms of later Neolithic–Early Bronze Age monuments survive in the North-East including a small number of HENGE MONUMENTS – enclosures defined by ditches with external banks surrounding burials or settings of timbers or megaliths within. The henge at Broomend of Crichie (Inverurie) surrounded an area that was used for burial in the Bronze Age. The burials stood in association with a series of standing stones. An avenue of stones entered the henge from the S and led from an area where a number of cist burials associated with Beaker pottery have been found. A more spectacular, though unexcavated henge monument, Wormy Hillock, survives in the Clashindarroch forest near Rhynie. A hoard of Bronze Age flat axes was found nearby in 1947.

We have even fewer settlements dating to the Chalcolithic and Early Bronze Age than we do from the Neolithic in North-East Scotland, but from the mid second millennium B.C. onwards there is a change in the character of the archaeological evidence. Rather than landscapes of ritual monuments and burial we have ones dominated by evidence relating to the settled landscape of houses and agricultural practices. From this time onwards a bewildering diversity of settlement forms emerged, but most were based on a tradition of architecture that came to dominate the settlement record for the next 2,000 years in the LATER BRONZE AGE and IRON AGE: the round-house. In the Lowlands and in North-East Scotland these ROUND-HOUSES were made of timber and turf and few survive above ground today. Some would have been monumental in their own right, using hundreds of trees in their construction and requiring a wide community to build and maintain them. These circular buildings measured from around 5 m. to 20 m. in diameter, based on a radial layout with a central hearth and wattle-and-daub timber partitions marking areas around the periphery of the round-house for sleeping, storage or keeping animals. One of the most common forms of North-East round-house was the ring ditch house, which included a sunken area (the ring ditch) between the inner roof-bearing posts and outer wall that may have been used for the over-wintering of animals. People may have slept above on a raised floor constructed in the eaves of the house.

We are missing much of the detail of Later Bronze Age and Iron Age lifestyles, which would have been defined by the routines of the household. Floor levels rarely survive in round-houses and the architecture has largely decayed away, leaving little evidence for internal furniture, décor and economy. These would have been mixed-farming economies in the main and some of the more curious archaeological monuments dating to the Iron Age are stone-built underground chambers known as SOUTERRAINS, which were probably built in association with round-house settlements and may have been used for storing agricultural produce such as milk, cheese, meat and grain. A rare survival of round-houses and field systems is visible at New Kinord (Dinnet) and good examples of souterrains can be seen at Culsh (Tarland), Kildrummy and in the grounds of Glenkindie House. Certain forms of round-house endured for centuries and this conservatism in architecture characterized communities where status and identity may have been closely tied to the house and household.

Status and community identity in the Late Bronze Age and Iron Age were also expressed in more monumental constructions that have been labelled with the descriptive, yet at times unhelpful, name HILL-FORT. In North-East Scotland these can range from modest sites defined by low stone banks and/or ditches (perhaps defining areas for settlement), to huge hilltop enclosures defined by massive stone and timber-laced ramparts. Traditionally these enclosures have been linked to increasing tensions in prehistoric society where warfare became endemic, but undoubtedly they had multiple roles and some of them, such as Tap O'Noth near Rhynie, may have been large-scale communal settlements. Tap O'Noth includes around a hundred house-platforms on the slopes between an Iron Age oval fort and an undated lower stone rampart found towards the base of the hill. It is uncertain if all of the house-platforms at such sites were in contemporary use and whether this was a permanent settlement or one used for periodic gatherings – perhaps summer fairs or important religious ceremonies. Indeed, the religious or ceremonial role of forts has been emphasized in recent scholarship and, while some may have had roles to play in Iron Age warfare and as markers of status of powerful groups, others may have had more spiritual significance. Oval Iron Age forts such as Tap O'Noth and Dunnideer, near Insch, for example, did not have defined entrance-ways through the ramparts and some simply contain features such as wells or ephemeral remains that give little away regarding function – these enclosures may have been as much symbolic or ritual as they were defensive. Other probable Iron Age forts in South Aberdeenshire include Barmekin of Echt, an example with multiple ramparts and a bewildering number of entrances.

Highlighting the potential symbolic and ritual rôle of forts is not to deny that warfare and conflict occurred in this period: cattle-raiding and inter-family feuds may have been a common part of later prehistoric life and at times enclosures such as hill-forts may have played a role in inter-community conflict and violence. Whatever the case, whether they were defensive or ritual enclosures, those who orchestrated the construction of these sites undoubtedly drew on the labour of a large community or workforce and would have ultimately drawn on networks of power and social status. Hill-forts may have been the ultimate expression of power in Iron Age landscapes, whether spiritually or militarily ordained.

The Roman period

In A.D. 79 the ROMAN army, under the command of Agricola, the Governor of Britain, entered Scotland. The expansion into northern Britain originally came at the behest of Emperor Vespasian, who had participated in the Roman invasion of Britain in A.D. 43 and was keen to expand the Empire northwards. In the first year of campaigning Agricola and his army got as far N as the River Tay. Tacitus records that the Iron Age tribes of southern Scotland disintegrated into warring factions, with some pro-Roman, others not. Over the next four years the Roman army proceeded to consolidate their control over southern Scotland with the construction of a series of forts, roads and outposts securing the area between the Forth and the Clyde and the routes into the Highland glens. The Roman military presence stretched up to North-East Scotland through forts built towards the Mounth, the most northerly being at Stracathro in Angus. In the following years there were subsequent seasons of campaigning northwards, culminating in A.D. 83 in the Battle of Mons Graupius. Tacitus records that, at that battle, 30,000 natives under the leadership of Calgacus the Swordsman succumbed to a disastrous defeat at the hands of the Romans, with a third of the native force killed. Shortly afterwards, Agricola's tenure as governor ended and he was recalled to Rome. The Roman army also suffered defeats on the Continent, leading to a withdrawal from the North; by the later C1 the Tyne–Solway line in northern England was reconsolidated as the northern frontier of the province of Britain.

Roman archaeology for North-East Scotland is limited to the presence of a number of MARCHING CAMPS that stretch from the Mounth into the North-East, following the Don and up towards the Moray coast. The camps almost certainly date to Agricola's campaign of A.D. 83. They were temporary fortifications that marked the lines of advance of the Roman army. They were generally spaced at distances of a day's march and were defined by a rapidly constructed rampart and ditch that marked out a secure area in which the army pitched its tents. Ancient military manuals suggest that camp space was ordered much like forts, with roads or paths through the camp and a hierarchy of settlement and tent location. The camps were generally defined by a V-section ditch and a turf and earth internal bank. Each *contubernium* (messing unit of eight soldiers) occupied a tent and there were also areas for draught animals, the baggage train and cooking.

In Aberdeenshire the Roman camps have largely been destroyed by ploughing, with the exception of some upstanding remains at Raedykes camp at Fetteresso that may have marked Agricola's first foray into the North-East. Many of the camps in the region were discovered by the archaeologist J. K. St Joseph through aerial photography. There are now known to be at least six large camps of probable C1 date and two smaller extending towards the Spey from Angus. The southernmost in Aberdeenshire lay near Balmakewan House, followed by one near Kair House. At Logie Durno (near Pitcaple) in the shadow of Bennachie in central Aberdeenshire, St Joseph discovered the largest camp in the North. He argued that, at 57 hectares, this was the mustering point for Agricola's troops during the Battle of Mons Graupius and archaeologists estimate that Logie Durno may have held a force of up to 30,000 troops (one much larger than Tacitus records). Our understanding of Roman marching camps has been hampered by lack of excavation and because many were assumed to be largely empty, but at Kintore, just to the S of Logie Durno, a 45-hectare camp has been the subject of extensive excavation: over 180 field ovens and 60 rubbish pits have been revealed – features that would have been essential for keeping the Roman army fed and the camp maintained during the brief occupation of the North-East.

Ptolemy's C2 map of Britain records the Taexali tribe occupying the area of North-East Scotland. The effect of the presence of the Roman army on the region is much debated: was it a brief inconsequential interlude or something more substantial and long-lasting? Direct Roman intervention in the North-East was probably restricted to Agricola's campaign and possibly an equally brief interlude in the early C3 when Emperor Severus came to Scotland to quell the troublesome natives N of the border.

Cassius Dio, the Roman historian, records that tribes in eastern Scotland did not abide by their promises to keep the peace and were accused of conspiring against Rome. He also records that, in the previous decades, Governor Virius Lupus had been compelled to buy peace for a large sum from the tribes of eastern Scotland. Severus arrived in the north in A.D. 208 to conduct a punitive campaign. This appears to have focused on the tribes of the Calidones and the Maiatai, who lived to a little to the S, but may have also proceeded northwards, perhaps as far as the Moray Firth. The Romans ravaged the countryside, burning crops and houses, but the campaign was undermined by the death of Severus in 211. His son, Caracalla, subsequently agreed treaties with the natives. The Roman marching camp at Kintore may have been reoccupied during Severus's war against the natives and Roman coin hoards at native settlements in North Aberdeenshire and Moray, such as at Birnie, near Elgin, are evidence of the ways in which the Romans 'bought' peace.

Native settlement changed little during the first centuries of the Roman Iron Age, but from the C3 onwards settlement becomes much harder to identify. Other traditions of architecture such as hill-fort construction also seem to have ceased by this period and may have ended prior to the Roman occupation. Severus's expedition was the last major Roman campaign in Scotland N of the Forth.

Pictish Aberdeenshire

In the late C3 A.D. Roman writers started to record renewed attacks on Britain's northern frontier. They called the aggressors *Picti*, or 'painted people', and throughout the C4 Roman military campaigns were waged against the Picts as they caused repeated trouble N and S of Hadrian's Wall. After the Roman withdrawal, during the early medieval period from the C4 to the C9, the kingdoms of the Picts became among the most powerful social and political groups in northern Britain. Their territories encompassed the entirety of North-East Scotland and at their height the Pictish kingdoms stretched from the Firth of Forth in the South to Shetland in the North. The Picts, along with the Scots, the Britons, the Anglo-Saxons and latterly the Vikings fought one another for control over northern Britain. Our knowledge of the social and political landscape of the Picts is vague, but in the North-East, the area of Aberdeenshire would appear to equate to the Pictish territory known as Cé, while Moray to the W may have made up the heartland of the most powerful Pictish kingdom, called Fortriu.

The political changes that occurred in the early medieval period in Scotland were part of a wider trend in Northern Europe during the second half of the first millennium A.D., towards more centralized authority and power over increasingly larger territories. This period formed the foundations for the medieval nation-state of Scotland. Yet it was also a time of constant flux in power structures and social and political alliances. Unfortunately, native historical documents for the Picts, like many of the early medieval kingdoms of northern Britain at this time, are scarce. The changes also occurred when the archaeological record becomes more diffuse and difficult to interpret. Pictish settlements are notoriously difficult to identify – everyday houses may have been largely built from turf and non-earthfast timber structures. No certain Pictish farms or everyday domestic sites are known from the North-East.

A little more is known about higher-status Pictish sites, but our knowledge is still limited. Accompanying the rise of new forms of social and political authority was a renewed focus on the construction and use of HILL-FORTS. The scant historical record mentions the use of forts as seats of kingship and their role in conflict, but few have been excavated on any scale. In the North-East one of the most important Pictish sites appears to have been a fort constructed on top of the hill named Bennachie. The historian Margaret Dobbs suggested in 1949 that the place name may have originally been *Benne Cé*, the 'mountain of the people of Cé'. In the Pictish King-lists, Cé is recorded in an origin myth as one of the seven sons of Cruithne, the father of Pictland; as noted above, Cé appears to have equated to the area of modern Aberdeenshire. The fort on the summit of Mither Tap, Bennachie (Oyne), has long been thought to resemble other early medieval complex hill-forts (known as nuclear hill-forts) in Scotland. It comprises two massive ramparts defining an upper and a lower fort; traces of collapsed walling around the prominent granitic tor of Mither Tap suggest that there may have been a third dramatic enclosure on top of the tor itself. The lower rampart was at least 8 m. thick and shows traces of a parapet and wall-head walk. Recent dating of occupation deposits within the hill-fort has confirmed occupation between the C5 and the C8, supporting the long-standing view that Bennachie is likely to have been a high-status Pictish centre.

Another massive fort at Burghead in Moray is also likely to have been a major Pictish stronghold; indeed, it is the largest Pictish fort known. Its complex defences included a triple rampart defining a distinctive promontory that juts into the Moray Firth. Within the fort there are upper and lower citadel enclosures and an impressive rock-cut well. Excavations and radiocarbon-dating suggest that the fort was in use from the C4 to the C9. Other recent excavations have identified more modestly defended enclosures dating to the Pictish period. These are smaller forts defined by stone or timber boundaries up to 60 m. across. One example is Maiden Castle, on the lower slopes of Bennachie, where recent excavations have found settlement deposits dating to the C5–C6, rich in finds including bone, metalworking debris and imported glass. Traces of at least two rectilinear buildings have also been found within.

Undoubtedly one of the most remarkable Pictish discoveries in the North-East in recent years has been a high-status settlement at Rhynie, s of Huntly. Rhynie was previously known for its collection of eight Pictish carved stones found in the village and

surrounding area from the earlier C19 onwards (*see* below). Exca- 9
vations in 2011–12 around the only stone now in situ, the Craw
Stane, found that this stone was originally part of a very high-
status settlement and fort, defined by both earthen ramparts and
ditches and a timber palisade. Centuries of agriculture mean that
only the Craw Stane is now visible above ground, but aerial photography first revealed the presence of significant buried remains
here. The settlement would have been enclosed by a monumental
timber palisade and wall-walk perhaps 4–5 m. high; inside, traces
of timber buildings built of squared oak beams have been located.
The settlement was a centre for the production of metalwork,
and finds have included bronze and iron pins and more remarkable items – wine amphoras imported from the Mediterranean
and glass drinking beakers from France. The finds are of the type
discovered on early royal sites in western Britain and Ireland, but
are the first of their type in Pictland. The place-name, Rhynie,
deriving from *rhynnoid*, 'a very royal place', suggests that it may
have been one of the early royal centres of the Picts in North-East
Scotland.

The most iconic monuments associated with the Picts are
carved stones, generally known as PICTISH STONES. Pictish stones
have been traditionally classified into types: Class I with animal
and abstract symbols on generally unworked stones as found at
Rhynie; Class II with Christian iconography, which can be carved
on much more finely worked and shaped stones; Class III, relief
crosses without symbols; and Class IV, stones with incised crosses.
The usefulness of such a scheme is now questioned by some, but
it provides a basic framework for the study of these monuments.
The difference between Class I and the other forms of stones may
be partly chronological, with the symbol-bearing slabs earlier
(perhaps emerging in the C5 or C6) and the more elaborate cross-
slabs and relief crosses later. Simple incised crosses may have a
wider chronological range. It has been argued that Pictish stones
may have emerged as a commemorative tradition associated with
the dead. This commemorative role has been supported by a
supposed association between symbol stones and burials; however,
a direct association between burial monument and symbol stone
has rarely been unequivocally demonstrated. Sculptured stones
obviously had other roles to play: six stones incised with bulls
survive from Burghead (Moray) from a much larger group found
in the C19 and may have been displayed within the fort or on the
ramparts. Similarly at Rhynie, the Craw Stane stood at the entrance
of an elaborate fortified settlement. The symbols on Pictish stones
also occasionally appear on metalwork and other more portable
material culture, as well as on the walls of caves – clearly the
symbols played diverse roles. Around thirty different symbols
were in common usage and included abstract symbols such as
crescents, double-discs (many with V- or Z-rods – a design
resembling a broken arrow or spear) and objects such as mirrors
and combs, as well as animal symbols depicting real and mythical
beasts. North-East Scotland has a distinct concentration of the
earlier stones that do not display Christian iconography.

In the C7 or C8 Pictish stones became more elaborate and monumental and the symbols appear alongside the Christian cross, marking the conversion of the Picts to Christianity. Some of the later sculpture gives further clues to what the symbols represent. The stones can include occasional depictions of individuals apparently 'labelled' with symbols and this strongly suggests that the symbols on these stones conveyed names or identities of some kind. The more elaborate monuments represent incredible investments in skill and resources, and the hunting and other elite activities depicted on some stones suggest that these monuments were strongly implicated in the emergence of new forms of rulership that characterized the rise of the early Pictish kingdoms in a post-Roman context. South Aberdeenshire has a magnificent array of Pictish and other carved stone monuments. These range from the impressive standing stone at Auquhollie (Rickarton) with its ogham (an Irish script) inscription to individual symbol stones to groups of cross-slabs and symbol-bearing stones. The most imposing symbol stones include those at Picardy (Insch), Rhynie and Brandsbutt (Inverurie). Impressive Class II stones include those at Dyce, Fordoun (Auchenblae church) and Migvie. The most impressive monument of all is the Maiden Stone, found on the lower slopes of Bennachie near Chapel of Garioch in the shadow of the Pictish fort at Mither Tap. On one side of the Maiden Stone is a faded but once majestic ring-headed cross; on the other is a series of figures and symbols including a centaur, a 'Pictish beast' and a mirror and comb. The stone probably dates from the C7 or C8.

Other than carved stone crosses with or without Pictish symbols, we know very little about the Pictish Church. There are no identified church buildings from this period. Sculpture from Burghead (Moray), which includes fragments of a cross-slab and shrine, suggests that an important Christian chapel was present in or near the Pictish fort here in the C8–C9. Other sites, such as Tullich and Dyce, that have clusters of carved stones may have been important early church sites or monasteries. Kinneddar (Moray), which has an impressive collection of sculpture, was the site of the episcopal seat in Moray in the C12, while Mortlach (Moray), where an unusual cross-slab and Pictish stone can be seen, may also have been an episcopal see of the North-East before that status was transferred to Aberdeen in the same century. The number and range of sculpture from Kinneddar is particularly impressive. In Elgin Museum, the current collection is fragmentary, but includes numerous examples of relief sculpture probably dating from the C7–C8. With one or two exceptions the stones are mainly fragments of interlaced cross-slabs without symbols, but there is at least one slab decorated with a crescent and V-rod. There are also slabs from shrines or sarcophagi, including a fragment showing Daniel rending the jaws of a lion – a very close match for the magnificent St Andrews sarcophagus in Fife, a more complete example of a royal shrine or burial monument. The Kinneddar assemblage includes unfinished pieces showing that sculpture was produced on site, underlining the importance of this site as an uninvestigated location of an early church that almost certainly attracted royal patronage.

By the C9 or C10 the Picts were absorbed in the expanding Gaelic Kingdom of Alba. Increasing Viking impact on northern Scotland from the C9 onwards appears to have weakened the powerful northern Pictish kingdoms, leading to the amalgamation of the Picts and the Scots. The forts that characterized the earlier Pictish kingdoms ceased to be constructed by the C9 and some, such as Burghead (Moray), may have been destroyed by Viking attacks. There is a fine cross-slab at Loch Kinord, near   11 Dinnet, which is probably C9. The carving of stone sculptures largely ceased, but some of the carved stone monuments, such as the remarkable Sueno's Stone in Forres (Moray), may be as late as the C10. In many ways the period from the C10 to the C13 is more of a 'dark age' than the Pictish period – settlement and material culture from this period are even more difficult to identify and are poorly represented in North-East Scotland. Yet this period was when the medieval kingdom of Scotland truly took shape. Aberdeenshire appears to have been part of Alba, but Moray continued to have important, and at times competing, roles to play in the rulership of early Scotland. The slaying of Mac Bethad mac Findláich (Macbeth) at Lumphanan and his son Lulach at Essie (Rhynie) by Malcolm III and his followers, however, allowed the Kingship of Alba to expand. The defeat of Macbeth and his son, whose power base lay in the north, marked the consolidation of royal power in central Scotland to the south.

ABERDEENSHIRE: SOUTH AND ABERDEEN*

MEDIEVAL CHURCHES
BY RICHARD FAWCETT

The only church in the area to retain visible work of the earlier C12 is Monymusk, which is thought to have accommodated both   13 the parishioners and a small priory of Augustinian Canons, the latter having had its origins in a Culdee community. It is a three-compartment structure with what was possibly an unusually extended rectangular chancel, a rectangular nave and a W tower. The chancel and tower arches remain in place, the former being of two orders with scalloped or cushion capitals to the jambs. Work of around the mid C12 has been found at Aberdeen's St Nicholas, where a semicircular apse located through excavation immediately to the E of the later crossing perhaps dates from before the time that the parish first comes on record, when it was confirmed to the bishop in 1157.

*Place names followed by (N) refer to sites in *Aberdeenshire: North and Moray*.

The earliest identifiable work to remain visible at St Nicholas, however, is of the late C12, and this is on a scale that suggests that it was one of the first churches of the major east coast trading burghs to achieve the great size that is such a striking feature of the later medieval burgh churches. The responds of the arches that support the central tower have a variety of crocket and leaf types which, although largely re-cut since a fire in 1874, appear to reflect the original forms. A combination of structural and archaeological evidence indicates that by around 1200 the church was cruciform, with a rectangular chancel, substantial transepts on each side of a central tower and an aisled nave. Work of this period is also to be seen at the rectangular parish church of Auchindoir, which, although of small scale, was finely detailed, the most handsome feature being the s door, which has crocket capitals to the outer order and a dogtooth-decorated hoodmould.

Little has survived from the C13, with the possible exception of the chancel at Arbuthnott and parts of the abandoned church at Kincardine O'Neil. The former has diminutive lancets in its flanks and what is probably a much-modified triplet of larger windows in the E wall. The latter was founded as a hospital before 1231; its chapel, which was also parochial, has a handsome door of four alternating continuous and shafted orders. The most significant recorded works of the earlier C14 were at the Cathedral, where major rebuilding was commenced by Bishops Henry Cheyne (1282–c. 1329) and William de Deyn (1344–50); but all evidence of this was lost when the second Bishop Alexander Kininmund (1355–80) started a further campaign of rebuilding. The account of the lives of the bishops by the first principal of Aberdeen's University, Hector Boece, which was published in 1522, is an invaluable source for the later building history of the Cathedral. Kininmund's work on the nave was continued by Henry de Lichton (1422–40), while Ingram de Lindsay (1441–58) roofed the nave and William Elphinstone (1483–1514) completed the central tower and started work on a new choir. We also know that Bishop Gavin Dunbar (1518–32) added spires to the w towers, worked on the transepts and inserted the nave ceiling. The choir, upper walls of the transepts and central tower were destroyed after the Reformation. The nave was retained in use for parochial worship, despite the fact that there was a nearby parish church, dedicated to St Mary of the Snows (St Maria ad Nives), of which nothing now remains in place. It can be seen that the cathedral nave had a number of innovative features that owed something to what had been observed through trading contacts with the Netherlands, including the complex crossing piers and the cylindrical arcade piers.

Apart from the works on the Cathedral, later C15 and earlier C16 Aberdeen witnessed a great amount of building activity. Plans for rebuilding the choir of St Nicholas were taking shape by the third quarter of the C15, and work may have started on the crypt that was required beneath the extended E end because of the steep fall of land. Quarrying for stone was in progress in the 1490s, and by 1495 the wright *John Fendour* was contracting for the roof. Apart from the crypt chapel, the choir was swept away in 1835–7, but drawings made before its destruction show that it had arcades carried on cylindrical piers comparable with those in the Cathedral, and a ribbed timber ceiling with sprigged bosses which, like the piers, suggest Netherlandish debts.

Bishop William Elphinstone was a patron of this work, which presumably explains why a similar ceiling was constructed over the chapel started in 1500 that was the main architectural focus of his new university foundation, at what came to be known as King's College. The basic form of this chapel, an apsidal-ended 21, 22 rectangle with a tower off one corner and a two-storey sacristy and treasury range along one flank, must have taken St Salvator's College Chapel in St Andrews (of 1450–60) as its main inspiration. But Elphinstone was a cosmopolitan figure who was unlikely to be satisfied with simple solutions, and his building shows the impact of a range of other architectural ideas. Like the sprigged bosses of the ribbed ceiling, the window tracery shows debts to the Low Countries, though for the main contributions to the splendid skyline he evidently looked to England. The flèche that rose from the roof above the screen was probably the work of *John Burwel*, the sergeant plumber to the King of England, who contracted for the leadwork in 1506, while the soaring arches of the crown steeple over the tower at the SW corner are also likely to be ultimately indebted to architectural achievements S of the border.

Apart from the churches in Aberdeen itself, the most ambitious project in the area was the addition of a finely detailed laterally projecting S aisle at Arbuthnott, which was built in 1505–6 by Sir 17 Robert Arbuthnott to house a chaplainry of the Virgin. Such lateral aisles were relatively common as a way of providing burial places and locations for prayers for the souls of prominent families. Arbuthnott's, however, was most unusual in having an apsidal termination, for which the only Scottish parallels are at Ladykirk (Borders) of *c.* 1500 and the Dominican church at St Andrews of *c.* 1516. It also had an upper chamber, above the barrel-vaulted main space, which perhaps functioned as a sacristy. It seems that there may have been unfulfilled proposals to remodel the rest of the church, possibly to a rectangular plan, on the evidence of tusking at the E end of the N nave wall, at its junction with the chancel.

Of other later rural parish churches, that at Kinkell is an unbuttressed rectangle. The date of its initial construction is uncertain, but it is attractive to suspect that its finest architectural feature – what must have been a large and presumably traceried E window – was inserted in the time of Canon Alexander Galloway, whose stall in the Cathedral was funded by the parochial teinds. From the later C12 it is likely that most parish churches were of simple rectangular plan, and that is also true of the churches housing communities of friars, though the degree of architectural enrichment might vary considerably. Two friaries in Aberdeen are known to have had such rectangular plans. Excavations at the site of the Carmelite house founded in about 1273 have exposed a church of this type with angle buttresses at the W end. A considerably more sophisticated variant was employed for the Observant Franciscan community, whose church was rebuilt in the early C16 for Bishop Gavin Dunbar, under the direction of Canon Alexander Galloway. It was originally a buttressed seven-bay structure with an impressive display of intersecting tracery, the seven-light E window having a particularly innovative pattern of interlocking intersecting patterns. Tragically it was demolished in 1902 to make way for the expansion of Marischal College, despite the fact that the architect, *Marshall Mackenzie*, produced designs demonstrating that it could have been retained. The only survivor of the church is the E window, which was rebuilt in the church that replaced it.

The area has retained some of the most significant church FURNISHINGS to have come down to us from medieval Scotland, with an extraordinary concentration in Aberdeen's King's College 23 Chapel. Finest of all are the early C16 ranks of choir stalls, which survive virtually complete, with their gloriously inventive displays of micro-architectural flamboyant tracery to the canopies and stall-ends. The return stalls back onto the screen, with its much remodelled entrance doors to the choir at its centre; the screen itself is severely plain, presumably because altars were placed against its western face. An altar *mensa* has survived through adaptation as a post-medieval memorial. Towards the E end of the N wall is the pulpit made for the Cathedral by Bishop William Stewart (1532–45), with the curved profile of its back panel designed to fit the Cathedral's crossing piers, and the pulpit itself decorated with heads in either roundels or lozenges to several of the panels. Since 1944 the chapel has also housed a fine late C15 Netherlandish timber carving of Sancta Maria in Sole, above the easternmost of the doors that once opened into the sacristy. The parish church of St Nicholas in New Aberdeen also had a set of stalls with more restrained carving than those in King's College Chapel, for which the wright *John Fendour* signed the contract in 1508; fragments of these are displayed in the National Museums of Scotland in Edinburgh, with other parts probably incorporated in composite assemblages of woodwork in the crypt chapel.

South Aberdeenshire has retained two particularly good sacrament houses: at Auchindoir and Kinkell. The former, with the initials of the rector, Master Alexander Spittal, is designed in the form of the monstrance in which the consecrated host would have been displayed, and the crucifix at its apex is a particularly remarkable survival. Kinkell, as the prebendal church of Canon Alexander Galloway, one of the great architectural patrons of the earlier C16, must have been particularly well equipped with liturgical furnishings. There the aumbry of the sacrament house is at the centre of a cruciform arrangement of panels, and the inscriptions include the date 1524, together with Galloway's initials. His other benefactions to his church included a relief panel of the Crucifixion dated 1525, now represented by a replica, and a font 20 with his arms that is now in St John's Episcopal church in Aberdeen.

19   Of the more common types of liturgical fixture, Auchindoir is supplied with a pointed-arched holy water stoup by the S nave door, and there are simple piscina and aumbry recesses in the

chancel. Arbuthnott has a pointed-arched piscina in the chancel and an ogee-arched piscina in the s chapel; there are holy water stoups by the nave and s chapel doors, the former round-arched and the later ogee-arched.

Among MONUMENTS, the most extraordinary tomb in the area must have been that erected before the high altar of King's College Chapel for Bishop William Elphinstone (†1514) by Bishop Gavin Dunbar, with the bronze effigy on the chest said to have been surrounded by candle-carrying angels, bedesmen, the four cardinal virtues, the three theological virtues with a figure of contemplation, and angels carrying Elphinstone's arms. Only the reconstructed plinth and ledger slab survive at the original location, but *Henry Wilson*'s magnificent reinterpretation   42
of the description, made in 1911–31, now stands to the w of the

St Machar's Cathedral, Bishop Dunbar's tomb.
By R.W. Billings, 1845–52

chapel. Of surviving monuments, the most ambitious canopied
tomb in the area is that for Bishop Gavin Dunbar (†1532) in the
s transept of the Cathedral. Its round-arched canopy, with cusped
cusping to the soffit and crocketing to the extrados, arcaded
tomb-chest and flanking buttresses were to be fascinatingly
restated in a Renaissance idiom for the tomb at Tarves (N) of
William Forbes of Tolquhoun (†1589). Representatives of a more
common type of tomb-recess may be seen in the N wall of the N
transept at St Nicholas, Aberdeen, and in the N wall of the
Cathedral's N aisle, where recesses have mouldings that run
unbroken around both the jambs and a segmental arch.

A number of LEDGER SLABS survive, including that of Gilbert
Greenlaw (†1411) at Kinkell, who is thought to have fallen at the
Battle of Harlaw, which bears his carefully incised armoured
likeness and which survived through being later reused. Several
high-quality EFFIGIES throughout the area provide invaluable
evidence for the details of armour and for both lay and ecclesiastical costume. The earliest armoured effigy is probably that
relocated within the s chapel at Arbuthnott, which is traditionally
identified with Hugo de Arbuthnott (†1282). Fine representations of both later armour and female costume are to be seen on
effigies at St Nicholas, Aberdeen, along with a rare depiction of
a figure in what is thought to be the costume of a lay magistrate,
said to be John Collison. In the Cathedral a number of effigies
have been relocated to the w end of the N aisle, including that of
Bishop Henry de Lichton (†1440), which used to be on his tomb
in the N transept. Of particular interest for the depiction of the
almuce that was the defining vestment of a secular canon are two
effigies of Cathedral prebendaries, that in an arched recess being
of Canon Walter Idyll (†c. 1468).

POST-REFORMATION CHURCHES
BY CHARLES O'BRIEN

The Reformation in Scotland can be dated formally to August
1560, when the Scottish Parliament forbade celebration of the
Mass according to Catholic usage, proscribed the recognition of
papal authority and adopted a Calvinist Confession of Faith.
This was the beginning of a period of dispute and turbulence in
the Church in Scotland which reached its peak in the C17, C18
and C19 and would last in one form or another until the C20.

The MONASTIC ESTABLISHMENTS of Aberdeenshire were
soon dissolved and abandoned, although their churches were
often retained. At Aberdeen, the church of the episcopal seat, St
Machar's Cathedral, was not abandoned but was maltreated and
greatly reduced in extent until in 1688 the collapse of its tower
and transept left only the nave in use for worship. The Greyfriars,
in New Aberdeen, resigned their property to the Town Council
in 1559 and their church was abandoned but then restored for

the college founded in the friary buildings by the Earl Marischal from 1593. It survived until 1902 (*see* below). By the end of the C16 the large Burgh church of St Nicholas had been divided into two parish churches: East (in the former chancel) and West (in the nave) and both adapted for Reformed worship.

Similar changes were played out also in the smaller BURGH AND VILLAGE CHURCHES where the new forms of worship were accommodated through a reorientation of the interiors of existing buildings so that equal emphasis would now be given to preaching, praying and Holy Communion. The first of these was given greatest importance and so evolved the pattern of church interior wherein every member of the congregation could see and hear the minister in his pulpit, while wooden tables were introduced for the by now only occasional celebration of Communion. In many medieval parish churches adaptation was a relatively uncomplicated matter: those of rectangular plan lent themselves to Reformed worship with relative ease, albeit greatly reordered to allow for the positioning of the pulpit in the centre of the long s wall or less frequently at the E end. Indeed, where a church is of rectangular plan and is aligned from E to W, and especially if it is significantly elongated on its E–W axis, it may be that at its core there is a medieval shell. An example is St Fittick's church at Torry (Aberdeen), which continued in use for worship until 1829. Where churches had chancels divided from the nave by an arch, it was often the case that these would be walled up and co-opted as burial aisles for the family of the local laird (whose pre-Reformation monuments might in any case already occupy this space), as at St Manir, Crathie. This practice was one means of getting around the Church of Scotland's proscription in 1581 of burial inside churches. In other circumstances the laird may have already built an aisle against one side of the church, doubling as a burial vault and loft for his family, looking into the church, and creating a T-plan building. Where new sites were later adopted for churches it is common to find post-Reformation burial aisles left behind in the old churchyard as the only reminder of the earlier church (e.g. the Botarg and Pitlurg Aisle of 1597 at Cairnie, the Marischal Aisle at Dunnottar of 1583, the Elphinstone aisle at Kildrummy, 1605, and the C17 Douglas Aisle at Kirkton of Glenbervie).

The SEVENTEENTH CENTURY was an especially uncertain time for the Church in Scotland. Nevertheless quite a large number of churches are on record as having been rebuilt or at the very least altered in this period and, for example, given new windows of rectangular pattern, as one can see in the shells of medieval churches at Auchindoir, Clatt, Kincardine O'Neil, Drumoak, Fetteresso and Kirkton of Glenbuchat. The other distinguishing addition was a BELLCOTE. The most popular form for the latter is the birdcage type (which carries on well into the early C19). In Aberdeenshire a significant number still contain their BELLS, the earliest and best of all of which is at Kirkton of Kinellar, dated 1612 and cast by *Peter Vanden Ghein III* of Mechelen. Other imported bells are at Keithhall, 1611 (originally at Culsalmond); Midmar, 1642 by *Peter Jansen* of Ostend (originally at Kinnernie); and by *Burgerhuys* at Rhynie (1620), Newmachar (1635), Leslie (1642) and Coull (1642). A slightly larger proportion of bells are mid-C18, signed by *John Mowat* of the Old Aberdeen bell foundry (e.g. Cluny, 1746; Durris; Gartly; Hatton of Fintray, 1751; Kildrummy, 1760; Kirkton of Skene, 1735); the last ever cast there, in 1788, is at Kemnay East Church.

But there is little physical evidence of rebuilding or new work in south Aberdeenshire from the mid C17 until the early EIGHTEENTH CENTURY, when Kinneff Parish Church was rebuilt (1737–8). The QUAKERS established their settlement in 1662 at Kinmuck, a suitably remote place in which to enjoy freedom of religion and reflective of the conversion to Quakerism of several of the important local lairds, notably Alexander Jaffray, Provost of Aberdeen, who owned nearby Kingswells (Aberdeen), the Skenes and the Forbes of Aquhorthies. During this period the Episcopalian cause within the churches was very largely eclipsed but there were also two SECESSIONS of ministers from the Church of Scotland: the first in 1733 (to form the Associate Presbytery) and the second in 1761 (forming the Relief Presbytery) and both in due course subject to their own splits (e.g. the Burgher and Anti-Burgher churches, *see* for example the West Church at Midmar, 1832) before reunion in 1847 as the United Presbyterian Church. Small traces remain of the Secession church at Lynturk (1762). An even smaller Protestant sect, the Bereans, founded in Edinburgh in 1773, followed a modified form of Calvinism and committed to 'searching the scripture daily'. They had a chapel at Sauchieburn, near Luthermuir.

Completely NEW CHURCHES are common from the settled period after *c.* 1760, either because changing patterns of settlement required a new site for the parish church or because the fabric of the medieval or C17 buildings was by now so decayed as to demand a fresh start. One of the earliest is Tarland (1762) though this is now just a shell. A better representative is the church for Keithhall & Kinkell parish at Keithhall, which was designed in 1768 and built 1772–3. It is a quintessential example of the T-plan type, with a N aisle for the Kintore family and the position of the pulpit on the S wall clearly denoted outside by the arrangement of the windows. Drumblade is exactly contemporary and with many similar features. Then there is a steady period of rebuilding in the rural parishes in the last two decades of the C18: Birse (1779), Logie Coldstone (1780–81), Maryculter (1786–7), Midmar (1786–7), Migvie (*c.* 1787), Cluny (1789), Rayne (1789), Coull (1791), Glass (1791), Newmachar (1791), Premnay (1792), Leochel-Cushnie (1797–8), Cairnie (1802), Towie (1802–4), Glengairn (1804), Oyne (1807–8). The basic pattern of these preaching-boxes remains unvaried (and for a very late example *see* Benholm, 1832), with pitched roofs, entrances in the E and W gables, and windows (usually arched but also straight-headed) in a row along the S wall. One of the most elegant examples is the former West Church at Alford of 1804–5, which is still rectangular but shorter than average and with just three round-arched windows on its s front.

This is an appropriate moment at which to mention the ROMAN CATHOLIC CHURCHES, because they are unusually significant. The break with Rome in 1560 was followed by a long period of suppression under the Penal Laws but in the North-East of Scotland a measure of protection was afforded by the presence of the Gordon family. In the wilder, remoter parts of the region there are still chapels erected for clandestine worship in Moray (e.g. at Tynet, disguised as a barn, and the former seminary at Scalan, deep into Glenlivet) and numerous chapels were tucked away in the loyally Jacobite district of Glengairn. With the death of the Young Pretender in 1766 and recognition of the Hanoverians by Rome, a series of Catholic Relief Acts followed in 1778, 1791 and 1829. From now on new churches could afford to be (a little) more visible. All the same, St Peter in Justice Street, Aberdeen, of 1803–4, shows that confidence took time to build and it is secreted away from the street in a tiny courtyard. Our Lady of Snows (N) built *c.* 1805 in the wild mountains near Corgarff maintains the clandestine C18 tradition. The Scalan seminary was expanded and re-established at the House of Aquhorthies (Kemnay) in 1798–9. Catholic worship which had taken place discreetly in Deecastle subsequently moved to Bogieshiel on the Ballogie estate at Birse, where the Roman Catholic Innes family were lairds.

An early C19 painting shows that St Peter's, Aberdeen, perhaps conscious of its status as the first new Catholic church since the Reformation, had GOTHIC windows with simple reticulated tracery,* in marked contrast with the new parish churches of the later C18. In fact the church at Kirkton of Skene, built in 1801, also has pointed windows, although only in the 'Gothick' sense, with a mullion forming a Y in the head of the arch with astragals designed in a basket-weave pattern, suggestive of intersecting tracery. The same occurs at Kildrummy (1805–6 by the local mason *William Minto*, with a lovely full-height bow for the gallery stair) and nearby at Echt in 1804–6, which is an even more attractive but unscholarly assay at a medieval style. A slight projection at the centre of the front for the bellcote and single windows either side imply a nave and aisles when it is still a piend-roofed box that stands behind. The most interesting of these Georgian Gothic churches is Stonehaven Fetteresso of 1810–12 by *John Paterson*, with its castellated appearance emphasized by a curved front with central tower and stair-turrets, a conceit no doubt inspired by Fetteresso Castle but ably suited to the provision of an auditory church within with U-plan gallery.

Advances in the architectural appearance of parish churches are, as one would expect, the preserve of the wealthier burghs. The large new parish church at Huntly of 1804 by *Alexander Laing* is a more consciously classical church than its rural

*Whether this tracery was timber or stone or simply fictive painting in blind arches is unclear.

counterparts, of fine dressed ashlar and with an entrance in a moulded and pedimented surround, as well as Diocletian windows in the gables. It is outdone in the same town, however, by the Catholic church of 1833–4 by *William Robertson*, the brilliant Elgin architect, and like much of his work in an extremely refined classical style. This has a tower of Spanish Baroque type and inside an octagonal-plan nave, with shallow coffered dome roof and pedimented recess for the high altar. Robertson designed it in collaboration with the Rt. Rev. *James Kyle*, a priest-architect who was ordained in 1812 and was appointed Vicar Apostolic of the Northern District of Scotland and subsequently Bishop in 1828. He was responsible towards the end of his career for Inverurie (1852), this time in concert with Robertson's nephews *A. & W. Reid*, also of Elgin (with whom Kyle participated in the design of Buckie, Moray, at about the same time). Contemporary with Kyle is the Rev. *Walter Lovi*, who also seems to have contributed to the design of some new Catholic churches in the North-East, and certainly supervised construction of the church at Braemar in 1839; this is a completely Gothic church with lancet windows and especially inside where it has a (false) rib-vaulted nave and chancel, similar to Lovi's earlier church at Dufftown, Moray.

But the most significant of the churches before *c.* 1830 is the
31 North Church in Aberdeen by *John Smith*, with its Ionic portico and stunning two-stage tower modelled on the Choragic Monument of Lysicrates. It must surely have been influenced by St Giles, Elgin, Moray, completed in 1828 by *Archibald Simpson*, Smith's rival in the Neoclassical rebuilding of Aberdeen. Neither of these architects were dyed-in-the wool classicists, however, and Smith had already designed the South Parish Church at Aberdeen in Gothic style before competing with Simpson for the rebuilding of the East Church (i.e. the medieval choir of the Kirk of St Nicholas), which was executed to Simpson's design in 1835, although without his intended spire over the crossing. Simpson had previously ventured into this style for the Episcopal chapel (now Cathedral) in 1816–17; he then rebuilt the churches at Forgue and Kintore in a Gothic style in 1819 and rehearsed the same design for Drumoak in 1835. The principal elevations are composed to imply a nave and aisles within but these are only superficial nods to medieval churches for the interiors remain preaching-boxes. The same is true of the designs by *John Smith*, who adopted a Tudor Gothic style in his churches, from Banchory (East) Church (1824–5), Glenbervie (1824–6), Footdee (1828), Nigg (1828) and Auchenblae (1827–9) to Keig (1834–5), Tough (1837–8), Inverbervie (1837–9) and finally Aboyne (1842) and St Andrew, Inverurie (1841–2). The majority of the earlier ones have towers and almost all sport pinnacled buttresses at the angles of the rectangular plan and spiky bellcotes; some of the later examples also experiment with Perp-style (timber) tracery.

For an unsullied impression of the INTERIORS of these C18 and early C19 churches, the West Church at St Nicholas,
26 Aberdeen, is the place to begin. It was rebuilt to designs by *James Gibbs* in 1751–5 and inside has galleries around four sides and a

magnificent classical pulpit, largely designed by the joiners *Archibald Chessills* and *James Heriot*. As the burgh church it also has a very fine pew for the Provost, baldacchino-style with a pediment, in the Town Loft. There was also a corresponding King's Loft and these lofts are the superior equivalent of the elaborately carved lairds' lofts which began to appear in the late C16 and C17 in parish churches, raised above the rest of the congregation. But if southern Aberdeenshire's churches ever had anything to compare with the lofts at Cullen (Moray) and Pitsligo (N) then they are long since lost. More typical perhaps is the C18 private pew at Kirkton of Maryculter's church, enclosed on all sides and with a balustraded top for further privacy. Among the humbler parish churches the most remarkable interior is Kirkton of Glenbuchat church, completely intact with pine box pews (including one that could be opened out for celebration of Communion), pulpit, precentor's box and a fine laird's loft of 1828 with painted and marbled front for the 4th Earl Fife. Benholm of 1832 also remains unchanged.

27

After the proscription was made in 1580 against burial inside churches, the graveyards around the churches became the site for MONUMENTS AND MEMORIALS. Those for the C17 and C18 are quite numerous, especially if one includes the large class of grave-slabs and table tombs and, particularly from the C18, head-stones for merchants, craftsmen and farmers, sometimes with lively and naïve decoration of emblems of mortality, time and the tools of the deceased's trade. The best individual MONUMENTS are unsurprisingly those of the major landowners. The end of the medieval tradition is represented by the low-relief effigies in Kildrummy Old Parish Church of Alexander Forbes in his armour, and his lady, of the 1550s. In the same church is an interesting grave-slab for John Reid †1563, which uses the Roman alphabet and Scots in preference to Latin. Then at Kirkton of Glenbervie in the Douglas Aisle, there is the tomb-chest for William Douglas †1591, with much lively armorial carving and lettering, although this ornament may be later as the chest has a backplate dated 1680. These are quite rare survivals.

There are rather more monuments from the C17, beginning with an outstanding example in the wall monument erected to Lady Mary Keith †1620 at Benholm. This is far from metropolitan standards of funerary sculpture but instead a large example of the artisan traditions of carving in the North-East with their weird figure-carving. At St Nicholas, Aberdeen, there is a fine brass to Dr Duncan Liddel, the benefactor of Marischal College, who became Physician to the Court of Brunswick. He is depicted as the very essence of a Renaissance scholar in his study. Memorial brasses are rare in Scotland; this was made at Antwerp by *Gaspard Bruydegoms* in 1622. For the post-Restoration period, there is the memorial at Kinneff Old Parish Church for the Rev. Robert Grainger †1663, who is credited with concealing the royal regalia here when Cromwell's forces besieged Dunnottar Castle (q.v.) in 1651; Elizabeth Forbes, Lady Thornton, †1661 in the Thornton Aisle at Aberluthnot church, Marykirk; and the backplate of 1680

24

p. 32

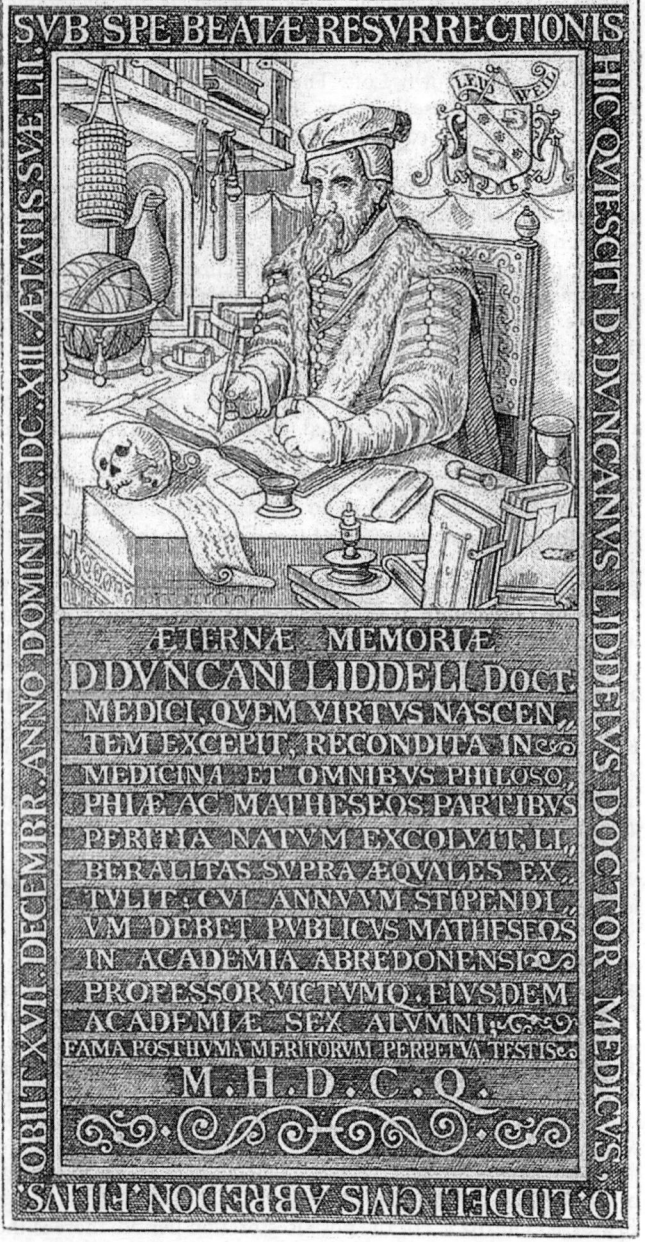

St Nicholas, Aberdeen, brass of Dr Duncan Liddel, 1622

to the Douglas tomb in the aisle at Kirkton of Glenbervie Old Church. These have crudely sculpted figures of angels and other emblems showing a basic understanding of Renaissance decoration and so too the rather remarkable remains of the monument to Alexander Garden, minister of Forgue and Professor of Philosophy at King's College, Aberdeen, †1674. Even the superior Baroque standing monument at St Machar's Cathedral to Bishop Patrick Scougal †1682, by *John Montgomery*, 1685, with its half-length portrait-bust in a frame – a typical style of monument for C17 clerics – is still very provincial in execution. So it is all the more remarkable to find at Benholm a large wall tablet, to Robert Scott †1690, which clearly shows in its design not only   25
the influence of publications of engravings of mid-C17 designs from France but also an awareness among local carvers of the best type of commemorative work by London sculptors.

There are no first-class monuments for the C18 in Aberdeenshire, even if one includes Aberdeen. Just two deserve attention and both are statuary monuments. The first is Ann Allardyce in the   28
West Church (St Nicholas), Aberdeen, by *John Bacon*, 1791; the second, the full-length figure of Bishop Skinner by *Flaxman*, 1820, in the Episcopal Cathedral. A little later, and very good, is the Grecian Doric monument to Robert Hamilton, Professor of Mathematics at Marischal College, of 1832–3 by *John Smith* in St Nicholas's churchyard, Aberdeen. MAUSOLEA of the C18 and early C19, as opposed to the fairly common walled burial enclosures for the lairds, are represented by three good examples: the fort-like Farquharson Mausoleum at Braemar, *c.* 1750; the exceptional Fraser Mausoleum at Cluny, designed by *James Byres*,   30
1808; and the powerful Neoclassical tomb of 1829 at Strathdon for the Forbes, very probably by *Archibald Simpson*, who designed Castle Newe for the family.

Churches after the Disruption

The DISRUPTION of the Church of Scotland occurred in 1843, when a significant minority of ministers (in fact all of the ministers in Aberdeen) and large numbers of ordinary worshippers left to found the FREE CHURCH OF SCOTLAND. A prediction of this split occurred in 1839 when the rejection of the appointment of the minister by the laird at Marnoch (N) led to the congregation walking out *en masse* and the construction of a new church at Huntly, which became the Free Church after the Disruption. The Triple Kirks at Aberdeen is the remarkable solution by *Simpson* to the exodus from the town's East, West and South Churches in 1843; in site, scale and appearance it is a very explicit challenge to the authority of St Nicholas's church, with each of the new Free churches housed in the three arms of the building and a mighty (brick) spire overall. Even in its partly demolished state it is impressive, and the confidence felt by the Free Church within a few short years may be judged from the building of the Free Church College in Alford Place in 1850 (by *Thomas*

Mackenzie). The wider objective, of an organization parallel with the Established Church, led the Free Church to provide a new church, manse and school in each parish. At Woodside, Aberdeen, the Frees actually returned to the pre-Disruption chapel of ease, while the Established Church built new accommodation. Sauchen was actually brought into being as a settlement by the building of the Free Church there. Its original church was by *James Henderson*, who with his brother William obtained almost all the Free Church work in Aberdeenshire in this period. Architecturally these churches are far from exciting. A good example is the former Free Church at Forgue (now Auchaber Parish Church) of 1843–4.

For the mid C19 attention should really be given instead to the activities of the SCOTTISH EPISCOPAL CHURCH, which after the Reformation had been in a position of conflict with the Established Church and damaged in the battles arising from the C17 Stuart kings' efforts to impose bishops and a new liturgy on the Scottish Church. Further tainted by their refusal to acknowledge William and Mary after 1688, the Episcopalians suffered, despite an Act of Toleration in 1712, for their Jacobite association. In the aftermaths of the risings of 1715 two-thirds of the Aberdeen Diocese's clergy were ejected and the 1719 Penal Act prevented ministry to more than nine worshippers at a time without declaring loyalty to the King. In 1745 the Episcopal chapels at Muchalls and Elsick and the chapel in the weavers' village of Drumlithie were burnt by Hanoverian forces in the wake of Culloden. Restrictions were enhanced to no more than four worshippers and by the time that the Penal Acts were repealed in 1792 Aberdeenshire was one of the few parts of Scotland with a significant Episcopalian presence (the first Episcopal bishop for the newly independent United States was ordained in Aberdeen in 1784); all the early C19 bishops appointed in the Episcopal Church came from the North-East. This explains the significance of the Episcopal Chapel (now Cathedral) at Aberdeen, designed by *Archibald Simpson* in 1816–17. In the rural areas there was an absolute shortage of Episcopal churches, and the revival can be traced in the new chapels established at Muchalls (1831) and Monymusk (1834, converted from the early C18 stone-polishing mill) and then by a sustained expansion from about 1845 until 1865 under Bishop William Skinner (whose father, Bishop John Skinner, led the Scottish Episcopalians in the late C18 and early C19). Important in the development and planning of the new churches was the influence of the Oxford Movement (or Tractarianism), which encouraged the introduction of vestments and ritual in the Anglican Church, and of the Ecclesiologists, who concerned themselves with reform in the design of churches. The Scottish Church, which had recognized the articles of the Anglican Church at the Synod of Laurencekirk in 1804, now followed suit.

In terms of church design the obvious difference in these churches is the presence of a chancel and the emphasis given to it, even in fairly modest buildings such as St Philip, Catterline, of 1848. Most of these early buildings are purely nave and lower chancel, without side aisles but with a central aisle inside, and with lancet windows and plate tracery and a bellcote, on the model of c13 E.E. (or First Pointed) or Dec churches approved by the Tractarians as the true representation of architecture in a purer age of faith. Christ Church, Huntly, by *Mackenzie & Matthews*, 1848, exhibits most of the features characteristic of these ecclesiologically 'correct' churches, including a pulpit integral with the wall of the chancel. The same firm designed the most elaborate Episcopalian church of this period at St John, Crown Terrace, Aberdeen, 1849–51, which has in addition a s aisle, porch and tower and inside the full complement of liturgical furnishings and decoration: aumbry, sedilia and a pulpit by the chancel arch. Of this partnership *James Matthews*, born in Aberdeen, had trained with George Gilbert Scott in 1839–44 and was among the first of the Scottish architects to design for the Episcopal Church. Another Aberdonian is *William Ramage,* architect of St Ternan, Banchory (1850–1) and St Margaret, Forgue (1856–8). The moving influence in the building of the estate chapel at Fasque was no doubt W.E. Gladstone M.P., who co-founded the Episcopal Trinity College, Glenalmond in 1847. The architect of both buildings was *John Henderson* and the Fasque chapel was opened by Gladstone's friend Samuel Wilberforce, newly appointed Bishop of Oxford. Henderson was the most prolific Scottish designer of new Episcopal churches at a time when many of the largest commissions for the Church were being handed to English architects. Another native with an impressive track record in this field was *Alexander Ross*. Although not heavily represented in southern Aberdeenshire, a good example of his work is St Laurence, Laurencekirk, 1871–2. But the most significant church is St Mary, Queens Cross, in Aberdeen of 1862–4, which makes use of structural polychromy in the contrasting colours of its masonry and is in an elaborate Continental Gothic style with patterned slates to the roof, wheel windows, rose windows, a flèche over the crossing, and (originally) a full polygonal apse. The designer appears to have been the incumbent, assisted by the local architect *Alexander Ellis*. The rebuilding of the Episcopal church at Stonehaven by *Robert Rowand Anderson* in 1875–7 is also immensely impressive, although part of its significance is due to later additions. Anderson's church also heralds the beginning of a consciously Scottish character for new churches by quoting, as Allan Maclean has noted, from the medieval nunnery at Iona, where Anderson was engaged in the consolidation of the ruins.

Meanwhile, it is interesting to note the effect of this Gothic Revival and Ecclesiology on the architecture of the PRESBYTERIAN CHURCHES. Strathdon Parish Church of 1852–3, again by *James Matthews* (who was himself a Presbyterian), is an especially good example of impeccable late c13 style with a cruciform plan, tower with broach spire and Geometrical tracery to the windows, yet inside still a traditional auditory arrangement. Also very notable for its spire in the Scott idiom is his former West Free Church in Union Street, Aberdeen, 1867–9. Yet just a few years earlier,

Matthews was still designing in an Italianate manner for Strathbogie Free Church at Huntly – perhaps an important way in which the Frees could still distinguish themselves architecturally from the Established Church (*see* also the extravagant Romanesque style of the former Congregational Church in Belmont Street, Aberdeen, of 1865 by *James Souttar*). Even so, the former Free Church (now Parish Church) at Braemar by *Robert Lamb* of Darlington in 1869–70 is very remarkable since it has a completely cruciform plan with spire, E apse and baptistery, i.e. externally it is absolutely indistinguishable from one of the more ambitious Episcopal churches. The Free churches at Lumphanan (1870 by *William Henderson & Sons*) and Aboyne (1868–9 by *J. R. Mackenzie*) have impressive towers with spires at the centre of their fronts; Mackenzie went even further at Glenmuick Parish Church, Ballater, in 1873–4, with a fully evolved Dec style with gabled apsidal front abutting a soaring tower with lucarned spire. His Rubislaw Parish Church at Aberdeen (1875–8) is similarly lavish and with an excellent interior of galleries on cast-iron columns and a pulpit with Gothic baldacchino and arches like sedilia as a screen across the purposeless apse.

The freedoms extended to the ROMAN CATHOLIC CHURCH in 1829 also produced a few more churches of confidently expressed identity. St Mary, Aberdeen, of 1858–60 by *Alexander Ellis*, became the Cathedral in 1878, when the Roman Catholic hierarchy was formally restored. As confirmation of that the splendid high Dec tower and spire were added to the church by *Ellis & Wilson*. At Stonehaven, the Catholic church by *J. R. Mackenzie*, 1877, is diminutive in comparison but thoroughly delightful with Geometrical tracery and spiky octagonal spire. The Relief Act of 1829 was followed by a move from the seminary at Aquhorthies, Kemnay, to Menzies House, Blairs, on the S side of the Dee. It grew significantly in the late C19 and embarked on a major rebuilding for both college (by *Ellis & Wilson*, 1892–1903) and chapel (by *Robert Curran*, 1899–1910). The combination of the college's Scots crown tower and the spire of the chapel is a memorable landmark on the South Deeside Road.

Churches after 1880

Towards the end of the C19 there is a significant rush of NEW CHURCHES of every denomination, especially in the rapidly expanding and wealthy suburbs of Aberdeen but also in those places where the advent of large numbers of summer visitors made acute the need for new places of worship. In terms of appearance the most notable aspect is a continued fidelity to Gothic but now less concerned with archaeological correctness of detail. Notable in this respect is the partnership of *Pirie & Clyne*, formed between *Arthur Clyne* and *John Bridgeford Pirie*, whose rogueish French Gothic manner reminds one of F. T. Pilkington but is altogether unique to this partnership. They finished off Rowand Anderson's church at Stonehaven in two

34

phases, 1885 and 1906, and also designed two other Episcopalian churches, both with idiosyncrasies: St Palladius at Drumtochty, in 1884–5, and St James, Union Street, in Aberdeen in 1887–8 (not fully completed). But the greatest work (including their church at Fraserburgh, N) is their first: Queen's Cross Church of 1879–81, which was designed for the Free Church, a reminder of the strength of the Frees in the late C19 and the wealth in the expanding suburbs of Victorian Aberdeen.

Roughly contemporary with the churches noted above, James Cooper, minister of the East Church in Aberdeen, founded the Aberdeen Ecclesiological Society. This was done in 1886, in concert with the architects *Charles Carmichael* (of *Matthews & Mackenzie*), *William Kelly* and the architect and metalworker *James Cromar Watt*. The purpose was the study of church worship, church architecture and the allied arts, with special reference to the Church of Scotland. The Society's foundation gave confirmation to practices already established in some new churches. Craigiebuckler Church, Aberdeen, of 1882–3, by *A. Marshall Mackenzie* (of *Matthews & Mackenzie*, the partnership he formed with James Matthews in 1877) is clear demonstration of the Ecclesiologists' influence in the interior layout of Presbyterian churches. It is cruciform, with shallow transepts (although for organ chamber and vestry) off an apsidal chancel, with the seating inside arranged collegiate-style. The church also derives some of the details of its features from local medieval examples, an important distinction from the essentially English sources of many Episcopal churches. This renewal of interest in the Scottish medieval churches was enhanced during this period by the publication of MacGibbon & Ross's survey of the *Ecclesiastical Architecture of Scotland* (in three volumes, 1896–7). There the claim was made that the late medieval churches formed 'a specially Scottish branch of Gothic architecture', and this respect for national examples of Gothic is found in Aberdeen's Holburn West Church of 1893 by *Brown & Watt*, where the pattern of three lancets and a vesica-shaped opening comes from the w front of Dunblane Cathedral (it is a motif that became very popular in many new urban churches of this date). It also comes out very clearly in Crathie Parish Church by *Mackenzie*, 1893–5, with motifs borrowed from Pluscarden and Jedburgh Abbeys. This church is also important as the parish church of the monarch of Scotland (Queen Victoria's first visit to Crathie's old church had been criticized by those who saw a conflict with her position as the Supreme Head of the Church of England but this is neatly resolved at Crathie by adherence to Presbyterian forms of worship while still allowing a chancel in the raised E end with high altar and a cruciform plan). Also significant is the design of Midstocket Parish Church (formerly St Ninian), Aberdeen, by *William Kelly*, 1898–1900. His antiquarian knowledge was further employed in the restoration of the medieval crypt of St Nicholas, Aberdeen, in 1898, with *Cromar Watt* executing the furnishings.

The above are all significant new works for the Established Church but most parish churches display the effect of ecclesiological reform in a spate of internal REORDERINGS, with the pulpit moved from the long s wall of rectangular-plan churches to the short E wall for a more 'traditional' E–W orientation, e.g. at Cluny (1893–4), Kirkton of Durris (1890s) and Drumblade (1900). Some go further with the addition of a full chancel for the communion table, as at Kintore in 1914–15 by *William Kelly*. The rearrangement at Dunnottar by *G. P. K. Young* of Perth in 1901–3 is especially ambitious, comprising not only a reorientation of the church but also an enlargement to a full cruciform plan. Several reorderings in Aberdeenshire churches were undertaken by *A. Marshall Mackenzie* and a few (e.g. Chapel of Garioch and Kemnay East Church, both 1920s) were given windows with intersecting tracery of the type found at Greyfriars Church, Aberdeen, which he rebuilt in 1901. It should be noted that some reorderings of this period (e.g. Auchaber Parish Church, Forgue) resulted from the reunions of denominations, for example the creation of the United Free Church in 1900 (formed by the union of the majority of the Free Church congregations with the United Presbyterian Church).

One other architect is of special importance for the late C19 in Aberdeenshire: *John Ninian Comper*. His father, John, moved from Sussex to Aberdeen and was ordained as a priest in the Episcopal Church. He became rector of St John's Church, the church designed by James Matthews (*see* above), and was an active member of the High Church group among the Episcopalians, advocating the revival of Scottish church liturgy and had Ninian educated at the Episcopalian College at Glenalmond. John Comper also founded St Margaret of Scotland in the Gallowgate slums in 1867, for which *Matthews* provided a simple chapel-cum-school in 1870. It was the rebuilding of this which gave Ninian Comper (in partnership with *Bucknall*) his first commission in 1889, although the full extent of his ambitions for the church remained unrealized and were confined to the addition of a W extension (St Nicholas's Chapel) with a genuine stone vault. His second commission in Aberdeen was the Conventual Chapel for the Episcopalian Community of St Margaret in 1891–2. The community had been founded by J. M. Neale in 1855 and brought to Aberdeen by John Comper. His son's work here draws very explicitly on late medieval Scottish sources, specifically the C15 choir of Holy Rood, Stirling, and this comes through even more forcefully in the Episcopal church at Braemar, 1899–1901, where he quotes from Pluscarden, Iona and the Greyfriars Church in Aberdeen. It is also evident in the essentially Scottish character of the s aisle added to St Margaret of Scotland, Gallowgate, in 1908.

Despite the prevalence of Gothic outlined above there are numerous CLASSICAL CHURCHES in Aberdeen, a style for which granite was arguably better suited. Typically for the period, there is a certain amount of freedom in the motifs. A good example is the former St Nicholas United Presbyterian Church on Holburn Street, Aberdeen, by *Ellis & Wilson*, 1887, and the same firm are also responsible for the Bon Accord Free Church on Rosemount

Viaduct, 1895–6, with its Thomson-esque domed towers. Others of note are the Melville United Free Church, Skene Street, by *Brown & Watt*, 1901–3, and the former Unitarian church (now Kingdom Hall), Skene Street, by *D. & J. R. McMillan*, 1905–6. But the best example is of course the former South Free (now St Mark's Parish) Church of 1892 by *Matthews & Mackenzie* with its grand Baroque dome and Corinthian portico, dominating the group of late C19 buildings along Rosemount Viaduct; also in a classical style by the same firm is Skene Street Congregational Church, 1885–6, and the former Trinity Free Church, 1890–2. In the wider area, there is the classical church at Lumsden (now Auchindoir Parish Church) by *R. Duncan* of Huntly, 1889–90. Standing completely outside either the Gothic or the classical tradition is the Salvation Army Citadel in Castlegate, Aberdeen, by *James Souttar*, 1893–6 which wholeheartedly adopts the Scots Baronial of contemporary public buildings.

One of the last of the fine new churches before the First World War is St Thomas (Episcopal) at Aboyne, 1907–9 by *Fryers & Penman* of Largs for the Laird of Glen Tanar, which faithfully copies a late C13 parish church in Leicestershire. The other is Sacred Heart (R.C.) at Torry, Aberdeen, 1910–11 by *Charles J. Ménart*, an exemplar of the emergence of the Romanesque as an appropriate style for the C20, valued at least in part for the possibilities of creating dramatic spatial effects inside without need for expensive decoration. The INTERWAR period offered few opportunities for new buildings. The major event was *Comper*'s reconstruction of the Episcopal Cathedral in Aberdeen, one of the last significant episodes in the Gothic Revival before the Second World War. Perhaps rather more typical of new churches in a Gothic idiom at this time is the spare style of the three churches at Aberdeen by *A. G. R. Mackenzie* of *A. Marshall Mackenzie & Son* (St John's Church for Deaf People, 1935–6; St Mary, King Street, Links, 1937–9; and St Ninian Episcopal Church, 1936) and of High Church, Hilton, Aberdeen, 1935–6 by *George Bennett Mitchell*. Mitchell was also responsible for several reorderings in parish churches in this period. Some of these are the consequence of the reunion of United Free Church congregations with the Church of Scotland in 1929, which elsewhere resulted in the redundancy of some older parish churches in favour of a more comfortable former Free Church (as happened at Kirkton of Glenbuchat and Braemar). One of the best remodellings of this period is the church at Echt. This was done by *William Kelly*, at a point in his career when he was largely retired, had been given an honorary doctorate by the University and contented himself with a role as consultant architect to Viscount and Lady Cowdray at Dunecht; his changes at Echt go hand in hand with his other works for them. The style of the ceiling at Echt is derived from the nave of St Machar's Cathedral, and Kelly's church work, including his restoration of King's College Chapel, 1930–31, is often distinguished by the quality of the panelling and other woodwork. The earliest POST-WAR church is South St Nicholas, of 1952 by *A. G. R. Mackenzie*, for

38

15

the new housing estate at Kincorth, Aberdeen. Externally it is remarkably domestic.

The defining feature of the new churches of the very end of the C19 and beginning of the C20 is the richness of their FURNISHINGS. This is particularly the case in the Episcopal and Roman Catholic churches, where a full array of liturgical furnishings might be designed in concert with the building or gradually acquired as gifts from wealthy parishioners. Superlative examples are the Episcopal churches in Aberdeen. St Andrew (now the Episcopal Cathedral), has fittings by *Lorimer* as well as *Comper*, notably the lavish baldacchino indicative of the Ecclesiologists' emphasis on the altar as the sacred focus of Eucharistic ritual. St John, also mostly by Comper, has an exceptionally interesting scheme of wall decoration of 1903 by *J. A. H. Hector*, a local painter who became principal Lecturer in Art at Aberdeen University following a period at the Académie Julian in Paris, where Les Nabis were formed – a connection which must explain Hector's precocious Divisionist technique. Chancel screens are an increasingly common feature in Episcopal churches from the late C19 onwards and none is finer than Comper's at St Margaret, Braemar, 1909–21 complete with rood loft. Other important Episcopal interiors are St Kentigern, Ballater; St Mary, Inverurie; St Thomas, Aboyne; and St James, Stonehaven; and, among the Catholic churches, Huntly, redecorated by *Earley & Co.* of Dublin, and the chapel at Blairs College, also originally painted by Earley but lavishly reworked in marble by C. J. Ménart. In the Presbyterian churches the principal furnishings, beside the galleries for the congregation, remained the pulpit, communion table, ministers' chairs and font. Nevertheless this could still result in rich furnishings, e.g. at Crathie where the donors were members of the royal family. The former Parish Church at Glass was given a fine set of furnishings in 1903 when it was extended by *John Robertson* of Inverness, principally a fine pulpit in Scots Gothic style with domed canopy, and pews with moulded ends.

STAINED GLASS appears from the mid C19 onwards, but to begin with is confined to the Episcopal and Roman Catholic churches. The majority of windows in Aberdeenshire and Aberdeen are at first by the principal English firms of glass-stainers, who had led the revival of techniques of staining from *c.* 1830. St Andrew's Episcopal church at Aberdeen was the first to include painted (rather than stained) glass in 1839, with a window depicting the Last Supper after Carlo Dolci, supplied by the London maker *William Collins*. It is now at St Devenick, Bieldside, Aberdeen. Then comes the glass at St John's Episcopal church, Aberdeen, by *Wailes* of Newcastle *c.* 1850–60 and later by *Wailes & Strang* at St Mary's (R.C.) Cathedral and Drumlithie's Episcopal church, non-figurative glass in the chapel at Fasque House and windows at Inverurie Episcopal church. Works by other leading English makers for Episcopalian churches include windows by *John Hardman & Co.* e.g. at St Andrew's Episcopal Cathedral, Aberdeen, 1881–3, 1899, 1902. One of the first glass-stainers in Scotland was *Daniel Cottier*, based in Glasgow, who

worked in the Pre-Raphaelite style he developed during his training in London in the 1860s with William Morris. Cottier supplied
the glass for the West Free Church (Langstane Kirk), Aberdeen,
in 1869, an early instance of glass in a Free Church but importantly it is purely decorative, free of overt religious iconography.
The first extensive use of figurative glass in a Presbyterian church
is, perhaps unsurprisingly, at St Machar's Cathedral, Aberdeen,
mostly of the early 1870s. The division of labour there was
between Cottier (exclusively depicting saints) and *Clayton & Bell*,
another of the major English firms, who designed the w window
with figures of Christ and the Apostles under Gothic canopies.
The same makers were also responsible for the 1870s windows
in King's College Chapel, combining Old and New Testaments
scenes, and windows at St James, Stonehaven. *James Ballantine*,
of Edinburgh, was another pioneer of Scottish glass. There is an
early window by him of the Good Shepherd (1875) in St
Margaret's Episcopal church at Forgue but his glass at the former
Carden Place United Presbyterian church, Aberdeen, 1882, again
avoids figures in favour of depiction of the flowers mentioned in
the Bible.

Only after 1880 is there a gradual softening in attitude among
the generality of Presbyterian churches towards Christian iconography in glass, partly as an appropriate medium for memorials.
An early instance, and significantly in a new church planned on
ecclesiological lines, is the glass of 1885 by *Morris & Co.* at
Craigiebuckler Parish Church, Aberdeen, again figures of saints,
to *Burne-Jones*'s design. There is hardly any work by the other
Glasgow firms who dominated Scottish glass production in the
late C19. Cottier's pupil *Stephen Adam* is represented in Aberdeen
only in the 1870s windows depicting the Seven Incorporated
Trades in New Trinity Hall, though the work there is up to his
usual standard. Adam's contemporaries were *W. & J. J. Kier*, who
executed a window in the same building; *Guthrie & Wells*, another
important Glasgow firm, are responsible for a single window at
Gilcomston South Church. There is also the glass by *Comper*,
designed in concert with his architectural work at St Margaret's
Convent, Old Aberdeen, and the Episcopal church of St Margaret,
Braemar, where the memorial window to Queen Victoria is a
good example of the contemporary taste for religious and historical figures of local significance. The same is true of the glass at
the rebuilt Greyfriars Church at Aberdeen designed by *C. E.
Kempe*, 1903, in the manner of medieval glass with the original
donor depicted. More good Kempe glass, or rather glass by his
firm, designed by *J. W. Lisle*, is at St Ninian, the Episcopal estate
chapel for Mar Lodge.

The quality of glass in Aberdeenshire's church windows only
becomes significantly more interesting about 1900 with the emergence of *Douglas Strachan* as the premier Scottish designer for
the first half of the C20. He was born in Aberdeen in 1875,
undertook a tour of Europe in 1898 and then returned to his
home town. He was initially a painter and examples of his
wall decorations survive in St Machar's Episcopal church,

Bucksburn, Aberdeen (and the Music Hall, Union Street, Aberdeen). His first foray into glass is the window in the crypt of the East Church (St Nicholas) executed with the encouragement of J. Cromar Watt, who was then at work on the restoration of the chapel. In the same space is the only work in Aberdeenshire by the brilliant designer *Christopher Whall*. Despite his misgivings about the St Nicholas window, Strachan's reputation grew quickly enough to secure him commissions across churches of all denominations: St James's Episcopal church, Aberdeen, 1899– 1900; the Boer War memorial window at the Holburn Chapel of Ease, Aberdeen, 1903; Queen's Cross (Free) Church; Midstocket Parish Church; Gilcomston South Church; then windows for St Machar's Cathedral from 1908; and, most importantly of all, King's College Chapel, for which he supplied windows over three decades, beginning in 1903. Of his approximately thirty windows in the area covered by this volume, most are found in the Aberdeen churches but a notable and early example of his work in the rural parishes is at Glass, paid for by the Chicago friends of the stupendously wealthy laird, Alexander Geddes. The single figure of David at Banchory Episcopal church, a war memorial of 1915, is also very fine. Late works apart from the King's College Chapel windows include the window at St James (Episcopal) Stonehaven of the Baptism of Christ, 1939.

Few other early–mid-C20 stained glass artists come close in quality but especially notable are the excellent 1937–53 windows by *J. M. Aiken*, another Aberdonian, in the West Free Church (Langstane Kirk), Aberdeen. The windows at Insch Parish Church by *William Meikle & Sons*, c. 1930, are agreeable examples of the early C20 Glasgow style of glass carried on, as is the 1930s Crucifixion by *James Steedman Hamilton* at St Mary, King Street, Aberdeen. Two artists working in the Arts and Crafts tradition, and always worth looking out for, are *Margaret Chilton*, a pupil of Christopher Whall, and *Marjorie Kemp*. They set up in partnership in Edinburgh in the 1920s but most of their work in Aberdeenshire is late 1930s and after (*see*, for example, their windows at Cults Parish Church, Aberdeen). Strachan's tradition is continued in the third quarter of the C20 by *Gordon Webster*, based in Glasgow, with the same use of small sections of intensely coloured hand-blown glass but a more abstracted approach to figure drawing, and *William Wilson*, a former pupil of Ballantine's in Edinburgh. Wilson's chief designer was *John Blyth* and he is probably responsible for the windows of the 1960s and 1970s in Aberdeenshire, by when Wilson had largely retired owing to blindness. The most important collection of work by Wilson is the series of Old and New Testament windows at Craigiebuckler Church, 1961–71, crowded with his familiar gaunt-faced figures, with much cross-hatching in the drawing and set against clear glazing. The continuation of this tradition comes to an end with the revolution in designing in a freer, more abstract and more symbolic style allied to new techniques of glass-making. The most important glass-stainers in the North-East of Scotland of the last fifty years have been the artists associated with the

Pluscarden Abbey workshop (e.g. at Huntly Parish Church), working largely with *dalles-de-verre*, the thick chunks of deeply coloured glass bedded in cement. Among current makers perhaps the most interesting is the Glasgow-trained *Shona McInnes*, who designed the Oilmen's window in St Nicholas Kirk, Aberdeen.

Finally, a review of the best C19 and C20 MONUMENTS. There are a number of the usual white-on-black tablets common to the mid C19 (e.g. at Strathdon) and a rather better example in the Episcopal Cathedral to Lt-Col. R. W. T. Gordon, †1886, with scenes of his Egyptian adventures. The memorial to Sir John Gladstone (†1851) in the chapel at Fasque by *Alexander Munro* is also notable, showing Sir John and his wife in pious contemplation: they were noted for their Low Church evangelicalism, in contrast to William Ewart Gladstone's High Anglicanism. There are good monuments in the municipal cemeteries of Aberdeen at Nellfield (e.g. William Alexander, by *J. Pittendrigh MacGillivray*, 1894) and Allenvale (James Saint †1890, by *J. B. Pirie*) and a fine late example of a mausoleum at Banchory-Devenick, for the family of the industrialist David Stewart, owner of the Comb Works on Hutcheon Street, Aberdeen, built in 1895. Of individual monuments in churches, churchyards and cemeteries the following are to be singled out: the wall tablet to the Rev. George Duncan at Maryculter by *Peter Macgregor Chalmers* with coloured mosaics and a frame in Glasgow style, 1901; *Comper*'s Calvary monument to his father, 1901, at St Peter's Cemetery, Old Aberdeen; then the superlative Elphinstone monument outside King's College Chapel by *Henry Wilson*, designed in 1911, as good a product of the 'New Sculpture' movement as one can find anywhere; war memorial tablets at Glass by *Lorimer*, 1916; the outlandish Italian-inspired Coats memorial at Aboyne, 1918, by *Percy Portsmouth*; the tomb chest to Viscount Cowdray (†1927) at Echt by *William Kelly*; headstones at Corgarff attributed to *Lutyens*; and the series of busts to the monarchs at Crathie by *Emil Fuchs* and *William Reid Dick*. 41

CASTLES AND TOWER HOUSES
BY DAVID W. WALKER

The earliest fortified places of which substantial remains survive are MOTTES raised from the late C12. Usually formed from mounds or ridges, enclosed by palisades or occasionally stone walls, their slopes were often steepened and earth excavated from around the base to form a defensive ditch. The lower part of a ridge, less stoutly defended, and known as the bailey, might provide secondary accommodation. Such ridges formed naturally within river confluences and were often selected as offering water and sanitation as well as protection. Some mottes became administrative centres for a wider area. Enclosed by the Don and the Urie, Inverurie's motte-and-bailey raised by David Earl of the Garioch *c.* 1180 survives within the churchyard where the

town once stood. At Huntly, capital of Strathbogie, the motte
survives within the confluence of the Deveron and the Bogie, the
bailey now the site of the present castle. At Kintore a motte – the
capital messuage, or *caput*, of the Thanage of Kintore – survived
until *c.* 1859. Prominent mottes survive at Cunningar (Midmar),
Durris, Fichlie (Glenkindie), Invernochty (Strathdon, the *capital
messuage* of the Thanage of Strathdon) and Lumphanan, and
there were formerly many others, their locations often of such
strategic value that they were developed in later centuries –
Caskieben (Keith Hall), Dunnottar, Fetteresso, Hallgreen and
Lesmoir (Rhynie). Such sites' defensive capabilities are occasionally recorded in a name such as Castlehill, Aberdeen or Castlehill,
Kildrummy, where the medieval township – although not the
church – has long since vanished.

The first STONE CASTLES date from the early C13. Kildrummy
was built by Alexander II's lieutenant in the North, Bishop
Gilbert of Moravia, some distance from the earlier motte on a
large promontory protected by sheer drops and with excellent
freestone nearby. It is a polygonal D-shaped enclosure, very big
by Scottish standards at 185 m. by 210 m. The entrance is in the
centre of the curve, with drum towers at the angles, each in itself
defensible. The largest towers at the rear were the bishop's own
– a French-style donjon based on that at Coucy – and that of the
castle warden. Between them a hall and kitchen extend across
much of the rear flank, and within the courtyard is a remarkably
large chapel, the more surprising since it was lit by tall windows
where its E end projected through the curtain wall. From *c.* 1303,
as a result of English occupation, Kildrummy had an English-
style gatehouse. Alexander II was probably also responsible for
Kincardine Castle (Fettercairn), 35 m. square. Although little
survives beyond foundations its deer dykes enclose 800 ha. After
Gilbert died in 1245 the Earls of Mar became custodians of
Kildrummy but, perhaps mindful of the threat that they might
pose, Alexander III granted part of Mar to the de Lundins. They
built Coull which, although much smaller (35 m. by 40 m.) and
constructed in rubble, was remarkably similar, a D-shaped
enceinte on a plateau with a donjon although without a comparable chapel; like Kildrummy it gained a gatehouse *c.* 1303.

Lauriston was built as a polygonal castle of enceinte *c.* 1260,
parts of its N and W walls being of that date; it was re-fortified
by Edward III in 1336. At Thornton a drum tower stands on
boulder foundations reputedly those of a predecessor belonging
to an early C14 fortalice. The much larger Dunnottar occupies a
peninsula which was fortified as an administrative centre for the
Mearns in the C7. During the early C13 there was a wooden tower
with palisade; a church (1276) and castle were burned by Wallace
in 1297 and the site re-fortified by Edward III in 1336. The gatehouse and curtain wall were begun in the 1390s, as was the tower
house within.

South Aberdeenshire has an exceptionally dense distribution
of distinguished TOWER HOUSES and the form persists as the
dominant symbol of lordship right up to the 1660s. The first

tower houses were perhaps built in the mid C13. They were simple rectangles with massively thick walls, small windows and the entrance often raised above ground, reached by a wooden stair. They had forecourts containing 'laigh [low] biggings' which provided more domestic accommodation. Dunnideer, on the site of the prehistoric hill-fort overlooking Insch, was perhaps built by the Balliols as the Garioch's *capital messuage* before 1260. This tower measured 15 m. by 12.5 m., its walls 2 m. thick; its very early date seems confirmed by the absence of internal vaulting. No tower houses appear likely to have been built during the Wars of Independence as Wallace and Bruce's policy was to destroy fortifications to prevent them from being garrisoned by their enemies, but afterwards it became important to defend communication routes into Moray. The tower of Drum on Deeside was probably begun by William Irvine *c.* 1323. This tower is 15.8 m. by 11.9 m. (a 4:3 ratio), its walls in well-coursed masonry 3.5 m. thick, with rounded angles but few openings; its entrance is at first floor. Internally it is vaulted for strength and fire resistance. The ground floor contains cellarage, the first floor the hall with a timber entresol providing further accommodation; the single turnpike stair enters the hall through a screens passage at the 'low' end, while the laird sat at the 'high' end with his back to the fire. Hallforest for Robert Keith *c.* 1324 is smaller, 14.5 m. by 9 m. with walls 2 m. thick, but again comprises two superimposed vaults – there may have been a third as at Drum – both of which probably had entresols. Again entrance has been above ground in the second vault, and there seems evidence of a SE turnpike, with the hall fireplace on the W. At Hallforest the kitchen hearth was in the E wall, the two fires ensuring even heat throughout the structure. Drum and Hallforest, together with the coeval but much-altered Skene,* guarded the routes between the Garioch and the Mounth. Although subsequently rebuilt, the comparable dimensions of the Leslies' Balquhain probably dates it to the early C14.

The North-East's largest rectangular tower was Kindrochit in Braemar, Robert II granting licence for its construction to his brother-in-law Sir Malcolm Drummond in 1390. It was 19.5 m. by 13 m., its walls 3 m. thick. Associated with it is the earliest HALL HOUSE (or PALACE-BLOCK) in North-East Scotland, where Robert stayed when using Kindrochit as a hunting lodge. It was originally 30 m. by 9 m., its walls again 3 m. thick, with square towers at its NW, NE and SW angles; the first-floor hall was raised over unvaulted cellars. About 1429–40 Alexander, 1st Lord Forbes also built a palace-block as an adjunct to the tower house of Druminnor Castle. Rising from a basement within embanked ground, it measures 22 m. by 10 m., a drum tower 5 m. in diameter within the castle courtyard containing one of the entrances and a broad turnpike stair. The walls are 2 m. thick, both basement and ground floor vaulted. Although the kitchen is at ground floor, a handsome fireplace within the 'Happy

*Skene is 11.9 m. by 7.8 m., like Hallforest a 3:2 ratio.

Room' at this level indicates that it formed part of the living accommodation. The main hall seemingly had its fireplace in the courtyard flank rather than the end gable. The builders at Druminnor, *John Kemlock* and *William of Ennerkype*, perhaps built the 1st Earl of Huntly's palace-block at Huntly Castle *c.* 1455–70. This again rose from a basement within embanked ground, its main block 23.2 m. by 11 m. but with two drum-towers, the larger 10.7 m. in diameter protruding outwith the courtyard, and entrance being gained by a smaller stair-tower within the court. This was the origin of the Z-plan which became common in tower houses later, but although the palace-block's walls were nearly 2 m. thick like Druminnor's it was never truly defensive.

The development of tower houses with one or two wings or 'jambs' extending from the main block to form L-, Z- or U-plans offered major practical advantages. Firstly they improved security, for the jambs protected the main block's flanks and *vice versa*, so attackers could no longer hide beneath overhanging parapets. Secondly, they offered more flexible accommodation. Thus overlooked, entrances could be formed within a jamb at ground floor rather than first, and a generous main stair could be provided rising to the principal (first-floor) accommodation. It became *de rigueur* to have a hierarchical sequence of principal apartments: a hall leading to an outer chamber and then an inner chamber – the laird's bedroom – often within a jamb, access to each determined by the laird himself. A much tighter turret stair within the angle between the entrance jamb and main block usually provided access to the upper storeys, the laird's wife sometimes having her own suite at second floor. Although North-East Scotland was fairly slow to adopt the new plans, the ingenuity of local masons resulted in distinctive variations. The first L-plans were built within existing fortified enclosures: Huntly's 'Auld Warke' (mid-C15, with main block 15.8 m. by 11 m. orientated E–W and SW jamb 7.9 m. by 5.8 m., their walls as much as 3 m. thick); Dunnottar (mid-C15); Elphinstone's Tower, Kildrummy (*c.* 1507–13) and Lauriston's tower house (1531). Elsewhere simple rectangles persisted, even for large tower houses, e.g. Castle Fraser (begun *c.* 1454) and Pitcaple (built for the Leslies *c.* 1470). Smaller examples include Kemnay *c.* 1540 and Corgarff *c.* 1546–60.

Wider adoption of L- and Z-plans occurs from the MID-SIXTEENTH CENTURY, when several factors encouraged tower house construction in the North-East. The Reformation split Scotland into broadly pro-English Protestant and pro-French Catholic factions; it also resulted in transfer of church lands to existing and new landowners. This, combined with reduced taxation under the regents who governed Scotland during the reigns of Mary Queen of Scots and the young James VI, resulted in propitious economic circumstances. Outwith existing enceintes, the earliest datable L-plan is Craig, built in 1548 for William Gordon. Its main block orientated N–S measures 12.8 m. by 10.7 m. and its NE entrance jamb 7.3 m. by 6 m. Its walls are near-blind, rising 12.2 m. to the wall-heads; it has a caphouse, but very early on (perhaps during construction) the wall-walks were roofed in. Craig is not only the first but the least altered of a group of tower houses identified by Douglas Simpson as having been built for prominent Catholics and which, through similarities of plan and detail, may be ascribed to the same master masons. Tradition suggests that these masons were the *Conns* of Auchry (N) and certain constructional features imply that they were either French or French-trained. At Craig as at Gight (a Gordon house), Delgatie and Towie Barclay (all N), the entrance leads into a small vaulted vestibule, carved with Symbols of the Passion; a corridor then leads to a turnpike centred between the main block and jamb against the long rear wall. Here, despite its considerable diameter, it can rise through the structure's full height rather than simply to first floor. At Craig the hall is altered but, assuming that it corresponded to other examples in the group, it probably had a vaulted entresol recess serving as an oratory. Colquhonnie (Strathdon) has the same plan-type and may also be by the *Conns*.

A much more radical development of the L-plan, again aimed at addressing the problem of the stair, was taken at Crathes and Monymusk *c*. 1550. At Crathes, the angle formed by the main block containing the first-floor hall and the jamb containing smaller rooms is almost completely infilled, resulting in a plan which is nearly – but not quite – square. The infill block contains the main turnpike staircase, relatively tightly planned, and an additional small room at each level. Monymusk represents a development of Crathes. It is broader and deeper, so the rooms within the infill block are more usefully sized. Its entrance is better-placed within the jamb's short flank, leaving attackers no place to hide. In the event of break-in, they would have had to fight their way around a corridor rather than finding themselves – as at Crathes – at the main stair's foot with access throughout the building. The Crathes–Monymusk plan appears only once more, at Balbegno (1569). Here the infill block is relatively small but the entrance and staircase arrangements are remarkably complicated, clearly designed to confuse intruders. From the entrance vestibule within the jamb, a cranked corridor leads back through the infill block to the main stair, rising to first floor. A turnpike then leads from first to second, and a tighter turret stair to the attic. The first-floor hall within the main block is groined and vaulted in two compartments, its dimensions near-identical to Towie Barclay's, and constructed in the same French manner, suggesting the *Conns'* involvement. Balbegno also has a sacrament house like that at Delgatie. That the Crathes-type plan does not appear again may reflect drainage problems inherent in big caphouses and wall-walks, it seeming significant that all three houses' upperworks have been reconstructed.

In the event, the Z-plan prevailed for many tower houses within our area. There are, however, only two C16 examples of a rectangular main block flanked by rectangular jambs, and these might hardly be considered typical. Both at the Douglases'

47

Tilquhillie (1576) and the Johnstons' Caskieben (Keith Hall), one jamb is small but the other is comparable in size with the main block. Both houses are plain, both have turnpikes in the angles and both are un-turreted. Caskieben's plan is similar to Arnage (N) before its reconstruction and has elevations of flat planes alternating with turnpike stair-towers as at Barra (N), features which suggest *Thomas Leiper* as master mason. Since at Tilquhillie as at Caskieben the entrance is in a flat plane set diagonally within one angle, it follows that *Leiper* may have been responsible for Tilquhillie also.

Much more common, however, and primarily associated with tower houses of the Gordon family, was a Z-plan with a square or rectangular jamb usually at the NW containing the doorway in the re-entrant flank and a main stair rising up to the principal (first) floor, and at the diagonally opposite angle a drum tower, consisting of bedchambers. The decisive influence on this fashion among the Gordons appears to have been Huntly Palace's lavish reconstruction by the 4th Earl – the second of its three phases of construction, in 1551–4. If we follow these houses' development, the main block progressively transforms from a long rectangle into a square; the entrance jamb grows with each iteration to provide further accommodation above the stairway rising from ground to first floor; and the drum tower reaches an optimum diameter and then expands no further. Thus at Beldorney, probably built for George Gordon in the late 1550s shortly after Huntly was remodelled, the three-storey main block 13 m. N–S by 7.5 m. deep has a NW jamb 3.5 m. square, and SE drum tower of 6.5 m. diameter. At the Leiths' Harthill *c.* 1554–70 the three-storey main block, 12.5 m. by 8.3 m., is flanked by a NE entrance jamb 6.8 m. by 5.3 m., and SW drum tower 6.8 m. in diameter. Then at Midmar, another Gordon house probably built by *George Bell c.* 1560–70, the four-storey main block 10 m. square is framed by a NW entrance jamb 6.5 m. square and SE drum tower 8.5 m. in diameter. At Castle Fraser, the original tower house of *c.* 1454, four-storey rectangular, was enlarged *c.* 1563–76 with a new NW entrance jamb 9.8 m. by 9.3 m. – i.e., almost as large as Midmar's main block – and SE drum tower again 8.5 m. across. Pitcaple was also remodelled in the mid C16: here the rectangular block of *c.* 1470 gained two circular jambs, the SE 3.5 m. in diameter containing the turnpike stair; the NW, although larger at 5.2 m., is modest relative to the other castles' drum towers, perhaps because the main block is so large.

Two smaller Z-plan towers built anew also have circular jambs, perhaps to reduce the requirement for freestone dressings. At William Gordon's Terpersie, 1561, the three-storey main block is only 8.5 m. by 5.4 m.; despite its size, its ground floor was originally vaulted. The main block contains the entrance in the E flank's S end, and the stair – a straight flight – is formed within the S end gable. The NE and SW jambs are identical at 5.1 m. diameter. At the Calders' Asloun the main block is 10.5 m. by 7.5 m., again vaulted at ground floor. Only the SE jamb survives, but it too is just over 5 m. diameter, and has contained the entrance and a turnpike to first floor. Although similarly small, Corse for William Forbes (1581) is a remarkable combination of the L- and Z-plans. Most of its accommodation was in the main block. The jamb contained the stair from ground to first floor, and the smaller of the two drum towers at the junction of the main block and the jamb contained the turnpike to the upper storeys.

In relation to these lesser tower houses we should consider Abergeldie c. 1560 and Pitfichie which is later C16. At Abergeldie, built for a branch of the Gordons, the four-storey main block is 10.8 m. by 8.7 m., both the ground-floor services and first-floor hall being vaulted; the entrance is in the long s wall near the angle with the s w drum tower, which is 4.5 m. in diameter and contains the turnpike.* At Pitfichie the main block's dimensions are only slightly different – 11.5 m. by 8 m. – but the drum tower is much larger at 7 m. The entrance was originally in the same position as Abergeldie's but the stair's planning is more sophisticated. It rises in the angle between the main block and the drum tower, diagonally opposite the entrance. It has been so cleverly considered beforehand that not until well above ground does it break out from the walls into a corbelled turret. Nevertheless after construction was well advanced the client, a member of the Hurrie family, decided that the entrance was too near the stair's foot for safety. Moving the entrance necessitated formation of a corridor cutting across the kitchen and guardroom. Balfluig and Lickleyhead are of similar size and date to Abergeldie and Pitfichie, but have rectangular rather than circular jambs. A distinctive feature is the manner in which these jambs rise considerably above the main block's wall-head, although the overall height of the roofs is kept consistent. The additional storeys within these jambs compensate for accommodation lost lower down in providing a big main stair rising from ground floor to first. In his analysis of Abergeldie, Douglas Simpson noted similarities with Balfluig and concluded that the two were probably designed by the same mason. A further resemblance between Balfluig and Lickleyhead – both for cadets of the Forbes of Monymusk – and with Monymusk itself appears evident.

Abergeldie and Pitfichie anticipate Birse (c. 1585) and Westhall (c. 1590). Birse, for Sir William Gordon of Cluny, has been much reconstructed. Its main block was relatively small (8.8 m. by 6.6 m.) but its ground floor was vaulted. The entrance was near the s e jamb, which was seemingly elliptical rather than circular, and contained a turnpike rising through its full height to second floor. Westhall for Sir Alexander Abercromby of Pitmedden may have been conceived identically, and the similarity of detail, particularly its key-pattern corbelling, implies that it was built by the same mason. Its main block measures approximately 9 m. by 5 m. and its elliptical s e jamb is 4.1 m. across its major axis. However, unlike Birse it has a second rectangular jamb at its s w angle, 4.3 m. by 5 m., which may be original, an alteration during

---

*Old Balmoral (dem. c. 1856) was apparently similar on plan.

construction or a very early addition, and which results in an extremely irregular U-plan. From these houses it would seem that by the late C16 the major upheaval of the Reformation had passed: the defensive qualities of jambs which had encouraged the Z-plans were much less necessary but they still served a useful purpose in providing smaller rooms off the main block. The Birse–Westhall mason has also worked at Allardice. It is unclear whether he was responsible for the L-plan in which entrance has, uniquely within our area, been gained not through a forecourt but through a pend in the main block;* but he is evident in the tower which bursts out above the pend in the angle with the jamb. It is supported on vigorous key-pattern corbelling, then corbels again into two separate turrets rising above the wall-head into conical spirelets.†

Kemnay was enlarged into a long L-plan c. 1590, but is quite different from Allardice. The modest rectangular tower house of fifty years earlier became part of the jamb. It was linked by a broad turnpike staircase to a new main block which contains the principal apartments. The mason was almost certainly *Thomas Leiper* since these additions correspond exactly to the turnpike and principal apartments at Tolquhon, known to be his work, and indeed to House of Schivas (both N). Kemnay was built either for William Douglas, who had recently succeeded to the Earldom of Angus and whose title was briefly challenged by James VI, or by his son William Jun. The choice of Leiper as master mason may not have been coincidence since James visited Tolquhon when it was nearing completion in 1589, and the construction of such a fine house at Kemnay was probably essential to prove the Douglases' worthiness of lordly status.

If a motive for Kemnay's reconstruction seems clear, the relationship between three important houses, two built new and one reconstructed, demonstrates the Gordons' success as the North-East's leading family but perhaps also hints at internal rivalry even at a time when their Catholic sympathies led to difficult dealings with the Crown. It is notable nevertheless that all three place their emphasis very much on display rather than defence. Glenbuchat was built for John Gordon c. 1590. Its three-storey main block is 14 m. by 8 m., the SW entrance jamb 6.6 m. by 6.9 m. and the NE jamb containing private apartments 6.7 m. by 7.3 m. The plan closely resembles Hatton Castle (Angus) but the *trompe* arches supporting the angle turrets on the N side are distinctly French. Still larger was Cluny Castle for Sir Thomas Gordon c. 1600–4. Its four-storey main block was 14.5 m. by 9 m. and its two jambs, which were circular rather than square, were each 7 m. in diameter with notably picturesque upperworks. But the most famous of these three houses is Huntly Palace itself,

67

---

* Cf. the much larger Doune (Stirling and Central Scotland). The Allardes were confirmed in their lands in 1426; a 'principal mansion' is recorded in the 1540s.
† Two other tower houses have this key-pattern corbelling: Fiddes, which is traditionally ascribed a date of after 1555, and Knock, of *c.* 1600. The latter incorporates its main turnpike wholly within the rectangular envelope.

which was reconstructed by the 6th Earl *c.* 1602–6 after he was pardoned by James VI for his part in the 'Spanish Blanks' Plot and the Battle of Glenlivet, and confirmed pre-eminent among the Gordons as a marquess. He did not build a new palace-block but rather reconstructed his forefathers' seat in still more magnificent form, engaging the English master mason *Ralph Raleyn* (or *Rawlinson*) to create a remarkably elegant suite of second-floor apartments for his wife, lit by oriels carved in polished ashlar. The entrance stair jamb had been demolished by the King as a token gesture: his real ire was directed towards the primitive but defensible L-plan tower house of 1452. The Marquess rebuilt the palace's entrance stair jamb with a unique heraldic display which asserted his triumphant return to grace and adherence to Catholicism in defiance of the Presbyterian Church. A hint of the magnificent interior is given by two surviving fireplaces, one carved with portrait roundels of the Marquess and Marchioness.

The general peace and prosperity of James VI's reign is expressed in the picturesque qualities of a key group of late C16 and early C17 Aberdeenshire tower houses. In each case a house built primarily for defence was enriched by a very elaborate heightening and remodelling of its upperworks. The results are first seen at Crathes, *c.* 1596–1603 for Alexander Burnett, where the tower of forty years earlier is enriched at attic level by small square and circular angle turrets supported on fine corbel courses with dummy water cannon; there are two more turrets on the E and W flanks. But the turrets on the N and particularly the S fronts are much more remarkable, being corbelled out from lower down at second floor and rising to the wall-heads; that on the principal S front rises telescopically through second and third floors before corbelling to the square as a clock stage just beneath the crenellated parapet formed between two chimney gables. These multi-storey turrets occur again at Castle Fraser, which was heightened for Andrew Fraser in 1617–18, the rectangular main block and square entrance jamb rising from three to four storeys beneath tall roofs, while the drum tower rose to seven storeys with a balustraded platform. A richly moulded, stepping corbel course supports the attic level of the main block and entrance jamb, their two-storey angle turrets rising into garret level under conical spirelets. The stair turrets rise within the Z-plan's angles, one between the main block and entrance jamb on the courtyard side six storeys from ground level to match the others' height, and the other on the rear side between the main block and drum tower, four storeys beneath an ogee domelet. On the courtyard front, the corbel course also supports a magnificent heraldic display, the Royal Arms set above those of Fraser, and beneath these, in recognition of his remarkable achievement, the mason *I. Bell* has been allowed to carve his own name, and the date.

The similarity between Bell's work here and the style of the Crathes upperworks has led to these and a number of contemporary tower houses being associated with the *Bell* family of masons. Of these *George Bell* †1575 whose gravestone lies in St

50

49

Nidian's graveyard, Midmar, is credited with the original construction of the Z-plan Midmar Castle *c.* 1560–70.* Its remodelling in the early C17 is similar in spirit to Castle Fraser but its
distinctive key-pattern corbel courses suggests that the Birse–
Westhall mason – perhaps another member of the Bell family, or
someone who worked with them – was responsible, using Castle
Fraser as his model. The main block and entrance jamb are again
four-storeyed, and the drum tower six-storeyed. Both the main
block and the entrance jamb have single-storey turrets; the tall
stair-turret rising in the angle between them on the courtyard
front is, however, corbelled from first floor, while that on the rear
side in the angle with the drum rises from ground level, and is
linked to it at third floor by a *trompe* arch.

48   At Craigievar the layout is not a Z-plan but a stepped L-plan.
It apparently began as a smaller example of the *Conn* type seen
at Craig, but during remodelling for William Forbes *c.* 1626 a tall
square entrance tower was formed within the L-plan's angle. The
result, as in a Z-plan, is that the principal frontage steps back in
three planes, but in a very concentrated form which makes the
new upperworks all the more effective. These upperworks are
carried on a stepping corbel course with dummy water-cannon,
the jamb gables – one forward-facing, one on the flank – framed
by two-storey turrets with conical spirelets, while the tower in the
angle has a three-storey turret rising to just beneath the balustraded platform. Overall, it is a formal but very striking composition. In the original L-plan structure, the long flank and rear
elevations were broken forward slightly to form two planes
midway across their length, partly for defensive reasons and
partly to extract additional space from the relatively small footprint. The remodelling exploits these features to excellent effect.
Within the break in the long flank a turret rises, its base remarkably corbelled from two different levels: it rises circular to the
corbel course and square thereafter into its own balustraded
platform above the wall-head. Then on the rear elevation, at the
opposite far end, another turret corbelled from first floor rises
above the wall-head not merely up to but actually *through* a
crowstep-gabled caphouse. Such are the similarities of detail with
Castle Fraser's remodelling that there can be no doubt that
Craigievar is also the *Bells'* work, but here as nowhere else they
seem to *play* with the centuries-old vocabulary of the Scottish
tower house. Inside, the small floor plans result in the private
apartments being stacked vertically rather than arranged as horizontal suites; within our area, the rich plasterwork is paralleled
only at Muchalls (*see* Country Houses below).

At Craigievar the entrance tower in the angle does not contain
the stair. Nevertheless, the building anticipates three other
stepped L-plan tower houses in which the stair is centred between
the wings. At Braemar (1628), for the 19th (and 2nd) Earl of
Mar, the central entrance tower is not square but circular and

*There is also a bond (in the Pitcaple Muniments) signed by David Bell, mason,
in 1607.

contains a turnpike. The short wings are of equal length, there being no distinction to show which contains the hall and which the small apartments. The angles once had two-storey turrets in the Bell style.

The Civil Wars resulted in a moratorium in castle-building, but two tower houses both on stepped L-plans were built shortly after the Restoration. Leslie Castle for William Forbes dates from 1661–4. It has a square six-storey entrance tower and two short four-storey jambs, one slightly longer than the other, both with single-storey angle turrets. The tower's scale-and-platt stair (cf. Innes, Moray) contained a remarkable innovation: a fireplace within its central newel to mitigate draughts from the doorway. Cluny Crichton for George Crichton, 1666, was similar, a tall square four-storey tower rising between three-storey wings, but very unusually the ground floor is unvaulted, and the tower's turnpike seems to have risen to first floor only, a smaller wooden stair in one wing presumably accessing the upper levels. The similarities between Leslie and Cluny suggest that they were both built by the same master mason.

Of the late C16 and early C17 tower houses just described, Crathes alone has exceptional interior painted DECORATION, even if some of it has suffered from over-enthusiastic restoration in the late C19. Particularly notable are three painted ceilings, one of which is dated 1599 and has figures representing Muses and Virtues. Another includes the Nine Worthies, popular 51 heroes in the medieval period who represent between them Classical Antiquity, the Old Testament and Christianity. The subject was adopted in late C16 plasterwork and first occurs in London ceilings, famously at the Old Palace, Bromley in 1606. Wooden moulds used by London plasterers seem to have found their way to Scotland in the early C17, probably for the royal houses, and roundels with heads of the Worthies, based on engravings by Nicholas de Bruyn, occur at Glamis Castle (Angus) in the 1620s, shortly before the same moulds were used at Muchalls Castle and at Craigievar. Some of the moulds seem 52 to have survived to be reused in the late C17 at Arbuthnott House.

COUNTRY HOUSES
BY DAVID W. WALKER

Country houses developed from tower houses – especially the longer L- and Z-plans built from the mid C16 – and the 'laigh biggings' within their forecourts. As tower houses evolved as a building-type, conventions were established in their planning which directly influenced several houses in the C17. These still had some defensive characteristics and tower house-like features but rose only two storeys, usually with an attic: they are horizontal rather than vertical in proportion.

A remarkably early example is Auchanachie (Ruthven, 1594), where most accommodation is within a two-storey laigh bigging, facing S, with a small three-storey tower behind it at one angle, linked to it by a stair-turret. But afterwards the unsettled conditions leading up to the Civil Wars resulted in a more cautious defensive approach. Muchalls (1619–27) for the Burnetts of Leys replaced a tower house of c. 1320, part of its fabric still surviving within the present structure. The C17 house is L-plan, with ranges N and E, but very horizontal rising only two storeys and attic. Its forecourt gateway is flanked by triple shot-holes characteristic of the *Leipers*. In true tower-house fashion, the gateway frames a view of the entrance to the house itself, set in the angle between the E range and a short stair jamb returned at its S end. Muchalls has tower-house features including corbelled turrets and bartizans. Its interior retains some of the finest plasterwork in the North-East.

At Drum the new house of c. 1603–19 added to the C14 tower has similar accommodation in a single long block with short jambs at each end, balanced but not symmetrical. Its present formal appearance with a central doorway at first-floor level dates from a partial remodelling in 1790. As first built it had a walled forecourt on the N. Like Muchalls, Monboddo (1635) was built on tower-house foundations. It is T-plan, turreted two storeys with a dormered attic; its entrance jamb containing the turnpike stair is overlooked by the main block. Mergie is another two-storey-and-attic T-plan, its ground floor containing services with the kitchen hearth at one end; the entrance jamb with its stair has been partially rebuilt. The first floor comprised a hall, its fireplace at the opposite end from the kitchen's – as so often the case in tower houses – and perhaps originally just one other room, a private chamber.* Mains of Hallhead, later C17, is a smaller simpler T-plan, still with its staircase jamb in original condition; Balbithan as first extended also conformed to this type before further enlargement into a very large L-plan (*see* below). 'Peill Castle', now forming Leith Hall's N range, was reputedly built as a country house on a rectangular plan c. 1650, but, given the troubled state of the Huntly area then, that would seem unlikely. Here the T- and L-plans of the earlier C17 are superseded by a simple rectangle with a central scale-and-platt stair. Its vaulted ground floor has a central doorway and slit-windows. Immediately behind the doorway it has an up-to-date scale-and-platt stair which opens onto a single room on each side at ground floor, first floor and second floor: the stair's side-walls are squint, probably to avoid obstructing pre-existing windows. A similar but much more sophisticated two-storey version of the same arrangement is to be seen at the S E wing of Glenkindie, a self-contained house built within the courtyard of an older tower house.

In the early years after the Restoration, symmetrical houses with towers projecting from their frontal angles became fashionable for the greater gentry. The earliest within our area is appar-

---

* Mounie (N) is of the same family.

ently the SE side of Culter House, Aberdeen, probably
c. 1660–70, which before early C18 alterations was similar to
Gallery in Angus (1677–80). Logie House (c. 1677–80) appears
to have been of the same type but with one or perhaps originally
two drum towers at the angles (cf. Kinnaber, Angus). Similar in
concept but on a smaller scale is Kingswells, Aberdeen, and the
Ha' Hoose at Raemoir. Kingswells was originally built c. 1666
but remodelled by *Alexander Jaffray* c. 1715 for his own use with
jerkin-roofed Dutch gables at the advanced end bays, and an
Ionic pilastered doorpiece with two oval lights above, the lower
horizontal and the upper vertical, again Dutch motifs. Raemoir,
presumably also by *Jaffray*, repeats the formula almost exactly
but without the pilasters and curvilinear gables, the projecting
end bays having simple piends.

SMALLER LAIRDS' HOUSES adopted a simple rectangular plan
without wings or jambs. Balnacraig (1673) is the earliest datable
example and Auchlossan (c. 1700; Lumphanan) is nearest to its
original condition. The entrance fronts are almost always symmetrical, of two storeys and five bays, the walls harled though
generally with good dressings, and the roof contains attic accommodation lit by windows in the end gables, which rise into coped
chimneystacks. They usually face S or W and have (or had) a side
wing – occasionally two wings – framing a semi-formal forecourt;
the kitchen wing stood separate to prevent fire spreading. The
main house is always single-pile; bedrooms were seemingly often
on ground floor with principal apartments on first for better
views. In certain examples (e.g. Maryculter Old Manse, and
Birkenbog (N)) the ground floor had only one window at each
end, the intermediate bays being blind, probably for security.
Indeed, a few houses (Aswanley, 1692, and Birkenbog) formed
laigh biggings for tower houses which continued in domestic use.

Developments to this basic house-type included a wall-head
gable providing central emphasis and improved attic lighting.
Craigmyle (dem.) had a huge three-windows-wide 'Dutch' gable
like those in Banff and Portsoy (both N): it reputedly dated
from the house's construction in 1676 but, unless a master mason
had been recruited from S of the Tay, it was more probably
an earlier C18 embellishment, like the much simpler one at
Balnacraig.* Another refinement was provision of a jamb at the
rear (Cushnie, 1707) so that the stair did not impinge on living
accommodation.

Other early C18 examples of this house-type include Edinglassie
(1726) and Skellater (1727) in remote Strathdon, both still following the Kingswells–Raemoir formula, although their projecting end bays rise into gables. They appear so similar as to suggest
that they were constructed by the same mason, but Skellater has
an elliptical light above the doorway, like Kingswells' and
Raemoir's. In good materials the simple two-storey five-bay
frontage remained fashionable for a long time to come. Mains of

---

* In this connection the large hemicycle gable of Frendraught, although not a house
of this type, is also of interest.

Shiels (1742) built in ashlar is perhaps by *John Middleton* for his own use – it retains panelling inside; while Inverernan (1764) and Bellabeg (Strathdon, 1765) were built identically in squared masonry with hemicycle gables. Forebank (Marykirk, 1757) is exceptional among these houses because it has a basement for the services and a double-pile plan.

LARGER LAIRDS' HOUSES of the late C17–early C18 present a much taller, more imposing appearance, although as a result of alteration or demolition only one example remains intact, Fordoun House, Auchenblae, *c.* 1712. Its three-storey five-bay front has the relatively tall narrow windows found in certain houses in north Aberdeenshire (e.g. Glack; Haddo House, Crimond) and its single-storey service wing survives. The most sophisticated example, however, was Newton (*c.* 1692), seemingly distinguished by a tall piended – rather than gabled – roof and central chimneystacks from the beginning. It was originally entered through its still-surviving courtyard on the N before its entrance was transferred to the S front in 1778, earth being banked up so that the ground floor became a semi-sunk basement while a stair led to a new entrance at principal (first) floor. This resulted in longer, lower proportions and better concealment of services, in similar fashion to Forebank, an innovation first introduced by 58 *Alexander Jaffray* at the NW front of Culter in 1721. Birkhall (1711–15) and Kinellar were seemingly altered in the same way.

Several of these three-storey houses were built as wings to earlier tower houses. The grandest was Fetternear, built in 1691–3 for the Leslies. It had a railed forecourt like Traquair (Borders) but was more probably influenced by the courtyard palaces that the Leslies saw while in the service of the Austrians. Their new house was substantially larger than the tower house, which was incorporated as a wing on one side, and partly duplicated on the other to give some impression of symmetry. Three-storey houses were also added to tower houses at Balbithan (1679) and Inglismaldie (probably *c.* 1693, with dormered attic; dem. *c.* 1882 but illustrated by MacGibbon and Ross), and were given angle turrets to blend in. Conversely at Skene the C14 tower house was remodelled to match the three-storey wing of 1680.

56   Keith Hall, built for the 1st Earl of Kintore in 1696–9, might seem the ultimate development of the Culter–Gallery type with its towers retracted into a single compact mass, but here wider Renaissance influences, including the earlier C17 Scottish Court School, distinguish it as a house akin to early works by Sir William Bruce and James Smith (cf. Caroline Park, Edinburgh, 1693–6). That its entrance is still at ground rather than at first floor suggests that it was designed by well-informed mason-builders rather than by an architect. Its centre block, three-storeyed and four bays broad, is framed by four-storey corner towers flush with the main frontage, each two bays with ogee domes: although much altered, Keith Hall's early Scottish classical profile still survives. It once had a Roman Doric pedimented doorway; above at first-floor *piano nobile* it retains a heraldic

display reminiscent of Huntly Castle's, and the corner towers are linked across the wall-head by a balustrade.

Further developments were driven by more up-to-date CLASSICAL impulses from the South, represented by *William Adam*'s Haddo (N) for the 2nd Earl of Aberdeen, designed in 1728. Although much more modest in scale, and subsequently altered with a portico and flanking pavilions, Whitehaugh (begun *c.* 1745) shows a keen awareness of contemporary sophistication. Built in granite ashlar it was originally two storeys and seven bays broad over a tall basement, its centre three bays pedimented; the piended roof rises low above a slim moulded eaves cornice and blocking course. At Wardhouse, begun in 1757, the homage to Haddo is very specific. Although built in coursed squared rubble rather than ashlar, its main block, like Haddo's, is three-storeyed and seven bays broad, the centre three bays projected and rising above the main wall-head into a pediment. The entrance is at ground floor, with a Serlian at first-floor *piano nobile*, and an oval niche above and between the smaller second-floor windows. The house is flanked by quadrants linking to pavilions. Wardhouse is an example not only of charming provincial Palladianism but also of a cadet Gordon following his leader, just as two centuries earlier Beldorney and Terpersie had followed Huntly. Arbuthnott (1755–7) reflects the ingenuity of one particular mason-builder, its very smart three-storey three-bay centrepiece in ashlar masonry with broad pediment framed between a pair of harled two-bay gables which are simply treated in the vernacular manner, the one on the l. built with the centre block to match that on the r. which, although remodelled, is essentially *c.* 1475–90. Arbuthnott is distinguished by its notably fine interiors.

61

Following such examples, in the mid C18 a new house-type emerged for more modest lairds. It was a taller two-storey height than the early houses, but a more compact three bays broad, the slightly projecting central bay carried into an attic chimney gable in imitation of the grander houses' pediments, and overlooking formal courts. Freefield with a triangulated gable has been harled, its quadrants linking to lower two-storey piend-roofed pavilions of some size; at Netherley *c.* 1750, the main block has a low curvilinear pediment and is tightly clasped between its wings at right angles. Menzies – now part of Blair's College – originally built *c.* 1740 as a small three-storey house on a rectangular plan, was almost immediately altered with a central projecting bay rising into an attic gable, its side wing being a predecessor house of the Balnacraig type; Corsindae, reputedly built in 1726, was remodelled in similar fashion *c.* 1750–60. Clova is exceptional, even though its original wings (if it had any) have been extended and rebuilt. Its main block is three storeys and four bays broad, raised over a service basement sunk almost completely beneath ground – an unusual feature in Aberdeenshire because of the difficulty of excavating into granite. Its doorway with open consoled pediment is approached by a broad railed stair, and a heraldic panel proclaims the Lumsdens, the attic window being round-arched. Dark red long-and-short quoins contrast against the harl, as they do at Corsindae.

Benholm c. 1760 is strikingly different – pure classicism of the John Adam school, excellent in its austere simplicity, proportion and ashlar masonry. It is three storeys and five bays broad. The pilastered ground-floor entrance is approached by a railed horse-shoe stair, and the bays on either side are relatively closely spaced together to express the internal arrangement of a hall and stair-way flanked by principal apartments. The *piano nobile* is on the tall first floor but all the windows are frameless, the only distinction being a band course. The bedroom-floor windows are square; there is a slim moulded wall-head cornice but the piended roof is kept so low as to be near-invisible, the twin chimneystacks punching into the sky as if from nowhere to complete a perfect composition of solid and void. Such sophistication is rare, approached only by the new house at Craig Castle, which rose into a very tall piended roof with centralized chimneystacks, now sadly altered. More typical of the North-East's provincial classi-cism was the now-lost three-storey seven-bay house at Lauriston Castle, still with gabled roof but made more fashionable with the addition of a pedimented centrepiece and balustraded parapet in 1789. Knockespock, two storeys and three windows wide, raised over a basement, has a railed stair leading to a transom-lit doorway deeply recessed within its opening. The gabled roof is tall but without window-lights even in the ends.

Balmanno (c. 1790) and Elrick (1789–92) represent an instruc-tive contrast with Mains of Shiels and Forebank. Both are two-storeyed and five bays broad but their scale is larger, and Elrick, raised over a basement, has set-back wings forming a rear court. In their fine proportions and squared masonry Balmanno and Elrick are essentially similar to the grander Aberdeen town houses in Schoolhill and Belmont Street. Straloch (c. 1790) also looks back fifty years but to the classical tradition of Whitehaugh, which it skilfully adapts to a more economical vernacular. It is two-storey-and-basement, five bays broad (rather than seven as at Whitehaugh), its pedimented centre bay slightly advanced with a railed stair leading to a fanlit doorway within a lugged achitrave. Its walls are harled, but with copious ashlar dressings. On plan it is double-pile, its depth expressed by a low M-roof with paired curvilinear end gables rising into twin chimneystacks to keep the proportions horizontal. Quadrants have formed links to pavilions enclosing a rear court, thus ensuring privacy and unobstructed views of the gardens.*

Of similar date, but a different hand, are additions to two houses belonging to the Leith family. Leith Hall's s range is tall three-storeyed with three broad bays, its outer windows tripartite with first-floor Serlians rising into flush pediments, a formula echoed in two-storey-and-basement form at Invery. A few years later, as Britain became immersed in the Napoleonic Wars, a still

---

*The resemblance to Dunlugas (N) is so strong as to imply some connection, possibly the same mason-builder.

plainer barrack-like vernacular classical style prevailed at Leith Hall's E range and Knockespock's N range. Its finest achievement was the impressive three-storey seven-bay Catholic seminary at Aquhorthies (1799), beautifully proportioned with a shapely piended roof and big chimneystacks.

From the EARLY NINETEENTH CENTURY country houses were no longer designed by mason-builders working in a vernacular tradition which responded to classical influences but by formally trained architects who were emerging as a recognized profession. This trend first appears to have been seen at Kair, probably c. 1788–90, a two-storey three-bay villa with single-storey pavilion wings, its pediment expressing the actual roof. It has a very early but unproven (and slightly improbable) attribution to the Adam office, but it is clearly the work of an extremely sophisticated designer. Next in seniority is The Burn (1791–6, much altered), its simple but stylish two-storey five-bay entrance front distinguished by fine ashlar, architraved windows and a balustraded parapet carved with swags. Kirktonhill House, Marykirk (c. 1795, dem.) was rubble-built but austerely elegant, its entrance sheltered by a peristyle colonnade encircling its three-windows-wide bow. All these houses were seemingly by Edinburgh (or London?) architects, The Burn having particularly fine interiors. A simplified version of Adam's CASTELLATED STYLE then gained currency, first at the remodelling of Fetteresso by *John Paterson* (1808) which has a big octagonal entrance tower. *Paterson* was probably also responsible for the symmetrical Fasque House (1808–12) which has remarkable classical interiors.

But thereafter the North-East nearly always remained loyal to extremely able men of its own, and c. 1810–50 the dominant figures were *John Smith* and *Archibald Simpson*, both London-trained exponents of the GREEK REVIVAL, whose prolific careers are well known. Smith was a capable and fluent designer in whatever style was prevalent at the time. He is first identified at Manar (1811) where his particularly suave handling of a tall and broadly spaced two-storey five-bay frontage, its centre minimally advanced with a distyle Greek Doric portico framing a finely detailed doorway, reflects his cosmopolitan background. Manar was the model for Smith's more sophisticated Phesdo (1814–15) and Dunecht (1820, subsequently remodelled), both with tetra-style Greek Doric porticoes, and the smaller and simpler Rickarton as late as 1829–32. Single-storey villas began to appear as a country-house type in the same years, the first being Torwood (Fettercairn, ruined) with a bowed Greek Doric portico, then Smith's Kirkville (1823–7) raised over a basement with a tetastyle portico of paired Doric columns. Smith was also adept at modernizing older houses as seen in his classical addition to Raemoir (1817). Like Smith, *Archibald Simpson* was an extremely accomplished exponent of Greek Revival whose best work challenges comparison with the Edinburgh masters. Park House (1821–2) is a tall single-storey villa with tetrastyle Doric pedimented portico, while Murtle House in Bieldside, Aberdeen (1823) is Greek Doric with a peristyle portico encircling its domed central bow.

Simpson's earliest-known commission in independent prac-
66 tice, Castle Forbes begun in 1814, is an ingenious castellated
composition. Its entrance front was designed to incorporate a
classical house of 1731 which he framed between a square tower
and a drum tower. Seen thus, it is asymmetric yet balanced, but
when viewed in perspective with its new wing of principal apartments the two together seem almost mirror image. Internally its
geometric planning reflects the influence of earlier designs made
for the house by *Paterson*. Simpson may also have been executant
architect for the castellated remodelling of Fetternear (*c.* 1815–
20), reputedly designed by his deceased master, *James Massie*.
Problems at Castle Forbes resulted in *Smith* being called in to
complete the job. Thereafter Smith rapidly developed the castel-
67 lated manner at Cluny (1818–36) where he re-cased the Z-plan
tower house of *c.* 1600–4 in granite ashlar and built another
identical to it in mirror image to produce a symmetrical entrance
front.

CASTELLATED was a romantic, picturesque style which
reflected the mood of a nation that had stood fast against the
threat of invasion: it evoked the world of Walter Scott and a new-
found interest in antiquarianism reflected in John Britton's
Architectural Antiquities of Great Britain (1805). The transition
from castellated classical to CASTELLATED GOTHIC is seen at
Drumtochty, where the Edinburgh architect *James Gillespie
Graham* built the original NW block *c.* 1810–12, a neat asymmetrical
composition of two and three storeys framed by slim square and
circular towers. It was almost immediately extended across the S
flank by *John Smith* – as architect or contractor? – in 1815–16,
Gillespie Graham returning as late as 1839 to build the E tower
with its porte cochère and Perp Gothic three-bay dining room
which completes the present entrance front.

The economic boom following the French Wars turned to bust
during the banking crisis of 1825–6 and this, together with the
increasing purchase of small estates by a growing class of successful professionals, encouraged smaller houses with an emphasis on picturesque qualities and – usually – economy. The only
substantial Neoclassical house built during this period is
Balmakewan, *c.* 1828, its two-storey five-bay frontage raised over
a semi-sunk basement, and its doorway within a segment-headed
recess framed by attached Greek Doric columns; rather more
typical are smaller, more economical villas such as Camphill
House (Lumphanan, 1827) and Kingsford House (Alford,
c. 1831). Williamston, by *Alexander Fraser* (*c.* 1825–30), shows the
familiar two-storey-and-basement five-bay front dressed in the
new ITALIANATE fashion, with a portico of paired Doric columns
(still Greek, without bases), cream harling imitating stucco, angle
pilasters and a low piended roof with the oversailing eaves
characteristic of such houses. *Simpson*'s Linton (1835) displays
his ingenious planning in very compact form, a two-storey
U-plan main block interlocking with a lower two-storey U-plan
service wing, the entrance being a round-arched open porch.
Further Simpson ingenuity is displayed at the equally Italianate

Thainstone (1835–6), where a mid-C18 house was largely concealed by a new range of tall principal-floor apartments, five bays
broad raised over a basement; the entrance is in one flank, a very
large arched porte cochère which opens onto a grand stair rising
between the old and new parts of the building. Either *Simpson*
or *Smith* must have been responsible for skilful additions to
another mid-C18 house, Haddo, Forgue (*c.* 1840), where the
porte cochère forms the lower stage of an Italianate tower.
Italianate assumed a much more substantial and expensive form
in 1855–9 when *William Smith* incorporated his father's Greek
villa at Dunecht into a much larger mansion for the scholarly
Lord Lindsay, its four-stage tower with Early Lombardic details
marking the break in the stepped s frontage where old work
meets new. Its Painted Staircase with an Alberti-type arcade is
decorated in the style of Raphael.

The most important NEO-TUDOR houses in our area are
Fettercairn by *William Burn*, 1826–9, and Ury by the Glasgow
architect *John Baird* (1855), closely modelled on Burn's Carstairs
with its big square entrance tower and porte cochère, and
mullioned and transomed windows. The most important NEO-
JACOBEAN houses included *Simpson*'s Castle Newe (1831,
dem.), Lessendrum (1837) and Pittodrie (1841), where additional
accommodation including a large entrance tower with balustrade
stands against an older tower house. The grandest Neo-Jacobean
survivor is Ecclesgreig (1844–6) by *H. E. Goodridge* of Bath. Its   70
s front is a near-symmetrical two storeys and five bays, with
windows mullioned and transomed in stone, a big crowstepped
central gable and smaller dormer gablets to each side, all clasped
by spirelet turrets; on its entrance (E) front is a robust tower
house pierced by a porte cochère.

The development of SCOTTISH BARONIAL was closely related
to a growing appreciation of the aesthetic merits of tower houses,
although their vertical proportions presented challenges in
respect of modern living and it would be decades before their
architectural traditions would be well enough understood for
additions to be built in corresponding styles. Nevertheless,
William Burn's modest but picturesque two-storey villa-like additions to Pitcaple of 1830, followed by *John Smith*'s still plainer
additions to Westhall of 1838, represented something of a turning
point. In 1847 – the last year of his life – *Simpson*, with his assistant *William Ramage*, produced the designs for a remarkably
picturesque remodelling of Skene for the antiquarian 4th Earl
Fife, transforming a C14 tower house with austere C17 and C18
courtyard extensions into a unified Baronial composition through
relatively modest additions of their own, all set off by an array of
slim towers rising into ogee domes and conical spirelets. The
magnificent interiors overseen by the twenty-year-old *Lady Agnes
Duff*, perhaps following a scheme by *David Ramsay Hay*, include
the scagliola entrance hall and the Great Stair with Jacobean
strapwork rising between Doric arcades, its ceiling with elaborate
heraldic décor; the complete heraldic achievement of Clan Skene
is on display in the Dining Room, while the Sitting Room and

Drawing Room still retain their C19 wallpapers. Simpson and Ramage's work at Skene was certainly prescient, anticipating the first published plates of Robert William Billings' *Baronial & Ecclesiastical Antiquities of Scotland*, sponsored by Burn, which appeared that year.

As the leading country-house practitioners, *John Smith* and his son *William* remained surprisingly conservative given the latter's London training, closely adhering to Burn's Tudor–Jacobean idiom of *c.* 1828–32 throughout the 1830s and 1840s – at Easter Skene (1832), old Balmoral (1834–8 and 1848–9), Banchory (now Beannachar, 1840) and probably Culdrain (1846–7), together with innumerable 'English rectory' manses, culminating in the new Balmoral of 1853–5 for Queen Victoria and Prince Albert. Balmoral's main block is laid out on a rectangular courtyard plan with another service court arranged diagonally behind it and an enormous five-storey tower as the focal point between them built in homage to a C16 tower house which it replaced altogether: Balmoral reflects both Germanic Romanticism and Germanic orderliness. Beyond Skene and Balmoral the best Baronial houses are Brotherton (now Lathallan School by *James Matthews*, 1866–8), and Ardoe (1877–8) by *Matthews* and his partner, *Alexander Marshall Mackenzie*, who with William Smith were the leading North-East practitioners during the later C19. Brotherton and Ardoe reflect not only Billings' influence but also that of *David Bryce*, the leading Baronial exponent in Edinburgh, who had remodelled Kingcausie in a simple symmetrical exposition of the style in 1852–3. Of smaller houses, Tertowie is by *James Matthews* (1867) as is Glenmillan's neat remodelling (1872) with a drum tower in the angle between two short ranges, and the remodelling of Tonley (*c.* 1891).

The cumulative effects of agricultural depression brought on by cheap American grain imports from *c.* 1870, industrial recession from *c.* 1873 and the City of Glasgow Bank crash in 1878 marked a significant watershed. Together with ever-increasing numbers of self-made men as against traditional landed gentry, they resulted in a rather different clientele which was reflected in country-house building in several contrasting ways. Ardoe had been built for a soap manufacturer and Brotherton with Indian money; so too was the original House of Glenmuick (1872–5), a pugnacious design by the contractor *Sir Morton Peto*. At a totally different architectural level is the biggest of mid-Victorian projects, *George Edmund Street*'s second phase of work at Lord Lindsay's Dunecht between 1870 and 1881. Its interiors once seen are never forgotten: the spiral stair built in the spirit of the C12, 5 m. in diameter and supported by forty-seven slim colonnettes; the unprecedented Library, 36 m. long, with cast-iron galleries and a magnificent fully glazed barrel-vault; and the 30 m. long Romanesque Chapel, its compartmented wagon roof rising 15 m. above the nave floor. But Dunecht is exceptional: just as tough as Glenmuick are Blelack (Logie Coldstone, 1881 and 1892) and Blairmore and Dinnet (both *Marshall Mackenzie*,

1884–5 and 1890), all three built with substantial new money and not especially academic. Contrasting with these are picturesque villas including Fawsyde House (Roadside of Kinneff, by *J.R. Mackenzie*, 1865–7) and Hopewell Lodge (Logie Coldstone, *c.* 1870). The engagingly idiosyncratic Tillypronie (*c.* 1867–8) in a North European manner is by the self-trained architect *Alexander Ogilvy* working with the diplomat *John Clark*, while Glen Tanar (*George Truefitt* 1874–9, with extensions, now mostly demolished) for the banker Sir William Cunliffe Brooks was much flightier still, and great fun with it.

A more scholarly attitude than in any of these came with the restoration and extension of Place of Tilliefour (1885–6) in an unturreted Arts and Crafts manner by *Hew Montgomerie Wardrop*, its long and varied new wing almost like a crowstep-gabled vernacular streetscape. Wardrop's work just anticipates MacGibbon and Ross's *Castellated & Domestic Architecture of Scotland*, much of which he had probably seen before publication in 1887–92. The transformation in understanding which MacGibbon and Ross engendered is well illustrated by comparing Invercauld with Glenkindie, both substantial remodellings of existing buildings. In each case the principal entrance front is expressed as a very large L-plan with a tower as the dominant feature, while a handsome courtyard lies at the rear. Invercauld House, added to by the London architect *J. T. Wimperis* in 1872–5, has a six-storey oblong tower rearing up in the angle between longer and lower wings extending from it on two adjacent sides. Built in granite, it is a simple bold composition, its principal features clearly expressed, and with regular fenestration, a marked contrast to the more elaborate Baronial designs of Matthews. Twenty-five years later Glenkindie, remodelled by *Sydney Mitchell & Wilson* in 1900, is clearly modern Scots Renaissance on its L-plan entrance front, where the tower rising from the longer of the two ranges was built to honour a tower house destroyed as long ago as 1644, but on the garden side it adopts a subtle Arts and Crafts manner to integrate two C18 wings into an equally satisfying courtyard design. 69 73

Marshall Mackenzie's Breda (1894) comprises a new-built three-storey three-bay tower house (with its entrance in a conically roofed drum tower at one corner) and a long two-storey wing, its rich red masonry only emphasizing its affinity with William Leiper's major houses on the West Coast. MacGibbon and Ross's influence had astonishing results at Aboyne Castle, where the hitherto idiosyncratic *George Truefitt* undertook a scholarly reconstruction of the Late Georgian front as a second Fyvie (N), alas never quite completed and subsequently demolished. Their influence is also seen at Kincardine House (1894–6), an enormous Scots château by the London-based *Niven & Wigglesworth*. Its very tall three-storey three-bay centre block with finely sculpted attic dormers is framed by two great towers, one like an early rectangular keep with crenellated parapet and crowstep-gabled caphouse, the other an overt tribute to the Seton Tower at Fyvie; there are, however, some very up-to-date London p. 64

Kincardine House.
Drawing by Niven & Wigglesworth, 1895

Neo-Baroque details and even hammer-dressed masonry suggesting an American brownstone influence, reflecting the architects' backgrounds. Much lower-key and closer in spirit to Wardrop's Tilliefour is *Robert S. Lorimer*'s granite-built Rhu-na-haven, Aboyne (1911–12); only traces remain of his work at Craigmyle in 1902. Besides these Scots Renaissance houses, Tudor returned in *Dan Gibson* and *T. H. Mawson*'s remodelling of Bracklay (now House of Glenmuick, 1895, extended by Mawson 1912), and English Neo-Jacobean in *Marshall Mackenzie*'s scholarly Kildrummy, completed in 1901, which replaced a Tudor cottage of *c.* 1835.

All this was a fine note for 'British' styles – Scottish and English – to go out on; but the increasing ability of architects to travel not only on the Continent but to North America, and still more particularly the publication in professional journals of drawings and photographs of architecture abroad, had a profound influence on country houses in the earlier C20. Thus *Marshall Mackenzie*'s Mar Lodge (1895–8), a large symmetrical two-storey U-plan in rock-faced pink granite with half-timbered attic gables and rosemary tile roofs seems less a reflection of English C16 architecture than the architecture of Central Europe. The same half-timbered style is found in *George Bennett Mitchell*'s Glenfarquhar Lodge (*c.* 1898–9) which was seemingly inspired by a Bavarian ski lodge, and his very similar Melgum Lodge, near Logie-Coldstone, of about the same date; indeed, the sheer breadth of their entrance gable fronts could never be considered English. Likewise *Sydney Mitchell*'s pink granite House of Cromar (now Alastrean House, *c.* 1902–4) for the 1st Marquess of Aberdeen appears to show the influence of Canada where the Marquess had been Governor-General. William Van

Horne had prepared a sketch for him of just such a house – in shingle-style timber – at Coldstream Ranch, British Columbia, in 1895.

Just before the First World War *Marshall Mackenzie* built the very stylish Coull House designed by his sons *Alexander* and *Gilbert Marshall Mackenzie*. Its two-storey three-bay centre block with ground-floor colonnade flanked by piend-roofed end pavilions was clearly inspired by contemporary French architecture. Between the Wars the only notable houses are by *George Bennett Mitchell*. At his Scots Renaissance Littlewood Park (1930–2) the entrance front is almost villa-like in its composition of three closely spaced gabled bays, but the garden front rises much taller with a conical-roofed drum tower at one angle and smaller turrets with spirelets. Whitehouse (*c.* 1937) is a big L-plan villa, reconstructed after a fire. The most significant works since the Second World War have been Birkhall's extension by *Andrew Graham Henderson* in 1953; Candacraig's reconstruction after fire by *A. G. R. Mackenzie* in 1956; House of Crathes by *Cowell Mathieson & Partners*, 1972; Glen Tanar by *Law & Dunbar-Nasmith*, *c.* 1975; and Inverey House by *Oliver Humphries*, 1983. Of the same date is the Neo-Georgian Ballogie (Birse). 58

In the later C20 several abandoned tower houses were restored and returned to domestic use. The pioneer was Balfluig's restoration by *John Lamb* of *George Bennett Mitchell & Son* for Mark Tennant in 1966–8. At Balfluig, Midmar (*John Harvey McLaren* and *Thomas Craig* for Richard Wharton, 1978–9) and Tilquhillie (*France Smoor*, architect, and *Slessor Troup*, mason, for John and Kay Coyne, 1985–8) the roofs had survived. At Harthill (*Bill Cowie* with *Slessor Troup* for Ann and Steve Remp, 1975–8) the shell was intact but the roofs had gone, though wall scars showed where they had been. At Pitfichie (*Cowie* and *Troup* for Colin Wood, 1978–96), Terpersie (*Cowie* for Lachlan Rhodes, 1983–9) and Leslie (*David* and *Leslie Leslie*, with *Troup* as mason, 1983–9) substantial masonry had fallen. At Aboyne *George Truefitt*'s alterations were demolished in the 1970s and the C16 core reconstructed by *Ian Begg* and *Alistair Urquhart*. 77

Estate buildings

DOOCOTS are among the earliest identifiable estate buildings but they continued to be built into the Late Georgian period. The beehive-shaped doocot at Fetteresso Castle is mid–late C16, unfortunately in poor condition. Muchalls's is early C17, small and square and built into a hillside. Those at Candacraig and Corsindae are also C17, rectangular with crowstepped gables; Candacraig's has a hearth venting into a chimney gable on its entrance front. Glenbervie's is also square with a pyramidal roof, dated 1736, and Balmakewan has two of this pattern, late C18. Inglismaldie's is of the double-chamber lectern type, mid- or late C18; Auchanachie and Manar are both circular. Disblair's, 1804, is rectangular with a saddleback roof.

Much the earliest surviving STABLES are at Dunnottar Castle, *c.* 1600. Purpose-built stable blocks coinciding with improvements to the roads were often built in conjunction with alterations to the big houses or their designed landscapes; whatever their plan form, the more important examples are almost always single-storeyed with hayloft openings beneath the wall-head. Kemnay has a very early coachhouse range of the mid C18, and there is another coachhouse in the offices of Candacraig, built before 1760. Leith Hall's stables, on a semicircular plan, are dated 1754; there was an intention to complete the circle in 1758. Castle Fraser's stables, polygonal with conically roofed drum towers, date from 1795, to an earlier design by *John Paterson*. All these stand a modest distance from their houses which – with the possible exception of Candacraig – had been begun earlier, but at The Burn, *c.* 1791–6, the stables lie immediately N of the main house as an asymmetric U-plan loosely enclosing a court; the principal N front is pedimented with a cupola. Keith Hall's of the early C19, perhaps by *John Smith*, are Greek Revival, a seven-bay frontage with a Doric pedimented portico and end pavilions.

During the earlier C19 stables are usually complete quadrangles: *Smith*'s at Dunecht are *c.* 1820, subsequently remodelled; Fasque's, probably by *Paterson*, have a pedimented principal front of seven bays; Learney's, by *Smith c.* 1838–40, also have a seven-bay pedimented front, but here it is asymmetric. At Durris *c.* 1838 *Archibald Simpson* built handsome Italianate stables on an H-plan with a slim octagonal tower rising above the centre. Drumtochty's stables are a castellated U-plan with a big square tower by *Matthews & Mackenzie*, 1850–1; Ury's are Tudor by *John Baird c.* 1855; and *William Ramage* was probably responsible for the robustly Baronial stables at Skene *c.* 1860, another U-plan with a still more massive clock tower rising into a caphouse. Balmoral's Scots Tudor stables, built by *William Smith* in 1857, are also U-plan, but here the 'open' W flank is entered through three four-centred archways, and there is a single-storey building within the court. Glen Tanar stables have *George Truefitt*'s predictably idiosyncratic detailing; Straloch's, 1872 in present form, are a Gothic H-plan with a bellcote. During the later C19 a stable court was built against the early C18 Kinellar House, the only instance of such an addition within our area. Place of Tilliefour's stables are Z-plan, *c.* 1885–6, with a tourelle answering the house. Mar Lodge's are quadrangular single-storeyed without a loft beneath the wall-head, *c.* 1893–5.

HOME FARMS coinciding with wider agricultural improvements (*see* p. 92) are generally plainer than stable blocks, though similar in scale, being usually single-storey and loft on courtyard plans. Good simple examples exist at Castle Forbes, Dunecht, Huntly Lodge, Kemnay and Williamston, but from the early C19 they can be of some distinction. Manar *c.* 1800–5 is exactly square, with a curvilinear gable and bellcote over its entrance pend. Leith Hall's pend is in a central tower with a Gothick first-floor window and crenellated parapet. *John Smith* built Keith Hall's Home Farm *c.* 1810; Monymusk's was built piecemeal from the mid C18, but its pedimented centre is by Smith *c.* 1825; at Newton, his impressive ten-bay frontage, again with a pedimented centre, is 1831. Fetternear, a large harled Neo-Jacobean quad with stables and a doocot tower, was built in 1841 in the style of *Archibald Simpson*. Wardhouse, Italianate with a pedimented archway, is perhaps also by Simpson, 1842. Glen Tanar has a distinctive barn designed by *George Truefitt c.* 1874.

Several houses have fine LODGES at their entrances, although none before the early C19, e.g. Keith Hall's octagonal lodge of *c.* 1810 by *John Smith.* A few take the form of miniature temples: Dunecht by Smith, *c.* 1820; Park by *Archibald Simpson, c.* 1822; Parkhill (Newmachar); Arbuthnott's of *c.* 1821; and the Mar Lodge gatehouse. Simpson's lodge for Thainstone *c.* 1836 is Italianate, complete with a tower. There are several Baronial lodges: Tower Lodge, Knockespock, is mid-C19, perhaps by *Thomas Mackenzie* (extended 1992); Dess's is probably by *James Matthews, c.* 1860; and the lodge to Dinnet House is by *A. Marshall Mackenzie,* 1890. The lodges at Aboyne Castle are by *George Truefitt,* and as delightfully eccentric as his extensive work at Glen Tanar. Craigmyle's by *Robert Lorimer,* early C20, is a combination of Dutch gable and semicircular staircase bay. *Sir Aston Webb* built the Neoclassical North and West Lodges at Dunecht in 1912; the exceptional Tower of Skene Lodges, also at   76 Dunecht, are a matching pair of full-size tower houses in granite ashlar built by *Marshall Mackenzie & Son* in 1923.

Early GARDENS sometimes had two-storey square-plan PAVILIONS, fitted with fireplaces which allowed the occupants to enjoy elevated views even in the winter. Muchalls has a very rare early C17 two-storey banqueting house, and pavilions survive in the walled gardens at Midmar and (altered) at Invery. The terraced garden at Arbuthnott has a very architectural pavilion of the 1680s and that at Mergie has two small square structures, one a pavilion and the other perhaps a doocot (*see* above), like the matching pair built by *Alexander Jaffray* at Culter in 1719–20. Fasque's pavilion (probably 1797) was seemingly built as an apple-house. There are two in the walled garden at Skene (C18–C19); Kinellar's is two-storeyed with a conical spirelet; Whitehaugh's is octagonal. A gazebo shown in old photographs of Tillypronie may have been formed so that John Brown could enjoy his meals apart from other servants. *Sir Aston Webb*'s garden pavilion at Dunecht *c.* 1913–20 has an Early Italian Renaissance doorpiece. The gazebo at Friendville in Great Western Road, Aberdeen, by *Fenton Wyness,* 1943, has Ionic columns supporting a wrought-iron dome. The most recent is Birkhall's pavilion by *Ben Tindall,* 2004, but in a traditional C17 manner. In the wider LANDSCAPES, many parks have BRIDGES of note to carry their drives to the house: that at Arbuthnott is of *c.* 1830 and fine enough to cross the Seine.

ROADS, RAILWAYS, HARBOURS AND LIGHTHOUSES
BY CHARLES O'BRIEN

There are scattered references in charters which give clues to the medieval system of tracks or ROADS in Aberdeenshire and in the southern area there was no doubt continued use of the roadway for wheeled traffic established by the Romans between the Tay and the Dee (for which *see* p. 15), crossing the North Esk into Kincardineshire and then to Stonehaven on the way to Aberdeen. Evidently there were several passes through the Mounth, the hilly terrain that separates (historic) Aberdeenshire from Kincardineshire, which were probably used to drive livestock south to markets. The army of the English King Edward I is said to have made its way from Perth to Aberdeen in 1296 via Cryne Cross Mounth, which led to a ford across the Dee at Durris. In 1644 Montrose also used this pass. Many of these passes were and are associated with crossings evenly spaced along the Dee between Braemar and Aberdeen that were either fordable or else served by ferries. The line of one of these roads is probably represented by the modern B974, which runs N from Fettercairn over the high pass of Cairn O'Mounth.

There is no evidence of MEDIEVAL BRIDGES over the rivers except at Aberdeen, where the Bridge of Balgownie, spanning the River Don N of Old Aberdeen, is the original link between the burgh and the northern territories of Aberdeenshire. The surviving bridge, with its pointed arch, may well date from the early C14, the period traditionally given for it, but was certainly extant by the mid C15 and remained the only bridge crossing on the Don until as late as *c.* 1830. There are over twenty bridges crossing the Dee today but as recently as 1800 there were just four and in the medieval period only the Brig O'Dee at Aberdeen; even here, where the river is wide, there was only a ford until the bridge was planned by Bishop Elphinstone and built by his successor, Bishop Dunbar, in the C16, with its triangular cutwaters and arches formed of ribs below the carriageway, a very distinctive form of medieval construction.* It still carries traffic into the city today.

In 1617 the Scottish Parliament set down minimum standards of width (20 ft) for roads between market towns and placed responsibility for their maintenance in the hands of the landowners in the parishes through which they passed. The Highways and Bridges Act of 1686 confirmed the powers of Aberdeenshire landowners as commissioners of supply or justices of the peace to oversee the roads and bridges and to use statute labour (i.e unpaid labour by parishioners) to make annual repairs. Examples

---

* It should be noted that this pattern of construction with ribbed soffits to the arches also appears in the Upper North Water Bridge across the North Esk at Pert, Angus, which was the principal crossing into Kincardineshire. It is C16 but was rebuilt in 1841.

of such improvements may be the Bridge of Dye (*c.* 1680) crossing the Water of Feugh on the Cairn O'Mount road a little s of
Strachan, and Ruthrieston Bridge, Aberdeen. In 1759 district
committees were established to supervise repairs funded through
taxation. However, the quality and extent of the road system as
a whole remained poor and badly financed, and statute labour
was difficult to organize. By the late c18 Aberdeenshire's roads
were perceived as a major impediment to effective agrarian
reform in the county. In the 1770s and 80s public subscriptions
or private individuals paid for the erection of new bridges such
as the seven-span North Water Bridge over the North Esk at St
Cyrus, designed by *Andrew Barrie* with advice from the engineer
John Smeaton and the architect *John Adam* (his father, William
Adam, had designed the Bridge at Cowie, Stonehaven, in 1732
but it has been replaced). Other examples of new bridges of this
period are at Banchory (Bridge of Feugh, 1790) and Inverbervie
(Old Bervie Bridge, 1799 by *James Burn*).

By this time the Aberdeenshire Turnpike Act had been passed
(1795) allowing turnpike trustees to raise funds through annual
assessments of landowners, supported by the borrowing of funds
and the levying of tolls. The resulting network of TURNPIKE
ROADS either overlaid the old parish roads, the remainder of
which continued under the supervision of the district committees, or was created afresh. Aberdeen's connections to the rural
parishes were greatly improved (and encouraged new suburban
developments along the roads to Alford, Inverurie, Skene and the
Deeside villages). *Robert Stevenson*'s fine four-arched Marykirk
Bridge (1811–14) bringing the turnpike road (now A937) across
the North Esk is an exemplary product of this period, with a
superb small toll house on the approach. Most other TOLL
HOUSES are much more routine, with canted bay or bow on the
face to the road, but the toll cottage by the river crossing at
Aboyne, 1830, is of a higher order altogether with channelled
ashlar façade.

Created in parallel with these developments on the parish
roads were the MILITARY ROADS, a direct consequence of the
Jacobite Rising in 1715 and still in progress by the time of the
second Rising in 1745. The first phase of road (and fort-building)
works was conducted under the supervision of General George
Wade but in Aberdeenshire the military roads belong to the
period after 1745, when *Major William Caulfeild* (1698–1767) was
in charge. He created the road from Blairgowrie (Perthshire) to
Fort George, Inverness (Highland), co-opting part of an existing
route crossing the w end of the Dee at Braemar and then along
the river's N bank before cutting through Glengairn to Corgarff
(where troops were garrisoned) to the high pass of The Lecht
(Moray). Bridges engineered by Caulfeild's men remain at
Invercauld, Braemar (Old Brig o' Dee) and Gairnshiel (Glengairn),
both with a familiar profile of road and parapet sloping upwards
to the crown of the arch. Caulfeild also improved the road across
Cairn O'Mount (B974) from Fettercairn and its continuation NW
towards Huntly (A980).

After the end of the Jacobite threat, maintenance of the military roads was passed from the army to the Commissioners of Highland Roads and Bridges established in 1803. *Thomas Telford* was their engineer and to him is due the design of Bridge of Alford (Alford, 1810–11), Potarch Bridge across the Dee (Birse, 1811–14, where it now made an effective link with the new turnpike roads along the N and S banks of the river) and Bridge of Keig (1817, again across the Don), on each occasion in collaboration with the local contractor *William Minto*. Telford's bridges are impressive but plain and serious. He had also provided the initial design for Union Bridge in Aberdeen (modified in execution) and then the Bridge of Don, Aberdeen (1827–30, in collaboration with *John Smith*).

Telford's bridge at Braemar, 1829, was completed just in time to be washed away by the Great Flood or 'Muckle Spate' of that year. This catastrophic torrent also destroyed several other bridges, including the bridge at Banchory and that at Aboyne, executed in 1828. The latter was a SUSPENSION BRIDGE and quickly rebuilt in the same form. This type of technology, excellently suited for achieving wide spans without need for a central supporting pier in the turbulent river, was adopted for the Wellington Bridge at Aberdeen, designed by the naval engineer and specialist in this field *Captain Samuel Brown* and executed by *John Smith* in 1829–31. What Smith learned in the process he applied to the footbridge he designed for the minister of Cults (Aberdeen) so that his parishioners could cross the Dee from the S bank to the N, but this was brought down by flooding in the C20 and is just a ruin. A smaller suspension bridge, for pedestrians, is at Crathie (1834). These bridges speak of the industrial revolution and the contribution of civil engineers and ironfounders, who dominated the C19 design and manufacture of bridges. One of the most important is the Girder Bridge of 1856 at Crathie, designed by *Brunel* and built at Prince Albert's command to carry traffic across the Dee to the gates of Balmoral; see also Invercauld Bridge of 1859. There are a number of very attractive light wire suspension footbridges along the Dee, manufactured by *James Abernethy & Co.*, ironfounders in Aberdeen (Polhollick, Ballater, 1892; Cambus O'May, 1905; Ballochbuie, Crathie, 1924). The designer of these bridges was *Louis Harper* of *Harper & Co.* who began as fence makers and diversified into light wire suspension bridges in 1865 (cf. Birkhall). Each has (or had) distinctive latticework iron pylons with crestings and finials. Abernethys also fabricated the splendid cast-iron Park Bridge of 1854 spanning the Dee at Drumoak, in partnership with the engineer *J. Willet*, a prolific designer of bridges (several in Strathdon alone).

Turnpike tolls were abolished in Aberdeenshire in 1865 by the Aberdeenshire Roads Act – a decade or so before the system was abolished nationally. After 1879 roads in Scotland became the responsibility of County Road Trustees and, from 1889, the newly created county councils. The C19 provision in Aberdeenshire meant that there was little new bridge-building until the interwar years, when the iron bridges at Aboyne (1937–41) and Dinnet (1935) on the Dee were replaced, and the Jubilee Bridge (1935) at Inverbervie built, all three engineered by *F.A. Macdonald & Partners*, specialists in reinforced concrete construction. The first two are slim elegant cantilevered structures spanning the river in a single arch, the latter an immensely powerful monument with seven arches and gigantic tapering piers.

The construction of an efficient road system from the end of the C18 contributed to the prosperity of rural Aberdeenshire but the improvements that it brought to wheeled transport, and the funds that produced for the turnpike system, were soon challenged by other modes of transport for goods and materials. The first of these was the ABERDEENSHIRE CANAL through Donside, authorized by Act of Parliament in 1796 and opened in 1805 (*John Rennie*, engineer) between Aberdeen and a terminus at Port Elphinstone, Inverurie, named after Sir James Elphinstone, one of the promoters. Although the scheme was intended to continue as far as Insch, it foundered; a proper connection with Aberdeen's harbour at Waterloo Quay was not made until 1834 and the canal closed in 1853. Almost immediately the line of the canal was filled in for construction of the RAILWAY by the Great North of Scotland Railway Co. (GNSR), which had been created in 1846 to connect Aberdeen with Inverness. The line was set out in 1852–4 between Kittybrewster (Aberdeen) and Huntly (and Keith in Moray, where it connected with the Highland Railway) and connected to the harbour in Aberdeen via the old canal route in 1856, so that freight to and from Aberdeenshire could be transported by sea. Meanwhile the Aberdeen Railway along the coast (from Guthrie in Angus) had reached Ferryhill on the s side of Aberdeen in 1850 and penetrated to its new terminus, and site of the present station, at Guild Street in 1854. Yet it was only from 1867 that the GNSR and the Aberdeen Railway were connected, by a line at Aberdeen along the Denburn valley and the creation of a joint station at Guild Street. The Deeside Railway, a commuter line running w along the river between the city and Banchory was constructed in 1852–3, before extension to Aboyne in 1859 and Ballater in 1866, but never as far as Braemar, partly owing to regal resistance. The line more or less superseded the coaching trade along the Deeside road, except beyond Ballater, and a bus station remains at Braemar as evidence of the need to transfer to road transport for the final leg of the journey for Late Victorian summer visitors. The line closed in 1966 and from this time forward the branch lines established in the 1850s and 60s to the towns of Banffshire and Buchan to the N (Turriff, Banff, Ellon, Fraserburgh and Peterhead) were also progressively closed to passengers and freight.

Besides the principal station at Guild Street, Aberdeen (rebuilt in 1913–15), very few RAILWAY STATIONS survive on the former Aberdeen Railway from the s, except at Stonehaven and Laurencekirk, both opened in 1849, although only Stonehaven's pleasant Italianate station is of that date. On the Aberdeen–Inverness line there is a good example at Kennethmont of the standard timber-clad stations erected by the GNSR in 1854 and a slightly more permanent station house at Insch, but the best is the long, low profile of Inverurie station, as rebuilt in 1902 by *James Lowson*, the GNSR's architect and *Patrick M. Barnett*, chief engineer, with a private waiting room for the Earl of Kintore. It is similar to Lowson and Barnett's Scots Baronial rebuilding of the (former) station at Aboyne in 1896, which had exalted status from its opening as the terminus in 1859 by virtue of its use by the royal party during their visits to Balmoral, and by the mid 1890s was rapidly emerging as one of the premier resort villages. The station at Ballater, as remodelled in 1886, is a classic of the Picturesque style which infected Deeside in this period.* By the time that Aberdeen's station was rebuilt in 1915, again by *Lowson*, the Classical Revival was in full swing; but alas the façade of this can no longer be easily appreciated following its overlay by the Union Square shopping centre. The only BRIDGES AND VIADUCTS of note are on the line s from Aberdeen where several rivers needed crossing, e.g. at Marykirk, with thirteen arches spanning the North Esk, built for the Aberdeen Railway. The viaducts on this line originally had timber arches between the piers, all replaced by steel girders in the 1880s. Otherwise only the GNSR's viaduct over the Deveron, a steel lattice girder crossing the river near Ruthven, of 1892 by their chief engineer, Patrick M. Barnett, is of interest.

The coast of southern Aberdeenshire (i.e. s of Aberdeen), where several small rivers run into the North Sea, proved hospitable to HARBOURS for fishing and cargo. Several are already recorded in the medieval period (Aberdeen, Catterline, Inverbervie) or C17 (Stonehaven and Johnshaven, where fishing boats could be pulled up onto the shore) but presumably of a fairly simple unsophisticated nature with jetties and tidal basins at best. Almost all the smaller harbours were reconstructed in the C19, with new piers at Catterline, Gourdon (by *Telford*, 1819), Inverbervie (also *Telford*) and Johnshaven (1884 and after). Stonehaven's C18 pier was reconstructed to form a safe enclosed harbour in the C19 (*Stevenson*) but it is still essentially a natural cove protected by piers and breakwaters. Only Aberdeen became a major harbour of the kind suited to the demands of foreign trade. The harbour was already trading with Scandinavia and the Baltic ports in the C16 but before the late C18 was comprised of wharfs along the mouth of the Dee. It was protected from silting up by a new pier in 1775 (it was silting that finished off Inverbervie's harbour in the earlier C19) and a series of quays were created to increase its capacity. But its formation into a proper harbour as one understands it now only began in the early C19 (the naming of the quays – Regent, Waterloo – gives the clue to the date) before construction of the Victoria Dock (the first enclosed dock) and in the 1870s the Albert Basin.

Beside the harbours, buildings for goods were erected but Aberdeen is somewhat unfortunate that the renewed significance

*In 2015 this was tragically destroyed by fire.

of its harbour as a centre for servicing the oil industry from the early 1970s caused most of the C19 buildings to be demolished. Nevertheless there are still numerous structures associated with harbour business and the welfare of sailors. One especially interesting group is the former warehouses in St Clement Street, built in 1828, which look very much like the grand classical terraces of houses being built in Aberdeen at this time. Regent Quay, which runs along the N side of the harbour, has not only the former Custom House of 1772–4 (No. 35, originally designed as a house) but also the grand Harbour Board offices by *A. Marshall Mackenzie*, 1883–5. The late C20 contribution is not without merit, especially the Marine Operations Centre on the North Pier of 2006 with its bow-fronted tower. It calls to mind the LIGHTHOUSES, of which Girdleness Lighthouse (at the entrance to Aberdeen Harbour, 1831–3) and the more modest Todhead Lighthouse (near Catterline, 1897) on the approach to Stonehaven are both good examples of the works executed by several generations of the 'Lighthouse Stevensons' for the Northern Lighthouse Board.

88

124

102

BURGH AND VILLAGE BUILDINGS
BY CHARLES O'BRIEN

An account of the secular architecture of the towns and villages of the southern area of Aberdeenshire is dominated by the presence of Aberdeen, Scotland's third largest city, with a population of approximately 227,000 people. From this the descent in scale to the next most populous settlement is dramatic, even if one includes the towns of north Aberdeenshire outside the area covered by this gazetteer: Stonehaven and Inverurie are the only proper towns, each of about 9,500 people; Huntly, a small market centre, is only half the size; and even places such as Banchory are little more than aggrandized villages, much of whose present-day expanse may be accounted for by a demand for housing since 1920. The relative lack of importance of towns in the settlement of Aberdeenshire is very much to its benefit, preserving a predominantly rural character throughout the area, which begins at the fringes of the city of Aberdeen and becomes increasingly wild as one progresses eastward toward the Highland.

Burgh and village buildings before the eighteenth century

In common with the northern districts of Scotland, from the medieval period until the last years of the C18, the majority of Aberdeenshire's population was engaged in agricultural activity and lived in fermtouns (that is, hamlets focused on the collective working of a farm) or in kirktons around a parish church. Several place names in Aberdeenshire retain their prefix 'Kirkton of', distinguishing them as the principal settlement of often large parishes. Along the coast there were evidently also fishing

villages: Gourdon is recorded *c*. 1315. A much smaller portion of
Aberdeenshire's inhabitants lived in burghs, a concept introduced to Scotland in the early C12 in the lowland areas. In these
royal burghs, where property and privileges were held directly
from the Crown, merchants exercised a monopoly of foreign
trade over a substantial area. Royal burghs spread north through
Scotland during the reign of David I and his successors. Aberdeen
(i.e. the port of New Aberdeen) was established as a royal burgh
before 1153. By the mid C13 at the latest a royal burgh had also
been founded at Kintore and this status was later conferred on
Inverbervie in Kincardineshire (1341) and Inverurie, capital of
the Garioch, in 1558. Only the last of these has maintained its
status as a significant town to the present day and even it was
hardly more than a single street until the end of the C18.

The other type of burghs were burghs of barony, under the
control of powerful local lairds, secular and ecclesiastical, where
privileges were more limited, extending only to rights to hold
markets for domestic trade and to house craftsmen. Besides Old
Aberdeen, which became a burgh in 1489, the most significant
of the burghs of barony in the central and southern area of
Aberdeenshire was Huntly, under the control of the Gordons,
which was erected as a burgh in 1488. s of Aberdeen, Stonehaven
was held under the superiority of the Keiths, Earls Marischal,
became a burgh of barony in 1587 and soon after assumed the
role of county town of Kincardineshire, succeeding the now
vanished castleton that lay near Kincardine Castle. Of the other
modestly size burghs, Fettercairn was erected into a burgh of
barony in 1504, Insch only in 1677, Laurencekirk as late as 1779.
It is informative to know that places which are now of almost
no significance were also granted this status: Kildrummy in
1377; Old Rayne from 1493 under the superiority of William
Elphinstone, Bishop of Aberdeen, for whom Clatt was also
erected a burgh of barony in 1501; Kincardine O'Neil in 1511;
Marykirk in 1543; Auchenblae (or Fordoun, as it was) in 1554;
Leslie in 1649; Tullich in 1661; and Tarland in 1683. This was no
guarantee of future importance and many of these settlements
remained very modest. The third class of burghs, apparently
unrepresented in Aberdeenshire, were burghs of regality,
granted to noblemen and giving them legal jurisdiction over a
wide area.

Medieval STREET PATTERNS can be discerned easily in the
layout of Old Aberdeen to this day. The street pattern of 'New'
Aberdeen, the heart of the modern city centre, has been overlaid
by the replannings and improvements of the C18, C19 and C20
but can still be recognized in the several streets ending in the
suffix 'gate' and the centrally placed former market place
(Castlegate) close to the site of the C13 castle. The layouts in Old
and New Aberdeen are exactly what one expects of medieval
burghs: a broad main street, usually doubling as market place,
from which long but narrow strips of land (burgage tofts)
extended on either side to provide the town burgesses with space
for dwelling at the front and ground for cultivation to the rear.

In time these plots were often subdivided and additional dwellings erected, to which access was provided by a passage, or 'close', reached via a pend on the street front. One may see the same pattern in Kintore, Huntly, Inverurie, Stonehaven, etc.

The earliest structures providing evidence of the rights of the burghs are the MARKET CROSSES. The majority of examples still to be seen are rarely earlier than the C16 or C17 and few are crosses in the true sense, usually sporting instead a variety of heraldic devices (e.g. lion, unicorn, burgh arms) at the head. Fettercairn's cross of *c.* 1504 is the earliest in southern Aberdeenshire and came from the vanished Castleton of Kincardine but was given a new top in the late C17 when the burgh's market charter was renewed. Similarly only the shaft of the C16 cross at Old Aberdeen bearing the bishop's arms survived its destruction at the Reformation. These crosses served more than one purpose and indicative of this are the sundial, ell measure and traces of attaching jougs on the Fettercairn cross. That Old Rayne was once a place of significance is indicated by the well-preserved late C17 cross there, even though there is hardly room around it to call a market place. Inverbervie's cross is dated 1737 and still stands in the market place (but the stepped base is perhaps earlier). Such renewal is quite common, so, for instance, Stonehaven's cross has a head of 1887 atop its C17 shaft. While these examples are representative of their kind and period, the most lavish example is, as one would expect, in Aberdeen. This is of 1686 and – somewhat remarkably for the date – the identity of its designer, *John Montgomery*, is known. In style it belongs to the largest class of such structures in Scotland, of which the other notable examples are at Preston, in Lothian (*c.* 1617), and Edinburgh (also 1617 but a C19 reconstruction), with a substantial drum podium, of polygonal plan, and open arcading supporting a platform from which the cross-shaft rises. The use of the Orders (Ionic and Corinthian) and the programme of heraldic decoration, with portraits of the C16 and C17 Stuart monarchs in wreathed surrounds, shows an awareness of Continental trends in Aberdeenshire.

Associated with these crosses, sometimes very directly in terms of placing, were TOLBOOTHS. These were the centre of civic and legal administration, providing rooms for collection of payments from market traders and for meetings of the burgesses, and lock-ups for miscreants. Their grandest architectural form was tall and slender, in character not unlike a church bell-tower crossed with the domestic tower house and thereby providing a most visible landmark for the burgh. Construction of Aberdeen's tolbooth was approved in 1393 but what remains is the stone-built Tolbooth steeple of 1616; it is partly concealed by its Victorian successor but highly visible is the top stage with battlements and Gothic belfry, surmounted by a lively spire added in 1630. In contrast, the Tolbooth at Stonehaven could not be simpler, perhaps because it was adapted for its civic purpose *c.* 1600 rather than newly built. The similarly domestic-looking Headhouse beside the market cross at Old Rayne was no doubt its tolbooth.

Most medieval burghs would have had their share of CHARI-
TABLE FOUNDATIONS, many of them associated with education
of the poor or provision of shelter and care for the sick and
elderly. The longest-lasting contribution of the medieval period
has been the COLLEGES. King's College, Old Aberdeen, founded
by Bishop Elphinstone in 1495, is early, even in national terms.
Post-Reformation the space formerly dominated by the church
became the gift of the wealthy burgesses and merchants, and
Marischal College in New Aberdeen was founded in 1593 by
George Keith, 5th Earl Marischal, and endowed with the property of the former Franciscan friary in Broad Street. Marischal
College was rebuilt twice in the C19 and there is only a little
post-medieval and C17 building left at King's, in the form of the
Round Tower of the C16 quad and the Cromwell Tower of 1658,
designed for student accommodation.

HOUSING from before the eighteenth century in southern
Aberdeenshire's burghs is a rare commodity indeed; even in
Aberdeen there is nothing surviving from before the late C16,
partly the consequence of clearance of the older streets of the
town in the C19 and C20. The earliest survival is Benholm's
Lodging (built c. 1588–1616) in Nether Kirkgate but since the
1960s banished to a site in Tillydrone Road in Old Aberdeen. It
is in every respect a small, indefensible version of the Z-plan
tower houses found in late C16 rural Aberdeenshire. A house of
a more truly urban character is in Shiprow (No. 48), one of the
high-status streets of medieval Aberdeen, and in spite of reconstruction in 1954 gives a good picture of forms of domestic
building for its date (1593) with a four-storey main block, set
back from the street, for principal accommodation over a ground-
floor kitchen but with a gabled tower to the fore on one side
containing the entrance and small chambers. Much larger and
more ambitious is Provost Skene's House in Broad Street. This
is an outstanding survival and an example of the tendency in
burghs by the C17 for the long medieval backlands to be subdivided and built up with additional houses. So the access to
Provost Skene's House was originally from the street at the front
of its plot via a pend in the property along the street itself. The
house itself appears to be C16 at its core but its full development
on a more fashionable courtyard plan was reached only in the
mid and later C17, again following developments in rural tower
houses for horizontal planning. Perhaps the most important
aspect of the building, however, is the preservation of its interior
decoration (though much restored in the 1950s), principally the
mid-C17 painted ceiling in the Long Gallery with its naïve painted
religious scenes, so surprising for the date and probably derived
from Flemish prints, and the late C17 plasterwork in other rooms.
In Stonehaven it is clear that its accession to the role of county
town c. 1600 resulted in new houses of some distinction (though
some were swept away in the mid C20), of which No. 51 High
Street with its corbelled turret and carved door surround is the
best.

Burghs and villages from 1700 to c. 1840

The C18 to the early C19 was a period of improvement. One of the first visible effects was the creation of PLANNED VILLAGES, set out by landowners on their estates with plots feued to incoming tenants to build houses and cultivate the land, though these are less common in south Aberdeenshire than in the north and Moray. Monymusk, one of the earliest, was created by Sir Archibald Grant from 1716 as part of the wider reform of his estate on improved agricultural lines (*see* p. 93). The second C18 innovator was the 3rd Duke of Gordon at Huntly, who in 1737 set about the creation of a weaving village. But the late C18, with its growing prosperity in land and industry, encouraged more ambitious schemes and Huntly was completely replanned by the 4th Duke in 1770 as a grid-iron pattern around a central square. This was the accepted pattern for several villages of this type and may be seen earlier in the layout of the Stonehaven New Town from *c.* 1759 for Robert Barclay of Urie. It occurs again at Ballater, begun in the 1790s by Farquharson of Monaltrie. While some planned villages were essentially started from scratch on virgin sites (e.g. the crofting and weaving village of Luthermuir), others were intended as a shot-in-the-arm to existing settlements by reviving them as centres of new industry. This is the case at Laurencekirk, reformed in 1765 by the Laird of Thornton Castle for linen weaving and boxmaking, and Auchenblae, set out by the 5th Earl of Kintore *c.* 1770 for flax spinning. Both Rhynie (*c.* 1795 for the Duke of Gordon) and the larger burgh of Inverurie (again for the 5th Earl of Kintore but *c.* 1800) were boosted by comprehensive replanning with new streets, houses and accoutrements of civic life. The coastal area also has a few planned fishing villages (e.g. Muchalls) but the place of major interest is Footdee near the Harbour in Aberdeen, which was created by the Town Council in 1808–9 and designed by *John Smith* with cottages – originally thatched – set around two squares, and which, despite alterations since the late C19, retains its rugged individualism. Perhaps the most extraordinary structure in these planned villages is the bell steeple at Drumlithie, erected in the late C18 to regulate the mealtimes of the local weavers. 86

Among PUBLIC BUILDINGS the most important Georgian item is Robert Gordon's College (originally Hospital) in Aberdeen, 84 founded in 1731 for the education of sons and grandsons of local burgesses. *William Adam* was the architect and this is the first formally classical building in the city. It is also among the earliest uses of granite ashlar in Aberdeen. Changing fortunes in the smaller burghs are often expressed by the replacement of the old vertical tolbooths with more commodious and horizontal buildings, even if the earlier steeple was retained as an emblem of continuity and civic pride. An example of this is the Town House (the more commonly used term for such civic buildings from the C18) at Inverbervie of 1719–20, which succeeded the tolbooth of 1569, and the Town House at Kintore built *c.* 1737–48. The latter 85

is an exemplar of its kind and date, partly funded by the
Convention of Royal Burghs (the assembly of merchants elected
to represent the common interests of the royal burghs). Its
appearance is essentially domestic, much like a mid-C18 two-
storey house but with a grand clock turret and elegant double
staircase towards the market place. Towards the end of the C18
87   there is also the new Town House at Old Aberdeen, by the
mason-architect *George Jaffray*, 1787–9, and that at Stonehaven
of 1789–90 by *James Rhind*. The Stonehaven building – a single
tower with spired roof – appears extraordinarily retardataire
when compared with the classically minded buildings at Kintore
and Old Aberdeen. County Buildings, i.e. the administrative
headquarters for the county of Kincardineshire, were built at
Stonehaven in 1767 (including a jail) and rebuilt by *John Smith*
97   in 1822. At about the same time the new Market Buildings were
erected as the landmark in the New Town at Stonehaven, which
had been developing since *c.* 1760.

Good examples of early C18 HOUSING in the burghs are Powis
Lodge, College Bounds, Old Aberdeen (of 1711), and Forsyth's
House, Huntly (of *c.* 1724–6), which introduces the motif of the
frontal gable, in this instance of Dutch form (possibly inspired
by its merchant owner's trade in cloth with the Low Countries).
Forsyth's House also has club skewputts, a feature shared by
numerous C18 houses of high and low status. Typically, housing
in the burghs and villages adopts a familiar form of rows of two-
or one-storey fronts, usually symmetrical with central door and
gabled ends with chimneys, e.g. Grant's Place, Old Aberdeen,
dated 1732, and the C18 rows in Castle Street, Huntly. Another
familiar kind of house in the towns is that which is set at right
angles to the street, showing only its gable, no doubt determined
6   by the narrow medieval plots they occupy, of which High Street,
Old Aberdeen, has characteristic examples. Towards the end of
the C18 elevations start to become explicitly classical: *see*, for
89   example, No. 81 High Street, Old Aberdeen, built *c.* 1773 as a
town residence for Maclean of Coll, or the detached houses built
in the Lochlands area of inner Aberdeen in the late C18.

In any rural parish the most prominent house after the laird's
house would have been the MANSE, the residence of the minister.
From 1663 the Scottish parliament required the landowners
(heritors) to provide a manse and offices, ranging in cost from
£400 to £1,000 Scots (*c.* £27–£85 sterling). But from 1760 the
upper limit was removed in the rebuilding of existing manses and
this explains the large number of late C18 and early C19 new
manses in Aberdeenshire. Typically two-storeyed plus an attic,
with a three-bay front and central door, they are very like detached
houses in the towns of the same date, but with one or two single-
storey ranges for offices/stabling at the rear or forming a court
in front, like some contemporary farmhouses. A superior example
is the former manse for Cairnie parish of 1784–5, its expensive-
looking classical style no doubt due to the marriage of the minister to the sister of the Duke of Gordon. A significant proportion
of the Aberdeenshire manses date from the 1790s and almost all

were subjected to alteration *c.* 1805 or *c.* 1820–30. In these second phases it is quite common to find the C18 manse relegated to the status of a wing to the new house.

Like manses, PARISH SCHOOLS were also the responsibility of the local landowners. The earliest now surviving in Aberdeenshire is that beside the burial ground at Kirkton of Fetteresso of *c.* 1778, comprising (as became the norm) a school and school house for its master under one roof. Like the former school at Towie of 1811 it is hard to distinguish from contemporary two-storey cottages.

For Aberdeen the period after 1790 was one of major URBAN IMPROVEMENT in which the creation of new streets was accompanied by new forms of housing and impressive civic and commercial buildings. Although modest by comparison with contemporary changes in Glasgow and Edinburgh, the first phase of the new classical formality in Aberdeen was the pioneering effort in 1766 to span the awkward changes in level across the town by laying out Marischal Street as a bridge, with houses on each side whose façades were executed to a standard design. From *c.* 1800 the creation of Union Street, again as a bridge street across the town's Denburn and several medieval streets, transformed the axis from small wynds leading down to the harbour to an immensely long horizontal E–W vista. This was accompanied by the building up of TERRACES of stern and regular four-storey tenements, without even mouldings to the window openings. The only variations on the straight terrace of the kind found in Edinburgh is Bon Accord Crescent, laid out from 1823 by 93 *Archibald Simpson* with two-storey terraces over basements. There are also two stately squares – Golden Square and Bon Accord Square – but neither forms part of a comprehensive formal plan. The new types of housing also begin to appear in suburban developments, e.g. the very fine Marine Terrace at Ferryhill, Aberdeen, of 1830–1 by *Simpson*. Here the terrace is single-storeyed, above a basement, except at its centre, and this single-storey form is also used in a number of detached villas in this period.

As will have become clear from the above, and in the previous chapters on churches and country houses, by the turn of the C19 and especially in the first three decades thereafter the identity of ARCHITECTS – as a profession distinct from masons whose names have survived in the records – was becoming increasingly important. Two figures already mentioned are of special significance in this period: *Archibald Simpson* and *John Smith*. Simpson was born in Aberdeen in 1790 to a clothier and practised almost exclusively in the city from about 1813 (following his training in London) until his death in 1847. Although much of his work was devoted to churches and country houses he also contributed the best of the city's early C19 public buildings to adorn the new pattern of streets, beginning in 1818–20 with the Medico-Chirurgical Society's Hall in King Street, the Union Buildings 94 (1819–22) and Assembly Rooms (now Music Hall, 1820–2) in 91 Union Street, and the Infirmary in 1832, followed by the rebuilding of Marischal College in 1837–44 and New Market in 1840–2, the last a major work now sadly lost. His urban work is almost exclusively in a restrained monumental classicism of the Late Georgian period and represents its high-water mark in the early Victorian years before the more eclectic styles take over after *c.* 1840. John Smith, who was the son of an Aberdeen builder-architect, also trained in London but was back in Aberdeen from 1804 and became the Town (or City) Architect in 1824. Like Simpson his style is grand Neoclassical, notably the great Ionic screen of 1830, known as the Façade, which divides St Nicholas's churchyard from Union Street, alterations to Robert Gordon's College in 1833 and the (former) Old Town School in Little Belmont Street with their giant portico. But Smith was not wedded to classicism and, as his nickname 'Tudor Johnny' implies, he was as much at ease designing in a notionally English C16 style, demonstrated by the former Trinity Hall in Union Street and King's College, Aberdeen, where his partial reconstruction of the college quad in 1822–6 is firmly Tudor Gothic and, if not inspired, is appropriate in its relationship with the medieval chapel. Smith's Gothicisim is more evident in his houses and the two sides to him can be appreciated in the contrast between his manses at Coull (1831–2) and Drumoak (1836), which are pristine Late Georgian examples of the Scots classical vernacular, and those designed by him at Keig (1834–5), Tough (1835), Skene (1840), Kincardine O'Neil (1844), Auchenblae (1844–5), Tarland (1846) and Hatton of Fintray (1847).

Victorian and Edwardian

The Victorian period was one of major change throughout the towns and villages of the area, at least in part the consequence of the arrival of the railways (for which *see* p. 71) and the building up of new large-scale industrial enterprises in Aberdeen. The city massively increased its population during this period and even in the smaller towns and villages there were consequences, most obviously in the increased scale of building to more than two storeys and the greater presence of purpose-built commercial buildings. In parts of Aberdeenshire from *c.* 1850 and until the end of the century the impact of tourism did much to enhance and develop places that were previously of quite modest charac-ter, notably along Deeside, where the decision of Queen Victoria and Prince Albert to acquire Balmoral in 1848 led to an influx of visitors and prompted the building of new hotels as well as houses for summer letting. Banchory, Ballater, Braemar and Stonehaven owe much of their character to this period.

The number of professional LOCAL ARCHITECTS proliferated hugely after 1840 and the following, concentrated largely but not exclusively in Aberdeen, deserve mention as they dominate the design of public and commercial buildings in the city and Aberdeenshire generally up to 1914: *Thomas Mackenzie, James Matthews, William Ramage, Alexander Ellis* (and later *R. G. Wilson*),

J. R. Mackenzie, James Souttar, Duncan McMillan (and later his son *J. Ross McMillan*), *A. Marshall Mackenzie* (and later his son *A. G. R. Mackenzie*), *George Watt* of *Brown & Watt, William Kelly, A. H. L. Mackinnon, George Coutts* and *George Bennett Mitchell*.

Among PUBLIC BUILDINGS there is a proliferation of new types, indicative of legislation in various areas of local government. The Great Reform Act of 1832, followed in Scotland by the Royal Burghs Reform Act of 1833, converted many royal burghs into parliamentary burghs with elected town councils, the first act in a series of efforts to reform the municipalities; the Burgh Police (Scotland) Act, passed in the same year, allowed burghs of barony to adopt new powers to cover policing, paving, lighting and sanitation. Huntly adopted this system almost immediately; elsewhere the burghs took on these powers more gradually. Banchory is the one place to add to the existing list of burghs at this time, adopting the police system in 1885. The creation of elected town councils is occasionally expressed architecturally in new MUNICIPAL BUILDINGS, so Stonehaven New Town's new council in 1856 decided immediately to erect the spire on the town's Market Buildings as a visible expression of civic authority. In Aberdeen the C17 Town House had been rebuilt more than once in the C18 and early C19 before achieving its present form in 1867–8 at the hands of *Peddie & Kinnear*, drawing together in one building the by now multifarious functions of the City and County Councils. Stonehaven's County Buildings, for administration of Kincardineshire, are a little earlier (1863–5 by *J. Campbell Walker*) and display the preference before the mid 60s for the Italianate. The same is true for Inverurie, which has the largest of the other Town Halls in Aberdeenshire, rebuilt in 1862 by *J. R. Mackenzie* but with the wholly unexpected feature of a large belfry of almost Spanish Baroque character. Like a number of other such town halls this also provided accommodation for the courts: the Sheriff Courts at Aberdeen are simply incorporated within the Town House complex.

In smaller burghs, a doubling up of premises for the council with PUBLIC HALLS for local assemblies and meetings of societies is quite common, so for example at Stonehaven, where the purpose-built Town Hall of 1878, opposite the Market Buildings, also included a newsroom and public hall. At Huntly, Stewart's Hall is of 1873–5 by *James Anderson* (though with a magnificent Scots Baronial tower on the Aberdeen Town House model added by *Matthews & Mackenzie* in 1886–7). The best of the other public halls include the quite ambitious but not entirely convincing Scots Renaissance-style Public Hall at Fettercairn of 1890–1 by *John Milne* and the much smaller but delightful Rannes Public Hall at Kennethmont of 1909 by *T. G. Archibald* of Huntly, borrowing its motifs from Leith Hall, where Archibald is thought to have worked a few years before. Probably the best is the last, the fine Arts and Crafts-style building at St Cyrus of 1911–12 by *D. Wishart Galloway*.

In the smaller places there is a perceptible spread of new VILLAGE HALLS in the last years of the C19 and the beginning of the C20. One impetus nationally was the desire to provide a suitable commemoration for Queen Victoria's jubilees in 1877, 1887 and 1897 and her death in 1901. At Braemar, this resulted in almost childish competitiveness between the two lairds, Farquharson of Invercauld and the Earl Fife at Mar Lodge; the Earl's Jubilee Hall, started second but finished first in 1879, is the more likeable, timber-clad with pretty bargeboards. There are not many others of note in the area except Auchenblae of 1870, surprisingly for Aberdeenshire entirely of brick, bestowing on it an almost Flemish character.

Other pieces of national legislation led to major reform in provision of healthcare. The urbanization of Scottish burghs and expansion owing to industrialization during the earlier C19 encouraged the building of new general HOSPITALS, many of which developed out of existing charitable medical institutions and free dispensaries. Aberdeen's Infirmary (founded *c.* 1740 and now part of Woolmanhill Hospital) belongs to this pioneering phase, being completely rebuilt in 1832–40 to accommodate over 200 patients in large open wards. The result is one of the best of the Neoclassical buildings by *Archibald Simpson* (*see* also above), with implied giant portico and small dome – easily the equal of other contemporary British hospitals in this style (and cf. Dr Gray's Hospital, Elgin, Moray). By the later C19 SPECIALIST HOSPITALS were attempting to deal with the limitations of treatment available in general hospitals, for children and women for example and the long-term sick. Treatment for infectious diseases required new forms of hospital planning, of which the former City Hospital, Aberdeen, of 1874–7 is an example (originally using concrete cast *in situ*). The setting, initially in spacious grounds outside the built-up area of Aberdeen, and the layout, of single-storey ward buildings with attached sanitary towers and a more impressive central block for administration and staff accommodation, are characteristic of such buildings in larger towns and guided by model plans issued to local government. Not all such initiatives were the preserve of local authorities. Private SANATORIA also belong to the latest years of the C19 and there is no better example than the former (and alas now derelict) Glen O'Dee Sanatorium established by Dr James Lawson in 1900–1 in the pine woods above Banchory for the treatment of tuberculosis and modelled on the pioneering establishment at Nordrach in Germany. The style is an interesting hybrid of Bavarian with Deeside's own distinct picturesque half-timbered style; like all such buildings it was designed to provide maximum access to fresh air and sunlight.

Among MENTAL HOSPITALS an early example was the Lunatic Asylum at Aberdeen of 1819–22 by *Simpson*. But advances in the treatment of mental illness over the course of the C19 gave rise to entirely new forms of planning of these institutions, which reached their apogee in the (former) Kingseat District Asylum erected near Newmachar, where a large site permitted the development of an expansive model establishment on the 'colony system', with villas or cottages for patients dispersed in an informal and picturesque pattern across the grounds and designed in an overtly humane style by *A. Marshall Mackenzie & Son*, 1899.

The Scottish Poor Law Act of 1845 updated the existing system of parish relief for the poor with funds raised through rates on property by elected parochial boards, who were also permitted to erect POORHOUSES to serve parishes or combinations of parishes exceeding 5,000 people. Stonehaven's poorhouse on Woodcot Brae by *William Henderson* (1865–7) is typically austere and exhibits the H-plan form widely adopted in buildings of this period. Aberdeen in fact had two houses, one for St Nicholas's parish (the East Poorhouse, *c.* 1847) and one for Old Machar (the West Poorhouse, *c.* 1849), eventually brought together as Oldmill Poorhouse and hospital (by *Brown & Watt* in 1902–7), a distinctly impressive establishment now in use as Woodend Hospital.

As the C19 progressed the extent of provision by burgh councils expanded to cover a variety of areas of cultural and intellectual life. Aberdeen ART GALLERY with its associated School of Art (both by *Matthews & Mackenzie*) opened in 1883 as an adjunct to Robert Gordon's College, to which it provided a grand Italian Renaissance entrance, but the outstanding aspect of the gallery is the later Sculpture Court, added by *A. Marshall Mackenzie* in 1901–5. These were places of education rather than leisure – the cast of the Parthenon frieze incorporated within the Art Gallery was intended to inspire and teach the monumental sculptors of Aberdeen's many granite yards – and such institutions were often provided by local philanthropists. Such is the case at Huntly, in the form of the Brander Museum and Library.

That free public LIBRARIES were a symbol of civic pride in the later years of the C19 is ably demonstrated by the prominent site given to Aberdeen's Central Library on Rosemount Viaduct by *Brown & Watt* in 1889–92, erected with funds raised through public appeal. It was given a fairly plain Renaissance character, which became quite popular for such buildings; the branch libraries in Torry (1902–3 by *Brown & Watt*) and Ferryhill (*Arthur Clyne*, 1903) are a good deal livelier. Among the villages and smaller burghs there is a very early example of a library at Monymusk, indicative of the activities of a progressive laird in his model village, with accommodation for the librarian. Most of the examples, however, date from the 1880s and after, some provided by local donors, e.g. the Anderson Library, Woodside, Aberdeen (1882 by *Arthur Clyne* and typically for him a little eccentric in its Baronial features), or as at Inverurie (1910–11) by local authorities under the Free Libraries Acts, which permitted financing from the rates and which were further supported through the largesse of philanthropists such as Andrew Carnegie, who also contributed to the Aberdeen Central Library.

New SCHOOLS are perhaps the most visible and numerous contribution of the Victorian years. The former Old Town School, Little Belmont Street, Aberdeen, by *John Smith*, 1840–1 is in a serious Neoclassical style with temple front – a relatively late example of the most favoured architectural expression for the best early C19 schools and academies. The Gordon Schools at Huntly, of 1839–41 by *Archibald Simpson*, favour instead a slightly impure Tudor-Jacobean collegiate style with central gatehouse crowned by an octagonal belfry – in fact, very similar in a diminished form to Simpson's contemporary rebuilding of Marischal College, Aberdeen (1837–44). The Huntly schools, executed for the Duchess of Gordon, are typical of larger Scottish burghs of this period in bringing together several formerly separate educational establishments under one roof. *James Matthews*'s rebuilding of Aberdeen's Grammar School in Scots Baronial style in 1861–3 succeeded the C18 school.

In the mid C19 the parish heritors continued to bear responsibility for new schools in the rural areas (e.g. Glass School of 1844 and the very typical design by *J. & W. Smith* for Hatton of Fintray in the 1850s) but the passing of the Education Act in 1872 transformed public elementary school provision, not only making education between ages five and thirteen compulsory but also placing the provision and maintenance of new schools in the hands of locally elected school boards (which might in any case include the heritor as one of the members). The Scotch Education Department was created to maintain educational standards and set standards for new buildings, favouring single-storey buildings with separate classrooms for infants and older pupils and a two-storey school house for the teacher. That at least was the model in the rural areas, and see for example the early results of the new legislation at Aboyne (1874) and Strachan (1876–7). In smaller burghs and suburban areas of Aberdeen (e.g. Commerce Street, the first such school in Aberdeen in 1875 and Old Aberdeen, 1874–5 (now St Peter's R.C. School), this could also be followed, but in the centre of Aberdeen – where space was restricted and numbers of pupils large – the more familiar three-storey type of urban school becomes the norm in the 1880s (notably Ashley Road School (1887), Mile End School (1899–1901) and Broomhill School (1893)), often with classrooms planned around a central hall. Very early Board Schools exhibit a few Gothic motifs but quickly a more secular style was adopted. By the turn of the C20 most burghs (and even some smaller places) were offering secondary education in 'higher grade' schools and so there are a good many more buildings from the period *c.* 1897–1914: *see*, for examples, additions to buildings at Aboyne, Huntly and Inverurie.

The design of schools was generally given out to a variety of local architects but from the early C20 one can see certain architects developing a specialism in this area of their practice, for example *J. A. Ogg Allan*, who was master of works and then official architect to the Aberdeen School Board from 1895 to 1905. The former Central School, in Schoolhill, and the Frederick Street School, with its rooftop playground, are the outstanding examples of his Aberdeen work before 1914 and show his aptitude for adopting the latest styles such as Baroque, Baronial or the Free Style, so there is much originality in his work. He continued to design the principal schools for Aberdeenshire into the period between the Wars.

The city also provided its own TECHNICAL SCHOOLS, which grew out of the Mechanics' Institutes, but from 1881 technical classes were offered at Robert Gordon's College and in its own buildings from 1910, laying the foundation for the modern Robert Gordon University. The late C19 also brought major changes with the bringing together of King's College and Marischal College as the UNIVERSITY OF ABERDEEN in 1860. The effect was felt first at King's, where in 1859–62 C18 rebuildings were swept away and replaced without much distinction, mainly by architects within *H.M. Office of Works*. Then in 1893–1906 *A. Marshall Mackenzie* was employed for a comprehensive reconstruction of Marischal College, around the core of 109 its buildings by *Archibald Simpson*, in a stunning Gothic tour de force, partly reminiscent of Pugin but with the freedom from archaeological observation of medieval detail that belongs only to the latest C19 and early C20. It is his masterwork and no doubt gave the University confidence in engaging him for the comparatively modest Gothic additions (New King's) at King's College in 1911–12. Here Mackenzie looked for historic continuity with the medieval parts in adopting the Flamboyant tracery of the Chapel as a leitmotif (rather as he had done in his churches by favouring the intersected tracery of the medieval Greyfriars Church and as would reoccur in the War Memorial Buildings at Aboyne in the 1920s and further inform his design for the larger Elphinstone Hall at King's in 1927–31). Away from Aberdeen the most impressive educational establishment in Aberdeenshire is the Roman Catholic seminary of St Mary's College, Blairs, of 108 1892–1903 by *R. G. Wilson* of *Ellis & Wilson*. The first seminary had been established in the year of emancipation in 1829, succeeding the more-or-less clandestine establishments at House of Aquhorthies (Kemnay) and Scalan in Glenlivet (Moray). No self-effacement was needed by the 1890s and the silhouette of the College's entrance tower with crown spire is a landmark on the South Deeside Road.

Among COMMERCIAL BUILDINGS, the BANKS AND INSURANCE OFFICES express themselves architecturally in a manner close to, and sometimes superior to, civic buildings. The Italianate palazzo, representative of mercantile success and suggestive of a long heritage and therefore probity, was the preferred model for banks throughout the whole of the period up to 1914. It begins in fact with *James Burn*'s Aberdeen Banking Co. premises of 90 *c.* 1801 in Aberdeen's Castle Street, and Aberdeen had one of the earliest joint-stock banks in Scotland, the Town & County Bank, Union Street, of 1826, in a building designed by *Archibald Simpson*. It is now demolished but Simpson's North of Scotland 92 Bank, 1842, in Castle Street is the best in the city and one of the best in Scotland, with its Soane-inspired corner elevation and sculptural enrichment that makes explicit the source of Aberdeen's earlier C19 prosperity in agricultural improvement of its hinterland. The contemporary bank by Simpson in The Square at Huntly is also highly distinguished. Banks in Victorian Aberdeen are more than usually restrained in their classicism, perhaps the inevitable result of working in granite; only *James Matthews*'s Clydesdale (former Town & County) Bank in Union Street, 1863, is more florid, Italianate with lavish interior. Even more impressive is the Northern Assurance Co. office by *A. Marshall Mackenzie*, 1882–5. The insurance companies, in contrast, seem to have been more willing to pursue styles of expression other than the Italianate, so for example the variations of Free Classical and Free Renaissance, e.g. the Scottish Temperance Assurance Co. in Union Street of 1899–1900 by *Jenkins & Marr*. In the smaller burghs and villages, the bank is often exceedingly hard to distinguish from a suburban classical villa; indeed it often sits in its own railed garden, e.g. Bank House, Laurencekirk (*c.* 1840), the Neo-Tudor former Town & County Bank, Alford (1859) or the banks in Insch.

Buildings for ENTERTAINMENT, redolent of the jollity of the Victorian and Edwardian years, have three excellent representatives in the form of the interior of the Music Hall, Aberdeen by *James Matthews*, 1859, complete with horseshoe gallery facing the stage; the Tivoli Theatre, by the specialist *C. J. Phipps*, which made a fascinating early use of concrete construction; and His Majesty's Theatre in Aberdeen, by *Frank Matcham*, theatre designer *par excellence*, who also remodelled the Tivoli at about the same date.

In terms of HOUSING, the mid–late C19 and early C20 make a handful of distinct contributions. The expansion of Aberdeen from the mid C19 resulted in the building of very large terraces of middle-class TENEMENTS in some areas, especially Rosemount. The type itself is not unusual – flatted buildings with a single entrance to a common staircase go back to the C17 – but the Late Victorian versions are on a massive scale and when composed along two sides of a street their flat, barely ornamented façades are immensely impressive. Very good examples line Rosemount Viaduct in Aberdeen, following its creation in 1884–5. Even without building on this scale these tenements can be attractive, especially in the years close to 1900. Terraces of the two-storey Late Georgian type continued to be built but now on a grander scale; indicative of their date they sport a variety of styles, e.g. Rubislaw Terrace by *Mackenzie & Matthews*, 1852, with two-storey canted bays and crowstepped gables. Detached VILLAS also now appear on a far grander scale and especially good examples can be seen in the western suburbs of Aberdeen for the length of Queen's Road and in Rubislaw Den South and North; particularly to be noted are those designed by *William Kelly*, *George Coutts* and most of all *Pirie & Clyne*, especially No. 50 Queen's Road and the semi-detached villas in Hamilton Place. The ubiquity of granite and the difficulty of carving enforces a monumentality on the largest of these Aberdonian villas that is unique to the city.

The extension of the railway system in the mid C19 (*see* p. 71) had an important effect on encouraging the building of villas in the villages outside Aberdeen for commuters, e.g. on Deeside, where Murtleden House at Bieldside is a fine example in the Arts and Crafts style of 1902 by *J. Coates Carter*. At Huntly the enclave of houses on Battlehill, close to the station, are similarly notable but their architects have not been identified. In the town there is also Howglen by *F. W. Troup*, who was born at Huntly. Stonehaven is also particularly strong in villas, partly because it drew large numbers of summer visitors. Especially good there is the house called The Lilies, Bath Street, by *George Gregory*, a local builder- 114 architect. Numerous country villas were built in the villages w along the banks of the Dee, especially at Aboyne, Ballater and Braemar, either by locals in need of a place to resort to in the summer and weekends or, increasingly, by well-to-do English visitors keen to have a residence close to good fishing, e.g. Ladywood Lodge, Aboyne, one of many by *George Bennett Mitchell*, *c.* 1900; Rhu-Na-Haven by *Lorimer*, also at Aboyne; Tullich Lodge by *A. Marshall Mackenzie*, 1897, as a sporting lodge for the Aberdeen advocate William Reid, and Craigendarroch House, Ballater. Something distinctive to these burghs along the Dee is the very large numbers of houses and cottages that were let out for the summer and were specially designed so that the resident owner could retreat to a self-contained annexe for the duration, e.g. the charming corrugated-iron-clad Elizabeth Cottage in Banchory, or Daisybank and Juniper Cottage at Braemar.

Finally, at the end of the century, the first examples of improved WORKING-CLASS FLATS appear in Aberdeen. The earliest lie between the Links and King Street in Aberdeen and were built under the 1890 Housing of the Working Classes Act. Their appearance is very severe. Examples of MODEL ESTATE HOUSING occur with distinction in three villages in the period *c.* 1870–1914 and are the consequence of enlightened, progressive and wealthy lairds. The first was the English banker William Cunliffe Brooks, Laird of Glen Tanar estate, who put the design of much new building for estate workers and others in the hands of *George Truefitt*, a very original and often eccentric designer, 75 active *c.* 1870–1900. This is most in evidence on the Glen Tanar estate itself but with some notable additions to Aboyne as well. At Monymusk in the late C19 Sir Arthur Grant employed *John Birch*, another English architect and proselytizer for the Picturesque, to embark on reconstruction of many cottages and other estate buildings. Then at Echt and Dunecht A. C. Pirie, owner of Dunecht House, erected new terraces of houses in a pretty style, with further enhancements for Viscount and Lady Cowdray in the 1920s by their regular architect *William Kelly*.

The attractions of parts of southern Aberdeenshire for visitors have been referred to but it is important to note that TOURISM did not begin in the Victorian period. One of the earliest draws to Aberdeenshire were its spas and springs, so popular with Georgian visitors elsewhere in Britain. At Tullich, towards the w end of the Dee valley, the wells at Pannanich were opened in the mid C18 and the demand led Francis Farquharson of Monaltrie to build an inn to capitalize on their custom and offer bathing in the waters. The Huntly Arms Hotel at Aboyne, the Burnett Arms at Banchory and the hotels at Braemar are collectively the best

representation of the effect of the growth of summer visitors to
Deeside and the Highlands after 1850, each one expanding to
meet ever larger demands. The Aboyne and Banchory hotels
were already active *c*. 1830 as coaching inns but once the Deeside
Railway had arrived in the 1850s their scale changed and also
their style. The same is true of the hotels at Huntly, which were
subjected to rebuildings in the 1890s. The Ramsay Arms Hotel
at Fettercairn is an interesting example of a rebuilding by *T. M.
Cappon* of Dundee, much inspired by the English Arts and Crafts
style. The c18 inn which it replaced had become famous as the
scene of an impromptu visit by Queen Victoria and Prince Albert,
know as their second 'Great Expedition' in 1861. The permanent
record of this royal outing is the nearby Royal Arch, erected in
1864–6 and designed by *John Milne*, a local architect.

This brings us to the subject of PUBLIC MONUMENTS, for the
presence of the monarch in Deeside from 1848 meant that a visit
to a town or village from Queen Victoria or Prince Albert would
usually result in some form of memorial, which is to say nothing
of the royal family's penchant for memorials across the Balmoral
estate. At the beginning of the sequence is, of course, the statue
to Prince Albert, 1862–3 by *Baron Marochetti*, which adorned
Union Street but is now at the end of Union Terrace. This is
followed by Victoria herself in the Town House at Aberdeen by
Alexander Brodie, 1866 (also originally in Union Street but superseded by a bronze of the Queen in her Imperial pomp in 1892
by *C. B. Birch*), and the sequence concludes with Edward VII by
Alfred Drury, 1910–14; the last is particularly outstanding. But
the first public statues of this kind were that in the Town House,
Aberdeen, of Provost Blaikie by *John Steell*, 1844, and in the same
year the statue for the 5th Duke of Gordon, erected in Castlegate
(but now in Golden Square) by *Thomas Campbell*, the Edinburgh
sculptor who also executed the fine portrait reliefs of the 5th
Duke and Duchess at the Gordon Schools, Huntly, 1841. The
Duke's statue is significant as an early instance of the technical
advances made in monumental sculpture by the Aberdeen gran-
ite-cutters. At Huntly is a statue of the 5th Duke by *Brodie*,
1862–3. For lesser citizens, MEMORIAL FOUNTAINS were a
particular enthusiasm, with quite distinguished examples at
Fettercairn (by *David Bryce*, 1869) and Huntly. Figures deserving
of commemoration were not always noblemen, so at Kemnay
funds were raised to remember a local carrier.

Buildings since 1918

The first category to address is that of civic WAR MEMORIALS.
The tour de force is of course the Aberdeen City memorial, in
Schoolhill, by *A. Marshall Mackenzie & Son*, which provides a
mighty curved colonnade as the site for civic remembrance. The
memorial is integral with the Cowdray Hall behind and a similar
strategy was pursued by the same firm at Aboyne in the design
of the splendid Memorial Buildings and Victory Hall (1920–1).

The majority of village and parish memorials are, however, familiar variations on Celtic crosses and only a minority include figure sculpture, notably the figures of Highland soldiers at Rhynie and Tarland by *Robert Warrack Morrison*, a sculptor employed at *D. Morren & Co.*, one of the many distinguished firms of masons active in Aberdeen at this time. The Inverurie war memorial is similar, carved by *James Philip* of *Arthur Taylor*'s granite yard, who famously carved the Edward VII memorial for Aberdeen in 1910–14. Indeed, the national demand for memorials of the most durable kind led to considerable growth in the exporting of monuments by the Aberdeen yards, often to their own design, notably by Messrs *Garden & Co.* (Laurencekirk) and *Stewart & Co.* (Tough). Among individual designers of non-figurative works, *William Kelly* stands out, especially for the quality of the lettering of his memorials (e.g. notably the woodwork in King's College Chapel, Aberdeen but also Banchory, Birse and the tablet at Finzean executed in collaboration with *Sir James Taggart*, who became a stone-cutter in Aberdeen aged sixteen and had his own works in the city from 1883). A foretaste of Kelly's skills as a memorial designer was given in his remarkable Harlaw Monument of 1911, near Chapel of Garioch. The Huntly memorial by the Arts and Crafts architect *F. W. Troup*, 1922, is a one-off and very original in its spare rectilinear design, making a virtue of the effects to be achieved in the contrast between light and dark granites. Similarly unique in its approach is the primitive circular Doric 'temple' on Black Hill, Stonehaven, by the local architect *John Ellis*.

A major preoccupation of the 1920s nationally was an increase in the supply of better HOUSING (following the passing of the Addison Act of 1919 and Wheatley Act of 1924, intended to provide 'Homes for Heroes'), although Aberdeen, like Edinburgh, suffered much less from the problems of overcrowding experienced in the major industrial centres of Dundee and Glasgow. The result in the smaller burghs is unremarkable bungalow-type housing but the public provision exhibits the influence of the low-density Garden Suburb, promoted before the War, with two-storey cottages in pairs set out in streets of geometrical patterns. The housing scheme at Torry, begun in 1920 in the outer southern district of Aberdeen, is the best representative, conforming to the orthodoxy of a radial pattern of curved streets and given presence by the hilltop site s of the Dee. The ready supply of granite meant that, even in pursuit of mass housing, the architectural character of these new schemes remained extremely robust. Smaller schemes of development of housing were also pursued by the burgh councils, especially in Banchory, Insch, Inverurie and Stonehaven, either by local architects employed by the councils or by their own surveyors and from 1930 by the Aberdeenshire County Architect.

The emphasis in the 1930s switched to clearance of slum areas – although again this was less acute in Aberdeen than elsewhere in Scottish cities – as part of a broader concern with improving public health. It produced the Rosemount Square housing (by the *City Architects*, 1938–48), a very good representative of the trend by the late 1930s towards patterns of design originated in the social housing schemes of Germany and Austria. A first step towards the style of Continental Modernism, with its emphasis on rational planning and unornamented surfaces, can be seen in the major reconstruction of HOSPITALS and especially in the design of the new Infirmary at Foresterhill, commenced in 1920 by *J. B. Nicol* of *Kelly & Nicol*, with *Pite, Son & Fairweather* (a practice that came to specialize in this field of design). It is nevertheless all of granite construction and in style perhaps best characterized as a stripped form of classicism, whereas the hygienic, white-walled, flat-roofed form of Modernism had been accepted by the time of the building of Inverurie's hospital by *R. L. Rollo* in 1936. SCHOOLS also become less historical in their motifs in this period in favour of a reduced classicism but only the Primary School at Tullos, Aberdeen, begun in 1939, exhibits the more radical tendency among younger architects before the Second World War. COMMERCIAL BUILDINGS tended to remain conservative, especially banks, but this is not a slur on them and the Royal Bank of Scotland, Union Street, of 1929 by *Jenkins & Marr*, is powerful Beaux Arts classical of the American type.

116

Buildings for LEISURE AND SPORT, especially where holiday-makers were expected, turned enthusiastically to the Art Deco, *moderne* and Modernist styles of the interwar period, notably the Beach Ballroom at Aberdeen (1926), the Northern Hotel, Kittybrewster, Aberdeen (by *A. G. R. Mackenzie*, begun 1938), the Bon Accord Baths, Aberdeen (1936–40 by the *City Architect*), the excellent Carron Restaurant of 1936 in Stonehaven and that town's Open Air Swimming Pool, and the Pavilion at King's College, of concrete construction with dramatic cantilevered balconies, astonishingly executed by *A. Marshall Mackenzie & Son*, 1939–41, just a few years after their highly traditional Elphinstone Hall.

117

118

After the Second World War the need for reconstruction in Aberdeen was less acute than elsewhere, but the North-East of Scotland as a whole was identified as an area for growth. The POST-WAR trend in the city towards decanting the population from the centre to the suburbs resulted in new estates of mixed (i.e. low-, medium- and high-rise) housing developments, followed by clearance of the congested inner-city slum areas and the construction of tower blocks. It should be said that Aberdeen's towers, slab blocks of maisonettes, though at their highest some nineteen storeys, are unusual among their mid-1960s contemporaries for being individually designed by the City Architect's Department, instead of factory-made components to designs by contractors, and they bear an unmistakably Aberdonian character in the use of rugged chunks of granite to the gable-ends. They contrast with the more routine system-built towers of the 1970s at Seaton.

The activities of the CONSERVATION movement also began in the 1950s, although the sensitive replacement of housing in Stonehaven from 1939 should perhaps be regarded as a first indication of a new approach. Provost Skene's House in Aberdeen was repaired in 1951–3. *A. G. R. Mackenzie* was also involved in the movement, partly through work for the National Trust for Scotland and partly through pioneering the concept of conservation areas. Old Aberdeen was among the first to be designated, in 1968, after extensive conservation work for the university by *Robert Hurd* and *Ian Begg*, funded by the MacRobert Trust from the 1950s. By then, however, much had been altered by the expansion of the University buildings (which began *c*. 1957). This confirmed the triumph of MODERNISM in public and civic buildings, initially in the humane timber-and-stone strain of Scandinavian post-war design, especially in the buildings that were completed according to the masterplan for the University developed by *Robert Matthew, Johnson-Marshall & Partners* in 1957 (e.g. Crombie Hall), and progressing through Brutalism 120 (the William Guild Building and attached Arts Lecture Theatre, both 1968–70), until by the time that the expansion programme was complete in the early 1970s the last buildings once more make reference to their historic surroundings, a harbinger of the Postmodern phase. Perhaps the most successful exercise in this field was the construction of the new riverside campus at Garthdee, in outer Aberdeen, originally for the Robert Gordon's Technical College's architecture school and Gray's Art School, with a new building for the latter in a rectilinear Miesian-inspired manner by *D. Michael A. Shewan* of *T. Scott Sutherland*'s practice, 1964–6.

The impact of new strains in architecture on the smaller burghs and villages in this period is minimal, with the notable exception of a handful of schools (e.g Inverurie), but Huntly in particular boasts a large collection of unaltered shopfronts of this era; the town was also helped by the decision to bypass it during this period. In the realm of COMMERCIAL BUILDINGS there is only one important event: the Brutalist Co-op department store building, now John Lewis, in Aberdeen's George Street, of 1967–70 122 by *Covell Matthews & Partners*. It expresses something of the contemporary preoccupation with highly integrated 'megastructures', bringing together several functions in one building, of which the Denburn Health Centre of 1969–76, by *Hugh Martin & Partners*, is another (grim) example. One of the most unexpected contributions of this high Modernist period is the New Trinity Hall, Aberdeen, by *Mackie Ramsay & Taylor*, 1966, which combines an orthodox cubic Modernist treatment of its elevations with Gothic tracery derived from its predecessor. Standing outside the Modernist stream of c20 architecture is the Camphill Hall, Bieldside, built for the Steiner community which established itself on Deeside in 1939 as refugees from the Nazis and whose Anthroposophical architecture has its roots in the Expressionism of early c20 Germany and Austria.

So far the patterns in the architectural narrative of post-war Aberdeen and Aberdeenshire are broadly similar to any city and rural county until the EARLY 1970s, when the impact of the discovery of North Sea oil in 1969 placed Aberdeen on a track of prosperity unshared by the declining industrial cities of Dundee and Glasgow. That impact was immediate in the city; oil actually began to flow into the refineries from 1975. New suburban areas were developed for housing and buildings to service the industry, including OFFICE BUILDINGS for the major oil companies, especially at Dyce, where the Airport (1977 by *Robert Matthew, Johnson-Marshall & Partners*) suddenly assumed major significance, and at Altens on the coast, where Shell's Exploration and Production complex was developed, along with headquarters for Chevron (now Total and Maersk) by *Jenkins & Marr*, who moved unexpectedly from an anonymous corporate Modernism in the first phase *c.* 1977 to a Neo-vernacular by 1979, a strong indicator of the path to be followed in architecture of the 1980s.

Otherwise it cannot be claimed that the later C20 amounts to much architecturally. Many of the housing areas, including expansion of older settlements, are boring dormitories, but outside the city boundary the boom gave impetus to the creation of Westhill, a remarkably late revival of the self-sufficient Garden City ideal by private developers. Further development of the smaller burghs in this period is no more exciting and the same must be said of the 1980s, which bestowed on Aberdeen's city centre the Bon Accord and St Nicholas Shopping Centres. The 1990s were altogether more promising, at least in part because of the emphasis given to new buildings for CULTURE, EDUCA-TION AND SPORT, so e.g. the extensions to the Maritime Museum in Aberdeen, 1996, and to His Majesty's Theatre, 2004–5, on both occasions by the City's own architects. More important are the major developments at Garthdee following the creation of Robert Gordon University, with two unusual tower blocks of student residences, 1992–3 by *Jeremy Dixon Edward Jones*, one of the most interesting practices of this period, although it is through the Aberdeen Business School and Georgina Scott Sutherland Library by *Foster & Partners*, 1997–8, that the university chose to broadcast its new status. Not to be outdone, Aberdeen University's Sir Duncan Rice Library was the subject of a competition in 2005 and built in 2009–12, the first time that a major new public building in Aberdeen and Aberdeenshire had gone to an inter-national practice: *schmidt hammer lassen* of Denmark. The same is true of the Maggie's Centre, one of the British network of respite centres for cancer patients, each designed by a different architect; Aberdeen's, on the Foresterhill Campus, is by *Snøhetta* of Norway, 2013, and, like many buildings of most recent years, adopts a wholly organic form.

RURAL BUILDINGS
BY CHARLES O'BRIEN

The rural economy of Aberdeenshire until the C18 was based on peasant agriculture, the land worked by tenants grouped in townships or communal fermtouns. Old Manse Inn Farm, Glass, is probably late C17 or early C18 and an unusually early survival of a farmhouse. But perhaps the most important is Nether Mains at Monymusk, where Sir Archibald Grant had set about a radical period of improvement on the impoverished estate his father had acquired in 1716 (*see* also p. 77). Grant drained and enclosed the land with stone dykes, practised rotation of crops and introduced the cultivation of turnips for winter feed for livestock and grassland for grazing. He also rebuilt his farms, but while Sir Archibald was a pioneer, this approach to Aberdeenshire's agriculture only became more widespread after a catastrophic harvest in 1782 which ruined many and determined the need for reorganization of farming practices. From this time, and following the precedent of the Lowlands, new larger farms were created with a single tenant farmer, often themselves incomers and active proponents of new methods. The fertile land was suitable for cereal and during this period Aberdeen was developing as a substantial market for the produce of the farms, which were helped by a rise in prices created by the blockades to imports erected during the Napoleonic Wars.

The changes wrought by existing and new landowners are represented in the *General View of Agriculture in Aberdeenshire* (1811) and the *General View of Agriculture in Kincardineshire* (1814), volumes commissioned by the Board of Agriculture. Wester Fintray Farm, near Hatton of Fintray, is a good example p. 94 of the type of well-organized steadings which met with approval. The forward-thinking tone of the times is nicely represented by the Ploughman's Society Hall at Old Rayne, a reflection of the growth in agricultural societies in these years. The most significant architectural change was the creation by the major landowners of MODEL STEADINGS leased for approximately nineteen years to the tenants (many of whom were incomers to Aberdeenshire) and practising crop rotation on arable land and winter food and shelter for livestock. Again, Monymusk provides a good example: Braeheads built *c.* 1830; there is also Kinbattoch near Towie. In these steadings, usually of the courtyard type, the buildings had clearly designed functions for each interdependent element of farming practice, from stabling to storage, shelter to threshing. Many of the rebuildings of the major country houses were also accompanied by model farm establishments, e.g. Barnyard of Midmar of *c.* 1796 in a castellated Gothic style and the Home Farm at Fetternear by *Archibald Simpson*. The Home Farm and adjoining offices and steading of 1792 at Arbuthnott House are in a very fine classical style (but not part of a simultaneous improvement to the house).

Aberdeenshire in the mid–late C19 was unusual for the survival of many farms of a traditional type let on long leases for low rent so that new land might be cultivated by their tenants. This allowed for the establishment of medium-sized new farms, also laid out in a rational, well-organized form. For the peasant farmers, however, the standard of cottage was still exceedingly simple. Auchtavan, in the hills above Crathie, is a remarkably important survival of an early C19 fermtoun, of a type that was

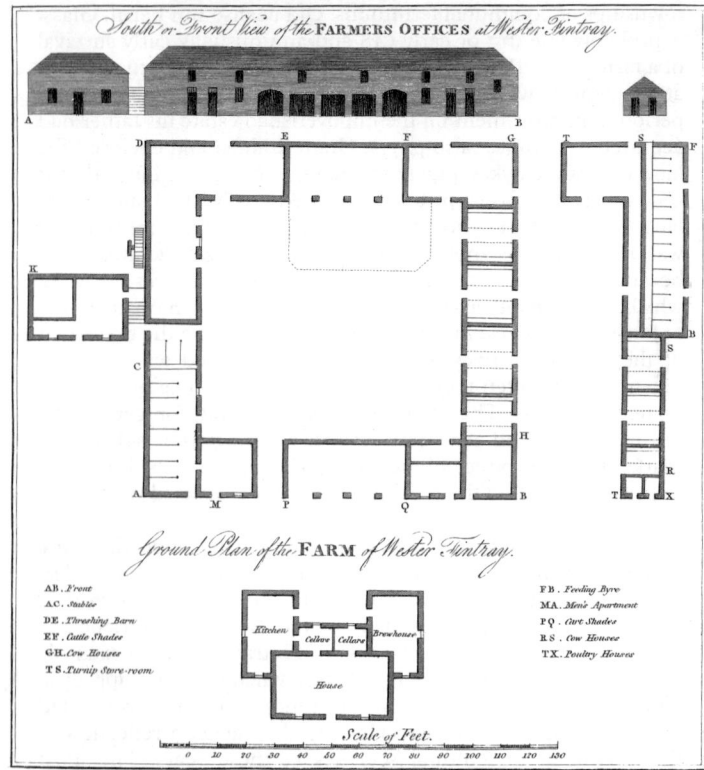

Wester Fintray Farm.
South front view and ground plan, 1811

largely swept away by the Improvers. Its croft is built from rubble and with a cruck roof originally thatched in heather. It also has a threshing barn, for threshing by hand as was common on the lowliest farms throughout the C19 but increasingly superseded by machinery elsewhere by 1800. Tomintoul Croft, outside Braemar, is equally precious, the farmhouse still with box beds and, like Auchtavan, a hanging lum over the fire.

The continued improvement of agriculture in Aberdeenshire in the C19 (*see*, for example, Mill of Sterin farmhouse on the Balmoral estate in Glenmuick) also included the introduction of notable cattle breeds such as the Aberdeen Angus (one of the first herds was farmed at Greystone Farm, near Alford, and the breed was developed by William McCombie, a farmer near Tillyfour, from 1824). Transport by steamship from Aberdeen to Edinburgh and thence to London at last brought their meat to Smithfield and the growth in this market required much larger buildings for keeping cattle. The 'Coo Cathedral' at Aboyne Castle of *c.* 1890 is, as its name suggests, the apogee of this type of farm building in Aberdeenshire, erected *c.* 1890 as one of the multiple estate improvements made by *George Truefitt* for Sir William Cunliffe Brooks. Similarly, at Aswanley House, Alexander Geddes, backed by the fortune made as the 'Grain King of Chicago', built an enormous steading. That these activities were carried on after the onset of the more general agricultural depression *c.* 1870 is a measure of the extent to which livestock farming, whether of cattle, or of sheep in the upland districts close to the Cairngorms, remained unaffected for some time after the decline of cereal growing had begun.

INDUSTRIAL BUILDINGS
BY CHARLES O'BRIEN

Without Aberdeen, the history of Aberdeenshire's industrial buildings would be more or less confined to those associated with agriculture and fishing. But the difference that Aberdeen makes is the range of manufacturing and extractive industries which developed from the late C18 and grew prodigiously through the Victorian period, adding paper mills, shipbuilding, textiles, granite yards, iron founding and engineering to the mix. Aberdeen is also of course unusual in the context of the later C20 in that, while the majority of Scotland (and Britain's) industrial cities, built on textiles, coal and steel, entered a terminal phase of industrial decline, the city transformed itself into the centre for servicing a wholly new industrial enterprise: North Sea oil and gas.

To begin with there are water-powered GRAIN MILLS, to which until the end of the C18 tenants of farms were obliged by law to bring their crops for threshing. From 1799 this could be avoided in return for money, and typically new farmsteads of the early C19 were equipped with their own mills, while some existing mills were upgraded. A fairly large number of such buildings survive, though in varying states of preservation, and a large proportion have been converted to other uses. In terms of the type, there is little significant evolution in the design of these mills once the basic layout had been adopted. The most distinctive feature is the kiln, in which the grain was dried, usually at one end, with its slender stove-pipe ventilator topped by a cowl. The best example, and still in operation, is the Mill of Benholm, predominantly early C18. Aberdeenshire also had a reputation for the quality of its oats, which were ground in MEAL MILLS. There are some small rural examples, e.g. Mill of Glenbuchat, but the scale of the C19 demand may be judged by the colossal, and still functioning, mill at Montgarrie, built *c.* 1882.

The other major industry of parts of rural Aberdeenshire and especially significant in the S, where there are considerable forests of Scotch fir and larch, is TIMBER. The area around Braemar is especially rich in this resource and before the arrival of the

railway in the mid C19 much timber was floated down the Dee
for export from Aberdeen. After the railway reached Banchory,
mills were established there to treat the lumber before transport
by rail to the city. Now the best examples of buildings associated
with this industry are at Finzean where, on the Water of Feugh,
there is the complete early C19 sawmill and turning mill at Percie,
and a remarkable bucket mill, both unique survivals and preserved by the Birse Community Trust. Some of the largest
Deeside estates, such as Glen Tanar, have sawmills as part of their
model complex of buildings. It might be added that after the
Napoleonic Wars brought to an end the historic timber trade with
the Baltic, Aberdeen's merchants switched their focus to the
Atlantic and British America, taking large numbers of emigrants
westwards (Aberdeen was second only to the Clyde as an emi-
grant port) and returning with Canadian timber.

Of TEXTILE MILLS we know for example that a cotton mill
was established at Woodside, Aberdeen, in 1785. The first mills
were for LINEN, made from flax (e.g. the small former flax mill
at the Earl of Kintore's planned village of Auchenblae). The most
important group of linen mills are the Broadford Works, in the
Lochlands district of inner Aberdeen. There the Old Mill of 1808
ranks among the most important and earliest surviving mills in
Scotland for its fireproof construction of cruciform iron columns
and beams supporting brick jack-arches and cased in a brick skin.
This form of construction originated in Shrewsbury and spread
thence to Leeds, Manchester and other major mill towns; indeed
the suppliers of the structure for the Broadford Mill may well
have been *Fenton, Murray, Wood & Co.* of Leeds. The flax mill at
Grandholm on the Don (Aberdeen) of 1792–7 also survives and
appears to have used cast-iron columns, but much of its structure
was still timber and only appears to have been remodelled with
greater use of iron beams and joists in 1812–26. The revolution
in scale created by the introduction of power looms is attested
by the rapid expansion of the Broadford Mills before 1840, the
additions again being of iron and brick construction. Steam
power was introduced at Grandholm in the 1840s.

Until the C19 WOOLLEN WEAVING was essentially a cottage
industry – see e.g. the cottages at Drumlithie and Huntly – but
the adoption of multi-storey weaving mills on the factory system
is apparent in Aberdeenshire from the late C18. The mills at
Cothal on Donside, near Hatton of Fintray, were in operation
from *c.* 1790 under the ownership of the Crombie family. This
became one of the largest concerns in Aberdeenshire, eventually
taking over the complex of mills at Grandholm and converting
them to woollen production. Crombie is (still) famous for its suits
and particularly coats, although they are no longer made in
Aberdeenshire. Garlogie's water-powered mill was established in
the early C19 by the Haddens, who also owned the Grandholm
Mills, and driven by water from Loch Skene, but *c.* 1830 steam
power was introduced and its beam engine, possibly by *Mitchell
& Neilson* of Glasgow, remains *in situ*, a rare survival. The mill

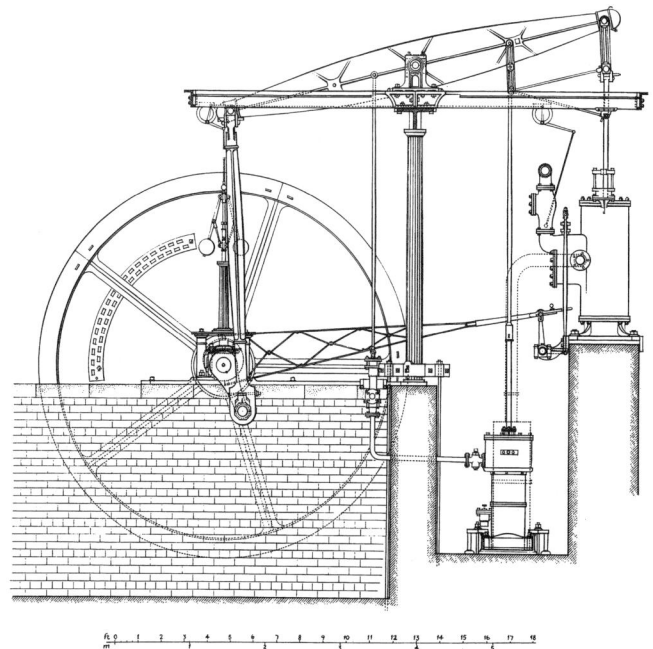

Garlogie Mill Engine House.
Elevation and part section of beam engine

complex is now smaller than as built, and from 1904 served instead as the generator house for electricity on the Dunecht estate. Other mills were built to restore life to villages where the handloom industries had died. So for example at Huntly, where weaving was in decline through the C19 but recovered after William Spence's woollen business was established in 1872, making gloves and socks, with the majority of work still done in the home; from 1878, however, it was mechanized and the large mill (now Huntly Business Centre) was developed, continuing in business until the late C20. Most of the mill buildings at the Broadford works are also early C20 by *Wilsons & Walker* and show the increasingly architectural character of the diverse elements of the largest mills and the refinements in the techonology of their construction, e.g. reinforced concrete.

PAPER MILLS, for making paper from rags, are also recorded quite early in Donside, probably from the C17 when new techniques were introduced from Holland and France and then revolutionized in the C18 by improved methods for mould-making to achieve smoother papers. Like other forms of mill they depended upon water to treat the fibres and power the stamps which reduced the rags to pulp. The paper mill at Stoneywood on Donside was established in 1710 and remains in operation;

104

indeed it is the only paper mill still working in Scotland.* Until the early–mid C19 paper making remained an arduous hand process; machines for rolling paper in continuous sheets were only progressively introduced in about 1805. By the late C19 paper mills were, as at Aberdeen, primarily concentrated into single large complexes close to sources of raw materials, good transport and labour, as well as a ready market in printworks and newspapers. The mills at Stoneywood were owned by the Pirie family, who in the later C19 also acquired and massively developed the single paper mill on the Dee at Peterculter (now demolished). It was served by the Deeside Railway. The success of the Piries' business can be gauged from the purchase of the Dunecht estate by A.C. Pirie in 1899.

Of the heavy industries, one of the earliest was SHIPBUILD-ING, carried on at the mouth of the Dee in Aberdeen. This was already an industry in the medieval period but construction of ships was confined to the riverbank and seashore until the development of the harbour (*see* p. 72) was accompanied by the creation of slips for builders. The busiest period for Aberdeen's shipbuilders was the early C19 when several clippers were built for the China trade by Alexander Hall & Sons and later for the Atlantic trade routes. William Duthie, who trained with Hall, and his brothers were active from *c.* 1816 and later generations produced the first iron ships at Aberdeen, as well as numerous vessels for the fishing industry. Although nothing significant remains of this or the other yards concentrated around Footdee on the river's N bank, Torry on the s and the Jamieson Quay in the main harbour, the gift of the Duthie Park to the Ferryhill area of the city is indicative of the considerable wealth produced by the Duthie yards by the late C19.

Associated with the above is the FISHING INDUSTRY, which in the C19 comprised white fishing, herring fishing and the export of salmon caught in the rivers Dee, Don and Spey (Moray). Much of the first two types of fishing was undertaken by the fleets launched further N along the Aberdeenshire coast (principally Fraserburgh and Peterhead). The southern Aberdeenshire ports were smaller but included Stonehaven, Cove Bay, Portlethen and Findon, whence came the traditional smoked Finnan haddock. The herring industry in particular was enormous in the mid C19, leading to larger harbours to accommodate the fleets of steam trawlers (*see* p. 72). Torry became a centre for FISH PROCESSING in the late C19 but little remains other than a C20 smoke house in Sinclair Road and other smoke houses cling on precariously in the area between the railway station and the Dee. Much better preserved are the early and late C19 buildings at Gourdon. Beside the coast at St Cyrus are two fishing stations,

---

*Paper mills were also erected at Inverurie in the mid C19, adapted from an earlier meal mill, which benefited from the immediate proximity of the river and railway there (*see* p. 71) but were closed in 2009 and demolished.

designed for the preparation of sea trout and salmon for export. It was the perfection of storage which made it possible for the industry to expand to meet demand in Edinburgh and London, so both stations have ice houses.

The needs of the mills for machinery, shipbuilders for engines and the railways for their infrastructure gave an increasingly important role to IRON FOUNDRIES and ENGINEERING WORKS in C19 Aberdeen. There is now hardly anything to show for it in terms of their once extensive working premises, except a large block of buildings near the harbour in St Clement Street, Aberdeen, although a very great deal in terms of the products of these works including railings, mill-wheels, bridges, etc. Some of the firms of ironfounders who are represented in this gazetteer are *James Abernethy & Co.*, *Blaikie Bros* and *John Duffus & Co.*

The GRANITE INDUSTRY was active from the late C18 and reached its peak in the mid C20. It is not yet extinguished but very little of it is devoted to granite for masonry construction. The sources of the stone, and their varied character across the whole of Aberdeenshire, are explained on p. 6 but what should be recorded here is that granite was first already being quarried at Rubislaw (Aberdeen) in 1700 for window sills etc. and that stone for paving was exported from Aberdeen to London in 1764. The figure behind this was *John Adam*, who leased quarries between Nigg and Cove, immediately s of Aberdeen. Granite from Aberdeenshire is also known to have been used in the construction of basins at Portsmouth and London Docks in the late C18 and early C19 and for Rennie's London Bridge in 1811–17 and the Thames Embankment. The creation of the Aberdeenshire Canal in 1805 facilitated the movement of stone from inland quarries along Donside to the harbour and this was further enhanced by the laying out of the railway system, which widened the choices of granite available for construction and monumental work. The branch line to Alford led to the wide export of granite from the Kemnay quarry operated from 1858 by John Fyfe, who also pioneered the use of a steam derrick crane to extract stone from his quarries and a suspension cableway (known as the 'Blondin') to remove stone from the quarry floor. A comparable revolution from the sculptural point of view was made in the 1830s by Alexander MacDonald of Macdonald & Leslie, who developed new machinery for cutting and polishing granite, finally making it useable for monumental sculpture. The statue of the Duke of Gordon now in Golden Square at Aberdeen was an early exemplar of the new techniques. By the early 1920s, when the demand for war memorials across Britain and its Empire was at a peak, the Aberdeenshire quarries and the associated masons' yards (notably *Arthur Taylor, James Taggart & Son, Morren & Co.* and *Garden & Co.*) were at the height of their activity, but with the advent of non-traditional building materials all were much reduced in number by 1970; Rubislaw, the last quarry in Aberdeen, closed in 1971. Again, as with the ironfounders, one is almost at a loss in seeking the traces of their premises and instead one should look to the index of this volume for (some) of their output.

Finally, the OIL AND GAS INDUSTRY, the most exciting built structures of which are, alas, miles out of sight in the North Sea (but *see* the model in the Maritime Museum, Aberdeen). The industry's most visible onshore architectural expression is the Gas Terminal at St Fergus (N) but in the area covered by this volume there are the headquarters and office buildings (*see* p. 92) and the industrial estates at Dyce, Altens and Tullos. Only Shell's Exploration and Production office complex (by *McInnes Gardner & Partners*, 1973–85) at Altens, however, is really a worthy monument to the industry's heyday. At the time of writing, the anticipated reduction of supply and the global price of oil mean that the future of the industry is in question for the first time since the first crude was piped ashore in 1975.

ABERDEEN

BY

JOSEPH SHARPLES

INTRODUCTION

3   With a population of *c.* 227,000, Aberdeen is the third largest
city in Scotland. It is also the cultural and commercial capital of
the North-East. Today it fills the whole area between the mouths
of the Don and the Dee, spreading into substantial suburbs
beyond both rivers, but it began as two quite separate settlements: Old Aberdeen, close to the s bank of the Don, and New
Aberdeen, occupying a cluster of small hills on the N bank of the
Dee. Both were in existence by the C12; their earlier origins are
obscure.

The present cathedral of Old Aberdeen was begun by Bishop
Henry Cheyne (1282–*c.* 1329), but it replaced an earlier building,
possibly founded in the C12. Manses for the clergy and a palace
for the bishop grew up around it, while to its N the Bridge of
Balgownie, possibly also built by Cheyne, linked both Old and
New Aberdeen with the country N of the Don. Old Aberdeen
became a burgh in 1489, and major developments followed at the
close of the C15 when Bishop William Elphinstone founded
King's College. By the time Parson Gordon of Rothiemay made
his detailed map of Old and New Aberdeen in 1661, Cathedral,
bridge and College were linked by an elongated Y of streets, the

tail forming the High Street lined with burgage plots. This plan remained essentially unaltered until the C20, and is still clearly recognizable today.

Ecclesiastical Old Aberdeen was outstripped and eventually absorbed by the trading settlement and port of New Aberdeen, its neighbour to the s. The latter was already significant when made a royal burgh by David I (1124–53). Its original centre is uncertain, but by 1393 Castlegate was established as the market place, taking its name from a castle – recorded in 1264, destroyed in the early C14 – which stood at the E end on what is still called Castlehill. Beyond the w end was the parish church of St Nicholas. Branching N was Broadgate – now Broad Street – becoming Gallowgate further N, while on the s Exchequer Row and Shiprow descended to the quay. Other surviving medieval streets are Nether Kirkgate, Upperkirkgate and Schoolhill, but no buildings remain from before the C16 except for parts of St Nicholas. Religious houses – the Blackfriars in the vicinity of what is now Robert Gordon's College, the Greyfriars in Broad Street and the Trinitarians and Carmelites near the Green – have left virtually no physical trace. Of the grandest dwellings of the late Middle Ages and Renaissance, the only survivors are the late C16 house of Provost Ross in Shiprow, and Provost Skene's C16–C17 house in Broad Street. The latter, despite its radically altered setting, gives some idea of the development of burgage plots and their backlands, which characterized the densely built-up central streets. The only other significant relics of this period are the Mercat Cross and Tolbooth.

It is important to understand the overland routes into New Aberdeen at this date, because their limitations were to determine the radical transformation of the city at the beginning of the C19. The approach from the s was via the Bridge of Dee (planned by Bishop Elphinstone and completed in 1527, some 3 km. sw of the Mercat Cross), then along the winding Hardgate and down the declivity of Windmill Brae, crossing the Denburn by the Bow Bridge, and entering the town through the Green. From here, Castlegate was reached by steep and narrow streets skirting St Katherine's Hill (the hill's summit was where Adelphi Court is now). Coming from the N, the narrow Bridge of Balgownie led via Don Street to the High Street of Old Aberdeen and thence over the hill of the Spital, before approaching New Aberdeen by Gallowgate and Broadgate.

From now on in this introduction we are essentially concerned with the growth of New Aberdeen. In the first half of the C18, architectural modernity was pioneered by a few projects which introduced classicism to what was still essentially a medieval town, but they had little impact on the wider urban setting: *James Gibbs's* West Church of St Nicholas simply occupied the site of its medieval predecessor, and *William Adam's* Palladian building for what is now Robert Gordon's College, though provided with generous formal grounds, was situated outside the convoluted old centre. It was not until the second half of the C18 that the first significant works combining architecture and urban

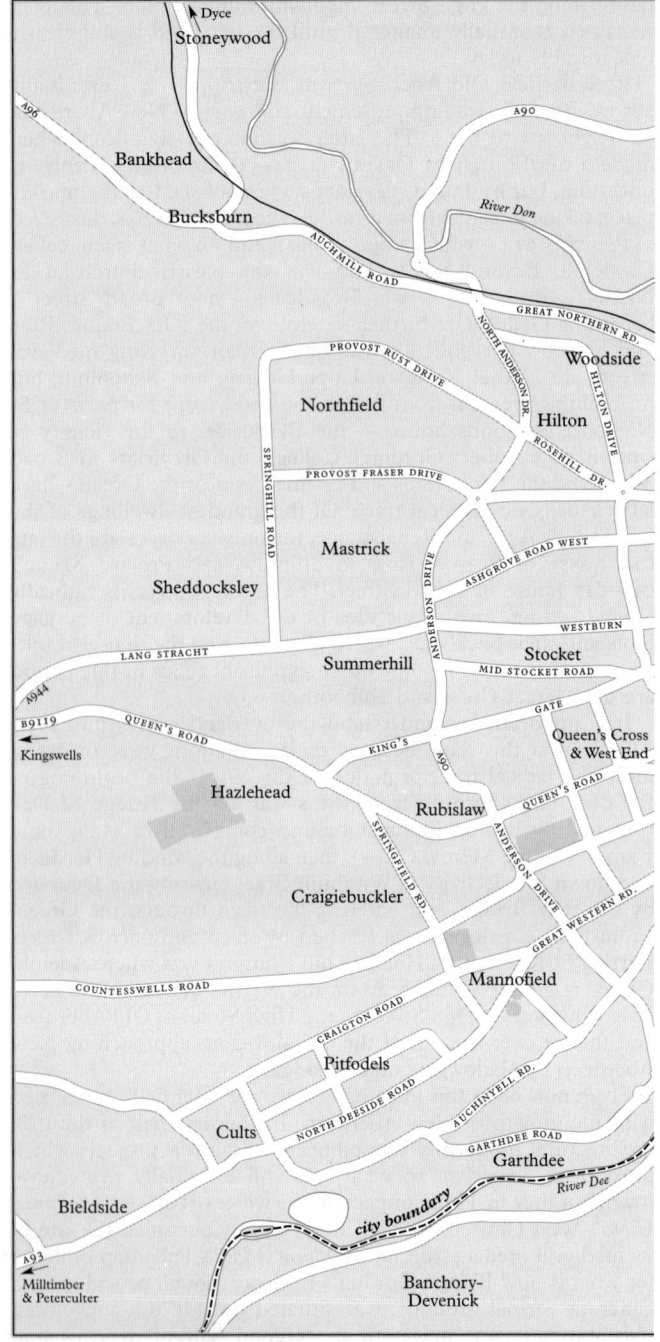

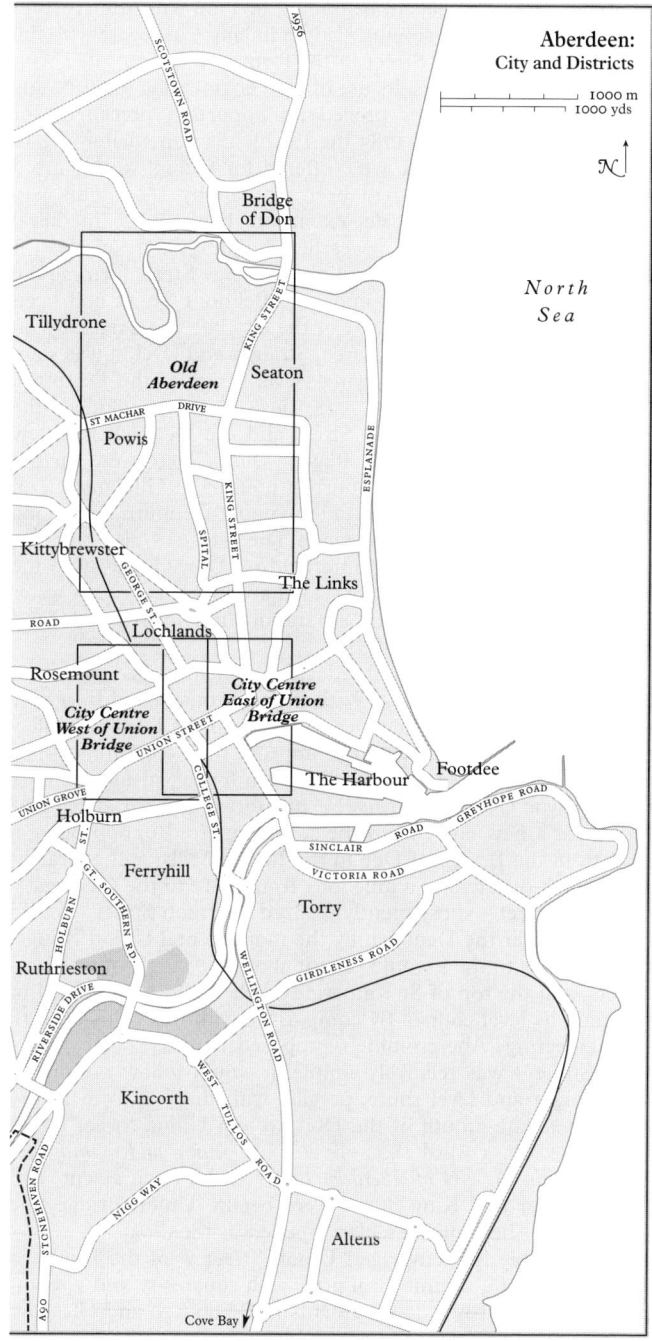

Aberdeen:
City and Districts

1000 m
1000 yds

N

North
Sea

Bridge
of Don

Tillydrone

Old
Aberdeen

Seaton

KING STREET

ST MACHAR   DRIVE

Powis

ESPLANADE

KING STREET

SPITAL

Kittybrewster

GEORGE ST.

The Links

ROAD

Lochlands

Rosemount

City Centre
East of Union
Bridge

City Centre
West of Union
Bridge

UNION STREET

COLLEGE ST.

The Harbour

Footdee

UNION GROVE

Holburn

GREYHOPE ROAD

SINCLAIR   ROAD

Ferryhill

VICTORIA ROAD

HOLBURN ST.

GT. SOUTHERN RD.

Torry

Ruthrieston

GIRDLENESS ROAD

RIVERSIDE DRIVE

WELLINGTON ROAD

Kincorth

WEST TULLOS ROAD

STONEHAVEN ROAD

NIGG WAY

Altens

A90

Cove Bay

planning were undertaken, beginning in 1766 with the creation of Marischal Street. A sloping viaduct linking Castlegate with the quay, it spans Virginia Street in the form of a flyover lined with uniform terraced houses. Its use of bold engineering to overcome topographical challenges proved an important precedent for future developments. In 1783 the Lochlands immediately NE of Robert Gordon's College were offered for feuing; work started c. 1790, and six streets had been opened by 1802. This was Aberdeen's first large-scale extension beyond its medieval boundaries and, although its earliest buildings were modest, it had an impressively regular grid plan, George Street forming the main axis. By the 1770s, fashionable Belmont Street had been laid out. It is now in the heart of the city but was originally on the very edge of the built-up area. Straight and level, it was soon lined with large houses enjoying views W across the Denburn. Other peripheral areas of C18 development included the Shorelands between Virginia Street and the Dee, where a few substantial houses survive in Regent Quay. There were further concentrations of humbler suburban housing at Gilcomston, an industrial hamlet clustered round the upper Denburn, and along Windmill Brae and the Hardgate. The late C18 also saw the beginnings of an industrial hinterland on Donside, away to the N, where the fall of the river provided a valuable source of water power: textile mills were built at Grandholm and Woodside, and a paper mill at Stoneywood.

By the end of the C18 Aberdeen's population had grown to between 17,000 and 18,000. With the city constrained by a hilly site, and hemmed in by the Dee to the S and the Denburn valley to the W, it was now essential to improve road communications and open up the area W of the Denburn for expansion. In 1794 the surveyor *Charles Abercrombie* put forward three alternative routes for a new entry from the S, his preferred option being a road from the Bridge of Dee to the Justice Mills, and a straight street three-quarters of a mile long from there to the Castlegate. This new street – subsequently realized as Union Street – would be carried over the Denburn by the monumental Union Bridge; lesser bridges to the E would raise it above the tangle of medieval streets, and the top of St Katherine's Hill would be flattened to maintain its level course. By comparison with this colossal work of engineering, Abercrombie's proposed N entry – the future King Street – was relatively simple: it would follow a more or less straight and level route, parallel with the sea, from a new bridge near the mouth of the Don, to join Union Street at the Castlegate. On 4 April 1800 *An Act for opening and making two new streets in the city of Aberdeen* received the royal assent, and Union Street and King Street were begun. Union Bridge, the vital link in Abercrombie's plan, opened in 1805.

Abercrombie had envisaged Union Street W of the Denburn as the S side of a symmetrical grid, with squares W and E, comparable to New Town developments in Edinburgh and Glasgow. In practice, however, the street itself became the principal focus of development, lined with large terraced houses with ground-floor shops, and punctuated by public buildings: the Assembly Rooms (now the Music Hall), the façade to St Nicholas's churchyard, the Advocates' Hall and Trinity Hall. The first stretch of King Street acquired an even richer collection of public and commercial architecture, and in both streets *Archibald Simpson* and the prolific Town Architect *John Smith* established a severe Neoclassicism as the architectural idiom of the expanded town. The vagaries of land ownership, however, meant that the areas N and S of Union Street were laid out and built up in a piecemeal fashion, with no comprehensive plan. The exception on the N side is Golden Square, planned by 1806, which does duty in place of Abercrombie's E square. On the S side, Simpson's Bon Accord Square and Crescent make a coherent but self-contained sequence of spaces, not formally related to Union Street at all.

More typical of the new residential areas opened up by the town's push westward are the irregular terraces and small detached houses of Crown Street, Dee Street and Bon Accord Street. Further W, progress was slow. The Alford turnpike was joined to the W end of Union Street *c.* 1802 to form what is now Albyn Place, and villas started to appear along its S side, but an ambitious scheme for a formal layout of streets on the N side languished until mid century. By this time Ferryhill was developing as a separate suburb S of the centre, with terraces overlooking the harbour. Further out still, the lands of Pitfodels were feued in the 1840s for large houses in extensive grounds overlooking the valley of the Dee. In 1840–2, Union Street was linked with the harbour by Market Street, a ramped viaduct on the model of Marischal Street, but much broader. This also gave access to the medieval Green, isolated by the construction of Union Street, and to a colossal new market hall, regrettably demolished in 1971. Market Street became a focus for other important public and commercial buildings, including Simpson's Post Office (since replaced) and Mechanics' Institute.

The maritime equivalent of these momentous urban improvements was the transformation of the estuary of the Dee into a modern harbour. A start had been made in 1775 with the commencement of the North Pier by *John Smeaton*. Reports commissioned from *Thomas Telford* in 1801–2 resulted in a sequence of quays along the N side of the estuary, stretching all the way from Market Street to Smeaton's pier, and in 1834 the Aberdeenshire Canal from Inverurie to Aberdeen was connected with the harbour at Waterloo Quay. A grid of new streets planned by Smith immediately behind these waterfront developments was only partly realized, but traces can be seen in the warehouses, shops and offices of St Clement Street, York Street and Waterloo Quay. Smith had earlier laid out the equally regular squares of small cottages that comprise the fisher village of Footdee, on the N side of the harbour mouth. The works proposed by Telford culminated in 1848 with the inauguration of the Victoria Dock by the Royal Yacht.

The railway from the s reached Aberdeen in 1850, and a station in Guild Street, adjoining the harbour, opened four years later. A line N to Huntly opened in 1854, following the route of the filled-in canal as far as Inverurie. N and s were eventually linked in 1867 by a new line through the Denburn valley, passing under Union Bridge. The Inverurie line tied the Donside industrial settlements of Woodside, Bucksburn and Stoneywood more closely to the city (Woodside was absorbed officially in 1891, the others later). Similarly, the Deeside Railway to the sw, opened in 1853, encouraged the growth of Cults, Bieldside and other Deeside villages as residential satellites (they became part of the city in 1975). In 1867, the expanded railway station was linked with Union Street by yet another sloping viaduct, Bridge Street, but the building of elevated roads to master the city's troublesome changes of level was to reach its spectacular climax in 1884–6, with the construction of the Rosemount and Denburn Viaducts. Along with the contemporary widening and rebuilding of medieval Schoolhill, these new thoroughfares created a direct route from the centre to the inner suburb of Rosemount, which became densely covered with tenements. They also provided worthy sites for a series of prestigious public buildings, including *Matthews & Mackenzie*'s Art Gallery and School of Art, and *Brown & Watt*'s Library. These speak of a burgeoning municipal pride, the main symbol of which had already been achieved a decade before the viaduct with the completion, in 1873, of *Peddie & Kinnear*'s Flemish-Gothic Town House at the E end of Union Street.

c19 Aberdeen was dense but small, with ready access to rural surroundings and to the Links and adjoining beach for recreation. As the city grew, however, landscaped open spaces were provided in the more affluent parts. In the 1870s came the modest Victoria Park to the N of Rosemount, and Union Terrace Gardens in the centre. They were followed in 1883 by the much larger and more ambitious Duthie Park overlooking the Dee. Contiguous with the park was the handsome Allenvale Cemetery of 1873–4, the two making an impressive set piece with sweeping Riverside Drive. Duthie Park stimulated the further development of Ferryhill as a residential suburb, but the undisputed focus of elite housing in the last quarter of the c19 was Queen's Cross and the West End. In 1874, the City of Aberdeen Land Association bought the entire district – the lands of Rubislaw – and laid it out with spacious, regular streets for feuing. Building now gathered pace, with villas and substantial terraces spreading W along Queen's Road and neighbouring streets, including many outstanding individual houses by leading local architects such as *George Coutts*, *William Kelly*, *A. Marshall Mackenzie* and the highly idiosyncratic *Pirie & Clyne*. Great Western Road developed in a similar way around the same time, and in both areas ambitious churches arose to serve the suburbanized middle classes. Meanwhile, the harbour achieved its present form in the 1870s with the diversion of the Dee into an artificial channel along the s side of the estuary and the construction of the Albert

Basin. Market Street was extended s across the land thus reclaimed from the river and, with the opening of Victoria Bridge in 1881, provided direct access to Torry on the Kincardineshire side. This former fishing village was swiftly transformed into a thriving and populous suburb, with streets of tenements, villas, schools and churches (the boundary extension of 1891 brought it within the city). The C19 preoccupation with street improvements ended in spectacular, if controversial, fashion when the N side of Broad Street, including the venerable Greyfriars Church, was demolished and replaced by the astonishing Gothic façade of *A. Marshall Mackenzie*'s addition to Marischal College, set well back from the old building line.

Transformation of the city in the first half of the C20 was dominated by house-building, both by the Town Council and by private developers. In the private sector, tenements gave way to the ubiquitous bungalows that fringe the inner city. Public housing, which had begun in a limited way in 1897–8 with the construction of municipal tenements in Urquhart Road, increased greatly as a result of interwar legislation. A first wave of four-flatted blocks was followed in the 1930s by numerous three-storey granite tenements, the corollary to slum clearances. Examples of both types are to be found at Hilton, Seaton, Torry, Powis and Woodside. At Torry, a hilltop site lent itself to ambitious planning, and was developed from 1920 with a radial layout focused on Torry Circle. It contrasts with the informal, picturesque plan for the Kincorth estate on the s side of the Dee, the result of a 1937 competition, implemented after the Second World War. A staunch advocate of public housing was Aberdeen's Medical Officer of Health, Professor Matthew Hay, whose other great project, begun in the 1920s, was the relocation of the city's hospitals and other medical facilities to a single greenfield site on the then outskirts at Foresterhill. New roads were also characteristic of this period. A dual-carriageway ring road – Anderson Drive – was completed in stages by 1931, linking the medieval Bridge of Dee (still the main approach from the s) with the Inverurie road to the NW. A W–E spur, ending with St Machar Drive, connected it with the Bridge of Don in 1921–2, ploughing its way destructively through the heart of Old Aberdeen in the process. Another major scheme of the interwar years was Great Southern Road, linking Holburn Street with the new King George VI Bridge giving access to Kincorth.

After the Second World War, the built-up area grew dramatically with the creation of large municipal estates on the fringes, notably at Northfield (from 1950) and at Mastrick (from 1952). These consisted almost entirely of low-rise houses and flats, but in the 1960s and '70s a mixture of low-rise flats and high tower blocks – designed by the City Architect, not bought in – became the pattern for peripheral council housing at Tullos, Balnagask, Tillydrone, Seaton and elsewhere. Decentralization also marked the expansion of the University of Aberdeen from the 1950s onwards, accomplished by extensive new building in Old Aberdeen rather than at city-centre Marischal College. A campus comprising teaching accommodation and student residences was created around King's College, but the historic character of the College buildings and the High Street was respected. Also in the 1950s, the School of Architecture moved from the city centre to the beautiful riverside setting of Garthdee, to be followed ten years later by Gray's School of Art, thus paving the way for the large-scale removal of the Robert Gordon University (a descendant of Robert Gordon's College) to new buildings at Garthdee in the 1990s.

In the centre, meanwhile, slum clearances resulted in a series of massive slab blocks of balconied maisonettes, generally in linked pairs with distinctive cladding panels studded with chunks of granite. These transformed the skyline and created major landmarks in the Gallowgate, Hutcheon Street, Rose Street and Castlehill. Bulky office buildings sprang up around the railway station, but the most significant development of this type was the building of St Nicholas House in the 1960s (demolished 2014), a sleek tower-and-podium of Council offices filling the w side of historic Broad Street, with Provost Skene's House forlornly preserved in its courtyard as a reminder of the area's former character. An intended civic square on the site of Broad Street itself was not realized at this time, but elsewhere covered shopping centres brought major changes to the historic street pattern. Protracted planning battles delayed the biggest of these schemes, and it was not until the 1980s that the St Nicholas Centre and the Bon Accord Centre, conceived many years earlier, were eventually built. They not only engulfed a large part of St Nicholas Street and its continuation, George Street, but also obliterated one of the city's major axial vistas, the great legacy of its early C19 development. Nor did the city centre escape destructive road schemes: an E ring road was created in the 1980s, following the line of South Market Street, Virginia Street and East and West North Streets, and doing much damage as it snaked its way through C18 Shorelands and across King Street to the giant roundabout at Mounthooly.

For the last forty years Aberdeen has been synonymous with North Sea oil. The first major discoveries under Scottish waters were made in 1969, and by the early 1970s the city had become the hub of Britain's offshore industry. The major international oil companies established themselves in Aberdeen, and numerous support industries followed in their wake, but the architectural results have on the whole been disappointing. Rapid but unpredictable growth meant that offices were built spasmodically, and the most prestigious were located well away from the centre, either at Rubislaw, or on new out-of-town industrial estates at Dyce, Tullos and Altens. The main infrastructural results were the complete modernization of the harbour for oil supply vessels, and the rebuilding and expansion of the airport at Dyce. However, the booming oil economy is reflected above all in the huge growth of suburbia. The Bridge of Don area was still largely fields in the 1960s, and Dyce was no more than a village, but both have expanded enormously, with industrial facilities set among swathes of public and private housing. The string of villages stretching w along the North Deeside Road – Cults, Peterculter, etc. – was absorbed into the city in 1975. At the same time, large and entirely new commuter settlements have been established at Cove Bay, Kingswells and Westhill (p. 763), the last being just outside the city boundary. And the pressure for further greenfield expansion continues.

In the following account it can be assumed that everything built before the Second World War is of granite, unless otherwise stated. No other British city – not even Bath – owes so much of its appearance to a single building material. The local granite was being used in ashlar blocks by the early C18, and by at least the 1840s Aberdeen was known as the Granite City. Confusingly for the historian, the extreme hardness of the stone means it shows no signs of wear: buildings of the early C19 are sometimes indistinguishable from those of the mid C20, and cleaning in the later C20 has added to the illusion of a city newly built, pristine and ageless. Not only has granite given Aberdeen its predominant greyness (on an overcast day it can feel as if one has strayed into the monochrome world of a black-and-white film), it has also largely determined its unique architectural character. As *The Builder* wrote in 1898, 'its hard and stubborn quality is a natural check against that over-exuberance of detail which is one of the most frequent sins of modern street architecture'. From the city's sudden expansion in the early C19 until the Second World War, severity and precision have been the hallmarks of Aberdeen's best buildings.

CITY CENTRE

EAST OF UNION BRIDGE

This was the medieval core. The boundaries are: on the w, the main railway line; on the N, Schoolhill, Upperkirkgate, Gallowgate and Nelson Street; on the E, the seaward spur of the railway, Beach Boulevard and Commerce Street; and on the s, Virginia Street, Trinity Quay and Guild Street.

CHURCHES

Former CATHOLIC APOSTOLIC CHURCH, Exchange Street. Opened 1877. So modest it might be taken for a mission hall. Outside, only the Gothic door and wheel window indicate its original purpose. Decorative open timber roof inside, but none of the architectural display for which the Irvingites were noted.

Former CONGREGATIONAL CHURCH, Belmont Street. Opened 1865. Officially the architect was *William Leslie*, though the young *James Souttar* was involved and probably supplied the design. A compact Romanesque building in grey granite, with

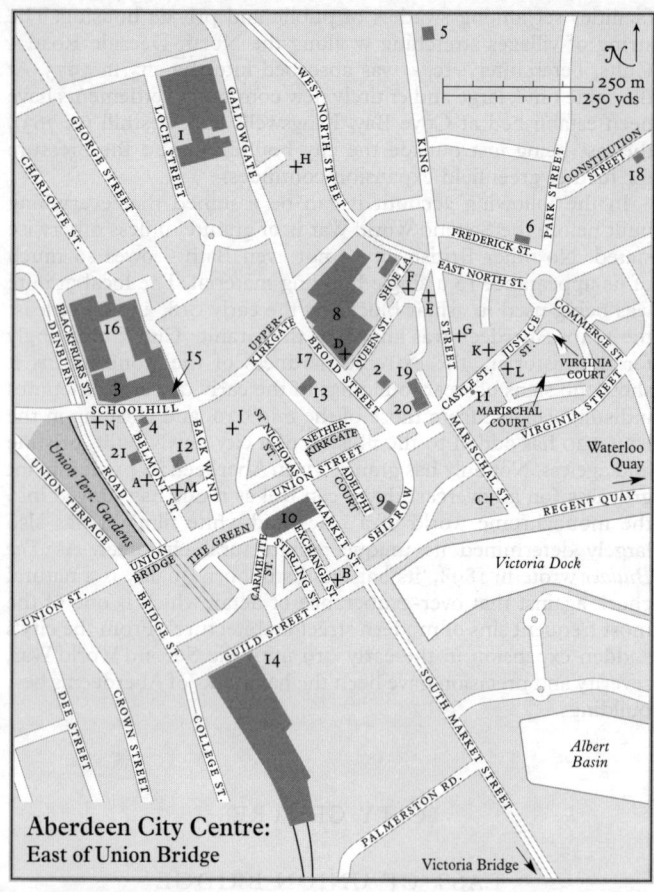

Aberdeen City Centre:
East of Union Bridge

A   Congregational Church
      (former)
B   Catholic Apostolic Church
      (former)
C   Elim Pentecostal Church
D   Greyfriars Parish Church
E   North Church (former)
      (now Aberdeen Arts Centre)
F   Queen Street Church
G   St Andrew's Episcopal
      Cathedral
H   St Margaret of Scotland
      (Episcopal)
J   St Nicholas
K   St Peter (R.C.)
L   Salvation Army Citadel
M   South Parish Church
      (former)
N   Triple Kirks (former)

1   Aberdeen College
2   Advocates' Hall

3   Art Gallery, War Memorial and
      Cowdray Hall
4   Central School (former)
5   Fire Station (former)
6   Frederick Street School (former)
7   Lemon Tree
8   Marischal College
9   Maritime Museum
10   Market
11   Mercat Cross
12   Old Town School (former)
13   Provost Skene's House
14   Railway Station
15   Robert Gordon University
16   Robert Gordon's College
17   St Nicholas House
      (now demolished)
18   St Peter's R.C. School (former)
19   Tolbooth Steeple
20   Town House
21   Trades Hall
      (now Belmont Cinema)

yellow Bannockburn sandstone dressings. Rectangular, gabled, with a round-arched corbel table all round and four octagonal turrets, set in from the corners and ending in open spirelets. E turrets frame the main door, with a wheel window above. Between the taller W turrets a segmental apse, its windows set in an arcade (this recalls Lund Cathedral in Sweden, where Souttar lived 1864–6). The ground falls steeply to the W, allowing for a schoolroom, etc., underneath, and giving the little church surprising prominence when seen from across the Denburn. Interior now in secular use, but not subdivided. Galleries on cast-iron columns on three sides, with arcaded fronts. – PAINTED DECORATION. On the rib-vaulted apse ceiling, Pelican, Lamb, etc., in roundels on a background of stars. On the apse walls, stylized trees, c. 1900. – STAINED GLASS. Apse windows contemporary with building, Gothic foliage without figures. E window similar, 1869.

ELIM PENTECOSTAL CHURCH (originally Trinity Parish Church), Marischal Street. *William Smith*, 1875–7. Converted from a theatre completed in 1795, variously said to have been designed by Henry Holland or a Mr Dodd of Edinburgh. Smith's façade has a gable right across, enriched with crockets and a bellcote at the apex. Three pointed doors and three windows above, with sandstone plate tracery. The church is continuous with the terraced houses on either side: a Gothic anomaly in the even classicism of Marischal Street. It extends back to form a bridge over Theatre Lane, which runs parallel with Marischal Street but lower. Simple interior with lancets down the sides and an E gallery with Gothic front. The basement is a series of low, brick-vaulted rooms with separate access from each side of Theatre Lane. Probably used originally for warehousing, they appear to be a survival from the theatre building.

GREYFRIARS PARISH CHURCH, Broad Street. *A. Marshall Mackenzie*, 1901. Visually part of Mackenzie's Marischal College scheme (*see* Public Buildings), and an effective S termination to it. It replaced the Greyfriars Church of c. 1525, which stood in the College courtyard and was demolished to make way for Mackenzie's monumental Broad Street façade. Majestic W tower, with long, narrow windows and soaring buttresses, carrying further the emphatic verticality of the College. Pierced battlements of brittle delicacy, and a needle spire, its supporting arches visible through the unglazed openings of the tower's cage-like upper stage. Nave with clearstorey; lean-to S aisle (the college abuts on the N) with stubby SW turret; hall and offices below. Shallow chancel with seven-light E window, its intersecting tracery salvaged from the old church, along with a weathered carving of Bishop George Dunbar's arms in the gable. The interior shows the influence of current ecclesiological thinking in the Established Church. Entry from W door under a deep gallery within the tower. Three wide, pointed arches on round columns of red sandstone between nave and aisle, with matching blind arcade on N. Chancel with altar-like marble communion table and seats for elders and readers facing inwards, like choir stalls. Red sandstone pulpit l. of chancel arch, with Christ and Evangelists' symbols inlaid in black, by *Lindsay Smith*: 'commendably small', thought the Scottish Ecclesiological Society, which deprecated traditional pulpit-dominated layouts. – WOODWORK. Carvings brought from the old church (but originally from St Nicholas, it seems), reused in chancel and gallery front: mostly heraldry and monograms, some dated late C17 and early C18. – STAINED GLASS. All 1903 by *C. E. Kempe*, in a rich late Gothic style. Six aisle windows with Marian scenes: Annunciation, Visitation, etc. E window with Crucifixion, Old and New Testament figures, Franciscan saints, and, top r., Bishop Dunbar accompanied by Sir Richard Vaus of Many, donor of the site, and Alexander Galloway, architect of the old church, holding plans.

31   Former NORTH CHURCH, King Street (now Aberdeen Arts Centre). *John Smith*, 1829–31. Smith's most impressive work, and Aberdeen's noblest classical church. Long flank facing King Street, consistent with neighbouring commercial and institutional buildings: giant pilasters and full-length, round-headed windows, horizontally divided at the level of the former gallery. The entrance front dominates the open space at the corner of Queen Street, with a massive Ionic portico of four columns supporting a flat balustraded entablature rather than a pediment. Above this, a lofty and graceful two-stage tower, the lower stage square with angle pilasters, the upper an elongated version of the Choragic Monument of Lysicrates, but with lotus capitals. David Hamilton used the same model for the tower of his Royal Exchange in Glasgow, but a much closer parallel is Archibald Simpson's church of St Giles at Elgin, completed 1828, which must surely have influenced Smith. Original interior destroyed during conversion to a performance space, 1963.

QUEEN STREET CHURCH, Queen Street. *William E. Gauld*, opened 1905. A large, asymmetrical block. Church offices on l., church on r., with pediment and Ionic semi-columns at first-floor level framing a Venetian window. Big, galleried interior, with shallow, segmental recess containing organ. – STAINED GLASS. Flanking the organ, Art Nouveau floral designs and heads of John Knox and Luther, by *James Mellis* of *Ferguson & Co.*, contemporary with the church. In the NE gallery, artificially lit, John Knox, 1912, by *Edward Copland*, brought from the former John Knox Parish Church, Mounthooly (*see* p. 209). Stairs in all four corners communicate with the HALL below (mural of Aberdeen buildings by *Edi Swan*, 1983–4) and other meeting rooms and offices. The church was influenced by Methodist central halls in England, with their generous provision for social activities alongside worship.

ST ANDREW'S EPISCOPAL CATHEDRAL, King Street. *Archibald Simpson*'s Episcopal chapel of 1816–17 (cathedral status only came in 1914) was given a chancel by *G. E. Street* in 1880, and

Robert S. Lorimer made further changes from 1911. Their work was completely eclipsed by *Ninian Comper*'s dramatic enlargement and remodelling of 1935–41. Simpson's gabled façade of Craigleith stone is slotted into the E side of King Street, set back slightly from the flanking terraces. It has Perp windows and octagonal, spired buttresses, marking the internal division into nave and aisles. Original central entrance now hidden by Lorimer's porch of 1911. After this unpromising front, Comper's interior comes as an uplifting surprise: lofty, spacious, white-painted, its austerity relieved by gilded and coloured ornaments in his trademark fusion of Medieval and Renaissance styles. The five-bay nave with its Tudor Gothic arcades is essentially Simpson's, from which Lorimer removed the galleries in 1910. Rather than scorning Simpson's un-archaeological work, as an earnest Victorian Goth would have done, Comper took it as his model. From 1935 he transformed the flat aisle ceilings by adding groined plaster vaults that echo the early C19 nave vault, emblazoning them with heraldic shields, wreaths, putti and arabesques, all modelled in relief: in the S aisle, Aberdeenshire Episcopalian families; in the N, the then forty-eight United States of America (American money paid for Comper's scheme, commemorating Aberdeen's historic links with the American Episcopal Church). Between 1938 and 1941 Comper lengthened and heightened the CHANCEL, so that only the Dec aumbrey and parts of the choir stalls remain from Street's work. The plaster vault – a clearstorey makes it higher than the nave vault – has further heraldic ornaments. E window with distinctive tracery, the point of the arch filled with a vesica (close to Comper's contemporary St Philip, Cosham). Dominating the chancel – and the whole cathedral – is the baldacchino or CIBORIUM, the climax of Comper's scheme. Four unfluted columns with idiosyncratic Corinthian capitals support the square superstructure, with statues of adoring angels at the corners. A crown of scrolly flying buttresses on top, with a statue of the risen Christ. Every inch is gilded and burnished, or painted in jewel colours, creating an impression of Byzantine splendour. Below the canopy, hanging PYX to hold the Blessed Sacrament, now unhappily converted to a light fitting: Comper attached special importance to this form of pyx. At the same time Comper added the SUTHER CHAPEL, a continuation of the S aisle, separated from the chancel by a three-bay arcade on octagonal piers, and again plaster-vaulted. It was reordered in 1976, when the altar was made free-standing and the reredos, moved here by Comper from the former high altar, dismantled.

FONT, in N aisle. Dec, stone, now painted, said to be *c.* 1845, by *George Gilbert Scott.* – SCREEN. 1911, by *Lorimer.* Originally in chancel arch, moved *c.* 1963 to the Suther Chapel, the ends canted to fit the narrower opening. Flowing Gothic tracery. *Lorimer*'s hanging ROOD – actually a cross without a figure – remains in the chancel arch. – PULPIT in nave, oak, by *Lorimer.* – CHOIR STALLS, with fleshy poppyheads and arcaded fronts, by *Street*, presumably. – LADY ALTAR, N aisle. *Lorimer* again, 1917. Reredos with much carving by *Clow Brothers* of Edinburgh in a rich late Gothic, Arts and Crafts manner, with statues of the Virgin and Child and flanking angels in niches at the top. Below, painting by *John Duncan*, Gethsemane, added *c.* 1919. – WAR MEMORIAL, S aisle, *Lorimer*, 1923. Gothic triptych with Crucifixion painted by *Miss Grant-Duff*. – STAINED GLASS. Chancel E window by Comper, Nativity below with Christ in Majesty above. Suther Chapel, glass of 1881–3 by *Hardman*, reused from Street's chancel: Apostles in side windows, Crucifixion in E window. S aisle, 2nd from W, Raising of Lazarus, 1899, and nave, W, Life of St Andrew, 1902, both *Hardman* again. – MONUMENTS. S aisle, Bishop John Skinner, †1816, by *John Flaxman*, completed 1820. Life-size, standing with a bible. Head and hands white marble, the rest darker stone. N aisle, W end, marble relief, painted, of Lt Col. R.W.T. Gordon in Highland dress against a background of the Pyramids and the Suez Canal. Designed by *Colonel Nightingale*, executed by *Edwards & Son*, London, 1886.

S of the Cathedral, former SCHOOL, 1865, by *Alexander Ellis*.

ST MARGARET OF SCOTLAND (Episcopal), Gallowgate. *James Matthews*, 1870; additions by *Ninian Comper*, 1889 and 1908. When founded amid the Gallowgate slums by the Rev. John Comper, St Margaret was hemmed in at the end of a narrow court. Now it stands exposed, a hilltop landmark. The 1870 building – a combined church and school – was a simple rect-angular box, still recognizable, lit by eight square-headed dormer windows in the open timber roof. Its one remarkable feature is Matthews's use of the steeply sloping site to raise the sanctuary high above the nave. In 1889 the founder's son made plans for an ambitious remodelling. It would have had a high vault carried on internal buttresses, pierced by low arches forming passage aisles, like Albi Cathedral and its C19 English derivatives. Only a small part was realized. This, Comper's first work, is ST NICHOLAS'S CHAPEL, a sort of narthex at the W end, lower than Matthews's building and awkwardly related to it externally. Inside, it has three unequal parts, divided by E–W arches and roofed with simple ribbed cross-vaults. Square central part, opening into nave, intended to have a 'tribune' above (a doorway meant to connect with this was built, but not the stair-turret). Shallow S part – the chapel proper – with altar against S wall behind a splendid Spanish-looking, wrought-iron SCREEN. N part, the baptistery, with internal timber porch on W, and holy water stoup based on a medieval one in King's College Chapel. The narrow arch opening into the nave from here, with elaborately inscribed foundation stone, would have been the commencement of the N passage aisle. In 1908 Comper made a second addition, simpler, but this time fully realized. This is the S aisle, or CHAPEL OF THE HOLY NAME, a memorial to his father. Outside, it has a Scottish flavour: buttresses of rock-faced granite, windows with simple inter-secting tracery and pantiled roof.

Inside, Comper opened up the S side of the nave to form a three-bay arcade. Shallow but fully furnished chancel with AUMBRY and PISCINA. Richly carved SCREEN with statues of St Helen and St Clement, in memory of the architect's mother. Wooden CEILING, almost flat, divided into lozenges and painted with the arms of St Margaret. At the same time Comper added the S PORCH, with a statue of St Margaret in the crowstepped gable. – FONT. Sandstone, with colonnettes to the bowl. Brought from Inverness Cathedral. – ROOD. Comper, 1898. – PULPIT, Comper also, 1924: octagonal with linenfold panelling, on a slender stem. – STAINED GLASS. Chapel of St Nicholas: r. of altar, Virgin and Child in Glory, Comper's first stained glass design, the figures influenced by C15 Netherlandish painting; w, four damaged lancets with reassembled fragments, including St John the Baptist and his burial; N, Sea Cadet Corps, modern, good. Chapel of the Holy Name: above the altar, and effectively serving as an altarpiece, Christ with St Margaret and St John, with the Rev. John Comper at prayer; its thorough medievalism contrasts with Comper's later Annunciation window, r., dated 1919 and incorporating Renaissance motifs. S aisle, W end, Naked and Ye Clothed Me, by *Martin Farrelly*, 2001, with lively portraits of two former clergy. Porch, Scottish saints, 1999, etc., by *William Stables*. Outside the porch, large CALVARY with gilded figure, by *Paul Waterhouse*, 1917 (a copy; original inside church).

CLERGY HOUSE by *G. G. Irvine*, 1908. Attached to the church, filling the angle between porch and nave, with the same pantiles as the S aisle. HALL, S, also Irvine, 1909.

St Margaret of Scotland.
Perspective by G.G. Irvine, 1909

p. 120

ST NICHOLAS, Union Street*. This was one of the largest of the medieval parish churches built for the great trading burghs, the group of buildings that together represents the most ambitious architectural enterprise of the Scottish later Middle Ages. It is the only one of those churches to have retained identifiable work from as early as the C12. Although relatively little medieval fabric remains visible, what has survived is of the greatest interest, while what has been lost closely conditioned what is now seen. The end result is a cruciform structure with a crypt chapel below the E chancel bay, and with an apsidal termination to both crypt and chancel; aisles run the full length of chancel and nave, and there is a crossing tower and spire flanked by asymmetrical transepts.

BUILDING SEQUENCE. The church comes on record in 1157, when it was confirmed as a possession of the bishop. There was probably already a substantial building in existence by then, for which an apse found immediately E of the crossing during excavations in 2005–6 is the chief evidence (this was previously located in 1837, although no record was made of its precise position). Transepts and a defined crossing were in existence by the later C12; by that stage there were evidently nave aisles but none to the chancel, since access from the transepts was initially only provided to nave aisles. The excavations of 2005–6 located the lower walls of a rectangular aisleless chancel, which was perhaps also part of the late C12 building; that chancel was extended a short way further E at some stage, possibly for structural reasons since the ground falls away sharply in the E part of the site. Foundations of an offshoot added on the N side of that chancel were presumably for a sacristy. Various works were in progress in the mid C14, evidently including the lengthening of the S transept in 1355 to house an additional altar; and the chancel was being paved in 1357.

An extended effort to create a more magnificent chancel began in the mid C15. As early as 1445 a donation to an altar in the N aisle of the Chapel of Our Lady of Pity suggests that the crypt below the E end of that chancel was under consideration, though it is unlikely that the crypt as now seen could have been built so early. (It would be difficult to accept that an apsidal termination to an aisled chancel could have predated that of Edinburgh Trinity College of c. 1460. The apse of St Nicholas is more likely to be closer in date to those seen at other major burgh churches: Linlithgow St Michael, of c. 1497–32, and Stirling Holy Rude, of c. 1507–46.) Further preparations for the new eastern limb are evident in a decision of 1448–9 that exports to Bruges were to be taxed to fund the church work, though it was only in the 1470s that major allocations of funding were made by both the bishop and the burgh. In 1484 *John Gray* was appointed master mason, and in 1493

---

*The account of the church is by Richard Fawcett, with advice from the Rev. James Stewart.

the masons *Alexander Stute*, *Thomas Barry* and *Matthew Wright* were contracted to quarry stone. The masonry fabric must have been nearing completion in 1495 when a contract was agreed with *John Fendour* for the chancel roof. There was a dedication by Bishop William Elphinstone in 1498, though much remained to be done. In 1508 *John Fendour* contracted for the choir stalls, while in 1510–11 the Kirk Master *George Bisset* was ordered to roof the church with lead, and the dates 1510 and 1515 are said to have been inscribed on the roof.

It is not known when the nave of the church reached its final form, though this may have followed on from completion of the chancel. A door was blocked and a 'fair wyndo' formed in the N transept in 1518–19, and it seems that the W front was rebuilt between 1537 and 1541. By then the church was the setting for services of quasi-collegiate splendour, based on regulations drawn up by Bishop Ingram de Lindsay (1441–58), with further regulations composed in 1519. A college was formally established in 1540.

St Nicholas has had a complex POST-REFORMATION HISTORY. In 1596 a wall was built between the nave and chancel to create two separate places of worship: the West and East Churches. By 1732 the West Church in the nave had to be abandoned because of structural failure, and *William Adam* reported on the remedial work required. In 1741 the Aberdeen-born *James Gibbs* provided two designs for its rebuilding, though the old church collapsed in the following year, before work began. It was eventually rebuilt in 1751–5 to Gibbs's design by the mason *James Wyllie*; Gibbs died before its completion. In 1835–7 the East Church was rebuilt by *Archibald Simpson*, on the lower walls of the medieval building but with the only medieval fabric remaining in evidence being the crypt chapel, and that only internally. Simpson's church was burnt out in 1874 and rebuilt in 1875–80, essentially to the same design, by *W. & J. Smith*, who also rebuilt the tower to a new design and heavily restored the crossing area. In 1898 *William Kelly* (of *W. & J. Smith & Kelly*) restored St Mary's Chapel in the crypt. A vestry was added against the N flank of the West Church in 1937. In 2005 the interior was cleared and excavated in advance of remodelling the East Church for community use to the designs of *Groves-Raines Architects*.

EXTERIOR. The five bays and apse of the EAST CHURCH stand on the footprint of the medieval chancel and incorporate parts of its lower walls internally. Now sheathed in squared grey granite dating from the rebuilding in 1835–7 by *Simpson* and after the fire of 1874, the bays are demarcated with buttresses with a single offset and capped by gablets at the wall-head parapet. At the lower level, rectangular three-light windows light the area that was below the galleries, except in the second bay from the W on each side, where a door flanked by single-light windows was inserted after 1874 (following unfulfilled proposals of 1835); at gallery level are tall arched two-light windows with a pair of mouchettes as tracery. At the E end and

Aberdeen St Nicholas from the south-east before rebuilding in 1835.
Engraving

around the apse are diagonal pinnacled buttresses. Lighting the
crypt chapel, above rectangular two- or three-light windows,
there are single lights onto the stairs added at the aisle ends, and
three-light windows with flowing tracery to the apse faces.

The S TRANSEPT (the Drum Aisle) owes its present extent
to the C12 and the southward extension of 1355, but its granite-
clad appearance is again all of 1835 and after 1874. The S face
has clasping buttresses with sunk angle rolls, capped by octagonal pinnacles, and there is an arched door with continuous
chamfers below a four-light window with flowing tracery. The
E wall is blank, but the W wall has three blind pointed window
arches above a door. The only externally visible medieval
masonry in the whole church is in the rubble-built N TRAN-
SEPT (the Collison Aisle), which is essentially of the later C12.
It has square clasping buttresses rising from chamfered base
courses at the outer angles, each with a single chamfered offset;
both are now capped by chimneystacks. There are traces of a
blocked round-headed door towards the W end of the N wall,
but the main feature of that wall is a four-light window with
intersecting tracery and a transom, presumably inserted 1518–
19. There is a single truncated and blocked round window arch
high in the E wall. The N transept is covered by a piended roof
with a leaded flat; hanging from the eaves of the N face is a
band of cast lead foliate cresting, replicating an original thought
to be of the C17.

Before the fire of 1874 the TOWER had one simple arched
opening to each face dating from c. 1785; until then there had
been two openings to each face, and the lead-sheathed spire,
which was still essentially late medieval in form in 1874, had

a pyramidal spirelet at each corner. Both tower and spire were rebuilt by the Smiths in granite and on a more ambitious scale after the fire. The belfry stage now has octagonal buttresses above gableted rectangular buttresses, which frame pairs of two-light windows to all faces, each with a quatrefoil between the light-heads. Rising between the octagonal pinnacles are crocketed gables with clock faces; the spire has two levels of decorated bands, with pinnacles rising from the lower level and lucarnes above the higher.

Gordon of Rothiemay (1661) shows the medieval NAVE as having had a crenellated parapet at least to the S aisle, with a porch projecting from near its W end. As rebuilt to Gibbs's designs in 1751-5 for the congregation of the WEST CHURCH, the keynote is monumental simplicity. Its five-bay flanks have a single round-headed window framed by a continuous architrave to each bay; below the window in the central bay on each side is a door with block rustication to the quoins and keystones rising up to a cornice. The W front, which has rusticated quoins to the outer angles, and the central part breaking forward, is capped by intersecting pediments. The windows at the aisle ends are like those of the flanks. The arched central window has block rustication and rises above a channel-rusticated salient framing the round-arched main entrance.

INTERIOR. The CRYPT CHAPEL, dedicated to Our Lady of Pity, provided a platform for the eastward extension of the late medieval chancel. Excavation in 2005–6 indicated that, together with the lower walls of the extended chancel, at least part of its shell had probably been built some time in advance of the main body of the chancel, and that initial working access had been down beaten-earth ramps against the inside of the S and N lower chancel walls. It is of three bays from N to S, with a five-sided apse on the E side of the central bay. On completion of the chancel the access was by way of stairs within the aisles, and through doors in the W wall of the N and S bays; those doors have reveals moulded with filleted rolls facing away from the crypt. It is now entered by doors in the E face of the S and N bays, at the base of enclosed flights of stairs added in 1835 to give access to the main space and gallery of the East Church. Within the crypt the bays are defined by arches with wave mouldings that rise from semi-octagonal responds with chamfered bases and moulded caps. There are ribbed vaults of basically quadripartite form with ridge ribs throughout, with the ribs of the central space and apse more richly moulded than those in the outer bays. The evidence has been confused by the extent of rebuilding of the responds at the entrance to the apse when the floor level of the central bay and apse was lowered to what was thought to be its medieval level in 1898, during restoration of the crypt chapel by *William Kelly* (of *W. & J. Smith & Kelly*). There appears to have been considerable difficulty in constructing those vaults, suggesting that their present form was not part of the first design. The diagonal ribs on the E side of the central bay and the W side of the apse rise

p. 122

Aberdeen St Nicholas, choir interior before rebuilding in 1835.
By Joseph Robertson, 1839

from figurative corbels that are sunk rather awkwardly between the respond caps, and that have all the appearance of being reused secondary insertions. One of those corbels is of particular interest for its carving of a crouching figure holding a scroll, a type of corbel that appears to have been introduced to Scotland by the Paris-born mason *John Morow*, in his work at Melrose Abbey, Glasgow Cathedral and Lincluden collegiate church. The way in which the vault springers are treated at the outer W corners of the N and S bays is especially awkward. The boss in the N bay bears the burgh arms, the central bay boss is decorated with the story of St Nicholas, and the S bay boss has arms thought to be of Alexander Chalmers, who was provost in 1478 and a master of the church works. Above the apse is a boss with the Virgin's monogram. – FURNISHINGS. The chapel's dado and furnishings are largely made up of relocated C17 PANELLING, installed to their present form in the campaign by *William Kelly* of 1898. One panel in the S bay is dated 1601, a N bay panel 1679 and a panel in the apse 1677. The CANOPIED PEW on the W wall of the central bay is inscribed for Provost Alexander Rutherford and dated 1606. It comes from the Town Loft in the West Church but the panelling along the desk front and the foliate cresting on the canopy is probably from *John Fendour*'s choir stalls of 1508; the parchemin decoration of the panels is closely similar to that on the chancel screen doors at King's College Chapel (*see* p. 191). Surviving parts of the choir stall canopies are now in the Museums of Scotland in Edinburgh. – COMMUNION TABLE, with heraldic panels by *J. Cromar Watt*. – FONT, designed by *William Kelly*, with panels by *Cromar Watt*. – STAINED GLASS. E window of 1899 by *Christopher Whall*. Presentation in the Temple, Deposition from Cross, Jesus with the teachers in the Temple. – In the S bay, another window of 1899, by *Douglas Strachan*, said to be his first stained glass commission, brought about through his collaborations elsewhere with Cromar Watt. Mary and Joseph and Mary with John at foot of Cross.

Nothing of the medieval chancel interior survived Simpson's rebuilding of the EAST CHURCH in 1835–7. Reconstructed after the fire of 1874, and reordered and re-furnished in 1936 by *A. Marshall Mackenzie & Son*, it is intended that the interior will be largely concealed as a result of alterations to be carried out by *Groves-Raines Architects*, to provide facilities for community use extending over several inserted floors. A view of the interior of the late medieval chancel in *The Book of Bon Accord* (1839) shows arcades carried on cylindrical piers, with clearstorey windows set above the pointed arch apices. A sketch of 1818 by James Logan shows galleries in the aisles and tie-beams below the ceiling, the latter presumably omitted from the view in *The Book of Bon Accord* as being inappropriate post-medieval insertions. The capitals are depicted as simply moulded, though surviving fragments have foliage decoration. The aisles were covered by open timber roofs. The central vessel and apse had timber barrel ceilings with ribs set out on the pattern of quadripartite vaulting, with sprigged bosses at the junctions of the ridge rib and the transverse ribs between the bays, and at the springing of the intermediate transverse ribs. The form of the apse ceiling is confirmed by a plan (undated but probably of the early C19) in the Hutton Collection in the National Library of Scotland. The ceiling, which, together with the roof, was presumably the work of *John Fendour*, shows close similarities with that over King's College Chapel (*see* p. 188). Elements of the chancel design, including the cylindrical piers and the ribbed barrel ceiling, may have been at least partly inspired by prototypes in the Low Countries. The ceiling inserted after 1874 over the rebuilt chancel is flat, supported along the N and S sides by arched braces terminating in pendants, and with a rectilinear grid of plaster ribs with sprigged bosses at the junctions – motifs derived from the medieval chancel ceilings and that of the cathedral. A gallery carried on cast-iron columns, and with an arcaded front, runs

p. 122

around the N, W and S sides, and was reached by stairs at the four corners. The E apse was entered through a tall and simply moulded arch. – STAINED GLASS. In the apse, the E window (Crucifixion, Resurrection, St Nicholas, Acts of Mercy) is by *Marjorie Kemp*, 1936; flanking this to N, the Birth of Jesus and St Margaret of Scotland, and to S the Baptism of Jesus and St Ninian, both windows by *Gordon Webster*, 1961. – N wall, Faith, Hope and Charity. – S wall, E window, Jesus and the children, by *Douglas Strachan*; second from E, Moses, Virgin and Child, Aaron; third from E, the archangels Gabriel, Michael and Raphael by *Shrigley & Hunt*, 1891.

12   Within the TRANSEPTS and CROSSING there is the only visible medieval fabric other than that in the crypt chapel. The plaster has been stripped from the walls and this, despite being historically inappropriate, allows a number of features to be seen. The crossing piers and arches were renewed after the fire of 1874, but surviving fragments and drawings suggest that the medieval forms were replicated as far as possible. However, the opportunity was taken in 1874 to remove casings of octagonal profile that had been added to the E crossing piers; these had cornices decorated with vine trails, above which the caps of the earlier responds had been left exposed. The responds have a stepped profile with engaged shafts in the angles and leading faces which, together with the waterholding bases, point to a late C12 date. This is confirmed by the capitals, which have a variety of crocket and simple leaf forms, while the round arches have sunk angle rolls. On the W side of the crossing, close to the W tower piers, are round arches of two unmoulded orders with simple imposts; these opened into the nave aisles. Of the same date as the crossing arches and the openings into the nave aisles must be a single blocked high-level window on the E side of the N transept; it has crocket capitals and an angle roll to the inner order. If those details are later C12, that might suggest that a number of simpler round-headed blocked window openings with splayed rere-arches in the flanks of the two transepts are rather earlier. However, it would be unexpected for an early C12 Scottish parish church to have transepts; furthermore, at least one of the blocked windows in the S transept is within the part that is presumed to have been extended in 1355. It may therefore be more likely that the blocked openings are later C12, and that their forms were followed in a new window in 1355 for the sake of architectural uniformity. In the later C15 large pointed arches were opened up into the new choir aisles, some of the caps of which have multiple mouldings and foliage trails. An inserted arch towards the N end of the E wall of the N transept was presumably the location of an altar. Since 1874 the N transept has been covered by an open-timber roof, while the S transept has a ceiling of polygonal profile with traceried panelling.

SCREEN AND FURNITURE in the N transept (Oilmen's Chapel). Sinuously curved skeletal designs in multi-hued hardwoods by *Tim Stead*, 1989. – STAINED GLASS. In the N transept N window, the Oilmen's window by *Shona McInnes*, 1989. – In the S transept, re-set panels with Christ walking on water, by *Walter J. Pearce*. – MONUMENTS. The church contains one of the most important groups of medieval monuments to have survived in Scotland. In the N TRANSEPT, N wall, a seg-mental-arched tomb-recess with continuous mouldings thought to have been made for John Collison, after whom the transept is named, but now containing an armoured effigy said to be of Provost Robert Davidson (†1411). A door was cut through the arch in the early C19 to give access to a boiler house, but has since been blocked. Various memorials have been re-assembled and set along the W wall: Andrew Cullen (provost in 1506 and 1535); Thomas Menzies of Pitfodels (provost in 1533–4, 1537–44 and 1547–75); Sir John Rutherford of Migvie and Tarland (provost in 1483–1500); Effemia Scheves (†1568). – In the S TRANSEPT SE corner, an armoured effigy of Sir Alexander Irvine of Drum (†1457(?)), after whose family the transept is usually named, and his wife, Elizabeth de Keith; this is below a relocated inscribed brass presumably cut before their deaths, since it gives the date simply as 14– (the canopy from this tomb is now in the chapel at Drum Castle, q.v.). On W wall eroded relief panel for William Leith of Barns (provost in 1351), a kneeling figure beneath an arcade, within a frame decorated with square flower.

The interior of the WEST CHURCH, which is shorter than the medieval nave that it replaced, is a sombre space of Roman magnificence. The square piers have projections to the lower stages that support the fronts of galleries within the aisles and at the two ends of the church. At the higher level the piers have Tuscan pilasters above the lower projections: those to E and W carry the heavy round arches that open into the upper aisles, which are covered by groined ceilings; towards the main vessel there are taller pilasters that support the transverse arches of the curved plaster ceiling. There are full entablatures above the pilasters themselves, but only the cornice runs between them. In the C19 the ceiling had a scheme of painted decoration by *Cottier & Co.*; this was refreshed by *Edward Copland* in 1898, but the present white ceilings are of 1949. Under the W part of the S gallery is a chapel formed in 1935. The C18 FURNISHINGS are largely intact, including box pews in the nave and the gallery fronts with raised and fielded panel-ling. The PULPIT, against the second pier from the E on the S side, only partly follows *Gibbs*'s design of 1741; it is an imposing work by *Archibald Chessills* and *James Heriot*. Semi-octagonal, with two stages of raised and fielded panelling, stair with turned balusters; large canopy with foliate frieze and dentilled cornice, carried to rear on three-quarter Corinthian columns. – PROVOST'S PEW, in the E gallery, designed by *William Crystall*, 1724. Classical baldacchino with fluted Corinthian columns carrying an entablature with foliate frieze and broken pediment with the arms of Aberdeen. – ORGAN, behind the provost's pew. Introduced in 1880, built by *Henry Willis* and enlarged by his firm in 1927 when the ORGAN SCREEN was designed by *William Kelly*. – CLOCK. Facing the pulpit, lacquered Chinoiserie case, by *Hugh Gordon* of Aberdeen, mid-late C18. – NEEDLEWORK PANELS, set on the W side of the draught screen. Acquired for the West Church in 1688 and said to have been hung on the King's Loft. They were purchased from Baillie George Aedie and are attributed to his wife, *Mary Jamesone*, possibly to designs by her father, the painter *George Jamesone* (†1644). They are large and depict the Finding of Moses, Jephthah and his daughter, Esther and Ahasuerus, Susanna and the elders. – STAINED GLASS. – W window. Annunciation, Nativity, Baptism of Jesus, Last Supper, Crucifixion, by *Burlison and Grylls*, 1884. By the same firm but *c.* 1886 is the Marriage at Cana window at the W end of the S aisle. – N aisle, W end, St Nicholas, by *Geoffrey Webb*, 1927. – MONUMENTS. In the S aisle window embrasures from E to W: first bay, John Collison (provost of Aberdeen 1521–2), a rare example of an effigy in costume assumed to be that of a lay magistrate; second bay, Margaret Setoun, wife of John Collison; fourth bay, armoured effigy of Gilbert Menzies (†1452); fifth bay, Marjory Liddel, wife of Gilbert Menzies. – S arcade, W respond. Brass to Duncan Liddel (†1613) by *Gaspard Bruydegoms* of Antwerp, 1622. He is portrayed at work in his study above an inscription. W respond, N arcade, Ann Allardyce (†1787) of Dunnottar by *John Bacon*, 1791. A large standing monument in white marble with figures of Piety and Benevolence flanking an urn swagged with a garland. Medallion below with the mourning husband and infant son at her deathbed. – WAR MEMORIAL. Set into the panelled front of the W gallery. By *William Kelly*, 1922; reinscribed for the Second World War.

CHURCHYARD with many C18–C19 slabs and table tombs. Some earlier mural monuments, architectural in scale, built into the W boundary wall: the Rickart family, dated 1696, Baroque, the inscription in a strapwork cartouche framed by Corinthian columns with a broken pediment and trumpeting angels above; William Guild, dated 1659, with paired Corinthian columns, harp, thistle, roses and the usual symbols of mortality; and George Davidson, †1663, similar motifs but simpler. In the SW corner near the entrance from Union Street, *John Smith*'s outstanding memorial of 1832–3 to Dr Robert Hamilton, Professor of Mathematics at Marischal College: a square Greek Doric aedicule, raised on a high base and originally enclosing an urn, now toppled from its place. Smith's own monument – a plinth with Greek detailing – is near the SE corner. Separating the churchyard from Union Street, the FAÇADE, by *Smith*, 1829. A screen of Ionic columns, with solid ends and central arched gateway, the spaces filled with cast-iron railings made at *Barry, Henry & Cook*'s Loch Street foundry. Conceived as a memorial to the philanthropist John Forbes of Newe. It resembles Decimus Burton's Hyde Park screen, and indeed Burton was commissioned by a private benefactor to make a design for the Aberdeen memorial. A model was prepared, but Smith's design was built instead. An obelisk in the churchyard was part of the memorial scheme but was removed to the Royal Cornhill Hospital *c.* 1838 (*see* p. 223).

ST PETER (R.C.), Chapel Court, Justice Street. 1803–4, by *James Massie*. Aberdeen's first post-Reformation Catholic church, erected ten years after the Catholic Relief Act, but still self-effacing to the point of near-invisibility. It owes much of its charm to its location in a tiny court, reached through a pend flanked by square columns carrying vases (apparently of 1828, when the tenement facing the street was rebuilt). Nave, a simple box with flat ceiling and pointed windows, separated from top-lit chancel by a heavy late C19 Tudor arch on brackets. W gallery on slender iron columns, erected or extended in 1814 to hold an organ. Originally it was reached by a wooden stair, but in 1817 the full-height lobby containing a stone stair was added, and the church's W end given battlements to match. Area under gallery screened off and marble font installed, C20; sanctuary reordered 1965 by *Charles W. Gray*, with free-standing marble altar. Former HIGH ALTAR and REREDOS still in place: Gothic, wood, elaborately carved with scenes from the life of St Peter, Belgian, 1890s. – LADY ALTAR similar, with statue of the Virgin and Child copied from a medieval original now in Brussels, but said to have come originally from the vanished chapel at the Bridge of Dee (*see* p. 259). – PULPIT. Gothic, wood, with saints in niches. – STATIONS OF THE CROSS. Small, sensitively modelled ceramic plaques by *Adam Kossowski*, 1963. – STAINED GLASS. Chancel, The Charge to Peter, by *Joseph E. Nuttgens*, 1956. Baptistery, Baptism of Christ with SS Andrew, Nicholas, Clement and Machar, by *Gordon Webster*, 1959. – PAINTING. On the gallery stairs, copy of *Albertinelli*'s Visitation, formerly used as the altarpiece.

Attached to the church is the early 1770s PRESBYTERY. Its ground floor was used for worship before the church was built.

SALVATION ARMY CITADEL, Castle Street. *James Souttar*, 1893–6. Full-blooded Baronial, appropriate both to the Church Militant and to the associations of neighbouring Castlehill. It dominates the view E along Union Street and bolsters the romantic medieval character established by Peddie & Kinnear's Town House, but there is something stagey about it: 'more pretentious than powerful' was *The Builder*'s verdict. Four storeys, crowned with a corbelled and battlemented parapet, with crowstepped gabled dormers above and conical-roofed tourelles at each end. Off-centre tower with oriel window and corner turrets, one fancifully higher than the rest. The big arched opening at the base led to the first-floor hall – originally galleried, now horizontally subdivided – with its three large windows of simple plate tracery. The ground floor was originally shops, the two ends tenement flats.

Former SOUTH PARISH CHURCH, Belmont Street and Little Belmont Street. *John Smith*, 1830–1. Less of a showpiece than Smith's contemporary North Church in King Street, but imposing nonetheless. Perp Gothic, almost square. N and S fronts gabled and divided in three by buttresses, the inner pair incorporating doors in little gabled porches. On the w, full-height projection containing gallery stairs, and tower with battlements, pinnacles and louvred bell openings under ogee hoodmoulds. Original interior obliterated; recent conversion to a theme pub has substituted a multi-level labyrinth, modelled on the set of a horror film.

Former TRIPLE KIRKS, Belmont Street and Schoolhill. *Archibald Simpson*, 1843. Partly demolished, partly ruinous, but still a major landmark. Built to house members of the South Church and the East and West Churches of St Nicholas who 'came out' in 1843 to form the South, East and West Free Churches. Simpson accommodated them in three hall-like buildings, self-contained, but joined to form a single, approximately cruciform mass, united around a lofty spire on the s side. Roughly the same size and shape as St Nicholas – comparison was perhaps invited – but of a gaunt austerity due in part to economy: Simpson's unadorned lancet style was carried out in granite rubble with brick and sandstone dressings, for a little over £5,200 (the North Church in King Street seated half as many and cost about twice as much). Of the three churches, the West Free has been completely demolished. It occupied the w end of the site, steeply sloping towards the Denburn, and was the most dramatic part of the composition. The roofless N end of the former South Free survives, facing Schoolhill. Tudor Gothic central doorway and flanking windows of sandstone, added by *William Kelly*, 1892–3, when it was taken over by the East Free as a church hall, the South Free having moved to its new building in Rosemount Viaduct, now St Mark's Parish Church (*see* p. 158). The East Free itself, at the corner of Belmont Street and Schoolhill, is just about recognizable as Simpson's, though in secular use. Ground-floor windows introduced below the original lancets in 1900 by *Kelly*, who at the same time added the semi-octagonal organ chamber at the E end (the pointed windows at its base date from 1974, when the church was converted to a restaurant and its interior subdivided; the ceiling of the former nave still has Kelly's decorative rib-vaults down the sides). The superb red brick STEEPLE survives – just: free-standing since the demolition of the West Free, it teeters on the edge of the dual carriageway. The tip is missing and the tower has lost its traceried parapet and the finials from its corner pinnacles, making it plainer even than Simpson intended. Nevertheless, the unusual (for Aberdeen) materials and the satisfying transition from square tower to octagonal spire make it memorable. The spire is of the helm type, but with an upper stage set in slightly above the gablets. It is closely based on the spires of the Elisabethkirche, Marburg.

PUBLIC BUILDINGS

ABERDEEN COLLEGE, Gallowgate. *D. J. A. Ross*, 1961–4. The site falls steeply from Gallowgate (where access is via a bridge) to Loch Street. Nine-storey curtain-walled slab, with lower, parallel, blocks facing each street, some granite-faced.

ADVOCATES' HALL, Concert Court. *James Matthews*, 1870–2. Built to replace the former Advocates' Hall in Back Wynd, to be nearer the courts behind the new Town House. Plain exterior belies a richly appointed interior. Entrance hall with scagliola pilasters and transverse arches, leading to a spacious staircase with coved ceiling. On the half-landing, stained glass by *Cottier & Co.*, 1872, a female figure of Justice with sword and scales. Good carved doorcases on first floor. The principal room is the library, with bookcases on two sides and galleries on carved brackets, an early work by *J. B. Pirie*. Granite chimneypieces at each end, brought from the old Hall. Well-preserved scheme of painted decoration in the Aesthetic taste on walls and ceilings, featuring stars and stylized flowers, probably by *Cottier*. Former dining room on ground floor now altered for court use.

ART GALLERY, GRAY'S SCHOOL OF ART (now part of Robert Gordon University: *see* below), WAR MEMORIAL and COWDRAY HALL, Schoolhill. Built over a period of forty years, but forming a unified block. First came *Matthews & Mackenzie*'s Art Gallery and School of Art, both 1883–5, linked by an archway forming the entrance to Robert Gordon's College (the School of Art was initially run by the College Governors). They are almost a pair, Italian Renaissance style, of grey Kemnay and pink Corennie granite, each with a centrepiece of engaged Corinthian columns and a pediment. Over the Art Gallery entrance, a bronze relief of putti representing Painting, Sculpture and Architecture, by *G. A. Lawson*. In 1901–5, *A. Marshall Mackenzie* extended the Art Gallery behind and reconstructed it internally to form the superb Sculpture Court, a coolly elegant space lit by a big oval skylight, surrounded by vaulted Quattrocento arcades. The polished granite columns were presented by the Aberdeen Granite Association to show the stone in all its variety, mostly from local quarries, but some from Norway: by this date Aberdeen was importing granite for polishing. An imperial stair leads to a broad balcony at first-floor level. Court and ground-floor galleries were designed for casts of sculpture, of which the Parthenon frieze and a few others remain, to educate carvers working in the monumental granite trade; top-lit first-floor galleries for paintings. Finally came *A. Marshall Mackenzie & Son*'s war memorial and Cowdray Hall, designed 1919, opened 1925. The Hall faces Blackfriars Street and essentially repeats the composition of the Gallery and School of Art. The war memorial, on the other hand, is a bravura piece of Beaux-Arts classicism, turning the corner with a concave screen of Corinthian columns against a windowless wall with inscriptions and coats of arms. Attic above, copper dome behind. The idea of an exedra containing a statue had been proposed as early as 1911, when it was intended for the Edward VII memorial. This gave way to the war memorial, with a noble granite statue of a lion designed by *William McMillan* occupying the recess instead. Double-height octagonal interior under the dome, lit from a glazed oculus, with first-floor balcony all round. In 2015 work commenced on a major scheme of alterations to the Art Gallery complex, including the addition of a second floor above the present roof level designed by *Gareth Hoskins Architects*.

112   Former CENTRAL SCHOOL, Schoolhill and Belmont Street. *J. A. Ogg Allan*, 1902. Big, suavely assured Baroque, with corner dome. Converted to a shopping centre by *RMJM*, 1990s, with a rear courtyard surrounded by fussy Doric colonnades.

Former FIRE STATION, King Street (E side, opposite St Clair Street). Won in competition by *A. H. L. Mackinnon*, 1897. Baroque, with raised voussoirs to the arched ground-floor openings (for fire engines) and giant pilasters to the firemen's living quarters above. Balustraded parapet, with open pediment and coat of arms. Pavilion-roofed tower behind, for drying hoses. Converted to student housing by *Acanthus Architects Douglas Forrest*, *c.* 2000. (Just behind in Jasmine Place is the eleven-storey ST CLEMENT'S COURT, 1984–5, the last high-rise council block to be built in Scotland. It was part of a programme of high-rise sheltered housing for the elderly, unique to Aberdeen.)

Former FREDERICK STREET SCHOOL, Frederick Street. *J. A. Ogg Allan*, 1903–5. Edwardian Free Style, with a pair of octagonal domed towers. The flat roof served as a playground. Now a business centre. Opposite, a former GRANARY with twin gables facing the street, probably by *James Matthews*, 1861.

LEMON TREE, West North Street. *Jenkins & Marr*, 1936. Originally St Katharine's Club for the YWCA, now a performing arts venue. Dudok-inspired Granite modernism, with a shallow oriel on the W side, acknowledging the adjacent Marischal College.

109   MARISCHAL COLLEGE, Broad Street. Aberdeen's most dazzling building, and one of the latest and most ambitious secular Gothic Revival projects in Britain. Founded as a second university in addition to King's College in 1593 by George Keith, 5th Earl Marischal, and endowed with the property of the former Franciscan friary in Broad Street. The old buildings had become inadequate by the C19, and *Archibald Simpson* produced alternative classical and Tudor Gothic schemes for replacing them. The latter was approved in 1836 and built 1837–44, and it survives at the core of the present complex: symmetrical, U-plan, open to the W, where the C16 Greyfriars church from the former friary still stood until 1902. Tower in centre of E range, flanked by vaulted cloisters, and N and S wings each with an ogee-capped octagonal turret at W end. A further wing projecting E from the back originally contained the hall. All this was hidden behind a row of old houses on Broad Street, and reached through an archway. Marischal College united with King's in 1860, forming the University of

Aberdeen, and between 1893 and 1906 a huge and elaborate extension scheme by *A. Marshall Mackenzie* engulfed Simpson's austere building. The original tower was heightened to form the 80 m. Mitchell Tower with its needle spire. The Mitchell Hall was added to the wing at the back, rising sheer from West North Street like the E end of a cathedral. At the front, the N and S wings were continued W, the N one ending in a second, lower tower (the S wing had already been doubled in width in 1889 by *W. W. Robertson*). To link the wings, Mackenzie provided a show front along Broad Street in place of the old houses and church, incorporating a monumental vaulted gateway to the now enclosed quadrangle. At its S end, the replacement Greyfriars Parish Church added yet a third tower (*see* Churches).

It is the array of towers and spires that makes the College such a memorable piece of scenic architecture, reminiscent of Pugin and Barry's Houses of Parliament. The Broad Street front is impressive too, but it was designed to be seen obliquely, and its impact was diminished by the widening of the street in the 1960s. Other parts, not meant to be seen at all, have been given unwelcome prominence by the demolition of surrounding properties in the later C20. The style is Perp of the most soaring kind: the buttresses largely unbroken by set-offs, jabbing their spiky pinnacles high above the parapets; the granite fretwork so thin that it looks alarmingly fragile. It echoes the campus Gothic of American universities, and looks forward to skyscrapers such as New York's Woolworth Building. Simpson's principal INTERIORS have survived. Main stair under the Mitchell Tower, two flights becoming one, with extremely tall and narrow Tudor sandstone arches carrying a plaster fan-vault. On the first floor, Museum and Library, l. and r., with former hall – now Picture Gallery – straight ahead, all with Gothic panelled ceilings. The Picture Gallery serves as vestibule to Mackenzie's Mitchell Hall, with timber lierne vault and Gothic canopy-work round the walls. E window, completely filling the wall above the stage, with stained glass by *T. R. Spence*, 1895, mostly heraldic. The University had withdrawn from most of the building by 2010, when almost everything W of Simpson's work was rebuilt behind preserved façades to house City Council offices. On Broad Street, equestrian bronze STATUE of Robert the Bruce by *Alan Beattie Herriot*, 2011.

MARITIME MUSEUM, Shiprow. The museum occupies two historic buildings – the former Trinity Congregational Church, l., and Nos. 48 and 50 Shiprow, r. – linked by a glass curtain-walled extension by the City's *Property and Technical Services Department*, 1996. The church, 1877 by *James Matthews*, is simple, gabled Gothic, with two big buttresses framing a trio of trefoil-headed lancets above its paired doors. Inside, only the stencilled wooden ceiling survives after comprehensive subdivision. Much exposed steel, both here and in the extension, which centres on a full-height circular atrium. This is planned round a stunning 8-metre-high model of the Murchison Oil Platform, almost a building in its own right, and as close as most *Buildings of Scotland* readers are likely to come to a type of structure intimately connected with the fortunes of C21 Aberdeen. The glass façade commands views of the harbour, which complement the displays. No. 48 Shiprow, known as Provost Ross's House, was acquired in 1702 by Provost Ross of Arnage. Dating originally from 1593, it was restored – and extensively rebuilt – from a state of dereliction by *A. G. R. Mackenzie* in 1954: the two dates are recorded in contemporary inscriptions on the gabled dormers, the earlier within a Gothic trefoil border. Granite rubble with freestone dressings. Three storeys, with a fourth in the roof, and a gabled four-storey turret overlooking the street. Main door in r. side of turret, narrow forecourt on l., behind a screen wall. The kitchen was evidently on the ground floor, where a big arched fireplace survives at the N end, but the original plan is otherwise hard to trace. Upper floors now have two principal rooms each, separated by stairs partly contained in a rear outshot (there is evidence of an earlier spiral stair here). Single small chamber on each floor of turret. Rooms on first floor have panelling, probably C18 in origin, restored in 1954. No. 50, now internally linked, is entered from the street through a double arch dated 1710. It may have been remodelled at this time. A large kitchen fireplace survives at the S end of the ground floor.

MARKET, Market Street. *Robert Matthew, Johnson-Marshall & Partners*, 1971. Notable only because it preserves the distinctive, apsidal plan of Archibald Simpson's colossal New Market of 1840–2, senselessly demolished to make way for it.

83   MERCAT CROSS, Castle Street. A splendid Renaissance monument, but still with medieval hangovers. Designed and built by *John Montgomery*, 1686. The hexagonal arcaded lower part has Ionic columns at the angles and segmental arches between, springing from pilasters. Bunches of fruit in the spandrels, animal gargoyles at the corners. The columns and a central pier support a twelve-sided platform with parapet. Two sides are carved with the arms of Aberdeen and the Royal Arms of Scotland, the rest with royal portraits in relief: Kings James I–V, Mary Queen of Scots, James VI, Charles I, Charles II and James VII, all enclosed in laurel wreaths, like Roman emperors. In the centre of the platform, a Corinthian column wreathed with thistles (a 1995 replacement) supports a unicorn and shield. The cross was dismantled and rebuilt by *John Smith*, 1821, when the roof was replaced in cast iron and the carving subjected to 'cleaning and polishing'. At the same time the arcade was filled in to serve as Aberdeen's Post Office. In 1842 the arches were reopened and the cross moved here from its original site in front of the Tolbooth.

Former OLD TOWN SCHOOL, Little Belmont Street, *John Smith*, 1840–1. Quite small, but exceptionally imposing. Single-storey, E-plan, with a central pedimented portico of four unfluted

Greek Doric columns, flanked by advancing wings with angle pilasters. Blocking course right across. Despite its limited size and restricted site, it is as monumental as any of the larger Greek Revival schools built in Scotland in the first half of the C19.

PROVOST SKENE'S HOUSE, Broad Street. C16–C17, restored as a museum by the *Aberdeen City Architect's Dept* (*A. Buchanan Gardner*, City Architect), 1951–3. Unique survival of a grand town house of the period, deprived of its original context by 1930s slum clearance and then marooned in the bleak municipal plaza of St Nicholas House (a block of council offices demolished in 2014). Built on the backland of a house in the now vanished Guestrow, access was by a pend from the E. Four-storey main block, lower gabled W wing at right angles, and full-height square stair-tower at SE corner, enclosing three sides of a courtyard. On the fourth side, entrance arch of 1673 from a demolished house in the Guestrow, rebuilt here in 1970. Granite rubble, exposed since the 1950s but no doubt harled originally, with freestone for windows, doors and corbelling. Dating is uncertain, and made more so by C20 interventions. The property is first recorded belonging to the Knollis family, from a date variously given as either 1545 or 1571, and it remained in their ownership until 1585. The barrel-vaulted ground floor of the main block is probably of this period. The W wing has the date 1626 carved on the E dormer, along with the arms of the then owner, Matthew Lumsden; however, it may have been built earlier than this, possibly as a separate dwelling. In 1669 Provost George Skene acquired the property, and it owes much of its present appearance to him. The main door in the SE stair-tower is carved with his arms, and the adjoining conical-roofed turret must be of the same date. The turret involved moving some adjacent windows: relieving arches show their former positions. A second turret – also Skene's? – is in the angle of the main block and the W wing, reached by an external stone forestair, now enclosed. A shallow corbelled turret on the N side may have contained a timber stair, linking the first and second floors of the W wing until superseded by the new SW turret. The roof of the main block is flat, a feature of only the highest-status buildings at this date, but curiously it has no parapet.

In one of the main rooms on the first floor is a stone chimneypiece with columns having alternate cables and flutes, and foliage capitals, perhaps early C17. Other rooms have moulded plaster ceilings with Restoration crowns, thistles, etc., dating from Skene's time (his initials are included in one on the first floor of the W wing), and C18 panelling (perhaps earlier on the first floor of the W wing). In a small room at the E end of the second floor, painted panelling with marbling and classical figures and landscapes in the borders, C18, possibly by *John Norie* of Edinburgh. The highlight is the long room filling the top floor of the W wing. Its timber CEILING, with flat central section and sloping sides, is painted with elaborate strapwork cartouches and *trompe l'œil* coffering, incorporating New

80,
p. 134

81

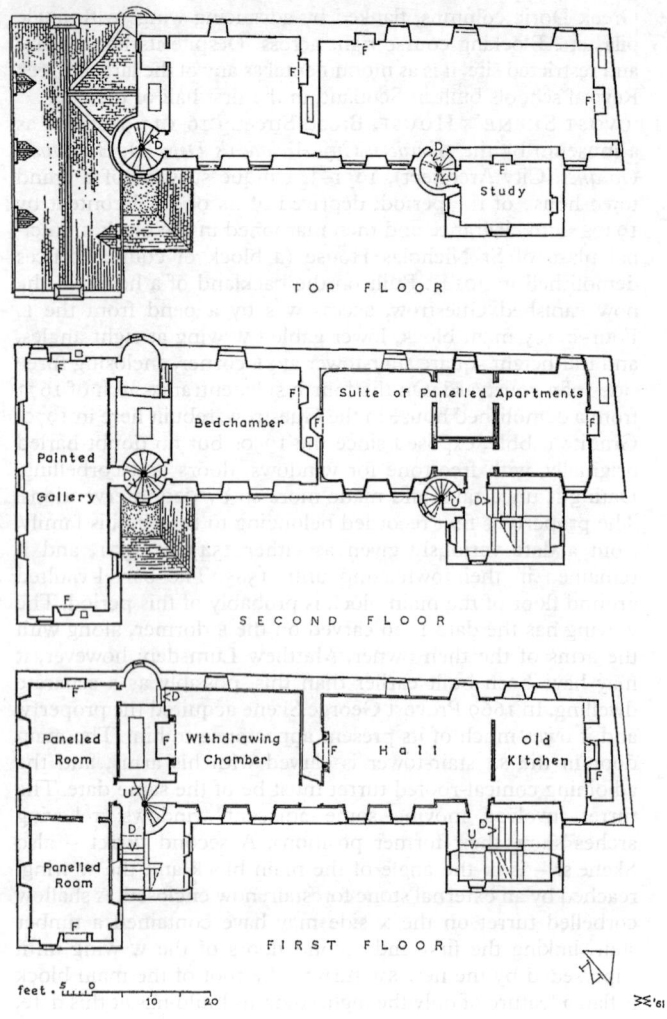

TOP FLOOR

SECOND FLOOR

FIRST FLOOR

feet ·   0   10   20

Provost Skene's House.
Plan of first, second and top floor by Edward Meldrum, c. 1958

Testament scenes in a naïve but vigorous style, probably based on Flemish prints. Eleven frames, but only five surviving scenes: Annunciation, Adoration of the Shepherds, Crucifixion, Entombment and Resurrection. Another, damaged, may show the Ascension. In the borders, cherubs with Instruments of the Passion, sacred monograms in Greek and Latin, and – a subject of particular devotion in North-East Scotland, persisting even after the Reformation – the *Arma Christi*, or Five Sacred Wounds. On the walls below, fragments of *trompe l'œil* Corinthian columns. Arms resembling Lumsden's are painted on the soffit of the sw dormer, indicating that the decoration may date from his tenancy, 1622–44. It has been suggested that the room served as a Roman Catholic chapel, but Lumsden's known religious allegiance makes this unlikely. Whatever its purpose, the very existence of such imagery so prominently displayed in Scotland at this date is surprising. Perhaps already hidden by partitions in the late c17, the ceiling was known in the c19, but not fully revealed again until the 1950s. Following the demolition of St Nicholas House, the future setting of Provost Skene's House is uncertain. There are plans to build shops, offices and a hotel, and to transform Broad Street into a public square. Perhaps space will be found for the bronze SCULPTURE by *T. B. Huxley-Jones* which was installed in a pool s of Provost Skene's House in 1970: Sea Fantasy, a naked woman and child gyrating ecstatically.

RAILWAY STATION, Guild Street. Aberdeen was first connected to the s by rail in 1850, the original terminus at Ferryhill being superseded by one on the s side of Guild Street in 1854. In 1867 the line through the Denburn Valley was opened, linking Guild Street to the N and necessitating through platforms. The present station is largely of 1913–15, by *James Lowson*, architectural assistant at the Great North of Scotland Railway Co. Beaux-Arts classical front building, originally containing booking office, etc., with round-arched openings between paired columns, mostly of Northumbrian sandstone. It can only be seen from inside the Union Square shopping development, which with utter contempt has been shoved right up against it. Most facilities are housed in the crisp, single-storey, granite-faced Travel Centre adjoining, N, 2008. Behind the original front building, impressive glazed concourse roof with gracefully curved steel trusses (large etched glass screen at N end, with imagery alluding to the sea, 1990, by *Elizabeth Ogilvie*). Platforms have individual roofs branching from central columns. Some, N of the concourse, levelled to serve as car parking. Guild Street is carried over the tracks on a steel-lattice bowstring bridge of two spans, 1904 by *P.M. Barnett*. At the bridge's SE corner, a granite arch encloses steps down to the station. At the NW corner (visually detached from the station proper, but actually standing on the most westerly platform), the former booking office for suburban services. 1909, Classical, single-storeyed above pavement level.

ROBERT GORDON UNIVERSITY, Schoolhill. (For the University's Garthdee campus, *see* p. 295.) In 1881, technical education classes were transferred from the Mechanics' Institute in Market Street to the reconstituted Robert Gordon's College (*see* below), where a Technical College was established in 1910. It separated from its parent institution in 1981,

becoming a University in 1992. The first purpose-designed
building, the Art School (*see* above), was reconstructed behind
the original Schoolhill façade by *Robert Leslie Rollo* in the
1920s, with much N-facing glazing. Behind it, filling the E side
of the quadrangle in front of Robert Gordon's College, is
Rollo's long TECHNICAL BUILDING, stripped classical of
1927–9; top floor added 1951.

84   ROBERT GORDON'S COLLEGE, Schoolhill. Robert Gordon
(1668–1731), a wealthy merchant of Aberdeen and Danzig, left
all his property for the erection and maintenance of a charitable hospital for the education of 'the sons or grandsons of
decayed burgesses of guild'. A design was at once commissioned from *William Adam,* presumably the one subsequently
engraved for his *Vitruvius Scoticus*. It had three storeys and a
central pediment with square clock tower and spire, but it was
too expensive for the Governors and Adam had to simplify it.
The resulting building, dated 1732 over the entrance and
known as the Auld Hoose, remains the centrepiece of the
College. Instead of a central triangular pediment, Adam substituted bell-shaped pediments (later altered) over the outer
bays. He also heightened the second floor and added another
in the roof, making a tall and rather forbidding façade. A
timber spire made by *William Crystall* in 1733 was substituted
for the intended tower. The material is granite ashlar – an early
example, though its smooth surface may be the result of pick-
dressing in the early C19 – with sandstone quoins and window
surrounds. The only ornament is a Serlian niche above the
entrance, with a full-length STATUE of the founder, commissioned from *John Cheere,* 1753, but possibly designed and
carved by *Roubiliac*. He holds a scroll and leans against a pedestal with a figure of Charity in relief: a fine Baroque work,
with twisting pose and drapery in weighty folds, unfortunately
painted. Substantial additions were completed in 1833 by *John
Smith*: two-storey advancing wings with Doric colonnades on
the ground floor, ending in pedimented pavilions. Smith also
altered Adam's top floor to match, replacing his curved pediments with triangular ones.
    Adam's entrance leads directly to a dog-leg stair in the centre
of the back, rising straight to the top. On each landing, paired
arches frame the upward and downward flights, those on the
lower floors with Doric half-columns (plus a full entablature
on the first floor), those higher up with rusticated surrounds.
Curiously, some of the arches have two intersecting curves,
descending to a cusp just below the keystone. There are similar
single arches on the half-landings. Adam's plan, with rooms
opening off W–E corridors, largely survives. At the W end of the
first floor, the GOVERNORS' ROOM has C18 panelling.
    In 1881 Gordon's Hospital became Robert Gordon's College,
a day school. Many additions have followed. On the W side of
the quadrangle, the MACROBERT HALL, with pediment,
cupola and wings of unequal length, by *Robert Leslie Rollo,*
opened in 1931. It was part of the same scheme as his Technical

Building opposite (*see* above). The most prominent late C20 addition is at the corner of Blackfriars Street and St Andrew Street, 1993 by *Gibson Pacitti Associates*: Postmodern, with a square cupola.

Former ST PETER'S R.C. SCHOOL, Constitution Street. 1833. Plainest classical, of two storeys, but long and low. E-plan, the larger central block with round-arched windows (sills lowered), inscription and pediment. It is linked to outer pavilions by single-storey Roman Doric porches. Two further blocks at right angles were added before 1855, serving as boys' and girls' orphanages, and enclosing a forecourt.

TOLBOOTH STEEPLE, Union Street. The wardhouse or gaol of the original Town House, incorporated into the E end of its C19 successor by *Peddie & Kinnear*. *Thomas Watson* was contracted to build it in 1616, and in 1704–6 it was extended N to provide an extra cell on each floor, with the advice of *James Smith* of Edinburgh. Granite rubble, four storeys, with battlements and corbelled angle turrets. S front largely hidden by Peddie & Kinnear's work, but parts of the E and N sides visible from Lodge Walk (the walls here belong to the early C18 addition, with some of Watson's masonry reused in the parapet). Above, and set back, is Watson's belfry stage, with Gothic twin-arched openings and balustraded parapet: it was probably for this that freestone was obtained from Kingoodie, 1622–3. Lead-covered spire dated 1630 (rebuilt 1739). The entrance was on the E side at first-floor level, reached by a forestair. In 1820 *John Smith* transferred it to ground level on the S side, removing the lowest internal vault to create a double-height entrance hall to his new court house on the N (demolished). This hall was stripped of its early C19 plaster, 1992–4, revealing an arcade embedded in the W wall at the old first-floor level, facing the original tunnel-vaulted entrance on the E. The arcade has semicircular arches with heavy mouldings, carried on pilasters carved with fluted columns in relief. A barrel-vault springs from carved corbels in the spandrels. The arcade may have opened into an adjoining room in the original Town House, W. Two spiral stairs in the thickness of the E wall give access to vaulted cells on the upper floors, a third to the roof. Several early doors with impressive iron reinforcements and locks.

TOWN HOUSE, Union Street and Broad Street. *Peddie & Kinnear*, p. 138 1867–73. Major Victorian town hall, built for county as well as municipal administration, and also incorporating courts. Gothic, acknowledging both the baronial architecture of the North-East and Aberdeen's medieval trade links with the Low Countries: a hugely significant stylistic departure for this site. Even so, its long, unbroken, horizontal lines defer to the established character of Union Street. Two four-storey wings, facing S and W, with ground-floor elliptical arches on massive, round demi-columns (the arches were originally to have been pointed). First-floor windows in continuous round-arched arcades. All the mouldings are big and simple, the emphasis

Town House.
Drawing by Peddie & Kinnear, published 1898

on broad, smooth masses of Kemnay granite rather than decorative detail. Union Street front divided in three by a pair of
corbelled turrets with conical roofs and, above the roof-line,
two huge, cliff-like chimneystacks; between them, long windows
with plate tracery show the position of the double-height Town
and County Hall. The shorter Broad Street front has angle
turrets. Pulling the wings together, a tremendous corner tower,
the square shaft with inset colonnettes at the angles, crowned
by four big, conical-roofed corner turrets, and a pyramid roof
ending in a short spire. It dominated the Aberdeen skyline until
the end of the C19 and is still a powerful presence, not least
from the harbour.

Entrance at base of tower leads via stone-vaulted vestibule to
an impressive octagonal flying stair in the angle of the two wings,
with cast-iron balustrade and heraldic stained glass. Second
entrance in centre of Union Street front leads via a vaulted
passage to Sheriff Courts in linked block at rear, and to imperial stair with more stained glass, giving ceremonial access to
civic suite on first floor: former Council Room, w, with heraldic
panelled ceiling; dining room, E, originally planned as a committee room for the County; between them, Town and County
Hall, with hammerbeam roof and minstrels' gallery along N
side. Within the tower, under a fireproof vaulted ceiling, is the
galleried Charter Room, lined with presses to hold the city's
archives. Light well between courts and Union Street block
covered with glazed space-frame roof, 1991 by the *Kennedy
Partnership*, to make an airily spacious atrium. – SCULPTURE.
Inside the tower entrance, Provost James Blaikie, 1844, an early

work by Aberdeen-born *John Steell*, said to be the first marble portrait statue executed in Scotland. Originally in St Nicholas, moved to the new Town House *c.* 1871. At the foot of the octagonal stair, Queen Victoria, full-length marble wearing plaid cloak, 1866, by *Alexander Brodie*; moved here from the corner of Union Street and St Nicholas Street, 1887, it retains its mighty plinth of polished red granite by *Alexander Ellis*.

Attached to the N end of the Broad Street wing, EXTENSION of 1975–7 by the *Aberdeen City Architect's Dept* (*T. Campbell Watson*, Chief Architect). It tries to mediate between the soaring lines of Marischal College and the broad, simple masses of Peddie & Kinnear's work, while staying thoroughly modern. Four storeys, the coupled verticals of the concrete frame, free-standing for much of their height, are clad in white mosaic, contrasting with the grey mosaic of the walls. Pilotis at N end, forming an undercroft. Inside, cantilevered stainless-steel staircase leading to double-height, wood-panelled Council Chamber with arrowslit windows.

Former TRADES HALL (now Belmont Cinema), Belmont Street. By *Ellis & Wilson*, 1896. Fitted behind pre-existing buildings on Belmont Street, and designed to be seen from the w instead. Here it reaches its full height of three storeys, a sheer-sided granite box relieved by a pair of domed angle turrets and a Venetian window. Ambitious painted decoration of the top-floor main hall (*Douglas Strachan*, 1898) apparently did not survive conversion to a cinema.

STREETS

ADELPHI COURT. In existence by 1808, it stands on top of what was St Katherine's Hill, flattened to make way for Union Street. A court of modest houses, mostly harled, with granite ashlar margins to the windows.

BACK WYND. Laid out 1594, but nothing earlier than the C18 remains. The wall of St Nicholas's churchyard runs all along the E side. W side, opposite the gateway to the churchyard, former Parish Rooms of the West Church of St Nicholas, rock-faced granite with ashlar pilasters and pediment, late C19. On the N corner of Little Belmont Street, a house dated 1787 on a skewputt. For the former Advocates' Hall, No. 1 at the s end, *see* Union Street.

BELMONT STREET. Before Union Bridge was opened in 1805, Belmont Street was effectively suburban. George Taylor's map of 1773 already shows some large, detached houses on the w side, with long gardens stretching towards the Denburn. Most of the other surviving houses had appeared by the time of Alexander Milne's 1789 map. They are now interspersed with C19 churches and Late Victorian commercial infill.

Starting at the Union Street end, No. 10, E side, is 1898 by *D. & J. R. McMillan*: a mix of Baroque and Jacobean details, with an octagonal turret at the corner of Gaelic Lane. For the former South Church on the other corner of the lane, *see* Churches. On the w side, Nos. 1 and 3 are early C19, perhaps by *Archibald Simpson*. Three storeys and plain, with round arches to the ground floor, but dropping to a dramatic five storeys at the back (visible from Union Bridge). Late C18 two-storey houses follow on this side, with a Baroque intruder of 1900 at No. 17, by *Ellis & Wilson* for the Aberdeen Electrical Company. Next door, No. 19 is now a pub, but the long ground-floor room of 1883 was designed by *Matthews & Mackenzie* as a showroom for the plasterer and encaustic tile merchant James Bannochie: each ceiling compartment is treated in a different style of plasterwork, illustrating the range on offer, with roundels of Queen Victoria and the late Prince Consort at the end. The floor (no longer visible) was laid with encaustic tiles in what must have been a migraine-inducing thirty-five different designs. No. 25 is larger, possibly *c.* 1786 by *James Massie*, extended on the r. Rubble walls, no doubt originally harled, with quoins and raised ashlar margins to the windows. No. 22, opposite, one of a row of three, retains an C18 open-well stair with simple turned balusters. The shop N of this group incorporates parts of the Gothic façade of Belmont Street United Presbyterian Church, by *James Souttar*, 1867–9, with his characteristic combination of white and blue granite. For the former Central School that completes this side (now the Academy shopping centre), *see* Public Buildings. Back on the w side, the former Belmont Street Congregational Church (*see* Churches) is followed by No. 37, the best house in the street, and one of the best of its date remaining in the centre. Pre-1773, built for George Moir of Scotstown, and later occupied by Menzies of Pitfodels, whose lodging in Castlegate was replaced by the Aberdeen Banking Co. Set back a little (originally a pair of pavilions stood forward on either side), five bays wide, with rusticated quoins and a moulded eaves cornice. Like the rest of the street it is now in commercial use, with a good 1990s classical shopfront by *Oliver Humphries* covering the centre of the ground floor. Inside, l., an open-well stair with twisted balusters, possibly altered. No. 47 is also pre-1773, No. 63 later C18.

CARMELITE STREET. At the sw corner, three-and-a-half-storey warehouse of 1883 by *Ellis & Wilson* for Thomas Ogilvie. The rounded corner has three windows on each floor, separated by piers from which embedded columns seem to be prising themselves free, a typically quirky Ellis touch.

CASTLE STREET. Not so much a street as a square, known also as Castlegate. It was Aberdeen's market place by the C14, and construction of a Tolbooth here was approved by Robert III in 1393. As the administrative and commercial focus of the medieval burgh, it was also the location of its most prestigious houses, but the development of Union Street drew the affluent westward after 1800, and Castle Street went down in the world.

Starting at the NW corner and going clockwise, for the Town House and Tolbooth, *see* Public Buildings. On the w corner of King Street, the former NORTH OF SCOTLAND BANK, completed 1842: the outstanding commercial work of *Archibald Simpson*, and one of the best Early Victorian banks in the country. The streets meet at an obtuse angle, elegantly accommodated with a curved, inset portico of four Corinthian columns. It echoes Soane's Tivoli Corner at the Bank of England, and the capitals are of the Tivoli type, but carved from granite with astonishing undercutting: the bank's masonry was an early triumph of the 'patent axe', or bush hammer, introduced from the United States in the 1830s. On top, terracotta statue of Ceres with a cornucopia, now painted, designed by *James Giles* and modelled by *Mr Nelson* of *Messrs Routledge, Lucas & Co.*, London. She represents the benefits of agricultural improvement in the North-East. The portico is a hinge between two higher blocks, which share its cornice but have balustraded attics above. The larger, facing Union Street, contained the ground-floor banking hall; the smaller, facing King Street, the board room and manager's residence. Strips of channelled rustication between the windows, with moulded bases like giant pilasters, and panels of chaste carving in the spandrels between ground and first floor. Much of the opulent interior decoration is due to *A. Marshall Mackenzie*, 1897–8, who added floors and revetments of polished granite and marble, and a gilded Parthenon frieze. Converted to a pub.

E of King Street, the N side is late C18–early C19, and therefore classical, but with pleasing variations in the height of individual buildings. No. 17 may be 1760s, since it resembles the nearby houses of that date in Marischal Street: windows with moulded and lugged architraves, and a round-arched pend. Nos. 19–23 perhaps similar in date, but with later Ionic pilasters between the ground-floor openings. For the Salvation Army Citadel filling the E side, *see* Churches; for the central Mercat Cross, *see* Public Buildings. The S side from Castle Terrace to Marischal Street is more regular, with some later C19 and C20 infill. The Old Blackfriar's pub, dated 1763 on a skewputt, has a vernacular front with paired windows in a central gabled dormer, but the side elevation to Marischal Street was evidently keyed in a few years later, and conforms to the Georgian terraced houses of the new street (*see* p. 146).

On the W corner of Marischal Street, the former ABERDEEN BANKING CO. (now Sheriff Court Annexe and High Court of Justiciary), *c.* 1801, by *James Burn*. Aberdeen's first building of fully dressed granite, and exceptionally imposing for a purpose-designed bank at this early date. It offers a foretaste of the refined granite classicism of the coming century. Three-storey, five-bay palazzo, with a rusticated blind arcade to the ground floor and giant Doric pilasters above. Handsome entablature and balustraded parapet. Matching extension facing Marischal Street, 1859, by *William Smith*, who also altered the interior; the Corinthian-columned former banking hall survived conversion to court use in 2005 by *Oberlanders Architects/David Murray Associates*, who added the obtrusive semicircular entrance ramp outside. No. 55 was seemingly built by the bank at the same time as its own premises, and is therefore probably also by Burn. A prototype for the standard terraced housing in King Street and elsewhere: three bays, three storeys, with round-arched openings to the ground floor (a later pub front has replaced the original windows). Behind it is Victoria Court, reached by a pend, where No. 54 occupies the l. side: classical, probably late C18, with a pedimented doorcase. It extends s beyond the court to end with a three-storey semicircular bow, only visible from Virginia Street. A grand room with Late Georgian plasterwork survived on the ground floor until subdivided in 2009. Back in Castle Street proper, opposite No. 55, a square stone WELL-HEAD with grotesque carved faces at the corners, c. 1706. The goldsmith *William Lindsay* was contracted to make a brass figure to stand on top, but cheaper gilt wood was adopted instead. The present lead statue, known as the Mannie, dates from 1852, when the well-head was removed from Castle Street to the Green. It was moved back in 1972. For Union Buildings, w side, *see* Union Street, p. 150.

EAST NORTH STREET. s side, backing onto St Andrew's Cathedral, former Corporation Lodging House by *Marshall & Dick* of Newcastle-upon-Tyne, opened 1899. Four storeys and very plain between arched ground-floor windows and crowstepped gables. Extensive demolitions and additions during recent conversion to flats.

EXCHANGE STREET. No. 23 is 1857–8 by *William Ramage* for the National Security Savings Bank, and as un-showy as such institutions generally were: two storeys, with unmoulded round-arched windows to the ground floor. It shows the austere granite classicism of Ramage's former master, Archibald Simpson, still flourishing into the second half of the century. For the former Catholic Apostolic church on the other corner of Trinity Lane, *see* Churches. Next door to this, at the corner of Guild Street, a big, gabled building incorporating the remains of the former Trinity Church of 1794, converted to a music hall after the 1843 Disruption.

GALLOWGATE. The N continuation of Broad Street, passing over the Porthill. Prestigious in the medieval period, by the end of the C19 *The Builder* called it 'narrow and evil-smelling', and slum clearance in the C20 has left little trace of its earlier importance. Of the characteristic medieval burgage plots, only the long, narrow strip occupied by St Margaret's church and former school, e side, is still evident. N of this are PORTHILL COURT and SEAMOUNT COURT, huge slabs of municipal flats by the *City Architect*, 1965–6. Raised on pilotis, with granite-studded cladding panels, now painted. The higher block straddles single-storey shops. The scheme includes a quadrangle of lower flats in Seamount Road, s, and a four-storey car park with spiral ramp in West North Street, built into the e side of the hill. The top of the car park is level with the Gallowgate flats, to which it forms a kind of podium or rampart. On the w side, opposite the flats, Aberdeen College (*see* Public

Buildings). s of this, No. 111 is the former offices of Ogston &
Tennant, all that remains of their important soap and candle
works. It was designed in 1922 by *J. L. Simpson* of Port Sunlight
(where Simpson worked extensively for Lever Brothers, who
acquired Ogston & Tennant in 1918). Single-storey granite
ashlar, with Doric columns flanking the door. On the same
side, between Berry Street and Upperkirkgate, a shop with an
outward-leaning green glass parapet, the frontage of an extension to the Bon Accord Shopping Centre (*see* p. 210) by *Archial*,
completed 2009.

THE GREEN. Possibly the centre of earliest settlement, serving
as the market place before Castle Street. Until the construction
of Union Street, those arriving from the s would descend
Windmill Brae, cross the Denburn, and enter the Green at its
w end. The onward journey to Castle Street would involve
skirting St Katherine's Hill, either to the s via Shiprow, or to
the n via Netherkirkgate. Nowhere gives a clearer impression
of how the narrow, steep and convoluted medieval streets were
overlaid by Union Street in the early C19: at the NW corner,
Back Wynd Steps rise two storeys to the level of Union Street,
while from the NE corner, Correction Wynd passes under it,
revealing its vaulted substructure. From the E end, East Green
runs parallel with Union Street before turning under it to
emerge at Carnegie's Brae on the N side. As for buildings, the
N side of the Green has the cliff-like backs of Union Street
shops. For the Market, E, *see* Public Buildings.

GUILD STREET. From E to W, beginning at Market Street. The
s side starts with St Magnus House, early 1980s by *Richard
Seifert & Partners*. A large corner block of seven-storey offices,
with glazed bays projecting between concrete piers. The rest
is mostly UNION SQUARE, a shopping centre on former
railway lands, incorporating hotel, cinema, bus station and car
parking, by *BDP*, opened in 2009. A glass-roofed area at the
w end abuts the railway station façade, making it an internal
façade of the shopping centre. For the station and the bridge
over the tracks, *see* Public Buildings. The N side is mostly Late
Victorian, after expansion of the railway station in 1867 made
Guild Street an important thoroughfare. Filling the block
between Exchange Street and Stirling Street, and extending
back to Imperial Place, is the ST MAGNUS COURT HOTEL
(originally the Waverley), dated 1870. By *James Souttar*, with
conical-roofed tourelles at the corners and flanking the centrepiece. On the opposite corner of Stirling Street is No. 28, now
the Custom House, but built as offices above shops by *Ellis &
Wilson*, 1896. Five storeys, with canted bay windows and giant
angle pilasters. C20 rear extension. Next comes the TIVOLI
THEATRE (originally Her Majesty's Opera House), 1872, by
the London theatre specialist *C. J. Phipps*, with *James Matthews*;
Frank Matcham made safety improvements in 1897 and remodelled the auditorium in 1909–10. It replaced the old Marischal
Street theatre (*see* p. 146) and marked a new era in Aberdeen
entertainment. Built of concrete cast *in situ* (the first such

theatre in Britain, it was said), its construction took just seven months. The concrete may originally have been exposed at the back in Trinity Street, but is now rendered and scored to look like masonry. The front is a polychrome Venetian Gothic palazzo and, except for the double doors filling the ground-floor arches, it does not look like a theatre at all. Polished Peterhead granite columns carry this arcade, with contrasting white granite and red sandstone used for the voussoirs here and above the arched windows of the two upper floors. Timber cornice on deep granite brackets. As modified by Matcham, the auditorium has juicy baroque plasterwork to the painted ceiling and the fronts of the two curved balconies, and boxes framed in shell niches on either side of the stage: the aim was no doubt to keep up with his own recently opened His Majesty's Theatre in Rosemount Viaduct (*see* p. 162). Opposite the station is the Station Hotel, *Ellis & Wilson*, 1901. It has a pair of shallow, canted bay windows running through two storeys, with mullions and arched transoms derived from the Sparrowe's House pattern popularized by Norman Shaw. Above, two big gables with little curvy pediments incorporating chimneys perched on top. Next door at No. 80, the former head office of the Great North of Scotland Railway Co., *Ellis & Wilson* again, 1892. Large and rather plain, except for the entrance, which has much carving, hovering somewhere between Greek Revival and Art Nouveau.

JUSTICE STREET. VIRGINIA COURT and MARISCHAL COURT, public housing by the *City Architect*, 1966–8. Two slabs of flats, one eight storeys the other eighteen, placed at right angles. Similar to the Hutcheon Street and Gallowgate schemes, the end walls with concrete cladding panels studded with chunks of granite. They stand on what was the Castlehill, latterly occupied by the militia barracks, and look suitably fortress-like, especially from the SE where the ground falls away sharply. From the W, however, their brutal silhouette blights the view along Union Street. SE of the flats, fragments of fortifications constructed by Cromwellian troops during their occupation of Aberdeen, 1651–2, including a bastion with rubble walls and roughly dressed quoins. Stone from the E end of St Machar's Cathedral was used.

KING STREET. Along with the wider Union Street, King Street was one of the two new streets proposed by *Charles Abercrombie* in 1794, to improve access and open up new areas for development (*see* Introduction). The necessary Act of Parliament was obtained in 1800. It leads N from Castle Street to the Bridge of Don, following a dead straight line for the first 1.5 km. Development began promisingly, but fashion favoured expansion westward, and King Street did not in the end achieve the sustained architectural quality of Union Street. Nevertheless, with impressive public and commercial buildings alongside handsome tenements, it made a grand beginning.

We start at the S end, at the junction with Castle Street. In 1804, *James Burn* drew up a scheme for symmetrical terraces on both sides, stretching from Castle Street to North Street, with higher pedimented centres and end blocks. Unfortunately, only an outline drawing of this by *Thomas Fletcher* survives, so it is unclear how far the executed buildings derive from Burn's proposals. In 1816, the middle stance on the E side was taken for St Andrew's Chapel, doing away with the possibility of a continuous terrace. Building on this side seems to have progressed very slowly, and on John Wood's map of 1828 just the chapel and the four-storey block at the corner of Castle Street are shown. The latter dates from *c*. 1811 and is almost certainly by *John Smith*, who had taken over from Fletcher as Assistant to the New Street Trustees in 1807. It has a quadrant corner, with tripartite windows divided by cast-iron mullions, and it consisted originally of three self-contained flats above three shops. For the rest of the houses on this side as far as North Street, there are minor variations in the design of individual fronts but they follow the same basic three-storey pattern with arcaded ground-floor shops.

On the W side, public and commercial buildings predominate, and very little of the terrace scheme was realized. For the former North of Scotland Bank on the corner, *see* Castle Street. Nos. 1–5 are the former North of Scotland Fire and Life Assurance Co., 1839, by *Archibald Simpson*: architraves to the windows on the upper floors, and a panel flanked by scrolls in the middle of the parapet. Next door, the former Commercial Bank of Scotland, by *James Gillespie Graham*, 1836. Five bays, the centre breaking forward slightly, with a temple front of two Roman Doric columns *in antis* above the ground floor. It is very like Graham's contemporary elevations for Moray Place, Edinburgh. Nos. 11–23, a short terrace of the standard pattern, are followed by *John Smith*'s former County Record Office, 1832–3, which is linked to *Archibald Simpson*'s Medico-Chirurgical Hall, 1818–20. The Hall housed the library, lecture room and museum of the Aberdeen Medical Society and, despite appearances, its pedimented portico of four giant Ionic columns comprises its full width. What look like recessed, three-bay wings are unconnected internally. They were built some years later, covenants in the leases requiring them to complement the Hall and make the whole block balance St Andrew's Episcopal Chapel, opposite. The s 'wing' was actually designed by Smith as the N half of his Record Office, the main block of which has four giant Doric pilasters and a balustraded parapet. A single-storey arched entrance, r., overlaps the join, matched by another, l. At least part of the interior was of fire-proof construction, with brick vaults and iron beams, to protect the records. This stretch of the W side ends with the former North Church (*see* Churches).

N of North Street (widened on its N side *c*. 1983, to form a dual carriageway), King Street continues for a while with early C19 three-storey houses incorporating arcaded ground-floor shops. No. 142, E side, a detached house with Greek Doric porch reached by a pend from the street, was built by *John Smith* for himself. Nos. 151–153, W side, were originally the County Hotel, 1894 by *Arthur Clyne*: the ground-floor windows have his characteristic horseshoe surrounds. From around this point, later C19 tenements with wall-head stacks take over from the consistent cornice levels of the earlier part of the street. For King Street N of the railway, *see* Old Aberdeen (W side) and Links and Seaton (E side).

MARISCHAL STREET. Aberdeen's first formally planned street: a ramped viaduct lined with regular terraced houses, designed by *William Law* in 1766 to provide a direct link between harbour and commercial centre. It replaced the steep natural drop S of Castle Street, spanning Virginia Street with the single arch of Bannerman's Bridge. Marischal Street is a seminally important example of a 'bridge street', the first in Scotland to be built with flanking houses. In the context of Aberdeen, it is the precursor not just of Union Street but of Market Street, Bridge Street and Rosemount Viaduct. As a pioneering example of a flyover, it is of European significance. The houses are mostly three storeys, but dropping another two at the bridge to ground level. John Home's survey of the harbour in September 1769 shows houses in existence on both sides N of the bridge; by the time of Alexander Milne's 1789 map, all the E side and most of the upper end of the W side were complete. The earlier houses have uniform, five-bay fronts of Loanhead granite, each with three doors, the outer pair giving access to ground-floor shops. All have cornices and windows with raised margins, and those on the E have doors with lugged architraves. Law presumably established the pattern for these houses, but No. 30 was built by the architect-builder *William Dauney*, 1770. *William Littlejohn*, wright and architect, is also known to have built a house in Marischal Street in 1779. The later houses at the lower end are recognizable by their lighter, more smoothly finished granite. Dauney worked here too, 1799–1800, and was responsible for the houses on the W side between the bridge and the church. Law's standard façade design was now explicitly abandoned, and Dauney was free to treat the fronts in whatever way he considered 'most commodious and advantageous . . . either as to doors or windows or any other part'. No. 44 is double-fronted, with elegantly simple cast-iron balconies. No. 46, similar, has inset granite Doric columns flanking the door. In 1983 Virginia Street was widened, resulting in the demolition of the southernmost houses in the upper half of Marischal Street, the rebuilding of their gable walls, and the replacement of Law's original Bannerman's Bridge in concrete. (For the former Town and County Bank at the SE corner, *see* p. 141.)

MARKET STREET. Constructed 1840–2 to link Union Street with the harbour, continuing the straight line of George Street and St Nicholas Street. Financed by a private joint-stock company formed for the purpose, the scheme included the erection of the Market Hall on the W side, the architect and engineer for the whole enterprise being *Archibald Simpson*. (Simpson's market, with its exceptionally severe Doric pilastered façade and its arcaded interior with nave and galleried aisles, was demolished in 1971: a great loss. It was one of the most ambitious C19 markets in Britain. For its unworthy successor, *see* Public Buildings.) Simpson provided a symmetrical 'gateway' from Union Street, where the flanking blocks had ground-floor arcades facing the new street. These have been replaced, but adjoining them was a pair of single-storey blocks with a trio of round arches, one of which survives, much altered, on the w side. The rest of the street has the kind of plain, three-storey terraces familiar from Union Street, interspersed with buildings of greater individuality. Directly opposite the Market, the former Mechanics' Institute, 1845, by *Simpson* and his assistant *William Ramage*, who made the drawings. Two-storey Italianate palazzo, with a rusticated, round-arched entrance and tripartite pedimented window above. The sills of the first-floor windows have been lowered. Arcaded ground-floor windows, some altered. Next door to this, s, the former City of Glasgow Bank, 1858, by *William Smith*. Italianate again, with a balustraded parapet. There are doors in the end bays, with heavy balconies over, the l. one leading originally to the bank, the r. one to the agent's residence. On the same side, further s, the Douglas Hotel. Partly 1840s, but the Art Deco façade with copper detailing to the recessed central windows belongs to a 1937 remodelling by *A. Marshall Mackenzie & Son*. Finally on this side, the former Post Office (now casino), 1873–5, by *Robert Matheson* of the Board of Works. The material was originally to be freestone, richly ornamented, but switching to granite resulted in simplification of the design. Only two visible storeys (a third is hidden behind the parapet), divided in three by Doric pilasters. Rounded corners to Shiprow and Trinity Quay, and a tripartite central entrance with good cast-iron gates.

On the w side, at the corner of Hadden Street, is the former Union Club, 1854: a solid, respectable palazzo by *Mackenzie & Matthews*, with alternating triangular and segmental pediments to the first-floor windows. This side ends at the corner of Guild Street with a good, four-storey, Edwardian Free Style block by *Sutherland & Pirie*, 1906. Originally a hotel, it has a well-preserved pub front of segment-headed windows between polished granite Ionic pilasters, and an octagonal timber cupola perched on top.

For Market Street s of Guild Street, *see* p. 254.

St Nicholas Street. Laid out in 1807–8 to connect with George Street. On the w side, at the corner of Correction Wynd, the former premises of Montague Burton, the 'Tailor of Taste' (name and motto are carved at the top), 1928 by *George Watt*. A good example of Burton's eye-catching Art Deco house style, made more serious by being in granite: large areas of glazing framed by tall arches with fluted voussoirs, and a Jazz-Gothic frieze along the top, all heraldic shields and zigzagging chevrons. On the e side, Marks & Spencer, 1964 by

Munro & Partners, clad in shiny grey and black granite, with first- and second-floor windows divided by granite fins and concrete spandrels. It is linked to the St Nicholas Centre, 1983–5 by *Thomson, Taylor, Craig & Donald*, a mostly single-storey shopping arcade which has absorbed the N half of the street, blocking what was an impressive vista along George Street. The arcade has a roof terrace reached by outdoor stairs, with three sculptures: *Moon Table*, by *Roland Piché*, 1985; *Two*, a large bronze relief of two faces by *Gavin Scobie*, 1984; and *Trumpet Leaf*, a carving in Clipsham limestone by *Paul Mason*, *c.* 1985. They do little to redeem a depressing environment of cracked paving and fussy landscaping, incorporating vents from the shops below.

SCHOOLHILL. An ancient street, many of its buildings the result of widening and straightening under the Aberdeen Extension and Improvement Act of 1883, when it became the approach to the new Denburn Viaduct. We begin at the upper (W) end. For the Art Gallery, etc., and the former Central School, *see* Public Buildings. In the triangular area facing the entrance to Robert Gordon's College, STATUE of General Gordon of Khartoum, bronze, 1887, by *T. Stuart Burnett*. Overlooking this space on the E side, and with another elevation facing S, a block by *A. Marshall Mackenzie* of *Matthews & Mackenzie*, 1887. Originally flats over shops. Italian Renaissance in pink and grey granite, matching the same architects' Art Gallery group, with pilasters and a pediment on the W side. Nos. 46–52, of the same date by *John Rust*, complete the block: grey granite with polished red granite surrounds to the windows, and a short square tower with pavilion roof set diagonally at the corner of Harriet Street. No. 61, S side, is James Dun's house, dating from 1769 and now dwarfed by newer neighbours. Two storeys, with raised window margins and lugged architrave to the central door, like the contemporary houses of Marischal Street but without a cornice. Set back, it was originally part of a terrace of three, but replacement buildings on either side have now pressed forward to the pavement edge. Conversion has obscured the C18 plan: original semicircular stair at the rear now leads to a single large room occupying the full width of the first floor, with an Adamish chimneypiece at one end. No. 57 is an impressive tenement, apparently of *c.* 1900, with a pair of wall-head stacks with battered sides, framing a pair of windows under a big broken pediment. E of Back Wynd, the boundary railings of St Nicholas's churchyard were set back to their present line in 1884–5, when the single-storey classical lodge by *John Smith*, 1833, was moved here from Robert Gordon's College. Back on the N side, Nos. 8–26 are by *Matthews & Mackenzie*, 1886: a long, symmetrical block of shops with battlements, crowstepped gables and drum-shaped dormers under conical roofs (the famously picturesque C16 house of the painter George Jameson stood here, removed for street widening and inadequately recalled in Mackenzie's Baronial detailing). Finally, at the corner of what was George

Street before the Bon Accord Centre engulfed it (*see* p. 210), a lively and eclectic former pub by *John Rust*, 1891, with a corner turret sitting on a squat classical column, and an array of shaped gables and pyramid-roofed dormers.

SHIPROW. Winding up from the harbour towards Castlegate, this was a prestigious medieval street, but only the C16 Provost Ross's House survives above ground from that period. (It is now part of the Maritime Museum: *see* Public Buildings.) The E side, from Exchequer Row to Shore Brae and extending E to Virginia Street, is CITY WHARF: shops, offices, hotel, casino and car parking behind a snaking curtain wall of grey cladding, by *SMC Davis Duncan*, 2010. Opposite, a nightclub and restaurant with black glass façade following the curve of the street. Immediately W of the Maritime Museum and on the same side are the remains of a house with what may be bits of medieval masonry built into its façade.

STIRLING STREET. CARMELITE HOTEL (originally Imperial Hotel), by *James Souttar*, 1869 with later extensions. Italian Gothic, in the subtly contrasted granites Souttar liked, with pointed windows and non-concentric extradoses. The earliest part is on the corner of Trinity Street. It originally had a symmetrical front to Stirling Street, with a central entrance under a small balcony (a second balcony overlooks Trinity Street, which had an open aspect until No. 28 Guild Street was built in 1896). Matching N extensions of 1871 and 1881, also by Souttar, include a square first-floor bay and a little round tower overlooking the Green, now lacking its conical roof. A further addition of 1885 along Trinity Street, by *William Henderson & Son*, is more Baronial than Gothic. Inside, the corner room in the earliest part has an arched entrance, divided by a central granite column. Stained glass window of St Andrew on stairs. Large former Coffee Room in 1885 wing, with elaborately moulded plaster ceiling. IMPERIAL PLACE, the short street opposite the hotel entrance, is apparently also by Souttar. The block filling the N side has corner tourelles.

UNION STREET. Built under the Act of 1800 for 'making two new streets in the City of Aberdeen' (*see* Introduction; the other street was King Street). Architects and engineers were invited to submit designs for constructing the streets, for the necessary bridges and for 'the proper heights of the fronts, and construction of the roofs, of the houses to be built along both sides'. *David Hamilton* of Glasgow was selected and *Thomas Fletcher* was appointed engineer by the New Street Trustees. The lynchpin of Union Street is UNION BRIDGE, spanning the valley of the now-culverted Denburn. The foundation stone of Hamilton's three-arched design was laid in July 1801, but mistakes over costs and levels led to its abandonment. Proposals by John Rennie for a cast-iron bridge and by Thomas Telford for a 150 ft-wide granite arch were considered, but in the end Fletcher's more economical scaling down of Telford's scheme was carried out. It opened in 1805. A relatively shallow segmental arch, it rises just 8.8 m. from springing to crown, with a span of 40 m. This was second only to William Edwards's 1755 hump-backed bridge at Pont-y-Prydd, and, as an urban viaduct, it was unsurpassed by any of the great schemes built subsequently in Edinburgh. Original niched abutments and balustraded parapet by *James Burn*. Widened in 1905–8 by *William Dyack*, the additions are carried on steel arches which mask Fletcher's and Burn's arch, though Burn's original abutments were reproduced on the new line. Cast-iron parapet designed by *William Kelly* and made by *Walter Macfarlane & Co.* (*Saracen Foundry*), with leopard finials ('Kelly's Cats') and a relief panel by *Sidney Boyes* representing the Arts. In 1963, shops were built along the s side, obliterating all sense of the bridge as a work of architecture in its own right (the parapet from this side was removed to Duthie Park, *see* p. 249). In addition to Union Bridge, there are lesser bridges over Correction Wynd and what was formerly Putachieside. The latter, reached from Carnegie's Brae and East Green, reveals the vaulted substructure of this part of the street.

We start on the s side opposite Broad Street with UNION BUILDINGS, 1819–22, by *Archibald Simpson*. Originally shops and flats, with the Athenaeum Club at the E end. It is the only example of a whole block designed as a unified composition. Short E elevation facing Castle Street, with a double-height tripartite window framed by four giant Ionic columns (the Athenaeum reading room behind it was horizontally divided after a fire in 1973). Round-arched ground-floor windows, both here and on the eleven-bay Union Street elevation, where the centre breaks forward slightly. Each front has a wall-head panel decorated with swags. w of Shiprow, the rest of this side is virtually all early C19, complete by 1828, but built piecemeal, with slight fluctuations in floor heights and cornice levels as the street follows a gentle downward slope. These granite tenements are the recurrent motif of Union Street: usually four storeys, their austerity relieved only by a simple cornice, with an occasional string course or wall-head stack. The original round-arched doors and ground-floor windows have largely given way to modern shopfronts. The misfit in this stretch is Crown Court, a six-storey Edwardian Baroque monster at Nos. 41–43 by *R. G. Wilson*, opened 1903. At Nos. 51 and 53 there is the broad, Tudor-arched entry to Adelphi Court (*see* above). Nos. 57–65 have gabled dormers and a balustraded parapet added by *William Kelly*, 1897. No. 67, now a shop, is by *G. M. Thomson* of Edinburgh for the National Bank of Scotland, 1877–8. Restrained Italianate, with round-arched ground-floor windows between pilasters; sympathetic grey granite extension along Market Street by *Hugh Martin*, 1985.

The N side begins at the corner of Broad Street with two Late Victorian commercial blocks, linked in the 1920s to form the department store Esslemont & Macintosh. The first, Nos. 26–30 by *Ellis & Wilson*, 1887, was originally offices for the Daily Free Press. Classical, with much fiddly ornament round the windows: dismissed by *The Builder* as 'cabinet-making on a large scale'. The second, Nos. 32–38 by *R. G. Wilson*, 1897, is bigger – six storeys – and bolder: two big Dutch gables, with oriel windows in styles from Elizabethan to Queen Anne piled on top of each other. Built for a draper and household furnisher. More adventurous at the back: three giant arches, the spaces between the thin piers filled with glass and iron. After this pair, Nos. 40–42, said to be *Archibald Simpson*'s first work, 1811, for Morrison of Auchintoul, but radically remodelled for the Bank of Scotland by *Peddie & Kinnear*, 1867. They appear to have opened up the centre with three big, two-storey arches to light the former banking hall, adding side doors with balconies over. Union Chambers, Nos. 46–50, was rebuilt 1895 by *William Henderson & Son*, with a pair of prominent wall-head chimneys. Finally, with a long return elevation to St Nicholas Street, the Clydesdale Bank (originally Town and County Bank) by *James Matthews*, 1863. Closer to the opulence of mid-Victorian architecture in other commercial towns than the usual Aberdeen austerity. Italianate, with giant Corinthian pilasters, round-arched windows grouped in threes, polished red granite to relieve the grey, and a lively balustraded skyline with vases and shell ornaments. Barrel-vaulted vestibule with polished granite columns, leading to top-lit banking hall with oval dome and more columns.

Staying on the N side, the superb ROYAL BANK OF SCOTLAND (originally Commercial Bank) takes full advantage of its corner site at the junction with a widened St Nicholas Street. By *Jenkins & Marr*, 1929. American-influenced classicism of a type more familiar in Glasgow. Emphatically cubic, with a pair of giant, three-storey Corinthian columns *in antis* to each front. The huge cornice corresponds to the height of C19 Union Street, but with a high, pilastered attic above. Next, Nos. 82–106, in existence by 1828 and typical of early C19 Union Street; then the bridge over Correction Wynd and the façade to St Nicholas's churchyard (*see* Churches). After this, at the corner of Back Wynd, the former Advocates' Hall of 1836–8 by *John Smith*. It was remodelled as a restaurant by *A. Marshall Mackenzie*, 1897–9, then converted to a cinema by *D. & J. R. McMillan*, c. 1913, and reconstructed internally after a fire by *Watt & Stewart*, 1936–7. Smith's treatment of the corner was a new departure for Union Street: instead of the simple inset quadrants of earlier blocks it is more generously curved and much more three-dimensional, with the entablature breaking forward over pairs of giant Ionic columns. The Back Wynd façade is comparatively flat, with pilasters and pediment above the rusticated ground floor, and windows with consoles to either side (they were blocked when it became a cinema). The smaller openings with Baroque surrounds are presumably Mackenzie's. Nos. 122–132, of 1830 by *Archibald Simpson*, are followed on the other corner of Belmont Street by Nos. 136–144, c. 1817, also *Simpson*. This block drops a further four rusticated storeys at the W end to the Denburn valley, as Union Bridge begins.

The s side of this stretch starts at the corner of Market Street with Nos. 73–77, Art Deco classical by *George Watt*, 1929–31. After this, mostly typical early C19 Union Street blocks. No. 93 was drearily rebuilt by *Robert Matthew, Johnson-Marshall & Partners* (*Kenneth Graham*), 1971, for British Home Stores. Nos. 117–119 have a row of round-arched windows with blocked surrounds on the first floor, inserted by *R. G. Wilson*, 1900. Opposite Belmont Street, the former TRINITY HALL, 1846 by *John & William Smith*: a Tudor Gothic intruder in the uniform classicism of mid-C19 Union Street. Originally the headquarters of the Seven Incorporated Trades, the style was no doubt an allusion to the guilds' medieval origins. It caught the eye of the Prince Consort and earned the Smiths the job of rebuilding Balmoral. Only the front block survives, absorbed into The Mall, a shopping centre by *Covell Matthews Partnership*, 1979–84. Ground floor largely gone, but the first floor has two-light traceried windows, battlements and a row of octagonal ogee-capped turrets. Inside, hall with hammerbeam roof and some Gothic painted decoration, recreated *c.* 1980; stained glass transferred to the new Hall (*see* p. 227). From here, there should be views N and S from Union Bridge, but the s side was built up in 1963. It was recently given a new façade with a row of sail-like awnings.

For Union Street W of Union Bridge, *see* p. 168.

UPPERKIRKGATE. Beginning at the lower (W) end, the clustered towers and spires of *A. Marshall Mackenzie*'s Marischal College extension (*see* Public Buildings) make a stirring climax to the view eastward. s side all rebuilt from the 1960s and now (2014) partly a cleared site (for the St Nicholas Centre, *see* p. 148). N side a pleasing jumble of late C17 to late C19 buildings, heavily restored or rebuilt behind preserved façades. It begins at George Street with Nos. 48–58: simple granite ashlar houses of 1823, with round-arched windows to the ground floors, and an inset quadrant corner. Next, Nos. 44 and 46, of more coarsely finished Loanhead granite, possibly later C18. The fabric of No. 42 is said to be early C18, but its form is older: the gable-end faces the street, and the original entrance would have been from the E, possibly reached via a pend in a neighbouring building. Nos. 24 and 26 have big, corbelled skewputts carved with sundials and dated 1694. Nos. 6 and 8 are 1899 by *R. G. Wilson*. Distinctive two-tier entrance, with a window framed by a Doric order above the door, copied from the Scots College in Paris. Various fragments from older buildings reused: at the front, triangular dormer gable dated 1680, and heraldic panel over the door; at the rear, a corbelled turret. There is also said to be a C16 doorway from Provost Robertson's house, which formerly occupied the site, and an armorial panel dated 1730. Finally, at the corner of Gallowgate, a lively Gothic block by *W. B. Coutts*, completed in 1878 as a drapery store. Most openings flat-headed, including the big shop windows, but from the corbel table upwards Medievalism takes over: dormers with crockets and pinnacles, and a two-storey gabled wall-head feature with a balcony overlooking Upperkirkgate, flanked by ogee-capped turrets derived from Archibald Simpson's work at Marischal College. An octagonal corner turret and another on the Gallowgate front originally had spires rather than domes. Later adapted as Aberdeen University Students' Union. Between 1938 and 1953, the first-floor union bar was decorated with murals by *Robert Sivell*, assisted by *Alberto Morrocco* and *Gordon S. Cameron*: the Journey of Life, including a scene of the Blitz.

WEST OF UNION BRIDGE

This was the New Town made possible after 1805 by Union Bridge, with Union Street as its main artery. Unlike C18 and C19 urban extensions in Glasgow and Edinburgh, however, comprehensive plans for a rational layout were never realized, so that behind the grand façades of Union Street lies a warren of irregular streets, reflecting the vagaries of land-ownership. The boundaries are, on the E, the railway; on the S, Springbank Terrace, Bon Accord Crescent and Justice Mill Lane; on the W, Alford Lane, part of Victoria Street, Thistle Place and Thistle Lane; and on the N, Skene Street (S side), Skene Terrace and the short stretch of Rosemount Viaduct with the library and theatre.

CHURCHES

ALFORD PLACE CHURCH, Alford Place. Originally a single-storey house, converted and extended at the back by *A. Marshall Mackenzie*, 1887, to be the library and museum of the former Free Church College across the road (*see* Public Buildings). Central entrance with Perp windows l. and r., and battlements. Two gabled dormers with carved bargeboards. Set at an angle to this front block, the former library is a long room with a polygonal apse and timber rib-vault. No windows in the side walls – presumably they were once lined with bookcases – only dormers with flowing tracery. Similar windows, but longer, in the apse. Used as a church since the 1980s.

CHRISTIAN OUTREACH CENTRE, Bon Accord Terrace. Originally Bon Accord Congregational Church. 1898, by *John Rust*. Three-storey façade with shaped gable and a confusing array of windows. The central arched one was originally the door to the church, raised above a ground-floor hall and reached by external steps, now removed.

CITY OF GOD JESUS HOUSE, Holburn Street. Built in 1836 as Holburn Chapel of Ease by *Alexander Fraser*, but much altered and extended. It later became Holburn Parish Church. Square tower, S, 1891 by *Jenkins & Marr*, of three stages, with an octagonal domed tempietto on top. Rebuilding of the Holburn Street front was planned by *Jenkins & Marr* at the same time,

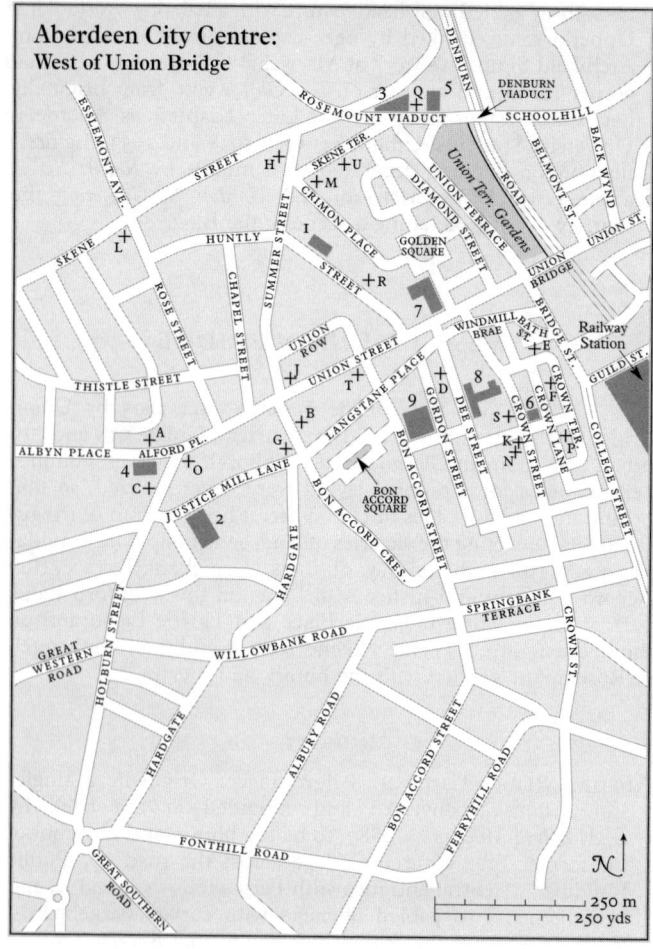

Aberdeen City Centre:
West of Union Bridge

250 m
250 yds

A   Alford Place Church
B   Christian Outreach Centre
C   City of God Jesus House
D   Congregational Church (former)
E   Crown Terrace Baptist Church
F   Crown Terrace Methodist
    Church
G   Free Holborn Church (former)
H   Gilcomston Parish Church
    (former)
J   Gilcomston South Church
K   Greyfriars Free Church
L   Melville United Free Church
    (former)
M   Original Secession Church
N   Quaker Meeting House
O   St James's Episcopal Church
P   St John's Episcopal Church

Q   St Mark's Parish Church
R   St Mary's R.C. Cathedral
S   Trinity Free Church (former)
T   Unitarian Church Centre
U   West Free Church
    (Langstane Kirk) (former)

1   Blind Asylum (former)
2   Bon Accord Baths
3   Central Library
4   Free Church College
    (former)
5   His Majesty's Theatre
6   Masonic Temple
7   Music Hall
8   Post Office (former)
9   Telephone Exchange

but apparently not carried out until 1903 (date inscribed in an oval plaque, along with the year of foundation). Pedimented gable with Doric pilasters on the first floor. Windows square-headed at ground level, segmental-headed between the pilasters. Interior horizontally subdivided and largely without original fittings. The main exception is the superb STAINED GLASS. Three E windows at former gallery level by *Douglas Strachan*, 1903, commemorate 242 Gordon Highlanders killed in the South African war. Religio-military subjects: Joshua and trumpeters before the walls of Jericho; the archangels Michael, Raphael and Gabriel casting out the dragon from heaven; and Sir Launfal and the beggar (from an Arthurian poem by J.R. Lowell). Multiple inscriptions are worked into the backgrounds, including the names of the dead on shields. The windows should read as a triptych, but later partitions mean Sir Launfal is now separated from the others and split between two floors. Six ground-floor windows with coats of arms against background quarries, by *Alexander Strachan*, form part of the same scheme. – MONUMENT. Ground floor, N wall: Dr McClymont, bronze mural tablet with relief portrait by *Pittendrigh MacGillivray*, 1929.

Adjoining, N, the former HALL by *W. & J. Smith*, added 1880–1. Simple classical, with round-arched first-floor windows. It was converted to a chapel in 1949, a likely date for the STAINED GLASS window, W, showing the Baptism of Christ.

Former CONGREGATIONAL CHURCH, Dee Street. In secular use. Opened 1860. Rectangular, Gothic, with a gabled façade flanked by buttresses. Three lancets above the door, the middle one with simple timber tracery.

CROWN TERRACE BAPTIST CHURCH, Crown Terrace. *James Souttar*, opened 1870. A gabled box. North Italian features include structural polychromy, non-concentric extradoses to the arched openings, and a pyramid-roofed campanile at the SE corner. These are mixed with Scottish elements: rock-faced blue and white granite laid in Aberdeen bond, and a big S window with flowing Dec Gothic tracery and prominent central mullion, reminiscent of King's College Chapel. Later central door (original entrance at base of tower). The gable has no coping, but each angled block overlaps the one below in a series of slight weatherings.

CROWN TERRACE METHODIST CHURCH, Crown Terrace. *James Souttar*, 1873. Another of Souttar's Italian Gothic efforts. Gabled façade with flanking octagonal spirelets. Shallow gabled porch with twin doors; four windows above. All the windows have arched ashlar surrounds with non-concentric extradoses. The middle two are united under another such arch, this time with alternating voussoirs of white ashlar and blue rock-faced granite, the same treatment as the doors.

Former FREE HOLBURN CHURCH, Bon Accord Terrace and Justice Mill Lane. In secular use. 1844, by *John Innes*. Gabled centre to Bon Accord Terrace, with three stepped lancets over the door and pairs of lancets to either side. More lancets to the gabled Justice Mill Lane front, the middle two with a round window over, united under a dripmould. Altered 1896 for the Catholic Apostolic Church.

Former GILCOMSTON PARISH CHURCH, Summer Street. *William Smith*, 1771; enlarged by *Duncan McMillan,* 1878–9. Originally a chapel of ease for the settlement of Gilcomston, N, from where its site on an escarpment appears commanding. Smith's building was a perfectly square, flat-roofed box, with four windows N and S. McMillan raised the walls, adding a steeply pitched roof and a substantial E extension with gabled centre and tower-like ends containing stairs. All the openings are round-arched, except for a wheel window in the W gable. McMillan's interior is lofty, light and spacious, despite deep galleries on three sides and a towering organ filling the fourth. The galleries are carried on slender cast-iron columns, with an upper tier of columns and round arches N and S. The capitals of the upper columns are level with the top of the walls, so the roof trusses are exposed above these side galleries. Above the level of the arches, the central space and E gallery have a high timber ceiling, divided into square compartments by ribs, with leaf ornaments at the intersections. – ORGAN. 1893 by *Wadsworth & Bros*, with a lacy classical case, brought from the former North Church in King Street. – MONUMENT. James Kidd, †1834. Marble tablet: a sarcophagus with an urn on top. Matching HALLS, S of the church, 1888–9.

GILCOMSTON SOUTH CHURCH, Union Street. By *William Smith*. Designs approved 1865, opened 1868; steeple completed *c.* 1870, belfry stage and spire rebuilt *c.* 1991. An exotic amid the uniformity of Union Street, its grey granite relieved with generous dressings of yellow freestone, its style Dec Gothic rather than classical. Arched entrance under steep gable, with wheel window above. Octagonal turret, r., with spirelet rising from an open arcade. Pinnacled corner tower, l., with two-light windows to belfry stage and 44 m. spire with lucarnes. Side elevation to Summer Street with buttresses and cross-gables, each bay having a two-light window above and three lancets below, signalling the presence of galleries. The interior has cast-iron columns between nave and aisles, and galleries on three sides with traceried fronts. Open timber roof over nave, transverse roofs over galleries. – ORGAN in apse, behind pierced Gothic wooden SCREEN and PULPIT, 1899, apparently by *William Kelly*; war memorial inscriptions added 1921 (by *Kelly*) and 1950. – STAINED GLASS. Above the organ, Ascension, 1907 by *Douglas Strachan*. W aisle, N, Faith, Hope and Charity, *Strachan* again, 1908. W aisle, second from S, SS Paul, John and Peter, 1899 by *Guthrie & Wells*, designed by *David Gauld*. – HALL at rear, with gabled porch and round window over, 1880.

Former GREYFRIARS FREE CHURCH, Crown Street. 1843. Now a motorcycle showroom. A very odd façade. What appears to be a large chimneystack runs up the centre, with the door at its base and an arched window above. It goes right through the middle of the pedimented gable, as if it were the side of a house, not the front of a church.

Former HOLBURN PARISH CHURCH *see* CITY OF GOD JESUS HOUSE

Former MELVILLE UNITED FREE CHURCH, Skene Street and Rose Street. *Brown & Watt*, 1901–3; converted to flats 1982 and renamed Melville Court. Classical, and mostly two-storeyed, but rising to three in the centre of the Skene Street front, where there is a round-arched window under a small pediment. The rest of the windows are square-headed, those on the first floor with architraves and central mullions in the form of slender, square piers. The main feature is the corner tower, with classical upper stage and pyramid roof, like a Venetian campanile (though the openings halfway up have anomalous curvy lintels, more reminiscent of contemporary Glasgow).

ORIGINAL SECESSION CHURCH, now Boys' Brigade Hall, Crimon Place and Skene Terrace. *William Smith*, 1885. A gabled rectangle with buttressed NW porch. Circular N window with plate tracery in a deeply splayed surround. Former vestry and session house at S end. Converted for the Boys' Brigade by *George Bennett Mitchell*, 1908, who added a transept-like wing to the W side.

QUAKER MEETING HOUSE, Crown Street. 1902, by *Kelly & Nicol*. Very simple, the main room with windows above eye level.

ST JAMES (Episcopal), corner of Union Street and Holburn Street. 1887–8, by *Pirie & Clyne*. Only the liturgical W front is visible from the street, squeezed between its neighbours, and not really rising to the demands of a corner site. It does not help that the intended spire was never built. 'Early French Gothic' in rock-faced pink granite. Gabled porch with deeply splayed doorway, flanking quadrant passages and stone roof. Above is a big, impressive circular window, recessed under a pointed arch, with chunky quatrefoils surrounding a multi-foil central light. The truncated tower, r., and an octagonal spirelet, l., are linked to the gable over the window by small trefoil-headed arches that show against the sky. Inside, five-bay wagon-roofed nave with narrow passage aisles (the S one added 1897–1900), divided by broad arches on octagonal piers without capitals or bases. Clearstorey with paired lancets. Two pilasters and a timber arch – part of the roof – mark the division between nave and chancel. Four-light Geometrical E window. – WAR MEMORIAL REREDOS by *William Kelly*, 1923, with pinnacles and pierced carving in late Gothic style. – PULPIT. Carved wood, Gothic. – STAINED GLASS. Excellent, strongly coloured E window of 1900–1, an early work by *Douglas Strachan*: Evangelists, Moses, Isaiah and Christ in Glory. Chancel, N side, Ascension, mid-C19, brought from the congregation's previous church in Crown Street. W window, Charity in the centre with other Virtues in surrounding quatrefoils, 1905 by *J. M. Aiken* and *John Whyte*.

ST JOHN (Episcopal), Crown Terrace. Dec Gothic in hammer-dressed granite with Burntisland freestone dressings. As built by *Mackenzie & Matthews*, 1849–51, it consisted of nave and s aisle only, plus N porch, chancel with N sacristy, and tower in the angle of aisle and chancel. In 1897–8 *Arthur Clyne* added the N aisle with a short N transept incorporating a bracket and canopy for a statue. The porch is presumably the original, reused. A polygonal extension to the sacristy is Clyne's too. Tower with shallow angle buttresses and paired bell-openings, and a battlemented top stage like an excessively deep parapet (a spire was intended). Four-bay nave with alternate quatrefoil and octagonal piers and open timber roof. Chancel with stone piscina and sedilia, now painted, and aumbry. – REREDOS by *J. Ninian Comper*, 1936. Italian Renaissance, lavishly gilt, with acanthus scrolls, *putti* and a roundel of the Virgin and Child with angels, after Botticelli. – FONT, W end of nave, C19 shaft supporting early C16 bowl from the church of Kinkell. Octagonal, with carving on each face, including *Arma Christi* and monogram of Alexander Galloway, rector of Kinkell *c.* 1516–52. – PULPIT, r. of chancel arch, stone, octagonal on clustered shafts. – ORGAN in base of tower, 1881. – Highly unusual MURAL PAINTING above chancel arch. The subject is taken from the Te Deum and shows choirs of angels, saints and martyrs, along with 'ordinary dwellers on earth' (fishermen hauling in their nets and shepherds with their flocks), but the remarkable thing is the Divisionist technique. It was painted by the Aberdeen artist *J. A. H. Hector*,★ and the date is 1903, incredibly early for Post-Impressionism in Britain, let alone North-East Scotland. – STAINED GLASS. Chancel windows all by *Wailes*, 1851. E, Our Lord as Salvator Mundi with the Virgin Mary and SS Peter, James the Great and John; NW, Mary at the feet of Jesus and Three Maries at the Sepulchre; NE, St Peter and St Andrew; s, St Margaret of Scotland and St Cuthbert. N transept, w, Presentation, Nativity and Adoration of the Magi, *c.* 1855; E, Martha and Mary, *c.* 1859; both probably also *Wailes*, and presumably re-set in 1897–8. N aisle, w, St Paul and St Timothy, 1875 by *Clyne*, also re-set. s aisle, E, Second World War memorial window, the empty tomb with SS Peter and John, *Chilton & Kemp*, 1947–9.

Former SCHOOL, s, 1862. Simple Gothic.

ST MARK'S PARISH CHURCH, Rosemount Viaduct. *Matthews & Mackenzie*, 1892, as the South Free Church. The church makes a handsome group with its secular neighbours, the library and theatre. Five-bay front block with pedimented Corinthian portico; pediments and pilasters to return elevations. The bow-ended rear part is a plain box with halls below, the ground dropping sharply to Skene Street. Above the portico, a dome on a high drum rises from an octagonal base. The drum has Doric columns breaking forward at the angles of the octagon, enclosing three-light windows with further

★The artist and date were discovered by Stuart Donald.

columns as mullions. Disappointingly, it does not light the church but forms a self-contained room above. Behind the portico, a vestibule with gallery stairs l. and r. leads to the main internal space, dark with heavily varnished woodwork. Giant arcades of three round arches across each end – fluted Corinthian columns to the N, Ionic to the S – with roundels of cherubs' heads in the spandrels. Galleries on three sides, with balustraded fronts. Panelled wooden ceiling, very slightly curved. The middle arch on the N frames the PULPIT, with the ORGAN above, added 1900. – FONT. Pink and grey granite, contemporary with the church. – STAINED GLASS. A rich and varied collection, much of it brought from elsewhere. Under W gallery, S to N: Conversion of St Paul, 1904; Christ blessing the children, by *Morris & Co.*, 1894, from a design by *Edward Burne-Jones* first used in 1874 (this and four windows of 1895–6 by *T. R. Spence* with Renaissance architectural borders were originally in Trinity Free Church, Crown Street); Presentation in the Temple (one of the *T. R. Spence* windows). Under E gallery, N to S: Charity, *J. M. Aiken*, 1927; Annunciation and Raising of Lazarus, both Spence. S gallery, Adoration of the Magi, Spence again. W gallery, Christ preaching to the sick, 1908. l. of organ: Miriam's celebration after crossing the Red Sea, and Christ with the centurion, both 1892. r. of organ: Peter and John healing the crippled man, 1892; Suffer the little children, by *Douglas Strachan*, 1900, with angel musicians in the borders. W gallery stair: The Light of the World (after Holman Hunt's painting), by *James A. Crombie* of the Abbey Studio, 1952. E gallery stair: Calling of St Matthew, *Gordon Webster*, 1963. The last two were originally in the Triple Kirks (*see* p. 128).

ST MARY'S R.C. CATHEDRAL, Huntly Street. *Alexander Ellis*, 1858–60. Angled to the street, so that the W end is seen obliquely, its parts picturesquely staggered. Dec Gothic with nave and lean-to aisles. Six-light Geometrical window above W door. No windows in aisles, only dormers. Clearstorey with lancets in threes, and a wheel window in E gable. NW tower with angle buttresses and paired windows under trefoil dripmoulds, completed 1876–7 by the addition of a belfry stage and richly decorated spire by *Ellis & Wilson*. It bristles with water spouts, multiple gablets and elaborate corner pinnacles set diagonally (the details recall William Burges). Sadly, the decorative exterior belies the interior, stripped of its rich C19 furnishings in a savage reordering of 1957–60 by *Charles W. Gray & Partners*, well before such destructive interventions became commonplace after the Second Vatican Council. Seven-bay nave entered under W organ gallery with wrought-iron balustrade. Square chancel with shallow flanking chapels, continuations of nave and aisles. Ellis's arcades are extraordinary for their date: the hexagonal freestone piers have no bases or capitals, their flat sides flowing uninterrupted into the chamfering of the arches and down to the floor. This would be noteworthy in the 1880s; for the 1850s it is amazing. Nave roof with scissor-braced trusses; lower wooden ceiling over chancel; aisle roofs supported on struts springing from arcade spandrels.

FURNISHINGS. Two late C19 side ALTARS with carved fronts survive from before the reordering; also the FONT, W end of nave, granite with incised decoration, perhaps late C19 or early C20. – ORGAN, by *James Conacher & Sons*, Sheffield, 1887. Other furnishings, introduced to mitigate the post-1960 bleakness, are mostly rather insipid. – RELIEFS above nave arcades, six scenes from the life of the Virgin Mary, fibreglass, by *Anne Davidson*, 1985. – ROOD, behind high altar, fibreglass, by *Charles Blakeman*. – PAINTINGS. Above the two side altars, seated Christ (N) and patron saints of Aberdeen (S), by *Felix McCullough*; on N and S walls of chancel, two very large murals of Scottish saints, 1998–9 by *Fiona Forsyth*. Better than these are the austere mosaic STATIONS OF THE CROSS, N aisle, 1969 by *Gabriel Loire* of Chartres, and the vigorous tapestry ALTAR FRONTAL with symbols of the Evangelists by Forsyth again. – STAINED GLASS survives from the late C19, all by *Wailes & Strang* of Newcastle: E wheel window, Gothic foliage; S aisle, W, Virgin Mary and St Theresa, 1876; Nave, W, Mysteries of the Rosary; under W gallery, SS Christina, John the Baptist and Andrew; base of tower, St Joseph and Tobias with the Angel, 1876; N aisle, W, Life of St Joseph.

CLERGY HOUSE attached on N, 1858. Former CONVENT and SCHOOL on S, already existing in 1860 (the 1863 datestone presumably refers to alterations).

Former SOUTH FREE CHURCH *see* ST MARK'S PARISH CHURCH.

Former TRINITY FREE CHURCH, Crown Street. Only the façade survives, 1890–2 by *Matthews & Mackenzie*, now fronting a restaurant with flats above. Pediment and four Corinthian pilasters raised on a high plinth, with a gap for the central entrance. In the manner of Palladio, the pediment is superimposed on another, lower and wider, of which only the ends are visible. Venetian window above the door; windows with cruciform mullions and transoms on either side.

UNITARIAN CHURCH CENTRE, Skene Terrace. Originally Church of Christ. *D. & J. R. McMillan*, 1903. Small gabled box. Central window with intersecting tracery.

Former WEST FREE CHURCH (Langstane Kirk), Union Street. *James Matthews*, 1867–9; conversion to a bar and casino by *Fitzgerald & Associates* completed 2007. Dec Gothic in pinkish Morayshire sandstone, with a landmark NE steeple 53 m. high. Asymmetrical entrance front set back the whole depth of the neighbouring house, making a forecourt on Union Street. Gabled centre with five-light window of Geometrical tracery above a moulded, arched doorway. Tower on l.; single bay on r. with two-light window and gallery entrance. Carved label stops, etc., a mixture of stiff leaf and naturalistic foliage. Six-bay side elevation to Bon Accord Street divided by buttresses, with windows in two tiers reflecting internal gallery. S end with wheel window. Three-stage tower with angle buttresses; broach spire with lucarnes and bands of carved decoration (tower pinnacles and aedicules above the broaches partly removed). Interior horizontally divided at gallery level to make a dark, low-ceilinged bar on the ground floor with the lighter, loftier casino above. It is surprisingly successful. Downstairs, round cast-iron gallery columns retained, the traceried gallery fronts making a frieze below the new ceiling. Large canopied pulpit retained at s end. Upstairs, quatrefoil cast-iron columns with foliage capitals supporting arcades. Flat ceilings with moulded ribs over former galleries. Timber nave ceiling, a shallow pointed arch with ribs in imitation of vaulting, modelled on King's College Chapel. Two-part Gothic organ case by *George Coutts*, 1898, moved from s to n. – STAINED GLASS. Filling the windows under the galleries, an outstanding series of twelve scenes from the life of Christ, 1937–53, by *J. M. Aiken*. Vigorous compositions crowded with expressive figures. Otherwise, glass of 1869 by *Daniel Cottier* of Glasgow: Gothic foliage in the s wheel and n window, and simpler quarries above the former galleries.

Attached at the back, two-storey meeting hall, session house, etc., with gables on three sides and mostly lancet windows. Adjoining this, and internally linked with the church, three-storey c20 addition, altered in connection with present use: asymmetrical gable, partly stone-faced, with large areas of glazing.

PUBLIC BUILDINGS

Former BLIND ASYLUM, Huntly Street. Now offices. 1841–3, by *John Smith*. E-plan, two storeys, the centre block with a consoled cornice above the door and a parapet with scrolls supporting a panel of chaste classical decoration. A rope walk and other workshops at the rear have been demolished.

BON ACCORD BATHS, Justice Mill Lane. 1936–40, a magnificent Art Deco temple of health and fitness by the *Aberdeen City Architect's Dept* (*A. Buchanan Gardner*, Chief Architect). Severe two-storey granite-faced front block, with central entrance framed by four projecting piers. This contains steam baths, club rooms, etc. The central wood-panelled lobby leads by a broad axial corridor to the cathedral-like 40-yard (36.6-m.) pool. Because of the fall of the site, the corridor enters on a level with the concrete diving platforms at the far end, and twin flights of stairs descend to the poolside. High vaulted roof on elliptical concrete arches springing from piers, with tall clearstorey windows between. Raked spectator seating in front of the piers, low aisles behind.

CENTRAL LIBRARY, Rosemount Viaduct. Two phases, 1889–92 and 1903–5, both *Brown & Watt*. The e half came first, set back behind a balustrade above a semi-basement. 'French Renaissance', but rather plain, and symmetrical apart from the entrances in the pavilion-roofed end blocks. Between ground-floor lending and first-floor reference departments, the latter with arched windows. Octagonal turret on roof. w addition containing enlarged reading room, in the same style but livelier, and nicely adapted to its long, triangular site. It has its own entrance where it meets the original building, with an arched and balustraded window above, and a pediment breaking the roof-line below a second turret. It then drops to a single storey, above which the return elevation of the higher part is semicircular in plan, with windows in threes. The lower part, with mullioned-and-transomed windows, tapers until it ends under a stone cupola at the acute angle between Rosemount Viaduct and Skene Street.

Former FREE CHURCH COLLEGE, Alford Place. 1850, by *Mackenzie & Matthews* (construction supervised by *William Henderson*). Collegiate Tudor Gothic, like the Free Church's slightly earlier New College in Edinburgh. Five bays and two storeys, with pointed windows to the ground-floor classrooms and square-headed ones to the hall above, all with cusped tracery. The first floor has a large oriel in each of the gabled end elevations. Diagonal buttresses with top-heavy pinnacles, and battlements. At the back is a high, battlemented tower with higher octagonal stair-turret, of pinkish, squared rubble laid in Aberdeen bond, unlike the grey granite ashlar of the main block. Now a pub, and altered internally. Seen obliquely, the whole group makes a picturesque termination to the view w along Union Street.

110 HIS MAJESTY'S THEATRE, Rosemount Viaduct. 1904–6, by *Frank Matcham*. Opulent Edwardian Baroque front, with richly blocked window surrounds and a copper-domed tower at one end. The entrance bay swells forward triumphantly under a scrolled pediment. Well-preserved interior, with plasterwork and stained glass in lobby and bars. Sumptuous horse-shoe auditorium with three galleries. Alabaster proscenium arch, flanked by pedimented boxes, with a frieze of classical figures by *W. H. Buchan* above. Attached on the E, EXTENSION by the *City Architect's Department*, 2004–5, providing enhanced front-of-house and back-stage facilities. It makes a stark contrast with Matcham's building. From the street, it is a two-storey glass box with an oversailing roof of green copper. The roof is flat on top but curved on the underside, which forms the ceiling of the double-height interior. Granite-faced and plainer at the rear, with few windows, and dropping a further three storeys to Lower Denburn.

113 MASONIC TEMPLE, Crown Street. 1908–11 by *Harbourne Maclennan* of *Jenkins & Marr*. A splendid English Renaissance design, replete with Masonic symbolism inside and out. Five-bay front, with rusticated basement and Gibbs surrounds to the ground-floor windows. The wider central bay projects, with coupled Ionic columns and an open pediment on the first floor. Leaded casements throughout. Timber cupola on the roof ridge, and a sundial on s gable chimneystack (similar to the one at Morden College, Blackheath, London), inscribed with the date 1912 in Roman numerals, according to the Masonic calendar. Entrance hall with chequered black-and-white

marble floor enclosing a circular mosaic of the Zodiac. Sumptuous oak chimneypiece, with flanking Ionic columns and four bronze figures by *W. H. Buchan* in niches above: Wisdom, Fidelity, Charity and Strength. Doors l. and r. of this lead to the Provincial Hall (with octagonal skylight) and Chapter Room. From a vestibule between them, a narrow stair descends to the smallest but most spectacular room, a subterranean domed chamber about 2.5 m. in diameter with a central altar. The decoration here is Italian Renaissance, with marble floor and pilasters and, between the pilasters, painted decoration resembling Cosmati work. A circular opening in the floor of the vestibule gives a thrilling view down through the crown of the vault into this secret, dazzling space. From the entrance hall, an open stair with cherubs on the newel posts leads to the first-floor landing, where an oak doorway surmounted by a figure of Hiram Abif, architect of Solomon's Temple, leads via a lobby to the Craft Hall. Oak-panelled, with C17-style cherubs' heads round the doors and Ionic pilasters between the windows down each side, it resembles the hall of a City of London Livery Company, except that the ribs of the segmental vaulted ceiling spring from very *fin de siècle* female herms with wings and Nordic plaits. At the E end, altar-like First World War memorial, with Italian Renaissance cherubs supporting an inscribed cartouche. In the entrance hall, bronze BUST of Alexander Wilson, 1911 by *F. Derwent Wood*. In the lounge, l. of the entrance hall, artificially lit STAINED GLASS window, Moses, 1909 by *T. F. Curtis, Ward & Hughes*.

MUSIC HALL, Union Street. Built as county assembly rooms by *Archibald Simpson*, 1820–2, the first major public building W of Union Bridge, and a statement of social aspirations for the New Town. An austerely elegant granite box, with a monumental portico of six Ionic columns and antae at the corners. A vestibule with steps leads to the Grand Saloon, parallel with the street. This has an elliptical coffered dome, pilasters and screens of paired Ionic columns at each end with anthemion necking. In the middle of the S side, between the doors from the vestibule, STATUE of Queen Victoria, *Alexander Brodie*'s original plaster model for his 1866 marble, now in the Town House (*see* p. 139). An axial corridor (or 'promenade') opens off the N side between two further columns, with segmental coffered ceiling and a dome halfway along. W of this are the refreshment room (square) and card room (circular, with a saucer dome and four elliptical recesses screened by Corinthian columns). All these spaces are top-lit. E of the promenade was formerly a double-cube ballroom with windows along Silver Street, now subdivided for cloakrooms and toilets. S of the Grand Saloon, a pair of smaller rooms flank the vestibule. A dining room, N, originally completed the interconnected suite.

In 1858 ownership was transferred to a company charged with building a public hall for concerts and large meetings. *James Matthews* replaced the dining room with the present Music Hall, opened 1859, and the rest of Simpson's building became its front-of-house. Matthews's hall is a plain rectangular block, with an entrance from Silver Street under a consoled cornice, and windows overlooking Golden Square (a single-storey extension was made here in the early C20 to improve access). Coved ceiling, galleries on cast-iron columns on three sides, and a segmental, arched recess for the organ behind the stage. The galleries have openwork fronts by *Walter Macfarlane & Co. (Saracen Foundry)*. In 1899, *Douglas Strachan* began an ambitious scheme of PAINTED DECORATION, only parts of which survive. On the walls, framed scenes from the Orpheus myth, with echoes of G. F. Watts in the rippling draperies. The E wall has a panoramic Orpheus crossing the Styx. The semi-dome behind the organ is more architectural in treatment, and thoroughly Secessionist in style: Apollo in the centre, the Muses curled in a bower of foliage above, and a frieze of figures on each side representing the 'various expressions of music', all against a gold background. The panel l. of the stage is a replacement of 1949 by *Hugh Adam Crawford*.

III   Former POST OFFICE, Crown Street and Dee Street – two distinct blocks in parallel streets, with a linking cross-range. By *W. T. Oldrieve* of *H. M. Office of Works*, opened 1907. Part Scots Renaissance, part Baronial, with Oldrieve's antiquarian interests much in evidence. The main front exploits the change of direction in Crown Street to make a picturesque composition, high and craggy like a tower house. Middle section symmetrical, viewed from E: a grand projecting entrance with blocked Doric columns and an open segmental pediment, flanked by mullioned-and-transomed windows, some with strapwork over. Oriel above the door, crowstepped gable above that. To the r. of this, and set back, a wing with conical-roofed tourelles and a secondary entrance (originally posting boxes) facing Union Street, and in the angle a fat round tower with a caphouse. To the l., another wing steps forward, culminating in a big round angle tower of the Holyrood-Falkland type, conical-roofed, with a corbelled and battlemented parapet that extends across all three parts, tying them together. The Dee Street elevation is flatter, following the line of the street, with central entrance and slightly advancing wings. It is symmetrical, apart from the details of the wings: the r. one has a crowstepped gable and angle turrets, the l. a caphouse and octagonal turret, linked by an arch. Now converted to residential use as NEW CENTURY HOUSE, with neighbouring four- and five-storey apartment blocks in both streets by *Macmon*, completed 2001. The new parts are granite-faced, with channelled rustication to the ground floor and a brise-soleil that does service as a cornice. Double-height entrances framed in darker granite. A satisfying C21 answer to early C19 Aberdeen classicism, and a good foil for Oldrieve's Romanticism.

TELEPHONE EXCHANGE, Bon Accord Street. *Leonard Stokes*, 1907. Three storeys and fifteen bays, the middle and ends breaking forward slightly. The whole of the ground floor, and bays two to seven and nine to fourteen of the first floor, are

pink granite. They look structurally as well as visually independent of the rest, which is grey granite and very plain. The
pink part has a cornice, and on the ground floor six deeply
splayed semicircular-arched windows – a favourite motif of
Stokes, used earlier at his Gerrard Street telephone exchange
in London – with scrolled keystones and raised voussoirs tied
into the surrounding banded rustication. The arches spring
from piers which are triangular in plan, and the front of each
pier is carried up as a vertical chamfered strip all the way to
the cornice (another familiar Stokes motif, dating back to his
1889 church of St Clare, Liverpool). On the first floor the strips
frame pairs of square-headed windows.

STREETS

BATH STREET. Royal Hotel, 1879–80 by *Daniel Macandrew*. It
follows the curve of the street, with a corbelled cornice and a
pointed octagonal roof at the corner of Bridge Place. Originally
a hydropathic establishment with Turkish baths.

BON ACCORD SQUARE and BON ACCORD CRESCENT. Along
with EAST and WEST CRAIBSTONE STREET, these were laid
out from 1823 on land owned by the Tailor Trade. Planned
by *Archibald Simpson*, who also designed the elevations, they
form the most coherent and architecturally satisfying development in the whole of the New Town opened up by Union
Bridge. Two-storey houses behind railed basement areas, with
no enrichment to doors or windows, and only a cornice to
relieve their severity. The Square – actually an oblong, with an
oval central garden – is entered in the middle of its short E and
W sides by the two sections of Craibstone Street. The houses
flanking the openings have wall-head stacks facing the Square.
In the centre of the garden, MONUMENT to Simpson, *c.* 1975:
a block of granite, just as it came from the quarry, with an
inscription. Extending S from West Craibstone Street is the
Crescent, a shallow curve of fifteen houses, plus straight terminal blocks, enjoying open views W over a steep, wooded
slope (once divided into garden strips for the houses, now a
public park).

BON ACCORD STREET. Plots here were feued by the Wright and
Cooper Trade in 1814, and – on the W side – by the Tailor
Trade in 1819. Pleasant houses of this period fill the stretch
from Bon Accord Lane to Springbank Terrace: far from
uniform, they vary between one and three storeys. At the N
end, some interesting later replacements. E side, on the S
corner of Langstane Place, former premises of Messrs
Campbell's Ltd, cab-hirers, converted to the GALLERIA
SHOPPING CENTRE by *Hendry & Legge*, 1990s. The original
1889 block by *Jenkins & Marr* extends back along Langstane
Place and round the corner into Gordon Street, where there
is a large 1890s addition. Utterly plain externally, the complex
was interesting for its internal structure and planning. The
ground floor was for carriages, the first and second provided

stabling for 168 horses, with stores for fodder on the third. A triangular courtyard – now roofed over at first-floor level for shopping – gave access to the stables via ramps and concrete galleries on cast-iron columns. The courtyard survives above the first floor, where the brick-faced stables have been converted to housing, but the original concrete galleries have been replaced with pre-cast units. Vehicular accommodation of a later date on the w side of Bon Accord Street, where the large former garage of Messrs Jackson fills the block between Langstane Place and East Craibstone Street. 1937 by *A. G. R. Mackenzie*, and typical of its period (horizontal metal-framed windows in long bands, rounded corners, etc.) but sensitive to its setting, the s side and back segueing smoothly into Archibald Simpson's Bon Accord Square. For the Telephone Exchange, *see* Public Buildings.

BRIDGE STREET. A sloping viaduct formed in 1865–7 (engineer *John Willet*), linking Union Street with the w end of Guild Street and the railway station. Nos. 20–28, w side, shops and flats by *Matthews & Mackenzie*, 1880–2. Five-storey Baronial with gabled dormers, rising to six storeys at the Bridge Place corner, making a rugged, semi-octagonal tower with a conical-roofed turret. Big windows at the rear in Bath Street, lighting the stairs. (In Bridge Place, the former Palace Theatre, 1897–8 by *John Rust*, with sparse classical details. Now a nightclub, the interior subdivided.) Nos. 32–52, Victoria Buildings, 1880 by *Ellis & Wilson*, with their typical mix of Greek and Egyptian detail. Fifteen bays, with giant pilasters and pedimented centre. s of Guild Street, Bridge Street becomes College Street, with St Machar House on the E side, an eleven-storey slab by *Mackie Ramsay & Taylor*, 1977.

CROWN STREET. Described in 1826 as 'lately' opened out of Union Street. The w side starts at the corner of Langstane Place with two tall, narrow tenement blocks by *George Coutts*: Nos. 6–10, dated 1900, with classical details but of no particular style, have a good contemporary pub front; Nos. 12–16, 1901, have a pair of four-storey shallow canted bays and elaborate Dutch gables. For New Century House, including the former Post Office, *see* Public Buildings. On the E side, Nos. 23–25 were built for Prudential Assurance by *Paul Waterhouse*, 1910. Georgian, with some odd Mannerist touches. Two-storey outer bays, stepping up to three, with a central attic making four. The three-storey part has giant Ionic pilasters over a rusticated ground floor, and a Venetian window and balcony above the round-arched entrance. Square panels between the first- and second-floor windows, with garlands and outsize guttae. Another of these panels is in the middle of the attic, flanked by close-set round windows like a pair of goggles, and two vases on the parapet. Nos. 27–29, in contrast, make up a very restrained classical block of 1932 by *A. Marshall Mackenzie & Son*. s of here, and in CROWN TERRACE, E, mostly two-storey terraced houses of the 1820s onwards (No. 13 Crown Terrace, s of the Baptist Church, is post-1867; it has

Doric columns of polished red granite flanking the door, and a matching band at first-floor level). For the Masonic Temple, *see* Public Buildings.

DEE STREET. Laid out 1806–7 but entirely rebuilt at the N end. Starting from Union Street, No. 11, E side, is a late C19 commercial block with painted terracotta ornament. For the former Post Office and New Century House, *see* Public Buildings. S of Academy Street is quite different, with charmingly irregular houses, mostly of the 1810s and 20s: some have long front gardens, some railed basement areas, and some are built right up to the pavement. Generally two storeys, but not consistent in height, they vary between rubble and ashlar. Among the developers active here was the builder *William King*. No. 57 is larger, with single-storey wings and a parapet added *c.* 1900. No. 77 is the OGILVIE BUILDING, 1898 by *W. & J. Smith & Kelly*. With its simplified classical details and absence of mouldings, it could be forty years later. Originally warehousing and manufacturing space for a hat and cap maker; now flats. Three storeys plus a mansard, with giant pilasters to the upper floors and a semicircular window in the pedimented gable. Long return to Dee Place. DEE PLACE takes its name from the detached three-bay house set back on its S side, on the axis of Dee Street. In existence by 1820, its extensive grounds were divided up for building after 1843. Of this date are two short flanking terraces, with cornices on simple consoles above the doors; another is round the corner in SPRINGBANK PLACE, W. The N side of SPRINGBANK TERRACE, S, may also be of the same date. It has one- and two-storey houses over basements, with long front gardens.

DENBURN VIADUCT. By *William Boulton*, Burgh Surveyor, 1886. It bridges the railway to link Schoolhill with Rosemount Viaduct. Originally three segmental arches; a fourth was inserted at the E end when Denburn Road became a dual carriageway, opened in 1994. Rock-faced granite with ashlar dressings. Ballustraded parapets.

GOLDEN SQUARE. Along with its tributaries SILVER STREET, DIAMOND STREET, etc. (the names reflect the ownership of the Hammermen Trade), this was the only attempt at a formal layout N of Union Street. Planned by 1806, built up after 1810. Two-storey houses behind railed basement areas, not quite uniform, but more or less consistent in design. Some have overthrows, some lamp standards (those at Nos. 4 and 5 incorporate the municipal arms). No. 1 has a single-storey office extension at the back, with an elaborate Romanesque doorway to South Silver Street, 1900, by *R. G. Wilson*. In the former central garden (now a car park) impressive STATUE of the 5th Duke of Gordon, leaning on his sword, foot raised on a broken cannon. Carved from a single block of Dancing Cairns granite by *Macdonald & Leslie* after a model by *Thomas Campbell*, and erected in Castle Street in 1844; moved here 1952. In the 1830s Macdonald had revolutionized the working of granite by his invention of machinery for cutting and polishing, and the statue was hailed as a pioneering demonstration of the stone's adaptability to monumental sculpture: 'the triumph of genius and art over difficulties which, since the days of the Ptolemies, have been deemed unsurmountable'. N of the square, set back from the W side of North Silver Street, is MIGVIE HOUSE. Early C19, three bays, the centre one recessed with a consoled cornice over the door. W of this, in Ruby Place, RUBY HOUSE, government offices by the *Property Services Agency, c.* 1979. Four storeys clad in pre-cast concrete panels: ribbed at the ends and on the inward-sloping top floor; smooth on the lower floors, except for the bush-hammered aprons of the first- and second-floor windows. North Silver Street ends at SKENE TERRACE, which has two-storey houses of *c.* 1800 on the N side. Nos. 48 and 50 share a four-column timber porch.

JUSTICE MILL LANE. W end, S side, former cinema by *T. Scott Sutherland*, 1931–2. Art Deco, granite, with red terracotta decoration. Opposite, at the junction with Holburn Street, columnar cast-iron VENTILATOR, *c.* 1905, by *Walter Macfarlane & Co. (Saracen Foundry)*. Glasgow Art Nouveau, with stylized plant forms to the cylindrical shaft, and an octagonal cap. It served a tunnel carrying electric cables from the Millburn Street generating station (*see* p. 248).

ROSE STREET. At the corner of Huntly Street, THISTLE COURT, fifteen-storey slab of flats by the *City Architect*, 1973–5. Raised on pilotis, with granite-studded concrete panels at either end. NE of here, between Huntly Street and Skene Street, extensive public housing of 1961, comprising the eleven-storey GILCOMSTOUN LAND, the Council's earliest city-centre high-rise scheme – plus several lower blocks. For Melville Court at the SW corner of Skene Street, *see* Melville United Free Church, above.

UNION ROW. No. 6, Investment House by *Jenkins & Marr*, dated 1925. Severely Neoclassical, two storeys, the centre breaking forward slightly with giant Doric pilasters and an attic. Curious Mansard roof – part of the original design – with deep eaves at the level of the top of the attic. On the E corner of Union Wynd, GRAMPIAN HOUSE, five-storey curtain-walled offices of 1982–3, said to be by *Glass Murray*. Bronze-framed windows with granite spandrels; top floor set back, with lead-covered pitched roof. Another façade to Huntly Street is slotted unobtrusively into a C19 terrace. On the skyline of the windowless service tower, stainless steel sculpture by *Doug Cocker*, Meridian, 1989. In sensitivity to its setting, Grampian House makes an instructive contrast with neighbouring UNION PLAZA by *Halliday Fraser Munro*, completed 2008, on the W corner of Union Wynd. An eight-storey monolith of speculative offices making three sides of a quadrangle, heedless of the surrounding street pattern. Black glazing with arbitrary areas of white render and pale green cladding. In the court-yard, a huge, free-standing gateway of the same pale green.

UNION STREET. The N side begins memorably at the corner of Union Terrace with the sumptuous former head office of the

NORTHERN ASSURANCE CO. by *A. Marshall Mackenzie* (the 101
drawings are signed by *Matthews & Mackenzie*), 1882–5. Italian
Renaissance, and much more richly modelled than most of
Mackenzie's classical buildings (money must have been plenti-
ful: it cost about £20,000). Quadrant corner with inset Doric
portico, an echo of Simpson's Castle Street bank (*see* p. 140).
Both elevations have windowless bays at each end, slightly
advanced. Ground floor with horizontally channelled rustication and windows with pediments on consoles. The first floor
has coupled Ionic columns between the windows, the lushly
ornamented main cornice breaking forward over each pair.
Above this is a recessed and balustraded attic – another
Simpson feature – with giant buttress-like scrolls between the
windows, in line with the first-floor columns. Sombrely imposing granite-lined vestibule with Doric columns against the
walls, leading to the main public office (now a pub). Screens
of pink granite Corinthian columns at each end with gilded
capitals, and wood-panelled walls with paired pilasters.

No. 150 (*c.* 1808–9 by *John Smith*) appears to be the oldest
surviving house on Union Street W of the Bridge, but the
chaste Neoclassical entrance and ground-floor windows are as
late as 1956, by *A. G. R. Mackenzie*. Typical early C19 Union
Street houses follow between here and the Music Hall, with a
couple of later interlopers rearing up above the standard
cornice height. No. 154 is of 1899–1900 by *Jenkins & Marr* for
the SCOTTISH TEMPERANCE ASSURANCE CO., and anything
but sober: Free classical, elliptical bay windows with columns
for mullions, and a pair of lively Dutch gables with obelisk
finials. No. 162 is of 1902 by *R. G. Wilson* for Lorimer & Son,
boot makers. Asymmetrical Tudor Gothic: gable on l., with a
three-storey canted bay; turret on r., with the entrance to the
upper floors under a little crenellated oriel.

The S side begins on the E corner of Bridge Street with the
Travelodge hotel. Large granite-clad block, built as a department store by *North & Partners*, 1956. W of Bridge Street is
mostly standard early C19 houses as far as Dee Street. An
exception is CANADA HOUSE on the E corner of Crown Street:
1893–4 by *Ellis & Wilson* for the North of Scotland Canadian
Mortgage Co. (hence the head of a Native American carved
over the door, from a design by *Pittendrigh MacGillivray*).
Italianate, with angle pilasters, central canted bay and balustraded parapet with urns. Staircase to chambers above with
stained glass. No. 213, THE GRILL, is a pub with a classical
bronze front of 1925 by *Harbourne Maclennan* of *Jenkins &
Marr*, who also did the wood-panelled interior with elegantly
moulded ceiling. W of Dee Street, No. 225, 1863 by *Alexander
Ellis*, still follows the basic Union Street pattern of fifty years
earlier, but with the addition of High Victorian details such
as incised foliage decoration over the first-floor windows and
the chamfering of the second-floor lintels. Nos. 245–255 are
the unusually large MACKINNON'S BUILDINGS, 1881–2
by *A. Marshall Mackenzie*. Canted bays, and dormers with

pedimented gables above the main cornice, rising to a higher, pavilion-roofed centre.

Back on the N side, between the Music Hall and Huntly Street is a three-storey block of 1963 by *Ian Burke, Martin & Partners*, built for the YMCA with shops below. Grey granite, with black granite details, including fins that divide the long band of first-floor windows. The W corner of Huntly Street has the Edwardian Baroque former ROYAL INSURANCE CO., 1910–11 by *George Bennett Mitchell*. Its octagonal corner dome echoes the company's Liverpool headquarters by James Francis Doyle (and more particularly Doyle's Prescot Street branch of the Bank of Liverpool in that city). After this comes a two-storey terrace of *c.* 1841, with consoled cornices to some of the first-floor windows, and, above the main cornice, a couple of lively upward extensions: Nos. 212–216 have an addition of 1901 by *Jenkins & Marr*, with two gables of sinuous Art Nouveau outline, while the upper floors of No. 220 (*c.* 1906 by *Sutherland & Pirie*) have exaggerated keystones to the windows and a semicircular broken pediment. Other parts of the terrace are little altered: at Nos. 222–224 is the only surviving basement area in the whole of Union Street, and at Nos. 226–228 is an Ionic porch, both reminders of the street's residential origins. W of Union Row, at Nos. 250–252, is AMICABLE HOUSE, an Art Deco office block by *T. Scott Sutherland*, *c.* 1933, the centre recessed in a series of overlapping planes.

On the S side, the former West Free Church (*see* Churches above) is followed by two- and three-storey houses of *c.* 1820–40. No. 343 has a nice late C19 doorway, apparently by *R. G. Wilson*, with Doric columns on plinths, and a semicircular hood on consoles enclosing an arched window. Nos. 373–377 were rebuilt by *John Rust*, 1901, with canted bay windows and a balustrade incorporating gabled dormers and a central round window. This stretch ends at the E corner of Bon Accord Terrace with what was originally a detached house, recessed behind its neighbours to the E and with four giant Doric pilasters evenly spaced across the front. It was perhaps by the London architect *G. O. Leicester* (a drawing for it by him is in the RIBA, dated 1831). In 1892 *Matthews & Mackenzie* rebuilt the façade further forward and gave it canted corners.

W of Summer Street and Bon Accord Terrace, Union Street was originally Union Place. Slightly narrower than the rest of the street, it was mostly built up by the 1820s with houses that are smaller and almost rustic-looking in comparison with contemporary buildings further E – a couple are even harled. On the S side, Nos. 419–421 have a peculiar off-centre Venetian window on the first floor. No. 431 is the former Capitol Cinema by *A. G. R. Mackenzie*, opened 1933. Smooth granite ashlar, fenestrated like a terrace of early C19 houses. Over the middle three first-floor windows there are panels of carving, above which the wall-head rises seamlessly to become a pediment. Most notable on the N side is the ponderous classical block at Nos. 478–484, built *c.* 1830 by *John Smith* to house a municipal cistern for water pumped from the Dee. Redundant by 1871, it was converted to a tenement. Channelled rustication from the original basement survives between later shop fronts. Above, pairs of giant Doric pilasters make an appropriate show of strength. Nos. 496–502, *c.* 1887, are the last significant block on this side, also terminating the view N along Holburn Street. Architraved windows to the upper floors and a pair of chimneys framing a dormer window with shaped gable.

UNION TERRACE. Transformed by commerce in the late C19, but retaining a few early C19 houses. It opens grandly from Union Street, flanked by the former Northern Assurance Co. (*see* Union Street) on the W, and the EDWARD VII MEMORIAL of 1910–14 by *Alfred Drury* on the E: colossal statue of the King in Garter robes – a tour de force of granite carving by the masons *James Philip* and *George Cooper*, of *Arthur Taylor*'s yard – flanked by bronze groups of Peace and Unity. The W side continues with Nos. 4–5, 1979 by *Jenkins & Marr*: granite clad, with tiers of shallow bay windows to harmonize with the neighbouring CALEDONIAN HOTEL by *A. Marshall Mackenzie*, 1891–2. After this some early C19 houses, then at No. 19 the former SAVINGS BANK by *William Kelly*, 1894–6. A three-storey, five-bay palazzo, sturdy but refined. First-floor windows with Gibbs surrounds, the middle one pedimented, with a balcony above the door. The cornice has modillions, each with a fleshy leaf ornament. N of Diamond Place, three more palazzi, now merged as DENBURN HOUSE. No. 20, built as Parish Council offices by *A. Marshall Mackenzie*, 1897–9, has a double-height doorway with Doric columns and an open segmental pediment. Rustication of the lower floors consists in every third course being raised, and these cut across the columns as blocking. Attached Doric columns between the second-floor windows. Next door is No. 22, the former Aberdeen School Board Offices, *Mackenzie* again, 1896–8. Originally three bays, extended to five 1900–1. First-floor windows framed by pedimented aedicules. Projecting between them are square buttresses, or piers – effectively slivers of wall, each with a full entablature returned down both sides. No. 25 is by *Sydney Mitchell & Wilson*, 1902, for the Scottish Life Assurance Co. Four storeys this time, with a central recess in the first and second floors framed by giant Ionic pilasters. Ground-floor windows set in rusticated round arches, each having a central Doric mullion and a shallow bell-shaped light above the transom. More early C19 houses follow, after which comes No. 40, for the SCOTTISH LEGAL LIFE ASSURANCE SOCIETY, by *George Sutherland*, opened 1901. Five storeys, with three double-height canted bays recessed within giant elliptical arches, and a Flemish gable. Finally, the former ABERDEEN UNION CLUB by *A. H. L. Mackinnon*, 1897–8. Baroque, with a broken pediment and obelisks on the parapet where it sweeps round into Skene Terrace.

The E side is open to UNION TERRACE GARDENS, laid out 1877–8 by *Matthews & Mackenzie*, with picturesque views across the railway to the churches of Belmont Street. The pavement was widened in 1891 (engineer *William Boulton*), supported on elliptical arches within the gardens. Halfway along, bronze STATUE of Robert Burns by *Henry Bain-Smith*, 1891. Within the Gardens, s, MEMORIAL to the Aberdeen-born African missionary Mary Slessor, by *Mary Bourne*, 2006–7: a granite vase in the shape of a Nigerian pot, containing bronze foliage. Two more bronze STATUES in the triangular space at the junction with Rosemount Viaduct. Prince Albert, 1862–3 by *Baron Marochetti*, moved here from the corner of Union Street where Edward VII now stands. Diminutive and lifeless on his outsize throne, like a marionette with its strings cut. He makes an amusing contrast with the colossal, histrionic William Wallace by *W. Grant Stevenson*, 1888, reared on a heap of granite boulders.

OLD ABERDEEN

Historically a separate entity from Aberdeen – both administra-tively, until absorbed by its larger neighbour in 1891, and physi-cally, until the city spread N to engulf it in the C20. Old Aberdeen did not become a burgh until 1489, but St Machar's Cathedral was established here in 1165 and a second great ecclesiastical foundation, King's College, followed at the end of the C15. Together they dwarfed what was little more than a village: even by 1636, the population of Old Aberdeen was probably no more than nine hundred. The medieval one-street town shown on James Gordon of Rothiemay's 1661 map, strung out between Cathedral and College, is still immediately recognizable, though lined now with mostly C18 and C19 houses (and jostled by later University buildings). The narrow frontages and narrower lanes between them reflect the original burgage plots. When the University is in session, it is Aberdeen's bustling Latin Quarter; at other times, a sleepily picturesque backwater. The prevailing granite is relieved with warm red brick, produced locally in the C18 and C19.

ST MACHAR'S CATHEDRAL*

14 Attractively set back within its own churchyard at the end of a tree-lined road of handsome villas, externally the Cathedral is chiefly memorable for its twin-towered w front, which compen-sates for its relatively small scale by the extraordinary monumen-tality of its massing.

An invaluable starting point for understanding the MEDIEVAL BUILDING CHRONOLOGY is provided in Hector Boece's history of the bishops of 1522. From that we learn that Henry le Cheyne

*This entry is by Richard Fawcett.

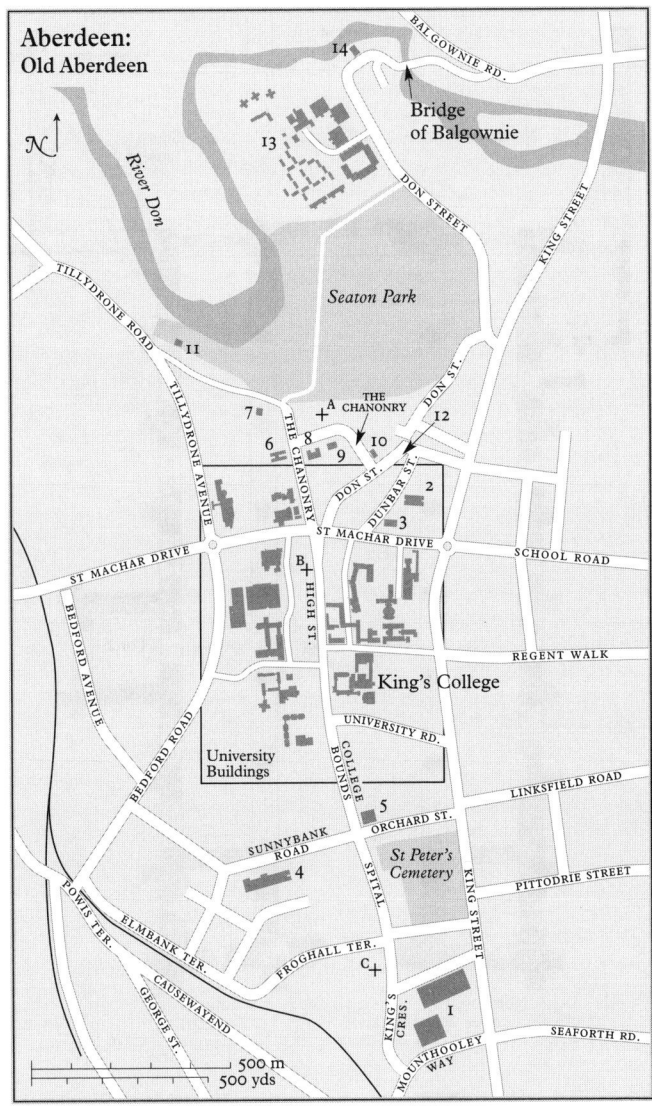

Aberdeen:
Old Aberdeen

A	St Machar's Cathedral	5	Orchard House
B	Old Machar Free Church (former)	6	Mitchell's Hospital
C	Convent of St Margaret of Scotland (Episcopal) (former)	7	Tillydrone House
		8	Chanonry Lodge
		9	Castleton House
		10	Chaplain's Court
I	Bus Depot	11	Benholm's Lodging
2	St Peter's R.C. School and Old Aberdeen House	12	Bishop's Gate
		13	Hillhead Halls of Residence
3	St Machar's Hall	14	Balgownie Mission Hall
4	Sunnybank School		

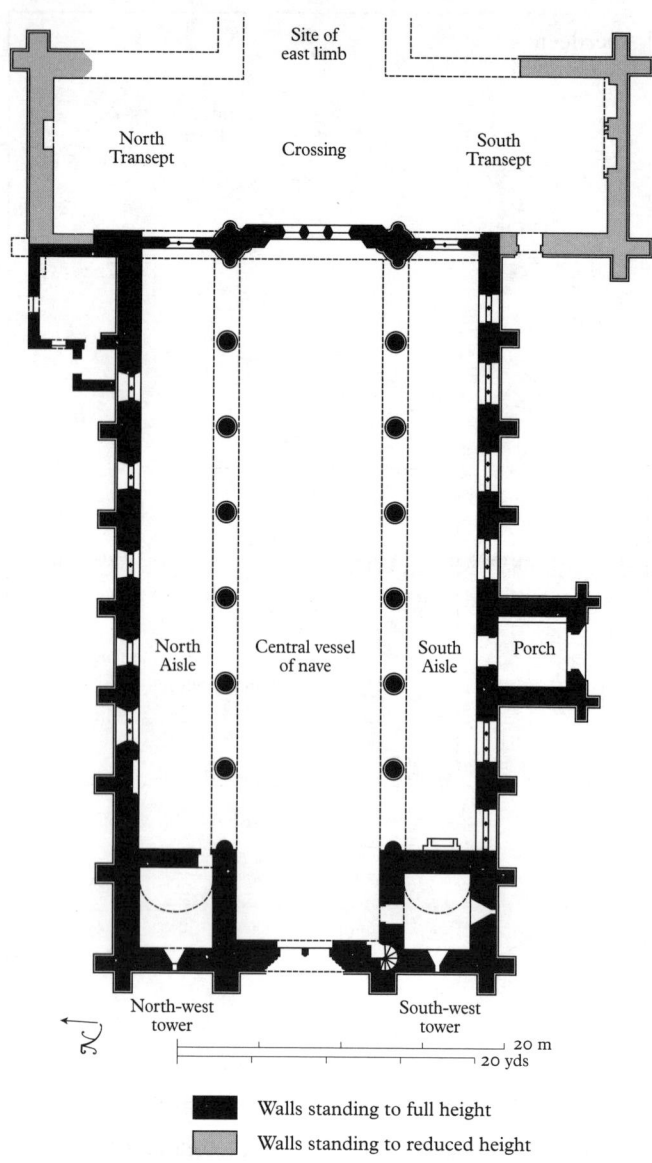

Site of
east limb

North
Transept

Crossing

South
Transept

North
Aisle

Central vessel
of nave

South
Aisle

Porch

North-west
tower

South-west
tower

20 m
20 yds

■ Walls standing to full height

▨ Walls standing to reduced height

St Machar's Cathedral.
Plan

(1282–*c*. 1329) started work on a new cathedral, that work was interrupted by the wars with England and that Robert I ordered the choir to be completed at the bishop's expense once peace was achieved. Alexander de Kininmund II (1355–80) started to build a new church (presumably meaning in this context the nave) and completed the arcades and towers to a height of 6 cubits (perhaps about 2.5 m.); he was buried before the high altar, suggesting that Cheyne's choir was still in place. Henry de Lichton (1422–40) completed the nave and w towers, but left the central tower unfinished; he was buried in the chapel of St John the Evangelist that he had built, which is assumed to be the N transept. Ingram de Lindsay (1441–58) inserted a ceiling and paved the floor. The main effort of Thomas Spens (1457–80) was directed towards furnishings, including a retable for the high altar and choir stalls. William Elphinstone (1483–1514) completed the central tower and began construction of a new choir. Gavin Dunbar (1518–32) decorated the ceiling of the nave with its extensive heraldic display. From other sources we know that Elphinstone gave orders in 1511 for his central tower and spire to be modelled on that of St John, Perth, with the timberwork to be carried out by *John Fendour*, who also worked at St Nicholas, Aberdeen (*see* p. 119). Dunbar added the spires to the w towers. The s transept was rebuilt on the existing base course by the mason *Thomas French*, whose memorial of 1530 on its w face records that he was 'mason of ... this isle'.

The nave and w towers are the only parts to survive complete: the choir is entirely lost and its form unknown, while only sufficient of the transepts was retained to serve as a burial enclosure. The nave is of seven aisled bays, with the w towers forming an eighth bay. Those towers are walled off from the rest of the nave, being accessible through small doors. The processional entrance is at the centre of the w front, and there is a two-storey porch over the door in the fifth bay from the E of the s aisle. There was previously also a door in the N aisle.

It might have been expected that the Cathedral would be abandoned after the Reformation in favour of the nearby church of St Maria ad Nives (the Snow Kirk), as tended to happen at other cathedrals when there was a separate parish church. Indeed, in 1568 the Privy Council ordered the lead roofing and bells of the Cathedral to be removed, though by a certain grim irony the boat bearing the spoil from Aberdeen and Elgin Cathedrals sank under the weight on leaving Aberdeen harbour. But in 1607 the roofs were re-covered with slates, and this was done again in 1642–4 after the building suffered further 'cleansing' in 1640. James Gordon of Rothiemay in 1661 and John Slezer in 1693 appear to depict the building largely complete apart from the choir, which is shown as a shell, and which may in fact never have been finished following the start of rebuilding by Bishop Elphinstone. Gordon and Slezer also both show the central tower with a saddleback roof, suggesting that Elphinstone's plans for a spire were never fulfilled. The situation changed dramatically in 1688, when the central tower fell, leaving the transepts and what remained of the choir in a devastated state. From that date only the nave remained in use for worship.

By the early C19 there were galleries in the aisles and the pulpit was against the N arcade. In 1832 a first restoration was carried out by *John Smith*, during which the N aisle outer wall was raised and a flat roof built over it with a ribbed plaster ceiling towards the interior; the interior was lined with lath and plaster. A more extensive restoration was carried out in 1867–8, following a report by *Daniel Macandrew*; *George Gilbert Scott* offered further advice, and the work was carried out by *James Matthews*. Against the advice of Scott, the roof was replaced, along with the boarding of the ceiling, and the lath and plaster was removed from the walls. In 1884 *Robert Rowand Anderson* inserted a new E window (now itself replaced), and in a further restoration of 1926–8 *A. Marshall Mackenzie* removed the plaster from the walls. In 1953 a new E wall was built within the W crossing arch by *A. G. R. Mackenzie*. In 1965–73 conservation and reordering were carried out by *Ian G. Lindsay & Partners*. In the most recent restoration, of 1976–91, by *Law & Dunbar-Nasmith*, the fabric was fully conserved.

DESCRIPTION

EXTERIOR. The pink granite ashlar N FLANK of the nave, between the NW tower and the N transept, was extensively reconstructed in the 1830s, when the aisle wall-head was raised and capped with crenellation, the upper parts of the buttresses reconstructed and the session house within the W end of the aisle replaced by a new structure against the E bay. (The line of the original slope of the N aisle roof is internally visible on the E face of the NW tower.) Some trouble was taken to perpetuate medieval details, and the reveals of all but the two windows in the W bays are of the same basic form as those along much of the S flank, with a roll on the outer angle of straight embrasures. The two-light windows in the four E bays have simple Y-tracery, while that in the fifth bay from the E, where there was evidently a door, is without tracery. In the three-light windows in the two W bays, which have reveals of three orders of chamfers (the outermost hollowed), all lights simply reach up to the window arch. The towers will be described with the W front (*see* below) but here it should be noted that on both sides of the nave the chamfered base courses of the aisles continue without break around the towers. At clearstorey level there are eight small round-arched windows. The pink granite ashlar N transept, which is attributed to Bishop de Lichton (1422–40), whose tomb was at the centre of the N wall internally, only survives up to the string course that was presumably at the base of the windows. The base course, which has a cavetto above a roll, is the most complex at the Cathedral.

The pink granite ashlar S FLANK, which appears to be still largely in its medieval form, presents a very complex picture. The inscribed tablet on the W face of the SW buttress of the transept suggests that the transept was rebuilt by the mason

Thomas French, who died in 1530, and a C16 date is supported by the location of Bishop Dunbar's tomb at the centre of the s wall internally. The only other feature of the transept is a doorway in the w face with mouldings of a chamfer, a sunk roll and an ogee. But it is likely that the C16 transept was rebuilt on the lowest courses of an earlier structure, work on which had continued into the E bay of the nave, since the transept's hollow-chamfered base course extends round to the first bay on the s side. There are other indications, both internally and externally, that the E bay of the nave aisle has earlier masonry than the rest of the outer wall on that side. In the Y-traceried window of the first bay this is seen in the change of mouldings from a filleted roll flanked by hollows and fillets in the jambs, to mouldings in the arch that are the same as in the rest of the s aisle windows. Below the aisle w of the first bay the base course changes to a simply chamfered profile, and the windows w of that first bay, all of which rest on a string course, have reveals like those in the windows of the E bays of the N aisle. Except for that in the E bay, all of the windows have three lights with intersecting tracery.

In the third bay from the w is a two-storey porch with gabletted angle buttresses and a crowstepped gable. The string course below the aisle windows extends along the flanks of the porch, but on the s face the string course is at the apex of the outer arch, which has continuous mouldings. Flanking the arch and at its apex are trifoliate-headed recesses, while there is a broken image corbel and a pair of canopies on each side of the central recess. On the central axis is a rectangular window that once had a mullion but now has intersecting timber glazing bars, and near the gable apex is a blind quatrefoil. The door within the porch has two orders of paired rolls linked by a hollow: the inner order has a three-centred arch framing the opening; the outer order is a pointed embracing arch. At clearstorey level of the s flank are ten small round-arched windows. Against the E face of the sw tower are masonry stumps at both aisle and clearstorey wall-head level, and there are blocked doorways that would have opened onto wall-walks. At aisle level, the masonry stump rises sheer from the lower face, suggesting that the aisle walls initially rose higher than we now see, with the stump representing the upward continuation of the wall. Supporting evidence for the reduced height of the aisle walls may be seen in the slightly uncomfortable way in which the aisle window apices extend up to the present wall-head, and also in the way that the doorway from the tower is at a higher level than is now appropriate. At clearstorey level there appears to have been a corbelled-out parapet.

The w FRONT is the great glory of the Cathedral and its most memorable feature. The pair of towers, which are almost identical, have heavy angle buttresses with a series of minimal offsets before being capped by gablets well below the wall-head, and there is a single string course at about two-thirds height. The windows are mostly no more than slits. The towers

terminate a short way above the gable base of the central vessel
with machicolated and crenellated parapets, the merlons of the
parapet being now truncated. Although ostensibly military features are not uncommon in church towers (e.g. the machicolated parapet on Dunfermline Abbey NW tower, the angle
rounds at Dunblane Cathedral, the shot-holes at Dysart Parish
Church and the almost universal use of crenellation as an
expression of high status), at Aberdeen the towers present a
rather more militaristic appearance than is seen elsewhere. Set
back behind the parapets are cubical blocks with stepped
crenellation and pinnacles at the angles, that over the S tower
being pierced by arched belfry openings. Rising from the
blocks are splay-foot spires decorated with two tiers of crenellated bands, with triplets of echelon-grouped lucarnes to the
lowest stage and a single small lucarne to each face of the
middle stage. At the lowest level of the W front between
the towers is a round-arched doorway framing a pair of
pointed-arched openings carried on a *trumeau*, and with a
blind vesica in the tympanum. The mouldings are reduced to
simple – almost crude – sequences of rolls and hollows, and
there are no more than block-like imposts at the arch springing. Resting on a string course above the door head is a grouping of seven slender attenuated round-arched trifoliate-headed
windows that rise through two-thirds of the height of the front
below the gable. The gable is set back behind a wall-walk that
has lost its parapet. There is nothing comparable to this W front
elsewhere, and there is a sense that the mason was responding
to the granite that was his building material by emphasizing
its intractability through massive and largely unarticulated
forms and greatly simplified detailing.

15   The INTERIOR has suffered from the removal of the plaster to
its walls in 1926; while the exposed rubble masonry with
recessed pointing allows details to be seen that would otherwise be covered, it undeniably detracts from the architectural
qualities of the space.

Three main building phases are evident in the masonry
fabric, the first two being both attributable to Kininmund in
the later C14, and the third dating from the second quarter of
the C15. Of the first phase are the piers and arch springers
at the E end, which supported the W side of the central tower,
together with the lower masonry in the E bay of the S aisle wall;
the second of Kininmund's phases embraced the lower parts
of the arcade piers and the towers. In the third stage the arcade
piers were completed and the arcades and clearstorey built.
The highest-quality work is to be found in the first phase,
which is constructed of fine pink sandstone. Although the
post-Reformation walls inserted at the E end of the central
vessel and aisles now make it difficult to see this, the W crossing
piers each took the form of a massive cylindrical core, with
large semi-cylindrical shafts in the cardinal directions that rise
to a variety of heights to support the arches of the arcades,
crossing and aisle ends. This most unusual pier type has no

close parallels in Scotland, but is found in several churches of the Brabant region of the Low Countries, as at St Gudule in Brussels in phases dating from both the C13 and C14. Of the surviving finely carved caps, some have carefully detailed foliage pushed up the bell to just below the abacus, while one (now only visible externally in what was the crossing area) has carefully individualized figures including a triton; as with the form of the piers themselves, these invite comparison with examples in the Low Countries. The arches springing from these caps have orders with rolls flanked by deep hollows and fillets. Because of later design changes, it is uncertain whether the aisles were intended to be vaulted in this first phase, though they certainly were not vaulted as completed. If there were to have been vaults, they would have sprung from the core of the pier rather than from the engaged shafts, and in fact the core of the pier at the NE angle of the S aisle's E bay does have a cap a short distance above the arches into the transepts and those of the arcade. But it is no longer clear what purpose that cap was intended to serve, since the supported wall has been thickened above a segmental arch that was presumably inserted to brace the central tower. As noted on the exterior, the E end of the S aisle's outer wall was started along with the S transept, and internally the jambs of the easternmost window are of a different form from those further W, as was the case externally (having a filleted roll flanked by hollows and fillets), while the arch is the same as the window reveals further W in having a heavy angle roll. There is also a string course in the E part of the bay that stops at the window.

The lower parts of the cylindrical nave arcade piers must have been built in the second phase of the late C14 campaign and they are of granite rather than the sandstone of the crossing piers. Taking account of that difference and of the changes at the E end of the S aisle wall, there must have been a break in operations following construction of the W crossing piers. Presumably largely because of the material employed, the arcade bases are treated with greater simplicity than those of the crossing piers. Along the aisle walls, W of the first bay, the S aisle windows have a heavy roll to their internal reveals. The same roll may be seen in the lower part of the first four windows of the N aisle, but not in their upper parts, which were rebuilt when that aisle wall was heightened.

There was to be even greater simplification of detailing than in the arcade bases in the third phase of work, when Bishop Lichton completed the piers and built the arcade arches. The arcade caps are very simply moulded, and there was no attempt to replace the arch springers that had been built along with the crossing piers, resulting in a clear change of profile above the springing point of those arches. There appears to have been some difficulty in accommodating the full width of the upper walls on the slender arcade piers, and the outer order of the arcades that was required to support the walls consequently starts a short distance above the caps. There is no string course to mark the base of the CLEARSTOREY, which was treated differently on the two sides. While it was relatively common for the clearstorey to be treated asymmetrically in buildings of middling scale, as in the burgh churches of Perth and Stirling for example, there are no precedents for the extent of disregard for symmetry and linkage between storeys seen at Aberdeen. Thus, in the N clearstorey there are eight windows, while on the S side there are ten, and in neither case is there any correspondence of rhythm with the seven bays at arcade level. There is also a sense that the arches on the inner sides of the wall passage at this level were being completed as economically as possible: while the splayed jambs are formed of dressed stone, the segmental arches are of rubble.

However, the eye tends to pass quickly over the clearstorey to the CEILING, which, after the W front, is Aberdeen's finest feature. It was remodelled to its present form by Bishop Dunbar in the years around 1520, and said by William Orem in the 1720s to be the work of the wright *James Winter*. Rising above a canted vertical frieze at the wall-head, which is articulated by small pinnacles, it is divided into square panels by a grid of longitudinal and transverse ribs, with a secondary network of diagonal ribs crossing each of those panels. At the junctions of the diagonal ribs are bosses from which sprigs of foliage project in the four cardinal directions. The sprigs are so like those still to be seen at King's College Chapel and that are known to have existed at St Nicholas's church, that it has been plausibly suggested that the name 'James Winter' was a distorted memory of the *John Fendour* who had worked at St Nicholas and who contracted for the spire at the Cathedral in 1511. The most striking feature of the ceiling is the series of forty-eight heraldic shields at the junctions of the longitudinal and transverse ribs. The central row represents the Church, starting at the E end with Pope Leo X, extending through the archbishops and bishops of Scotland and ending with the prior of St Andrews (Scotland's senior regular cleric) and the University of Aberdeen. The S row represents the kingdom of Scotland, commencing with James V and St Margaret, passing through the dukes and earls of Scotland and ending with the royal burgh of Aberdeen. The N row represents wider Christendom, with the Holy Roman Emperor heading the rulers of Europe and ending with the burgh of Old Aberdeen. This programme has been aptly characterized by David McRoberts as 'a vision of the political situation of Scotland and of Christendom'. Cleaning in 1990 revealed that the restoration of 1867 had been more invasive than previously assumed, with the boarding of the ceiling having been replaced, together with the scrolls that accompany the shields, while at the same time the shields had been re-tinctured.

FURNISHINGS. SANCTUARY AREA. COMMUNION TABLE. Two panels of Gothic arcading and foliage trails, with a ciborium chalice and host, by *A. Marshall Mackenzie*, 1928. – LECTERN AND PRAYER DESK, brought from Old Machar Free

Church in 1943. S AISLE. WHEEL-HEADED CROSS-HEAD. Pink sandstone, remounted on its present shaft by *Alistair Urquhart* in 2000. One face has radiating ribs to the three surviving cross-arms and a central rosette; the other face has rosettes to the arms and central boss. Probably late C12–early C13. The closest parallels are with a cross at St Helen, Kelloe (Co. Durham). N AISLE. HOLY WATER STOUP, to W of blocked door, rectangular recess, with what appears to be a re-set font basin. – FONT, tapering cylindrical bowl with relief carving of St Machar baptizing, on circular step, by *Hew Lorimer*, 1954. W END. SCREEN, relocated between the towers, *c.* 1830s(?). – CROSS-SLAB, early Christian incised cross on irregularly shaped slab, fixed to E wall of NW tower.

STAINED GLASS. An instructive artistic range from the historicism of *Clayton & Bell*, through the aestheticism of *Cottier* and the attempt to establish a new idiom by *Strachan*, to the bright palette of *Chilton* and *Kemp*. W FRONT, Christ and his Apostles, by *Clayton and Bell*, 1870. S AISLE, from W: St Machar, by *Douglas Strachan*, 1908; war memorial, by *Strachan*, 1924; Jesus, the Virgin and St Joseph, *Clayton & Bell*, 1877; Bishops Kininmund II, Lichton and Elphinstone, by *Strachan*, 1913; Faith, Hope and Charity with heads of three Aberdeen artists, by *Daniel Cottier*, 1874; St John the Baptist and St Peter, again by *Cottier*, 1871; St Luke and St John, also *Cottier*, 1871. N AISLE, from W: parable of the talents, 1949; Nativity, 1946; Dorcas and Bishop Gavin Dunbar, 1947, all by *Marjorie Kemp*; brazen serpent and Crucifixion, by *Margaret Chilton*, 1947; 24th psalm, also by *Chilton*, 1947; St Cecilia, by *Daniel Cottier*, 1873; St Mary Magdalene and St James, by *Cottier*, 1871. E WINDOW, Last Supper, Crucifixion and Road to Calvary, with Scottish saints, by *William Wilson*, 1953. – Bellringers' window, *Emma Thompson*, 1989.

MONUMENTS. S AISLE. Towards E end, mural tablet for Canon Simon Dods (†1496), low-relief representation within cusped ogee arch. Below monument to Dods, inscription for Alexander de Rynd (†1432). Relocated to W end of aisle, Bishop Patrick Scougal (†1682), *John Montgomery*, 1685. Large aedicular monument with broken segmental pediment pierced by heraldic achievement; flaming urns above broken forward entablature of composite columns and above pediment, flanked by balusters; relief portrait of Scougal within segmental arch at centre flanked by prophet figures. – FIRST WORLD WAR MEMORIAL. Tablets by *J. Cromar Watt*, 1924. – Archdeacon John Barbour, poet (†1395). A triptych of arched timber reliefs and an inscription, by *Roland Fraser*, 1997. – N AISLE. In arched recess towards W end, effigy of Canon Walter Idyll (†c. 1468), wearing mass vestments and almuce (the distinctive fur hood of a secular canon). On modern polished granite slab, weathered relief effigy and inscription of Bishop Henry de Lichton (†1440), wearing mass vestments and carrying pastoral staff; relocated from N transept. On modern polished granite slab, weathered relief effigy of a canon, wearing mass vestments and almuce, again relocated from the N transept. – S TRANSEPT, W WALL EXTERIOR. Inscribed tablet on SW buttress for Thomas French, the 'mason of ... this isle' (†1530). – S WALL INTERIOR. At centre, canopied tomb-recess of Bishop Gavin Dunbar (†1532); tomb-chest with blind arcade of cusped and crocketed ogee arches with eroded figure in central arch; round-arched canopy with multiple-cusped cusping to soffit, square flower within mouldings and crocketing along extrados; flanked by buttresses and capped by cornice with miniature corbelling and crenellation; arms of Scotland and Dunbar in the spandrels. To E, tomb-chest with blind arcade of cusped and crocketed ogee arches; segmental-arched canopy with foliage trails and square flower; flanked by buttresses. N TRANSEPT, N WALL INTERIOR. At centre, tomb-chest of Bishop Henry de Lichton (†1440); arcaded front flanked by bases of buttresses, recess now bridged by a brick segmental arch.

CHURCHYARD with many C18 and C19 MONUMENTS. Beside the NE corner of the Cathedral, Hector Munro Macdonald, mathematician, †1935: squat headstone carved with foliage and an inscription in Ogham.

CHURCHES

Former CONVENT OF ST MARGARET OF SCOTLAND (Episcopal), Spital. Now in secular use. Like St Margaret's church, Gallowgate (*see* p. 116), this owed its foundation to the Rev. John Comper, and again his son was employed as architect. *Bucknall & Comper* made designs for a long N–S range in Scots Gothic with crowstepped dormers, but only the chapel and one bay at the S end were built, in 1891–2. They are all the more impressive for being a fragment. The site is a wooded outcrop, high above the road, and the battlemented polygonal apse of the CHAPEL – modelled on the Church of the Holy Rude, Stirling – seems to grow out of it like a fortified tower. It has buttresses at the angles and two-light Dec windows between, with a statue of St Margaret in a niche below the E one. The rock-faced granite is laid in a rough version of Aberdeen bond, the set-offs barely noticeable amid the general ruggedness. S side simpler, with more two-light windows; W end with a square, pyramid-roofed porch and a concave-sided triangular window with tracery high up in the gable. In the angle where the N side meets the convent, a polygonal turret contains the organ gallery stair. The interior – a single vessel, high and narrow – comprises a choir with a short ante-chapel at the W end and apsidal sanctuary at the E. The CHOIR has STALLS down each side and across its W end. A screen with flowing Gothic tracery divides it from the ante-chapel and supports an organ loft with Jacobean-looking fretwork balustrade. Above the N stalls, a triangular oriel looks in from the first floor of the convent next door. Choir and organ loft have a continuous painted wooden CEILING, while the marble-paved SANCTUARY, divided from the choir by a deeply moulded

Apse of St Margaret's Convent.
Drawing by W. Curtis Green, 1898

arch, has a rib-vault with PAINTED DECORATION. Behind the
altar is a screen wall with ogee-headed doors l. and r. into a
rear vestry. Originally it supported a richly painted wooden
reredos and gilded figures of angels on corbels holding tapers.
SEDILIA and PISCINA, r., and a highly elaborate stone SACRA-
MENT HOUSE, l.: a recess behind a grille, flanked by relief
carvings of the Crucifixion and Entombment. Above this is a
coloured STATUE of the Virgin and Child under a spire-like
stone canopy rising all the way to the vault. Set into the chancel
arch beside the entrance from the convent, a holy water STOUP
in a nodding ogee niche. Typical *Comper* STAINED GLASS: large
figures of saints with rich canopy-work, and much white glass.
The NE sanctuary window includes a portrait of the Rev. John
Comper at prayer. In the sacristy, a window of 1964 by *Sebastian
Comper* commemorates John Mason Neale, founder of the
convent's mother house at East Grinstead. The adjoining fragment of Bucknall & Comper's convent range has a two-storey
triangular oriel with mullioned-and-transomed windows. If
continued N as planned, it would have replaced the two adjoining C19 houses. No. 19 Spital, immediately N of them, was built
as St Martha's Home for Young Women, 1886–7, by *Arthur
Clyne*. Pink and grey granite, with a traceried window in the

front gable, and a conical-roofed tower in the re-entrant angle of the N and E wings.

Former OLD MACHAR FREE CHURCH, High Street. 1845–6, by *Archibald Simpson*, with amendments by *William Henderson*. A plain, gabled façade, with angle buttresses and three lancets over the door. Shallow gabled porch with Romanesque doorway – an addition? Converted and extended for the University's Geography Department.

KING'S COLLEGE
College Bounds

Founded by Bishop William Elphinstone in 1495, with the support of James IV and a bull granted by Pope Alexander VI. It is the third oldest university in Scotland, after St Andrews and Glasgow.

Chapel*

King's College Chapel is the most complete academic collegiate church to survive in Scotland, and its design reveals a fascinating blending of ideas evidently drawn from both Scotland and wider afield in order to meet the requirements of a discerning cosmopolitan patron, Bishop William Elphinstone (1483–1514). It is additionally significant for having retained a uniquely important set of medieval furnishings.

Elphinstone received papal permission for his *Studium Generale* (the basis of the University) in 1495, and by 1497–8 was purchasing materials from the Low Countries for use in preparing the site. An inscription cut into the masonry of the W front, N of the doorway, says that the church was started on 2 April 1500, though parallels with the foundation of Solomon's Temple may indicate that this date had been selected for symbolic associations. By 1504 work was well advanced: this date is inscribed on a tablet with the arms of James IV on the NW tower buttress, while the arms of James, Duke of Ross and Archbishop of St Andrews, who died in that year, are above the N door. There is also heraldry associated with Alexander Stewart, Archbishop of St Andrews (1504–13), and Queen Margaret, to whom the King was married in 1503. On 21 October 1506 a contract for the leadwork of the roof was signed with *John Burwel* (or *Burnel*), Sergeant Plumber to Henry VII of England, and the chapel was dedicated in 1509, indicating that the main body was structurally complete. In 1522 the crown steeple over the SW tower was referred to in Hector Boece's history of Aberdeen's bishops, so must have been nearing completion by then. Bishop William Stewart (1532–45) built a sacristy, library and treasury range along the S flank,

---

*This entry is by Richard Fawcett.

and placed his arms on it. This is the only structural element of the building that has been lost: it was largely rebuilt in 1725–6 but was demolished fifty years later. Of other major structural interventions, the crown steeple was partly reconstructed by *George Thomson* in 1634, and there have been a number of restorations, most significantly those directed by *Robert Rowand Anderson* in 1891 and by *William Kelly* in 1931–2.

The PLAN consists of an elongated aisleless rectangle of six bays, with a three-sided apse at the E end; buttresses define the bays and the angles of the apse. The tower projects from the S side of the W bay, where it continues the line of the W front. Despite being internally of square plan, externally the tower is longer from N to S than from E to W; however, the S buttress of the W face is set in from the SW angle, resulting in a slight awkwardness in the relationship between tower and crown steeple. There are doorways in the W front, in both flanks in the second bay from the W, and on the S side in the second bay from the E. The two doors on the S side, despite now facing outwards, were probably always intended to open into the sacristy range. The principal model for the apsidal-ended unaisled plan, the single asymmetrical tower and the elongated sacristy range was presumably St Salvator's College chapel at St Andrews University (Fife), founded fifty years earlier. It was there that the unaisled apsidal plan may have been first introduced into Scotland from France.

EXTERIOR. The walls, which are mainly of buff, pink or grey sandstone, rise from a chamfered base course, and there is a string course below the windows. An unexplained feature on the N flank is a stepping up of the wall and string course into the middle of the window in the fifth bay from the W; this   22

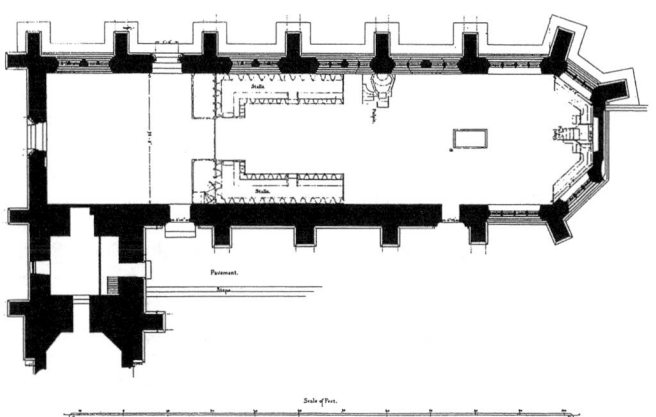

King's College Chapel.
Plan by J. C. Watt, 1885

presumably reflected some intended provision at the E end of the N rank of choir stalls. Around the wall-head is a cavetto cornice, the line of which continues along the W front as a string course, above which the crowstepped gable is slightly set back. Early views show a crenellated parapet around the flanks and apse. The buttresses have multiple offsets in their upper parts, and those along the N side and around the apse have the rather stunted pinnacles characteristic of late medieval work in Scotland. Along the S flank there has been extensive refacing in grey granite along with the addition of buttresses, following the removal of the sacristy range; the upper parts of the buttresses may embody parts of the lost parapet. The doorways have three-centred arches, with continuous mouldings which, in the case of those in the W and N walls, rise from bases. On the S side, above the site of the sacristy, are two- or three-light windows in which all of the trifoliate-headed lights extend up to flattened or slightly segmental arches. There are four-light windows in the W front, in all but the second bay from the W along the N flank, and in the E bay of the S flank, while around the apse the windows are of three lights. The arch forms of these windows vary: most are pointed, but the W window and the window in the fifth bay from the W on the N side have arches of almost semicircular form. The windows in which the tracery is still essentially in its medieval form are those in the W front and in the first, third, fourth and fifth bays from the W of the N flank. Their most striking feature is a massively constructed pier-like central mullion that rises up to the arch apex, on each side of which the tracery takes the form of rather loose groupings of dagger forms. While a Scottish precedent for the tracery can be found in windows likely to be of the 1470s at St Monans (Fife), the combination of the tracery and the extended central mullion has closer parallels in the Low Countries, as in a window of the Domproosten Chapel in Utrecht Cathedral. The trading port of Aberdeen had very close contacts with the Low Countries, while the highly cosmopolitan Bishop Elphinstone knew the area well, having bought some of his building equipment there, and having travelled through in 1495 on an embassy to the Emperor. He would have been well aware of many buildings in that area.

Other aspects of the design display a renewed interest in architectural developments in England, at a time of growing rapprochement between the two countries, with the leadwork contract of 1506 with the English royal plumber *John Burwel* being particularly significant in this. In addition to the roof itself, *Burwel* was presumably responsible for the lead-sheathed hexagonal flèche, known as the little steeple, which rises over the fourth bay from the W, marking the original W end of the choir internally. Above a vertical base is a spirelet flanked by six pinnacles, though much of what is now seen dates from a reconstruction by *William Scot* in 1655, incorporating panels with the initials of Charles I that probably date from the re-foundation of the college in 1641.

The most obviously English-inspired feature of the building is the CROWN STEEPLE over the tower at the SW corner. It was one of a number of crown steeples built in Scotland in the years around 1500, the others being at St Giles, Edinburgh, and St Michael, Linlithgow (the latter now demolished), while they were evidently also planned for St Mary, Dundee, and St Mary, Haddington. These virtuoso displays of masonry, in which a lantern stage is projected skywards on quadrant flyers, have come to be regarded as a particularly Scottish manifestation. They are best understood as one of the most delightful culminations of a long period of experimentation across Europe with the extreme structural possibilities of masonry construction; it must be conceded, however, that Scotland appears to have played little previous part in those experiments. It was probably in England, at St Nicholas, Newcastle (post-1474), and at St Mary-le-Bow in London (pre-1512) that the idea of the crown steeple was first perfected.

The Aberdeen example has four flyers that rise steeply from diagonally set sections of wall capped by two stages of pinnacles at the angles of the tower wall-head. The flyers are decorated with large-scale foliate cresting and have a small pinnacle at mid-height. The lantern is a solid octagon with cusped arches to the faces and three-quarter colonnettes at the angles that support higher arches; at the summit is an open imperial crown, the arches of which reflect those of the crown steeple itself. The imperial crown was an important element in the iconography associated with the Scottish monarchy at this time, and it is also seen on a fountain in the courtyard of

King's College Chapel.
North elevation, by J. C. Watt, 1885

Linlithgow Palace of about 1532, and on the conical turret roofs of James V's chamber tower at Holyrood Palace of 1528–32. Whether or not the crown steeple with its imperial crown was part of the original design of 1500 at Aberdeen, it was certainly nearing completion by 1522; some of the detailing, however, and particularly the solidity of the lantern stage, may date from the partial reconstruction of 1634.

INTERIOR. The sense of spatial progression within the chapel was considerably modified when the choir stalls were moved westwards by one bay in 1873, following the removal of the library that had been installed in the nave in 1773; this reduced the ante-chapel to little more than a vestibule. It also meant that the original architectural arrangements associated with the rood screen and loft made no obvious sense. Thus, the section of blank wall to the w of the window in the fourth bay from the w on the N flank, which marked the point where the screen abutted that wall, has lost its purpose, while the (already blocked) door from the upper floor of the sacristy range was no longer adjacent to the rood loft. Within the presbytery area, on the site of the high altar there is now a re-set medieval *mensa* that had been re-used as a grave-slab. The altar location was emphasized by a foliate image corbel on each side.

Most of the internal features to be discussed will be covered under the furnishings; the exception to this is the timber CEILING. It is of depressed three-centred profile, and is decorated with ribs on the pattern of a quadripartite vault, the seven bays of which bear no direct relationship with the six bays of the walls. There is a horizontal ridge rib, and transverse ribs define the bays and cross at the mid-point of bays. Extended foliate sprigs decorate the junctions of the ribs along the ridge and the bases of the mid-bay transverse ribs. The ceiling rises from a cornice with dropped cusping, which Billings shows as also having had foliate cresting in the mid C19; at the w end on the S side, where the presence of the tower meant that the ceiling could not rest on the wall-head, Billings shows it as carried on corbels, though this is no longer the case. In the use of foliate sprigs there are similarities with the ceiling of the nearby Cathedral, which was installed by Bishop Gavin Dunbar (1518–32). There were even closer similarities with the ceiling recorded over the nave of the parish church of St Nicholas in New Aberdeen, which was presumably constructed along with the roof contracted for by the wright *John Fendour* in 1495. In view of the similarity between the ceilings, and the fact that in 1511 Bishop Elphinstone contracted with Fendour to build the steeple at the Cathedral, it must be seen as a strong possibility that Fendour was also responsible for the King's College ceiling.

The design of the King's College and St Nicholas ceilings reveals a fascinating admixture of ideas. A number of Scottish timber ceilings were constructed from the mid-fifteenth century onwards, though none is known to have had ribbing on a quadripartite pattern. However, a number of stone barrel-vaults with such a pattern of ribbing were being built from the later fifteenth century, as at Seton collegiate church and St Mirin's aisle at Paisley Abbey. But the foliate sprigs, like the window tracery, may suggest an awareness of work in the Low Countries, where large numbers of timber barrel ceilings were constructed in the later Middle Ages. Sprigs of this kind are to be seen at the church of St Giles in Bruges, where Scottish artisans resident in the city had a place of worship in the chapel of St Andrew. The ribs of that ceiling are not arranged on a quadripartite pattern, though that arrangement is to be seen in several ceilings in the city of Ghent, and it was presumably once a more common pattern. The Aberdeen ceilings may thus represent a fusion of ideas found in both ceilings and vaults within Scotland, and in ceilings within the Low Countries.

FURNISHINGS. – Medieval ALTAR MENSA of Tournai marble(?), with three of the five incised crosses still partly visible. Reused as a ledger slab for Peter Udny (†1601), who was briefly appointed chancellor of the diocese in 1589, and now re-set on stone legs on the site of the high altar. – COMMUNION TABLE. 1898, three panels wide, with figures of Apostles within tabernacles at the bay divisions, the tabernacle heads interconnected by dropped foliate cresting; vine trail cornice. – PULPIT, on N side, to W of sanctuary. An extremely rare example of a medieval pulpit, although moved and extensively reconstructed on five or more occasions. Originally made for the Cathedral in the time of Bishop William Stewart (1532–45), the form of the back-board indicates that it was positioned against one of the crossing piers. It was brought to the chapel in 1844 but its present form dates partly from a reconstruction by *William Kelly* in 1933. The body of the pulpit has two levels of panels, the upper level having heads in roundels or lozenges and the bishop's arms, and the lower level foliage within reticulation units. A curved panel with the Royal Arms has been re-set within the balusters of the stair. The back-board, curved to fit against the Cathedral crossing pier, has four levels of panelling; of the two upper decorated levels, one now has the arms of Stewart, while the others have foliage trails. The sides of the polygonal tester are decorated with blind tracery capped with foliate cresting, and with pinnacles at the angles. – DESK, on S side, to W of sanctuary. A much remodelled piece dated 1627, designed for Bishop Patrick Forbes (1618–35) as the bishop's seat at meetings of diocesan synods. Initially located on the site of the high altar, it was adapted for other uses after 1823 and removed from the chapel in 1931, only being returned to its present position in the mid C20. It now has a desk front with two levels of three panels, a back with three levels of three panels and a quadrant canopy. The formalized relief designs of the panels are paralleled in work at St Nicholas and Greyfriars in New Aberdeen. – CARVING. A relief panel, above the SE door. Sancta Maria in Sole, accompanied by scenes prefiguring her virginity: Moses, Ezekiel, Gideon and the Emperor Augustus with the Tiburtine Sibyl. Attributed to the circle of

Arnt Beeldesnider, late C15. Given to the chapel by Douglas Strachan in 1944.

The CHOIR STALLS, the most complete set in Scotland and the great glory of the chapel, were in place by 1522 when they were referred to by Boece; they were moved westwards one bay in 1873. On each side the upper rank has twelve lateral stalls, and three return stalls against the screen; the lower rank has nine and two stalls respectively. The most inventive feature is the canopies. Above each stall is a multi-cusped and crocketed ogee arch set against a panel of highly complex openwork tracery framed by miniature pinnacled buttresses; above each of those panels is a pair of smaller traceried panels topped with foliate cresting, again framed by miniature buttresses, and with

King's College Chapel, choir stalls and screen.
By R.W. Billings, 1845–52

paired pinnacles rising above the buttresses. A number of these traceried panels have been repaired and reconstructed. The seat cappings of both ranks of stalls, which curve forward without break over the stall shoulders of the standards, are carved with bands of foliage, and the seat backs of the lower rank have linenfold decoration. The cheeks of the curved stall elbows of both ranks have foliage decoration, and there are miniature buttresses at the base of the leading edge of the standards. The stall ends are decorated with complex flamboyant relief tracery; in the upper stalls they are surmounted by panels with openwork foliage trails and tracery; there are miniature tabernacles on the leading edge. The misericords are decorated with a range of foliage and other motifs including the sacred monogram and crowns. Additional stalls, based on the design of Bishop Forbes's desk, were added to the E of the medieval stalls by *Robert Rowand Anderson* in 1891, and further stalls within the sanctuary area by *William Kelly* in 1931–2. One traceried panel on Kelly's NE sanctuary stall is all that remains from the choir stalls in St Machar's Cathedral.

The lower part of the SCREEN facing W towards the ante-chapel is simply – almost roughly – framed and panelled, and was presumably initially expected to be obscured by the retables associated with the altars of the Virgin and of St Germain located to N and S of the processional entrance. By contrast, the two doors of that entrance are extremely elaborate. At the bottom level of each are two panels decorated with parchemin motifs; above that are two panels with openwork tracery; occupying the top half are three openings with tracery supported by pinnacled buttresses. These doors show similarities with those from the screen in Fowlis Easter collegiate church (Angus). Towards the E the doors are framed within a series of traceried panels, and immediately above the opening is a flattened ogee arch with multiple cusping and crocketing, though this may not have been the original arrangement. Rising above the solid part of the screen is known to have been an openwork screen of uncertain date that was dismantled in 1873. Parts of this were relocated and reconstructed in 1891, albeit with an organ at their centre. They were again dismantled in 1960 when a new organ was installed on the loft, though the quadrant ceilure capped by foliate cresting was retained and reinstalled directly above the processional entrance. The present ORGAN on the loft, dating from 2004, is by *Bernard Aubertin*. 23

A small three-sided timber structure currently attached to the interior of the W wall, was earlier fixed to the W side of the screen above the door. It originally served as part of a decorative parapet and frame for statues of Christ and the apostles. Rising from a string course with vine-trail decoration and dropped foliate cresting, the open arches on each side have foliate cusping and the angles are decorated with tabernacles.

STAINED GLASS. The only fragments of the medieval glazing programme are two quarries re-set in the W window. By the later decades of the C19, at a time when figurative stained glass was beginning to be deemed more acceptable in Scottish churches, the removal of the library from the w bays and the relocation of the choir stalls one bay westwards in 1873 offered the opportunity to introduce glass as funding became available. The result is a group of windows ranging in date from the work of *Clayton & Bell* in 1875 to that of *William Wilson* in 1963, but it is of particular interest for demonstrating the artistic and technical development of the Aberdeen artist *Douglas Strachan* over thirty-five years. Chronologically earliest are the w window and the window in the westernmost bay on the N. w window, Old and New Testament scenes with a didactic theme and the history of the University, by *Clayton & Bell*, 1875. N flank: fifth bay from w, Solomon and the Queen of Sheba, and Adoration of the Magi, *Clayton & Bell*, 1880; sixth bay from w, four prophets (Isiaah, Ezekiel, Jeremiah and Daniel), by *Morris & Co.*, 1897, adapting a design of 1875 by *Burne-Jones*; sixth bay from w, Adoration of the Magi, Plato and Virgil, by *Douglas Strachan*, 1903; fourth bay from w, Virgin and Child, Presentation in the Temple, by *Douglas Strachan*, 1904; third bay from w, life of Bishop Elphinstone, by *Douglas Strachan*, 1912; first bay from w, war memorial, by *Douglas Strachan*, 1921. – Apse: NE bay, hymn of praise, by *Douglas Strachan*, 1938; E bay, Christ the King, by *Douglas Strachan*, 1938; SE bay, Creation, by *Douglas Strachan*, 1938. S flank: second bay from w, University arms, badge of Gordon Highlanders and St Andrew, by *William Wilson*, 1963.

MONUMENTS. WAR MEMORIAL. 1929–30, by *William Kelly*, forming part of the panelling around the S, w and N sides of the ante-chapel, a canopied recess in the S wall housing the roll of service. – FOUNDER'S TOMB, on the central axis in front of sanctuary area, a composite piece of 1931, combining a Tournai marble(?) plinth and ledger slab from the original tomb of Bishop William Elphinstone (†1514) with a new brass commemorative frieze added between the two pieces by *William Kelly*. The tomb was made after Bishop Gavin Dunbar expressed concern that the chapel's founder was not properly commemorated, and a description of it in the college's 1542 inventory said that there were candle-bearing angels at the head, bedesmen carrying the epitaph at the foot, and Theological and Cardinal Virtues together with a representation of Contemplation along the sides. – Several Tournai marble(?) slabs are set into the floor on each side of Elphinstone's tomb. A large matrix stone on the S side is recorded as marking the burial place of Hector Boece (†1536), first Principal of the University and historian of Aberdeen's bishops.

To the w of the chapel, the ELPHINSTONE MONUMENT, under discussion from 1910, commissioned from *Henry Wilson* in 1911 but only finished in 1931; initially intended for the site of the founder's tomb, but on completion it was deemed overlarge for the interior and was relocated to its present site. A fine Arts and Crafts reinterpretation of the description of the tomb in the 1542 inventory. The masonry plinth and sarcophagus are largely lost to sight within the sinuously modelled high-relief bronze sculpture cast by *Munaretti* of Murano. Lying on the chest is Elphinstone's effigy in episcopal mass vestments, while along its sides are representations of the Virtues conquering the Vices. There are heraldic wreaths at the centre of the long sides and the W end, with a wreath framing an inscription at the E end. Angels stand at the W corners and bedesmen to the E.

Other buildings

In addition to the chapel on its N side, the QUADRANGLE of the C16 College comprised the Common Hall above the Schools on the E, masters' and students' rooms on the S, and the

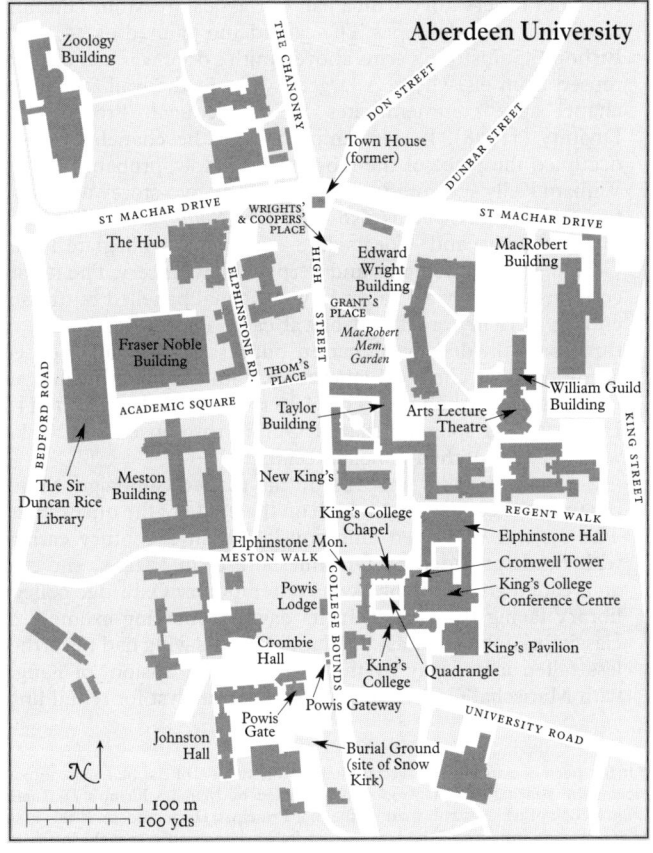

Principal's accommodation on the w.* The SW and SE corners had round towers, which by the mid C17 carried timber and lead spires. Of these buildings, only the granite rubble ROUND TOWER that marked the SE corner survives, not visible from within the quadrangle but embedded in the E side of the C19 E range. Utilitarian, with small, irregular openings (now blocked), it was completed in 1525. It has been shorn of its spire and has a shallow conical roof. According to the inventory of 1542, one of its rooms contained the original library. At the quadrangle's NE corner, beside the chapel apse, is the only other pre-C19 survival, the so-called CROMWELL TOWER. Stark, square and battlemented, it was begun in 1658 (an inscription on the W side records the date) using stone from the former Bishop's Palace. It contained twenty-four student bedrooms (plus a billiard room) on six low floors. In 1822–6 *John Smith* reconstructed it internally to make a basement and three floors of loftier classrooms (blocked original windows are clearly visible on the N and W sides). He also added a higher projection at the SW corner, containing a granite stair and a top-floor observatory, with a pair of classical freestone columns to support the telescopes. The carved and painted PANEL with Bishop Elphinstone's arms above Smith's door was presumably reused from elsewhere. A larger PANEL in the wall facing the chapel apse commemorates Henry Scougal, Professor of Divinity (†1678). It was removed from the chapel, where it occupied the place of the blocked E window, probably during William Kelly's restoration of 1931–2. The two-storey W RANGE facing the High Street is also 1822–6 by *Smith*. It is of freestone in an attractive and – for its date – competent collegiate Tudor Gothic, with battlements and Perp window tracery. The N part contains the gateway, flanked by octagonal panelled buttresses ending in richly crocketed ogival caps. The higher S part, of three bays divided by pinnacled buttresses, originally housed a ground-floor chemical laboratory, with a double-height galleried museum above. The latter is now the DIVINITY LIBRARY, its splendid glazed Gothic cases used for books, with a Tudor-arched panelled ceiling.

So to the E and S RANGES. In his 1822–6 campaign, Smith repaired the C16 Common Hall on the E side of the quadrangle. The S range had been ambitiously rebuilt a century earlier, with funds provided by Dr James Fraser in 1724–5, and had an arcaded ground floor like a contemporary Oxbridge college library facing the chapel. In its day a pioneering example of classicism in North-East Scotland, Fraser's wing had nevertheless fallen into decay by the mid C19. The 'fusion' of King's with Marischal College in 1860 was the catalyst for rebuilding,

---

*It has been convincingly suggested that the orientation of the buildings, in particular the s-facing students' rooms, was guided by Marsilio Ficino's *De Triplici Vita*, a copy of which was owned by the first Principal, Hector Boece. If this is so, it is a striking instance of the influence of Italian Renaissance thought in the far north.

and in 1859–62 both Fraser's wing and the Common Hall were demolished and replaced with classrooms by *Robert Matheson* of the Office of Works. They follow the Tudor model established by Smith but are of a rather uninspired plainness: two storeys, crenellated, with two-light, square-headed windows relieved by cusping. The ends of the S range are marked by three-storey battlemented stair-towers on the side facing the quadrangle, and by canted bays on the S side (this range was extended E in 1894). Inside the S door of the E range is an early C18 TABLET recording Fraser's benefaction, re-set. In 1868–70, Matheson added the Library (now the KING'S COLLEGE CONFERENCE CENTRE), an elongated T projecting E from the centre of the E range, its entrance flanked by shield-bearing statues of a lion and unicorn (externally, its N and S elevations are largely obscured by C20 additions). It was lengthened in 1881–4 by *Walter Wood Robertson* of H.M. Office of Works, who added a further transept with an E window modelled on those of the chapel. Conversion by *Edward Taylor*, 1990–1, reinstated the impressive double-height interior with its timber barrel-vault (again modelled on the chapel), but obscured other features. The transept is now an auditorium, to which Matheson's original library serves as a foyer, the JAMES MACKAY HALL. In the auditorium, at gallery level, MEMORIAL to George Macdonald (†1905), incorporating a cast of *Alexander Munro*'s 1858/9 bronze portrait medallion of the writer. In the James MacKay Hall, MEMORIAL of 1904–5 to the Principal and classical scholar Sir William Duguid Geddes, a white marble relief portrait with chaste Greek ornament by *Pittendrigh MacGillivray*.

Facing the N side of the chapel across a spacious lawn is NEW KING'S, a block of lecture rooms by *A. Marshall Mackenzie*, 1911–12, with attached Sacrist's House at No. 24 High Street. Scots Gothic in sandstone, with decorative details such as window tracery derived from the chapel. Full-height oriels at each end contain stairs. In front of the W end, a free-standing ARCHWAY to the High Street dated 1912, with painted heraldic carvings. At the E end, a bronze STATUE, Youth with Split Apple, 2005 by *Kenny Hunter*. Enclosing the lawn on the E, and making the third side of a quadrangle open to the High Street, is *Mackenzie*'s ELPHINSTONE HALL, designed with the involvement of his son, *A. G. R. Mackenzie* – as late as 1927–31, but still taking its cue from the medieval setting. Once again of sandstone, in this case salvaged from Archibald Simpson's demolished Castle Newe (Strathdon). The crowstepped gable of the Hall faces the lawn, linked visually with the Cromwell Tower and chapel by a Gothic arcade with carved and painted shields in the spandrels. The arcade piers have no capitals, and the arch mouldings continue down to the base. However, the outermost order of each arch stops just above the springing and joins its neighbour to form one continuous moulding from end to end of the arcade – a feature adapted from the nave of St Machar. Two oriels on the N side, overlooking Regent Walk, the W one containing an elegant concrete stair. Panelled interior, with a fine open timber roof. A plain sash-windowed range of 1952 by *George Bennett Mitchell & Son* links the E end of the Hall with the transept of the former library (*see* above).

Just E of the 1894 extension to the S range of the quadrangle is KING'S PAVILION, 1939–41 by *A. Marshall Mackenzie & Son*. The University's first Modernist building, and a world away from the same practice's Elphinstone Hall, opened eight years earlier. Steel-framed and flat-roofed with walls of rendered brick, but granite-faced on the sides that face older neighbours. Above the ground-floor swimming pool and changing rooms, a cantilevered canopy serves as a balcony to the first floor, which has generous windows overlooking the playing fields. For the University's post-war buildings, dispersed N and W of King's, *see* the Description below.

PUBLIC BUILDINGS

BRIDGE OF BALGOWNIE, Don Street. Until 1830 this ancient bridge was Aberdeen's only road link with the North. Though traditionally said to date from *c.* 1320 and to be the work either of Bishop Henry Cheyne or Robert the Bruce, the earliest documentary reference is to repairs carried out in 1443. By the start of the C17 it was ruinous, and between 1607 and 1611 it was substantially reconstructed by the masons *Andrew Jameson* and *William Massie*. A fund for future maintenance had been established in 1605 by Sir Alexander Hay: an inscribed tablet commemorating this is on a buttress at the SW corner. The bridge is a single Gothic arch of sandstone, 10.5 m. high and 20.4 m. wide, with a granite rubble parapet. Unlike the Bridge of Dee (*see* p. 259) it is traffic-free and has not been widened, preserving its medieval character to a remarkable degree. The wooded setting and the winding, buttressed approaches (extensively rebuilt in 1877 and 1912) make it highly picturesque.

BUS DEPOT, King Street and Mounthooly Way. Long, Baronial front range, 1861 by *William Ramage*, with conical-roofed corner turrets, loopholes (now blocked) and a central arched entrance. Originally a depot, and later barracks, for the Royal Aberdeenshire Militia.

ST PETER'S R.C. SCHOOL and OLD ABERDEEN HOUSE, Dunbar Street. The earliest part – originally the Board School of Old Aberdeen – is actually on King Street: single-storeyed and minimally Gothic, by *William Henderson & Son*, 1874–5. In 1898–1900, *J. A. Ogg Allan* built a much larger new school behind, facing Dunbar Street. Classical, with four pediments down each side, and big, four-light windows. Overlooking King Street, a life-size STATUE of the Rev. Charles Gordon in mass vestments, by *A. Brodie*, carved in granite by *John Panton*. It was first erected in 1859 in front of the Roman Catholic school in Constitution Street (*see* p. 137).

ST PETER'S CEMETERY, King Street. Main entrance probably *c.* 1843, flanked by simple gabled Greek Revival lodges, each with primitive acroteria and a window with inward-sloping sides. Latticework cast-iron gates with skull-and-crossbones roundels – the appropriately funereal badge of the Moir family of Scotstown, who owned the land and evidently developed it as a cemetery. The older part (at the W end, adjoining the Spital) is on a higher level. Here is the Moir enclosure, a roof-less rectangular building of granite rubble with shallow pediments and other Greek details in freestone. It occupies the site of a vanished church associated with St Peter's Hospital, a foundation of the late C12 from which the Spital derives its name. Some MEMORIALS of interest. Near the SE corner of the upper section, William Walker, †1868, an obelisk with a good portrait relief in bronze. Near the SW corner of the lower section, the Rev. John Comper, †1906 by *J. Ninian Comper*: a Portland stone Calvary over 4 m. high, with the Pelican in her piety on top.

ST MACHAR'S HALL, Dunbar Street. By *Ellis & Wilson*, 1886, in a style derived from the nearby Cathedral. Pink and grey Aberdeen-bond granite, with a crowstepped gable and four round-headed lancets over the door.

SEATON PARK, Don Street. Formed from the grounds of Seaton House, an C18 brick mansion, burnt down in 1963.

SUNNYBANK SCHOOL, Sunnybank Road. *J. A. Ogg Allan*, 1904–6. Three storeys, with a long, two-storey E extension of the 1930s.

TOWN HOUSE, High Street. By *George Jaffray*, 1787–9, replacing buildings of the C17 and early C18. Freestanding in the fork at the N end of the street (adjoining buildings on the N were demolished *c.* 1921 for St Machar Drive), it makes a handsome terminal feature. Three bays and three storeys. There are quoins to the angles and centre bay, which breaks forward slightly under a pediment. Short clock tower with corner urns and an octagonal domed belfry, lead-covered. Over the door, a panel carved with the burgh arms and dated 1721, reused. An old dormer pediment carved with thistles and the Scottish Royal Arms is built into the E wall. Inside, stairs in the middle at the back lead to a single large room on each of the upper floors. The second-floor room apparently served as the council chamber and has a coved ceiling with original plasterwork. In front is the MERCAT CROSS, cast down at the Reformation and re-erected in 1951. The shaft is C20, but the damaged octagonal knop is C16, with the shields of Bishops Elphinstone, Dunbar and Stewart, and the lion of Scotland, still more or less legible. William Stewart's episcopate – 1532–45 – gives an approximate date.

87

DESCRIPTION

King's Crescent to St Machar Drive

Old Aberdeen's linear plan means that it is best explored by following the main street from S to N (*c.* 1.25 km.), with occasional detours. This ancient route begins at Mounthooly Way, from where KING'S CRESCENT leads N. Nos. 17–21, W side, plus the adjoining No. 1 Jute Street, are an 1875 terrace of Italianate houses by *Daniel Macandrew*. Superficially unremarkable, they are an early example of concrete construction, disguised under scored and painted render. No. 33 on the same side, originally a detached house of 1838 with consoled cornices to the windows, is now bookended by extensions. From here, King's Crescent becomes the SPITAL, and starts to climb. On the E side, opposite St Margaret's Convent (*see* Churches), a model tenement block of 1934 by *John G. Marr* of *A. Marshall Mackenzie & Son*, erected by the Aberdeen Voluntary Housing Trust. Severely plain, but elegant, with windows grouped in threes, and access balconies at the rear. No. 49, set back on the W side, gable to the street, is mid-C18, its gateway flanked by a pair of lodge-like shops. Opposite is public housing of the early 1970s, harled, with distinctive rounded stair-towers. Descending towards the cloistered precincts of the University, the Spital becomes COLLEGE BOUNDS, and tarmac gives way to granite setts. No. 2, E side, was formerly ORCHARD HOUSE, *c.* 1800, but with a skewputt dated 1770 built into the SW corner. In the high wall lower down on the W side is a blocked ARCH with the mitre and arms of Bishop Elphinstone above. It may have served as entrance to the precinct either of the Snow Kirk (*see* below) or of the C16 manse of the Grammarian of King's College, the successor to which is No. 19, a house of 1818–19 hidden behind the wall. College Bounds continues N, with modest but pleasingly varied C19 (and possibly C18) houses, until the fantastical POWIS GATEWAY, dated 1834, appears on the W side. Built by John Leslie as the entrance to his residence, Powis House, 0.5 km. W (*see* Powis Community Centre, p. 214), it seems to have been designed by *Alexander Fraser*, 'architect and landscape painter', and consists of two tall conical-roofed round towers of harled brick with granite dressings. Near the top are battlemented balconies on elaborate lobed corbels, and between them an arch under a shaped gable with a heraldic panel on each side (the W one, older, has the arms of Fraser impaling Moir of Scotstown and was moved here from the E wing of Powis Lodge: *see* below). The towers look like minarets, an impression reinforced by the crescent moons on the weathervanes, but these are apparently taken from the Fraser arms.

Inside the gateway, the L-shaped POWIS LODGE, immediately NW, has an uncertain history. The E wing is a granite rubble house fronting College Bounds, dated 1711 on the skewputts. It was probably built by Alexander Fraser, Sub-Principal of King's, who acquired a large site opposite the College in 1691 and erected several cottages and houses. The larger W wing looks late C18 or early C19, with a two-storey polygonal bay in the middle of the S front. It was 'completely altered' in 1829 and further extended in 1830–3 by the architect *Alexander Fraser*, who presumably added the ornamental round tower at the SW corner, similar to the gate towers. The present entrance is to the r. of the bay. It opens straight into a narrow hall, completely filled by an imperial stair at right angles to the s front. The half-landing gives access to the E wing, while the return flight leads to the main first-floor room of the W wing, with delightful Batty Langley-ish Gothick woodwork extending into the bay. Can all this really be as late as 1829?

Just SW of the gateway is a handsome house of 1855–6, built as a manse for the Sub-Principal of the day, and now confusingly called POWIS GATE. It has channelled quoins and deep eaves, and was designed by 'Mr. Leslie' – probably *William Leslie* (1802–79). It faces S towards the brick boundary wall of a small and almost hidden BURIAL GROUND, one of the most evocative sites in Old Aberdeen. The simple rectangular enclosure with canted corners at the E end occupies the apsidal footprint of the vanished Snow Kirk, the church of St Maria ad Nives founded by Bishop Elphinstone in 1498 as the parish church of Old Aberdeen, which fell into ruin after the Reformation. It has continued to be used for Catholic burials, among the MONUMENTS being the heraldic slab of Sir Gilbert Menzies of Pitfodels, †1669.

100 m. W of the Powis Gateway is CROMBIE HALL, a loosely quadrangular group of student residences with an attached dining room. Designed by *Robert Matthew & Johnson-Marshall*, 1953–6; built 1957–60. The first mixed-sex hall of residence in Scotland, it embodies the approach that Matthew was to recommend in his masterplan for the University's Old Aberdeen site, commissioned in 1957: keeping large developments away from the historic High Street and breaking them down into 'small related groups and open spaces'. Varying between two and five storeys, the residential blocks allude to vernacular tradition in their pantiled pitched roofs and harling. Squared sandstone rubble is used for the gable-ends of some blocks, while elsewhere timber cladding gives a Scandinavian flavour. The block running W–E in the middle is more overtly modern, with a monopitch copper roof and windows in horizontal bands. But the most striking is the single-storey dining room, projecting E from the entrance block. Largely timber-clad inside and out, it has a concave S front and a roof that slopes up to a fully glazed E wall, framing a view of King's. JOHNSTON HALL, immediately S and by the same architects, followed in 1964–6: two accommodation blocks and another dining hall make three sides of a square, harled, with corrugated metal spandrels.

Back on COLLEGE BOUNDS to the N, Nos. 50 and 52 on the E side are a semi-detached pair, with cherry-cocking and lugged architraves to the doors, built in 1773–5 for professors. The principal contractor was 'George Jeffrey, wright' – presumably *George Jaffray*. No. 53, W side, is a handsome three-bay detached house of 1839–42 – still perfectly Georgian – by *John Smith* for the Professor of Medicine. For King's College and New King's, E side, *see* pp. 184–96. N of here, College

120

6   Bounds becomes the HIGH STREET, with a picturesque
     assortment of mostly C18 and C19 houses, many with gables
     facing the street. At the rear of No. 7, the Catholic Chaplaincy,
     a pair of fine rococo wrought-iron gates, brought from else-
     where. They look C18, but with later alterations. Nos. 57–61 on
     the w side, dated 1821, have a central wall-head stack contain-
     ing a small arched window with Gothick glazing. Opposite is
     the University's TAYLOR BUILDING, 1961–4 by *George Bennett
     Mitchell & Son*. It presents a deceptively modest gable of harl
     and granite to the High Street, but it is large, zigzagging all the
     way back to Regent Walk and crossing Dunbar Street on a
     sandstone arcade. The two westernmost wings make a quad-
     rangle with a terrace of refurbished houses and a former
     brewery fronting the High Street, the setting for a 2007 bronze
     SCULPTURE, Case, by *Steve Dilworth*.
         The Taylor Building leads into an area dense with University
     buildings of the 1960s and 70s. To its N is the EDWARD
     WRIGHT BUILDING, 1973–5 by *Robin Dunn* of *George Trew
     Dunn Beckles Willson Bowes*. It follows the E side of curved
     Dunbar Street, set back behind a band of preserved mature
     trees, its long, harled façade punctuated by rounded stair-
     towers. It was the last major outcome of the University's rapid
     post-war expansion, and the most successful in terms of its
     sensitive response to the Old Aberdeen setting. E of it are the
     WILLIAM GUILD BUILDING and attached ARTS LECTURE
     THEATRE, both 1968–70 by *Matthews, Ryan, Schwerdt & Hill*.
     The former is calmly rectilinear, the latter an aggressive
     hexagon walled with raking slabs of ribbed concrete. S of this
     group are undistinguished administrative offices; E, at the
     corner of St Machar Drive and King Street, the MACROBERT
     BUILDING (originally Agriculture), by *Robert Matthew,
     Johnson-Marshall & Partners*, 1965–8. A nine-storey slab faced
     with white pre-cast concrete, but far enough from King's and
     the High Street to do little visual damage.
         We return to the HIGH STREET where we left it and cross
     to the w side, where the narrow wynd of THOM'S PLACE leads
     w to Elphinstone Road, beyond which is another cluster of
     post-war University accommodation. Earliest is the very large
     MESTON BUILDING, 1949–52 by *Pite, Son & Fairweather*.
     Originally for Chemistry, it is a five-storey cruciform block
     faced with pink and grey granite, with a weedy copper spire
     over the crossing. A large and dreary L-shaped addition of
     1961–7 extends S from the E wing. The Meston Building was
     conceived in 1947 as part of a formal group, to be approached
     axially from the High Street by a broad new avenue, a destruc-
     tive intervention which happily did not materialize. In the
     paved area which takes the place of this avenue – now called
     ACADEMIC SQUARE – are two SCULPTURES: 'Evolutionary
     Loop 517', an enormous abstract bronze by *Nasser Azam*,
     2013; and 'Waterlines', two incised stone uprights by *Marian
     Leven* and *Will Maclean*, 2012. Directly facing the Meston

Building across the Square is the more interesting FRASER NOBLE BUILDING (originally Natural Philosophy) of 1960–3 by *J. Douglass Mathews & Partners*, with *Cyril Blumfield & Partners* as structural consultants. At either end of its granite-faced podium are parallel teaching and research blocks, with vertical glazing and thin concrete mullions (a third curtain-glazed block behind is a later addition). Between them sits a billowing concrete sail dome, 30 m. in diameter, on six glazed arches, covering the entrance hall and a lecture theatre.

The axial focus envisaged sixty years earlier was eventually achieved with the completion of the SIR DUNCAN RICE LIBRARY in 2009–12, won in competition by *schmidt hammer lassen* of Denmark in 2005. An eight-storey glazed cube, approached up a ramped forecourt from Academic Square. Some of the greenish glazing is clear and therefore appears dark from outside, while some is translucent and milky, the contrasting tones making a jagged zebra-stripe pattern. The recessed ground floor is fully glazed and the exterior paving flows right through, so for such a monumental building it sits lightly on its site. Immediately inside, the eye is drawn up through a glorious full-height atrium, each floor being pierced by a softly curved triangular opening. These openings become smaller as they rise and are not vertically aligned, but recede gradually from the entrance front, floor by floor, each successive triangle rotated through a few degrees. The result is a dynamic upward spiral, as exhilarating as a Baroque church (disadvantages are the sacrifice of usable floor space on the upper levels and some noise penetration from the ground-floor café). It is an uplifting space, one in which to meet and socialize as well as study, and open to the world outside rather than cocooned from it.

NE of the Fraser Noble Building, at the corner of Elphinstone Road and St Machar Drive, is THE HUB, originally the central refectory and staff club, 1965–9, refurbished 2005–6 to house an expanded range of student services.

We return once again to the HIGH STREET at the point where we left it and continue N to No. 70 on the E side, which with two segmental bows looks early C19. No. 81, opposite, is the detached town house of Maclean of Coll. In existence by 1773, it is the grandest in the whole street. Set well back behind screen walls and handsome gatepiers, it has quoins and an arched window with Gothick glazing pushing up into an open pediment. Similarities with the later Town House (*see* Public Buildings) suggest that the architect may have been *George Jaffray*. The screen walls are brick, and at the back in Elphinstone Road are brick service buildings enclosing a court. Back on the High Street's E side, opposite the former Free Church (*see* Churches), are GRANT'S PLACE – a short terrace of pantiled single-storey cottages, end-on to the street, with a lintel dated 1732 – and parallel WRIGHTS' AND COOPERS' PLACE, with two-storey houses. Both rows were restored in 1963–6 by *Robert Hurd* and *Ian Begg*, who also designed the

MacRobert Memorial Garden, just E of the houses. This enclave is followed by No. 96 High Street, with a damaged skewputt which may have borne the date 1623 or 1723. In any case it was largely – perhaps entirely – rebuilt *c.* 1952–3. Here the street widens in front of the Town House to form the market place, with the Cross at its centre (*see* Public Buildings). Nos. 108–110, E side, are dated 1751. Larger houses on the w side, with more regular fenestration, are perhaps late C18.

The Chanonry

At the Town House the High Street splits, the l. branch leading to St Machar's Cathedral, the r. to the Bridge of Balgownie. Both were rudely interrupted in 1921–2 by St Machar Drive, a busy stretch of ring road ploughing w–e, right behind the Town House. Taking the l. branch and crossing the Drive, one is straight away in The Chanonry, the Cathedral precinct where the medieval canons had their manses. These were gradually demolished in the course of the C17 and C18, but 'of late years', writes William Kennedy in 1818, 'many people of fortune, besides the members of the college ... have chosen [Old Aberdeen] as a place of residence; and have built upon the west side of the chanonrie several beautiful villas.' Today, such Late Georgian houses predominate.

First on the w side (actually No. 23 St Machar Drive) is a late C19 house with additions for the University, surrounded by the Cruickshank Botanic Gardens. At the w end of the gardens (beside a good wrought-iron gate with vines, lilies and roses, by *McHardy*, 1916) is the University's Zoology Building, normally entered from Tillydrone Avenue: a two-storey plinth and five-storey slab clad in white concrete, 1966–70 by *Mackie Ramsay & Taylor*. On the w side, the uprights of the plinth branch out into inverted pyramids. In the ground-floor museum, an exquisite Memorial Tablet of 1900 to the naturalist William MacGillivray (1796–1852), originally erected in Marischal College. Repoussée copper with a border of birds, designed by *C. R. Ashbee* and made by the *Guild of Handicraft*. Back in The Chanonry, No. 8, w side, is distinguished by a pediment and finely dressed ashlar. Next is Mitchell's Hospital, a former charitable institution, founded in 1801 by David Mitchell of Essex and Old Aberdeen, to house five widows and five unmarried daughters of burgesses or gentlemen. Single-storey H-plan block with central bellcote. The front wings were originally dormitories, the cross-bar a refectory. It was converted to self-contained cottages in 1924 by *A. H. L. Mackinnon*. A little further along, on the opposite side, is the sw Gate of the Cathedral churchyard. The flanking lodges, originally built by *George Jaffray* in 1812, seem to have been given their present form by *John Smith* in 1832: polygonal fronts, round angle towers at the back, and simple pointed windows. Beside the l. lodge, a former well,

pyramid-topped, with a ball finial. Here The Chanonry forks.
A short way along the l. branch is early C19 TILLYDRONE
HOUSE, No. 12, single-storey-plus-basement, with the entrance
in a canted porch. The r. branch has bigger houses. CHANONRY
LODGE is harled, late C18, with later gabled wings enclosing a
forecourt. No. 14 is also basically C18, but with a late C19 porch
and E wing. CASTLETON HOUSE looks early C19: originally
two storeys with gable-ends, but now raised to three, with a
flat roof. No. 16 is of 1936 by *A. Marshall Mackenzie & Son*
(*A. G. R. Mackenzie*), but reuses some older materials. Finally,
No. 20, CHAPLAIN'S COURT, incorporates the only surviving
C16 fragments in The Chanonry, including a moulded arch
with the arms of Bishop Gavin Dunbar in an ogee-headed
niche above.

One interesting outlier: from Tillydrone House, Tillydrone
Road leads to BENHOLM'S LODGING in Tillydrone Avenue,
0.25 km. NW. This small Z-plan tower house, built by Sir
Robert Keith of Benholm between 1588 and 1616, originally
stood at the angle of Nether Kirkgate and Carnegie's Brae. It
was dismantled to make way for an extension to Marks &
Spencer, and re-erected by the *City Architect's Department* on
this superb site overlooking the Don in 1965. Much of the
stonework was evidently renewed in the process. The NE tower
has a corbelled stair-turret in the re-entrant angle, an armorial
panel and a life-size relief sculpture of an armed figure, possibly Sir Robert.

Don Street

From the Town House, the r. branch of the High Street continues N of St Machar Drive as DON STREET. Nos. 20–22, E
side, have an arched pend leading to a corbelled stair-turret at
the back, with a plaque, difficult to read, but said to be dated
1676. No. 45, W side, is three-bay early C19 with a Greek Doric
porch; No. 55, SW corner of The Chanonry, is late C18. Back
on the E side, No. 78 is C17 BISHOP'S GATE, harled, with
painted margins to the irregularly placed windows. After this,
Don Street skirts Seaton Park (*see* above), with nothing much
of interest for 1 km. (the University's HILLHEAD HALLS OF
RESIDENCE, 1965 onwards, are on the l.) before descending
steeply to a cluster of cottages that form an attractive prelude
to the Bridge of Balgownie (*see* Public Buildings). On the N
side, Nos. 245–247 make up a harled L-plan house with sandstone dressings. A heraldic plaque over an archway, l., has the
date 1655 and the initials GCBH. It is probably the house
known to have been built by George Cruickshank for use
during the fishing season, with stone from the demolished
Manse of Clatt in The Chanonry. No. 1 Rocky Bank, next
door, is dated 1722. After this comes the former BALGOWNIE
MISSION HALL of 1884, now a dwelling, with crowstepped
gables, before the road turns towards the bridge.

INNER DISTRICTS: NORTH

KITTYBREWSTER

A populous suburb in the second half of the C19, centred round extensive railway yards and a cattle market, now vanished.

NORTHERN HOTEL, No. 1 Great Northern Road. *A. Marshall Mackenzie & Son (A. G. R. Mackenzie)*, 1938–48. Stylish Art Deco in granite and concrete, on an acute triangular site. Bands of metal-framed windows sweep round the curved corner, which houses a circular bar. In the first-floor ballroom, plaster coving flows smoothly round the sensuous violin-shaped space, concealing the electric lighting.

KITTYBREWSTER PRIMARY SCHOOL, Great Northern Road. 1897–9 by *Brown & Watt*. Round-arched ground-floor windows with alternately blocked voussoirs, flanked by squat little bar-rel-shaped columns. Windows on the first and second floors have column mullions.

LINKS

The Links, the common lands bordering the beach, have been immemorially dedicated to outdoor recreation. The beach itself was promoted as a place of amusement from the 1890s. The Esplanade was begun at the same time and completed all the way N to the Don in 1923. Public housing began to colonize the area between the Links and King Street in the late C19 and early C20, and large buildings for retail and leisure use encroached on the s end in the late C20.

CHURCHES

KING'S COMMUNITY CHURCH, King Street and Urquhart Road. Originally St Andrew's United Free Church. *D. & J. R. McMillan*, 1901–3. Gabled front with large Perp window and octagonal corner pinnacles.

ST MARY, King Street and Regent Walk. *A. Marshall Mackenzie & Son (A. G. R. Mackenzie)*, 1937–9. Vestigially Gothic, but purged of overt medievalism and composed of almost cubic shapes. w tower with four long windows – little more than slits – with the merest hint of triangular tops to make them lancets. Two round arches cut out of the NW corner make a porch – the only curves anywhere. The w end of the nave is slightly wider than the tower, but it becomes narrower towards the E, with more lancets down the sides and very low passage aisles. Inside, the ceiling rises to a central ridge and there are wide, shallow-pointed arches between nave and aisles. – STAINED

GLASS. Contemporary with the building. In the three E windows, a strikingly stylized Crucifixion with Mary and St John, by *James Steedman Hamilton* of Gray's School of Art. Elsewhere mostly clear, with thin horizontal bands of colour. Attached HALL at NE corner.

PUBLIC BUILDINGS

ABERDEEN SPORTS VILLAGE, Linksfield Road. *Reiach & Hall*, with *KSS Design Group*, 2008–9. A cavernous aircraft hangar of a building. Behind the modest entrance front, a 210 m. walkway-cum-viewing gallery runs from end to end on two levels, with a full-size indoor football pitch on one side (portholes allow spectators to watch matches) and a straight running track and nine-court sports hall on the other. The curved roof of the pitch runs parallel with the main axis on tubular steel trusses, while a series of vaults at right angles covers the sports hall, track and other facilities. Translucent polycarbonate cladding in pale blues and greys lets in plenty of daylight, and at night has a mysterious, unearthly look from outside when artificially lit. Immediately N, and linked by a pedestrian bridge, is the ABERDEEN AQUATICS CENTRE by *Faulkner Brown*, opened 2014. Two interlocking blocks. One – soberly rectangular, with dark, vertically ribbed cladding and slit-windows – contains the 50 m. pool. The other – square, with rounded corners and battered sides – is taller and more dramatic, its windowless walls covered in fish-scale tiles of stainless steel. It contains a 25 m. swimming pool, which can be transformed for diving by lowering the bottom. This explains the great internal height, with diving platforms projecting at different levels from one of the walls.

BEACH BALLROOM, Esplanade. *Thomas Roberts & Hume*, 1926. The octagonal roof is a seafront landmark, a red tiled pyramid crowned by a tempietto. Single-storey classical façades of cream faience, with an angular rooftop extension of 1962–3 overlooking the sea. Inside, the octagonal ballroom has coupled Ionic pilasters, with a continuous balcony behind and clearstorey above. A flat ceiling has sadly replaced the original domed one. Earlier seafront structures have left little trace, but *c.* 1 km. N of the Ballroom are four cheerful SHELTERS of *c.* 1963, of reinforced concrete, built into the retaining wall behind the lower promenade. The splayed walls have porthole openings, and the roofs rise steeply from back to front, projecting to form canopies which curl up at the edge.

Former BOYS' AND GIRLS' HOSPITAL, No. 352 King Street. *William Smith*, 1869–71. Built as a residential school for poor children; now converted to flats. Italianate, symmetrical, with gabled wings. A pair of belvedere towers with open, arched tops flank the central entrance.

Former CITY HOSPITAL, Urquhart Road. Originally built 1874–7 by *William Smith* as a fever hospital, with four parallel ward blocks of concrete, for ease of cleaning. The existing

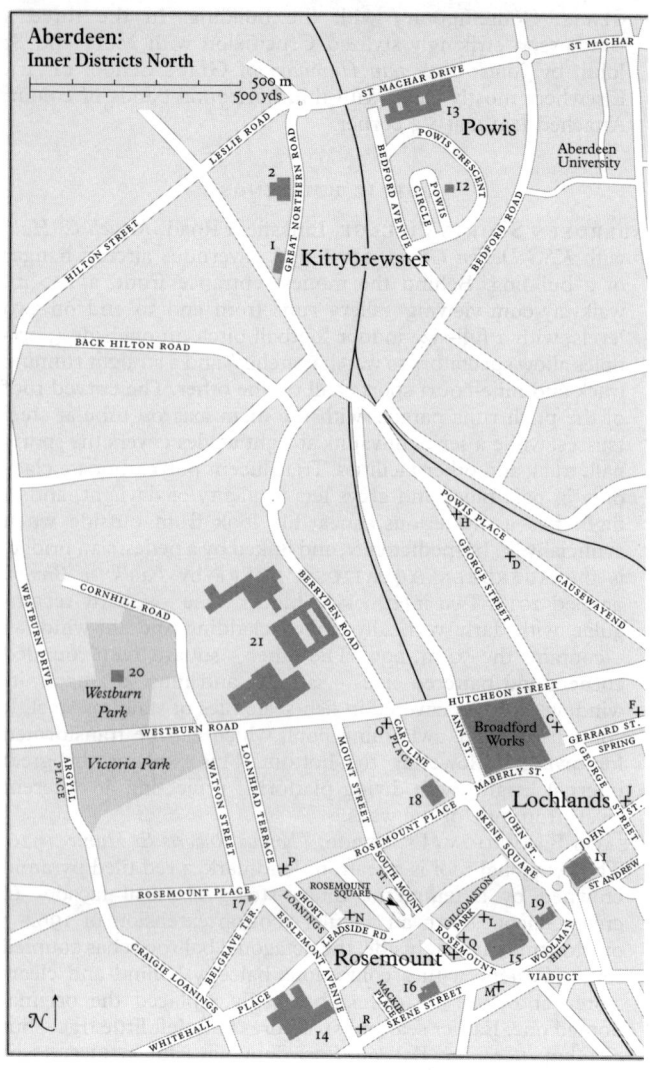

Aberdeen:
Inner Districts North

500 m.
500 yds

ST MACHAR

Powis

Aberdeen
University

13

12

2

1   Kittybrewster

ST MACHAR DRIVE

POWIS CRESCENT

POWIS CIRCLE

BEDFORD AVENUE

BEDFORD ROAD

LESLIE ROAD

GREAT NORTHERN ROAD

HILTON STREET

BACK HILTON ROAD

POWIS PLACE
H

GEORGE STREET
D

CAUSEWAYEND

CORNHILL ROAD

BERRYDEN ROAD

WESTBURN DRIVE

21

20
Westburn
Park

HUTCHEON STREET

CAROLINE PLACE
O

ANN ST

Broadford
Works
C

GERRARD ST.
F

GEORGE SPRING

WESTBURN ROAD

Victoria Park

ARGYLL PLACE

WATSON STREET

LOANHEAD TERRACE

MOUNT STREET

18

MABERLY ST.

ROSEMOUNT PLACE

SKENE SQUARE

JOHN ST.

Lochlands
J

JOHN STREET

11

ST ANDREW

ROSEMOUNT PLACE
17   P

ROSEMOUNT SQUARE

SOUTH MOUNT ST

SHORT LOANINGS

ESSLEMONT AVENUE

BELGRAVE TER.

LEADSIDE RD

N

GILCOMSTON PARK

ROSEMOUNT

L
Q
19

15

WOOLMAN HILL

VIADUCT

M

CRAIGIE LOANINGS

WHITEHALL PLACE

MACKIE PLACE

SKENE STREET

R
16

14

N

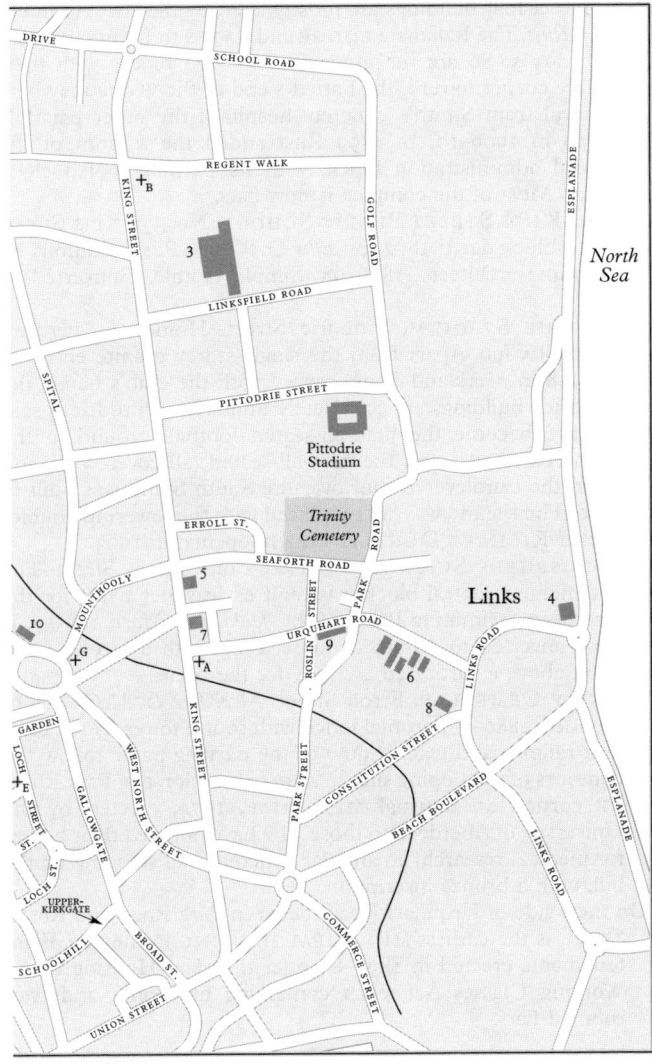

1   Northern Hotel
2   Kittybrewster Primary School
3   Aberdeen Sports Village
4   Beach Ballroom
5   Boys' and Girls' Hospital
     (former)
6   City Hospital (former)
7   King Street Public School
     (former)
8   Stratosphere Science Centre
9   Municipal Housing
10 Causewayend Primary
     School (former)

11 Robert Gordon University,
     St Andrew Street building
12 Powis Community Centre
13 St Machar Academy
14 Aberdeen Grammar School
15 Denburn Health Centre
16 Gilcomstoun School
17 Rosemount Community
     Education Centre
18 Skene Square School
19 Woolman Hill Hospital
20 Westburn House
21 Royal Cornhill Hospital

granite ashlar buildings are mostly later, by the City Architect
John Rust. The Italianate LODGE and GATES to Urquhart Road
are 1893–5. So are the inner pair of ward blocks with their
square corner towers (the harled S end of the W one may be a
survival from Smith's concrete hospital); the outer pair followed in 1909–10. In 1899 Rust added the N front of the
central administration block, with its pavilion-roofed clock
tower. Most of the complex is now flats.

Former KING STREET PUBLIC SCHOOL, No. 338 King Street.
Front block dated 1882, by *Ellis & Wilson.* Rear additions by
the same architects, 1886–98. Simple Gothic. Converted to
flats.

PITTODRIE STADIUM, Pittodrie Street. Home of Aberdeen
Football Club. Apart from the single-storey granite entrance
of 1928 in Merkland Lane, carved with the club's name, the
red brick buildings are completely utilitarian. Pittodrie is said
to have become the first all-seated football ground in the
country in 1973, and the first all-seated, all-covered ground
when the cantilevered roof over the South Stand was built in
1980. The E stand was later replaced with the towering double-
decker RICHARD DONALD STAND, opened in 1993.

STRATOSPHERE SCIENCE CENTRE, Constitution Street. The
pedimented central block was built as seawater baths for the
Aberdeen Swimming Bath Co. by *Jenkins & Marr,* 1885–7. It
was converted to a tram depot, *c.* 1901, with a second pediment above a rusticated archway for the trams.

TRINITY CEMETERY, Erroll Street. *McKelvie & McCulloch* of
Dundee, 1880–1. Baronial lodge with round tower. Good cast-
iron railings and gates. Some of the curving paths follow the
contours of the sloping site. In a later extension E of Park Road,
NE corner, an unusual MEMORIAL, 1974, erected by the
University of Aberdeen to those who have donated their bodies
for medical research: an angular concrete wall stepping up the
hill, with a bronze inscription.

On the S side of Urquhart Road, between Park Road and Roslin
Street, is the earliest MUNICIPAL HOUSING in the city. Eight
tenements erected in 1897–8 under the 1890 Housing of the
Working Classes Act, each containing nine one- and two-
roomed flats.

LOCHLANDS

Lying just N of Robert Gordon's College and the medieval core,
Lochlands was an expanse of marshy ground with an E boundary
recalled in the curve of Loch Street. In 1783 the area was offered
for feuing by James Staats Forbes, according to a grid plan by
the surveyor *Colin Innes,* and became Aberdeen's first large-scale
extension beyond its medieval boundaries (*see* Introduction).
Development was continued N to Hutcheon Street by the lawyer

and property speculator Hugh Hutcheon, and the area N of Hutcheon Street as far as the end of George Street has much the same character. Around 1800 it was decided to make George Street the Aberdeen end of the turnpike road from Inverurie, and it became a bustling commercial thoroughfare. Late C20 developments have tended to undermine its importance. NE of the Lochlands, the historic street name of Mounthooly now attaches to a vast 1970s roundabout, the focus for a handful of older buildings.

CHURCHES

ABERDEEN CHURCH OF CHRIST, No. 393 George Street. Built as the Aberdeen Savings Bank by *Kelly & Nicol*, 1906–8. Small – just one storey – but exquisitely refined. The entrance is in a lower block, l., with a finely moulded architrave round the door. The bank proper has a high, smooth, windowless basement in alternate bands of dark and light grey granite. Above this are four pairs of Roman Doric engaged columns (the outermost square), against a background of channelled rustication. The centre columns frame a Venetian window, and above the cornice is a balustrade. Serene, square interior, with four Ionic columns of pink granite, polished to a dull sheen, supporting a shallow coffered dome with central skylight.

GERRARD STREET BAPTIST CHURCH, Gerrard Street. Built 1899–1900 by *George Coutts* as the John Knox Free Church, replacing the congregation's previous building on the same site. Quite an impressive façade. Rock-faced granite, with four giant pilasters of horizontally channelled ashlar. The outer pair are returned to form square corner piers, finished off with little pointed domes. Pediment above the middle pair, raised on short, tapering pilasters and buttressed by scrolls. Keystone of the main door carved with head of Knox. Secondary entrances in the rubble side elevations, with ashlar surrounds incorporating round-arched windows. HALL, l., 1889 by *Ellis & Wilson*, built in connection with the earlier church. Gothic, with a three-light window in the gabled street elevation. It has a blind tympanum with dripmould over.

Former JOHN KNOX PARISH CHURCH, Mounthooly. *Wilsons & Walker*, 1911. Classical, with a pediment and a heavy balcony above the door. Now converted to flats. It replaced a church of 1832–5, the graveyard of which survives behind the present building, laid out by *Alexander Fraser*.

Former POWIS PARISH CHURCH, George Street and Powis Place. Right at the N end of George Street. 1894–5 by *A. Marshall Mackenzie*. As it stands, not really big enough for its prominent corner site: its four bays were intended only as the nave of a more ambitious building, but planned transepts and apse were never realized. Gothic, of a more distinctly Scottish type than Mackenzie's earlier churches. Its simple intersecting tracery was based on the old Greyfriars church,

soon to be demolished to make way for Mackenzie's own
Marischal College extension. Converted to flats.

Former ST GEORGE'S PARISH CHURCH, John Street. 1877–8,
by *John Smith*. Gothic, with a steeply gabled s end facing the
street, topped by a bellcote. The centre breaks forward slightly,
with three doorways under linked dripmoulds, and a large
window with sandstone plate tracery. On each side, a trefoil
and a small lancet light the 'aisles'. Interior subdivided.

ST STEPHEN, Causewayend (originally Causewayend Free
Church). 1881–2 by *Duncan McMillan*; extensively rebuilt
1949–51 after war damage. Classical. Square clock tower l. of
gable, with domed tempietto on top.

Former ZION CHAPEL, John Street. Opened 1841. A flat, classical façade of five bays, the middle three with a pediment.
Round-arched windows above the altered ground floor. Now
a pub.

PUBLIC BUILDINGS

Former CAUSEWAYEND PRIMARY SCHOOL, Causewayend. By
William Smith, dated 1876, with a big SE addition by *W. & J.
Smith & Kelly*, 1892. A surprisingly grand statement by the
new School Board, who were accused of having built 'a large
castle in the midst of a gutter'. Smith's original part is indeed
Baronial, with a massive square tower ending in a balustraded
parapet, and a round, corbelled turret at one corner. 1892
extension simpler.

ROBERT GORDON UNIVERSITY, St Andrew Street Building.
1914–20, by *J. A. Ogg Allan*. Originally a teacher training
centre. Classical and very large, filling the entire block bounded
by St Andrew Street, North St Andrew Street, John Street and
Charlotte Street. Thirty-one-bay s entrance front, with a pair
of giant Doric columns above the door. The other elevations
are plainer.

For ABERDEEN COLLEGE, Gallowgate, *see* p. 128.

DESCRIPTION

Most things of interest can be seen by following GEORGE
STREET from s to N, with occasional detours w and E. The s
end has been swallowed by the BON ACCORD CENTRE, a large
shopping complex with associated multi-storey car parks,
1987–90 by *Jenkins & Marr*. It hides behind preserved buildings on Schoolhill and Upperkirkgate. The exposed N side is
granite-clad, the car parks mildly Postmodern with pedimented
gables. A two-level glass-vaulted mall zigzags through it, widening out into a domed atrium near the centre. Introspective
and disorientating, it makes a mockery of the historic street
pattern. Outside the George Street entrance, the monolithic
JOHN LEWIS store fills the E side from Loch Street to St
Andrew Street. Built as a department store for the Northern
Co-operative Society by *Covell Matthews & Partners*, 1967–70,
it was converted for John Lewis and connected to the new

shopping centre by a glazed link, reopening in 1989. Four storeys plus roof-top car park. Continuous shop windows at ground level, but each floor above is faced with vertically ribbed concrete, with just a narrow glazed strip at the top. The concrete facings have a triangular profile, with a short outward slope at the bottom and a longer inward slope above, and they wrap smoothly round the building's curved corners like giant caterpillar treads. The first floor overhangs the pavement to make a canopy, but the floors above are progressively set back, so the whole block is slightly pyramidal. It is by a long way the most distinctive and impressive contribution of the 1960s to the city centre. Opposite, Nos. 119–125 are the former CENTRAL BAKERY of Messrs A.B. Hutchison, 1899 by *Brown & Watt*. Five storeys, with shopfronts on the ground floor. Giant arches at each end enclose canted bay windows, with crowstepped gables above. Another canted bay in the middle has chimneystacks on either side, linked by a flying arch above the roof-line. (Turning E along St Andrew Street leads to Loch Street, and the C18 former GATEWAY of the demolished St Paul's Episcopal church. The church was by *Alexander Jaffray*, 1721, but the gateway is said to be *c.* 1750. A semicircular arch, flanked by blocked Doric pilasters. Originally on Gallowgate, it was re-erected here *c.* 1990, in meaningless isolation.)

GEORGE STREET N of St Andrew Street has mostly plain two- and three-storey granite houses with ground-floor shops, some perhaps of *c.* 1800. No. 207, 1905 by *Brown & Watt*, incorporates two splendid Greek Revival scrolls at attic level, possibly reused from the Unitarian church previously on the site. The neighbouring No. 213 – chaste classical with Doric pilasters and a pediment – would not look out of place in Union Street. It is by *William L. Henderson*, 1882, for the Aberdeen and Northern Friendly Society. The NW corner of John Street has a Free Style block by *Brown & Watt*, 1899, with a little domed turret. On the NE corner is the former North of Scotland Bank, 1883 by *Matthews & Mackenzie*. Rusticated pilaster strips at the angles, and giant Ionic columns framing the corner entrance. Nos. 261–265 on the W side are the former CHURCH OF SCOTLAND TRAINING COLLEGE (for training teachers), by *A. Marshall Mackenzie*, 1874. Round-arched on the ground floor, Gothic above. The octagonal corner tower ends in a short, cylindrical top stage with a conical roof. An addition fronting parallel Charlotte Street was completed in 1887 by *Matthews & Mackenzie*. It has crocketed pinnacles and a lead-covered spire, and above an archway, l., a statue of John Knox, originally on top of the George Street tower. Both buildings have been converted to flats. Back on George Street, on the NE corner of Spring Garden is the former TOWN AND COUNTY BANK, 1880, by *J.R. Mackenzie* (of *Mackenzie & McMillan*). Segmental-headed ground-floor windows treated as an arcade, with polished red granite columns between.

From here, Maberly Street leads W to the huge BROADFORD WORKS, a dense C19–C20 industrial complex of linen mills and

104, p. 212

Broadford Works.
Drawing by J. Bulloch, 1898

warehouses, like a citadel with its gates and towers. It started
in 1808 with a flax mill for Scott Brown & Co.; this was taken
over in 1811 by John Maberly, and in 1834 the site passed to
Richards & Co. A temporary stoppage in 1898 led to the formation of a joint stock company, followed by much new building in the early C20. At one time Aberdeen's largest employer,
the works eventually closed c. 2003. Buildings of all periods
survive, weaving sheds with sawtooth roofs filling the spaces
between multi-storey mills and stores. The earliest make up an
irregular N–S range, granite-built, occupying the centre of the
site opposite the Maberly Street gate. They are of three phases:
Scott Brown & Co.'s seven-bay OLD MILL of 1808 in the
middle, flanked on the S by the eight-bay SOUTH MILL of
c. 1820 and on the N by the fourteen-bay NEW MILL of
c. 1850–60 (the roofs were renewed in 1922–3, when brick
towers containing stairs and toilets were added on the W). All

are of fireproof construction, with brick-arched floors on cast-iron columns. The columns are generally cylindrical but in the Old Mill they are cruciform. This – the oldest surviving iron-framed mill in Scotland, and among the oldest anywhere – may have been designed by the Leeds engineers *Fenton, Murray, Wood & Co.*, who were certainly responsible for the original machinery. Just E of these early buildings, and parallel, are the NEW NORTH and SOUTH MILLS, a very large brick range by *Wilsons & Walker* with slight Baroque touches, dated 1914. Just SE of this is a multi-storey granite FLAX STORE, early C20, with three gables. The flax was hoisted in; workers' access was by narrow external walkways across the façade, reached by a cast-iron spiral stair. Also at the E end of the site are two distinctive round TOWERS: the earlier – brick with a flared top – was built *c.* 1918 for ventilation, and adapted in 1958 for applying latex linings to canvas fire hoses, an important part of Richards & Co.'s business; the other – concrete – was purpose-built *c.* 1961 for the same process. At the SW corner of the site, between the main gate and Ann Street, is an L-shaped granite building of *c.* 1860, reconstructed *c.* 1900, where heckling (the separation of long and short fibres) was carried out.

Opposite, on the S side of Maberly Street, is a mighty fortress-like four-storey flax store of 1911–12 by *Wilsons & Walker*, converted to flats by *Architectus* of Dundee, *c.* 1995, and renamed the BASTILLE BUILDING. Reinforced concrete with red brick exterior. The square-headed windows date from the conversion, the segmental-headed ones were originally taking-in doors. Access to each floor was by external gantries, now removed, reached by stairs and a lift in a pair of thin, round turrets at the corners. The crenellated projection on the roof contained the tank for the sprinkler system. Ann Street forms the W boundary of the site. It is overlooked by the brick and concrete WEAVING AND WEFT WINDING MILL, reconstructed 1912 by *Wilsons & Walker*, just E of which, and parallel, is the granite SEWING MILL of 1904 by *R. G. Wilson*. Ann Street leads to Hutcheon Street, the N boundary, where a high, square, brick chimneystack is said to be dated 1862. (Further W on Hutcheon Street are two late C19 cast-iron SEWER VENTILATORS.)

Back on GEORGE STREET, a few better-class early C19 houses were originally set back from the street, but their front gardens were later built on: an example survives behind the shops on the W side, immediately N of the Aberdeen Church of Christ (*see* Churches). On the NW corner of George Street and Hutcheon Street, the BUTCHERS ARMS is a Free Style pub of *c.* 1901 by *Brown & Watt*, with a corner dome. Extending W from here along Hutcheon Street were the slaughterhouse and the Hide and Tallow Market, both of 1908 by *John Rust*. Flats have taken their place, but two gabled bays of polychrome rock-faced granite survive, attached to the pub, and round the corner in Fraser Road, W, is a preserved entrance arch carved with the arms of the Flesher Trade. HUTCHEON STREET E of

George Street has HUTCHEON COURT and GREIG COURT
on the S side, 1973–7, the last and largest of the Council's
high-rise city-centre flats. There are one or two houses of the
very early C19 towards the N end of George Street, including
No. 595, with a Venetian window.

POWIS

A 1930s estate of mostly three-storey granite tenements with
concrete dressings, built over the grounds of Powis House (*see*
below). The layout is concentric: an outer, outward-looking loop
of tenements facing Powis Crescent and Bedford Avenue; an
inner, inward-looking loop facing Powis Circle.

POWIS COMMUNITY CENTRE, Powis Circle. Built as POWIS
HOUSE by *George Jaffray*, 1802–4, for Hugh Leslie. Classical,
harled with ashlar dressings. Giant angle pilasters, pediment
and a four-column Roman Doric porch with a Venetian
window above. This window has Gothic glazing bars and lights
a room with a plaster Gothic vault. Otherwise, the interior has
been thoroughly institutionalized.
ST MACHAR ACADEMY, St Machar Drive and Bedford Avenue.
1936, by *J. A. Ogg Allan*. Long, smooth front to St Machar
Drive, with flat-roofed centre and piended wings. Identical
horizontal windows all along, except near each end where the
staircases come.

ROSEMOUNT

A large inner suburb dominated by late C19 tenements, lying N
of the centre and W of the railway. Westburn Road marks its N
boundary; to the W of Craigie Loanings it gives way to the more
spacious West End. Scattered villas in their own grounds were
replaced by streets from the mid C19, and more intensive development followed the creation of Rosemount Viaduct in the 1880s.
Rosemount absorbed the settlement of Gilcomston – part industrial village, part rural retreat – which grew up along the Denburn
in the C18 and early C19; few traces of it now remain. Woolmanhill
lies at the SE corner of our area, presided over by C19 hospital
buildings.

CHURCHES

BON ACCORD FREE CHURCH, Rosemount Viaduct. By *Ellis &
Wilson*, 1895–6. An ambitious and impressive classical façade.
Asymmetrical, with a small pediment and flanking scrolls, and

Bon Accord Free Church.
Drawing, 1898

not one but two domed towers, standing boldly forward on each side. The l. one has an octagonal top stage, the r. one, much higher, ends in a balustraded belvedere. Between them, a tripartite doorway framed by Corinthian pilasters, with an elongated Diocletian window above. More carved ornament was originally intended. Completely preserved interior, with pulpit on w side and galleries on the other three. ORGAN, in an arched recess behind pulpit, added 1922–3. – STAINED GLASS. E window (brought from the former St Paul's U.P. church, *see* below), Suffer the little children, 1897. Ground level is 5 m. lower than the entrance from the Viaduct, so HALLS are accommodated under the church.

CITY CHURCH, Gilcomston Park (originally Gilcomston Park Baptist Church). By *Brown & Watt*, 1893–4. Grey Kemnay granite, with red dressings from Hill of Fare. Gabled front, framed by a pair of flat, gabled buttresses. Trios of small lancets flank the central door, with three large, stepped lancets above. Interior with gallery at entrance end. Wood-panelled ceiling on segmental transverse arches. Original seating removed. As with nearby St Mark and Bon Accord Free Church, the hall is under the church.

KINGDOM HALL OF JEHOVAH'S WITNESSES, Skene Street. Originally Christian Unitarian Church. *D. & J. R. McMillan*, designed 1898, but not built until 1905–6. Classical, though not at all conventional in its details. Two sheer, square, pyramid-roofed towers, with quoins and simple cyma recta cornices of an Arts and Crafts type. Each has a rusticated round-arched doorway, a three-light window above and a Diocletian window at the top with a curvy apron (all the mullions are unmoulded). The façade between the towers is framed by a pair of giant Doric pilasters with entablature. In the middle, a curious elongated tripartite window, again unmoulded, but flanked by Ionic pilasters for two-thirds of its height. These support a solid panel that cuts across the window with a little semicircular balcony. Above the main entablature is a further storey, pedimented, with a large arched window flanked by niches. Interior modernized and subdivided.

NEW LIFE INTERNATIONAL CHURCH, Leadside Road and Short Loanings. Apparently built as Northfield Mission Hall by *Charles Forrest Jun.*, *c.* 1938. It looks more like 1838: just a gabled box, with three lancets at each end, and otherwise mostly square-headed windows. Did Forrest re-erect a dismantled building from elsewhere?

Former ROSEMOUNT PARISH CHURCH, Caroline Place. By *William Smith*, opened 1877. Converted to secular use. Prominent on its elevated island site, it would be a landmark if the tower had received its intended spire. Cruciform, the nave with a very steeply pitched roof, the transepts lower. The stump of the tower is in the angle of nave and S transept. Single-storey vestibule across E end, with three stepped lancets above, framed by thin buttresses ending in pinnacles. Paired lancets down the sides. Each transept has a round window and a dormer, both with freestone tracery, originally to light galleries. Another round, traceried window in the W gable. Below this is a single-storey apsidal projection for session house, vestry, etc. Matching HALL, 1889–90 by *Jenkins & Marr*, attached at the NW corner.

Former RUTHERFORD FREE CHURCH, Rosemount Place and Loanhead Terrace. By *W. Henderson & Son*, opened 1870. Disused. Originally a gabled oblong with lancets, plus a tower and broach spire at the SW corner. The tower has diagonal buttresses and large louvred openings with timber tracery to the belfry stage. In 1896 *Ellis & Wilson* raised the side walls to accommodate galleries, and added transepts with windows of simple Y-tracery. FIRST WORLD WAR MEMORIAL, exterior of W wall, moved here from Rosemount Parish Church: a granite tablet with Celtic interlace. A subsidiary building, E, with lancets in threes, was presumably the 'neat and commodious' session house and vestry added by *Henderson* in 1875. It is now in secular use.

Former ST PAUL'S UNITED PRESBYTERIAN CHURCH, Rosemount Viaduct. By *Ellis & Wilson*, 1896–7. An odd design, hovering somewhere between Baroque and Baronial. Three-bay front with shaped gable, the higher central part flanked by tourelles with bulbous little domes. Similar gables, but lower, to the first bay of each return elevation. Converted to flats.

Former SKENE STREET CONGREGATIONAL CHURCH, Skene Street and Esslemont Avenue. By *Matthews & Mackenzie* (*A. Marshall Mackenzie*), 1885–6. Classical, rectangular, with a semicircular apse at the N end. The Skene Street front has four Ionic pilasters and a pediment, raised on a rock-faced basement and framed by narrow rock-faced strips at the corners. Two tiers of windows between the pilasters, with slender square columns as mullions. A single-storey former porch, l., was intended as the base of a domed tower. Side elevation and apse are squared rubble, but with an ashlar entablature and long windows with ashlar frames and cornices. Halls under the church. Converted to offices.

PUBLIC BUILDINGS

ABERDEEN GRAMMAR SCHOOL, Skene Street and Esslemont Avenue. After an abortive competition among invited architects in 1856, *James Matthews* was eventually appointed to replace the Grammar School's inadequate C18 building in Schoolhill. His Scottish Baronial design was exhibited in 1861 and the building opened in 1863. S-facing, it forms the middle part of today's much extended school. E-plan, with projecting central entrance bay and flanking wings. The wings have crowstepped gables and a single tourelle each at the inner corner. The entrance bay has rounded corners, corbelled out to make a square top stage with another crowstepped gable. A conical-roofed turret tucked into its l. side is just about the only asymmetrical element in the entire plan. The two-storey wings were originally classrooms, with the double-height Public School between, lit by long, square-headed windows and distinguished by a corbelled and battlemented parapet. Matthews provided two further short wings at either end, parallel to the front but set back, each with a tower in the re-entrant angle with the main block. Despite the general symmetry, the contrasting towers make a lively skyline. The l. one – square, becoming round, with a higher round turret ending in a dome – was intended as an observatory (Matthews's monogram is proudly carved on the dormer gable to its l.). The taller r. one has rounded corners, becoming square, and a corbelled and battlemented parapet, caphouse, and conical-roofed turret (the date 1631 and monogram PD on the s face record the valuable bequest of Dr Patrick Dun). These wings were extended at right angles in 1913 by *J. A. Ogg Allan*, who had added a N wing in 1905, all matching Matthews's work. The interior was almost completely destroyed by fire in 1986, and reconstructed behind preserved façades by *Robertsons* of Elgin, 1992, who introduced an additional floor. On a high plinth in front of the main building, bronze STATUE of Lord Byron (he attended the Grammar School in Schoolhill) by *Pittendrigh MacGillivray*. Modelled in 1914, cast in 1920, but not installed until 1923. LODGE on Skene Street, presumably by Matthews.

NE of the main building is the former WESTFIELD SCHOOL, by *A. Marshall Mackenzie*, 1898–1900, built as a Board School but taken over by the Grammar School and remodelled by *J. A. Ogg Allan* in the 1920s. Baronial, symmetrical, with conical-roofed tourelles flanking the entrance, and three short spirelets on the roof ridge. Just N of this on Esslemont Avenue is the former CHALMERS SCHOOL, now also absorbed into the Grammar School. It began as a charitable foundation 'for poor girls in Gilcomston', and looks the archetypal village school. S wing of 1866–7 by *William Henderson & Son*, Dec Gothic, with flowing tracery in the four-light gable windows and in the smaller windows of the s elevation. N addition, similar but simpler, perhaps by Mackenzie.

DENBURN HEALTH CENTRE, Rosemount Viaduct. 1969–76, by *Hugh Martin & Partners*. A large, multi-purpose development lying in the valley of the culverted Denburn. Two storeys of car-parking form a podium clad in vertically ribbed concrete panels. On top sits the health centre – a group of one- and two-storey linked blocks – around which the car park roof is treated as a piazza with low-walled enclosures and planting. It is a desolate space, abandoned to vandalism and decay. Ramps give access to it from the varied levels of the surrounding streets. Adjoining on the N, and also part of the scheme, is DENBURN COURT, a twenty-two-storey residential tower.

GILCOMSTOUN SCHOOL, Skene Street. The oldest part is by *J. R. Mackenzie*, opened 1878. Steep roofs and gabled dormers, but no particular style. At the E end, a mid-C20 addition with large E windows.

ROSEMOUNT COMMUNITY EDUCATION CENTRE, Rosemount Place and Esslemont Avenue. Handsome former Board School by *James Souttar*, opened 1887. Square, classical, with piended roof and deep eaves. Windows in groups, with Doric pilasters between. Top-lit central hall. SW additions, beginning with one by *J. A. Ogg Allan*, 1902.

SKENE SQUARE SCHOOL, Skene Square and Rosemount Place. Buildings of several phases. The school began in 1861 as a charitable institution, endowed by Dr John Brown and designed by *James Matthews*. Part of this may survive at the N end of the main block, embedded between W and E extensions of 1879 for the School Board by *Duncan McMillan*. The mildly

Tudor elevation to Skene Square looks right for 1879, but the end to Forbes Street has evidently been altered again since. The much larger classical extension fronting Rosemount Place was added in 1891–2. It originally had gables each side of the main entrance, but the l. one was lost when this side was raised a storey in the C20. The impressive central hall survives inside, top-lit and galleried. Finally, N, a completely separate three-storey block of 1912 with Baroque details.

VICTORIA PARK, Westburn Road, between Argyll Place and Watson Street. Aberdeen's first suburban park, laid out in 1872. Simple bargeboarded Gothic LODGE on Watson Street. In the centre, columnar FOUNTAIN of multicoloured granite with chunky, angular Greek Revival details. Designed in 1878 by *J. B. Pirie* for Union Terrace Gardens, but erected here instead in 1881. It was given and executed by the Master Masons' Association, whose members' monograms are inscribed on it.

WOOLMANHILL HOSPITAL, Woolmanhill. The earliest part is the s block, built 1832–40 as the INFIRMARY by *Archibald Simpson*. It is both a little-altered survival of a major early C19 hospital, and the noblest Neoclassical public building in Aberdeen. A mid-C18 infirmary previously stood on the site. Simpson's majestic three-storey replacement has an H-plan and a low hemispherical dome over the centre. Thirteen-bay s front, with horizontally channelled rustication to the ground floor and a centrepiece of six Doric pilasters and pediment (the cornice extends round the entire block). On the ground floor and between the pilasters the windows are unmoulded; elsewhere they have architraves and, on the first floor of the wings, consoled cornices. The main entrance was originally on this side, but the central doors were seamlessly transformed into windows in the 1890s. E and W fronts simpler, each breaking forward in the centre with four Doric pilasters and a pediment. N front simpler again, and altered in 1893–4 when *William Kelly* inserted a single-storey kitchen block between the wings. At the same time he converted the INTERIOR to house the admissions department, nurses' home, etc. However, the W–E corridor of Simpson's plan survives on each floor, with NW and NE staircases in their original positions. In the middle of the N side on the ground floor is Simpson's MANAGERS' HALL, a dignified classical room with shallow coffered ceiling, pilasters and a pair of Roman Doric columns flanking the door (the opposite pair has been removed). On the top floor, the dome covers a rotunda which was the original operating theatre, presumably with tiered seating for students, now subdivided. At the foot of the NE stair, MEMORIAL to Alexander Kilgour, †1874: a marble relief portrait by *J. Hutchison*, erected *c.* 1892.

N of the Infirmary is a long, triangular court enclosed by two late C19 ranges, W and E, projected in 1887 to commemorate Queen Victoria's Golden Jubilee. Granite-faced, with fenestration which is more or less Georgian, they make a very satisfactory adjunct to Simpson's work. First came the four-storey

Surgical and Pathology Departments (w), opened in 1892 and extending along Spa Street. By *H. Saxon Snell & Son* of London, with *W. & J. Smith & Kelly* of Aberdeen. The inner side has gabled projections with balconies between, originally open but glazed since 1927. The pathology block at the n end also housed the hospital laundry, its distinctive timber-framed top floor serving as a drying loft. Between the s end and Spa Street, a four-storey square tower containing operating theatres was added in 1910–11 by *Kelly & Nicol*. Oddly Gothic-looking diagonal buttresses are pierced at each floor by openings which must have given access to narrow balconies, presumably for window cleaning. s is the boiler house, with a high brick chimney. The e range, overlooking Woolmanhill, is the Medical Block by *W. & J. Smith & Kelly*, dated 1896. Four-storey centre with three-storey wings, the s one ending in a semicircular bow. Quite plain except for the ground-floor openings of the bow, flanked by Doric demi-columns. The side overlooking the central court has Italianate touches and more glazed-in balconies. Next to the gap between the e wing and the Simpson building is the Porter's Lodge, also *Simpson*, moved here in the 1890s from its original position further s. Channelled rustication, to match the main building.

DESCRIPTION

The best place to start is at the s end of Rosemount Viaduct, a mighty elevated roadway by the Burgh Surveyor *William Boulton*, 1884–5, crossing the steep-sided ravine of the Denburn n of Skene Terrace. It was planned along with the Denburn Viaduct (*see* p. 167) to link the growing n suburb with the city centre. Only a single segmental skew arch over Upper Denburn is visible, brick with granite facings. The rest is concealed by embankments and flanking buildings.

Rosemount's most interesting Tenements line the Viaduct's grand uphill sweep. They are higher than usual for Aberdeen: four and five storeys above street level, with shops on the ground floor, but dropping a further two storeys below the street at the Upper Denburn arch. Best of all is the first block, Nos. 1–27 (s side up to Skene Street). Of 1897–9 by *Brown & Watt*, it is the only one that bears comparison with its Edinburgh and Glasgow contemporaries. Five storeys, though the top one is really a mansard, with dormer windows and wall-head chimneys making a lively skyline. Rounded corner at the acute angle with Skene Terrace, corbelled out and becoming polygonal higher up, before ending with a tall conical roof. Concave façade to the Viaduct, rippling with shallow canted bays topped by curious balustrades: the balusters have the usual vase-like silhouette, but they are flat, not cylindrical. Higher up on this side, between Upper Denburn and the Bon Accord Church (*see* above), a succession of four-storey-plus-attic blocks, beginning with a polygonal domed turret at the s end. The most northerly of this group is dated 1894. Gilcomston Park, leading off on the E, was laid out before the Viaduct in 1871. Of this date must be the three houses on its N side, including the unusually elaborate Park House at No. 34, with column mullions and foliage capitals to the ground-floor bay windows. Back on the Viaduct, Nos. 96–120 between Gilcomston Park and Baker Street are of 1887 by *James Souttar*. Baronial, with Gothic touches, in rock-faced Syllavethy granite with bands of Kemnay.

At this point Rosemount Viaduct becomes SOUTH MOUNT STREET, on the W side of which is ROSEMOUNT SQUARE: municipal flats by the *Aberdeen City Architect's Dept* (the job architect is said to have been *Leo Durnin*), designed in 1938 but not completed until 1948 (their wartime origins are reflected in the provision of basement air raid shelters). One of a number of 1930s schemes in British cities (e.g. Quarry Hill, Leeds) that show the influence of recent Viennese and German public housing. A four-storey quadrangle, curved at the S end to make an elongated D, with archways W, S and E leading to an inner courtyard. Granite-faced – said to be the last such tenement block erected in Aberdeen – except for the prefabricated lintels, sills and other dressings, and the concrete balconies overlooking the courtyard. The smooth, sheer walls are punctured by rows of identical, horizontal windows. Decorative mouldings are eschewed but over the S and E archways are excellent figurative relief carvings by *T. B. Huxley-Jones*, representing those Aberdeen perennials, Wind and Rain. (Comparable housing of the 1930s by the City Architect nearby in Short Loanings, W, this time incorporated into a traditional street terrace.)

South Mount Street continues N of Rosemount Place as MOUNT STREET, where the single-storey No. 1A is worth a glance. Built for himself by the granite master *James Wright*, 1860. A remarkably self-important front, despite its modest size: all of Peterhead granite, partly rock-faced, but with polished and channelled dressings round the windows and door, and incised anthemion and palmette ornament on the lintels. The *Aberdeen Journal* saw it and recognized the architectural potential of the distinctive pink stone: 'Considering the very durable nature of this material, and that it is at the same time ornamental, it is likely we may see it used frequently in our buildings'. On the N side of ROSEMOUNT PLACE, just E of Mount Street, is ROSEMOUNT HOUSE. In existence by 1810, it gave its name to the surrounding area. It is a survivor of the type of detached suburban villa that gave way to denser tenements in the late C19: eventually its grounds were built on, and it is now hidden behind No. 30 and reached by a pend. Two storeys and three bays, extended later to make a short terrace. Handsome doorcase with fanlight and Doric columns.

Rosemount Place W of Mount Street is lined with late C19 tenements, and there are many more (plus some houses) in streets branching off on either side. The better-quality ones

tend to be concentrated at the top of the hill and around
Victoria Park. An uphill walk of 750 m. brings us to ARGYLL
PLACE, overlooking the park from the w, which has particularly attractive houses of 1884–5 by *Pirie & Clyne*: pink and
grey granite, with quirky Greek Revival details to the doorways
and eye-catching sunflower finials on the prominent dormers.
The Grammar School provides another leafy focus for affluent
housing, with grander tenements at the s end of ESSLEMONT
AVENUE (railed basement areas) and in WHITEHALL PLACE
(canted bay windows), and even a few large villas in BELGRAVE
TERRACE (No. 42, with Baronial touches, is by *John Rust*,
1896; No. 44, *W. & J. Smith and Kelly*, 1887; and No. 46, *Ellis
& Wilson*, 1886). More impressive than the architecture of
individual houses, however, is the consistency and relative
completeness of the densely built-up whole.

A few early C19 houses – relics of the non-industrial aspect of
Gilcomston – cluster round the Denburn, N and E of the
former Skene Street Congregational Church (*see* Churches).
On Skene Street itself, SKENE PLACE is a short two-storey
terrace of four houses, the middle two doors united under a
segmental arch, with the name displayed on the parapet above.
Down in the hollow behind is MACKIE PLACE, where Nos. 4
and 5 are a small and quite delightful semi-detached pair of
c. 1812. They have quoins and bell-shaped pediments, and
paired front doors on the *piano nobile*, reached by curving
forestairs. No. 3, E, was evidently similar, but has been rendered and extended. Finally, just W of the Grammar School
but still in Skene Street, is CARDEN HOUSE: a simple late-C18
or early C19 house, livened up with fancy gabled dormers,
probably in the late C19.

WESTBURN PARK

The park was formed in 1901 out of the grounds of WESTBURN
HOUSE, a small mansion of 1839 by *Archibald Simpson*. Single-
storey stuccoed brick on a granite plinth, with a four-column
Roman Doric portico and pediment on the W entrance front.
The s side has a central bow, hidden by a huge early C20 cast-
iron veranda, added when the house became the park's refreshment room.

ROYAL CORNHILL HOSPITAL, Westburn Road. *Mackie Ramsay
& Taylor*, from 1988. A determinedly informal and non-
institutional-looking psychiatric hospital. Predominantly
single-storey buildings, linked together around small, open-
ended courtyards and interspersed with trees. Red tiled roofs,
varied window shapes and walls of render and artificial stone
give the feel of a bungalow suburb. The contrast with the
former Victorian hospital buildings, which survive cheek by
jowl, could not be greater. Immediately N is the disused C19

and early C20 Lunatic Asylum. Originally built by *Archibald Simpson*, 1819–22; extended by him, 1845–6; further extended by *William Ramage*, 1856; and again by *J. & W. Smith* from 1870; it is difficult to tell what, if anything, survives from these earlier phases. A major remodelling was carried out from 1899 by *William Kelly*, and there were further changes later. Axial plan, originally bi-partite (the W side has been demolished) with minimal classical details. N of the Asylum is the former Hospital Division, now the UPPER OLD HOSPITAL, of 1893–6 by *Kelly*. Here the details include mullioned-and-transomed bay windows. W of the Upper Old Hospital, a red granite OBELISK of 1830 by *John Smith*, originally erected in St Nicholas's churchyard along with Smith's façade (*see* p. 126) as a memorial to the Asylum's benefactor, John Forbes of Newe. It was moved here *c.* 1838. *Ramage*'s Italianate ASYLUM LODGE of 1856 is No. 32 Westburn Road; a second LODGE by *Kelly* dated 1899 is on Cornhill Road. ELMHILL HOUSE, 0.25 km. NW of the new hospital in May Baird Avenue, is also by *Ramage*, of 1860–2. Formerly part of the Asylum, but intended for better-off private patients; now flats. Handsome Italianate S front, with pedimented centre and a square tower and semicircular bow at each end.

Nos. 37 and 39 WESTBURN ROAD, a dignified pair of granite ashlar semis at the W corner of Mount Street, were originally built near Guild Street as the offices of the Aberdeen Gas Light Co. in or after 1824. In 1865 the site was needed in connection with the Denburn railway scheme, and the offices were dismantled and re-erected here as houses. The curvilinear gables and dormers seem to date from the rebuilding.

INNER DISTRICTS: WEST

HOLBURN AND GREAT WESTERN ROAD

Holburn, immediately S of the W end of Union Street, is the starting point for the major thoroughfare of Great Western Road.

CHURCHES

HOLBURN GOSPEL HALL, Holburn Street. *Alexander Brown*, 1891. Originally a mission hall of Holburn Free Church (when it was still in Bon Accord Terrace). Aberdeen-bond granite, with a round-arched window flanked by two circular ones in the gable.

HOLBURN WEST CHURCH (originally Holburn Free Church), Great Western Road and Ashley Park Drive. *Brown & Watt*, 1893. Conventional late C19 Gothic at first glance but much more idiosyncratic on closer inspection. The gabled S front has

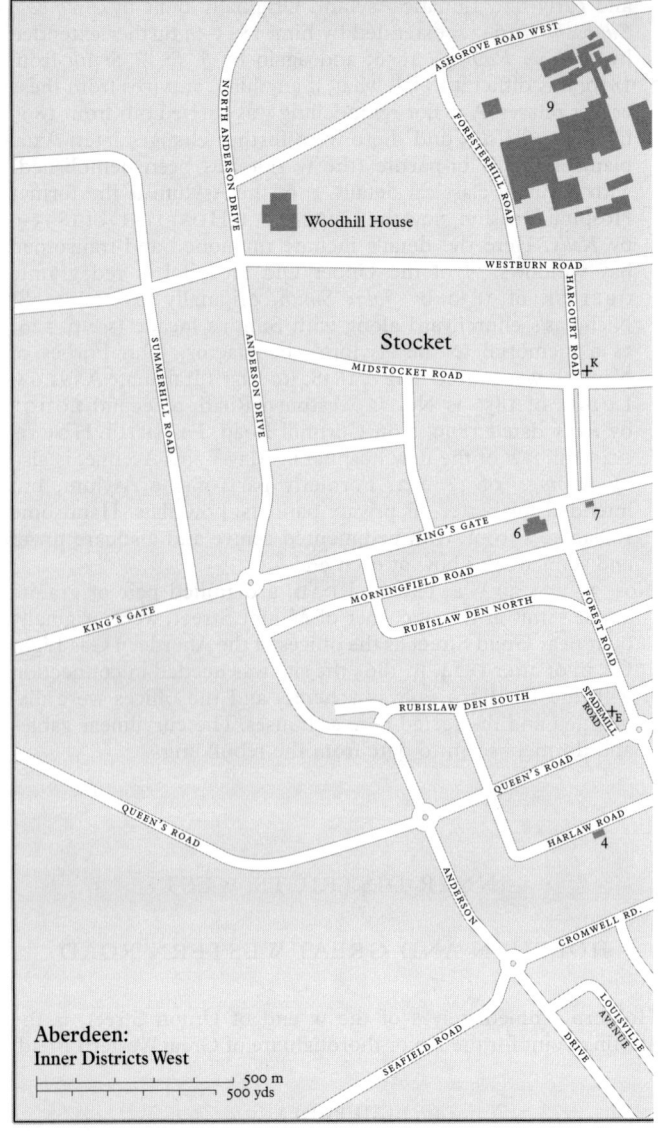

Aberdeen:
Inner Districts West

500 m
500 yds

A   Holborn West Church
B   St Nicholas United Presbyterian
    Church (former)
C   Holburn Gospel Hall
D   Carden Place U.P. Church
    (former)
E   Christian Community
F   Queen's Cross Church
G   Rubislaw Parish Church
H   St Mary (Episcopal)
J   Beechgrove Church
K   Midstocket Parish Church

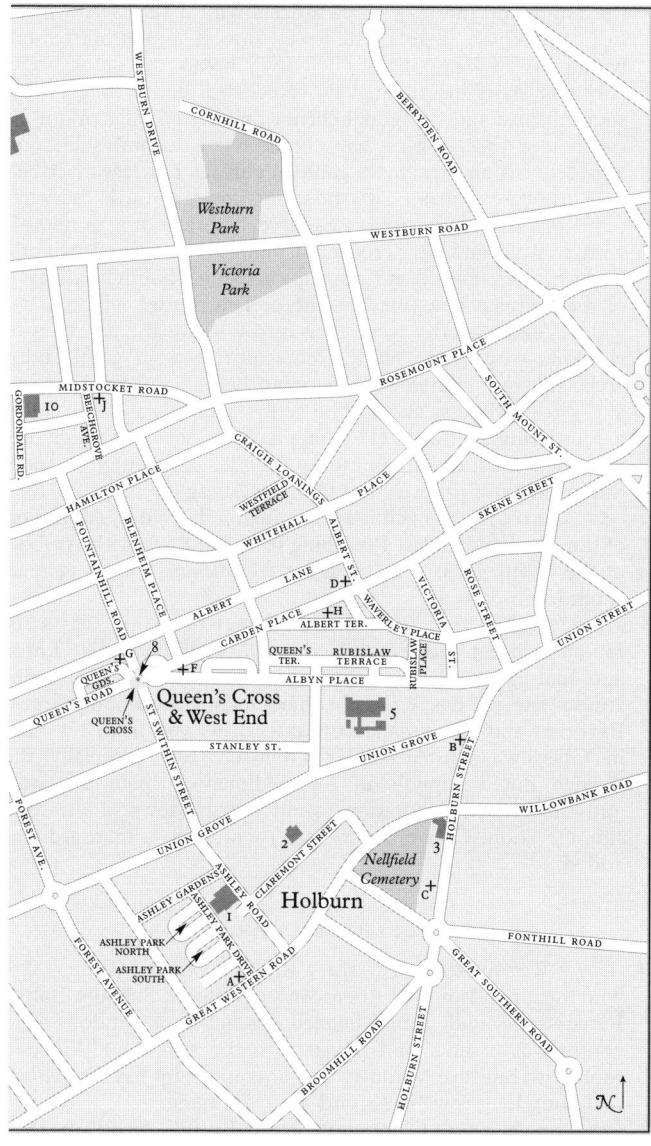

1   Ashley Road School
2   Nazareth House
3   New Trinity Hall
4   Aberdeen Grammar Rugby
    Club Pavilion
5   Harlaw Academy
6   Morningfield Hospital
    (former)
7   Rubislaw School (former)
8   Statue of Queen Victoria
9   Foresterhill Medical Campus
10 Mile End School

the Dunblane motif of three lancets with a vesica above. To its r. is a lofty SE steeple. The tower, smooth and unbuttressed, with pairs of long, slit-like windows below the clock stage, contains stairs to the gallery. Recessed belfry stage, with soaring spire and octagonal corner pinnacles. Balancing it on the l. is a cross-gabled bay containing a second stair, and between this and the main gable, a curious buttress inscribed with the date. It has no set-offs, but slopes towards the wall-plane in a barely perceptible S-curve, before ending in mid-air with a gable and tiny crocketed pinnacle. A second, slightly lower buttress joins it at right angles, rising from the wall-head of the staircase bay. Interior with arched timber ceiling and s gallery (side galleries were envisaged – hence the two tiers of windows – but never built). Recess at N end – a giant Tudor arch, stilted – containing the organ behind a fretted screen, and a rose window above. The central pulpit was removed in a reordering of 2003. On either side of the arch, high up, darkened MURALS in Giottesque style, apparently c. 1905: Suffer the little children and Christ washing the disciples' feet. – STAINED GLASS. s window, Crucifixion flanked by Adoration of the Magi and Christ Preaching from the Boat, with symbols of the Evangelists, 1923 by *Douglas Strachan*. HALLS at rear, extended 1962.

Former ST NICHOLAS UNITED PRESBYTERIAN CHURCH, Holburn Street and Union Grove. *Ellis & Wilson*, 1887. Large and hall-like, set back behind a forecourt on a prominent corner site. It has Wilson's characteristic fusion of Greek, Egyptian and Renaissance ornament, derived from his time in Glasgow with Alexander Thomson. See especially the strange fluted capitals of the pedimented main doorway, and the incised decoration round the windows of the long side elevation. Converted to flats 1978, when a mansard was added.

PUBLIC BUILDINGS

ASHLEY ROAD SCHOOL, Ashley Road. *Jenkins & Marr*, 1887. The most handsome of Aberdeen's C19 Board Schools. Italian Renaissance, with round-headed ground-floor windows in a continuous arcade, and pilasters to the first floor. Piended roofs with bullseye windows. C20 alterations by *J. A. Ogg Allan*, including long rows of second-floor dormers.

NAZARETH HOUSE, Claremont Street. By *Ellis & Wilson*, 1871 with later additions. A Roman Catholic charitable institution, originally run by nuns. It housed destitute children, the elderly poor and an 'industrial school' for girls. The confined site exaggerates its forbidding appearance: approached from the street through a windowless lodge, relieved only by a Gothic gable carved with the date, the main building rears up quite suddenly. Three storeys, with advancing gabled wings at each end and the entrance in a narrow, tower-like central projection under a short spire. Statue of the Virgin and Child in a canopied niche high up. Some of the windows are Gothic, the rounded corners and heavy parapet more Baronial. NW wing dated 1890 and larger NE wing said to be 1900, but both matching the original part. Main stairs immediately behind the entrance, and beyond them on axis the CHAPEL, forming a rear wing. Gothic, cruciform, with pink granite arcades between nave and aisles, some of the octagonal piers curiously flattened. It was enlarged in 1897, a plausible date for the arcades, transepts and square chancel. – STAINED GLASS. Late C19, with figures of saints. Abutting the W boundary wall of the site, a range of workshops imaginatively transformed into a soup kitchen by *David Murray Associates*, 1992. At its S end, the now roofless MORTUARY with Gothic gable.

NELLFIELD CEMETERY, Great Western Road. A commercial venture by one William Wood, laid out in 1834 with central and perimeter paths, and graves in straight rows. Extended SW *c.* 1874, over the site of Nellfield House and its grounds. LODGE by *James Souttar*, 1881: Baronial, with an open-sided porch in the angle of the two wings, on which a conical-roofed tower sits like a rocket. Several MONUMENTS of interest. Opposite the entrance, against the SE wall, the author William Alexander, †1894: a bronze bust by *Pittendrigh MacGillivray* in a classical granite niche. Further SW on the same wall, John Thomson Rennie, †1878, a pedimented aedicule with the kind of Thomsonian Greek details found in the work of *J. B. Pirie* and *Ellis & Wilson*. Opposite, against the entrance wall, Alexander MacDonald, †1860, founder of the Aberdeen granite polishing industry, commissioned by his son in 1871, with a bronze relief portrait by *George Anderson Lawson*.

NEW TRINITY HALL, Holburn Street and Great Western Road. *Mackie Ramsay & Taylor*, 1966. Headquarters of the Seven Incorporated Trades of Aberdeen, and a surprisingly modish design for so venerable a body, although it reuses elements from the old hall in Union Street (*see* p. 152). The ground floor is taken up by shops, except for the ceremonial entrance at the canted corner, which leads via a broad axial stair to the first-floor committee and function rooms. The main hall is expressed externally as a rectangular box, its long axis bisecting the acute angle of the plan, projecting over the entrance to form a porte cochère. It has Gothic windows, copied from the Union Street building to receive its C19 stained glass. The rest of the first floor, which also overhangs the pavement, is mostly either harled or concrete-clad with narrow clearstorey strips, so maximizing the internal wall space for the Trades' remarkable collection of paintings and artefacts. – STAINED GLASS. In the main hall, seven two-light windows, each with the arms of a Trade alongside a relevant biblical or historical scene. The Hammermen's window, 1878, is by *Messrs Kier* of Glasgow; the rest, 1877, are by *Stephen Adam* of *Adam & Small*. Heraldic glass from the old building is displayed on the landing, artificially lit, along with fragments of a C17 carved LINTEL from the gateway of the former house of the Trinity Friars, near the present Trinity Street. It commemorates the gift of the friary buildings by Dr William Guild in 1633, to serve as the first Trades hall.

DESCRIPTION

HOLBURN STREET connects Union Street with the Bridge of Dee. Laid out according to *Charles Abercrombie*'s plan (*see* Introduction) and completed *c.* 1807–8, it was the essential final link in Aberdeen's new road system, but there was no attempt to give it architectural coherence in the manner of Union Street or King Street. At the N end, late C19 and early C20 tenements give an urban character. Nos. 26–38, W, are a handsome pilastered block of 1887 by *Matthews & Mackenzie*. UNION GROVE leads W from here, lined with late C19 tenements and modern variations on the same theme. No. 163 Holburn Street is TALISMAN HOUSE, a very large L-shaped office block by *Jenkins & Marr*, 2000, with roofs that describe long, wave-like curves.

Architecturally, the major artery is the old Deeside turnpike road, known since 1883 as GREAT WESTERN ROAD. It leads SW from New Trinity Hall (*see* above). Until the 1870s it was fringed with widely spaced villas in extensive grounds, but denser housing of good quality spread along both sides in the late C19, turning it into a handsome boulevard. Behind the later houses a few earlier villas survive, shorn of their grounds. Near the Holburn Street end is the best, the yellow freestone GRANTON LODGE. It was built *c.* 1829 for John Ross of Grenada, the fruits of a career as a West Indian sugar planter. Now sandwiched between tenements and approached side-on from Great Western Place, it originally faced the main road across a garden and carriage drive. Square, with a canted bay facing W, and consoled cornices to the ground-floor windows. Further W, in Ashley Road, is FRIENDSHIP FARMHOUSE, perhaps incorporating parts of a building of *c.* 1798. Parallel Ashley Park Drive leads N from Holburn West Church to early C19 ASHLEY HOUSE, of granite rubble with red granite margins to the windows. During and after the First World War its former grounds were laid out for housing by *D. & J. R. McMillan*, creating ASHLEY GARDENS and ASHLEY PARK NORTH and SOUTH, which they lined with pleasant cottage-style houses for Northern Garden Suburbs Ltd.

Beyond Holburn West Church, the houses on Great Western Road become grander, and at the junctions with cross streets there are occasional turrets and other Baronial details (for instance No. 327, at the corner of Salisbury Terrace; more such villas are on the W side of Salisbury Terrace itself). In FOREST AVENUE, N, Nos. 32 and 34 are a curious pair of square, early C20 semis. Each has a flat-topped gable on three sides, and piended corners, so that the roofs above this level are octagonal. Further W again, in Louisville Avenue, the single-storey-plus-attic LOUISVILLE was apparently in existence by 1804. *A. & W. Reid & Mackenzie* made additions in 1859, a possible date for the dressed granite façade: two canted bays with a pair of Doric columns between, united under a continuous cornice and blocking course. Near its w end, Great Western Road is intersected by the early c20 ring road, ANDERSON DRIVE. For this, and Great Western Road w of Anderson Drive, *see* Mannofield, p. 284.

QUEEN'S CROSS AND WEST END

The Lands of Rubislaw, stretching w from the w end of Union Street for over 2 km., became Aberdeen's most prestigious residential district during the c19. At first, under the proprietorship of James Skene of Rubislaw (1775–1864), building progressed only slowly, but by mid-century the town was pushing westward. Sir Alexander Anderson, dynamic lawyer and man of business, bought the estate in 1860, and in 1874 it was acquired by the City of Aberdeen Land Association, set up by Anderson and others to feu land for suburban house-building. Queen's Road and its eastward continuation Carden Place–Carden Terrace (the old Skene turnpike road) form the principal thoroughfare, dead straight for almost 2 km., with Albyn Place making a southern spur to connect with the w end of Union Street. They are lined with imposing villas and terraces. Some of the secondary streets N and S have villas scarcely less grand, but the housing here is on the whole simpler. A cluster of exceptionally ambitious churches was built to serve this affluent community.

CHURCHES

Former CARDEN PLACE UNITED PRESBYTERIAN CHURCH, Carden Place and Albert Street. 1880–2, by *Ellis & Wilson*. Cruciform, Gothic, the S end flanked by a high tower with short spire, r., and a lower tower with saddleback roof, l. Short transepts and small N apse, with attached building behind containing session rooms, vestry, etc. The whole church is very lofty, and made more so by being raised above a basement hall. Geometric freestone tracery in transept and aisle windows, and in the central S window, which is flanked by lancets. Twin-arched S door under a gabled porch, with canopies either side for (non-existent) statues, reached by a rather secular-looking branched stair of two curving flights. – STAINED GLASS. 1882, by *James Ballantine & Son*. Religious texts, with trees, fruits and flowers mentioned in the Bible. Interior subdivided and converted to offices.

CHRISTIAN COMMUNITY, Spademill Road. *Camphill Architects*, 1991. W end flanked by single-storey wings set at an angle. Several non-rectilinear windows – characteristic of the architects' Rudolf Steiner-inspired work.

QUEEN'S CROSS CHURCH (originally Queen's Cross Free
  Church), Carden Place and Albyn Place. An outstanding work
  by *John Bridgeford Pirie* of *Pirie & Clyne*, and one of the most
  singular churches of its date in Scotland. Built 1879–81, dwarfing the recently completed Rubislaw Church opposite (*see*
  below), it glories in its splendid corner site. The components
  – rectangular nave and shallow transepts with galleries on three
  sides, plus a high SW steeple – are conventional enough, but
  the lofty proportions and soaring verticality are thrilling, and
  the mix of early French and Dec Gothic is laced with idiosyncrasies. The basement has a slight batter, which with the exaggerated splaying of the sills gives a general sense of upward

Queen's Cross Church.
Drawing by J.B. Pirie, *c.* 1880

thrust. There are numerous peculiar details: the dripmould over the big Geometric W window, for instance, has label stops like seahorse tails; the same motif recurs inside, as do the trumpet-mouth paterae in the interstices of the tracery and elsewhere; the gabled W porch has two orders, the inner colonnettes of normal proportions, the outer ones hugely fat and squat; what appears to be a cross on the crowstepped W gable is in fact a five-pointed star; and so on. Most extraordinary of all is the open porch at the E end of the Albyn Place side, added by Pirie in 1888, with what was originally an organ chamber above. Its tympanum is composed of almost vertical voussoirs tied together by scroll-shaped joggles, their soffits forming a succession of wave shapes. The outer pair rest on brackets of unfathomable derivation – animal? vegetable? – and the gable above has a similarly bizarre finial and small, two-light opening. The mutation of organic forms into abstract decoration brings to mind late C19 Barcelona. 'Although there may be differences of opinion regarding the precise value of the work,' declared the Aberdeen Ecclesiological Society, 'all competent judges must acknowledge its originality and expressiveness, and recognise the refinement with which all points of accentuation are treated.' The geometry of the steeple is fascinating. The soaring angle buttresses of the tower have no set-offs. At ground level they die into elongated pyramids of masonry; at the top, squinches transform them into octagonal pinnacles. The short, conical spire rests on an open colonnade so compressed that the shafts are barely taller than the capitals.

INTERIOR sadly much altered. Immensely lofty nave (now without pews) with arcades on slender cast-iron columns. The elaborate pulpit and inward-facing stalls at the E end have been removed, and some of the STALLS repositioned against the E wall. Arched and panelled nave CEILING of polished wood with gilt stars, but the rest of the joinery – vestibule, gallery stairs and inner doors, with much turned decoration and Pirie's ubiquitous trumpet-mouth motif – is all now painted. Original PEWS survive in the gallery, with bench-ends in the form of seahorse tails. – ORGAN. Moved from its 1888 position to the W gallery in 1957, hiding the W window. Pirie's amazing Greek-Gothic case does not survive. – STAINED GLASS. E window, Noah's Ark surrounded by symbols of Providence, *Douglas Strachan*, 1920. Gallery, N side, second from W, the Three Maries at the Tomb, *A. L. Moore*, c. 1910; third from W, Christ sowing and an angel reaping, *A. Ballantine & Gardiner*, c. 1901; S side, second from W, Christ in the house of Martha and Mary, *Strachan*, 1904; third from W, two angels with the Lamb of God, c. 1887. Under the S gallery, E end, a small window by *Vanessa Thoms Oyama*, 1980; a corresponding window by the same artist, 1989, is under the N gallery. SESSION HOUSE and HALLS attached at E end, extended 1937–9 by *J. A. Ogg Allan*.

RUBISLAW PARISH CHURCH, Queen's Gardens. *J. R. Mackenzie*, 1875. Dec Gothic, 'with a bold, but attractive combination of the old Scottish'. Its pinkish Elgin freestone makes it stand out. Nave plus aisles, with shallow transepts and a round apse. Tall SE clock tower – part of the original design, but not completed until 1878 by *Mackenzie & McMillan* – with gables, a lead-covered pyramid roof and octagonal corner turrets with spirelets. Each aisle bay has a crowstepped cross-gable, and the s entrance front and transept gables are crowstepped too. Halfway up the s front is a trefoil-headed blind arcade, with a corbelled and battlemented parapet over, which continues round the tower. Wheel windows in the gables, two-light Dec tracery in aisles and tower. Unusually well-preserved interior, complete with pews. Cast-iron nave arcades with foliage capitals, and timber colonnettes in the spandrels supporting the roof trusses. In 1877–8 galleries were added in the transepts and the organ gallery extended across the s end. The fronts of the transept galleries are in line with the nave arcades, so they cut across the aisles, the space between gallery and aisle ceiling filled with timber arcading. Extending right across the chancel arch on the N side of the crossing is the timber PULPIT, an octagonal Gothic canopy flanked by trios of gabled Gothic arches, making an elaborate screen. Beyond it is the apse, mysteriously hidden like the Holy of Holies, though it actually serves no liturgical purpose. – ORGAN, 1889–90 by *Henry Willis*, enlarged 1899. – COMMUNION TABLE, oak, late Gothic, 1893, and eagle LECTERN, 1912, both by *A. Marshall Mackenzie*. – STAINED GLASS. Directly facing each other across the nave, two windows by *Douglas Strachan* from opposite ends of his career: W, Crucifixion, with Moses and the brazen serpent, 1901–2; E, the Supper at Emmaus, 1940s, lighter and brighter, without the dark stippling of the earlier window. In the apse, floral designs in Aesthetic taste, 1901–2 by *John Whyte*. HALL, N, added 1877–9 by *Mackenzie & McMillan*.

ST MARY (Episcopal), Carden Place and Albert Terrace. 1862–4. Scottish-Italian Gothic, to a 'general plan and design' by the incumbent, the *Rev. F. G. Lee*, with professional assistance from *Alexander Ellis*. The first impression is of colour, for among the monochrome surrounding streets this is a startling essay in structural polychromy: walls of squared pink and grey granite rubble, with tracery, voussoirs and other dressings of contrasting red Turriff and orangey-yellow Kenmuir freestone, and dark grey granite (from an early date it was popularly known as the Tartan Kirkie). The rectangular, aisleless nave has a steeply pitched roof with coloured slates in fish-scale patterns. W front with crowstepped gable, flat buttresses and three round windows with plate tracery above a gabled porch. Pairs of lancets alternate with round windows down the sides; cross-gables at the E end make quasi-transepts, with larger round windows over groups of lancets, and wrought-iron corner finials. There was originally a flèche over the crossing. All the windows are high up, with big expanses of blank wall below. The polygonal apse with gables and small rose windows to each face was completely rebuilt and simplified after war damage by *John Alistair Ross*, 1950–2. W porch leads to an inner doorway with capitals naturalistically carved with lilies by *Brodie*.

Interior walls of the same granite rubble as the exterior, with the same coloured dressings, but here red brick is added to the palette. Open timber roof with arched trusses; diagonal trusses intersect over the crossing. It is extremely high and picked out in colour. The choir is a raised platform projecting W from the polychrome chancel arch, enclosed by a dwarf screen of granite columns with stone coping and latticework wooden GATES. The chancel is higher again. Apart from the wooden Gothic communion rail, dated 1923, its furnishings are post-war: granite ALTAR (the original ALTAR PAINTING is now in the crypt: a triptych of the Crucifixion by *N. H. J. Westlake*, 1864), AUMBRY, PISCINA and wooden SEDILIA. – FONT. At W end of nave. Gothic, granite, octagonal. – PULPIT. Wood, with chunky trefoil-headed arches. – CLERGY STALLS. 1913 by *William Kelly*, carved with Christ and St Thomas, and Job, after models by *William Banbury*. – ROOD and ROOD BEAM. Polychrome wood. – CHAMBER ORGAN. By *Samuel Green* of London, 1778. – MURAL. N wall of nave, W end, a monumental painting of the Annunciation by *Allan Sutherland*, 1908, on canvas stuck to the wall. A series of six was intended, but the other panels remain empty. Attached to the S side of the church, matching pavilion-roofed VESTRY and PARISH ROOM, added 1905–6 by *Arthur Clyne*. Rounded corners corbelled out to become square. Three-sided S apse with crowstepped gables.

PUBLIC BUILDINGS

ABERDEEN GRAMMAR RUGBY CLUB, Harlaw Road. *J. A. Ogg Allan*, 1923–4. Single-storey classical pavilion with colonnaded centre and piended, tiled roof with dormers. This being Aberdeen, the Roman Doric columns are granite monoliths.

HARLAW ACADEMY, Albyn Place. The impressive central block of 1837–40 is by *Archibald Simpson*, built as a charitable institution for orphan girls at the expense of Mrs Elmslie. Pedimented ends (originally dining room and schoolroom, with dormitories over) flank the pilastered middle part (administrative and domestic, with more dormitories above). In 1891–2 it was converted to a school by *W. & J. Smith & Kelly*. On either side, set well forward, are two former villas. The E one, in existence by 1828, has a four-columned Greek Doric portico; the W one, later, is similar, but the portico is Tuscan. From 1937, *J. A. Ogg Allan* built linking blocks between the villas and the former institution, absorbing them into a more or less symmetrical, unified composition.

Former MORNINGFIELD HOSPITAL, Morningfield Road and King's Gate. *William Henderson & Son*, 1883–4; additions and alterations by *W. & J. Smith & Kelly*, 1902. For incurables. Quite plain, with gabled centre and piend-roofed wings. Now flats.

Former RUBISLAW SCHOOL, King's Gate, opposite Richmond-hill Place. 1874, extended by *W. L. Henderson*, 1879, and again by *Ellis & Wilson*, 1890. Single-storey Board School, converted to flats.

STATUE OF QUEEN VICTORIA, Queen's Cross. Bronze, 1893, by *C. B. Birch*. First installed at the corner of Union Street and St Nicholas Street, where it replaced Alexander Brodie's marble statue of the Queen (now in the Town House). Moved here in 1964.

DESCRIPTION

The description moves broadly chronologically from E to W, following the main route of Albyn Place–Queen's Road, with detours N as necessary.

Albyn Place to Queen's Cross

ALBYN PLACE was formed shortly after 1802, but it was many years before the then proprietor of the lands of Rubislaw, James Skene, could attract house-builders in significant numbers. An 1819 scheme by *Archibald Elliot* for laying out the triangle between the N side and Carden Place with an Edinburgh-style grid proved overambitious. Just two houses were built in 1820 by Skene himself, to set the ball rolling – probably the pair now combined with a single entrance at No. 6 Albyn Place – but the rest of the surrounding short terrace seems not to have followed until the 1830s. By now *Archibald Simpson* was in charge, having replaced Elliot's proposals with a new plan *c*. 1828. However, comprehensive development of the triangle did not properly get under way until 1849, to a layout which is probably largely by *James Forbes Beattie* (he widened and straightened Queen's Road–Carden Place at the same time, and made a new feuing plan). The streets have charming small-scale terraces. At the N end of VICTORIA STREET, two-storey houses on the E side face single-storey-plus-attic cottages on the W. The houses are rubble but with finely dressed margins, and the cottages have consoled cornices to doors and windows. Parallel ALBERT STREET has the same cottage-versus-house arrangement and similar architecture, though here the fronts are all finely dressed and some houses have sunk basements (the E side of RUBISLAW PLACE, s, is very similar). Building in Albert Street was under way by 1851, with *Mackenzie & Matthews* designing at least two cottages, though the major developer seems to have been *William Henderson* (*William Henderson & Son* by 1853). ALBERT TERRACE – rubble again – has similar cottages, and the Hendersons were active here too, but the biggest player in this street was *William Keith, Jun.*, who built eighteen cottages in 1862–3. The *Aberdeen Journal* summed them up as 'very excellent homes for unambitious folks in comfortable circumstances'. The same basic house type was still being built by *James Henderson* in CARDEN TERRACE in 1867, and even a decade later, on the s side of CARDEN PLACE, where No. 47 is dated 1876. An anomaly among the surrounding terraces is a pair of large semis, now No. 22 on the N side of WAVERLEY PLACE, linked by a quadrant corner. They are *c.* 1851, by Simpson's former assistant *William Ramage*. Meanwhile, from 1849 the N side of Carden Place was developed with villas by *William Henderson*, mostly to a single-storey-plus-attic-and-basement formula, with canted bay windows. Later arrivals include Nos. 38 and 40, a pair of Gothic semis of 1884 by *George Coutts*. No. 1 Carden Place, dated 1900, was remodelled in that year by *William Kelly*, who had already transformed No. 12 in 1897, giving it a handsome Italian Renaissance front with triple-arched first-floor windows.

Contrasting with the cottagey back streets, the N side of Albyn Place itself, w of Rubislaw Place, has terraces of a grandeur previously unknown in Aberdeen. First, from 1852, came RUBISLAW TERRACE, raised up and separated from the road by a broad strip of pleasure grounds. With its two-storey canted bays with balustraded tops and crowstepped gables, it also marked a stylistic departure, taking its cue from 'the renowned Abbotsford House – a combination of the Scottish and Elizabethan orders'. The architects were *Mackenzie & Matthews*, with some input from 'Mr Giles, artist', presumably *James Giles*, who may have laid out the original pleasure grounds (these have since been transformed into a municipal garden with a curious granite FOUNTAIN of *c.* 1971: a classical baluster squeezed into an S-curve between two boulders). Continuous with the w end of Rubislaw Terrace is QUEEN'S TERRACE, begun in 1871 by *J. R. Mackenzie*. It has the same two-storey bays but reverts to a flat, classical roof-line. Ten houses, the end two and middle pair distinguished by an extra storey and chamfered quoins. w of Queen's Terrace, but started earlier (No. 3 was already complete in 1867), is ALBYN TERRACE by *James Matthews*. It is set forward again to the line of Albyn Place, throwing into prominence the short E elevation with massive half-round corner towers under conical roofs, more French than Baronial. The w end is the same; the long s elevation is plainer, with a pair of central gables and another at each end, and round-headed dormers.

So to the s side of Albyn Place. This was always intended for VILLAS, with rear gardens stretching down to the Justice Mill burn. A few had appeared by 1828 and all sites had been filled by the 1860s; many of the houses have been remodelled and extended, and nearly all are now in institutional use. The following deserve special notice, from E to w. No. 9, said to be *c.* 1820 and often attributed to *Archibald Simpson*, with a semicircular Tuscan porch and windows in blind arches on

98

each side. Wings demolished. Well-preserved interior with curving stair, l. For Nos. 18 and 20, now the wings of Harlaw Academy, *see* Public Buildings. In front of No. 24 is the U-plan granite ST JOHN'S WELL. The inscription records its rebuilding in 1852. Originally sited between Skene Street and the Denburn, it was moved here in 1955. No. 25, with pedimented wings and Doric porch, could be *c.* 1830; likewise No. 26, a single-storey-plus-basement cottage, but dignified by angle pilasters and a Greek Doric porch. No. 28 – said to be 1838 by *Simpson* – is also single-storeyed, of squared rubble, with a four-column Greek Doric porch and wings with piended roofs. T-shaped, top-lit central hall, with scrolled plaster frieze. No. 33 was altered by *Brown & Watt*, 1897: theirs is presumably the half-timbered first floor with three gabled oriels. Nos. 35 and 36 are a pair of mid-C19 Italianate semis, with a triple-arched porch between the wings. No. 40 has semicircular bows linked by a columned porch, and No. 41 repeats the formula but with canted bays. Finally, at the corner of Albyn Place and St Swithin Street, is the altered but still splendid No. 1 QUEEN'S CROSS of 1865, traditionally ascribed to *J. R. Mackenzie*, for the eminent photographer George Washington Wilson. A flamboyant break with Aberdonian convention, influenced perhaps by French domestic architecture. Two bay-windowed wings, parallel with the two streets, branch from an octagonal, pavilion-roofed entrance tower, its skyline enlivened by a conical-roofed turret and a crown of *Walter Macfarlane & Co.*'s effervescent ironwork. Granite-faced rear extension by *Mackie Ramsay & Taylor*, 1970s.

From the Queen's Cross roundabout, FOUNTAINHALL ROAD heads N. The corner building, comprising No. 2 Queen's Cross and No. 2 Fountainhall Road, is an ingenious double villa with Tudor Gothic details, built between 1868 and 1876. Fountainhall Road itself has terraced houses of the 1870s onwards. Several are by *George Coutts*, the most enterprising being Nos. 44 and 46, 1884–7, with a domed corner turret and segmental bows under differently shaped pediments. Nos. 58–64 have concave buttresses to the chimneystacks and distinctive lintels over the doors: they look like the tops of Egyptian pylons and suggest the hand of *Pirie & Clyne*. The latter were certainly responsible for the house of rock-faced granite at the NW corner of the junction with Hamilton Place. It has an almost windowless elevation to that street, but the Fountainhall Road front has weirdly detailed ashlar pediments above the first-floor windows, rising above the eaves. This gives a fore-taste of HAMILTON PLACE itself, the N side of which, from Fountainhall Road E as far as the junction with Whitehall Road, consists entirely of houses by *Pirie* for the builder John Morgan, in pink and grey granite. Mostly semis, each pair different, they show Pirie's extraordinary inventiveness in manipulating Greek detail and combining it with Gothic and even Baronial elements. Beyond Whitehall Road, much more conventional houses, including a few Tudor and Baronial. S of and parallel to the E end of Hamilton Place, *James Henderson* was laying out WESTFIELD TERRACE by 1868, where he built a series of large semis with Jacobean gables.

Finally, in BLENHEIM PLACE, leading S from Hamilton Place, No. 130 on the E side is the harled, five-bay FOUNTAINHALL HOUSE. In existence by 1773, with a rounded granite porch added *c.* 1830, it now finds itself incongruously attached to a late C19 terrace. The gatepiers carry Adam-esque iron vases.

Queen's Cross to Anderson Drive

Until the City of Aberdeen Land Association acquired the lands of Rubislaw in 1874, building had barely progressed beyond Queen's Cross. From this date, however, the march of stately houses moved unstoppably westward, at the same time spreading S and – especially – N of Queen's Road. Only a few call for individual comment: once again, it is the overall impression of late Victorian prosperity that impresses.

QUEEN'S ROAD W of the Cross starts with a continuation of the terrace pattern established by Rubislaw Terrace. QUEEN'S GARDENS, a symmetrical row of ten houses on the N side with continuous cast-iron balconies, was begun by *J. R. Mackenzie* in 1877. It was only completed in 1884–93, by *Ellis & Wilson*, who may have been responsible for the end houses with their canted bays and pediments. Apart from this, VILLAS are the norm, mostly detached, occasionally semis, and in some cases very large. Many are now in commercial or educational use, the spaces between filled with link buildings. Sober classicism predominates, along with Baronial, and there are occasional excursions into livelier styles, but on the whole there is little in the way of ostentatious individualism. The S side begins with the Italianate No. 3 Queen's Cross, built for the accountant Robert Fletcher. It is now the R.C. BISHOP'S HOUSE, linked to neighbouring St Joseph's School. In existence by 1867, it was the only new house W of the Cross before the advent of the Land Association. Six bays, with quoins, deep eaves and a porch of four Roman Doric columns. Nos. 9 and 11 are both symmetrical, the former – dated 1878 – with Jacobean strapwork over the porch, and shaped gables; the latter – 1875 by *James Matthews* for James Saint – Baronial with corner tourelles and crowstepped gables. No. 23, 1879, now part of Albyn School, is one of the largest houses. It occupies the E side of the junction with Forest Avenue, balanced on the W by No. 3 Queen's Gate, 1882. Both are Italianate, by *Matthews & Mackenzie*.

Immediately W of the Forest Avenue–Forest Road junction, on the N side, is the single-storey bull-nosed TOLL HOUSE of 1837. It is a legacy of Queen's Road's origin as the Skene turnpike, and a survival from before the road was widened by the Land Association. Just beyond it is No. 50, the most

106

remarkable Victorian house in Aberdeen. Dated 1886, it replaced a mansion of 1675 which stood in the way of the road's realignment. It was designed for the builder John Morgan by his friend *J. B. Pirie* of *Pirie & Clyne*. Morgan – a traveller and bibliophile who collected the works of Ruskin and Morris – was much more than the archetypal self-made businessman, and the house reflects his discerning patronage as well as Pirie's fertile imagination. The style is a late flowering of muscular High Victorian Gothic, fusing medieval and Baronial with idiosyncratic details that have no obvious historical source. Rock-faced granite contrasts with smooth ashlar dressings and carved decoration of exceptional quality. Filling the l. gable of the entrance front is a first-floor oriel, which grows out of a buttress bearing Pirie's and Morgan's monograms. Its mullions have capitals composed of two curling fronds of foliage back to back, more like an Aolic capital than anything Gothic. The top forms a balcony for the second-floor window, under a chunkily carved blind arch of pink granite. The angle turret r. of the entrance is even more original. It features a tripartite window made up of a rectangle flanked by two quarter-circles, separated by a pair of stubby foliage capitals; but no description can do justice to the strangeness of the shapes. The way that the smooth corbelling of the turret emerges from the rough surrounding stone makes the granite seem almost malleable. The entrance itself is recessed under a Gothic arch, with a dripmould incorporating highly stylized organic forms. Visible on the r. return elevation is the semicircular stair-tower. The flanking pairs of semis, Nos. 46–48 and 52–54, were built by Morgan at the same time and are also by *Pirie & Clyne*.

Nos. 60–64, 1901 by *John Rust*, have glazed lanterns to light their attic billiard rooms. On the same side, further w, No. 82 is of 1898 by *A. Marshall Mackenzie*, in pink and grey granite with a curvy pediment over the door and triangular gabled dormers. There follows a varied group of *c.* 1900 by *George Coutts*. No. 88, 1902, is classical, with the central entrance bay carried up into an elaborate pedimented dormer with a round window. TARROBANE, 1905, combines Gothic windows with half-timbered gables *à la* Norman Shaw. The most individual of the bunch is HAMEWITH, 1906, of red and grey rock-faced granite, with a red tiled roof, and an off-centre mullioned-and-transomed window above the timber porch. No. 94, 1899, classical again, has a steeply pointed roof above the central dormer, making a kind of tower. This stretch ends at the corner of Anderson Drive with EARL'S COURT, 1898 by *Ellis & Wilson*. Big, with vaguely Jacobean details, and a porch with stubby columns tucked into the angle of its two wings. (For Queen's Road w of Anderson Drive, *see* Rubislaw, p. 289.)

Retracing our steps E, FOREST ROAD leads N from Queen's Road, lined with further large houses. Nos. 2–12, 1877 by *Matthews & Mackenzie*, make a thirteen-bay terrace with a corner turret. After this come semis and detached villas, including several with the sunflower paterae that mark them out as *Pirie & Clyne*'s. Nos. 13–19 are a pink granite pair with shaped gables, of 1899 by *Walker & Duncan*. Others worth a look are No. 26, 1908 by *William Beattie*, with a timber balcony below its deep eaves; No. 28, 1895 by *Brown & Watt*, with a conical-roofed turret; and, opposite, No. 31, Callan Lodge, 1899 by *A. Marshall Mackenzie*.

Branching off from the W side of Forest Road at this point are Rubislaw Den South and Rubislaw Den North, two streets laid out *c.* 1883–4, flanking the wooded valley of the North Burn of Rubislaw. The houses backing on to the Den itself enjoy an especially favoured setting. The N side of RUBISLAW DEN SOUTH begins with *Pirie & Clyne*'s No. 2: pink and grey granite with the entrance in a giant blind arch flanked by chimneystacks. Bigger houses are at the upper (W) end, the grandest being two neighbours on the N side by *Brown & Watt*: No. 32, of 1897, has a square entrance tower with battlements that step up at one corner; No. 34, 1900, is also mildly Baronial, but with Gothic timbering to the gables, and a recessed balcony. On the S side, just W of the junction with Bayview Road, No. 57 is 1908 by *Sutherland & George*. Back on the N side, No. 72 is the Baronial former DUTHIE PARK LODGE of *c.* 1883 (*see* p. 249), rebuilt here *c.* 1947.

The largest houses are on the S side of RUBISLAW DEN NORTH, beginning splendidly with a multi-gabled extravaganza of 1908 by *George Coutts* at No. 1. No. 5 is low, rambling Tudor of 1900 by *William Ruxton*. Braco Lodge at No. 11, 1928, is one of two Voyseyesque houses by *Clement George*, with its main front facing S over the garden rather than the street. The other is Glenburn Lodge of 1929 at No. 15. Between them is No. 13, Glenburnie Park, 1885 by *Matthews & Mackenzie*, with Aberdeen-bond ground floor, squared-rubble first floor, and carved bargeboards and timber framing to its multiple gables. Cramond House, No. 17, is 1884 by the same architects, but classical, with a pediment. No. 21 resembles No. 13, but is as late as 1907, by *W. Henderson & Son*. Finally on this side comes Rubislaw Den House, a mansion rather than a villa, built in 1881 for the granite merchant and speculative house-builder William Keith Jun. It stands on the site of an earlier house, predating the street. A mishmash of bays and battlements, with short Romanesque columns halfway up its square Baronial tower. The architect is said to have been *Duncan McMillan*, but did Keith himself have a hand in it? The motto of his namesake, founder of Marischal College, is carved over the S entrance. On the N side at this upper end the houses are smaller, the dominant style being a refined version of the Domestic Revival, adapted to the hardness of Aberdeen granite. Nos. 60–64, all of 1895, are subtle variations on the same basic pattern by *William Kelly* (*W. & J. Smith & Kelly*), No. 62 being his own house. In 1901 he added No. 58. No. 68, with a Gothic doorway dated 1905, is by *Coutts*. No. 72, with half-timbered gables and an oriel, is of 1913 by *Jenkins & Marr*.

Forest Road continues N to KING'S GATE, where No. 54, the ATHOLL HOTEL, closes the view. It is the most shamelessly showy house in the West End. The original l. half is Baronial, apparently of *c.* 1890, with a segmental bow under a hugely tall pavilion roof with three gabled dormers. To the r. is a completely discordant Gothic addition of 1895 by *Brown & Watt*, as big as the original house: mullioned-and-transomed ground-floor windows, linked by panelling to first-floor tracery of the King's College Chapel type, and ball finials on the gable above. It was built for the draper William Morrison. Continuing E, King's Gate has more large villas. Mid-C19 RICHMONDHILL HOUSE on the N side has battlemented canted bays with mullions and transoms, flanking a Roman Doric porch. It is largely hidden by C20 sheltered housing built over its grounds. No. 14, KING'S ACRE, is probably of *c.* 1880, with crowstepped gables and a square, pavilion-roofed entrance tower.

GORDONDALE ROAD leads off N at this point, with pairs of semis in rock-faced dark grey granite with bands of pinkish ashlar (for Mile End School, N, *see* p. 244). They are *c.* 1880 by *James Souttar*, who was probably responsible around the same time for Nos. 12 and 8 King's Gate, where the same distinctive materials are used (the latter was his father's house). On the S side, this stretch of King's Gate has detached and semi-detached villas of the 1880s and 90s, quite large but closely packed together. No. 21, 1897 by *Brown & Watt*, has ball finials; No. 19, 1887 by *George Coutts*, a square tower. *Coutts* probably also did the semis at Nos. 13–15 and 7–9.

STOCKET

An area of scattered estates until the late C19, occupying the site of the former forest of Stocket. Now overlooked from the N by the huge Foresterhill hospital complex.

CHURCHES

BEECHGROVE CHURCH, Beechgrove Avenue and Mid Stocket Road. *Brown & Watt*, 1898–1900. Disused. Cruciform, lancet style. The high NW tower and spire are particularly graceful, the belfry stage a lofty cage of granite tracery. More traditionally detailed than the same architects' slightly earlier Holburn West Church (*see* p. 223), but the arch mouldings die into the chamfered doorways in the same end-of-the-century manner. The buttress r. of the entrance has a curious window-shaped carving of intersecting tracery.

MIDSTOCKET PARISH CHURCH, Mid Stocket Road and Harcourt Road. Formerly St Ninian. A very good building by *William Kelly*, 1898–1900, in a refined version of Scots Gothic. It demonstrates Kelly's antiquarian knowledge and

Beechgrove Church.
Design by Brown & Watt, published 1903

ecclesiological principles, and makes a striking contrast with
the exactly contemporary Beechgrove (*see* above). Nave with
clearstorey and lean-to aisles, plus shallow transepts and a
fairly deep chancel. SW battlemented tower with pyramid roof,
balanced by SE stair bay. Between them, the gabled S front is
framed by buttresses, one carrying a SUNDIAL, with the central
door recessed under a broad segmental arch. Apart from the
triple lancets above this door and the three chancel windows

with their flowing tracery, all the windows are square-headed (those in the clearstorey have blind ogee heads). Inside, S gallery with glazed lobby underneath. Three-bay nave with cylindrical granite columns carrying very broad, segmental arches, simply chamfered. A chamfered pointed arch without capitals separates it from the raised chancel. Open timber roofs to the aisles, segmental timber ceiling to the nave and chancel.

Harmonious FURNISHINGS by Kelly throughout. In the panelled chancel, COMMUNION TABLE, PULPIT (to r. of chancel arch) and canopied REREDOS incorporating First World War memorial. – LECTERN. The Angel of St Matthew with outspread wings, with small figures of Melchizedek, Moses, David and Isaiah round the base, 1902. – ORGAN CASE, in two parts, each side of the gallery, 1906. – STAINED GLASS. N window: Christ cleansing the Temple, preaching from a boat, raising the widow's son and carrying the Cross, with symbols of the Evangelists below, by *Douglas Strachan*, 1903. E transept, Martha and Mary, Christ with Mary Magdalen, and St Peter with Dorcas, 1951 by *Marjorie Kemp*. E aisle, N end: the Good Samaritan, by *Fr Ninian* of Pluscarden Abbey, 1971. E aisle, second from N, early C20 cherubs' heads with scriptural texts, brought from Beechgrove Church, 2007. W transept, scenes from the life of St Ninian, by *J. A. H. Hector*, 1923. W aisle, more cherubs from Beechgrove. Attached HALL at N end, 1956–7 by *A. M. Stewart*. (Opposite the church in RICHMONDHILL GARDENS is early C19 MOREFIELD HOUSE, once a secluded suburban villa.)

PUBLIC BUILDINGS

FORESTERHILL MEDICAL CAMPUS, N of Westburn Road. Aberdeen's pioneering Joint Hospital Scheme was launched in 1920, with the aim of uniting all the city's hospitals on one site, alongside medical teaching and research. The s-facing slope of Foresterhill was chosen, and over a period of eighty years it has been more or less covered with buildings. The complex is vast (56 hectares) and visually confusing. What follows is less a suggested itinerary than a broadly chrono-logical and thematic account. At the centre is the ABERDEEN ROYAL INFIRMARY of 1928–36, replacing the one at Woolmanhill (*see* p. 219). The four-storey buildings – severely classical, of granite with artificial stone dressings – comprise three linked U-shaped blocks, open to the S, entered through a larger courtyard block in the middle of the N side. Later accretions make it difficult to appreciate the crisp geometry and monumental plan. The architect was *J. B. Nicol* of *Kelly & Nicol*, with *Pite, Son & Fairweather*. The E block was extended N in similar style by *Pite, Son & Fairweather* in the 1950s, but after this, granite was abandoned. Very large additions on the W by *George, Trew & Dunn* are of two phases, 1963–6 and 1971–9, the earlier with an exposed concrete frame and white tiled infill panels, the later a nine-storey ward block with balconies surrounding each floor.

Teaching and research are concentrated along the upper edge of the site, N of the Infirmary. The cruciform UNIVERSITY MEDICAL SCHOOL at the NE corner is by *Pite, Son & Fairweather*, 1936–8, but with later modifications. The concrete structure is more frankly expressed here than in Nicol's work, and there are only small areas of granite, used as a smooth decorative facing. In 1966–70 a five-storey block by *George, Trew & Dunn* linked it to the Infirmary. W of the link is the MEDICAL LIBRARY, AUDITORIUM & MEDICAL CHIRURGICAL SOCIETY, 1971–3 by *George Trew Dunn Beckles Willson Bowes*, and N of this, the INSTITUTE OF MEDICAL SCIENCES, five-storey research laboratories of 1995–6 by *David Murray Associates*. The forbidding exterior, clad in gunmetal grey panels, gives no hint of the pleasant, light-filled atrium, with much natural wood. Office windows open directly into it. Immediately W, the new ROWETT INSTITUTE FOR NUTRITION AND HEALTH by *Halliday Fraser Munro* is under construction 2014, replacing the original buildings at Bucksburn (*see* p. 266). S of this is the SUTTIE CENTRE FOR TEACHING AND LEARNING IN HEALTHCARE, 2009 by *Bennett Associates*. A four-storey timber- and glass-clad square. Steel uprights surround it, supporting external steel walkways and timber brise-soleil at each floor, so it seems to sit inside a cage. The interior has an atrium overlooked by balconies, with a spiral stair to the first floor. Rising through the stairwell to the full height of the space, an intriguing ARTWORK by *Marilène Oliver*, Doctor–Patient, 2009: magnetic resonance imaging scans of two men (one the Aberdeen inventor of MRI), printed onto acrylic discs and threaded onto steel cables. The result is a translucent column with shadowy human forms, head to head, locked inside.

NW of the Suttie Centre is FORESTERHILL HOUSE, the C19 harl-and-granite dwelling whose lands were colonized by the Joint Hospital Scheme. Neighbouring ASHGROVE HOUSE, at the W edge of the site, was originally a nurses' home, by *Nicol* again, the same date and style as the first phase of the Infirmary. Between it and the 1960s wing of the Infirmary, a SCULPTURE, Breathing, by *Hideo Furuta*, 1992: a granite column with figures in relief emerging from the roughly hewn stone. 100 m. E of the Infirmary is the 1934–7 MATERNITY HOSPITAL, also by *Nicol*, and much like his other buildings on the site, but with later additions. Among the smaller buildings S of the Maternity Hospital is OCCUPATIONAL HEALTH, a four-storey Aberdeen-bond granite block designed as housing for medical students by *Pite, Son & Fairweather*, 1939–41. Directly S of the Infirmary is the CHILDREN'S HOSPITAL of 2001–3 by *Mackie Ramsay Taylor*. It tries a bit too hard to be playful and friendly. In the middle of the S front, a round tower with oversailing V-shaped roof; square stair-towers at the four corners have roofs of the same form. On a site between it and the original Infirmary buildings is the MATTHEW HAY BUILDING for emergency care, completed 2012 and also by *Mackie Ramsay Taylor*.

Against the big, blocky, sometimes oppressive buildings that dominate the campus, the small MAGGIE'S CENTRE (for cancer care and support) sits beside the helicopter landing site on Westburn Road like something just arrived from another world – a gentler, more enlightened world. Designed by the Norwegian practice *Snøhetta*, it opened in 2013 and takes the form of a pale, pebble-shaped concrete shell with sections cut away. This shell forms the walls and roof and also embraces a little garden. In the open-plan interior, timber contrasts with the smooth, overarching walls and ceiling – the inner surface of the shell. More intimate enclosed spaces are located below a mezzanine, and everything is washed with daylight from a cluster of circular openings in the roof and from glazed walls where the shell is cut away.

107 MILE END SCHOOL, Gordondale Road. *A. H. L. Mackinnon*, 1899–1901. Three-storey Board School with very shallow, pedimented wings. Blocked surrounds to first-floor windows, pilasters between second-floor windows. (For the rest of Gordondale Road, *see* p. 240.) A new MILE END SCHOOL, 2009–10 by *Aedas*, has been built at the W end of Mid Stocket Road to replace the Gordondale Road building.

WOODHILL HOUSE, Westburn Road. Headquarters of Aberdeenshire Council. 1975 by the *Council Architects Dept*. Vertically ribbed concrete (partly refaced in 2007 with blue cladding) above a granite rubble plinth. Concave E front with mosaic-covered fins between vertical window strips. In the foyer, a 6ft high boulder with Pictish carving of the fearsome axe-wielding 'Rhynie Man', discovered at Rhynie (q.v.) in 1978.

INNER DISTRICTS: SOUTH

FERRYHILL

Ferryhill has all the natural ingredients for a select C19 suburb – an elevated site, river views and proximity to the centre – yet its growth was only gradual. A handful of mid-century villas survive but most early development was in the form of terraces. Of industrial uses that colonized the low-lying strip by the river, few traces apart from the Aberdeen Railway viaduct remain. Building gathered pace from the 1870s, with two churches and a swathe of substantial Late Victorian and Edwardian housing, including tenements and semi-detached villas. The opening in 1883 of Duthie Park – a municipal showpiece – hastened the transformation from hinterland to fully fledged suburb.

CHURCHES

FERRYHILL PARISH CHURCH, Polmuir Road and Fonthill Road. By *Duncan McMillan*, opened 1874. Originally Ferryhill Free Church. It stands at the highest point of the district, its tall steeple a landmark. Broad nave, shallow transepts and a round apse. N front with rose in gable and small windows with plate tracery l. and r. of entrance. Porch with squat columns added 1883. The main feature is the three-stage NW tower with angle buttresses and big, pyramidal pinnacles round the octagonal spire. Interior (reordered by *Oliver Humphries*, 1990s) with wooden nave ceiling on transverse segmental arches. N gallery with Gothic timber front, extended down both sides in 1897, now cut back, with a glazed foyer under. – FONT. 1927, wooden, octagonal, with Late Gothic carving. – STAINED GLASS. Rose window with Burning Bush in centre, 1883; nave, E side, St Peter and St John, and w, Martha and Dorcas, plus St Margaret round the corner in the w transept, all 1925 by *Alexander McLundie* and all originally in the former Ferryhill Parish Church (*see* below); r. and l. of apse, Victory and Courage, First World War memorials, 1919 by *A. L. Moore & Son*; in the centre of the apse, three-light Nativity, 1903–4 by *Gordon & Watt*, again from the old parish church and now framed and artificially back-lit; pairs of lancets on each side, 1897, with symbols of the Evangelists and maps showing the four quarters of the globe, like pages from a school atlas; E transept, two notable windows by *Jane Bayliss*, 1994 and 1999, the former a memorial to the 1988 explosion on the Piper Alpha oil platform, the latter a surprisingly erotic Adam and Eve (the small trefoil window over the N door is by the same artist). HALL, W, added by *McMillan*, 1885. The space between it and the church has been roofed over to make an atrium.

Former FERRYHILL PARISH CHURCH, Ferryhill Road. 1875–7 by *William Smith*. A good deal humbler than its Free Church rival at the top of the hill. Gothic, T-plan, with a shallow gabled porch and buttresses to the main, E, front. Round window above the door with cusped sandstone tracery. A projection with stepped lancets, N, contained the gallery stair. Converted to flats.

PUBLIC BUILDINGS

ALLENVALE CEMETERY, Allenvale Road. Designed 1873 by *J. R. Mackenzie* and opened the following year, though work continued for some time after that. Cruciform paths meeting at a *rond point* divide the site in four, the larger SW segment spreading out into a cluster of intersecting circular paths. The most notable feature of the layout is the S edge, a gently concave terrace following the curve of the river, lined with monuments looking outward. Grandest of all are the monuments against the E boundary wall, backing on to Great Southern Road, the best being that of the Union Street

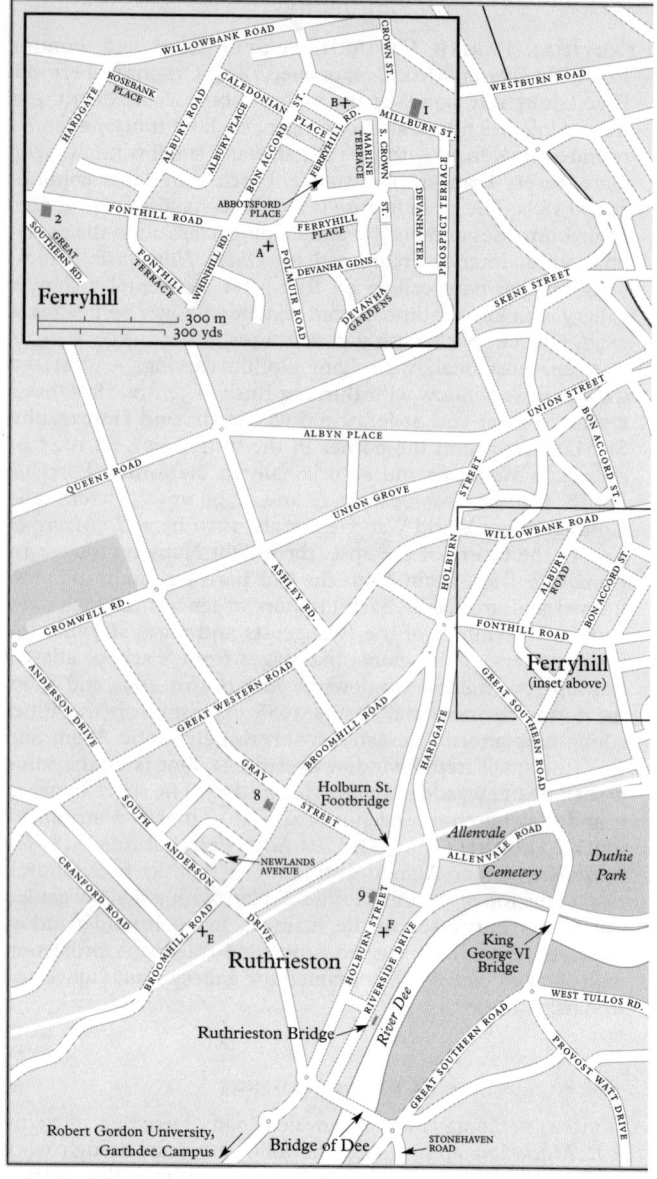

Ferryhill

300 m
300 yds

Ferryhill
(inset above)

Holburn St.
Footbridge

Allenvale
Cemetery

Duthie
Park

Newlands
Avenue

King
George VI
Bridge

Ruthrieston

Ruthrieston Bridge

River Dee

Robert Gordon University,
Garthdee Campus

Bridge of Dee

Stonehaven
Road

A   Ferryhill Parish Church
B   Ferryhill Parish Church
     (former)
C   St Clement's Parish Church
     (former)

D   Mission Hall
E   Ruthrieston West Church
F   South Holburn Parish
     Church

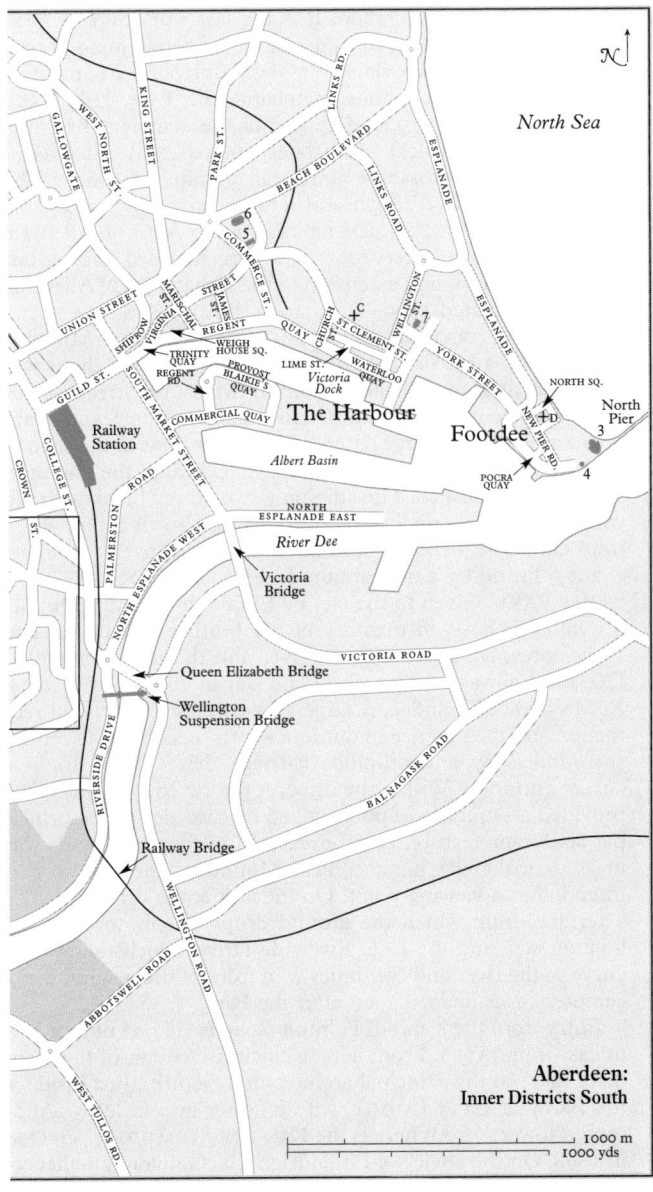

North Sea

GALLOWGATE

WEST NORTH ST.

KING STREET

PARK ST.

LINKS RD.

BEACH BOULEVARD

LINKS ROAD

ESPLANADE

ESPLANADE

COMMERCE ST.

6
5

UNION STREET

SHIPROW

MARISCHAL ST.

VIRGINIA

STREET

JAMES ST.

REGENT

WEIGH
HOUSE SQ.

TRINITY
QUAY

REGENT
RD.

PROVOST
BLAIKIE'S
QUAY

GUILD ST.

SOUTH MARKET STREET

COMMERCIAL QUAY

QUAY

CHURCH ST.

ST CLEMENT ST.

LIME ST.

WATERLOO
QUAY

Victoria
Dock

WELLINGTON ST.

YORK STREET

C

7

ESPLANADE

NORTH SQ.

NORTH
Pier

3

D

Footdee

NEW PIER RD.

POCRA
QUAY

4

The Harbour

Railway
Station

Albert Basin

CROWN

COLLEGE ST.

ST.

PALMERSTON

ROAD

NORTH ESPLANADE WEST

NORTH
ESPLANADE EAST

River Dee

Victoria
Bridge

VICTORIA ROAD

Queen Elizabeth Bridge

Wellington
Suspension Bridge

RIVERSIDE DRIVE

BALNAGASK ROAD

Railway Bridge

WELLINGTON ROAD

ABBOTSWELL ROAD

WEST TULLOS RD.

Aberdeen:
Inner Districts South

1000 m
1000 yds

1	Corporation Electricity Works (former)	5	Commerce Street Public School
2	Ferryhill Library	6	Hanover Street School
3	Marine Operations Centre	7	York Street School (former)
4	Round House	8	Broomhill School
		9	Ruthrieston Community Centre

outfitter James Saint, †1890. It is the last work of *J. B. Pirie*, and wildly idiosyncratic in its use of Greek detail. Just s of this, an austerely impressive slab with Gothic surround commemorates the wife of the granite merchant John Fyfe, †1889, and also Fyfe himself, †1906. The rest of the cemetery has rank upon rank of classical headstones, interspersed with veiled urns and Celtic crosses – almost all granite, of course. The general standard of design and lettering remains remarkably high into the mid c20. LODGE by *Jenkins & Marr* on Allenvale Road dated 1889: steep roofs and bargeboarded gables, but classical details. Large extension to the cemetery N of Allenvale Road, consecrated 1900.

Former CORPORATION ELECTRICITY WORKS, Millburn Street. 1901–3 by *Stewart Milne*. The offices were in the three-storey pavilion-roofed block fronting Millburn Street. It has some rudimentary classical details, but the main features are the name carved in large letters and the city arms in the shaped gable above. The rest of the complex, including the chimney, has been demolished. The adjoining two-storey block with big windows and two pediments overlooking Crown Street was a tram car repair depot. Both buildings were converted to flats *c.* 2005, linked by a new granite-faced corner block.

DUTHIE PARK. Given to the city by Elizabeth Crombie Duthie, a wealthy heiress, in memory of her brother and uncle. The 18 hectares, lying between the river and the now-dismantled Deeside Railway of 1853, were laid out in 1881–3 by *William R. McKelvie* of Dundee. A large grassed area 'for general recreation and the practice of outdoor sports' occupies the centre, surrounded by a continuous carriage drive linked to four corner entrances. Within the drive, at the sw corner, McKelvie provided a sequence of pools linked by cascades as the principal landscape feature. Earth excavated to form the pools was used to make the high, conical Mound at the NW corner, intended as a viewing point. On the s side, the drive becomes a terrace, from which the ground drops steeply towards the boating lake and the Dee. Riverside Drive, which follows the curve of the river and continues w in front of the neighbouring cemetery, was formed soon after the Park.

Entry from the s end of Polmuir Road is via one of four sets of cast-iron GATES. From here, a clockwise circuit of the main drive takes in the principal architectural features. Just inside is the Baronial EAST LODGE, with its door in a little pyramid-roofed tower. s from here is the DUTHIE MEMORIAL, erected in 1898. On the advice of Pittendrigh MacGillivray, an allegorical design was preferred to a portrait. A squat Corinthian column supports a statue of Hygeia, Greek goddess of health, from a model by *John Cassidy* of Manchester. She denotes the sanitary benefits of Miss Duthie's gift. Four red granite lions surround the base, like a miniature Nelson's Column. At the se corner of the drive is a granite FOUNTAIN designed by *Alexander Macdonald* of *Macdonald, Field & Co.*, the upper bowl supported by four swans. Dominating the s side of the park, a 22 m. OBELISK of Peterhead granite commemorates Sir James McGrigor (†1858), Director General of the Army Medical Department. Designed by *Alexander Ellis* and *James Giles*, it was first erected in the quadrangle of Marischal College in 1860, and moved here in 1906 when the College was extended. W of this, a BRIDGE with granite piers and cast-iron balustrade carries the drive over the lowest of McKelvie's pools. Near the park's NW corner are the domed granite TEMPERANCE FOUNTAIN and the WEST LODGE, a 1938 rebuild made necessary by the widening of Great Southern Road (for its predecessor, *see* p. 239). N of the lodge, a triangular OBELISK of 1898 by *W. & J. Smith & Kelly* commemorates Gordon Highlanders who served in the Indian campaign. The N side is mostly occupied by the DAVID WELCH WINTER GARDENS, a complex of tunnel-vaulted glasshouses opened in 1970, replacing a domed 1890s palm house. A glazed entrance pavilion with sandstone façade was added *c.* 2003. In and around the glasshouses are features salvaged from demolished Aberdeen buildings, notably the cast-iron parapet from the s side of Union Bridge (*see* p. 150), including, in an inner courtyard garden, *Sidney Boyes*'s bronze relief panel representing Aberdeen's trade and industries. SE of the Winter Gardens, a CELTIC CROSS commemorates Gordon Highlanders who died in the Egyptian campaign of 1882. The octagonal cast-iron BANDSTAND at the centre of the park is by *McDowall Steven & Co.* of Glasgow, 1893.

FERRYHILL LIBRARY, Fonthill Road. *Arthur Clyne*, 1903. Small and picturesque, with a quirky mixture of Gothic and Jacobean details: the pointed tympanum of the reading room's N window is filled with strapwork, and the gable-ends in a miniature spire composed of classical scrolls.

KING GEORGE VI BRIDGE, over the Dee. 1936–41, by the City Engineer, *Thomas F. Henderson*, with *Considere Constructions Ltd* (consulting engineers) and *Frank C. Mears* (consulting architect). Three elliptical arches of reinforced concrete, clad in rock-faced granite. Designed to link with the projected suburb of Kincorth (*see* p. 298). Great Southern Road was widened to form the bridge's N approach and equipped with handsome cast-iron lamp standards, also by Mears.

QUEEN ELIZABETH BRIDGE, over the Dee, N of Wellington Suspension Bridge. By *Grampian Regional Council Road Department*, with *Considere & Partners* as consulting engineers. Opened 1984. Three shallow-arched spans of pre-stressed concrete.

RAILWAY BRIDGE. Opened 1850. By *Locke & Errington*, engineers for the Aberdeen Railway. The seven masonry piers originally carried wooden arches, later replaced with steel trusses.

WELLINGTON SUSPENSION BRIDGE. Built 1829–31, the first 103 bridge over the river since the medieval Bridge of Dee. *Samuel Brown* (pioneer of chain-supported bridges) was the engineer; *John Smith* was responsible for the masonry. The flat-link chains are carried by battered pylons of rock-faced granite, pierced by round arches for the carriageway. The cast-iron-framed wooden deck was replaced in steel in 1930. *William Boulton* made the elliptical arch in the W approach in 1886, when Riverside Drive was constructed.

DESCRIPTION

A good starting place is MARINE TERRACE in the NE of the suburb, the earliest planned development in Ferryhill and architecturally speaking the most ambitious. Designed by *Archibald Simpson* in 1830–1, but only Nos. 9 and 10 were built during his lifetime, in 1837. Work did not resume until 1877–82, to a slightly revised design by *Duncan McMillan* and *J. R. Mackenzie*. Set behind a railed basement area, the nine houses stand on an artificial embankment facing E to the harbour. Just one storey plus basement and attic dormers, except for the middle pair, which have a first floor. All are three bays wide, generally with the door to one side, though the two earliest have central doors. Smooth granite ashlar, with eaves cornice and blocking course, and moulded architraves to the ground-floor openings (No. 9 has a consoled cornice over the door). McMillan and Mackenzie intended double houses at each end, rather than the two-storey terminal blocks originally planned by Simpson, but in the end neither was built, and lamentably inappropriate buildings of the late 1960s now stand in their place.

Just W of Marine Terrace's N end is CALEDONIAN PLACE, with classical terraces of the late 1860s by *Duncan McMillan* on each side. Two storeys on the S, one on the N, with sandstone dressings. From here, BON ACCORD STREET leads uphill, passing FERRYHILL HOUSE (now a hotel) on the E: perhaps late C18, square, harled, with quoins and granite margins to the windows. 'Great additions' were being made in 1811. They may have included the two large segmental bows on the S front. At the top of the hill are more C19 terraces. The site of FERRYHILL PLACE, E, was offered for feuing by the Shoemaker Trade in 1848, houses appearing from *c.* 1850. Building took place at both ends, but there were still large gaps in the middle of each side in the late 1860s. Single-storey cottages at the W end, with basements and attic dormers, rising to two storeys at the E end where the ground level is lower. The W end – earlier? – is mostly squared rubble, with ashlar used for the consoled cornices over the doors, but further E the granite is more finely dressed. Front gardens, coupled with modest height and unpretentious architecture, create a character more rustic than urban. MARINE PLACE continues the line of Ferryhill Place eastward, and was feued at the same date. A charming short terrace of single-storey cottages, it overlooks a triangular railed green. More such houses lie E of here in SOUTH CROWN STREET, DEVANHA TERRACE and PROSPECT TERRACE (where No. 70, a detached cottage, is the C18 Old Ferryhill House). Another little group is N, in ABBOTSFORD PLACE. More urbane are Nos. 1–7 POLMUIR ROAD, adjoining the W end of Ferryhill Place and facing the church. Described as 'recently finished' in 1852, they are severely plain and recall Archibald Simpson's Bon Accord Crescent and Square.

Polmuir Road leads S to Duthie Park, lined with villas, mostly late C19 semis but a few detached. No. 11, E side, has both Gothic and Arts and Crafts touches, and is by *Wilsons & Walker* for the salmon merchant John Hector, 1906. No. 16, Rotunda Lodge, is *c.* 1859 and said to have good classical plasterwork behind its unassuming exterior. Further down on the same side, Nos. 22 and 24 are a Baronial pair with crowstepped gables. Back on the E, Clifton Villa with lacy bargeboards is *c.* 1870, while its harled neighbour, No. 27, looks like a more modest version of Ferryhill House, and might be early C19. Just before the dismantled bridge of the Deeside Railway and the Park gates, Nos. 62–64 are of 1900 by *George Sutherland.* He was a pupil of Pirie & Clyne, whose influence is evident in the horseshoe arches round the doors. (Polmuir Road continues E from the Park gates, passing under the railway viaduct to join RIVERSIDE DRIVE, where C19 industry has given way to new blocks of flats with river views. The only survivor is part of the former DEVANHA DISTILLERY, S of Polmuir Road. Masked by a new façade on the E side, its granite rubble walls are still visible from the railway.)

Back uphill near the N end of Polmuir Road, DEVANHA GARDENS leads E to DEVANHA HOUSE, the grandest villa in the area. It now lies along the street, its original extensive grounds built over in the early C20. Basically a five-bay house of 1813, with a Greek Doric entrance porch on the N side and a single-storey segmental bow with a veranda on the S. It was enlarged *c.* 1857 for the ship-owner William Henderson, who added full-height semicircular bows with giant Doric pilasters to the end elevations. The whole is rendered and scored to look like masonry. Immediately W, No. 2 DEVANHA GARDENS WEST is good Arts and Crafts of *c.* 1900 by *John Ross McMillan.* Harled, with granite dressings, and a pleasing variety of windows placed with studied irregularity.

From the N end of Polmuir Road, FONTHILL ROAD runs W. The Cowdray Club Nursing Home, immediately W of the church, comprises a modest house of 1874 by *Duncan McMillan* and a much larger one with a pavilion-roofed central tower of *c.* 1884. Linking them is a harled addition by *Kelly & Nicol* with mullioned-and-transomed windows, dating from 1927 when the property became a residential and social club for nurses. Further W, No. 17 is Eastbank, an asymmetrical Tudor villa of *c.* 1850. FONTHILL TERRACE leads S from here, where No. 1, Whinhill, 1900 by *Brown & Watt*, combines Baronial and Gothic in a squared-off, 'modern' way. The transom of the canted bay window is treated as a cornice, cutting across the square mullions. Nos. 2–14 make up a good terrace of 1901 by *D. & J. R. McMillan*, with square and polygonal bays and gabled dormers. Leading N from Fonthill Road is ALBURY ROAD, with 1870s *cottages ornés* by *Duncan McMillan* on the W side. An outlying group of villas lies further W along the E side of Hardgate, the main route into town from the S until Holburn Street was laid out. Much the grandest is WILLOWBANK, now approached from Willowbank Road. A simple, flat-fronted Georgian house, squeezed between two large and unequal wings added by *J. & W. Smith*, c. 1843. The wings have shallow-pitched gables and deep Italianate eaves, and the W one has a semicircular bow on the side. Alien both to the wings and the original house is a massive Greek Doric porch, but this is also said to be Smith's. (On the opposite side of Willowbank Road, granite council flats of 1936.) Immediately S of Willowbank in Rosebank Place is ROSEBANK, which seems to be shown on Milne's map of 1789. Now embedded in a late C19 tenement terrace, but the harled C18 house with tripartite windows on the first floor is unmistakable. S again, on Hardgate itself, is MILLBANK, another simple Georgian house, completely swamped by ugly late C20 extensions.

THE HARBOUR

W of its narrow entry to the sea, the estuary of the Dee was a 500 m.-broad expanse of shifting channels and sandbanks until the C19. A quay near the bottom of Shiprow was extended eastward in stages from the mid C15 to the mid C17, and in 1775 a pier by *John Smeaton* was begun on the N side of the river mouth to combat silting. However, it was not until *Thomas Telford* reported for the Town Council in the first decade of the C19 that the estuary began to be transformed systematically into a harbour. Under Acts of Parliament of 1810 and 1829, Trinity Quay, Regent Quay and Waterloo Quay were built. A further Act of 1843 resulted in the enclosed VICTORIA DOCK, opened in 1848. In 1871–3 an artificial channel was cut, confining the Dee to the S side of the estuary and diverting it along its present course. This permitted the creation of the ALBERT BASIN, roughly where the main channel had been, and the extension of Market Street southward across reclaimed land to the new Victoria Bridge and Torry. Comprehensive reconstruction from the 1970s onwards has removed almost all earlier dockside structures. The most conspicuous new arrivals are ranks of cylindrical storage tanks for 'mud' – a chemical lubricant used in offshore drilling.

The boundaries are, on the W, the railway; N, Trinity Quay, Virginia Street, Commerce Street and Beach Boulevard; E, Links Road and the sea; and S, the Dee. For features of the harbour on the S side of the Dee, *see* Torry (p. 302).

CHURCHES

Former ST CLEMENT'S PARISH CHURCH, St Clement Street. Disused. *John Smith*, 1828. It replaced a church of 1787 on the same site, which had itself replaced a chapel of medieval origin. Now the community of which it was the focus has vanished. Gothic, with a dignified w tower, battlemented and pinnacled. Rectangular nave with buttresses between windows; E wheel window. Interior not seen, but a photograph of 1987 shows a conventional arrangement with side galleries, the pulpit and organ in an arched recess at the E end. CHURCHYARD with a good collection of monuments and headstones, mostly C19, a few C18, many with maritime associations. A carved plaque on the N churchyard wall states that it was paid for by George Davidson, 1650. Midway between tower and street, a cast-iron monument to members of the Farquharson family, apparently *c.* 1836: a sloping-sided classical plinth with a tiny urn on top.

MISSION HALL, North Square, Footdee. *William Smith*, 1870. A gabled granite box with brick dressings.

PUBLIC BUILDINGS

Former COMMERCE STREET PUBLIC SCHOOL, Commerce Street. *Duncan McMillan*, 1875. Now offices. The first school built by the newly created Aberdeen School Board. Very plain, with segmental-headed windows, two little square spires on the roof and other minimally Gothic details.

HANOVER STREET SCHOOL, Beach Boulevard. *Arthur Clyne*, 1898; refurbished and extended by the *City Council's Architects*, 2007–9. Three pedimented square bays front and back. New entrance in angular w extension with oversailing roof.

MARINE OPERATIONS CENTRE, North Pier. *SMC Parr Architects*, completed 2006. Five-storey, D-plan service tower of white concrete. Wrapped round its flat, seaward side is a faceted curtain wall of dark glass, also D-plan, but wider towards the top, giving panoramic views over the harbour and its approaches. Boldly functional, it follows worthily in the tradition of C19 lighthouses.   124

ROUND HOUSE, Pocra Quay. Predecessor of the Marine Operations Centre, and a distinctive landmark perched on the quayside. Payments for a 'new house' at the North Pier in 1797–8 provide a likely date for the octagonal lower stage of harled rubble with granite dressings. A flat-roofed, first-floor extension on thin legs was added to the s side in 1947. The slated, bell-shaped upper stage with glazed top came in 1966.

Former YORK STREET SCHOOL, York Street. *Pirie & Clyne*, 1881, with additions. Single storey. Narrow gabled façade to street, with three blind-headed lancets. A church-like, pyramid-roofed tower with battered sides and open bell stage rises from the apex of the roof.

DESCRIPTION

We begin at the N end of Victoria Bridge (for the bridge, *see* Torry). Heading N along Market Street, on the corner of North Esplanade West a rectangular classical former TRAM SHED by

W. Dyack, Burgh Surveyor, 1903–4. Grey granite, with pink granite pilaster strips and a pediment. Except for the high, round-arched entrance, it might be taken for a chapel. (w of Market Street, as far as the railway viaduct, was reclaimed from the estuary when the Dee was diverted. Older buildings here, many associated with fish processing, have largely given way to late C20 industrial sheds and early C21 offices. An isolated survivor is on North Esplanade West, between Russell Road and Old Ford Road: *c.* 1890s, with a shaped gable and a triangular-plan oriel. On the SE side it includes a later kiln for smoking fish, one of a handful remaining in the area, recognizable by their rooftop vents. The railway viaduct was rebuilt in its present form in granite, 1902–4.) MARKET STREET (a noisy stretch of ring road at this point) continues with commercial buildings of *c.* 1900 on the w side, a few of which stand out: No. 182, for the Seaton Brick and Tile Co., but of granite, is by *Ellis & Wilson*, 1897. Three gables, and arched first-floor windows with blocked surrounds. Then, turning the corner of Palmerston Road, the FERRY HOTEL, originally Seamen's Mission, 1925–6 by *Pite, Son & Fairweather*. Three storeys rising to four at the chamfered corner, making a kind of squat tower with a shallow, rustic-looking pediment to each face. On the other corner of Palmerston Road, the lively and eclectic Grimsby Chambers, 1902 by *Brown & Watt*. Round inset corner tower flanked by taller contrasting gables and still taller chimneystacks. Nos. 162–166, 1903, are by *Jenkins & Marr*: shallow canted bays recessed between giant Ionic pilasters, and an elaborate curvy gable incorporating a wall-head stack.

On the E side of Market Street, COMMERCIAL QUAY leads into the dock compound and to REGENT ROAD, running between the Albert Basin and Victoria Dock. Of C19 buildings here, only a block of three-storey warehouses survives, overshadowed by *Mackie Ramsay & Taylor*'s twelve-storey Salvesen Tower of 1977: concrete cladding panels, each making a bevelled frame for a recessed window. Just E of this, on PROVOST BLAIKIE'S QUAY, a small, single-storey building of polychrome, rock-faced granite with two Dutch gables, built as offices for the granite merchant John Fyfe, 1890, and evidently an advertisement for his wares. The details recall Pirie & Clyne.

Returning to Market Street and turning N brings us to Trinity Quay, which leads E to REGENT QUAY and an attractive variety of C18 and C19 harbourside buildings, aligned with the distant tower of St Clement (*see* Churches). The HARBOUR OFFICES by *A. Marshall Mackenzie*, 1883–5, are classical but not symmetrical. Originally only the r. part was for the harbour board, with domed clock tower above pediment and pilasters; the rest was offices and warehousing for a separate client, though conforming in design. Arcaded ground-floor windows right across, with decorative blocking. Facing the E side, on the corner of Weigh House Square and Virginia Street, a plain

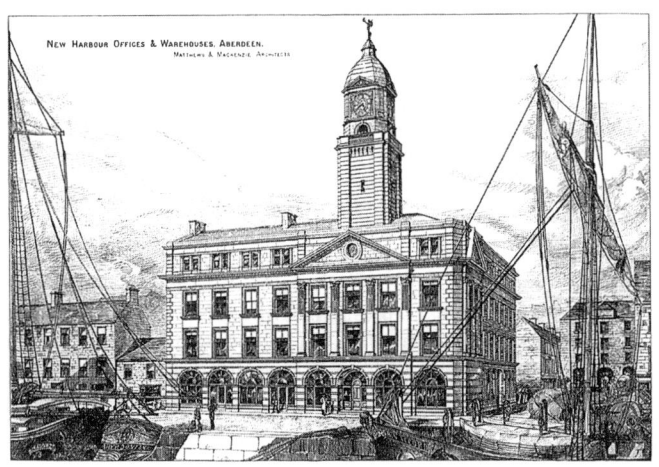

Harbour Offices.
Design by A. Marshall Mackenzie, 1883

four-storey warehouse block for the Shore Porters Society with taking-in doors in vertical rows, 1865. (E of this on Virginia Street is another block for the Society dated 1861: originally shops and dwellings, converted to warehousing 1891. Just E of the Marischal Street bridge is yet another of their warehouses, dated 1897 on the turreted corner of Virginia Street and Shore Lane.) Back on Regent Quay, on the SE corner of Marischal Street, the excellent former TOWN & COUNTY BANK, 1901, by *R. G. Wilson*. Seven-bay palazzo front to Marischal Street, with giant Ionic pilasters above a rusticated basement. Just one bay wide to the quay, where the basement has a round-arched door with coved surround. Pairs of giant pilasters and a pediment above, framing a first-floor window with broken pediment and balcony,

No. 35 Regent Quay, described as 'lately erected' in 1772, 88 is the best surviving house of its date in the centre. Possibly by the mason *Alexander Kennedy*, who feued the land in 1766. It became the CUSTOM HOUSE in 1774. Five bays, three storeys plus a basement, with a sunk area in front. Moulded cornice, rusticated quoins to angles and raised margins to windows. Door with Gibbs surround and pediment. Open stair opposite entrance, with wrought-iron balustrade. Next door, E, Regent House, 1898–9 by *A. Marshall Mackenzie*. Originally offices for William Williams & Sons, distillers. First floor almost filled by a shallow, serpentine bow window on carved brackets, with flanking urns and a balustrade on top. The two floors above are set back, the centre breaking forward with a pediment and attached Ionic columns framing the windows. After this, houses of *c.* 1780 as far as James Street, with varied window treatments: No. 42 has Gothic glazing bars at the rear, No. 43 balustrades below the first-floor sills and No. 49 a couple of Venetian windows. No. 52, on the other corner of James Street, is also C18 but was raised another storey in 1896–7 by *Ellis & Wilson* for use as a hotel. Nos. 73–75 are Torridon House, offices converted from a six-storey warehouse, after which Regent Quay ends at No. 76 with an early C19 granite ashlar corner block, with arcaded ground-floor windows.

This brings us to WATERLOO QUAY. On the N side, just E of Commerce Street, was the terminus of the Aberdeenshire Canal, connected with the harbour via a lock in 1834. In 1853 the canal between here and Kittybrewster was drained and railway tracks were laid along its bed, but there is no trace of the station buildings of the Great North of Scotland Railway Co., which existed here before the line through the Denburn valley opened in 1867. E of Church Street, Waterloo Quay has buildings erected by the Northern Agricultural Co. for processing and storing animal feed and fertilizer. *William* and *James Henderson* designed some in 1854–5, parts of which may survive towards the Church Street end of the site. More impressive is the five-storey block on the SW corner of Waterloo Quay and Lime Street, perhaps 1870s, with giant pilasters to the upper floors. A similar block is on the SE corner. Further blocks extend along the W side of LIME STREET: the gabled one with square-headed windows is by *W.B. Coutts*, 1881, for milling locust beans; its neighbour at the corner of Clarence Street with semicircular windows is by *George Coutts*, 1907, for manufacturing manure. All were converted to offices from the mid 1970s, a fairly early case of the adaptive reuse of historic industrial buildings, though interiors were not retained.

Back on Waterloo Quay, at the corner of Wellington Street is a refined three-storey classical house with architraves to the first-floor windows, commissioned in 1837 from *William Knight* as the headquarters of the Aberdeen Steam Navigation Co. N of here, *John Smith* had earlier envisaged a grid of streets round a large central square – a planned suburb in association with the developing harbour – but instead the area grew in a piecemeal way, with industry predominating. The most impressive early C19 remnant, perhaps by Smith, is a block begun in 1828 on the S side of ST CLEMENT STREET between Wellington Street and York Place. Three-storey corner pavilions contain shops and dwellings, with warehousing between, the same height but four storeys. The warehouses (now converted to flats) have smaller segmental-headed windows and a central cart entrance, but the whole reads as a unified classical terrace, given gravitas by three slab-like wall-head pediments. Facing it across St Clement Street, a big utilitarian block of engineering works extending back to York Street, with a row of five gables to Wellington Street. The site was an iron foundry in the mid C19, which may be the date of the granite rubble walls, but the internal steel structure must date from after it became part of the Hall Russell shipyard in the later C19.

York Street continues SE to POCRA QUAY, which ends at the harbour mouth. For the Round House, *see* Public Buildings. W of it, the Footdee WAR MEMORIAL, a granite obelisk with small bronze reliefs of a sailor and a Gordon Highlander, 1919, designed by *James Gordon Milne* and carried out by *Caie & Rettie*. From the quay below the Round House projects a hook-shaped jetty, completed in 1878. Along with a corresponding pier on the Torry side, it was designed to break the strength of heavy seas entering the harbour. It incorporates part of the earlier Abercrombie's Jetty – constructed according to Smeaton's design, 1788–90, and intended to address the same problem – the original datestone of which is set into its W side. N of the Round House is the single-storey former CUSTOMS WATCH HOUSE (now a restaurant, and raised a storey above the original battlemented parapet), 1871 by *William Smith*. The brick obelisk between it and the Marine Operations Centre (*see* Public Buildings) is a ventilation shaft for the main outfall sewer of 1867. Beyond the Marine Operations Centre is Smeaton's NORTH PIER, 1775–80. It was extended by *Telford*, 1811–16, with *John Gibb* superintending the work (the end was twice destroyed by the sea, before being successfully rebuilt in 1816 with its base spreading outwards). A final extension in concrete was added by *William Dyce Cay*, 1874–7, with *John Hawkshaw* and *James Abernethy* as consultants. The octagonal cast-iron LIGHTHOUSE at the end, designed by *Messrs Stevenson* and made by *Abernethy & Co.* of Ferryhill, was erected in 1865 at the head of the Telford part, and moved to its present location in 1877.

New Pier Road leads N from the war memorial. Between it and the sea is FOOTDEE, a planned village of fishermen's cottages and one of the sights of Aberdeen. As originally designed by *John Smith* for the Town Council, 1808–9, the cottages were single-storeyed and thatched, forming two large inward-looking squares. In 1837 Smith added Middle Row, bisecting South Square. A separate terrace – Pilot Square – was built *c.* 1854 between South Square and Pocra Quay, the gaps at each end being closed with taller tenements in the 1870s. From this date the cottages began to be sold to their occupiers, resulting in upward extensions of one or more storeys. Sheds of various shapes and sizes, originally for fishing gear, had already started to colonize the open spaces, and the Mission Hall (*see* Churches) joined them in the middle of North Square in 1870. The transformation of Smith's orderly plan by quirky individualism is a delight.

RUTHRIESTON

Despite the presence of the C16 Bridge of Dee, Ruthrieston remained a peripheral area of scattered villas until the late C19

and early C20, when speculative housing pushed S from Great
Western Road and along Holburn Street.

RUTHRIESTON WEST CHURCH (originally Ruthrieston Free
Church), Broomhill Road. An ambitious building of 1900–1
by *Brown & Watt*, consisting of nave, shallow transepts and an
inset tower and spire at the NW corner. Its much simpler predecessor of 1876 by *James Matthews* survives, attached to the
E end: Aberdeen-bond rubble with paired lancets, it serves as
a hall, but from the outside reads as a chancel. The present
church is Aberdeen-bond too, above a rock-faced basement.
Windows mostly of intersecting tracery, lancets at the W end.
The main feature is the tower: not especially tall, but powerful
and sturdy, with big diagonal buttresses. The short spire with
exaggeratedly long lucarnes is surrounded by four smaller
spirelets, set close in behind the corbelled parapet to make a
memorably spiky silhouette. At the tower base, paired doors
under a broad, shallow arch open into a square vestibule with
Gothic woodwork. Broad interior with W gallery (the space
underneath enclosed by a glazed screen, 2000). Pitch-pine
ceiling – a trefoil arch in section – with tie-beams. – PULPIT
in centre of E wall, Gothic, 1889, moved here from the old
church. – COMMUNION TABLE and other furnishings, Gothic,
1920s. – STAINED GLASS. N transept, Christ as shepherd with
Moses and a female saint, 1903; nave, S side, Christ flanked
by two saints, by *James A. Crombie* of the Abbey Studio, 1957.
Other windows have pleasing Art Nouveau foliage patterns in
pale colours, contemporary with the building. The former
SCHOOL of 1876 stands just N of the old church.

SOUTH HOLBURN PARISH CHURCH (originally Ruthrieston
Church), Holburn Street. *Matthews & Mackenzie*, 1890–1.
Shaped by ecclesiological principles, like Mackenzie's slightly
earlier church at Craigiebuckler (*see* p. 277): correct E–W orientation, nave and chancel distinguished by their separate
steeply pitched roofs, W gable with bellcote and cross, and a
generous S porch. Large W window to the street: five lancets,
alternately pointed and trefoil-headed, the middle three stilted.
More trefoil-headed lancets down each side, in ones and twos.
Inside, the nave is lofty and very long for its width, with a
segmental arched timber ceiling. Steps and a chamfered,
pointed arch separate it from the chancel, with a small timber
Gothic PULPIT on the r. side rather than in the centre. The
reordered chancel has an open timber roof, and originally had
stalls facing inward on each side. Transept-like projection on
the N, originally for organ and vestry. – COMMUNION TABLE.
Classical, a First World War memorial brought from Holburn
Parish Church (*see* p. 153). – STAINED GLASS. E window, the
Supper at Emmaus, brought from an unrecorded church in
Edinburgh, 1990. HALLS of 1904 with additions of 1971,
attached at right angles, S.

PUBLIC BUILDINGS

BRIDGE OF DEE, Anderson Drive South and Stonehaven Road.   3, 79
Projected by Bishop William Elphinstone, who gathered materials but died in 1514 before construction could start. His successor Bishop Gavin Dunbar began building – the earliest
datestone is 1520 – and completed the bridge in 1527, formally
handing it over to the Town Council in 1529. *Thomas Franche*
was master mason and the work was overseen by Alexander
Galloway, Rector of Kinkell, who may have acted as architect.
Predominantly freestone with some granite. Seven semicircular arches with triangular cutwaters, from which semi-
hexagonal buttresses rise to form pedestrian refuges in the
parapet. The undersides of the arches have deep, chamfered
ribs. The datestones show that work began at the S end, then
the N, before the two parts were joined in the middle.
Extensively rebuilt in 1718–24 by the master mason *Alexander
Riach*, who 'supplied the Place of ane Architect after the first
Schem was drawn by Mr Alexander McGill'. Widened in
1841–2 by *John Smith*, with *James Walker* of London as consultant. Proposals to build outwards on each side using granite or
cast iron were rejected in favour of preserving the structure's
historic appearance: Smith extended it by 11 ft 6 in. (2.1 m.)
on the W side only, the original facings being carefully reinstated (although from underneath the new ribs can be distinguished from the old). Heraldic carvings are a notable feature,
the arms of Bishop Dunbar being the most prominent.
Contemporary inscriptions on the W side record the C18 and
C19 changes. At the SW corner, a SUNDIAL dated 1719. A
chapel existed in connection with the bridge before the
Reformation.

BROOMHILL SCHOOL, Broomhill Road. 1893, by *Alexander
Mavor* (*Harvey Mennie*, his chief assistant, is said to have been
responsible); alterations by *J. A. Ogg Allan*, 1936. A big Board
School – three storeys – the main front divided into pedimented bays of tripartite windows with sparse Renaissance
details.

HOLBURN STREET FOOTBRIDGE, Holburn Street and Gray
Street. Opened 2004. Engineers, *Halcrow Group*. A suspension
bridge, with cables anchored to a single strut that passes
through the bridge deck at an angle. The deck widens towards
the middle of the span. Part of a footpath and cycleway along
the route of the defunct Deeside Railway.

RUTHRIESTON BRIDGE, between the Dee and Riverside Drive,
near the junction with Ruthrieston Road. Built over the
Ruthrieston burn in 1693 to link the Bridge of Dee road with
Hardgate. It stood 32 m. W of its present site until relocated
in 1923. Three semicircular arches, the middle one bigger, with
triangular cutwaters and weathered heraldic panels on the E
side. The l. one shows the arms of Aberdeen, the r. one those
of Robert Cruikshank, provost when the bridge was built. The
stepped parapet is C20.

RUTHRIESTON COMMUNITY CENTRE, Holburn Street (opposite South Holburn parish church). The former Ruthrieston Public School, 1875, by *William Henderson & Son*. Extended 1883.

DESCRIPTION

A few C19 villas survive, their grounds built over with suburban streets. In Cranford Road is CRANFORD, with gabled dormers. Probably built in the early 1860s for the ironmonger David McHardy, it is now a nursing home, swamped by later extensions. 0.5 km. E, marooned between the roaring traffic of South Anderson Drive and mid-C20 housing in Newlands Avenue, is NEWLANDS: a substantial Baronial-Gothic villa of 1889 by *Alexander Brown*, with a conical-roofed corner tower. Built for the spirit dealer William Murray, whose monogram is over the door. The triangle between Holburn Street, the Dee and Riverside Terrace was offered for feuing in 1875, to a plan by *James Forbes Beattie & Son*, river views making it an attractive site for large villas. One survivor is DEEFORD HOUSE, in existence by 1886, at the corner of Riverside Terrace and Riverside Drive: Baronial, with Gothic touches and a pyramid-roofed tower. Another is the classical No. 74 Riverside Drive, 1885 by *Matthews & Mackenzie* for the shipbuilder William Hall.

OUTER DISTRICTS: NORTH

BRIDGE OF DON

The name denotes the large suburban sprawl which has grown up N of the river Don since the 1960s, a mix of housing and industrial estates. A few earlier buildings of interest lie close to the river or along Ellon Road, the northward continuation of King Street.

ABERDEEN EXHIBITION & CONFERENCE CENTRE, Ellon Road. The main front, with a swooping roof like a ski jump, is part of a gimmicky remodelling of 2001 by *Mackie Ramsay & Taylor*. An arched opening in the glazed façade makes the S end into a bridge, leading to a viewing tower.

ABERDEEN SCIENCE & TECHNOLOGY PARK, Balgownie Road and Balgownie Drive. Spread across three campuses, with High-Tech sheds set among generous tree planting. In the middle of Campus Three, on the S side of Balgownie Drive, is BALGOWNIE LODGE. Probably built soon after 1798, when the exceptionally beautiful site above the Don was leased by Thomas Leys, of Leys, Masson & Co. (*see* Grandholm Mill below). A single-storey house, originally called Polgownie Cottage but altogether grander and more sophisticated than that suggests. Square, with a sandstone portico of four unfluted Ionic columns on the N and a segmental bow with veranda on the W. Harled walls, with long windows reaching from just below the eaves to just above the granite plinth. Inside, a corridor with pilasters runs parallel with the entrance front. The heart of the house is a splendid saloon with oval-domed ceiling and pendentives, lit from a skylight. The room with the bow opens off it. It has painted decoration in the Aesthetic taste, almost certainly by *Daniel Cottier* for John Crombie, a later owner of Grandholm Mill, to whom the Lodge was feued in 1871. There is STAINED GLASS of the same date in the front door: Dante and Chaucer. (Crombie was surely following the example of his neighbour John Forbes White, friend and patron of Cottier, whose GLENSEATON LODGE, 500 m. S at the end of Kettock's Mill Road, is said to contain the remains of a scheme by the designer. Cottier also worked at BRIDGEFIELD HOUSE, No. 64 Balgownie Road, a building probably of *c.* 1800, but his decoration of the apsidal mid-C19 drawing room there has been covered up.)

COTTOWN OF BALGOWNIE. Picturesque terraces of mostly single-storey cottages, lining the E approach to the Bridge of Balgownie (*see* p. 196). Heavily restored *c.* 1960.

GRANDHOME HOUSE, 2.5 km. NNW of Persley Bridge. A mansion of great charm, in a matchless setting overlooking the Don. The present E-plan is the result of an 1859 addition, which occupies the courtyard of what was previously a U-plan house of three wings. The history of these pre-C19 wings is difficult to understand. The N one seems to contain the oldest fabric and may stand on the foundations of a medieval tower. Its walls are thick and there is a gunloop and a built-in stone sink in the ground-floor room at the E end (though the huge round-arched fireplace here is evidently C19 or C20). There are bolection-moulded chimneypieces at each end of the first floor, and a lean-to addition on the N side has a skewputt dated 1731. The S wing – perhaps at one time a separate building – has a rubble ground floor and ashlar first floor, indicating at least two phases of construction; blocked windows in the gables suggest that it was once higher still. In the S front is a panel dated 1686 with the arms of George Paton of Ferrochie, who acquired the property in 1673. Until 1859, the main entrance to the U-plan house seems to have been here, via a pedimented doorway with a Gibbs surround, identical with the one of *c.* 1770 at No. 35 Regent Quay (*see* p. 255). A ground-floor chimneypiece inside this part is dated 1722. Connecting the N and S wings, the five-bay W wing has a low ground floor and a much higher *piano nobile*, said to have been added in 1780. It originally ended with a S gable, which suggests that the heightening of the adjoining S wing (or at least the W end of it) must have come later. In 1859, the W wing was doubled in depth on the

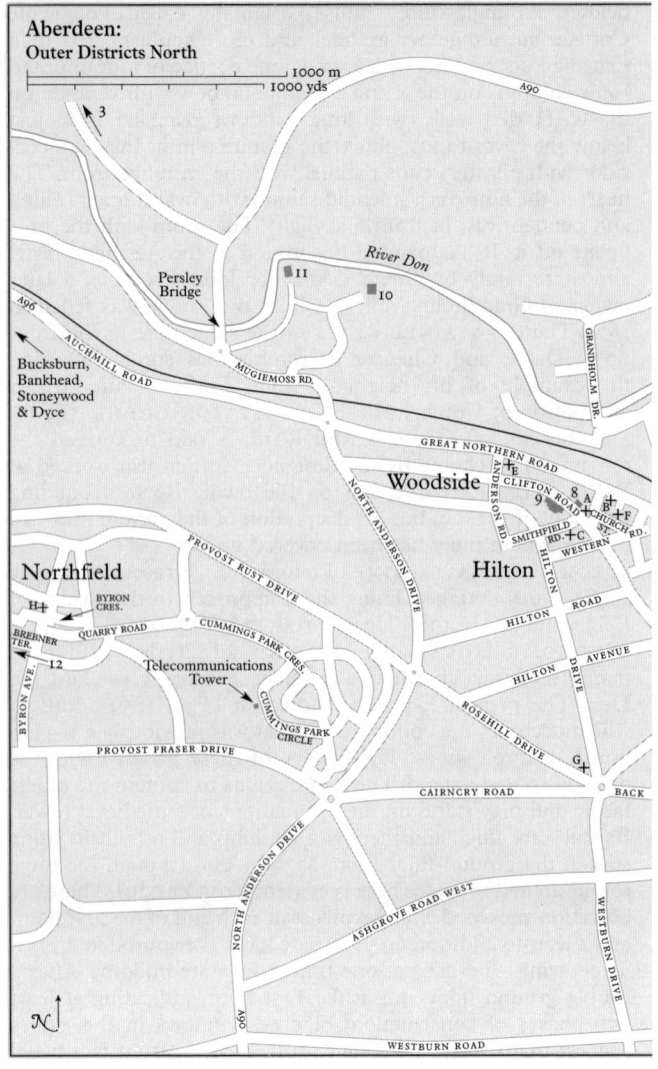

Aberdeen:
Outer Districts North

1000 m
1000 yds

A   Chapel of Ease (former)
B   Congregational Church (former)
C   St John's Church for Deaf People
D   St Joseph (R.C.)
E   United Presbyterian Church
     (former)
F   Woodside Parish Church
G   High Church
H   Northfield Parish Church
J   St Ninian (Episcopal)
K   St George's Church

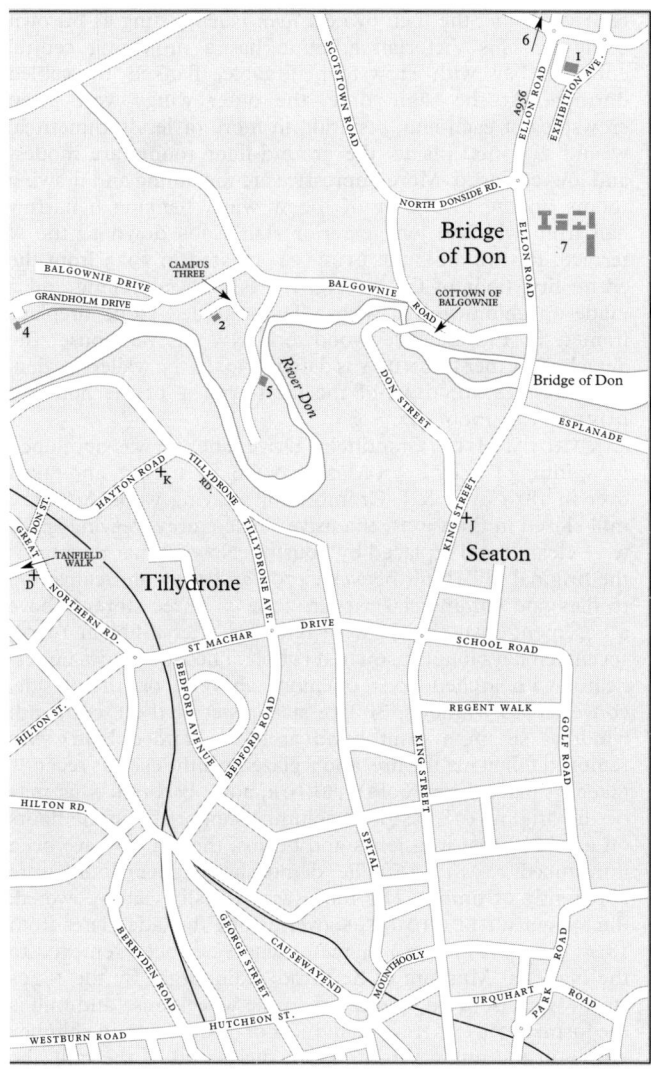

courtyard side, the then owner, *John Paton*, acting as his own architect. This Victorian addition has a projecting central entrance bay with crowstepped gable, flanked by gabled dormers. At the same time, the outer wings were given crowsteps at each end, resulting in more or less symmetrical W and E fronts. Inside, the ground-floor rooms are modest and low-ceilinged. More impressive are the dining and drawing rooms on the first floor of the W wing, flanking a narrow hall from which a long exterior stair leads down to the W terrace. Best of all is the LIBRARY, created in 1923 from the entire first floor of the S wing. It has a coved ceiling and a made-up chimneypiece with a Tudor-arched stone fireplace framed in Empire-style woodwork. NW of the house, the detached former LAUNDRY is dated 1736. In the walled garden, a C17 or C18 SUNDIAL of the facet type. E of the house, a DOVECOT of 1709.

GRANDHOLM MILL, Grandholm Drive. The site was developed for spinning flax by Leys, Masson & Co. from 1792, and taken over in 1859 by J. & J. Crombie for weaving wool. After the mill closed in the 1990s, extensive single-storey weaving sheds were cleared and replaced by housing. Now all that remains is the original mill, built between 1792 and 1797 and converted to flats and commercial uses in 2002–5. Three storeys above a basement (two storeys were removed after a fire in 1900), seventeen bays long, in squared rubble. The lade passes underneath, with arched hoist openings above it on the N side, converted to windows. Square stair-tower at the E end, with windows set in a giant blind arch. Its domed belfry was removed following the fire, and a glazed penthouse has recently taken its place. Fireproof INTERIOR, now obscured; what may be the original C18 cast-iron columns support flagstone floors on a grid of cast-iron joists and beams, thought to have been introduced *c.* 1812–26. The demolished upper floors were apparently of timber. The mill was originally water-powered: the former WHEELHOUSE, S, overlooking the lade, dates from 1826; the 25 ft (7.6 m.)-diameter wheel has been removed to the National Museum of Scotland, Edinburgh. By the 1840s steam was also used, and between the wheelhouse and mill is the former ENGINE HOUSE, the scar of its demolished chimney visible in the mill's S front. From the W end of the mill, the single-storey WING MILL extends S. It was originally used for heckling.

KETTOCK'S MILL, Kettock's Mill Road. C19 corn mill, converted to flats.

MILL OF MUNDURNO, 2 km. N of the Exhibition Centre, on the W side of Ellon Road. An early C19 rubble-built corn mill with overshot wheel and timber lade.

TERRITORIAL ARMY BARRACKS, Ellon Road. Built 1932–5 by the *War Office* for the Gordon Highlanders, replacing their previous barracks on Castlehill. A variety of separate blocks, some with Baronial touches, grouped around the large parade ground. Additions by *Alison & Hutchison & Partners*, 1962.

BUCKSBURN, BANKHEAD AND STONEYWOOD

Paper mills along the River Don were the main employers here in the C19.

CHURCHES

BUCKSBURN STONEYWOOD CHURCH, Oldmeldrum Road. Originally Newhills Free Church. 1844, probably by *William Henderson*. The canted gable to the street has three windows with simple timber Y-tracery, and a square bellcote topped with a little spire. This is the pulpit end, and what looks like a porch below the windows is actually the vestry. Inside, galleries on three sides on cast-iron columns, pulpit and organ (installed 1924) on the fourth.

ST MACHAR (Episcopal), Oldmeldrum Road. *Mackenzie & Matthews*, 1878–80. Simple but dignified, in Aberdeen-bond granite rubble with ashlar dressings. Nave with lower apsidal chancel flanked by short transepts containing vestry (N) and organ (S) – a prototype for Mackenzie's Craigiebuckler church (*see* p. 277). The W front has diagonal buttresses, lancets on either side of the door and a small sexfoil window in the gable. Simple plate tracery in the nave windows; lancets in the apse and transepts. Inside, arched timber ceilings to nave and chancel, separated by a sandstone chancel arch (W end divided off to make a meeting area, late C20). – FONT. Polished granite, baluster-shaped. – ORGAN, 1902. – PAINTED DECORATION by *Douglas Strachan*, 1901, with echoes of late Burne-Jones: on either side of the chancel arch, angels against a background of trees; above the chancel windows, a frieze of kneeling angels and an inscription; between the windows, four paintings on canvas, applied to the wall: Adoration of the Magi, Transfiguration, Crucifixion and Resurrection. – STAINED GLASS. Apse E window, the Good Shepherd, *John Hardman & Co.*, 1880, with matching windows to either side, presumably also by Hardman, of St Andrew, r., †1901, and St Machar, l., undated. Apse N side, St Margaret of Scotland, 1948, by *Douglas Hamilton*; s side, Christ carrying a child, 1955, *J. M. Aiken*.

Former STONEYWOOD PARISH CHURCH, Bankhead Road and Bankhead Avenue. *William Henderson & Son*, 1878–9. Gothic, with a corner tower ending in an octagonal belfry and spirelet. Cross-gables to the nave and twin gables to the transepts, all with unusually tall windows of timber tracery. Interior subdivided for secular use.

PUBLIC BUILDINGS

BEACON COMMUNITY CAMPUS, Kepplehills Road. Under construction 2010. School, library, sports facilities and other community services in a mixture of new and refurbished buildings. Render, with corrugated metal and timber cladding. In front of the school on Kepplehills Road, granite WAR MEMORIAL: a lion with a shield on a hexagonal column.

MEAL MILL, Howes Road (1 km. S of the Beacon Community Campus). On the Bucks Burn, opposite Bucksburn House. C18, roofless.

ROWETT INSTITUTE OF NUTRITION AND HEALTH, Greenburn Road. Established in 1913, it became part of the University of Aberdeen in 2008. STRATHCONA HOUSE, 1930–2 by *A. G. Ingham* of the Department of Agriculture, was built as living accommodation and a place for the Institute's scholars to mingle. Plain Scots vernacular in rock-faced red sandstone with gabled dormers. The main block has two short S wings with a loggia between. Behind is a double-height oak-panelled dining hall with an inglenook in the middle of the N side. Over the fireplace a PAINTING, The Pioneers, 1932 by *Alexander Gibson*: a procession of purposeful agricultural workers. Several heraldic STAINED GLASS windows commemorate Imperial links, the earlier, darker ones by *James S. Hamilton*, the later ones, with larger areas of clear glass, designed by *William Kelly* and made by *Alexander Strachan*. The REID LIBRARY, N, established in 1923, is plain granite with a gabled centre and later C20 additions. Over the door, a good carved panel designed by *Kelly* and a little oriel. Inside on the landing, a three-light STAINED GLASS window by *Kelly* and *Alexander Strachan*, 1938, illustrating the work of the Institute: a scientist in the laboratory, a farmer with his livestock, and students in the library.

Former SCHOOL, Nos. 101–109 Stoneywood Road. Provided in 1864 by Alexander Pirie & Sons of Stoneywood Paper Mill (*see* below): their monogram and the date are on the S front. A single-storey Gothic range, harled with granite margins. Bellcote on the central gable, porches either side, plus a two-storey teacher's house at each end. Now all in residential use.

STONEYWOOD PAPER MILL, Stoneywood Terrace. A sprawling industrial complex on a riverside site where paper has been made since 1770. It was operated for much of its history by the Pirie family. The oldest surviving buildings – of granite, some in existence by 1848 – are in the centre of the site, bordering the W side of the tail race. Facing the mill lade further N, a long, three-storey range dated 1871 has continuous bands of windows divided by cast-iron mullions, with brick infill between the floors. Dominating the N end of the site, a giant warehouse of 1914–15 by *Harbourne Maclennan* of *Jenkins & Marr*: two storeys, of reinforced concrete construction, with pitched roofs, steel windows and a square corner tower. The former CANTEEN of 1898 has pyramid-roofed corner pavilions. It stands apart from the factory, W of Stoneywood Terrace. 250 m. N is STONEYWOOD HOUSE, 1849–50 by *James Matthews* for Alexander Pirie II. Jacobean, with a triple-arched portico between bay-windowed wings, shaped gables and an ogee-roofed NE tower. 300 m. SW of the Canteen is WATERTON HOUSE, another large mid-C19 Pirie residence, with a Jacobean gable and segmental bow window. Its LODGE – a *cottage orné* facing the former school on Stoneywood Road (*see* above) – is now cut off from the house by the realignment of the road.

DYCE

A railway village originally, but now synonymous with Aberdeen's airport. The oil boom of the 1970s saw the enormous expansion of the airport, the construction of a large industrial estate to its W and the transformation of Dyce into a populous suburb.

CHURCHES

DYCE PARISH CHURCH, Victoria Street. *George Scott*, 1894–5. A rock-faced granite box with a semicircular pediment crowning the W gable. It was built as a mission hall for the former Parish Church of 1871–2 (now demolished). The parish HALL on the opposite side of Victoria Street, dated 1894, was originally the Free Church mission hall.

ST FERGUS. The roofless shell of the pre-Reformation parish church stands proudly on a bluff overlooking the River Don, 3 km. N of the airport. A simple gabled rectangle, much altered and restored, the principal medieval features being two blocked Gothic doorways in the S side and one in the N. NW skewputt carved with an animal head. Bellcote on the W gable. FONT outside the W door, broken. Inside, E end of N side, carved sill of a SACRAMENT HOUSE, said to have been dated 1544, with the initials of Alexander Galloway, Rector of Kinkell, but now illegible. In a modern shelter within the W end are six Pictish SYMBOL STONES. Of the two largest, the earlier, thought to be C6, is incised with a beast, double-disc and Z-rod. The later, perhaps mid-C9, has relief carvings of a cross with interlace ornament, double disc and Z-rod, and an Ogham inscription. Churchyard with WATCH HOUSE.

PUBLIC BUILDINGS

ABERDEEN AIRPORT. Main terminal by *Robert Matthew, Johnson-Marshall & Partners*, opened 1977. Long and low, with off-white metal cladding. More assertive is the CONTROL TOWER by *McAlister Armstrong & Partners*, a stepped pyramid with octagonal glazed top, completed in 1978.

BP HEADQUARTERS, Stoneywood Road. 2006–7, designed and built for BP by developer *Akeler*. A three-storey linear atrium with seven radiating wings, three on one side, four on the other. The wings end with emergency stairs in detached towers with rounded ends, clad in perforated metal. The building superseded BP's previous office complex in Burnside Road, N, built in phases, *c.* 1975–1980s, of which at least the later five-storey blocks are by *Mackie Ramsay & Taylor*.

LIDDEL'S MONUMENT, off Pitmedden Road, 0.75 km. SSW of St Fergus. A square stone pillar with a pyramid-topped upper stage bearing inscriptions and a ball finial. It was erected in 1637 to the memory of Duncan Liddel (1561–1613), who vested the surrounding land in the Town Council of Aberdeen to endow bursaries at Marischal College.

SKENE ENCLOSURE, off Riverview Drive, just SE of Cordyce Residential School. Walled burial ground, laid out in 1689 beside the now demolished house of the Skenes of Dyce. Remodelled in Greek Revival style in 1837, with angle pilasters and a pedimented entrance with acroteria.

WALTON EXPERIMENTAL FARM, Walton Road (1 km. SW of the airport). Farmhouse of finely dressed granite ashlar, dated 1795 on the SE skewputt.

WAR MEMORIAL, Gordon Terrace. *William Kelly*, c. 1920. A square granite cenotaph in the middle of the road, the W face carved with a cross copied from one of the Pictish stones at St Fergus (*see* above).

PITMEDDEN HOUSE, Pitmedden Road. Described in 1857 as 'recently erected'. Large, asymmetrical, with Jacobean touches. The main feature is a viewing tower, looking out across the Don valley. Unsympathetic late C20 additions.

HILTON

HIGH CHURCH, Hilton Drive. *G. Bennett Mitchell*, 1935–6. Big, cruciform and very prominent on its corner site, in a round-arched style somewhere between Gothic and Romanesque. Nave with low aisles and a deep clearstorey, transepts and chancel. The aisles have distinctive sloping buttresses which extend across the lean-to roofs and continue upwards between the clearstorey windows. Inside, the broad nave with its open timber roof is impressive, but the aisles are just passages behind arcades punched through its walls, and the buttresses make no appearance. – STAINED GLASS. Three chancel windows: First World War memorial in the centre, an angel and a knight in armour, brought from the Triple Kirks in Schoolhill (*see* p. 128); Second World War memorial either side, Christ, l., and St Michael, r., by *James A. Crombie* of the Abbey Studio, 1950. Attached HALL, N.

NEWHILLS

Much of the parish of Newhills is still completely rural, though lying within the City boundary.

NEWHILLS PARISH CHURCH. *John Smith*, 1829–30 (it replaced the OLD CHURCH of 1662–3, the roofless, rectangular shell of which survives, 500 m. W). A big, gabled rectangle with round-arched windows of simple timber tracery. Greatly extended on the N side in 1989 to provide halls and meeting rooms. Inside, PULPIT with ogee-domed tester in the middle of the S side; galleries on the other three, on quatrefoil cast-iron columns. The arcaded gallery fronts are canted at the corners to make a semi-octagon, and incorporate painted COATS OF ARMS of the Earl Fife and Hay of Seaton. The gallery PEWS survive, some with names of farms and estates painted on the ends. – STAINED GLASS. Flanking the pulpit, windows of 1928–30 with figures of St Catherine of Siena, r., and St Francis, l. Set into these windows are five earlier roundels, possibly pre-Reformation, with symbols of the Evangelists and the Arma Christi: their provenance is a mystery.

ST MARY'S CHAPEL, c. 2 km. NNW of the Old Church. Founded 1367. Only the rectangular outline of the foundations remains. The surrounding burial ground contains a holy well.

NEWHILLS HOUSE, 150 m. SW of the church. Originally the manse, it started off as a two-storey-plus-attic house in granite ashlar, built between 1769 and 1775, modelled on the recent manse at Pettens (N). This is now the W wing, partly reduced to a single storey, its central door replaced by a window. In 1858–9, *William L. Henderson* added a bay-windowed E wing, which he extended N in 1883 to provide a new entrance and staircase. An earlier addition by John Smith appears to have been demolished.

TYREBAGGER SCULPTURE TRAIL, Tyrebagger Wood. S side of the Inverurie Road, c. 1 km. W of St Mary's Chapel. Site-specific sculptures commissioned by the Forestry Commission Scotland, installed from 1994 onwards. Widely scattered, in some cases they blend seamlessly with their setting. They include: Earth Chamber for the Trees and Sky, 1994, by *Chris Drury*, a domed underground room which acts as a camera obscura, projecting an image of the outside world onto a circular table; Beacon, 1994, by *Allan Watson*, a tree-like form of polished steel; Stepping Stones, a functioning footbridge by *Simon Beeson*, 2000; and Tyrebagger Circle, 2003, by *Gavin Scobie*, a shrine-like structure of three concentric wooden enclosures, becoming higher and more solid towards the centre.

CLINTERTY HOUSE, c. 2.5 km. SW of St Mary's Chapel. 1916–20, by *W.J. Devlin*. A tall, gaunt, crowstepped house on the W slope of Elrick Hill, with a round-arched loggia and terrace on the garden front. Gabled dormers, alternately polygonal and pointed-arched.

NORTHFIELD

Aberdeen's first major post-war housing estate, begun in 1950. In contrast to Kincorth (*see* p. 298), granite was abandoned in favour of non-traditional construction. Community buildings are grouped round Byron Square.

NORTHFIELD PARISH CHURCH, Byron Crescent. What is now the hall – harl and granite, 1952–3 by *George Bennett Mitchell & Son* – served as the church until the present main sanctuary was built by *William Coutts Youngson* in 1963–4. The 1960s flat roof was replaced with a pitched one in 1994.

HEATHRYBURN SCHOOL, Howes Road. Completed 2009. One of two Northfield schools by Icelandic practice *Designa Arkitektar*; the other is MANOR PARK SCHOOL, Danestone Circle, 2010. Both are low and linear, of laminated wood construction. Natural light reaches corridors and teaching areas from roof-lights and high-level s windows.

TELECOMMUNICATIONS TOWER, Cummings Park Circle. 1966. The defining landmark of Northfield, visible from all over the city. A 60-m. latticework tower, square below, pointed at the top.

SEATON

A cluster of seventeen- and nineteen-storey residential towers of the 1970s dominates the Links just s of the Don. Also much interwar municipal housing in the form of three-storey granite tenements (N of School Road) and two-storey flatted blocks (between School Road and Regent Walk). For Seaton Park, *see* Old Aberdeen.

ST NINIAN (Episcopal), King Street and Livingstone Court. By *A. Marshall Mackenzie & Son*, 1936, in a squared-off Gothic similar to their contemporary St Mary, further s on King Street (*see* p. 204). Granite rubble. Side windows in threes with triangular tops. w front unsympathetically altered – 1980s? – with a tile-hung gable and round-arched window instead of the original three lancets.

BRIDGE OF DON, King Street. 1827–30, by *Thomas Telford* and *John Smith*. A replacement for the medieval Bridge of Balgownie (*see* p. 196) on the line of early C19 King Street. Five segmental arches of rock-faced granite, with semi-octagonal buttresses that become pedestrian refuges in the parapet. It was doubled in width on the seaward side in 1958–9, replicating the original structure and reusing the original parapet.

TILLYDRONE

Almost entirely municipal housing of the 1960s and 70s, including five nineteen-storey tower blocks of 1964–8 on Auchinleck Road. For Benholm's Lodging, see p. 203.

Sᴛ Gᴇᴏʀɢᴇ, Hayton Road. *Mackie Ramsay & Taylor*, 1970–1.
Triangular, of harled brick, with a clearstorey window strip
below the overhanging, shallow-pitched roof (a replacement
for the original flat one). A concrete flue doubles as a belfry.
Designed for multiple uses, with movable seats and a partition
to subdivide the main space.

WOODSIDE

A water-powered cotton mill on the River Don was established
here in 1785 by Gordon, Barron & Co. but it does not survive.
Grandholm Mill on the other side of the Don (*see* above) was
accessible by pedestrian bridge, and quarries also provided
employment. Absorbed into Aberdeen in 1891, in the interwar
period Woodside saw the construction of much new housing to
replace overcrowded and insanitary city-centre property. Further
public housing followed in the later C20. Amid urban decay and
the roar of traffic along the Great Northern Road, a surprisingly
attractive core of C19 churches and public buildings remains.

CHURCHES

Former ᴄʜᴀᴘᴇʟ ᴏғ ᴇᴀsᴇ, No. 352 Clifton Road. *Archibald
Simpson*, 1829–30. A granite rubble box, extremely plain but
nobly proportioned, with round-arched windows down the
sides. The ᴇ end has a pedimented gable, arched doorway and
flanking windows, and makes an effective termination to
Queen Street. Converted to flats in 1985, with the loss of the
galleried interior. 1880 addition at the sᴡ corner.
Former Cᴏɴɢʀᴇɢᴀᴛɪᴏɴᴀʟ ᴄʜᴜʀᴄʜ, Great Northern Road (ᴡ
side, between King Street and Queen Street). 1867, financed
by *William Leslie*, who may also have designed it. Plain lancet
style, gabled, with four pinnacled buttresses. Later ʜᴀʟʟ, ʀ.
Disused.
Sᴛ Jᴏʜɴ's Cʜᴜʀᴄʜ ғᴏʀ Dᴇᴀғ Pᴇᴏᴘʟᴇ, Smithfield Road
(originally All Saints Episcopal Church). By *A. Marshall
Mackenzie & Son*, 1935–6, and closely related to the practice's
contemporary King Street churches, St Mary (*see* p. 204) and
St Ninian (*see* p. 270). Cruciform, in roughly squared, random-
coursed granite, with tall, narrow windows. *The Builder*
described it as 'unfettered by stylistic detail and superficially
applied ornament, relying for its effect on quiet dignity
of proportion'. It has been disfigured by unsympathetic
additions.
Sᴛ Jᴏsᴇᴘʜ (R.C.), Tanfield Walk. Opened as a school, 1842. A
simple rectangle of squared granite rubble with segmental-
headed windows. Alterations by *Victor Mitchell* in 1899 probably included the polygonal chancel with glazed lantern.
Attached house, ᴡ, by *Ellis & Wilson*, 1880.
Former Uɴɪᴛᴇᴅ Pʀᴇsʙʏᴛᴇʀɪᴀɴ Cʜᴜʀᴄʜ, Great Northern
Road (s side, behind Nos. 585–593). *Ellis & Wilson*, 1881.

Gothic, with a bellcote and three lancets under a dripmould above the door. Originally it overlooked the road, but houses have been built in front. Converted to offices.

WOODSIDE PARISH CHURCH, Church Street. *Archibald Simpson*, 1845–9. Unusually, it was the Established Church who erected this new building after the schism of 1843, while those who had 'come out' returned to the pre-Disruption chapel of ease (*see* above). Simpson produced another box for them, this time with deep Italianate eaves and elliptical-arched windows. Entrance and gallery stairs are in a w narthex (a later addition?), but the principal elevation is the E tower, closing the view up steeply sloping King Street: above a rectangular base with big angle pilasters is a short square stage, becoming octagonal, then cylindrical, before ending in a dome. Interior with galleries on three sides, on thin cast-iron columns. Chancel formed in 1938–9 by dividing off the E end with a semicircular arch. – STAINED GLASS. E wall (artificially lit), 'Come unto me all ye that labour', *H. S. Danks*, 1930, from the former chapel of ease.

PUBLIC BUILDINGS

ANDERSON LIBRARY, Clifton Road. *Arthur Clyne*, dated 1882. Given by the Woodside-born engineer Sir John Anderson. Baronial, with crowstepped gables and substantial buttresses, one of which grows out of the s porch and blossoms into a tall, conical-roofed turret. Interior with open timber roof. E extension of 1931.

PERSLEY BRIDGE, Mugiemoss Road. Five granite arches, built 1891–2 (though the drawings are dated 1888). The engineer was *P. M. Barnett.*

WOODSIDE PRIMARY SCHOOL, Clifton Road. 1902 by *J. A. Ogg Allan.* Free classical, with two prominent domed turrets. It replaced a Board School of 1874 by *W. L. Henderson,* which stood on part of the site. This led to phased construction, reflected in the asymmetrical plan. Comparatively long and only two storeys, unlike compact three-storey Board Schools on constricted city-centre sites. (The predecessor to Henderson's school, *c.* 1837, survives as the BURGH HALL, opposite.)

1.25 km. NW of the Parish Church, between Mugiemoss Road and the Don, is WOODSIDE HOUSE, *c.* 1859 by *William Knight.* Roman Doric porch, consoled cornices to the windows. An C18 wing survives at the back. 300 m. w of the house is PERSLEY CASTLE, the current name for a curious battlemented building with Gothic windows and corner turrets. The central carriage arch makes it look like a stable block, but it is said to have been built shortly before 1797 to accommodate child workers at Gordon, Barron & Co.'s mill (*see* above). If this is so, it is surprisingly ornamental for the purpose. Both it and the house are now nursing homes.

OUTER DISTRICTS: WEST

BIELDSIDE

INTERNATIONAL BAPTIST CHURCH, Earlswells Road. *G. R. M. Kennedy & Partners*, 1984. The square, harled church is preceded in early Christian fashion by an atrium, or garden court. The court's enclosing walls were designed to be load-bearing, so that if required it could eventually be roofed over to double the church in size.

ST DEVENICK (Episcopal), North Deeside Road and Baillieswells Road. *Arthur Clyne*, 1902. Rugged Scots Gothic in irregular, squared grey granite, with red granite dressings and rock-faced quoins. Aisleless nave, choir and chancel under one roof, plus short S transept. Intersecting tracery in transept and W and E windows; simple Y-tracery down sides. Transept and chancel have string courses which step up and over the windows before rising into the gables and branching to become crosses. Battlemented SW tower, square and sheer, with a semi-octagonal stair-turret, E, and an arched doorway, S. The shaft has numerous small windows: lancets and a quatrefoil near the bottom, mullioned-and-transomed squares above, and arrow-slits dotted here and there higher up; larger openings with Y-tracery in the belfry stage. Simple lean-to porch at W end. Interior with wooden ceiling on round, transverse arches. As at Clyne's St James (*see* p. 157), a thicker timber arch and stone pilasters mark the division between nave and choir. W gallery, 2000, glazed below. – REREDOS, a war memorial, 1920. Gothic, carved by *David K. Graham*. Also matching STALLS and COMMUNION RAILS. – FONT. Stone, Gothic, 1908. – ORGAN, S transept, 1910, by *Wadsworth & Brothers*, with simple Gothic case. – STAINED GLASS. Chancel, Crucifixion, 1928, designed by *John Ives*. S transept, E side, Christ at the Last Supper, supplied by *William Collins* of London, 1839 (originally the E window of St Andrew's Cathedral, King Street). A rare survival in Scotland of Collins's pictorial glass. The artists he employed copied their designs from paintings, in this case a work by *Carlo Dolci*. Ten years earlier, Collins supplied the almost identical E window at Christ Church, Hilderstone, Staffordshire.* Nave, N side, W end, Adoration of the Shepherds, 1955.

DESCRIPTION

BAILLIESWELLS ROAD leads N from the church, with large houses among the woods at its upper end. After 1 km. on the E side is DALHEBITY, *c.* 2007–10, an enormous imitation of a Victorian mansion, complete with conical-roofed corner tower and balustraded balconies, for the house-builder Stewart Milne. A bit higher up, W side, is LITTLEWAYS, 1934, by *David*

---

*Information from Michael Kerney.

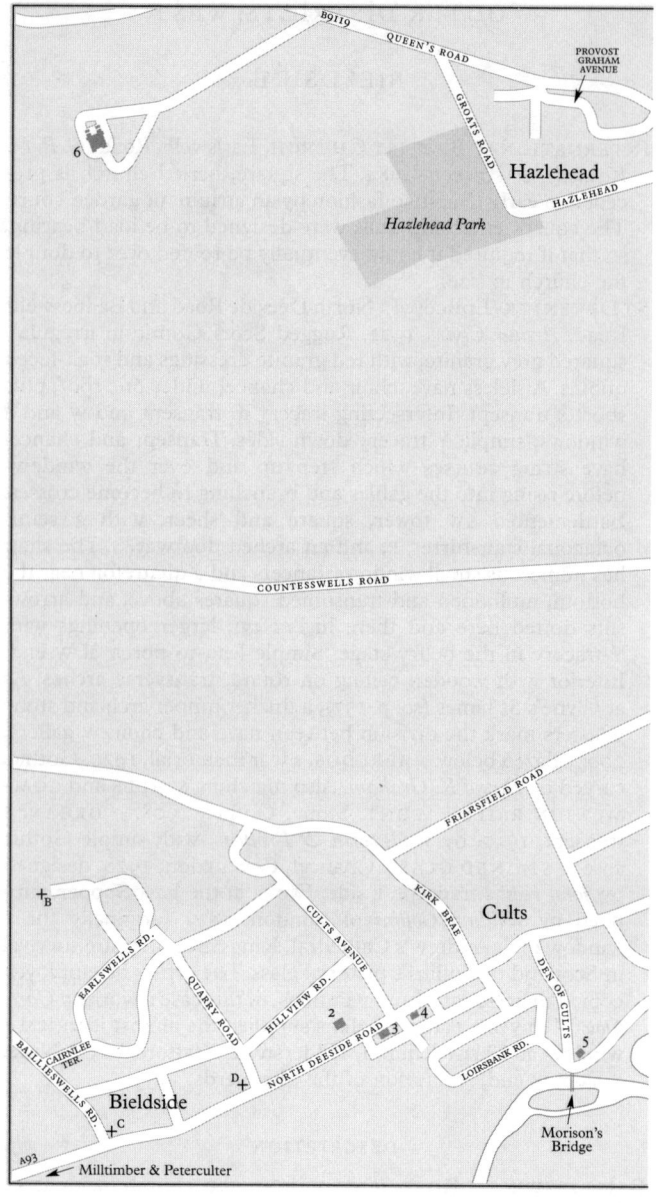

A Craigiebuckler Parish Church
B International Baptist Church
C St Devenick (Episcopal)
D Cults Parish Church
E Mannofield Parish Church
F St Francis of Assisi (R.C.)

1 Macauley Land Use Research Institute
2 Outreach Centre (former Cults United Free Church)
3 Cults School (former)
4 Cults Library

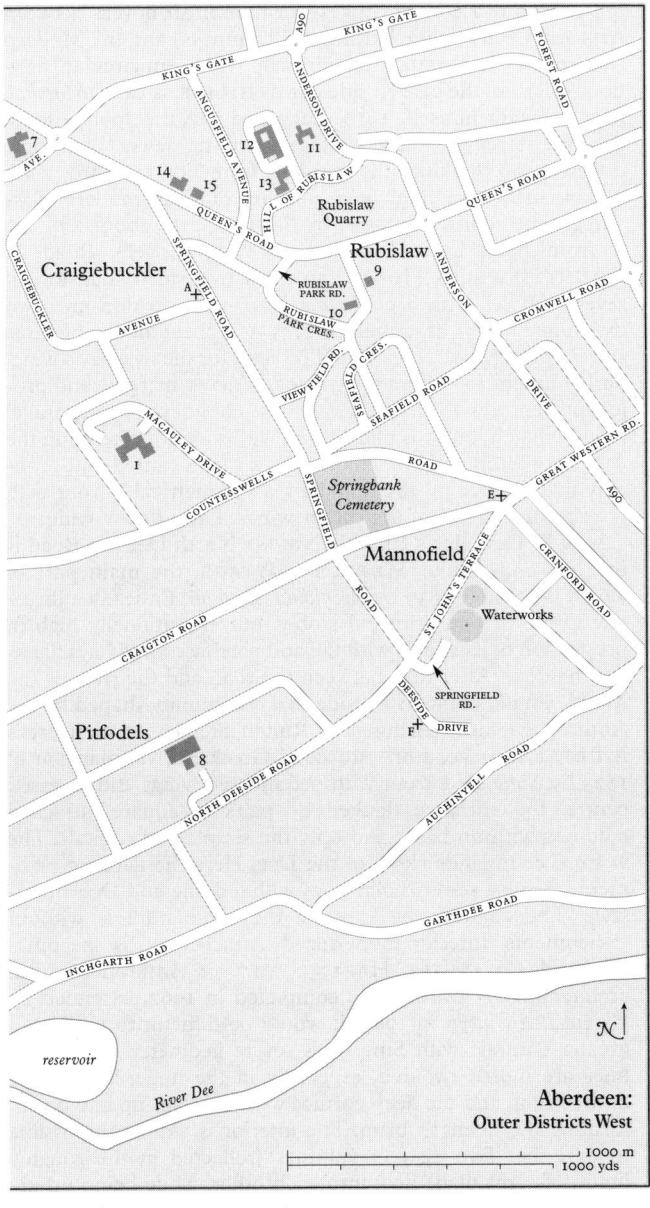

**Aberdeen:
Outer Districts West**

1000 m
1000 yds

Stokes (son of Leonard Stokes) for himself. It hovers between Arts and Crafts (white harling, tall chimneys) and the Modern Movement (horizontal, rectilinear), with semicircular first-floor oriels on the garden side. LADYHILL, E, is by *A. Marshall Mackenzie* for himself, 1912. Long and low, the apotheosis of the one-storey-plus-attic cottage, with no fewer than nine dormers overlooking the garden from its mansard roof. Colonnaded segmental bow, plus restrainedly modern glass and granite addition at N end by *Bob Fitzgerald*, 2009. 0.75 km. N from here, at the W end of Countesswells Road, is COUNTESSWELLS HOUSE, an attractive small mansion of several phases with a confusing plan, now divided into two dwellings. It was described in 1741 as a 'new' house of three storeys plus garrets. This would be right for the five-bay S wing, harled except for its granite quoins, window margins and pro-jecting centre with shaped gable. The chimneys of the parallel N wing match, but it is plainer and was evidently altered in the C19. Between is a higher linking block with a canted bay, prob-ably in existence by 1808, making a symmetrical E front with the flanking gables of the earlier wings. Later C19 W wing.

W of St Devenick's Church, No. 151 North Deeside Road is the harl-and-granite MURTLE COTTAGE, the main part of which is possibly 1839 by *Archibald Simpson*. Basically a three-bay house of one principal storey, but exceptionally high in proportion to its width, with tall and narrow canted bays flank-ing the door. After this, between the road and the river, is the Murtle estate, home to a residential community shaped by the Anthroposophical teachings of Rudolf Steiner. At its heart is MURTLE HOUSE, a fine stuccoed Greek Revival mansion of 1823 by *Simpson*. E front with pedimented wings and recessed centre, the entrance flanked by pairs of square, attached columns with no bases and only the simplest of capitals. The W front commands views of the Dee. Here the flanking pedi-ments frame a semicircular bow, with a dome and Doric peri-style. The columns have bases; the entablature is without enrichments. Interior modernized. Attached, N, is the pink-rendered CAMPHILL HALL, a work of Anthroposophical architecture by *Gabor Tallo*, completed in 1962, extended by *Camphill Architects* in 1985. It would be difficult to imagine a greater contrast with Simpson's severe geometry. Horizontal lines are mostly avoided, especially in the huge, helmet-like domed roof, and the deep cornice which zigzags up and down, forming the helmet's brim. The interior is almost impossible to describe. Two distinct volumes (reflected in the roughly figure-of-eight plan) flow into each other, while being utterly different in character. One has a pitched timber ceiling and a proscenium stage, the other a higher floor and a much higher ceiling – the great dome itself. Seen from the lower level, the top of the domed space is out of sight, so it seems infinitely high, and is flooded with light from concealed windows. An altar and stained glass windows, coupled with the apsidal form, give it the feel of a chapel. Long flights of stairs attached to the curving walls meet above the altar to form a kind of singing loft or minstrels' gallery. More buildings by *Camphill Architects* are scattered across the estate.

Just w of the Murtle estate lodge on North Deeside Road is the WATERWHEEL INN, converted from the mid-C19 Mill of Murtle, and much altered in the process. The water wheel remains in place. 0.5 km. w again, Murtle Den Road leads N to MURTLEDEN, a very good Arts and Crafts house of 1902 *p. 278* by *J. Coates Carter*. Squared granite rubble ground floor, harled above, with granite ashlar dressings and green slate roofs. The N entrance front is all gables and deep eaves. Divergent wings – billiard room and bedrooms, l.; service wing, r. – extend a welcoming embrace, while artfully grouped casements and high chimneys reinforce the message of homely comfort. The s side overlooks sweeping grounds and has a large veranda, now glazed in. A harled corner tower with semicircular bedroom oriel marks one end, a granite canted bay the other. Dog-leg stair off entrance hall, with slatted screening. Excellent panelling, doors and joinery throughout. Murals in dining room (scenes of medieval chivalry) and billiard room (yachts), recent, but quite in keeping.

300 m. E of St Devenick's, on the s side of North Deeside Road, is BIELDSIDE HOUSE. Early C19, with a gabled upper storey added by *George Watt* (of *Brown & Watt*) in 1903.

ROUND CAIRN, Cairn Crescent, 0.4 km. NE of St Devenick's church. Almost entirely surrounded by housing, this huge round cairn is a rare survival in the suburban areas of Aberdeen, composed of large boulders and smaller stones and measures almost 20 m. in diameter. There are traces of possible kerb stones around its perimeter. It is unexcavated and undated, but is likely to date to the Chalcolithic or Early Bronze Age and may cover burials of that date. (GN)

CRAIGIEBUCKLER

CRAIGIEBUCKLER PARISH CHURCH, Springfield Road. Built in 1882–3 on what was then the semi-rural fringe of the city, for an affluent community of extra-urban villa-dwellers. The founder was John Cardno Couper, who had made his fortune shipbuilding in Hong Kong. He gave the site and half the building costs. *A. Marshall Mackenzie*'s design is an important early example of the impact of ecclesiological thinking on Presbyterian architecture. Nave, polygonal chancel with shallow transepts, and s porch, all clearly distinguished by separate roofs. Mostly lancets, with plate tracery in the chancel. There are hefty buttresses to the porch and at the angles of the chancel, and a double belfry on the E nave gable. Some features are adapted from Scottish medieval buildings – the three lancets of the w front from Kildrummy Castle, and the transept

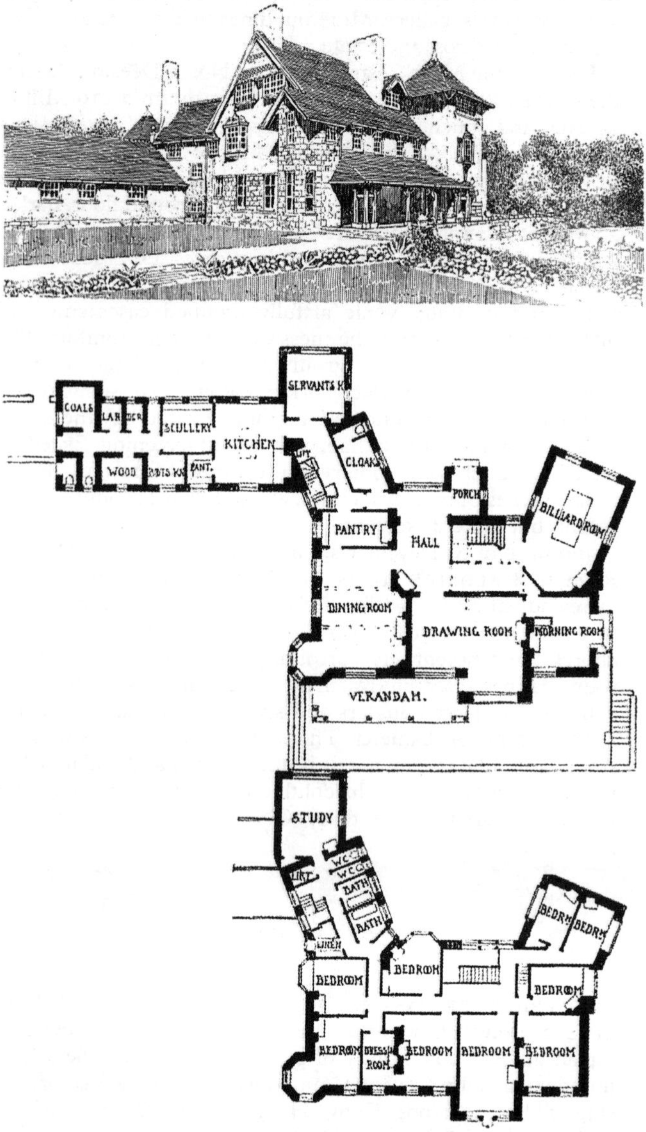

Murtleden.
Plan and perspective by J. Coates Carter, 1902

windows from Pluscarden Abbey (N) – and the masonry is Aberdeen-bond granite; but the overall effect is of an English village church such as Butterfield might have designed.

Inside, round chancel arch with moulded piers of freestone. Within the chancel, round arches N and S open into what were originally organ chamber and vestry ('purists', said the Aberdeen Ecclesiological Society, 'might take exception to the symmetrical and transeptal treatment'). The chancel stalls are 1950s but the inward-facing arrangement is original. Nave and chancel have round-arched wooden ceilings with scriptural texts in Gothic letters, added in 1892 as part of a decorative scheme devised by the portrait painter *George Reid* of nearby St Luke's (*see* p. 289). – PULPIT. Octagonal, oak, with carved panels of scenes from the life of Christ, 1887, given by Couper. Originally it stood on the chancel steps against the N pier. Detached VESTRY, N, 1965, with glazed link to church. – STAINED GLASS. A rich collection. Apse windows by *Morris & Co.* to designs by *Edward Burne-Jones*, given by Reid. In the centre, Mary's salutation to Elizabeth, 1885 (the design was first used at Speldhurst, Kent); on either side, SS Matthew and Mark and SS Luke and John, 1892 (designs first used at Jesus College, Cambridge). The nave windows all date from 1960–71 and are nominally by *William Wilson*, though Wilson's failing eyesight at this time means that they are probably the work of his partner and successor, *John Blyth*: Old Testament prophets on the N, scenes from the life of Christ on the S, and the Last Supper, Crucifixion, Resurrection and Supper at Emmaus combined in the three W windows. In the door leading to the vestry, the Good Shepherd and St Margaret of Scotland, 1995 by *Josefa von Furstenberg*. At right angles to the church, matching HALL of 1891 by *Mackenzie*, lengthened 1910; further additions 1979.

The surrounding C19 villas have mostly been demolished, living on only as street names in what is now amorphous C20–C21 suburbia. Couper's own house, the mid-C19 Craigiebuckler, survives in Macaulay Drive as part of the MACAULAY LAND USE RESEARCH INSTITUTE. Large, but disappointingly plain, it is outshone by its magnificent wooded grounds. The even lovelier JOHNSTON GARDENS in Viewfield Road, a public park since the 1930s, was created from the grounds of another demolished house.

CULTS

'Picturesque Deeside begins at Cults', wrote the *Aberdeen Journal* in 1886; 'nowhere is the Aberdonian craze for building houses – fine houses too – more forcibly illustrated'. There were a few houses here by the early C19, but it was the opening of the Deeside Railway in 1853 that began the transformation of this agricultural village into a commuter suburb. The railway closed in 1966, but the view s to the unspoiled landscape of Kincardineshire is as alluring as ever, and Cults has continued to grow.

CULTS PARISH CHURCH, North Deeside Road and Quarry Road. 1915–16 by *A. Marshall Mackenzie*. The previous church by *George Marr*, built as a mission hall 1882–3, and raised to a separate charge in 1888, faces onto Quarry Road and now serves as the HALL. It is just a gabled box, with Dec E window, lancets down the sides and a bellcote. Mackenzie's church – not especially large, but imposing – proudly overlooks the main road. Nave with very broad, lean-to aisles, square s tower and shallow N chancel. The tower has a corbelled and battlemented parapet and a short spire. A barrel-vaulted porch with splayed reveals tunnels deep into its base, and there is a long, round-headed mullioned-and-transomed window in each face. Three-light gabled dormers with simple Y-tracery light the nave. Aisle windows are more domestic-looking, wider than they are high, and divided into three square-headed lights; chancel window with intersecting tracery. Entrance under organ gallery within the tower. The interior – pink Corrennie granite, in contrast to the grey Kemnay exterior – is exceptionally wide: three-bay nave and aisles together make a square, divided by round arches on slender octagonal piers, without capitals or bases. Mackenzie's pews have sadly been replaced by moveable seating. – STAINED GLASS. Chancel: the Ascension, First World War memorial by *Alexander Strachan*, 1920. E aisle, N to s: St Margaret, *Margaret Chilton*, 1937 (a memorial to Mackenzie); St Columba, *Marjorie Kemp*, 1950 (Second World War memorial); the Aberdeen skyline, 1986. w aisle, N to s: St Ninian, 1937, *Kemp*; 'Christ in the beauty of Nature', 1971, *Sadie McLellan*; centenary window showing the 1880s church and its C20 replacement, 1988, *G. Mackinnon*. s end: Spring, Summer, Autumn and Winter, 1980, *John Blyth*.

OUTREACH CENTRE (former Cults United Free Church), North Deeside Road. A church of 1902–3 by *D. & J. R. McMillan* was largely destroyed by fire in 1941. Only the sw steeple and octagonal SE stair-tower survive. A replacement church by *George Watt & Stewart* – now the Outreach Centre – opened on the same site in 1959. Drab, rendered exterior, but inside is a good, vigorous s window of 1967 by *Crear McCartney*: Christ with St Cecilia and St Luke.

Former SCHOOL, North Deeside Road (opposite Outreach Centre). 1896–7 by *Ellis & Wilson*, and almost identical with their slightly earlier school at Peterculter, but only one principal storey instead of two. Converted to housing.

LIBRARY, North Deeside Road. 1966, by the County Architect, *J. C. Arnott*. Butterfly roof.

MORISON'S BRIDGE, Inchgarth Road. 1836–7, by *John Smith*. A suspension footbridge, known colloquially as 'the Shakkin' Briggie'. Built at his own expense by Dr George Morison, minister of Banchory-Devenick on the s side of the Dee, in whose parish Cults then lay, to make it easier for worshippers to attend church. Now a ruin, but an impressive one. The cast-iron pylons are pairs of unfluted Greek Doric columns with heavy entablatures, standing on high stone piers.

WATERWORKS. Former PUMPING STATION on Inchgarth Road, opposite the N end of Morison's Bridge, 1864 by *William Smith*. Single-storey pedimented engine house with attached dwelling, all now in residential use. Granite, with freestone dressings, including rock-faced quoins and a consoled doorway. It supplied water to a high-level reservoir at Pitfodels. A later PUMPING STATION is on the N side of the North Deeside Road, just W of the Cults Hotel. Dated 1885, with pediment and pilaster strips, it is by the Burgh Surveyor, *William Boulton*. It conveyed water to a new high-level reservoir at Slopefield. The brick chimney was demolished after conversion to electricity, 1920s.

DESCRIPTION. A few houses are worth singling out. CULTS HOUSE, on the W side of Cults Avenue, is one of a small number predating the railway. Basically C18, it was altered by *William Henderson* in 1859: the two-storey canted bays and square porch on the S front may be his. The symmetrical, three-bay WESTERTON OF PITFODELS, Westerton Road, is perhaps also C18. In the grounds is a former WATER MILL, lacking its machinery. An unusually large house of the post-railway years is GLENDARROCH (originally Dunmail) in South Avenue, built *c.* 1876 for the photographer Edmund Geering. Tudor, with a pyramid-roofed tower. Recent single-storey extension by *Arc Architects*: partly faced with glass and granite, partly wrapped in a curving trellis of stainless-steel wires to create a living wall of foliage. At the W corner of North Deeside Road and Netherby Road, NETHERBY is an attractive Arts and Crafts house of *c.* 1905. 0.5 km. N, at the corner of Craigton Road and Friarsfield Road, is *Archibald Simpson*'s GREENRIDGE (originally Morkeu). In existence by 1844, it was a modest, L-shaped villa with diagonally set chimneys, decorative bargeboards and gabled first-floor windows pushing up into the roof. In 1910 it was richly Edwardianized by *George Watt* (of *Brown & Watt*) who added a huge Baronial porte cochère, S-facing terrace and loggia, and dark panelling inside. The enormous LODGE, with timbered gables and conical-roofed turret, is presumably *Watt*'s too. At Hillhead of Pitfodels, 0.5 km. NW of Greenridge, is an attractive Arts and Crafts COTTAGE by *William Pyper*, dated 1905. Twin gables, steep roofs and Voysey-ish angle buttresses.

HAZLEHEAD

CREMATORIUM, off Skene Road, N of Hazlehead Golf Course. 1973–5 by the *City Architect*. Low and spreading, with copper-covered mansard roofs, inward-leaning walls of pre-cast

concrete panels, and four spacious portes cochères. Separate
MEMORIAL CHAPEL in the beautifully landscaped grounds.

HAZLEHEAD PARK, Hazlehead Avenue. Formed out of the
grounds of Hazlehead House, a 1775 mansion demolished in
1959, which stood on the site of the present restaurant. Only
the early C19 Tudor lodge and stables survive, both by *John
Smith*. SW of the restaurant, in the centre of a formal rose
garden, the PIPER ALPHA MEMORIAL by *Sue Jane Taylor*,
1991, commemorates the victims of the 1988 fire on the Piper
Alpha oil platform. Three bronze statues of oil workers in stylized, almost ritualistic poses, on a high granite plinth inscribed
with the names of the dead. Adjoining on the W is the Queen
Mother Rose Garden, with a statue, Freedom, 1953, by *Richard
Robertson*. There are more sculptures N of here, the most interesting a SUNDIAL by *Ian Hamilton Finlay*: a low, table-like slab
of stone, with text in high relief. Others include an abstract
construction in painted steel by *James Reid*, 1969, and Division,
a horizontal yellow-painted beam-like structure about 15 m.
long, close to the ground and partly embedded in a fallen tree,
by *Gerald Laing*, 1971. On the S edge of the park, in Hazledene
Road, a FOUNTAIN in a Gothic niche, restored 1884. Between
the park and Queen's Road, an attractive HOUSING scheme of
1961 by the *City Architect*. Four twelve-storey blocks, with
lower blocks and terraces coherently grouped around them.

HAZLEHEAD SCHOOL, Provost Graham Avenue. 2008–10, by
Aedas. The main feature is a large rotunda containing the
entrance.

KINGSWELLS

KINGSWELLS CHURCH, Old Skene Road (originally Kingswells
Free Church). 1857–8, by *J., W.H. & J. M. Hay* of Liverpool.
Largely financed by Francis Edmond of Kingswells House (*see*
below). Built from locally gathered fieldstones – John Hay
spoke of Kingswells as 'the land of stones' – with hammer-
dressed window surrounds, etc. A single vessel with a W porch
and a bellcote on the N gable. Trefoil-headed windows, mostly
with diamond panes. Open timber roof. – STAINED GLASS. S
wall, Crucifixion and Resurrection, 1958 by *Douglas Hamilton*.
Side windows, Baptism and Communion, 2008 by *Shona
McInnes*. HALLS, attached at S end, 1998.

KINGSWELLS HOUSE, Skene Road. Its present Baronial appearance is due to a remodelling of 1855 for Francis Edmond – the
year is inscribed on a tablet over the door, along with 1713 and
1666, though the significance of the earlier dates is unclear.
The date of the original house is not known but there was
formerly a stone over the door with the initials of *Alexander
Jaffray*, 4th Laird of Kingswells, who succeeded to the estate
in 1701, and his wife, Christian Barclay, whom he had married

the previous year. It seems likely that Jaffray – a gentleman-architect who went on to design the N front of Culter House (*see* p. 287) – was the author of his own house, or else remodelled what he inherited. A painting of 1841 shows the W front before its mid-C19 transformation. It had a shallow U-plan, with a central door framed by Ionic pilasters, and two oval windows above, one upright, one on its side – very like Ha' Hoose, Raemoir (*see* p. 705). This central part has been completely changed, but the wings survive. They have jerkin roofs and fairly correct classical scrolls on either side of the gables. Such Baroque details were not common in early C18 North-East Scotland but Jaffray was no doubt influenced by architectural publications (by 1719 he owned a plan and elevation of fellow Aberdonian James Gibbs's St Mary-le-Strand, London). In 1855 Edmond built the towered entrance bay in the middle of the W front – rounded below, then corbelled out to become square, with a crowstepped gable – and single-storey lean-tos filling the spaces between it and the wings. At the same time the roof was raised, and gabled dormers and a conical-roofed SE turret added. All this recalls David Bryce's 1851 transformation of Kingcausie (*see* p. 603). The shallow wing projecting from the middle of the E side evidently predates these changes. Running W–E *c.* 500 m. N of the house is the extraordinary CONSUMPTION DYKE, an immense wall built to 'consume' stones removed from the surrounding agricultural land. It is *c.* 450 m. long, 2 m. high and 10 m. wide, with a path running along the top, and was probably completed under Francis Edmond in the middle of the C19, though its origins are older.

MANNOFIELD AND PITFODELS

CHURCHES

MANNOFIELD PARISH CHURCH, corner of Craigton Road and Countesswells Road. *Jenkins & Marr*, 1881–2. Gothic, cruciform, with a slender SE tower and spire. Timber tracery, except for the granite W window. Interior reordered in 1968, when the organ was moved from the chancel to the E gallery. Timber ceiling with elaborate trusses, approximating to a hammerbeam roof. – STAINED GLASS. W window, Christ with Martha, Mary and Lazarus, *Clayton & Bell*, 1892; S transept, They that sow in tears shall reap in joy, 1989; N transept, The calming of the storm, *Shona McInnes*, 1999.

ST FRANCIS OF ASSISI (R.C.), Deeside Drive. A happy combination of tradition and modernity, thoroughly at home among suburban bungalows. The simple hall of 1960 was used for worship until the new church by *Oliver Humphries* was added at the S end in 1982–3, at a lower level because of the sloping site. Its plan is two superimposed squares, making an eight-pointed star, with the hall abutting on one side. Harled walls and red tiled roof. The roof is basically an octagonal pyramid, but with steep-sided triangular dormers extending to the W, S and E points of the star (they are the only windows, except for some tiny Mackintosh-derived square lights in vertical rows below). A segmental-arched doorway, E, leads via a narthex to the fan-shaped nave with S chancel. Attached presbytery, W.

PUBLIC BUILDINGS

INTERNATIONAL SCHOOL OF ABERDEEN, North Deeside Road. By *Halliday Fraser Munro*, 2009–10. Surrounded by the new buildings is PITFODELS HOUSE, a villa of *c.* 1860 with two-storey bows linked by a veranda. Just E of the house, a square, three-storey FOLLY tower. It incorporates a carved panel with the dates 1633 and 1692, possibly brought from elsewhere.

SPRINGBANK CEMETERY, Countesswells Road. Laid out by *Brown & Watt*. Lodge dated 1891 with octagonal domed tower. Just S of the Springfield Road entrance, a good monument to the notable Aberdeen builder John Morgan (†1907) and his wife (†1906): a granite monolith carved with a Celtic cross in relief and a fine inscription.

WATERWORKS, St John's Terrace. Two circular reservoirs. The E one formed part of *James Simpson*'s scheme to bring water from the Dee, 21 miles (34 km.) upstream at Cairnton. It was opened by Queen Victoria in 1866. The W one was added by *James M. Gale*, 1885–8. In 1913–14, both were roofed in reinforced concrete and grassed over by the Water Engineer, *Cecil H. Roberts*. This is presumably when the two central, keeplike structures were added. Battlemented and white-painted, one round and one square, they face each other like outsize chess pieces.

DESCRIPTION

Immediately N of the Parish Church is THORNGROVE, No. 500 Great Western Road. Now absorbed into a housing complex, the original part is of 1867 by *J. R. Mackenzie*, with steeply gabled wings and other Gothic touches. Just E of it, at the corner of Great Western Road and Thorngrove Avenue, is FRIENDVILLE, a five-bay house of 1773 with central wall-head stack, plus a back wing of 1812. It was restored in 1943 for the antique dealer William Bell by *Fenton Wyness*. He added the pantiled roof and incorporated various architectural fragments into the house and its delightful walled garden, including a gazebo of Ionic columns with a wrought-iron dome. This short W stretch of Great Western Road was separated from the rest (*see* p. 228) in 1900 by ANDERSON DRIVE, a broad road linking with King's Gate, 1.5 km. NW (from 1927 the drive was extended S to the Bridge of Dee and N to Great Northern

Road, forming a ring road). There is a run of good BUNGA-
LOWS on the E side, just N of the junction with Great Western
Road, of which the best is the exceptionally large No. 4, of
1902 by *G. Fordyce*.

W of the church and reservoirs (*see* above), NORTH DEESIDE
ROAD for 1.5 km. between Mannofield and Cults has big C19
and early C20 villas facing S across the valley of the Dee. The
grandest are set in extensive wooded grounds on the N side,
on sites offered for building in 1846 by the trustees of John
Menzies of Pitfodels. WOODBANK is the most ambitious.
Evidently a fairly plain, square house originally, it was given
showy classical additions in 1881 by *Ellis & Wilson*: a large,
circular bow with a truncated conical roof and iron cresting,
and a campanile-like tower containing the main door. Various
additions in connection with its present use as a training
centre. In the boundary wall on the main road, a WAR MEMOR-
IAL fountain of *c.* 1920. Further W is WELLWOOD, a symmetrical twin-gabled house of the 1840s with a higher E wing,
probably added in 1894 by *A. Marshall Mackenzie*. Tudor
details, plus a Jacobean W porch. Recent new housing in the
grounds. There are further large houses N of here and S of
Craigton Road: AIRY HALL in Airyhall Road, now flats, looks
mid-C19 Tudor, with a big square tower.

MASTRICK AND SHEDDOCKSLEY

The large council estate of Mastrick was begun in 1952. It has
its own shopping centre and community facilities on Greenfern
Road, and consists mostly of low-rise flats and houses, plus the
fourteen-storey Mastrick Land of 1961–3 (the tallest building in
the north of Scotland at that date), NE of the shops. Sheddocksley,
immediately W and half the size, followed from 1974. Housing
here is more informal, much of it grouped around cul-de-sacs,
with generous provision of grassed areas and many trees.

HOLY FAMILY CHURCH (R.C.), Upper Mastrick Way. 2004–5,
by *Oliver Humphries* of *GPA Humphries Architects*. An exotic
amid the repetitive surrounding housing. More or less a Greek
cross, harled, with an octagonal red tiled pyramid roof that
pays homage to the Beach Ballroom (*see* p. 205). The N and S
arms (sanctuary and porch) have pitched roofs with gables,
creating an axis. Windows are arched, with classical surrounds
and Georgian glazing.

ST CLEMENT (Episcopal), Mastrick Drive. *Ivor Ll. B. Hopkins*,
1958–60 (it replaced a church in Regent Quay by William
Kelly, 1928, which had itself replaced a former Free church
taken over in 1889). Rectangular, in pink and grey artificial
stone, with a fully glazed W end. The oversailing roof is a
shallow pointed arch in section. Battered SW tower with

domical roof. Interior subdivided, with only the w end now used for worship. – FONT. Granite. A square bowl on a squat round column, the base ornamented with waterleaf. 1925. – STAINED GLASS. Three C19 windows, said to be *Clayton & Bell*, incorporated into the w-end glazing: Scourging, Crucifixion and Deposition. Also a smaller window in storage, The Controlling Purpose (an angel-geometer brooding over the celestial sphere), by *Douglas Strachan*. This last came from Regent Quay; the other glass and the font are probably also from the predecessor churches.

MILLTIMBER

On North Deeside Road at Binghill Road is the former TOR-NA-DEE HOSPITAL, of 1898–9 by *R. G. Wilson*. Originally a hydropathic institution. Large, E-plan, with two-storey bay windows of contrasting design in the outer wings. Converted to flats 2009, with steel balconies added to the preserved façade, and large additions at the back and in the grounds.

PETERCULTER

PETERCULTER PARISH CHURCH (originally Peterculter Free Church), North Deeside Road. *John Rust*, 1894, replacing a church of 1843 on a different site (both dates are inscribed on the front). A standard preaching-box but in 'Norman' dress, with semicircular apse and NW battlemented tower. Wheel window above s door. Buttresses between side windows, with unusual convex set-offs. The broad interior has the shallowest of transepts – no more than recesses – and an open timber roof on corbels. The apse is raised up behind the communion table and pulpit, and framed by a semicircular arch and columns with foliage capitals. Seating for the choir, in a curve against the wall, was added in 1903. – STAINED GLASS. Three apse windows, Faith, Hope and Charity, 1894; N wall, r. of apse, the Good Shepherd, †1911.

ST PETER, Howie Lane. The former parish church, now St Peter's Heritage Centre. Built 1779 by *William Fleming*, mason, and *William Knowles*, wright, replacing an earlier church. Originally a simple rectangle, with a Venetian window and bellcote at the w end, and chamfered, round-arched side windows. It was repaired and altered by *James Matthews*, 1874–6. In 1895, *Alexander Brown* added a large and externally discordant N aisle in red granite, making a T-plan. Organ chamber added to s side, 1914. Inside, galleries W, N and E, with pulpit and organ against the s wall. Open timber roof.

– STAINED GLASS. W window, the Good Shepherd, 1894, *Gordon & Watt*. In the churchyard, SE, MONUMENT to Patrick Duff of Culter House, †1763. A flaming urn on a marble plinth. W of the church, iron and timber HALL. Formerly used as an Episcopal church at Ballater, it was re-erected here in 1907. W again, the former MANSE of 1726–9, enlarged in 1767 and 1776. The three-bay front part is an addition of 1826 by *John Lyon*.

CULTER SCHOOL, School Road. By *Ellis & Wilson*, 1895–6. Aberdeen-bond granite. Venetian windows, and gables with C17 details. C20 extensions.

ROB ROY BRIDGE, North Deeside Road, where it crosses the Culter Burn. Widened in reinforced concrete by *Walker & Duncan*, 1926. STATUE of Rob Roy on the E bank immediately N of the bridge, unveiled July 1926 and replaced a number of times since.

WAR MEMORIAL, North Deeside Road (200 m. W of Rob Roy Bridge). A square, battered tower of fieldstones, high above the road, with pink granite battlements and rock-faced quoins.

WAULKMILL BRIDGE, over the Culter Burn (200 m. N of the North Deeside Road, 1 km. W of Rob Roy Bridge). A semicircular arch with chamfered voussoirs. Square, chamfered recess in S side dated 1710.

DESCRIPTION. The Culter Burn S of Rob Roy Bridge was long associated with industry. Extensive paper mills originating in the C18 have been demolished, but in Kennerty Mills Road is the disused and derelict UPPER KENNERTY MILL (for corn), dated 1838 and 1942. SE in Burnside Road is LOWER KENNERTY MILL, later C19, rebuilt as a dwelling from 1940 by *W. L. Gavin*. An attractive pastiche of salvaged fragments, in which the original form of the mill is difficult to make out.

CULTER HOUSE, Culter House Road. The highlight of Aberdonian Deeside: a real country house, with woods and policies, magically secluded from its suburban surroundings. There are two main phases: the towered SE side appears to be basically C17; the Georgian NW side is 1721 by *Alexander Jaffray*, who at the same time remodelled the earlier part. Jaffray's client was Sir Alexander Cuming, M.P. (who also consulted James Gibbs). The other important date is 1910, when there was a fire. The house is entirely harled, which gives visual unity but makes analysis difficult. The SE side is the place to start. Culter's appearance before 1721 is not recorded but it seems to have been a gabled block, 5.5 m. from front to back, with a square tower at each end of the garden front. These C17 elements survive – the walls of the three-storey main block sheer and cliff-like; the towers to the same height, with a pronounced batter, and projecting beyond the gables – but it is not clear to what extent they were altered by Jaffray. His letters to Cuming show that he made significant changes to the old house, demolishing two round turrets and a stair, which he thought spoiled the roof-line. A painting of the 1730s shows the towers with sharply pointed, spire-like roofs (C17, or added

59

by Jaffray?) but now they have shallow pyramid roofs and eaves cornices that match the rest of the house, probably of 1910. Apart from the towers, the most memorable feature of the SE front is the heroic central chimneystack, corbelled out above the door, with the Cuming arms in a carved panel at its base. It becomes broader at the second floor, broader again above the eaves, before ending, trident-like, with three square, diagonally set flues, the outer two overhanging the sides of the stack. Fenestration to either side is regular, and may be C17, but the windows on the double-height second floor have C18 proportions, the two adjacent to the chimneystack with segmental tops.

So to the Georgian phase. In transforming Culter's plan from single-pile to double-pile, Sir Alexander's modest ambition was 'to build the addition of my house for conveniency & not for grandeur (tho' I would have everything regular & decent about it) & to make the rooms of the same height and the floors on the same level with the old building'. Jaffray's four-storey NW block is accordingly plain, though it would have been less so before his central cupola was removed. As it is, the only ornaments are the eaves cornice and the lugged architrave round the door, both of which look early C20 but follow the original. At seven bays, the addition is longer than the C17 block. The site slopes up from SE to NW, but the levels are made to work by sinking the lowest floor and having steps up to the door at first-floor level. The two-storey wings enclosing a forecourt are of 1910, by *W. D. Ironside* of *Walker & Duncan* for Theodore and Margaret Crombie (a plaque on the SW elevation of the old block has the date and clients' initials). They resemble Jaffray's wings, which they replaced, but are linked to the main block by convex quadrants on the SE side.

Inside, fire damage and decades of institutional use have taken their toll. The 1721 addition has SW–NE corridors where it joins the C17 part, with doors punched through the dividing wall. Jaffray's stone dog-leg service stair at the SW end (reusing steps from its C17 predecessor) survived the 1910 fire, but the timber open-well staircase between first and second floors is a C20 replacement. It leads to the grandest room, filling the double-height second floor of the C17 block. Remodelled by *William Adam* for Patrick Duff of Premnay, who acquired Culter in 1729, it was reconstructed after the fire by *William Kelly*. Pairs of full-height Roman Doric pilasters frame the fireplaces at each end and the three doors from the corridor. Adam's drawing shows another fireplace between the pilasters in the centre of the window wall, corresponding with the great chimneystack. The coved ceiling has a post-fire re-creation by *Allan Sutherland* of *William Mosman*'s 1735–6 ceiling painting, itself a copy of *Guido Reni*'s famous Aurora, done in Rome. On the SE side of the house is a formal walled GARDEN, overlooked by a TERRACE with matching GAZEBO and DOVECOT, both square with pyramid roofs. *Jaffray* was already working on these in 1719–20, before starting on the NW front.

0.5 km. E of Culter House on North Deeside Road is KIPPIE
LODGE, by *A. H. L. Mackinnon*, 1940. Harled Neo-Georgian
with a piended roof and segmental-headed ground-floor
windows.

RUBISLAW

At the SW corner of Queen's Road and Anderson Drive are
the former grounds of KEPPLESTONE, recently built over with
tall blocks of flats. The HOUSE itself was extended and remodelled in the mid 1870s by *J. R. Mackenzie* for the granite
magnate Alexander Macdonald, partly to accommodate his
growing art collection. It was badly damaged by fire, 2013. The
interior had rich decoration by *Daniel Cottier*. Kepplestone
backs on to Viewfield Road, on the opposite side of which is
the house formerly known as St Luke's, now the GORDON
HIGHLANDERS MUSEUM. The oldest part is the harled SE
wing, originally a single-storey cottage of *c.* 1800 with canted
bays. It was extended *c.* 1890 for the portrait painter Sir George
Reid, who added the large studio wing at right angles, of white-
painted granite with big leaded windows and a circular stair-
tower. The design of this has generally been attributed to
William Kelly. STAINED GLASS in the oriel of the cottage staircase: Dawn and Dusk, probably by *Douglas Strachan*. Other
windows have fragments of C17 and C18 painted glass.

On the N side of Queen's Road, opposite Viewfield Road, is
the immense chasm of RUBISLAW QUARRY. The source of
much of the granite used to build C19 Aberdeen, it finally
closed in 1971 after more than two hundred years of production. Now fenced off and flooded, there is little to indicate its
importance in the city's history. Just N of it, between Hill of
Rubislaw and Anderson Drive, is a cluster of three large, low-
rise oil company offices, developed from 1978. MARATHON
HOUSE, built originally for Conoco by *Thomson, Taylor, Craig
& Donald,* faces Anderson Drive and has concrete cladding
panels with chamfered window surrounds. It is less interesting
than its contemporaries at Altens (*see* p. 291). Dreary SEAFIELD
HOUSE, W, has ugly ribbed concrete panels. CHEVRON
HOUSE, S of the latter, was completed as recently as 2007 by
Bradford Robertson. It has much green glazing and widely
spaced columns to the upper floors.

Queen's Road W of the quarry has superior interwar bungalows on the S side and houses on the N. No. 226, close to
Northburn Avenue (N side), is ANGUSFIELD, rich Georgian
Revival of 1902 by *R. G. Wilson*, with pedimented wings,
quoins and consoled eaves cornice. The rusticated arched
doorway has a broken semicircular pediment and a round
window with garlands above. It makes an interesting contrast
with the Arts and Crafts charm of BAIGLIE at No. 222 (entered

from Westholme Avenue). This dates from 1909 and is by *Wilsons & Walker*, a partnership formed by Wilson and his son in 1906. Asymmetrical mullioned-and-transomed windows, without mouldings, and a shaped gable pushing up through the eaves at one end.

SUMMERHILL

WOODEND HOSPITAL, between Queen's Road and Eday Road. Built 1902–7 as Oldmill Poorhouse by *Brown & Watt*. Long, axial drive from Queen's Road, flanked by pairs of LODGES and handsome single-storey former PROBATIONARY WARDS with Venetian windows. A VIADUCT carries the drive over the Denburn, after which the former NURSES' HOME, W, is vernacular Georgian, harled above a granite basement, with crowstepped gables. The POORHOUSE itself – three-storey centre, with long, two-storey wings – has a high, Free Style CLOCK TOWER with square corner domes, pyramid roof and square cupola. Two small polygonal buildings in front, with conical roofs and curious mushroom-shaped window openings, were originally privies serving the male and female yards. NW is the former poorhouse HOSPITAL: H-plan, the two ward blocks with pavilion-roofed corner towers linked by a glazed corridor to the administrative block, sitting between them like a large villa. W of this group is a three-storey U-shaped block of

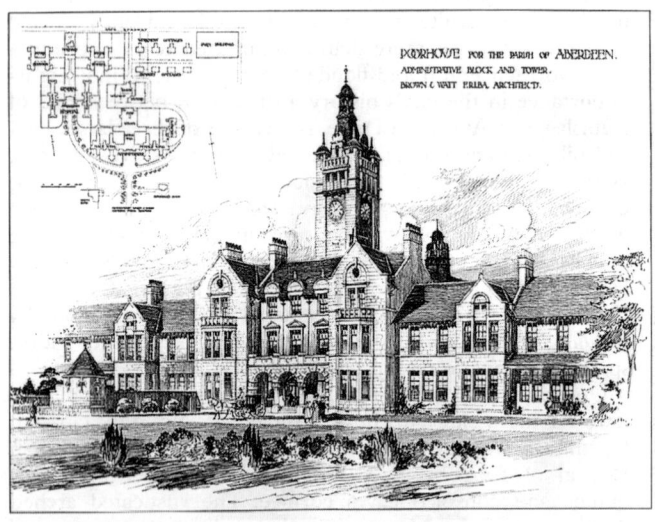

Woodend Hospital.
Plan and perspective by Brown & Watt, 1908

NURSES' HOUSING by the *City Architect*, 1937–40, severely rectilinear, softened only by a gentle bowing of the central entrance.

HOTEL, Lang Stracht, corner of Summerhill Road. By *Baxter, Clark & Paul*, 1964. A three-storey Brutalist megastructure with shops on the ground floor and more shops behind, grouped round a court. Prominent bellows windows. The upper floors of the hotel jut out in wedges at each end, giving the whole building the appearance of a stranded ship.

SUMMERHILL HOUSE, Anderson Drive at Maryville Place. A typical two-storey, three-bay C18 house, completely engulfed by C20 suburbia.

OUTER DISTRICTS: SOUTH

ALTENS

The largely oil-related industrial estate at Altens was built *c.* 1976–7. It dwarfs its older neighbour, Nigg, which consists of little more than a handsome church with manse and school.

Former NIGG PARISH CHURCH, Nigg Kirk Road (disused). *John Smith*, 1828–9. A replacement for the old parish church of St Fittick (*see* Torry), built beside the new turnpike road to Stonehaven in anticipation of an increase in population after the opening of the Wellington Bridge. A gabled box with angle buttresses and Tudor-arched windows, similar to Smith's St Clement (*see* p. 252) but better sited and more elegantly proportioned. Entrance in the slender NW tower, which has battlements and diagonal buttresses ending in pinnacles. Interior inaccessible but said to contain a war memorial E window with STAINED GLASS by *J. A. H. Hector*, 1920. N of the church is the former manse, 1848–9, extended 1861–2; and S, on Wellington Road, the former school, 1847–9, with master's house attached. Both Tudor, by *Mackenzie & Matthews*.

On the opposite side of Wellington Road from the church – actually in Tullos – is SHELL EXPLORATION AND PRODUCTION. This very large office complex by *McInnes Gardner & Partners* was built in five phases between 1973 and 1985, and the rather muddled result reflects the dizzying growth of the offshore oil and gas industry during these years. The last and largest phase is the most distinctive; indeed, it is the only one of Aberdeen's oil buildings to express the heroic, elemental character of the industry. The steeply raking entrance front of ribbed concrete overlooks the city imperiously, with window bands of bronze glass – black gold? – recessed behind slanting concrete struts. The same raking treatment is used for the side elevations of the rear half.

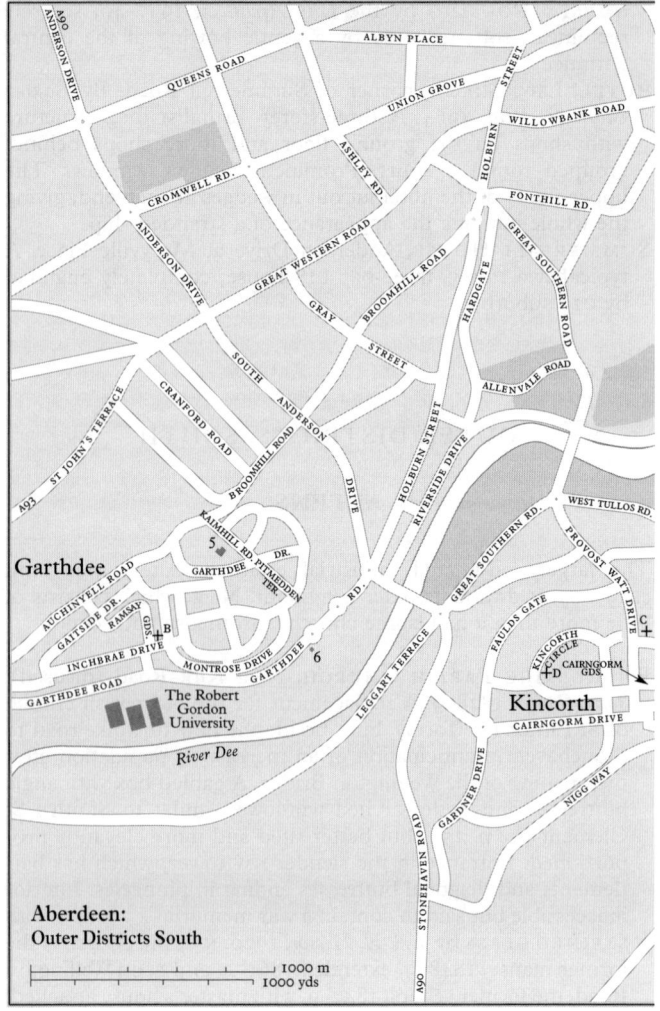

Aberdeen:
Outer Districts South

1000 m
1000 yds

A	Nigg Parish Church (former)	F	St Fittick's Church (former)
B	Garthdee Parish Church	G	Torry St Fittick's Parish Church
C	Our Lady of Aberdeen	H	St Peter (Episcopal) (former)
D	South St Nicholas	J	Torry Free Church (former)
E	Sacred Heart (R.C.)	K	Torry United Free Church

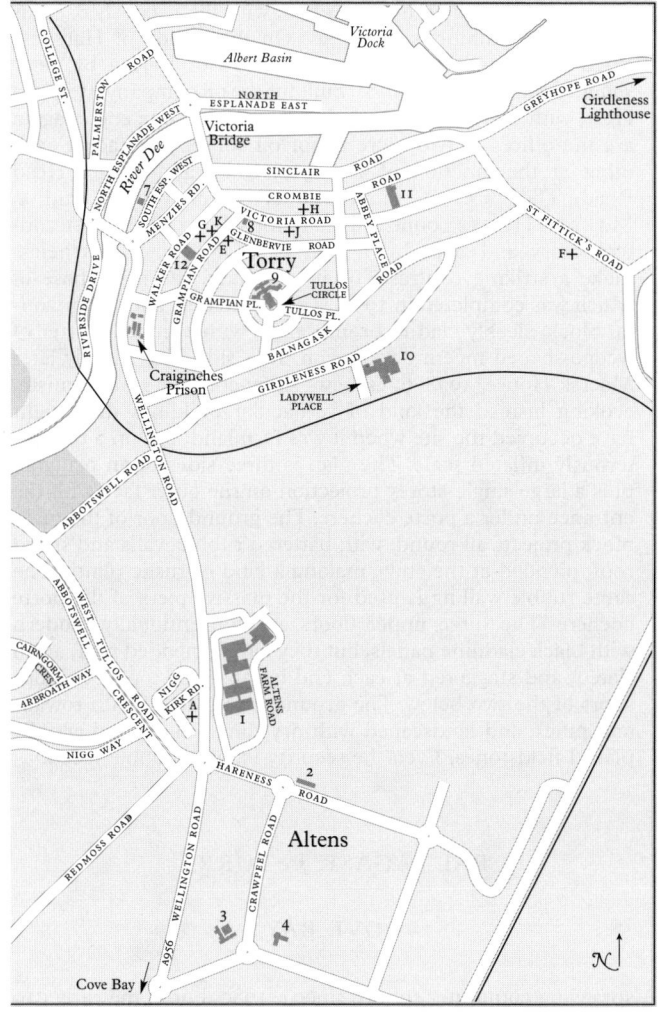

1 Shell Exploration and
  Production
2 Nexen House
3 Headquarters of Total
4 Maersk House
5 Crematorium (former)
6 Pump House
7 Aberdeen Boat Club
8 Library
9 Torry Academy
10 Tullos Primary School
11 Victoria Road Primary School
12 Walker Road Primary School

The Altens estate extends s from here with the usual sheds, plus three more ambitious buildings. On the N side of Hareness Road is the white-clad NEXEN HOUSE of 1991–3 by *Percy Johnson-Marshall & Partners*, built for the oil company Amerada Hess, with the entrance in a glazed atrium at one end. S again are the offices of two more major oil companies, facing each other at the junction of Crawpeel Road and Souter Head Road. They are, w, the headquarters of TOTAL, and E, MAERSK HOUSE (built originally for Chevron). Almost contemporary and both by *Jenkins & Marr*, they nevertheless make a striking contrast. Total's building, the first phase of which was completed in 1977, is dominated by a long horizontal block, sleekly clad in bronze glass, with a linked cluster of wedge-shaped meeting rooms on the s side. The slightly later Maersk House, 1978–9, eschews shiny corporate Modernism, evoking instead the kind of vernacular buildings that might have occupied the site when it was farmland, but on a preposterously inflated scale. The plan is three sides of an octagon, plus a large single-storey projection on the outer face with the entrance under a porte cochère. The ground floor of the main block projects all round, with battered rubble walls and slated roof, piended at the ends, making a kind of rustic plinth. The same rubble walling is used for the massive piers of the porte cochère. The three upper floors are conventionally modern with black cladding panels, but they have a piended roof, again slated, and staggered at each end because the top floor stops short of the two below. The grounds are planted with rowans and pines, and landscaped with drystone walling and artfully placed fieldstones. Even the security lodge is rubble-faced.

BALNAGASK *see* TORRY

COVE BAY

A sprawling commuter suburb since *c.* 1980, but in the early C19 a small fishing village and the site of a coastguard station established by the Scottish Customs Board to combat smuggling.

ST MARY (Episcopal), Loirston Road. *Alexander Ellis*, 1867. Built as both school and chapel. Oblong, with a three-sided apse at the w end and a lopsided E front with the door in a lean-to porch, l. Circular window in E gable, with pointed dripmould above, and housing for a bell at the apex. Dormers are the only other windows. Open timber roof inside; simple wooden rood screen between chancel and nave, with widely spaced uprights (a curtain closed off the sanctuary when the nave was being used for teaching). C19 painted decoration on the apse walls – texts, sacred monograms, etc. – and an Italian Renaissance-style Virgin and Child over the altar.

Along Loirston Road are several identical COTTAGES built in 1820 for the Customs Board's personnel, with simple Gothic doors and windows. Terraces of FISHERMEN'S COTTAGES survive just E of the bridge over the railway, in and off Colsea Road, with gable-ends facing the sea. Also in Colsea Road is the HOTEL, perhaps altered after the railway opened in 1850, but apparently older; and, near the S end, overlooking the harbour, the altered coastguard WATCH HOUSE with its simple boathouse close to the water's edge below. The concrete PIER and BREAKWATER were built in 1878 and improved in 1883 (engineer *G. G. Jenkins* of *Jenkins & Marr*). On Cove Road the former school, now COMMUNITY CENTRE, is dated 1865. 750 m. W in Charleston Road is CHARLESTON SCHOOL, 1998–9 by *Aberdeen City Council Property and Technical Services Department*. Y-plan, with two single-storey wings for teaching, and a higher general-purpose hall with curved roof in the third. White render and timber cladding with silvery metal for the roofs. Windows in a variety of playful shapes.

GARTHDEE

GARTHDEE PARISH CHURCH, Ramsay Gardens. *J. A. Ogg Allan, Ross & Allan*, begun 1952. Cruciform, with a shallow octagonal lantern over the crossing. The rendered exterior is stamped all over with semicircles, like inverted fish scales. Granite tympanum over main door, carved with dove and burning bush. The nave was designed to double as a hall: a stage at the S end can be closed off with folding shutters.

Former CREMATORIUM, Kaimhill Road. 1935–8, *Rollo & Hall*. A dignified, flat-roofed block, in pink and grey rock-faced granite. The higher central chapel has upright clearstorey windows. Surrounding it on three sides is the Hall of Remembrance, a columbarium lined from floor to ceiling with wooden niches and memorial tablets.

ROBERT GORDON UNIVERSITY, Garthdee Road. Higher Education came to the beautiful riverside setting of Garthdee in 1957, after the architect Tom Scott Sutherland gave Garthdee House and its grounds to Robert Gordon's Technical College for its School of Architecture. Gray's School of Art moved here from the city centre a decade later. From the 1990s, the newly constituted Robert Gordon University has aimed to concentrate its activities at Garthdee, and several major buildings have resulted.

The campus can be seen in more or less chronological order by entering at the W end, beside the Neo-Tudor WEST LODGE of Garthdee House (1870 by *William Smith*; there is a matching East Lodge). Just inside is GRAY'S SCHOOL OF ART, 1964–6 by *D. Michael A. Shewan*, an elegant and beautifully sited structure of exposed steel and glass (the model was Mies van der Rohe's 1956 Crown Hall for the Illinois Institute of Technology). It encloses three sides of a quadrangle. The fourth was originally open to the s and the quadrangle enjoyed glorious views of the Dee, until with unbelievable crassness it was shut off by a row of prefabs. Marble BUST of John Gray in the entrance hall, 1885 by *H. Bain-Smith*. Further E, facing the Art School across sweeping lawns, is *William Smith*'s Garthdee House, a substantial mansion of 1870 for the provision curer John Moir Clark. It is now the SCOTT SUTHERLAND SCHOOL OF ARCHITECTURE & BUILT ENVIRONMENT. Tudor exterior with variously shaped gables and canted bays. The interior by contrast is classical, centred on a double-height top-lit hall, arcaded on the first floor, with the stairs in a recess off one side. In 1877 the house was described as 'done up internally' by *Daniel Cottier*, and the stained glass window of Ceres on the stairs is no doubt his. The ground-floor rooms at the sw corner are linked and have pairs of Corinthian columns between. Large extensions for the School of Architecture – a glazed rear wing by *Scott Sutherland*'s own practice, 1956–7, with further harled additions by *Thomson, Taylor, Craig & Donald*, completed in 1971 – together form a quadrangle. Just s of the house is the SQUARE TOWER, one of two excellent blocks of student flats by *Jeremy Dixon Edward Jones*, 1992–3. The other – the ROUND TOWER – is SE, overlooking the river. Picturesquely sited like C18 follies in their parkland setting, they also evoke the tower houses of the region (both are finished with pink harling). Squeezed between the School of Architecture and the river is the rectangular CENTRAL SERVICES building by *RMJM*, completed 2008. Two timber-clad storeys above a glazed and recessed ground floor, with a further recessed floor on top. The timber-clad part has a big expanse of glazing in each end elevation, deeply recessed to form a cavernous balcony.

E of the School of Architecture is KAIM HOUSE, a harled villa of 1910 by *A. Marshall Mackenzie & Son*, with two bows on the side facing the river. E of this is the key building of the Garthdee campus's recent transformation, the very large ABERDEEN BUSINESS SCHOOL AND GEORGINA SCOTT SUTHERLAND LIBRARY by *Foster & Partners*, 1997–8. The University wanted a landmark building by a leading architect, and they got it. The site slopes steeply to the river and the six floors step down from N to s in a series of internal terraces under the huge overarching curve of the aluminium roof. Side walls are clad in a grid of polished granite and silvered metal, with recessed, black-framed glazing higher up towards the roof. Inside, the N end is a four-storey atrium which serves as foyer, thoroughfare and informal meeting place. The library floors, s, are linked by a central, open stair and provide work stations which are surprisingly human in scale, despite the immense roof-space above. (Interior altered following opening of the new library in Riverside East building: *see* below.)

Foster & Partners made a masterplan for the campus which envisaged a succession of similar buildings, linked by a pedestrian street threading through their upper ends. Only the neighbouring SPORTS CENTRE by *Thomson Craig & Donald*, completed 2005, has adopted the street idea – it runs through a winter garden at the N end, with views into the swimming pool, S – but externally it is a rather dull, metal-clad box. Further E is the FACULTY OF HEALTH AND SOCIAL CARE by *Halliday Fraser Munro*, opened 2002. Closely modelled on the Business School, it is if anything more successful in its relationship with the landscape. Rock-faced granite is used for parts of the exterior, with narrow gantries passing in front of the glazing on the W and E elevations. Inside, an atrium runs N–S, an immense canyon descending through the heart of the building, its glass roof drawing the eye to the river views. E again is the largest of the University's buildings, the huge RIVERSIDE EAST by *BDP*, opened in 2013 (a further addition is under construction in 2014). A linear, snaking block, parallel with the Dee, it is clad in silvery metal panels, with the green glass drum of the nine-storey library tower anchoring its SW corner. Inside, an atrium winds its way from end to end, an echo of the pedestrian street envisaged in Foster & Partners' masterplan. The base of the library tower is a circular space with informal tiered seating for performances, while the top floor commands a near-360° panorama of the city and Deeside. At the E end of the site, a HEALTH CENTRE and NURSERY opened in 2004: cedar cladding and render, with opposing monopitch roofs.

PUMP HOUSE, Garthdee Road (*c*. 300 m. SW of the Bridge of Dee). A squat granite rotunda with machicolated coping and conical roof, associated with the 1830 water works which supplied river water to the Union Place cistern (*see* p. 170) via an engine house at the Bridge of Dee. It appears to have been moved from its original site nearer the river.

DESCRIPTION

N of Garthdee Road and S of Auchinyell Road was developed as a municipal housing estate from 1938. Kaimhill Gardens and Kaimhill Circle were laid out at this date: attractive semis with a mix of slated and red tiled roofs, on axis with the crematorium and symmetrical about a central green. Of the same date are some attractive timber houses and flats with shingled upper floors, behind the crematorium in Auchinyell Gardens. Postwar housing further W is less interesting. S of Garthdee Road, the picture is completely different. Garthdee House was the last of four neighbouring villas built on choice riverside sites feued by the Pitfodels Land Company. Going W, the next is NORWOOD, built 1861 and remodelled in 1881 by *J. R. Mackenzie* for James Ogston (now a hotel, a recent large extension, W, has doubled it in size). Harled, with freestone dressings. Finely moulded classical architraves and pedimented

tripartite windows contrast with the more florid details of the
E wing, which has Ogston's initials on the gable. Did he also
add the similar square w bay and Doric porch? Sumptuous,
burnished late C19 interiors (also 1881?) by *W. Scott Morton*,
encrusted with the firm's Tynecastle tapestry and much carved
woodwork. Imperial stair under square, coffered dome and
skylight. Two LODGES on Garthdee Road, the w one a *cottage
orné* with carved bargeboards. Adjoining Norwood on the w is
DRUMGARTH, *c.* 1858, probably by *A. & W. Reid & Mackenzie*.
A WINDMILL with a 1680 lintel and 1760 weathervane is said
to be in the grounds, brought here from Windmill Brae near
the Green. Finally, w again, is INCHGARTH. A house was built
here *c.* 1862, part of which may remain, but what meets the
eye now is *A. Marshall Mackenzie*'s work of 1897. Handsome
S front with pediment and urns, and a semicircular Ionic
portico, so large it is almost a veranda.

KAIMHILL *see* GARTHDEE

KINCORTH

A large housing estate, the subject of a 1937 planning competition
won by *Robert Gardner-Medwin*, *Clifford Holliday* and *Denis
Winston*, with a design embodying Garden City ideals. The
Second World War intervened, and construction to a modified
layout did not begin until afterwards, but the essential features
of the winning design were implemented: the broad sweep of
Provost Watt Drive leads uphill from the purpose-built George
VI Bridge (*see* p. 249) to the civic centre at the top, with a large
open space for recreation adjoining. This channels traffic away
from the residential streets, which follow the contours of the hill
and look out over the city and the valley of the Dee. The earliest
houses are in pairs and short terraces, granite-built and of traditional design. The civic centre with shops, clinic and octagonal
library did not come until the 1960s, accompanied by denser
housing in modern materials.

OUR LADY OF ABERDEEN (R.C.), Cairngorm Crescent. 1963–4.
A rendered box, narrower towards the altar end, with SW
porch. Entrance front with shallow gable, the centre filled by
a large concrete window. More such windows at the sides.
SOUTH ST NICHOLAS, Kincorth Circle. *A. G. R. Mackenzie*,
1953. Church and hall are attached to form an L, set back from
the street behind a green. Granite with artificial stone dressings, and steep slate roofs with low eaves. Mullioned windows
to the church, dormers and a gable stack to the hall. The
traditional forms, materials and grouping match the first phase
of housing at Kincorth and reflect Mackenzie's involvement
with the incipient conservation movement at this date.

NIGG *see* ALTENS

TORRY

Historically part of Kincardineshire, Torry was no more than a fishing village on the s bank of the Dee until the late C19. In 1874 the Aberdeen Land Association purchased Torry Farm with a view to house-building, but serious development only began after the opening of Victoria Bridge in 1881. Amalgamation with Aberdeen in 1891 gave further impetus, and by 1899 Torry had become 'the newest and most growing of the suburbs of Aberdeen', with tenements advancing rapidly uphill from the bridge. After the First World War, large-scale public housing schemes colonized the top of the hill before spreading s to Tullos and e to Balnagask.

CHURCHES

SACRED HEART (R.C.), Grampian Road. *Charles J. Ménart*, 38 1910–11. Splendidly sited, high above the street. This is the most impressive church in Torry and one of the best in Aberdeen. French Romanesque, in contrast to the Roman High Renaissance of Ménart's slightly earlier St Aloysius, Glasgow. Cruciform, with a massive, squat crossing tower, the width of nave and aisles combined; short transepts; and a round apse with lower ambulatory. Red tiled roofs (including a low-pitched roof over the tower), and walls of rock-faced red granite with ashlar dressings. The stones are not coursed and look more like vertical crazy paving than rubble. w front and N transept have rounded corners, corbelled out near the top to become square – a Scottish touch – and there are small rounded porches tucked into the angles of transepts and aisles. Interior plastered and painted. Vestibule under w choir loft, leading to a two-bay nave with cruciform piers and passage aisles. More such piers form an arcade of stilted arches between apse and ambulatory, enclosing a marble baldacchino over the high altar. Nave and aisles open into the crossing as one very large arch flanked by two much smaller ones, mirrored by apse and ambulatory. The motif is repeated for the transepts but the arches here are just a screen, since there are no aisles. Four big windows in each face of the tower flood the central space with light. The attached PRESBYTERY is a continuation of the s transept under the same roof. A rounded stair-turret marks the junction with the church but otherwise there is nothing medieval about it.

Former ST FITTICK, St Fittick's Road (ruin). Situated just outside the present built-up area, but originally much more isolated, it served a rural district stretching as far s as Cove Bay. A church was dedicated here in the 1240s. The present remains – a roofless rectangle abandoned in 1829 when the new church at Nigg opened (*see* p. 291) – are perhaps C17 or c18. Bellcote on E gable, said to be dated 1704 but now over-grown. Walled churchyard (permission to rebuild the walls was granted in 1862) with monuments from the c17 to the c19.

Former ST PETER (Episcopal), Victoria Road. *Kinross & Tarbolton*, 1897–8. Gothic, with a very tall, narrow nave and aisles, and cliff-like walls faced with blocks of red granite the size and shape of bricks. It lies parallel to the street, slotted between tenements. Austere S elevation relieved at one end by a porch with crowstepped gable, and at the other by a three-bay chapel and unfinished tower. Circular window in W gable with flowing tracery; pointed windows to aisles and chapel. Square-headed clearstorey windows with panels of carving, doubled in 1985 during conversion to housing. At the same time dormers were added, and the interior subdivided.

Former TORRY FREE CHURCH, Victoria Road. *D. & J. R. McMillan*, 1889–90. Raised above the street. Gothic, mostly lancets. Short NW tower with octagonal belfry and spire.

TORRY ST FITTICK'S PARISH CHURCH, Walker Road. *A. H. L. Mackinnon*, 1898. Gothic. Grey granite nave with bands of pink, and trefoil-headed lancets in pairs. Mackinnon planned a cruciform building with semicircular apse. Instead, a very simple N end was eventually added to the nave. It is the same width, but rendered, with cross-gables rather than transepts, and no apse. Interior with open timber roof. – STAINED GLASS. N window, 1995, Christ overlooking the harbour, with one of the leading lights (*see* below). – BELL from old St Fittick, 1759, by *John Mowat*. – MODEL SHIP. One of several votive ship models made for Aberdeen churches, it was presented to Nigg Parish Church by Capt. Affleck, 1829, and originally hung in the nave there.

TORRY UNITED FREE CHURCH, Grampian Road. By *W. E. Gauld*, 1932, though if the date were not inscribed on the foundation stone, it would be impossible to believe: it looks thoroughly conventional late c19 Gothic. The congregation did not follow the majority of the United Free Church into union with the Church of Scotland in 1929, and the new building deliberately emphasized continuity with the past.

PUBLIC BUILDINGS

ABERDEEN BOAT CLUB, South Esplanade West. *Michael Rasmussen Associates*, 1982; doubled in size 1993. Two parallel A-framed structures – a hint of upturned hulls – with boat storage at ground level and club facilities above. Circular corner balcony added *c.* 2003.

CRAIGINCHES PRISON, Grampian Place. 1889–91, presumably by *H. M. Office of Works*; new gatehouse, 1970s. The original plan had parallel cell blocks, male and female, with a linking corridor. Both survive, though altered, within the high perimeter wall. The larger, male block has crowstepped gables and big octagonal flues with corbelled tops. Gothic dormers at the N end indicate the first-floor chapel.

LIBRARY, Victoria Road. *Brown & Watt*, 1902–3. Small but dignified. Tripartite façade like a Renaissance church, the higher
central bay pedimented and flanked by concave buttresses,
framing a Diocletian window. Other windows mullioned and
transomed. Handsome classical interior.

TORRY ACADEMY, Tullos Circle. *J. A. Ogg Allan*, 1926–7. Low
and spreading, unlike earlier multi-storey urban schools such
as Walker Road, Torry (*see* below). The classrooms occupy two
very long, single-storey wings, zigzagging out from the central
block. Their symmetry is now unintelligible because of a huge,
bunker-like extension attached to the front in 1977.

TULLOS PRIMARY SCHOOL, Girdleness Road. By *D. J. A. Ross*,
as chief assistant to *J. A. Ogg Allan*. A stylish modernist design
of 1939, not completed until after the Second World War, and
marred by later additions. Central block with cylindrical glazed
stair-tower, flanked by long wings with flat roofs and rounded
ends, the E one lower because of the sloping site (the plan
suggests that Machine Age icon, the aeroplane). The S front
of the W wing is almost fully glazed on the ground floor, the
classroom windows opening onto a terrace under a glazed
canopy.

VICTORIA BRIDGE. Five segmental arches of rock-faced granite
with rounded cutwaters and solid parapet, by *Edward L. I.
Blyth*, opened 1881. Long contemplated, it was eventually built
after the acquisition of development land on the Torry side by
the Aberdeen Land Association in 1874, and the disastrous
capsizing of a ferry in 1876.

VICTORIA ROAD PRIMARY SCHOOL, Victoria Road. Disused.
The earlier part on Abbey Road, facing N towards Old Torry,
is by *William Henderson & Son*, 1878. The gabled end blocks
were originally houses for male and female teachers. A large
addition by *J. A. Ogg Allan* dated 1904 faces S to the newly
important thoroughfare of Victoria Road.

WALKER ROAD PRIMARY SCHOOL, Walker Road. Huge central
block of 1895 by *Ellis & Wilson*, reflecting the rapid growth of
Torry in the last decade of the C19. Three storeys, with four-
storey domed corner towers and a parapet with little arches
and pediments. Large early C20 additions by *J. A. Ogg Allan*, N
and S. By 1938 this was the biggest school in Scotland, with
over 1,600 pupils.

DESCRIPTION

Housing

Torry housing falls into three categories. First, there are the
sparse remains of the fishing settlement of 'Old Torry', dating
in their present form mostly from the later C19. Abbey Road
is the focus, with a square of fishermen's houses of 1870 by
J. & W. Smith, one with a forestair. Then there are the tenements and semi-detached villas of 'New Torry', built after the
opening of Blyth's Victoria Bridge (*see* above). Victoria Road is

the main artery here, curving uphill from the bridge, with Menzies Road and Walker Road branching off, apparently laid out by *Blyth*; Grampian Road, Oscar Road and Glenbervie Road followed from 1896, laid out by *Walker & Duncan*. One block worth singling out is at the curved SE corner of Victoria Road and Sinclair Road, with shaped gables to the dormers, probably by *Ellis & Wilson*, 1897. Finally, there is C20 municipal housing, extending S and E to Tullos and Balnagask. The earliest – a mixture of semi-detached houses and flats in small blocks – was begun in 1920 and occupies the top of the hill (the layout of concentric and radiating roads is by the Burgh Surveyor *John Gordon*, with *William Kelly* and *Harbourne Maclennan* as consultants). S of the prison and E of Mansfield Road are granite-faced 1930s tenements with gabled entrance bays. On the S side of Girdleness Road, just W of Tullos School, a short flat-roofed interwar terrace makes a contrast with its pitch-roofed neighbours. The rest, as far E as St Fittick's Road, is mostly low-rise housing of the 1960s and 70s with a few tower blocks.

Harbour

Sinclair Road leads E from Victoria Road, passing the RIVER DEE DOCK, built 1909–15. Opposite at Nos. 82–84 is a C20 brick SMOKE HOUSE, an isolated survivor of a building type associated with the historically important Torry fish-processing industry. W and E of the junction with Baxter Street are two LEADING LIGHTS, tapering octagonal iron beacons aligned with the navigation channel, erected in 1842 to guide vessels into port. On the quay near the W light is a small, octagonal, domed SYPHON HOUSE of 1906, and facing it across the channel at Point Law a matching building, both for transmitting sewage from N of the Dee to a new outfall at Girdleness.

Beyond St Fittick's Road, Sinclair Road continues E as Greyhope Road, with several features of interest strung out along its considerable length. First on the l. is an early C19 CAPSTAN JETTY, and next to it a curving concrete PIER completed in 1878, built along with its counterpart at Pocra Quay on the N side to protect the inner harbour from heavy seas. Further E on the S side of the road is TORRY POINT BATTERY, a ruined fort of 1858–60 commanding the entry to the harbour. Only the landward side of the diamond-shaped enceinte survives. It has loopholes and a bastion at the SW angle, and an imposing round-arched entrance with dated keystone and heavy, corbelled top. Inside are the remains of gun emplacements and the roofless guardroom. Below the battery is the OLD SOUTH BREAKWATER, planned by *Telford* and built under *John Gibb*, 1812–15, but reduced in length when the much longer SOUTH BREAKWATER of 1869–73 was built further E by *William Dyce Cay*. Cay's breakwater is entirely concrete: liquid concrete laid under the water in jute bags for the foundations, then large pre-cast blocks, then liquid concrete cast *in situ* for the upper part, including the roadway. In 1937 a breach near the N end was repaired with block work, and the widening of the whole structure on the seaward side was begun in 1939. The smooth curves of the terminal concrete LIGHTHOUSE – like an elongated egg in an eggcup – look utterly C20, but it too is by *Cay*.

Greyhope Road continues to the headland, and the most splendid of all the harbour structures: *Robert Stevenson*'s GIRDLENESS LIGHTHOUSE of 1831–3. A tapering tower with two corbelled balconies, one at the top, the other a third of the way up. There were originally lights at both levels, but in 1890 the upper one was improved and the lower one dispensed with. Access to the tower is between two symmetrical, single-storey keepers' houses, plainest classical, linked by an archway bearing the date of completion. Between the lighthouse and the sea is the FOG SIGNAL of 1902 (known affectionately as the 'Torry Coo'), a concrete base supporting the horn, with cylinders for compressed air behind; on the shore below, the classical 1906 VALVE HOUSE of rock-faced granite, built in connection with the Girdleness sewage outfall.

102

TULLOS *see* TORRY

ABERGELDIE CASTLE

2090

2.6 km. E of Crathie

The site has been in the hands of the Gordon family since 1482. It must have existed in some form by 1594, when orders were given to tear it down, but it is not clear how much damage was done. A fire of 1816 burnt the 'principal part of the mansion to the ground' with only the tower intact, but by 1832 when the *Aberdeen Journal* described it as ready to let, the house had a considerable extension to the W, accommodating a large service area, the dining room and many bedrooms. *James Henderson* is associated with further work in the early 1840s. The royal family leased it from 1848 to 1970 and made further changes. It became the favoured resort of the Duchess of Kent, Queen Victoria's mother. All these accretions were completely removed in 1970, when the C16 fabric of the tower was recovered and restored by *George Bennett Mitchell and Son*.

Of granite rubble and pink harl, the tower has a four-storey rectangular plan, and a circular stair-tower on the SW corner similar to the plan of Pitfichie and Birse Castles (qq.v.). The stair-tower corbels out at the wall-head, to provide a square, flat-topped viewing platform, reached by a secondary minor staircase, level with the roof ridge. On the N side there is a small corner turret with three pistol-holes on the NE corner, springing from subtle rounded and square corbels. The chimneys on E and W gables have bold talus-moulded copings. The arched entrance, with its yett hooks, is on the main block, adjacent to the tower. A decorative iron 'tirl-plate' of openwork is on the modern door. On it are the initials AG and EG, Alexander Gordon (8th Laird, 1655–94) and his wife, Euphemia Graham. There are two notable C19 Italianate additions to the S façade: a wide Venetian window at dormer height and a classical cupola on top of the tower.

Inside there is a vaulted ground floor of kitchen, cellar with gunloops and prison pit. There is no internal kitchen fireplace but the restoration discovered one on the exterior of the w wall,

*Places marked (N) have entries in the gazetteer for *Buildings of Scotland: Aberdeenshire: North and Moray*

implying a subsidiary lean-to wing. It is not clear how this kitchen communicated with the main block but a doorway at the back of the kitchen hearth corresponds to an intramural staircase from the screens end of the hall to the W cellar. At the head of these stairs is a small intramural garderobe. The edge-roll of the entrance doorway corresponds to that of the hall fireplace on the first floor. The hall has a segmental arched vault and large fireplace. On the second floor are two chambers, each with their own garderobe and fireplace. On the third floor, now two rooms, there is only one fireplace and garderobe.

ABERGELDIE SUSPENSION BRIDGE. By *Blaikie Bros*, 1885. Built at the expense of Queen Victoria to improve access to Abergeldie Castle, across the Dee from the A93. Slender iron suspension footbridge between iron pylons on granite piers. Currently in poor condition (2014).

ABOYNE

What one will always remember about Aboyne is its immense village green, which lies along the road from Aberdeen to Braemar and continues SW down to the bank of the Dee, with the spire of the former Free Church proudly placed on one side. It is a scene that seems strikingly English. There was a medieval settlement at Formaston, 3 km. NE, in the possession of the Gordons of Tilphoudie, but the village was largely created in 1676 as a burgh of barony by Charles Gordon, 1st Earl of Aboyne, the policies of whose castle begin immediately N of the village. Officially known as Charlestown of Aboyne, it became a centre for livestock markets and until the mid C19 was the terminus of both the turnpike road along the N bank of the Dee and the railway, bestowing an importance on it as the last settlement of significance for tourists before the Highlands, and scene of the annual Aboyne Highland Games from 1867. It also became an attractive place of resort with fishing lodges and villas for businessmen by 1900; as in Banchory and Braemar (qq.v.), a significant minority of Aboyne's villas were built specifically for summer letting by entrepreneurs who would inhabit purpose-built 'back houses' for the duration. The character of many of the village's late C19 buildings was determined by the influence of the Manchester banker Sir William Cunliffe Brooks, who from 1869 leased the Glen Tanar estate (q.v.) from the 11th Marquis of Huntly, to whom Brooks married his daughter in the same year and from whom he also acquired Aboyne Castle in 1888. Brooks's architect was the Englishman *George Truefitt* but after 1900 almost all new work in the village was in the hands of *George Bennett Mitchell*, who made his own home here. After 1945 and again in the most recent decades there has been a good deal of development for housing around the fringes of the village, but with few exceptions the Late Victorian and Edwardian tone predominates.

CHURCHES

ABOYNE-DINNET PARISH CHURCH, Huntly Road, at the SW
end of the green. An enchanting small design of 1842 by *John
Smith* in his version of Gothic, the motifs of the uncusped
tracery Perp. Rectangular, with pinnacled buttresses at the four
corners and also framing the centre of the gabled W front,
which projects slightly and has a large window under an ogee
moulding and a bellcote with gables, nook-shafts and spirelet.
Inside, the 1840s galleries around three sides have Gothic
panelling. The entrance to the HUNTLY VAULT (N side) is
dated 1761 with weathered Gordon armorial over. It was
retained from the previous church on this site (1759–63). –
CHURCH HALL by *Jenkins & Marr*, 1902.

BURIAL GROUND, Formaston, 3 km. NE. Just the footings of the
medieval parish church of St Adamnan, granted to the Knights
Templar in 1232 by Walter Bisset, Lord of Aboyne. Covering
the E end a burial aisle containing a C17 tomb-slab, bearing a
skull-and-crossbones and armorial shield with central crescent
and three animal heads, possibly boars for a Gordon of
Tilphoudie.

Former FREE CHURCH, Charlestown Road. The landmark of
the village, beside the green's SE edge. 1868–9 by *J.R.
Mackenzie*. In 1946 it became the Masonic Hall and it is now
in community use. Nave-and-aisles-pattern Gothic front with
fine broach spire to the angle-buttressed central tower. Gabled
lucarnes at the base of the spire. Lancet windows with lattice
glazing. – STAINED GLASS. E window, 1901 by *Swaine Bourne
& Son*.

ST MARGARET (R.C.), Ballater Road. Close to the gates of
Aboyne Castle, and of 1874 by *Alexander Ogilvy*, who became
the Marquis of Huntly's clerk-of-works in 1871 (cf. Tillypronie
House, q.v.). Although small, with nave and chancel in one
and apse at the W end, there is a degree of originality in the
Gothic details; see for example the quirky moulding of the N
door. Refurbished inside in 1970 by *Leo Durnin* following a
fire; much use of varnished pine. Presbytery attached to the S.

ST THOMAS (Episcopal), Ballater Road, 0.5 km. W of the green
in a pine wood. A remarkable design of 1907–9 for George
Coats, the Paisley cotton thread manufacturer who became
Laird of Glen Tanar (q.v.) in 1905 and Lord Glentanar in 1916.
His architects were *Fryers & Penman* of Largs, Ayrshire, a firm
frequently employed by the Coats family and also engaged in
the rebuilding of Glen Tanar House. The notable fact is that it
is based on St Mary, Burrough-on-the-Hill, Leicestershire,
where the Coats also owned property. So the style is late C13
and Dec with chancel, S organ chamber, nave with clearstorey,
and N and S aisles embracing the buttressed W tower with its
spire behind its parapet. The material is of course granite,
silvery grey from Kemnay. The tracery mostly Dec, flowing in
the E window. Inside, nave arcades with C13-style circular piers
and chamfered arches, the chancel arch in the same manner.

– FITTINGS all of 1907–9, mostly with Gothic tracery, and very
nicely carved e.g. the ORGAN CASE with its trumpeting angel
supporters (the instrument originally by *Abbot & Smith*, but
rebuilt by *Harrison & Harrison*, 1924, and *Paul Miller*, 2008).
– Also (numbered) rush-seated CHAIRS instead of pews. –
FONT. Portland stone. By *H. H. Martyn & Co.*, copying the
C13 original at Burrough, with dogtooth to the base and shafts,
and crude stiff-leaf around the bowl etc. – STAINED GLASS.
Chancel E (Passion, Crucifixion and Resurrection) in C13 style,
by *William Morris & Co.* of Westminster. Chancel lancets
(emblems of the Passion) and tower window with quotation 'I
have set thee for a tower among my people' (Jeremiah 6:27)
also by Morris & Co. – Aisle windows have C15–C17 British
and Continental fragments of heraldry and saints, arranged by
Morris & Co. – Organ chamber window, by *Michael Zappert*
of Aboyne, 1995. – MONUMENT. George Coats, 1st Lord
Glentanar †1918. An astonishing piece, by *Percy Portsmouth*,
1923, replicating in Carrara marble the Carpaneto monument
in the Campo Santo (Staglieno cemetery), Genoa, of 1886 by
Giovanni Scanzi. It depicts the Angel of Hope furling the sail
of a boat reaching the shore. The architect credited for the
work, so perhaps the author of the finely lettered plinth, is
Robert S. Lorimer (*Building News*, 28.9.1923).

PUBLIC BUILDINGS

ABOYNE ACADEMY, Bridgeview Road. By the *Aberdeen County
Architect*, *c.* 1972. As part of the same scheme, the adjoining
cluster of community buildings: library, swimming pool and
theatre. Immediately S is the PRIMARY SCHOOL of 1979.

ABOYNE BRIDGE, across the Dee 1.8 km. S of Aboyne Castle,
where until 1828 there was a ferry crossing. 1937–41 by *George
Bennett Mitchell* and *F.A. Macdonald & Partners*, in reinforced
concrete with 52 m.-wide low segmental arch over the river
and two flood arches beyond the S bank. At the N end is the
former TOLL HOUSE (now Bridgend Cottage) built *c.* 1830 to
serve the suspension bridge of that year, the suspension bridge
of 1828 having been washed away in the floods of 1829. It is
of an exceptionally high standard for such buildings, no doubt
due to the influence of the Earl of Aboyne, who paid for the
bridges. Rusticated granite ashlar, the front of three bays with
windows and door in segmental-arched recesses. Inside, one
fine room to the l. overlooking the river and small office for
the tollkeeper to the r. Piended platform roof.

ABOYNE HOSPITAL, Bellwood Road. The former isolation hospital of 1897 by *Jenkins & Marr*. Three very simple single-
storey pavilion blocks, the principal one with attic and jerkin
roof, but much poor infilling in the spaces between.

Former ABOYNE SCHOOL, encroaching on the Green along
Huntly Road. Now a business centre. 1874–5 by *George Truefitt*,
rather nicely done in rock-faced squared pink granite with
half-timbered gables in the N side. Extended E in 1901 by

Jenkins & Marr with bellcote in the gable-end and a s wing with double gables prettily linked by a circle across the roof valley. The single-storey wing to the SE with two gabled ranges is of 1911 by *G. Bennett Mitchell* as the Higher Grade Dept. The N end of this addition, with Gothic window and diagonal chimneys may be the earlier C19 Female School incorporated.

POLICE STATION, Charlestown Road. Cottage-style police house, dated 1859, extended by *William Henderson & Son*, 1896. Of one storey and attic, with later two-storey extension to N. Remarkably large kitchen garden in front.

Former STATION, Station Square. Closed in 1966, now commercial units. The Deeside Railway was extended from Banchory to Aboyne in 1859. The original station building, then considered 'commodious and imposing . . . the last word in design', was the terminus until 1866 when the line was extended to Ballater. The present building, on a grand scale, is of 1895–6 by *James Lowson*, and *Patrick M. Barnett* architect, chief engineer, of the GNSR. It has a satisfyingly long front, single-storeyed but with a higher centre for the entrance under a low slate roof with carriage canopy in front, anchored at the outer corners by circular towers with Baronial cone roofs with fish-scale slating.

WAR MEMORIAL BUILDINGS, Ballater Road. 1920–1 by *A. Marshall Mackenzie & Son* as Aboyne and Glen Tanar's memorial to its war dead and survivors, the cost largely met by Thomas Coats, 2nd Lord Glentanar. On the granite front a loggia of chamfered arches with shields in the spandrels and a three-sided apsidal projection to the l. with flamboyant tracery, recalling the firm's work at New King's, Aberdeen University (1912), and anticipating the canted bay and loggia concept of the University's Elphinstone Hall (1927). Inside the bay is the memorial shrine: stained glass by *J. Dudley Forsyth*, 1926, with seated figures symbolic of Valour, Patriotism etc. below mouchettes of cherubs. The stair inside to the upper floor makes an elegant sweep. The building contained a reading room and billiard room with the public hall (the VICTORY HALL) to the rear. – Inside, a fragment of a PICTISH CROSS-SLAB (the 'Formaston Stone'), combining Ogham inscription with a mirror symbol and Celtic interlace. Probably late C9. It was found at the Burial Ground, Formaston (*see* above), and from the late C19 until the 1970s was at Aboyne Castle.

DESCRIPTION

The appropriate place to begin is the NE tip of THE GREEN at the HUNTLY ARMS HOTEL, which although now of distinctly C19 appearance, with cusped bargeboarding to its gabled wings and porch and a veranda along part of the E front, is in fact a large Georgian coaching inn set beside the former turnpike road. The original part is the five-bay centre in roughly squared and coursed pink and grey granite with raised surrounds to the windows. Blocked semicircular carriage arch at the W end of the N wing. Attached to the S wing is a major addition of 1892 but completely refronted and raised to three storeys *c.* 1920 in a flimsy castellated style; it accommodates a banqueting hall inside. The lounge bar is a period piece of *c.* 1950, smoothly panelled in walnut veneer with tile fireplace still in Deco style. Large stained glass window of the same date celebrating the Aboyne Games and its co-founder Donald Dinnie (1837–1916), champion athlete. In the garden a memorable rustic GAZEBO, which was here by 1867 but is probably early C19. It is octagonal, surrounded by a veranda of log columns supporting the roof, which sweeps up to a pointed finial. Lattice windows. Inside it was lined with compressed moss and paved with inverted bottles. Restored from 2002.

E of the hotel is the extensive STATION SQUARE, which served the cattle market before and after the opening of the Station (*see* above). On the N side an interesting group of shops including a BUTCHER S SHOP of *c.* 1867 and a long row called CHARLESTON COTTAGES, built in the unmistakable and eccentric Arts and Crafts style of *George Truefitt* for Sir William Cunliffe Brooks, whose monogram is carved on the concave curve of the building's corner. Rugged local granite walls, chimneys rising directly from the wall face and the piend roofs of the dormers are tropes familiar from Glen Tanar (q.v.). At the W end a truncated cone roof on broaches with horseshoe weathervane, so presumably for the blacksmith's shop.

The buildings of interest around the Green are well spread out; along CHARLESTOWN ROAD, SW of the former Free Church, are villas in spacious gardens. BIRSE LODGE, W of the Green and S of the Parish Church, is one of the largest, dated 1861 and built originally as Huntly Lodge, the dower house for Aboyne Castle. In the picturesque manner very characteristic of mid-Victorian Deeside, with walls of coursed rock-faced local granite, mullioned windows and steep roofs carried over the eaves on brackets and with trussed gables. The porch has tree-trunk columns, a popular motif in Victorian houses in the village. So, for example in BALLATER ROAD, N of the Green, is CHARLESTON, very ambitious with a full rustic veranda, its columns retaining branches to form cob-webby spandrels. The house itself is symmetrical with canted bays and almost certainly by *G. Bennett Mitchell*, who designed its similar neighbour TIGH-NA-GEALD in 1901, here with its veranda placed between the canted bays. Further W, HAZLEHURST is a former lodge to the Castle policies, with some of the same quirky motifs as the R.C. church (*see* Churches) so also probably *c.* 1874 by *Alexander Ogilvy*. Then beyond that an attractive small house called THE COTTAGE of *c.* 1900 by *Mitchell* in English Arts and Crafts style, two storeys but the upper one contained in the attic, with the gabled dormer spanning the width of the house. The eaves of the fish-scale-slated roof form a pentice over the entrance between canted bays. There are several more houses by Mitchell between Ballater Road and Charlestown Road, e.g.

in St Eunan's Road and Huntly Road, variously treated. In
BRIDGEVIEW ROAD, on the corner with Charlestown Road
and overlooking the Dee crossing, is DESSMUIR, a large villa
of 1901 by *J. M. Pirie*, with walls of Cambus O'May granite
and steep and sharply gabled slate roofs with half-timbering
and a smaller, sharper gable over the entrance in the angle
between the two wings; this is a slight variation on the design
(*Building News*, 27.12.1901) which had a stone octagon with
spire expressing the form of the hall and smoking room inside.
GLEBE HOUSE, 200 m. w, is the former parish manse of
1790–1: three storeys with a basement and attic; at right angles
to it a lower s addition of 1835. Altered and renewed inside by
Matthews & Mackenzie, 1892–3.

To the w, bounded by the river, is LADY WOOD for which
a feuing plan was made for Cunliffe Brooks by *Thomas Mawson*
c. 1895. RHU-NA-HAVEN ROAD runs in a dog-leg through it
and at the N entrance from Ballater Road are heavy GATEPIERS
with pyramidal tops as one finds at the entrance to Glen Tanar
(q.v.). At the E end of Rhu-na-Haven Road by Bridgeview
Road is LADYWOOD LODGE of 1903–4 by *G. Bennett Mitchell*,★
for Lady Jane Cunliffe Brooks, Sir William's widow. Very
English-looking with a façade covered in a grid of black-and-
white half-timbering and red tile roofs, including the log-
columned veranda that runs along the garden front with its
canted bay and continues out to the street as a covered walk.
w of Rhu-Na-Haven Road, where the houses have grounds
running down to the river, is LYS-NA-GREYNE, also by
Mitchell, 1914, designed for Sir Francis Outram. Rock-faced
granite walls, mullioned windows and square gabled bays on
the garden front embracing a single-storey bow. BALNACOIL,
N of this, was originally built as a fishing lodge but is now flats.
Mild Baronial, by *A. Marshall Mackenzie & Son*, 1913, with a
round tower.

At the far s end of the road, set on the bend in the Dee, is
RHU-NA-HAVEN itself, built as a fishing lodge for J. Herbert
Taylor by *Robert S. Lorimer*, 1907, and extended by him in
1911. It is low and wide, in granite, and accordingly a little less
homely than one hopes for from Lorimer. The earlier part
comprises the s end, L-plan with the service wing projecting
on the s side of the E front and the entrance in a tower in the
re-entrant angle with crowstep-gabled attic. The gables of the
main wings are shaped with scrolled skewputts inspired by
Craigmyle House of 1676 (near Torphins q.v.), which Lorimer
had added to in 1902. On the w front, facing the river, a fine
two-storey canted bay for the drawing room. The dormerheads
for the second storey have scrolly shaped heads. The N extension added a commodious library, in the same style as the rest,
with a projection on its E front, and in the space between this
and the porch Lorimer set an arcaded loggia. (Inside, the study

★ *Mitchell* also designed a smaller version of this house for himself at Birsemore, on
the B976 along the s bank of the Dee opposite Aboyne. It is called CEAN NA COIL.

has excellent plasterwork of vine leaves decorating the ceiling beams and the frieze above the panelling.) The outbuildings have Lorimerian hallmarks e.g. bell-shaped roofs. Especially good wrought-iron entrance gates are presumably by *Thomas Hadden*, Lorimer's usual smith.

ABOYNE CASTLE

77   The Gordons acquired the lands of Aboyne in 1449 through the marriage of Alexander Gordon, 1st Earl of Huntly, but the first building of which any structure remains is the tower house built by Charles Gordon, 1st Earl of Aboyne, *c.* 1671. This evolved into a colossal E-plan mansion, reaching its apogee in the C19 with extension in 1801 (and again in 1835 by *William Burn*) for the 5th Earl, who claimed the title of 9th Marquess of Huntly in 1836 on the death of the 5th Duke of Gordon and left considerable debts on his death in 1853. The 10th Marquess (†1863) had made his principal residence in England, at Orton Hall near Peterborough, and borrowed yet more money against the Aboyne estate.* This and his own unwise expenditure caused the 11th Marquess to advertise Aboyne Castle for sale in 1885, 1886 and 1887 and finally to sell to his father-in-law, Sir William Cunliffe Brooks of Glen Tanar (q.v.), in 1888. *George Truefitt*, who had already rebuilt the castle's service wing in 1869, was engaged to begin some improvements in a Baronial style but they were incomplete by the time Brooks died in 1900 and the castle was sold on by his grandson, Ean Cecil. It was recovered in a decayed state in the 1970s by Granville Gordon (now 13th Marquess) who, assisted by *Ian Begg* of *Robert Hurd & Partners*, stripped away all but the structure of the original tower and remade it, work completed in 1974–82.

The result is a clever conceit, because at a distance where it is seen against the backdrop of a deep pine forest it might easily be mistaken for one of the local brand of Renaissance tower houses. It is harled, its rectangular main range of five storeys with crowstep-gabled ends topped by chimneys and a frontal stack more or less centre on the S front, its breast carried on corbelling above the first floor. The windows are randomly set, following the original pattern of the C17 windows before they were blocked in the later remodellings. Attached to the NW corner is a round stair-tower, given a traditional gabled cap-house in the 1970s in place of a square top, and a balcony to its r. with a balustrade of saltires. On the rear elevation a stunningly tall six-storey square tower, also gabled with crowsteps, with matching cylindrical stair-turrets with dome tops pressed into its inner re-entrant angles. The interior is a complete recreation within the shell, by *Alistair Urquhart*, mason, and

---

*The newly ennobled 10th Marquess entertained outlandish plans for remodelling in 1854; surveys for the sale in 1885 by J. Russell Mackenzie show the layout of the house, including the kitchen wing rebuilt by *Truefitt* in 1869.

with some moulded plasterwork ceilings in Jacobean style by *Albert Cramb*.

Besides the castle itself the building of principal interest is the 'COO CATHEDRAL', i.e. the cattle shed but one on a breathtaking scale, eloquent both of Cunliffe Brooks's zeal for model farming but also of its architect *George Truefitt*'s unconventionality. It was done in 1889. Large round-arched openings (now glazed) along the front; low clearstorey of horizontal windows and a broad piended roof over all, with gablets l. and r. below the ridge. The building is aisled on three sides and on the N and S sides the aisles extend forward as little pavilions with piended and jerkin roofs. Inside, the aisles are fronted by arcades, the arches in rough grey granite. Fine open roof, of six bays with trusses carried from corbels on raking struts.

In the steading courtyard a BELLCOTE which comes either from the earlier parish church in Aboyne or its predecessor at Formaston (*see* Burial Ground, above). BELL by *John Mowat* of Old Aberdeen, 1753.

The WEST LODGE, on the Tarland road, and the SOUTH LODGE on Ballater Road in Aboyne village are both by *Truefitt* for Cunliffe Brooks, the latter dated 1889; emphatically Baronial with cone-roofed round towers, less Arts and Crafts than his Glen Tanar work, but with many original notes, e.g. the massive bracket supporting the round tower of the West Lodge.

NORTH BALNAGOWAN, 3.8 km. NNW. A steading with humorous castle pretensions, converted and enhanced in 1977 by *Alistair Urquhart*, master mason of Aboyne Castle (*see* above). The former cattle byre has a single-storey turret, and whimsical decorated jambs for windows and doors. Cast sandstone dormer pediments celebrate the mason AJU with tools of the trade, and his wife, Mary, MAJU.

GLEN TANAR. *See* p. 512.

ALASTREAN HOUSE   *4000*
1 km. ENE of Tarland

Built *c.* 1902–4 as House of Cromar for the 1st Marquess and Marchioness of Aberdeen by *A. G. Sydney Mitchell* of *Sydney Mitchell & Wilson*. It was sold to Sir Alexander MacRobert, 1st Baronet of Cawnpore and Cromar, in 1918 (cf. Douneside House, Tarland) and from 1943 was used as an airmen's leave centre. Reconstructed in much-modified form by *D. M. Hall*, 1958, following a fire in 1952, it is now a residential care home.

Although the details are Scots Renaissance, as first built the house had North American overtones in its general concept, particularly at the tall piended roof punctuated by big chimneystacks and at the circular tower bays, their conical-roofed profiles drawn from that of the shingle-style house the Aberdeens had planned to build at the Okanagan lakeside, British Columbia, in 1895. The N ENTRANCE FRONT and its forecourt have been much altered. The tall single-storey porch is framed by rock-faced pilasters and projects forward between twin conical-roofed drum towers; its doorway is flanked by refined pilasters which are blocked and fluted. The apex of its gable was once crowned by a magnificent armorial now at Haddo House (N); in its place is the MacRobert crest and an inscription commemorating Sir Alexander and Lady MacRobert's three sons, all of whom were killed while flying: Sir Alasdair (†1938) and Sir Iain and Sir Roderic (both †1941). Above the main wall-head the towers formerly framed a curvilinear attic gablet but this has gone and the roof pitch has been reduced. The billiard room flanking the forecourt on the W was originally single-storeyed but was heightened to two storeys and matched by a corresponding E wing. These have since been extended to the N: by the residential and care block on the E in 1985–8, and by the new NW block in 2001–2.

The GARDEN FRONT is less altered. It has a five-bay centre framed by two pairs of conical-roofed drum towers but its profile has been diminished by the lower roof, the reduction of the chimneyheads and the loss of dormers. It overlooks a low-walled terrace garden which extends on the W into the ITALIAN GARDEN. The garden's central feature is a spiral-fluted sundial column; it is sheltered by raised terraces on the N and W. The W terrace with its pergola survives intact but the N terrace lost its rubblework upper level when the house's NW wing was built in 2001, the fine sculpted term of Pan being relocated. A summer water-course ran through the garden, supplying the alcove fountain at the terrace below the house. Within the woodland is the pink granite MACROBERT MAUSOLEUM known as the Cairn.

The INTERIOR is almost wholly c. 1958 with plain timber panelling and plasterwork, the original Jacobethan panelling with pilasters and strapwork surviving only in the billiard room.

ALFORD

Although a kirkton first recorded in the Middle Ages became the focal point of a prosperous farming community, the modern village stands some distance E of the kirkton and the crossroads formed with the Old Military Road because landed interests would not allow the Vale of Alford Railway to build its terminus any nearer.

HOWE TRINITY PARISH CHURCH, Main Street. Designed as a Free Church by *James Souttar*, 1866–7. First Pointed in dark grey granite, with quoins, voussoirs and horizontal bands in a much lighter grey. First Pointed, the tall N gable front lit by stepped triple lights and vesica, five-bay flanks with lancets. The NW entrance tower was never completed. Interior reordered in 2001 by *William Lippe Architects*. Open roof supported on arched scissor trusses resting on corbels. STAINED GLASS. Burning Bush by *Jennifer-Jane Bayliss*, *c.* 2000. Adjacent MANSE also by *Souttar*, 1869–70, and CHURCH HALL by *William Lippe Architects*, 2007–8, with double-curve roof.

ST ANDREW (Episcopal), Donside Road. By *James Matthews*, 1868–9, its SW tower and broach spire added by *George Watt* in 1929–30; the vestry a recent addition. Matthews's church is predominantly Early Dec with some E.E. elements, modest but well detailed, and set within a large churchyard which has retained its railings. Nave and slightly lower narrower chancel built in pinned granite with polished dressings. Timber-traceried wheel window in the W gable; the nave flanks have two-light windows with simple plate tracery, and the chancel has lancets. Inside, the same pinned granite walls. Pointed chancel arch. The nave's open herringbone roof is supported on arched braces resting on corbels and the chancel roof on braced scissor trusses with a polygonal profile resting on the wall-heads. A segmental opening on the chancel's N side has been intended for an organ. – PULPIT. *c.* 1920 with fine low-relief woodcarving. – ALTAR. An 'English' altar of 1948; but the trefoiled ALTAR RAIL original. Elaborate late C19 OIL LAMPS over the altar and at the choir stalls. – STAINED GLASS. All by *J. Powell & Sons*. E window, 1896: in the centre light the Crucifixion, SS Peter and Paul, Hosea and King David within Gothic niches; in the l. light Our Lady and in the r. St John. Other windows of 1899, 1902 and 1903.

WEST PARISH CHURCH, Kirkton of Alford. Built by *William Minto*, mason, with *Andrew Marshall*, wright, in 1804–5. Originally a small square-plan church with two tall round-arched windows on its S front and entered through a bowed N projection containing the gallery stair. In 1826 Minto added one matching bay to the E and re-set the ball-finialled bellcote (bell by *John Mowat* of Old Aberdeen, 1761) on the W gable. E porch by *George Watt*, 1928–9. Inside, the gallery is supported on Doric columns. – PULPIT, COMMUNION TABLE and FONT of 1929. STAINED GLASS. Central S window, Good Shepherd, 1952. – MONUMENTS. Re-set in the outer walls, a slab to George Melville, †1678; the burial aisle of Mary Forbes of Balfluig (q.v.), †1728(?), its eroded inscription panel flanked by dwarf supporters and surmounted by a nude female angel; plinth sculptured in low relief with a laid-out skeleton and skulls.

Former PARISH MANSE, W of the Parish Church. Built in several stages, resulting in a T-plan. The entrance (W) front is two-storeyed and semi-symmetrical, its harled two-bay centre flanked by granite ashlar wings, that on the N slightly stepped back with a railed stair to the door in the angle. The centre is the manse of 1718, heightened by the Aberdeen mason *William Fleming* in 1776. N wing by *William Minto* in 1831–2, the S wing matching it is later. Alterations including rear kitchen block by *George Marr* (of *Jenkins & Marr*), 1898–9.

DESCRIPTION. The Vale of Alford Railway, authorized 1856, connected with the Great North of Scotland Railway at Kintore (q.v.). It built a station (replaced) on the Aberdeen road near Greystone Farm, where the Reid family were important cattle breeders and dealers, with one of the first Aberdeen Angus herds in the country. The village's early development focused a little W of the station, and even before the railway opened in 1859 *James Matthews* had designed the Station Hotel (now the HAUGHTON ARMS) in the fork between Greystone Road and Donside Road, near the market stance; within a few years Donside Road was built up with villas. The former ABERDEEN TOWN & COUNTY BANK at the corner of Greystone Road and Bank Terrace is by *William Smith*, 1859, a handsome Neo-Tudor cottage villa set in well-kept grounds with original railings; its central porch and wall-head dormer gablet are flanked by broad gable fronts with traceried bargeboards and three-light windows.

BRIDGE OF ALFORD, 2 km. NW, is a small village which grew up where the Old Military Road (A944) crosses the Don. The handsome BRIDGE was designed by *Thomas Telford*, surveyed by *William Minto* and built by contractor *W. Farquharson* in 1810–11, its cost met by the Commissioners of Highland Roads and Bridges. It was repaired after the Muckle Spate of 1829. Built in dressed granite and gently hump-backed, it is 39 m. long. It comprises three segmental arches, that in the centre of 14.6 m. span and those flanking it to either side 12.2 m., which rise from low piers with half-hexagonal cutwater buttresses between them forming pedestrian refuges at parapet level.

ASLOUN CASTLE, 3.7 km. WSW. A mid-C16 to early C17 tower house, owned by the Calders and later the Forbes; partly demolished c. 1750. Asloun was a Z-plan with two round jambs, built in loosely pinned rubble with granite dressings, but only the SE entrance jamb survives substantially intact, c. 5.2 m. in diameter, together with a fragment of the main block's E wall. The main block was c. 10.5 m. long E–W by 7.5 m. deep, and its walls 1.2 m. thick. Its ground floor was lit by slit-windows and at least partly vaulted but of the first-floor great hall very little survives. Protected by two wide-mouthed shot-holes in its base, it contained the entrance at ground floor on the S, somewhat unusually adjacent to the gable rather than the main elevation. The SE jamb, 5.2 m. in diameter, contains the roll-moulded doorway; above, the first of two empty field-panels, the second higher up stairway above a slit-window; there is another empty field-panel with a square window on the E. Within is a turnpike stair crowned by a shallow domical vault, formerly with a cable-moulded sandstone pendant, which led directly up to the hall. A string course demarcates two upper floors above the stair. These were reached by a turret stair corbelled out in the E re-entrant angle; that at second floor has aumbries and garderobe. At the wall-head are moulded corbels which once supported a parapet. Beside the ruins is CASTLETOUN FARMHOUSE, a two-storey, three-bay house of *c.* 1830 in cherry-cocked ashlar granite over a semi-sunk basement. Splayed approach stair to round-arched doorway, now sheltered by a curvilinear open porch.

ANNFIELD FARMHOUSE, 2.25 km. W. Built *c.* 1800, presumably by the mason-contractor *William Minto*, tenant of Annfield and Nether Auchintoul. Neat two-storey front, three windows wide with mid-C19 lying-pane glazing, built of whinstone with grey granite dressings, moulded eaves course and gabled roof with coped end stacks. Outbuildings to N form a loose court including a small MILL powered from the Leochel Burn. Two-storeyed in red rubble, heightened in granite to form a larger loft; flanked by its kiln on one side and forestair on the other.

KINGSFORD HOUSE, 1.8 km. SW. Seemingly built for Benjamin Lumsden *c.* 1831 but remodelled and extended by *J. F. Beattie* in 1849. Georgian Survival, raised on an embanked terrace with balustraded stairway to the lawns beneath. Two-storey three-bay entrance front in granite ashlar with distyle Roman Doric portico and astragalled sash-and-case windows. Gabled roof with deep machine-cut skewputts and end stacks; three canted dormers. Behind, off-centre to the r., rises a square four-storey square tower with blocky crenellated parapet, presumably by Beattie. Substantial two-storey-and-attic rear wing parallel to main house and enclosing a court.

BALFLUIG CASTLE. *See* p. 342.

BREDA HOUSE. *See* p. 394.

HAUGHTON HOUSE. *See* p. 520.

WHITEHAUGH HOUSE. *See* p. 764.

ALLARDICE CASTLE   K   *8070*
1.75 km. NW of Inverbervie

Allardice Castle lords it above a tight meander of the Bervie River, with spreading terraces of gardens to the SW and a narrow causeway behind, to the NE. Original access came up from the river via a bridge or ford, while the modern drive approaches from the N. The barony of Allardice was confirmed to John de Allerdes in 1426, and the family may have been here earlier; in the 1540s a principal mansion is mentioned here; by 1600 this is called a 'fortalice'. The estate left the Allardice family in 1872 and the house was in poor condition by 1969 when it was bought and restored by its present owner, *William Cowie*. The W wing was gutted by fire in 1975, and restored.

The house began as a stubby L-plan enclosed by a courtyard. Although the barmkin has gone, there is evidence of a doorway at first-floor level, leading out from the great hall to a wall-head walk like that at Muchalls Castle (q.v.). The Allardice heraldic plaque in the courtyard, dated 1542, was created by Cowie. At ground level, the hall (E) block has a vaulted store, separated from the entrance wing by a round-arched pend which emerges on the N side with a well-fortified gateway, guarded by gun-loops and sockets for a draw-bar. Most effective and arresting is the compressed series of label corbels supporting the stair-case which rises in the re-entrant angle and then meanders outwards to form a second stair-turret and slender window turret flanking the caphouse. This intense curving sculpture is bolstered by the adjacent projecting wall-head chimney of the great hall. Such label corbels, bristling like knuckles, are only echoed to a lesser degree at Westhall (q.v.) and Birse Castle (*see* p. 381).

The original entrance was a low round-arched doorway, now blocked and replaced by a more substantial Georgian doorway, adjacent. This new entrance was created in order to improve circulation within the house. The early C19 improvements removed a tight spiral staircase immediately inside the original front door and installed a spacious new stair curving up two storeys, with delicate cast-iron balusters. A service stair from the vaulted undercroft to the low end of the great hall was also removed. This opened up a lobby inside the front door which facilitated entry into the kitchen (W) wing. Although the kitchen wing culminates in an enormous segmental arch over a deep hearth, and its walls are thick on the ground floor, all its floors are wooden (renewed after 1975) and its upper floors have thin walls and Georgian sash windows. Within the hearth is a doorway to the base of the W tower. This was originally a cupboard but Cowie installed a stone spiral staircase to the first floor, using treads recycled from Flemington Castle (Angus). There are several masons' marks in the hearth area. This W wing may have begun as a separate block as its linking corner, with curving wall and squinch to the N, is awkward, and its upper storeys are a later addition.

Upstairs all the rooms have an early C19 appearance. The great hall retains its massive Renaissance fireplace, with long moulded stone lintel, but has been partitioned into dining room and bedroom. At first floor, the original staircase took a dog-leg and resumes within the re-entrant tower. The attic bedroom of the W wing has a panelled ceiling painted by Cowie in the 1970s with heraldry relating to the castle's owners, and whimsical pets associated with the house. The pedimented dormer above the hall is original; those on the W wing were replaced after the fire.

AQUHORTHIES HOUSE *see* KEMNAY

ARBUTHNOTT   K

Ancient, charming kirkton first documented in the C12. It now consists of just the church along with the former manse and school.

St Ternan.* The combination of a laterally projecting two-storey apsidal chapel and a conically capped w bellcote, rising above the stepped roofs of the chancel and nave, makes Arbuthnott one of Scotland's most visually memorable rural medieval parish churches. There was probably a church here by the later C12, and certainly by 1242, when Bishop David de Bernham carried out one of his many provisional dedications. Before 1447 it had been appropriated to the college of St Mary on the Rock in St Andrews. In 1505 a chaplainry of the Virgin was established, and the s chapel that housed it was said in the Arbuthnott Missal to have been built in 1506. In 1869–70, after a long period of poor maintenance, the nave alone was reordered, with galleries around three sides and the pulpit against the s wall, to the designs of *William Smith*. Following a major fire in the nave in 1889, restoration by *A. Marshall Mackenzie* brought the whole building back into use. There was a further restoration in 1952–3.

The church has three main elements: a small rectangular chancel, a larger rectangular nave and an apsidal chapel projecting laterally from the s side of the chancel. The earliest part is the unbuttressed C13 chancel. Its E wall, evidently reconstructed in the later Middle Ages, rises from a chamfered base course. It is pierced by three restored square-headed windows with ogee-flips to the lintels of the two side windows, all three rising from a chamfered offset, and there is a second offset at the base of the gable; there are segmental rear-arches internally. Mackenzie considered that there was evidence for a previous echelon arrangement of windows. There were probably originally three lancets in each of the chancel flanks, but the w lancet on the s side was lost when the chapel was added; the E lancet on each side has been restored. Below the w lancet on the N side is a lintelled doorway of uncertain date. Tusking at the E end of the N nave wall suggests that there were proposals to rebuild the chancel as an extension of the nave.

The nave has doorways in both s and N walls. The s wall is lit by three rectangular windows with a single mullion, framed by a broad chamfer; although they are of 1890 as now seen, Mackenzie considered he had found evidence for their form. The w wall, rising from a chamfered base course, was rebuilt around the same time that the s chapel was added: it has broad diagonal buttresses, each with an ogee-headed niche below the offset. There is a small restored lancet window on each side of a three-sided buttress at the centre of the wall. The buttress carries a circular, conically capped bellcote; its w face, with an ogee-headed niche at the lower level, rises up through the bellcote, with the projecting curves on each side corbelled out from its diagonal faces. Two bells were donated by Sir Robert Arbuthnott in 1505, suggesting that work was nearing completion by then.

*This entry is by Richard Fawcett.

The most striking feature of the church is the ashlar-built
17 apsidal S chapel of 1506. There is a pair of laterally projecting
apsidal chapels at Ladykirk (Borders), of *c.* 1500, and there
was a single laterally projecting apsidal chapel at the Dominican
Church in St Andrews (Fife) of *c.* 1516, but lateral apses were
never common in Scotland and that at Arbuthnott differs from
the others in being of two storeys. It has a chamfered base
course and there is a string course at a higher level around the
buttresses and apse, but not the E and W walls. The buttresses,
which are capped by pinnacles, have well-detailed corbels and
canopies for images, the corbel of the E buttress being decorated with the Arma Christi. At the junction of the chapel's W
wall with the S wall of the nave is a polygonal stair-turret
topped by a circular conically roofed caphouse. The chapel's
crowstepped N gable rises well above the adjacent chancel. A
round-headed doorway with continuous mouldings gives
access through the W wall and there are cusped single-light
windows in four faces; a rectangular window in the E face is
displaced to the S, presumably to allow space for a retable. The
upper chamber, usually referred to as a priest's room, was
perhaps a sacristy; it is lit by rectangular windows in the W,
S and SE faces.

Internally, the pointed chancel arch is of two continuous
orders of chamfers rising from simple bases. The roofs of 1890
have collar-beams in the chancel, and there are collars and
arched braces in the nave. The chapel is entered from the
chancel by a wide arch with semi-octagonal responds, moulded
caps and a semicircular arch with two orders of cavettos. It is
covered by an unribbed barrel-vault of rounded profile. The
upper chamber is open to the roof timbers and is equipped
with stone benches in two of the three window embrasures.

FIXTURES AND FURNISHINGS. CHANCEL. PISCINA, below
S wall E window. A pointed-arch recess, basin cut back. – COM-
MUNION TABLE. Pine, 1890, arcaded base of standard type.
– CHOIR STALLS. Pine with poppyheads and raised and fielded
panelled front. NAVE. PULPIT. Octagonal with raised and
fielded panels. – FONT. Circular, pink granite on circular stem
with octagonal base. – STOUP, E of the S doorway, largely
hidden behind a pew. CHAPEL. PISCINA. Ogee-headed recess
in E wall. – STOUP. Moulded ogee-headed recess below SW
window of apse. There is a second STOUP within the entrance
to the chapel's upper level. Inside is an AUMBRY. – SCULP-
TURE. Statues of Christ, St Peter and St John, copies of those
by Bertel Thorwaldsen in Copenhagen Cathedral. – CARVED
FRAGMENTS. Built into the centre of the nave S wall, a shield
charged with two mullets and a heart. Built into the nave N
wall near its E end, a stone with initials AL and AR, arms of
Arbuthnott and date 1573. – STAINED GLASS. Chancel E
windows, figures of Faith, Charity and Hope, by *Daniel Cottier*,
1890. – MONUMENTS. CHAPEL: below S window, knight's
effigy with armour of C13 type, traditionally identified with
Hugo de Arbuthnott, †1282. It rests on a later tomb-chest

carved with arms of Douglas, Arbuthnott and Stewart. – NAVE:
to N of chancel arch, a medieval slab with disc-head cross on
stepped base, shaft flanked by two shields, one with sword
behind; set into the N wall, a fragment of grave-slab with date
1662 and initials IMS.

CHURCHYARD. Memorial to Catharine Hunter, †1812, with
fine relief depiction of a sailing ship. In the extension to the W
a memorial to James Leslie Mitchell (the author Lewis Grassic
Gibbon), †1935, and his wife. Grey granite, an open book on
a lectern.

ARBUTHNOTT HOUSE   K   7070
0.75 km. NW of Arbuthnott

Few homes can boast an uninterrupted succession since the C12
by more than twenty-five generations of the same family. Hugo
de Swinton acquired the estate and in 1206 his son Duncan took
the toponym 'de Aberbuthnot', meaning 'the mouth of the little
holy stream'. This refers to the most dramatic feature of the site:
above steep banks on two sides, the house is constrained on a
ridge by the confluence of the Bothenoth Burn and the Bervie
Water.

Understanding of the house relies on documents that include
an account of the history of the family and house written in 1567
by Alexander Arbuthnott, first Protestant principal of Aberdeen
University and nephew of the 14th Laird, and a contract for
improvements in 1754 that contains information on both the old
and new structures. H. Gordon Slade has provided an initial
survey of its development, amplified by family documents,[*] but
when the harling was stripped from the walls during restoration
in 2010, more complex phasing and reworking were revealed.[†]
Reconciling some of the visual with the documentary evidence
remains difficult.

The house is essentially a cluster of buildings around a trap-
ezoid courtyard aligned E–W, with the N and S ranges pressed
against the rim of the steep riverbanks below. It is possible that
the square footprints of the (former) kitchen, terminating the S
range, and the E block are remnants of C12 towers, once joined
by a curtain wall. Another trace of the medieval house is the
distinctive chamfered plinth which survives below the N block
outside the N wall of the courtyard. This is similar to the plinth
of Arbuthnott church (q.v.), consecrated in 1242, which therefore
relates to Hugh de Arbuthnott, 3rd Laird. Hugh Arbuthnott, 9th
Laird, began the hall house up to the first floor, along the S
perimeter in 1420. He was prompted to strengthen his defences

---

[*] *Proceedings of the Society of Antiquaries of Scotland* 110 (1978–80).
[†] The findings at this time were analysed in an unpublished report by Professor
Charles McKean.

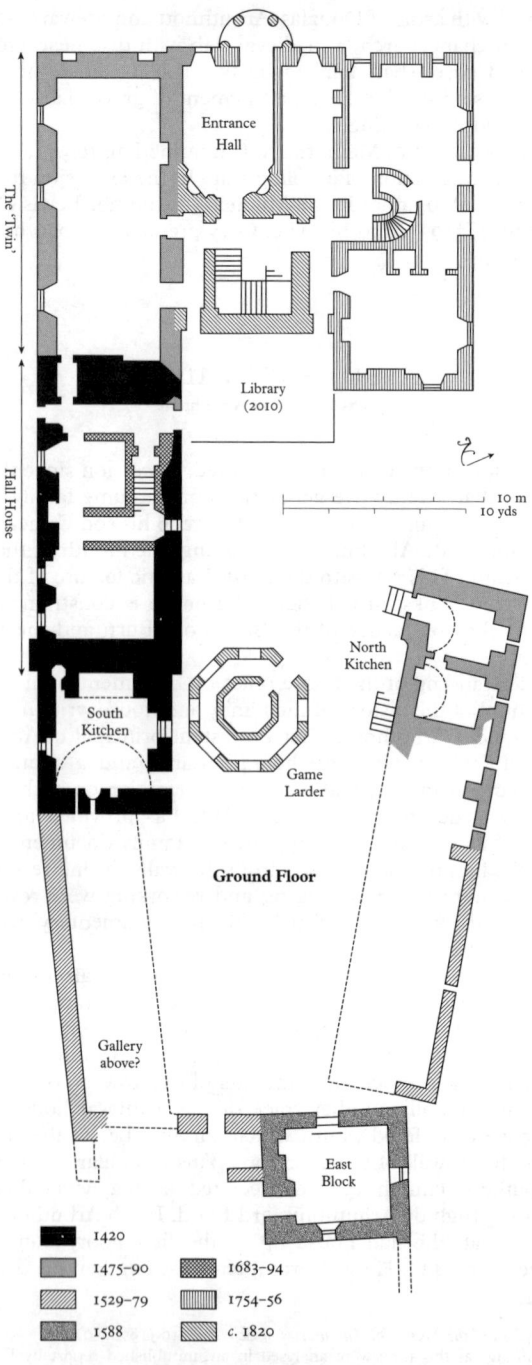

The 'Twin'

Hall House

Entrance
Hall

Library
(2010)

10 m
10 yds

North
Kitchen

South
Kitchen

Game
Larder

Ground Floor

Gallery
above?

East
Block

■ 1420
1475–90 ▨ 1683–94
▨ 1529–79 ▨ 1754–56
1588 ▨ *c.* 1820

Arbuthnott House.
Plan of ground- and first-floors

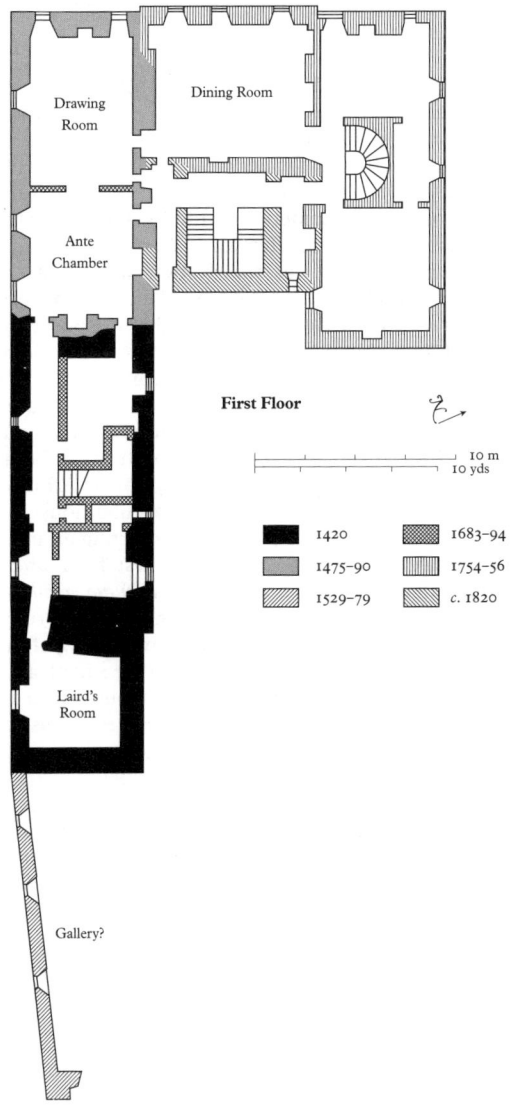

First Floor

Drawing Room

Dining Room

Ante Chamber

Laird's Room

Gallery?

10 m
10 yds

	1420		1683–94
	1475–90		1754–56
	1529–79		c. 1820

at this stage because he had taken part in the outrage of killing John Melville, the sheriff of neighbouring Glenbervie, boiling his victim and supping the resulting broth.

Sir Robert Arbuthnott, 12th Laird, completed the hall house *c.* 1475–90 and, according to Principal Arbuthnott, 'decorated the wall-head with eaves, galleries and battlements as is the custom in castles'. He added the adjacent block to the w, called the 'Twin', which was formerly vaulted on the ground floor. Immediately N (i.e. closing the w side of the courtyard) he also created a fore-tower, namely a vaulted gatehouse with chamber above. Against the N perimeter, Sir Robert built the vaulted cellar with kitchen above. It was this Robert who built the aisle at Arbuthnott church and commissioned the missal, prayer book and psalter which are now in Paisley Abbey. Robert Arbuthnott, 14th Laird, completed the roof of the fore-tower between 1520 and 1529. Andrew Arbuthnott, 15th Laird, put his initials AA and the date 1588 on the skewputt of the square E block. Otherwise Arbuthnott missed out on the building boom between 1560 and 1630, during which so many of the neighbouring tower houses were crowned. Around 1683–94, Robert Arbuthnott, 20th Laird and 3rd Viscount, gutted the 1420 hall house by opening a new entrance door on its N side and inserting an internal staircase with two new chambers on the first floor and two attic bedrooms. In the Twin, he developed a *piano nobile*, creating a polite drawing room and antechamber with elaborate plastered ceilings. He also carried out the major landscaping of the gardens, creating the exquisite sloping terraces on the s flank and the Dark Avenue, a new formal approach to the house from the w. His ambitious modernization was probably linked to his marriage in 1683 to Lady Anne Sutherland Gordon, daughter of the Earl of Sutherland.

By this stage, the house was a series of disconnected, inconvenient buildings linked by the medieval battlements and gatehouse straggling across the w of the yard. This problem was taken in hand by John Arbuthnott, 5th Viscount and 22nd Laird, who succeeded in 1710. An inveterate Jacobite, he nonetheless survived the rebellions without forfeiting his estate, but politics postponed his building works until *c.* 1754–56 when, aided by the contractor *John Ferrior* of Montrose, he refashioned the w front, sweeping away the medieval gatehouse and reworking the large block on the NW corner of the yard, where the contract specified 'taking down an old house on the North Side of the Close ... [which] is joined to the South wing by an entry wall'. Aiming for symmetry and a classical air, the w gable of this N block approximately matches the w gable of the 'Twin', and the two are joined by the pedimented centrepiece, with an open entry below and dining room above. One final step was required to link all parts of the house on both sides and at all levels: the installation of the central staircase block and conversion of the mid-C18 entrance passage into an enclosed hall with a porch. In the absence of documentary evidence, these are ascribed to John Arbuthnott, 7th Viscount and 24th Laird, 1795–1800, but might more probably be the contribution of the 8th Viscount, who succeeded in 1800 and died in 1860, giving ample scope for building campaigns. His main achievement was to create a stately entry into the domain, building the NE gate with its fine lodge, and the monumental classical bridge over the Bothenoth ravine. Painted by David Wilkie *c.* 1840, he sits proudly in front of his bridge, park and house.

The estate was heavily in debt by 1849, and by 1919, following decades of low maintenance, no electricity or sanitation, a breakup of the estate was contemplated. However, the house survived the C20 and underwent a substantial restoration programme in 2010, by Keith Arbuthnott, 17th Viscount, executed by *GLM* chartered architects.

A chronological tour of the EXTERIOR should proceed from E to W. The EAST BLOCK has, as has been said, a skewputt dated 1588 and the initials of Andrew Arbuthnott, but its thick coarse bouldered walls suggest an earlier origin and it holds the key strategic position commanding the E point of the ridge. Its S doorway was forced through a small fireplace and its gable windows have glazing grooves. By the C16 it could have served as lodging for a senior household member. It is approximately the same size as the SOUTH KITCHEN block at the E end of the S range, which is substantially built with a vault on the ground floor, a long narrow window formerly on its E wall and an entrance originally on its NW corner. The massive medieval fireplace and chimney appear to be a subsequent insertion, breaking through the vault. Very oddly the fireplace arch has voussoirs chamfered on the inside, and the bread oven is set in the W wall of the kitchen rather than inside the fireplace. That this kitchen block is earlier than the adjoining Hall which it serves is indicated at first floor by a passage, from the Hall into the Laird's Chamber above the kitchen, which has been slapped through the wall at an angle. Running E of the kitchen block is a wall with traces of windows on two storeys overlooking the park, implying that it was perhaps a GALLERY, although how it was accessed or linked to the other buildings is not known.

The HALL HOUSE adjoining the South Kitchen to the W was begun *c.* 1420 and on the N and S sides its walls are set back, with a sloping ledge at first floor, a C15 feature also found at House of Druminnor (q.v.). A buttress projects at the SE corner. The windows are now Georgian sash-and-case, but a large pointed archway at ground-floor level was revealed towards the SW end of the Hall House when harling was removed. Too large for a window and too exposed to danger for a significant entrance, it looks onto the rim of the steep slope; it could have been a recess rather than a structural feature. On the Hall House's N side there are three evenly spaced windows above, and a narrow one at the W end, plausibly the original entrance to the screens passage from an external stair. The roof, which fits poorly against the E gable, is clearly a later alteration: inside its currently windowless garret are two gable fireplaces, indicating living rooms on the second storey which must have required at least dormers if not a higher wall-head as well.

The NORTH KITCHEN block of 1475–90, on the N side of the inner courtyard, has two barrel-vaulted cellars of dressed ashlar, like that in the South Kitchen. Its gunloops are a crosslet type, with short head and arms and roundlet at the base. This unusual form is found at Ravenscraig Castle (N), licensed in 1491, and the later group of tower houses at Towie Barclay, Gight and Craig (also N). Although described as a kitchen by Principal Arbuthnott, and furnished with slop chutes, it lacks a hearth and chimney.

The 'TWIN' range built in 1475–90 had its upper parts altered c. 1653 by Sir Robert Arbuthnott, 18th Laird and 1st Viscount; its dormer windows have changed both in height and location, indicated by traces of blocked openings beneath the harling. In their original narrower form, they may have fitted their florid but abraded C17 pediments more accurately. One of these showed the initials VV RA and apparently KA (no longer clear), for Katherine Arbuthnott, wife of Robert, 1st Viscount (m. 1653, †1655). The lower parts have a jumbled arrangement of windows, revealing numerous changes within. On the first floor, the windows are unevenly spaced, dictated by the arrangement of the Antechamber (E) and Drawing Room (W) created inside in the late C17. Later panelling in their reveals indicates that they were lengthened in the C19. On the ground floor there were three sash windows by the C18; a fourth (second from E) was added in 2010.

61 The W gable of the 'Twin' belongs to the WEST FRONT of 1754. This was a bold attempt to create a symmetrical façade from the medieval buildings but its old-fashioned style is perhaps a consequence of the political preoccupations of the 5th Viscount earlier in the century. A three-bay and three-storey sandstone ashlar pedimented centrepiece is squeezed uncomfortably between two traditional, harled 'gable-enders', each of two widely spaced bays with stone margins to the windows and with chimneys topping the gables. This is similar to many old townhouses in Montrose but the gable-ends also recall Balcaskie (Fife, by William Bruce, 1670–4) and the draft made by William Adam for Fasque House (q.v.) around the 1720s or 30s and illustrated in *Vitruvius Scoticus*. The central first-floor windows, with moulded and lugged architraves and a dentil cornice, are taller than the rest, expressing the greater height of the Dining Room within. Above are square attic windows, also with moulded surrounds. The pediment, with heraldic blazon, is topped by urns. The semicircular Doric portico was added in the early C19 when the C18 passage entrance was modified to form a hallway. The N gable-ended wing of this front may contain remnants of the 'old house' mentioned in the 1754 contract. Evidence for this may be its width, which does not precisely match the existing 'Twin' to

the S; its E and W walls, which are of different thickness; and the ashlar plinth which binds the three sections of the W front but does not continue around either corner. Its principal access from the Hall is also skewed.

Discrete additions in 2010, E of the main stairs, include a library and convenient back entrance to the yard. In the yard itself is an early–mid-C19 GAME LARDER.

A chronological tour of the INTERIOR begins on the N flank of the 1420s Hall, where Robert, 3rd Viscount, developed his Baroque processional circuit of chambers, c. 1683–94. Now filled with smaller rooms, there is little evidence of the medieval hall which must have had a substantial fireplace, presumably in the E gable. If the ground floor was for storage, then the hall was on the first floor, witnessed by ashlar window reveals with half-round and fillet profile, on the S side. The current ceiling cuts the old jambs, indicating that the attic with its little fireplaces is a later alteration. The LAIRD'S ROOM with its C17 bolection-moulded panelling was originally the medieval chamber, with access slapped through the thick E wall of the Hall. A dignified moulded C17 doorway and modest but formal stone staircase lead from the N side of the Hall to the first floor, where a passage was cut through into the Twin. Here the ANTECHAMBER AND DRAWING ROOM are clad in honey-coloured bolection-moulded panelling, amply lit by the elongated S windows. Their PLASTER CEILINGS are among the finest in Scotland. They are deeply moulded with rich sprays and swags, of crisp, high-quality workmanship. While these were fashionable in the period, and are found at Brodie (N) and Kellie (Fife), the folk art filling the spandrels and margins reflect an earlier rustic age, with limbless creatures and Jack-in-the-Green. The spreading foliage in some spandrels is closely matched by that at Fyvie Castle (N), where the work was carried out by Robert White of Edinburgh in 1683. The two BEDCHAMBERS upstairs, clearly also 1680s, have simpler plaster ceilings, with similar oak leaves, acorns and vines, but they also have portrait-heads in cartouches like the 1620s ceilings at Craigievar and Muchalls (qq.v.), suggesting the survival of old moulds. This plasterwork replaced mid-C17 painted decoration, contemporary with the dormer pediments installed by Robert, 1st Viscount. In the stair lobby to the attic is the painted remnant of a winged head, and some wavy graining which appears to be interrupted for the placement of bookshelves, slender evidence for a library.

The DINING ROOM forms the centrepiece of the first floor of the W front, part of the 1754 campaign, with panelling of that period but rather shallow classical ceiling plasterwork and a fireplace of the (mid?) C19. It leads into the staircase block, finally constructed c. 1820 to judge from the style of the simple decorative iron balustrade to the cantilevered stone steps. Elegantly top-lit with a glass cupola. The ENTRANCE HALL sums up the compromises and quirky history of the house. The front door is not opposite the doorway leading to the stairs: perhaps the latter related to a previous structure. As specified in 1754, the entry was a corridor leading from front to back, with a narrow lodge or store to either side; the one on the N remains but c. 1820 the S partition was removed and the present arrangement of niches and columns installed. The principal alteration in 2012 was the creation of a kitchen on the ground floor of the 'Twin', formerly the location of the LIBRARY, which is now contained in the addition E of the staircase.

The TERRACED GARDENS with their sloping paths were laid out by Robert, 3rd Viscount, 1683–94. Intensively cultivated at the top, they shift to greater informality towards the lade at the bottom. Backed by a garden wall on the N side, the GARDEN HOUSE was begun at this date, with richly moulded doorpiece and rusticated quoins. C19 polygonal SUNDIAL. A new picturesque entrance to the house from the E was constructed around 1821. This included the imposing GATEWAY, flanked by a faux Greek temple on one side and another designed as a lodge, decorated with compact pilasters, pediments and acroteria. The BRIDGE, of theatrical proportions with pierced parapet, curving wings and great vases, crosses the Buthenoth Burn. – The HOME FARM and its steading, inscribed 1792, are made from exquisitely cut ashlar, with refined joints and dressing. The farmhouse is nobly framed by a pilaster on each corner. The Tudor-style EAST LODGE, with its decorative chimneys and exaggerated finials, resembles lodges at Ury House (q.v.) which were designed by *John Baird*, c. 1855.

The former DOWER HOUSE is now Fordoun House (*see* Auchenblae, p. 333).

8000

ARDOE HOUSE   K
1.4 km. WSW of Banchory-Devenick

Built in 1877–8 by *Matthews & Mackenzie* for Alexander Milne Ogston, an Aberdeen soap manufacturer whose father bought the estate in 1839. On high ground above the Dee, the house is Scots Baronial, expensive-looking but slightly stark in grey granite dressed with silvery quoins and margins of the same. Four-storey tower at the NW corner of the main front with a slender turret rising higher still and concluding in a slated cone. Projecting from the base of the tower a hefty ashlar porte cochère with pepperpot turrets. The rest of the house is three storeys, with the usual panoply of crowstepped gables, bay windows and bartizans. A hotel from 1947, with feeble 1980s ballroom addition. Other large but architecturally insignificant additions to E.

The sumptuous interior dates from 1883, also by *Matthews & Mackenzie*. Porch vestibule with a rib-vault and mosaic floor, and beyond this a spine corridor, darkly panelled and with lavishly carved doorcases in Free Renaissance style. Strapwork ceiling. Staircase behind an arcaded screen with painted decoration around the arches and good Aesthetic Movement glass in the stair windows depicting the Four Seasons and Ogston's arms. In the principal rooms, similar decoration and several Jacobean-style ceilings.

LODGE. 1897 by *A. Marshall Mackenzie*.

ASWANLEY HOUSE
1 km. ESE of Glass

4030

A two-storey L-plan house, long and low in pink harl. Its N range is essentially late C17 (a recorded datestone suggests 1692) with bolection-moulded doorpiece, chamfered windows which have formerly been barred, moulded skewputts and sturdy coped chimneystacks at either end. As originally built it appears to have belonged to the first generation of vernacular classical houses, symmetrical, five bays broad with a S forecourt enclosed by single-storey wings on E and W. Its rear (N) elevation is almost blind, but projecting from it slightly off-centre is a circular tower containing the original turnpike stair: that this stair rises well above the main wall-head indicates that the attic once contained living accommodation. Its ogee roof is by *Law & Dunbar-Nasmith*, 1960, but re-creates that shown in James Giles's view of 1838. In the early C18 the N end of the W wing was rebuilt to two storeys, the windows again in chamfered surrounds and formerly barred. The N range was extended W to join it and at this time its doorway was moved to its present position and a jamb inserted in the re-entrant angle between the ranges, providing a new entrance and stair. The W range was partly demolished before 1901 (along with the corresponding E range) and reconstructed in its present form in 1975–80 by *Ian Begg*, with two dormerheads facing the court; the roof and gable of the stair jamb are also of this date. Three late C17 dormerheads re-set in the walls bear the initials of George Calder of Aswanley and Isabel Skene. Inside the N range, the original kitchen fireplace survives with salt-boxes in its cheeks and the hinge for a swey. The turnpike stair within the round tower and the scale-and-platt stair within the early C18 jamb are original and both are of stone.

Part of the FORECOURT WALL, a low drystone dyke, remains standing, but the small round building in its angle, random rubble with a conical roof, was rebuilt in 1975–80. The forecourt wall terminates in a large GATEWAY with a moulded round-arched opening which once rose into a gablet. This is perhaps a relic of a more defensible predecessor house. Overgrown foundations suggest that there was once an outer court to the S.

STEADING, 50 m. E. Dated 1890–1900. Perhaps by *George Sutherland*, who produced plans to radically redesign Aswanley

House for Alexander Geddes (*see* Blairmore Lodge, Glass); few but 'the Grain King' could contemplate such a handsome complex during the agricultural depression which American grain had brought about. Central gabled bay with round-arched pend, first-floor window and attic oculus; asymmetric flanking wings, on the l. single-storeyed with dormered loft and gabled end bay, on the r. plain single storey.

Site of the kirkton of Fordoun, already established as an early Christian settlement in the C5. A chapel was built here in 452 to receive the shrine of St Palladius, early Apostle of the Scots, and remained a popular site of pilgrimage through the Reformation. The medieval settlement was erected a burgh of barony in 1554. Beginning *c.* 1770, the 5th Earl of Kintore laid out a village on a large T-plan to promote the spinning of flax. The population continued to grow through the mid C19 but is still little more than 500.

PARISH CHURCH. Also known as Fordoun Parish Church. Elevated on a mound overlooking the Luther Water, and long viewed as the 'mother church' of the Mearns. The present church is by *John Smith*, 1827–9, replacing at least five other buildings on the site (*see* below). Good Neo-Perp of reddish sandstone with a square tower rising up the centre of the w front (cf. Inverbervie and also Fettercairn). Tudor-arched entrance, two-light window and louvered belfry with crocketed ogee hoodmould, all flanked by diagonal buttresses. Five-bay flanks with wooden Y-tracery and stepped buttresses in between; pinnacles linked by a very tall, blank parapet. Wide rear gable with a rosette window.

Simple, wide interior with ribbed, coomb ceiling (restored, 1889). Smith's original octopartite rib-vault in the porch. Full U-plan GALLERY with canted angles and clusters of four shafts below. Cinquefoiled panelling. – ORGAN. In the gallery. Good Dec case by *Messrs. P. Larg & Co.* of Aberdeen, 1899. – STAINED GLASS. E window, 1877. Good Shepherd in the centre and foliage in the spokes. – In the vestibule is the FORDOUN STONE, a large PICTISH CROSS-SLAB discovered in 1788 and used as the base of the pulpit in the previous church. Relocated here in 1966. It displays a hunting scene on the same face as an interlaced but damaged cross. A double-disc and Z-rod are carved under the hunting scene. An Ogham inscription is on the edge of the stone and an inscription in minuscule is on the upper l. side of the front face; these are undeciphered. (GN)

In the CHURCHYARD are the remains of ST PALLADIUS'S CHAPEL, standing on the site of the cell built by the saint in the C5. Rubble rectangle, *c.* 11.9 m. by 5.5 m., unroofed *c.* 1928

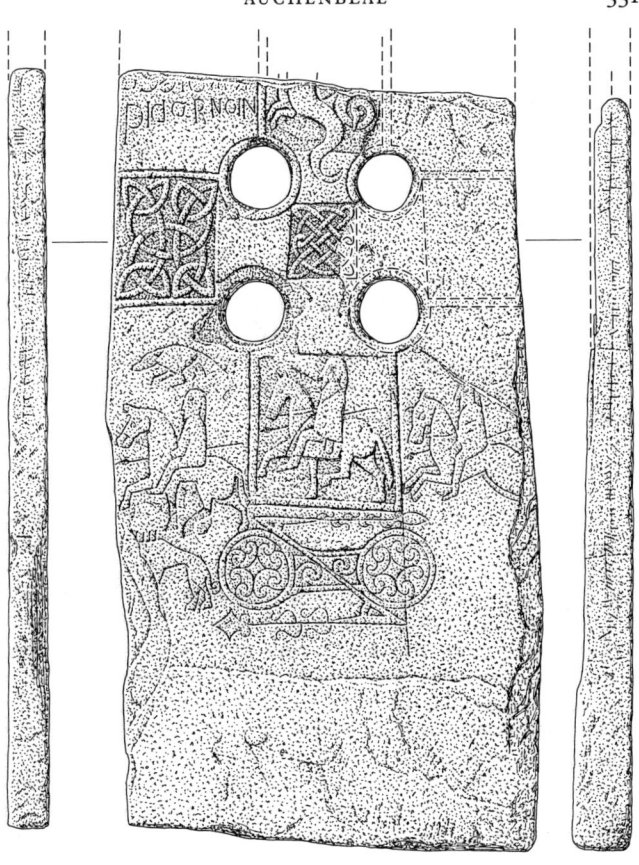

Auchenblae, Fordoun Stone.
Ink drawing by John Borland

and restored in 2006. The masonry appears to be an early C16 reconstruction of a late C12 chapel that was consecrated by Bishop David Benham in 1244. Chamfered round entrance set low on the N flank; taller one on the W. Three chamfered rectangular windows on the S flank. Below and to the r., a low opening into a shallow burial chamber that is submerged below the E end. Inside the main chapel, a large, round-headed recess in the E gable, said to have held the shrine of St Palladius but much more likely a tomb-niche inserted in the C17. Small pointed piscina to the r. and square aumbry on the N wall. The three S windows have segmental rere-arches. – Large TOMB-CHEST for Captain Robert Irvine, †1652, and his wife, Elizabeth Douglas, builders of Monboddo House (q.v.). The top has good heraldry and a monogram. Side carved with initials, Latin inscription and *memento mori* with skull-and-crossbones.

St Palladius (Episcopal). *See* Drumtochty Castle, p. 458.

Primary School. Confident Scots Renaissance by *John Sim*, 1889–91. Big crowstepped U-plan of hammer-dressed stone, the advanced ends with round angles corbelled into squares. Shafted tripartite windows, the central lights taller with little segmental pediments.

Village Hall, Monboddo Street. Cutting a fine and colourful profile, its red brick – a refreshingly unusual choice of material – contrasted by beige margins and quoins. Original section on the l. by *John Johnstone*, 1870. Two crowstepped gables straddling an arched doorway studded with nailhead. Five-bay extension, 1903, with slightly jettied dormerheads.

War Memorial, Gilbert's Hill. By *Charles Davidson*, 1919–20. Square pier with a sword, leaf and swag on one face. Corniced capital with a ball finial.

DESCRIPTION

The Parish Church and St Palladius's Chapel (*see* above) form the nucleus of the ancient kirkton. Just to the sw is the Parish Hall, a little harled rectangle built as a school in 1740–2 and remodelled as a poorhouse in the early–mid C19. S of this, the former Manse (now Kirlytham), 1844–5 by *J. & W. Smith* and incorporating the previous manse of 1779. Harled, Neo-Jacobean with mullioned-and-transomed windows and sharply gableted dormerheads with ball-and-spike finials. Inventive chimneystacks with diamond shafts corbelled into square tops and set at an angle.

N of the church, a brief l. at the fork reveals the former Schoolhouse by *George Croll* of Laurencekirk, 1852–3. Much tamer Jacobean here with L-plan front and tall lying-pane glazing. The fine Primary School (*see* above) lies to the E. The road then leads down to an idyllic view of the Luther Water, after which Burnett Street turns to the l. Second on the l. is the converted Den Mill, a flax-spinning establishment founded in 1801 and rebuilt as a corn and sawmill in the mid C19. Kiln with pyramidal roof and pagoda ventilator added by *Charles C. Doig* in 1896–7 to enable use as a distillery.* On the rear gable is an eight-spoke overshot water wheel. Beech Villa, across the street, was built as the Free Church school in 1845. Pinned, squared rubble and sharply corniced porch. The church itself (built 1843 and dem. 2012) is now represented by just the finial of its E gable at the end of the block. There the road turns to the r. and becomes Monboddo Street, passing the fine, polychromatic Village Hall (*see* above). After it, gatepiers and railings for the former Craig House (now The Bank House), built *c.* 1840 for the banker James Farquharson and later converted into a Clydesdale Bank. Two storeys of pinned, coursed rubble by *George Croll*,

---

*But short-lived, as whisky production was discontinued in 1926.

the r. side slightly advanced. Lying-pane glazing and big ashlar porch with ball-finialled parapet and armorial plaque.

KINTORE STREET then leads l., climbing the hill in a straight line. It then broadens out to form the small and strangely unassertive MARKET SQUARE, its upper limit marked by the granite BRUCE FOUNTAIN (1910). Four columns supporting pediments incised with tulips and a mini-rotunda with a peristyle of six colonnettes. To the l. is THE HOLLIES, 1790–1, preceded by thin channelled gatepiers with renewed ball finials.

KILVAXTER, 140 m. ESE of the Parish Church. The former Free Church manse, 1847–8 by *George Croll*. A pleasing house in a beautiful, elevated setting, and harled in yellowish cream. Piended roof with end stacks and a wide, extremely depressed block pediment on the wall-head. Portico with unfluted Greek Doric columns, corniced architrave and stepped blocking course.

FORDOUN HOUSE, 1.6 km. SSE. Built 1712 as the dower house for Arbuthnott House (q.v.). Severe and imposing, rising up like a sheer bulwark with little of the finesse that was to come in the Georgian period. This is still what one would expect of a laird's seat of the C17, although the spacing of the bays shows an incipient sensitivity. Harled three storeys and five bays, the outer pairs of windows set off from the centre and indented from the ends. One has the dated lintel. Terrible modern porch in the centre; single-storey range advanced on the l., mid–late C18. – 250 m. to the E, a well-preserved medieval MOAT, roughly rectangular (*c.* 75.9 m. by 34.7 m.) and indicated by a group of trees. The ditch is about 7 m. wide and the external bank survives on the E (*c.* 3.7 m. wide and 0.6 m. high).

DRUMTOCHTY CASTLE. *See* p. 456.

GLENFARQUHAR LODGE. *See* p. 506.

MONBODDO HOUSE. *See* p. 675.

AUCHERNACH

3.8 km. NW of Strathdon

3010

AUCHERNACH HOUSE, built in the early C19 by Nathaniel Forbes of the East India Co., was demolished in 1945. Forbes reputedly laid out its remarkable castellated WALLED GARDEN as a reminiscence of the fort of Vellore in NE India. Rectangular and falling steeply to the S, it gives the impression of a large medieval castle of enclosure, roughly 70 m. deep N–S by 50 m. broad, its pinned rubble walls 6–7 m. high appearing genuinely defensive. Its focal point is at the centre of the N wall, a slim square tower in coursed squared granite with a crenellated parapet which is approached by a flight of stone stairs and once contained an ingenious clock mechanism of 1787. Two lower circular towers built in rubble, again with crenellated parapets, stand midway within the E and W curtain walls, that on the E with a basement in a sharp fall of the ground. The s wall flanked by pavilions at each far end contains the main entrance; it has been partly breached, as if by attackers. The elaborate pipe-system which fed the garden from a reservoir immediately to the N has been destroyed but restoration is intended.

AUCHINDOIR

Former AUCHINDOIR PARISH CHURCH. A shell since *c.* 1970. Built 1811, its design evidently modelled on Towie (q.v.) of 1802–4 but an early example of the Gothic style in Aberdeenshire. For the present parish church *see* Lumsden.

Former MANSE, 0.35 km. WSW. Built 1843 with a lintel dated 1765 reused from the previous manse.

ST MARY, 0.5 km. W.* A roofless but otherwise structurally complete rectangular shell displaying an unusually high degree of architectural refinement. In 1236 its patronage was disputed between the bishops of Aberdeen and Moray, but in 1361 it was added to the prebend of Invernochty in Aberdeen Cathedral; in 1514 it became a prebend of King's College, Aberdeen. Initially built *c.* 1200, with the liturgical arrangements of the chancel area modified in the early C16; the E end was again remodelled in 1638 and there were repairs and additions in 1664. It was abandoned for the new church (*see* above). The walls are pink rubble with ashlar dressings. A double-chamfered base course (now only partly exposed) runs around the whole building; it is set at a higher level along the w wall. Cavetto wall-head cornice along the N and s flanks. Doorways of *c.* 1200 are set towards the w end of the N and s walls. The N door is a simple round-arched opening with chamfered surround, beneath a relieving arch. The round-arched s door is altogether finer: a continuous roll-moulded inner order is framed by an outer order with keeled and rounded roll mouldings to the arch, carried on (renewed) detached shafts with crocket capitals; around the arch is a hoodmould decorated with dogtooth. The only original window (now blocked), towards the N wall's E end, is a small lancet framed by two continuous orders of chamfers.

As part of the early C16 reordering of the chancel area a new priest's doorway was inserted towards the s wall's E end; the rectangular opening is framed by a quirked and filleted roll moulding, and the lintel has the partly defaced initials M.A.S., probably for Master Alexander Spittal, rector *c.* 1529–38. Rather confusingly, a tablet within an ogee recess with those same initials carved in relief was evidently reused when a window was formed over the doorway, with the tablet re-set

*This entry is by Richard Fawcett.

above that. A fresh inscription was cut into the tablet stating NEC TIBI NEC MIHI (Neither Thee nor Myself) and the date 1638. That date is also inscribed on the heraldic S skewputt of the E gable, together with initials WMD and the Davidson arms, for the minister Mr William Davidson, pointing to a general remodelling of the E end in the mid C17, when a large rectangular window was cut at the E end of the S wall, a doorway surmounted by a square window was cut through the E wall, and the upper part of the E gable was rebuilt with the apex surmounted by a cross. A small (blocked) window near the S wall's mid-point may also have been inserted then, presumably to light the pulpit. The last identifiable structural addition was a rectangular bellcote on the W gable, capped by a pediment with pinnacles at the angles, and with the date 1664 on its S face transom. Shortly before then the church was said to be ruinous, and this was presumably part of the repairs.

Inside, most of what is seen is part of the early C16 liturgical reorganization or of the *c.* 1638 reordering; sockets in the W wall presumably mark the location of a C17 gallery. – FURNISHINGS. The finest and most fascinating is the SACRAMENT HOUSE, near the N wall's E end. The locker is framed by a relief depiction of a monstrance with trifoliate base, flanked by pinnacles and with a pyramidal tiled roof capped by a crucifix. The locker's sill has the initials M.A.S., for Master Alexander Spittal, and a scroll on the roof is inscribed HIC E[ST] CORP[US] D[O]MI[NI]CVM (here is the Body of the Lord), in reference to the consecrated host it was designed to hold. – STOUP. S wall E of priest's door. Recessed basin framed by a small arch with chamfered surround – PISCINA. Rectangular recess with a reused sill as the lintel; a small roughly formed rectangular AUMBRY to its E. A second rectangular AUMBRY towards the E wall's N end. – HERALDIC PLAQUES, towards N end of E wall. A pair of small framed panels with arms of William Gordon of Craig and his wife, Clara Cheyne, the former framed by foliate bands and dated 1557, the latter framed by balusters. – MONUMENTS. E wall, towards N end: re-set heraldic ledger slab with initials IG (for James Gordon?) and date 1580; towards S end: large aedicular monument with archaizing detail for family of James Francis Gordon Shirrefs Gordon, 1887. – S wall, E of SE doorway, wall tablet with heart-shaped pediment and *memento mori*; between doors, Tuscan aedicular monument for the Rev. James Reid, †1842.

CRAIG CASTLE. *See* p. 427.

19

AUCHLUNIES HOUSE
3 km. E of Kirkton of Maryculter

K   *8090*

A late C17 or early C18 house, but much altered or rebuilt in 1768 when it was described as 'new' by the *Edinburgh Evening*

Courant. Subdivided into flats in the mid C20. The original house was two-storeyed but relatively low, harled with a gabled roof and coped chimneystacks. Its original entrance front may have faced w, the modest gabled bay in the centre of the E side built to contain a stair. The present E entrance front was formed later in the C18. The original house was lengthened at each end, the additional bays standing slightly taller and extending into two projecting wings so forming an E-plan. The central bay contains the simple doorway, which is transom-lit. At the far l., beyond the S wing, a long single-storey range contained the services and kitchen. w elevation now almost blind, except for a broad deep canted bay added in the mid C19 (before 1865). Internally, the entrance front's central bay forms a small porch. It leads through a stone doorway into a spinal corridor running down the E side of the house at ground floor. This in turn opens onto a simple stair of C18 appearance. The principal apartments were probably at first floor, where some early panelling and cornices survive. The bay-windowed room on the w rises into a coved ceiling.

AVOCHIE

2.1 km. E of Ruthven

AVOCHIE HOUSE. Late Baronial by *Matthews & Mackenzie*, 1888, remodelling and enlarging an earlier house. Comfortable villa-like character, built of granite with ashlar dressed work. The N flank remodelled with a three-storey tower and an oriel at the NW angle in 1916 by *A. Marshall Mackenzie & Son*.

AVOCHIE CASTLE, on the Braes of Avochie overlooking the Deveron, is C16–early C17, ruinous but a unique survival of a house-type which must once have been more common. Small and rectangular, single-storeyed with end gables rising into a tall double attic; flank walls reduced almost to ground level, formerly with a turret at the SE corner.

BALBEGNO CASTLE   K

1.3 km. WSW of Fettercairn

A fine building set on a long-standing strategic site, as the vitri-fied fort (*see* Fettercairn, p. 488) 0.9 km. SW shows. James IV granted the land to Andrew Wood in 1488, and John Wood and his wife, Elizabeth Irvine, built an L-plan tower house in the early C16. The same couple then carried out a grand remodelling in 1569, including the insertion of a new stair-tower in the old re-entrant angle. At the same time a Great Hall was constructed with a fine stone vault, and a parapet added that was studded

with sculpture. Both are rare features and of very high quality.
The estate passed to the Ogilvy family in 1710 and in 1795–6
Walter Ogilvy of Clova (*de jure* 8th Earl of Airlie) built an addition
to the E. Sir John Gladstone, 1st Baronet of Fasque (q.v.), pur-
chased Balbegno in 1846 and his grandson Sir John Robert
Gladstone (3rd Baronet) carried out restorations in 1899–1901.

The MAIN FRONT is to the S. Both mighty and refined, it shows
all three building campaigns, the original L-plan TOWER
HOUSE on the l. half. Its design is closely related to Craig (q.v.)
and also to Delgatie, Gight and Towie Barclay (all N), all of
which are probably the work of the same master mason (and
attributed by Jervise to the *Conns* of Auchry). The tower's main
wing runs N–S and has a gable on the S front. Elliptical shot-
hole on the ground floor; three tall storeys above with a few
original slit-windows. A parapet was removed in the early–mid
C18, when the crowsteps of the gable were renewed and its
pyramidal-roofed chimneystack added. Between this wing and
the contemporary NE jamb is the stair-tower of 1596, which is
brought out to the line of the S wall of the main block, with a
result very like that achieved at Crathes Castle and Monymusk
House (qq.v.). Unusually the stair-tower is carried up one
storey higher than the main block and crowned with a caphouse, while the attic and parapet are accessed by a stair-turret
corbelled out on the third floor in the angle with the jamb. The
caphouse's S window is flanked by shafts and has a cable-
moulded sill. Huge heraldic plaque below it; on top of it, a
sculpted panel with two men raising their r. hands and a
woman emerging from an urn in the centre, similar to sculpture at Tolquhon Castle (N, 1584–9). The gable above is asymmetric, its l. side crowstepped and the r. covering a corbelled
round angle with another elliptical shot-hole. Heraldic tablet
above it with inscriptions for the Wood and Irvine families.
Around the corner, facing E, the parapet is carved with a
remarkable fictive mullioned window with half-length figures
in each opening. Just beyond it, the rounded re-entrant angle
has the remains of another coat of arms with Wood inscriptions. Then, over the main entrance, is a round medallion
carved with the figure of a man, who appears to interact (or
eavesdrop) on the figures in the window diagonally opposite.
Similar medallions originally encircled the entire building and
were brightly painted and gilded, as at Craigston (N) and the
Marchioness's fireplace at Huntly (q.v.). So the whole parapet
was a boisterous conglomeration of socializing and conversation, welcoming the late C16 visitor to one of the most urbane
tower houses in North Scotland.

The entrance to the tower is now masked by a single-storey
entrance added in 1795, with doorcase of Venetian-window
type. It is contemporary with the addition of the Georgian E
WING, a house of two storeys and three bays. Its l. pair of
windows is placed asymmetrically: a strange, satisfying genu-
flection to the proportions of the original tower house. Tall,

steeply pitched roof with panelled chimneystacks on the ends. Wide E flank and, behind it, two more of the late C16 medallion portraits, the l. of a woman and the r. of a man. Remains of another rounded angle on the end, abruptly truncated on the rear of the façade.

The INTERIOR of the Georgian wing is unexpectedly fine. DINING ROOM on the ground floor with beaded-panelled dado, doors and window shutters. Anthemion-palmette frieze on the ceiling and a good, vigorous wooden chimneypiece with streamlined shafts and large, swagged urn in the centre. Two more Adam-style chimneypieces in the lower BEDROOMS. Dog-leg staircase to the DRAWING ROOM, its ceiling decorated with a tripod frieze under acanthus cornice. The chimneypiece has fluted Corinthian columns and a flower-spilling urn flanked by palmette, all on a ground of Wedgwood blue.

In the ground floor of the tower house are the remains of several CELLARS, the best one now serving as the Billiard Room and covered by a segmental barrel-vault. The glory of the interior is the GREAT HALL on the first floor, sumptuous and lofty under the stone vault of 1569. The room is composed of two continuous cells, each c. 9 m. long and 6 m. wide and covered by an octopartite rib-vault. The dimensions are almost identical to those of the rib-vaulted hall at Towie Barclay (c. 1550–80) and it is vaulted in the same French manner, i.e. with the stones of the vault webbing set parallel to the ribs. The vault is carried on six corbels, the central ones carved as grotesques and the corners with foliage and/or coats of arms. The two main bosses have shields and leaf ornament. Even more impressive is the survival of the PAINTED DECORATION added by Andrew Wood and Helen Stewart c. 1585, now much decayed and renewed by *Alfred Nixon* in 1900. It commemorates the removal of the Regent Morton in 1581, each individual cell of the vault painted with a motto and the name of an Earl who participated: Argyll, Bothwell, Crawford, Eglinton, Errol, Huntly, Lennox, Marischal, Moray, Orkney, Rothes, etc. In between the painted texts are helms flanked by pairs of beasts, Hercules or elaborately dressed women. The palette was originally very bright with red, blue and green.

In the N wall of the Hall is a good, large AUMBRY with ogee head. Close to this, in the E wall, the shafted l. jamb of the original fireplace, now truncated but with square salt-locker intact. The upstairs chambers are unoccupied and in poor condition, but the final staircase still leads out onto the parapet, allowing the 'real' spectator to become part of the virtual conversation that unfolds to the l. and r.

Fine landscape surrounding the Castle, with WALLED GARDEN slightly sunk out in front of it. Ball-finialled GATEPIERS, again c. 1795, axially aligned with the front porch. – In another wall, a sculpted LUNETTE showing the sea captain Sir Andrew Wood †1515, cousin to the 1st Laird of Balbegno. His three extended fingers commemorate the number of English ships he captured in a celebrated battle in 1488.

Balbegno Castle.
Survey of painted ceiling in hall, by Thomas Bonnar

DOOCOT, 90 m. EE. Crowstepped rectangle of red sand-stone, a good survival of the C17. Original door in the W gable; rat course above with five little semicircular flight-holes perched on top.

BALBITHAN HOUSE

8010

1.1 km. SW of Kinmuck

A stepped L-plan house of substantial size, within a secluded valley of the Don. Unusually, it is strongly horizontal rather than vertical, the result of its complex building history between the mid C16 and early C19. Built by the Chalmers, it was recon-structed by a branch of the Gordons, who acquired the estate in the early C18.

The house is of three storeys, harled in sandy-pink with granite dressings. It consists of two ranges at right angles facing into what is now an open forecourt. Its E range is 22 m. long, but with only two generously spaced windows towards the fore-court; it incorporates the original mid-C16 rectangular tower house. The N range is a C17 addition, 17.5 m. long but with five windows facing the court. Both ranges have corbelled

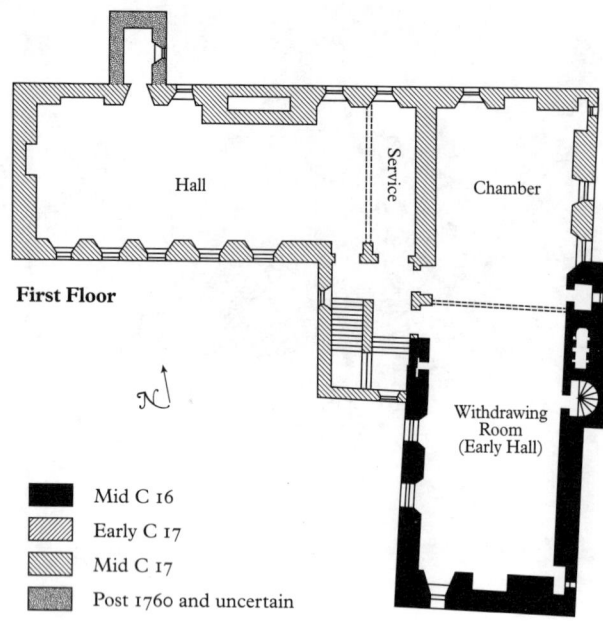

First Floor

Hall

Service

Chamber

N

Withdrawing
Room
(Early Hall)

Mid C 16

Early C 17

Mid C 17

Post 1760 and uncertain

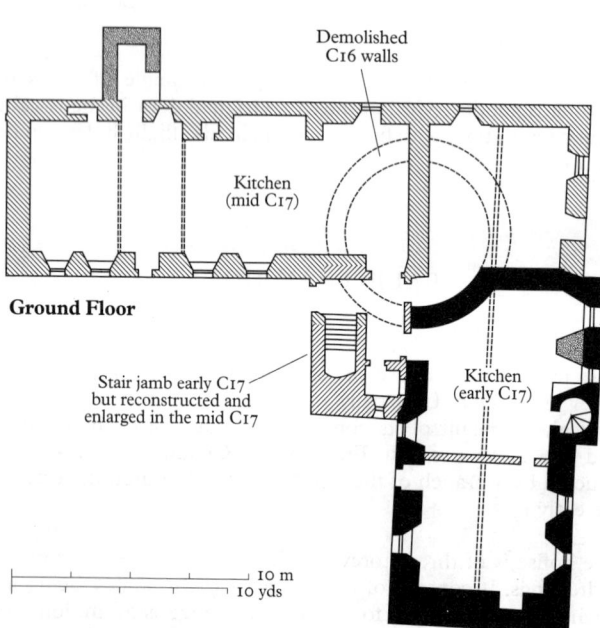

Demolished
C16 walls

Kitchen
(mid C17)

Ground Floor

Stair jamb early C17
but reconstructed and
enlarged in the mid C17

Kitchen
(early C17)

10 m
10 yds

Balbithan House.
Plan of ground and first floors

angle turrets rising high above their eaves to clasp their end gables and chimneyheads. Within the re-entrant angle between them is an oblong stair-tower 5.5 m. wide, with the main entrance on its W face and an oddly asymmetric roof running parallel with that of the E range. In the jamb's western re-entrant a circular stair-turret with a neat conical spirelet is corbelled out at second floor on a deep corbel course with a crude mask as its label stop; a blind field-panel must once have contained a coat of arms. At ground floor the house may originally have been vaulted, although its relatively slim walls (only 1 m. thick) make that appear unlikely.

The E RANGE is of two dates. Its southern two-thirds represent the original house. It comprised a main block 15 m. by 7.5 m., and a big drum tower 8 m. in diameter at its NW angle, a segment of which remains within the ground floor. This plan is reminiscent of Pitfichie (q.v.) but its walls are thinner, necessitating a large kitchen chimney-breast incorporating the service stair at the N end of its near-blind E wall. This has been altered but it still contains its small turnpike stair which, modest in diameter between ground and first floor, becomes still tighter when it rises from first to second.

The drum tower appears to have been demolished comparatively early, when the rectangular block was extended N and the stair-tower built, producing a classic early C17 T-plan arrangement with a long bar and a short stalk (cf. Mounie, (N), and Hallhead, q.v.). The stair-tower then contained a wheel stair, some of its winders being reused in the present stair, and probably had a turret stair to the upper floors in one of its re-entrant angles as in the other houses of this type.[*]

Later in the C17 the N RANGE was built and the stair-tower reconstructed on an enlarged plan with a scale-and-platt stair, the stair-turret being removed and rebuilt within the new W re-entrant angle, resulting in the house achieving its present elongated stepped L-plan form. The N and E ranges and the stair-tower all rose rather higher than they do now: both ranges may have been lit by attic dormers and the stair-tower rose a further storey, with apartments at second floor and attic level. In the later C18 or early C19 the wall-heads were reduced and the attic storey eliminated, probably during improvements made by William Forbes Gordon, who inherited in 1803, resulting in the horizontal roof-lines.

A kitchen occupied the E half of the ground floor of the new N wing and a hall or dining room the first floor, the old hall in the E range being subdivided into private apartments. The provision of two doors at the 'low' E end of the hall nearest the stair indicates the position of the servery, the hall fireplace being at the 'high' W end. These arrangements led Harry Gordon Slade to assume a date of *c*. 1630 for the N wing, but

[*]Harry Gordon Slade's assumption (*see* 'Balbithan House, Aberdeenshire' in *P.S.A.S.* vol. civ (1971–2), pp. 257–67) that it was at its NW angle – i.e. its present position – seems unlikely.

it may have been built as late as 1679, the date of the sundial on its SW turret and one which Douglas Simpson accepted at face value.

The oldest surviving element of the INTERIOR is the scale-and-platt stair, built in stone up to first floor and timber above, with semicircular arches over the half-landings. The rooms are very simple, having been re-partitioned in the mid C18 for Gen. Benjamin Gordon and again refitted c. 1803, but one internal doorway linking the stair-tower with the N wing at ground floor has a checked and rolled chamfer. It appears to have once been the main entrance, deconstructed and reused in the C17 works.

Following a period of neglect the house underwent a further major repair for Benjamin Abernethie Gordon from c. 1840. After its purchase by Mary McMurtrie it was tactfully restored from 1960 by *A. G. R. Mackenzie*. The bolection-moulded fireplaces in the library, dining room and drawing room are all Mackenzie's; so too that in the music room on the N range's second floor, where the ceiling was lowered to its original height. During the restoration some masons' marks were discovered, and fragmentary C16–C17 décor in indigo, white and grey with scrolls and arabesques.

BALFLUIG CASTLE
1.3 km. SE of Alford

A distinctive small tower house on a stepped L-plan; built by a cadet branch of the Forbes of Corsindae (q.v.) and dated 1556. Balfluig was sold by the Forbes to the Farquharsons of Haughton (q.v.) in 1753 and ceased to be regularly occupied c. 1800. The Tennant family acquired it in 1966 and by 1968 had restored it to designs by *John Lamb* of *George Bennett Mitchell & Son*.

The tower house comprises a three-storey-and-attic main block 10.5 m. long N–S by 7.5 m. deep with a jamb 4.5 m. square hinged from its SE corner, the doorway being at ground floor of the main block close into the re-entrant angle between them. The jamb is of five storeys, and rising above the height of the main block's wall-head its rounded angles are corbelled to the square beneath a double-height caphouse rising into a chimney gable. Behind the jamb, in the re-entrant angle formed with the main block's S gable, a round tower 3.5 m. in diameter contains a wheel stair rising through the three main storeys before it too corbels to the square at the top, the upper storeys being reached by a narrow turnpike within a slender turret.

Construction is in rough pinned boulder rubble, harled with dressings in both granite and sandstone. The main doorway is chamfered and round-headed, and its approach is well

protected by two wide-mouthed shot-holes in the jamb's flank.
At ground floor the walls are near-solid with only small slit-
lights but at first-floor hall level there is one large window in
the centre of the main block on the entrance (E) side, two on
the W side and one on the S gable with smaller windows at
second floor. Their dressed surrounds have been drilled for
iron bars, but the triple shot-holes – a motif characteristic of
the work of *Thomas Leiper* – are really for ventilation. High up
on the E front, two corbels once supported a brattice or platform overlooking the doorway. The gables have straight skews
and appear to have been altered, perhaps after Balfluig was
burned by the Marquis of Montrose in 1645. They have
moulded skewputts and their massive chimneystacks are
simply coped; that over the main block's S gable is much taller
than the others and, rising against the caphouse of the stair-
tower, is progressively stepped inwards. At the main block's
NW corner a small pepperpot turret corbelled out from attic
level was removed some time after the castle was depicted by
James Giles in 1840 but has since been reinstated.

On PLAN the ground floor is vaulted. The main block contained a cellar and a kitchen still with its stone sink and drain,
and a hearth well over 2 m. wide within the N wall. The jamb
contained another cellar or guardroom, and the round tower
behind it the main stair with a small chamber (perhaps a pit-
prison) beneath. An intramural service stair in the cellar's SW
angle allowed for drink to be brought up separately to the hall.
Although the hall was not vaulted, Forbes's room within the
jamb was. The main block's second floor seems originally to
have been one chamber.

BALLATER   3090

Flanked by craggy peaks, Ballater straddles the junction of three
rivers, the Muick and Gairn, with Tullich Burn just to the E, all
joining the River Dee. Up to the C18, there were three separate
settlements with medieval churches but they were all abandoned
when the town of Ballater was created by Francis Farquharson
of Monaltrie, and later his nephew William Farquharson, to
service visitors taking the waters at Pannanich Wells (*see* Tullich).
A prerequisite for his town was an effective bridge, the first of a
series being built in 1783, linking the flat settlement plain to the
wells on the S side of the river. Houses grew up around the central
parish church, begun in 1798. The house plots and streets were
laid out in a grid plan based on an open square and green in the
centre. Ballater's popularity rose when Queen Victoria and
Prince Albert acquired the Balmoral estate nearby in 1852, and
the town began to prosper after the railway arrived in 1866,
becoming a burgh in 1891. It is primarily residential, catering for
holiday-makers, and combines an attractive mixture of neat rows

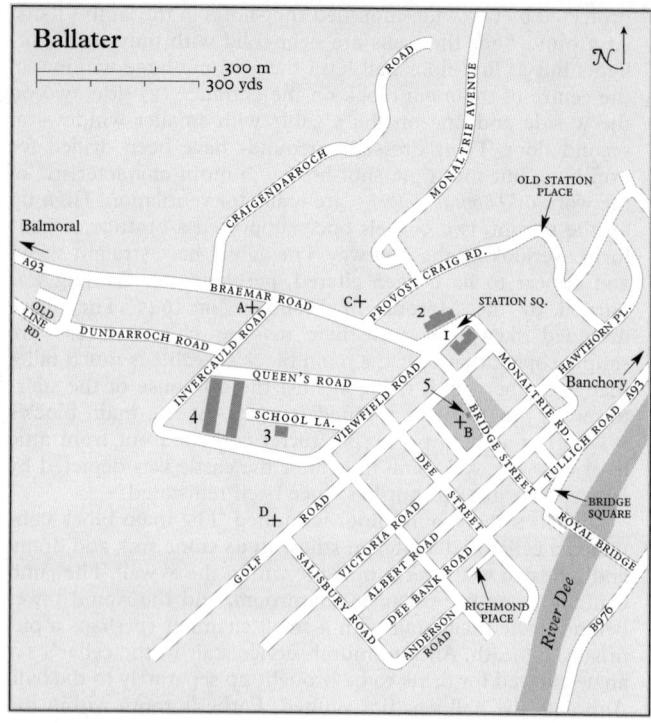

A   Free Church (former)
B   Glenmuick Parish Church
C   St Kentigern
D   St Nathalan (R.C.)

1   Albert Memorial Hall,
    Victoria Hall & Gordon Institute
2   Ballater Station (former)
3   Old School
4   Victoria Barracks
5   War Memorial

of low granite cottages with exuberantly bombastic Baronial villas. Sir Patrick Geddes (1854–1932), pioneer of building preservation and town planning, was born in Ballater.

CHURCHES

Former FREE CHURCH, Braemar Road. Now The Auld Kirk B&B. 1869 by *William Duguid & Sons* of Ballater. A prominent three-stage tower dominates both the E front and the road junction. It is framed by its stepped corner buttresses. A single archway, without orders, forms the entrance; above is a large window with Y-tracery, and above that plain triple lancets, capped by a stone broach spire with gabled lucarnes. The corners of the façade are marked with buttresses and pinnacles.

The relatively discreet conversion in the 1990s, by *Stewart Anderson*, inserted an extra floor and two rows of windows along the nave but little of the interior survives.

GLENMUICK PARISH CHURCH, Church Square. The datestone of 1798 on the E front is a reminder of the original foundation, a small box with wooden spire by *James Massie* (for the previous church, *see* Glenmuick). The present building, by *J. R. Mackenzie*, 1873–4, is far grander than one would expect for a small highland township, dominating the surroundings with its massive tower and stone steeple. It is similar in detail to his Rubislaw Church, Aberdeen (p. 231). The E front thrusts forward a double-height canted porch, with gabled entrance and three spacious windows of geometric tracery above. The SE tower is tacked on awkwardly, rising from a plain base to triple lancets and pinnacles below the spire. The stone is rock-faced pink and grey granite with dressed copings. On the N and S sides there are gables over each of the five aisle bays, with a plainer church hall at the W end.

The interior is airy and light, the transverse barrel-vaults of the aisles supported by slender cast-iron columns, the nave covered by a wagon roof. The pulpit, communion table, font and lectern form a mellow suite of C19 liturgical furnishings. Pine E gallery with traceried fascia; original pews. A particularly esteemed ORGAN, by *Foster & Andrews*, 1889, fully occupies the canted W apse. – BELL, located in the porch. Made by *Pat Kilgour* in 1688. A gift from St Machar's Cathedral in 1798, it is one of the largest survivors from the Old Aberdeen Foundry. – STAINED GLASS, N aisle starting from E, twin lights: for Rev. William Middleton, 'Suffer the little children' and the Good Shepherd, after 1920; the Walker window is by *Margaret Chilton* and *Marjorie Kemp*, 1953, Christ in the Carpenter's shop; The Middleton window, *Sax & Christian Shaw*, 1986, St Margaret of Antioch and St Luke; the window for Michael Sheridan, master butcher, is by *Jennifer-Jane Bayliss*, 2006 (after a painting by *Howard Butterworth*), 'I am the light of the world', featuring Ballater bridge and village with the butcher's delivery van.

ST KENTIGERN (Episcopal), Braemar Road. Dedicated to St Saviour until 1945. By *A. Marshall Mackenzie*, 1907, to replace an iron church of 1897 (now at Peterculter, Aberdeen, p. 287).

Dignified and crisp, the understated exterior hides many decorative delights within. Single storey with N aisle in snecked Cambus O'May granite, the chancel marked by a simple buttress. Plain narrow lancets increasing from one to three in the progression E, with the E wall stacked with two below and one above, like Mortlach Church, Dufftown (Moray), a reminder of the origins of the See of Aberdeen. Inside, the wooden barrel-vaulted ceiling combined with the rich stained glass produce a dark enclave, but the shining silver granite of the chancel arch and three bays of the N aisle, on plain circular

piers, creates a lift. The N aisle ALTAR RETABLE was made
in 1875 for St Nathalan (*see* House of Glenmuick) by *Mayer*
of Munich. Figures in gold and blue enamel of SS Margaret,
George, Andrew, Patrick and Elizabeth. – HIGH ALTAR. Given
by the ecclesiologist Francis C. Eeles and made of wood from
the altar of the previous iron church; the wooden shelving
behind the altar came from Dinnet House (q.v.). The other
FURNISHINGS are chiefly by *James Ogilvie & Sons* of Aberdeen,
who made the altar rails, lectern, pulpit and font cover. –
Contemporary FONT by the local builder *George Hall.* – ORGAN
by *Harrison & Harrison*, 1960s, handed on from King's College
Chapel, Aberdeen University, in 2004.

The STAINED GLASS creates a mysterious, jewel-like
atmosphere. Chancel E, Nativity, Agony in the garden and
Ascension, by *T. F. Curtis, Ward & Hughes*; chancel s, to Mrs
L. M. Barclay-Harvey of Dinnet House, Jesus with children,
Give me meat, Give me drink, by *Thomas F. Firth* of *Ward &
Hughes*, 1908. – s wall, proceeding from E: for Charles Malcolm
Barclay-Harvey of Dinnet House, St Machar, St Kentigern
with heraldry, shield of Barclay-Harveys, Grand Lodge of
Scotland, Order of St John of Jerusalem and state badge of
South Australia, by *Gordon Webster*, 1971; for John Francis
Gaskell of Cambus O'May, St John and St Francis, by *Morris
& Co.*; it was originally destined for Christ Church, Oxford,
with three figures by *Burne-Jones* (†1898), but completed by
Henry Dearle in 1910, who made the lower St Francis. – St
Kentigern, given by Canon W. E. Adam, by *C. C. Powell* of
Highgate. – w window for Sir Allan Mackenzie of Glenmuick,
St George, by *Albert Ernest Child* from the *Tower of Glass*,
Dublin studio, 1907. – N aisle from w: for Ceal Shirras, St
George, by *C. C. Powell*; St Cecilia by *H. W. Laxford* of New
Barnet; John Skinner Bishop of Aberdeen, by *William Wilson*,
1965.

N of the church the sympathetic addition of a wooden HALL,
2005.

ST NATHALAN (R.C.), Golf Road. Glengairn had a strongly
Catholic, Jacobite population and the current church, by
Archibald Macpherson, 1905, is a successor to several ruined
sites up the glen. Scots Gothic with attached presbytery to s,
in rock-faced pink granite with fine grey dressings. The church
has a three-sided apse, small transepts, nave and porch.
Approached from the E, the chancel's sheer rugged walls feel
like the prow of an approaching barge. With small side
windows, the solid E face of the chancel has a statue of St
Nathalan in a niche breaking into the dressed crowstepped
parapet, topped by a Celtic cross. The major light source is
from the w gable where there are two pairs of twin lancets and
a round window above, all quirkily framed by hoodmoulds.
Inside, a simple open roof, chancel and transepts emphasized
by fine wooden dado panelling below blue walls sparkling
with gold stars. The w gallery railings and severely plain green-
and-white stained glass have a pleasing Arts and Crafts

restraint. – FONT. C20, on polished marble columns. The treasure is the small square stone early medieval BOWL FONT marked with a small cross in the bowl, which was rescued from Inchmarnock, a flooded island in the Dee, near Cambus O'May. – STATIONS OF THE CROSS. Given by Maria Buxton in the 1930s.

PUBLIC BUILDINGS

ALBERT MEMORIAL HALL, VICTORIA HALL and GORDON INSTITUTE, Station Square. The buildings form part of a U-shaped square, providing a dignified public amenity comprising a hall, post office, reading room, library, learning centre and billiard room. The Albert Memorial Hall is of 1874–5, the Victoria Hall and Gordon Insitute of 1896, both by *William Duguid & Sons* of Ballater, and sponsored by Alexander Gordon, a prosperous brewer. The buildings are mainly two storeys, pink granite with grey dressings, featuring a high gable, square tower with crenellated parapet and consoled balconies over main entrances.

BALLATER STATION. Opened in 1866 by the GNSR as the terminus of the Deeside Railway, and at that time the closest station to Balmoral, but now as remodelled in 1886. Built of clapboard with deep eaves forming a canopy of decorative bargeboards and a slender porte cochère, decked in cream and red livery. It was temporarily painted black and gold in 1896, for the arrival of Tsar Nicholas of Russia. The unique royal waiting room was complete down to its floral-design toilet bowl. It had a plaster strapwork ceiling with Adam details, Ionic timber pilasters and timber mantelpiece with mirror and tiled cheeks. Decorative leaded glass windows. (It closed in 1966, happily restored as a tourist attraction in 2000 by Aberdeenshire Council, but severely damaged by fire in 2015.)

OLD SCHOOL, School Lane and Abergeldie Road. 1877 by *William Duguid & Sons*, a good example of the type of school recommended in the 1872 Education Act. Attractive vernacular complex with double-height classroom and two school houses, resulting in a cottage-style grouping of gables and pedimented dormers.

ROYAL BRIDGE, across the Dee. 1885 by *Jenkins & Marr*. The struggle to maintain a bridge here indicates the extremes of climate experienced in Ballater. The first was built in 1783, destroyed in 1789; the second, by *Thomas Telford*, was destroyed in the 'Great Flood' of 1829; a wooden successor lasted from 1834 to 1885. The present structure has four segmental arches with bull-nosed cutwaters and rectangular refuges on a solid parapet.

VICTORIA BARRACKS, Queen's Road. Built in 1860 or 1869 by the *War Office Department* as housing for the Royal Bodyguard, the barracks consist of five Tudor cottages with steeply pitched roofs and sweeping bargeboards, yellow crested roof tiles. Set in a fenced parade ground, they nonetheless maintain the exuberant holiday tone of the village. Additional late C20 boxy blocks.

WAR MEMORIAL, Church Square. 1922, by *Sir J. J. Burnet*. Tall Kemnay granite Celtic cross on a base which forms a seat.

DESCRIPTION

A short description of the town's other buildings can start at the bridge in BRIDGE SQUARE. First, in a prime location beside the bridge, is the former MONALTRIE HOTEL, built after 1870, on the site of an earlier 1830s coaching inn. This imposing building is large, rambling and Victorian Tudor in style, featuring numerous gables and dormers with overhanging eaves. It has been extended eastwards in stages. Mainly white-harled, but with the generous bay windows in dressed granite. Conversion to flats in 2005 has restored its exterior presence on the riverbank. In BRIDGE STREET, first on the l. the BANK OF SCOTLAND (formerly Union Bank) of 1870 by *William Henderson*. Stugged granite classical style, with pilastered doorpiece and rusticated quoins. The rest of the street is mostly one- and two-storey frontages of modest character. Off Bridge Street to the w is CORNELLAN SQUARE, a successful and discreet conversion of a C19 stable courtyard into housing by Churchill Developments, 2003, reusing the original granite.

The oldest houses are w of Bridge Street; generally three bays, one or two storeys. In DEE STREET is FORD HOUSE, early C19, long and low, in an ample garden facing the river. Three bays, two storeys, gable-end chimneys with coped stacks. Originally the school, with master's accommodation as wing to rear. Also in Dee Street, DEEBANK HOUSE, the land for which was bought in 1858 by the local builder *William Duguid* but not erected until after 1866. A fine small classical mansion, three bays, two storeys, granite with ashlar dressings. Simple but stylish details of plain, raised window margins, string course between floors, pilastered doorcase, dressed quoins, piended roof with broad modillioned eaves. Garden wall entrance through classical arch. The interior has some fine plasterwork and classical fireplaces in the principal rooms. In DEEBANK ROAD, NE of Dee Street, INCHLEY (No. 11) is a house marked in this location on a map of 1808, with large garden towards the river, now built up. Three bays, two storeys, piended roof. A rustic Doric portico made of carved tree trunks.

The smarter VILLAS vie for grandeur along BRAEMAR ROAD. CRAIGENDARROCH HOUSE, No. 36 Braemar Road, of 1869 was the home of the Hall family of local builders; aggrandized in 1920 by *George Hall*, for himself. Originally L-plan, with a broad plain gable face to the E. A prominent square tower was added in the re-entrant angle. This is of finely tooled granite rescued from the demolished Union Bridge in Aberdeen, with corbel table and balustrade on the fourth storey, and an open archway to an entrance lobby below. The door is flanked by a remarkable pair of granite stags' heads, reputedly from House of Glenmuick, set above garlanded stained glass windows. The w corner ends in a slender conical-roofed turret. The interior has a fine oak-panelled staircase and carved balusters, with original plaster-work in principal rooms. OAKHALL was built in 1890 for Dr Alexander Ogilvie, headmaster of Robert Gordon's School, Aberdeen. Tightly massed Baronial villa, crammed with detail, with even a castellated 'sitooterie' on a castellated terrace. The L-plan s front has three crowstepped gables, two-storey bays, and two slender towers – one for the stairs, the other for the entrance – topped with corbel table and crenellations. There is a further conical turret on the w. Interior has fine cornice plasterwork and some decorative encaustic tiles. THE OLD COACH HOUSE, No. 50, was built for Oakhall in the early C20. Pert yet lavish, the simple coach entrance, flanked by two windows, occupies the centre of the house. The first floor is separated by a wandering string course, topped by two dormers with segmental pediments and one with crowstepped gable. Cheeky candlesnuffer turret corbelled out on SE corner. Accommodation for grooms and chauffeurs in domestic range to rear. The joy of turrets and crenellations for small villas can also be seen at GLENBARDIE, No. 42.

DARROCH LEARG HOTEL. 1888 for Dr Hendry. An English-looking mansion of restless variety. The high Scottish granite walls are topped by half-timbered gables and dormers, clad in fish-scale tiles, with every window subtly different. Interior damaged by fire, 2015. A follower of Norman Shaw's Cragside (1870–85) and precursor to Marshall Mackenzie's half-timbered gable house, Mar Lodge (1895) (q.v.).

SLUIEVANNACHIE, Old Line Road. One of the oldest houses in Ballater, of 1836 by *Peter Mitchell*, a local builder and farmer. Unusually stylish for a farmhouse, perhaps influenced by the Gothic style of John Smith of Aberdeen. Gothic pointed doorway to entrance porch, delicate fanlight; tall pedimented dormers breaking the wall-head, and distinctive ornamental chimneystacks, set on the diagonal. Cheese press. Milk house in basement.

MONALTRIE HOUSE, Monaltrie Avenue. 1782 by *James Robertson*, master mason, for Francis Farquharson, a staunch Jacobite who spent twenty years as a prisoner in England following the Battle of Culloden in 1745. Having lost his Monaltrie home at Crathie, he set about developing the Pannanich Wells (Tullich) and built a seat for his family beside his new town. The house has an unusual plan for this date: nine bays wide, two storeys high, piended roof, with rear wings forming an internal courtyard. The principal SE elevation is articulated by crenellations above the end bays and the bowed central bay.

Old photographs show the main door entered through the central bay, now occupied by a staircase, and the room to the l. is large enough to be a hall. In the w wing is a double-height drawing room with bowed front; kitchen in E wing. On the N side, flanked by two pavilions with pyramid roofs, was a range of sheds and offices, now mostly derelict and demolished. With its long, low elevation and sequence of small narrow rooms, Monaltrie resembles the Farquharson inns at Pannanich and Inver. Almost derelict by the 1970s, the house is now extensively refurbished with few original details.

POLHOLLICK BRIDGE, across the Dee, 2.5 km. WNW. Designed by *Louis Harper* of *Harper & Co.*, erected by *James Abernethy & Co.* in 1892. Rivetted latticework pylons and balustrade. 54.4 m. (178 ft 6 in.) span. The first of two iron suspension footbridges over the Dee (*see also* Cambus O'May) erected with funds provided by Alexander Gordon, a native of Ballater who made his fortune as a brewer and settled in Hildenborough, Kent. He also funded the Albert Memorial Hall, Victoria Hall and Gordon Institute at Ballater.

6060   BALMAKEWAN HOUSE   K
                   2 km. WNW of Marykirk

An austere Neoclassical design of *c.* 1828, the crisp, chocolate-brown ashlar contrasted with pristine white courses of mortar.* Two storeys and five bays over a semi-sunk basement, the centre minimally advanced with a segmental-headed entrance. Doorpiece with two engaged Greek Doric columns (lower third unfluted) and a sharp, corniced architrave. Window above it in a segmental recess. The ground floor has corniced windows with simple aprons and thick band courses running above and below. Less refined masonry on the flanks, and then a rear extension of *c.* 1860 forming an L-plan in a similar style. Inside, the centre is filled with a full-height rectangular hall, much remodelled in the late C19 when its staircase was removed. The swagged garlands around the base of the cupola are original.

160 m. N of the house are the late C19 former KENNELS (now shop and tea room; restored by *John D. Crawford Ltd*, 2006–11). Of brick, the middle section two-storeyed under a jerkin-headed gable with weathervane. – Twin DOOCOTS, 350 m. SW of the house, late C18. Charming little squares with straight-headed entrances. Pyramidal roofs with catslide dormers pierced by flight-holes.

---

*Thomas Gillies, the patron, commissioned a design from *John* and *Robert Adam* in 1789, but nothing was ever done.

BALMANNO HOUSE *see* MARYKIRK

BALMORAL CASTLE   *2090*
0.9 km. w of Crathie

Balmoral is the private residence of the Sovereign in Scotland,   71
as distinct from a royal palace primarily concerned with affairs
of state. It was designed in 1852–3 for Queen Victoria and Prince
Albert by the Aberdeen architect *William Smith*, its main block
being completed in 1855 and the Great Tower, service court and
Ballroom in 1856, although the Ballroom was not fitted out
internally until 1857–8.

Victoria and Albert first visited the Highlands in 1842, staying
at Taymouth Castle (Perth & Kinross) as guests of the Marquess
of Breadalbane, who introduced them to deer-stalking. They
made further expeditions to the Highlands in 1844 and 1847, on
the latter occasion cruising around the West Coast and visiting
Fingal's Cave before staying with the Duke of Argyll at Inveraray
Castle (Argyll & Bute) and then renting the shooting lodge of
Ardverikie where the weather proved dreadful. Reports from Dr
James Clark, Victoria's physician-in-ordinary, of magnificent
scenery and much better weather at Balmoral on the Dee where
his diplomat son John (*see* Tillypronie) had been recuperating as
a guest of Lord Aberdeen's brother, Sir Robert Gordon, encour-
aged them to take the remainder of Sir Robert's lease on 17
February 1848, after his unexpected death; the neighbouring
Abergeldie estate was leased in 1848 and Birkhall purchased in
1849 (qq.v.).

The existing castle at Balmoral was a rectangular three-storey
tower house with wall-head parapets and caphouse, built in the
early C16; it was extended in the late C16 or C17 and again as a
hunting lodge for Sir Robert Gordon in 1834–9 during his transformation of Balmoral into a sporting estate. However, it was still
much too small for the royal family and their court. In 1848–9
Victoria and Albert therefore commissioned Sir Robert's architects, *John* and *William Smith*, to build a new service court which,
with other additions intended as part of a larger scheme, doubled
the house in size. By 1851, however, Albert was giving thought
to a completely new house, although Osborne (Isle of Wight) had
only just been finished, and he purchased the Balmoral estate
freehold on 22 June 1852; the high price of £31,500 demanded
by the Earl Fife's trustees was perhaps met by proceeds from the
sale of Brighton Pavilion which were realized that year. The possibilities of building a new house at Balmoral were transformed
when almost immediately afterwards Victoria received a £500,000
bequest from John Camden Nield, a total stranger. Albert held
detailed discussions with William Smith on 8 September 1852,
and corresponded with him about every aspect of the design
thereafter. The first drawings were produced by December when
they were sent to *Thomas Cubitt*, with whom Albert had designed
Osborne; Cubitt was entrusted with Balmoral's plumbing

arrangements and may well have advised on other matters. Working drawings were issued in 1853, when James Giles was commissioned to paint perspectives.

The site chosen lay 100 m. NW of the old castle, nearer the Dee and with better views of the river valley and mountains. Substantial earthworks were required for both the house and gardens before the Queen laid a foundation stone monogrammed with the initials 'V.A.' on 28 September. The new castle was built in pale grey – originally near-white – granite from Glen Gelder on the Balmoral estate. Although work progressed swiftly under the supervision of *Alexander Clark*, the clerk-of-works, with *John Beaton* in charge of the masonry, the granite proved so hard to cut and polish that more than once it provoked the masons to down their tools; the mouldings and most of the ornament were carved on site. The main block was finished and the royal family moved in on 7 September 1855, the servants remaining in the old castle until the service court was completed a year later. A photograph by George Washington Wilson and a watercolour by F. Colebrooke Stockdale show both castles together, the new castle dwarfing the old, which was demolished shortly after. The final cost of the new castle was some £100,000.

Giles's perspectives show the particular importance attached to the SE view from the approach drive. From here the castle's main block can be seen in perspective together with its service court stepped back diagonally behind it and the Great Tower between them forming the focal point of the design; since the entrance is at the main block's far W end visitors have ample opportunity to admire the full length of the frontage from every angle before they arrive. The main block's Tudor-Jacobean is familiar from the Smiths' earlier work and derives from that of William Burn, from whom they had learnt much after taking over his commissions at Fintray (1827–31, dem.) and Auchmacoy (N, 1831–3).* However, the Great Tower itself, although patently a homage to the demolished C16 tower house in its profile, has no obvious precedent among new-built houses in Britain. Its purpose was primarily scenographic: it had no private family access either to its grandly balconied window or to its platformed roof, its interior comprising the wine cellar and a barrack for the pages. It may have been influenced by Charles Barry and G.P. Kennedy's proposals for Drummond Castle (Perth & Kinross), which Victoria and Albert had visited in 1842, although there the tower was ancient, but the colossal scale of the Balmoral tower perhaps owes more to German Romanticist castle projects from the mid 1820s onwards.

The MAIN BLOCK is a near-square courtyard plan, 37 m. broad by 38 m. deep. It is predominantly three-storeyed across its

---

* Burn sought an interview with Albert, probably to complain that, as at Osborne, the royal family had shunned the leading members of the Royal Institute of British Architects, which had received its charter in 1837, an important step in recognition of the profession. Smith had resigned from the RIBA in 1847.

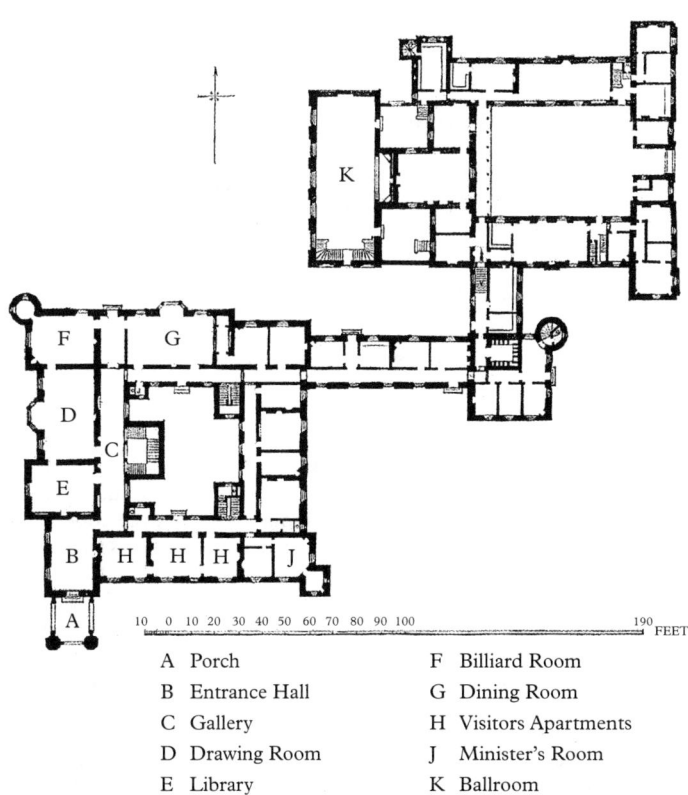

K

F G

D

C

E

B H H H J

A

10 0 10 20 30 40 50 60 70 80 90 100   190 FEET

A	Porch	F	Billiard Room
B	Entrance Hall	G	Dining Room
C	Gallery	H	Visitors Apartments
D	Drawing Room	J	Minister's Room
E	Library	K	Ballroom

Balmoral Castle.
Ground-floor plan by William Smith, 1855

SOUTH FRONT but has two taller storeys at its far W end where
it is entered through a porte cochère.* This porte cochère has
three archways, that in the front semicircular and those for
carriages in the flanks semi-elliptical: they are clasped by slim
octagonal corner bastions rising from splayed bases into steeply
battered sides with blind crosslets. The arches were enclosed
(either by *Robert Rowand Anderson c.* 1902–3 or by *Alexander
Marshall Mackenzie & Son* 1911–12) with an astragalled
window in the front face and four-leaf doors in the flanks. An
elaborate key-pattern corbel course supports the porte cochère's
crenellated parapet, which has a small marble panel displaying
the Royal Arms of Scotland inset at its centre, notably in pre-
1603 form with two unicorns as supporters, their standards

---

* Strictly speaking, the entrance front faces SSE, but the orientation has been simplified for ease of understanding.

displaying the lion rampant and saltire. The porte cochère forms a roof terrace for the Queen's apartments, accessible from her dressing room. Angle turrets with double-keyhole gunloops, arcaded eaves and fish-scale-slated spirelets with thistle finials frame the crowstepped and ball-finialled gable. At the E end of the S front, the entrance bay is balanced by a slimmer but taller angle tower, broached above the wall-head into an octagonal stage again with key-pattern corbel course, crenellated parapet and a caphouse with tall ogee domelet and wrought-iron weathervane. The seven intermediate bays are very regular in appearance, their large windows with timber mullions and transoms; at each level square windows (three panes wide by three panes deep) alternate with narrower windows (two panes by three). Some at ground floor have stepped hoodmoulds; at first and second floors the bays immediately flanking the centre are minimally corbelled out and break through the eaves into crowstepped gablets with escutcheon panels and ball finials, shallower dormerhead gablets without crowsteps rising over the end bays. The chimneystacks over the roof ridge are plain rectangles with simple copes.

The SE angle tower turns the corner into the EAST FRONT, framed between the gables of the S and N ranges, the latter with a diagonally set square turret at its NE angle. The E front is near-symmetrical, essentially similar to the S front with four main bays between the gables, two of which are corbelled out at first and second floor to rise into gablets. The LINK BLOCK connecting its N gable with the service court and the great tower is two-storeyed and four bays broad. Its windows have lying-pane glazing, the ground floor's being set within four-centred arches and the first floor's rising into segmental dormer pediments with ball finials and escutcheons with gilt motifs.

At the link block's E end the GREAT TOWER is almost exactly 11 m. square, and rises to 24 m. height; at its NE angle, a slim round tower with balustrade rises higher still, over 30 m. above the ground. The great tower's ground storey is of hammer-dressed rusticated masonry; immediately above, on the S side, a carved panel bears the Royal Arms of Scotland, again pre-1603. The upper stages are in lightly stugged ashlar, their angles rounded. The fourth stage's S-facing window has an arcaded balcony; at fifth stage, the clock dials are framed by double-keyhole gunloops. A very deep arcaded corbel course supports the crenellated parapets, and double-height turrets with conical spirelets mark the SE, SW and NW angles. On the E flank is the luggage entrance, surmounted by a square panel carved with a round cartouche bearing a commemorative inscription; it is flanked by hounds and surmounted by a stag's head, with an array of hunting horns and spears.

Concealed from the main approach drive, the WEST FRONT expressing the principal apartments on ground floor and Victoria and Albert's rooms on first floor is much more private, and finer in its detail. It consists of two broad crowstep-gabled bays alternating with recessed wall-planes. Both gabled bays are flanked by turrets, but that at the N end abuts a three-stage corner tourelle, its conical roof with a spike finial; above first floor the gables themselves are jettied out slightly on stepped corbel tables. The wall-plane between them has a five-light canted bay inset with marble *alto-relievo* panels: in the centre St Hubertus – patron saint of hunters, popular in the Middle Ages, with a particular following in Germany – praying before a stag with the Crucified Christ between its antlers; on the l. a valiant Albert as St George in chain-mail slaying a dragon, and on the r. St Andrew with his cross. These and other sculpted panels were by *John Thomas R.A.*, who also worked at Windsor Castle (Berkshire). The canted bay is crowned by a ball-finialled balustrade at parapet level. The wall-plane at the S end has a first-floor oriel boldly corbelled out at its centre with cast-metal heraldic emblems, and a quarter-drum turret in the angle with the adjacent gable.

The principal feature of the NORTH FRONT, which rises from a basement terrace, is a central two-storey canted bay with a shapely bellcast prismatic roof, crowned by a lion sejant at its apex. The main block's downpipes bear the V.A. mono-gram, dated 1855.

The BALLROOM stands on the lower ground to the NE of the main block. Accessed from the N front's terrace, it is aligned N–S in parallel with the service court's W range and was originally entered by the centre of three arches in its S gable, the outer two being blind; the short corridor from the link block was inserted sometime before 1871. The Ballroom is just over 22 m. long by 9 m. broad. Its exposed W elevation is lit by five tall windows which rise into four-centred arches with timber Y-tracery. Corbels support a cornice and crenellated parapet inset with an *alto-relievo* panel by *John Thomas* repre-senting the royal family – Albert standing in relaxed pose in full Highland dress, with Victoria seated next to him and their children nearby – watching muscle-bound locals engaged in athletic games, the bagpipers behind them completing a display of unity between monarchy and people.

The SERVICE COURT standing diagonally to the NE of the main block is of closely similar size in terms of ground plan, 39 m. by 35 m., but appears much more modest since it is set well back, stands on lower ground and is substantially con-cealed on the S by both the link block and the Great Tower. It was originally two-storeyed throughout with a basement on the N side, but the S side was raised to three storeys *c.* 1902–3 by *Robert Rowand Anderson*, who replicated the wall-head with its upper-floor windows breaking into gableted dormers and a larger gable at the far E end. The entrance is on the E flank, a four-centred archway which was originally framed by two small single-storey blocks giving the impression of a gatehouse before it achieved its present two-storey gabled form prior to 1871.

The main block's PLANNING owes something to the Smiths' Forglen (N, *c.* 1839–40), particularly the circuit corridor running round the internal courtyard, the main stair projecting into the courtyard behind the principal apartments, and the service stairs in two of the courtyard's angles. The specialized accommodation required by the royal family was, however, very much determined by Prince Albert. In its provision and sequence it bears close resemblance to the unexecuted proposals for the old castle prepared by the Smiths in 1848–9, with greater accommodation for visitors and staff and a more private disposition of the principal apartments. Indeed, the over-riding sense of order, although perhaps inevitable in a house of such a size, appears particularly German. Like Osborne, Balmoral was advanced in its construction, with fireproof floors on malleable iron beams.

The original INTERIORS and their oak, maple and birch furniture were almost wholly the work of *Holland & Sons*, who also worked at Osborne; they were recorded by James Roberts, William Corden (Jun.) and Egron Lundgren on completion. Within the porte cochère, three steps lead to a round-arched, roll-moulded doorway with panelled and studded double-leaf doors flanked by ornate wrought-iron lanterns. Inside, the ENTRANCE HALL was originally lined in plain wood, then granite ashlar, then (from 1902–3) in Ballochbuie pine; its marble floor, with pale eight-pointed étoiles contrasted against dark cruciforms, was echoed in its panelled ceiling. The fireplace was flanked by warriors (attributed to *Trotter's* of Edinburgh) bearing an oak mantelshelf, the only known retrieval from the 1834–9 work at the old castle; a new chimneypiece carved with the Royal Arms copied from the Great Seal of Scotland was introduced in 1902–3. Continuing the martial theme, the niche in the N wall contained a bronze statue of Malcolm Canmore by *William Theed*, electrocast by *Elkington & Co.* in 1861.

But, although the principal interiors were distinguished by armorial shields and low-relief sculpture (including another St Hubertus) and had certain Neo-Gothic elements, their general treatment was restrained classical, and indeed bright, airy and colourful, inspired by the 'Deeside Décor' pioneered by Lady Agnes Duff at Corriemulzie (Mar Lodge, q.v.). The Entrance Hall provided a cranked access to the GALLERY – forming the W side of the circuit corridor – so protecting the house from draughts. The Gallery walls were originally marbled (later they were panelled), its ceiling with a pattern of interlocking octagons; it had semi-elliptical arch recesses, mirror-backed, at each far end on its W side for sculpture. It provided access to the public apartments, the Library and Drawing Room, arranged on this W side to enjoy fine outlooks towards the Dee Valley and Lochnagar. Both apartments were entered through doorcases with finely moulded cornices, the DRAWING ROOM's flanked by small round-headed niches. Inside, the Drawing Room had a Neoclassical fireplace in white marble (carved like all the others by *Mr Wright* of John Street, Aberdeen), its ceiling with a shallow cornice and central pendant. Its walls were papered in rich blue with gilt thistle motifs and its carpet was Royal Stewart tartan. This décor extended into the LIBRARY on the S, fitted out with handsome bookcases, its fireplace again in white marble; perhaps surprisingly it also extended to the BILLIARD ROOM – traditionally part of the male domain – at the main block's NW corner, so forming a unified three-room suite.

The Billiard Room could be accessed from the Gallery through an ANTE-ROOM with a lozenge-patterned ceiling which also opened onto the DINING ROOM centred on the N flank. The Dining Room, originally in green with deep red curtains, had a Tudor-Gothic fireplace in Peterhead granite; its E-end sideboard recess was framed by marble pilasters with gilt Composite capitals, and its ceiling had a central roundel. Above the sideboard, a mirror recessed within a four-centred arch surround was answered by another four-centred mirror at the opposite W end: their repeated reflections suggested an endless series of apartments stretching to infinity in either direction. The SERVICE ROOM used as a CHAPEL was lined, sometime after 1878, with Ballochbuie pine; it had a pulpit carved by a local woodworking class, and a stained glass window of an angel (1899) commemorating Marie, Princess of Leiningen.

On the Gallery's E side, a screen of three pointed archways on slim columns with foliate capitals, somewhat German in character, opened onto the marbled MAIN STAIR projecting into the courtyard with a large triple-light on that side, and two smaller lights in the N and S flanks; the stair itself rising in three cantilevered flights to first floor had elegant cast-iron balusters, painted black with gilt detailing. It was convenient not only for the public rooms but also for the VISITORS' APARTMENTS ranged across the S front with outlooks towards Craig Gowan, a MINISTER'S ROOM being provided at the SE corner. LADIES-IN-WAITING and MAIDSERVANTS' ROOMS on the E overlooked the approach drive.

At FIRST FLOOR the CORRIDOR was again marbled, with three similar arches overlooking the stair, its ceiling plain. The QUEEN'S SITTING ROOM was arranged directly above the Drawing Room and was very similar in appearance, although the fireplace was of a different design, its slips and cast-iron register decorated with thistles; this room, too, was carpeted in tartan. The QUEEN'S BEDROOM next to it on the S was very simple, its walls originally papered in dark blue with gold thistles; the DRESSING ROOM beyond with en suite bathroom was still more modest in plain blue, but carpeted in blue Stewart tartan. N of the Sitting Room, the PRINCE CONSORT'S DRESSING ROOM (doubling as his study) was pale green to match its carpet in Hunting Stewart. The PRINCESSES' ROOMS were arranged nearest their mother on the S above the visitors' apartments, and the PRINCES' ROOMS nearest their father on the N, their sitting room with a balcony overlooking the River Dee; rooms were also provided for their tutor and for the artist-in-residence whom Victoria and Albert appointed each year. The SECOND-FLOOR rooms on the S and E were mostly occupied by personal servants.*

The BALLROOM is accessed across the N terrace, twin stairs in timber leading down to the dance floor. Its concept was that of a Tudor great hall (cf. the Banner Hall at Taymouth, Perth & Kinross) and its decoration was largely the work of the theatre designer *Thomas Grieve* in 1857–8. The granite ashlar walls partly timber-lined and once draped with brocade were articulated into five bays by the Tudor-Gothic windows festooned with tartan curtains on the W side; the timber arch braces springing from the side walls supported a shallow-pitched compartmented roof from which hung three magnificent multi-jet gasoliers. On the E side, a Gothic royal alcove with a daïs was framed by slim shafts rising into a four-centred arch. At its lower level the alcove's canted sides were richly traceried with niches, and above it was carved with heraldry, all designed by Grieve with Smith's assistance; from very early on it was fitted with mirrors to reflect light and give it a jewel-like quality. Across the Ballroom's N side ran a balustraded timber balcony. Food was provided from the double-height top-lit kitchen immediately adjacent on the W side of the SERVICE COURT; the kitchen's arrangements were based on those at Windsor Castle, the stewards' room being in the service court's N range and the servants' hall in the S.

The STABLE COURT, COACHHOUSE AND ESTATE OFFICE are 150 m. ENE. Scots Tudor by *William Smith*, 1857. Two storey U-plan, its open end facing W, with a central single-storey range within the court. The W front is symmetrical: the court is entered through three four-centred archways beneath a stepped parapet with clock dial; they are connected by short link bays to two-storey three-bay house blocks advanced at each end, their centres slightly projected under curvilinear gables and with tourelles at the inner angles rising into spike-finialled conical spirelets. The PONY STABLES to the immediate E are by *J. & W. Smith*, 1851, i.e. for the previous castle.

Beyond the stables is a handsome group of copious larders for game, all with their ventilators and pagoda roofs on top. The VENISON LARDER, by *J. & W. Smith*, 1850, is circular with stugged ashlar granite base, harled walls and lintel band course above dressed arrow-slit windows. Antler trophies at intervals between. Timber bracketed overhanging eaves. Adjacent are two timber piend-roofed grouse larders and a rectangular deer larder, later C19.

S of the stables is the IRON BALLROOM, which was erected at Balmoral in October 1851, in time for the gillies' ball, but moved here in 1882 to become a workshop following construction of the present Ballroom at the castle. The prefabricated

---

*A SMOKING ROOM described by the *Building News* as 'commodious and highly finished' was fitted up in 1866.

iron structure, from the Eagle Foundry, Manchester (*E. T. Bellhouse & Co.*) and shown at the Great Exhibition as a warehouse intended for emigrants to Australia and Canada following the Highland Clearances. Cast-iron columnar frame with lotus-leaf capitals infilled with corrugated iron. Decorative bargeboards. This is the earliest remaining corrugated-iron building in Scotland and possibly in Britain.

E of these, KARIM COTTAGE is of 1893, built for Munshi Hafiz, Abdul Karim, Queen Victoria's secretary, and added to in 1899. A simple timber bungalow with overhanging eaves. External shutters provide a nod to the colonial connection.

The POLICIES are an outstanding example of a C19 designed landscape, incorporating formal gardens around the house, picturesque paths along the river and up the hills which are densely populated with memorial cairns and statues, plantations of amenity trees and fine estate buildings. Whatever their function, these last are characterized by a robust if eclectic Tudor style. They feature high-quality granite masonry, crowstepped gables, Tudor arches, hoodmoulds, occasional crenellation, some mullions but also generous Victorian bay sash windows. Minor houses keep the tight Scottish roof, while more prominent houses adopt the Picturesque chalet style, with lower roof pitch and overhanging eaves. The Ordnance Survey map of 1868 shows that the vision of Prince Albert, assisted by *James F. Beattie* and *James Giles*, was swiftly carried out after the purchase of the estate in 1852. Plans for the parterres were drawn up by *J. & W. Smith* and *John Thomas*.

Key to the integrity of the estate was building a new bridge over the River Dee at Invercauld in 1859 (q.v.). This enabled Prince Albert to divert the Old Military Road from the S bank of the river to the N, thus removing traffic from the Balmoral policies. At the same time he obtained an Act of Parliament for *Brunel* to build the bridge across the Dee E of the castle (for which, *see* Crathie), so transporting visitors from the main road directly into the royal domain. The entrance thus created is heralded by an effective but low-key group, beginning with the GATE LODGE, probably by *William Smith*, 1858. Restrained Scottish and Tudor style with crowsteps, corbelled bay window and arcaded loggia with four-centred arches. Opposite is the similar BRIDGE LODGE (originally built as a sanatorium, now police barracks), 1870–1, with later additions. The GATEPIERS with cable mouldings and ball finials are by *William Smith*, 1858, but have wrought-iron, C18-style gates dated 1925, with monograms GVR and MR for King George V and Queen Mary, by the *Waverley Foundry*.

By the bridge is the WAR MEMORIAL for the estate workers. 1922, designed by *William Kelly*, carved by *Sir James Taggart*. Slab with Celtic cross and sword. Swastikas, the Sanskrit sun symbol, on the base.

Flanking the house to W and E are PARTERRES, flush with flowers timed to coincide with the royal season, with further vistas merging into forest and fell. On the W parterre a

FOUNTAIN BASIN of *c.* 1855, and late C19 lifelike STATUE (painted 1929) of a chamois deer on a rocky outcrop, cast by *M. Geiss*, Berlin, who also supplied statuary for Osborne. W is a sunken garden, *c.* 1855, with shell-shaped drinking FOUNTAIN: panelled back and shell pediment. In the E parterre a SCULPTURE of a roe deer, also by *Geiss*, and PUTTO FOUNTAIN, 1859, standing above a large circular granite basin. There were originally two statues of the FLORENTINE BOAR, *c.* 1855, on the W terrace, but now there is only one, placed S of the house.

Away from the house, 200 m. S on lower ground is the SOUTH GARDEN, entered through locally made iron gates, initialled GR MR 1923, in honour of King George V and Queen Mary. It was originally laid out in 1876 as the Outside Flower Garden and many of the garden houses and greenhouses date from this date and later, the area being refashioned by Queen Mary. The Duke of Edinburgh has overseen the development of a water garden near Garden Cottage and shrubberies towards the river.

GARDEN COTTAGE, W of the South Garden in the trees, is by *William Duguid Jun.*, the Ballater builder-architect, 1895. An airy summerhouse built for Queen Victoria's grandchildren, to replace her private retreat of 1863. Single storey with the eaves sweeping down over the surrounding rustic veranda. Barley-sugar chimney cans. Precocious wall construction using shuttered and harled concrete panels.

0.75 km. SE of the house, on the drive towards Easter Balmoral, are the DAIRY and DAIRY COTTAGES. Inspired by the Windsor Castle dairy at Frogmore by John Thomas, 1858, these were completed in 1862–3 by *William Smith*, fulfilling the concept of Prince Albert. The dairy honours milk products with a new level of aesthetic delight, though far simpler and more practical than its Windsor model: there is only one panel of ceramic floral decoration. The cottages flank the dairy itself, which is a two-storey octagon shaded by a Tudor-arched arcade and topped by a ventilator with ogee dome and finial above. Above the tiled floor and milk shelf are stained glass windows of nature's bounty, while timber corbels support an ambitious panelled ceiling with arch braces and pendants.

Further S is BAILE-NA-COILLE, the house begun for Queen Victoria's servant John Brown but incomplete at his death in 1883. Probably designed by *Smith*, in 1877, but added to by *Sir Robert Rowand Anderson*, 1904–5, and further altered in 1923–4. Gabled, two-storeyed, of rectangular plan with projecting service wings to rear. The busy façades are articulated by rock-faced quoins, a bold string course between the floors, and corbelled chimney-breasts. The Germanic roof has overhanging eaves enhanced by pendant finialled timber brackets and scroll-flanked kingposts to broader gables, while there are cusped bargeboards to the swept dormerheads. Handsome porch with pointed-arch doorway and cast-iron brattishing above corniced parapet. Behind the house is the bronze STATUE of John Brown, kilted with cap in hand, by *Sir*

J. E. Boehm, 1883. Commissioned by Queen Victoria to her 'Friend more than Servant, Loyal, Truthful, Brave, Selfless than Duty even to the Grave'. Originally sited near the Queen's Garden Cottage, her descendants removed it to this less-prominent position.

Throughout the policies are drystone MEMORIAL CAIRNS, usually conical. Many are clustered around Craig Gowan and commemorate the marriages of Queen Victoria's children. The first to be joyfully erected was the PURCHASE CAIRN, 0.7 km. S of the house, to celebrate the acquisition of the estate in 1852. All the family and guests laid stones, accompanied by piping, reels and whisky. The cairn-building tradition lapsed until a new one was created for Queen Elizabeth's diamond jubilee in 2012, gifted by the estate employees.

PRINCE ALBERT'S MEMORIAL CAIRN, Creag an Lurachain, 1.7 km. S. Conspicuous from a great distance, this simple yet eloquent pyramid of dressed granite is inscribed '21st August 1862. To the Beloved Memory of Prince Albert, the Great and Good Prince Consort, Erected by his Broken-hearted Widow, VICTORIA. R.' Prince Albert had died suddenly of typhoid at Windsor Castle in December 1861.

ALBERT MEMORIAL OBELISK, 200 m. E of the dairy. 1862. Granite obelisk sited on raised ground, on stepped dais and square, ashlar pedestal with billetted cornice crowned by Greek block pediment and acroteria to each face, designed by *John Beaton*, the Balmoral clerk-of-works. Presented by the estate tenants as 'humble tribute to the affection of their beloved master'. It is a partner to the QUEEN VICTORIA MEMORIAL OBELISK, 250 m. NNW near the Gate Lodge, likewise erected by the tenants in 1901. Nearby in the rocky woods are STATUES of the royal couple. The bronze of Prince Albert (cast by Elkingtons) is by *William Theed*, 1867, based on a marble statue of the Prince in the Castle, made in 1862. Theed made Prince Albert's death mask in 1861. Here he stands with kilt and plaid, hands on hound and rifle. Queen Victoria's statue is by *Boehm*, sculptor-in-ordinary to the Queen, presented by her tenants in 1887, in honour of her golden jubilee. Bronze, in Tudor-style costume, holding orb and sceptre.

DRINKING FOUNTAIN, by the golf course. A memorial to Edward VII, by *Mr Taggart* (i.e. *James Taggart*), 1911. Handsome granite fountain with fluted bowl, flanked by curved benches inscribed ER 1901 and 1910.

BALNACRAIG HOUSE
2.75 km. ENE of Birse Parish Church

5090

Built 1673 by either the Chalmers or the Davidsons, and thus the earliest datable example of the first generation of Aberdeenshire country houses. The arrangement of the house's main block with near-symmetrical flanking wings enclosing a forecourt (as formerly at Aswanley and Fetternear, qq.v.) seems to have been original and follows central and southern Scottish patterns; forecourts with a single W wing as protection from the prevailing wind were more usual in late C17 and early C18 Aberdeenshire. A major reordering of the main block for the Innes family took place in 1735 and enlargement of the wings in the late C18 and c. 1900; the house was restored in 2002–3 and again by *Laing Traditional Masonry* in 2014.

The house's main block, in common with other early examples of this type, is a simple rectangle. The entrance front facing S is two-storeyed and five bays broad in harled pinned rubble. Its central moulded doorway with carved lintel is inscribed I.I. (James Innes) I.H.S. (Iesus Hominem Salvator) C.G. (Catherine Gordon) 1735; the windows are deeply recessed in chamfered surrounds. The wall-head is kept low, just above the first-floor windows; the skewputts are moulded and the end stacks deeply coped. The central bay breaks through the wall-head into a steeply raked attic chimney gable, its window with a bowtell-profiled arched lintel; this gable is apparently part of the 1735 works and characteristic of the mid C18 (cf. Bellabeg House, Strathdon, p. 739). The rear (N) elevation is almost blind, and the end gables have pairs of blocked attic windows with sills at floor level.

Inside, the central stair is flanked by square rooms, one to each side at ground floor and first floor. Examination by Thomas Addyman has revealed how such early houses were once furnished. Five fireplaces were found of which three were bolection-moulded, one of these being marbled; the first-floor rooms have box beds and plain plastered panels within wooden framing, probably of 1735 and intended for fabric hangings. The present timber panelling and stair are excellent modern work.

The W WING was originally a separate structure, but remodelled and deepened on plan in the late C18. It is a rubble-built single storey with a tall dormer-less attic, pronounced skews and coped stacks. It contains a large kitchen hearth in its S gable. The E WING was similarly reconstructed in single-storey and dormer-less attic form and was restored to its late C18 profile in 2014. Its N gable has a projecting brick chimney-breast flanked by two pointed windows, opened up when a private Catholic chapel was formed by the Innes family; its birdcage bellcote is now at the nearby early C19 CATTLE COURT.

On the W side of the S approach there was once a FORMAL GARDEN with a screen of timber railings between monolith piers with ball finials, an arrangement reminiscent of that at Gallery (Angus). The piers survive but the woodwork was lost by the mid C20. GATEPIERS. Square-plan, V-jointed with ball finials, probably once on the axial approach to the house.

BANCHORY

Deeside's largest town but that only proves how modest are the settlements along the river. Indeed much of the size is entirely due to the second half of the C20 and it was a rural village until the railway in 1853 brought the prospect of tourism and realized its potential as a place of resort for summer visitors. Burgh status came in 1885. The old kirkton by the parish church (dedicated to St Ternan, from whom the parish takes its full name, Banchory-Ternan) lies at the E of the modern town by the river but once the old road along the Dee had been turnpiked and moved to higher ground (now the A93) in 1802, a new settlement (also known as Arbeadie) grew up and from 1805 the present heart of the town formed around the junction of the High Street and the road S to the Bridge of Dee.

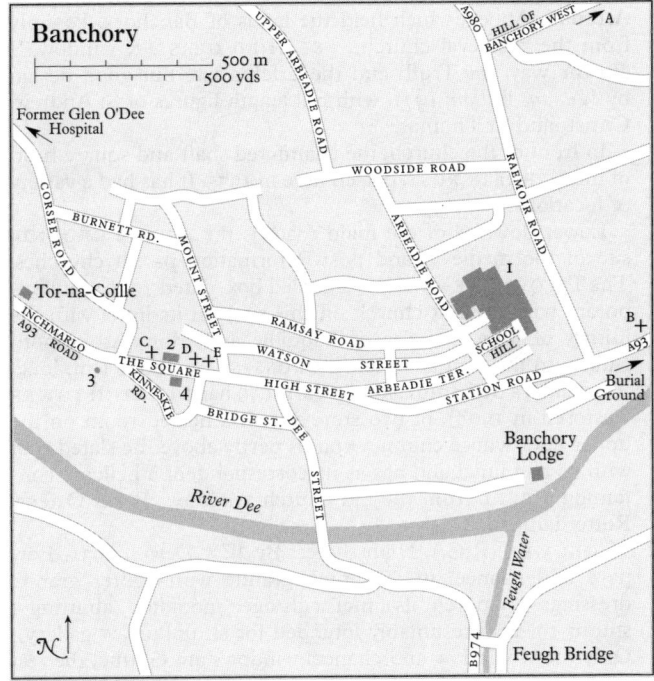

A	Christian Fellowship Church	1	Banchory Academy
B	East Parish Church	2	Burgh Offices and
C	St Columba (R.C.)		War Memorial
D	St Ternan (Episcopal)	3	Gordon Highlanders Memorial
E	West Parish Church	4	Town Hall

CHURCHES

CHRISTIAN FELLOWSHIP CHURCH, Burn of Bennie, 2.5 km.
NE of the town centre. 2010 by *Davis Duncan Architects*
(Director in charge *Ray Davis*; Project Architect *Michelle
Farrell*). Two admirably simple gabled units for church and
smaller hall with a low link between. Larch cladding and
render.

EAST PARISH CHURCH, Station Road. 1824–5 by *John Smith*,
succeeding the previous parish church but on a new site. A
pleasing design in a still-Georgian Gothic, rectangular with a
pinnacled tower over the S porch. The sliding sash windows
have pointed arches and their original tracery except those on
the S side, which are blocked. In 1929–30 *George Bennett
Mitchell* added the chancel with trigonal apse to the N end, with
Perp windows, flanked by a vestry and choir room. Inside,
Mitchell removed all but the S gallery. In the apse E wall, the
ORGAN, with good case, made by *Wadsworth*, 1932. In the
vestibule, a rough granite FONT carved with the arms of
Arbroath Abbey, which held the lands of Banchory. Possibly
from the medieval church. – STAINED GLASS. N window, 'I
am the Way, the Truth and the Life', a late but good design
by *William Wilson*, 1971, with full length figures of St Andrew,
Christ, and St Thomas.

In front of the church, the chamfered shaft and square head
of the MARKET CROSS, placed here in 1975. It has had a variety
of locations.

Lower down, S of the main road, is the BURIAL GROUND,
site of the medieval and post-Reformation parish churches.
The TILQUILLIE VAULT is a gabled box, dated 1775 (contemporary with the last church on this site) on its lintel with the
initials of John Douglas of Tilquillie and Mary Arbuthnott.
Built into the wall is a Pictish CROSS-SLAB, about 1 m. long.
Alongside, a delightful circular early C19 harled WATCH TOWER
(restored in 1998), of two storeys with a heated room on the
upper floor whose chimney stands pertly above the slated roof
with its ball finial and has as its correspondent a bellcote containing a BELL from the old church made by '*Petrus* Ostens,
Rotterdam, 1664'.

ST COLUMBA (R.C.), High Street. By *W.J. Devlin*, 1931. Low
nave and chancel in one, pink granite with lighter granite
dressings. SW porch, its lintel with ogee moulding, abutting a
stubby tower (presumably intended for an unbuilt W gallery).
Only the W window and chancel windows are Gothic, the rest
round-arched. – Monolithic granite ALTAR and other fittings
of 1978.

ST TERNAN (Episcopal), High Street. By *William Ramage*,
1850–1, and largely paid for by John Michell, the English
owner of Glassel House (q.v.). Tiny and simple with steep
roofs over the nave and lower chancel, narrow lancets only and
a small W bellcote above a buttress. Vestry and hall added 1904

on the N side. Good roofs inside with prominent saltire-bracing and chancel arch with C13 mouldings. SEDILIA in the chancel. – FONT. Caen stone, nicely carved foliage in the panels of its sides. – Brass eagle LECTERN by *Hart, Son, Peard & Co.*, 1894. – ORGAN by *Wadsworth*, 1904. – STAINED GLASS. E lancets *c.* 1934, signed by *Shrigley & Hunt*. Central light after Holman Hunt's Light of the World, with the Good Shepherd (l.) and Good Samaritan (r.). Chancel S, St Michael by the *Abbey Studio, c.* 1945. – Nave S wall. St Michael and St George, 1909 by *A. K. Nicholson*; an excellent figure of David with strong but subtle colouring as a war memorial to a son of the Innes family of Raemoir (†1915) by *Douglas Strachan*; and St James Major again by *A. K. Nicholson* but *c.* 1928. – Nave N wall: St Margaret and St Francis of 1952, again by the *Abbey Studio*, with their mitre monogram. Also St Ternan, unsigned.

WEST PARISH CHURCH, High Street. The former Free Church by *James Souttar*, 1879–80, and a landmark of the town by virtue of its magnificent tall SE tower topped by battlemented clock stage with gargoyles and short splay-footed spire. The church itself is an uncomplicated gabled pink granite box with to the High Street an austere window of stepped lancets and below this a row of tiny lancets, expressing the position of the gallery within. – ORGAN. N wall. 1924, by *Ingram & Co.* – Good carved oak COMMUNION TABLE and CHAIRS of 1920 (war memorial). – SCULPTURE. By the porch. The Good Shepherd by *George Cruickshank*, 1970.

PUBLIC BUILDINGS

BANCHORY ACADEMY, School Hill. At the heart is the former Central School with three fingers of classrooms jutting forward under strict gables. The middle finger with a bellcote and the spine range is of 1877–8 by *James Thomson*; the flanking wings, the E and W extensions with shaped gables and the enlargement of the main range N are of 1912 by *Wilsons & Walker*. Substantial post-war and later additions between Arbeadie Road and Raemoir Road.

BURGH OFFICES, The Square, High Street. Built as a school in 1838, succeeding one of 1750 and endowed by Lady Burnett of Leys. Simple Tudor style with a bellcote on the gable to the l. over the entrance. Converted 1911. In front, the WAR MEMORIAL by *William Kelly* (of *Kelly & Nicol*), 1923. Polished granite rocket with open spire. Finely lettered.

GORDON HIGHLANDERS (VII BATTALION) MEMORIAL, Inchmarlo Road. 1920 by *William Kelly* (of *Kelly & Nicol*). A handsome stripped classical exedra in silvery granite inscribed with the names of First World War battles and a central ceno-taph bearing the Gordon motto.

TOWN HALL, High Street. 1872–3 by *James Thomson* of Crathes. Rather lifeless.

DESCRIPTION

At the centre of HIGH STREET at the corner with Mount Street is the BURNETT ARMS HOTEL of *c.* 1830, all white with granite margins, lying-pane glazing and slate roofs with deep eaves on brackets. The main part is of five bays with the eaves of the roof forming a central pediment above the centre three and with an Ionic porch. The eaves also oversail on the side elevation and it must have looked like a comfortable villa originally. Large coat of arms in the centre, of the Duchess of Kent and Strathearn, mother of Queen Victoria, whose summer residence was Abergeldie Castle (q.v.) from *c.* 1850. Projecting forward to the r. two late C19 wings, the larger one with half-timbered gable but also a stylish granite ashlar turret above the corner entrance to the bar lounge, ending in an octagonal top stage with an ogee cupola and thistle finial. It was built after 1908 and is distinctly Glasgow in style. Possibly by *Brown & Watt*, the motif of strips of stone around the windows is similar to their Central Bakery, George Street, Aberdeen, and the firm worked for the Burnetts at Crathes. Probably of the same time the charming wrought-iron hotel sign with the Burnett horn. The rest of High Street is in a much lower key, except for the former POST OFFICE (s side, now Cook and Dine) of 1909–10 by *Sutherland & George*, with moulded surrounds and triple keystones and canted bays in the upper floor continued as attic dormers; the CHEMIST'S (No. 67) is the outstanding item, still with its mortar and pestle sign. Roughly opposite, turning its façade towards the river, is BELLFIELD (retirement home), a villa of *c.* 1900 in red granite, mildly Baronial, with a spired tower.

s of High Street is the interesting enclave of SCOTT SKINNER SQUARE by *James Hammond*, 1993, for mixed residential and commercial use but also including the town library and museum. The style is a coarse Postmodern Scots vernacular, with gables, harled walls, arcading along the street and boxy oriels.

High Street continues E as STATION ROAD; further out No. 45 (now Aberdeenshire Council Social Work offices) is a grand former BANK (probably the Town & County Bank of 1902 by *R. G. Wilson*) executed in Aberdeen bond in a refined Baroque style, with the shallow roofs projecting deeply on brackets.

0.3 km. E, in the area of the old kirkton and on the s side of the road, is CELTIC CROSS HOUSE, the former PARISH MANSE of 1793, a formulaic three-bay and two-storey house but with an emphatic single-storey addition along the s front, probably *c.* 1830. Set into the wall facing Station Road a Pictish CROSS-HEAD, discovered in the churchyard. Opposite the church the school (now offices) of *c.* 1854.

The streets climbing in parallel lines above the town centre begin with ARBEADIE TERRACE, close to the junction of High Street and Dee Street, with a former CHURCH HALL making a big display of lancets and wheel window in the front gable.

In spite of the style it is of 1904. Nicely converted to housing by *James Hammond* of Banchory, 1994. There are a number of villas in the streets ranged along the hillside to the N in an area otherwise extensively built up in the earlier and mid C20. Above High Street, reached from WATSON STREET above, CASTLE AIRY is a tall but shallow early C19 three-bay house, plain and straightforward but with panache in the wall-head dormers which are gently bowed and set on curved sills. There are larger Victorian villas in the streets to the N but the best are to the w in CORSEE ROAD, which climbs gently uphill from High Street, and here the houses take advantage of the position for the views across the Dee valley. They have large plots secluded by fir trees, although the C20 has seen much new building in their grounds: WYNNDUN, set back at the first bend in the road, is later C19 and in the manner which one is tempted to call Deeside Picturesque. Harled walls, asymmetrical front with a gabled bow to the front and a square tower with cone roof that has a timber platform for taking the view. Balustrade of saltire bracing. Uphill to the w, first DRUIMDARROCH of *c.* 1890–1900 in a Baronial style, which was occupied by Dr David Lawson, founder of the Nordrach-on-Dee Sanatorium (*see* below). Large round tower on the garden front where the ground descends downhill and another containing the main entrance which seems to be part of additions made by *George Bennett Mitchell c.* 1910–21. In the garden a picturesque timber summerhouse. Its neighbour, BALNACRAIG of 1887, has a stout castellated tower above the porch; nice entrance gate.

Much of the top of the town is a mid-C20 and later story of development for council housing but in WOODSIDE ROAD is ELIZABETH COTTAGE, a late C19 timber-framed bungalow clad in corrugated iron with frilly bargeboards and an uncommonly pretty veranda along the front. Just two rooms l. and r. of the porch and hall and kitchen wing at rear. Of special interest is that it was clearly designed to be let out by its owner during the summer; a room for her with its own fireplace for cooking and (formerly) with its own entrance from the rear is built in the angle with the rear wing. Nicely handled two-storey addition clad in red cedar shingles, 2008.

DEE STREET runs S from High Street to the river. It is disappointing and disfigured by the incoherent development of a car park and leisure buildings on the E side. The KING GEORGE V MEMORIAL PARK was formed from the policies of BANCHORY LODGE, off Dee Street's E side by the river. Begun in the early C19 by Lt-Gen. William Burnett, the unmarried youngest son of Sir Thomas Burnett of Leys, but incorporating an early C18 inn that stood on the old Deeside road. Harled white walls with grey granite margins, of two storeys above a deeply sunk basement. Five-bay w front with a two-storey canted bay in the middle for the door, whose pedimented surround is made up from miscellaneous granite pieces but has its original fanlight. In the middle of the S front,

overlooking the river, an elegant full-height bow. Now a hotel
with additions to the N of 1980 by *Jane Durham* with polygonal
tower in the angle. The entrance hall has an apsidal end within
the canted bay and some good plasterwork. The doors to the
rooms N and S have elegant Regency woodwork with reeded
pilasters with Tower of Winds capitals and lions masks at the
corners.

s of the entrance to Banchory Lodge, BRIDGE OF DEE was
built in 1798, its construction encouraging the development of
the new town. It originally had a timber central span between
the outer granite arches but the wooden section was replaced
in cast iron after the floods of 1829 and further remade in the
C20 before its present reconstruction and widening in reinforced concrete in 1983–5. Immediately s of the bridge on the
W side are the former BLACKHALL CASTLE GATES, a single
arch beneath a crenellated parapet flanked incongruously by
screens of classical columns. The arch once carried a large
statue of a goat (symbol of the Russells of Blackhall) and the
screen terminated in square lodges with lancet windows but
its extent was radically curtailed in 1945 when the Baronial-
style lodge was added by *Walker & Duncan*; this now has a
small Modernist addition of 2012 by *Fiddes Architects*. The
castle, which stood about 2.8 km. WNW, was in its final iteration of 1884 by *Charles Brand* but was demolished in 1949.

0.5 km. SE of the castle gates is the BRIDGE OF FEUGH,
built in 1790 by the Russells to span a turbulent rocky passage
of the Water of Feugh running N into the Dee. Three round
arches, the widest over the centre, with V-shaped cutwaters
carried up as refuges. Aligned to the W a TOLL HOUSE with
the familiar canted-bay projection to the road. Between the W
bank of the Feugh and the s bank of the Dee is RIVERSTONES
(at the time of writing in a state of neglect). Fine s front of
c. 1800 with a recessed centre and two-storey canted bays with
piended roofs l. and r. But the core is earlier and appears to
have begun as a U-plan house facing N to the Dee; Jane Geddes
notes the thick walls of the E wing, which has a vaulted ground
floor, as evidence of probable C17 origin and this was no doubt
always a good strategic site for a house.

TOR-NA-COILLE (Hotel), off Inchmarlo Road, 0.8 km. WNW
of the centre in woods. A considerable villa of 1873 in a slightly
French style, with walls of coursed rock-faced granite blocks,
mansard roof and originally iron crestings. Two large canted
bays on the side elevations and encompassing the square front
a cast-iron veranda with balcony over. Large service wing.
Conversion to a hotel *c.* 1905–6 seems a natural role for it.

Former GLEN O' DEE HOSPITAL, Corsee Road, 1 km. NW. Now
disused and deplorably neglected. This was the Nordrach-on-
Dee tuberculosis sanatorium, designed by *George Coutts*,
1900–1, for Dr David Lawson on the model of the pioneering
establishment of 1888 at Nordrach, Bavaria. The elevated site

among pinewoods on the Crathes estate was considered exceptionally beneficial to patients. It is stupendously long, of three storeys and of distinctly Germanic character, with a granite base, timber-clad walls and detached half-timbering in the gables. At the centre of the s front a mighty ashlar entrance tower with machicolated top for the water tank under an elegant saddle-backed roof. The end pavilions (partly added later) have canted bays framing sun balconies. There was also a veranda stretching the length of the façade. Pretty glazing patterns of small panes in the top lights. Stairs and corridors were placed on the N side so that the wards could face s for sunlight and fresh air. Dining room to E and recreation blocks extending downhill to s. Former kitchen range also to the E. The sanatorium became the Glen o' Dee Hotel in 1934 and a hospital in 1945. Closed 1990. The present hospital lies behind and is nothing remarkable.

(BIRKWOOD HOUSE, 1.5 km. NE of the Bridge of Feugh, on the s bank of the Dee. An early C19 fishing lodge orné with exquisite veranda of cast-iron lattice uprights and tent roof. Sensitively extended 2005 by *Gary Grant*.)

(CAIRNTON HOUSE, 4.75 km. w, close to the Dee. A substantial fishing lodge of 1921 for Arthur H. Wood (of Glassel House, q.v.), who pioneered the greased (i.e. floating) line technique for salmon fishing. Modest Arts and Crafts style with gables. Wood designed the handsomely appointed timber-clad and timber-lined FISHING HUTS and ROD ROOM.)

CLUNY CRICHTON CASTLE, 4 km. NNW by Cluny-Crichton Farm. A ruinous small L-plan tower house, dated 1666 over the door, with a square tower in the angle between the two parts. Built by George Crichton of Cluny and his wife, Jean, daughter of Robert Douglas of Tilquhillie. Originally of three storeys but only the tower remains to its full height. It is thought to be the last tower house built anew in Scotland.

KNAPPACH HOUSE, 3 km. ESE. Built c. 1840. On the E front a two-storey central bow but also square towers with piend roofs at the ends. Extended 1999 in matching fashion.

MILL OF HIRN, 5 km. NE. An eye-catching C19 group comprising the miller's house, granite-walled in Aberdeen bond, with a decorative pattern of saltire-bracing below the eaves and trussed gable-ends, and the mill itself with crowstepped gables and the kiln poking up at the w end. Now residential, with recording studio in the mill.

BURNETT'S TOWER, Scolty Hill, 2.5 km. SW. A landmark in views from the town. Erected 1842 by the tenants of Lt-Gen. William Burnett of Banchory Lodge (†1839). Circular, nearly 15 m. high. The spiral stair inside is a reinstatement of 1992.

THE NINE STANES, Mulloch Wood, 5.25 km. SE. A Recumbent Stone Circle. When the site was excavated in 1904, a central ring cairn with cremation deposits was found. (GN)

GLASSEL HOUSE. *See* p. 505.

INCHMARLO. *See* p. 546.

INVERY HOUSE. *See* p. 568.

RAEMOIR HOUSE. *See* p. 704.
TILQUHILLIE CASTLE. *See* p. 751.

BANCHORY-DEVENICK

A scattered settlement s of the Dee and remarkably rural given
the presence of the suburbs of Aberdeen less than a kilometre
away to N and E.

ST DEVENICK'S OLD PARISH CHURCH. Site of an early
church, just beside the bank of the Dee and dedicated to a
follower of Columba. In its present form of 1821–2 by *John
Lyon*, a wright of Holburn, Aberdeen. Simple gabled box with
W bellcote and pretty Gothic windows of intersecting timber
tracery. The E window in this style is of 1929–30 by *A. Marshall
Mackenzie & Son*, who removed the galleries and moved the
pulpit and organ from the s to the E wall. Contemporary N
vestry and the shallow vaulted ceiling with ribs.
  s of the church a C19 WATCH HOUSE and to its W a cast-iron
MORT SAFE, early C19, for placing over coffins to secure them
from bodysnatchers.
  MANSEFIELD HOUSE, 0.2 km. W, is the former parish
manse, by *J. & W. Smith*, 1847. Restrained Italianate in white
render with granite margins. Impressive W front with two-
storey projecting wings with pedimental gables embracing a
granite porch. By the entrance, former OFFICES by *William
Smith*, 1874–5.
Former FREE CHURCH (St Devenick's-on-the-Hill), 1 km. SSE.
1843–4 by *Cousin & Gale* and not attractive. Converted to flats,
1989. – In the burial ground a MAUSOLEUM 'erected by David
Stewart of Banchory-Devenick and Leggart 1895' according to
the finely lettered frieze. Stewart was owner of the Comb
Works on Hutcheon Street, Aberdeen. Stone slab roof with
dormers and cross finial. Over the Tudor-arched entrance a
fine bronze of the pelican in her piety.
  The former MANSE (Gregellen House), 0.25 km. NE of the
church, is by *John Henderson*, 1844.
BANCHORY HOUSE (Beannachar Camphill Community),
0.9 km. E. Built in 1839–40 by *John Smith* for Alexander
Thomson, gentleman polymath and collector, whose library
was donated to the Free Church College in Aberdeen and is
now at the University. The mansion is on the site of an earlier
house, whose datestone of 1621 is incorporated. It became a
residential Rudolph Steiner training centre for young adults in
1978.
  Jacobean-style elevations, with on the entrance (s) front to
the r. two gabled bays of two-storeys and a porch in the centre,
adjoining a lower wing to the l., with a variety of shaped and
straight gables, quite lively in their treatment. This lower range

fronts the w service wing. The principal rooms are in the e and n ranges and at the ne corner is a remarkable octagonal tower with a balustrade lookout platform at the top. On the n and w fronts also nice turrets with cone roofs. At the se angle a late c20 conservatory, replacing a Victorian predecessor. All of the best interiors were destroyed by fire in 1981.

Of the buildings added for the community the following are of note: ROSE HOUSE of 1994 has a butterfly plan, with curved roof-lines and shallow bow and chimneys slightly projecting from the harled wall face; PADDOCK HOUSE, 2008–9, also has two low wings for community hall and games room, of straw-bale construction, under low curved sedum roofs with timber and glass link between. Both are by *Camphill Architects*, and the avoidance of straight lines inside and out is something very characteristic of the organic anthroposophical architecture in the Steiner communities.

Within the WALLED GARDEN (1853) are re-set several PICTISH STONES brought from Dunnicaer (a site on the coast near Stonehaven) with double-disc, symbols, Z-rods, a fish, etc. OBELISK, 0.4 km. ESE, on Tollohill, with outstanding prospects of Aberdeen. Erected in memory of the Prince Consort's visit, 1859.

ARDOE HOUSE. *See* p. 328.

BELDORNEY CASTLE

4030

2.3 km. s of Glass

Standing on a rise of ground above the River Deveron, a Z-plan tower house built by George Gordon, 1st Laird of Beldorney, probably in the late 1550s. Originally it may have resembled the Old House of Carnousie (N) built *c.* 1577 by the Ogilvies, to whom the Gordons of Beldorney were related by marriage, but its earlier date is reflected in its much smaller entrance jamb. Its forecourt on the w dates from *c.* 1679, and further alterations were probably made *c.* 1715–30 after the estate was acquired by Alexander Gordon of Tirriesoule. A long two-storey wing on the forecourt's N side was remodelled in the early c19, then again by *A. Marshall Mackenzie* (of *Matthews & Mackenzie*) in the 1890s. Beldorney was restored twice in the later c20, first in the 1960s and then by *Ian Begg* in 1982–8 with *Alistair Urquhart* as master mason.

(The TOWER HOUSE comprises a rectangular main block of three storeys, 13 m. long N–S and 7.5 m. broad, with a round tower 6.5 m. in diameter embedded in its se corner and a 3.5 m. square tower attached to the NW corner at a slight angle. The latter contained the original entrance and a wheel stair 2.5 m. in diameter. This distinctive Z-plan reflects the influence of the 'New Warke' at Huntly Castle (q.v.) remodelled by George

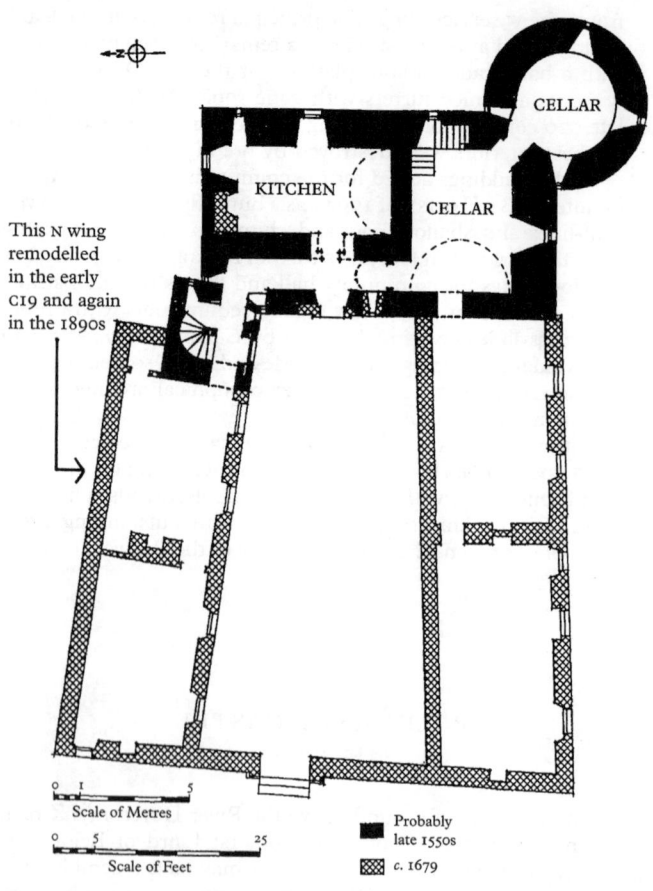

This N wing
remodelled
in the early
C19 and again
in the 1890s

KITCHEN

CELLAR

CELLAR

0   1   5
Scale of Metres

0   5   25
Scale of Feet

Probably
late 1550s

c. 1679

Beldorney Castle.
Ground-floor plan

Gordon, 4th Earl of Huntly, in 1551–4, and soon to be repeated
at Terpersie (q.v.), another Gordon tower house of 1561,
where both towers are circular.

The appearance of Beldorney has been significantly altered
since the mid C16. The original doorway (now a window) in
the square tower's S flank is set within a finely moulded architrave in red freestone and protected by shot-holes, one within
the tower itself and one in the main block's W flank. Above its
lintel are two empty field-panels. Other than this doorway the
ground floor of the castle was once almost blind, lit only by
very small windows; the doorways in the main block's E and W
flanks are both later. The first-floor windows have been
enlarged, either in the late C17 or early C18; the much smaller
second-floor windows may formerly have broken through the
wall-head as dormers. The gable skews have been remodelled

but the main block's roof appears original; if it is, Beldorney is a very early example of a tower house built without wall-head parapets. The NE skewputt is carved with a scallop shell.

The square tower rises into a gable with a sculpted dog finial. In its N re-entrant angle there is a quarter-drum stair-turret and a gargoyle for a water chute. The round tower is defended by gunloops at ground-floor level. String courses encircle its second and attic floors, where small lights break through the wall-head under catslide roof dormers. Above the wall-head the round tower rises into a broad gable chimneystack; its roof has clearly been altered and may once have been crowned by a conical roof rather than the present ridge roof. Within the angle between the round tower and main block on the S side, a stair-turret rises from first floor over corbelling with a grotesque mask as a label stop. The turret, which has itself been altered, bears a shield charged with the 1st Laird's arms and initials.

The present doorway in the main block's W flank, set in a red freestone surround carved with rosettes in its lugs, dates from c. 1679 when the forecourt itself was formed. Next to this doorway is a re-set Gothic window, and above it a former sacrament house, its ogee top carved with a winged angel's head, mantling with fleur-de-lys, and a string course with tablet flowers; the fleur-de-lys are repeated on either side of a thistle at its base. It probably derives from the Pre-Reformation St Walloch's Kirk which stood NE on the Deveron and as such is an expression of the Gordons' continuing loyalty to Catholicism during the most difficult of times. The division of the great hall and insertion of a new fireplace in the late C17 or early C18 resulted in window alterations, the flue rising into a wall-head chimney gable on the W side. It has an attic oculus and a fleur-de-lys carved on one of the skewputts.

On PLAN the square tower's original doorway once opened onto the still-extant wheel stair which rises directly to the great hall. At ground floor the main block contains a kitchen and cellar, both accessed off a passage, with another cellar in the round tower. All the ground-floor rooms are vaulted: the kitchen vault frames the segmentally arched hearth at the N end. Food was carried up the wheel stair to the 'low' end of the great hall, but a second intramural stair rises from the cellars and opens out at the 'high' end. In the hall's NE corner was a closet and possibly a garderobe. The great hall's division into two apartments in the late C17 or early C18 was reversed during *Ian Begg*'s restoration, although the panelling and the bolection-moulded stone fireplace* installed at that time were retained. The original position of the fireplace is no longer clear. Panelling also survives in the round tower, formerly the laird's private chamber.

Both the wheel stair and the turret stair rise to the second floor; the wheel stair may originally have risen to first floor

---

*This was slightly reduced in width in the C19.

only, but the quarter-drum stair-turret in its re-entrant angle indicates that its present form is C17 at the latest. It leads to a small chamber over the main stair within the square tower.* The main block's second floor may once have been a single space open to the rafters before the attic floor was formed; it had fireplaces at either end.

The semi-formal FORECOURT comprises a two-storey N range, its upper floor originally containing three family apartments, while its (altered) ground floor was devoted to services, as was the low single-storey S range, which contained a new kitchen. The forecourt is entered through a handsome Renaissance GATEWAY with its round-headed arch framed between plain pilasters which support a pulvinated frieze and cornice: these in turn support a pediment with finials. The keystone is dated 1679 and initialled A.G. I.G. for John Gordon, 5th Laird of Beldorney, and his wife, Anne. Since the N range follows the line of the old house's square tower, which stands at a slight angle to the main block, the forecourt itself is not quite rectangular on plan. The modest two-storey N WING at right angles to it is probably C17 or C18, remodelled in the early C19 and then by *A. Marshall Mackenzie* during the 1890s. STABLES by *R. Duncan* of Huntly, 1889.)

BENHOLM

Good example of a kirkton, nestled between two burns in a woodland setting. Benholm is first documented in the late C12 and has managed to retain most of its quiet charm.

Former PARISH CHURCH. Built in 1832, and a late instance of the usual Georgian box. Closed 2004 and now cared for by the Scottish Redundant Churches Trust. It is plain and harled, the S flank with four tall arched windows, the N side blank. Simple pediments on the gables. The present building replaced a much-altered church on the same site, consecrated in 1242 by Bishop David de Bernham.[†] Interior with original layout and pulpit in the centre of the long side. – Five-sided GALLERY with LAIRD'S BOX marked by little fretwork screens. – SACRAMENT HOUSE, re-set in the E wall, from the earlier church. Late C15 or early C16. Pointed, roll-moulded locker with thistle keystone and stylized crocket pilasters. Interior carved with a winged soul, crossbones, hourglass and the initials D.L. and I.R. (for David Lundie of Benholm Castle and unknown wife; *see* below).

---

*Harry Gordon Slade in *PSAS*, 105, 1972–4 suggests that there were once two chambers occupying the upper storeys of this tower, the lower one of which was destroyed during alterations in the C19 when the wheel stair was extended up to second floor.
[†]The new church was built on an arched platform so as not to disturb the graves below the floor of its predecessor.

On the s wall are re-set a pair of superb MEMORIALS from
the previous chancel. – The MONUMENT to the five-year-old   24
Lady Mary Keith, †1620, daughter of George Keith, 5th Earl
Marischal, and his wife, Countess Margaret Ogilvy, dates from
1621. It is carved in four tiers in the most primitive and splendid Jacobean way. On the bottom, a triple arcade with skeleton
piercing the hearts of the Earl and his wife with long spears.
The former holds a sword and a huge gun; the latter has out-
landishly long, pretzel-like arms and a massive headdress.
Heraldry above with a 'woodwose' (wild man holding a staff).
Latin inscription above it ('That I may live with Christ makes
it sweet for me to die') and triangular pediment with monograms and angels. – In complete contrast is the shimmering
marble TABLET to Robert Scott of Benholm, †1690, a rare   25
Scottish example of local carvers following contemporary
London fashions. Its design copies that in an engraving in
Robert Pricke's *The Ornaments of Architecture* (1674), itself a
reversed version of an engraving in *Les Epitaphes Inventes par
N Blasset d'Amiens*, i.e. the sculptor Nicolas Blasset (1600–
59).* Cartouche on the apron; putti flanking a Latin inscription and then a broken segmental pediment with reclining
angels.

The former MANSE, to the SE, was built 1826. Harled two
storeys and three bays with a piended roof; full-height, rectangular bay window on the l. added in the late C19. Very long
double-walled garden to the s with ice chamber in the outer
w wall. To the rear of the house, a slender circular fruit store,
late C19, topped by a tall witch's-hat roof. Stable block beyond
of *c.* 1791, given a big Tudor arch for the gig house in the late
C19.

The hamlet is entered via the large BRIDGE over the Castle Burn
with datestone of 1774. Imposing semicircular arch (*c.* 12.2 m.
high and 4.9 m. wide) with long approaches on either side.

BENHOLM CASTLE
1.2 km. N

Built in three principal campaigns, and sited on a strategic peninsula that once held commanding views of the countryside. Sir
John Lundie and his wife, Isabel Forrester, began a tower house
on the site *c.* 1475. This passed to the Keiths Marischal at the
start of the C17,† and *c.* 1660 the estate was purchased by the
Scott family. They added a Georgian mansion *c.* 1760, which was
originally free-standing and set off to the s of the tower. Tower
and house were then linked by a rear extension *c.* 1790. The
buildings were dilapidated after *c.* 1940 but have been beautifully
restored since 1990. In 1992 half of the tower house disastrously
collapsed, and this counts as one of the greatest architectural
losses in Kincardineshire.

*This information was kindly supplied by Geoffrey Fisher.
† *See also* Benholm's Lodging in Aberdeen, built by Sir Robert Keith of Benholm
c. 1613 (p. 203).

Benholm Castle.
Engraving by D. MacGibbon & T. Ross, 1887

The Georgian MANSION faces s, as built by David Scott and his
wife, Margaret Brown. Fine courses of cherry-cocked ashlar,
everything trim and austerely elegant. Three storeys and five
bays, the centre wider with a four-pilaster doorpiece and corniced architrave. The band course to the l. and r. is the only
other form of decoration. Longer windows on the first floor
and square ones on top; piended roof with two longitudinal
chimneystacks.

To the rear of the l. flank, the meagre remains of the rear
block of c. 1790, mostly destroyed in the collapse of 1992 and
now taken up by a fountain. It was originally taller than the
mansion in front, and its central bow (still visible on the
ground floor) once swept up three storeys. Attached to the l.
are the remains of the original TOWER HOUSE, originally a
four-storey rectangle c. 11.5 m. by 8.7 m., of dark red sandstone

rubble with ashlar quoins. Only the w wall, along with half of the s wall and a spur of the n, are intact after the collapse. On the w, a straight-headed entrance inserted *c.* 1790 with a reused lower l. jamb. Tall, plain parapet (not crenellated) supported on lobed corbels. Round bartizans in the sw and nw corners, originally open to the air but the former given its own little crowstepped caphouse in the late c16 or early c17.* On the exterior of the s face is the original arched entrance of *c.* 1475, blocked *c.* 1790 when the Georgian link was added.

However tragic, the collapse now allows for a good 'cutaway' examination of the interior. Tall w wall topped by a crowstepped gable and with the bow of the turnpike staircase running up the s re-entrant angle. The ground floor originally contained two vaulted cellars (cf. the curvature on the n side). The great hall occupied the entire first floor, the w wall with a bench-lined window in a segmental rere-arch. Aumbry to the r. of it; chamfered entrance on the n wall leading to the former garderobe. The upper two floors featured accommodation, the second with mirrored windows to the n and s, the former now with only its l. jamb and a seat ledge intact.

On the back of the Georgian mansion, a big thermal and Venetian window, much restored after the collapse and the removal of the rear block. Stretching back on the l. side is another rear wing of *c.* 1790, also originally three-storeyed and taller than the main house. It is now a single storey with former service buildings stretching beyond.

Inside, the kitchen features a cusped, ogee-headed AUMBRY re-set from the first floor of the tower house after the collapse. The jambs are modern. The FIREPLACE opposite combines two old relics. Triple-shafted jambs from the former great hall, good Gothic of the late c15 with filleted central shaft and double abaci. The lintel is dated 1618 and was formerly plastered over in the rear wing. It commemorates the year that Benholm's barony was reconfirmed by James VI. Heraldry, crowns and paterae carved with admirable gusto; initials for George Keith, 5th Earl Marischal, and his wife, Margaret Ogilvy. It was made three years before their daughter's monument in the parish church (*see* above) and four years before Margaret ran off with Alexander Strachan to plunder £16,000 of 'surplus treasure' from Thornton Castle (q.v.).

MILL OF BENHOLM, 260 m. SE. One of the only water-powered corn mills still in operation in Scotland, and thus a rare survival. Restored 1986–95 and now run as a tourist attraction. Two-storey, piended L-plan of the early c18, much altered in 1817 (*see* the door lintel in the re-entrant angle, signed 'William Davidson').† Kiln with little vent attached to the w gable, early–mid c19. Overshot water wheel on the e gable by

---

* *See also* the similar stair caphouses at Comlongon Castle (Dumfries and Galloway) and Newark Castle (Borders).
† Another datestone of 1711 is now completely faded.

Whittaker Engineering of Stonehaven, *c.* 1992. Internal machinery (including cast-iron gears) mostly rebuilt 1991–4. – Former MILLER'S HOUSE (now the café) to the w. – Piend-roofed BYRE set at a right angle to it.

BERVIE *see* INVERBERVIE

BIRKHALL
3.5 km. sw of Ballater

Secluded and intimate, Birkhall looks over the winding course of the River Muick, its neatly hedged terraces of roses, topiary and vegetables leading down to the tumbling water. The house was built in 1715 by Charles Gordon of Pitchaise, who had married Rachel Gordon, the 10th laird of Abergeldie (q.v.). A later Charles Gordon set about improving the estate in the 1780s and 90s, contemporary with the development of Ballater (q.v.). Prince Albert purchased Birkhall in 1849, after he leased Balmoral (q.v.). Although gifted to the Prince of Wales in 1852, he preferred to stay at Abergeldie so Queen Victoria purchased Birkhall from him in 1884. In time it came to the Duke and Duchess of York (George VI and Queen Elizabeth) and was a favoured residence of the Queen Mother. It now belongs to Prince Charles, Duke of Rothesay.

The pink-harled house enjoys a spectacular outlook s over steeply falling ground to the river, and then across a broad moor towards Craig Vallich. The original part is a single pile of five bays, three storeys on the N, and on the s two storeys over a semi-sunk basement, with a railed approach stair and bolection-moulded doorway at first floor, its lintel carved with Charles and Rachel Gordon's initials and the date 1715. Above the door a panel for heraldic arms. Chamfered windows. Steeply pitched roof, with a stone coping to the ridge, moulded skewputts and end stacks. It appears that this became the formal entrance front in the late C18, coinciding with improvements to the estate, changes illustrated on a map of 1788 which shows the original drive to the N front and detached service block to the NW and a smaller block to the SE, forming an open courtyard, typical of early C18 houses. It also shows a central projection on the N side of the house, presumably for a staircase, which would have been required once the entrance had been moved to the s. The style of the cast-iron balustrade of the approach stair to the s door is also late C18 or early C19 and the carriage drive to this front was only possible once the bridge at Ballater had been built in 1783 (cf. the similar changes made at Newton (q.v.), also for the Gordons).

The two-storey NE wing was built in 1839, with round staircase tower linking it to the main house: the old N staircase tower was removed at this time. The wing now has the formal entrance in its centre, part of the alterations in 1851 by Prince Albert who constructed a new service driveway from the N. The commodious log-columned porte cochère is a little later. Before 1891 a single storey was added to the W end of the S front but subsequently replaced by the present two-storey range, with small bell-roofed tower, that links this front to the large bow-fronted SW wing, added by *A. G. Henderson* in 1953 when this became the Queen Mother's summer residence. Its style honours the harled Scots vernacular but with Modernist overtones. E door moulded in imitation of the S door of 1715, but with characteristic mid-C20 crispness. The rear part is three-storey, with a semicircular bow at the W flank's N end. Further additions were made in 1980 by *Andrew Wright* of *Law & Dunbar-Nasmith*.

E of the house on the terrace is a GARDEN PAVILION of 2004 by *Ben Tindall*. Square, set on the diagonal, with bolection-moulded doorpiece and a slated ogee roof surmounted by a ball finial, like the late C17 pavilions in the Great Garden at Pitmedden (N). Adjacent WALL, in random rubble of different colours heavily mortared with heather-thatch coping.

From the terrace in front of the house the GARDEN falls sharply down to the river in a productive bell-shaped plot. Enhanced by the Queen Mother in the 1950s, the planting continues to evolve under her grandson. Topiary hedges give it structure even during the winter. The WENDY HOUSE was installed in 1935 by the Duke and Duchess of York, for their daughters Elizabeth and Margaret. On an islet in the river, a snug SUMMERHOUSE of cob and thatch, with a rustic porch, given to Prince Charles on his sixtieth birthday in 2008. A SUSPENSION FOOTBRIDGE by *Harper & Co.*, 1885, for Queen Victoria leads to the opposite riverbank.

The STABLES, 50 m. WSW of the house, were built *c.* 1800. Their principal (N) front is near-symmetrical, single-storey and loft, its broad central bay with pedimental gable containing a segment-headed carriage arch and the flanking three-bay wings being slightly set back.

BIRSE

A large and very scattered rural parish S of the Dee.

PARISH CHURCH. Built 1779. Simple rectangular plan. Entrance W gable with doorway and round-arched gallery window, attic oculus and moulded skewputts. Ball-finialled birdcage bellcote with semicircular pediments, dated 1722. Four-bay S flank, its round-arched windows checked for shutters. Renovated by *James Matthews* 1855 and 1890, further reconstructed by *George Bennett Mitchell & Son* in 1934–7 when the four round-arched

windows were formed in the N flank and the church lengthened. Chaste interior entirely by the Mitchells; they moved the
pulpit from the S wall to the E end and inserted the chancel
arch and minister's door in the S wall. Small-paned leaded
glazing. – STAINED GLASS. E window, Christ on the Road to
Emmaus by *Douglas Strachan*, 1910, originally in the S wall. – N
window, Christ with Simon Peter and Andrew, 1972; the style
suggests *William Wilson*'s studio.

Former PARISH MANSE. A two-storey house of the earlier
C18, with a taller two-storey E wing of the 1790s, and a S wing,
very broad with a pedimental gable projecting still more boldly
forward, inserted in the angle in 1834; these wings' gables, and
a plain classic single-storey porch in the W re-entrant angle,
form the present S entrance front.

FOREST OF BIRSE CHURCH, 7 km. SSW, isolated on the road
to Birse Castle (*see* below). Built 1891. Small with two lancets
and gabled porch on the S flank. Large round W window,
stepped triple lancets at E.

BALFOUR HOUSE, 1 km. S. Picturesque cottage style, built 1845
for Francis Cochran, an Aberdeen advocate. Principal front
facing E is asymmetrical. The main house is at the S end, two-
storey L-plan with its shallow projecting gabled bay containing
a console-corniced doorpiece. It is repeated on a smaller
scale by the service wing at the N end, its luggage entrance
sheltered by a log-column veranda. Simple but distinctive
detailing, pale golden harl with ashlar dressings, mullioned-
and-transomed lying-pane casements. Low-pitched roof with
carved bargeboards; diagonally shafted chimneystacks. Garden
elevation near-symmetrical, its three-windows-wide centre
flanked between broad gables, that on the r. with a ground-
floor canted bay.

BALLOGIE HOUSE, 2.4 km. SE. Neo-Georgian, by a Mr
Patterson, dated 1983. Two-storeyed, five bays broad. Central
doorway with sidelights and fanlight. Pinkish harl with grey
dressings, piended roof. It succeeded a house by *James
Matthews*, 1852–5 for James Dyce Nicol, who made improvements to the estate. The WALLED GARDEN survives from an
even earlier house, known as Tillysnaught, which was a property of the Roses of Kilravock, followed by the Forbes in the
C18 and then by the Innes family; both of the latter were
Roman Catholics.

BOGIESHIEL LODGE, 0.75 km. SW of Ballogie House, was
begun as a chapel after the Roman Catholic mission moved
here from Deecastle (q.v.) in 1815. It was rectangular with an
apsidal S end. A slightly taller two-storey house hinged to its
NW angle was built *c.* 1850; then a further addition built against
the chapel's N gable by *Walker & Duncan* in 1874 formed a link
to a pre-existing steading. The chapel, built in harled rubble,
may have been heightened during conversion to residential use.
Its E flank presents the principal entrance front, two storeys
and three bays broadly spaced, with a later timber columnar
porch rising into a gable. The S bow is lit by two pointed

windows with basket tracery at ground floor and twelve-pane
sash windows at first, a very tall chimneystack rising over the
wall-head between them. To the N, *Walker & Duncan*'s addition
is slightly set back but adopts the same two-storey three-bay
pattern, the end wall of the steading to the far N being expressed
in coursed rubble. The house of *c.* 1850 is only visible on the
rear side, where it forms an irregular T-plan.

At MAINS OF MIDSTRATH, 3.4 km. SSE, is an early C19 LIME-
KILN. Three-bay front, its advanced centre boldly battered and
side-bays curved. Dry granite rubble with dressed long-and-
short quoins, round-arched firing-holes at base; built into a
slope and loaded from the top.

MUIR CROFT, 2.4 km. ESE on the B976, is a standard late C18
cottage but next to it is a timber-boarded SOUTER'S SHOP,
built *c.* 1897 for James Merchant. Corrugated metal roof with
brick chimneystack. An extremely rare survival, with complete
interior.

POTARCH BRIDGE, 5 km. E, crossing the Dee. Designed by
Thomas Telford, engineer to the Highland Roads & Bridges
Commission, and built by *William Minto* in 1811–14 as a
larger version of their Bridge of Alford (q.v.); partly funded
by the government and partly by the Inneses of Balnacraig
and Ballogie (qq.v.). Three magnificent segmental arches in
coursed grey granite, ashlar voussoirs and cutwater piers rising
to form refuges at parapet level, the approaches splayed.
Central span 21.3 m., outer spans each 19.8 m.

WAR MEMORIAL, on B976, Corsedarder Hill, 5.3 km. SE. By
William Kelly, 1921. Broad obelisk-shaped cenotaph in rock-
faced pink and grey granite. Beautiful lettering cut by *Messrs
Henry Hutcheon*.

BIRSE CASTLE
7.5 km. SSW

A tower house built by Sir William Gordon of Cluny, who feued
the Forest of Birse from 1585; closely related in plan and dimensions to Westhall (q.v.). Burnt 1640, a sheep-cot in 1792.
Reconstructed in simplified form by *George Bennett Mitchell* for
J.R. Heaven 1905–6, but his work was altered and substantially
extended in 1929–30 by *William Kelly* for Annie Pearson,
Viscountess Cowdray.

The TOWER HOUSE comprised a three-storey-and-attic main
block, orientated E–W, with a drum tower containing the main
stair at its SE corner. The main block was not quite rectangular.
Its entrance (S) front was 8.8 m. in length but its N side was
9.2 m. long because the W end gable stood at a slight angle,
the depth being 6.6 m. The walls, built in granite rubble and
formerly harled, were 1 m. thick at ground floor to support
internal vaulting, but progressively diminished from level to
level, the wall-heads being 8.5 m. above ground. The original
doorway was immediately next to the drum tower which was

originally slightly elliptical on plan and contained a turnpike
stair rising to the second floor, as at Westhall. Just above the
second floor it was corbelled into a two-storey square caphouse
set on the diagonal. The elaborate stepped corbels which supported these turrets – those at the NW and presumably the SW
angles rising from second floor, that at the NE angle from attic
level – are further indicators of its relationship to Westhall (and
indeed to Allardice and Knock qq.v.). Together the caphouse
and turrets clasped the main block's tall crowstepped gables
with moulded chimneystacks. The entrance was protected
internally by an iron yett, and the windows, mostly small, had
iron grilles; there were 'gun-ports at every convenient place'.
The ground floor presumably contained the kitchen, the first-
floor hall was reached by the main turnpike and by the service
stair from the kitchen in the NE corner. James Giles's drawing
of c. 1840 shows a large segmentally arched window in the E
gable between them, the 'high' end and fireplace being on the
W. Giles's drawing also shows remains of a courtyard against
the near-blind N wall. When Robert Dinnie examined Birse
c. 1865 the S wall and W gable had largely collapsed.

In Mitchell's RECONSTRUCTION of 1905–6 the main block
was rebuilt, its new walls less thick since the ground-floor vault
was not reinstated. In the centre of the S front, between the
new windows at first floor and second floor, a round-arched
niche was formed for a statue. The doorway, with an armorial
above its lintel, was transferred to the drum tower, which was
rebuilt exactly circular, 3.2 m. in diameter; although Mitchell
suggested reinstating the caphouse, it was given a bellcast
conical roof. The angle turrets were reinstated, with the
distinctive corbelling shown by James Giles and David
MacGibbon. A single-storey service outshot was formed on the
site of the N court, proposals for a three-storey jamb with a
second stair-tower on the W flank being passed over.

During *Kelly's* alterations of 1929–30 the entrance was transferred to its original position in the main block, and Mitchell's
SE tower was rebuilt with a two-storey caphouse. The two W
turrets were increased in height to match, their upper levels
expressed by ovoid lights just beneath the eaves of their spirelets. But this was only part of Kelly's ENLARGEMENT of Birse
which trebled it in size. Mitchell's addition was demolished
and a three-storey range matching the height of the old main
block was built against its N side, forming a substantial E
wing, ending in a tall chimney gable flanked by matching
two-storey turrets; the NE turret now was corbelled from the
angled plane between the old and new ranges. (Inside, a new
entrance hall was formed within the main block where the
kitchen had been; the drawing room occupied the first floor.
Mitchell's stair was gutted out from the SE tower and a new
one formed at the W end of the new N range, which at its E
end contained the kitchen and, at first floor, the dining room.
In the 1990s *William Brogden* reworked the first floor and
formed a new Baroque stair; the decoration was carried out by

Willa Elphinstone and a beamed ceiling was richly painted by *Jennifer Merredew*.)

Beyond Mitchell's terraced garden are his 1905 KENNELS, honoured with witty Baronial splendour, including a drum tower rising into a bellcast conical roof.

BALNACRAIG HOUSE. *See* p. 361.

BLACKBURN

8010

A village founded *c*. 1800 when Adam Wilson of Glasgoego built a coaching inn on the new turnpike road between Aberdeen and Inverurie just W of the bridge over the Black Burn. Then *c*. 1820 he built a distillery and workers' cottages, forming a pool at the village's W end as a water supply, but fierce competition and illicit hooch rendered him bankrupt a decade later. The distillery was converted into a Free Church in 1843 (now in other uses). Blackburn's growth was encouraged by construction of the railway nearby and a granite quarry at Little Clinterty. More ambitious development *c*. 1960 was prompted by its proximity to Aberdeen and Dyce airport.

Former FREE CHURCH MANSE, Fintray Road. By *James Henderson*, 1844. Cottage style.

KINALDIE HOUSE. *See* p. 597.

KINELLAR HOUSE. *See* p. 602.

TERTOWIE HOUSE. *See* p. 746.

BLAIRDAFF

6010

A small village, rather spread out.

Former PARISH CHURCH. Built 1838–9, but reduced to a shell in the later C20. A simple Gothic preaching-box, in coursed pinned granite rubble with ashlar dressings. End gables have slightly projected centres containing pointed doorways and gallery windows. Pyramidal finials and arched birdcage bell-cote over W end. Four-bay S flank. Session house on N.

PARISH (SCLATTIE) CHURCH, 1 km. SE. Built as a Free Church of 1850. SW gable in pinned rubble with round-arched doorway and flanking windows, gallery window above. Pyramid finials and arched bellcote with pyramid spirelet echoing those of the Established church. Three-bay flanks. Well-crafted interior divided into nave and aisles by very attenuated timber colonnettes of polygonal profile which rise into depressed arches supporting the compartmented ceiling. – MANSE. 1879.

Two-storey L-plan, with a broad gabled bay stepped out on the r. Reconstructed after fire in 1916.

GRANT LODGE, beside the road close to the parish church, is dated 1827. Reputedly built as charitable housing. Two-storey five-bay in coursed squared granite. Doorways on each side of the central bay, three windows at first floor. Broad wall-head chimney gable.

BLAIRS

ST MARY'S COLLEGE. In 1827 John Menzies of Pitfodels, last surviving member of an old Catholic family, gifted Menzies House, seat of the Blairs estate, and 1,000 acres for use as a seminary to educate boys for the priesthood, the first students being admitted in 1829. It was so successful that in 1890 its rector, Aeneas Chisholm, later Bishop of Aberdeen, inaugurated a campaign to build a new college and chapel. Much of the funding was provided by Chisholm's friend, Monsignor James Lennon of Liverpool. The College was extended in 1928 but a falling roll contributed to its closure in 1986. At the time of writing (2014) proposals are well advanced to convert the buildings into a hotel, leisure and conference centre, but St Mary's Chapel will remain in religious use.

The COLLEGE was designed by *R. G. Wilson* (of *Ellis & Wilson*), and seemingly begun by 1892, although its foundation stone was only laid in 1896; the first part was opened in 1897 but it was not completed until 1903. The construction of St Mary's Chapel immediately to the E, and the substantial extension of Wilson's work to the W in 1928, results in an impressive composition of 140 m. total length. Wilson conceived the College as a U-plan quadrangle, predominantly three storeys and basement in granite ashlar, the principal front facing N with an impressive entrance tower of five stages. It has corbelled angle turrets, a crown spire rising into a miniature peristyle, and a finely carved orb with a crucifix finial. Its lowest stage is an open porch, with pilaster buttresses clasping round-headed arches: their pedimented triple key blocks are carved with the arms of Pope Leo XIII (centre), Aeneas Chisholm (l.) and Menzies of Pitfodels (r.). Flanking the tower, three-storey three-bay links rising from a rusticated basement plinth end in slightly projecting pavilions. That on the l. is rather broader than that on the r., and their fenestration is irregular, but both break up into crowstepped gables to acknowledge the matching E and W wings behind them which enclose the open courtyard to the S. The W EXTENSION of 1928 is also built to match: three storeys in ashlar over a rusticated basement, its considerable length broken by being stepped out slightly towards the r. end. Within the tower porch an ornamental red tile floor, and the doorway framed by Ionic pilasters. This doorway is perhaps by *John Henderson*, who was responsible for the ENTRANCE HALL's panelled dado in pitch pine and angle pilasters rising up to a panelled ceiling. The double-height former LIBRARY is mostly wainscoted with a balustraded gallery, its ceiling again compartmented. Within the E wing the former REFECTORY, over 24 m. long and 10 m. wide, has a coffered ceiling and is lit by six windows in each long flank.

Standing immediately next to the College, ST MARY'S CHAPEL by *Robert Curran* of Warrington, 1899–1901, is of substantial size and very unusually is orientated facing W rather than E. Predominantly Geometrical with some Perp elements in grey granite ashlar, it comprises a nine-bay nave with a NE tower and spire 45 m. high, a single NW transept and a three-sided W apse, all with crenellated parapets and stepped buttresses rising into pinnacles. The tower is of three stages, the lowest providing the porch, its doorway with two orders of marble shafts under a gableted niche; the third stage has two-light windows and the granite spire has two tiers of lucarnes in alternate faces. Impressively large windows, that at the E gable of six lights and that at the transept of five. On the S side the ashlar is pinned; the buttresses fly over a cloister with a gabled porch, linking the chapel with the College.

Inside, the church had rails and gates to separate a congregation in the nave from 200 students singing in the choir, but it is now open from end to end. The walls' original decoration by *Earley & Co.* of Dublin was destroyed by dry-rot soon after opening and instead they were panelled by *C. J. Ménart* in fine coloured marbles beneath the window arches, with niches in the piers between them. The eye is drawn irresistibly towards the apse, which is marble-faced for its full height, and to the polygonal timber-boarded roof on arched trusses springing from wall-shafts. – ALTAR of white Carrara marble, carved with the Last Supper, and framed by colonnettes in richly veined black and honey-gold by *Pearse & Son* of Dublin. – HIGH ALTAR, by *Ménart*, also Carrara marble, inlaid with deep red panels; sacrarium with a brass door and a crucifixion under a canopy. Flanking this are SEDILIA within the canted angles of the apse, framed by elaborate crocketed and canopied timber niches containing statues of saints; the crescendo is a magnificent timber ogee arch culminating in a crown forming the baldacchino over the high altar. – LECTERN. The former pulpit, converted in 1983–4 – half-hexagonal, its central face with a seated Christ in low relief; colonnettes with foliate capitals at the angles, the other faces with blind Gothic tracery. – The nave PEWS are arranged in collegiate style. – STAINED GLASS. The apse windows by *Mayer* of Munich, scenes from the life of the Virgin in the W window. – ORGAN. Originally by *E. H. Lawton*, 1903.

MENZIES HOUSE at the time of writing has been reduced to a shell. It was probably built *c.* 1750, its entrance front originally three storeys high and seemingly three bays broad, built in coursed, squared and cherry-cocked rubble: to keep up with fashion, the centre bay was built out *c.* 1760–70, three storeys rising into a full-height attic with a round-arched window beneath a shallow-pitched chimney gable. The house was subsequently extended symmetrically to each side. The l. wing has been concealed by the chapel and Menzies's apartments (*see* below). The house's unusual orientation, facing uphill to the s, was seemingly determined by the desire to incorporate what appears to be a previous house of *c.* 1720–40 as its E wing. This is a simple late example of the Birkenbog type, two storeys, rubble-built on a simple rectangular plan, with moulded skewputts. The entrance elevation almost certainly faced W, its central ground-floor window having perhaps been formed from the original doorway. The N gable was demolished when the new main block was built, and a chimney gable was seemingly inserted slightly off-centre, but the s gable retains its original skewputts. Projecting from this gable is the SERVICE RANGE, a low two-storey L-plan, extending twelve bays to the E, although the coachhouse at the E end may be an addition. The service range may have provided shelter for a large walled garden. What had become a DOOCOT by 1865 was probably once a two-storey pavilion, with large openings at both ground floor and first floor.

Projecting forward from the l. of the main block, a short three-storey two-bay wing contained MENZIES'S APARTMENTS, built by *John Gall* shortly after 1829. Beyond stands the CHAPEL: it comprises a central block, with three blind openings, tall and round-arched, and a loft with three small square lights, also blind, beneath a broad pedimental chimney gable. A short range linking to Menzies's apartments on the r. is balanced by the l. wing, with three round-arched windows. Although rubble-built on the E flank, to their W overlooking the walled garden the apartments and chapel are built of reddish-brown brick in very slim courses, with grey granite dressings.

LODGE. Probably by *Ellis & Wilson*, *c.* 1900.

BRAEMAR

Crathie and Braemar is an extensive conjoined rural parish, mainly protected by the Cairngorms National Park owing to its exceptional highland scenery of mountains, rivers, tundra and relics of the Caledonian pine forest. Whereas Crathie (q.v.) developed no commercial centre, Braemar lay at a strategic junction of wild mountain routes leading through to Angus, Perthshire, Inverness-shire and down the Dee to Aberdeen. According to the St Andrews Foundation legend, written in the C12, it was here at '*Doldauha*, now called *Kindrochit-Alian*', that the relics of St Andrew were brought to the C9 Pictish King Hungus for veneration, and he built a church dedicated to the saint here, even before a church was built at St Andrews. The medieval church was sited in the graveyard by Braemar Castle.

The visible medieval settlement was based around Kindrochit Castle, at the crossing point of the River Clunie, *Kindrochit* meaning 'bridgehead' in Gaelic. This Castletown was a completely independent settlement from Auchendryne on the w bank of the river: the joint name of Braemar only began to be used in the C19. The rivalry between these two communities and their lairds is a striking element of the local architecture. Auchendryne was staunchly Catholic with its own church, school, village hall and Fife Arms Hotel; while Castletown of Braemar, with its royal medieval castle, became Protestant and had its own hall, church and Invercauld Arms Hotel.

The joined parish of Crathie and Braemar has no fewer than twenty-five churches and chapels, testimony both to its scattered settlements and to their sectarianism. Architecture is dominated by the patronage of the three big estates: Balmoral, owned by the royal family since 1852; Invercauld, seat of the Farquharsons; and Mar Lodge, purchased in the 1730s by William Duff, Earl of Fife. Four types of building characterize the area. Owing to their remote location, some primitive vernacular crofts still survive. The great houses are predominantly Victorian thanks to the surge of investment which followed the revival of the Braemar gathering (highland games) in 1832 and the arrival of the royal family in 1848. The lairds developed their land with model estate houses, which in turn influenced the style of more modest villas and cottages. They used the handbooks of picturesque architecture such as those produced by P. F. Robinson. A mélange of Swiss chalet (with overhanging eaves, low roof pitch and decorative bargeboards) and Tudor (with mullioned windows, tall chimneystacks and hoodmoulds) was considered appropriate for the location. Lastly, there was a strategic investment in bridges from the suppression of the Jacobites in 1745 onwards. Given the dramatic terrain, many of these are visually significant.

CHURCHES

Former **BRAEMAR PARISH CHURCH**, Invercauld Road, Castleton. Originally a chapel of ease built in 1832 by *Alexander Fraser*, it became the parish church, then the United Free Church, then a theatre and was finally tactfully converted to flats in 1997. The T-plan chapel of yellow/brown rubble was oriented N–S. To this was added in 1878, by *Matthews & Mackenzie* the dignified E façade in stugged grey ashlar, with three large lancets flanked by pinnacle buttresses, and a small tower with a ring of gabled lancets at the base of a spire.

BRAEMAR PARISH CHURCH, Cluniebank Road. Originally built as the Free Church in 1869, by *Robert Lamb*, this was an ambitious undertaking for a small divided community which had just completed a new parish church in 1832 (*see* above). It became the present parish church in 1946. Cruciform, with apse, tower, stone spire and baptistery. Snecked and coursed whinstone rubble contrasts with granite ashlar dressing stones and quoins. Tower in two stages with louvred lancets for belfry, and angled pinnacles above. Gabled clock panels to each face at base of broached spire. The lofty interior has an exposed hammerbeam roof springing from stone corbels. Short transepts are divided by polished granite columns. The main emphasis is on the apse, fronted by a traceried table and dominated by a large central pulpit. The apse windows are delicate geometric and floral design. The fiery minister Hugh Cobban, who instigated this building, died just before its completion and is buried in the apse, with this memorial: 'If any man preach any other gospel unto you, than that ye have received, let him be accursed'. Nicely treated door ironmongery and dated water hoppers.

ST ANDREW (R.C.), Auchendryne Square. Built in 1839, an early example of Catholic Gothic Revival. Lady Carmarthen, a holiday-maker at Mar Lodge, was the patron and building works were supervised by the priest-architect Father *Walter Lovi*. The completion was celebrated with 'merry pibrochs of the hardy Highlanders' and a 'bumper of mountain dew'. Narrow S (entrance) façade, with clasping buttresses, corner pinnacles, slim lancets and a bellcote. The interior has a plaster rib-vaulted ceiling with foliage bosses, dado panelling and pews with fleur-de-lys ends. Vigorous MOSAIC on vestibule floor of St Andrew, designed by the parish priest Canon Paul, executed by *Minton, Hollister and Co.*, 1901. – ALTAR with gilded reredos depicting saints, surrounded by screen and angels. – STAINED GLASS. A worthy ensemble of Scottish saints and exemplars, single figures under Gothic canopies, produced by *Louis Grossé* of Bruges in 1901–3. Anticlockwise from SE end: Bishop Chisholm of Aberdeen, King David of Scotland, St Nathalan, Malcolm Canmore, St Ninian; over the altar, St Margaret, Crucifixion, St Andrew; St Columba, St Gregory, St Machar, St Bride, Bishop Elphinstone. – Early Christian boulder FONT on pedestal outside entrance, apparently from the demolished Catholic chapel at Arderg. These are rare examples of pre-Romanesque work, found elsewhere in the district e.g. at Tullich.

ST MARGARET (Episcopal), Castleton Terrace. Now in the care of the Scottish Redundant Churches Trust. Following Queen Victoria's adoption of Deeside in 1852, English tourists flocked to Braemar for the summer season, including Bishop Lightfoot of Durham. In 1880 a small wooden Episcopal church by *Arthur Clyne* was built on this site, and later the stone-built Lightfoot aisle was added for restricted winter worship. This forms the S transept of the present stone church, built in 1899–1901 by *J. Ninian Comper*; he was recommended by Dr Wickham Legg, antiquarian and liturgist of the Ecclesiological Movement, who was a summer visitor to Braemar. The cost was mainly financed by Miss Eliza Jane Scholfield.

Braemar is arguably Comper's finest church in the Scottish style, excelling even Kirriemuir, Angus, in grace and beauty.

It combines spirituality, pellucid light, spaciousness, timeless harmony and pin-sharp acoustics. It is a sublime space in which the liturgy is enclosed as a visual feast. While deeply rooted in designs of the Scottish late Middle Ages, it leavens that certain heaviness with a delight in sparkling detail. On the outside, the church has a low harmonious profile, with no feature dominating another. Nave and chancel have a similar roof pitch, separated by a squat buttressed tower, based on Iona Abbey. Generous open porches preface the nave and Lightfoot aisle. The stones are a joyous display of all the different colours of rock found in the vicinity of Glen Callater, while the Scotch slates were recycled from old Mar Lodge (q.v.), demolished in 1895. The intersecting tracery of the E window derives from Greyfriars, Aberdeen; the square windows of the tower recall those at Iona; while those in the Lightfoot aisle are based on lancets at Pluscarden Abbey (N).

The NW porch has a Perp oak ceiling, and firm oak door, bench and serpentine hat rack. The nave, a double square with plain white walls and large tracery windows on all sides, is flooded with light. It was completed in two stages, with plaster in the W bay slapped straight on the wall where elsewhere it rests on battens. Wagon roof with castellated tie-beams. The crossing opens up full height to a rib-vault, pulling in light from the tower windows to fall on the rood screen. The crossing arches are simple mouldings without columns or capitals. A stair-tower rises inside the SE corner of the crossing, leading, rather inconveniently, to a stone pulpit set in the wall. Above it is the doorway to the rood loft. The Lightfoot aisle has a roof similar to the nave, and a stone altar. The chancel, framed by the open rood screen and large low windows on all sides, was intended to appear 'as a lantern, and the altar is a flame within it'. Its wagon-vault is enriched with flowers in the bays above the altar. At the time of writing the SRCT plan to add the N aisle originally envisaged in Comper's designs.

FURNISHINGS. For Comper, the architecture was merely a protection for his ecclesiologically designed furnishings: these give the instant impression of entering an East Anglian medieval church. The ROOD SCREEN, a memorial to Eliza Scholfield †1909, is a delicate evocation like that at Ranworth, Norfolk. It has six bays of paired solid-traceried panels at the base. From these rise six open-traceried lights, with an ogee arch at the centre forming the door. The loft rests on timber coving which is fronted by pendant traceried arches and a delicate openwork balustrade. The ROOD of the Crucifixion surrounded by golden fire was consecrated with the screen in 1921. – CHOIR STALLS, in the chancel, with poppyheads and traceried fronts to match the screen. Around the granite altar are RIDDEL-POSTS carrying gilded angels. – SACRAMENT HOUSE, a revival of a common feature in medieval Aberdeenshire churches (e.g. Auchindoir) for the reservation of the host, plus AUMBRY and PISCINA. – Comper's STAINED GLASS adds an ethereal atmosphere to the church: he used clear translucent glass to admit light rather than exclude it, and retains a scheme of silvery-gold and blue, delineated with the delicacy of the Wilton Diptych. In the nave, the W and N lights are plain, to bring in natural light. Nave S: The Visitation, 1914; Christ and the children, 1827. Chancel, anticlockwise starting from SW: SS Stephen and Decuman, 1914; St Monica, St Perpetua, St Thecla, after 1908; E window, lower tier, scenes from life of Christ; middle tier, the Risen Christ flanked by Evangelists; top tier, Virgin and Child flanked by St Moluag, St Margaret, St Andrew and St David; Annunciation in tracery tops. – Handsome wrought-iron LAMP STAND and GATEWAY ARCH from the previous church, 1894, by *Walter Mcfarlane & Co.*

BRAEMAR GRAVEYARD, 0.8 km. N, near Braemar Castle. Bishop Regulus, carrying the relics of St Andrew, was supposed to have met the Pictish King Hungus at *Doldauha*, 'land of the water meadow', an appropriate description for this site, and the first church dedicated to St Andrew in Scotland was built there. All trace was removed after the parish church moved up to the village in 1832. – FARQUHARSON MAUSOLEUM. Like a miniature keep with blank ashlar walls topped by small corner turrets and a pediment like a sarcophagus lid. Plaques inside commemorate members of the family from John Farquharson, 9th Laird, †1750. – Table tomb just to the E commemorates the many Catholic priests who served this area, from 1708 onwards.

CASTLES

BRAEMAR CASTLE, 1 km. NNE. Commanding a sweep of the River Dee, from a distance this looks like a toy-town castle, bristling with five flat-topped crenellated turrets, so different in outline from the Deeside tower houses. These alterations reflect its dramatic history. It is basically an L-plan with a five-storey round tower in the re-entrant angle and two-storey angle turrets at the top of each wing. It was built in 1628 for John Erskine, 19th (and 2nd) Earl of Mar, as a hunting lodge. In 1689 it was attacked and burnt by his Jacobite neighbour Colonel 'Black' John Farquharson of Inverey, to prevent it falling into the hands of General Mackay, a supporter of William of Orange. In 1715 'Bobbin' John Erskine, 23rd (and 6th) Earl of Mar, raised the standard of Jacobite rebellion at Braemar, and forfeited his estates following defeat. The castle, still ruinous, passed to John Farquharson of Invercauld who leased it to the government as barracks from 1748 to 1797. Troops were stationed here and at Corgarff (q.v.) to pacify the Highlanders after the 1745 Jacobite rebellion. At this stage, *John Adam* rebuilt the roofless turrets with crenellations and erected the star-shaped curtain wall, according to the design theories of the French military engineer Sebastien de Vauban (1633–1707). In the C19 the castle was converted to domestic use by the Farquharsons of Invercauld (q.v.) and today gives the predominant impression of a cosy Victorian country house run, since 2007, as a museum by the Braemar community.

Braemar Castle.
Drawing by David M. Walker, 1961

The castle is entered through a yett in the wide re-entrant tower, which houses the principal staircase. Some windows retain their original iron bars. The ground floor is vaulted with three principal chambers. On the way to the kitchen is a pit-prison. The kitchen originally had a wide arched hearth but this has been subdivided to make way for a C19 service staircase leading up to a vestibule at the low end of the hall. It was probably 'Piccadilly Jim', James Ross Farquharson, the great socialite Laird of Invercauld, who enlarged the kitchen area to cater for royal and distinguished visitors to the Braemar Games. He built a new kitchen in the back yard, against the military wall, and installed an iron cooking range there, using the exterior of the old kitchen chimney. This kitchen and its eleven service rooms were removed in 2007. Upstairs, the castle is basically designed around a large hall wing and smaller chamber wing on each floor. Their visible décor and plasterwork is C19, with some early bathrooms and Farquharson furniture originally at Invercauld House. In the military phase, soldiers occupied the long wing, leaving plenty of graffiti, and officers used the smaller rooms.

KINDROCHIT CASTLE, in the centre of the village, on Balnellan Road. Perched on a rocky crag above the E bank of the Cluny Water, the castle guards a narrow crossing point of the river. Documents reveal that King Robert II regularly stayed at Kindrochit between 1371 and 1388, accompanied by a substantial household. In 1390 Robert III licensed Sir Malcolm Drummond, his brother-in-law, to build a tower here.

Excavations by Douglas Simpson corroborated these main
phases in the ruinous walls which survive.* The original structure was a long hall, more than 30 m. by 9 m., over unvaulted
cellarage. At each corner except the SW are the remains of
square corner towers. This unusual structure reflects the
'palace-wise' construction of some early Scottish houses, in
which the hall is more important than a tower. On a slightly
different alignment a massive keep was intruded on the SW
side, presumably from 1390. At 19.5 m. by 13 m., with walls
3 m. thick, this is the largest tower in North-East Scotland,
greater than Spynie (Moray) and Drum (q.v.). It had three
cellar chambers, the central one with a postern gate leading to
the bridgehead. Beside the postern gate is an intramural staircase leading to a hall above. All dressed stone was fine sandstone, brought from Kildrummy. It is not clear how these two
structures operated together, but they were both utilized in the
scheme for the new bridgehead, and an additional E porch was
added to the old hall after the tower was built. The castle fell
out of use under James V and was 'in rubbish' by the mid C16.
It is now in the care of Aberdeenshire Council.

PUBLIC BUILDINGS AND HOTELS

VICTORIA HALL, Glenshee Road. By *J. B. Pirie* of *Pirie &
Clyne*, 1880. An ambitious and patriotic public building for a
tiny village, set in a prominent central location. Ground-floor
windows with horseshoe architraves; doorway topped by consoled balcony; walls of rock-faced granite. Central oriel on
upper storey flanked by very tall windows with shallow pedimented heads. Erected by the Farquharsons of Invercauld
(q.v.), it posed a challenge to the Earl Fife, who responded by
rapidly constructing the timber JUBILEE HALL (Village Hall),
Mar Road, on the opposite bank of the river at Auchendryne,
which overtook the Victoria Hall project and was completed
in 1879. This is a joyous red and white confection of swirling
bargeboards, drooping eaves and perky finials.

Former OMNIBUS STATION DEPOT, Castleton Place, off
Invercauld Road. Weatherboarded, a cheery addition to the
streetscape. Opened *c.* 1900 by the Great North of Scotland
Railway, its sign a reminder that for most of the holiday visitors
trains stopped at Ballater (q.v.) and a bus service was required
to connect Braemar with the station. Nice reeded doorposts
and margin-paned glazing. Four-bay garage in the rear wing.

PRINCE ALBERT'S OBSERVATORY, Glenshee Road. Prominently located on the village green. Octagonal, with nice detailing, particularly on the slates and louvred cupola. An
appropriate donation from Prince Albert in 1855, as Braemar
records the coldest temperatures of any British village.

Next to the Celtic cross WAR MEMORIAL, Cluniebank Road, by
George Bennett Mitchell, 1920, is the Bristol Pegasus engine

---

* See *Antiquaries Journal* 8, 1928.

from a bomber that crashed locally in 1942 on a training mission. Literally an *objet trouvé* found on the hillside, this produces a powerful sculptural form, mounted in 2004.

INVERCAULD ARMS HOTEL, Invercauld Road. A dominating presence which dictates the Highland streetscape at the entrance to Castleton. On this site John Erskine, 6th Earl of Mar, raised the standard of the Jacobite rebellion in 1715. There was already a substantial house, probably an inn, shown here on the Invercauld estate map of 1775 but the present core appears to be mid-C19. By 1850 there was a three-bay central block, with lower matching wings to each side and Tudor chimneys set at an angle. Later, matching bay-fronted wings, decorative bargeboards and rustic pillared verandas were added. At the centre is a three-storey porch, with crowstepped gable flanked by thimble bartizans, added by *J. T. Wimperis* in 1886 and characteristic of his work at Invercauld House (q.v.). Considerable extension to the N, by *Jenkins & Marr*, 1903. The interior has some decorative plasterwork and pine panelling.

FIFE ARMS HOTEL, Mar Road. The landmark of Auchendryne. By 1850 there was a building of seven bays, two storeys and dormers. Traces of this original construction can be seen at the back centre, with sash windows of Early Victorian proportions. The E wing, of whinstone with plate-glass sashes, also looks like part of an early phase. In 1897–8 *A. Marshall Mackenzie* created the splendid front range and added a storey. This is in pink granite ashlar, characterized by busy gables with curly bargeboards, bay windows with multi-paned upper sashes, and Tudor mouldings. The castellated porch with double arches and the Fife coat of arms was added in 1905 by Mackenzie, with rustic timber verandas to either side. In 1906 *Kelly & Nicol* of Aberdeen rebuilt the W wing in a similar style but of grey granite with pink margins. Unassuming interiors with some pine panelling and Art Nouveau coloured glass on the staircase. STABLES, 1897, discreetly modernized in 1990 by *John McRobert* for Grampian Regional Council, as a visitor centre.

DESCRIPTION

S of the Fife Arms on Cluniebank Road is KLINGRAHOOL, a house by *Peter Mulvey*, 2007, in a challenging and picturesque location clinging to the cliffs of the gorge of the Cluny Water. This is an intelligent and dramatic reuse of a dank turbine shed originally built to supply electricity to the Fife Arms Hotel. The resulting home, of glass and granite with copper pyramid roof, is flooded with light, not water. Slightly further down, THE GRANARY (formerly Mill of Auchendryne) is late C18 with a C19 N addition. Late C20 conversion to a house retained its picturesque wheel by the riverbank. A popular postcard view in the C19.

Many houses in Braemar were designed for the holiday season, when owners would retreat into a nearby cabin and let

out the main building. DAISYBANK, Fife Brae, from the later
C19, is one of the best-preserved examples of a single-storey-
and-loft, with alcove for box bed, and bell-pull system for the
visitors. The 'Wee House', added about 1890, retains its internal panelling, cooking range, original sinks and cast-iron
washing tub. Another example, JUNIPER COTTAGE, Mar
Road, has Glen Callater slates on the roof.

TOMINTOUL CROFT, 1.3 km. SSW, off Cluniebank Road. A
miraculous time capsule of C19 rural life. It is of three bays,
single storey and loft, with corrugated iron roof over heather
and turf thatch. The short chimneystacks project from within
the roof ridge. Internally, these are 'hanging lums', wooden
cowls suspended over a low stone hearth. Several fitted box
beds and panelled wall cupboards. The attic sarking is lined
with C19–early C20 newspapers, and walls in the rest of the
cottage are pasted with many contemporary art posters and
advertising from *c.* 1900. Undergoing restoration in 2014.

FRASER'S BRIDGE, Glen Clunie, 5 km. S on the Old Military
Road. By *Lt-Gen. William Blakeney*, for the Board of Ordnance,
1748–50. Two rubble-built segmental arches over Clunie Water.
On the parapet coping, initials and dates of 1862/1863 may
refer to masons carrying out repairs to the road instigated by
Prince Albert.

OLD BRIG O'DEE, across the Dee at Invercauld, 3.5 km. ESE.
1753 by *Major W. Caulfeild*. A magnet for artists and anglers.
Military bridge originally built to link Blairgowrie with Corgarff
and Inverness. Hump-backed, with seven segmental arches,
increasing in size towards the centre but piers irregularly
spaced according to the availability of foundations. Massive
V-shaped cutwaters. Rubble, with solid parapet, now pedestrian use only. One of the oldest bridges across the Dee (apart
from Brig O'Dee in Aberdeen), where most were swept away
by the Great Flood of 1829.

INVERCAULD BRIDGE, over the Dee, 150 m. N of the Old Brig
is by *J. F. Beattie*, 1859, at the expense of Prince Albert. Three-
span segmentally arched bridge with smaller flood arches at
each end, and roundels set within the spandrels. The Old
Deeside Road had run along the S bank of the river, directly
through the Balmoral policies. Having purchased the estate in
1852, Prince Albert made use of the Ballater Turnpike Act of
1855 to divert the road onto the N bank from Crathie to this
point, replacing the Old Brig.

INVERCAULD HOUSE. *See* p. 555.

5010

BREDA HOUSE

3 km. WNW of Alford

A Scots Renaissance country house by *A. Marshall Mackenzie*,
dated 1894, and in a similar idiom to William Leiper's houses
on the West Coast. Built in red granite, the principal S frontage
comprises a compact three-storey, three-bay main block, tower

house-like in profile with a large circular entrance tower crowned by a conical roof at its w end, and a two-storey, five-bay wing extending towards the E, its big ground-floor windows regular in arrangement and those at the upper floors breaking through the eaves into gableted stone dormerheads with scrolls; turrets are corbelled out at the angles, and the roof-line is punctuated by tall chimneystacks. The main entrance and first-floor window above are recessed within a moulded surround, and set between them is a sculpted panel displaying the McLean arms; the main block's second floor is slightly projected on a corbel course, the window of the circular tower being framed by colonnettes and its pedimented and finialled dormerhead carved with the initials of the builders. Behind the entrance tower rises the crenellated parapet of a taller square tower, punctuated by tall chimney-breasts and a turret, but the rear elevation is comparatively plain. Until 1963 a harled vernacular house of the later C18, much smaller in scale, stood against the main block's w flank. On plan the principal apartments are ranged across the ground floor's entire length, but with the drawing room in the main block at first floor. The stair itself is very handsome with turned balusters and elaborate finials. The more important interiors include the corridors distinguished by fine woodwork with panelled dadoes, richly carved fireplaces with overmantels and plasterwork ceilings.

MAUSOLEUM, 0.4 km. WNW. Derelict. Built to contain the remains of Andrew Farquharson of Breda (†1831). A two-storey classical front, very plain in granite ashlar with a band course, large square inscription panel and blocking course raised at the centre for a funereal urn; it screens the single-storey mausoleum with its roof of stone slabs. The mausoleum stands within a circular enclosure, entered through a round-arched ashlar gateway with wrought-iron gates.

BROTHERTON CASTLE *see* LATHALLAN SCHOOL

THE BURN   K   *5070*
5.6 km. WSW of Fettercairn

A long house built in four campaigns, although now mostly of the late C18 and early–mid C20. It was originally built for General Lord Adam Gordon, governor of Edinburgh Castle in 1791–6, and his house remains the nucleus at the S end of the building. After Gordon died in 1801, Alexander Brodie of Arnhall (*see* p. 487) extended it two bays to the N. In 1836, General William McInroy built a new service wing further N and reorientated the house to be entered from the W. The estate was purchased in 1921 by George Hubert Russell, who demolished both of the C19 additions and replaced them with a long block by *J. A. Ogg Allan*, 1933–6. In 1949, The Burn was donated to the Dominion

Students' Hall Trust (now managed by Goodenough College, London) and is run as an academic centre for student retreats.

Gordon's house is of two storeys and three bays, all in coursed brown ashlar. The ground floor is as remodelled in the late 1830s, when the main entrance was resited here from the S. Pilastered doorway topped by lintel with alternating fluting and medallions. In front of it is McInroy's porte cochère, slightly over-large, with three Roman Doric columns in the far angles and a tall, corniced architrave with blocking course, orginally balustraded. Tripartite windows to l. and r. remodelled in the same fashion, and slightly sunk in big, semicircular arched recesses. Below them are the upper margins of the windows that once lit the original Georgian service area, showing that the basement was originally exposed on this side (*see* below). Plain windows on the first floor as built by Gordon, the central one tripartite. Bad modern platform-piended roof.

The new wing of 1933–6 sweeps to the l., very long and generically similar enough to avoid causing real offence. Multipane glazing, the first section slightly recessed with five dormers. Of the same date are the two wide bow windows on the ground floor of the house's S flank. The wall-head on this side originally featured a wide pediment with glazed oculus. To the rear, Gordon's block was originally arranged 1–3–1 with the main entrance in the centre, now with the centre blind on both floors. It was topped by swagged and balustraded parapet, now re-set over the entrance to the stables (*see* below).

The glory of the INTERIOR is the rectangular ENTRANCE HALL, which rises full height to two storeys. Excellent late C18 plasterwork ceiling, all in exemplary Adam style on a ground of Wedgwood blue. Massive circular fan in the centre with anthemion at the end of the spokes. Quarter-fans in the corners and, in the panels flanking it, a big stag's head (symbol of the Gordons). The corners have a collection of muskets, sabres, bows and arrows – all symbols of the General's illustrious military past. Cantilevered staircase below it, now facing backwards to accommodate the original entrance. DRAWING ROOM on the ground floor with walls covered by beaded panelling of different sizes. Plaster frieze with swagged garlands and maidens' heads; similar overdoor with urns and dentils added. White marble chimneypiece recessed to the S, re-set here when the original entrance was blocked in the mid C19. Charioteer on the lintel and more bows and arrows as per the ceiling. One BEDROOM on the first floor with another good Adam-esque chimneypiece, of yellow-brown marble with thistle pilasters and swag. The inside of Allan's 1930s wing is drably institutional, but the BASEMENT of the old house retains the original Georgian servants' block and hall, before they were relocated to the N.

SCREEN WALL to the N of the house with two pedimented entrances (the l. now blocked, the r. topped by part of the former E balustrade). Courtyard on the other side, its N side bounded by Gordon's STABLE BLOCK, again late C18. Big U-plan of red sandstone with ashlar pediment in the centre over three straight-headed carriage entrances. Good octagonal cupola on top covered by a leaded dome. The r. wing has a jerkin-headed gable, modified *c.* 1935 when it was converted into a chauffeur's house.

Good designed landscape surrounding the house, begun by Lord Gordon in 1786, a full five years before the house was started. It is filled with embankments, ha-has and walks cut directly out of the rock, all praised in 1801 for their 'most wonderful and Romantick beauty'. Rectangular WALLED GARDEN, 0.5 km. N of the house, early C19. It is charmingly bisected by the Burn of Kirktown, with a little footbridge to pass over. Two ruined FOLLIES are hidden away in the woods: IMRIE TOWER, 0.3 km. SE of the garden, is just a wall fragment from a circular tower of *c.* 1785, already in ruins by the mid C19; GANNOCHY TOWER, 1.1 km. SSE of the house, is two storeys of cherry-cocked sandstone, originally cruciform and now gutted. Big, round keystoned arch to the NW, later blocked.

The MAIN ENTRANCE, 0.7 km. SSE, is again *c.* 1795, with circular GATEPIERS with fluted capitals flanked by low, mirrored LODGES. Each has a timber-bracketed eave overhanging a tripartite window. Screen walls extend up to GANNOCHY BRIDGE, which crosses into Angus over the rushing waters of the North Esk. Wide segmental arch of red sandstone, *c.* 15.8 m. wide, the original half paid for and built in 1732 by a local farmer, *James Black.** Three square ribs on the intrados – big, bold engineering and a daring effort for its time. The bridge was doubled in width for Lord Gordon in 1792 (see the central datestone) to accommodate larger carriage traffic, the treatment here simpler without ribs.

Former LOUPS BRIDGE, 0.4 km. W. Derelict suspension foot-bridge over the North Esk, *c.* 1825, probably by *Justice & Co.*, blacksmiths of Dundee. A rare and fine survival, notwithstanding its poor condition.

CAIRNIE   4040

A small village with school, hall and housing (mostly mid-C20) stretching along one side of a long main street, and with a much older kirkton at its E end.

Former PARISH CHURCH. By *Thomas Smith*, mason in Huntly, 1802–3. Entrance gable with round-arched doorway, square-headed gallery window and ball-finialled birdcage bellcote. Long S flank lit by four round-arched windows with shutter

---

*Black was assisted by a 'local mason' for the arch ring, but did much of the work himself.

hinge-pins, Y-tracery added mid C19. Session house at E end; N wall blind. Brown rubble with grey dressings. Interior with pulpit centred in s wall and gallery extending around three sides. FONT, 1955. ORGAN installed 1902.

The CHURCHYARD has perhaps been significant since pre-Christian times; some lying slabs and a table tomb remain. The roofless BOTARG AND PITLURG AISLE, 1597, survives from the previous St Martin's church, rebuilt in 1868 for Charles Elphinstone Dalrymple of Kinellar Lodge, whose wife was a Gordon of Pitlurg. Square enclosure, with round-arched entrance incorporating three dressed stones excavated during the works, inscription panel above. Inside, a further inscription – 'Sir Iohne Gordone of Petlurg knycht caust / big this ile in remembrans of his / predicessouris quha ar bureit / heir and to be and to be [sic] ane / burial to him and his successouris / sa lang as it pleisis God thay conteneu. 1597.' Above the arch, a half-length statue of St Martin; also within the aisle, a slab with incomplete incised figure of a knight, and a human figure tearing open his breast to reveal his heart.

Former PARISH MANSE. Unusually distinguished, built in 1784–5 for the Rev. Alexander Chalmers, who married the 4th Duke of Gordon's sister Anne Gordon in 1782. Classical, two storeys and three bays broad with pedimented projecting centre, built of dark squared whinstone with golden sandstone dressings for contrast. Roman Doric pilastered doorpiece, finely moulded architrave window surrounds and pronounced long-and-short quoins. Refined wall-head cornice and low blocking course, gabled roof with coped end stacks, later pedimented attic dormers. Rear extension c. 1868; interior much altered. Within the walled garden's SE corner a cobbled floor of medieval origin, close to St Martin's Well.

DAVIDSTON HOUSE, 6.8 km. W, near the Davidston Born. Dated 1678, altered late C18. Low three-storey L-plan house. One wing altered as a three-bay entrance front, with doorway and windows set in dressed margins against a background of harled rubble, the other wing with a tripartite window formed at first floor and outsize corner turrets at second floor where the windows break up through the eaves as small dormers; tall steeply pitched roof with crowstepped gables, solid coped chimneystacks, the elevations within the angle almost blind. NE turret corbel carved with mask and inscription 'I. G[ordon] I. A[bercrombie] builded this house' and date. Very low single-storey ranges extending from each wing enclose square court-yard with doocot. Restoration by *Jack Meldrum*, 1973–4; further restoration 1981–2.

CAMBUS O'MAY

STATION (now CAMBUS COTTAGE). Built on the Deeside Line in 1876 to service the local granite quarries. A picturesque

vernacular building, weatherboarded and covered by a polygonal bell-tipped roof with overhanging eaves and decorative
ridge tiles. Line closed in 1966, and the station converted
c. 1980s.

SUSPENSION FOOTBRIDGE, across the Dee. An elegant landmark, designed in 1905 by *Louis Harper* of *Harper & Co.* and
made by *James Abernethy & Co.*, replacing the previous treacherous ford and ferry. Paid for from the same legacy left by
Alexander Gordon that funded Polhollick Bridge, Ballater
(q.v.), this has the Harper firm's same trademark iron lattice
pylons and balustrade to a rigid-truss bridge of 49.9 m. (164 ft)
span and 4 m. (13 ft 1 in.) width.

CAMBUS O'MAY HOTEL, N of the bridge. A fishing lodge built
in 1874 by *George Truefitt* for Henry Gaskell, who was married
to Alice, sister of William Cunliffe Brooks of Glen Tanar (q.v.).
Less elegant than Fasnadarach (Dinnet), the s front has triple
gables fronted by a rustic wood veranda, facing the river. The
property retains its essential complement of fine dog kennels
and stabling, with Aberdeen-bonded stonework and fish-scale
slates.

BIRKELUNN, 0.9 km. SW of the bridge. Little Norway on
Deeside, set in a shimmering birch wood. A typical Norwegian
farmstead in log-cabin style, with local stone foundations,
mighty Norwegian timbers from Trøndelag and a flowering
turf roof. Good detailing, with carved door jambs and traditional casement windows, all with fine handmade decorative
iron fittings. It was given by Thor Thoreson of Oslo in 1938
to his daughter Grete Dagbjørt, wife of Thomas, Baron
Glentanar.

CAMMACHMORE K 9090

A hamlet close to the coast, W of the A90.

Former FREE CHURCH. Built 1843–4 and now a house. Harled
box with four arched windows to the N (the second lowered to
form a door). Ball-finialled, birdcage bellcote on the E gable
with small former vestry beyond.

BERRYHILL HOUSE, 0.7 km. NNW. The two-storey, three-bay
central block was built c. 1760 for a Rev. Gordon of Aberdeen.
Lower, symmetrical wings added at the start of the C19, battlements at the end of the C19. The red harling dates from the
late 1930s. – Around the house, the remains of a mid-C18
designed LANDSCAPE, including long s green terraced by
ha-has.

ELSICK HOUSE. *See* p. 480.

CANDACRAIG HOUSE
2 km. sw of Strathdon

Scots Vernacular, recast by *A. G. R. Mackenzie* in 1956 after a fire. Prior to that date it was larger and Neo-Jacobean, principally by *John Smith*, 1835–6, for Alexander Anderson, who had recently succeeded to the estate, but incorporating fabric from an earlier house, perhaps that recorded in 1579. A w wing was added for Alexander Falconer Wallace by *George Gordon* of Inverness in 1900–1, the enlarged house being remodelled internally by *George Bennett Mitchell c.* 1928. Smith's house comprised a two-storey main block rising into dormerheads, attic gables and clustered chimneystacks, its focus being a four-stage entrance tower with a ball-finialled balustrade on the E. Its porte cochère with four-centred archways was replaced by an iron veranda in the early C20.

The present house incorporates elements of the old but is quite different in character, an elongated, irregular composition of fairly consistent two-storey height, harled in cream. Its s front divides into two parts. A three-bay block, but with four windows at first floor breaking into stone dormer gablets, constitutes most of what survives of Smith's main block, much remodelled by Mackenzie. It is flanked by drum towers rising into conical roofs at its NW and SE corners, cleverly designed to give the impression of a small Z-plan house. The NW drum tower is original and forms a link with Gordon's surviving w wing, which, progressively stepping back, consti- tutes the remainder of the s front, its mullioned-and- transomed bay window and the banded first-floor windows being evidently later work. The SE drum tower forms the s corner of the entrance forecourt. This is two-storeyed and enclosed on two sides only, that on the w partly reconstituted from the remains of Smith's main block, and that on the N from the large L-plan wing which stood to the rear of Smith's house, its two-bay gable front rising into tall ashlar chimney- stacks on the N side. Within the re-entrant angle Mackenzie formed a large ogee-roofed quarter-drum which contains the main doorway.

The principal apartments are arranged across the s front. The dining room occupies the fragment of the old main block, its doorcases with broken pediments and simple ceiling cornice being Mackenzie's work. In the w wing the drawing room's wood panelling and strapwork plaster ceiling must date from Mitchell's time, although the finely carved Tudor fireplace may be earlier. The library beyond is also panelled, as is the first- floor master bedroom.

OFFICES (50 m. wsw). Mid-C18 (before 1760), with alterations *c.* 1835. Rectangular courtyard plan. An early COACHHOUSE forms the s range, single storey and dormered attic, three depressed arches in the centre framed by taller single arches at each end. N and W RANGES single storey and attic, E RANGE single-storeyed only. Cream-harled, now residential.

DOOCOT, 240 m. E. C17. Small square-plan with crowstepped gables E and W. Small central wall-head gable with lozenge opening rises into moulded chimneystack. Inside, ground-floor room with hearth.

TEMPIETTO, 110 m. ESE. By *Ian G. Lindsay* with *Wattie Cooper*, mason, 1963. Roman Doric columns reused from the demolished Altyre House in Moray, raised on a stepped plinth and supporting an entablature.

CASTLE OF FIDDES   K   *8080*
5.4 km. NW of Catterline

Four-storey tower house built for Andrew Arbuthnott, who acquired the land in 1555. Construction was complete by the end of the C17 – a time of dynamic experimentation – and the result is a fine and bizarre variant of the usual L-plan. Crowstepped main block running N–S with wing projecting to the E. The main S gable is lost amid thick protrusions, each attached like massive barnacles threatening to take over their host. In the l. angle, a circular tower rising up diagonally below a square, corbelled caphouse. Opposite is the castle's greatest eccentricity: a circular stair-tower bursting out of the re-entrant angle, projecting well beyond the confines of the building like an independent donjon. The upper crowsteps are swept around in a strange, pleasing curve, and beyond it a balcony corbelled out which originally served as the guards' WATCHING PLATFORM. That feature too is very rare. Roll-moulded, segmental entrance in the next re-entrant angle, with a circular shot-hole to the l. and r. Shallow, machicolated projection over it (originally with a large heraldic plaque) to discourage intruders.

The jamb stretches to the r. with a stack of four windows. The upper one has a lintel dated 1592 and then a triangular dormerhead with 'Laus Deo' ('Praise God') and a thistle finial. Plain E gable with central chimneystack flanked by a corbelled, roofed tourelle; shot-holes pointing downwards. In the centre of the N side, a narrow stair-tower is very shallowly corbelled out and made square on top. The W front faces the garden, its l. angle featuring a two-storey tourelle as a foil to the bulky SW tower.

The interior was remodelled twice in the C20 and has few original features. Barrel-vaulted wine cellar in the main block with service staircase to the hall above. In the basement of the jamb, a big C17 fireplace arch. For all its heft, the re-entrant stair-tower leads only to the first floor and a small chamber over the entrance.

CASTLE FORBES
1 km. E of Keig

66   A castellated house by *Archibald Simpson*, his first commission,
begun in 1814 for Gen. James Forbes, but completed 1821 by
John Smith after difficulties arose during construction. Forbes
had previously commissioned *John Paterson* to produce two
designs in 1807 and 1811, the first symmetrical castellated and
the second a Neoclassical scheme which incorporated the plain
three-storey Putachie House (built 1731) into a remarkable triangular plan with an ingenious geometrical layout of the internal
accommodation: this Paterson subsequently carried out at Lennel
(*see* Borders) in 1820. Simpson's design similarly incorporated
Putachie into its entrance front. It combined Paterson's geometrical planning with more up-to-date developments in the
Castellated style, in which the elevations were asymmetrically
composed for greater picturesque effect, as in the work of John
Nash and Simpson's own London-based master, Robert Lugar,
who had recently designed Tullichewan (1808, dem.) and Balloch
(1809), both in w Dumbartonshire.

Simpson's commission for Castle Forbes was an extraordinary
achievement for a man of twenty-four, newly established in independent practice and already working for the premier baron of
Scotland. As Forbes was still insisting on the retention of Putachie,
which faced s w and had relatively low ceiling heights, Simpson's
concept was to incorporate it into his entrance front and build a
new block at right angles facing s e with two tall storeys in the
height of Putachie's three to provide the grander principal apartments required; a tall circular tower at the s salient angle avoided
any direct incompatibility in scale or floor levels, the composition
being balanced by lower rectangular towers at the n w and n e.
Building began with *Alexander Wallace* as mason, but fairly early
in the contract Putachie suffered subsidence and had to be
demolished. Enough had been built, however, for Forbes to be
committed to Simpson's scheme, Putachie's s w front being
rebuilt in a three-bay format rather than the original five. The
house as completed by *Smith* is all of a piece in squared granite,
with only small details hinting that it is the work of two
architects.

The ENTRANCE FRONT is essentially a composition of simple
geometric masses with corbelled and crenellated parapets
dominated by the tall circular four-storey s tower on the r.,
balanced by the lower rectangular n w tower on the l. Between
them is the three-storey three-bay centre which replaced
Putachie, still in the Adam–Paterson Roman castellated
manner, with an arched recess sheltering the first- and second-
floor windows at the advanced centre bay. Projecting from it
is the central porch with dummy angle turrets, the hoodmoulded round arch of its doorway echoed in the tall ground-
floor windows of the circular s tower. The detail is otherwise
sparing, with hoodmoulds only at the second-floor windows

and at the central second-floor window of the circular tower, where there are robustly carved headstops of a medieval knight and his lady.

The SE FRONT is similar but reversed, the circular S tower on the l. balanced by the three-storey NE tower on the r., the latter with a canted bay and a two-storey four-bay centre, all with tall windows from which to admire the landscape as it rolls down to the banks of the Don. As the SW entrance front and the SE flank are of almost identical length, when seen together from the S they present a balanced composition receding back from the circular tower, which has clearly been drawn from Paterson's triangular plan. Small but significant details differentiate Simpson's work on the SE and Smith's on the SW. Only the SE elevation has the carved heads of muzzled bears and hounds just below the central block's parapet, the particularly savage-looking dog with razor-sharp teeth nearest the circular tower evidently a waterspout for draining the roofs; and while the turrets of the SE elevation's rectangular tower have double-keyhole gunloops, those of its counterpart on the entrance front have simple slits.

The NW FRONT is shorter, with a lower three-storey block behind the entrance front, and then the walls of the SERVICE COURT, still in coursed squared rubble with crenellations, entered through a round-headed archway on the NE SIDE, with blind fenestration suggesting ground and low first floors. Within the court the service accommodation was single-storeyed, the tall triple chimneystacks, diagonally shafted, identifying the location of the former kitchen. After the Second World War the service ranges were demolished to enlarge the court for recreational purposes.

The PLAN ranges the principal apartments across the SW entrance front and SE garden front. Behind them are two main staircases which enabled the SW and NW apartments with their lower ceiling heights to function separately from the remainder in winter. In contrast to Tullichewan, their decoration is classical throughout, perhaps reflecting Smith's lack of experience in Gothic work at that date.

The ENTRANCE HALL, which occupies the r. bays of the centre block on the SW front, has a simple Neoclassical chimneypiece and (as befitted a general) a deep frieze with victory wreaths, its fine eight-panelled doors within reeded doorcases a measure of the high-quality finishes of the interior as a whole. Two deep doorway recesses lead into the much taller bicameral DRAWING ROOM, which occupies the circular tower and most of the centre block on the SE front: the circular saloon in the tower has a saucer-domed ceiling decorated with rosettes while the larger apartment has a simple Greek chimneypiece in white marble, doorcases with lions' heads and consoles, a deep reeded dado and a Neoclassical frieze. It links through a short passage into what was formerly the DINING ROOM in the NE tower: this has a canted bay but has been altered, since as designed by Simpson it had a distyle *in antis* columnar screen at its inner end. The l. bay of the entrance front contains the former MORNING ROOM, also somewhat altered, while the NW tower contains the LIBRARY, which remains intact with slim colonnettes framing its chimney-breast and still fitted with its original bookcases. The SE staircase is approximately square on plan, simple but very handsome with cast-iron balusters and top-lit from a coffered dome; the NW staircase is also top-lit and even more simply detailed, but of a splendid elliptical form which is a refinement of the oval staircase proposed in Paterson's plans of 1811.

Behind the house the DAIRY (50 m. ENE), either by *Simpson* or *Smith c.* 1815–20, reflects the main house's geometrical interests – Y-plan single storey, ashlar-built, with three arms each a single bay in length extending from a central castellated drum. Its entrance front facing the house has a concentric timber porch supported on slim clustered colonnettes which frame three finely panelled doors; the wings have blind windows (painted dummies) and shallow-pitched roofs with crowstepped gables. The central drum is kept relatively low with round-headed dummy lights beneath a boldly crenellated parapet; the rear elevation is comparatively plain.

Simple HOME FARM (250 m. NNW) in coursed rubble laid out around a square courtyard, the E range single storey and loft with the farmhouse at its S end rising into gableted stone dormers. The N and W ranges together form a single-storey L-plan. The S range was rebuilt in the C20 and subsequently demolished.

Castle Forbes stands at one end of the Alford Valley on Bennachie's SW slopes, centred in its POLICIES on the banks of the Don. Their layout dates from the C18: driveways approach from the B992 on the W and a minor road, 'The Laird's Throat', on the N, one of the western drives crossing a round-arched BRIDGE in coursed squared rubble across a small burn. A SUSPENSION FOOTBRIDGE at Craigpot, mid-C19, with cast-iron pylons and chains and a timber walkway, crosses the Don itself into the dense woodland on the E side.*
Well protected by shelter-belts, the house enjoys a fine outlook over rolling parkland to the S and W, with the Bridge of Keig (q.v.) in the distance.

Within the policies, 350 m. SW, is KEIG OLD PARISH CHURCH. C17. Roofless rectangular plan; five-bay flank, now with alternating doorways and windows. The W window is unusual in that it is narrower above its transom. E wall with memorial to James, 16th Lord Forbes (†1804); C18 stones in the graveyard.

On the policies' W edge, the former MANSE (now Oakbank, 500 m. SW), 1774. Simple attractive two-storey three-bay house, harled with exposed dressings and margins, gabled roof with end stacks.

---

*Seemingly pre-1868, as a suspension bridge is shown in the 1st Ordnance Survey, published in that year.

CASTLE FRASER

2.8 km. NE of Sauchen

Castle Fraser is one of the great masterpieces of the Scottish   49
Renaissance. Striking from whichever angle it is observed, its
architecture appears consistently of the early C17. It was, however,
constructed in at least four separate building campaigns, and
over the past two hundred years the leading historians of North-
East architecture have tried to establish its building history, culminating in the detailed study published by Harry Gordon Slade
in 1977, which has so far withstood the test of time.

Thomas Fraser was granted the barony of Stoneywood and
Muchall by James II in 1454, and there is now a general presump-
tion that the central block – the earliest fabric of the House of
Muchall-in-Mar, as Castle Fraser was once known – dates from
that time. It was a simple rectangle and did not remotely resemble the magnificent tower house we see today: that began to take
shape between 1563 and 1576, when Michael Fraser laid out the
basic Z-plan by extending the original rectangle and adding a
smaller square tower – the Michael Tower – at its NW corner, and
a circular tower at the SE. The castle was then only three-storeyed, probably like the Old House of Carnousie (N) completed
c. 1577, and possessing distinctive motifs pointing to *Thomas
Leiper*'s authorship. The tower house achieved its present form
when it was heightened for Michael's son Andrew in the early–
mid C17, the elaborate panoply of its upper storeys dated 1617–18
and signed by *I. Bel*, traditionally interpreted as *John Bell* of the
family of master masons active in Aberdeenshire. *James Leiper*
was commissioned to undertake further works, including the
laying out of a geometric floor (like that at Thomas Leiper's
Tolquhon, N) but early absconded and was outlawed, being 'put
to the horn'. The forecourt on the N, the master mason for which
is unknown, was seemingly constructed c. 1631–3 when Andrew
Fraser, possessed of broad estates and an exceptional new house,
was elevated by Charles I as the 1st Lord Fraser, and recognized
as pre-eminent in his clan.

The House of Muchall passed to the Frasers of Inverallochy
(N) in 1717, and was seemingly renamed Castle Fraser at about
that time. Miss Elyza Fraser inherited in 1792; by 1794 she had
decided that the Castle should not be approached through its
forecourt on the N but that a new carriage entrance should be
formed on the S. The S-side windows were enlarged, with a bright
outlook over the policies, which she and her friend Mary Bristow
improved; her architect was probably *John Paterson*, who produced designs for the entrance hall and stables. Another of her
friends, *James Byres* of Tonley (*see* Tough), who designed her
mausoleum (*see* Cluny Old Churchyard), may also have been
involved. Miss Elyza's great-nephew Col. Charles Mackenzie
Fraser seemingly commissioned *William Wilkins* c. 1819 to
instigate a more radical Tudor remodelling but this was not
carried out, *William Burn* being called in to make minor internal

alterations. Then *c.* 1829 and 1837, with *John Smith* as his archi-tect, Col. Fraser formed a new stair hall on the N side of the central block and extended the forecourt.

After the Frasers sold the castle to Sir Weetman Pearson, 1st Viscount Cowdray, in 1922, his second son, Clive, asked *Sir Robert S. Lorimer* to survey the structure, but despite – or perhaps even because of – Sir Robert's enthusiasm to enlarge the castle as a family home, from *c.* 1928 Clive engaged the scholarly *William Kelly* to undertake a conservative, archaeologically led restoration which continued until the Second World War. Kelly died in 1944, and in 1946 Clive Pearson passed the castle to his daughter Lavinia and son-in-law Major Michael Smiley. They continued the restoration by clearing the forecourt of its C19 accretions, and in 1976 they presented the castle to the National Trust for Scotland.

To visitors approaching by the Broad Walk, as the 1st Lord Fraser would have done, the gently falling slope and trees on each side reveal the castle's N FRONT only gradually, first enticing with its turreted upperworks, then its upper storeys until, in almost theatrical fashion, the whole tower house emerges as if out of the ground, with its courtyard in front of it.

It is the largest Z-plan tower house in North-East Scotland, 30 m. measured diagonally across from the NW corner of the four-storey Michael Tower, through the four-storey central block, to the opposite far curvature of the Round Tower stepped back on the SE, which rises seven storeys to a balus-traded platform roof. The turrets marking the corners of the central block and Michael Tower, and that over the slim stair-tourelle in the re-entrant angle between them, are unusual in that they are two-storeyed – attic and garret – under their spirelets. At the central block, two pedimented attic dormers and one above them in the garret frame a very large heraldic panel which, although eroded, remains a fine piece of carving in red freestone, formerly tinctured and gilded: above, the Royal Arms as used in Scotland between 1603 and 1707, encir-cled by a garter, and beneath Lord Fraser's arms flanked by supporters, a falcon *dexter* and heron *sinistra*, both still visible. Beneath the heraldic panel, a much smaller panel is carved with the inscription 1617 I BEL MM♡F. MM may stand for Master Mason, the heart for loyalty to Fraser, or it may be Bell's own symbol, since it reappears at Craigston (N).

The turrets, dormers and heraldic panel all rise from a deeply sculpted corbel course with individual corbels, cables, rope moulding and dummy water cannon. This is stepped down where it supports the turrets and panel, and is carried across both the Round Tower and the Michael Tower, tying all these elements together. There is a further corbel course around the Round Tower's wall-head, and on the Michael Tower's N face there is a stepped moulding between the turrets, hinting that it once had a crenellated parapet.

During the C20 restoration it was decided to leave the central block's C15 rubble work exposed to show the archaeological evidence of its building history, although the C16 Michael Tower and Round Tower are still harled with ashlar dressings, as was the whole castle until the 1950s. For much of its height the central block's N elevation is now blind, with only two small windows high up on the third floor; but in the centre of the wall at first floor is a blocked opening which seems originally to have been a window but was formed into a mid-C17 doorway with diamond-pattern rustication of which traces remain, and which was approached by a grand stair removed to build the new stair hall in 1829–30.* It was certainly not the original doorway: in Michael Fraser's time, as a Z-plan house of only three storeys, access was through the doorway still surviving in the Michael Tower's re-entrant flank, just as at Carnousie. This doorway was once protected by *Thomas Leiper*'s distinctive triple gunloops, other examples of which may be seen in the Michael Tower and Round Tower. High up in the same flank is a panel displaying the Arma Christi, suggesting that the Frasers adhered to Roman Catholicism for some time after the Reformation.

The two-storey FORECOURT RANGES, extending forward to conical-roofed drum towers at their outer corners, were built *c.* 1631–3; the single-storey crowstepped 'lodges' and segment-headed gateway in front of these through which the forecourt is now entered are part of *John Smith*'s work for Col. Fraser in 1836–9, one of the bellcotes (E) having originally graced Cluny Parish Church. The forecourt is very much a formal approach. The ground-floor rooms once contained services but those at first floor contained galleries and were much more distinguished: their windows face into the courtyard and out across the policies and rise into tall dormerheads with alternately triangular and segmental pediments. These are carved with Andrew Fraser's initials and those of his two wives, his son Andrew and his daughter-in-law, proof of his links to other NE families and the future of his line; the W range is slightly older, dated 1631 with initials A.F. for Andrew Fraser, while the E range, with initials L.A.F. (Lord Andrew Fraser), must have been completed after he was ennobled.

The S SIDE – Miss Elyza's entrance front from 1795 – rises tall and sheer from the lawn, the original tower house the central block with the Round Tower projecting boldly forward on the r., the Michael Tower set back on the l., and the long two-storey courtyard ranges stretching back to conical-roofed drums at the rear. Elyza's new entrance is a welcoming cavetto-splayed round-arched and key-blocked doorway entered at ground level with minimal formality. At first floor she lowered the sills of the three windows lighting the great hall, the broad

*The suggestion that this stair is the one now at Meldrum House, Oldmeldrum (N), is now known to be incorrect.

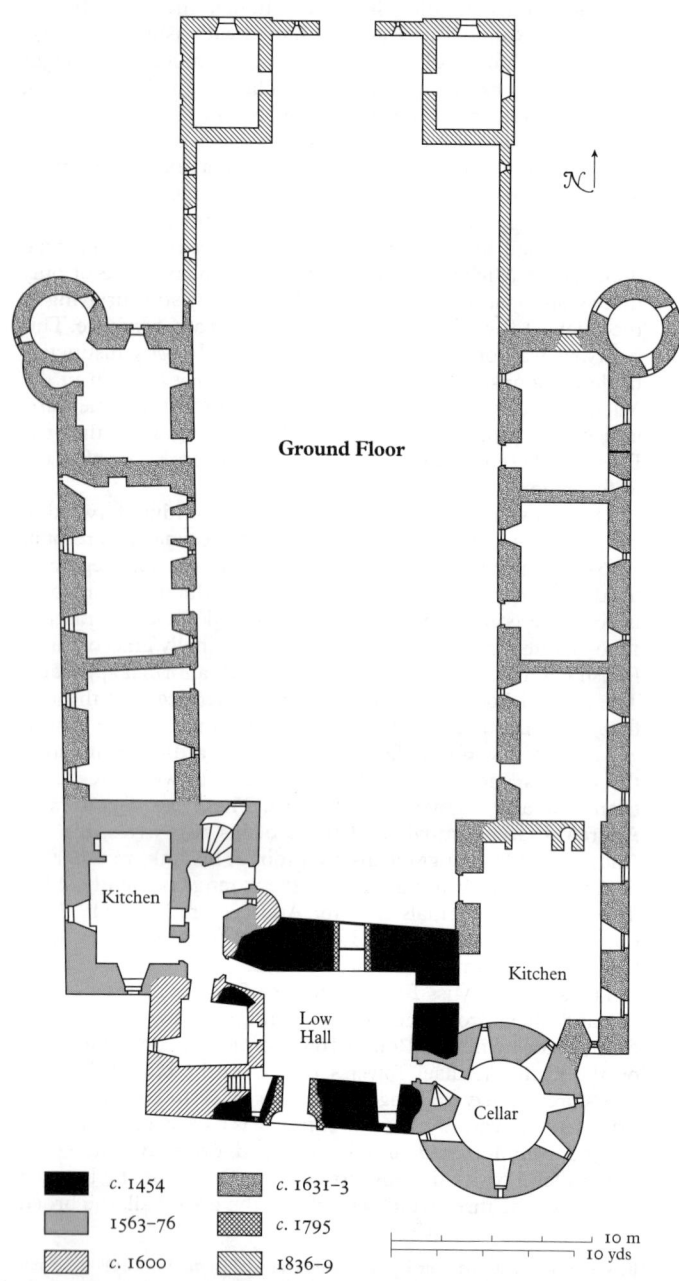

Ground Floor

N

Kitchen

Kitchen

Low
Hall

Cellar

■	*c.* 1454	▨ *c.* 1631–3
▦	1563–76	▧ *c.* 1795
▨	*c.* 1600	▨ 1836–9

10 m
10 yds

Castle Fraser.
Plan of ground and first floors

expanse of rubble masonry above expressing the height of its vault; then four smaller windows at third floor, beneath the pedimented attic dormers supported – as on the N front – by a deeply moulded corbel course. The roof-line is punctuated by spirelet corner turrets, and within the junction between the centre block and the Round Tower a four-storey stair-turret is corbelled out, rising above the Round Tower's balustrade into an ogee domelet and weathervane.

A few earlier, smaller windows have survived. Inserted into the walls by Miss Elyza are three tablets: the Royal Arms dated 1576; the arms of Charles, 4th and last Lord Fraser, dated 1683

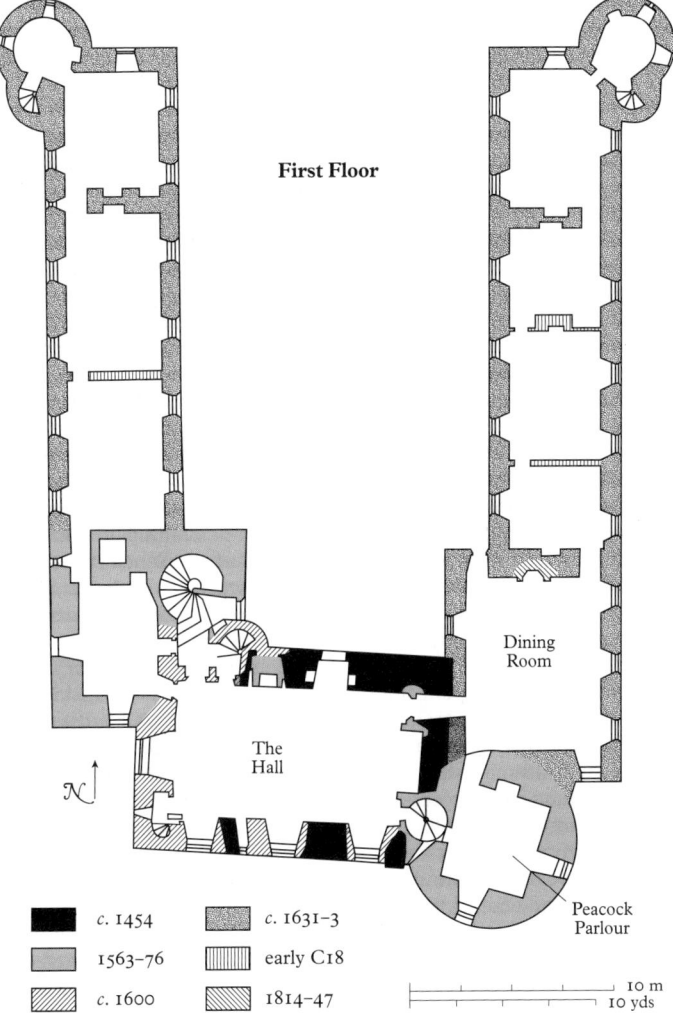

First Floor

Dining Room

The Hall

N

Peacock Parlour

■ c. 1454		▨ c. 1631–3	
▨ 1563–76		▥ early C18	
▨ c. 1600		▨ 1814–47	

10 m
10 yds

(both transferred from the N front); and her own arms, dated
1795. To the l. of the entrance is a single inverted keyhole
gunloop, quite different from Leiper's, dating from the mid
C15.

On the W SIDE the central block was not always so long as
it is now. Its westward enlargement (*see* below) is evident at its
junction with the Michael Tower, the windows of which are
pressed close in to the angle; the large window lighting the
great hall's W end was reputedly formed – or more probably
enlarged – so that Miss Elyza could enjoy the sunsets.

On PLAN the original tower was apparently a rectangular structure 12 m. by 10 m., its walls 2 m. thick, and both its ground-
floor low hall and first-floor great hall vaulted. The entrance
was seemingly at first floor on the N side, but to the w of the
C17 central doorway, superseded by the present ground-floor
entrance when the Michael Tower was built. Allowing for a
stair, of which there is now no visible trace, it provided only
modest accommodation for Thomas Fraser and his retainers
in the mid C15, although more may have been provided in the
barmkin. The Michael Tower is nearly square, 9.75 m. by
9.25 m., over walls just 0.5 m. thick, vaulted at its ground and
second floors only. It differs from most entrance jambs of the
same vintage in being unusually wide to accommodate, on the
ground floor, a vaulted kitchen as well as the main stair. This
led Douglas Simpson to conclude that it might have been the
original tower house, but it seems hardly big enough even if
its kitchen and stairs to all levels would have allowed it to
function as such. Its square footprint is typical of Leiper, who
used square plans elsewhere, e.g. at Arnage, possibly at
Carnousie, and in the entrance jamb and courtyard at Barra
Castle (all N). The Round Tower, again vaulted at ground
floor, is more solid: 8.5 m. in diameter over walls 1.8 m. thick.

The complexities of Castle Fraser's building history are
reflected in the planning of its stairs generally. When the Z-plan
was first laid out by Michael Fraser in the mid C16 and the
Michael Tower became the entrance jamb, its broad turnpike
stair rising from the ground-floor entrance to the first floor was
the main means of access to principal floor level as in most
other L- and Z-plan houses. It serves that purpose again now
that the grand external stair built by Andrew, 1st Lord Fraser,
and the stair hall built by Col. Fraser to replace it have both
gone. Although his analysis has since been disputed, Slade
concluded that access to the upper floors in Michael Fraser's
time must originally have been by a smaller turnpike stair in
the Michael Tower's SE corner at its junction with the original
W gable of the central block; this turnpike had been demolished
when the central block was extended westward, and replaced
by a completely new stair built into the re-entrant angle, blocking the Leiper triple gunloop which had hitherto guarded the
main entrance. Slade believed that this was a slightly later
development sometime after 1588; Thomas Addyman believes
it to be part of the works of c. 1563–76 as access from the

original main block to the new Michael Tower would otherwise have been too constricted. The E turnpike stair rising through all three floors within the junction of the central block and the Round Tower is certainly part of Leiper's works of c. 1563–76, but to give access to the new upper floors at the latter Bell provided a further turnpike corbelled out at attic level immediately above it.

The INTERIORS are relatively simple. As the 1st Lord knew them they lasted less than ten years after his death since the 2nd Lord was a prominent Covenanter and the castle was sacked by the Earl of Aboyne in 1644. Decorative features, such as the window shutters carved with portraits of Scottish kings – which must have been similar to those at Craigston (N) – have long since been lost. The only features surviving from that time are the finely carved MAIN STAIR newel in the Michael Tower, and the GREAT HALL's Early Scots Renaissance fireplace. The very large fissure in the Great Hall's vault shows clearly the point from which the central block was extended westwards: the blocked opening in the N side with small aumbries and hinge-pins was formerly a doorway. Evidence has been preserved of a tightly planned SW service stair rising up from the Low Hall. In 1815–16, Col. Fraser engaged *William Burn* to design a Gothic ceiling for the Great Hall's vault in its transformation into the Drawing Room; during the course of the colonel's works throughout the castle – from c. 1829 entrusted to *John Smith* – many original features were damaged or destroyed, including the 'Laird's Lug' formed above the Great Hall vault, so called because it was once thought to be a secret listening chamber in which the Frasers could eavesdrop on their guests. Most of Col. Fraser's alterations were reversed in the C20.

In the DINING ROOM, which opens off the Great Hall on the first floor of the E forecourt wing, the simple Early Georgian woodwork and the slim plain cornice supporting a coved ceiling have survived, but the room's present appearance dates from 1977 when David Learmont and Lavinia Smiley removed Smith's Peterhead granite chimneypiece and inserted the present marble bolection one salvaged from an English demolition. On the central block's third floor above the great hall, the LIBRARY with ribbed canted ceiling was formed by *Smith* in 1839 where the Fore and Back Great Chamber had been; it still retains its original Tudoresque wallpaper and classical broken-pedimented bookcases purchased in London.

Within the Michael Tower, the ground-floor KITCHEN retains its massive segmentally vaulted range, complete with bread oven. The second floor contains two rooms, one probably an ORATORY since the Arma Christi are set in the outside wall beneath its window sill; the VAULTED CHAMBER next to it has a central boss bearing the initials M.F. and a secret under-floor compartment. The third floor contains the WORKED ROOM, named after the needlework bedhangings, curtain and seat furniture reputedly made by Elyza Fraser and her companion Mary Bristow; its has a C17 doorcase, as does another adjacent BEDROOM.

In the Round Tower, the PEACOCK ROOM is named after its early C19 wallpaper; the GREEN ROOM wallpaper is late C19, while the PINK ROOM is modern reproduction. The rooms commemorating the Smileys are decorated in their own taste.

The Forecourt ranges contain services at ground floor and living accommodation at first floor. Originally the longer E range contained a dining room with a gallery of six bays beyond. The W range consisted of a four-bay gallery with Lady Fraser's chambers occupying the N end and drum tower, a narrow turnpike staircase leading to an attic-level 'wardrop' or dressing room above. Examination by Thomas Addyman has demonstrated that the dining room and the galleries once had barrel-vaulted ceilings in timber. The present divisions of these wings dates from the earlier C18.

The POLICIES extend over 150 hectares from Alton Brae Wood on the N to Miss Bristow's Wood on the S, and from the shelter-belt on the E to the boundary wall running along the minor road behind the stables to the W. In the C17–C18 the castle was enclosed by the Doocot Yard's walls and dykes on the W, the Cherry Yard next to the castle itself and the formal gardens to the S. The E and W avenues ran along the N side of these, the Broad Avenue to the N being the axial approach to the castle, and extending beyond it as the South Avenue. Of this approximately cruciform formal layout only the BROAD WALK of sycamores survives, albeit replanted and now with some ash. What seems to be the oldest feature of all, visible from Broad Walk, is a STANDING STONE 200 m. NW of the castle, traditionally said to have been erected in celebration of I. Bell *c.* 1618, but more probably of prehistoric origin, a natural boulder partly hewn to form an obelisk, its granite capstone added centuries later, and once with a ball finial. About 650 m. WSW of here stands a fine RECUMBENT STONE CIRCLE, which consists of seven standing stones, recumbent and flankers. Cremated bones were found in the centre during C19 excavations.

The Picturesque LANDSCAPE was begun by Elyza Fraser and Mary Bristow on the basis of *Thomas White (Sen.)*'s plan of 1794, which they adapted. Further improvements took place under Col. Fraser between 1815 and 1840, perhaps assisted by *James Giles*. Clive Pearson, his daughter and son-in-law enhanced the policies between the 1920s and 1970s, with the assistance (among others) of *Lanning Roper* and *James Russell*, and the National Trust for Scotland has continued to develop them since. The woodlands suffered badly in the Great Gale of 1953 and have been substantially replanted. The large rectangular WALLED GARDEN – 80 m. by 50 m., lying 150 m. NNE of the Castle – was part of *White*'s scheme and was formed in 1795; the N wall was heated by steam pipes running between its outer face of granite and the inner brick lining. The complex lectern SUNDIAL in freestone is C17, although its tapering granite shaft appears later. *White* was also responsible for an artificial serpentine LAKE to the SE of the Castle, subsequently improved by Col. Fraser but infilled between 1846 and 1850. The lake in Alton Brae Wood was created later to encourage wildfowl-shooting.

The STABLES, which stand on a rise of ground overlooking an ornamental pond 250 m. WSW of the Castle, are themselves a focal point, built in 1795 to earlier designs by *John Paterson*. Their polygonal entrance front, two-storeyed in coursed squared granite, has taller cylindrical angle towers with spired roofs, nodding to the Castle without in any way challenging it. The central segmental archway opens into a courtyard which is almost square. Above this archway is a C17 carved panel of a rearing horse; above the archway on the far side of the courtyard is a lion's head.

In Miss Bristow's Wood the MOSES WELL (900 m. SSE) is a low vaulted chamber probably *c.* 1795, with bas-relief sculptures of Moses striking the rock and on Mount Sinai, perhaps obtained by *James Byres* acting as a dealer; its fountain is a reused dormer from the castle.

CATTERLINE K   *8070*

Small village perched over a bay scooped out of the Mearns coast. From the C12 it served as a natural harbour, and 'den houses' for sailors are documented at the end of the C14. Little had changed by the early C19, when the rubble pier was constructed, jutting straight out with solid parapet on the seaward side. Nos. 1–10 SOUTH ROW are single-storey three-bay cottages from *c.* 1820, of whitewashed rubble with slate roofs. They include a former washing house and fishermen's store.

ST PHILIP (Episcopal), 0.5 km. N. Buttressed, lanceted box by *Charles Brand*, 1848, with slightly lower chancel and SW porch. Stepped triplet in the E gable; elementary plate tracery in the w. Scissor-brace roof in the nave. – Octagonal stone FONT, *c.* 1906, carved with Instruments of the Passion. – STAINED GLASS. E window, mid-C19 Crucifixion flanked by SS Philip and James. – To the N are Brand's former PARSONAGE, built 1848, and SCHOOL, 1850. The latter has additions, 1901.

OLD BURIAL GROUND, 250 m. NW. Site of the medieval parish church dedicated to St Catherine (Katerline), first recorded in the late C12 and superseded in the mid C18 by the Old Parish Church at Kinneff (*see* p. 606). Nothing remains except its former AUMBRY, re-set on the inner wall to the r. of the entrance. Depressed ogee with a spiked centre, probably C15. Above it, a late medieval SLAB incised with cross and sword.

TODHEAD LIGHTHOUSE, 1.2 km. S. By *D. & C. Stevenson*, 1897; light with Fresnel lens made jointly by *Henry-Lepaute* of

Paris and *Milne & Son Ltd*, Edinburgh (discontinued, 2007).
Thick, rather squat cylinder with slight entasis, the bright
white harling contrasted with beige margins. Row of stout
corbels supporting the upper walkway. Large domed light on
top with lattice glazing and ball finial. – Blocky, flat-roofed
KEEPERS' COTTAGES behind. Entrance with dedication on a
block-pedimented lintel. – Two-storey detached KEEPERS'
HOUSE also of 1897, meant to house three families.

EAST MAINS OF BARRAS, 2.6 km. NNW. Embedded in the
garden wall is the SE base of a tower house built by the Ogilvies
of Barras in the late C17 (dem. *c.* 1862).

CASTLE OF FIDDES. *See* p. 401.

CHAPEL OF GARIOCH

A village on a ridge above the Urie valley. A private chapel dedicated to the Virgin was founded by Robert Bruce's sister Christine
before 1357. A new parish church – a presbytery seat – was built
after Chapel of Garioch and Fetternear parishes united in 1599.

PARISH CHURCH. By *Alexander Wallace*, mason in Drumnaher,
and *William Sangster*, wright in Oldmeldrum (N), 1813.
Gothick. A simple rectangular plan in coursed red granite,
partly cherry-cocked, unusually tall and broad for a rural
church of its date. Its size is reflected in the shallow pitch of
its gabled roof, with a small ball-finialled birdcage bellcote at
its W end. Four big S windows. Transom-lit E and W doorways;
matching gallery-level windows probably formed by *Kelly &
Nicol c.* 1914–15. Original glazing with basket-weave tracery
throughout. Reordered *c.* 1922–3 when *A. Marshall Mackenzie*
added the shallow but broad N chancel rising from low walls
into a tall gabled roof; its five-light N window has intersecting
tracery of Aberdeen Greyfriars type (*see* p. 113). Small outshots
to either side by *McCombie & Mennie*, 1968. The remodelled
INTERIOR AND FURNISHINGS are very much *Mackenzie's*
work. Raked galleries with panelled fronts supported on square
columns extend across the nave's E and W sides, partly obscuring the S windows. – FONT. Slim octagonal pedestal, finely
crafted with the Leslie crest. 2014. – ORGAN by *Evans & Barr*,
Belfast, 1923. – LAMP in the form of the Burning Bush by local
craftsmen. – STAINED GLASS. Chancel N window, 1931. Virgin
and Child, Holy Grail and Crown of Thorns, four scenes
from the Old Testament, Life of Christ, Crucifixion, and
Evangelists. – MONUMENT. Robert Farquhar, †1787. Classical
wall tablet.

The previous CHURCH of *c.* 1600 is represented in the
churchyard by its S aisle, a coursed rubble rectangle, preserved
as a burial enclosure. Inside, a panel crudely carved with a
Calvary cross. In the churchyard's E wall, PITTODRIE'S
GATE, dated 1626, but perhaps not *in situ*. Roll-moulded

round-arched opening beneath a moulded gable; three carved finials on top are perhaps from the old church's belfry.

BALQUHAIN CASTLE, 1.9 km. ESE. Ruinous tower house on rising ground above the Strathnaterick Burn, sheltered by Bennachie. A Leslie seat from at least the early C14: a tower house was reputedly burnt by John Forbes of Druminnor (q.v.) *c.* 1420 and in 1441 John Leslie contracted with *David Hardgat, David Dun, Roger Masoun* and *Gilbert Masoun* to complete its reconstruction. Burnt again by the Forbes in 1526, it was rebuilt by Sir William Leslie *c.* 1530, its surviving architectural features being consistent with that date.

The Leslies abandoned Balquhain for Fetternear (q.v.) in 1710. It was stripped to a shell by John Clerk, advocate in Aberdeen, in 1749, but as depicted by James Giles in 1839 its walls survived substantially intact. Consolidation was carried out *c.* 1870. When MacGibbon and Ross surveyed the site its rear (N) wall and part of the W gable had fallen. Proposals by *George Bennett Mitchell* (then of *Davidson & Garden*) to restore Balquhain in 1897 came to nought, and by the 1920s the courtyard had been largely reduced to its foundations.

The TOWER HOUSE's simple rectangular plan, its massively thick walls and its original entrance at first floor rather than ground floor all suggest that it incorporates substantial fabric of the structures burnt *c.* 1420 and 1526. It measures 13.8 m. by 8.8 m., built in local granite rubble, partly coursed, with carefully wrought quoins, the E gable being more tightly constructed than the rest. The long S front still rises four storeys to a wall-head some 14 m. above ground, although the fourth storey is an addition, the previous wall-head above the third storey having risen flush into battlements.* At ground floor, lit only by loopholes, the walls are 1.8 m. thick and contain two vaulted chambers; a masonry set-off marks the crowning of their vaults. It is unclear whether there was any access from ground floor to first, although there may have been a service stair in the SW corner. The first floor was the hall, its two large S-facing windows blocked during the later C19 consolidation, and its fireplace in the E gable. A turnpike in the NE corner, beginning at this level, gave access to the upper floors. These rested on corbel courses, their smaller windows being barred; inside, they had segmental rere-arches and side benches, and there are two garderobe chutes. In the collapsed N wall, the position of a first-floor doorway is indicated by footings of a scale-and-platt stair in the courtyard which enclosed that side.

This COURTYARD was roughly square. Its entrance is unclear but there was a postern transe to the Strathnaterick Burn. Giles's perspective shows the ruined gable of a large HALL almost 6 m. broad over walls 1.2 m. thick, which stood at right angles to the tower house on its W side. The hall's original length is unclear as it was seemingly curtailed by a later N gable

---

*Strictly the tower house is orientated NE–SW; the orientation given here has been simplified for ease of understanding.

and DRUM TOWER 3.8 m. in diameter, the surviving fragments of which suggest an early C17 date. Foundations of a possible COURTYARD HOUSE, also C17, stand at an acute angle to the old court on the E side. Beyond the hall to the W are the remains of TERRACED GARDENS, perhaps mid-C19. A date-stone of 1677 with initials I.H.S. (Iesus Hominum Salvator) and M.R.A. (Maria Regina Angelorum) was re-set in a cottar-house at Mains of Balquhain, testament to the Leslies' enduring adherence to Catholicism.

HARLAW HOUSE, 2.9 km. ENE. Formerly the Free Church manse, built *c.* 1843. Two-storeyed with dormerheads and three bays, its doorway with a stepped hoodmould; harled with slim margins. The timber canted bays and slim spirelet corbelled out from one angle are additions, the latter of 1883 when Alexander Collie, an Aberdeen slate merchant, enlarged it and added within the re-entrant angle of the rear wing the tall entrance tower from which he could overlook the battlefield of Harlaw. The tower is of granite ashlar with Gothic windows, a crenellated and bartizaned parapet, and a spirelet tourelle. Over its doorway is a commemorative tablet to the men of Aberdeen who fell at Harlaw in 1411.

HARLAW MONUMENT, 3.3 km. E. By *William Kelly* for the Burgh of Aberdeen, 1911, to commemorate Provost Robert Davidson and others killed at the Battle of Harlaw in 1411. A robust, unsentimental Late Scots Gothic tower rising almost 14 m. high from a rough boulder base. Hexagonal, with slightly battered sides above the set-off of its plinth, it is solidly built in coursed hammer-dressed whinstone with red Corennie granite dressings; its prismatic ashlar roof has waterspouts and vestigial crockets. Boldly projecting heraldic shields at the angles and finely lettered inscriptions.

INVERAMSAY BRIDGE, 2.5 km. ENE. Built *c.* 1850 to carry a minor road over the Urie. Now a rare example of its kind. Main span of three segmental cast-iron pierced-arch girders, each cast in two parts and bolted at the centre. The parapets are thin cast-iron plates. Abutments in coursed squared granite, simple girder flood-span on the w.

10 MAIDEN STONE, 1.3 km. WNW, in the shadow of Bennachie. Perhaps Aberdeenshire's most impressive Pictish symbol stone. Tall pink granite slab with an elaborate but faded ring-headed cross with a human figure and two fish-monsters above on one face and a series of figures and symbols on the other. These include the mirror and comb at the bottom, a 'Pictish beast', a notched rectangle and Z-rod and a group of centaurs and other four-legged beasts. (GN)

PITTODRIE HOUSE. *See* p. 701.

PITTODRIE HOUSE. *See* p. 701.

5020   CLATT

A small village, erected as a burgh of barony for Bishop William Elphinstone in 1501.

Former PARISH CHURCH. Stands on a knoll above the Gadie Burn, site of St Moluag's church which was attached to Aberdeen by 1157. The w end was built or rebuilt in 1640 or 1662; the earlier date is carved on the bellcote, with spirelet and pinnacles, which was transferred from the w gable to the E in 1778 when the simple rectangular plan was extended to its present length. The crowsteps were added in 1886, the date in the keystone of the round-arched, transom-lit E doorway. The two tall round-arched s windows are in their present form probably of *c.* 1820–30 when alterations were made. Smaller window near the E end lighting the vestibule and gallery stairs. Incorporated below this window a stone carved with a shallow recess, perhaps a medieval aumbry or piscina. Above the window a heraldic panel, with escutcheon and initials A.D. The SE skewputt bears an escutcheon and initials A.S., perhaps for Alexander Spittal, Canon and Prebendary of Clatt in the 1530s. w door blocked when the interior was reordered, probably in 1886; the w gable now has two slim round-arched windows. N flank absolutely blind, the internal galleries having once extended across this side; the NW skewputt (different from the others) is initialled I.T. Very chaste interior, now with a single gallery at the E end; the PULPIT was lowered and simple PEWS altered to form the present central aisle *c.* 1935. Early C20 TABERNACLE and PISCINA sculpted in rough-hewn stone by *Alexander Tawse* of Rhynie, doubtless to match the FONT unearthed in 1886.

The CHURCHYARD runs down the knoll to the s, E and w and is enclosed by retaining walls of 1828. A PICTISH STONE carved with a beast and an arch or horseshoe, discovered 1905, has been incorporated into the churchyard wall on the w. Two other Pictish stones were found in the graveyard, one subsequently transferred to Knockespock House (q.v.).

CLOVA HOUSE

1.9 km. w of Lumsden

4020

Of at least three distinct phases: the original vernacular classical house facing E, built for the Lumsdens of Auchindoir (q.v.) and Clova and dated 1760 over its doorway; on its l. a wing tripled in size in 1888 to form, in effect, a second house with a new entrance front facing s; and on the r. of the old house a two-storey N wing built *c.* 1780 but remodelled in 1922, the three ranges together forming an asymmetrical open court, all harled with red ashlar dressings. The original house is the most impressive of its size, date and type in Aberdeenshire, tall and upright in its proportions. Three storeys and three broad bays raised over a low basement plinth, its slightly advanced centre breaks up through the wall-head into an attic chimney gable. The centre bay contains a doorcase with open pediment on consoles, two windows at first- and second-floor and a round-arched attic window; centred between the first- and second-floor windows is a heraldic panel. The outer bays have single windows, those at ground floor enlarged to bipartites. Long-and-short quoins. Subtly bellcast roof with straight skews and big ashlar end stacks. Much of the interior was replaced after a fire c. 1810 but the original stone stair has survived. As first designed, the house was to have had right-angled corridor links to square-plan two-storey and basement pavilions with gable-fronts answering that of the main block, but only that on the SE was built. In 1888 this became the eastern two bays of the new S WING, its S-facing entrance front two-storey and basement in the height of the original house's three and six windows wide, the centre bays closely spaced and rising into a pedimental gable. This S front has a tetrastyle portico of banded Roman Doric columns crowned by a balustrade. The N WING is two-storeyed over a semi-sunk basement, with tall pedimented windows at ground floor and those at first floor breaking through the eaves into piended dormers. The most notable feature of the interior is a DOOR, which incorporates panels from the pulpit of the medieval church at Auchindoir (q.v.).

The STABLES, 120 m. W, dated 1819 but altered by *James Henderson* in 1846, have a Gothic tower with turrets and gablets.

6010

CLUNY

PARISH CHURCH. Built on a new site in 1789. Rectangular plan with arched windows. Granite ashlar E flank, its centre windows rising slightly taller than the outer pair; all four have long-and-short surrounds, shutter hinge-pins and Y-tracery. Ball-finialled birdcage bellcote with obelisks, the bell by *John Mowat*, 1746, from the previous church. NW vestry added in 1893–4 by *Duncan McMillan*; he also reorientated the interior to the N, removing the N and W sides of the original horseshoe gallery which had faced the E wall and inserting the polygonal ceiling on stone corbels. – ORGAN by *H. S. Vincent & Co.*, c. 1911.

The OLD CHURCHYARD walls were rebuilt by *William Ramage* in 1852–3 and extended W by *McMillan* c. 1895. – FRASER MAUSOLEUM. Designed by *James Byres* of Tonley (*see* Tough) for Elyza Fraser of Castle Fraser (q.v.), dated 1808; Byres's will expressed a wish that he should be buried in a monument of identical design. It is perhaps the finest sepulchral monument in Aberdeenshire: a Neoclassical Roman rotunda constructed of massive granite ashlar blocks, with lugged door architrave surmounted by Elyza's coat of arms, inscription frieze and a tiered dome with central oculus. The wrought-iron outer gate, almost fanciful in nature, is composed of hearts; double-leaf timber inner doors with small glazed windows, and inside the mausoleum a large semi-recumbent cross and memorial panels set into the walls. Nearby, the LINTON ENCLOSURE. Simple Neoclassical, probably by *Archibald Simpson c.* 1830. In the NW corner, an elaborate Early Italian Renaissance MEMORIAL to Marie Claudine Nardin (†1897) with a terracotta portrait bust. Former PARISH MANSE, 200 m. NW, by *Ramage*, 1852.

CLUNY CASTLE

Massive castellated Neo-Tudor externally and Neoclassical within, built to *John Smith*'s designs for Col. John Gordon 1818–36, and financed by Gordon's West Indies estates. It incorporates within its granite ashlar structure a Z-plan tower house of *c.* 1600–4, possibly by *I. Bell*. Col. Gordon died in 1858 and from *c.* 1866 his son John enlarged the service quarters into a rear court, behind which he built a chapel by Smith's son *William Smith*, 1870–2. The rear court and chapel were severely damaged by fire in 1926 but reinstated much as they had been by *George Bennett Mitchell* for John's widow.

The house that *John Smith* built attempted – like earlier proposals by *Robert and James Adam c.* 1790–3 and (perhaps) by *John Paterson c.* 1814 before him – to duplicate the distinctive plan and form of the early C17 tower house, but in an early C19 idiom.* The TOWER HOUSE consisted of a four-storey rectangular main block 14.5 m. long N–S by 9 m. deep E–W, with turnpike stairs concealed in the NW and SE angles linking to two very large drum towers at diagonally opposite corners: the four-storey NW tower was 7.5 m. in diameter and the five-storey SE tower very slightly smaller. The attribution to *I. Bell* derives from the remarkable upperworks: the SE tower rose into a crowstep-gabled caphouse with an oriel, the NW tower into a semi-conical roof and a tall slim square tower with crenellated parapet and pencil stair-turret, and angled out from the NE and SW corners were small square bartizans with pitched roofs. The NW tower's details were seemingly very similar to those on Bell's addition to the round tower at Castle Fraser (q.v.), but its balustraded platform roof (if it ever had one) had been replaced by a pitched roof by 1789.

In PLAN AND FORM *John Smith*'s design comprises, in effect, two Z-plan tower houses – the old Z-plan tower house, reconstructed and refaced in grey granite ashlar to the W, linked by a central block to a mirror-image Z-plan tower house with thinner walls to the E, so forming a twin-towered symmetrical entrance front. Its style reflects the attitudes of its time, when Old Scots work was appreciated for associations with heredity rather than for architectural characteristics which were then neither understood nor appreciated. In consequence, Cluny Castle is uncompromisingly a Picturesque gentleman's seat of

67

---

*A design for Cluny of about this date has been found among other drawings attributed to *William Wilkins*, but Paterson's authorship of this scheme seems far more likely.

the early C19, meeting expectations and requirements of that age, and whatever regrets there may be for the old tower house it must be recognized as such.

The handsomely proportioned ENTRANCE FRONT faces S. Its three-storey, three-bay centre block is flanked by the four-storey drum towers of the original Z-plan tower house re-cased by Smith in ashlar on the W, and his mirror-image tower house on the E. The Castellated character is emphasized by the cren-ellated parapets, those of the drum towers being boldly machicolated, but the Tudor hoodmoulded windows have Late Georgian sashes as in Paterson's Castellated houses. The central entrance doorway is within a three-bay semi-elliptical arcade between the drum towers. The ground-floor windows are round-arched, the taller first-floor windows and those at second and third floors being square-headed with hoodmoulds.

The FLANK ELEVATIONS are similar to one another but not identical. The W flank encasing the old tower house is of two bays with the NW drum tower rising through five storeys – the ground floor with round-arched windows the same height as in the main block, first and second floors rather lower, and the third and fourth floors corbelled out slightly and crowned by a crenellated parapet. The E flank is of three bays and is con-sistently three-storeyed, its drum tower having a diamond-pattern frieze beneath its parapet, and a small octagonal turret at its rear as a partial answer to the C17 square turret on the W. The SERVICE COURT as altered by *William Smith* is rela-tively low at two storeys, the centre of the rear elevation pro-jecting as a big canted bay; an outshot on the N corner contains the kitchen. At the S end, *William Smith*'s Perp CHAPEL of 1870–2) is five bays, correctly orientated E–W with a canted apsidal chancel.

On PLAN the ground floor comprises the entrance hall in the centre block, with the male domain arranged across the S front: billiard room on the E side, and gun room and smoking room on the W within the C17 tower house; the remainder of this floor consists of services. The main stair rises to first floor, with library in the centre, drawing room to the E, morning room in the entrance front's E tower and dining room within the C17 tower house's former great hall on the W.

The INTERIORS are simply finished, but in materials of high quality. The ENTRANCE HALL is lozenge-shaped: flanking the main entrance, its windows are set within deep panelled reveals framed by Roman Doric pilasters with polished granite shafts, the floor laid in black-and-white marble, the ceiling shallow but coffered. The doorways are set in low-profile surrounds but the doors themselves are very wide and reeded down the centre. The entrance hall opens into the ground-floor corridor and STAIR HALL, which is almost square on plan, and lit from the rear court – this is perhaps the richest interior, having a magnificently carved Neo-Caroline balustrade and fine pan-elled dadoes installed in 1867–8. The stair opens onto a very grand first-floor corridor of three broad bays which are divided off by coupled Corinthian pilasters. The DRAWING ROOM has a richly detailed Neoclassical ceiling and the lozenge-plan LIBRARY above the entrance hall has handsome architectonic bookcases, while the DINING ROOM windows are set within broad reveals, slim colonnettes supporting their segmental heads beneath a coffered ceiling. The MORNING ROOM in the entrance front's E tower is particularly remarkable in that its ceiling is tented, Regency in character although the silk probably dates from redecoration *c.* 1870.

The CHAPEL interior was carefully restored by *Mitchell* after the fire in 1927–8. The nave's N and S walls have Tudor arches framing tall windows with Perp tracery (the S side is partly blind with one window obscured by the organ⋆). Between the arches, slim wall-shafts carry the trusses of the open timber roof. Tall chancel arch, of moulded and dressed stone. PEWS, with poppyheads, and CANDELABRA, both fine Neo-Gothic craftsmanship. – STAINED GLASS. In the chancel apse windows, scenes from the Life of Christ and the Passion, remade to the original designs by *Clayton & Bell* in 1872. Heraldic glass in the nave windows, originally by *Cottier & Co.* who also supplied the original furnishings and mural decoration destroyed by the fire.

COOKNEY   K   *8090*

Former PARISH CHURCH. Large and lofty E.E. By *Mackenzie & McMillan*, 1881–5.† It is visible as a landmark for miles around. W gable with a small porch, rosette window and two corbelled pinnacles poking up like quasi-tourelles. Gableted bellcote above with datestone and carved cross. The flanks have lancets, the first two swept up into big gables with wheel windows to light the W gallery. Quatrefoils in plate tracery. – WAR MEMORIAL. Celtic cross by *George Bennett Mitchell*, 1919.

CORGARFF   *2000*

Former PARISH CHURCH. By *James Daniel*, 1834–5, replacing a church of 1762. Plain Georgian Gothic four-bay coursed-rubble rectangle. Entrances in the N and S gables beneath pointed

---

⋆The first organ for the chapel was given to All Saints Episcopal Church at Buckie, Moray, *c.* 1877. Its successor was destroyed by the fire.
†It replaced the original chapel of ease to Stonehaven, built 1816–17 and enlarged in 1838–9.

transom-lights, small spheric triangle gallery windows above, both with V-tracery; blind openings to either side at mezzanine level and a birdcage bellcote with spike finials at the N end. E flank lit by tall windows with timber Y-tracery, w flank completely blind. The handsome galleried interior survived intact as late as 2012.

OUR LADY OF THE SNOWS (R.C.), 1.5 km. ESE in a remote situation on the Ford of Tornahish, but near the Old Military Road (A939). Built *c.* 1805, a tacit acceptance of Catholicism some twenty years before Emancipation. Small, rectangular, rubble-built, with a stone porch at its liturgical W end and round-arched E window. Very simple interior with coved ceiling. – ALTAR TABLE. *c.* 1860, behind decorative wrought-iron ALTAR RAILS. – TABERNACLE. Wood, carved with *Agnus Dei* and Cross in front of a gilded Sun. – STAINED GLASS. E window. 2003 by *Maureen Ross*. Cottage presbytery at right angles to the chapel.

CORGARFF CEMETERY, 0.6 km. E on the A939. Rubble-walled enclosure, laid out in 1869. – Three simple Neoclassical stones to the Tennants of Edinglassie (q.v.): the statesman Harold John Tennant (†1935); his wife, May, who was a pioneer social reformer (†1946); Lt.-Col. Archibald Tennant (†1955) and his wife, Diana (†2011), all to a uniform design reportedly by *Edwin Lutyens*.

60 CORGARFF CASTLE, 2.5 km. W. A small tower house, built either for Robert, Master of Elphinstone, following his marriage in 1546, or for John Forbes of Towie (q.v.), who assumed the tenancy before 1561. Isolated on moorland, it was perhaps originally a hunting seat for the Forest of Corgarff, but as the only fortified site for a considerable distance around it has always possessed strategic significance. It is surrounded by burns and rills, and commands the Dee, Don and Avon valleys; and from the first it has had a troubled history. The ballad *Edem o'Gordoun* recounts that during the Marian War in 1571 the Gordons burnt it with Margaret Forbes, her family and servants inside. It was briefly seized by Highland thieves and local ruffians in 1607 and ravaged in 1609. Derelict when occupied by Montrose for the Royalists in 1645, in 1689–90 it was burnt by the Jacobites to prevent it from being occupied by government forces. During the 'Fifteen the Earl of Mar recruited his forces there, and it was again occupied by the Jacobites during the 'Forty-five. After Prince Charles Edward's retreat from Derby it became an arsenal in preparation for mountain warfare but was burnt yet again in the face of a Redcoat raid. The government acquired the castle in 1748 to stamp out any remaining Jacobitism and unauthorized whisky distilling and smuggling, the *Board of Ordnance* reconstructing it as a barracks with new wings and a curtain wall; the military road from Blairgowrie (Perthshire) to Fort George (Highland) was routed nearby in 1753. As peace returned, Corgarff's importance diminished and it was periodically let as a shooting lodge and farmhouse, but pressed back into service against

illicit distillers *c.* 1826, the last troops – two or three invalid soldiers – leaving in 1831. It remained inhabited until 1912, but by then its condition had deteriorated. Entrusted to state care in 1961, its restoration was completed *c.* 1976 by *J. Douglas Hogg* under the supervision of *William Boal.*

The TOWER itself, orientated E–W, is rectangular, 11 m. long by 7.5 m. deep. Its harled walls rising with a gentle batter for 10 m. to the wall-head are built mostly in schistose rubble in slim courses, but infilled with pink granite boulders and with loose use of pinnings. The entrance is on the S side near the E end at first floor, some 1.8 m. above ground; its chamfered granite jambs are original but its lintel has been renewed. Originally it appears to have been accessed by a removable wooden stair, subsequently replaced by a steep stone forestair rising against the S wall, and finally by the present L-plan or dog-leg stair during government occupation. The ground floor contains two vaulted cellars lit by slit-lights with broad reveals in the 1.5 m. depth of the walls. Until 1748 the tower had a double-height hall with a barrel-vault rising 4.5 m. above first-floor level; it was lit by windows protected by iron bars and had a fireplace in the W gable. A kitchen, once with large hearth and sink, was partitioned off the E end, with an entresol (perhaps a steward's room or oratory) above. The tower's third storey contained the withdrawing room and bedroom, the traditional layout of hall, outer chamber and inner chamber thus being effectively laid out over two levels.

In the *Board of Ordnance* reconstruction the hall's vault, the kitchen and entresol were all demolished and a new floor inserted so that the tower now contained four storeys, all roughly equal in height. On the entrance front the first, second and third floors were each lit by two large windows, roughly formed without chamfers or mouldings, but regular in arrangement and of classic Georgian proportions, fitted with shutters; the first-floor window sill on the W side is a tread from the old newel stair reused. All trace of the previous fenestration is concealed by harling, but on the plainer N front some windows are Georgian and others much older. The original crowsteps of the steeply pitched roof were replaced by straight skews with curved skewputts sometime after 1690, and the gable chimneystacks were modified in 1748–50. But two large corbel brackets just beneath the wall-head on the S front are early features, the wall between them being raked back; they would once have supported a *chambre mâchicoulis* (a machicolated chamber) overhanging the entrance directly beneath. The gabled caphouse marking the head of the turnpike stair at the SE corner is also early. A timber scale-and-platt stair was introduced *c.* 1748, the E flank's slit-windows being of that date. There was probably a small turret at the NE corner.

The single-storey WINGS of 1748 have their own well-wrought doorways (the jambs are reused, presumably from the laigh biggings), and before the restoration they were roofed in stone slabs. The W wing was originally intended to contain a brewhouse and bakehouse, and the E wing a guardroom and prison; in 1827 they became, respectively, a powder magazine and kitchen.

The CURTAIN WALL is similar to that at Braemar Castle (q.v.) and 3.5 m. high. It extends 30 m. in length by 16 m. in depth, but beyond this on each side is a triangular projection – a right-angled salient – so that the overall plan is star-shaped, there being a single doorway in the S flank. Long narrow slits widening out within the curtain's 0.6 m. depth provided multiple fields of fire, the salients ensuring that there was no place to hide.

WEST TORNAHAISH, 1.25 km. E. Late C18 former inn, near the Old Military Road and a ford (subsequently bridged) across the Tornahaish Burn. It is single-storeyed, of three bays, in coursed squared rubble, its gabled roof with end stacks. Exceptionally well-preserved interior including a very large kitchen hearth – a feature of several houses in Strathdon – and box beds. Timber-lined attic floor.

CORSE see LUMPHANAN

6000

CORSINDAE HOUSE

2.5 km. SW of Sauchen

A complex building history stretching over 400 years. The S front seemingly divides into two clear parts. To the E is a near-symmetrical U-plan house of three storeys with a central attic gablet. This looks later C17 but is actually of several dates. It was reputedly begun in 1484, when Corsindae was granted to James Forbes, as a small rectangular tower house. It appears to have had a ground-floor doorway in its S wall's W end and a hatch opening to the first floor. It was subsequently enlarged with a slim SW jamb and a circular stair-turret in the angle, the latter heightened c. 1800. In 1848 *J. & W. Smith* added the matching jamb and turret at the E end to produce the present near-symmetrical façade. The W end of the S front is a house added to the existing tower in 1726 but reconstructed c. 1750–60. It is two storeys and three bays broad over a semi-sunk basement, its projecting centre with Gibbsian doorway breaking up into a crowstepped chimney gable. Long-and-short quoins contrast against the harl. The slim canted bays in the flanks of the projecting centre are mid-C19 as, perhaps, are the crowsteps. The entrance front rises significantly taller than the rear elevation, seemingly as a result of the alterations of c. 1750–60. At the rear is a two-storey-and-basement wing with a bowed end, built c. 1800 to provide new dining and drawing rooms. The tower house is vaulted at ground floor but the rooms otherwise are mostly by the *Smiths c.* 1848. Some mid-C18 panelled rooms survive and in the C18 house the entrance hall has a tightly planned stairway with early C19 cast-iron balusters. Dining room with Neoclassical chimneypiece; the drawing room fireplace has anthemion capitals.

DOOCOT, 90 m. SE. Late C17. Rectangular plan, rubble built with rat course. Crowstep-gabled roof with moulded skewputts.

COTHAL *see* HATTON OF FINTRAY

COULL

5000

The 'Kirk of Cula' was granted by William the Lion to his newly founded Arbroath Abbey in 1188–99. This, together with the now-ruinous Coull Castle, established in the C13, constituted the civil and religious centres of a small township of which only church, manse and mill still survive.

PARISH CHURCH. Reputedly built by the *George family c.* 1791. Its W gable is said to incorporate C17 masonry. Doorway with flat arch of dressed voussoirs is flanked by slim round-headed lights, big roundel above. Reused birdcage bellcote with pediments and ball finials (cf. Aboyne Castle, Birse and Kincardine O'Neill, qq.v.) contains a bell by *Michael Burgerhuys* dated 1642, which displays the arms of its donor, Alexander Ross. S flank in fine coursed squared rubble has four large windows, round-arched and once fitted with shutters, all but the W window (altered *c.* 1947) with astragalled sashes. E porch and N outshot both of 1876 (the latter's boiler-room air duct seems to be a reused shot-hole, perhaps from the castle, *see* below). Stone-ridged roof. Austere interior with stained matchboard dado and a coved ceiling. At the W end, a railed platform PULPIT perhaps 1876; MINISTER'S BOX with canted front and tall back-board with festoon-type war memorial *c.* 1920. – COMMUNION TABLE with central cruciform and flanking cusp-headed Gothic panels; plain open-backed PEWS fitted with brass oil-lamps seemingly installed in 1925. – STAINED GLASS. W window, above the pulpit. Crucifixion by *J. Dudley Forsyth* in memory of Gilbert Marshall Mackenzie, architect, killed in 1916. In the two flanking lights, Jesus receiving the little children, and Preaching to the faithful, both 1930. Still more vibrant, the war memorial window in the S flank, by *Marjorie Kemp, c.* 1947.

Large rubble-walled GRAVEYARD with lying slabs and table tombs, C18 onwards. Near the path, James Middleton (†1751), with angels, hourglass, crossbones, coffin and a skull of unusual design, similar to those at Migvie and Tarland (qq.v.) implying that the same mason worked there. – MORT-HOUSE, early C19. Low, gable-fronted. Granite walls 0.6 m. thick, barrel-vaulted inside, turfed over. On the churchyard's E side, two pairs of GATEPIERS: those to the N with conical caps, seemingly *c.* 1831 but very old-fashioned for that date.

Former PARISH MANSE (Kirklands of Coull), 80 m. N. By *John Smith* 1831–2. Late Georgian vernacular. Entrance front two storeys and three bays, door recessed between slim inset timber pilasters supporting an elegant transom-light; ground-floor windows much taller than first. Crisp white harl setting off the pale granite dressings, exposed rubble gables with ashlar end stacks. Rear elevation also exposed rubble with bowed projecting stair-bay and attic dormers.

Former SCHOOL, 0.8 km. N. *c.* 1860. Plain Jacobean. Tall single-storey T-plan, coursed squared red granite with grey granite dressings. Large astragalled sash-and-case windows, the wings rising into broad dormerhead gablets.

Former SPRINGBANK MILL, 0.9 km. N. Late C19. Simple rectangle, still with threshing machine in excellent condition. Cottage with attached timber shop. Restored *c.* 2009 by *Ben Addy* of *Moxon Architects*.

COULL HOUSE, 1.8 km. SE in woodland. Built in 1914 by *A. Marshall Mackenzie* after he purchased the Coull estate in 1912 but largely designed by his sons *A. G. R. Mackenzie* and *G. Marshall Mackenzie*. A stylish stripped classical villa in sparkling white harl with pale grey granite dressings. Entrance front facing S comprises a centre block which was originally flat-roofed, a very modern – probably French – concept for its date. It is two storeys and seven windows wide, the casements with lying-pane glazing and fronted at ground floor by a Roman Doric colonnade that once opened into a large winter garden. Single-bay pavilions slightly projected at each end have first-floor windows segmentally arched and key-blocked with elegant wrought-iron balconies, and rise into piended roofs in dark grey slate with oversailing eaves. At first floor the centre is lit by just three windows, the wall-head over which has been raised, perhaps when *A. G. R. Mackenzie* formed the present pitched roof with simple piended dormers in 1937. He also added the two-storey-and-attic two-bay wing slightly set back on the r. Inside, the living hall occupies the centre block, with drawing and dining rooms in the pavilions; the stair at the rear has stylized balusters rising to the first-floor bedrooms. The finishes are very simple: there are no cornices, but the floors are in Appalachian oak, and the same wood is used to veneer the doorways; the moulded fireplaces are carved stone. Restoration in 2002. The POLICIES overlooking the Howe of Cromar have largely been replaced by commercial forestry but the giant sequoia avenue reportedly planted *c.* 1937 as a driveway to the house survives.

COULL CASTLE, 250 m. SSE. Scant ruins of one of the largest and most fully developed of the early stone-built castles of enclosure in Scotland, standing on a granite knoll overlooking the Howe of Cromar. It was probably built in the C13 by the

1. Donside, view from Keithhall (p. 6)
2. Deeside, Falls of Garbh Allt (p. 445)

3. Aberdeen, Bridge of Dee, view looking N towards Aberdeen (p. 259)
4. Aboyne, view E across the green (p. 309)

5. Stonehaven Harbour (p. 727)
6. Aberdeen, Old Aberdeen, High Street (p. 200)

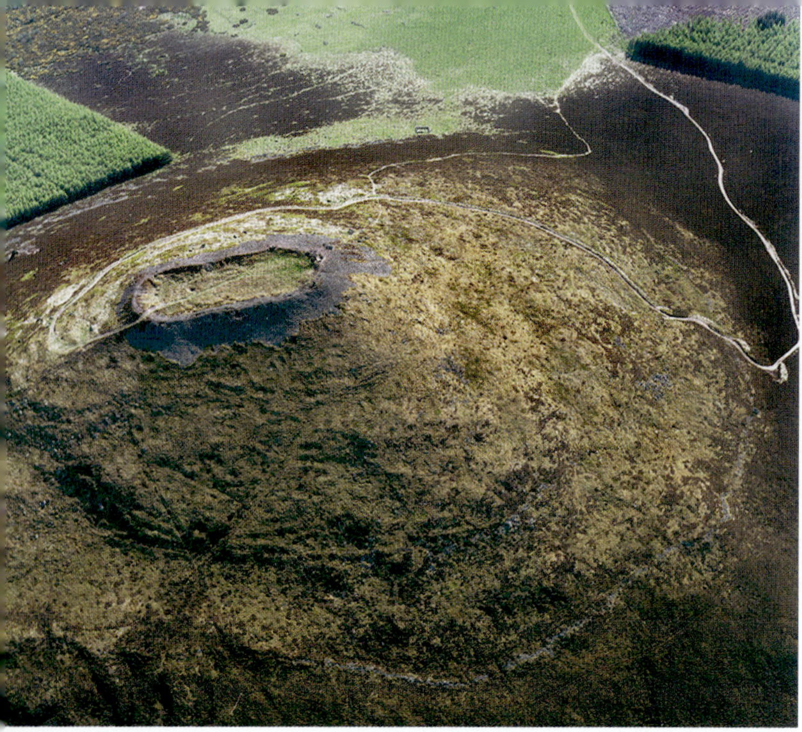

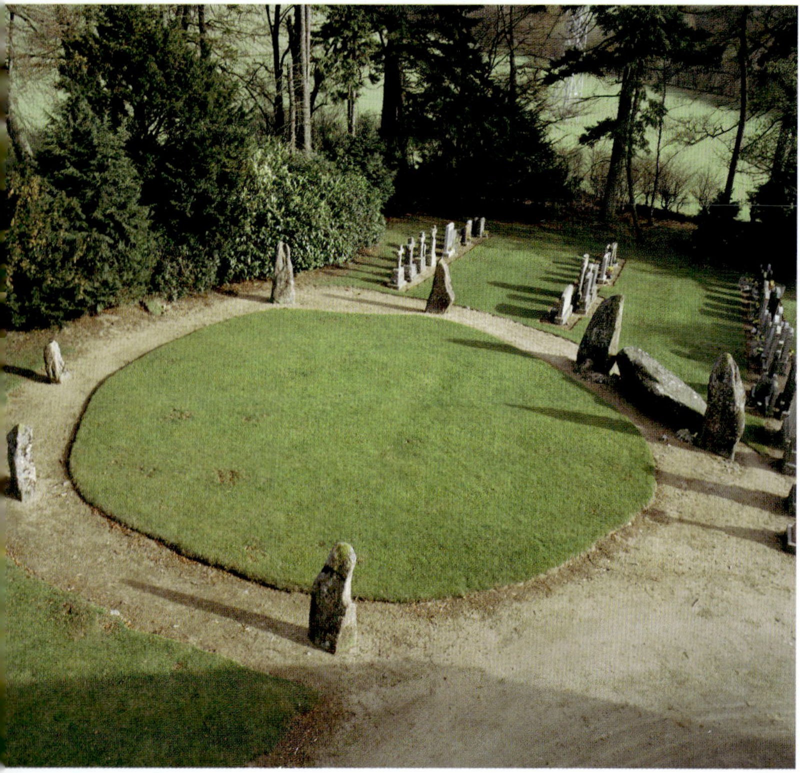

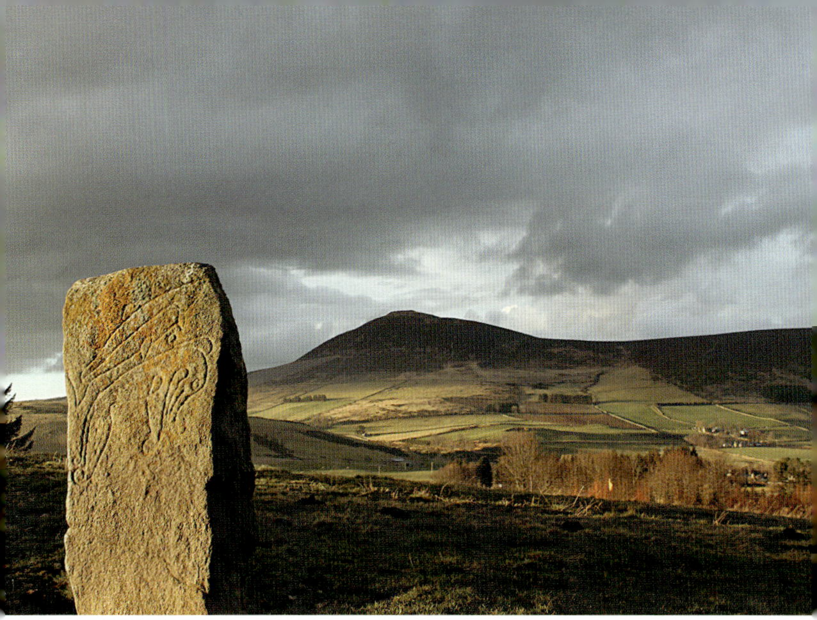

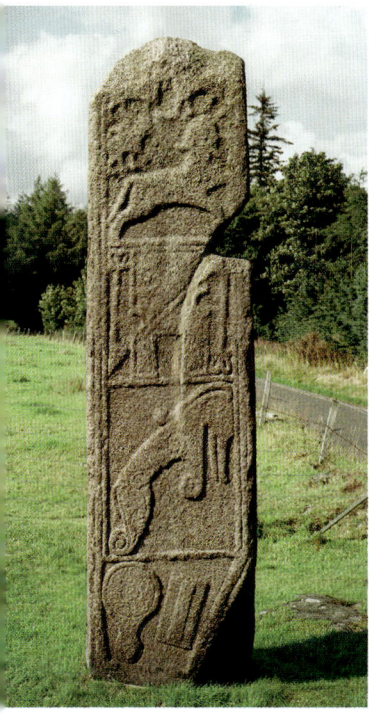

7. Rhynie, Tap O' Noth vitrified fort, aerial view from the NE, Iron Age (p. 708)
8. Midmar, Recumbent Stone Circle, Bronze Age (p. 668)
9. Rhynie, Craw Stane, Pictish (p. 706)
10. Chapel of Garioch, Maiden Stone, Pictish (p. 416)
11. Dinnet, Loch Kinord, cross-slab, probably c9 (p. 447)

7 | 9
8 | 10 11

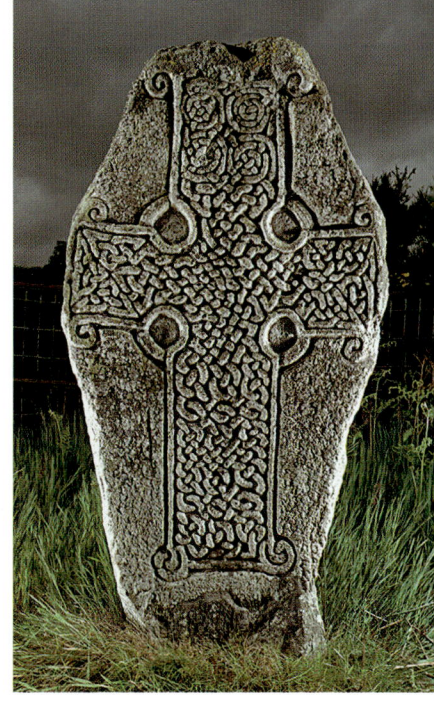

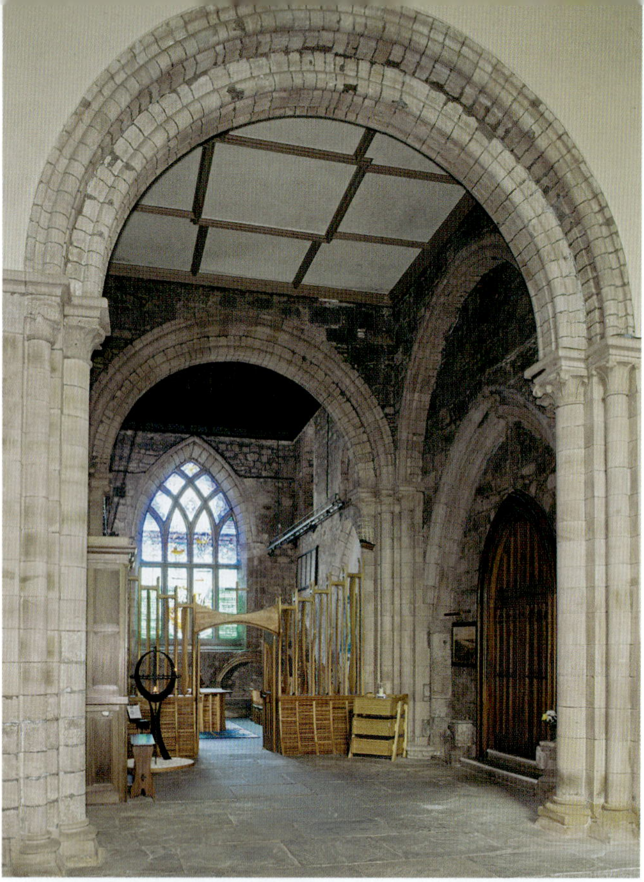

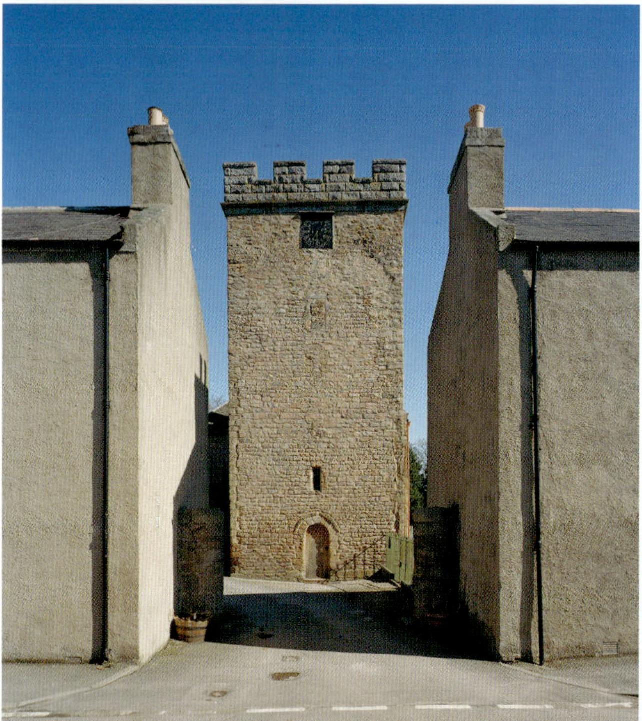

12. Aberdeen, St Nicholas, interior of N transept and crossing, late C12, restored 1874 (p. 124)
13. Monymusk, Parish Church, W tower, C12, lowered 1822, parapet 1891 (p. 677)
14. Aberdeen, Old Aberdeen, St Machar's Cathedral, W front *c.* 1355–80, completed *c.* 1422–40 (p. 172)
15. Aberdeen, Old Aberdeen, St Machar's Cathedral, nave, interior, later C14 and earlier C15 (p. 178)

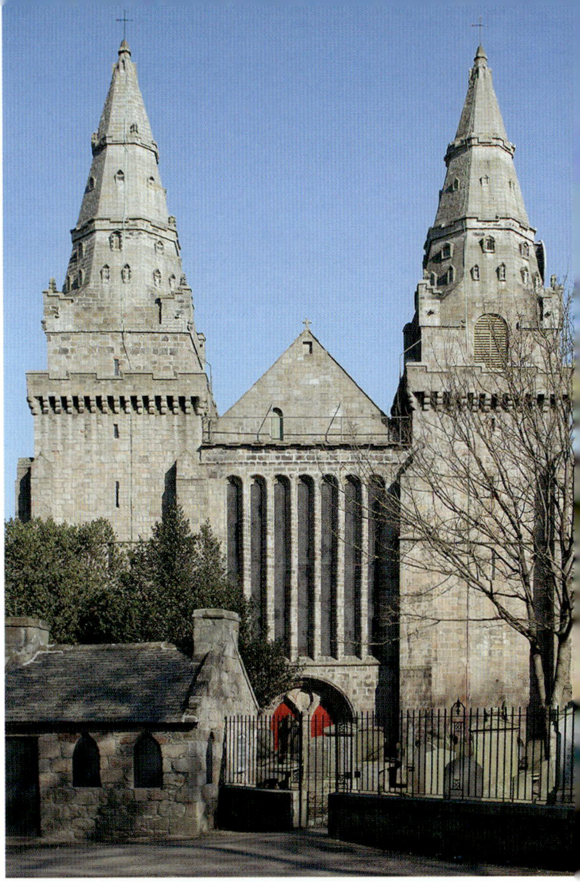

12	14
13	15

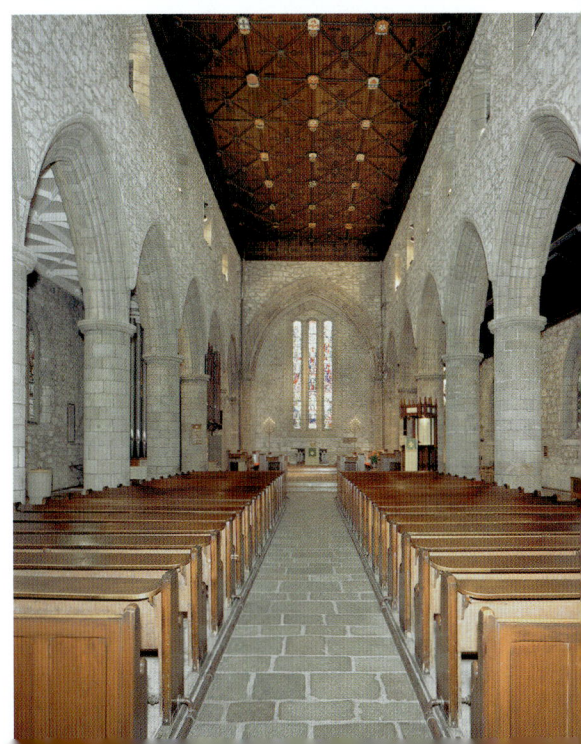

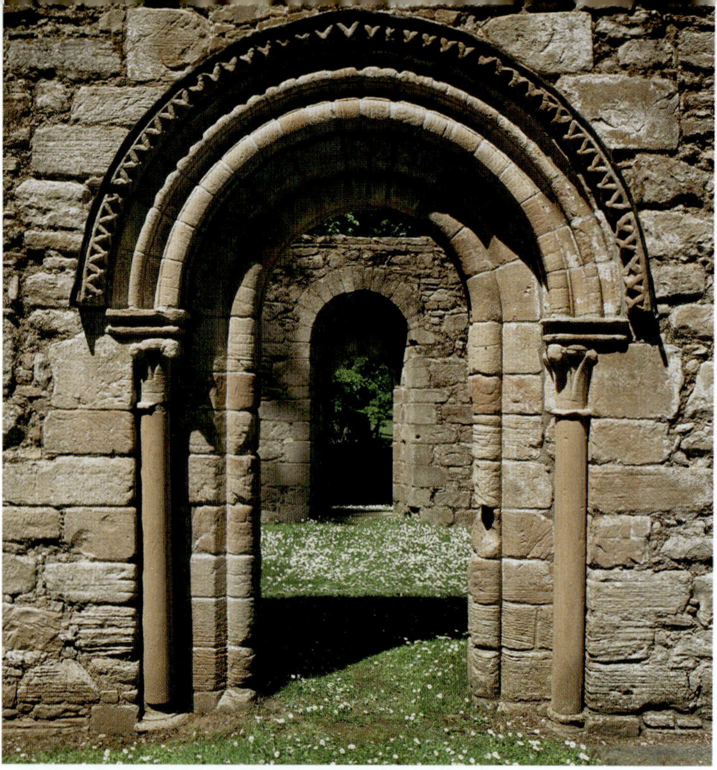

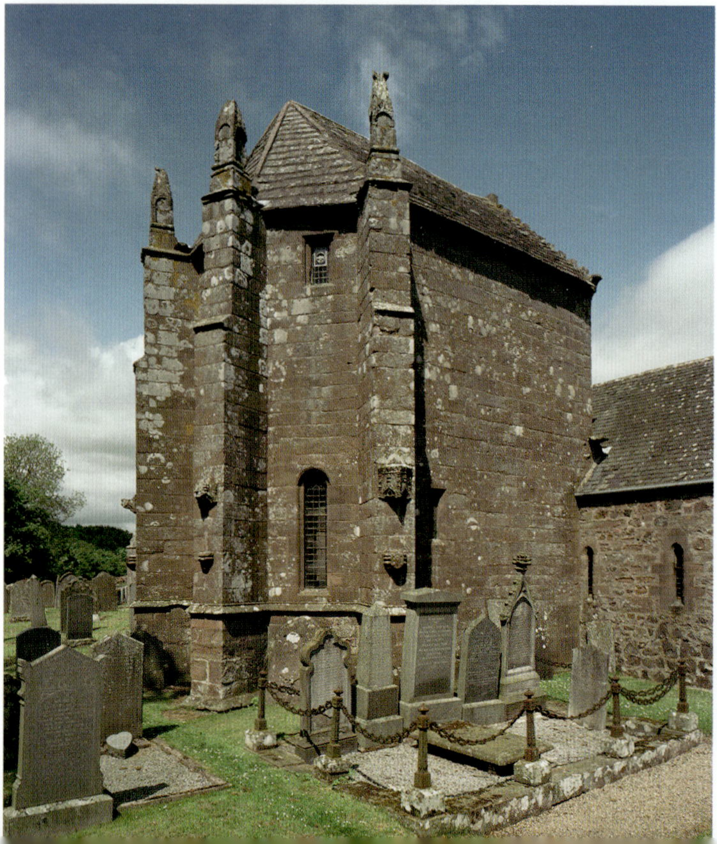

21. Aberdeen, King's College Chapel, w front, begun 1500, completed
    c. 1522 (p. 186)
22. Aberdeen, King's College Chapel, N flank (p. 185)
23. Aberdeen, King's College Chapel, interior, ceiling, choir stalls and
    screen, early C16, organ, 2004 (p. 188)

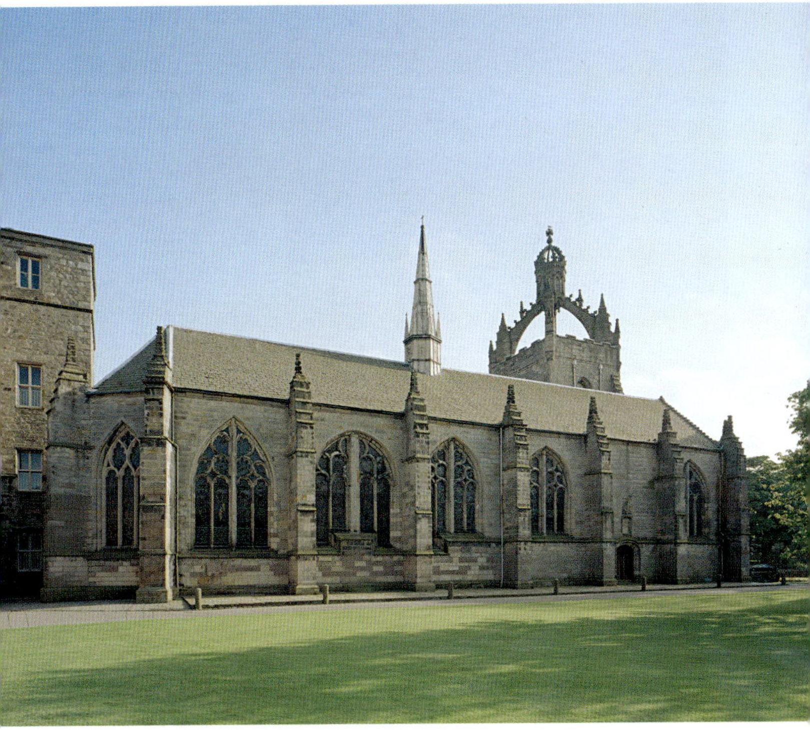

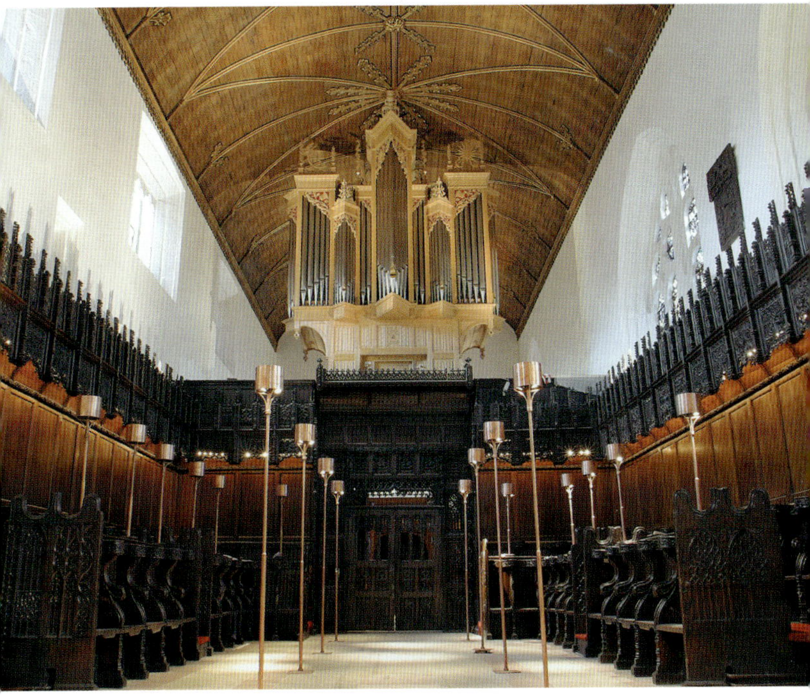

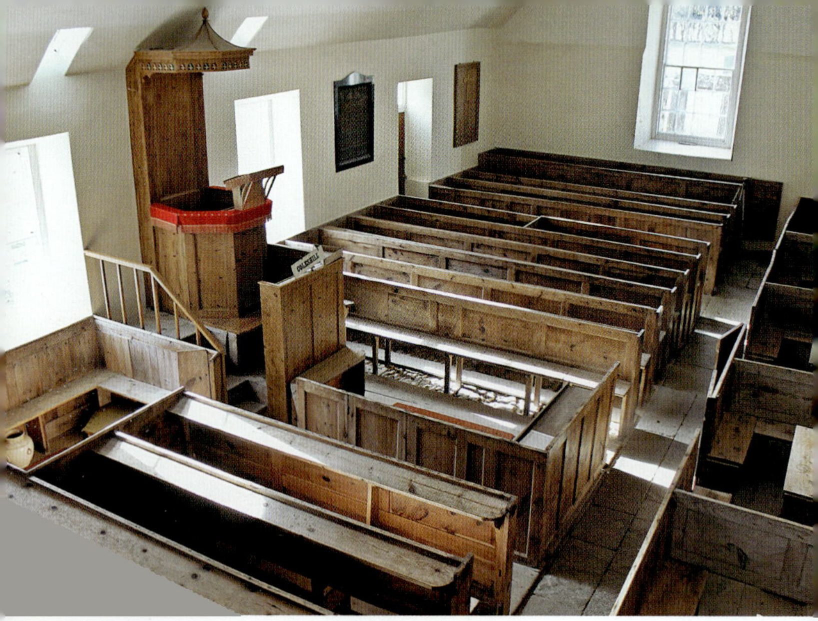

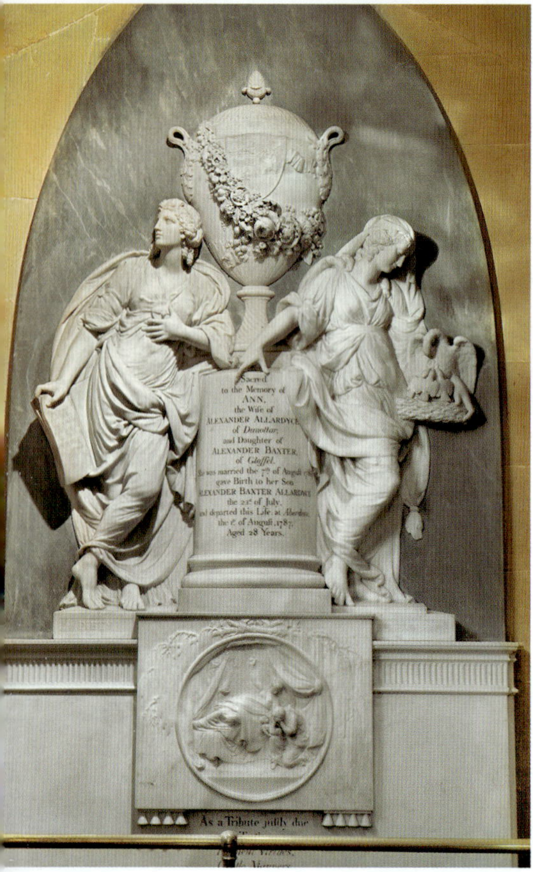

27. Kirkton of Glenbuchat, Old Parish Church, interior, remodelled by William Minto, 1828 (p. 622)
28. Aberdeen, St Nicholas West Church, Allardyce Monument, by John Bacon, 1791 (p. 126)
29. Echt, Parish Church, w front, 1804–6 (p. 477)
30. Cluny, Old Churchyard, Fraser Mausoleum, by James Byres, 1808 (p. 418)

27 | 29
28 | 30

ECHT PARISH CHURCH

JOHN PATERSON J.P.
WILLIAM HENRY
HELEN MARY MAVER
PATERSON

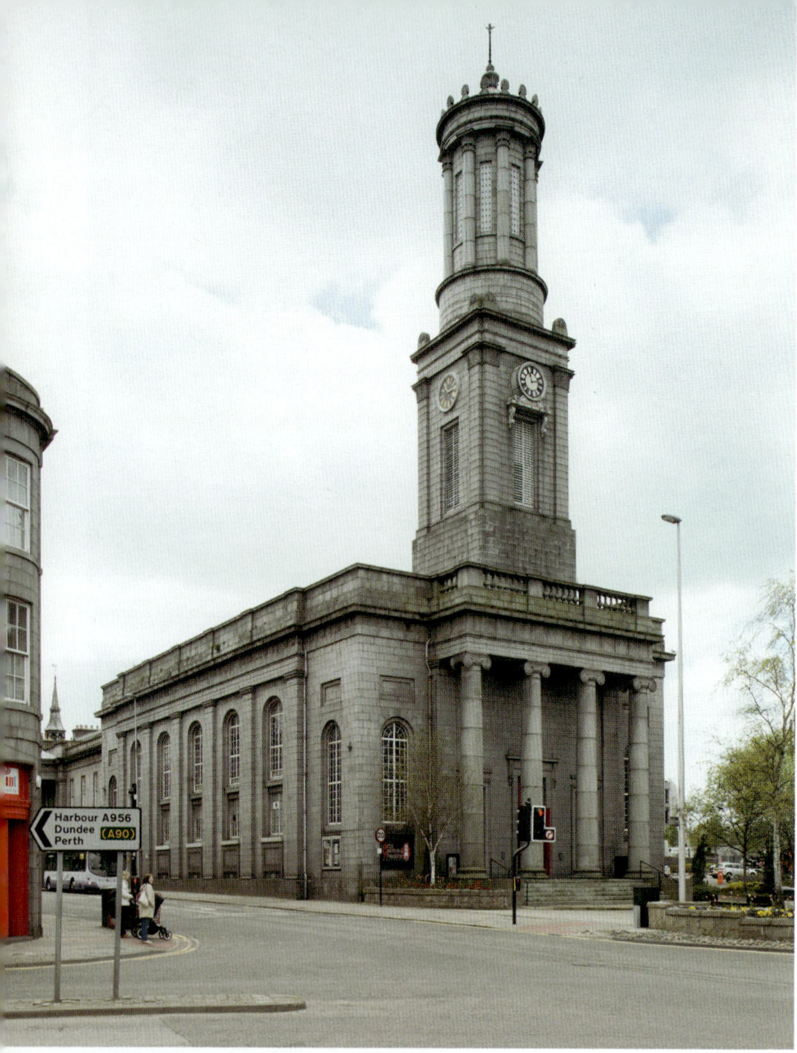
Harbour A956
Dundee (A90)
Perth

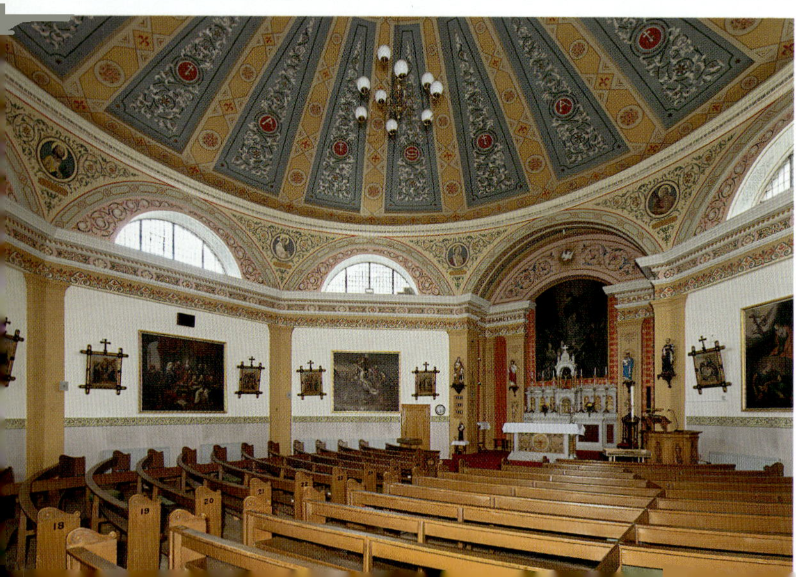

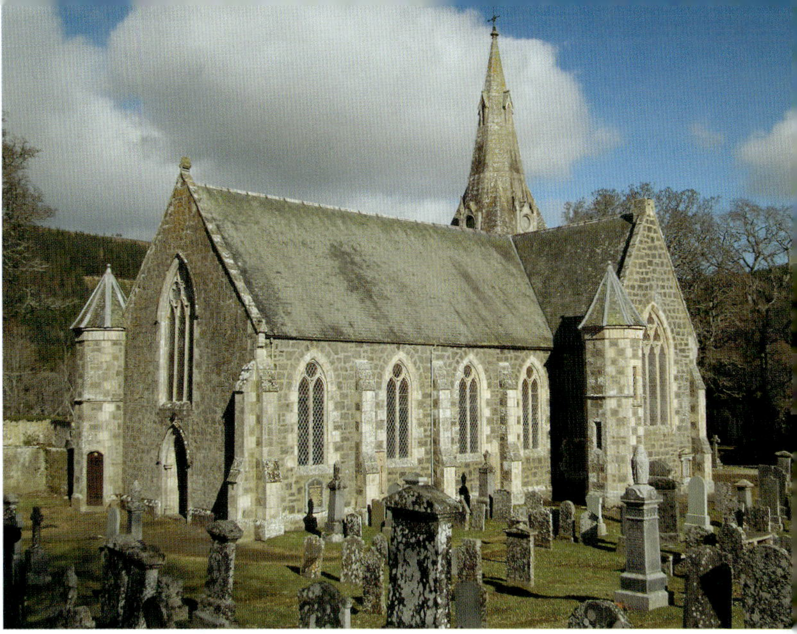

31. Aberdeen, former North Church (now Aberdeen Arts Centre), by John Smith, 1829–31 (p. 114)
32. Huntly, St Margaret (R.C.), by William Robertson and Rev. James Kyle, 1833–4, interior, painted decoration by Earley & Co., 1905 (p. 529)
33. Strathdon, Parish Church, by James Matthews, 1853 (p. 737)
34. Stonehaven, St James (Episcopal), by Robert Rowand Anderson, 1875–7, additions by Arthur Clyne, 1885 and 1906 (p. 722)

31	33
32	34

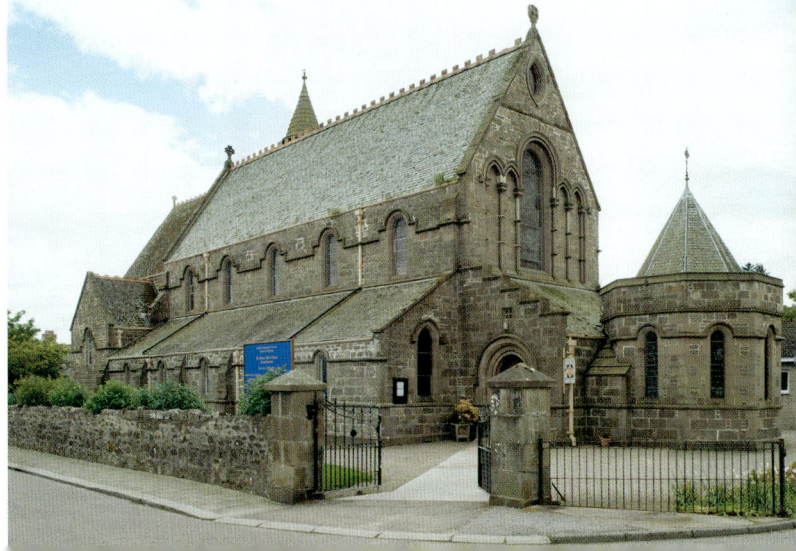

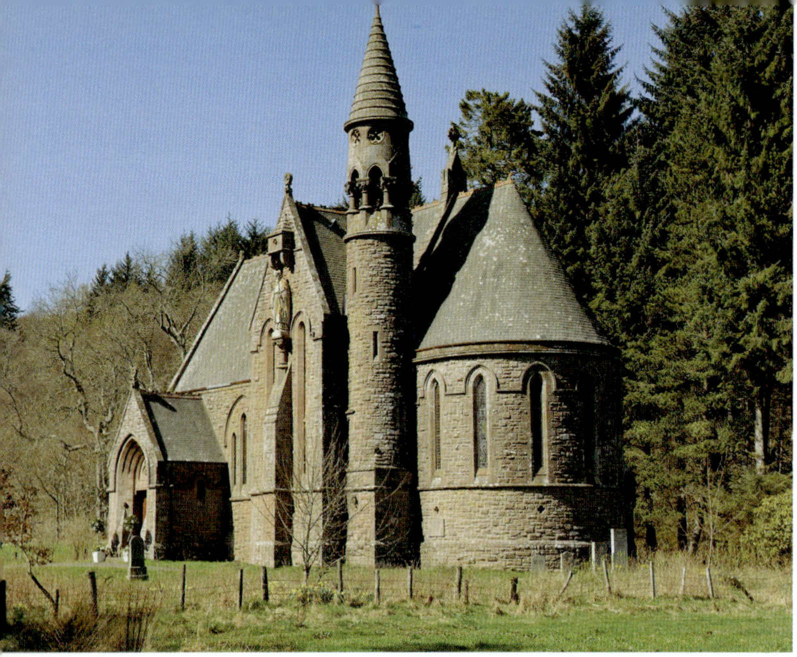

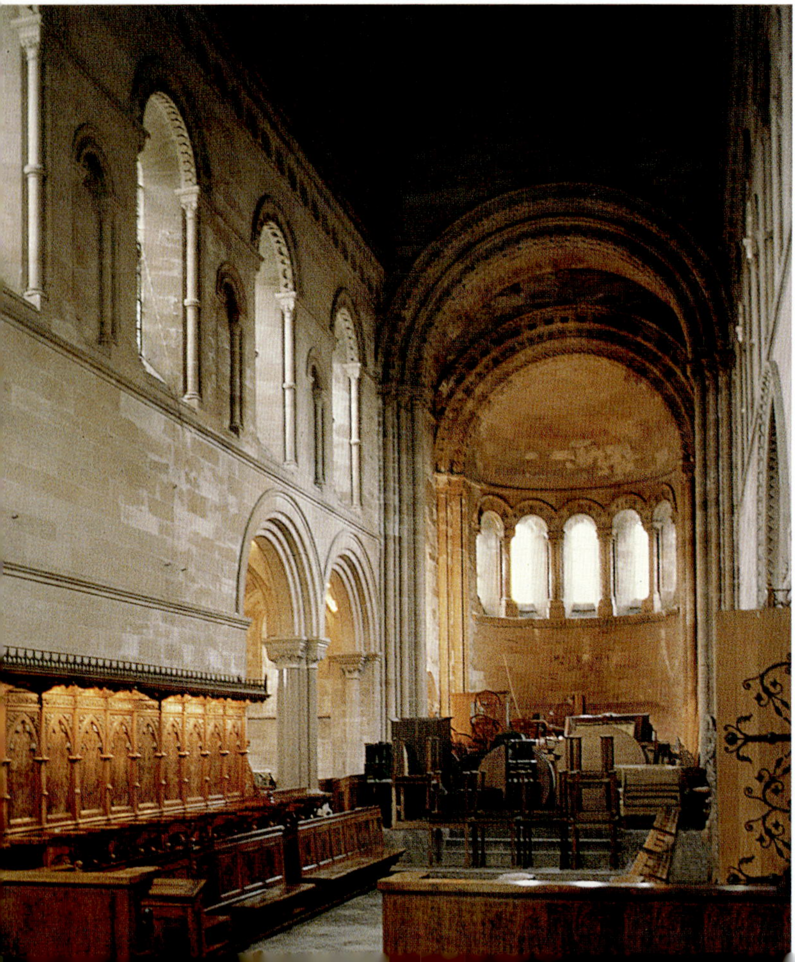

35. Drumtochty, St Palladius (Episcopal), by Pirie & Clyne, 1884–5 (p. 458)

36. Dunecht House, chapel, interior, by G. E. Street, 1870–81 (p. 462)

37. Aberdeen, St John (Episcopal), wall decoration by J.A.H. Hector, 1903 (p. 158)

38. Aberdeen, Torry, Sacred Heart (R.C.), by Charles J. Ménart, 1910–11 (p. 299)

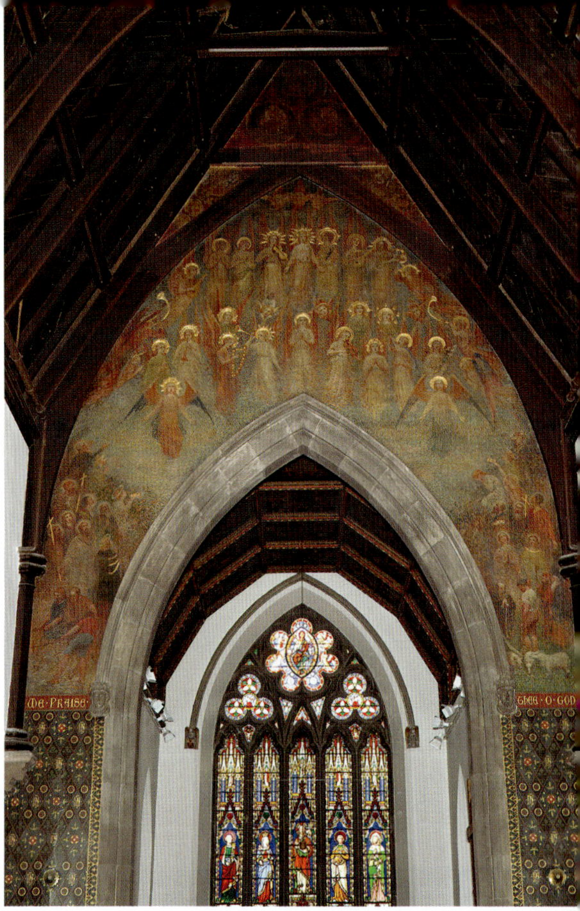

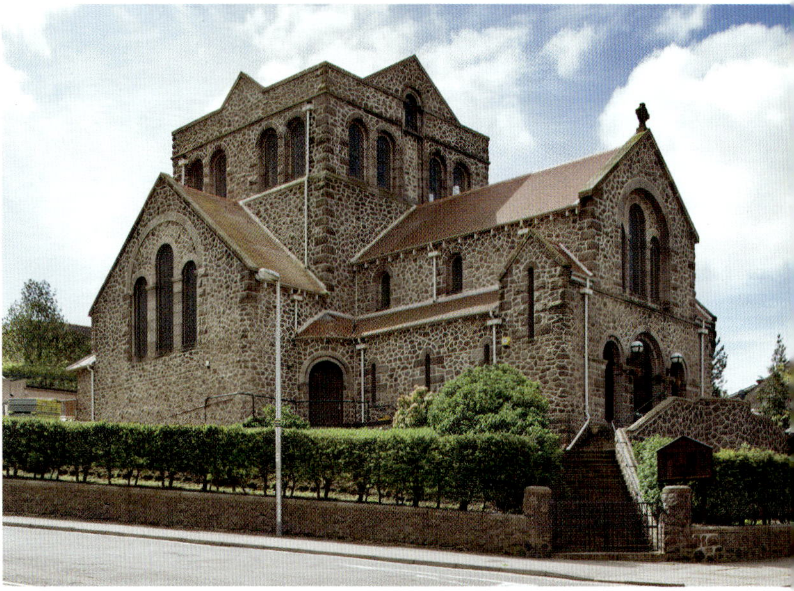

35 | 37
36 | 38

39. Braemar, St Margaret (Episcopal), rood screen, by J. Ninian Comper, 1909–21 (p. 389)
40. Aberdeen, King's College Chapel, war memorial window, by Douglas Strachan, 1921 (p. 192)
41. Aboyne, St Thomas (Episcopal), monument to Lord Glentanar, †1918, by Percy Portsmouth, 1923 (p. 308)
42. Aberdeen, King's College, Elphinstone Monument, by Henry Wilson, 1911 (completed 1931) (p. 192)

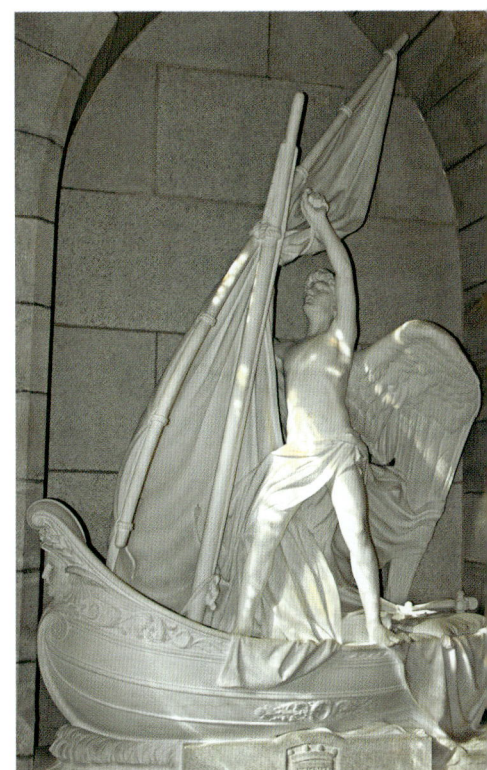

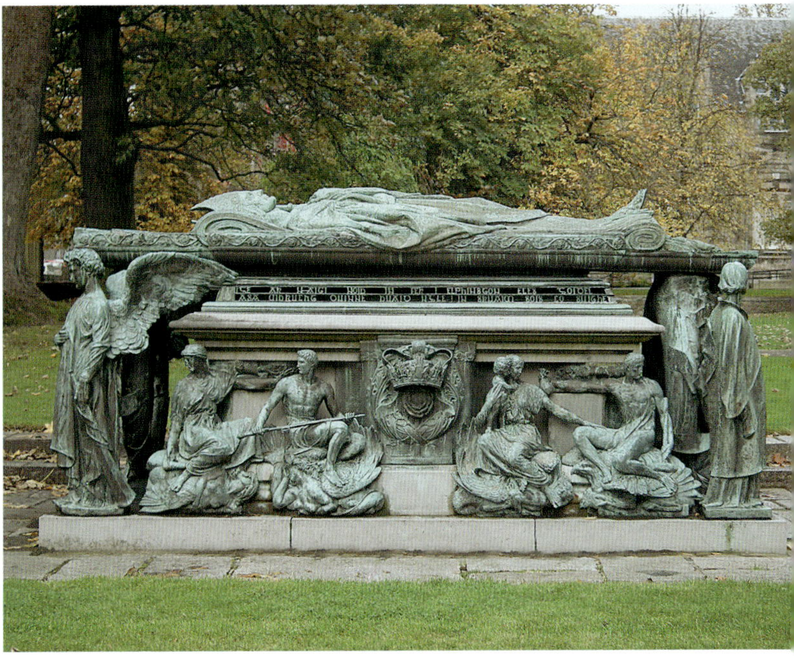

39	41
40	42

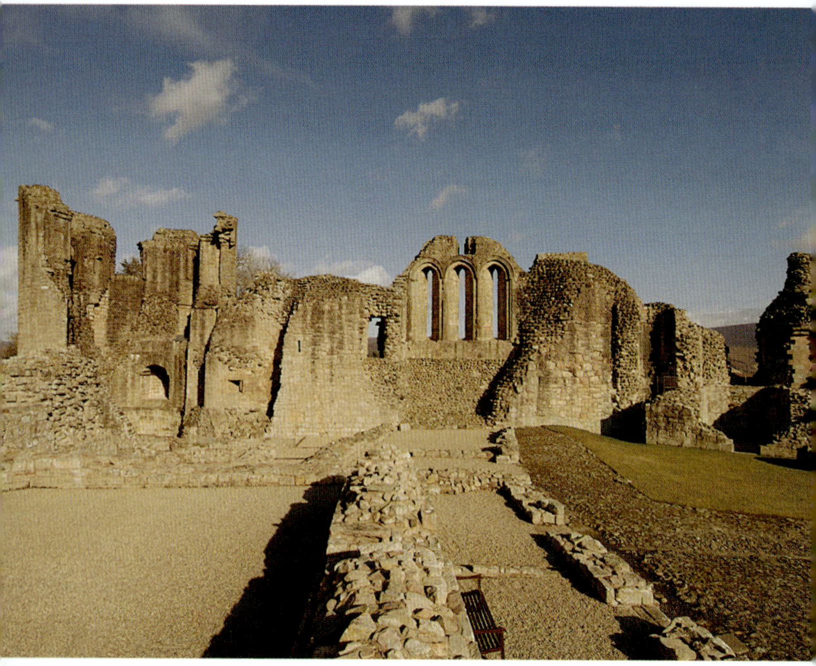

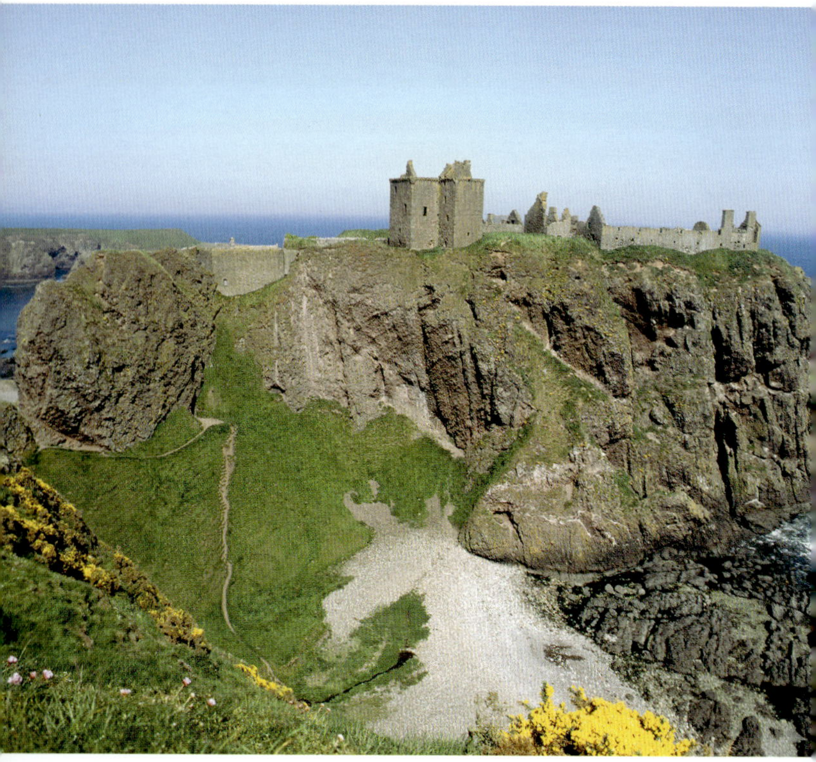

43. Kildrummy Castle, view E towards chapel window, early C13 and later
(p. 588)
44. Dunnottar Castle, from the NE, late C14 to late C16 (p. 469)
45. Drum Castle, tower, early C14 (p. 448)

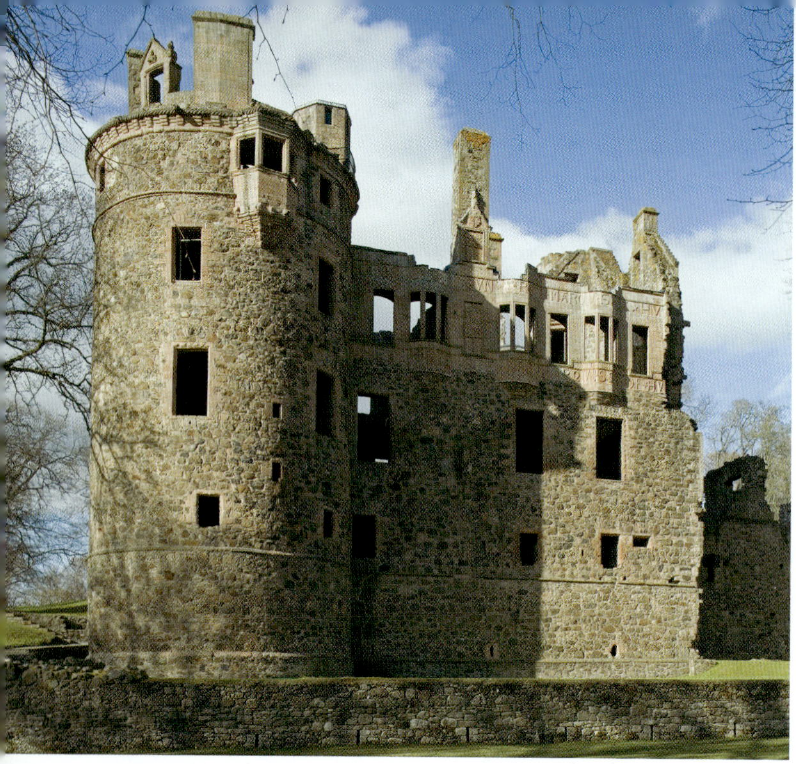

46. Huntly Castle, 'New Warke', view from the SW, mid C15, mid C16 and early C17 (p. 538)
47. Crathes Castle, view from the SE, mid and late C16; wing reconstructed by W. Schomberg Scott, 1971 (p. 437)
48. Craigievar Castle, S front, lower storeys mid-late C16, upperworks completed c. 1626 (p. 432)
49. Castle Fraser, view from the S, late C16, enlarged c. 1617–18; courtyard wings c. 1631–3 (p. 405)

46	48
47	49

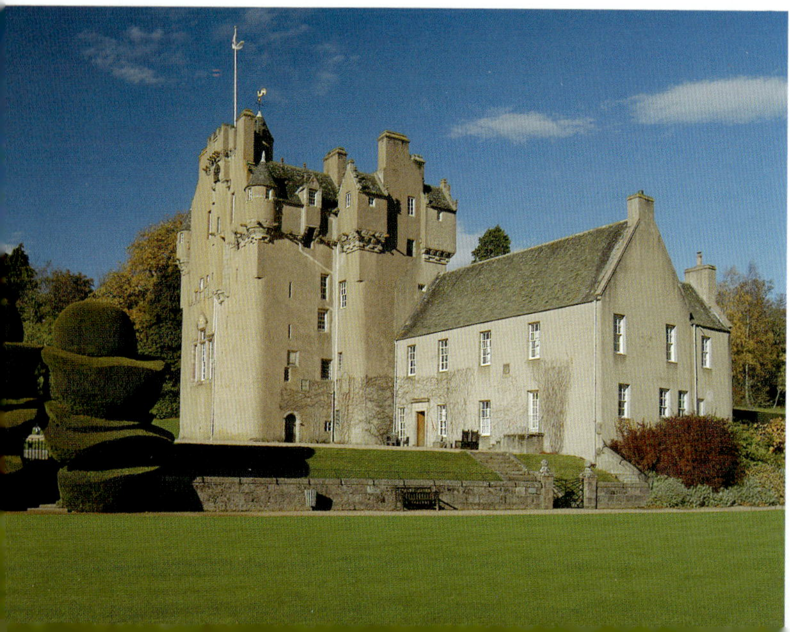

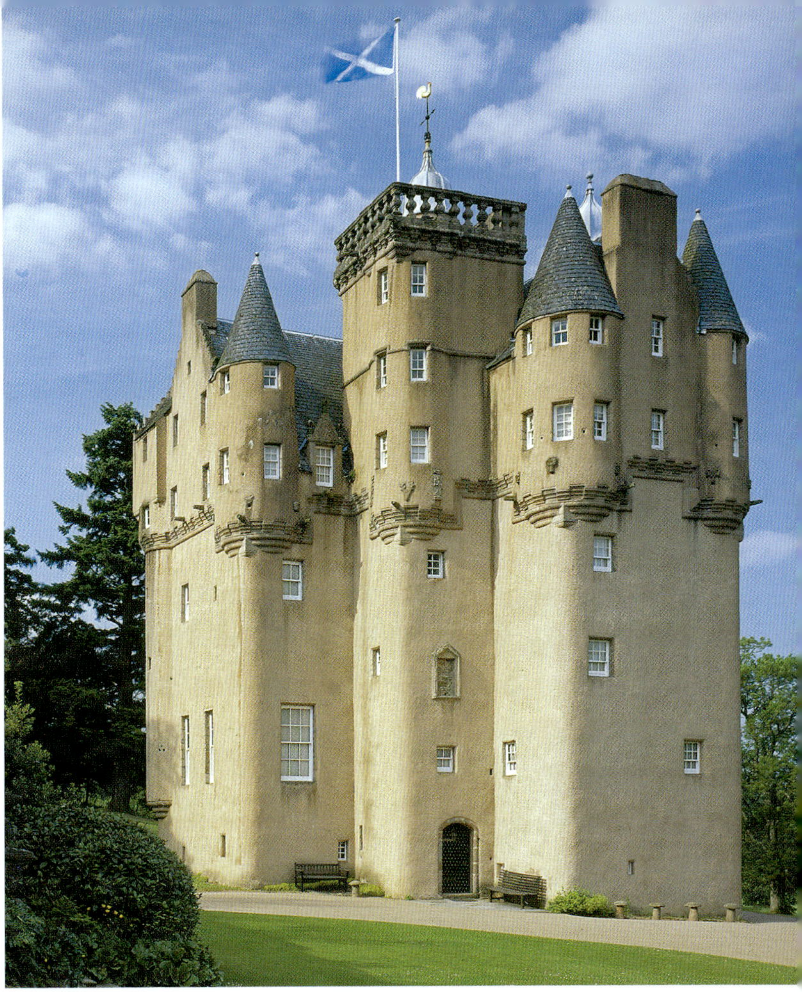

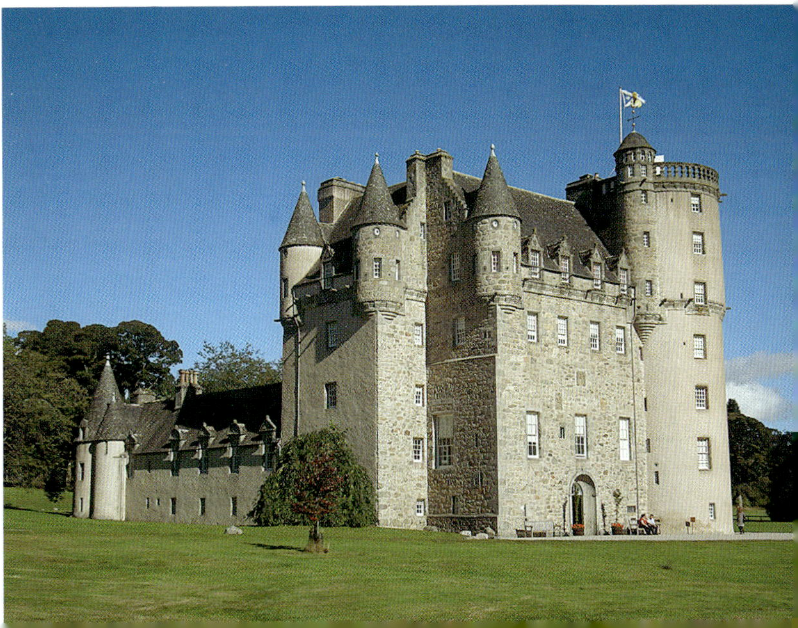

Hector
of Troy
Julius Cesar
Josue the noble
Chiftan of Israell

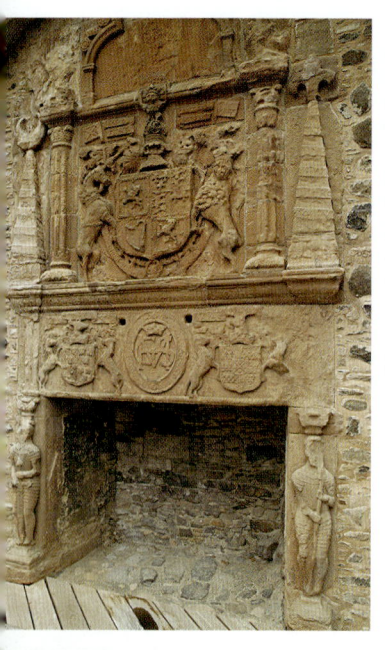

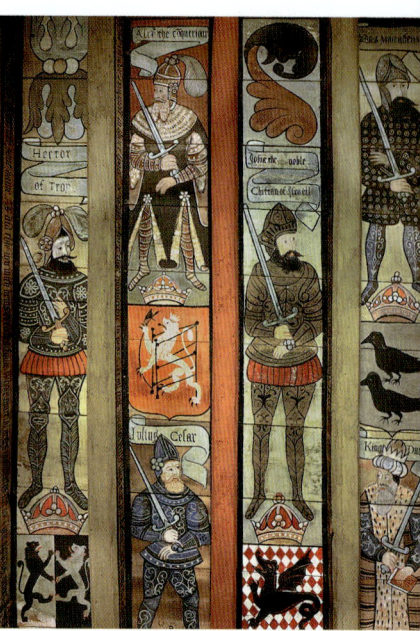

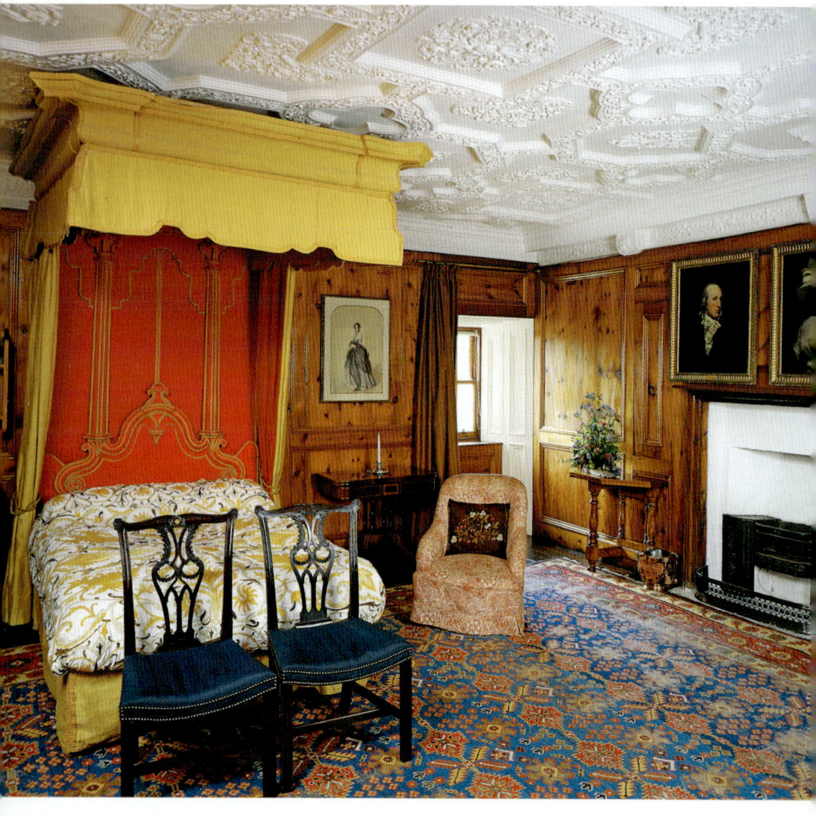

50. Huntly Castle, Marchioness's Hall, fireplace, early C17 (p. 542)
51. Crathes Castle, Room of Nine Nobles, painted ceiling, *c.* 1599 (p. 442)
52. Craigievar Castle, Queen's Room, plasterwork, early C17 (p. 436)
53. Crathes Castle, Long Gallery, ceiling, early–mid C17 (p. 442)

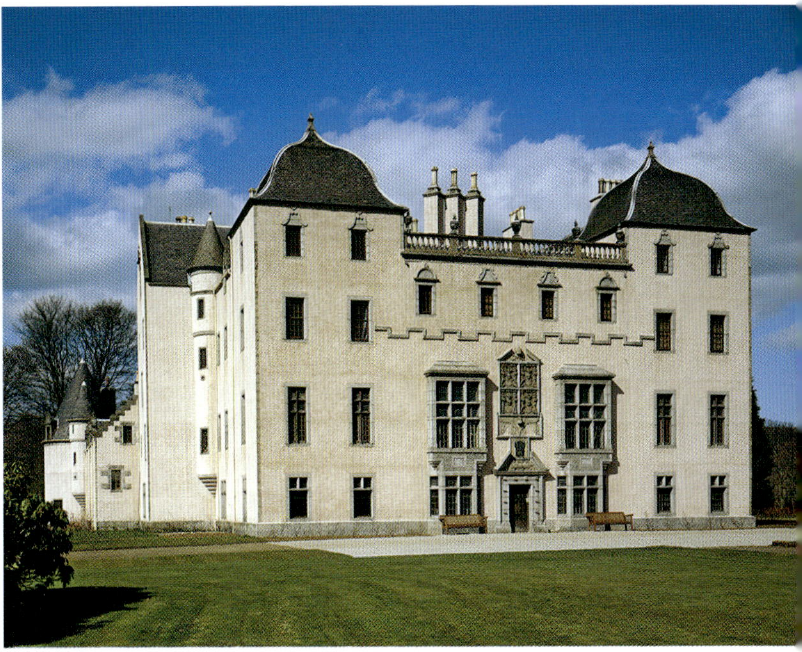

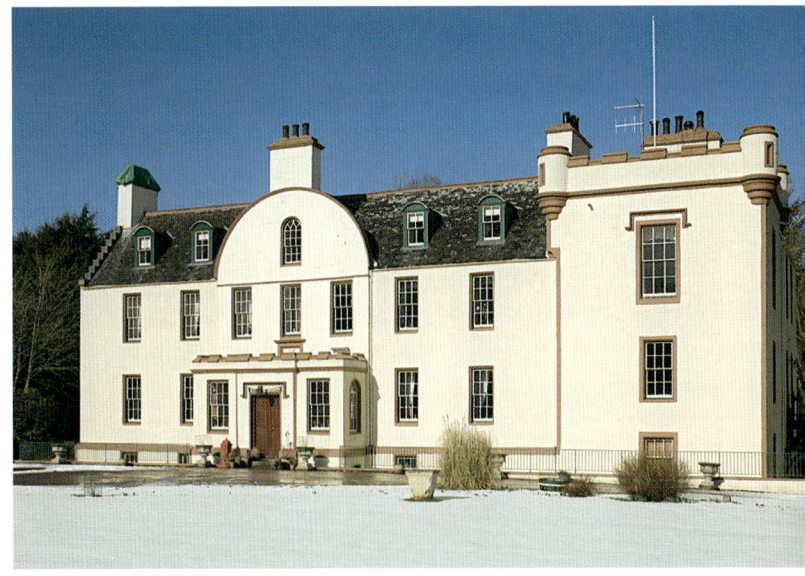

54. Glenmuick, Knock Castle, view from the SW, *c.* 1600 (p. 511)
55. Leith Hall, view from the NW, N range *c.* 1649; W range remodelled 1868 (p. 642)
56. Keith Hall, view of S front, 1696–9, altered by Sydney Mitchell & Wilson, from 1897 (p. 574)
57. Frendraught House, S front, 1656, remodelled *c.* 1753 and extended (r.) 1841–2 (p. 499)

54 | 56
55 | 57

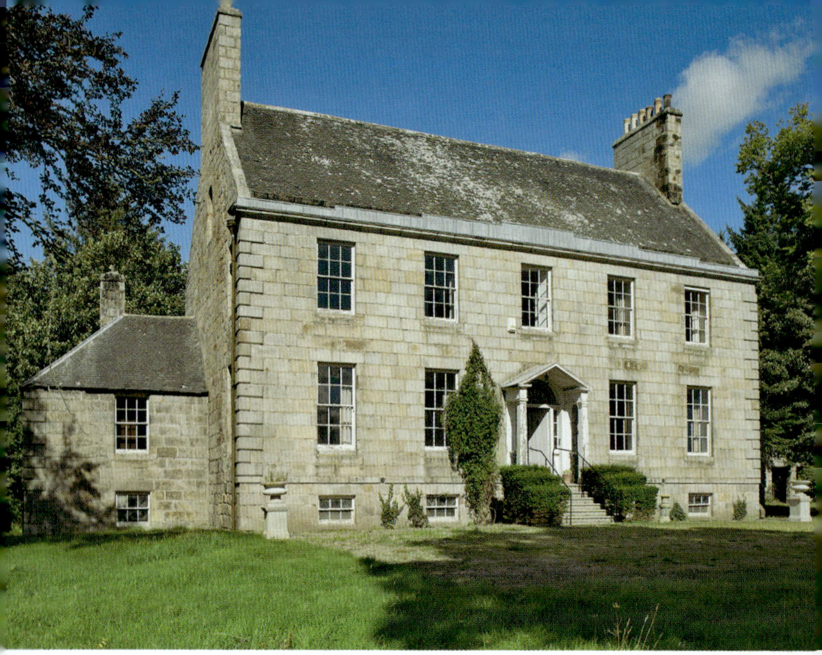

62. Elrick House, S front, 1789–92 (p. 480)
63. Manar House, Home Farm, *c.* 1800–5 (p. 662)
64. Fasque House, Stair Hall attributed to John Paterson, 1808–10 (p. 482)
65. Park House, SE front, by Archibald Simpson, 1821–2 (p. 696)

62	64
63	65

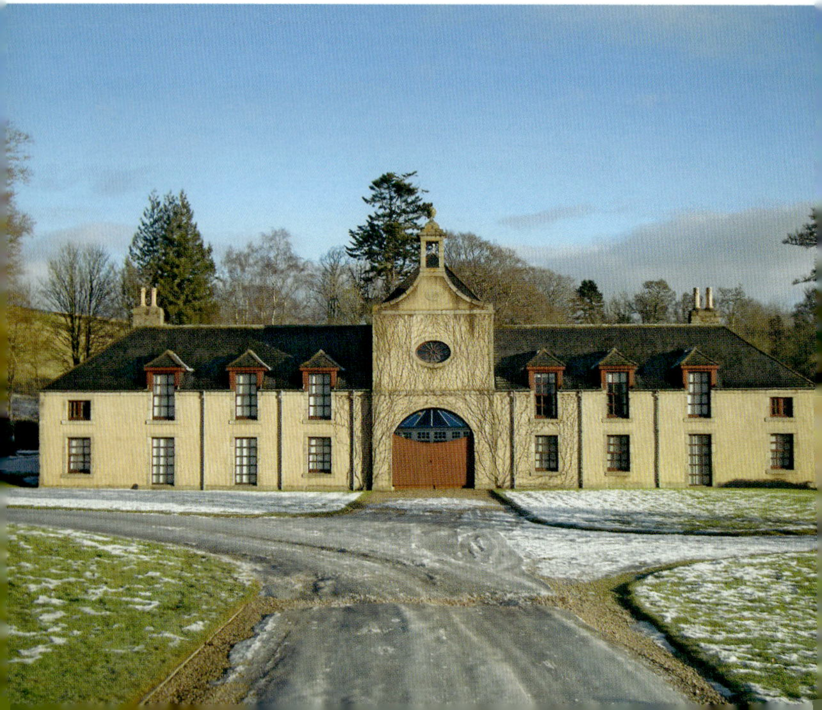

66. Castle Forbes, begun by Archibald Simpson 1814, completed by John Smith, 1821 (p. 402)
67. Cluny Castle, aerial view, by John Smith, 1818–36 (p. 419)
68. Drumtochty Castle, hall ceiling, by James Gillespie Graham, 1839 (p. 457)
69. Invercauld House, view from the W, C15–C18, remodelled 1840s and 1872–5 (p. 556)

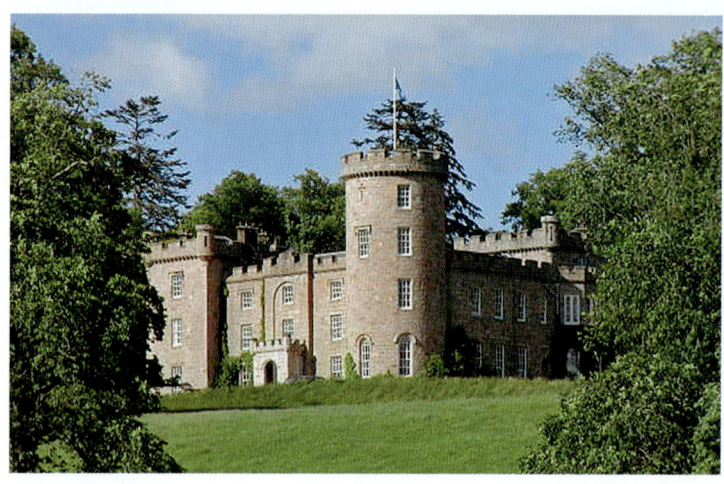

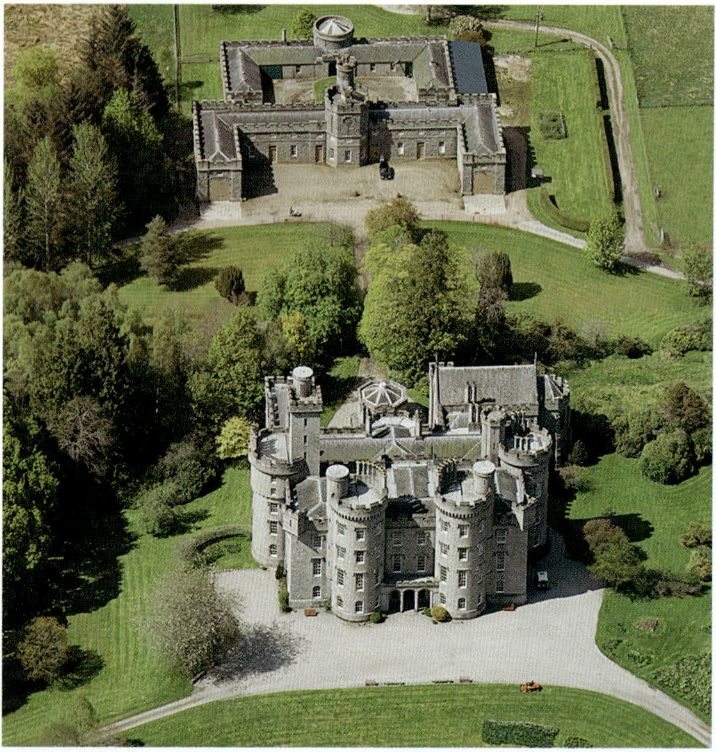

70. Ecclesgreig House, s front, by Henry Edmund Goodridge, 1844–6 (p. 477)

71. Balmoral Castle, view from the ESE, by William Smith, 1852–8 (p. 351)

72. Dunecht House, library, by G. E. Street, 1870–81 (p. 461)
73. Glenkindie House, s front, c16–c18, remodelled by Sydney Mitchell & Wilson, 1900 (p. 508)

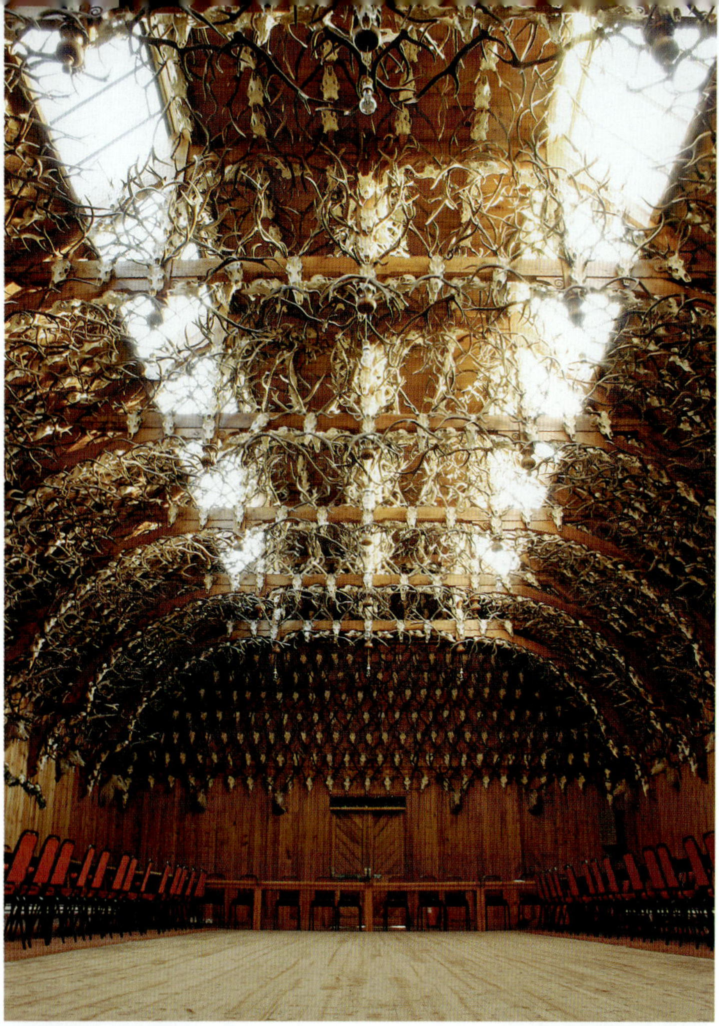

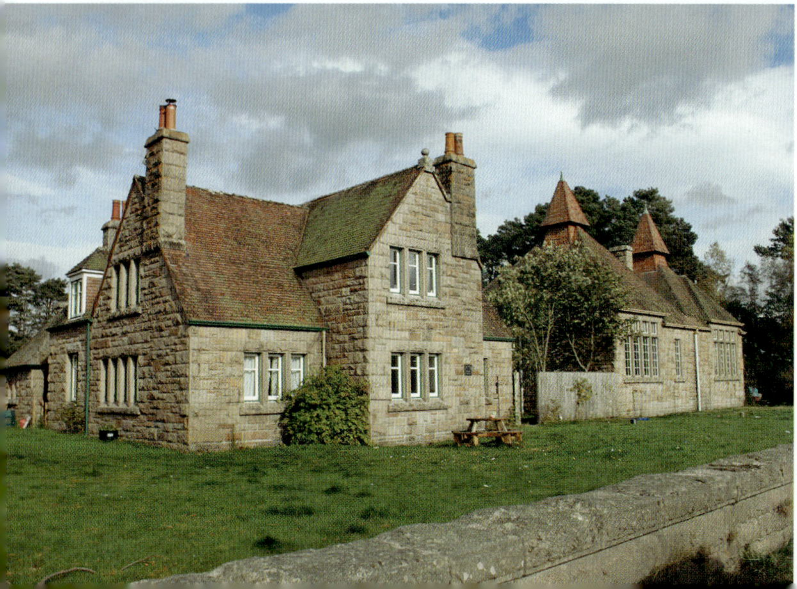

74. Mar Lodge, ballroom, mid C19, reconstructed 1895 (p. 663)
75. Glen Tanar, Board School, by George Truefitt, 1896–8 (p. 514)
76. Dunecht House, Tower Lodges, by A. Marshall Mackenzie & Son, 1923 (p. 466)
77. Aboyne, Aboyne Castle, view of s front, reconstructed by Ian Begg, 1974–82 (p. 312)

74	76
75	77

78. Aberdeen, Old Aberdeen, Bridge of Balgownie, early C14, reconstructed 1607–11 (p. 196)
79. Aberdeen, Ruthrieston, Bridge of Dee, 1520–7, partly rebuilt 1718–24, widened 1841–2 (p. 259)
80. Aberdeen, Provost Skene's House, exterior, C16–C17 (p. 133)
81. Aberdeen, Provost Skene's House, gallery ceiling, possibly 1622–44 (p. 133)

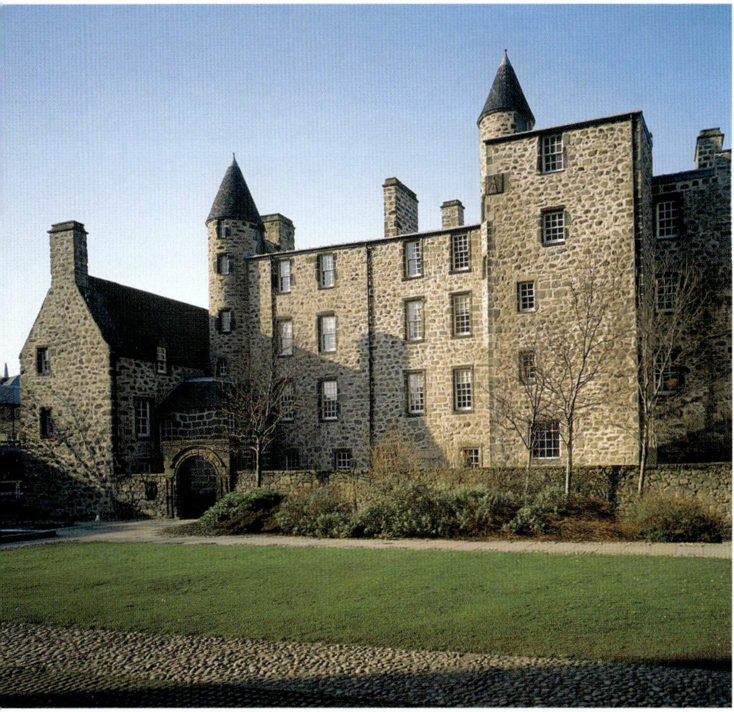

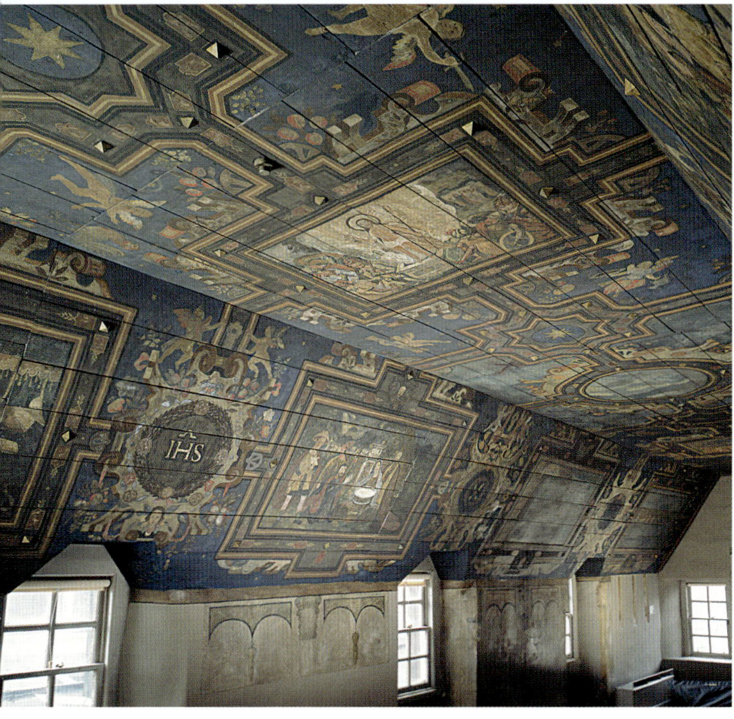

78 | 80
79 | 81

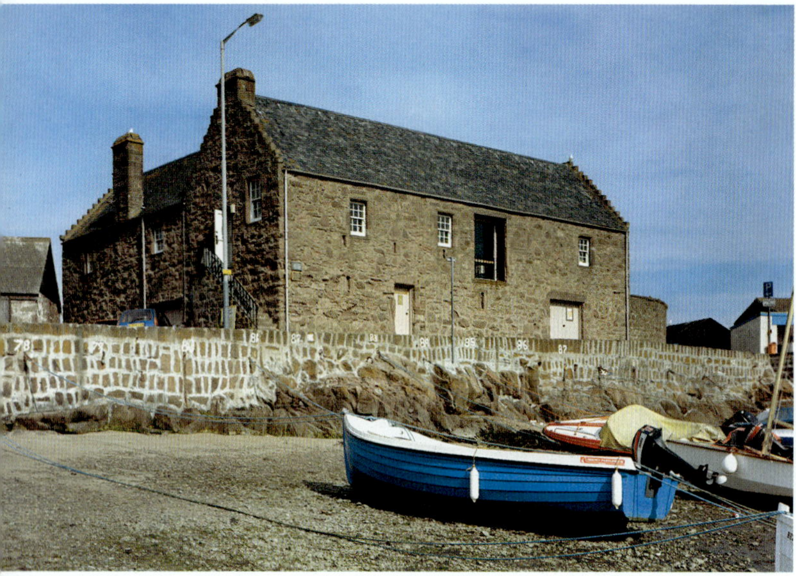

82. Stonehaven, Tolbooth, late c16 and early c17 (p. 726)
83. Aberdeen, Mercat Cross, by John Montgomery, 1686 (p. 132)
84. Aberdeen, Robert Gordon's College, by William Adam, 1732 with additions by John Smith, 1833 (p. 136)
85. Kintore, Town House, 1737–48, completed by John Rind (p. 609)

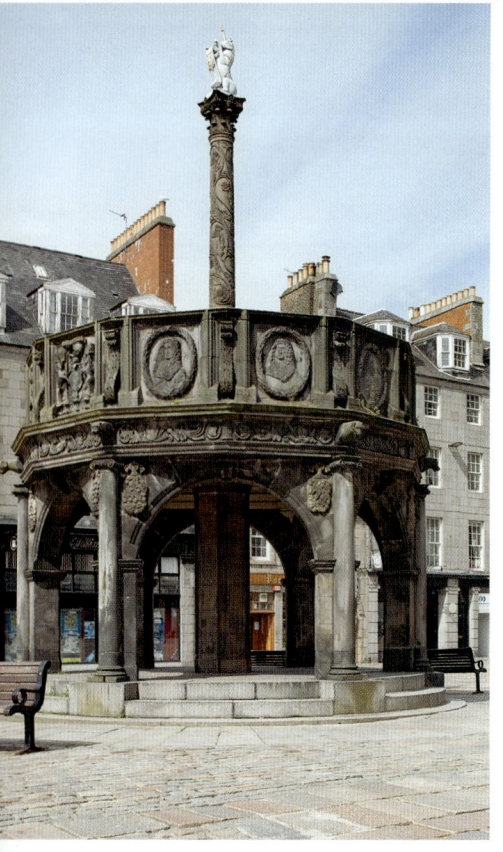

82 | 84
83 | 85

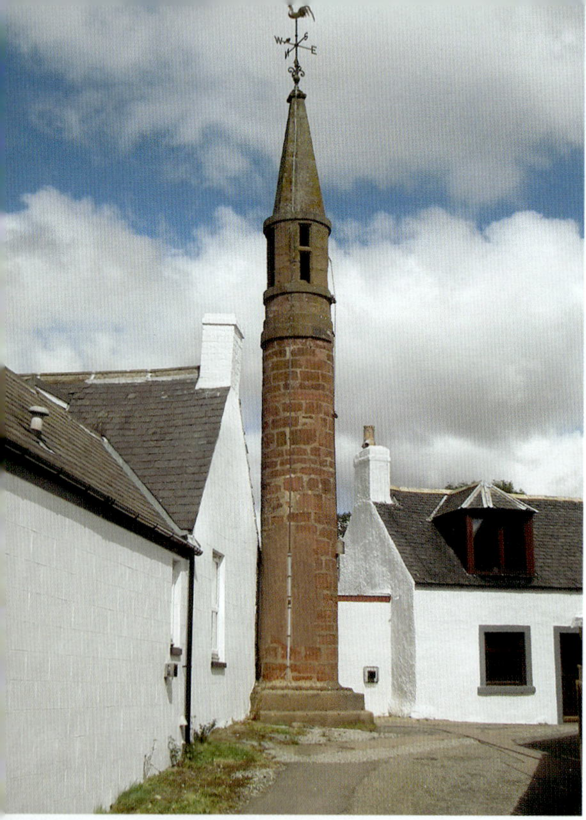

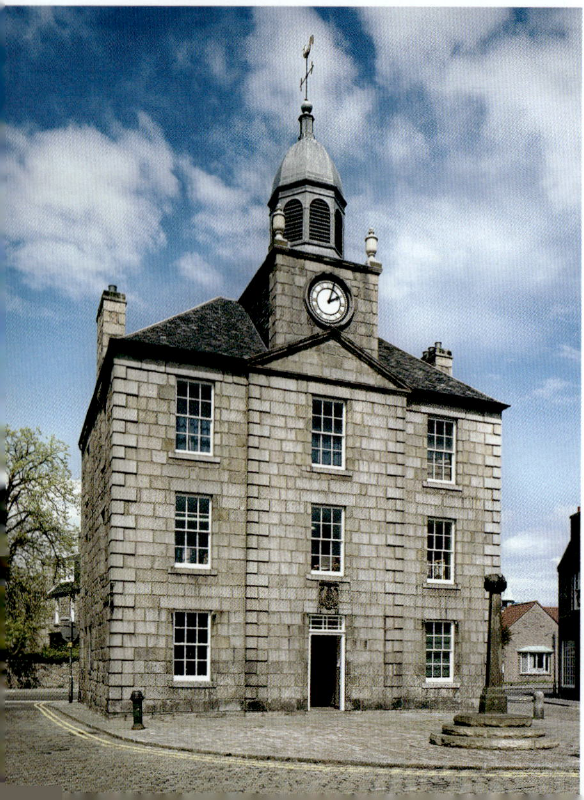

86. Drumlithie, Steeple, 1798, renovated C19 (p. 455)
87. Aberdeen, Old Aberdeen, Town House, view from the S, by George Jaffray, 1787–9 (p. 197)
88. Aberdeen, No. 35 Regent Quay, possibly by Alexander Kennedy, *c.* 1772 (p. 255)
89. Old Aberdeen, 81 High Street, possibly by George Jaffray, before 1773 (p. 201)

86 | 88
87 | 89

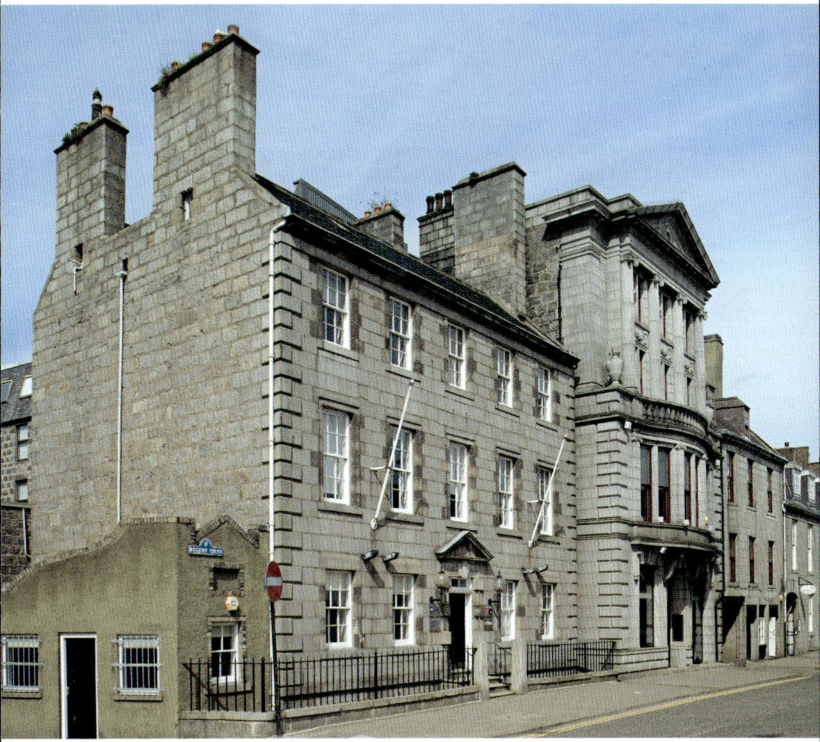
REGENT QUAY

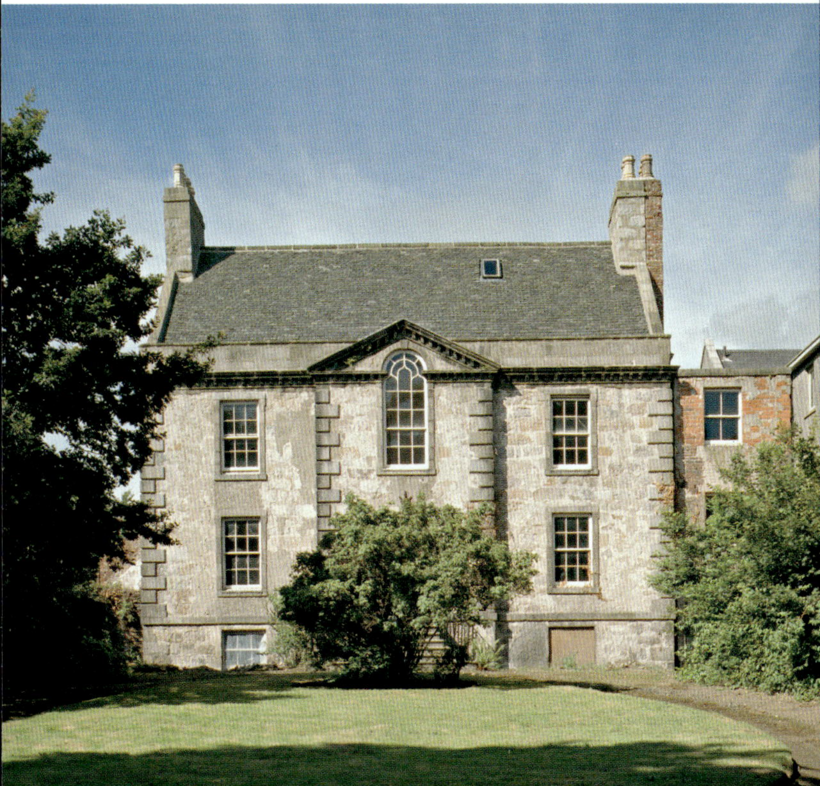

90. Aberdeen, Castle Street, Former Aberdeen Banking Co., by James Burn, *c.* 1801 (p. 141)
91. Aberdeen, Union Street, Music Hall, by Archibald Simpson, 1820–2 (p. 163)

92. Aberdeen, Castle Street, Former North of Scotland Bank, by Archibald Simpson, 1842 (p. 140)
93. Aberdeen, Bon Accord Crescent, by Archibald Simpson, 1823 (p. 165)

94. Aberdeen, King Street, former County Record Office by John Smith, 1832–3, Medico-Chirurgical Hall by Archibald Simpson, 1818–20 and North Church by Smith, 1829–31 (p. 145)
95. Aberdeen, King's College Divinity Library, by John Smith, 1822–6 (p. 194)
96. Huntly, Gordon Schools, view of the main block from the SE, by Archibald Simpson, 1839–41 (p. 531)
97. Stonehaven, Market Buildings, by Alexander Fraser, 1826, spire built 1857–8 (p. 725)

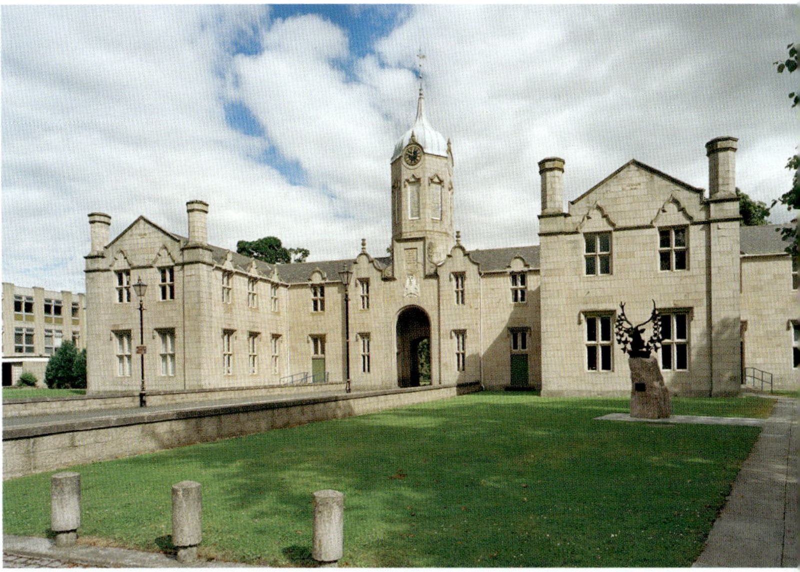

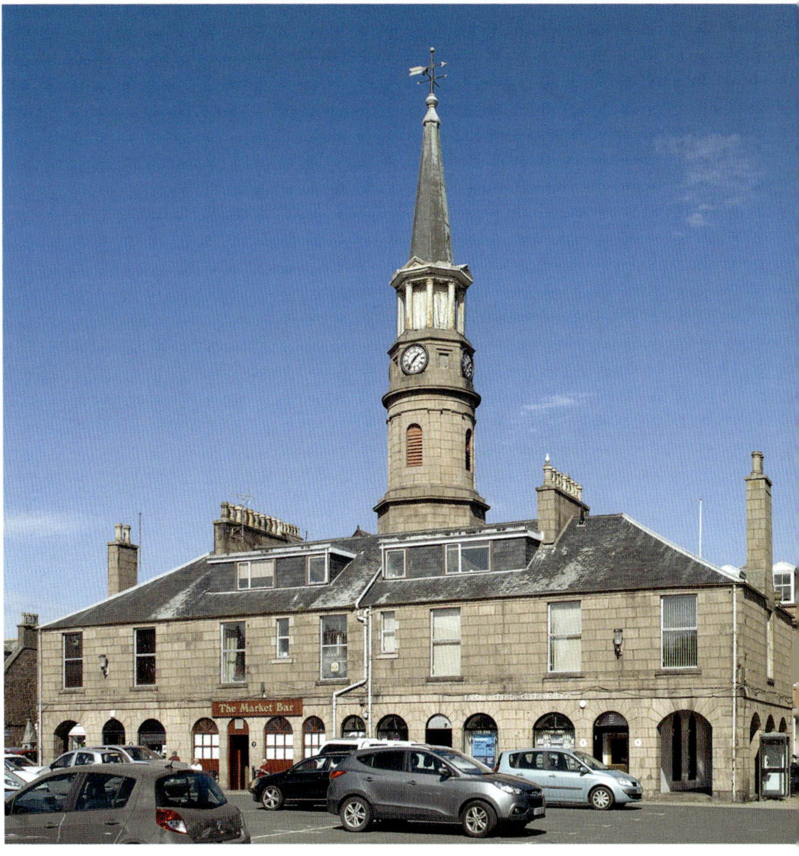

94 | 96
95 | 97

98. Aberdeen, Rubislaw Terrace, by Matthews & Mackenzie, 1852 (p. 235)
99. Inverurie, Town Hall, by J. R. Mackenzie, 1862 (p. 565)

100. Aberdeen, Advocates' Hall, library, by J. B. Pirie, 1872 (p. 129)
101. Aberdeen, Union Street, former Northern Assurance Co. offices,
    by A. Marshall Mackenzie, 1882–5 (p. 169)

102. Aberdeen, Torry, Girdleness Lighthouse, by Robert Stevenson, 1831–3 (p. 303)
103. Aberdeen, Wellington Suspension Bridge, by Samuel Brown and John Smith, 1829–31 (p. 249)

104. Aberdeen, Broadford Works, view from the SSW, C19–C20 (p. 211)
105. Marykirk, North Esk Viaduct, view from the ESE, 1861–5 (p. 667)

106. Aberdeen, No. 50 Queen's Road, by J. B. Pirie, 1886 (p. 237)
107. Aberdeen, Mile End School, by A. H. L. Mackinnon, 1899–1901 (p. 244)

108. Blairs, St Mary's College, by R. G. Wilson, 1892–1903, chapel by
Robert Curran, 1899–1901 (p. 384)
109. Aberdeen, Marischal College and Greyfriars Church, by A. Marshall
Mackenzie, 1893–1906 (p. 130)

110. Aberdeen, Rosemount Viaduct, His Majesty's Theatre, by Frank Matcham, 1904–6 (p. 162)
111. Aberdeen, Crown Street, Former Post Office, by W. T. Oldrieve, 1907 (p. 164)
112. Aberdeen, Schoolhill/Belmont Street, Former Central School, by J. A. Ogg Allan, 1902 (p. 130)
113. Aberdeen, Crown Street, Masonic Temple, by Harbourne Maclennan, 1908–11 (p. 162)
114. Stonehaven, Bath Street, The Lilies, by George Gregory, 1897 (p. 734)

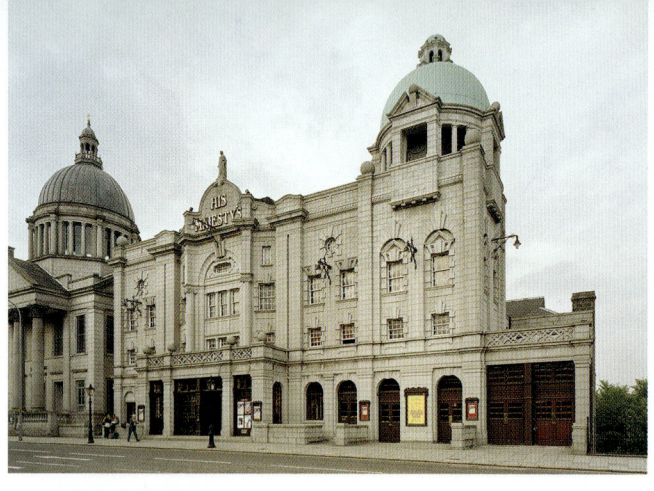

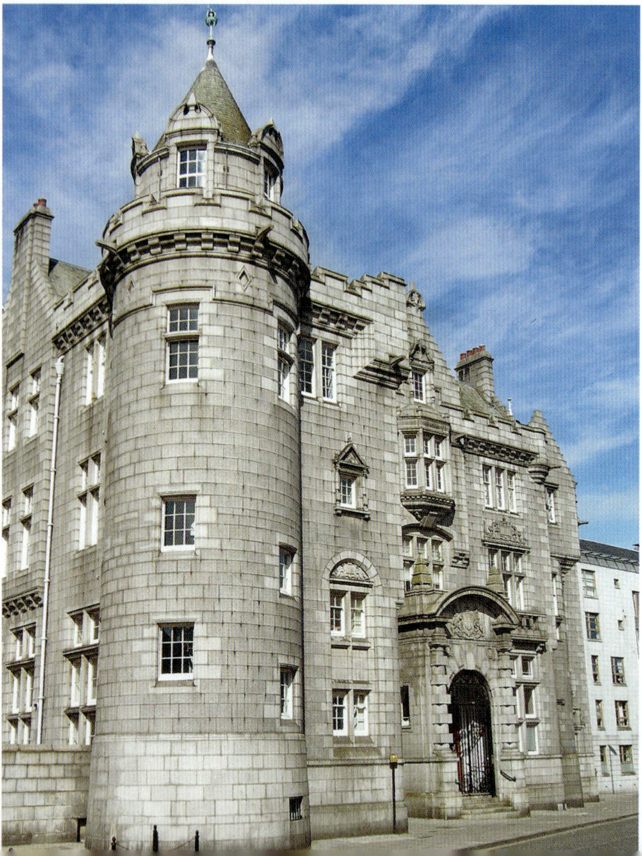

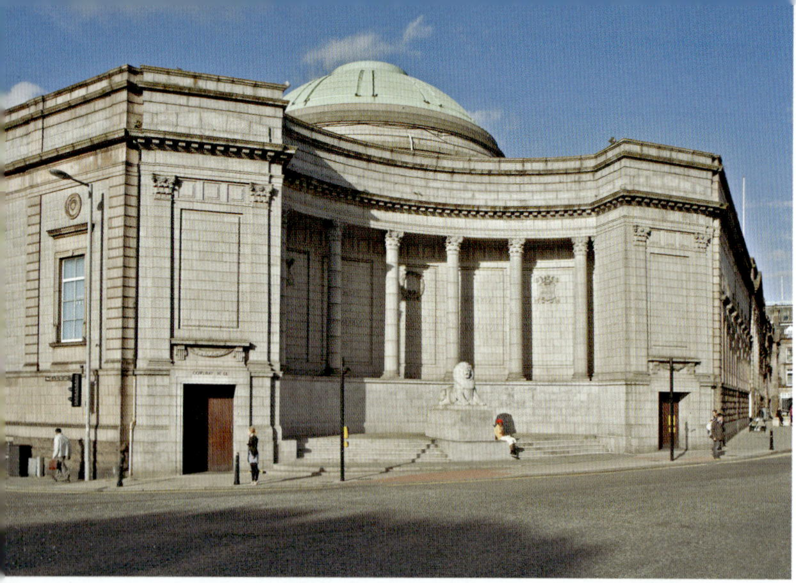

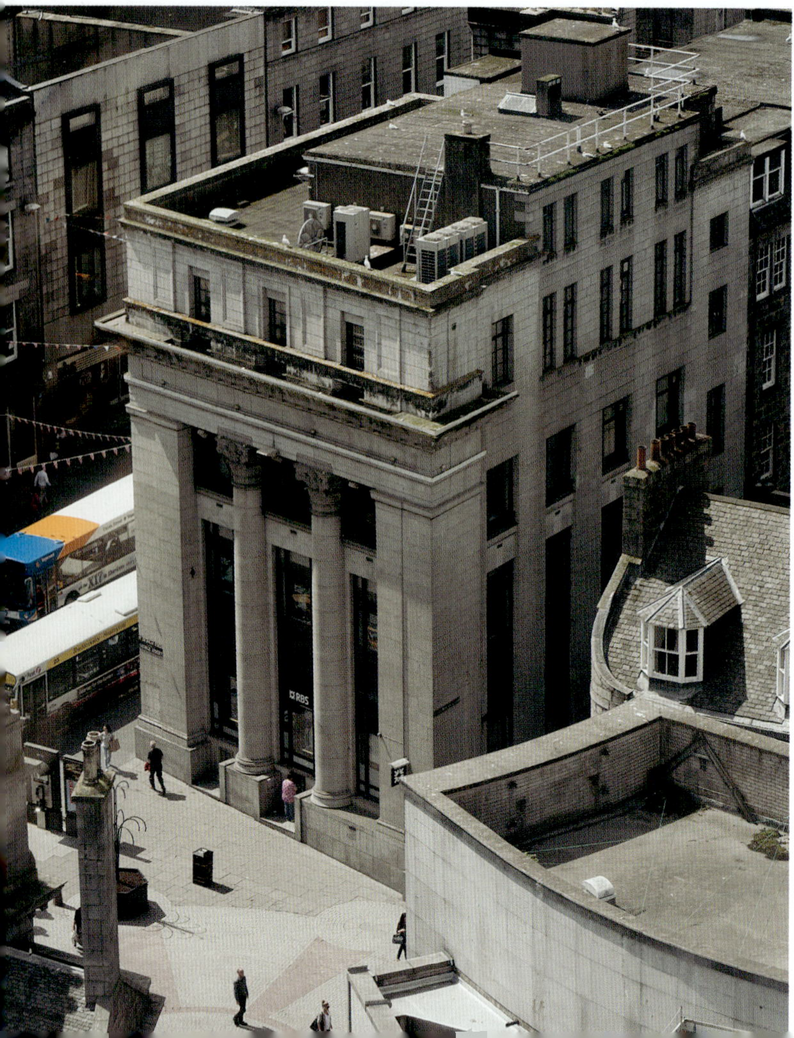
RBS

115. Aberdeen, Schoolhill, war memorial, by A. Marshall Mackenzie & Son, 1919 (p. 129)
116. Aberdeen, Union Street, Royal Bank of Scotland, by Jenkins & Marr, 1929 (p. 151)
117. Stonehaven, Carron Restaurant, by Tawse & Allan, 1936 (p. 731)
118. Aberdeen, King's Pavilion (University Swimming Pool), by A. Marshall Mackenzie & Son, 1939–41 (p. 196)

| 115 | 117 |
| 116 | 118 |

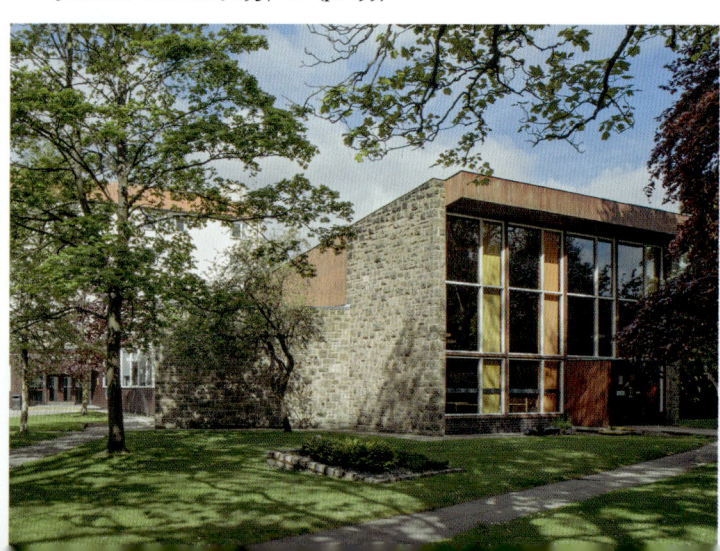

119. Aberdeen, Rosemount Square, detail of entrance archway, carving by
T. B. Huxley-Jones, 1948 (p. 221)

120. Aberdeen, King's College, Crombie Hall, by Robert Matthew &
Johnson-Marshall, 1957–60 (p. 199)

121. Aberdeen, Gallowgate, Seamount Court and Porthill Court,
by the City Architect, 1965–6 (p. 142)
122. Aberdeen, John Lewis, by Covell Matthews & Partners,
1967–70 (p. 210)

127. Aberdeen, King's College, Sir Duncan Rice Library, interior, by schmidt hammer lassen, 2009–12 (p. 201)

de Lundins (known as Durwards) after Thomas de Lundin challenged the legitimacy of Duncan, Earl of Mar, and King Alexander III divided the Celtic palatinate between them. Although Kildrummy Castle (q.v.) which the Earls held on the Crown's behalf was much the biggest and most architecturally distinguished stronghold in the Dee valley, Coull was the next most important and closely resembled it in situation, plan and development. Like Kildrummy, it was conceived as a D-shaped pentagonal courtyard, approximately 34 m. N–S by 40 m. E–W (compared to 185 m. by 210 m. at Kildrummy), with thick walls rising from battered bases and drum towers protecting the angles; the largest tower with the thickest walls was a French-style donjon, 8.8 m. in external diameter. In each case the main living quarters, including the great hall, were arranged furthest from the entrance and overlooking a deep ravine; and in each case the entrance itself was protected by an English-style gatehouse some 21 m. broad, with a drawbridge and a pend flanked by two roughly circular towers, probably built c. 1300 by supporters of Edward I and Balliol. The castle was almost certainly destroyed on Robert Bruce's orders during his Aberdeenshire campaign of 1307. Its ruins were re-discovered in the C18, the findings recorded in the *Old Statistical Account*. The first proper excavation was begun by A. Marshall Mackenzie who had purchased the Coull estate in 1912 (*see* Coull House, above) but he was interrupted by the First World War. More detailed excavation was directed by Dr W. Douglas Simpson in the years immediately afterwards. From what remained it was evident that the castle's walls had been quickly and crudely constructed mostly in local red granite but fragments of high-quality Kildrummy freestone were also found, some with masons' marks, and one initialled M.S. in Gothic letters.

CRAIG CASTLE

0.75 km. WNW of Auchindoir

4020

Craig Castle is the most complete member of a group of four mid–late C16 tower houses – the others being Gight, Delgatie and Towie Barclay (all N) – which were identified by Dr Douglas Simpson as being so similar in concept, plan and even certain details as to strongly imply that they were all the work of the same master mason. They were all relatively conservative for their date, genuinely defensive and built for closely related families who remained staunchly Catholic during the Reformation. Tradition suggests that they were built by the *Conn family* of master masons based at Auchry. Their exact dates are not known for certain. Craig may have been built for William Gordon, 2nd Laird of Craig, c. 1550, or more probably his son William, 3rd Laird, c. 1560–75. Although its interior was refitted in the late

C17, a separate three-storey house was built in the early–mid C18 immediately E of the old tower, which thereafter became an annexe. An extension of 1832 provided a new entrance hall, dining and drawing rooms, its details suggesting that *Archibald Simpson* was its architect; a further extension was added in 1908.

The TOWER HOUSE is a four-storey L-plan. Its main block, orientated N–S, is 12.8 m. by 10.7 m., and its NE jamb 7.3 m. by 6 m.: the length-to-breadth ratio in each case is exactly 6:5.* The doorway is in the main block's E face, within the re-entrant angle. It is roll-moulded and segment-headed, and the stout oak door is original or early, still with iron handle and knocker, and protected by shot-holes, one wide-mouthed on the l. and the other smaller on the r. in the juncture with the jamb. Above the entrance is a row of three armorials (*see* below) which are again roll-moulded, that in the centre square and those either side with depressed ogee heads. Above these again is a large window, secured by an iron grille, providing light at the hall's 'high' end. The second floor is blind, but at attic level a turret with a conical roof is corbelled from its SE angle, while the wall-walk is slightly jettied out on filleted brackets and a cable moulding, the only section of the parapet so treated. The jamb's S flank within the re-entrant angle also has first- and second-floor windows lighting the private chambers but the long N and W walls are much more solid, partly to prevent heat loss but mostly for defence: unlike most tower houses in continuous habitation, Craig's fabric has remained virtually unaltered over the centuries. Its walls still have their original massive strength, and rise above a base course with a slight batter sheer and almost unbroken to 12.2 m. height. They retain nearly all their original ground-floor openings, widemouthed shot-holes, arrowslits and, on the N, a single crosslet with an oilette, although a few have been blocked on the S side; even at the upper levels the original windows in red sandstone surrounds are modest in size. There is no ornament of any kind, and it is hard even to determine the floor levels.

This remarkable sense of a protective shell is reinforced by the way in which either during construction or shortly afterwards the roofs of the attic caphouse were swept over the wall-walk, thus sealing it in, the small square windows lighting it now having originally been intended as crenels; a circular opening on the W flank is a doocot flight-hole. One of the caphouse skewputts (on the jamb gable) has been carved with initials V.G. (William Gordon). The height of the finely coped ashlar chimneystacks, either rising tall from the side walls of the enclosed caphouse just above the eaves or from the crowstepped end gables, is 17.2 m.

---

* Strictly speaking, the main block is orientated NE by SW, and the windows in the re-entrant angle thus have ideal SE and SW aspects.

The HERALDIC PANELS above the doorway represent, centre, the Royal Arms of Scotland – a declaration of loyalty to the young Queen Mary, and perhaps also implying that the Gordons held Craig directly from the Crown. The sole of this panel has a scroll which has not been lettered. On the r., arms and initials of the 1st Laird, Patrick Gordon, and his wife, Rachel Barclay of Towie, are combined with their son the 2nd Laird William, and his wife, Elizabeth Stewart of Laithers. Two allounds rampant act as supporters, 'Ioīsleis' referring to Johnsleys, a house which stood near Insch. On the l. are the arms of the 1st Laird and his wife combined with William the 3rd Laird and Clara Cheyne, again supported by allounds and dated 1548 (MD48) in mixed Roman and Arabic numerals.

PLAN AND INTERIOR. The wall thicknesses vary but at their strongest, notably on the W side, they are over 2 m. at ground floor. The entrance is protected, behind its oak door, by an iron yett with two strong bolts. This opens onto a small vestibule with groined vault, the ribs springing from corbels: the central boss displays the Royal Arms with crown and supporters, the NW corbel the Gordon arms and (formerly) initials V.G., and the SW corbel the Five Wounds. The vestibule forms part of a corridor extending along the main block's E flank from S to N where it meets the main newel stair. This is 1.3 m. in diameter and rises through the tower's full height at the junction of main block and jamb. The corridor accesses two vaulted cellars and a SE pit-prison in the main block and the kitchen in the jamb. The arched kitchen hearth fills the jamb's E gable: in its N end are two shot-holes and in its S a recess, presumably for keeping salt dry. The ground floor is paved throughout, but the paving stones are not original, and the floor is at a rather higher level than formerly.

At first floor the hall within the main block was remodelled in the later C17. Originally it had a very broad near-central fireplace in its W flank. It was entered by means of a short flight of steps opening off the newel stair into the cheek of a window recess at the 'low' (or N) end; in the opposite cheek, a second flight in the NW angle was used to carry food and drink from the N cellar. Above the window was a vaulted musicians' gallery, entered off the newel stair, with an elliptical archway opening into the hall. During the Reformation it served another more important purpose, as a venue for Catholic worship – with a curtain closed over the arch, as a private oratory, or open, when the priest officiated to a congregation in the hall beneath, all much as at Towie Barclay except that the vault is not ribbed. Gordon himself entered the hall at its 'high' (S) end through an antechamber and bedchamber (both within the main block's E wall), which connected to a square-plan private chamber in the jamb.

During the late C17 or very early C18 the hall's N end was partitioned off as small serving rooms, the fireplace width reduced and the ceiling height lowered, these changes obscuring the gallery. The heraldic panel at the hall's S end contains arms of the 7th Laird, Francis Gordon, and Agnes Ogilvie. Another panel above the doorway linking the antechamber to the bedchamber represents the arms and initials of John Gordon, the 4th Laird, and Lilias Barclay; this coat of arms, like the bedchamber fireplace, is seemingly early C17. Within the jamb the private chamber had a vault which was concealed when the room was panelled in the late C17–C18. It had a closet and garderobe and its own fireplace in the N wall. The second floor was presumably the Gordons' wives' apartment. It followed the same basic layout as the first floor but with lower ceilings; here the corbels are still visible. It had no oratory, but the vestibule between the upper hall and its private apartment also opened into what seems to have been a strongroom within the wall thickness on the main block's E side. As at first-floor level the hall has been partitioned, the N end into a small bedchamber and closet and the S end into a large square room with chimneypiece inserted in the S wall.

The GATEWAY is in channelled red ashlar sandstone. Its round-headed arch is framed by pilaster-buttresses rising above a bolection moulding into obelisks and ball finials. These flank a heraldic panel framed by scrolls and crowned by another obelisk and ball finial, which represents the arms of Francis, 8th Laird, and his three wives, Elizabeth Barclay, Anne Forbes and Katherine Campbell. They are supported by allounds and crowned by an esquire's plumed helmet and the stag's head of the Gordons, with the motto 'Bydand' on a raised scroll. The initials of all four individuals, together with the date 1726, are incised beneath. Another panel on the gateway's plain inner face, dated 1667, represents the Gordon arms in its first three quarters and Menzies in the fourth, signifying Francis the 6th Laird's marriages to Elizabeth Menzies and Jean Gordon. Next to the gateway, a half-length SHOTPUTTER, carved C16–C17.

The early–mid C18 HOUSE is built of red cherry-cocked ashlar sandstone. It is a shallow rectangle on plan, three storeys high, the top floor originally being a low attic under a tall piended roof. Its entrance front faced W, the doorway near the S end still extant but concealed by the 1832 addition (*see* below), and the windows set in raised margins. It had a moulded eaves cornice and a piended roof with two big chimneystacks over its ridge, but its original profile was lost when the house was reconstructed after a fire by *John MacLennan* (of *Jenkins & Marr*) *c.* 1946, the wall-heads being raised over the eaves cornice and the roof pitch being flattened.

The EXTENSION concealing the S half of the C18 house's entrance front was added in 1832. A tall square-plan single storey, it provided a new entrance on the N side, facing into the courtyard. The arms over the doorway are those of the builders, James Gordon, 11th Laird, and Anne Elizabeth Johnstone; their initials and date also appear on the canted bay with curvilinear gable overlooking the grounds on the S side. Certain details, including the plasterwork of the new entrance hall, dining room and drawing room, suggested to Douglas Simpson that the architect was *Archibald Simpson*, on the basis of their resemblance to those at Castle Newe (dem.). Another EXTENSION further to the W, plain two-storeyed with crenellated parapet, was added in 1908, concealing much of the old tower house's S face.

The rectangular WALLED GARDEN immediately to the N and E probably preserves some of the original courtyard and garden layout. Part of the W wall nearest the castle is in coursed pinned rubble apparently of C16 or C17 date; the gateway (which is later) incorporates a heraldic panel of 1667. The remainder seems to be the same date as the C18 house; within the garden the SUNDIAL was carved by the local mason *John Montgomery* but its metal dial is by *Peter Hill* of Edinburgh, 1821. The layout of THE DEN in picturesque fashion with rustic bridges and paths linking together through the woods is attributed to John, the 10th Laird, and corresponds to a survey drawing of 1777, although it was subsequently augmented by James, the 11th Laird, during the early C19.

CRAIGIEVAR CASTLE   5000
3.6 km. ESE of Leochel-Cushnie

Standing high up within the valley of the Leochel Burn, Craigievar – 'the Rock of Mar' – has long been celebrated as the most elegantly composed of all Scottish tower houses. As it appears now it was completed *c.* 1626 for William Forbes, the merchant 'Danzig Willie' who was scion of a noted Protestant family and brother of Bishop William Forbes of Corse (q.v.). There is little doubt that in its final form it is the work of the *Bell family* of master masons, of whom I. Bell signed his work at Castle Fraser (q.v.) in 1617–18, its magnificently composed upperworks being characteristic of their style. However, Craigievar was begun by the Mortimer family, who remained Catholic after the Reformation and were obliged to sell their estate in 1610. Although more complex on plan, with a smaller footprint, it has been convincingly suggested that certain features of the Mortimers' house bear very close relationship to the group of four (or more) deliberately conservative and defensive castles which include Craig (q.v.), and Gight, Delgatie and Towie Barclay (N), all built by prominent Catholics during the Reformation, their master masons traditionally identified as the *Conn family* of Auchry. Although the supreme skill and confidence of the Bells' remodelling presents a perfectly unified composition, the plan reveals clear evidence of alteration. In many ways Craigievar is a hybrid in which tradition and modernity are both in tension and in fusion – externally, in a composition in which martial towers and turrets vie for dominance with domestic gables; on plan, where elaborate conventions of social hierarchy are reflected both horizontally and vertically;

and in the magnificent interior of a Protestant merchant which overlays but does not quite conceal the earlier Catholic origin of the castle's basic structure.

48 The ENTRANCE (S) FRONT at first appears to correspond to the classic stepped L-plan of many C17 tower houses. Its main block stands with its jamb projecting boldly forward on the r., and with its square entrance tower built into the angle between them. For their first four storeys the walls (harled with pink granite dressings) rise almost entirely plain, though with a gentle batter. The roll-moulded entrance is segmentally arched, with a pedimented second-floor field-panel above it, while the position of the Great Hall, at first floor within the main block, is identified by one window much larger than the others. Otherwise the windows are relatively small – those at ground floor particularly so – and the angles are softly rounded until at the main wall-head a boldly profiled corbel course with dummy water cannon zigzags its way around the entire building to support the Bells' superstructure. Inset into the walls immediately above the corbel course are low-relief sculptures including animal and gargoyle heads concealing shot-holes, and a lion and unicorn rampant. The turrets are either circular or slightly ovoid, and as so often in the Bells' work rise through two storeys into steep conical spirelets. The S front has one at the main block's W end with a pedimented and finialled stone

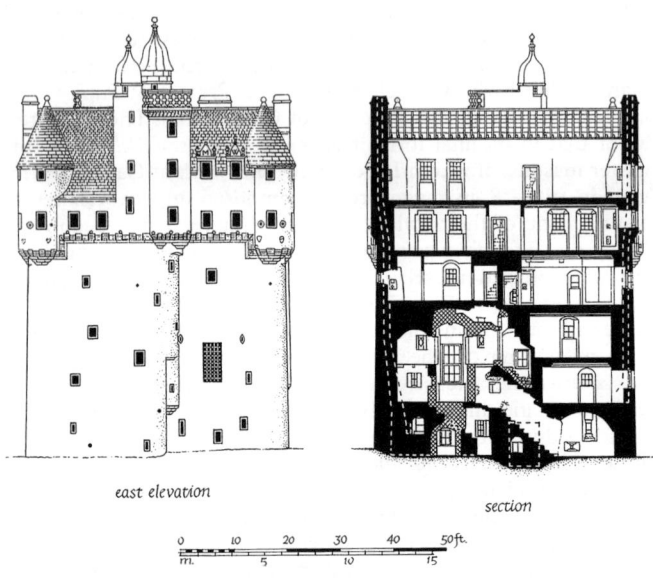

east elevation

section

0   10   20   30   40   50 ft.
m.   5   10   15

Craigievar Castle.
Elevation and section of east front

dormer next to it (the initials M.V.F. stand for Master William Forbes), while the jamb has two turrets which frame the coped chimney gable between them so tightly that the gable element is asymmetric with only a very few crowsteps. Above the wall-head, the square entrance tower extends back across the roofs of the main block and jamb, and rises a further three storeys: its outer (SW) angle swells out like another turret to echo those which flank it on either side, but instead of being crowned by a conical spirelet it corbels to square again just beneath the tower's chunky balustrade, the most classical feature of the composition as a whole. The steep roofs were originally clad in sandstone tiles, which remarkably for a house so deep within the Aberdeenshire hinterland were obtained from the Carmyllie district of Angus; the present Foudland slates date from 1824–6 when the castle was re-roofed by *John Smith*.* They are now drained at the angle between the entrance tower and the main block by a delightful weeper in the form of a dog with its paws over its ears; this, the equally charming bearded piper over the main block's pedimented dormer, the field-panel commemorating both the Forbes and the Mortimers, and the twenty replacement water cannon (which in their finely sculptured form represent the castle's history and setting) all date from the National Trust for Scotland's major restoration of 2008–9, the work being undertaken by fourteen of *Laing Traditional Masonry*'s apprentice stonemasons, directed by *Andrew Allan* and *Steven Harper*.

The N and E FLANKS are similar in character to the S front. Both are vertically broken into two planes: these breaks may have been designed to provide the best fields of fire rather than for any picturesque effect. The E flank's division marks the juncture between the main block and the jamb: within it, from first-floor level, a round turret rises up to the corbel course before continuing as a very slim square tower of three storeys crowned like that on the entrance front by a balustrade and slightly angled to the N. To the r. the main block's roof ends not in a gable but in an unprecedented two-storey superstructure which continues the roof of the jamb behind the tower and over the main block's E end to accommodate the long gallery, resulting in a very skilfully balanced composition which once had dormers on the l. as well as on the r. On the N side, at the E end, the kitchen hearth and flue swell out slightly to rise above the corbel course into this superstructure, its gable merging into the NE angle turret. At the NW corner the inter-relationship between turret and gable reaches its final synthesis: the stair-turret corbelled out at first floor rises right through the main block's roof into a two-storey caphouse to which another much smaller stair-turret at its NE angle gives access, the caphouse crowsteps being simply swept around it. The castle's memorable roof-line is completed by the lead ogee

* Smith was also responsible for Craigievar's distinctive pink harling; before his time it had been harled in cream.

domes of the two stair-turrets which give access to the tower rooms; one has a weathervane crowned by a cockerel, the heraldic crest of William Forbes. These are Victorian restorations, *Smith* having heightened them with balustraded platform roofs.*

It is only when the PLAN AND INTERIOR are examined in detail that the anomalies revealing the original Mortimer structure begin to emerge. The main block is 12 m. broad E–W by 8.5 m. deep. The jamb is 6.7 m. broad by 8.5 m. deep again, and as already noted steps out slightly beyond the main block's E gable. Within the angle, the walls of the entrance tower do not stand quite square with those of the main block and jamb: rather they are angled so as to allow as much light at possible to enter the small ground-floor windows, which, were they pushed further towards the corners, would be of less use in lighting the rooms within. Behind the studded entrance door (which is comparatively modern), the castle is protected by a yett with interwoven iron bars. The ground floor is entirely vaulted, and contains a kitchen and cellar in the main block; there is another cellar in the jamb which, in 1825, was partitioned to form a larder, the shot-hole which once guarded the main doorway being altered to a window.

The MAIN STAIR arrangement is very unusual. It is not in the entrance tower as might be expected but rises in a single flight across the junction of the jamb with the main block to first floor. It was only by raising the ground floor of the entrance tower, with short flights of steps running down to the lower floor levels of the kitchen and cellars, that the rake of the main stair could be reduced enough to be manageable, clearly indicating alteration and an element of compromise. Some evidence survives of the earlier main stair of the Mortimer house. Within the jamb's NE corner, adjoining the main block, the short flight of curving steps which now link the kitchen with the pantry beneath the present main stair, and the curve of the stairwell at first-floor level, imply the former existence of a turnpike 1.8 m. in diameter, accessed by a corridor from an entrance in the jamb's W flank in similar fashion to the Conn houses. In the 1620s this corridor became the route of the new stair, connecting it with the old just below first-floor level to enter the S end of the screens passage at the Great Hall's E end in exactly the same way.

At first floor the GREAT HALL occupies the main block and the drawing room the jamb. Within the double-height Great Hall the screen on the E forms a continuation of the arcaded oak panelling which extends round the three other sides of the room, its vigorous design and skilful carving a testament to

*A small but very revealing difference between the mid-c16 work and that of *c.* 1626 is the treatment of the window dressings: those of the Mortimer period are chamfered and those of the Forbes period have rounded arrises. This reflects a general change in fashion from the late c16 onwards rather than any difference between individual masons.

the Early Renaissance spirit that had infused the craftsmen. That spirit is perhaps still more evident in the magnificent Renaissance plasterwork covering the stone groin-vault over the hall, a relic of the Mortimer house now transformed into something altogether different in concept. On either side of the central of three pendants it displays the arms and initials of William Forbes and his wife, Marjorie Woodward, daughter of Nicol Woodward, an Edinburgh provost. However, many of the moulds used for the geometric pattern of enriched ribs and medallions of the Worthies had already been used at Glamis (Angus) in 1620 and Muchalls (q.v.) in 1624. In the s wall the granite fireplace with salt-box in one cheek dates from the Mortimer period, its jambs with a Gothic quirked edge-roll supporting an exceptionally broad lintel. It has been partly disguised by a heavy stucco Renaissance cornice, above which is an enormous display of the Royal Arms as used in Scotland, one of the finest examples of heraldic plasterwork anywhere in Britain. The arms are flanked by their supporters, a rampant lion *sinistra* and unicorn *dexter*, and by male and female cary-atids rising into the arc of the vault. Beneath are the collars of the Order of the Thistle and the Order of the Garter. These arms, signifying that William Forbes held his lands directly from the Crown and was responsible for the administration of justice on the Crown's behalf, would once have been richly tinctured and gilded. Elsewhere, William Forbes's arms dated 1610 may be seen over the doorway.

The Great Hall is lit by two large windows at its 'high' w end, one in the s side again near the w end, one in the centre of the N flank and one in the E. Stair-turrets rise through the height of the castle from the hall's NW and SE corners. The SE stair accesses a timber musicians' gallery above the screens passage: this is one of two galleries lit by vesicas (which suggest a North European influence) to either side of the main E window, the NE gallery having no access. In the course of restoration in 1973 it emerged that the E window had been deepened by Smith, for which he had cut the gallery into two parts; and this stair, together with the hall's groin-vaulting suggested to Ian Bryce, almost certainly correctly, that in Mortimer times the stair had opened into a much larger masonry gallery used for performance of Catholic rite as in other houses of this type, the E wall here being very thin to accommodate it. More of this gallery may have survived prior to Smith's intervention of 1824–6. Its so-called 'secret chamber', where John Paton of Grandholm supposedly hid after the 'Fifteen Rising, more probably had some sort of reli-gious purpose.

The NW and SE stairs access two distinct suites of apart-ments, arranged not horizontally but vertically. All the ceilings are plastered in similar style to the hall, though some are evi-dently of later C17 date. The SE stair is conveniently placed for the first-floor room in the jamb – the WITHDRAWING ROOM or 'BOUDOIR', its C17 panelling in Memel pine – which is clearly of a feminine character since the central motif of its ribbed plaster ceiling (dated 1625) represents St Margaret. From this it seems that the SE rooms constituted Forbes's wife Marjorie's apartments, and the NW rooms accessed off the 'high' end of the hall through a bow-fronted door those of Forbes himself. In a study of the Bell houses with specific reference to Craigievar, Dr Matthew Davis has suggested that the Boudoir acted as equivalent to the inner hall of older castles, with the SECOND-FLOOR 'TARTAN BEDROOM' above equivalent to a private chamber, the Forbes arms reappearing in plaster over the fireplace and the fine ceiling complemented by a particularly attractive frieze; both the Withdrawing Room and the Tartan Bedroom had small side rooms within the main re-entrant tower. Similarly in Forbes's suite the third-floor room directly above the Great Hall vault, although now known as the 'QUEEN'S ROOM', probably served as his inner chamber, its pine panelling similar in style to that of the Boudoir but actually C19 reproduction. Remarkably, the hall's vault is strong enough to support the masonry partition with its fireplaces and flues for the upstairs rooms which was formed or added in the 1620s. Within the upperworks at fourth floor where the walls are much thinner and projected out above the corbel course, the accommodation is noticeably more spacious, and well lit by the many windows in the angle turrets.

The fifth floor was accessed by two very tight turnpike stairs separate from, although immediately adjacent to, the stairs which had risen up from the first floor. That next to the SE stair gives convenient access to the LONG GALLERY. It was probably once panelled and must like the other rooms have had a richly ornamental plaster ceiling but these were lost to leaking roofs before 1824. The same SE stair continues up to access the balustraded platform of the small E tower; another small stair rises up to the platform of the entrance tower.

The castle stands within what was the FORECOURT'S NE corner. It was entered through a doorway in the rubble-built W wall which still survives – although heavily buttressed internally during the C19 or early C20 – together with a small drum tower crowned by a conical roof which is apparently of later date than the wall but which marked the court's SW corner. The segmentally arched and moulded doorway is protected on each side by round shot-holes; its studded timber door bears a metal plate incised with initials of William Forbes's grandson 'Red' Sir John. An estate map prepared by *George Brown* in 1776 shows the forecourt still complete, with laigh buildings against the N and S walls and a square tower at the NW corner, but these had been cleared away by the time another plan was produced in 1791. Excavation by Moira Greig in 1990 revealed scant evidence for these laigh buildings except post-holes which may suggest that they were timber-framed, although fragments of stone roofing slab were also found. The survey plans also show a large U-plan courtyard steading some 50 m. SW of the forecourt and a walled formal garden, not quite rectangular, lying immediately W and NW: both were gone by the later C19.

CRATHES CASTLE

7090

4 km. ENE of Banchory

One of the celebrated group of C16 castles of Aberdeenshire, along with Midmar, Castle Fraser and Craigievar. It stands near the top of ground that rises gently uphill from the N bank of the Dee and is, or rather was, the seat of the Burnetts, who are thought to have come to Scotland from Arlesey, Bedfordshire, during the reign of David I (1124–53). Alexander Burnard was the Forester in the Royal Forest of Drum and helped enclose the park in 1318 before losing his position to William Irvine of Drum (q.v.) in 1323. In that same year Burnard, who already held some forest lands, was granted the land of Leys, N of Banchory, by Robert the Bruce. From the time of the 5th Laird the family was known as the Burnetts of Leys; the Barony of Leys was created in the late C15 for Alexander, 6th Laird.

The BUILDING HISTORY of the present tower house begins in 1543 with the marriage of Alexander Burnett, 9th Laird, to Janet Hamilton, daughter of Robert Hamilton, a canon of Arbroath Abbey, which held extensive prebendary lands in Kincardine, part of which became her dowry. Further property in Banchory-Ternan was granted in 1545 by the Abbot of Arbroath. The first phase of construction is dated to 1553 by a panel containing the arms of Burnett and Hamilton above the E door to the Castle and the final phase of building by a second stone dated 1596 with the initials of Alexander Burnett, 12th Laird, and his wife, Katherine Gordon, of Lesmoir. Furthermore we know from analysis of the roof timbers that oaks were felled for their construction in the spring of 1589 and 1591; and high up an attic dormer carved with the lion and unicorn supporters of Scotland and England gives a *terminus ante quem* of 1603. Clearly the whole of the upper storeys, with their emphasis on display and greater sculptural enrichment, belong to the 1590s and it is the motifs of these parts, with their obvious similarities to contemporary work at Craigievar, Midmar and Castle Fraser (qq.v.), which has led to their attribution to the *Bell* family of masons.

With the exception of the interior of the long gallery created by Sir Thomas Burnett, the 1st Baronet (in the Baronetage of Nova Scotia), from 1626, there is also no evidence of significant embellishment until the early–mid C18, when a substantial E wing was added to the tower, perhaps as a state apartment on the site of an earlier building. The interior of the tower house was refitted and to some extent restored for Sir Robert Burnett, who became the 11th Baronet in 1876. It was during his time that much of the Renaissance painted decoration was rediscovered. His brother and successor Thomas, 12th Baronet, continued this work from 1896 and seems to have instigated the last significant change, adding a large family wing by *Brown & Watt* to the NE of the Georgian wing. All this survived until the castle was given to the National Trust for Scotland in 1951, after which the Victorian wing was retained by the Burnetts for their own use. A calamitous fire in 1966 destroyed all of the C19 parts, gutted the C18 wing but miraculously spared the C16 tower; and from the shell of the C18 part *W. Schomberg Scott*, the Trust's architect, produced a slightly smaller wing in a sensitive Georgian style. The ruins of the Victorian part were demolished and the Burnetts built their new house in the policies (*see* House of Crathes, below). The principal repairs and restoration for the Trust were undertaken in 1975.

Like many C16 tower houses the PLAN FORM of Crathes is a stepped L with a stair-tower in the angle between the two wings. But Crathes is slightly unusual in that this stair-tower fills almost the whole of the space between the two wings and has its S wall in line with that of the hall block, resulting in the impression of a nearly square tower house except for a short jamb projecting E.

The EXTERIOR of the tower is powerfully tall, in a light-coloured render. The lowest storeys, containing the cellars and first-floor rooms are plain, with rounded corners and large vertical windows except at the SE corner where there are slit-openings lighting the spiral stair and close to the re-entrant angle where there are windows lighting mezzanine rooms. But from the beginning of the second floor the rounded corners are corbelled on little squares of granite to form right angles and from here upwards to the peak of the attic roof there develops a delightful profusion of ornament. In the centre of the S front a stair-turret projects in a half-circle as far as the apex of the roof, where it transforms first into a flat square and then a crenellated viewing platform between the chimneyed gables of the roofs. The base of this platform is carried on elaborately moulded continuous corbelling of the false-machicolation type. The same occurs at the base of the stair-turret and to the l. this is continued across the wall face as a string stepping up and down around panels of the Royal Arms flanked by armorial shields (dated 1553 and 1596 but both late C16 work) and then runs vertically up the wall to meet the base of a circular bartizan at the SW corner of the attic storey. Something similar occurs on the other side of the stair-turret, where the corbelling first runs upwards like five thick cables and then horizontally to support a projection in the wall face and stepping over a window before continuing as a corbel course around a second bartizan at the SE corner and then along the E wall.

Besides the circular attic turrets there are others that are larger square ones, also richly corbelled, at the NW angle of the main block and the NE and SE angles of the E wing. These bristle with individually carved cannon spouts and have gabled roofs topped by moulded finials. In the centre of the N front, a bowed stair-turret that serves the rooms above first floor is corbelled at the attic level for a gabled caphouse. The attic dormers of the W and E fronts have carved and moulded triangular heads, again with finials, and there are finials on the roof ridge also, as well as the carved figure of a little man atop the SW bartizan. The gable-ends of the roof are crowstepped and behind the square turret in the centre of the S front is a cylindrical tower with cone roof and weathervane. The dormer in the centre of the W front is bowed and is now as restored in 1975 when a chimney that had its stack atop the dormer was removed. Its flue projected from the wall at the level of the hall fireplace and its scar may still be seen in the harling. A view by C. J. Hullmandel, after a painting by Hugh Irvine of Drum, shows this chimney already in place c. 1820 (but neither Billings in 1845 nor MacGibbon & Ross in 1887 were prepared to record it).

The W windows lighting the hall seem to have been blocked in the late C19 but reinstated during the early C20. The hall's S window in its present form is probably of 1877 when the hall at this level was refitted (*see* below), tripartite with the central light taller and crowned by a pediment with the Burnett hunting horn in carved relief. Early C19 views show it as three tall graduated lancets: probably a Gothick alteration. In the S wall of the E jamb is a fine armorial plaque with vine surround for Sir Thomas Burnett, 1st Baronet, with his initials and those of his second wife, Dame Jean Moncrieff (i.e after 1621). It was brought from Muchalls Castle (q.v.), the building of which was completed by Sir Thomas.

The E wing, the so-called QUEEN ANNE WING, is (as has been stated) a reconstruction of 1971 after the fire but broadly emulates the scale and appearance of a two-storey wing added to the tower in the early C18. It was raised to three storeys in the early C19 and its roof-line may still be seen on the E wall of the tower. It has a re-set armorial. Of the Victorian wing the only remnant appears to be the footings of a circular turret remade as a terrace and stair to the gardens (*see* below).

The visitor now enters the INTERIOR by the S door in the Queen Anne Wing; indeed where the main entrance was from the C18 onwards. The original door to the tower survives at the base of its E wall and retains its iron yett at the foot of the spiral stair to the hall. At this level are three vaulted rooms, comprising the kitchen (with its fireplace in the projecting part of the tower's E jamb), a larder to its W and adjoining this to the S a cellar or guardroom. From the cellar there was a small turnpike stair in the S wall connecting this room with the High Hall above. Deeply splayed window reveals. At the head of the winding stair is a granite arch of roll mouldings drawn to a point at their springing.

The HIGH HALL fills the W side of the tower and is the finest room in the house, although only in part authentically mid-C16. The room has a high barrel-vault and dropping from

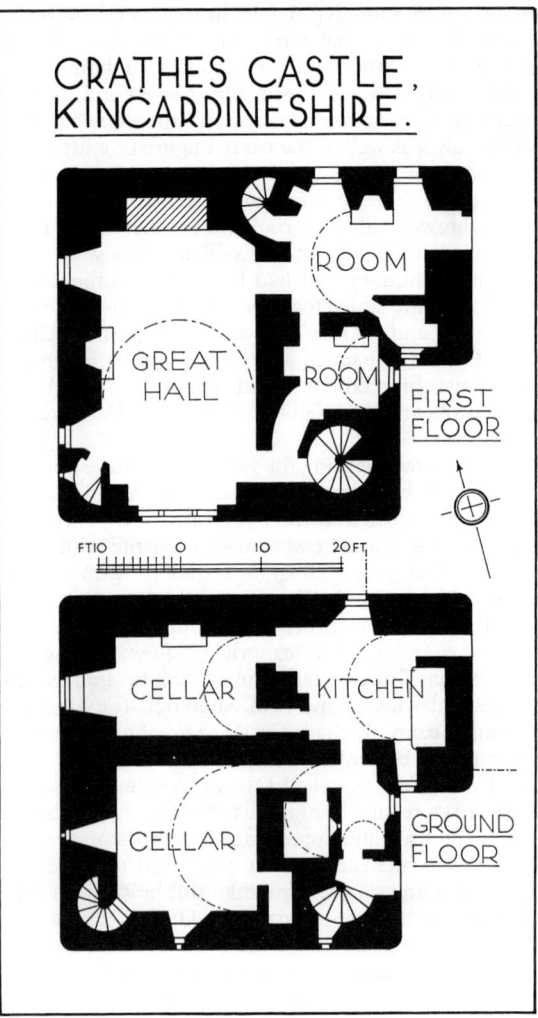

Crathes Castle.
Plan of ground and first floors

the crown of it are three remarkable long pendant bosses, the centre one dated 1554, and decorated with the holly leaves emblematic of the Burnetts and five-petalled flowers for the Hamiltons. Within a recess above the fireplace in the w wall a substantial fragment of painted decoration in grey, green, black and red, broadly imitative of ribs springing from corbels with guilloche patterns and a roundel painted with the Burnett arms. In the window recesses of this wall are semi-domes painted with Burnett/Hamilton armorials in floral surrounds. The central recess was clearly originally always a tall window and subsequently blocked for the fireplace. As was noted outside this seems to have been at the latest an alteration of *c*. 1820, the C16 fireplace having been in the N wall behind the dais. However, the hall was refitted as a dining room in 1877 by *Wallace & Flockhart* and at that time the fireplace was in the E wall, but when the room was 'restored' in 1930–2 by *Fenton Wyness* for Sir James and Lady Burnett the present stone chimneypiece was introduced and set in the W wall again. It is a magnificent Jacobean item, stone carved with caryatids and strapwork decoration. Wyness also stripped the stone walls and vault of late C19 embossed and gilded leather hangings (a fragment is preserved in a screen). The National Trust reinstated the present painted plaster surfaces. The S window is, as has been said, of *c*. 1877 and contains a charming stained glass roundel with a portrait of Sir Robert Burnett, 11th Baronet (†1894).

Opening off the Hall's NE corner (i.e. at the high end) and set within the E jamb above the kitchen is the STONE HALL, a private chamber, also vaulted but about half the height of the Hall. It has a small closet incorporated within its S side, with significant remains of painted decoration, imitating hangings, though now only quite faintly discernible. From the NW corner of the Stone Hall, and contained within the wall thickness, is a private stair to the upper floors.

Above the High Hall are two rooms formerly an outer and inner chamber for the laird but in their present form (Victorian Bedroom and the Laird's Bedroom) they are as altered in the C18 or C19. In the LAIRD'S BEDROOM there is a CARVED PANEL with a square frame and sunk centre carved with typical late C16 patterns of linked circles and squares and a leaf pattern in the centre. It probably comes from a lost ceiling. Corresponding with these rooms in the E half of the tower is the MUSES' ROOM, probably the bedchamber of Katherine Gordon, which has the first of a series of superior figurative, moral and allegorical painted ceilings of the late C16. These were uncovered in 1877 and were unfortunately too enthusiastically restored in bright colours but are nevertheless one of the most important schemes of their date, rare evidence of what was no doubt a widespread taste in Scottish Renaissance interiors. On the flat of the ceiling are female figures of the nine Muses and seven Cardinal Virtues playing musical instruments etc. and accompanied by poetic maxims on the beams. One of the beams is dated 1599. Painted frieze of oak leaves twining around a rod, a motif also to be found in late C16 and early C17 woodwork. Adjoining this, and formerly connected with it, is the STAIR CHAMBER, reached from the spiral stair, with painted decoration painted all over the joists and boards of its ceiling, with chevron patterns in black and red and moral aphorisms in blackletter. Around the top of the wall, patterns of red and white like twisted rope.

From this level upwards, the rooms in the E part are partly placed at a mezzanine level, beginning with the ROOM OF THE NINE NOBLES (a.k.a. the Nine Worthies). Between the beams here are full-length figures in a pattern 1:2:1:2:1 beginning with the Ancient heroes: Hector of Troy, Alexander the Great, Julius Caesar; three worthies of the Old Testament: Joshua, Judas Maccabeus and King David; and finally Charles the Great (i.e. Charlemagne), King Arthur and the Crusader leader Godfrey of Bouillon. Around them foliage work and coats of arms. Running along the sides of the beams are their stories, related in Gothic script. The adjoining room to the NE is called the GREEN LADY'S ROOM, and it too has writing running along the sides of the beams, mostly moral aphorisms, some full-length figures but also *grotteschi*, garlands and on the soffits of the beams decorative interlacing patterns. Also some surviving wall painting in the form of a frieze of bayleaves etc.

At the attic level, the climax of this floor is the LONG GALLERY, which runs the length of the tower's N side and has small closets or studies in the square bartizans of its NW, NE and SE corners. There may have been a long gallery in the late C16 house (cf. the later Craigievar) but its present appearance was formed in the mid C17 and has a panelled oak ceiling of canted profile overlaid with ribs of low moulded profile forming a pattern of linked squares and diamonds, alternating with bosses that have diagonal spurs of holly leaves and unicorns emerging from scroll tails. Along the flat of the ceiling the bosses have the Royal Arms of Scotland, the arms of Sir Thomas Burnett (†1653), who created the gallery, and also the arms of his father, Alexander (†1619), who completed the house, and of an eminent member of his kin Alexander Seton, 1st Earl of Dunfermline, the great Renaissance remodeller of Fyvie Castle (N). The arms of the Marquess of Hamilton and of Gilbert Burnett, Bishop of Salisbury, were added during the restoration of the gallery in 1896 by *Brown & Watt*; of the same time presumably the painted shields on the subsidiary ceiling bosses and most of the doorcases. The N wall's doorcase with rosettes in the panels over is original and conceals the privy N stair. Opening off the S side and filling the SE corner of the attic floor with a closet in the circular bartizan is the GALLERY BEDROOM. The other room, on this floor's W side, is called the FAMILY ROOM. It too has a coved ceiling but is otherwise remodelled.

Of the courtyards which preceded entry to the tower in the C16 and C17 nothing survives above ground but excavations in 2014 have revealed substantial remains of the S courtyard, which appears to have been terraced downhill. A two-roomed building has been found in the SW corner and the possibility of another pairing it in the SE corner.

The GARDENS to the S and E of the house are arranged as a series of subdivided rectangular enclosures descending in terraces to the large walled former kitchen garden. They are now as formed after 1926 by Sir James and Lady Sybil Burnett but probably incorporate earlier gardens, and a recent survey appears to indicate that the flat lawn s of the castle overlies a parterre of C16 or C17 date. It is edged with manicured yew hedges of C18 and early C19 vintage. Attractive iron gates, by *A. & J. Main* (*Clydesdale Iron Works*), Glasgow. There are few garden structures to speak of other than a rustic Victorian SUMMERHOUSE and a charming granite-walled DOOCOT in the walled garden's SE corner with pyramid roof. It was rebuilt in the 1930s and contains a re-set carved panel, said to come from the Palace of Westminster.

Finally, NW of the castle, the former STEADING court. The principal range, along the s side has a circular mid-C19 former horse mill (now the shop). The café building opposite is an adaptation and extension of 2005–6 by *Leslie F. Hunter Architects*.

Within the policies of the castle, 0.45 km. SW, is the successor HOUSE OF CRATHES, built for Sir Jamie Burnett in 1972 after the fire destroyed the private wing of the castle. Designed by *G. M. M. Thomson* of *Cowell Mathieson & Partners*. Essentially Scots traditional in the same idiom as the Queen Anne Wing. 100 m. SW is KASHENTROCH, a self-build, timber-framed, low-energy house of 2006 for Alexander and Vinny Burnett by *Gokay Devici*, Professor at the Scott Sutherland School of Architecture, and extended to his designs *c.* 2009. The earlier part has a pitched copper roof and gabled projection in the centre that is fully glazed. Larch cladding. The later part to the l. has a barrel-vaulted roof over the width of the building, carried forward as a veranda.

EAST LODGE. At the public entrance to the policies, on an approach formed in 1854. Dated 1858. Single-storeyed, heavily Baronialized.

CRATHIE

Crathie is an entirely rural parish split by the River Dee. The standing stone at Rinabaich, with surrounding burial ground, may mark the first settlement by St Manir, patron saint of the parish. Thereafter the focus of activity has moved upstream to the area of Brunel's bridge, where the current parish church is located and access provided to the estates of Balmoral and Abergeldie (qq.v.) on the s bank.

CRATHIE ST MANIR. Ruins of the old church lie close to a ford on the River Dee. The walls of random rubble stand up to gable height at w end; site of the E wall is covered by the burial enclosure of the Farquharsons of Invercauld and Monaltrie. Of medieval origins, this church is first mentioned in 1574 and was abandoned by 1804 for its successor (*see* below). In the graveyard are many Victorian royal household retainers, including John Brown (†1883), 'the devoted and faithful personal attendant and beloved friend of Queen Victoria', his memorial simply decorated with a thistle, by *Macdonald, Field and Co*.

CRATHIE PARISH CHURCH. Prominently situated on a bluff 0.25 km. NNE above the old church of St Manir. The first church on this site, a simple design of 1804 by *William & Andrew Clerk*, was totally replaced in 1893–5 by *A. Marshall Mackenzie*. His church is cruciform with apse, crossing tower, squat spire, three-bay nave and a lean-to timber porch across the W end. The walls are grey rock-faced granite, topped by steeply pitched roofs of red clay tile (replacements of 1903). The outline is austere and dignified from all sides, with restrained external detailing limited to shallow corbels around the tower parapet and a rose window at the W end. The S transept provides a private entrance for the monarch, with its own wooden porch, triple lancets and vesica window above. Several motifs – the vesica, S doorway, shallow corbels – derive from Pluscarden Abbey (Moray), while the Dec nave tracery is based on windows at Jedburgh Abbey (Borders). The unadorned E end has simple narrow lancets above a plain string course. Surrounded by mountains and larch trees, with its high-pitched roofs, steeple and timber porch, it has the outline of a Norwegian stave church, but is also reminiscent of the early wooden Episcopal church at Braemar (dem. *c.* 1899). The church provides a subtle compromise between the severity of Presbyterian worship and, with its chancel steps and marble communion table, a fitting setting for the Supreme Governor of the Church of England.

Inside, a ruggedly local impression is created by the exposed rough granite walling and natural pine. Plain ashlar walls with reeded dado panelling in the nave, and lofty wooden ribbed wagon roof; wide ashlar Romanesque crossing arches. Mackenzie also designed the furnishings which were gradually presented by members of the royal family. The modest S transept is reserved seating for the royal family, distinguished by crowns on the end of the benches. A parclose tracery screen creates a vestibule at the S end. The front pew is faced by panels of Gothic quatrefoils and the imperial monogram of Queen Victoria. The N transept is panelled with heraldic shields of local notables. There is a fine wooden REREDOS, 1910, copied loosely from the choir stall canopies at King's College Chapel, Aberdeen (q.v.), made from 300-year-old oak taken from a Leicestershire country house. – COMMUNION TABLE, 1910, of Iona marble. – PULPIT, 1895, made of eighteen types of Scottish granite and pebbles collected by Princess Louisa on Iona. Its CANOPY is of 1903, Gothic openwork with emblems of the Evangelists. – FONT, 1895, Kemnay and Rubislaw granite. ORGAN in the loft at W end, with delicately carved woodwork, by *Henry Willis & Sons*, 1895. – STAINED GLASS, clockwise N–W: St John's eagle, 2011 by *Jennifer-Jane Bayliss*; Baptism of Our Lord, 1929 by *Clayton & Bell*; Transfiguration, 1913, also by *Clayton & Bell*; N transept, Moses by *R. Douglas*

McLundie, 1956; Diamond Jubilee window (King David flanked by Miriam and Deborah), by *Clayton & Bell*, 1898; chancel, St Margaret of Scotland, St Andrew, Christ, St Columba, St Bridget, 1895; the S transept windows are all by *Clayton & Bell*: an angelic figure rising from the sea, 1897; the Risen Lord with angels bearing armorial shields, 1895; Duke of Clarence as the Black Prince, with a fetching handlebar moustache, 1898; by the same firm also the W rose window, Praise, 1897. – MONU-MENTS: under Gothic canopies integral with the crossing arches, BUSTS of Queen Victoria, 1903, by *Emil Fuchs*; George V, 1938, by *Sir William Reid Dick*; George VI, 1957, also by Reid Dick, and beneath him, free-standing, Queen Elizabeth the Queen Mother, †2002.

CRATHIE MANSE. Double pile, rear wing of 1789 with gable and coped stacks. Front wing of 1866–73 with moulded stack caps and skewputts; the resemblance of its plan and elevation to Tarland Manse (q.v.) suggests *J. & W. Smith* as architects. A good example of a country manse getting an upgrade owing to royal proximity at Balmoral.

CRATHIE SUSPENSION BRIDGE, 0.6 km. S of the church. By *J. Justice Jun. & Co.* of Dundee, 1834; partly renewed in 1884 by *Blaikie Bros* of Aberdeen. Instead of metal cable, this bridge, with its delicate lattice pylons, is suspended from paired flat-link chains. It provided the original vehicular access across the Dee to Balmoral. 0.75 km. NNE along the river it is supple-mented by the supremely robust CRATHIE GIRDER BRIDGE of 1856–8, by *I. K. Brunel*, leading to the Castle entrance. Single span, wrought-iron plate-girder bridge 40 m. long between granite abutments with regularly pierced iron-plate parapets and prominent riveting (the ironfounders were *R. Brotherhood* of Chippenham, Wilts., who collaborated with Brunel else-where). Commissioned by royal request, it was possibly the earliest wrought-iron girder bridge in Scotland.

BALLOCHBUIE BRIDGE, 8 km. WSW, across the Dee from the A93 road to the Balmoral estate (q.v.) on the river's S bank. Iron suspension footbridge, spanning 179 ft (54.5 m.) between latticework pylons on stone abutments. By *James Abernethy & Co.*, engineers, 1924, its design almost identical to their Polhollick Bridge (Ballater) of 1892.

GARBH ALLT FALLS BRIDGE, 8.5 km. SW in Ballochbuie Forest, 1878, by *Blaikie Bros*, Aberdeen. Cast-iron segmented arched bridge with lacy parapet of circular openwork motifs. Leading to nowhere, this eloquent bridge frames the foaming falls and was a favourite painting spot for Queen Victoria.

AUCHTAVAN, 6 km. WNW. A clachan set high and remotely up Glen Feardar, with outstanding views towards Lochnagar, and frequently above the snowline. It is recorded on Roy's Map of 1747–55. The CROFT is late C18–early C19, a rare survivor. Walls of alternating courses of large and small rubble stones with large rubble quoins. Turf and heather thatch beneath a corrugated iron roof, the roof itself of jointed and pegged crucks set into the walls but ending above ground. It has a 'hanging lum' cowl made of vertical timber boards over the low hearth. Immaculately laid cobbles in the 'animal end' of the house and a 'warm' sleeping loft above. The THRESHING BARN and GRANARY also survive, with outdoor horse walk. The families who lived here supplemented their subsistence farming by working a series of nearby limekilns. The buildings were restored in 2008 by Braemar Community Ltd. Adjacent is the 'Queen Mother's Picnic House', an improved mid-C19 farm workers' home, with tongue-and-groove panelled walls, and swey over the hearth. Belonging to the Balmoral estate, it was a favoured destination for the Queen Mother and is now available for community educational use.

MILL OF COSH, Girnoc, 6 km. E. Mid-C19 and later. A two-storey corn mill with integral drying kiln and well-preserved equipment by *Duncan Thomson & Son*, Inverurie, including timber buckets and paddles on the wheel, timber elevators, hopper and trap doors, the mill stones and an interesting device to channel water into the lade. Used until the 1970s.

4090

DEECASTLE

CHAPEL HOUSE. Outwardly an apparently simple three-bay two-storey Georgian house. Internally, the almost 2 m. thick walls in the NW corner indicate the remains of a possibly C16 hunting lodge, Kandechyle, which belonged to the Earls of Aboyne and was burnt in 1641. Small, low-ceilinged rooms downstairs open up to a single spacious room on the first floor, created in the 1960s restoration. In the late C17 it became a Catholic priest's house, with chapel below and residence above, until the Catholics moved their services to Bogieshiel, Birse (q.v.) in 1815.

4090

DINNET

DINNET AULD KIRK. Built in 1875 as a chapel of ease for Aboyne, following the construction of the railway halt in 1866. Dinnet became a parish in 1881. Rectangular buttressed box with vestry and E porch (both 1890); the main E elevation has a steep pitched roof, triple lancets in the gable and a bellcote, of squared snecked granite. Gatepier inscribed WCB 1899, and pebble garth wall mark the patronage of Sir William Cunliffe Brooks of Glen Tanar (q.v.). Converted to domestic use in 2005, but retaining the original fine hammerbeam roof.

DINNET HOUSE, 1.2 km. SW of the church. Built as an opulent shooting lodge by *A. Marshall Mackenzie*, 1890, for Charles H. Wilson, M.P. Following a fire, *Mackenzie & Son* lowered the roof, restored the two upper floors and added a colossal square tower to the N entrance façade, 1905–11. The three- and four-storey house is still enormous but the extensive w and service wings were demolished in 1976. The house looms majestically above terraced gardens overlooking the Dee, externally dominated by two large round towers on the eastern corners, while on the N front the square tower defines the new entrance porch. The house is a muscular combination of Baronial features: corbels, crenellations, crowstep and Dutch gables, bay and oriel windows, set in Aberdeen-bonded granite. Its large plate-glass sashes give a gaunt appearance. The plan delivers the required Victorian sequence of public rooms: a gentlemen's cloakroom by the porch, a spacious lobby with elegant oak doors from which proceed the morning room and dining room (both oak-panelled by *Waring & Gillow*), the Adam-style drawing room with plastered ceiling, breakfast room and billiard room. Top-lit staircase with understated woodwork. – EAST LODGE, s of the church. By *Marshall Mackenzie*, 1890. A compact, petite version of Dinnet House with lavish Baronial detail. The quality and guts of the NORTH LODGE, also *c.* 1890, with massive square Baronial caphouse, also suggest the same architects.

DINNET BRIDGE, crossing the Dee. A stylish and monumental cast-concrete construction by *F.A. MacDonald & Partners*, engineers, 1935. Sharply geometric Art Deco forms include the square piers with pyramid coping, the triangular cantilevers, parapets lined like cast clapboard, and curved shelves beyond the parapet.

FASNADARACH, 0.5 km. E of Dinnet Bridge. Begun in 1874, by *George Truefitt*, as a simple fishing lodge for William Cunliffe Brooks with the barest dining room, kitchen and caretaker's room perched on a terrace directly above the river. Extended in 1900 for his daughter, Lady Frances Cecil, by *Charles Ewen*, retaining the Glen Tanar style. The s entrance front has all the busy grouping of forms found on Glentanar estate houses, with piend roofs, crowsteps, dormers juggling the roof-line, and above, complex roof-lines with strong overhanging eaves. The N (river) face is equally asymmetrical along its nine-bay frontage, advancing and receding, rising and falling, in rugged pink and grey granite. Many interior details remain, including good Art Nouveau door furniture.

HUT CIRCLES AND FIELD SYSTEM, New Kinord, 3 km. NW of Dinnet Church. An extensive set of field and track systems and groups of hut circles. The hut circles are defined by low stone walls which probably surrounded timber round-houses. Some of the hut circles have attached souterrains. The field systems are defined by low stone banks and clearance cairns. The settlement system is not directly dated, but may date to the 1st millennium B.C. or the early centuries of the 1st millennium A.D.

CROSS-SLAB, Loch Kinord, 2 km. NW of Dinnet Church. Fine stone cross carved with interlace, probably C9. 11

DRUM CASTLE K

2 km. NNE of Drumoak

Drum presents one of the most satisfying architectural ensembles among the Deeside castles, each stage in its evolution from medieval tower to Jacobean country house to Scots Baronial mansion clearly delineated in its fabric.

A considerable portion of the Royal Forest of Drum – that part not already given to the Burnetts (*see* Crathes) – was granted in 1323 by Robert the Bruce to William Irvine, in the office of forester, and erected into a barony for him in the same year.* The tower that he built, from which he could have monitored activity in the forest and controlled one of the fording points across the Dee from the S, is shown on Pont's map of *c.* 1590 with its barmkin. Major additions were made following the succession in 1603 of Alexander Irvine, 9th Laird, resulting in an entirely new house, apparently largely complete by 1619 and one that seems surprisingly advanced for its date in Aberdeenshire in adopting a rectilinear form that owes nothing to the tower house tradition of e.g. nearby Crathes. In the C17 civil wars the house was twice captured – by General Monro and by the Marquess of Argyll – and there followed nearly a century of decay and loss of the estate until the time of the 18th Laird, also Alexander, who, following his marriage in 1775, seems to have brought the Jacobean house up to date. Finally Drum was substantially remodelled and extended by *David Bryce*, succeeded after his death in 1876 by *John Bryce*, for Alexander Forbes Irvine, the 20th Laird, in 1875–82. That is the state in which it was bequeathed in 1975 by the Irvines to the National Trust for Scotland, for whom it was repaired and restored in 1983–4 by *Cunningham Jack Fisher Purdom*.

The castle buildings are arranged around a courtyard. The earliest part is the powerfully vertical but compact rectangular TOWER HOUSE on the courtyard's E side, which was probably begun soon after 1323, making it among the earliest surviving in Aberdeenshire. The walls are a sheer mass of rubble masonry of large and small blocks but quite evenly coursed and very elegantly rounded at the corners, topped by a corbel course and battlements of broad merlons. Close inspection of the structure has shown evidence of four stages of building, each representing a season's work. The lowest two stages – with walls 3.7 m. thick – are of the first phase; the upper floor may have been added a little (perhaps only a few years) later. Until the early C19 at the latest there was also a caphouse. There are scarcely any visible openings, the few windows randomly disposed across the wall face (except the large C19 arched E window at first floor) and close to the corners (originally

45

*Traditionally thought to have been a clerk in the royal chancellery, it is now believed that this Irvine came from Dundee and was in the service of the Abbot of Arbroath who held much of the neighbouring land along Deeside.

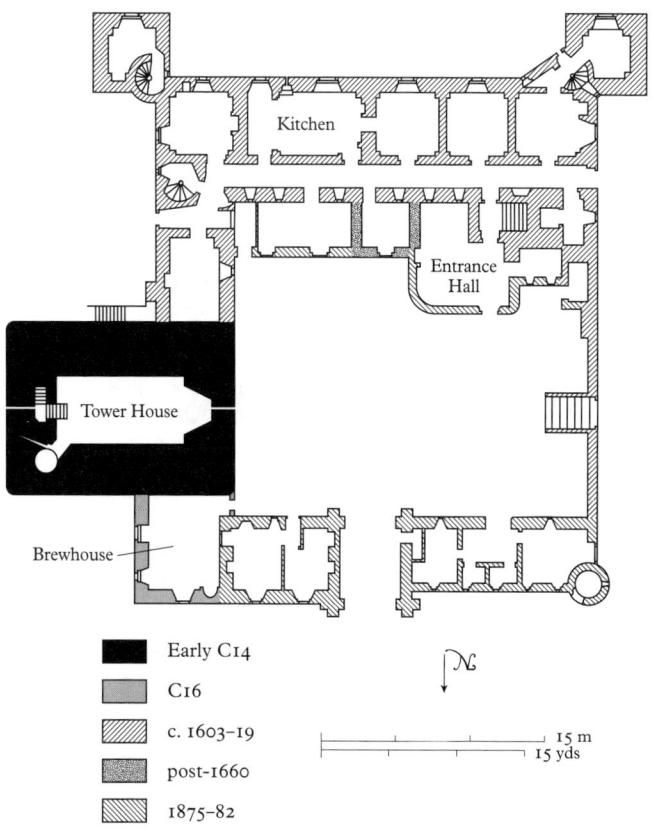

Early C14

C16

c. 1603–19

post-1660

1875–82

Kitchen

Entrance Hall

Tower House

Brewhouse

15 m
15 yds

Drum Castle.
Ground-floor plan

lighting garderobes and other closets within the walls) are tiny lancets. At the SE corner slits for the spiral stair. In the usual way access was at first floor, the former ladder or timber forestair on the S side now replaced in stone.

Within the tower house there is at ground floor a barrel-vaulted former STOREROOM, with a recess in the NE corner for a well and basin, and a ceiling hatch which would have served the screens passage of the HALL above, a barrel-vaulted room which was tall enough to accommodate a second floor or entresol, probably for sleeping accommodation. The door from the entrance lobby into the screens passage of the hall and the door to the entresol further up the SE turnpike stair was blocked however when the hall was converted for the library in the early 1840s and the large E window was inserted (for the description of its interior, which is reached from within the main house, *see* below). Investigation has revealed the existence of two mural chambers in the NE corner, interpreted as

buttery and pantry, and an intact garderobe chamber in the
NW corner originally accessed via a passage from the high end
of the hall; both spaces are indicated externally by one of the
tiny lancet openings.

Above is the LORD'S CHAMBER, largely preserved in its
medieval state with pointed barrel-vault, bench seats in the
recesses of the N and S windows, a deep window reveal
(blocked) in the E wall and large fireplace with red Kildrummy
freestone voussoirs to its arch in the N wall. In the NW corner,
following the pattern of the floor below, another mural garderobe with latrine and window (now blocked). Within this
space too there was an upper floor of rooms and in the W wall
can still be seen the fireplace for this entresol as well as two
small (blocked) windows close to the head of the vault. Only
the wall-walk of the caphouse remains but its level is higher
now than originally. Of an unusual type with stepping to aid
drainage and niches for archers between the merlons, as well
as a privy corbelled out at the NW tower.* Also perhaps earlier,
of late C15 or C16 date, is the BREWHOUSE attached to the
keep's NW corner; there was a building alongside it, running
across the N wall of the keep, now lost but indicated by a corbel
in the N wall. The formation of the W court as the entrance to
the castle is probably of about the same time.

There is a little evidence that a S wing was added to the
keep.† Pont c. 1590 appears to show such a range but its date
can only be a matter of speculation. The harled range now
attached to the SW angle of the tower is three storeys high but
about half the height of the keep and known as the CROSS-
CHAMBER RANGE. Its roof timbers, of oak taken from the
Forest, have been dated by dendrochronology to between the
last years of the C16 and 1612 and so undoubtedly the range
belongs to the major reconstruction under the 9th Laird, but
attached to its S end is a four-storey tower, with a newel stair
inside and crowstepped W gables. It seems structurally distinct
from the rest and just might be earlier than the C17. Its individual identity seems even clearer on the S front of the S RANGE
where it is incorporated at the E end but separated from the
rest by a thick cross wall with crowstepped gable, large chimney
and slightly higher roof-line. The rest of the S front has a two-
storey centre over a basement and each end is flanked by
gabled square towers of the same height tenuously attached at
the SE and SW corners, the joins partly masked by flat sections
containing passages and spiral staircases; the granite corbelling
below the angle with the SE tower is of stepped profile with a
roll moulding and a square corbel of a kind found also at

*The cesspit serving the stack of latrines at the tower's NW corner has been found,
and pottery discovered within it supports a C14 date for construction.
†At the time of writing this evidence is only gradually emerging but suggested by
discovery of traces of a scar of a building in the keep's S wall. Some miscellaneous
artefacts and roof timbers reused in a staircase dated to c. 1400–40 may be evidence
of a C15 date for this lost range. The provisional interpretation of this is as a new
hall range for the earlier tower.

Crathes. The stair in the re-entrant angle with the SW tower is revealed above second floor in a circular turret with conical roof.

The first floor or *piano nobile* of the main part contained the Great Hall of the Jacobean house and above this was a long gallery. This phase is dated to 1619 by the heads of the wall-head dormers, pediments decoratively carved with the date and initials of Alexander Irvine and his wife, Lady Marion Douglas. One of these however is inverted, so they may have been re-set and if so, this may have been done in 1790–2 when the S façade was re-formed into one of greater classical symmetry and an entrance with plain cornice and flying stair created in its centre to supersede the entrance to the Jacobean house, which was from the N courtyard. The door occupies the position of a former window and simultaneously the other windows were blocked and replaced, more or less evenly spaced across the façade 1:3:1.

To the courtyard the S range is overlaid entirely by later additions. The first in date is the centre bay, which originated as a square jamb projected from the centre of this front and which dates probably from after 1660. According to an inventory of 1761 this jamb contained bedrooms but as it stood in line with the S entrance created in 1790–2 it appears to have been made into the staircase tower at that date. The remodelling by Bryce removed the stair and added W of the jamb the present Baronial-style ENTRANCE TOWER with round-arched doorway on the curve of its corner with comically literal rope moulding. It is topped by a caphouse, and adjoining is a two-storey part with battlemented parapet. The Bryces infilled to the E of the entrance with a three-bay section containing service rooms with a corridor over. In the re-entrant angle with the E wing is a turret. The new parts are of coursed granite.

The W side of the courtyard is the screen wall of c. 1615–20 with an arched gateway. A star-pattern cresting is re-set above. The present N RANGE containing the entrance to the courtyard below a crowstepped gable is a remodelling by Bryce, also incorporating the C16 brewhouse (*see* above). W of the arch are offices, terminating in a small round tower with candlesnuffer roof.

The INTERIORS of the tower house have been described. The rest can be taken roughly in the order in which they are seen by the visitor. The ENTRANCE HALL is Bryce's creation and is on two levels. At the higher level it overlays the Jacobean entrance to the S range, which is still preserved with its iron yett. This entrance opens into a lobby at the foot of the main stair, a single flight of granite steps running at right angles to the entrance up to a landing originally at the entrance to the former Hall (S) and also to a room in the lost W range (N), an arrangement also found at Craigston Castle (N) of 1604–7, a house attributed to the *Bell* family of master masons. On the opposite side of the stair lobby from the entrance door a second door leads into the basement of the S range. This has an axial SERVICE CORRIDOR running E–W; at the W end, just inside the entrance is a BENCH or SHELF. The corridor continues around the corner, where it continued into a W wing, now lost. Here, tucked below the stairs to the first floor, is a recess known as the PORTER'S BED. The bull-nosed mouldings around the openings in this part of the corridor and also around a blocked door in the S wall in line with the kitchen fireplace are reminiscent of work associated with the Bells. Along the corridor's S side are three square groin-vaulted cellars etc., with the larger kitchen, also groin-vaulted, at the E end and a fifth vaulted room beyond that. The last of these is in that part of the E end of the S range which could be pre-Jacobean and the vaulted room may have been the earlier kitchen; there is some evidence that the flue of the present kitchen fireplace originally served one on this side of the wall and that would agree with the large chimney seen outside. Next to this room is the turnpike stair serving the first floor and continuing upwards to the attic floor. There are further vaulted cellars in the SW and SE angle towers.

At first floor, the Jacobean house is thought to have been divided into a hall and withdrawing room. The late C18 rearrangements reformed these into a dining room (W) and drawing room (E) separated by an entrance lobby behind the new S door. But the Bryces reversed the arrangement in 1882 so their DRAWING ROOM comes first. It has a Jacobean-style oak compartmented ceiling and ornately carved oak chimneypiece, both by *John Bryce*, 1879–80, but also to the l. of the fireplace an original door with chamfered granite surround to a private newel stair to the gallery and other rooms on the upper floors, and at the room's SW corner is a door to the stairs from the cellars and a door into a passage to a room in the SW tower. Between the C18 S windows are the reveals of the C17 windows with rounded jambs and segmental arches and there is also a larger arch of this type in the W wall which may have been a serving recess before it became a window in the C19. The DINING ROOM to the E was created by incorporating the 1790s entrance lobby with the former drawing room. It has an oak ceiling, like that in the Drawing Room, and a chimneypiece copied by Bryce from an C18 one in the Gallery above. In the NE corner is the entrance to a diagonal link to the E wing. S of this is the BUSINESS ROOM, with original roll-moulded fireplace, and CHARTER ROOM in the SE tower with a private stair linking it to the cellar below. The CROSS-CHAMBER in the E wing provides the link with the C14 tower at first floor via an entrance cut into the W window embrasure on the tower's S flank. This leads into the LIBRARY formed in the early 1840s inside the tower's Lower Hall. Its barrel-vault has a ribbed plaster ceiling with moulded corbels and painted heraldic shields. Fine oak bookcases and chimneypiece on the W wall. Running along the N side of the principal rooms in the S range is a GALLERY created by Bryce, with his grand STAIR-CASE to the second floor towards the W end. This has a closed string and turned balusters. At the far end of the Gallery is a funny arched recess with a stove and two little bench seats. On the second floor of the S range, there are C18 bedrooms created from the early C17 Long Gallery. The room in the SE tower also has mid-C18 panelling.

The CHAPEL, SW of the house, is a tiny granite box with crowstepped gables. The round-arched E and N doors and the three small rectangular S windows with chamfered margins are original, but the enlarged W window and cross finial and the arched E window and bellcote date from the chapel's restoration in 1857–64 when the roof was replaced and the N and S walls extensively scraped and repointed. The tusking N and S of the E front shows it was tied into the C17 garden walls? Two small, perhaps C17, heads also re-set in the NE angle. – ALTAR SLAB. Said to have been brought from Dalmaik church (*see* p. 455) in 1820, but possibly originally in the choir of St Nicholas, Aberdeen (dem. 1490). It may be C15 and has five incised consecration crosses. – FONT. A memorial to two sons (†1856 and 1875) of the 22nd Laird. After the C12 Tournai font at Winchester Cathedral. – SCULPTURE. A large silver figure of the Virgin, from Augsburg, introduced in 1897. – STAINED GLASS. W window, Crucifixion, by *Hardman*, *c.* 1864. – E window. Deposition from the Cross, again a memorial to the 22nd Laird's sons, so presumably *c.* 1875. – MONUMENTS. The canopy only of the tomb of Sir Alexander Irvine (†1457), originally in the Drum Aisle of St Nicholas, Aberdeen, where his and his wife's effigies remain (*see* p. 125). Brought here after the fire at St Nicholas in 1875. Three orders of moulding and typical Perp foliage around the outside. Keystone with finely carved crest. Angel supporters at the base.

The area of the early C17 WALLED GARDEN was discovered on the S lawn during excavation in 2008.

DRUMBLADE

PARISH CHURCH. A simple five-bay rectangular plan, built 1773, with a later and lower porch and session-room block of some length extending out from the W gable, harled throughout. The windows in its S flank are square-headed with grey granite margins checked for shutters, of which the hinge-pins survive; moulded skewputts, SW dated; square windows in both gables lighting a gallery, and over the W gable a birdcage bellcote from the previous church of 1641, crowned with gablets and obelisk finials. The annexe, piend-roofed at one end so as not to obscure the W gallery window, but gabled with a short chimneystack at the other, is also harled, with small square windows and a simple recessed doorway. The INTERIOR has been remodelled, in 1829 and 1900. The pulpit once stood near the centre of the S wall with a U-plan gallery extending on three sides around it; in 1900 this gallery was removed and a smaller W gallery erected facing the octagonal PLATFORM PULPIT at the opposite E end. – COMMUNION TABLE. From Drumblade Free Church, closed in the 1930s. – FONT. Given 1954. – ELDERS' STALLS, CHOIR STALLS and PEWS, all in pitch pine, date from 1900. – ORGAN in dark stained timber probably slightly later, by *Wadsworth & Brother*; next to it a TRIPTYCH displaying the Ten Commandments, and on the N wall monuments to the Bissetts of Lessendrum (*see* below). The Art Nouveau STAINED GLASS is 1900, replacing original small-paned sashes.

The CHURCHYARD is an L-plan, with some lying slabs. In the angle, a memorial (erected 1995) to the author George MacDonald (*see* Greenkirtle, near Huntly, p. 537), and his wife, Louisa; close by, Rev. Robert Troup and Margaret MacDonald, and other family members, including the Arts and Crafts architect Francis Troup.

LESSENDRUM HOUSE, 1.7 km. NNW. Burnt 1928, ruinous, partly collapsed. Jacobean on a courtyard plan, a substantial enlargement and remodelling by *Archibald Simpson* for Walter Bissett, 1837, of an L-plan house probably C17, in turn deriving from a tower house of 1470. Principal (NW) front is all Simpson's work, two-storey asymmetric with gable bay and tower at the N end balanced by a larger canted bay gable with octagonal buttresses at the S: the impressive scale of the main apartments can be judged from the size of their first-floor windows. Rubble-built, formerly harled, with diagonally shafted chimneystacks. Ruined STABLES, the surviving sections with Simpson-like proportions.

HOUSE OF CORSE, 1.5 km. E, settled into the folds of its landscape within a park bounded by ancient trees. Charming early C19 farmhouse, two storeys, three windows wide, rubble-built with tall piended roof and big coped end stacks; single-storey side wings, again with piended roofs. Pedimented Greek Revival porch added *c.* 1830, tripartite doorpiece with elegant fanlight framed by anta-pilasters, all in timber. Flanking rectangular bays with tripartite ground-floor windows are of similar date, ashlar-built with mutuled cornices. The OLD HOUSE OF CORSE (60 m. NW) survives as the E range of a three-sided courtyard steading – a long low two-storey rectangular building with a tall roof, crowstepped at one end, and a 1733 datestone with initials P.H.Y.M./M.S.Y.M.S. Chimneys removed and somewhat altered, but inside at the N end a fireplace of some distinction, with carved pilasters supporting a heavy entablature.

DRUMINNOR CASTLE *see* HOUSE
OF DRUMINNOR

DRUMLITHIE   K   7080

A village which grew up as a parish centre in succession to Glenbervie, a chapel being recorded here in 1585. By the early C18 it was dominated by Episcopalian weavers, whose chapel was burnt by government forces in 1746. A row of single-storey WEAVERS' COTTAGES survives in School Road, and there are two-storey houses, also of C18 date, in Kinmonth Road, Croft Road and Glenbervie Road, the last with a single-storey blacksmith's range adjoining. Directly opposite the present-day inn is its predecessor, an C18 coaching house standing with its gable to the street. A remarkable feature is the 'STEEPLE' built   86 in 1798 to regulate the weavers' mealtimes: a tall slim round tower in squared red sandstone rising from a stepped base, its bellcote and pyramidal spire with weathervane renewed in the later C19.

ST JOHN THE BAPTIST (Episcopal). Now closed. By *Charles Brand* of Fordoun, dated 1863. Simple E.E., built in fine ashlar masonry, stugged, snecked and pinned. Nave with gabled SW porch and two pairs of triple lights beneath a very tall roof with filigree brattishing, gableted double bellcote over the W window. Lower chancel with lancets. (STAINED GLASS. The E window (Baptism of Our Lord, the Crucifixion and Our Lord healing) and a chancel lancet (Raising of the widow's son) by *Wailes & Strang* of Newcastle, 1874. – Also in the chancel, Our Lord blessing little children, erected 1891.)

Former BRIDGE OF MONDYNES, 1.3 km. SSW, next to the A90. Early C19, by *William Smith* of Montrose. Three arches over the Bervie Water, the central one semicircular and the others segmental. Triangular cutwaters.

COURT STANE, 2.3 km. SW by Mains of Mondynes on the W side of the railway. Standing stone, *c.* 2.1 m. tall and leaning to one side. It is said to commemorate the death of Duncan II, murdered near this spot in 1094 (GN).

DRUMOAK   7090

Former DALMAIK CHURCH, 2 km. ESE of the village on a wonderful secluded site by the Dee. This was the place of ancient settlement. Roofless, rectangular plan with gables E and W. Probably predominantly C17* but the E window on the S side has a moulded frame which may be late medieval and looks as if it has had a pointed arch curtailed by the present lintel. There is also what may be a former aumbry in the N wall inside and a former stoup by the S door. The W gable's bellcote again looks C17 (BELL of 1790) but raised on an earlier base above

---

*The Listing description of 1971 notes in the N wall the initials of Alexander Scroggy, minister 1607–21, but these are no longer visible.

the W window, which has a deep reveal. There is a forestair and doors in the N wall, possibly for the Laird of Drum's loft, and a stair to a door made through the former E window. Corbels survive for a W gallery. All this may date from *c.* 1737 when the interior was reoriented and the pulpit moved to the S wall (*see* the S windows of this period).

Former DRUMOAK FREE CHURCH (DRUMOAK COMMUNITY HALL), 0.5 km. SW at the hamlet of Park. By *Ellis & Wilson*, 1880. Built of grey and pink granite. The Gothic S front reads as nave and transepts with bellcote over the S gable. Lancets to the main body.

DRUMOAK PARISH CHURCH, Sunnyside Drive. By *Archibald Simpson*, 1835–6, to succeed the old church at Dalmaik. Gothic carapace to a standard preaching-box (cf. Kintore), harled except for the granite of the gable bellcote and thin buttresses of the S front with crocketed pinnacles, and the chamfered surrounds of the lancet windows. The latter have lattice glazing but Perp-style tracery for the S window. Plain interior with W gallery (infilled below) on classical columns, oddly. Late C19 furnishings. – STAINED GLASS. Christ the Good Shepherd. 1959 by *Douglas Hamilton*.

DRUMOAK HOUSE, 0.8 km. SE of the parish church, is its former manse. By *John Smith*, 1836, and an exemplar of its date. Crisp two-storey S front with an attic, rendered except at the margins. Three bays, the central door with sidelights and fanlight of vertical-pattern glazing. Bowed stair at the rear.

PARK BRIDGE, 1 km. SSE. A handsome road bridge, built in 1854 by the Great North of Scotland Railway to permit access from the S bank of the Dee to their station at Drumoak (dem.). By *J. Willet*, engineer, and *James Abernethy & Co.*, ironfounders of Aberdeen. Spanning the river are two wide and shallow cast-iron segmental arches each of 36.5 m. (120 ft) springing just 4.3 m. (14 ft) to the head of the curve from central granite pier and granite abutments. Each span is cast in four pieces. Spandrels of open arcading below the deck.

BELSKAVIE TOWER, 3 km. ENE. A small castellated turret on a granite rock. It appears to be an early C19 Picturesque folly and had two floors inside.

DRUM CASTLE. *See* p. 448.

PARK HOUSE. *See* p. 696.

DRUMTOCHTY CASTLE   K
3.1 km. WNW of Auchenblae

A highly picturesque setting, simultaneously elevated on its own terrace and nestled in a deep, romantic glen. George Harley Drummond (of Drummond's Bank, London) purchased the estate in 1810, where he found nothing but a 'snug and unpretending cottage' covered in thatch. *James Gillespie Graham* built a new house *c.* 1810–12 in restrained castellated style, which now survives as the NW wing. Three years later, this was already insufficient and large additions were made in 1815–16, again by Gillespie Graham but with *John Smith* as executant architect. These consisted of most of the S front and its return face around the W block. More additions – again by Gillespie Graham – followed in 1839, by now for Andrew Gammell, whose grandfather James Gammell, a Greenock banker, purchased Drumtochty *c.* 1820. This phase included the dining room (completing the E entrance front as it now stands) and masterful top-lit hall inside. In 1841–2, the whole of the E front and half of the S front were veneered in new sandstone ashlar from Dundee. Sir Sydney Gammell let out Drumtochty from *c.* 1905 and dereliction followed in the C20; the house served as a prep school from 1948 to 1968. Restoration by *Jenkins & Marr* in 1974–5 has been supplemented by excellent work from 1997 to 2004, and the house is now used as a venue for weddings and corporate events.

The EXTERIOR has many stylistic variations, but all are generically Gothic and united by a crenellated parapet. The E front is courageously asymmetric, the far l. section dating from the second campaign of 1815–16. Tall, square turret on the end with dummy cruciform arrowslit on top. One bay of plain Tudor-arched windows to the r. and then the work of 1839, with a taller, slightly advanced tower pierced by triple lancets. Shallow but mighty porch in front of it with big Tudor entrance arch and octagonal pinnacles to the l. and r. Then the three-bay dining room, lower but beautifully proportioned and given wide, three-light Dec–Perp windows. Raised crenellations in the centre and rectangular (former) stair-tower on the far r. end. The S FRONT is plainer – more castellated, less Gothic – and presents a serenely powerful façade to the glen below. In the centre is a three-storey rounded bow, the highest part of the building; octagonal tower further recessed above it, originally serving as a water reservoir. The windows to the l. (long and Tudor on the ground floor, lanceted on the first) are set in long, slightly recessed panels. In the SW corner, a fanciful four-storey tower of quatrefoil plan, based on the C14 Caesar's Tower at Warwick. The NW WING sits recessed beyond it and is the original house of *c.* 1810–12, of much flakier sandstone as it was never re-veneered. Big, three-storey square, the style again asymmetric with rectangular Perp windows facing W. Tall octagonal tower in the l. corner and a shorter square one on the r.

The INTERIOR has a long hall running down the centre with public rooms in the ground floor of the S wing and the original dining room to the r. Just inside the porch, an entrance lobby with octopartite rib-vault and glazed screen wall with Gothic details. The HALL, straight ahead, is subdivided into four sections by transverse arches. The low height near the entrance allows the second section to come as a tremendous surprise, flying up three storeys with a thrilling sense of weightlessness. It is one of the finest effects that Gillespie Graham ever

68

achieved. Long cinquefoiled panelling on the first floor, glazed on one side and balustraded elsewhere. Conventional lancets in the upper storey, and then a quadripartite rib-vault sub-divided with stylized fan-vault and pendant boss. It is the perfect conclusion to the upward propulsion of all the long, thin mullions below. At the far end is the STAIR HALL with a cantilevered, dog-leg staircase and extremely fine iron railing with gigantic scrolls of rinceau. Big three-light window on the half-landing with the Gammell motto, 'Moriens sed invictus' ('Dying, but unconquered').

The DRAWING ROOM is to the l. of the entrance, very opulent with beaded-panelled dado and windows sweeping all the way to the ground. Excellent rinceau frieze (coeval with the staircase) and attenuated ceiling rose with foliage. More good foliage in the corners. On the overmantel, fluted pilasters flanking urns and anthemion. Cantilevered shelf divided into a mini-colonnade for displaying statues. The former RECEPTION ROOM follows to the S, its three windows nicely seated at the bottom of the bow. Jet black chimneypiece with acanthus accents. The original DINING ROOM is to the r. of the entrance, long and very spacious.* Fine, massive transomed windows allowing for a full cascade of light. Tudor-headed chimneypiece of polished Peterhead granite. The second floor of the S bow has an elliptical BEDROOM with a stair up into the old water tower, ingeniously converted in 2013.

S of the castle, a long TERRACE with screen wall and alternating round, triangular and polygonal projections. – On the approach to the entrance, good SCULPTURES of lions set on little rusticated bases.

ST PALLADIUS (Episcopal), 0.8 km. ESE. Originally built as the estate chapel, and largely endowed by the laird, the Rev. James Stewart Gammell. The design is by *Pirie & Clyne*, 1884–5, broadly E.E. but with all the personal oddity of the firm's style. Tall but compact cruciform plan,† the short chancel with semi-circular apse under the same roof as the nave. Steep gables and craggy rock-facing. Most memorable is the tall circular bell-turret shooting up the E re-entrant angle, its conical spirelet carried on shafts with gigantic stiff-leaf capitals. The tympanum of the porch is carved with vigorous flowers and foliage by *Dawson & Strachan*. S transept high and narrow, its buttress topped by a massive statue of Palladius by *Harry Hems*, 1886. He is robed and holds a crozier below a cantilevered rectangular tabernacle. The nave has lancets under arched hood-moulds, the chancel cusped lancets.

Inside, a ceiled pointed barrel-vault subdivided into panels by ribs and a chancel arch rising the full height of the church. The chancel lancets have deep rere-arches with suave roll mouldings; the nave triplets are perched on a string course. – Original FURNISHINGS. – ALTAR by *Hems* with shafts of

35

---

*The original ceiling was removed in 1945.

† The N 'transept' is lower and serves as a vestry.

polished Devonshire marble and stiff-leaf. – Metal COMMUN-
ION RAILS with little spiral columns and metal flowers. –
Chunky square FONT, also by Hems, set on low, stubby shafts.
Excellent stiff-leaf. – STAINED GLASS. W windows. Foiled
oculus with Lamb of God and angels; two lancets of Christ
meeting John and Peter. – In the apse lancets, Christ's crucifixion and single figures of Saints, 1901.

HALL and LODGE to the W, 1888 and also by Pirie & Clyne.
Former STABLES and COACHHOUSE, 260 m. WSW. A fine design
by *Mackenzie & Matthews*, 1850–1, now converted into flats.
U-plan with projecting gables topped by double chimneystacks. Square tower over the former entrance arch with mightily corbelled, crenellated parapet and octagonal stair-turret.

DUNECHT *see* DUNECHT HOUSE

DUNECHT HOUSE
3 km. NNE of Echt

7000

Dunecht! This extraordinary house was enlarged and embellished over a period of one hundred years to reflect the interests,
aspirations and achievements of its succession of plutocratic
owners. It began in 1820 as a Greek Revival mansion, two storeys,
attic and basement, square on plan with a Greek Doric porch on
its E side, built to designs of *John Smith* for William Forbes, whose
family could trace their tenure of Echt back to 1469; work was
completed after Forbes's death by his son James. But that
Dunecht is quite unrecognizable today. In 1845 it was purchased
by James Lindsay, 7th Earl of Balcarres, whose riches derived
from coal on his estate at Haigh, Lancashire, since he needed a
Scottish seat to pursue his claim to the Earldom of Crawford.
That claim was allowed in 1848, and in the same year he conveyed ownership of Dunecht to his son and heir, Alexander
Lindsay, a bibliophile, a noted scholar in several fields, author of
Sketches of the History of Christian Art, and a passionate enthusiast
for early Italian architecture. In 1855–9, with John Smith's son
William Smith, who had just rebuilt Balmoral (q.v.), Lord Lindsay
remodelled Dunecht completely. The square-plan house of 1820
was transformed and doubled in size, the extended principal
front to the South Lawn being stepped with a tall square tower
separating the old work from the new. The style was no longer
Greek but simple Italianate, a new porte cochère replacing the
old Doric porch on the E side.

In 1867 Lindsay commissioned *G. E. Street* to build a Library
forming a new and much more ambitious Franco-Italian
Romanesque W range to the house, ending on the N with a tall
private chapel correctly orientated E–W. These additions together
with the existing house formed a large open entrance court, the

redundant porte cochère on the E being replaced by a belvedere or garden entrance tower; construction took from 1870 to 1881, partly because of Street's slowness in issuing the drawings and partly because of a dip in Lindsay's income. Within this court-yard, surrounded by buildings of almost daunting scale, and all in solid granite, a circular entrance tower containing a new main stair was formed in the angle between William Smith's South Block and the new W range of the Library. But the Lindsays lost interest in Dunecht after Balcarres came back into their posses-sion and the transformation was not completed until the early years of the C20, under the ownership of the paper manufacturer A.C. Pirie, when the S block's courtyard front was remodelled by *George Bennett Mitchell* to match Street's work, a new dining room being formed on the courtyard side and a conservatory extended out from the E front.

That was not all. In 1909, after two years as Pirie's tenant, the fabulously wealthy contractor Sir Weetman Pearson, afterwards 1st Baron and then 1st Viscount Cowdray, purchased the Dunecht Estate. He engaged *Sir Aston Webb* to make alterations and addi-tions, including the conversion of Mitchell's conservatory into an arcaded loggia, a screen wall across the entrance courtyard and a new boiler room; and between *c.* 1924 and 1932 *William Kelly* made further alterations to the interiors for Annie, Viscountess Cowdray so that they more than matched those of the family's English houses. Although the Estate Office removed Mitchell's dining room and Webb's courtyard screen in the 1950s, the house has survived largely intact. On its E approach facing the broad gravel terrace of the gated forecourt it can feel rather forbidding but from all other angles, particularly the NW, it is almost unworldly; it certainly has a remarkable sense of place and atmos-phere, a testament partly to its architects but still more so to their clients.

The PRINCIPAL ELEVATION, facing the South Lawn, is predominantly two-storey-and-basement, a stepped frontage with its central four-storey tower standing in the angle between the old *John Smith* house – the East Block – of 1820, recessed back on the r. and remodelled in a simple Italianate style by *William Smith* in 1855–9 to match the South Block, which is advanced boldly forward on the l. The five-bay East Block and five-bay South Block are almost exactly equal in length: there is a sense of balance if not symmetry, even though the East Block has been reconstructed with a single central canted bay, while the South Block has advanced ends with four-light canted bays. The house rises from an excavated basement area, its service storey being fully sunk and once screened by a chequerwork parapet. Construction throughout is in grey granite ashlar, rusticated at basement level and polished above, the parapets plain except at the canted bays, where they are balustraded.

The four-storey TOWER rises some 30 m. high, its profile evidently suggested by those at Osborne on the Isle of Wight.

At ground floor it has a single big round-arched and key-blocked window in each exposed face, then at second stage a smaller single light in its S flank and triple lights facing E, the quoins at these levels being heavily rock-faced. Above the wall-heads of the main house, the tower's third stage is lit by Early Italian two-light windows with blind tympana. At the fourth stage, arched triple lights on each side open onto balustraded balconies supported on brackets; the stage has a mutuled cornice on an arcaded corbel course beneath the eaves of its low platformed roof.

The other dominant element in the composition is *Street*'s BELVEDERE, the broad three-storey garden entrance tower projecting from the E ELEVATION, which had formerly been graced first by *John Smith*'s porch and then by his son *William Smith*'s porte cochère. This belvedere has tall twin chimney-stacks on its N and S flanks and, at its NE angle, a round turret corbelled out from the second floor rising into a conical spire-let. The large lead URNS with bas-relief sculptural decoration which flank the entrance on this side are much older than the house itself, perhaps C17. At its NE corner the E front extends into the five-bay arcaded LOGGIA originally built in 1899–1900 by *George Bennett Mitchell* as a conservatory and then rebuilt to its present form by *Sir Aston Webb c.* 1913–20 with a school-room for the Pearsons' children at its far end.

The Library and Chapel built by *G. E. Street* between 1870 and 1881 are totally different in character from William Smith's work, being Franco-Italian Romanesque with some François Premier Renaissance elements and genuinely monumental in their sense of weight and sheer scale; they are faultlessly constructed in grey granite ashlar. On the W elevation the LIBRARY is linked to the main house by additional family accommodation at its S end, much more adventurously composed than the belvedere with mullioned-and-transomed windows and a conical-roofed cylindrical bay in its re-entrant angle. The Library front itself, raised over a basement, standing as tall as the main house and of extraordinary length, is symmetrical – its middle three bays projecting as a reading room and entrance vestibule, with a central semicircular bow and a François Premier gablet flanked on each side by spired stair-tourelles with ascending string courses. The steps leading up to the Library from the gardens are guarded by a pair of very handsome but impassive sphinxes of *c.* 1800, stock still yet seeming ready to come to life and speak, forbidding the ignorant and unworthy and challenging the intelligent to enter. To each side, the three flanking bays of the Library are expressed by blind arcades; above are robustly detailed chequerwork parapets (their significance is heraldic★) with the Lindsays' motto 'ENDURE FORT' emblazoned in huge letters.

72

★The Earl of Crawford's arms contain *fesses chequées* in argent and azure, represented in the parapets by the grey of the granite and the roof slates which show through in blue.

36

At the far N end of the Library is the W gable of the six-bay CHAPEL with which *Street* partly enclosed the N side of the entrance court. The Chapel is immensely tall, its undercroft being wholly above ground, making it not so much double- as triple-height. The W gable itself has a finely carved Italian Romanesque columnar porch in pink Peterhead granite, with triple round-arched windows above and a large, deeply recessed mincer-plate wheel window; framing these on the S is a buttress, and at the NW angle a slim circular tower rising high above the eaves into a belfry of close-spaced columns bearing its granite spirelet. The Chapel is lit by a continuous clearstorey of round-arched lights but it is not symmetrical: towards the E end of its N flank it has a two-aisled side chapel with parallel roofs and paired crowstepped gablets, while on its courtyard flank it has an organ chamber rising into a broad gable with interlaced arcading and an aisle-like vestry. The very short chancel is only slightly lower than the nave itself, and has an arcaded semicircular apse beneath the towering height of which visitors had to pass on their way into the Entrance and Service Courts. For those who felt less than sure of themselves, to arrive at Dunecht must have seemed an intimidating event, still more so after *Sir Aston Webb*'s ADDITIONS on the NE approach, the single-storey boiler-house range with corner drums giving it a semi-fortified appearance.

The ENTRANCE COURT is 42 m. deep by 19 m. broad and enclosed by tall grey granite ranges on all four sides, conveying a truly palatial sense of scale. Approaching at an angle from the E end of the Chapel, the visitor is confronted by the great breadth and height of the Library front expressed above the basement as a blind arcade, its parapet and tall wall-head chimneystacks emphasizing that height still further. The great expanse of the courtyard is quite austere – it appears never to have been planted. Within the court a tall NW stair-tourelle hinges the organ chamber to the Library, and in the SW angle stands *Street*'s entrance tower. It is of substantial girth with a gabled main entrance doorway of François Premier derivation, big mullioned-and-transomed windows which express the ascent of the spiral stair within, and a conical slated roof of graceful profile. Diagonally opposite on the E side of the court it is answered by a semi-cylindrical bow, its first floor a big mullioned-and-transomed window. As on the W front, Street's stone-carving is of the very highest quality.

As refitted by *Sir Aston Webb* and *William Kelly* in the years during and after the First World War, the INTERNAL PLANNING of the house was divided so that the gentlemen's apartments occupied the South Block built by *William Smith* in 1855–9. Separated from the gentlemen by the dining and drawing rooms on either side of the Long Gallery, which runs across the South Block's N flank, the ladies' apartments occupied the East Block built by *John Smith* in 1820 and remodelled by his son, with all the rooms of both suites facing across the

South Lawn; the children's rooms also occupied the East Block, but their rooms looked out over the East Lawn, sheltered by the loggia on the N side. The privacy and comfort of the sexes and generations was thus absolutely respected: only *Mitchell*'s Dining Room had windows facing N into the Entrance Court – too high for prying eyes to see – and the ladies' and gentlemen's apartments could operate quite independently if so desired, each with their own entrances and stairways leading to the twenty-two bedrooms and dressing rooms on first floor and the extensive services sunk in the basement, well lit and ventilated but with no view of any kind. The Library and Chapel could both be entered separately, without any need to admit visitors to the rest of the house.

The COURTYARD ENTRANCE TOWER is remarkable for its spiral stair over 5 m. in diameter – as fine as anything that the French master masons of the C12 could produce – which, supported by forty-seven tall colonnettes, winds around a hollow core towards its rib-vaulted top. This tower opens into *William Smith*'s LONG GALLERY, 36 m. in length and 5 m. wide, which runs across the N side of his South Block into his father's East Block. The Gallery is lit chiefly by five windows facing N into the Entrance Court, the paler light on this side ideal for preserving the magnificent tapestries which graced its walls. There are two fireplaces. That centred opposite the windows is a simple bolection-moulded surround of dark polished marble; its Caroline overmantel mirror framed by high-relief foliate swags of the Grinling Gibbons school has been inserted by either *Webb* or *Kelly*. That at the far W end, which forms an ante-room to the Library, is an Early Italian extravaganza by *Street*, very similar in spirit to his chapel porch – a semicircular fireplace opening framed by columns and with a multitiered overmantel of arches and gablets supporting a low-relief figurative roundel and a heraldic motif. It was still awaiting assembly when its architect died. Both the Long Gallery and its ante-room have elaborately compartmented plaster ceilings composed of rectangles and octagons which appear to be *William Smith*'s work of 1859.

As first built in the 1850s the symmetrical South Block with bay windows at each end probably contained the classic sequence of dining room, library and drawing room following Burn–Bryce precedent. But after the building of the new Library by Street and the new Dining Room by Mitchell, *Webb* divided the large W-end apartment to become LORD COWDRAY'S ROOMS. The central square apartment became the BILLIARD ROOM, with a C15 English screen and spectators' gallery installed *c.* 1920. In the E apartment, the DRAWING ROOM is lined with Jacobean woodwork with marquetry panels up to a pilastered plasterwork frieze and pendant ceiling. Its fireplace is exceptional, Ionic timber pilasters supporting the mantelshelf and framing the overmantel with a tinctured and gilded coat of arms flanked by niched aedicules, and a fretwork crest above its cornice. The drawing room is lit by bay windows facing to both S and E; on the E side, an arcaded screen opens into an ante-room, later the SMALL LIBRARY.

Within the original East Block the *pièce de résistance* is the top-lit PAINTED STAIRCASE. This stair is square on plan with cantilevered flights and elegant cast-iron balusters: it was inserted by *William Smith* during the remodelling of his father's house. It rises, at first-floor level, into an Alberti-type arcade supporting a coved ceiling and cupola. It takes its name from its richly coloured decoration, the arcade with Neoclassical motifs and the ceiling with figurative scenes in a Raphaelesque manner by unknown Italian artists *c.* 1860, with additions *c.* 1900.

Street's Library and Chapel interiors are on an altogether grander scale than any of the Smiths' apartments. The LIBRARY (in Cowdray times the BALLROOM) is 36 m. in length by 8 m. in breadth, and is based on the model of the South Kensington museum halls (cf. Fowke's Royal Scottish Museum, Edinburgh). At ground level its walls are bare for the display of pictures, the bookshelves being above at two gallery levels, accessed by the spiral stairs on the W elevation and in the NW angle of the court. The lower gallery in decorative cast iron is cantilevered out on slim iron colonnettes and spandrel-brackets; then a second tier of colonnettes supports the upper gallery with an arcaded oak balustrade; a third tier rises up into the ribs of a magnificent fully glazed barrel-vault 12 m. high with clear and patterned glass. The Library is richly decorated, and is distinguished at its S end by a lunette painted by *James Pryde*, Annie Pearson's favourite artist. On its W side a triple-arched and pilastered screen gives access to the READING ROOM and garden entrance, and another triple arch at the N end frames the doorway to the Chapel.

Finally the CHAPEL itself: not quite so long as the Library (30 m.) but massively built, its walls of bare ashlar masonry and its compartmented wagon roof rising 15 m. above the nave floor. Twin arches with richly sculptured capitals open into the NE side chapel, a single broader arch on the S once contained the organ, and at clearstorey level the lights are shafted and round-arched. At its E end the nave opens through an immensely tall arch rising from clustered columns into the slightly raised chancel, then through an identical second arch into the vaulted semicircular apse with five arcaded lights illuminating the altar. Inside the NE side chapel the woodwork is C16. The stalls in the nave with their superb inlaid Florentine woodwork are by *Street*, 1877, supplemented by furnishings designed by *Kelly*. The organ, a water-powered instrument made by *Ingram & Co.* of Edinburgh, is now in Echt Parish Church (q.v.).

The raised TERRACES which enclose both the South Lawn and the North Forecourt were formed by *Webb*, 1913–20. The South Terrace has, at its SE corner, a lead-domed GAZEBO with an Early Italian Renaissance doorpiece in bronze and marble;

also fountains, an armillary sphere and a pair of Neoclassical lions guarding the steps leading up to the lawn. The North Forecourt is approached at either end through identical GATEWAYS: carriage gates in wrought iron display beaten metal sculptures of the Cowdray Arms with their supporters, an underwater diver and a Mexican *peón* in low relief, their overarch also with a heraldic cresting; lantern standards and side gates between grey granite piers with the Cowdray griffins; then balustrades link to small circular PAVILIONS with stone roofs crowned by thistle finials. Near the West Gates, a small granite ARCHWAY flanked by summerhouses, also by *Webb*, dignifies the separate approach for visitors to the Chapel and the Library.

The POLICIES – which form only a small part of the much wider Dunecht Estate – extend to some 700 hectares, being enclosed on the N side by the A944, on the W by the B977, and by minor roads to the S and E, and embracing gardens and parkland, three lochs (including Loch Skene), woodland shelterbelts which enclose the house on all sides, and a number of estate buildings of considerable architectural merit. Several are older than the House itself: these include the much-altered remains of the previous seat of the estate, HOUSEDALE (570 m. NE). The ground floor of its five-bay entrance front with a cartouche of 1705 survives within the E flank of the large rectangular WALLED GARDEN. Its C18 flanking pavilions were altered out of recognition into two ESTATE HOUSES by *Walker & Duncan c.* 1912. Another carved stone with date and initials 1723 I.F. M.F. survives in an outbuilding. On the S side of the Walled Garden, the HOME FARM STEADING has a segmentally arched pend within a broad gable leading into the central court, with single-storey-and-dormered-attic cottages for the farm workers on either side. The DOOCOT is rectangular with a piended roof supporting an octagonal cupola, mid-C18.

The PARKLAND itself, however, really began with the present house *c.* 1820 when William Forbes planted 145 trees – oak, ash, beech, elm, gean, plum, lime, thorn and maple – over an area of 12 hectares on the basis of a plan prepared by *Sir Henry Steuart* of Allanton. As a designed landscape the policies had almost reached their present extent by 1868, but they were extended E to take in Loch Skene in the early C20. Much of the present coniferous woodland is replanting by the Cowdrays after the Great Gale of 1953. The WILD GARDEN immediately to the W of Dunecht House has a truly magical quality; the pair of classical bronze sculptures of a HUNTER AND HUNTRESS are signed by *Lillian M. Wade*, 1916.

The STABLES (250 m. ENE) were built by *John Smith* perhaps *c.* 1820 but remodelled afterwards – the entrance front not quite symmetrical, with a round-headed pend arch crowned by a clock face, framed between single-storey and dormered attic blocks built in squared rubble.

Two of the LODGE HOUSES are also by *John Smith c.* 1820: DUNECHT LODGE (900 m. ENE) is a miniature Greek Doric temple, corresponding in style to that of the original Dunecht House; SOUTH LODGE (800 m. S) is a single-storey rectangle subsequently deepened on plan, its doorway in the three-bay front elevation facing the drive. It is simple but stylish, harled with ashlar pilasters and dressings, its low piended roof with broad eaves and low stacks. The WEST LODGES (930 m. WNW) and NORTH LODGES (1 km. NE) are by *Sir Aston Webb* – each a pair of classical single-storey T-plan lodge houses, harled with ashlar dressings, canted bays and tall piended roofs with chimneystacks. Although the West Lodges are dated 1910 this refers to the date of Sir Weetman Pearson's baronetcy: they were designed in 1912. The DUNECHT GATES (1.2 km. NNE) – rusticated granite gatepiers crowned by griffins, with wrought-iron gates, overarch cresting and lanterns – are by *Kelly* 1924–5 and face his restoration of Bridgend (*see* below); they lead to an avenue lined with magnificent copper beeches.

The most remarkable approach to the estate, however, is through the TOWER or SKENE LODGES (3.5 km. E) by *A. Marshall Mackenzie & Son*, 1923, which even by the standards set by Aberdeenshire constitute the purest romantic fantasy. They were built by Annie, Viscountess Cowdray (it is said) after her husband had asked Col. Forbes-Sempill if he could buy Craigievar (q.v.) and the colonel had bluntly refused. On the banks of Loch Skene, within a broad approach densely surrounded by trees, two massive mirror-image tower houses frame gatepiers surmounted by fierce Cowdray griffins and an elaborate wrought-iron gateway with heraldic crest which gives entry to what was once the principal driveway of the Dunecht Estate. Each tower house is of four storeys, square on plan in solid grey granite ashlar, with a circular corner turret rising full height into a spirelet at the wall-head parapet and crowstepped caphouse. They are visible above the treetops for some distance, making them a prominent landmark. The S tower stands on a basement terrace which provides a viewing platform and contains a tea house and boathouse guarded by a portcullis water gate. The terrace looks over the water to a RUINED TEMPLE (3.1 km. ESE of the House) – Doric columns with entablatures on the banks of Loch Skene, originally the porte cochère of *John Smith*'s Dunecht House of 1820, re-erected as a propylaeum at Skene Gates *c.* 1859 and moved *c.* 1923 when replaced by Marshall Mackenzie's tower house lodges.

The estate village of DUNECHT, 1.4 km. N, has its origins in the earlier village of Waterton. It assumed its present name at the beginning of the C20 when THE TERRACE was formed, a long row of cottages set well back from the N side of the road in large gardens. These were built by *George Bennett Mitchell* for A. C. Pirie after he bought the estate in 1899. They are arranged as six semi-detached pairs with a larger house separate at the E end, and two at the W. All are in the same style, single storey and attic in squared rubble, glazed porches with bargeboarded gables, timber-gabled dormers and square chimneystacks, and the overall effect is very picturesque.

The Terrace was only the first phase of Dunecht's development as a model village. Viscount Cowdray's factor *David Morris* provided The Terrace with SHOPS in 1923 (more were added in 1936) and a GARAGE in 1925, utilitarian but decently built in granite with a central archway. By that date Viscountess Cowdray had begun taking an interest in the village, advised by *William Kelly*, who was then in semi-retirement with ample time to devote to it. The next phase was the earlier village of WATERTON, E of The Terrace at the road junction for Kintore. Here the two-storey JASMINE VILLA, in the style of Pirie & Clyne *c.* 1885, was allowed to remain, but opposite Kelly's Dunecht Gates of 1924–5 (*see* above), BRIDGEND – a three-sided quadrangle of late C18 estate cottages sunk below the road level – was remodelled with thatched roofs to *Kelly*'s designs in 1925–7. Annie Pearson was delighted with the result, but they were remodelled again with more practical slate roofs by the *Dunecht Estate Office* in the 1950s.

At the W end of The Terrace, at the road junction for Echt (q.v.), the ESTATE OFFICE is also by *Kelly*, 1925–7, semi-symmetrical Scots Georgian with a few C17-style details. A two-storey U-plan, the central range is flanked by gabled end bays which extend back as wings, harled in grey with dressings in pale granite ashlar. Doorway with segmental heraldic pediment in the l. gable, the r. gable containing the hall with a big Serlian window; large Cowdray coat of arms set into the middle of the central range. The WORKS YARD is by *Morris*, 1922: a very long single-storey symmetrical range with projecting crowstep-gabled wings in rock-faced grey granite with shouldered vehicular openings. DUNECHT SCHOOL is a smaller and much simpler version of the Estate Office, a single-storey range with flanking gabled end bays lit by Serlian windows, built in grey granite ashlar and dated 1928, presumably the work of the County Council in consultation with *Kelly*.

The village grew considerably when *c.* 1990 a new development of houses was designed by *John Cattanach* for *Bancon Homes*, a few lining the main road but rather more arranged to the N around TILLYBRIG; although clearly modern their design borrows from Mitchell's estate cottages, single-storeyed with porches and dormers.

DUNNOTTAR K   *8080*

There is no village, only the church and a few houses separated from the SW surburbs of Stonehaven by the Carron Water.

PARISH CHURCH. A venerable location, and the site of a church
built by Sir William Keith at the end of the C14 and dedicated
to St Brede or Bridget.* That building was reconstructed in
1593 and nothing of it survives except its former – and slightly
earlier – s aisle (*see* below).

The present church was built in three campaigns, the earliest
part a Georgian oblong aligned E–W and erected in 1782.
Arched windows and a w gable with a ball-finialled birdcage
bellcote. E gable extended by *William Smith* in 1862–3. In
1901–3 however *George P.K. Young* demolished Smith's N aisle
and made the present cruciform plan by adding a new, long
N–S arm for nave and chancel and converted the Georgian
church into the transepts. Young's chancel and nave are simple
but good E.E., the latter with aisles and polygonal stair-turrets
in the transept angles. Broad entrance façade to the N with
large triple lancets, the central light with Y-tracery. Narrow
lanceted gable to the l. screening off the E aisle.

Good interior as remodelled by Young. Stepped triple arches
to the chancel and nave arcades carried on circular piers.
Chancel ceiling painted blue with fleur-de-lys stencilled in
gold; over the rest, a fine trussed wooden roof with semicircular
braces in the centre. – GALLERY to the N, moved forward one
bay in 2005–6, when the glass wall was inserted and the final
nave arch blocked. Original glass screen to the lobby, early C20,
reinstated below it. – ORGAN in the chancel by *Wadsworth &
Bro.*, 1903. – STAINED GLASS. S (liturgical E) window, early
C20. Suffer the little children, Blessed are the pure in heart and
Consider the lilies of the field: Parable of the talents in the
bottom centre. – Four windows by *John Blyth*, 1948 (E chancel
wall): Agony in the garden, Betrayal, Flagellation, Christ carrying the Cross. – In the E transept, Psalm 65:9 ('You care for
the earth and make it fruitful') by *Shona McInnes*, 2006–7; Tree
of Life with swirling flights of birds; dark silhouette of
Dunnottar Castle off in the distance. – Some good MEMORI-
ALS from the late C16 church. By the organ, a triangular pediment with initials for James Keith, minister of Dunnottar from
1593 to *c.* 1654. – Cartouche for Elizabeth Keith †1695 (s nave
wall). – Large upright slab for William Ogilvy †1650 and
Catharin Straquhan †1651 (E transept gallery stairs).

Large GRAVEYARD containing the small, rectangular
MARISCHAL AISLE, built in 1582 by George Keith, 5th Earl
Marischal (†1623) and founder of Marischal College, Aberdeen.
It was originally attached to the s side of the medieval church
and featured a burial chamber beneath the floor, 'the hoarse
sea winds and caverns of Dunnottar singing vague requiem to
his honourable line'. So relates the inscription added when the
aisle was re-roofed and much rebuilt by *Young* in 1913–14 following dereliction; the cost was met by Aberdeen University.

---

*This in turn replaced the two churches dedicated to St Ninian sited at Dunnottar
Castle (*see* below).

Original entrance lintel with datestone and monogram topped by roll-moulded frame for a missing plaque. Crowstepped gables with tripartite windows, the upper half all early C20 masonry. Inside, blind semicircular recesses and a stained glass panel with 'Veritas Vincit' ('Truth prevails'), the motto of Clan Keith. Also some good FRAGMENTS of memorials, including one with the Royal Arms and a Marischal stone with excellent carving of birds, dragons and crown.

Outside the door, a semicircular PEDIMENT with crown and sceptre, dated 1663. – Just to the s is the COVENANTERS' STONE, commemorating nine prisoners who died at Dunnottar Castle in 1685 – seven inside the Whigs' Vault and two on the cliffs while attempting to escape.

DUNNOTTAR HOUSE, s of the church. The former manse, and not to be confused with the demolished country house (*see* below). Two storeys and three bays facing s, built 1786. Large nepus gable in the centre; full-height canted bay window to the l. by *William Smith*, 1885–7, in smooth ashlar. His also the large rear block forming a double pile.

DUNNOTTAR HOUSE, an austere Neoclassical house built 1798–1804 for Alexander Allardyce (newly rich from booming sugar plantations in Jamaica), was demolished in 1959. It stood about 0.35 km. s of the church and its WALLED GARDENS survive nearby, fine designs of 1809 by *John Paterson*. One very large garden to the N, the walls so tall that they could be surrounding a military compound. Smaller nursery garden attached to the s, both with bowed s corners – a nod to Paterson's signature geometry. (*See also* the interior of Fasque House (q.v.))

SSE along the Burn of Glaslaw is a small SHELL HOUSE, built *c*. 1810. Hexagonal red brick base with little dome on top. Interior restored and re-shelled by *Diana Reynell* in 1999–2000, now glowing like a miniature baptistery in Ravenna.

DUNNOTTAR CASTLE   K   *8080*
2.7 km. SSE of Stonehaven

Justly famous for its spectacular setting – a supremely theatrical position and certainly among the most impregnable in Europe. The castle sits high on a promontory over crashing waves, with sheer cliffs surrounding it on three sides and the only connection to the mainland a very narrow, tortuously steep approach. The strategic site has a long history of occupation. St Ninian founded a missionary station here in the C5, and by the early C7 Dunnottar had become the administrative centre of the Mearns. A fort on this site was besieged in 681, again in 694, and then destroyed by the Vikings at the end of the C9. King Donald II died here in battle in 900, and so 'upon the brink of the wave in the east he sleeps in his gory bed'. A castle with palisaded mound and wooden tower is documented in the reign of William the Lion

(1165–1214), and referred to as 'le castil de Dunostre' in the early
C13 *Roman de Fergus*.

A church on the site was dedicated to St Ninian and consecrated by Bishop William Wishart of St Andrews in 1276. It and
the castle were burned by William Wallace in 1297, then re-fortified by Edward III in 1336. In 1346, William de Moravia, the
5th Earl of Sutherland, received a licence from David II to build
a fortalice, but he seems not to have done anything. In 1392, the
estate was firmly under the control of Sir William Keith, Marischal
of Scotland, and remained in his family for the next three centuries. He began building a stone castle but was excommunicated
by the Bishop of St Andrews for building on sacred ground, i.e.
too close to the parish church. In 1395 the dispute was ended by
Papal bull and the parish church moved closer to Stonehaven (*see*
Dunnottar, above). Of this date (the late C14), the big keep and
front curtain wall survive. In 1581, George Keith received the title
of 5th Earl Marischal and set about redesigning the medieval
fortress into a proto-Renaissance palace built for comfortable
living. His quadrangle with its deluxe rooms was begun *c*. 1585
and completed by the 7th Earl in the mid C17.

Dunnottar was besieged only once, in 1651–2 by Cromwell's
forces, when the Regalia of Scotland were secretly removed to
the parish church at Kinneff (q.v.) for safe-keeping. In 1715, the
10th and last Earl Marischal, George Keith, was convicted of
treason for his role in the Jacobite uprising and forced to surrender his title and estate. The castle was partly dismantled in
1716–18 and the floors and roofs removed. In 1919, the dilapidated complex was bought by the 1st Viscountess Cowdray, who
undertook extensive restorations and opened the buildings to the
public. The consolidation and restoration was by her usual architect *William Kelly*, advised by W. Douglas Simpson, and completed *c*. 1930.

From the car park, the approach path is perilously thin and
treacherous, winding across the tiny land bridge connecting
the castle to the mainland. It ends at the mighty GATEHOUSE
complex, its front curtain intact from the late C14. This is a
tall, sheer wall *c*. 10.7 m. high, bonded into the cliff on the l.
and completely filling the only cleft in the rock. It was originally defended by big crenellated parapets. The original gate is
a semicircular arch, *c*. 1.7 m. wide, reduced in size and made
rectangular in the C17. Angled out to the r. of it is the similarly
tall, sheer BENHOLM'S LODGINGS, built by the 5th Earl at
the end of the C16. Five storeys, the lower two with four and
then three gunloops set in elliptical embrasures. One more
above it flanked by slit-windows; then two larger upper storeys
to accommodate guards and servants.

Everything beyond the curtain wall also dates from the end
of the C16. In the pend is the slot for the portcullis. Then steps
leading up, ending in four more gunloops arranged in a
rectangle and surrounding a square one in the centre. They

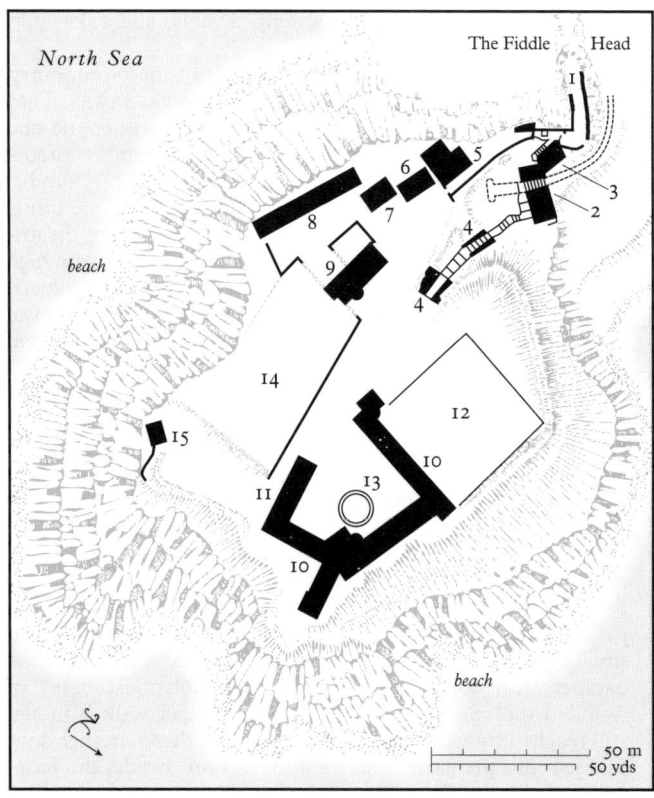

The Fiddle Head

North Sea

beach

beach

50 m
50 yds

1	Entrance	6	Storerooms	11	Chapel
2	Gatehouse	7	Smithy	12	Bowling Green
3	Benholm's	8	Stable Range	13	Cistern
	Lodgings	9	Waterton's	14	Burial Ground
4	Passages		Lodging	15	Sentry Room
5	The Keep	10	The Palace		

Dunnottar Castle.
Block plan

are, surprisingly, rebated for glass, so the idea of invaders actually penetrating this far could never have been seriously contemplated. To the r. is the BARRACK ROOM, a long barrel-vault
excavated deep out of the rock. Off the l. of the middle of the
passage is a former STORE with barrel-vault, two small windows
and an aumbry. Across from it, a chamfered door frame to the
former GUARDS' ROOM, originally ceiled in wood, and from
here a door into the bottom of Benholm's Lodging. A side stair
(by the present ticket booth) leads to the wall-walk over the
main entrance and to the upper storey of Benholm's Lodging,

which has been restored.* Crowstepped gables and a skewputt with worn Keith heraldry.

The main path leads up to the summit of the promontory, which is reached by two arched, tunnel-like PASSAGES. They are each *c.* 7.9 m. long, originally with doors at either end and entrances defended by more parapets. The first pend is entered via a chamfered semicircular arch, originally with a sundial above (*see* below). Walking through creates a sense of mounting constriction and the effect could not have been more theatrically managed: the final emergence onto the high plateau, high in the sky with the sea spinning out, is one of the finest experiences in Scotland. Buildings are scattered around the top of the plateau, although it must be admitted that none of them is of sufficiently high quality to challenge the scenery.

The KEEP lies in the SW corner of the platform and originally sat in isolation. The Papal dispute means that it must have been begun in the late C14, but the presence of typically late features (a continuous stair from ground to parapet, thin walls and inwardly projecting stair-turret) suggest that it was not completed until the mid C15. It is a four-storey L-plan, rather squat, with re-entrant angle facing the cliffs; as a result, the entrance is not there but, rather surprisingly, in the NE corner. Round-headed recess above it for holding an effigy or armorial panel. Many of the windows are larger, later insertions but two small originals remain in the basement of the jamb. Corbelled parapet with some indication of machicolations; bases of rounded tourelles in the corners. The parapet walk is intact, still reached by a small caphouse, and from there another door that led into the garret and its wooden roof. Inside, the basement of the keep's main wing originally served as a storage cellar but was converted into a KITCHEN *c.* 1500, in turn replacing the original kitchen at first floor. New fireplace on the l. wall, somewhat crudely inserted, with two small stone seats and a large aumbry. Window over the sink and drain on the W wall; window above it to light the wooden loft that formerly divided the room. At the same time as the kitchen conversion, the N wall was given a window and its old loophole converted into a door. The ground floor of the jamb has the usual vaulted store, and tucked under the stairs is a prison cell with latrine and aumbry.

The stair rises straight to the first floor and then turns into a newel. The main wing, as per usual, featured the GREAT HALL, which is now gutted and open to the sky. The fireplace in the W gable is not the original one, but reuses older material. On the r. wall, a segmental recess for a cupboard and a window seat with benches. Another one on the opposite wall with a small room flanking the latrine. The E end of the Hall was originally the screens passage and had its own entrance off the staircase, now partially blocked. The second floor above served

---

*Although not quite correctly, as Slezer shows dormers facing N.

as a more private hall, with another window bench and a good trefoiled PISCINA in the NE corner. The first floor of the wing was converted into a WITHDRAWING CHAMBER when the kitchen was moved to the basement, although the original segmental fireplace was retained and just made smaller. Old sink and drain in the angle to the r. of it; another window bench and large garderobe beyond.

The new kitchen in the basement created a lack of cellarage, and so new STOREROOMS were built just off the E side of the keep at the same time. These have two vaulted cellars in the basement and two servants' chambers above (now roofless), once entered by the forestairs on the ends. The ruined SMITHY lies beyond, described as an 'Ammunition House' in the mid C17 as it was used to produce cannonballs in addition to horseshoes. Massive fireplace flue in the W gable and a lone arch screening off the front room. Beyond it is the long STABLE RANGE, built for the 5th Earl c. 1600 and split internally into five chambers. The central one is large and could accommodate up to twelve horses. On the far E side are two chambers for the head retainers, with double-decker fireplaces and rectangular chimneystacks. Next to the l. door, a tiny C13 recess reused from the Chapel (see below).

Across from the stables is the so-called WATERTON'S LODGING, built in the late C16 by William, eldest son of the 4th Earl, and his wife, Elizabeth Hay. It was a complete, independent family home so that his father – the well-named 'William o' the Tower' – could remain undisturbed in the Keep. It is of two sections, the junction marked by a circular staircase-turret corbelled into a square caphouse; another turret in the rear re-entrant angle. Ground floor formerly with a hall (see the fireplace) and private apartment. Chambers above for the servants.

And so to the PALACE, built by the 5th Earl to showcase his nobility and cosmopolitan taste to the full. It provides luxurious living for a new age, one in which cramped tower houses were simply incompatible with ideals imported from Continental houses. The buildings are arranged as an asymmetric quadrangle around a central courtyard, a very unusual form. There is nothing like it in Scotland, although a larger, more complicated version was begun at Kirby Hall (Northamptonshire) in the 1570s. Construction took place in four campaigns. The WEST WING came first, probably begun right after the death of the 4th Earl in 1581. On the ground floor, a long range of seven GUEST CHAMBERS, each with a fireplace, door and window. Rounded buttresses in between corbelled into pilasters and then tall, free-standing chimneystacks above. The upper floor is now roofless but formed a grand GALLERY over 35 m. long, with a private room at the N end and balcony overlooking the sea. There was originally an oak ceiling with collar-beams. Access was provided by the so-called SILVER HOUSE, a square, crowstepped tower attached diagonally to the SW corner. Wide, bolection-moulded doorpiece at the

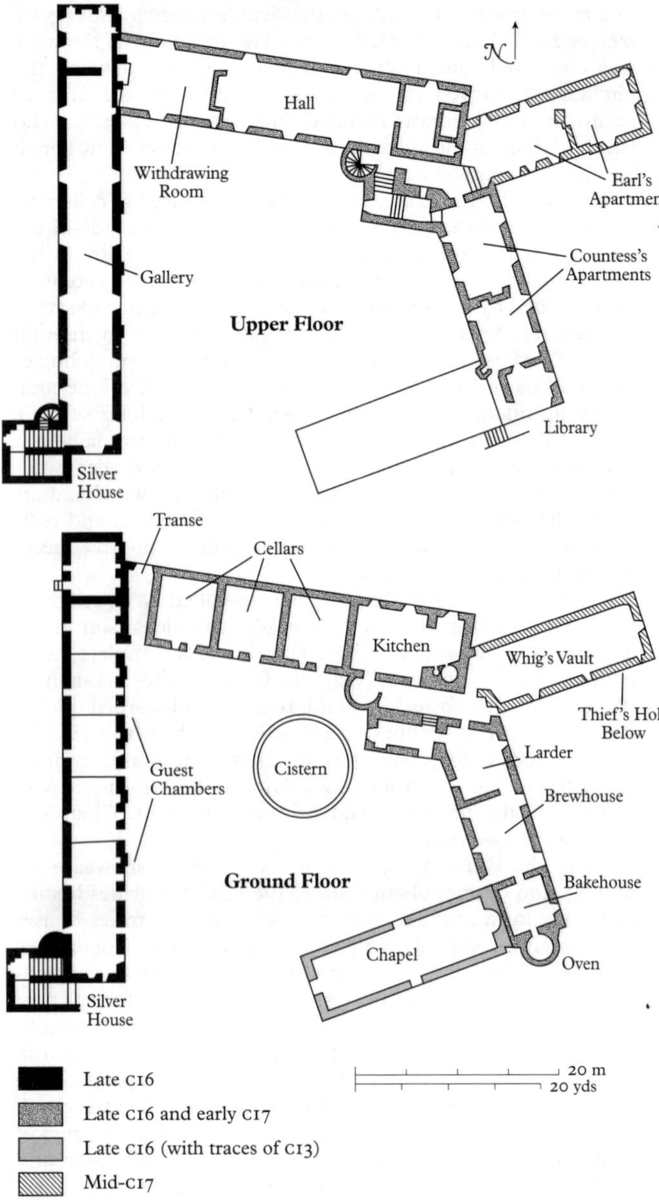

Upper Floor

Hall

Withdrawing Room

Gallery

Earl's Apartments

Countess's Apartments

Library

Silver House

Ground Floor

Transe

Cellars

Kitchen

Whig's Vault

Thief's Hole Below

Larder

Brewhouse

Bakehouse

Guest Chambers

Cistern

Chapel

Oven

Silver House

Late C16

Late C16 and early C17

Late C16 (with traces of C13)

Mid-C17

20 m
20 yds

Dunnottar Castle.
Floor plan

entrance leading to a dog-leg (not newel) staircase. The flat, grassy area to the W was used as a BOWLING GREEN in the C17; excavation in 1970 revealed that the escarpment beyond was the MOTTE of the original C12 castle, and was oval in form.

The NORTH WING post-dates the W range, indicated by the fact that the final living chamber of the earlier wing had to be blocked off and given a new entrance on the W side. The ground floor here has, first of all, a transe leading out to the cliff edge, and then three cellars, identified in 1694 as the wine cellar, ale cellar and larder. Beyond them, a long KITCHEN with enormous fireplace, two dome-vaulted ovens, sink, drain and a service hatch for passing out food. The ground floor of the EAST WING, also built c. 1600, is divided into three chambers: first a larder, then a brewhouse (with kiln and big vat intact) and BAKEHOUSE on the end with oven spun out beyond the wall. In between this and the N range, a new addition was made in the mid C17, stretched out to the NE and perilously close to the cliffs. The ground floor was meant as a long, vaulted cellar, but is now much better known as the notoriously grisly WHIGS' VAULT, where over 150 Covenanters were imprisoned and tortured in 1685.* Underneath it (accessed via the door at the end of the kitchen passage) is the THIEFS' HOLE, a much smaller chamber where forty-two of the Covenanters were crammed and took turns breathing what little air was available.

The FIRST FLOOR of the N and E wings is accessed by a broad staircase in the NE angle. It is a wide scale-and-platt (cf. Innes House, Moray), now renewed but proclaiming the Earl's advanced taste and sophistication. At the top, the very long HALL (or Dining Room), so much more capacious than the original one in the tower house. Fireplace in the far gable and flash line of the former roof. WITHDRAWING ROOM beyond, re-roofed in the early C20. Its panelled CEILING, with canted sides, was designed by *Kelly*, and a scholarly evocation of late C16/early C17 types, with ribs linking diamonds and spurs of foliage to the bosses (cf. Crathes Long Gallery, King's College Chapel, Aberdeen). The ceiling is now as restored in 2007. The doors flanking the modern fireplace are now blocked but once led to the Gallery and its private chamber. To the E of the Hall was the servery.

Over the Whigs' Vault are two private chambers for the EARL'S APARTMENTS. The first one has a fireplace on the far end and – out of the r. windows – a view of a window sill painted red with the phrase THAY HAF SAID: QUHAT SAY THAY: LAT HAME SAY ('What others say of me is of none of my concern'). Smaller chamber beyond with shot-hole in a latrine turret and the sundial formerly over the first pend (*see* above). Above the fireplace, a reused triangular DORMERHEAD

---

*There is a memorial at Dunnottar Church (p. 468) to those who died and fell off the cliffs while attempting to escape.

dated 1645 with the arms of William Keith, the 7th Earl, and his first wife, Elizabeth Seton.

The first floor of the E range was divided into three rooms, two for the COUNTESS'S APARTMENTS and a LIBRARY on the far end. The S end of the quadrangle is taken up by the CHAPEL, much altered since its consecration in 1276 and burning by William Wallace in 1297. Only the lower courses of the S wall and its two little lancets survive from the C13, as the rest was rebuilt in the late C16 along with the W range. Large rectangle, 17.4 m. by 4.6 m., with door on the W gable under Gothic hoodmould. Window above it and then the base of the missing bellcote. Inside on the E end, a fireplace recess on the E and next to it a window that was blocked when the E range was inserted.

Much of the courtyard is taken up by the vast CISTERN, sunk into the earth as a deep conical trough of stone. Facing the Chapel is a long wall, formerly marking off the BURIAL GROUND. Although now levelled, mounds of graves were still visible in the early C19. There is now only one little PLAQUE, pathetically commemorating a nine-year-old boy who died with the Covenanters in 1685. To the SE – on the far corner of the plateau – a ruined SENTRY ROOM overlooks the sea.

LODGE, 0.5 km. W by the car park. By *William Kelly*, 1925. Crowstepped gables, re-entrant drum tower and dormerhead with the cheery exhortation to 'Do it with thy might'. Rock-faced GATEPIERS.

DURRIS HOUSE *see* KIRKTON OF DURRIS

ECCLESGREIG HOUSE   K
1.6 km. NW of St Cyrus

The site was originally known as Criggie and is first documented in 1357. The Strachans of Lauriston (q.v.) acquired it in 1541 and built a tower house here, of which there is now no trace except a plaque dated 1635. The present house dates from 1844–6, built for William Forsyth Grant in grand-scale Baronial style by *Henry Edmund Goodridge* of Bath. It is his only surviving work in Scotland.* Although the house now sits abandoned and in very poor condition, it is still among the finest buildings of its kind in Kincardineshire. While all of the detail is fantastical, it is firmly controlled and does not lapse into the wild flights of fancy that so often tempted Scottish architects.

---

*Goodridge, through his work for William Beckford in Bath, obtained the commission in 1842 to alter Hamilton Palace, Lanarkshire (dem.), for the Duke of Hamilton, Beckford's son-in-law.

Symmetrical s front of five bays, the centre taller and mini-   70
mally advanced. Stack of big mullioned-and-transomed
windows; crowstepped gable on top with balcony and slender
tourelles. To either side, pairs of good Dutch-gableted dormerheads with mottos for Clan Forsyth ('Instaurator ruinae' or
'Restorer of ruin') and the Grants ('Stand fast'). Another
tourelle corbelled out on the far corners. The E flank has a
huge shaped gable and, recessed beyond it, a colossal two-stage
TOWER with mightily corbelled balcony and oriel. The top is
a faux crenellated caphouse, while the bottom is hollowed out
as a porte cochère. Lofty Tudor arches and buttresses. The
back of the former service court is ranged out beyond it. On
the W flank, a full-height rectangular bay window and a bizarre
projecting tower added *c.* 1853 by *David Mitchell* of Montrose.
It starts square (see the dummy cruciform arrowslit) but is
then broached into a circular tower with gableted lancet and
very high conical roof. The latter is encircled by a cast-iron
widows' walk, restored *c.* 2007, to provide sweeping views out
to the sea.

TERRACE in front of the house bordered by a pierced balustrade of *c.* 1845. – Beyond it, the GARDENS are still immaculately maintained to their mid-C19 plan with double parterres
and statues surrounded by hedges, shrubs and topiary. It is like
a stage set, waiting for the party that will never come.

ECHT   7000

Echt with its parish church is centred on the junction formed by
the roads linking Aberdeen to Ballater and Banchory to Kintore
(qq.v.). The former Kirkton of Echt is strung out along the
Banchory Road some distance to the s, while the remains of the
Old House of Echt stand on a hillside to the w.

PARISH CHURCH. A very early Gothick church in Aberdeenshire,   29
built 1804–6 for the 3rd Earl Fife and reflecting his family's
antiquarian interests. Attractive three-bay W front, its slightly
advanced centre rising into a concave-curved gable and ball-
finialled bellcote. Pointed doorway with basket-weave tracery
in its transom-light and an oval spoked *œil de bœuf* at gallery
level; tall windows in the flanking bays with pointed arches and
reeded mullions. Four-bay end elevations with the same tall
windows, all with original basket-weave tracery and glazing,
rear elevation with single *œil de bœuf*. Grey harl with polished
granite dressings, tall piended roof. Later session house. The
interior was originally arranged with its pulpit in the centre of
the s flank surrounded by a horseshoe gallery but in 1929–30
William Kelly reorientated it with the pulpit at the E end and
a single W gallery displaying the arms of the Cowdrays which
reuses the Doric columns and panelled front of its predecessor.

The timber ceiling is Kelly's, modelled on that of St Machar's Cathedral, Aberdeen (q.v.); also Kelly's are the PULPIT, COMMUNION TABLE, FONT STAND and LECTERN, purest Arts and Crafts, all of which were intricately carved in oak by the Dunecht Estate workers in 1930; the lectern is incised with the names of the leading craftsmen; all purest Arts and Crafts. – ORGAN, within the gallery. By *Ingram & Co.* of Edinburgh, originally for the Chapel at Dunecht House (q.v.), given to the church in 1930. – STAINED GLASS. In the oval E window, two angels worshipping either side of a Chi-Rho.

In the GRAVEYARD, a Neoclassical SARCOPHAGUS with block pediment and volutes to the 1st Viscount Cowdray (†1927), guarded by the Cowdray lions raised on obelisk-like pedestals: the design by *William Kelly*. – WAR MEMORIAL. A Highland soldier in bronze, signed by sculptor *William McMillan* and founder *Giovanni Mario Manenti* of London, 1921, the rock-faced base designed by the Dunecht estate factor, *David Morris*.

DESCRIPTION. E of the church, the SCHOOL of *c.* 1875, Gothic. On the other side of the road, opposite the churchyard, the former ABERDEEN TOWN & COUNTY BANK of *c.* 1850, single storey with dormered attic between taller gabled ends, built in rock-faced granite ashlar. The GARAGE is similar to that in the estate village at Dunecht (*see* p. 467), by *David Morris*, 1925.

To the W, the VILLAGE HALL, apparently by *William Kelly*. Dated 1931, it incorporates an earlier school. Of the ESTATE COTTAGES on the N side, two on the junction forming an L-plan were built as a single early C20 house by *George Bennett Mitchell* but altered by *Kelly* in 1932; beyond them THE TERRACE is a row of five single-storey three-bay cottages built in granite with bargeboarded porches and dormers, by *Mitchell* for A.C. Pirie (cf. The Terrace in Dunecht village).

KIRKTON OF ECHT CHURCHYARD, 0.3 km. S, overlooking the Gormack Burn. Ruins of the Pre-Reformation church granted by Thomas de Lundin to Scone Abbey in the early C13 were removed in 1966. Gravestones, including lying slabs and table tombs, from the C18. Adjoining is the former PARISH MANSE built by *James Tough*, *William Minto* and *Alexander Adam* in 1805. Simple, handsome, two storeys and three bays broad, the entrance front in ashlar, with a distinctive nine-panelled doorway, transom-lit; gabled roof with end stacks and later canted dormers. Large three-bay rear wing added to designs by *William Smith*, 1855, may incorporate offices of the previous manse erected *c.* 1793; internal alterations by *John Smith II*, 1877.

OLD ECHT, 0.5 km. WNW. Remains of HOUSE OF ECHT of C16 and C17 date, seat of the Forbes family who could trace their tenure back to 1469. Former courtyard now incorporated into a steading with the large round-headed moulded archway of its forework protected by a shot-hole; on the r. a two-storey remnant with a marriage stone T.F. MF. 1733 indicates extension or remodelling at that time, the tower house itself long gone. To the N the large rectangular enclosure was formerly the orchard, and on the E a wall of the former forecourt.

MILL OF ECHT, 0.8 km. SSW. A corn mill of impressive proportions, very late C18 or early C19, converted to domestic use in 1979. Rectangular plan, three storeys and five bays in pinkish squared granite rubble, the top floor kept very low beneath a tall piended roof; two smaller rear outshots, one a kiln with tall ventilator. Formerly contained an all-iron internal wheel 3.5 m. in diameter, powered by the mill lade which was controlled by a large sluice still surviving in the garden.

GREENTREE LODGE, 1 km. W. Built *c.* 1840 for Mrs Greentree of Midmar Castle (q.v.), set well back from the road on an elevated site. A single-storey, three-bay villa raised over a semi-sunk basement, its porch (now glazed) framed by square columns and a pediment. The roof has gabled dormers typical of the Dunecht Estate *c.* 1900. Distinctive cylindrical gatepiers with coped tops.

STONE CIRCLE, Cullerlie, 5 km. ESE. An unusual monument, related to recumbent stone cirlces, but of a slightly different form. A circle of eight stones surrounding eight miniature cairns, some of which contained cremated human bone. (GN)

HILL-FORT, Barmekin of Echt, 2 km. NW. Multiple ramparts enclose a prominent hill overlooking the village. It is unusual in having so many ramparts and entrances. Four outer ramparts are earth-defined while the two inner are made of more substantial drystone walling and may be of more recent date. (GN)

DUNECHT HOUSE. *See* p. 459.

EDINGLASSIE HOUSE

2.6 km. WSW of Strathdon

3010

A vernacular classical laird's house dated 1726, very similar to nearby Skellater (q.v.), although Edinglassie has extensive additions of the C18 and C19, built in the same pale red granite rubble, snecked and squared. The entrance (S) front of the laird's house is two-storeyed, five bays broad, the projecting end bays rising into gables with tall chimneystacks. Central double-leaf doors (partly glazed) and traceried transom-light within raised surround. Ground-floor window to l. enlarged as two-light opening, dormers with pedimental stone gablets in the E roof pitches of both projecting bays. The earliest extension, built later in the C18, is the lower two-storey three-bay asymmetrical block to the E; its central ground-floor canted bay with crenellated parapet was added *c.* 1850. Of similar mid-C19 date, a short link connects to the broad two-bay end gable of the E wing; on the W the original house was extended into a short wing lit by a two-storey canted bay rising into a stone gablet. Restoration after a fire in 2011 resulted in internal changes:

during the works a very large round-arched kitchen hearth and an oven were discovered within the E bay of the 1726 house.

The GATE LODGES are early C19, a single-storey pair, harled with ashlar dressings, piended roofs and tall coped chimney-stacks rising over the ridges. Single-bay S elevations facing the approach have arched window heads and panelled angle pilasters of identical design to the gatepiers.

STABLES, 100 m. E of the house, early C20, and GARAGE built slightly later, designed to match, facing each other across a yard between them; their style is modelled on that of the lodges.

ELRICK HOUSE

8010

1 km. SSW of Newmachar

62 Elrick, with Straloch (q.v.), represents the climax of achievement of the Aberdeenshire master masons of the C18. A late vernacular classical house, built 1789–92 for James Burnet of the East India Co., it incorporates the pavilion wings of a previous house built *c.* 1765. The beautifully proportioned entrance front, facing S, is two-storey and five windows wide in silver granite ashlar, raised over a semi-sunk basement. Central doorway with sidelights and finely detailed fanlight approached by a short flight of stairs. The pedimented timber porch looks early C20. Long-and-short rusticated quoins, slim wall-head cornice. Deep double-pile plan expressed by broad end gables rising into tall chimneystacks. The single-storey single-bay wings have been refaced in ashlar granite to match the main block: E wing slightly earlier than W wing but both with bellcast hipped roofs. These enclose a shallow rear court where the basement of the main block is fully exposed.

The interior survives remarkably unaltered, with mahogany doors, doorcases and brass locks. Entrance hall lined out as ashlar. Cantilevered stone staircase with iron rod balusters. The principal rooms have refined cornices and wood-and-gesso chimneypieces. Large room in the E wing, with coved ceiling and bolection-moulded stone fireplace. Its earlier C18 panelling reputedly derives from Hilton House, Aberdeen (dem.).

ELSICK HOUSE   K

8090

1.4 km. W of Cammachmore

Site of a castle built for the Earls of Fife after they acquired the land in 1382. The present building is long, harled and two-storeyed, the original section built after a fire in 1754. It incorporates a thick s wall from its predecessor and there is a C17 bolection-moulded doorpiece re-set to the rear. Much restoration 1968–74 by *Thomson, Taylor, Craig & Donald*, including a new w wing and porch.

WALLED GARDEN to the w, late C18 with upper sections of brick. – Foundation walls of a former Episcopal CHAPEL, 360 m. E of the house. Possibly of medieval origin and burned in 1746, just like the chapel at Muchalls Castle (q.v.). – NEWHALL (900 m. SW of the house), a 'modern mansion' of the late C18, now serving as the Estate Office. Two storeys and three bays, harled and elegantly spare. Minimally advanced centre swept up into a square attic window and topped by gable with chimneystack.

FASQUE HOUSE
2 km. NNW of Fettercairn

K   6070

A very large and symmetrical mansion, built in 1808–10 for Sir Alexander Burnett Ramsay, who brought himself to financial ruin by spending over £30,000 on it.* The style is castellated Georgian, achieving its effects via monumentality and proportion rather than through architectural finesse. The name of the architect remains unknown, although the restraint of the exterior and the predilection for geometric forms inside has led to attributions to *John Paterson*. In 1829 the house was purchased by John Gladstone (later Sir John and 1st Baronet), who was born at Leith but made his fortune in Liverpool as a corn merchant, importing sugar from his West Indian plantations. He made several changes to the house, and until his death in 1851 the house was the annual autumn retreat of his son William, M.P. and later Prime Minister. William's elder brother inherited Fasque and the house remained in the Gladstone family until 2007 when the contents were sold. Since 2010 it has been thoroughly restored by Douglas and Heather Reid Dick with *@rchitects Scotland Ltd* (project architect: *Paul Fretwell*); it now serves as a wedding venue.

The MAIN FRONT is long and regular, nineteen bays of red sandstone. Main block of three storeys and eleven bays; longer windows on the first floor and square ones on top. Crenellated parapet on the wall-head. The l. and r. angles are marked by projecting octagonal turrets that rise slightly higher than the main roof. A wide and canted bay rises up the very middle, originally three-storeyed but given an additional floor in 1829. The bizarre entrance portico with crenellated cornice and architrave carried on quasi-Roman Doric columns was added

*He demolished the C17 house which stood just to the w. An earlier Alexander Ramsay had commissioned *William Adam* c. 1750 to extend that house but nothing seems to have been carried out.

South Prospect of Faskie House toward the Court the Seat of the Hon.ble S.r Alex.r Ramsay of Balmain in the County of Mairns Extract, 163

Fasque House.
Unexecuted design by William Adam, 1750

by John Gladstone. The columns have octagonal blocking and the abaci are eight-sided as well. Beyond the main block are two-storey mirrored wings, again ending in octagonal angle turrets. Off the r. flank is the L-plan SERVICE WING, its top storey added in 1902. Tudor entrance arch leading to the rear façade, which still retains its original disposition of three floors in the centre. Another canted bay window on the l. flank.

The INTERIOR comes as a surprise and forms a complete contrast to the austerity outside. Long and rectangular ENTRANCE HALL, the first bay with rounded niches set in blind segmental arches. Beyond them are mirrored doorways, each topped by a pediment. The l. leads into the BUSINESS ROOM, with panelled window shutters and pilastered chimneypiece of grey marble. Very thick ceiling frieze of swagged garlands. SNOOKER ROOM beyond it with one D-ended wall. The r. door leads into the DINING ROOM, featuring big panelled dado and cornice with brackets over egg-and-dart. Ornate white chimneypiece with consoles and delicate foliage and rinceau on the lintel.

Straight ahead from the main hall is the dramatic, full-height STAIR HALL, set out in the form of a shallow ellipse. Cantilevered imperial staircase, the first branch very short and then sweeping off to the l. and r. in a smooth, delicious curve. Fine plaster rose high above; three rectangular windows on the first floor which retain their original etched glass. The sills are perched on a band course of Greek key, and above them a little frieze of acanthus separated by miniature Gothic fan-vaults. Balusters with lozenges and attenuated quatrefoils. At the top landing, the two sides of the staircase meet at a triple-shafted entrance leading into the UPPER HALL. This is a tighter ellipse rising up to a top-lit quasi-dome decorated as the spokes of a huge fan. Jettied upper landing with more Greek key ornament and cast-iron railings with arrowhead finials. Back at floor level are three segmental arches with trabeated lintels carried on Corinthian columns. The s one leads into the massive DRAWING ROOM, originally two separate rooms but joined together by Sir John Gladstone, 3rd Baronet, in 1902. Thick ceiling frieze of scrolled rinceau. Fine white marble chimney-piece with goddesses pouring wine out of urns.*

The POLICIES are structured around a designed LAND-SCAPE, also *c.* 1808–10 but retaining some features made by the Ramsays in the C18. – Large LAKE, 0.9 km. SSW of the house, dug out for Sir John *c.* 1830. It occupies a total area of *c.* 7.9 hectares, with three small islands and also a boathouse on the N shore. – Double WALLED GARDEN, 370 m. SSW, and probably built in 1792. Two roughly equal brick compartments with castellated entrance in the centre of the S. Ruinous green-house range on the N wall. The dividing wall is straddled by a charming two-storey PAVILION, originally built as a cubical Apple House with pyramidal roof on top. Original flat elevation to the S, but on the N a broad, depressed bow added by *John Paterson c.* 1810, further cementing the theory that the main house is by him. His also the flanking octagonal towers with Y-glazed lancets and blind quatrefoils. – 420 m. W is an octagonal Gothic FOLLY, originally built as a gazebo for playing cards but now ruinous. Lancets with big voussoirs.

ST ANDREW (Episcopal), 160 m. E of the house. E.E. box by *John Henderson*, 1847, built as a private chapel for Sir John Gladstone and consecrated by Samuel Wilberforce, Bishop of Oxford. W gable with pointed entrance and diagonal buttresses. Stepped hoodmould around a plate-tracery window with quatrefoil; good gabled bellcote with shafted, trefoiled arch. Three lancets to the S flank separated by buttresses, and a vestry poking out on the N. Slightly lower two-bay chancel added by *Alexander Ross* in 1867–9 to commemorate Sir John's son Captain John Neilson Gladstone, who died at sea in 1863. E gable with stepped triple lancets under a blind trefoil (reused from the original wall). Underneath the church is a crypt with a BURIAL VAULT containing eight coffins for the Gladstones.

Good interior as restored by *Alexander Ross & Son* in 1925–7. Wooden roof carried on corbels (coomb over the nave and arch-braced over the chancel). Double-chamfered arch to the chancel and another on the l. with organ and the vestry behind. – In the chancel, a Gothic dado as well as STALL SCREENS and ALTAR RAILS pierced with attenuated, cusped vesicas, *c.* 1869. – BARREL ORGAN by *Hamilton* of Edinburgh, 1846. Crenellated pinnacled case. – STAINED GLASS. Mostly memorials to the Gladstones. Chancel E lancets, *c.* 1869, in appropriate C13 style with St Andrew and emblems of the four Evangelists in medallions. – In the N and S windows angels with musical instruments, for two Gladstone daughters †1885. – Nave S wall, two windows, *c.* 1866, with good Dec micro-architecture: St John the Evangelist with the Virgin (above) and Christ (below); Woman anointing over Noli me tangere. – Nave

*This may well be the chimneypiece commissioned *c.* 1816 from *John Gibson* for Gladstone's Seaforth House, Liverpool, which had 'two female figures in alto-relievo' and which Gibson had been told had been taken by Gladstone to Scotland (*Memoir of the Life of John Gibson R.A.*, 1870).

N wall, Christ and two little children (for daughters of Sir Thomas †1853) and female figure (for Anne Mackenzie Gladstone †1829). – W window (for Robert Gladstone †1835). – MEMORIAL. Sir John Gladstone †1851 and his second wife, Ann MacKenzie Robertson, †1835 (N nave wall). Large tablet of white marble in high relief. Both figures praying within a semicircular niche. By *Alexander Munro*, 1854–5.

Quadrangular STABLE BLOCK, 280 m. NNW of the house. An excellent survival of *c.* 1810, restored and converted into flats by *@rchitects Scotland Ltd*, 2012–13. Spare, patrician S façade of seven bays, the centre wider and minimally advanced with a broad elliptical courtyard arch (now glazed over). Pediment above with a blind oculus. Triplets of arched windows to the l. and r. and then a blocking course with piended roof.

FAWSYDE HOUSE *see* ROADSIDE OF KINNEFF

FETTERCAIRN   K

First documented in the C11 but almost certainly occupied in the Pictish period. Fettercairn was made a free burgh of barony in 1504 and endowed with both a weekly market and an annual fair (dedicated to St Mark). The village was plundered by the Marquis of Montrose in 1645.

PARISH CHURCH. Sited on an elevated, elliptical mound, and so probably occupied from the early Christian period. The medieval parish church – dedicated to St Mark and probably built in the C13, but not documented until the C15 – was sited just to the S of the present building.* The present building began as the usual wide, gabled rectangle with arched windows, built 1803–4 of red sandstone. Slightly advanced central tower of ashlar added during renovations by *John Henderson*. 1838. Diagonal buttresses clasping a Tudor entrance arch, Y-tracery window, round clock face and gableted, louvred belfry. The angle pinnacles of the latter were removed after a storm in 1879. Octagonal stone spire on top. Y-tracery windows to the l. and r. as renewed during a second wave of renovations by *George P. K. Young* in 1924–6. Four more of them on the long SE flank, which is tall and long. His also the stepped buttresses in between and the gableted pinnacles set very low over the wall-head. Slightly lower chancel as added by Young, with two Y-tracery windows and a pair of lancets sturdily buttressed against the terrain. On the W flank, a tall projecting transept

---

*No remains above ground, but the vault of the C17 Balbegno Aisle attached to its N side was still accessible in the early C20.

added in 1838, sticking out with rather awkward asymmetry. Canted stair-turret off its re-entrant angle, 1924–6.

The interior is as recast by Young. In the nave, a ribbed coomb ceiling with wide, segmental arch braces over faux hammerbeams. Corbels underneath it. In front of the chancel is a Gothic 'triumphal arch', its centre a wide arch with narrower, smaller arches to the l. and r. Tall triple arcade into the original transept, extended by Young into a longer aisle. The piers of the latter are octagonal or chamfered squares and have no capitals. – Original GALLERY over the entrance with its original straight-backed PEWS. Replica in the aisle, 1924–6. – FONT with round, partially translucent marble bowl, 1929. Swagged garlands around the outside. Acanthus leaves on the stone base. – ORGAN, 1886. Exposed pipes taking up the whole NE chancel. – STAINED GLASS. Two N (liturgical E) windows by *A. Ballantine & Son*, 1927. Four scenes of charity (hunger, thirst, sickness, hospitality).

The GRAVEYARD has a good collection of late C17 and C18 TOMBSTONES, the earliest one dated 1615. – Just outside the door, a HEADSTONE carved with a fine primitive Temptation, showing Eve about to hand the apple to Adam. Figures (now headless) covering their nakedness, with the tree in between.

ST ANDREW (Episcopal). *See* Fasque House, p. 483.

DESCRIPTION

At the SW end of the burgh is the RAMSAY ARMS HOTEL, replacing the original Eagle Inn founded in the late C18. Harled, asymmetric Arts and Crafts by *Thomas Martin Cappon*, 1896–7, with red tiled roof and multi-paned mullioned-and-transomed windows. Jacobethan wooden porch with baluster posts and, inside on the ground floor, original carpentry including high, panelled dado. Diagonally across is the hefty ROYAL ARCH, built 1864–6 to commemorate a clandestine visit here by Queen Victoria and Prince Albert in 1861. The couple left Balmoral by pony in the morning and stayed overnight at the Ramsay Arms, dressing in disguise to avoid detection. In 1862, the villagers commissioned several designs for a public monument, and the Queen personally selected *John Milne* as the winner. His style is triumphal Rhenish Romanesque. Big semicircular arch in the centre and crumbling inscription of 'Victoria & Albert'. 'Sept' and '1861' (now eroded) in the spandrels. Crenellated parapet above with raised, segmental centre featuring a crown. Thick octagonal buttresses to the l. and r., themselves buttressed at the bottom. Good foliate label stops and then slightly recessed octagonal pinnacles topped by gableted, pyramidal spirelets. Crocketed capitals and big iron finials lending an extra sense of height.

Just beyond the arch, a short BRIDGE over the Burn of Cauldcots, built in 1864 along with the arch. Iron parapet with Gothic detailing, after which the short MAIN STREET follows.

First on the l. is GLENGOWAN, early C20, with three piended dormers and an original shopfront on the r. with bracketed fascia and dentilled cornice. Next door is THE BANK HOUSE, built *c.* 1915 with curvilinear cornice over the door and multi-pane glazing in the upper third of the windows. Three pedimented dormers through the wall-head. Across the street, THE BAKERY HOUSE, late C18, of rough red sandstone with a nepus gable in the centre. At the far corner (on the s side of the roundabout) is the PARISH CHURCH HALL by *David Wishart Galloway*, 1901. Crowstepped L-plan with two-light plate-tracery window and little ventilator with concave pyramidal roof. It has a metal Art Nouveau finial. A short walk E leads to THE GRANGE, built as the Manse in 1867–9 by *John Johnstone*. Semicircular keystoned entrance and slim sub-Italianate windows on the first floor. The L-plan former offices (now converted) were built 1764–6 for the earlier manse on the site.

Back at the roundabout is the large PUBLIC HALL, 1890–1 by *John Milne* and built on the site of an early C19 Temperance hotel. Lacklustre Scots Renaissance with a large crowstepped gable and dummy tourelle in the l. angle. Square, crenellated tower on the r. with a little square stair-turret poking up. In front of it is the Eleanor-Cross-style FOUNTAIN by *David Bryce*, 1869, commemorating Sir John Forbes. Good Dec carved by *John Rhind*, the square base with blind trefoiled arches over shafts with stiff-leaf. Marble basin below with a lion's head; octagonal spirelet above with gableted mini-tabernacles and a crocket-studded pinnacle.

THE SQUARE lies to the NE, a long rectangle lined with buildings of the mid C18 to early C19. In the middle lies the MARKET CROSS, originally made for the county capital of Kincardine (*see* below), but moved here by 1670 after the latter had fallen into swift decline. Square, stop-chamfered shaft, carved *c.* 1504 and topped by a moulded cornice. One side is incised with the Scottish 'ell' (official unit measuring three feet and one-and-a-half inches) and there was formerly an iron ring for fastening the jougs. Cubical capital on top carved in 1670, when the right to hold weekly markets in Fettercairn was reconfirmed by royal charter. Datestone on the N face; scars of a former sundial on the S. On the W side, a lion rampant with crown and on the E the coroneted initials for John, 1st Earl of Middleton, builder of the original Fettercairn House (q.v.). Underneath, a tall octagonal plinth with six steps. At the far NE end of The Square, a long early C19 housing block with full-height canted bays to the l. and r. of centre.

FETTERCAIRN DISTILLERY (Whyte & Mackay), Distillery Road. First established in 1824, and so one of the very earliest in Scotland founded after the Excise Act of 1823. Now one of the only 'lowlands' distilleries still in production. Originally built in 1825 by Sir Alexander Ramsay of Fasque House (q.v.), who converted a mid–late C18 corn mill on the site. Current complex mostly of 1888–90 by *Robert Milne* of Fettercairn, following a fire in 1887. Pleasing contrast of white cement-rendered walls and black roofs, with tall modern chimney silhouetted against far-off hills. The iconic pagoda kiln ventilator is a sham, set anachronistically over a warehouse but giving the necessary imprimatur.

INCHDOWRIE HOUSE, S end of Burnside Road. The former Free Church manse, 1845–6 by the mason *Alexander Jamie*.* Harled two storeys and three bays with piended roof. Segmental window in the upper centre flanked by strange eaves-course fragments that look like little inverted crenellations. Two big corniced, canted bay windows, late C19. – Gothic-panelled GATEPIERS. – Original GATE with fleur-de-lys.

KINCARDINE CASTLE, 2.6 km. NE. Wooded hillock with the foundations of a royal castle, probably built for Alexander II between 1217 and 1227. Quadrangular plan with curtain walls (*c.* 35 m. square), now mostly reduced to footings. Former main entrance on the S with gatehouse and a postern on the N. Ranges of domestic apartments on the N, E and S sides. – Sprawling out to the NW are the remains of an outstanding medieval DEER PARK, by far the finest example to have survived in Scotland. It was probably built in the late C12 by William the Lion and extended by Alexander III in 1264, when fencing for a 'New Park' is recorded. It consists of a vast earthen bank, especially well defined on the N and originally enclosing *c.* 8 square km. Intact dyke around the perimeter, originally lined with timber palisades and high, open intervals that forced the deer to turn in the middle of the chase.

SW of the Castle once lay the CASTLETON of Kincardine, which was elevated to a burgh of barony in 1504 and made the county capital in 1531 but succeeded by Stonehaven in 1600. The whole settlement had virtually disappeared by the mid C18. For its Market Cross *see* above.

KIRKTON OF BALFOUR, 4.9 km. W. Site of the vanished church of Newdosk, dedicated to St Drostan and abandoned *c.* 1658. – HEADSTONE carved with a wonderfully primitive angel, the head nearly round and the wings looking like big, flapping sails covered in feathers. Leggy, stylized flower to the l. and r. Helm, monogrammed shield and 'Memento Mori' on the bottom. – HEADSTONE for Margaret Dury †1735 and Margaret Duncon †1740, the front with an armorial plaque and the rear dated 1747 under stylized egg-and-dart. The two naked women's corpses are perched on the upper rim, sleeping peacefully and stroking their husband's hair while they await the Last Judgment.

ARNHALL HOUSE, 5.8 km. SW. Harled two storeys and three bays of the mid–late C18, built on the site of the early C17 Aurinhall House. Longer windows on the first floor; tall, steep attic with three canted dormers added *c.* 1840. They have

---

*The Free Church (1843–4 with additions by *Robert Milne*, 1864–5) formerly lay 500 m. to the NW.

bowed roofs and big fifteen-pane glazing, so much more generous than the usual kind added in the late C19. Inside, a stone dated 1622 with the initials C.E.S., now reused as a chimney-piece lintel.

Former TORWOOD HOUSE, 4.4 km. wsw. Ruins of a single-storey, Neoclassical cottage, built *c.* 1829 in a surprisingly urbane style. Wide, bowed centre with tetrastyle Greek Doric portico (lower columns unfluted). Flanks also nicely curved forming a double-bow-ended plan.

LONG BARROW, Capo Plantation, 7.4 km. ssw. A large Neolithic long barrow 80 m. long, 2.5 m. high and 28 m. wide at the E end. The mound is likely to overlie wooden structures and mortuary deposits as have been found at other excavated examples. (GN)

VITRIFIED FORT, 2.1 km. sw, by Cairnton of Balbegno. Roughly oval mound on a low knoll, originally *c.* 45.7 m. long and 18 m. wide at the centre. Rampart walls intact most of the way around. Gap in the NE for an entrance.

BALBEGNO CASTLE. *See* p. 336.

FASQUE HOUSE. *See* p. 481.

GANNOCHY BRIDGE. *See* p. 397.

FETTERCAIRN HOUSE

0.7 km. NE of Fettercairn

A long and comparatively low house, everything disposed horizontally rather than via the usual drive to build higher and higher. It seems a strange choice for a country house, but the explanation is simple: the core of the present building is a rectangular hall house built in the mid–late C17 for John, 1st Earl Middleton (†1674), and its low proportions set the pattern for everything that followed. The Carolinian building was remodelled 1826–9 by *William Burn*, who reorientated it and doubled its width by adding an entirely new entrance façade to the w. That work was carried out for Sir William Forbes of Pitsligo (7th Baronet), who died in 1828, and completed for his son, Sir John Stuart Hepburn-Forbes (8th Baronet). In 1874–7, *Wardrop & Reid* added a quadrangular service court for Charles Hepburn-Stuart-Forbes-Trefusis, the 20th Baron Clinton, who had acquired the estate in 1866. It sits in the NE corner and forms a big L-plan. Later, in 1898, he commissioned *Sir Robert Lorimer* to redesign the library, and this remains the glory of the house.

The WEST FRONT is entirely as built by Burn, imposingly aloof and in a forthright Elizabethan style. Nearly symmetrical main block, three very wide bays. Tall, square tower advanced in the centre with straight-headed entrance approached by short flight of steps. Neo-Jacobean balustrade and ball-finialled newel posts flanking it. Above it, a blank heraldic shield corbelled into a big canted oriel; octagonal buttresses to the l. and r. extended into pinnacles with faceted, leaded domelets. Tall Dutch gable in between them, the *leitmotif* of Burn's work at Fettercairn. The side bays have full-height rectangular bay windows, mullioned to the semi-sunk ground floor and with big, five-light mullion and transoms at first-floor level. Shaped gables on top with Tudor chimneystacks (the l. now missing, and its wing slightly advanced). Four more bays are spun out low to the l., the first three with alternating triangular and shaped dormerheads. Nice little skyline of diamond chimneystacks above and a tall canted bay window on the end.

The junction between the old and new work is best seen on the SOUTH FLANK. On the l., another of Burn's full-height canted bays with Dutch gable and diamond stack. Next to it is the original wide flank of the C17, its ends slightly advanced and squared. Only the inner one is authentic, both of them topped by Burn with square turrets under good ogival slated roofs. The EAST FRONT is a splendid sight, facing the garden and in a wholly different style to the other side. Long, rectangular core with good rubble masonry of the mid–late C17, sensibly left exposed by Burn. His additions are in greyer or redder ashlar, adding bits of 'historical' detail that he believed the 'real' building had lacked. Original square stair-tower advanced on the r., its chamfered door frame topped by a lintel dated 1666 with the monograms IEM (for the 1st Earl) and GCM (for his wife, Grizel Durham). Cantilevered balconies to the l. and r. with balustraded parapets by Burn; his also the ogee dormerheads above. Two original small C17 windows survive to the l. with, in between them, Burn's tall canted bay window corbelled out over a door frame and with his crowsteps above. Authentic C17 window to the l. of it, originally breaking the wall-head under a stepped string course. It is now topped by one of Burn's dormerheads; his also the crowstepped gable to the l., with long C17 blank masonry below.

On the far r. side is the SERVICE COURT of 1874–7, set at a right angle and of snecked, redder stone. Drum tower in the re-entrant angle topped by big conical roof with fish-scale slates. Three Dutch gables, originally part of Burn's much smaller service wing and re-set here when the latter was demolished in 1874. Long, tall SCREEN WALL attached to it and leading down to the garden.

The INTERIOR of the house is very fine, and like the exterior has two completely different personalities. Burn's work is concentrated in the w half that he built. Shallow but surprisingly tall ENTRANCE LOBBY, a nicely theatrical manipulation of space. It is topped by a square lierne vault with bosses of Dec foliage. In its centre, an octagonal pendant fan-vault lit by the main oriel over the door. A short wooden flight of steps with turned, key-blocked balusters passes through a tall Tudor arch and straight into the ENTRANCE HALL.* Coomb ceiling ribbed

---

* *See* the small butler's door sunk low to the r. of the staircase.

with rectangular panels and more foliate bosses. Big top-lit glazing panel in the middle. DRAWING ROOM to the r. with geometric strapwork on the ceiling and a cornice decorated with Dec seaweed. White marble chimneypiece with two caryatids, their arms outstretched and doubled back over their heads in defiance of the loads above them. DINING ROOM on the other side of the hall with ribbed, panelled ceiling and flowing, crocket-esque cornice.

And so to the LIBRARY, occupying half of the upper floor of the original hall house. It is very long but manages to be cosily inviting at the same time. Thick frieze on the ceiling with wavy vines, leaves and birds. Four bursts of foliage in the corners. Wooden panelling on the s wall flanked by pairs of windows seats; in between them, a door into the C17 stair-tower, its newel staircase winding up in a tight curve. Bolection-moulded chimneypiece on the far wall, of excellent green marble striated like malachite. Long wooden bookshelves on the W and s walls. The latter is topped by a series of faux ancestral portraits, their costumes convincingly Georgian enough to appear authentic from a distance. Pilaster strips in between carved with painted heraldry, names and mottos. Underneath the ends are two delightful ALCOVES with segmental barrel-vaults, decorated with quintessential Lorimer foliage and birds. They are thickly textured, and perfect for studying close up. In the l. one, a stained glass panel with heraldic plaque and the mottos 'Mercy is my desire', 'Nec timide, nec temere' (Neither timidly nor rashly) and 'Avant' for the Hepburn, Stuart and Forbes families.

FETTERESSO *see* KIRKTON OF FETTERESSO

FETTERNEAR
1.25 km. NNW of Kemnay

Lying within the confluence of the Marshes Burn and the Don, Fetternear has been of importance since the early C12. In 1157, a Papal Bull of Adrian IV confirmed that the Bishop of Aberdeen held the church and township in a free forest. Charters indicate that by the mid C13 Fetternear had become an episcopal seat, additions being made by Bishop Peter de Ramsay in 1256. During the 1330s it was rebuilt by Bishop Alexander Kyninmund as an EPISCOPAL PALACE, one of the largest in Scotland, its courtyard enclosed by a moat and a timber palisade which was quickly replaced by a stone curtain wall.* Fetternear with its 'palace, tower and fortalice' was leased first by Bishop William Gordon

---

*Archaeological excavation *c.* 1900 turned up First Pointed mouldings and tracery in Kildrummy freestone.

to his relative the 4th Earl of Huntly in 1549, then the following year to John Leslie of Balquhain (*see* p. 415); in 1566 Bishop Gordon granted the lands outright to John Leslie's son William, who had protected St Machar's Cathedral and the Chanonry from a Protestant mob.

Within the site of the palace the Leslies built the HOUSE OF FETTERNEAR. Now in perilous condition, it is in its present form a near-symmetrical Castellated mansion of *c*. 1815–20. Its entrance (s) front comprises a central block, three storeys high and six windows wide, flanked by slim drum towers and standing slightly in advance of non-identical wings at each end.

Most of Fetternear's fabric significantly pre-dates the early C19. Its BUILDING HISTORY is unusually complex, for it was once much more extensive than it is now. The oldest part is the E wing and the adjoining drum tower, which appear to be the tower house built by John Leslie sometime after 1570. Its main block 11 m. by 6 m. orientated E–W was of three storeys, its vaulted ground floor containing kitchen and cellar, and the first floor the hall. The drum tower, 3.5 m. in diameter, contains its turnpike stair. This tower house was subsequently extended W into what is now the central block. As originally built the central block was of two storeys and stood flush with the front-age of the tower house. A three-storey W wing with just one window on each floor was built to create a semi-symmetrical appearance, the central block's original roof-lines being still visible in a raggle in the tower house's W flank. An estate plan of 1838 and the 1st Ordnance Survey of thirty years later show another large block at the far E end which may also have dated from this time but which had been demolished before the 2nd O.S. was published in 1900. The mid-C17 house must still have been defensible as it was twice besieged by the Covenanters, who appear to have resorted to cannon. Two shot-holes were repositioned in the old tower house at that time.

In 1691–3 Patrick Leslie transformed this much-extended house into something approaching a Continental palace by rebuilding the central block as the N side of a symmetrical cobbled forecourt with flanking office ranges on the E and W and railings and gates on the s, all much as at Traquair (Borders). Patrick's elder brother and uncle had served as marshals of the Holy Roman Empire and Patrick acquired a fine collection of pictures. To house these pictures he rebuilt the central block on its present line slightly forward of its wings and raised it to three-storey height, but with a lower eaves line than the present parapet. The central doorway and three small windows to either side are still much as he built them but the first-floor windows have been deepened and the second-floor windows originally rose through the eaves as heraldic dormer pediments. Although the now-vanished forecourt seems to have been symmetrical, full symmetry was not quite achieved at the house itself, the original E drum tower still having a caphouse while the later W one had a conical roof; nevertheless the ensemble probably formed the model for Faichfield and the other Aberdeenshire and Banffshire houses with formal and semi-formal forecourts.

The dates of Patrick Leslie's reconstruction can be surmised from three CARVED PANELS above the doorway. Between the second-floor windows two small panels display initials I.H.S. (Iesus Hominum Salvator) and M.R.A. (Maria Regina Angelorum), together with the initials of Patrick and his wife, Mary Irvine of Drum (q.v.) and the date 1691: a reflection not only of the Leslies' Catholic faith but of the Counter-Reformation cult of Holy Names and somewhat hazardous even in North-East Scotland, probably tolerated only because of Patrick's international standing. Beneath, his heredity is expressed much more boldly – a magnificent panel 1.8 m. high displaying his arms impaled with those of his wife, supported by griffins and surmounted by a helmet, mantling and crest, dated 1693; the coronet above is presumably that of a Count of the Holy Roman Empire. By 1762 the Leslies were crippled by litigation; they were obliged to lease Fetternear to their factor David Orme, an Edinburgh advocate. He demolished the forecourt and stripped the house and estate of all their assets when forced to relinquish the lease in 1775.

The s front of the house achieved its present appearance when it was reconstructed for John Leslie. According to G.M. Fraser, his architect was the Roman Catholic *James Massie*, †1816: Massie's designs were presumably executed by his former apprentice, *Archibald Simpson*, who had returned from London three years earlier. In the course of these works the central block's wall-head was raised to its present height by the mason *Alexander Wallace* of Cluny, and the drum towers – shorn of their caphouse and spirelet – were raised still higher. All were crowned with corbelled and crenellated parapets finely cut in grey granite by *William Robertson*. The first-floor windows were significantly enlarged by dropping their sills. At the rear, behind the stairwell, a two-storey wing was built containing a ground-floor kitchen and first-floor dining room, with a bow at its E end.

In about 1850 Charles Leslie appears to have commissioned *Thomas Mackenzie* to produce a scheme returning the house to something like its C17 appearance, and of this an unsigned sketch elevation survives. The two-storey L-plan wing hinged from the W end of the entrance front appears to have been a first instalment of this proposal, as it has characteristic Mackenzie details, but its lower floor is earlier, built by John Edward Leslie in 1841–4. The proposal was not pursued, a broad porch with a railed first-floor balcony being built instead as can be seen in Victorian photographs. The house was completely gutted by fire in 1919.

As replanned by Patrick Leslie in the 1690s the interior had a square entrance hall opening to a staircase, again square on plan and built out on the N at the rear. At first floor there was an enfilade of four principal apartments extending the full length of the entrance front, one in the w wing, two in the central block and one in the hall of the original tower house. These interiors appear to have been remodelled in the 1815–20 works, the cantilevered main stair dating from that time. The remains were first surveyed by Harry Gordon Slade in the late 1960s. His findings were revised by Dr Penelope Dransart, Dr Nicholas Bogdan and others, who re-examined the entire site – including the medieval palace – from 1995, the preceding account being a synthesis of their findings.

HOME FARM STEADING, 330 m. N. Probably by *Archibald Simpson*, 1841. One of the most impressive buildings of its type and date in Aberdeenshire. Large harled Neo-Jacobean quadrangle which included the stables, its w range domestic with a square doocot tower at its sw angle.

ST JOHN THE EVANGELIST (R.C.), 0.75 km. NNW. By *George Goldie*, 1859, for the Leslies of Fetternear, whose heraldic crest is incorporated within its walls. Mid-Pointed. Liturgical w gable front in coursed dark granite with red dressings, massively buttressed to suggest a nave and aisles; central gabled entrance porch, its pointed opening with a hoodmould, tall three-light window with cinquefoil roundel tracery in an arched recess, and gableted bellcote with wrought-iron crucifix. Four-bay N flank with two-light windows; three windows on the s; at the fourth bay an L-plan PRESBYTERY hinged on the liturgical SE corner with a shouldered doorway and windows and a pointed-arch porch in the re-entrant angle; one window mullioned and transomed. Chancel arch with granite shafts on corbels, open-roof scissor trusses with collars giving a polygonal profile.

FINZEAN

5090

BIRSE & FEUGHSIDE PARISH CHURCH. Built *c.* 1863 as a mission church in Birse parish, paid for by Francis Farquharson, Laird of Finzean. Simple Gothic, five-bay, in pale golden harl with ashlar margins. Gabled porch centred in s flank with hoodmoulded doorway. Two lancets in w gable, monogrammed with Farquharson initials and the date in metal. Gableted bellcote. Transverse vestry at E end by *George Bennett Mitchell* 1933–4; stepped triple lancets in its s gable. The church porch is echoed in an archway formed in 2010 between the church's E end and Mitchell's vestry. – First World War MEMORIAL TABLET in polished grey granite designed by *William Kelly* and cut by *Sir James Taggart*; Second World War tablet designed to match.

TILLYFRUSKIE, 2 km. E. A very early survivor of a small laird's house, built for David Ochterlouny in 1733. Harled vernacular entrance front facing E, two-storeyed, three bays very broadly spaced, central transom-lit doorway and relatively small windows in dressed surrounds. Gabled roof with moulded skewputts carved with Ochterlouny's initials and date; coped chimneystacks. Inside, the ground-floor plaster detailing may be C18. The house stands within a high-walled court with a single-storey wing on its s side, also 1733. Courtyard walls (themselves rare survivors) on E and N, original ball-finialled gatepiers on N side.

EASTER CLUNE, 1.3 km. SSE. Dated 1719. Built for Alastair Irvine, who purchased this small estate six years earlier, a very rare survivor of a house-type which must once have been more common. Two storeys, three bays very broadly spaced. Boulder foundations, rubble construction with sandstone dressings now concealed under brown harl. Central doorway, marriage stone A.I.♡M.S. Windows relatively narrow, those on first floor with gableted dormerheads. Stone roof ridge and coped end stacks. Extended to l. by *Peter Young* 1988, with single-storey entrance bay linking to a much taller block at right angles, designed to match. Nearby, a fragment of the C16–C17 tower house reputedly built as an episcopal seat in association with a church and burial ground.

SAWMILL AND TURNING MILL, 1.3 km. SW at Percie. Earlier C19, built to process timber from Glen Ferrick pine woods. A very rare survivor, its machinery still in working order. Standing on the Feugh Water, most of its structures are timber on granite rubble bases, with corrugated-iron roofs. From w to E, the SAWMILL, a single-storey rectangle approached by a timber walkway and with a cast-iron-framed start-and-awe wheel 4.9 m. in diameter at the rear. GENERATOR HOUSE with its own wheel powers the TURNING MILL, a two-storey rect-angle built into sloping ground with a 3 m. wheel and smaller buildings at right angles forming an L-plan. At the E end, the KILN, square, rubble-built with dressings, pyramid roof, cast-iron firebox within an outshot; brick CHIMNEYSTACK nearby and timber-framed SMIDDY adjoining. Nearest the Feugh, three LADES, all rebuilt: one in concrete powering the sawmill, and two in timber, stacked vertically, the upper for the genera-tor and the lower discharging into the tail race of the others, their combined fall driving the turning mill. The small timber building with slated pyramid roof nearest the road was for-merly a BUS GARAGE, surprisingly small, and supported under-neath by wooden stilts. On the far side of the road, the MILLER'S COTTAGE, single-storeyed, three bays with a gab-leted porch and attic dormers, together with ancillary buildings.

MILL OF CLINTER, 0.9 km. SE. L-plan, originally single-storeyed, built 1819; low second storey added 1886. Predom-inantly coursed granite rubble, but ashlar-built on the s, the low-breast eight-spoke water wheel projecting from the jamb on this side. It is 3.6 m. in diameter, with timber paddles. A much smaller six-spoke wheel is later, used for wood-turning.

Ventilator stump on roof.* Inside, complete machinery of 1886 survives.

BUCKET MILL, 3 km. WSW, beside the Water of Feugh. An exceptionally rare C19 survivor of a once-common rural industrial building, probably built *c.* 1830 by *Alexander Duncan*, millwright, for production of timber buckets and tubs; the machinery was reconstructed by *Peter Brown* immediately after he took over in 1853 and is still in working order. The MAIN BUILDING is an L-plan single storey and attic, predominantly timber-boarded but rising from a granite base, with corrugated iron roofs; granite chimneystack rising from far end of longer range. Lean-to sawmill standing against long range within the angle. Against the rear elevation, a double-framed cast-iron start-and-awe wheel, 4.1 m. in diameter, powered by a timber lade. Close by the KILN, small, rubble-built with timber-boarded gables, corrugated-iron roof, brick chimneystack; entrance door approached by ramp, cast-iron firebox beneath. STABLE AND CARTSHED again timber-framed with corrugated-iron roof. MILLER'S COTTAGE on opposite side of the road.

GRAIN KILN, Haughend, 2.3 km. SW. Late C18, restored in 1986 by *Robert Callander*, Master Dyker and Drystane Dyker to H.M. The Queen. Circular, in pink granite rubble with battered sides, and built into sloping ground, a ramp of granite and earth allowing it to be loaded from the top. Originally one of two such kilns associated with a small crofting settlement which survived until *c.* 1830.

FORDOUN

Small village that developed around the toll road in the mid C18, and not to be confused with the ancient kirkton (*see* Auchenblae, q.v.).

REDHALL HOUSE, 1.3 km. NW. Harled main block of two storeys and three bays, built *c.* 1764. Original window margins on the first floor topped by cornice and blocking course. Canted bay windows and porch added in the late C19. Very fine wing to the l., built *c.* 1830 with a full-height, three-bay bow window facing S. – Single-storey LODGE at the end of the drive, again *c.* 1830. Wide bow on the l. flank with semi-conical roof. Bad pebbledash.

PITTARROW, 2.5 km. WSW. Once the site of a fine tower house, probably built in the C16 and dem. in 1802. The great hall contained a late C15 or early C16 painting cycle of the Pope leading a procession into Old St Peter's, Rome. – On the rear of the farmhouse, a re-set DORMERHEAD dated 159[-] with

---

*Its pig weathervane, a reminder of the pig which the millers once paid the landowners in part-rental, is preserved on site.

the initials I.D. (for the Douglas family) and 'ISCH' (for the Wishart family, who acquired the land in the mid C13). – On the SW gable of the Mains, a head CORBEL, C15 or C16.

FORGUE

AUCHABER PARISH CHURCH, 4.4 km. SSE. Originally a Free Church, by *James Henderson* 1843–4. Simple T-plan. Broad N gable front with tall roof rising to a ball-finialled bellcote. Round-arched doorway with windows slightly stepped up on each side, central Serlian window above, harled walls with slim margins. Three-bay E aisle slightly lower with square-shafted chimneystacks. A minister's room was added at the rear *c.* 1869; in 1908 the aisle was divided off to become a hall and the interior recast. Inside, a very wide single-span space, the roof trusses braced with tension rods. At the S end, the Gothic PLATFORM PULPIT is probably 1908, dark-stained with a canted front and twin approach stairs; behind it the arched recess of the original pulpit, framed by slim fluted colonnettes rising into unusual foliate capitals. – COMMUNION TABLE in stripped pine, remodelled *c.* 1920. – Oak FONT mid-C19 – PEWS probably 1908. – STAINED GLASS. S gable, with emblems of the Free and United Presbyterian Churches commemorating their union in 1900, the roundel above with a dove. By *Comper*, 1901.

Former MANSE, *J. & W. Smith*, 1847–9. Simple two-storey three-bay house, still Late Georgian in character, cream-harled with railed stair to central doorway; dormers look original.

OLD PARISH CHURCH. By *Archibald Simpson* 1818–19, closely similar to his Kintore Parish Church (q.v.). Entrance W front with centre boldly stepped forward to suggest tall slim nave with flanking aisles. Splayed pointed doorway and stepped triple lancets with Y-tracery rising to pedimental gable and gableted bellcote with pyramid spirelet. S flank with three large Neo-Perp windows, alternating with four roundels at the level of their arches. E gable with two Neo-Perp windows. N elevation blind, with a single door originally for the minister. Built of squared grey rubble with granite dressings throughout; timber tracery with zinc diamond-pane glazing. A simple rectangular interior, with some of the original painted decoration of 1819 still surviving, including the Greek Revival ceiling and, just faintly visible, stencilled acanthus-patterned borders around the walls. Rearranged in 1872 and 1926. W gallery with panelled arcaded front is of the later date but its clock is 1870 and the cast-iron columns and panelling have been reused from the original U-plan gallery. The octagonal PULPIT, altered and repositioned from the N wall to the E gable, is also arcaded; the PEWS were altered in 1872 and rearranged 1926. – ORGAN, also of 1872, and reportedly the first in an Aberdeenshire kirk since the Reformation, is an early example of the work of *Peter Conacher* – a tripartite Gothic case with decorated pipes. Detached single-storey SESSION HOUSE *c.* 1859, extended by *Duncan & Monro* 1911.

GRAVEYARD. No trace of the earlier ST MARGARET'S CHURCH is now evident, but its T-plan foundations are shown on the 1st Ordnance Survey *c.* 1870. The Morison of Bognie BURIAL ENCLOSURE contains two wall monuments formerly in the old church. Particularly fine is that to Prof. Alexander Garden with arms and inscription framed between Corinthianesque half-columns with garlanded shafts, a gablet top carved with Scottish thistle, angels, skull and sandglass: it dates from 1674.

Former PARISH MANSE. Mid-C18, enlarged 1830. Entrance front symmetrical, two-storeyed, its centre doorway framed between taller and broader gable-ends. The N gable is the original C18 manse, cream-harled with ashlar dressings. (Cf. Cuminestown Manse (N), also enlarged 1830 in exactly the same way.)

ST MARGARET (Episcopal), 0.5 km. S of Forgue. Designed by *William Ramage*, built by *John Thomson*, mason, 1856–8. A classic E.E. Tractarian church. Five-bay nave with SW porch, slightly lower and narrower two-bay chancel, all buttressed with hoodmoulded lancets and roofs steeply pitched; on the chancel's N side, a square-based three-stage tower with louvred belfry openings and broached stone spire 33 m. high; on its S side a lean-to sacristy over the basement heating chamber; all built in brown and grey pinned rubble with Auchindoir dressings. The spire lucarnes were added by *James Duncan* of Turriff in 1886 to accommodate the clock, its two copper dials painted black with gilt hands and numerals. – Oak REREDOS containing figures of Our Lord and the Evangelists, 1896. – EAGLE LECTERN, again in oak, by *Jones & Willis*, 1889. – ORGAN. By *Merklin, Schütze & Co.*, 1857. – STAINED GLASS. Nave W lancets; SS Luke and John, by *James Ballantine & Son*, 1874. – Two-light N windows by *Wailes & Co.* of Newcastle, the Parable of the Talents, and Our Lord's charge to St Peter and Blessing the little children, 'recently erected' in 1873. – In the S wall another two-light, the Nativity and Resurrection, designed by the *Ven. Maurice Fenwick-Bisset*, 1872. Also in the S wall, Our Lord as Good Shepherd, by *Ballantine & Son*, 1875; another Good Shepherd by *John Hardman & Co.*, 1891; and St Margaret of Scotland, by *Ballantine & Gardiner*, 1899. – In the chancel's E gable, the stepped triple lancets represent, centre, the Passion and Crucifixion, with scenes from the life of St Margaret in the sidelights, by *Wailes & Co.*, 1877. – Chancel N, the Supper at Emmaus, and S, the Risen Lord appearing to St Thomas, both by *Bucknall & Comper*, 1901; two further chancel windows dedicated 1902, and the Risen Lord by *Norman Macdougall* of Glasgow, 1907.

SCOTT'S HALL, 0.4 km. SE of the Old Parish Church. By *A. Marshall Mackenzie* 1885, financed by Walter Scott, tenant of Boynsmill House and Glendronach Distillery (*see* below). Scots Renaissance, a small version of the Great Halls at Edinburgh and Stirling Castles.

GLENDRONACH DISTILLERY, 1.8 km. SE in the Forgue valley. Founded 1825–6. The Dronagh Burn is channelled through the centre of the site and once supplied the distillery with power. On the N side, the three-storey COURTYARD BUILDING in random rubble contains the maltings, mash house, tun room and kiln, which has been increased in height with a pagoda roof at the NE corner. On the S side, a STILL ROOM of 1966–7, two-storeyed with four big copper stills clearly visible through a large first-floor picture window, and the chimney rising up behind; nearby a STABLE BLOCK with gabled centre and flanking wings, arcaded across its length, part-ashlar, part-rubble, now the visitor centre and restaurant. In the late C19 the site was taken over by the Glendronach Distillery Co., which engaged in substantial rebuilding including new BONDED WAREHOUSES designed by *C. C. Doig*. The distillery manager's residence, DRONAGH HOUSE, is early C19, two storeys, three windows wide, built in rubble.

BOYNSMILL HOUSE, immediately next to the distillery, was built for James Allardyce, one of the founders, *c.* 1835. Picturesque Neo-Jacobean. Single-storey-and-attic L-plan, with tall hoodmoulded ground-floor windows and gableted dormers, all with lying-pane glazing, and diagonally shafted chimneystacks. E wing with entrance porch is an earlier house built for William Allardyce 1771, remodelled when the N wing was added, but still bearing a datestone with its first occupant's initials. All built in squared rubble, the N wing with red sandstone dressings. Encloses a pleasant small forecourt with trees and shrubs, and to the rear a fine formal garden separating the house from the distillery.

CONZIE CASTLE, 1.6 km. W. A ruinous shell but a landmark on the plain. The house was built for Viscount Frendraught, perhaps to replace an earlier fortified residence, but reputedly left unfinished on his death in 1698. Principal (S) elevation tall and symmetrical, three-storeyed, four windows wide, originally with a steep roof drained by water cannon and a dormered attic of which only sills remain. E gable rises into a chimneystack, fireplace openings still evident internally, and at first floor a small aumbry; fragments of W gable and rear elevation, all in pinned rubble, dressed stones long since removed. Small-windowed and single-pile plan, seemingly with a N corridor; modest ceiling heights. If completed, in its time a distinguished and comfortable house.

COBAIRDY HOUSE, 3.8 km. WSW. Georgian Italianate Survival by *A. & W. Reid*, built for Robert Simpson *c.* 1855–60. Entrance E front two storeys and seven bays, near-symmetrical with gabled entrance bay boldly stepped forward, very tall ground-floor and smaller first-floor windows, cream-harled with ashlar dressings, slim margins, piended roofs and tall chimneystacks. Principal apartments on six-bay S front with central single-storey bow; N front lower two-storeyed and single-storeyed; rear elevation plain. Simple dignified interiors, some doorcases with sopraporta panels. Closely similar to Knockleith House near Auchterless (N).

DRUMBLAIR HOUSE, 2.9 km. SE. Begun C18, early C19 addition, remodelled in castellated style 1877. Long two-storey front with original three-bay house on r., two-bay addition on l. and a crenellated square tower in the re-entrant angle between them; slim circular angle towers with slated spirelets at each far end. White-harled, granite margins. Interior mostly 1877. Circular DOOCOT.

DRUMBLAIR COTTAGE to the S is three storeys, three windows wide, with gabled roof, built c. 1780. Remodelled c. 1845 with single-storey bow-fronted flanking wings linked together across the main block by an entrance hall corridor.

HADDO HOUSE, 1.5 km. NE. The tragic ruin of an Italianate country house formed c. 1840 by deft additions to a vernacular classical house of the early–mid C18. The style suggests either *Archibald Simpson* or *John Smith* as architect. Entrance front to W. The original house is in the centre, three storeys and three bays, rubble-built. The S addition of similar height, but only two storeys, provided a new principal apartment suite. Handsome projecting entrance tower with round-headed arches rising into an upper stage with triplets of small round-arched windows and a low pyramidal roof. At the N end the service court is also two-storeyed, with twin gables curving concavely into stepped ashlar chimneystacks. Although the house thus comprises three parts they come together as a surprisingly unified whole. The entrance tower opens into a fine hall-corridor with pilasters and niches for sculpture; this in turn opens into the large dining room projecting on the S and the drawing room on the E side with a big three-window bow facing the gardens. Interior derelict and dangerous but within the dining room the Neoclassical décor survives: painted panels with sphinxes and an elaborate gilt ceiling rose; the doorcases have *trompe l'œil* cornices, the doors themselves ten-panelled. The central core is completely gutted. Only simple fireplaces and the foot of a spiral stair remain.

FRENDRAUGHT HOUSE   6040

3.5 km. SSE of Forgue

Frendraught House has its origins in a hall house reconstructed   57
in 1656 and recast in the early–mid C18, probably 1753. Vernacular classical entrance (S) elevation, long two-storeyed, seven windows wide, with the central three bays slightly projected beneath a very large hemicycle pediment; tall roof inset with small attic dormers. Railed basement area. Crowstepped porch incorporates 1688 datestone but is actually an addition

of 1841–2. Square tower at E end, formed at same date by heightening the S end of the house's late C18 E wing; it has a low battlemented parapet and pepperpot angle turrets. Except for this tower, the fenestration is regular; the round-headed windows in the attic pediment and the porch's flanks have basket-weave tracery. Harled in cream with ashlar dressings, chimneystacks rising from the pediment, and end gables simply coped. The W gable has a moulded set-off at ground floor and is crowstepped: two of its windows, small and simply chamfered, are seemingly C14.

The entrance front, a late C18 NE wing, the two-storey three-window block dated 1753 to the N of it, and the low N range form a three-sided court, enclosed on the W by a wall with square gatepiers at the entrance. The 1753 block was formerly a W addition to the lost tower house and may be older, its datestone being re-set; on its W elevation are voussoirs of a blocked archway. Mid-C18 interior, altered 1841–2. Dining room in E wing c. 1790.

GARLOGIE

A village extending on one side only along a straight stretch of the B9119.

A short distance W stand the remains of a spinning and weaving complex first recorded in the C16 and operated in the earlier C19 by Hadden & Sons of Aberdeen. It employed 120 workers. The VILLAGE HALL & MUSEUM OF POWER is a tall single-storey block with piended roof and lower wings extending back along each flank: formerly the boiler and engine house of a complex of two-to-three-storey mill and factory buildings, originally powered from Loch Skene and occasionally supplemented by a beam engine which still survives. The mill closed in 1904, hydro-electric generating equipment was installed for Dunecht Estate (q.v.) in 1923, and after the two large mills were demolished the engine house was restyled with a Diocletian window and converted to hall use by the factor *David Morris* in 1931. The BEAM ENGINE in a rear outshot is reputedly the only Scottish example still *in situ* – a rotative beam engine installed during the late 1830s, perhaps by *Mitchell & Neilson* of Glasgow, whose engines had similar characteristics. Supported by a cast-iron Doric column, the beam is 4.95 m. in length, with double-acting cylinder, separate condenser and air pump. In the adjoining room, ELECTRICAL EQUIPMENT driven by Loch Skene includes a 90 kW water turbine constructed by the Swiss firm *Escher Wyss & Cie* in 1923 and a 60 kW *English Electric* generator providing power to the whole Dunecht Estate.

GARTLY

A small village founded by the Duke of Gordon on the Old
Military Road near its junction with the A97.

PARISH CHURCH, 2.8 km. N. Disused. Built for the Rev.
   Alexander Anderson to designs by *Andrew Thomson* of Fife-
   Keith (Moray), 1879–81. Big simple Gothic, rectangular plan,
   whinstone with pale granite dressings. Entrance E gable has
   double-splayed pointed-arch doorway flanked by vestibule
   lights; gallery roundel with trefoil glazing and small lancet
   immediately beneath its robustly detailed bellcote (dated) with
   wrought-iron finial. Five-bay flanks with timber Y-tracery,
   steeply pitched roof. W gable has similar roundel and lancet,
   the session house built against it approached by a railed
   forestair from the falling ground. Its gablet is crowned by a
   fine Renaissance bellcote from the previous church, its openings framed by colonnettes and rising into three tiers of pinnacles, dated 1515 but almost wholly of 1621 when the church
   was rebuilt.*
DESCRIPTION. Gartly's development began when the Great
   North of Scotland Railway opened a STATION on the
   Aberdeen–Inverness line in 1854. Its associated WAREHOUSE
   stands 40 m. S, and on the High Street's N side is the former
   STATION HOTEL, originally a single-storey rubble-built
   cottage, raised to two storeys in coursed masonry *c.* 1880 but
   still very plain. At the village's W end the cast-iron BEAM
   BRIDGE with solid side panels is an outstanding example of a
   type common in North-East Scotland. Constructed by *James
   Abernethy & Co.* of Aberdeen and dated 1884, it spans some
   12 m. between granite abutments across the Bogie Burn.
Former PARISH MANSE, 0.3 km. NNW of the church. Built 1821,
   perhaps based on plans of 1802. Entrance (S) front two-
   storeyed, three windows wide over a railed basement, with
   flyover stair to the doorway. Coursed squared whinstone,
   pinned and cherry-cocked, with pale granite ashlar dressings,
   original woodwork and piended roof with end stacks. Tall
   piended stair-bay at rear, single-storey wing with attic and
   basement added *c.* 1830. OFFICES (40 m. NE), perhaps 1757–8.
   Very neat single storey on open courtyard plan, rubble-built,
   with segmentally arched cartshed openings.
CULDRAIN HOUSE, 1.5 km. N. An asymmetrical Tudor cottage
   built for Maj.-Gen. John Gordon in 1846–7, probably by *John
   Smith* on the basis of its resemblance to Easter Skene (Kirkton
   of Skene, q.v.). It was very neatly raised in height during the
   later C19, probably by John's son *William Smith*, without any
   detrimental effect on its picturesque profile. Entrance front
   originally single-storeyed with gabled central porch, the

---

*Its bell (now removed) is by *John Mowat*, 1758.

broad l. bay more modestly advanced but rising into a much bigger gable with a canted bay at its ground floor. Services sunk in the basement; clusters of tall diagonally shafted chimneystacks rising from behind the roof ridge. The original design was to have been more ambitious, with drum towers. The later C19 alterations increased the wall-heads slightly to provide accommodation at attic level: thus the l. gable bay rises taller than it did originally, while the r. bay has two gablet dormerheads, all very much in the Smiths' style; the chimneystacks still feature prominently. Simple fine detailing, round-arched doorway with elegant transom-light, and the bay window with timber mullions and transoms, original glazing throughout; a well-finished house inside. Restored by *Marion Coats Donald* (of *John & Marion Donald*) in 1981. Former STABLES AND COACHHOUSE (50 m. N) are also 1847, L-plan single-storeyed, rubble-built with broad-eaved roofs, now converted to domestic use.

COYNACHIE MILL, 3.7 km. NW. Mid-C19. Rubble T-plan, built into falling ground. Main block tall two-storeyed with loft rising into piended roof. Smaller two-storey side wing, also piend-roofed, with cast-iron overshot wheel (4.5 m. diameter) in the junction between them. When not in use, a trap diverted the water into a flume above the wheel, whence it discharged directly into the tail race. A rope drive once powered a threshing and sawmill at a higher level.

GARVOCK

Small collection of buildings near a hilltop overlooking the Howe of the Mearns.

Former GARVOCK PARISH CHURCH. On the site of a church founded *c.* 1282 by Sir Hugh le Blond (first of the Arbuthnotts) and once a dependency of Arbroath Abbey (Dundee and Angus). The present building is a simple rubble rectangle built 1777–8. Closed in 2003. Birdcage bellcote on the W gable with two tiers of Renaissance-moulded balusters and ball finial on top. Pair of lancets on the S flank subdivided by Y-tracery; low porch in between them with Tudor-headed entrance, *c.* 1830. It replaced the original door on the E gable. Plain interior as renovated by *George Gregory* of Stonehaven, 1912. – Above the ceiling, a re-set MONUMENT to Robert Keith †1666 and other C17 FRAGMENTS, originally on the E gable of the previous church.

Near the porch, a LEDGER SLAB for Richard Lason †1723, decorated with a heart and a primitive, oversized winged soul. – S of it, a fine SLAB for William Greig †1643, featuring robust capital letters and a panoply of his blacksmith's tools.

Former MANSE (now Collardo House) to the SE, a white L-plan by *William Henderson*, 1865–6 with several later additions. The U-plan former offices date from *c.* 1788 and incorporate a tombstone of 1603.

TOWER OF JOHNSTON, 2.2 km. SW, Hill of Garvock. Architectural folly built *c.* 1812 over a Bronze Age cairn, by James Farquhar of Johnston Lodge (q.v.). Circular tower, *c.* 9.1 m. high, its buttresses pierced with open lancets. Corbelled parapet.

GLASS

4030

Former PARISH CHURCH (ST ANDREW). Begun as a simple rectangular plan in 1791. Renovated by *Alexander Reid* (of *A. & W. Reid*) in 1883–5, who added the E porch and vestry, then enlarged in 1903 to form a T-plan with the addition of a N aisle by *John Robertson* of Inverness for Alexander Geddes of Blairmore (*see* below). The aisle windows are all slightly pointed in moulded surrounds, with three stepped lancets in the broad N gable. Entrance is by a lean-to porch in the W angle with a round-arched doorway approached by a railed forestair. Robertson also gave the four original arched windows in the S flank their stone tracery (two cusp-headed lights) and blocked the W door, replacing it with a single long window. The finialled birdcage bellcote with small pediments appears C17, reused from the previous church.

The interior was completely remodelled by Robertson with timber arches supporting flat panelled ceilings. The pulpit in the centre of the S wall faces the majority of the congregation in the N aisle through a triple-arched screen on clustered shafts. The PULPIT is tall, its back panelled with colonnettes supporting a richly decorated Gothic arch and a still more elaborate ogee-domed sounding-board with crockets and finials rising into a cross. – FONT. Like a marble champagne flute but with a pale wooden cover with combined cross and dove for a handle, it commemorates Alexander Geddes's wife, Frances (†1933), but the designer is unknown. – PEWS simple, but with zither-type ends. – ORGAN. Given by *Sir Frederick Bridge* of Cairnbarrow, composer and organist at Westminster Abbey, in memory of his wife. It was built to his own specifications by *Alfred Kirkland* of London, 1906. Superb fretwork. – The church's greatest glory is its six brilliantly composed and coloured STAINED GLASS windows by *Douglas Strachan*. In the S wall, two early examples of his work erected in memory of Alexander Geddes in 1904, their cost met by friends in Chicago – to the W, the Nativity; E, the Ascension. In the E gable, the Flight into Egypt, 1912, rather different in character. In the aisle's N gable, Faith, Hope and Charity on earth and in

heaven, dedicated in 1915. – l., the C8 St Wallach baptizing a
brave yet contemplative Pictish chieftain in the Deveron; r., St
Andrew as fisher of men; in the centre Our Lord blessing little
children. – WALL MONUMENTS. To John and Alexander
Geddes, both killed 1915, a finely lettered bronze tablet with
crests of their regiments (the Canadian Scottish 79th and the
Royal Scottish Fusiliers), set in a pale stone carved frame with
maple leaves and thistles, and with the Geddes coat of arms
above, designed by *Robert S. Lorimer*, 1916. Another wall
plaque to Sir Frederick Bridge (†1924), a carved and gilt oak
panel with vine surround and symbols of the Evangelists,
designed by *William Kelly*.

Former PARISH MANSE. By *Thomas Mackenzie*, 1843. Two-
storey double-pile L-plan. Asymmetrical Tudor entrance front
with previous manse of *c.* 1772–4 remodelled as wing on r.

GLASS SCHOOL AND SCHOOL HOUSE, 1 km. W. By *Thomas
Mackenzie*, 1844. Tall single storey with gables. Additions by
Morrison of Glass, 1889.

BLAIRMORE LODGE, 0.25 km. SE. By *A. Marshall Mackenzie* (of
Matthews & Mackenzie), 1884–5, for Alexander Geddes, who
was born in Glass parish but made his fortune as 'the Chicago
Grain King' and bought Blairmore in 1876. Exceptionally
robust, blocky Tudor in dark rock-faced granite, dressings in
pale Kemnay granite ashlar for contrast, originally with crenellated parapets and now with a late 1960s mansard. Massive
two-storey four-bay (entrance front) with rounded angles corbelled to the square at first floor. Big ground-floor porch with
canted angles and bold crenellation, its four-centred doorway
in one flank approached by a side stair with solid parapets.
Tall mullioned-and-transomed windows, heavy square turret
slightly corbelled out at first floor on the l. side; thrusting water
cannon across the wall-head parapet. Large two-storey-and-
basement wing rising from lower ground at rear, similar design
but with conventional gabled roofs and big chimneystack;
additions and alterations mid–later C20.

OLD MANSE INN FARM, 0.5 km. N. Latest C17 or early C18. An
exceptionally rare, perhaps unique survival of a house of this
modest size and date in North-East Scotland. Entrance front
facing S, single storey and attic, five bays broadly spaced with
alternating windows and doorways, rubble-built and harled in
sandy-gold; slated roof (formerly thatched?) with stone ridges
and simple chimneystacks. Seemingly built in two phases, the
three W bays original and two E bays only slightly later as all
the ground-floor windows have roll-moulded surrounds. The
end gables are roughly crowstepped but the internal gable has
straight skews above the slating. The attic-floor openings have
been raised into timber dormers. Near-blind on rear side.

MILL OF INVERMARKIE, 1 km. SW on the Deveron. Earlier C18
corn mill, heightened in the late C18–early C19, and altered
during residential conversion in 2002. Rubble-built L-plan
with single-storey-and-attic main block and rather taller piend-
roofed wing which contained the drying kiln, still identified by

its roof-top ventilator. Eight-spoke cast-iron overshot wheel, 3.8 m. diameter.

BELDORNEY CASTLE. *See* p. 371.

GLASSEL HOUSE*

6090

5.5 km. NW of Banchory

Splendidly isolated in its own extensive woodlands and cattle pastures at the S foot of the Hill of Fare. The house wears an Edwardian aspect but its still-visible core is the mid-C18 five-bay, two-storey laird's house erected for the Baxters, a merchant family of Aberdeen who traded in Russia. Walls of dark grey field boulders. The Michells (of Forcett Hall, Yorkshire) inherited the house and estate in 1823 but neglected it until the late C19. They then first added a service wing to the N, with a crowstep gable (dem. 1960) before building the flush-fitting wings in lighter granite ashlar, which form the asymmetrical garden front of nine bays. The E wing of 1902 is in a half-hearted Neo-Romanesque style (by *Jenkins & Marr*) with projecting entrance tower with roll-moulded monumental E doorway. This superseded the C18 S door which, along with the two windows immediately to its l., has been transformed into a floor-length window. The W wing when it was built in 1912 was a return to the Baronial by *George Bennett Mitchell*, but after Arthur H. Wood, chairman of B.S.A. and the leading fly-fisherman of his era, purchased Glassel in 1915 he had *Mitchell* strip it of its Scots motifs, leaving it blandly suburban in the Aberdeen villa mode. The best room is the part-panelled C19 LIBRARY that takes up the S half of the Georgian block's ground floor.

The ROCK GARDEN, which Wood's mistress *Nancy Robinson* designed, is the estate's most celebrated component: a naturally occurring rock field taking up much of the area between the house and bridge, falling dramatically 30 m. vertically in 75 m. and piped for artificial streams (fed from a *c.* 1920 PUMP HOUSE, designed by *Mitchell*). The couple were devoted scientifically and financially to curing Isle of Wight bee disease, and had Mitchell design a bee house, immediately W of and longer than the actual house, with monumental doorways, sundials and Latin inscriptions (mostly dem. 1960). The flowering alpine plants in the garden were intended in part to provide a varied food supply for the bees. An innovative BEE WELL has recessed pointing along which a continuous but strictly limited supply of water flows, and from which bees can drink. The rock garden and bee well, including their hydraulics, were completely restored in the early C21 by *Mike Flatters* for Moir

*This entry is by Daniel MacCannell.

Lockhead and Audrey Lockhead. The bridge was restored at about the same time by Flatters and *Alistair Urquhart*.

GLENBERVIE *see* KIRKTON OF GLENBERVIE

GLENFARQUHAR LODGE   K
2.9 km. NNW of Auchenblae

Chalet-style mega-villa by *George Bennett Mitchell*, 1898–9. It was built for Sir Sydney Gammell, who had admired a similar ski lodge in Bavaria. Gammell inherited Drumtochty (q.v.) in 1899 and after 1905 Glenfarquhar was let out and used almost exclusively for grouse shooting. Ground floor built of granite; first floor slightly jettied out above it, of concrete criss-crossed with timber framing. Everything but the wooden beams is harled, so there is a nice swatch of white overlaid with a grid of painted red. Spiky profile of gables along the top. L-plan S front with a full-height rectangular bay window on the l. side; rectangular oriel to the r., breaking through the attic with mullioned-and-transomed glazing. Veranda wrapped around to the E flank.

Small STEADING to the NE, also 1899 by Mitchell. Little cupola with concave pyramidal roof. – Former GARAGE next to it, *c.* 1905, necessary as Gammell purchased one of the very first cars produced by Rolls-Royce.

GLENGAIRN

A straggling community which begins at the confluence of the Gairn with the Dee and continues with few isolated buildings up a long wild valley.

GLENGAIRN OLD PARISH CHURCH, Bridge of Gairn, at the junction of the Rivers Gairn and Dee. Ruins on a medieval site, a rectangular box with ivy-covered footings and some plain granite rubble walling. Disused by 1800, after the new church was built in Ballater (q.v.). – FONT. Medieval. Simple dressed circular stone, with shallow bowl.

GLENGAIRN PARISH CHURCH, 6.5 km. NW of Bridge of Gairn between the N bank of the Gairn and the A939. Opened 1804. Simple box plan, triple lancets below ball-finialled bellcote on W gable. Two-bay nave with classical round-topped windows; shouldered heads to arches in E porch. Plain white plastered interior.

DALPHUIL, 0.25 km. SSW of the Parish Church by the Gairn. Early C18. Known as the 'Teapot House' because of its cosy proportions, it has a square plan and two storeys under a generous piended roof. Although it is made with barely dressed stone, the disposition of its windows around a spacious stone porch produces a building of classical charm. Two coped chimneystacks peak up like ears at the rear. Formerly used as a manse and school, now a hunting lodge.

GAIRNSHIEL BRIDGE, 0.5 km. SW of the Parish Church. Built *c.* 1749 on the section of Military Road from Blairgowrie to Fort George completed by *William Caulfeild*. Elegant, sweeping rubble bridge across the Gairn with high arch and solid parapets, set in dramatic landscape.

RINETON, 3 km. WSW of the Parish Church. Early–mid-C18, built for the Macdonalds of Rineton. The main two-storey harled house looks unassuming but its small irregular windows and gabled stacks with thack stanes indicate an early thatched building. In the lower E wing is a traditional open hearth with swey. The substantial steep-roofed outhouse may have been a detached kitchen, with majestic hearth, massive granite jambs and lintel.

GLENGARDEN, 0.4 km. NW of Bridge of Gairn. 1902 by *Rudolph Christen*, a Swiss artist, for himself. Tudor-style villa with granite base and half-timbered first floor, under low-pitch chalet eaves. Good interior fittings of wood panelling, carved architraves, brass door furniture. Artisan stained glass panels in door and upper corridor ceiling. Double-height dining room with open timber roof and gallery. Carved wood and marble fireplaces.

MOINE-NA-VEY, 1.25 km. W of Bridge of Gairn. Built in 1922, with alterations and additions by *Jenkins & Marr* in 1930. The house has an unusual three-pointed star plan, with complex bell-canted roof-lines over white harled ground floor. The plan allows the service and ancillary rooms to cluster around the front door on the N side, leaving all the main rooms to survey the splendid views to E, S and W. The wings are punctuated by tall stacks and eyelid dormers. Art Deco interior with geometric balustrades on the staircase and original bathroom fittings.

ABERGAIRN CASTLE, 0.7 km. NE of Bridge of Gairn. A small ruined hunting lodge built in 1614 with a round tower in the NW corner. The interior is barely 3 m. by 3 m. Only the lower courses survive.

GLENKINDIE

4010

A small village, mostly C20, straggling along the A97 near the banks of the Don.

GLENKINDIE ARMS HOTEL, 0.7 km. E. Built as St Andrew's Masonic Lodge 1820–1, but probably always intended to serve as an inn, and certainly used as such before 1840. Surprisingly old-fashioned appearance, looks early–mid-C18. Two-storeyed, five bays very broadly spaced. Central doorway and architrave-framed square field-panel at first floor above. Harled, with ashlar dressings and margins, deep plan with gabled roof and end stacks. STABLES opposite by *Walker & Duncan*, 1883.

PEEL OF FICHLIE ('BURGESS' MOUND'), 2.6 km. E between Glaschul Hill and the Don. Possibly raised by Alan de Lundin (i.e. Durward) or his descendants after he was granted a large portion of Mar in 1228. In 1828 Alexander Laing recorded that the motte rose over 18 m. high to a summit 39 m. long N–S by 61 m. deep E–W; remains survived of a tower 'built of unhewn pebbles, and partly vitrified'. The motte was surrounded by a fosse partly natural and partly artificial, ranging from 3.5 m. broad on the E and S to 12.5 m. broad on the N, and between 2.5 m. and 10.5 m. deep. A triangular spur of ground to the E of the motte may have served as its bailey. The motte's size appears to have been curtailed since then, its summit now *c.* 39 m. square.

4010

GLENKINDIE HOUSE
1.3 km. WNW of Glenkindie

73   Large country house, part early–mid-C18 classical and part Scots Renaissance, which achieved its final form as the result of substantial remodelling and enlargement by *Sydney Mitchell & Wilson* for Capt. Alexander Henry Leith* in 1900.

The house takes the form of an h-plan with its long central block running E–W and three wings at the SE, SW and NW. It has two entrance courts: the original three-sided one of the C17–C18 on the S and the two-sided forecourt of 1900 facing N. The original S approach to the house now runs through formal gardens, a new driveway to the E being formed in 1900.

The two S WINGS which enclose the forecourt on that side are the oldest elements, and the circular drum towers at their SW and SE angles may be even older. They formed the forecourt of a tower house reputedly built by William Strachan in 1595 and destroyed in 1644, and then of an early country house built by Peter Strachan and Jane Forbes in 1711 and rebuilt *c.* 1785–7. Both wings are symmetrical, two storeys and three windows wide, built in coursed and cherry-cocked whinstone rubble. Their diminutive doorways and windows are framed by flat-arch voussoirs and long-and-short quoins in fine ashlar sandstone for contrast. Although they are a matching pair, the masonry of the SE wing looks older, as indeed it is. Its doorway is carved with the initials A.L. C.D. for Alexander Leith and

*Afterwards Lt-Col. the 5th Lord Burgh.

Christian Davidson, the date 1735 and the Leith family motto, 'Trusty to the end'; the initials reappear on one of the skewputts. The SW wing displays the Leith arms impaled with those of Garden for their son Alexander and his first wife, Jane Garden of Troup, and the date 1741, as well as initials A.L. C.S. for Alexander Leith and Christian Scott, dated 1785. Both the SE and SW wings have small catslide dormers in the roofs, their tall coped ashlar chimneystacks having clearly been renewed. The conical roofs of the drum towers had stone pineapple finials with Ionic volute bases until the later C20.

Sydney Mitchell & Wilson's CENTRAL BLOCK takes both its style and material from these wings but rises considerably higher and extends beyond them to the E and W. Its three-bay centre is broadly similar to the predecessor 1787 house – it may incorporate some of its masonry – but its r. bay rises a further storey into a two-windows-wide tower with a wall-head parapet, angle bartizan and caphouse, an evocation of the lost tower house of 1595. Drum towers echoing those of the fore-court on a grander scale link the new work to the old at the re-entrant angles. Both have the same ashlar crenellated para-pets as the tower, that on the W having a conical roof with a finial. The new work reuses details from the two older houses on the site, the door lintel of the previous house being re-set over the new. It bears initials A.L. M.E.G. for Alexander Leith and Mary Elizabeth Gordon and the date 1787. The E drum incorporates a triangular dormerhead lettered in random fashion with the name Velam Straquhem (William Strachan) and the date 1595 (M VC LXXXXV), which survived the demolition of the tower house. A shield-panel in the W drum represents a stag with the initials V.S. Sydney Mitchell & Wilson's work is altogether remarkably successful, both pictur-esque and formal in carefully crafted materials and enormously enhanced by the formal gardens, a skilful upgrading in 1900 of the original C17 and early C18 layout (*see* below).

Outwith the courtyard on the W FRONT, another Sydney Mitchell & Wilson drum tower links the 1787 wing to the far W end of the new central block, which has a broad bay window at ground floor; although on a smaller scale than the principal fronts, the W front is an elaborately stepped and richly varied composition, punctuated by the addition of a smaller stair-tower at the SW wing. The E FRONT is rather simpler with fewer Sydney Mitchell & Wilson additions, but has great charm, the formal topiary garden giving it a very atmospheric setting; here the central range has an octagonal angle oriel with a prismatic roof corbelled out at first floor, echoing those at Well Court (*see The Buildings of Scotland: Edinburgh*).

The N FRONT is entirely of 1900. This very grand court is far more consistent in its early C20 Scots Renaissance style, again drawing from previous Sydney Mitchell & Wilson projects. It is straightforwardly constructed of snecked rubble sandstone masonry in contrast to the whinstone on the S, the roof-line neatly concealing the changes of masonry on the flanks of the tower. The venerable atmosphere of the S and E fronts is completely absent. At the centre bays the tower is offset to the l. and has a stronger emphasis than it does on the S side, being slightly stepped forward so that its height and bulk are more fully apparent. The main entrance is correspondingly bold, a single-storey porch with doorway angled to the NE framed by columns and crowned by a balustrade, a detail reminiscent of that at Craighouse (Edinburgh).

The NW service wing is both continuation and contrast. It is of the same two-storey scale but with a lower wall-head, its first-floor windows rising into dormer pediments, and towards its far end a round-arched pend at ground floor is flanked by drum towers with bellcast conical roofs framing a big wall-head gable, a feature echoing the now-lost main entrance at Duntreath (Stirling & Central). Beyond the pend, in the angle between the centre block and the NW wing, is a rather more utilitarian two-storey block containing the kitchen, its somewhat incongruous mansard roof seemingly an afterthought to provide servants' bedrooms.

The most remarkable of the EARLIER INTERIORS is the STAIR-CASE in the E wing, its foot immediately behind the door. Although tightly planned and modest in scale with rather short narrow flights, it is distinguished by the very handsome stone half-columns at the ends of its spine wall. These have richly detailed Ionic capitals, moulded bases and tall dosserets; even the undersides of the stair treads are finely moulded. It is distinctly Caroline in appearance and so may pre-date the E wing's remodelling, but the field-panelling and lugged door surrounds in the ground-floor OLD DINING ROOM, first-floor OLD DRAWING ROOM and BEDROOMS all seem to be of 1741, notwithstanding the Ionic columns on tall pedestals which frame the fireplace in one of the bedrooms and its scrolled overmantel surmounted by a scallop shell. Both the dining and drawing room overmantels contain romantic classical landscapes in the style of *James Norie*; in one of the bedrooms there is a tripartite portrait of girls with a doll. The dining room panelling conceals an oven, perhaps for keeping food warm.

The LATER INTERIORS in the central block are all *Sydney Mitchell & Wilson*'s. The ENTRANCE HALL is spacious double-height with a first-floor gallery on the N, and lies within the three centre bays of the S front. Its gallery has a semi-elliptical arcade of Roman Doric columns and a finely turned wooden balustrade. The timber panelling is of high quality and is carried into alcoves with inbuilt seating in the drums at the angles of the S front. On the W side a big semi-elliptical archway opens into the cantilever MAIN STAIR, which has a matching balustrade and a coved ceiling with a big decorative roof-light. The far W end of the central block contains the BILLIARD ROOM at ground floor and the DINING ROOM at first floor, the latter in restrained good taste with a Neoclassical chimneypiece, panelled dado and a shallow segmentally arched

sideboard recess. The other principal apartments are both at
first floor to the E of the hall. The DRAWING ROOM is richer,
with a semi-elliptically arched arcade which continues the
theme of that in the hall; its chimneypiece with segmentally
arched overmantel is framed in very attenuated Ionic colonnettes. These are answered by those at the wide semi-elliptical
archway to the LIBRARY at the far E end, more like a relaxed
sitting room in character but with inbuilt bookshelves at the
SE oriel.

FORMAL GARDENS. The original approach from the S leads
through an avenue of trees to a long walled outer court which
must be C17 or earliest C18. Its GATEPIERS are mid-C18: tall
square ashlar piers with fluted shafts and moulded bases and
capitals crowned by elaborate urn finials, still with the original
wrought-iron gates. To the E the topiary garden is c. 1900.
There are two SUNDIALS, one a Doric column dated 'Leith
Hall 1722', and the other a finely moulded baluster dated 1892.

EAST GATES (0.5 km. ESE). By *Sydney Mitchell & Wilson*,
1900. Modelled on those of the main avenue, six square piers
of ashlar partly fluted, with very pronounced slim cornices and
decorative urn finials; they frame carriage gates, footgates and
low convex wing walls. The WEST GATES probably of the same
date and by the same architects but the LODGE is the early C19
TOLL HOUSE with bowed-out centre beneath a tall piended
roof, its windows commanding both sides of the tollbar (cf.
Poldhullie toll house, Strathdon, q.v.).

In the grounds of the house is a well-preserved later Bronze
Age or Iron Age SOUTERRAIN comprising a main chamber and
passage and side chamber. The walls and roof are made from
impressive blocks, some over 2 m. in length. (GN)

GLENMUICK   *3090*

ST MARY. Sited at the confluence of the Rivers Muick and Dee,
the church was 'very old and thatched with heather' when it
burned down in 1798, and was replaced by the new church in
Ballater (q.v.). Only a kirkyard remains. Scattered houses
including Birkhall (q.v.), mainly belonging to the Balmoral
estate, are found along the tumultuous valley which leads up
to Loch Muick.

KNOCK CASTLE, 1.4 km. W. Owned by the Gordons of Abergeldie   *54*
(q.v.) in the C16 and C17, the present castle erected c. 1600.
Set on a commanding eminence overlooking both the Dee and
Muick valleys, the walls of this compact pele tower survive but
the four-storey interior is ruined. The ground floor was vaulted,
with two newel stairs leading up to the hall. Each window is
protected by three shot-holes. Circular angle turrets in the NW
and SW corners are supported on key-pattern corbels. Above

the door, a square caphouse on meandering corbel projects above the roof-line. Remains of the courtyard may still be traced.

MILL OF STERIN SCHOOL HOUSE, 2.4 km. SW of the church. Early 1850s. T-plan with schoolmaster's cottage at W, and longer schoolroom projecting at rear to NE. The sash windows with a pronounced central astragal mimicking casement windows are a trademark of *J. & W. Smith* from about 1830–48.

MILL OF STERIN FARMHOUSE AND STEADING. 1862 by *John Beaton*, the Balmoral clerk of works. Three-bay single storey and dormers with rustically scrolled bargeboards to the gables and porch. The dormers with their up-swept roofs, formerly braced by wooden consoles and topped by tiered finials, were like little pagodas. L-plan Tudor-detailed steading of the same date.

GLAS-ALLT-SHIEL, 19 km. SW of the church. A rather staid but beloved royal lodge in a sublime location among pine trees on the shores of Loch Muick, beneath the Falls of Glasallt. Begun as a single-storey stalkers' cottage by *James Henderson* in 1851. After Prince Albert's death, *John Beaton* extended it for Queen Victoria in 1866–9, with cellars, stables, and U-plan gabled house. She came here with her companion John Brown.

ALLT-NA-GIUBHSAICH, 13 km. SW of church. Starting before 1806 as a single-storey cottage, this collection of buildings was enlarged under the patronage of Queen Victoria and Prince Albert, for whom it was a favourite retreat. The porch, *c.* 1860, of the East Cottage has a swept roof supported by log pillars, joined by cusp-headed timber railings. Pagoda-like GAME LARDER, late C19.

BIRKHALL. *See* p. 378.

HOUSE OF GLENMUICK. *See* p. 524.

4090

GLEN TANAR
6 km. SW of Aboyne

The estate of Glen Tanar, spread along the valley of the Water of Tanar, a tributary flowing into the Dee from the S, belonged to the Aboyne Castle estate but was let in the mid C19 by the Gordon Earls of Aboyne, first to the Earl of Southesk as a shooting tenant and from *c.* 1869 to the Manchester banker Sir William Cunliffe Brooks, who purchased it outright from his son-in-law, the 11th Marquis of Huntly, in 1874.

GLEN TANAR HOUSE, which lies about 3.25 km. upstream from its entrance gates off the south Deeside road, had already been enlarged as a sporting lodge for the Earl of Southesk but grew like Topsy under Brooks's ownership with extensive additions and remodelling in 1874–9 by *George Truefitt*, the London architect who designed Brooks' Bank in Manchester in 1868 and enjoyed his client's patronage here until the end of his life.* Further additions were made to the house by *Fryers & Penman* in 1906 for George Coats, the Paisley cotton thread magnate who became Lord Glentanar in 1916, and more was done for his son Thomas, the 2nd Baron, by *George Bennett Mitchell*. The result was sprawling and eccentric, its character dominated by the peculiarities of Truefitt's deeply personal style. It lasted until the death of Lord Glentanar in 1971, when most of it was pulled down and replaced by the present, comparatively modest, house designed by *Law & Dunbar-Nasmith*, completed *c.* 1975. Attached to it however is the former BALL-ROOM, which excels in Truefitt's wayward style with at one end a deep bow (formerly the bowling alley) with a clearstorey lighting a musicians gallery inside, abutting a chimney that carries above the wall-head and curved roof. To the r. of this two windows with arched heads in the glazing and straight-head sidelights as one finds in houses *c.* 1650. Inside, the main part has an open timber roof carried on arched braces with cusping and rafters studded with stags' heads. At the far end a substantial Baronial fireplace.†

The ballroom's fish-scale slate roofs, the feature of a little piend roof straddling the main roof ridge, the exaggeration of the chimneys and the rock-faced character of the masonry are all motifs found in abundance in the ESTATE BUILDINGS designed by Truefitt before 1874 when they were described in the *Aberdeen Journal* (9th September). They lie to the w of the house and collectively combine the appurtenances of an expensive model establishment with wild fantasy, including among other buildings the SAWMILL, GAME LARDER, STABLES, a row of COTTAGES and uphill the former KENNELS for the deer hounds, with cottages for the keepers that have on the E side roofs descending in catslides and on the w front also a fairytale tower with conical roof for the house of the estate deer-stalker. HOME FARM, an existing farmhouse made picturesque by the addition of a dairy – again with pyramid roof – has also one astonishing BARN with a slated piended roof with squat octagonal ventilator on the ridge at one end and aisles to the barn under spreading roofs of shallower pitch. The only later building is the RECREATION HALL of 1926, designed by Thomas Coats, 2nd Baron Glentanar, and constructed from pine felled in Glen Tanar forest. Clad with shingles imported from Matane, Quebec.

The entrance to the estate is not easily forgotten; it begins at the BRIDGE OF ESS, crossing the Water of Tanar in a heavily wooded small ravine; this has a re-set late C18 datestone but a pretty Victorian cast-iron cresting. Presiding over the crossing

*Truefitt officially retired in 1890, handing his practice to his son G.H. Truefitt, but he retained his role as Architect to the Glen Tanar Estate until Brooks's death.
†The organ which was placed in the ballroom in 1927 by the 2nd Lord Glentanar was given to the Temple Church, London, in 1950.

is the TOWER OF ESS, Truefitt's fantasy of a tower house, four storeys with a corbelled top stage and a stair-turret poking up at one corner wearing a petite bell-shaped roof. It has a little garden with a semicircular lookout in one corner that is contiguous with the ENTRANCE GATES, two solid square piers with pyramidal tops of overlapping stone slates and symbols in roundels on each face, including the monogram of William Cunliffe Brooks. The date of these is probably *c.* 1895, part of re-landscaping by *Thomas H. Mawson*, who described Brooks in his memoirs as 'the most generous yet the most tyrannical client for whom I have ever worked'. Further SW along the drive is the BRIDGE OF TANAR, a fine example of a mid-C18 bridge with a stilted arch carrying the road on a steeply sided hump across the Water of Tanar. Mawson may also be credited with the lakes etc. in the policies and probably the BOAT-HOUSE by the pond S of the house, with its turf roof and cobbled walls.

Between the entrance and the main house along the drive there are numerous ESTATE COTTAGES, exhibiting many of the same originalities of design as the other buildings, e.g. GREYSTONE COTTAGE, a square plan under a deep piend roof with a prow-like attic dormer cutting through it. One corner is cut out for a porch beneath the roof, the supports painted pine-tree trunks.

On the other side of the Tanar Water, about 0.5 km. NE of the house, is ST LESMO'S CHAPEL, adapted by *Truefitt* in 1871 from the remains of a small house or inn called Braeloine. This he remade into a standard gabled box but preserving a chimneystack which he moved from the E to W gable. A puzzling stub of wall with a fine ashlar arch also remains attached to the W, in front of the extraordinary vestry of 1938 with flowering turf roof. Transeptal organ chamber terminating in a doocot like tower with pyramid roof, also 1938 by *A. Marshall Mackenzie & Son*. Inside, the roof structure is composed of rustic pine trusses and was originally '... 'powdered' with lead stars, gilt, and with small mirror in the centre of each ...'. BENCHES. Also rustic with deerskin seats. – STAINED GLASS. N window. Cunliffe Brooks portrayed as St Lesmo. Attributed to *Clayton & Bell c.* 1900 (P. Cormack). – MONUMENT. Grethe Dagbjørt, Lady Glentanar †1940. A tablet by *A. G. R. Mackenzie* with *T. B. Huxley-Jones*. – HEADSTONE for Sir William Cunliffe Brooks (†1900) by *George Bennett Mitchell*, copying the Pictish Kinord cross-slab (*see* Dinnet)

The estate covers territory as far N as the Dee. About 3.4 km. WNW of Bridge of Ess is the former BOARD SCHOOL, one of the best and last of the estate buildings by *Truefitt*, 1896–8. The schoolrooms are joined into one building but covered by two steeply pitched and red tiled roofs which at their peak are saddled by tiled ventilators like the kilns of a distillery. Between the roofs a stone chimney sprouts. At the corner of the enclosing wall, a strange MEMORIAL FOUNTAIN to Queen Victoria's Jubilee, 1897, of a round arch with dome finials. In the wall to the r. a single stone is left undressed – 'Shape thyself for use. The stone that may fit in the wall is not left in the way' reads the bizarrely lettered inscription.

CRAIGENDINNIE, 1.5 km. E of Bridge of Ess. (The house seems to be by *Truefitt* from 1894 – rock-faced granite walls, stepped gables etc. – but was remodelled 1929–30 by *G. Bennett Mitchell & Son* for the Dowager Lady Glentanar. The same firm reduced the house to its present size in 1956–7.) Very pretty Gothick cast-iron entrance gates.

GOURDON   K   *8070*

Small cove on the North Sea, first documented as a fisher-town *c.* 1315. In 1506, there were formal complaints that the people of 'Gordoune' were illegally exporting fish, salt and hides. By the early C19, the new harbour had supplanted the one at Inverbervie (q.v.). Manufacturing brought additional growth in the C19, when most of the cottages were built.

The HARBOUR remains the nucleus of the village and is still surprisingly active. Long, straight pier in the centre by *Thomas Telford*, 1818–19, originally the only protection offered; canted pier to the W added in 1842, now extended to the S in concrete. A shorter, secondary harbour was created to the E in 1859, now in poor condition and with a very long, sinuous breakwater stretching out into the sea.

Between the E and W harbours is the hulking FISH PROCESSING FACTORY, built in two separate campaigns. The rectangular, three-storey section on the E with piended, corrugated-iron roof was opened as a granary *c.* 1830. Three gables set transversely to it, added 1896 by the fish merchant John S. Boyle.* At the same time, the ground floor of the earlier section was converted as a store for ice delivered from the Baltic Sea. In front of the factory, a polished granite MEMORIAL to Lt William Farquhar of Hallgreen Castle (q.v.), lost at sea in China in 1864. Barometer on its N face by *David & Co.* of London, 1871, topped by a metal cross and finial.

The main street of the village was originally known as Shorehead but was renamed WILLIAM STREET in his honour. To the E, the MAGGIE LAW MARITIME MUSEUM sits in the middle of the road, built in the early C19 as a Coast Guard apparatus shed. Segmental arch facing W and corbelled, canted dormer to the S. Further down the street (on the r.) is the former LIFEBOAT HOUSE, 1877–8 (closed 1969). Segmental arch in the gable originally for unloading the boats but now infilled with windows.

*He later moved his business to Glasgow and endowed a large park in Forfar (Angus).

The two brick buildings at the far end of the street are all that remain of the former SELBIE WORKS, built 1908 and dem. 2008; until 1997 they were the last surviving operational flax spinning mills in Britain. BRAE ROAD leads uphill out of the village, past the late C19 UPPER LEADING LIGHT. Cylindrical tower, whitewashed brick with conical roof over sawtooth. Projecting lantern window facing the harbour.

HADDO HOUSE *see* FORGUE

HALLFOREST CASTLE *see* KINTORE

8070   HALLGREEN CASTLE   K
570 m. SSE of Inverbervie

Originally held by the Dunnett family, who built a castle here in the C14. A datestone of 1376 was still visible in the mid C19. In the C15 'Hawgrene' passed to the Rait family, and David Rait was granted full ownership in 1472 by the burgesses of Aberdeen. The present building is large and rather amorphous, but the nucleus is a good late C16 L-plan tower house. Later wings added to the N and W have resulted in a U-plan straddling a narrow courtyard. Exterior re-harled in the 1990s, when there was much restoration.

The Raits' original tower house sits on the S and E sides, three storeys with exposed long-and-short quoins. Segmental, roll-moulded entrance arch in the re-entrant angle. Ogee-headed recess above it; to the l., two fine double gunloops allowing a full field of fire without deep embrasures. Crowstepped W gable with corbelled tourelles under conical roofs. The N wing was added in the late C17 but over an earlier structure and then much modified in the C19. Chamfered doorway to the court-yard and a MARRIAGE LINTEL dated 1687 with initials for William Rait and his wife, Helen Crichton. Opposite is a SERVICE WING added *c.* 1806 after the estate was acquired by James Farquhar of Johnston Lodge (q.v.). It stands in the footprint of a C16 ancillary building and was again much Victorianized (upper storey removed in the 1990s). The court-yard is now entered by a fanciful crowstepped arch with flank-ing tourelles, entirely work of the late C20.

The original tower house is best seen from the S side, where its chocolate-brown stone is unharled. More double gunloops and a blocked access arch that led out of the barmkin. E gable crowstepped with coped chimneystack and another tourelle. In the SE angle, a projecting buttress to defend against the sharply declining terrain, all of which was no doubt exploited as a motte from an early date. Surprisingly, the whole NE angle of the Castle was empty space until the bland Edwardian extension was inserted *c.* 1905.

Heavily restored INTERIOR with two vaulted cellars on the ground floor. They retain much C14 work, and a C16 chamfered fireplace arch had to be slapped into a pre-existing vault. The original turnpike stair was removed from the W jamb in the C18. In the great hall on the first floor, a massive lintelled fireplace with roll moulding and salt-box.

HARTHILL CASTLE   *6020*
1.5 km. ESE of Oyne

A Z-plan tower house, one of several following the 'New Warke' at Huntly Castle (q.v.) in having a main block with an entrance tower at one corner answered by a round tower at that diagonally opposite. Harthill's plan form may date from the mid C16, begun after the New Warke's remodelling of 1551–4 but before the sale of the estate '*cum castro, fortalicio et manerie ejusdem*' by Patrick Leith to Robert Arbuthnott in 1570. Harthill was subsequently re-acquired and remodelled by the Leiths, a recorded datestone of 1601 suggesting works were carried out in that year. Confusion over another datestone, now lost, leaves doubt as to whether John Leith, a prominent Royalist, engaged in substantial alterations in 1638 at the outset of the Civil Wars, which would explain heavy borrowings from relatives at about that time. In 1643 John burnt Harthill to prevent its capture by Covenanting forces, or perhaps because it was about to be granted to George Leith of Overhall in settlement of debt. An alternative reading of this stone with a date of 1658 would suggest that Harthill was rebuilt after the Civil Wars before again being abandoned. Remarkably, its rubble shell survived the centuries virtually intact; even the courtyard gatehouse, although fragmentary, is still extant, an unusual survival. Restoration was undertaken by Ann and Steve Remp in 1975–8 with *Bill Cowie* of *Datum Design Associates* as architect and *Slessor Troup* as master mason, their work recognized by a Saltire Award in 1979. The castle has a neat garage block in mid-C18 coachhouse guise.

Harthill consists of a three-storey-and-attic rectangular main block with a four-storey-and-attic entrance jamb built out from the NE corner, and a four-storey-and-attic round tower built out from the SW.* Its footprint is closely similar to Old House of Carnousie (N, *c.* 1574–7) but Harthill rises much taller, with wall-heads 14 m. above ground, and consequently its character

---

*Strictly, the main block lies NE by SW, with the entrance jamb at the N and the round tower at the S, but for ease of understanding the orientation has been simplified.

is emphatically more vertical and defensive. It is a tightly drawn composition of harled rubble walls with chamfered window dressings, very simple and robust at its lower levels, the ground floor being almost blind; it has, however, a picturesque C17 skyline of tall coped chimneystacks, crowstepped gables, corbelled angle turrets with small spirelets and a big conical roof over the round tower.

On plan it is very sophisticated for its date. The entrance jamb is almost square, 6.8 m. deep N–S and 5.3 m. across its S front, with corbelled angle turrets at its NE and SE corners. The door is on the S face within the re-entrant angle. It is round-arched and roll-moulded as at Carnousie and flanked by slit-windows, that on the r. having a wide-mouthed shot-hole beneath; above, beneath the first-floor window, is a blank panel which once displayed the Leith coat of arms. Within is an entrance passage and a straight flight of steps to the turnpike stair serving all five floors, which is neatly tucked into the shallow re-entrant angle on the N. This very tight and economical planning enables the jamb to accommodate a ground-floor guardroom, a first-floor private apartment with a sizeable closet and garderobe, and bedchambers on the floors above.

The main block, 12.5 m. by 8.3 m., is deeper than at Carnousie. Its vaulted ground floor contains a kitchen at the N end and cellar at the S, accessed from a passage running down the E side, a right-angled continuation of the passage in the entrance jamb. The arched kitchen hearth occupies the N wall's full width, and has a small recess in one cheek with a shot-hole; there is a sink and slop-hole on the W, and a service hatch opens onto the passage. Both kitchen and cellar have intramural service stairs within the W wall leading to the first-floor great hall, the kitchen stair entering at the 'low' end and the cellar stair at the 'high' end. The great hall was never vaulted, having always had a simple timber ceiling supported on joists. Its fireplace was not at the high end but in the E flank, a common feature of the Huntly group of Z-plan castles; its lintel is a single enormous slab of granite almost 3.5 m. long and 0.5 m. deep and is seemingly C15, reused from an earlier tower house which probably stood at Old Harthill, near Oyne Parish Church. Like the jamb, the main block has small turrets at its SE and NW corners.

The round tower is 6.8 m. in diameter and contains a domed cellar at ground floor opening off that within the main block; this cellar has three wide-mouthed shot-holes guarding the main block's S and W flanks. Above it contains a single bedchamber on each upper floor, separately accessed by a private stair within its splayed junction with the main block. This stair is lit by slits and has a further shot-hole at ground level. Although the walls are up to 1.5 m. thick, there are only small areas of solid masonry at the upper levels, the walls being extensively hollowed out for stairs, fireplaces, closets and recesses, all showing a further refinement of what had been achieved at Carnousie. The simple interior finishes throughout the castle date from the restoration of 1975–8.

The ruined GATEHOUSE is two-storeyed: a round-headed arch which was once the entrance to the forecourt, with a small upstairs room supported on a corbel course and lit by a window between two empty fields which contained heraldic panels; the base of a gable is just visible. This upstairs room could be reached directly from the tower house's great hall along the parapet walk of the right-angled wall enclosing the courtyard at the SE, reinstated from modest remains during the 1975–8 works.

HATTON OF FINTRAY

PARISH CHURCH. By *John Smith*, dated 1821. Plain Tudor, tall rectangular plan with unusually broad end gables, and relatively shallow-pitched roof. Four large windows in S flank with timber Y-tracery. The gables were originally identical, each with a four-centred doorway, triple gallery lancets and quatrefoil, but the W doorway is overlaid by a link to the later hall. Birdcage bellcote at W end with spirelet and pinnacles (bell by *John Mowat* of Old Aberdeen, 1751). The interior is unusually well preserved: horseshoe gallery with panelled front on cast-iron quatrefoil colonnettes, facing the PULPIT on the S side with a canted front and tall back rising into an ogee-domed sounding-board. – ORGAN. By *Dulsanell*, mid-C20.

The CHURCHYARD was consecrated in 1715, shortly after Sir William Forbes built the church of which only the W gable survives. – MORT-HOUSE. Ice-house-like, with iron door and granite lintel dated 1830, vaulted interior.

Nearby is the former PARISH MANSE. 1853 by *William Smith* (of *J. & W. Smith*). Plain Tudor in his English rectory manner.

Hatton of Fintray was the estate village of FINTRAY HOUSE, which was demolished in 1952. It was designed for Sir John Forbes-Sempill by *William Burn* in 1827, and built in 1829–31 with amendments by *John Smith*. The Tudor-style WEST LODGE survives, on the B979 at the entrance to the Lairds Park housing development, together with a few other mid-C19 buildings including the coachhouse and stables. The former village SCHOOL, 0.35 km. S of the church, is by *J. & W. Smith*, 1850. Tudor, a smaller simpler version of the manse (*see* above).

WESTER FINTRAY, 2.9 km. W. A vernacular farmhouse of *c.* 1800, referred to extensively in George Skene Keith's *Agricultural Survey of Aberdeenshire* (1811) but remodelled *c.* 1840. Two storeys, three windows wide, over a very low raised basement, harled with granite ashlar dressings. Transom-lit doorway with console-cornice, astragalled windows, gabled roof with end stacks. Rear elevation almost blind, framed by single-storey wings forming a small back court. Quadrangular steading with semi-elliptical arches built 1800.

St Meddan's Churchyard, Cothal, 3.4 km. e on the banks of the Don opposite Dyce church (see p. 267). Granted by David Earl of Huntingdon and the Garioch to his Abbey of Lindores c. 1190. The Forbes of Fintray burial enclosure incorporates the remains of the medieval church, ruinous by 1732, including its red sandstone sacrament house. The near-square locker is carved with what is possibly a monstrance, above which a smaller plaque represents Christ crucified with two flanking figures in low relief.

Nearby are the remains of Cothal Mill, once famous for high-quality woollen cloth and tweed, founded c. 1798 and developed by John Crombie from 1806. Steam- and water-powered, the mill employed over 100 workers. Although progressively superseded by the Crombies' Grandholm Mills at Bridge of Don (see Aberdeen, p. 264), Cothal remained in use until the early C20. Originally three large blocks on a steeply sloping site, the upper mill is now demolished and the centre and lower mills converted to domestic use. Each is two storeys and six windows wide, built in coursed granite with straight skews.

5010

HAUGHTON HOUSE

1.2 km. nne of Alford

Once a Farquharson seat, built c. 1800, remodelled and enlarged c. 1860. Entrance front of the original house is three storeys, three bays broad over a sunk basement in granite ashlar, the centre bay slightly projecting. Ground-floor windows round-arched with apron panels, first- and second-floor in plain surrounds; long-and-short quoins. The entrance porch, curvilinear wall-head gable and the rear range which runs parallel to the original block and extends beyond it on either side are also built of granite ashlar but are of c. 1860. The porch's central doorway, flanking niches and side windows are all round-arched and key-blocked. Plain gables, all two windows wide, with big coped stacks. Interior subdivided at first and second floor but some features are retained.

About 160 m. nnw is a group of c18 cottages, surprisingly distinguished of their kind. L-plan single storey in coursed squared and cherry-cocked masonry. Chamfered windows (some formerly barred). Pronounced skews and moulded skewputts, graded slates, stone roof ridge and sturdy, finely coped chimneystack. Diptych sundial built into one angle.

– ICE HOUSE (120 m. NW), *c.* 1800. Barrel-vaulted and turfed over, with off-centre entrance gable.

HOUSE OF CROMAR *see* ALASTREAN HOUSE

HOUSE OF DRUMINNOR

5020

1.6 km. ESE of Rhynie

The House of Druminnor comprises the surviving palace-block of Druminnor Castle, once the chief seat of the Forbes family, most of which was demolished in 1800. Sketches and plans show that the castle was then laid out around a series of three courts – a forecourt to the W; a main court, entered through a two-storey gatehouse with an arched pend, with the tower house on its N side and the palace-block on its S; a service back court with laigh biggings to the E; and the church of Kearn further to the E. The tower house may have been begun at any time from the late C13, but was probably substantially strengthened after raiding in the mid C15, King James II granting a licence to fortify in 1456. It was rectangular on plan, roughly 20 m. long with walls almost 3 m. thick at ground floor, and of substantial height with a crenellated parapet and a circular turret rising from its SW corner.

The palace-block's origins are well documented. On 4 July 1440 Alexander, 1st Lord Forbes, paid 151 out of 200 merks promised to *John Kemlock* and *William of Ennerkype* for 'ye makyn ye House of Drumynnor'; Kemlock had recently been engaged on work at Kildrummy Castle (q.v.) for the King, perhaps at Forbes's instigation since he was then Baillie of Mar. The lower (less-altered) storeys of the palace-block at Huntly Castle (q.v.) resemble Druminnor in several respects, and have the same maon's marks: indeed, the 1st Earl of Huntly's daughter was married to Lord Forbes's grandson, and John Kemlock was his chaplain and lawyer in 1471. Druminnor Castle was damaged during the Marian Wars in 1572 and rebuilt by William, 7th Lord Forbes, *c.* 1577. During the Civil Wars it was captured by the Royalists and defended against its Forbes owners between 1645 and 1647, requiring further rebuilding by William, later 11th Lord Forbes, in 1660–1. In 1770 James, 16th Lord Forbes, was obliged to sell Druminnor to the Forbes of Newe. They sold it to John Grant of Rothmaise whose son married Newe's daughter, but their son Robert demolished most of the castle in 1800 and the church of Kearn in 1810. In 1841–3 Robert's son-in-law Captain Alexander Foulerton-Grant engaged *Archibald Simpson* to enlarge the surviving palace-block with a Jacobean villa at its NW end, but in the process its upper floors were substantially altered to conform with the new work and many original features were

concealed behind lath and plaster. In 1954 Druminnor was purchased by Margaret Forbes-Sempill. From 1960 she engaged *Ian
G. Lindsay & Partners* to reverse as far as possible the changes
made since Druminnor passed out of the family. They demolished Simpson's villa but work stalled when both Forbes-Sempill
and Lindsay met untimely deaths in 1966. Further restoration
was carried out by *Harry Mantell* (of *Meldrum & Mantell*) in
2004.

The PALACE's principal front facing N into the lost courtyard is
22 m. in length and two tall storeys in height with a dormered
attic in its steeply pitched roof. The main entrance is within
a big drum tower 5 m. in diameter at the NE angle: this contains the stair and is corbelled out into a massive square-plan
caphouse. Within the re-entrant angle with the main block is
a slim stair turret which rises higher into a conical roof.
The tower, its caphouse and its stair turret date from the
reconstructions of 1577 and 1660. There are two separate
doorways, one slightly off-centre within the main block and
one facing not quite N in the tower, its five-pointed arched
head described as 'almost unique' by MacGibbon and Ross
and probably part of the 1577 works. Above it are three field-
panels displaying heraldry – in the centre, William, Master of
Forbes; l., William, 7th Lord Forbes, and Elizabeth Keith,
dated 1577; r., Jane Campbell of Calder, Mistress of Forbes
(1648–60).
   The main block has a set-off at first-floor level. The height
of blind wall above the three first-floor windows reflects the
major alterations of 1841–3, as do the gableted attic dormers,
for prior to that date there were three full storeys beneath the
eaves. The roof is now simple, with coped ashlar chimneystacks over crowstepped end gables and the internal gable
between the hall and the private apartment. The E windows
are Lindsay's, the wall there being rebuilt when the Simpson
wing was demolished.
   The main block is 10 m. deep. Being built on steeply sloping
ground, on its S side it reveals a tall basement, wholly invisible
on the N front. Rising from a deep base course it is very plain
in appearance, though the set-off is carried round between the
entrance and principal storeys. It was formerly four generously
spaced windows wide but the window second from l. was
blocked by a turnpike stair formed behind it in 1660–1. The
window surrounds in dressed red sandstone are early, and
traces remain of holes drilled for iron grilles, but the individual
stones are not all in their original positions. The stair itself has
a triple shot-hole of the Leiper type, evidently re-set: the openings have different carved decoration – a rope moulding, strapwork and quatrefoil. Above Simpson's wall-head, some of the
sculptured attic dormers have been reused: that on the l. with
a fleur-de-lys has been carved with mason's tools arranged to
suggest the letters V.F. for William Forbes and date 1661; the
next is dated 1869; next again, scrolled with initials I.M.F.,

John Master of Forbes, its scallop shells a traditional symbol of welcome to all peaceful visitors.

PLAN AND STRUCTURE. The wall thickness at basement and ground floor, some 2 m., and the fact that both floors are vaulted would appear to confirm that they are mid-C15. Even above the set-off, much of the first-floor masonry is of the same thickness, and the repetition of basement- and ground-floor masons' marks on the circular stair-tower suggests that it too was part of the original plan. The entrance is protected by an iron yett which was reputedly stolen by the Forbes from Craig Castle (q.v.), although more probably it came from Lesmoir, another Gordon stronghold nearby.

The BASEMENT is accessed by a straight flight of stairs descending within the main block from immediately behind the round tower down to a corridor running along the N side. This opens onto three large cellars and a pit-prison beneath the tower itself which is secured by two external drawbars and has access to neither air nor light. The GROUND FLOOR also consists of three large vaulted rooms, but without a corridor. As late as 1960 each room had its own external entrance off the old castle court which could be secured internally, and they did not open into one another, as they do now. The E and W doorways were converted by Lindsay into windows but the central doorway with a guardroom in the depth of its reveal was retained. Internal doorways were formed between the rooms, their carved candelabra bosses being restored at that time by *Ann Henderson*. The E room was the kitchen, with a hearth some 3.5 m. wide and 1.5 m. deep in its end gable. This room has a garderobe in its SE angle, services adjacent to the stair, a small store which opens off the hearth's N cheek and a sink in the S wall. The W room – the so-called 'Happy Room' after the remains of an inscription found there – has the unusual distinction for a ground-floor room of a fireplace with a salt-recess, string mouldings in stone and again its own garderobe, indicating that it was part of the living accommodation.

The FIRST FLOOR is reached by the broad turnpike stair, 3.4 m. in diameter, within the entrance tower. The newel post at its top appears to be part of the 1660 works. The first floor was originally divided into two rooms, the hall at the E end being much larger than the outer chamber on the W, although not quite so large as it is now. Both were once lit by two windows in the S wall but in 1660–1 a spiral stair was formed within the W room's E window recess and the partition was rebuilt slightly to the W. Within this rebuilt partition one jamb remains of the fireplace in red sandstone which once warmed the 'high' end of the large E room; the original fireplace may have occupied a prominent recess in the N wall. The fireplace in the W room, within the end gable, is C19. During Simpson's alterations the E room was subdivided into two chambers and the ceilings raised. This subdivision was reversed in the 1960s but the ceilings remain at the same height as Simpson left them, the lower parts of the second-floor doorways and fireplaces now being exposed in the upper parts of the walls to indicate what has happened.

The rubble-built GARDEN WALLS to E and W of the palace are probably C18, partly remodelled by *Simpson*, but may incorporate some material from the old castle courts. – CEMETERY, 250 m. NNE, with CROSS by *George Bennett Mitchell*, 1900. – EAST LODGE, 280 m NE, also by *Mitchell*, 1907–8. Half-timbered.

HOUSE OF FETTERNEAR *see* FETTERNEAR

3090

HOUSE OF GLENMUICK
1.1 km. S of Ballater

The original House of Glenmuick was built in 1870–2, designed by *Sir Morton Peto* and executed by *William Henderson & Son* for Sir James Mackenzie, an Aberdeen silk mercer who made his fortune with indigo from India. It was in a free Tudor style, distinguished by a massive square tower and porte cochère. Demolished in 1948, its name was transferred to the present mansion, which had been the dower house, a short distance to the E. It was called Brackley House and stands on a splendid eminence dominating the Ballater Plain from the S (a site once occupied by BRAIKLIE CASTLE, now untraceable but attacked in 1715 and 1745; and where a house is marked on Roy's map of the 1750s). On the recommendation of Sir William Cunliffe Brooks of Glen Tanar (q.v.) Sir Allan Mackenzie commissioned *Dan Gibson* and *T. H. Mawson* in 1895 to reconfigure the house in a Tudoresque style, with service wing added by Mawson in 1912.

The *Gibson & Mawson* work is characterized by striking red Penrith sandstone mullioned windows and leaded panes, within walls of random-sized grey granite. Their plinth is usually two courses high. The N entrance front, eight bays and two storeys, is articulated by a castellated porch with round-arched entrance and stepped hood moulding above. However, the earlier dower house can be recognized within the complex plan, on the W and part of the S sides, by its plinth of single large stones, Aberdeen bond on the walls, a plat band above the ground floor and below the eaves, and Victorian sash windows framed in granite. The sandstone mullions on the W bay of the N front are insertions into the older house. The INTERIOR retains its Gothic, Tudor and classical elements, in fine plasterwork, timber panelling, mantelpieces and decorative carved staircase. Landscaped with great terraces in 1895. The WALLED GARDEN has a decorative iron gate and a pavilion with pyramidal bell-canted roof. ESTATE BUILDINGS, stables and kennels continue the Tudor theme.

St Nathalan's Episcopal Church, 1 km. w. Built for the estate in 1875 by *James Matthews* with nave, chancel and fine NW tower, but only the last survives, finely detailed in white Glenmuick granite. The rest was demolished in 1961.

HOUSE OF KAIR *see* KAIR HOUSE

HOUSE OF KINGCAUSIE *see* KINGCAUSIE HOUSE

HOUSE OF MONYMUSK *see* MONYMUSK

HUNTLY

5040

Huntly probably began with a few houses straggling along the ridge of ground still traced today by Old Road and Lennox Terrace. 'The Raws' or Milltown of Strathbogie, as it was once known, was not always the most important settlement in the district, the earliest churches being established at Dunbennan and Kinnoir, where they remained for a millennium. However, in a bid to subdue the rebellious northern tribes, in the late C12 William the Lion granted Strathbogie to Duncan, Earl of Fife, who recognized The Raws's strategic importance and built his castle there.

Duncan's descendants lost Strathbogie to the Gordons of Huntly in Berwickshire in 1318–19 and during the tumultuous years of the mid C14 they made strenuous efforts to gain it back before their male line failed in 1369. But afterwards Sir John Gordon transferred his principal seat to Strathbogie from the Borders and the new interest which he and his descendants took in their northern estates resulted in greater prosperity and the Raws's development as a market town; in 1488 it was erected a burgh of barony by King James III. During the C17 Huntly became an important centre of spinning and weaving and an Act of 1695 granted further markets.

From a population beneath 300, Huntly developed considerably in the early part of the C18. In 1737 Cosmo, 3rd Duke of Gordon invited the Belfast linen manufacturer Hugh McVeagh to set up business in Huntly, with new houses being built for the weavers; and after 1745, when the Gordons were debarred from holding lucrative government offices, Alexander the 4th Duke turned to improvement of his estates to generate an income, offering new feus within the town. Its core was by then well established with The Square at its centre and streets extending from each side: Castle Street – then the main commercial thoroughfare – running broadly N to the Deveron and ultimately to Elgin and Inverness, Gordon Street approaching from Aberdeen and the S, Deveron Street leading W and Duke Street to the E, this last continuing

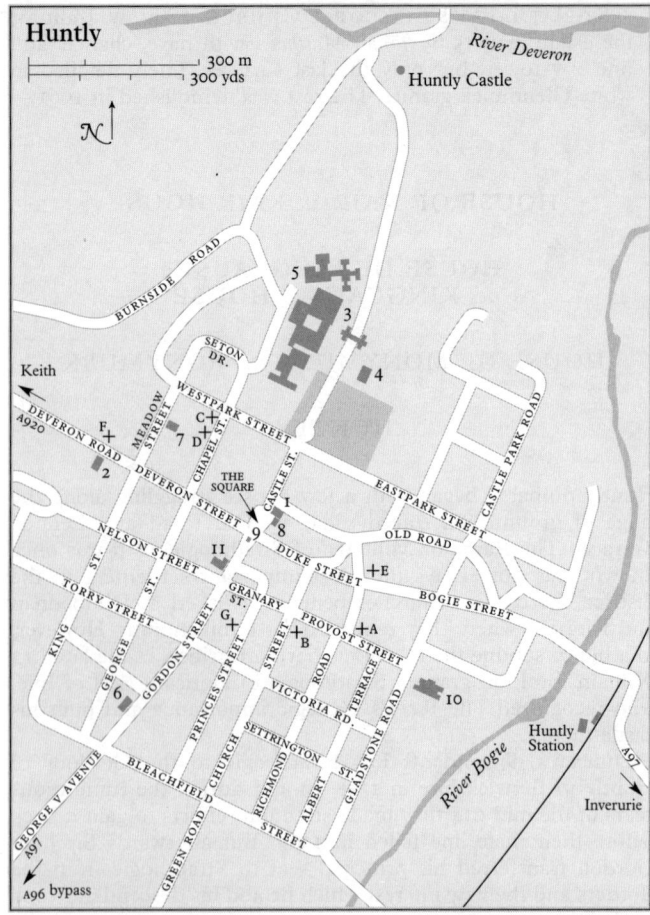

Huntly

300 m
300 yds

River Deveron

Huntly Castle

A Christ Church (Episcopal)
B Parish Church
C St Margaret (R.C.)
D Presbytery House
E Strathbogie Parish Church
(former Free Church)
F Free Church Manse (former)
G United Presbyterian
Church (former)

1 Brander Museum and Library
2 Volunteer Drill Hall (former)
3 Gordon Schools
4 Elementary Department
(former)
5 Higher Grade Department
(former)
6 Huntly Business Centre
7 Masonic Lodge
8 Post Office
9 Robertson Fountain
10 Scott's Hospital/Institution
11 Stewart's Hall

down through Bogie Street and over the Bogie Bridge. Huntly also profited from the military roads built after the 'Forty-Five, and in 1770 Duke Alexander commissioned *Mr Milne* to lay out the town on a gridiron plan, many of the new feus being taken up quickly for houses and manufactories. Communications improved further with turnpikes first to Fochabers (*see* Moray (N)) and later to Dunbennan and Rhynie (q.v.). The countryside prospered as the marshes were drained and farmers adopted improved agricultural techniques. By the end of the century the population must have been around 2,000.

The Great North of Scotland Railway reached Huntly in 1854. Although by this date the textile industry was waning, the town diversified into a thriving industrial centre and grew rapidly on both sides of the N–S axis formed by Castle Street, The Square and Gordon Street, with modest one- and two-storey houses built to the W in such irregular fashion as to give remarkable variety to the long straight lengths of King Street and George Street and the minor roads running between them. In the later C19 the 'New Feus' were laid out for smart villas within easy reach of the station, and an exclusive retreat developed on Battle Hill just E of the river. Huntly's long association with the Gordons came to an end after the 8th Duke died in 1935. His son concentrated his interests on his English estate at Goodwood, West Sussex, and sold the Huntly Estate, including feudal superiority over the town itself and 12,000 acres (5,000 ha.) of farmland, in 1936. During the 1960s a bypass protected Huntly from the growth in traffic between Aberdeen and Inverness. This has helped preserve Huntly's historic character largely intact.

CHURCHES

CHRIST CHURCH (Episcopal), Provost Street. By *Thomas Mackenzie* (of *Mackenzie & Matthews*), 1848; one of the earliest Episcopal churches in Aberdeenshire to acknowledge the influence of the Ecclesiologists. Modest E.E. with one-bay chancel and taller nave of four bays with gabled porch and slim SW tower with octagonal spire of early C13 type. Simply treated interior, although evidence of painted decoration shows it was formerly richer. W organ gallery, with arcaded screen forming a narthex below. – PULPIT, by the narrow chancel arch and entered through the wall from the vestry, as approved of by the Tractarians. – ALTAR. Gothic, carved by *Miss E. Logan*, 1897, with three panels representing the Lamb of God worshipped by the Heavenly Host (Revelations 5:12). – BENCHES. Ends carved with simple fleur-de-lys. – ORGAN. A beautiful chamber organ, by *R. Mirrlees & Sons*, Glasgow, *c.* 1863, with Gothick case and fretwork panels. Restored by *David Loosley* in 2013 when it was brought from the old parish church at Kinneff (q.v.). – STAINED GLASS – Chancel E (Ascension), 1873. – Three nave S windows (scenes from the life of Christ).

PARISH CHURCH, Church Street. Replaced the first parish church of 1727, which stood on the Gordon Street–

Upperkirkgate junction. *George Burn*'s plans approved by
Presbytery in 1802 were superseded by *Alexander Laing*'s
scheme of 1804. Laing envisaged a temple-fronted building but
the 4th Duke of Gordon demurred at paying for a portico, with
the result that the sw gable while austere and dignified is
plainer than the more sophisticated flanks. Nevertheless the
church is monumental in scale and detail, its construction in
good rough ashlar. Its sw doorway is very tall and deep, with
elongated fanlight; two windows in arched recesses light the
gallery stairs, and three gallery windows brush the band course
and plain pedimental gable with thermal opening. Birdcage
bellcote evidently reused from the old church. Five-bay flanks,
with central round-arched and key-blocked entrance set in
Roman Doric pilasters and pediment, and wheel window
above; tall arched and key-blocked windows on either side with
simple late c19 tracery; moulded cornice at the wall-head. NE
gable with tall twin round-headed lights, low vestry of 1836–7
at rear.

Broad open interior with flat ceiling of impressive span and
large U-plan gallery with its panelled fronts on fluted Doric
columns; additional iron supports were inserted after the
gallery of Kirkcaldy Parish Church collapsed in 1828. The
present furnishing dates from *c.* 1914 and was probably carried
out by *A. Marshall Mackenzie & Son*. At the w end, the PLAT-
FORM PULPIT with twin stairs (possibly reused). The Neo-
Baroque COMMUNION TABLE (probably 1898) with fluted legs
and console brackets supporting its top, and FONT with four
fluted Ionic columns bearing a bolection-moulded basin are
probably Mackenzie's. – ORGAN CASE behind the pulpit by
Matthews & Mackenzie, 1893; the instrument itself is by *Eustace
Ingram*, overhauled by *Rushworth & Dreaper* 1961. – STAINED
GLASS. w wall flanking the pulpit. By *Pluscarden Abbey*, 1964:
on the l. the Nativity, with shepherds, kings and angels in
attendance; r., the Crucifixion and Ascension. – In the vestibule a MEMORIAL to the Rev. Adam Semple (†1914), surrounded by brass plaques commemorating casualties of the
First World War, by *A. Marshall Mackenzie*, 1921.

The HALL, dated 1927, represents all that was built of an
ambitious scheme by *A. Marshall Mackenzie & Son c.* 1913–14,
in which it would have projected much more boldly forward,
linked to the church's sw gable by an impressive Neoclassical
tower.

Former ST JOHN (R.C.), Meadow Street. Built for Charles
    Maxwell of Gibston, 1787. Discreet low-key cottagey vernacu-
    lar, like all Catholic churches at that date. Arched openings at
    the gable. It became the MASONIC LODGE from 1887.
ST MARGARET (R.C.), Chapel Street. Built 1833–4 by *William
    Robertson* and the *Rt Rev. James Kyle*, largely funded by the
    Gordons of Wardhouse (q.v.), who made a fortune in the
    vineyards of Jerez. A monumental Hellenic temple front sup-
    porting a soaring Hispanic tower forms the triumphant fron-
    tispiece to an octagonal church with a magnificent interior.

Approached between square gatepiers, the temple front is built of massive ashlar masonry, its doorway very tall, set in a lugged surround with shallow block pediment and acroteria. Pairs of giant antae carry the heavy entablature with dedication to Sãnta Margarite, the crowning pediment with plain tympanum and acroteria. The Baroque tower is square-based and in three stages – first a panelled plinth supported by giant console scrolls; then a tall blind stage with Corinthianesque pilasters at its canted corners; and finally an open belfry with concave sides and smaller scrolls, surmounted by a crucifix on further scrolls, the whole rising 25 m. above the ground. This ashlar frontispiece forms a contrast with the nave itself, mostly built in dark snecked granite rubble: it is lit by thermal windows with ashlar voussoirs, the prismatic roof kept low.

The octagonal nave, with its elaborate PAINTED DECORA-TION carried out under the supervision of *Earley & Co.* of Dublin in 1905, is firmly focused on the altar recess directly opposite the entrance and organ gallery. The recess, with a large ALTAR PAINTING of the Ascension by *José Maria Romero*, 1842 (installed 1843), is finished in sandy gold with rich stencilled decoration, whereas the flank walls with six pictures of the late C18 Spanish School (probably installed in the mid 1850s) are white between pilasters set into the angles. Their entablature, window arches and spandrels are also stencilled. The saucer dome is divided into twelve compartments, predominantly dark blue-grey as a contrast against the ribs in lighter sand. Within the spandrels are eight roundel-portraits: SS Andrew, Ninian, Joseph, Patrick, Charles Borromeo (later renamed as Louis IX of France), Peter, Columba and Margaret. – Further additions carried out in 1905 included a new oak PULPIT by Huntly cabinet-maker *James Anton* with full-length high-relief figures of the Evangelists. The front of the white marble ALTAR, with marble-shafted corner columns, is inset with mosaic panels depicting the Sacred Heart on a cross of gold. Behind the altar, the Italian Romanesque REREDOS is again in marble, with mosaic panels in its upper stage and an aedicule above the sacrarium which contains a Crucified Christ. – FONT. *c.* 1870. Octagonal stone basin with Holy Monogram in a quatrefoil panel, on clustered marble columns bearing a single foliate capital. – COMMUNION RAILS (now set in front of the pews). Oak, carved by *Garvie & Sons*. The PEWS are arranged in a gentle curve which, with their spare open design, gives the nave floor a strong sense of geometric order. – ORGAN, originally by *Conacher*, 1871. The church was restored in 1978 and 1989–90.

PRESBYTERY HOUSE on Chapel Street 1900, two-storey-and-attic replacing a single-storey predecessor. Immediately w of the church, the former SCHOOL, built 1848 and reconstructed in a simple Scots Renaissance manner *c.* 1900.

STRATHBOGIE PARISH CHURCH, Bogie Street. The former Free Church. An Italianate entrance front with tower, by *James Matthews* 1862–3; behind it is the harled pre-Disruption church of 1840–1, built as a result of the 'Marnoch Case' (*see* p. 33). Matthews's entrance front is a tall nave-and-aisles design, its pedimented nave stepped slightly forward and a square-based tower on the r. concealing the E aisle. Grey squared granite, semi-elliptical central doorway framed by Roman Doric pilasters and pediment; the tower and W aisle with smaller square-headed doorways under console cornices. Very tall upper level lit by small-paned round-arched windows, the central nave window larger and framed by paired Roman Doric pilasters carrying a shallow entablature and pediment. Tower rises into a clock stage, then into a loftier belfry with triple-arched and pilastered openings, long-and-short quoins and eaves brackets at the low pyramidal roof. Flanking it on the r. the tall single-storey PRAYER HALL projecting boldly forward on the E is an addition by *Sander & Archibald*, masons, adopting Matthews's motifs, three round-arched lights in a pedimental gable front.

The interior is of 1840 but as remodelled by *William Kelly* with *Thomas G. Archibald* in 1911–12. It has a spare but refined character accentuated by the light of its big clear-glass windows. Its U-plan gallery with simple panelled fronts is supported on very slim colonnettes which continue up into graceful timber arches carrying a panelled timber ceiling. Although the colonnettes appear to be of timber, they are so slim that they must have iron cores. At the ritual E (N) end is the PLATFORM PULPIT and above this the ORGAN LOFT built out from the N gable with a triple-arched Neoclassical lattice screen case of 1903, the instrument itself by *Lewis & Co.*, 1904. – In the vestibule (formed 1870) a very large bell formerly in Kinnoir Parish Church (dem.) bears the names of Iohne Hamiltovn Gordovn and Adame Gordovn with the date 1605 in a frieze around the top; then under Hamilton Gordon's name a further inscription '*coft me for Kinnoir 1653*'.

The former FREE CHURCH MANSE, Deveron Road, was built *c.* 1852–4 for the celebrated Robert Rainy (later Principal Rainy of New College, Edinburgh), an early incumbent. Cottage style, asymmetric two-storey two-bay house, very much in the manner of *Thomas Mackenzie*. Stylish octagonally shafted chimneystacks.

Former UNITED PRESBYTERIAN CHURCH, Princes Street. Now Scout Hall. Built *c.* 1850, replacing an earlier church of 1809; closed 1917. Gable-fronted in squared granite, large window with simple intersecting tracery, pronounced skewputts, porch with canted corners and moulded doorpiece later. Four-bay flanks in coursed rubble with dressed quoins and margins, simple rectangular window openings with paired pointed-arch lights, diamond-pattern glass. The former MANSE is a handsome two-storey three-bay house in grey granite ashlar, *c.* 1810–20.

PUBLIC BUILDINGS

BRANDER MUSEUM AND LIBRARY, The Square. By *John Rhind*, 1883–5, the gift to his native town of William Brander, a member of the London Stock Exchange. Neo-Perp. An impressive two-storey-and-attic gable front containing the main entrance from The Square, with a narrow stair bay slightly set back on the r., and a five-bay flank to Castle Street, all in snecked Kemnay granite with red Auchindoir freestone dressings. Four-centred doorway is simply moulded, its quatrefoil spandrels sheltered by a hoodmould with sculpted heads representing John Knox (Religion) and George Buchanan (Learning) by *D. & A. Davidson*; single lights to either side, and heraldic arms in an apron band above. Large four-light mullioned-and-transomed library window framed by monogram panels at first floor; fleur-de-lys finial at the gable apex. Castle Street elevation has mullioned-and-transomed two-lights, wall-head parapet and a gable over the far end. Steeply pitched roof with dormer ventilators and chamfered square-shafted chimneystacks. Interior similar in character: fine timber stair, open library roof. The jewel-like quality of the leaded glass and the ornate Gothic detailing inside and out suggest a precious treasure-casket filled with memories and knowledge.

Former DRILL HALL, Deveron Road. Now HUNTLY FAMILY CENTRE. 1901–2 by *George Sutherland*. Tall two-storey gable-fronted structure, flanked l. by three-stage tower, and r. by a two-storey bay, with porch at far r. end. Simple Free Renaissance in grey granite ashlar with pink Auchindoir dressings. Tower and porch with crenellated parapets.

GORDON SCHOOLS, Castle Street. By *Archibald Simpson*, 1839– 96 41, for Elizabeth Brodie, dowager Duchess of Richmond and Gordon, in memory of her husband, the 5th Duke, and as a replacement for the old castle gatehouse. Jacobean, two-storey H-plan in pale ashlar sandstone with mullioned-and-transomed windows and an octagonal tower over the central pend. Within the pend, flanking an inscription panel, recessed roundels with marble busts of the Duke and Duchess, signed by *Thomas Campbell* and dated 1841. The front elevation is nine bays wide, its centre five bays recessed between wings two bays wide and three bays deep. Round-arched double-height pend simply moulded with the Gordon arms above. The tower has a dedication panel flanked by scrolls, slim louvred belfry openings and roundels with ogee heads on alternate sides, but only those to front and rear have clock faces; above, a leaded ogee dome with thistle finial and weathervane. Flanking the pend, narrow bays rising into curvilinear gables and dormerheads at the outer bays. The wings have shallow-pitched roofs and stilted gables framed by broad angle pilasters rising into stout octagonal chimneystacks. Rear elevation similar, but here the pend is single-storeyed only, with a blind bell-shaped first-floor panel. The matching rear wings added for the School Board (who took over in 1886) are of 1888 by *A. Marshall Mackenzie* (of *Matthews & Mackenzie*). (WAR MEMORIAL. Stained glass window by *J. A. H. Hector*, the Aberdeen painter. Two panels with names and four others with representations of the men called into service. At the top figures of poetry, consolation, history, justice, peace and epic poetry. Further window of 1950 by *Robert Jamieson Troup*.)

Immediately E is the former ELEMENTARY DEPARTMENT (now LINDEN COMMUNITY CENTRE), by *Robert Gordon Wilson* (of *Ellis & Wilson*), 1903–4. Neo-Baroque in granite ashlar with Elgin freestone dressings. Two-storeyed, its central entrance bay flanked by twin gablefronts with tripartite windows, their first-floor centre lights crowned by semicircular broken pediments containing obelisks.

To the W, the former HIGHER GRADE DEPARTMENT by *Kelly & Nicol*, 1910–12. Distinctive asymmetrical Neo-Jacobean. Two-storeyed grey granite with freestone dressings, upper floor rising into tall wall-head gables. Mullioned-and-transomed windows arranged as paired or triple-lights. It is now largely concealed by the PRIMARY SCHOOL, ASSEMBLY HALL and DINING ROOM, which are of *c.* 1954–8 but still 1930s Modern; further extensions of the 1970s.

HUNTLY BUSINESS CENTRE, No. 85 Gordon Street. Formerly the woollen mill of William Spence & Co. Later C19, substantially altered by *George Bennett Mitchell* in 1910–12. Three storeys, seven bays with tall paired windows, pilastered main entrance in fifth bay towards r. end. Grey granite ashlar with rock-faced giant-order pilastrade framing first and second floors. Low hipped roof with overhanging eaves on simple brackets. HUNTLY LEARNING CENTRE. Single-storeyed with ogee gable front, once part of the mill.

SCOTT'S HOSPITAL (Eventide Home), Gladstone Road. Also known as Scott's Institution, founded for the elderly destitute with a bequest from Dr Alexander Scott (†1833). The original Jacobean edifice by *William Smith*, 1853–5 and extended 1868, is concealed by the impressive Scots Perpendicular front added by *A. Marshall Mackenzie*, *c.* 1899–1901. This is symmetrically balanced about a tall central tower stepped out from the three-storey, three-bay centrepiece, short links connecting to advanced two-storey, four-bay wings with gabled projections at each end. Built in snecked pink granite with Auchindoir dressings, the design is given interest by its mullioned-and-transomed windows, the battlemented parapets of the tower and projecting bays, crowstepped gables of varying heights breaking up the wall-head, and tall clustered chimneystacks across the roof ridge; the pinnacles of Smith's earlier spires are just visible behind. The tower is of four stages: a porte cochère with four-centred arches, first and second floors relatively modest, but the tall upper stage is entirely brown Auchindoir masonry. This upper stage has four traceried Perp lights on each side, and simply detailed fleur-de-lys and gargoyles just beneath the arcaded parapet. Smith's surviving elevations at the rear are harled and very plain.

STEWART'S HALL, Gordon Street. The design for the town hall was won in competition by *James Anderson*, 1873, and built 1874–5 but reconstructed in 1886–7 after a fire, with a redesigned tower by *Matthews & Mackenzie*. Symmetrical, two storeys and seven bays broad with crenellated parapet, the central entrance bay rising into a Scots Baronial clock tower 24 m. high. Belfry gablets and corbelled turrets with slated spirelets clasp the central pavilion roof, with patterned slates and brattishing. Doorway dignified by pilasters and an exuberant cast-iron lamp fitting, original flanking shopfronts with large plate-glazed windows in shouldered openings, channelled end pilasters.

DESCRIPTION

Since 1770 Huntly has been laid out on a gridiron plan orientated NNE–SSW, its earlier nucleus around The Square lying towards the N end of the central axis, which comprises Castle Street to the N of the Square and Gordon Street to the S: the latter is not quite parallel with the other streets in the grid because it remained on its pre-C18 alignment at its S end. On the WNW–ESE axis THE SQUARE is divided into four equal quarters by Deveron Street on the W and Duke Street on the E. It is still the heart of the town and near its centre is a STATUE of the 5th Duke of Richmond and Gordon by *Alexander Brodie*, 1862–3, in Redland freestone, the Duke wearing the uniform of the Sussex militia, of which he was colonel. But the site was important long before The Square itself was formed. At the foot of the statue are two STANDING STONES which once formed part of a circle 12–15 m. in diameter. One has been carved with a Pictish horseshoe now eroded away. In the S half of The Square is the ROBERTSON FOUNTAIN by *Matthews & Mackenzie*, 1882 (masons *Macdonald, Field & Co.*), a memorial to James Robertson, distiller and bank agent. The design is based on the early C17 Scots Renaissance well-head at Pinkie House (Lothian) with a ribbed spire and Doric arches on four sides, all in polished granite.

The Square must have assumed its present form not later than the early C18 for on the W side, towards the N end, is FORSYTH'S HOUSE erected *c.* 1724–6 for Alexander Forsyth, who made a fortune trading cloth in the Netherlands. Three storeys and six bays broad in grey granite ashlar, it has a big 'Dutch' wall-head gable rising into a chimneystack, club skewputts and moulded chimney copes. At ground floor it has a central round-arched pend, but the other bays have been altered for shop windows, probably *c.* 1900. The adjoining building to the l. seems to have been of the same general appearance but has been truncated at its S end by reconstruction in 1875 as CRUIKSHANK'S, a shop with flats above in Scots Baronial of the Matthews school. This has its first floor corbelled out slightly and a telescopic angle turret rising into the attic as a spirelet with fish-scale slates. Its gambrel roof has nicely detailed piended dormers, the ridge with brattishing. The other early building is No. 4, at The Square's SE corner, which is of 1736 but so altered as to be unrecognizable.

The later buildings around The Square begin at the S end with the CLYDESDALE BANK of *c.* 1842 by *Archibald Simpson* for the North of Scotland Bank. A handsome Neoclassical frontage with Italianate details in grey granite ashlar, two storeys and three bays broad. Principal entrance deeply recessed and framed by Doric pilasters with round-headed transom-light encompassed beneath a moulded arch. Large astragalled windows, those on the ground floor altered. The flank to Gordon Street is four bays, but with triple-light arcade on ground floor again set between Doric pilasters. The design is bound together above the wall-head by a simple cornice and deep blocking course, rising over the entrance front into a panelled parapet with scrolls, and thence into a tall broad chimneystack. Facing this on the W side of Gordon Street, and clearly influenced by it, is a two-storey building of *c.* 1844, with a relatively broad two-bay ashlar frontage rising into a blocking course and panelled gable. Next to this, on the square's W side, the GORDON ARMS HOTEL. There has been an inn here since at least the mid C18 but the present structure was built *c.* 1820 and substantially remodelled in the High Victorian style by *Francis D. Robertson c.* 1893. The set piece is the centre bay, which has a pilastered entrance sheltered by a (later) glazed canopy, and a broad five-light bay window at first floor; the Gordon arms are set in a round-headed panel over its cornice. Pavilion roof distinguished by filigree ducal coronet in cast and wrought iron; and pretty jerkin-headed dormers.

Less showy, but replete with Victorian holiday atmosphere, is the HUNTLY HOTEL at the N end of The Square, which was built in 1900–3 by *Robert Duncan* of Huntly. Its entrance is framed by polished grey granite columns supporting a flattened semi-elliptical key-blocked arch over a nine-panelled transom-lit door, with a fine cast-iron balcony above. The hotel provides the foil to the Brander Museum and Library (*see* Public Buildings) on the opposite side of Castle Street, which itself makes an engaging ensemble with the excellent POST OFFICE in the square's NE corner. This is by *H.M. Office of Works*, 1934–5, striking a fine balance between homage to provincial classicism and the architecture of state. Neo-Georgian, three storeys and five windows wide in grey granite ashlar. Channelled ground floor, panelled double-leaf doors with deep transom-lights in the two l. bays. Centre window recessed between fluted Greek Doric columns, plain entablature with Egyptic lettering. Upper floors austerely elegant, gabled roof with coped end stacks.

CASTLE STREET leads to the Castle Parks, with late C18 and early C19 houses on its W side. Two groups stand out, Nos. 8–10 of 1793 and Nos. 20–22: both two-storey, four-bay, long low buildings with broad arched pends off-centre opening into rear courts, gabled roofs with club skews and coped stacks. At the far end, No. 30, its entrance front two low storeys, three windows generously spaced, built in squared golden granite, end gables in rubble. Round the corner in West Park Street,

BALVENIE HOUSE *c.* 1835 is classic Late Georgian. Two storeys and three bays, harled with margins, pedimented porch with anta-pilasters, railed front area. The view along Castle Street is focused on the WAR MEMORIAL, a very remarkable design of 1922 by *Francis W. Troup*, who was born in Huntly. An austere, elegant obelisk 12 m. high in palest grey Kemnay granite, raised on six square columns forming an elongated hexagon; the names are carved on panels of polished dark granite set between the columns, with further panels added for the Second World War.

In DEVERON STREET, off The Square's W side, the best house is No. 29, early C19, two storeys and three bays broad in granite ashlar with cavetto-splayed entrance (cf. 6 Church Street), moulded cornice and coped chimneystacks. GORDON STREET, S from The Square, was named after Alexander, the 4th Duke. On the E side, beyond the Clydesdale Bank (*see* above) is the BANK OF SCOTLAND by *William Henderson*, 1863. Austere Late Georgian Survival. Two storeys, three windows wide, grey granite ashlar, doorway sheltered under console cornice. Then the CROWN BAR, dated 1898. Two storeys and two bays with panelled gable-fronted attic. Canted corner with entrance on Richmond Lane junction, corbelling to square on first floor. Ground-floor windows inset with coloured glass lights; tall first-floor windows and scrolled gable with paired attic lights and date. More stained glass panels inside. Diagonally opposite, beyond Stewart's Hall (*see* Public Buildings), at the corner with Nelson Street, a simple but sophisticated commercial building of *c.* 1820. Classical two-storeyed in grey granite ashlar, symmetrical entrance front with seven-bay arcade at ground floor, and three broadly spaced windows on the first. Bowed corner; plain frieze, slim cornice and wall-head parapet extend across both elevations, with console scrolls above the bow.

Now E from The Square along BOGIE WYND, a single street which begins as DUKE STREET and becomes BOGIE STREET further downhill. Close to the top on the S side, Nos. 3–7 is another Dutch-style house, early–mid-C18 with the characteristic central hemicycle gable with club-moulded skews and surmounting coped chimneystack. Beyond it stand much larger buildings of *c.* 1900, including Nos. 25–27, dated 1908 – two storeys and five bays broad in granite ashlar with lighter sandstone dressings; central wall-head chimneystack with pedimented attic dormers in mansard roof with brattishing. Next to it, No. 29, a baker's shopfront, fascia consoles detailed with wheatsheaves. Opposite, and more lavishly detailed, is Nos. 32–36 of *c.* 1897, a two-storey six-bay block in grey granite ashlar with brown sandstone dressings. Fine central doorpiece with twin doors under single transom-light inset with coloured glass; above, a curvilinear pediment raised on pilasters. Both the original shopfronts survive. Well detailed, with central chimneystack and timber dormers. At the end of this row and set at right angles to the street, overlooking what is effectively a small square, is the ROYAL OAK, originally built for William Petrie, burgess, in 1726.

The street descends quickly downhill and towards the bottom is LOGGIE BUILDINGS (Nos. 1–3 Bogie Street), an eye-catching design by *Thomas G. Archibald*, 1906–7, facing Strathbogie Parish Church. A bold, freely styled block of shops and flats, two storeys and a tall attic with a fine cast-iron balcony across the first floor. Paired arched entrances to flats at centre, flanked by polished red granite columns. Shopfronts in flanking bays with slim cast-iron colonnettes framing recessed doorways and plate-glazed windows. At first floor the end bays are canted; a boldly profiled, rippling cornice, attic dormers with curvilinear pediments in the mansard roof. The chimney-breast rising through the central bay has the Masonic square and compasses, the monogram of William Loggie and the date. The rest of the street is a picturesque ensemble of houses of mixed dates including No. 15, simple earlier C19 in coursed squared rubble with consoled doorpiece and long-and-short quoins, and single-storey piend-roofed wings on either side. Then, set well back from the street within its garden on the N side SPRINGBANK, of *c.* 1880, an assured two-storey symmetrical villa in fine-cut silver granite ashlar with a shallow tetrastyle portico. Lastly, on the N side before the river, JAKE FORBES CLOSE, opening off the main thoroughfare between two low contrasting gables, one whitewashed, one cherry-cocked rubble with club skews, the latter on the r. (dated 1793) belonging to a two-storey house built into the banks of the Bogie. Restored 1996 by the North-East Scotland Preservation Trust. The BRIDGE over the Bogie was rebuilt in 1807 to make it more suitable for wheeled traffic, and widened in 1895.

Back to CHURCH STREET (formerly Tannery Street), leading off the s side of Duke Street, long and varied street with two-storey houses of the late C18 and early C19. On the E side, No. 6 is taller than the norm, with a fine simple frontage in cherry-cocked ashlar granite. Three windows generously spaced, the entrance round-arched and cavetto-splayed with railed approach stairs; separate coachhouse. No. 8 is another big two-storey three-bay house, perhaps slightly later and certainly more sophisticated, its front of polished ashlar and the doorway with elegant rectangular fanlight approached by a railed stair. The w side is lined with more modest vernacular houses, but Nos. 15–17, WRIGHTS' HALL, dated 1797 is five bays and much taller with a moulded cornice.

Sloping downhill between Church Street and the Bogie are the 'New Feus', which were laid out with affluent villas in the last quarter of the C19. Three main streets – Richmond Road, Albert Road and Gladstone Road – run N–S, with a number of shorter streets running E–W. Of these villas only a selection can be mentioned here. In RICHMOND ROAD, No. 10, at the corner with Settrington Street, is Free Style in grey granite with exuberant dripmoulds at the entrance and Baroque pediments over ground-floor bays. In QUEEN STREET, THE COTTAGE is of *c.* 1835, stripped classical, single storey and three bays, with centre rising into low attic gable. Lying-pane glazing, slim surrounds, and gently pitched roofs with eaves bracketing. In GLADSTONE ROAD the best house is HOWGLEN, 1898, by *Francis W. Troup* for his father, the Rev. Robert Troup. It is in his highly personal Arts and Crafts style, two storeys, harled in white with slate-hung first-floor cantilever bay sheltering the entrance and rising into a tall gable in front of the main roof. Ground-floor bay on l. flank with nice filigree detail. Short diamond-plan chimneystack on roof ridge. Rather more conventional Old English, close to Scott's Hospital (*see* Public Buildings), is THE GABLES, *c.* 1900.

A separate and particularly exclusive enclave of larger houses lies E of the Bogie on BATTLE HILL, close to the railway station. They were mostly built for military men and factory owners. Off the Aberdeen road, first ALDIE HOUSE, built for the Sellars family, who developed a self-adjusting plough. Symmetrical, two-storey three-bay house, grey granite framed by crowstep-gabled ends. Further up is BATTLEHILL LODGE for Col. Mellis, 1887. Scottish Baronial, two-storeyed with segmentally arched entrance flanked by single-storey bow window and two-storey canted bay, the latter rising into an octagonal slated spire. Varied wall-head gables, inglenook and slim corner turret; large set-back wing. BATTLEHILL HOUSE is of *c.* 1885, late Baronial for Mr Dunn. It is laid out on a complex stepped plan, two-storeyed in grey granite rising into crowstepped attic gables, single-storey porch in re-entrant angle, service wing built into higher ground at rear. Higher up, MARYFIELD of *c.* 1883 for Mr Porter. Two-storey L-plan frontage, crowstepped projecting bay on r. lit by bay window rising through both storeys which forms a balustraded balcony for attic room in the gable. Finally, DALHOUSIE, for Commander Simpson *c.* 1884. Cottage style, long and stylish single storey with projecting end bay rising into broad gable. Predominantly dark granite with lighter stone dressings, log-column porch with rustic latticework in the angle, attic dormers and gable with nicely carved bargeboards, two-bay log-column veranda on the flank, fine roof-ridge brattishing.

GREENKIRTLE, 0.8 km. SSE of the town centre, on the other side of the A96 bypass. 1824. Childhood home of the author George MacDonald, and a classic example of a villa type particularly characteristic of North-East Scotland. Single-storeyed, of three bays, in cherry-cocked squared rubble raised over a basement. Elegant central doorpiece approached by a neat railed stair and astragalled sash-and-case windows set in slim surrounds, grey granite dressings.

HUNTLY CASTLE

This strategic site within the confluence of the Bogie and the Deveron, a crossing point on one of the chief routes into Moray, was once the principal seat of the Gordons, for centuries the dominant family in North-East Scotland. The impressive Z-plan palace-block, with a drum tower at one corner and stair-tower diagonally opposite, can trace its origins to the mid C15, and was probably influenced by French châteaux. But it was never a truly defensive structure, for it was built only after the defeat of the Gordons' main rivals, the Earls of Moray, during the Douglas Rebellion of 1452. Henceforth the Gordons were established as the new adjutants of the Crown, but after the Reformation their adherence to Catholicism, and their substantial wealth, presented a threat which neither fledgling Kirk nor Royal House might possibly ignore: and the Castle was slighted twice, then each time rebuilt within a few years more splendid than ever previously, so that by the early C17 it was unequivocally palatial. Ultimately, its downfall was brought about not by Kings but by Covenanters. It was abandoned after the Civil Wars and is now roofless, although its shell survives substantially intact.

For a long time before the palace-block was built, the site had been genuinely fortified. On the W, a large mound was formerly the MOTTE of a motte-and-bailey castle, probably constructed c. 1190 by Duncan, Earl of Fife. His descendants lost Strathbogie to the Gordons of Huntly in Berwickshire after Bannockburn, but only after 1376 when the old Fife male line died out did the Gordons actually move north.

The Gordons' own male line failed with Sir John Gordon in 1407, and he was succeeded by his brother-in-law Sir Alexander Seton who died in 1440 or 1441. Seton's son, also Alexander, was created 1st Earl of Huntly in 1444 or 1445. It is not clear which of the two Setons built the very large TOWER HOUSE known as the 'Auld Warke' in the centre of the bailey which thereafter became the castle court. Its L-plan was very modern for its time, the main block orientated E–W being 15.8 m. long by 11 m. deep and its SW jamb 7.9 m. by 5.8 m. over walls 3 m. thick. The younger Seton assumed the name of Gordon c. 1457. On the S side of the court he built a new and more comfortable hall block – 'the New Warke' – construction on the site continuing until after his death in 1470. In 1594 Huntly Castle was slighted by James VI after the 6th Earl was first implicated in the 'Spanish Blanks' plot and then humiliated the Crown by defeating a Protestant army under the 7th Earl of Argyll at Glenlivet. The Auld Warke was rendered uninhabitable, blown up by powder lent by the burgesses of Aberdeen. Its ruins stood until 1731, when they were reduced to foundations, still visible today.

46 How the 'New Warke' – the PALACE-BLOCK – fared in the wake of this destruction is not entirely clear, but it was not the first time that it had faced the Royal anger. It had its origins in the hall built next to the Auld Warke in the mid C15 but was substantially reconstructed and heightened by the 4th Earl, who was Lord Chancellor of Scotland and a nephew of James IV. Here he entertained the Queen Regent, Mary of Guise, with

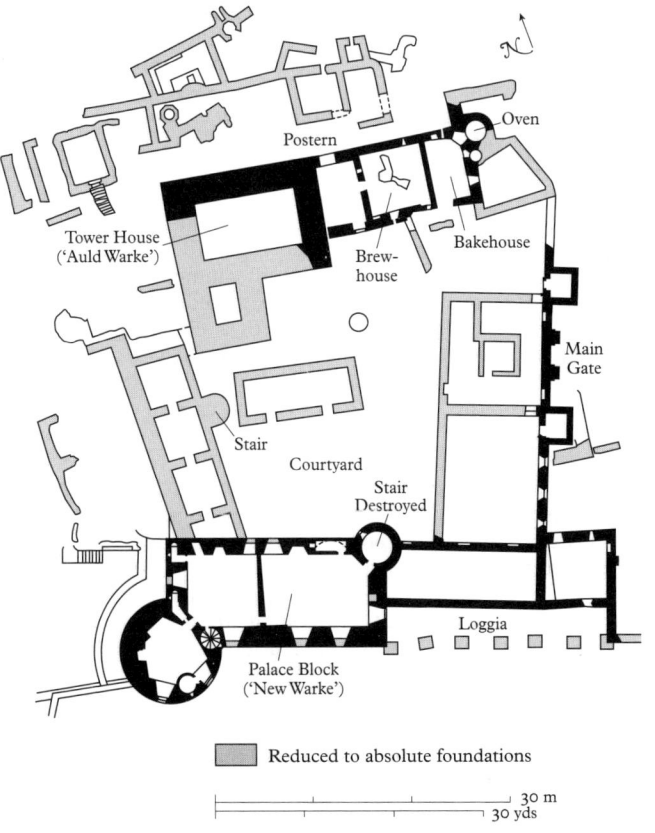

Huntly Castle.
Plan

Reduced to absolute foundations

30 m
30 yds

such indulgence and aplomb that her countryman the French ambassador dubbed him the 'Cock o' the North' and urged her to clip his wings. After Mary died and her daughter Mary, Queen of Scots succeeded, under pressure from her Protestant lords she engaged the 4th Earl in battle at Corrichie (1562), following which he died of apoplexy. His son John and six other family members were executed, the lands attainted and the castle looted of its treasures and burned; but in 1565 the titles were restored to the 5th Earl and the castle was rebuilt. When James VI blew up the Auld Warke in 1594, the New Warke as a less defensible structure escaped comparatively lightly: only the entrance tower on the courtyard elevation was destroyed, allowing it to be easily rebuilt. The King forgave the Earl in 1597 and elevated him as 1st Marquess of Huntly in 1599. Thereafter, the castle's name was changed from Strathbogie to

Huntly by Act of Parliament, rendering the Gordons, their title and their family seat synonymous and indivisible. Thus the New Warke was set for its final and most magnificent transformation.

The basic design – a giant four-storey tower house (23.2 m. by 11 m.), with its principal elevation facing s and incorporating a drum tower (10.7 m. in diameter) at its sw angle – dates from the 4th Earl's reconstruction of the original stone hall in the mid C16. The likelihood that its inspiration might be French is all the greater since the Earl accompanied Mary of Guise on a visit to France in 1550, although the immediate prototype is now thought to be Druminnor (q.v.). Built in pinned brown granite rubble, the s FRONT's length is closely similar to its height, resulting in a massive composition of square and cylinder. The splendid treatment of the upper storey with its delicate oriels and boldly lettered friezes is later, carried out for the 1st Marquess *c.* 1602–6, seemingly by the English master mason *Ralph Raleyn* or *Rawlinson*: at that date the 'New Warke' must have appeared even taller and more impressive than it does now, its wall-head lined with a further range of dormers and oriels in the steeply sloping roofs, the tall chimneystacks rising between them to carry their smoke clear above the ridges.

The lowest storey – the foundations of the former hall – is actually a basement built into sloping ground, and its walls are absolutely solid, 1.8 m. thick, save for inverted keyhole gun-loops. It accommodates three vaulted cellars with a corridor running across the N side, the drum having been divided by a mezzanine providing either a prison or a store. The walls of the mid-C16 upper storeys are much less substantial – 0.6 m. – and lit by windows in dressed surrounds. Small square windows, formerly barred, on the ground floor express the kitchen flanked by two stores in the palace-block itself, and the steward's room within the drum. These are vaulted like the basement but larger, and they communicate without a corridor.

The first and second floors are much taller, the latter raised in height by the 1st Marquess to create a suite of apartments for his wife which would be still more splendid than his own: they were probably influenced by what he had seen during his brief period in exile. The first-floor hall and great chamber windows are again set in dressed surrounds, the fixing holes for their iron grilles still visible although infilled. But the real magnificence is at second floor where the walls were rebuilt in pale red ashlar sandstone, the Marchioness's apartments being lit by triple-light oriels with single-light windows between them. Above was a splendid attic floor lit by an upper tier of dormer oriels with the prismatic roofs recorded in John Claude Nattes's drawing of 1798. At such a height defensive grilles were unnecessary; the glazing pattern, a fixed light with shutters under, survives in the pedimented dummy window which carries the theme across the chimney-breast. Above and beneath the oriels are two large friezes in raised Roman letters:

GEORGE GORDOVN FIRST MARQVIS OF HUNTLY 16
HENRIETTE STEVART, MARQVISSE OF HUNTLY 02

In each case the end of the inscription has been lost through collapse of the square two-storey turret formerly at the SE corner, but the message remains clear – an assertion of rights reinstated by the Sovereign and enshrined by Parliament after the rough-and-tumble of the past few years. This turret evidently had its own smaller inscription, of which only the first letter Q and last letter T survive.

Inside, the upper storeys were arranged identically, each a hierarchical sequence of rooms including a hall and outer chamber at first floor, linking to an inner chamber (i.e. a bed-chamber) in the drum. The halls were entered off the stair in the NE entrance tower, but there were also two spiral stairs in the wall of the drum itself, one linking the steward's room with his master's and one rising through the whole height of the drum between the outer and inner chambers to the attic bedrooms. The drum's top (fifth) storey also features an oriel, and has a rich corbel course with rope moulding around its wallhead, once crowned by the conical roof shown in Nattes's drawing; of this too a pedimented dormer and tall chimney-stacks survive, together with a polygonal lookout post.

The COURTYARD ELEVATION is plain save for the NE entrance tower, which rose circular for its first two storeys before corbelling to the square at top floor and attic level; the outer face of this two-tier caphouse has unfortunately been lost. The tower was erected by the 1st Marquess as part of his early C17 remodelling, its predecessor having been destroyed by James VI. As part of their reconciliation, the Marquess had nominally embraced the Protestant faith, but the tower's iconography made it clear that nothing had really changed. The doorway itself is finely moulded, with string pilasters, shaft-rings and tiny capitals supporting a heavy lintel: this is carved with four escutcheons bearing the arms of Huntly, the Marquess and Marchioness's monogrammed initials, the arms of her family – Lennox – and the date 1602, with deer-hounds (the Huntly supporters) between them. But the real message was in the elaborate display of sculpted panels rising up the tower's shaft.

These begin with the arms of the Marquess and his wife flanked by their supporters, a Gordon deer-hound and a Lennox wolf, with the Gordons' stag-head and the Lennox bull-head in the crest above. Then come the arms of the King and Queen, I.R.6, Jacobus Rex Sextus and A.R.S., Anna Regina Scotorum, flanked by the Scottish unicorn and Danish wyvern, and with the Scottish crest, a front-face lion – all well and good. But then came two more panels with strong Counter-Reformation overtones, in the context of which the inclusion of these arms was much more dangerous. First, an unusually comprehensive set of Symbols of the Passion – the Cross with Christ's pierced heart, hands and feet, the Crown of Thorns, the clothes for which the Roman soldiers drew lots and the instruments of the Crucifixion – with the Scottish motto *In Defens* beneath, suggesting that the interests of the Scottish Crown and the Counter-Reformation were one and the same. Above the Passion, *Absit Nobis Gloria Ri Nisi in Cruce Domini Nostri Iesu Christi* (from Galatians 6:14, 'God forbid that I should glory save in the Cross of our Lord Jesus Christ'). The Passion was flanked by two figures whose identity is now unclear. Further above the Passion, a roundel represented the head of Christ in Glory after the Resurrection – *Divina Virtute Resurgo* ('I rise again with Divine Power'), an explicit reference to the Marquess's own return to greater glory after the period of his darkness in exile, which, even as it began, it was fordained must end. But the most provocative element of all was the small figure which crowned the ogee head of this sculptural display: St Michael – God's field-commander – standing on a serpent crouched into a ball, having slain it with his spear.

Both the 4th and 6th Earls of Huntly had been elevated as members of the French chivalric Order of Saint-Michel, the 4th Earl by Henri II in 1548, and the 6th Earl by Henri IV in 1594. The 4th Earl had subsequently died a martyr at Corrichie, forced into opposition against Queen Mary – a Catholic Sovereign, appointed by Divine Grace – by scheming Protestant nobles; many of his followers had been executed and there had been a period of forfeiture. The 6th Earl had in the same way been driven to rebellion against King James, but after banishment he had returned, raised by that King into a position of supreme glory.

That the 6th Earl should be honoured by Henri IV in the year of his victory at Glenlivet was particularly appropriate since Henri, like James, had been born a Catholic yet raised a Calvinist: but when he ascended the French throne in 1589, he had deemed it prudent to abjure his Protestant faith – *Paris vaut bien une messe*, he had reputedly remarked, 'Paris is well worth a mass'. King James's own grandfather, James V, who had died after the English victory at Solway Moss in 1542, and his father, Henry Stewart Lord Darnley, had also been members of the Order of Saint-Michel. Far more, then, than just a brilliant gesture of defiance, the sculptural display at Huntly, once richly tinctured and gilded, was a personal manifesto of religious and political belief, and one that could not be silenced after King James VI had left for England: there can be little doubt that the Marquess designed it himself, and indeed nothing else quite like it exists anywhere else in the British Isles. Its 'popish' imagery was chiselled off by Captain James Wallace when a Covenanting garrison was billeted at the Castle in 1640, although notably its heraldic motifs remained untouched.

Likewise, the chief surviving work of sculpture within the building, the FIREPLACE in the Marchioness's Hall, has only partly been defaced. Two swordsmen in armour act as Atlantes to support a mantelpiece carved with monogrammed initials

50

of the 1st Marquess and his wife, flanked by their arms (his l., hers r.); a top moulding bears a verse based on Romans 8:28, 'Sen God doth us defend, Ve sal prevail unto the end. To thaes that love God Al thingis virkis to the best.' Above the mantel the Royal Arms supported by lion and unicorn are framed between fluted columns with ornate capitals, and flanked by obelisks with crescent and fleur-de-lys finials at the corners. The columns support an upper trefoil-headed panel, its subject obliterated by the iconoclasts. A second fireplace in the outer chamber displays medallion portraits of the 1st Marquess and Marchioness.

The ruined remains of the COURTYARD BUILDINGS, excavated *c.* 1923–33, once contained a chapel, but its location remains unclear. It has been suggested that it occupied the upper storey of the fragmentary E WING built out from the New Warke by either the 1st or 2nd Marquess between 1600 and 1643, at which latter date *George Thomson* (who rebuilt the lantern of King's College tower, Aberdeen, q.v.) was working on the site. An alternative theory is that the chapel occupied the small rectangular building in the centre of the courtyard, now reduced to its foundations. Both possibilities may be correct, as it is known that work was carried out in the chapel in 1607, and it may have moved to the E wing then. In front of the E wing are square stone footings of what was once a vaulted LOGGIA affording views over the Castle Parks.

The lesser ranges enclosing the courtyard are so ruinous that the castle's overall plan is not entirely clear. The W RANGE was of real distinction – stone-built, two storeys in height as evident from the roof-raggles in the N elevation of the palace-block's N elevation, and extended from it at a slight angle to skirt past the Auld Warke. It had a semicircular tower containing a stair-way, and a bakehouse at the far end. Of the N RANGE little can be discerned with certainty, but it contained a bakehouse with two ovens, and a brewhouse of which the vat's seat has survived. The E RANGE with its gatehouse was apparently being constructed by the 2nd Marquess in 1643 when the Covenanters arrived, and consequently was never finished. Trouble had clearly been expected as a RAVELIN was formed in front of the E range as a shelter for defending artillery and protection against bombardment.

The castle was held for the Royalists by Montrose in 1644 but in 1647 James Gordon of Newton, commanding it for the 2nd Marquess of Huntly, was starved into surrender by General David Leslie. Many of Newton's 'Irish' retainers were summarily executed; Newton himself was hanged for treason in Edinburgh and the 2nd Marquess beheaded in 1649. After the Restoration the family preferred to live at Gordon Castle (Moray), the 3rd Marquess becoming Duke of Gordon in 1684. Huntly remained the residence of their chamberlain and baron-bailie who represented them in dealings with the town, but maintenance was not a priority and the castle fell into decay, a process exacerbated by its use as a Hanoverian fort in

1745. In the 1750s some of its fabric was requisitioned by Katherine, the 3rd Duke's widow, and her consort, Staats Morris, for reconstruction of Huntly Lodge (*see* below), other materials being purloined by lesser hands. The New Warke's SE turret and loggia had collapsed by 1799, although the main roof still held and visitors noted surviving painted decoration in the family apartments and the chapel; only fragments of cornice now survive. When the 5th Duke married Elizabeth Brodie in 1813 she requested that the castle be restored for their use but its deterioration was thought to make that impracticable. The 7th Duke entrusted the castle to state care in 1923, and over the next decade the site was cleared of débris, consolidated and excavated: the terrace on which the castle stands was unearthed and the Auld Warke's foundations in the courtyard exposed.

The CASTLE PARKS have been divided for a variety of uses. The 1st Marquess probably created the Pleasaunce when he reconstructed the castle *c.* 1600 and even after the Gordons left in the mid C17 the grounds were maintained, the avenue of linden trees through which the castle is approached today being planted in the 1840s shortly after the Gordon Schools (*see* p. 531) were built. The Richmond & Gordon Estates allowed Huntly Cricket Club to use the upper East Park nearest the town from *c.* 1890, the Club building its PAVILION in 1920. Part of the lower East Park near the Castle was laid out as a nine-hole golf course by *Tom Morris* in 1892. The remainder was subsequently sold to the Town Council in 1925 as a recreation ground, financed by Alexander Cooper of New York in whose honour it was named; the memorial gates to him date from 1934. After the Second World War, school extensions and housing around Seton Drive partly overran the West Park; the former Castle garden (later Show Park) survives as playing fields.

HUNTLY LODGE
(Castle Hotel)
0.6 km. N of the Castle

A large and austere classical country house which openly acknowledges its piecemeal construction between the mid C18 and earlier C19. After the death of Cosmo, 3rd Duke of Gordon, in 1752 his widow, Catherine, decided to reconstruct Sandieston Farmhouse as a tall three-storey house of the John Adam school for her own use. It still survives, largely concealed by later extensions. Huntly Lodge was sold by the Richmond & Gordon Estates in 1924 and opened as a hotel in 1946.

The S entrance front divides into two clear parts. At the E end, a simple two-storey three-bay block in squared granite, ground-floor windows taller than first, was built *c.* 1769 as an extension to Sandieston by Catherine and her new husband, the American Staats Morris. Some materials were reused from the old castle as doubtless they had been for the original 1750s works. The long symmetrical block in grey granite ashlar constituting the rest of the entrance front on the w was built by George Gordon, 8th Marquess of Huntly (later 5th Duke of Gordon) either in 1800 or *c.* 1814–20 after he married Elizabeth Brodie, the Lodge having become the seat of the heir. It is the same height as the 1760s wing but three storeys rather than two. It has a four-bay centre recessed between shallow canted bays four windows wide at either end, very unusual in design with ground-floor doorways and blind openings in the canted planes at first and second floor. The 1760s wing was heightened slightly in different stone to match it, but the two blocks have separate piended roofs with tall coped chimneystacks, both rising from within plain parapets with no cornices.

The E flank is the original entrance front. Behind the 1760s part is the original farmhouse, reputedly incorporating a C17 core although the visible parts of its elevations are mid-Georgian, built of squared granite, with ground-floor windows taller than first, and small oblong windows at second floor beneath a tall piended roof. The house and its 1760s frontal wing are matched in height, but their gables are stepped. Against the N front *Archibald Simpson* built *c.* 1832 another two-storey block at right angles, rubble with dressed margins and quoins, again with the same wall-head but shallow on plan with a lower piended roof, and in the re-entrant angle thus formed he provided a single-storey porch with a very simple architraved doorpiece. A low two-storey service range with square first-floor windows behind Simpson's N range encloses the service court. Prominently displayed near the entrance within one of the ground-floor windows are two SCULPTURAL FRAGMENTS retrieved from Huntly Castle: a cartouche with coronet and monogram, and supported on this, an Ionic pilaster capital with foliate decoration.

The INTERIOR is generally simple with a good cantilever stair, the 1760s wing containing a distinctive chimneypiece with pulvinated frieze.

The CASTLE BRIDGE over the River Deveron – here known as the Devil's Chair – is quite exceptional, as befits its remarkable situation. A single round arch of 12 m. span, its spandrels splaying out towards the foundations, it is rubble-built with neatly dressed scrolled and chamfered ashlar voussoirs and the intrados also in ashlar: the gently hump-backed carriageway is over 2.5 m. wide between coped parapets with more generous approaches. This bridge has all the appearance of C17 or earlier work (some of its stones bear medieval masons' marks) although it has been repaired since, iron bands having been applied in the C18 and the S side of its W pier strengthened with rubble buttressing by *Master-mason Elgin c.* 1800.*

Behind the Lodge lies the HOME FARM with much-altered courtyard steading and big DOOCOT probably built in the 1750s or 60s. Telescopic type with two rat courses and truncated conical roof, pinned boulder rubble with red sandstone

---

* Its W side has recently partially collapsed.

dressings; the nails bristling from its joints were a novel protection against the rats.

INCHMARLO   K

3 km. WNW of Banchory

Begun in the late C18 as a two-storey house for John Douglas of Tilquhillie. The present squared-off and severe classical appearance is the result of remodelling in 1823 by *John Smith* for the banker and merchant Walter Stevenson Davidson and the addition *c.* 1850 by *John & William Smith* of a third storey with balustraded parapet in place of a piended roof with pediment over the slightly projected centre of the five-bay front. There was a central Doric porch and from the 1880s wide canted bays to l. and r. and an E wing but these features were removed in 1949. The present two-storey E wing, matching the rest, was built in 1986–7 by *G. R. M. Kennedy & Partners* (architect-in-charge *Russell Parker*) when the house was refurbished as a care home.

Many buildings in the grounds for the RETIREMENT VILLAGE, a then-pioneering concept in Scotland, beginning with QUEEN VICTORIA PARK, also by *Kennedy & Partners*, with polygonal rows of apartments containing one and two bedrooms and forming two squares that interlock around a central garden like a figure-of-eight. Nice timberwork balconies in the local tradition and brown pantile roof. The later neighbourhoods are predominantly houses and bungalows of traditional type.

Pretty SOUTH LODGE, probably *c.* 1823 and sensitively enlarged in 1923 by *Walker & Duncan*.

INGLISMALDIE CASTLE   K

2 km. SSW of Luthermuir

A sprawling and impressive building, with a complicated history of at least five major campaigns. The nucleus is an L-plan tower house, probably begun in 1588 when James VI granted the land to John Livingstone of Dunipace. He soon adopted Inglismaldie as his principal seat. In 1693 the estate was sold to David Falconer of Haulkerton Castle (*see* Mains of Haulkerton, Laurencekirk, p. 638) and it was probably he who added the three-storey, five-bay wing to the l. of the tower – a laird's mansion at its most severe. Around the year 1730 a piended wing was also spun out to the r. A fire led to a major restoration by *Matthews & Mackenzie* in 1882–4, including the demolition of the laird's block and the conversion of the castle into a proper Victorian house. In 1907 the Georgian wing was itself demolished and replaced with a new group of buildings.

The Victorian and Edwardian work straddles the original castle like a pair of overgrown bookends, but the C16 TOWER HOUSE still blazes in the centre, built of the most extraordinarily vivid red sandstone. It is impossible to imagine that it could have ever been harled. w front of four storeys, rising up flat as the jamb lay to the rear. Present entrance inserted in 1882–4 with segmental arch topped by a heraldic plaque. Double shot-hole to the l. (cf. Hallgreen Castle, q.v.) under two slit-windows. A strange broken string course runs across the top of the first storey. Three tourelles are corbelled out above, the middle one placed unusually off-centre so as not to encroach on the gable. The bases share the same moulding as the string course. Everything above is by *James Matthews*, including the tall candlesnuffer roofs, the C17-style dormerhead with griffins and the gable (unfortunately not crowstepped).

To the l. is Matthews's late C19 wing, running N–S and of comparatively dingy brown stone. Crowstepped gable facing W and, to the N, four bays with more dormerheads carved with monograms, coronets and thistle finials. A similar elevation wraps around the rear of the castle. To the l. of it is the large SERVICE WING added in 1907, its red sandstone a pale nod to continuity with the original building. Big drum tower in the re-entrant angle; crowsteps on the gables and dormerheads. A similar block extends around the whole s flank, where it is advanced to the r. of the original tower house.

The INTERIOR has several features of note. The current entrance leads straight into the original CELLAR, featuring segmental barrel-vaults and a former guardroom tucked under the turnpike stair. The latter is a good specimen with roll mouldings on the underside of the treads. The whole base of the N wing is taken up by Matthews's long Drawing Room. It

Inglismaldie Castle.
Engraving by D. MacGibbon & T. Ross, 1892

has a good wooden chimneypiece and also incorporates the original C16 ENTRANCE, a segmental arch picked out in thick roll moulding. In the Library is a collection of wooden PANELS featuring some of the finest medieval carving to have survived in northern Scotland. They were originally made in the mid C16 for a chapel (then known as 'Egglismaldie') that was incorporated into the rear of the tower house. Matthews demolished it to build his service wing but – thanks to his intense antiquarianism – reused the panels on cabinets and doors. They are a virtuosic display of mouchettes, daggers, strapwork, consoles and foliage – all excellent examples of Flamboyant tracery.

Former DOOCOT, 340 m. SW in a field. Large double-chamber lectern, now roofless. Built in the mid–late C18, and of the same ruby-coloured stone as the castle. Straight-headed entrances with rat course above. Every inch of the interior is crammed with nesting boxes, totalling over 1,500. – For the former Dower House *see* Forebank House, near Auchenblae (p. 666).

INSCH

From Gaelic *innis*, a meadow; a small market town in the Garioch's NW corner.

Situated on the Shevock Burn's N bank and sheltered by surrounding hills, Insch is first recorded in the late C12 in connection with a church granted by David, Earl of Huntingdon and the Garioch to the abbey he founded at Lindores in Fife. In 1677 the town was erected a burgh of barony for Charles Erskine, 21st (and 4th) Earl of Mar. Although the Aberdeenshire Canal never reached Insch as intended, its terminus at Port Elphinstone (*see* Inverurie) was close enough to encourage agricultural improvement during the earlier C19, and the quarrying of fine blue roofing slate at Foudland Hill. Nevertheless Insch's development remained confined to the immediate High Street–Market Street area until 1869, when its increasing prosperity resulted in the Public Hall in Commerce Street; this began the expansion SW towards the railway station at Rothney, which continued after the First World War. During the interwar years Insch's development N and W was driven by housing by the Aberdeen County Architects *George Gray* c. 1929 and *Edwin Williamson* c. 1934, and then by *W. Liddle Duncan* from 1937.

CHURCHES

CONGREGATIONAL CHURCH, High Street. *See* St Andrew's Masonic Lodge (Public Buildings).

OLD ST DROSTAN, High Street. Ruinous rectangular plan church on a much older site. The tall W gable in granite rubble is probably of 1769, its square-headed doorway and round-arched gallery window in dressed surrounds formed during renovation by *Matthew Daniel*, square-wright and carpenter, in 1793–4. One broken skewputt is carved with initials A.R. and an unclear date. Elaborately pedimented and finialled Scots Renaissance bellcote, dated 1613, initials M.I.L. (Magister Iohannes Logie) on S side; bell by *Albert Gely* 1706 removed in 1971. The remainder of the church has largely been demolished. Near the doorway, two BURIAL MONUMENTS – the Radulfus Stone *c.* 1200, incised with Celtic cross and inscription *Orate Pro Anima Radulfi Sacerdotis* ('Pray for the Soul of Radulf the priest'); next to this the head and shoulders of a carved knight *c.* 1300, details almost completely eroded.

PARISH CHURCH, Western Road. Built at the instigation of the Rev. Archibald Storie to designs by *Matthews & Mackenzie* 1881, completed 1883. Gothic, rectangular plan. Simple tall gable front in pinkish-gold squared granite with golden dressings, lit by three stepped windows, the tall central one two-light with geometric tracery. Sturdy pencil entrance tower at l. corner, beginning square before broaching to octagonal and rising into a belfry with clock gablets on alternate sides of the stone spire, its details simplified in 1914. Five-bay flanks in pinned granite rubble, simple pointed windows with diamond-pane glazing. Rear gable with small rose window above the session house; big roof with gablet ventilators. Broad open interior with shallow arched ceiling, divided into bays by slim ribs with bosses; deep gallery at the entrance end on cast-iron columns, panelled arcaded front with clock by *D. & J. Riddel*, Aberdeen. The dominant features are the ORGAN at the N end by *Wadsworth & Brother* 1906, and the STAINED GLASS – four windows by *William Meikle & Sons c.* 1923–8, l.–r. Christ carrying the Holy Grail; King David with his harp and as a shepherd; Christ as Light of the World carrying a lamb; and the Virgin and Child, with scenes of industry and charity. Either side of the pulpit are two windows from St Ninian, Oyne (q.v.), of Christ and St Andrew. In the vestry the stone FONT from Old St Drostan (*see* above), dated 1517. CHURCH HALL opposite by *James Duncan & Son* of Turriff 1901, altered by *W. Liddle Duncan* 1925.

ST DROSTAN (Episcopal), Commerce Street. By *Alexander Ross* (of *Ross & Macbeth*), 1894–5. Very simple E.E., described at the time as Early French. Four-bay nave with SW porch and two-bay chancel, all in reddish-gold snecked granite with sandstone dressings and sturdy angle buttresses. Steeply pitched red tiled roofs with bracketed eaves; over the nave's roof ridge near the W end, a slated timber bellcote with broached spirelet, cruciform finials at the E gables only. Plain W gable with three stepped lancets. Paired lancets at the nave and chancel, three lights in the chancel's E bay to illuminate the altar; small vestry outshot at the nave's N flank, and organ chamber on the chancel's N side. E gable with single large pointed window containing cinquefoil roundel. Good cast-iron gates, railings and finely detailed lamp standard.

The nave impresses through its excellent exposed stonework, open timber roof supported on arched trusses, and segmental rere-arches over its twin lancet windows. – FONT designed by *Ross & Macbeth*, sculpted by *D. & A. Davidson* 1892. – Oak CHANCEL SCREEN, 1904. – STAINED GLASS in the chancel – cinquefoil E window focuses on the Crucifixion; smaller windows in the chancel flanks represent the Virgin and Child with shepherds and magi, the Baptism in the Jordan, and St Andrew; all by *J. Powell & Sons*, 1898.

RECTORY to immediate S. CHURCH HALL by *Speirs & Co.* of Glasgow, 1901–2.

PUBLIC BUILDINGS

HOSPITAL, Rannes Street. By *George Bennett Mitchell*, 1922, built as a war memorial by public subscriptions; enlarged by Mitchell *c.* 1933. Cottage-scale, single-storey U-plan in coursed granite. Frontal wings have low piended roofs with oversailing eaves and tall chimneystacks.

PUBLIC HALL (now COMMUNITY CENTRE), Commerce Street. By *James Matthews*, 1869. Simple classical, with pilastered and pedimented segment-headed doorway.

RAILWAY STATION, Gordon Terrace. An unusually complete example of a late C19 country station, built on the Great North of Scotland Railway's main line between Aberdeen and Keith, and opened in 1854. On the 'Up' platform the main STATION BUILDING dated 1880, Neo-Jacobean, a tall single storey of three bays with its centre slightly projected under a gable. Harled in white, simple bold detailing, entrance with console cornice, windows mullioned and transomed. Two wings projecting at rear, small outshot on one side; the station clock, wall-mounted drinking fountain and simple interior have all been preserved. On the 'Down' platform, a timber-and-glass SHELTER to a standard GNSR pattern, now the last of its kind remaining; FOOTBRIDGE also to standard design at E end. Timber SIGNAL BOX to W with semaphores in clear view. Opposite, the WATER TOWER.

RUSSELL LIBRARY & INSTITUTE, Rannes Street. Late Arts and Crafts by *T. Scott Sutherland*, dated 1928, opened 1929. Single storey with centre bay projecting under steeply raked gable.

ST ANDREW'S MASONIC LODGE (No. 228), High Street. Former Congregational church, *c.* 1875. Simple gable front with pointed-arch doorway, lancet windows and roundel in dressed ashlar surrounds once set against a harl background, spike finial over apex; two-bay flanks. – STAINED GLASS by *George Donald & Sons*, Aberdeen, 1897. Vestry annexe behind.

SCHOOL, Alexander Street. By *George Sutherland*, 1898, with additions by Sutherland 1909. Granite ashlar entrance front E-plan single storey with gables rising into tall chimneystacks, the centre windows in the short linking bays with piended dormerheads. Blocky porch and rear wing later. Large E extension by *George Bennett Mitchell & Son*, 1933.

DESCRIPTION

Apart from churches and public buildings, the chief works of architecture are the surprisingly impressive BANKS, reflecting the importance of Insch's markets. The former ABERDEEN TOWN & COUNTY BANK in High Street by *William Smith* (of *J. & W. Smith*) was built in 1867, two-storey Italianate with a distyle Roman Doric portico off-centre crowned by a balustrade, and its telling room with a three-light segmentally pedimented window. Next to it is the former NORTH OF SCOTLAND BANK, Scots Renaissance by *Matthews & Mackenzie c.* 1883, tall two storeys and dormered attic, its ground floor pilastraded and its entrance bay on the r. rising into a full third storey under a gable.

Former PARISH MANSE, No. 1 Western Road. Entrance front comprises original two-storey, three-bay house built 1771, extended by a slightly projecting gabled bay in 1824–5. The original manse's centre doorway has been moved l. near the angle, and the gabled addition is lit by a ground-floor canted bay. w wing by *J. R. Mackenzie*, 1870.

BRIDGE, Wardhouse, 4 km. W. A single arch across the Shevock Burn with dressed chamfered voussoirs but without parapets, probably C17 and once the approach to Wardhouse Castle, which stood 150 m. E.

DRUMROSSIE HOUSE, 0.8 km. E. Probably by *J. & W. Smith c.* 1840. A very unusual country house, seemingly built for an invalid, either Miss Mary Gordon or Robert Abercrombie. Entrance front facing s comprises a single-storey five-bay centre block flanked by pavilion wings forming an H-plan almost 40 m. long, rubble-built and formerly harled with ashlar dressings. Georgian sash-and-case windows in the centre block, its roof punctuated by two tall chimneystacks; the wings have canted bays originally with lying-pane glazing and rise into shouldered Jacobean gables with escutcheon panels and enormous spike finials. The entrance is in the angle between the centre range and r. wing, its glazed porch being a later addition. Inset into the l. wing is a heraldic tablet bearing the arms of Gordon of Lesmoir, date 1687 and eroded motto ... *Pax vel bellum.** Behind the centre block, and linked it to it by a corridor, a second service range with female servants' bedrooms in the dormered attic, and behind this again a very large walled garden, originally with glasshouses against its rear wall.

Although the close similarities to post-Crimean hospital planning suggest a later C19 date, the interior can be no later than *c.* 1840. A small elliptical entrance hall, its doorcases fluted with lions' masks and the doors themselves elegantly bowed, opens into a drawing room with Neoclassical fireplace and dining room where an Art Nouveau fireplace has been inserted *c.* 1920; both rooms have coved ceilings rising into the roof-space. A spinal

---

*Probably from Cicero, *Pax vel iniusta utilior est quam iustissimum bellum* ('Peace however unjust is of more use than the most justified war').

passage running the house's full length is lit from the rear by Gothic windows with diamond-pane glazing and basket-weave tracery, and rises into a shallow four-centred vault. Another fireplace has been salvaged from Beaton Hall, Methlick (N).

Tudor COACHHOUSE, *c.* 1840; DOOCOT, small square-plan with one canted angle, its truncated pyramidal roof with over-sailing eaves. The landscape PARK was described by Samuel Lewis in 1846 as 'finely situated on a gentle acclivity on the northern bank of the Shevock, beautifully ornamented with wood, the approach from the village being particularly admired'. Much survives but the artificial LAKE is later C20.

CASTLE OF DUNNIDEER, 1.95 km. W, on Hill of Dunnideer. At the hill's summit is a HILL-FORT, a vitrified oblong with a well at the W end and further down a series of ramparts with entrances to the W. The oval fort is of similar character to the better preserved Tap o'Noth, Rhynie.

Within the main enclosure and mostly built of stones reused from it is a medieval TOWER HOUSE of which only the W wall survives to a substantial height. It rises from a battered base, the ragged opening of its great hall window at first floor making it a prominent landmark in the low-lying countryside. It was rectangular on plan, 15 m. broad E–W by 12.5 m. deep N–S; a narrow blocked opening survives at ground level within the W wall, and evidence of a window within the remnants of the E wall. The immense solidity and closely packed, striated con-struction of its rubble masonry (nearly 2 m. thick), together with the apparent lack of any vaulting as found in later tower houses, strongly implies that it was built by the Balliol family in the C13: indeed it is similar to the Balliols' Red Castle in Angus, and to Boharm (Moray). It may be the castle referred to in an agreement of 1260 preserved in the Chartulary of Lindores, and if so it is perhaps the earliest tower house in mainland Scotland of which any fabric still survives. It was the *capital messuage* of the Garioch during the mid C16 but a par-tially collapsed ruin when Adam de Cardonnel drew it for his *Picturesque Antiquities of Scotland* published in 1788. Rather more survived then than now.

CHRIST'S KIRK, Rathmuriel, 2.7 km. WSW. Foundations of a church granted to Lindores Abbey in either the late C12 or mid C13 and united with Kennethmont *c.* 1630. One notable GRAVESTONE of 1767, Death standing on a sphere with scythe and hourglass in outstretched arms.

The PICARDY STONE, 2.5 km. NW of Insch, is an impressive pillar of whinstone with prominent veins of quartz. On one face there is a mirror, snake and Z-rod and a double-disc and Z-rod. Fine views of Dunnideer hill-fort can be obtained from here. (GN)

Site of a monastery from at least the late C10, and a significant town by the mid C13, when it is shown (as 'Enderburie') on the

Gough map. King David II made Inverbervie a royal burgh in 1341, having landed at Bervie Bay on his return to Scotland after exile. A large Carmelite friary was established on the outskirts in the early C15 (now no trace). A large harbour was in operation from the early Middle Ages, rebuilt in the mid C18 and improved by *Thomas Telford* in 1819. By *c.* 1830, however, the mouth of the Bervie Water had been blocked by shingle and trade activity relocated to Gourdon (q.v.).

CHURCHES

BERVIE CHURCH, King Street. Big Neo-Perp oblong by *John Smith*, 1837–9, built to replace the previous church in the Burial Ground (*see* below). It is large and accomplished – a proper kirk for a proper burgh – but the design perhaps a bit too bookish. Gabled SE front with three-light windows and tall crocketed pinnacles. Advanced central tower of four stages with angle buttresses and Tudor-headed entrance. Window above with a crocketed ogee hoodmould; crenellated parapet over the louvered belfry. Four-bay flanks with more wooden tracery.

Big interior with a shallow coomb ceiling by *A. Clark & Son* of Montrose, 1890. Smith's octopartite rib-vault remains inside the porch. – Canted GALLERY panelled with cinque-foiled arches. It retains its original PEWS (those on the ground floor removed in 1964). – ORGAN by *E.H. Lawton*, 1904. Huge canted case with rectangular PULPIT in front of it, again 1904. – STAINED GLASS. In the vestibule, two lancets from the former Free Church, 1893. Lilies, Burning Bush and Pelican feeding her young. – Panels in the lobby doors, 2000–1.

ST DAVID OF SCOTLAND (Episcopal), Victoria Terrace. Gabled box of galvanized iron by *Mills & Shepherd*, 1922.

OLD BURIAL GROUND, Kirk Burn. Site of the medieval parish church, consecrated in 1242 but probably built in the late C12. It was rebuilt on at least three occasions after the Reformation, for the last time in 1781. Of this, only the W gable remains, now overgrown. Pointed, lintelled entrance arch under a lancet. Platform for bellcote above. Interior wall with original plaster and joist pockets to the former gallery.

DESCRIPTION

At the S edge of the burgh is the GATE to Hallgreen Castle (*see* p. 516), and then Montrose Road extends straight ahead. Up on the l., just before the junction with Victoria Terrace, is HAZELGROVE, *c.* 1890, recessed from the street and the only real villa in Inverbervie. Off-lime harling; full-height rectangular bays with balustraded segmental arch in between. Key-blocked gatepiers on the road with pulvinated architraves. The building to the l. was built as the coachhouse *c.* 1912, with round-headed former carriage entrance and an open pediment with big modillions. Victoria Terrace angles off to the l., ending at the large former DRILL HALL, late C19 and converted into commercial premises *c.* 2010. Snecked, rock-faced E façade. Aberdour Place angles back to the r. and ends at the quadruple-gabled former FREE CHURCH MANSE, built 1843–4 and extended in the late C19.*

King Street continues NE as the main route through the burgh. A turn N down CHURCH STREET leads to the former TOWN HOUSE (now LIBRARY), originally of 1719–20 but said to have been altered in the mid C19. Restrained classical design of two storeys and five bays, the centre minimally advanced under a pediment with belfry platform. Datestone on the E gable from 1569, re-set from the earlier town hall on Market Square (*see* below). Back on KING STREET, the intersection with Church Street features a two-front mini-villa of *c.* 1840 with bowed corner. Across from it, on the corner with Kirk Burn, is the POST OFFICE and CLYDESDALE BANK, 1883. Across is Bervie Church (*see* above) and to the r. of it, the former MANSE. It was originally built in 1737 by *James Burness* and given a large double-pile rear extension by *William Fettis* in 1876–7. Refronting of the narrower old section by *Carver & Symon*, 1916–18.

Further up, a r. turn on High Street leads to the rectangular Market Square with the MARKET CROSS holding pride of place. Chamfered shaft, *c.* 4.3 m. tall, ending in a cone-shaped finial incised with the date 1737. Big, stepped octagonal plinth below it.

At the end of King Street is the memorial SCULPTURE to the Cutty Sark, 1997, a full-scale replica of the ship's original figurehead. The designer of the famous clipper, Hercules Linton, was born in Inverbervie in 1837. Beyond it extends the delicious swerve of the JUBILEE BRIDGE, engineered in 1935 by *F. A. MacDonald & Partners* of Glasgow (*Charles Dick & Son* of Monifieth, contractors). Good specimen of interwar design, with seven spans of reinforced concrete arranged in a curve over the Bervie Water. Tapered rectangular piers between the arches, each featuring an original metal lamp standard. The bridge's lilting path allowed for the survival of the OLD BERVIE BRIDGE, built in 1799, and now sitting disused to the NW.[†] Huge segmental arch, *c.* 31.4 m. wide and 24.4 m. high, built of rubble with finely dressed voussoirs. Blind oculi in the spandrels; huge abutments, the lower stage rusticated with vaulted cellars inside. Dated cast-iron parapet.

ALLARDICE CASTLE. *See* p. 317.
HALLGREEN CASTLE. *See* p. 516.

---

*The Free Church, built 1843–4 and rebuilt by *Hutcheson & Henderson* in 1892–4, was dem. in 1982.
[†] It was itself the replacement to a two-arched bridge built in 1696.

INVERCAULD HOUSE   *1090*
2.5 km. ENE of Braemar

The gleaming, predominantly Victorian, silver mansion occupies a prominent site facing s directly onto the River Dee, flanked in front and behind by towering pine-clad mountains. This craggy wilderness, teeming with deer, reaches almost to the door. The house became in many ways an ambitious rival to its neighbour Balmoral. The Earl of Mar settled here about 1494, but the Farquharson family has been responsible for most of its built history.

A barrel-vaulted undercroft in the heart of the building may be its oldest element, followed by a plaque inscribed AF [Alexander Farquharson] 1674, now over the entrance. In 1679 the same Farquharson made a contract with William and Francis Gordon 'for buildings at Invercauld, according to plans submitted to them'. No further information survives from this stage, but by 1715 John Erskine, 23rd (and 6th) Earl of Mar, could refer to the house as 'a suitable place for residence and commodious'. He was staying at Invercauld when he mustered John Farquharson, 9th Laird, and the Jacobites to raise the standard for the 1715 rebellion in Braemar. Erskine was the prodigious architect and landscape designer of Alloa (Stirling & Central Scotland), and Margaret Stewart suggests that he may have been responsible for the ambitious design of the Invercauld policies visible on Roy's Map (1747–55).* These involved cutting vistas through the forest to focus on stupendous geological and historical features such as Lion's Face and Braemar Castle (q.v.). Oddly, Roy's map shows no building at the heart of this radiating scheme. Likewise, a neat estate plan of 1753 showing a house facing N, six bays wide flanked with wings attached by quadrants forming a courtyard, may reflect a structure never completed, although its central block is apparently under the footprint of the present tower.

A print of 1784 depicts a substantial L-shaped building which corresponds more closely to the surviving structure, with a three-storey SE wing. The house was at that time approached from the s, with the main entrance in the w front of the SE wing. A further addition was made to this wing in 1794 to bring it to its present extent but in 1843 the whole house was made over for James Farquharson, 12th Laird, by *John Smith*, in the same Scots Tudor style of his work at Balmoral. Further additions were made in 1847 by *James Henderson* (who also designed lodges on the estate in the style of P.F. Robinson). An engraving of 1848 shows that the house had now become an extended Z-plan with N service wings, a long s elevation facing the river with Dutch gables and the SE wing, two storeys high, at right angles to the main block. But its final lofty presence was achieved in 1872–5 for Lt-Col. James Ross Farquharson (a socialite known as 'Piccadilly Jim')

---

*M. Stewart, 'On regenerating a Highland Heritage, 1700–32', *Architectural Heritage* 18(1) (2007), pp. 127–8.

by *J. T. Wimperis*, who had already designed his London residence at No. 20 Park Lane. Wimperis reconfigured Invercauld on a vast Baronial scale, keeping 'the old house preserved as far as possible; new work on old foundations' but raising the dominant central tower at the intersection of the main block and the SE wing. The strength of his design is in the massing of blocks rather than meticulous detail. Plate-glass sash windows add to the external severity.

69   EXTERIOR. Many of these documented phases can be recognized in the stonework. Plans show the thickest walls, possibly C15–C16, are beneath the tower and include the vaulted store with arrowslit window SE of the tower, forming a small L-plan. In these areas, on the lower two storeys, the masonry is small random rubble and the window lintels have a slight chamfer (all the sills are replaced, possibly to enlarge the openings). In the 1784 engraving, the SE WING ended in a chimney gable, marking the S extremity of the lower and upper halls. The entrance was on the W side, in the vicinity of the current garden door, providing a natural access to the main dining hall on the ground floor, just to the l. of the entry. The S end of this wing now ends in a bow front, containing the library below and drawing room above, but this is evidently later (the library is on a lower level than the adjacent low hall) and was added by James Farquharson in 1794. Sir William Forbes refers to it in a letter in which he calls the house '… a poor one, not worth the keeping up. I think he would have done better to have pulled it down, and built a new one'. The third storey of the S wing, capped by twin tourelles, corbels and crenellations, is of 1890, part of the last phase of alterations, carried out by Alexander Haldane Farquharson and his wife, Zoe Musgrave, again to designs by Wimperis.

Invercauld House.
Drawing by F. Walkins, 1875

The lower two storeys on the S front of the MAIN BLOCK also have 1840s chamfered window surrounds but here the changes made by Wimperis are clear to see. He removed a bay window at the W end (its large relieving arch may still be seen) and replaced the frilly Dutch gables by Smith with the present two crowstepped gables; he joined the two eastern gables into one, linking their separate bays with a stilted arch. However his most distinctive contribution is the TOWER at the intersection of the main block and its SE wing, which he created by heightening the existing walls of the old main block to six storeys. It is four bays wide but only two narrow bays deep, with crenellations and turrets on top, and dominates the entire composition. To create a dramatic approach, the drive was switched from the S to the E front of the S wing, where Wimperis added his bold square castellated PORCH projecting forward at an angle from a new entrance hall. The N wall of this entrance hall incorporates the remains of an E wing which was visible on the 1784 engraving. Both the entrance hall and vestibule are of rough-cut, squared grey granite, but fit together so poorly in terms of detail that the addition in 1890 of a third polygonal structure immediately adjacent to the S, containing a boudoir, merely makes the entry more discordant and jumbled. Wimperis's medieval-style hand-wrought ironwork to exterior doors and stylish rainwater hoppers and brackets are attractive.

The NE and NW SERVICE WINGS were built or reworked completely in the 1840s. They are separated from the old main block by a long corridor which runs E–W for the length of the house. They are characterized by tall chimneystacks set on an angle (a trait of Smith's), a dressed chamfered plinth, a moulded course at the wall-head, squared blocks of masonry and window reveals chamfered on all sides.

INTERIOR. The VESTIBULE inside the porch has a pyramidal roof and vaulted ceiling. The entrance hall, with manly Doric polished granite fireplace, sets the scene with a staircase swinging around a newel post which reaches floor to ceiling, a great tree from the local Ballochbuie forest, festooned with shields and carved with eclectic Jacobean motifs including four tiled aedicules at the base, and griffins on corner posts. Portentous moulded doorways open off the landing, the greatest with polished marble columns leading on to the UPPER HALL. This has a Jacobean-style fireplace of marble and crenellated pine, and heraldic stained glass by *Gibbs & Moore* of London. The bow-ended DRAWING ROOM in the SE wing is 1890s, with plaster strapwork ceiling, mantelpiece and doorcases in delicate Gothic style. The polygonal BOUDOIR opens off this space as a retreat. On the ground floor, the LIBRARY, also in the SE wing, and the DINING HALL at the core of the central block are warmly panelled.

The OFFICES around the back and sides of the house are 1870s–90s. GUN ROOM with game larder above, square with chamfered corners and external iron staircase. Pyramidal roof with

deep bracketed eaves. Former DOG KENNELS, a clapboard
shed graced with tetrastyle portico and pediment made with
rustic tree-trunk columns; scalloped bargeboards. DAIRY,
square plan with pyramidal roof, deep bracketed eaves and
louvre at apex of roof. Cottage S of dairy, simple three-bay
house enhanced with large polygonal entrance porch (the old
dairy) with pyramidal bellcast roof, consoled classical doorpiece and nicely panelled door. – BALLROOM, 1861, a shed
as at Balmoral. Weatherboarded, six-pane windows with
glazed pediment above. To the W of the house, with exceptional
views, a SUMMERHOUSE of lozenge boiserie with rare heather
thatch.

ALTDOURIE, 0.8 km. NW, the former factor's house, is an unusual
design, single storey with dormers, five bays long with bowed
end bays and central porch covered by bell-canted conical
roofs, facing a spectacular view of the River Dee. With an
M-profile roof, the rear of the house is darkly Gothic style with
crowstepped dormers. It may date from early C19 estate
improvements by Margaret Carr, wife of James Farquharson.

INVERERNAN HOUSE

3 km. SW of Strathdon

Vernacular classical laird's house of 1764, remodelled 1828, then
returned to something near its original appearance by *George
Bennett Mitchell* in 1934–5. As a result of Mitchell's remodelling
it closely resembles Bellabeg House (Strathdon) and, given
their close proximity and their very similar proportions, they
were probably built by the same master mason and once
looked near-identical. ENTRANCE FRONT (facing S) is two
storeys and five windows wide, built in squared red granite
rubble: as at Bellabeg, the centre bay is slightly wider than the
flanking bays. Its hemicycle gable with a round-headed attic
light is however a hypothetical Mitchell reinstatement, reusing
a finely carved urn finial, and was probably based on evidence
found in the roof. Even the panel over the doorway, dated 1764,
is an insertion of 1934–5, Mitchell having removed the tetrastyle Doric portico which was the main feature of the 1828
works. He also removed a slim wall-head cornice and blocking
course of that date (though the raised skews remain) and coped
the chimneystacks. The NE REAR WING comprised a three-
storey E range rather taller than the original house of 1764 with
a canted bay at its N end, and a predominantly two-storey N
range, which together enclosed a central court with a large
greenhouse on the W. Mitchell demolished this greenhouse,
replacing it with an additional masonry bay. The INTERIOR
was replanned with the drawing room on the W side of the
original house and the dining room in the additional bay

directly behind it, the third principal apartment being the smoke room on the E side of the house.

INVEREY HOUSE   *0080*
7 km. WSW of Braemar

By *Oliver Humphries*, 1983, for Captain Ramsay of Mar. The roof-line, broken into three blocks of different height, and narrow proportions to the rooms and windows create the impression of an authentic C18 laird's house. From its imposing location above the Ey Burn, it overlooks the remains of Inverey Castle, now only a line of foundations on the other side of the road.

INVERURIE   *7020*

At the confluence of the Don and the Urie, and a fording point on the route from Aberdeen through Huntly (q.v.) into Moray, Inverurie has been inhabited since Neolithic times. Small tributaries flow into these rivers and a Culdee Church ('the Rocharl Kirk') once stood near St Pollinar's Burn. A natural mound, 'the Bass', provided a defensible location, and when David Earl of Huntingdon received the Garioch from his brother William the Lion *c.* 1180 he transformed it into a Norman-style motte and bailey. A burgh is first mentioned in 1195 and as late as 1774–5 the Bass's chapel served as the parish church. But in the later Middle Ages, as the Don flooded more often and the art of fortification developed, the Bass fell into disrepair. The Earls moved to Ardtannes and the burgh population occupied the ridge between the Don and the Urie, so forming the High Street.

In 1558 Mary of Guise granted Inverurie a new charter affirming royal burgh status, confirmed by James VI in 1587. From the Reformation it was a presbytery seat, and it was admitted to Parliament in 1612. The town built its first modest tolbooth in 1660, was admitted to the Convention of Royal Burghs in 1661, and its position as the Garioch's capital was confirmed by Parliament in 1663, but its isolated situation between the Don and the Urie left it eclipsed by Oldmeldrum (N). During the mid C18 Inverurie still only consisted, as William Roy's map shows, of a single long street with the tolbooth and market cross (erected 1671) near the present-day 81 High Street. During the later C18, the town's population fell while Oldmeldrum's rose.

In an attempt to revive Inverurie's fortunes, the Powtate Loch was drained to form the Market Place and houses were built along the Huntly road, now West High Street. But what really

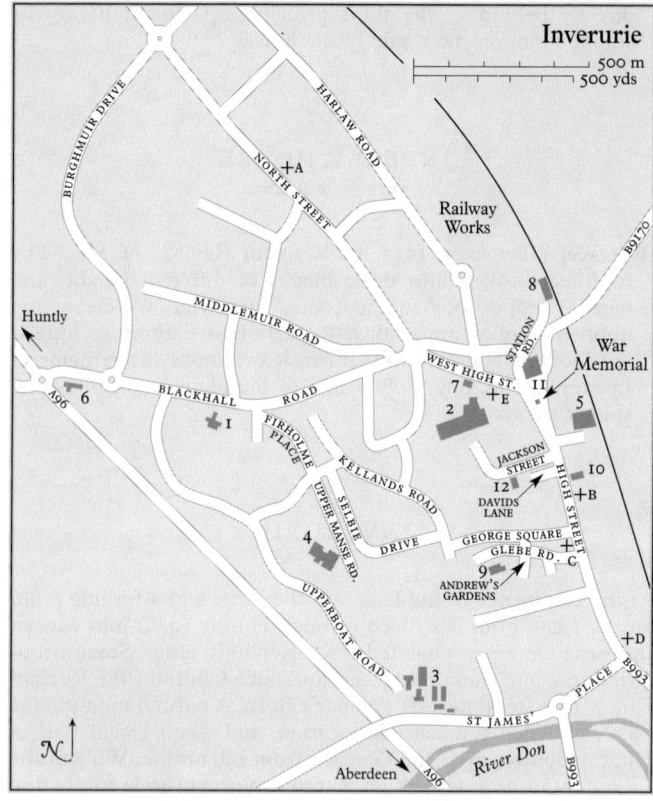

Inverurie

500 m
500 yds

Huntly

Railway
Works

War
Memorial

A   Church of the Immaculate
    Conception (R.C.)
B   Gospel Hall
C   St Andrew
D   St Mary (Episcopal)
E   West Church

1   Gordon House
2   Inverurie Academy
3   Inverurie Hospital
4   Kellands Primary School
5   Market Place School
6   Police Station
7   Post Office
8   Railway Station
9   St Andrew's School
10 St Anthony's Masonic Lodge
11 Town Hall
12 Wyness Hall

drove growth were the improvements in communications
prompted chiefly by the 5th Earl of Kintore and the Elphinstones
of Logie (qq.v.): the construction of a bridge over the Don
by *James Robertson* in 1789–91, the Aberdeen–Huntly turnpike
which reached Inverurie in 1802, and then – most importantly
– the opening in 1805 of the Aberdeenshire Canal at Port
Elphinstone, s of the bridge. A new town hall was built in 1803.

The turnpike and canal, together with three further bridges built over the Urie between 1809 and 1839, facilitated the import of fertilizers to transform the Garioch's agriculture, so encouraging the export of produce beyond the immediate area. The population growth brought a wide variety of commercial enterprises which ultimately included banks, hotels, brewing, weaving, wood- and grain-milling, a gasworks, paper manufacture and quarrying at Port Elphinstone. The town's markets were of major importance, livestock – especially beef cattle – being despatched as far south as London.

Inverurie reclaimed its position as the Garioch's capital when the Great North of Scotland Railway built much of its main line to Inverness along the canal route in 1854, the original station being on the High Street's E side. By 1900 the town had developed through the Burgh Muir along Constitution Street and particularly North Street where the railway had sidings, but the station did not move to its present site near the Market Place until 1902, following a decision to transfer the railway's locomotive, carriage and wagon works from Kittybrewster (Aberdeen) to Inverurie. The new Works (*see* Public Buildings) cost £40,000 and transformed the town into a centre of heavy industry. The railway also built housing for over 100 employees at a cost of £60,000, extending the town northward around Harlaw Road, King Street, Queen Street and Princes Street: it was such a distinctive community – not least because it was lit by electricity – that it was known as the 'Colony'. All this was designed by the railway's own staff under *Patrick M. Barnett*, its chief engineer, but Inverurie's dominant architect from the 1890s was *George Gray*, appointed Aberdeen District Architect for schools in 1920. It was probably he who built the first council housing, beginning in Westfield Gardens that year, before the appointment of *William Connor* as Burgh Surveyor by 1932; Connor remained in post until after the Second World War. The Works closed in 1969 but Inverurie retains its key advantages of a rich agricultural hinterland and excellent communications to Aberdeen, which have resulted in remarkable growth between the confines of the railway to the E and the A96 to the W.

CHURCHES

CHURCH OF THE IMMACULATE CONCEPTION (R.C.), North Street. By *A. & W. Reid* of Elgin, with *Bishop James Kyle*, for Father Charles Tochetti: completed 1852 'in strict medieval style … a parish church as it was in the goode olde Catholic tymes'. A small rubble-built chapel with a side-porch and a token tower at the rear concealed by the steep roof combines with an L-plan presbytery to form an interesting composition of geometrical masses, very simple in detail. Chapel's w gable is lit by stepped triple round-arched lights, with a blind oculus beneath a cruciform finial at the apex. Short two-bay flanks with porch on the S side, and tower with a low pyramidal roof on the NE. Behind the E gable the PRESBYTERY is two-storey and attic with the same eaves-line as the chancel but a much lower roof ridge. The chapel interior is, by virtue of its height relative to its small area, intimate and imposing at the same time. Tall round-headed chancel arch and narrow barrel-roofed chancel. A w gallery has been removed. Simple furnishings, the pews reconstructed to provide a central nave aisle. – STATIONS OF THE CROSS. Painted by the Benedictine Nuns of Turvey Abbey, Bedfordshire. Installed 2005. – STAINED GLASS. w window roundel of a dove in *dalle-de-verre*, *c.* 1965.

GOSPEL HALL, High Street. Former Wesleyan Methodist Church. First Pointed, looking *c.* 1870 but actually 1890s. A simple gable front in rough granite ashlar with a relatively tall roof, and a neat square entrance tower at one corner broaching to an octagonal belfry and tall stone spire. Pointed doorway with nave window above; the tower has a small wheel window with polychrome voussoirs, spheric triangles and tall lucarnes at its belfry. Three-bay flanks and polygonal chancel. Rainwater goods of notable quality.

ST ANDREW, High Street. By *John Smith* 1841–2, replacing a church of 1774–5. Handsome Neo-Perp gable front in granite ashlar, articulated into nave and aisles by slim stepped buttresses rising into tall pinnacles. Central pointed doorway with boldly profiled hoodmoulding, finely panelled double-leaf doors; three-light gallery window with timber tracery of elegant cusped lights and ogee hoodmould, simpler two-light glazing in the aisles. The very wide aisleless interior with canted ceiling reflects a major reordering of 1964–5 with a w gallery and new chancel formed at the E end, its round-headed chancel arch weakly detailed with long-and-short voussoirs; the glazed Gothic screen under the gallery (incorporating the Chapel of St Apollinarius) was designed by the *Rev. Graeme Longmuir* in the early C21. – PULPIT. *c.* 1965, carved with St Andrew in his fishing boat. – COMMUNION TABLE. *c.* 1921. War memorial with brass plaques commemorating the Fallen. – ORGAN (w gallery). Presumably that installed *c.* 1899 by *Conacher*. Elaborate Gothic case.

Nearby in Glebe Road, the former PARISH MANSE, Georgian Survival by *Matthews & Mackenzie*, 1854.

ST MARY (Episcopal), High Street. By *James Ross*, 1840–2, very similar to his church at Portsoy (N) which had been admired by Bishop William Skinner of Aberdeen. Miniaturized Gothic, tiny cruciform plan in granite ashlar. Entrance gable has a slightly projected centre with doorway and pointed window with Y-tracery, its tall open belfry suggesting a tower and spire. Three-bay flanks with token central transepts. The long Early Dec chancel and its N aisle were added by *William White* in 1857. Very simple interior, the nave with only a plain coved ceiling, the chancel rather less austere with sedilia and E window of three stepped lights in an arched recess. – PULPIT. Octagonal, oak with Perp carving and shields. Installed 1947. – TILES. In the chancel, encaustic, by *White*, 1857. – Octagonal stone FONT dated 1847, with cover of 1910. – Brass LECTERN by *Jones & Willis*, 1888. – SANCTUARY LAMP. Probably by the *Warham Guild*, *c.* 1945. – ORGAN by *E. H. Lawton*, 1900, repaired by *Rushworth & Dreaper*, 1966. – STAINED GLASS. The chancel's E and S windows both *c.* 1857 in C13 style with vesica-shaped medallions. The small two-light chancel window to SS John and Mark, *c.* 1882, is much finer, as are the nave windows. S wall, l. to r. the Virgin with St John the Evangelist by *J. Ninian Comper* (signed with trademark strawberries) 1930–3; the big three-light Madonna and Child, with the Annunciation and Visitation, by *Heaton, Butler & Bayne*, 1910; and SS George and Michael, commemorating two young men killed during the Second World War, signed by *J. M. Aiken*, 1948. – N wall, Christ in Majesty receiving a devoted follower, early C20 signed by *Franz Mayer* of Munich.

WEST CHURCH, West High Street. Former Free Church, by *Duncan McMillan*, 1874–7. Big simple Early Dec. A broad gable front with square corner tower buttressed at the angles in pink and grey granite, its louvred belfry breaking up into steep jerkin-headed gablets and a broached stone spire with lucarnes 32.5 m. high. Twin doorways with trefoils in their pointed heads, a large four-light gallery window with timber mullions and quatrefoil roundels, and a two-light window in the tower which once lit the stair. Five-bay flanks and rear gable with geometric wheel window in squared rubble. Hall by *George Gray*, 1905–6; chapel also by *Gray*, 1935–6; apse 1950. Glazed porch of 2008, contemporary with the division of the interior horizontally. Restaurant at ground floor and the church itself at gallery level, the gallery's cast-iron clustered columns with stiff-leaf capitals still supporting the queenpost roof. – COMMUNION TABLE 1919; COMMUNION CHAIRS by *James Buchan*, 1935. – STAINED GLASS. Geometric window in deep rich blues of 1877 with the handsome ORGAN CASE beneath it following its curvature: Art Deco Perp by *Rushworth & Dreaper*, 1935. – WAR MEMORIAL, on the stair, by *Morris & Co.*, 1920.

CHURCHYARD, Keithhall Road. Probably the original site of the burgh and, judging from archaeological evidence, occupied since Neolithic times. Within the churchyard are the BASS and LITTLE BASS, the remains of a motte and bailey of *c.* 1180. The Bass itself, a natural mound which has been scarped, was joined to the Little Bass until excavations and landscaping in 1883; both were once surrounded by a defensive moat or ditch. Abandoned by the later Middle Ages, the Bass's chapel survived until 1774–5. Four PICTISH SYMBOL STONES are grouped together nearby. All but one is damaged, a charismatic horse carved on a small standing stone. The other three have more abstract symbols including double-discs and a crescent and V-rod, although a serpent does makes an appearance on the largest stone of the three (GN). Next to these a GRAVE-STONE for Walter Innes of Ardtannes †1616.

PUBLIC BUILDINGS

ABERDEENSHIRE COUNCIL OFFICES (Gordon House), Blackhall Road. By *Aberdeen Construction Group*, 1982, originally for Gordon District Council. L-plan, two storeys of precast concrete panel cladding with vertical ribbed pattern above a rusticated plinth. Nuclear BUNKER added 1991.

INVERURIE ACADEMY, School Lane. The present Academy site comprises several schools which were originally distinct institutions. The three largest buildings stand together in a row, some 200 m. in total length, overlooking playing fields to the S. At the E end is the PUBLIC SCHOOL by *A. Marshall Mackenzie*, built 1902–3 to accommodate the children brought to Inverurie by the Railway Works. Tall single storey, granite-built, with broad central gable bay and lower flanking wings with three-light windows breaking into dormer gablets, severely damaged and rebuilt in 1904 after a fire. Next to it, the HIGHER GRADE SCHOOL by *George Gray* 1908–9, again single-storeyed but with three curvilinear gables and a central glazed rotunda with dome and peristyle. Both schools are of simple robust construction with minimal enrichment to appease the ratepayer. At the W end is the large NEW SCHOOL of 1965–7, a good design of rectangular masses laid out on an elongated courtyard plan with the front range kept relatively low and the rear range rising much taller behind it, with pavilion blocks at each far end and even a token tower; construction is in stone, glass and enamelled panels. The approach from School Lane is through good early C20 cast-iron GATES.

Extending from the rear of Mackenzie's school is an earlier, plainer EXTENSION *c.* 1953–7; facing this across the yard is the DOMESTIC SCIENCE BLOCK by *George Gray* dated 1910, a MANUAL DEPARTMENT being opened in 1911 and new classrooms *c.* 1934, both also by *Gray*. The oldest part of the complex is the former FREE CHURCH SCHOOLS – a single-storey range with broad gabled ends, progressively built from 1848 and evidently by *William Henderson*, who designed the first Free Church. In Chelsea Lane is WILLIAM CLARK'S FREE SCHOOL, 1871, which provided for the poorest children until 1903.

INVERURIE HOSPITAL, St James's Place. Designed by *Robert L. Rollo* 1936–7, opened 1940. Modernist – the rational stylish architecture of health, bright, clean, efficient, markedly influenced by Thomas Tait's Hawkhead Hospital, Paisley (Renfrewshire). Facing the road, a neat lodge, two-storeyed with cantilevered canopy over its door. Two-storey administration block, again with canopy in the centre and deeply shaded single-storey bow windows towards each far end. The ward blocks and nurses' home were laid out as a large formal rectangle – single-storey blocks (for scarlet fever and diphtheria) E and W, and shorter two-storey blocks (general diseases and nurses' home) N and S; general diseases was demolished *c.* 1985.

KELLANDS SCHOOL, Upper Manse Road. Single storey in brick, glass and enamelled panel, 1974–5. NURSERY SCHOOL, 1987.

MARKET PLACE SCHOOL, Market Place. Probably by *Alexander Ellis, c.* 1862. Altered by *Duncan McMillan,* 1875, and secondary school wing added in 1895 by *Ellis & Wilson.* New dining hall and classrooms, 1955.

POLICE STATION, Blackhall Road. By *Aberdeenshire Council Architects' Department, c.* 2005. Three-storey centre block with 'floating' segmental roof, single-storey wings.

RAILWAY STATION, Station Road. By *James Lowson,* the Great North of Scotland Railway's architect, and *Patrick M. Barnett,* chief engineer, 1902; cf. Aboyne. 'An admirable example of everything a station should be, having ample offices and long, wide and high platforms, very adequately sheltered by veranda roofs.' Long single-storey centre block in red granite ashlar with a piended roof and slightly lower gabled wings. The N wing rises into an elegant cupola and weathervane at its far end. Good interior woodwork, once with private waiting room for the Earl of Kintore. Glazed awnings on cast-iron columns and spandrels; cast-iron drinking fountain still in place. FOOT-BRIDGE dated 1902. Timber SIGNAL BOX and semaphores.

In Harlaw Road the former RAILWAY WORKS was also designed by *Barnett* with *William Pickersgill,* the GNSR's Locomotive Superintendent, in 1898 when a merger was being contemplated with the Highland Railway. It reflected an increasing tendency among even the smaller railway companies to build their own engines and rolling stock. The Works was once the Garioch's largest employer with a staff at its peak of 500 men. The CARRIAGE & WAGON SHOP and FURNACE, SMITHY & FOUNDRY, both 1898–1900, are still standing, together with the GENERAL OFFICE *c.* 1902–5; the Boiler & Erecting Shops and Paint Shop have been demolished. A late example of a railway works, employing granite-clad steel-framed construction, and very advanced for its time, powered by electricity. Closed 1969. WORKS MANAGER'S HOUSE stands off Mortimer's Lane, and the Works' HARLAW PARK football ground in Harlaw Drive.

ST ANDREW'S SCHOOL, Glebe Road. Opened 1954. Extension by *Jenkins & Marr c.* 1967–71.

ST ANTHONY'S MASONIC LODGE, High Street. By *William Allan,* 1881, with a much-eroded PICTISH STONE in its N flank.

TOWN HALL, Market Place. Built 1862 by *J. R. Mackenzie,* on the site of a predecessor of 1803. Provincial Neo-Baroque palace-block. Two-storey entrance front, seven bays broad in granite ashlar with projecting end pavilions and central cupola. Its five central bays are articulated by giant-order Roman Doric pilasters; channelled masonry, tripartite doorway and round-headed windows at ground floor, taller arched windows at first floor, wall-head balustrade. End pavilions have plain pilasters, square-headed windows and panelled parapets with couchant lions. Diagonally set timber and lead cupola, Spanish

Baroque in character, supported on a base of hemicycle clock pediments; tall lattice belfry openings framed by colonnettes and pinnacles, and domelet surmounted by a peristyle. The interior originally contained a courtroom and other chambers, reconstructed *c.* 1930 by *George Gray* after a fire. Large hall with coupled Ionic pilasters extending across its flanks and a coved ceiling. The CARNEGIE LIBRARY & MUSEUM added to the w flank is by *Harbourne Maclennan* (of *Jenkins & Marr*), 1910–11.

WYNESS HALL, Jackson Street. Built 1896 by *George Gray* as the Volunteers' drill hall. Granite ashlar, simple and robust. Broad Neo-Baroque gable front with large pedimented entrance porch, segmental pediment with spike finial at apex.

DESCRIPTION

The MARKET PLACE is the centre of the town: a long triangle linking three roads, the old High Street leading s to Aberdeen, West High Street leading NW to Huntly (q.v.) and the B9170 leading towards the NE coast. Notwithstanding the new bypass, Inverurie is a busy town like none other in Aberdeenshire: traffic convolutes in front of the Town Hall (*see* Public Buildings) with its Spanish Baroque cupola. The Market Place was open ground until the First World War but became a garden after the WAR MEMORIAL was erected in 1921. This is by *James Philip* of *Arthur Taylor*'s yard in Aberdeen and has a gallant moustachioed Highlander in Rubislaw granite, standing on a square battered plinth and stepped base. Hidden on the E side of the market place, a near-symmetrical group of vernacular buildings *c.* 1800, now known as CROSSLET COURT, with their own sense of modest formality. Their central block is two storeys and seven windows wide, rubble-built with a segmental pend; on each side slightly lower there are two-storey three-bay wings in squared rubble, all with dressed quoins. By way of contrast, No. 56 further down is mid-C19 Late Georgian Survival, with a glazed ground-floor arcade. Market Place's w side must have been similar to Crosslet Court but has suffered from shop conversions.

HIGH STREET extends almost straight and level for 700 m., the two-storey scale which predominates near the Market Place gradually descending to single-storey. Beyond the Established, Methodist and Episcopal churches and a couple of solid villas of *c.* 1900, a few buildings stand out, including No. 4 (E side) which is very similar to No. 56 Market Place. There are two near-identical banks: on the w side No. 3 is the former NORTH OF SCOTLAND BANK, probably by *Matthews & Mackenzie c.* 1850, and further down on the E side is the former UNION BANK OF SCOTLAND (No. 80) by *John Henderson & Son* 1857, both rather grand Neoclassical two-storey five-bay frontages with distyle Roman Doric porticoes and railed areas, constructed in fine granite ashlar with apron panels beneath the windows. The North of Scotland Bank has long-and-short quoins and pedimented dormers. Opposite the Union Bank, the KINTORE ARMS is by *William Ramage*, 1854, built by the 8th Earl of Kintore to take advantage of passengers alighting at the old railway station, which opened that year. It is two storeys and seven bays broad with a Roman Doric portico and a handsome carved and painted armorial. Harled with lying-pane glazing, its canted bays were added *c.* 1875–80. Next to this, EARLSMHOR is a prosperous villa by *George Gray c.* 1905, an amusing amalgam of Old English gable, Baronial turret and Art Nouveau glass. Further on, set back from the road on the E side, HOLLYBANK (No. 100) of *c.* 1770 is a pretty two-storey three-bay house with polished ashlar doorpiece and slim window margins, formerly harled.

WEST HIGH STREET is also long and straight – some 300 m. – and most densely built up near the Market Place, where the simple two-storey buildings again date from the earlier C19. The former GORDON ARMS is old-fashioned Matthews-school Baronial, near-symmetrical with a central crowstepped gable flanked by dormers and a tall turret corbelled out from the r. corner; designed by *George Gray*, it was built as late as 1901–2 to cater for the new Station (*see* Public Buildings). But the dominant feature of West High Street is the West Parish Church with tower and spire (*see* Churches), while on the N side the CLYDESDALE BANK (originally the Aberdeen Town & County Bank) was built *c.* 1845 as a stylish Italianate villa, two-storeyed with a solid pilastered entrance porch, lying-pane glazing and a steep roof with bracketed eaves; its long rear wing has a console-cornice doorway for the bank house. Roughly opposite, the POST OFFICE with adjoining shop and flats above, commissioned by George Mellis & Son from *George Bennett Mitchell*, 1908–9. Granite ashlar, with original glazed shopfront to the post office; broad chimney gables and flat-roofed dormers, all with carved eaves brackets. At the street's far end is the VICTORIA CINEMA, now a bar, designed by *T. Scott Sutherland*, a partner in the Inverurie Cinema Co., and opened in 1934.

The catalysts for development of ST JAMES'S PLACE, with villas overlooking the Don built from *c.* 1930, were the purchase of Kellands Park and increasing car ownership. Amid such salubrious surroundings, at the far W end is Inverurie Hospital (*see* Public Buildings). The Old Bridge which had sparked the resurgence of Inverurie in 1791 was replaced by a new DON BRIDGE designed by *Tawse & Allan*, engineers, in 1923 and completed by *William Tawse* in 1925. It comprises three shallow semi-elliptical arches (the centre arch of 19 m. span and the outer arches 17.5 m.) in reinforced concrete, providing a much wider and stronger deck.

On the bridge's far side PORT ELPHINSTONE is a modest village strung out along Elphinstone Road with side streets off, but it was once a hive of industry with a brewery, grain mill, granaries and sawmills, and on higher ground a quarry and reservoir. In the centre of the village is BLYTHEWOOD HOUSE, a large grey granite villa built *c.* 1890, now a care home. Here at its terminus the ABERDEENSHIRE CANAL (designed by *John Rennie*, begun 1796 and opened 1805) still survives complete with a sluice, the railway which followed much of its path entering Inverurie by a different route.

PICTISH SYMBOL STONE. Now in the middle of a housing estate in the road called Brandsbutt, this stone was broken up for a field dyke in the C19. It has a crescent and V-rod, a serpent and Z-rod, and an ogham inscription on the front. The stone may have been associated with and reused from a stone circle that stood nearby. (GN)

HENGE MONUMENT, Broomend of Crichie, at the s edge of Port Elphinstone. Later Neolithic or Early Bronze Age, consisting of an external bank and internal ditch enclosing a central area with standing stones. The circle was originally approached by an avenue of standing stones which have almost entirely been removed. A PICTISH SYMBOL STONE displaying a 'Pictish beast' and a crescent and V-rod has been moved into the circle from its original site, which was nearer to the River Don. (GN)

RECUMBENT STONE CIRCLE, East Aquhorthies, 4.7 km. W. Well-preserved stone circle, consisting of eleven uprights and recumbent stone. Traces of a low cairn survive within the circle. This may cover a cremation pyre, but the site is unexcavated. (GN)

6090   INVERY HOUSE   K
                         1.7 km. s of Banchory

A vernacular classical country house built in five phases framing an irregular U-plan court on its N, E and S sides, and open to the rear on its W.

The original house which now forms the low N range has seemingly been an early example of the first generation of country houses in the North-East, probably built for the Douglas family of Tilquhillie (q.v.) in the 1680s. Its surviving windows are small, and the fenestration was presumably once regular. Inside, a stair directly opposite the s door led to the principal apartments at first floor. The wall-head may have been slightly reduced in the mid C18 when the original gabled roof was replaced by a piended one. This was to match that of a new three-storey, piend-roofed house with its entrance elevation facing E (now the central range) erected at right angles to the earlier house by a Mr Rose. He may also have been responsible for a low and irregular s wing (dem.), the whole forming an approximately symmetrical arrangement.

Invery began to achieve its present appearance *c.* 1795 when it was 'further embellished' by a Mr Leith. He deepened the mid-C18 central range (still partly visible on the N gable) to a double-pile plan and refronted it as two tall storeys over a semi-sunk service basement, closely resembling the s front of Leith Hall (q.v.) with a central window at ground floor flanked by two Serlians, their arches with keystones. The central window was the entrance doorway until the early C20. The first floor unusually has four windows evenly arranged, with a very broad floating pediment beneath an ashlar chimneystack in front of the piended-platform roof. Filling the NE and SE re-entrant angles of this front are elegant single-storey-and-basement quadrants which seem to have been built *c.* 1800 for the antiquary and artist James Skene of Rubislaw. The SE quadrant links to a single-storey-and-basement pavilion inserted into the s range at the same date and also now contains the entrance, framed by slim pilasters and with an elegant Neoclassical transom-light, which was formed after 1903 when the house was altered for the Kerr family, of Kerr-Clark the thread manufacturers. It may be by *William Kelly* whose practice, *Kelly & Nicol*, subsquently added the s range beyond the pavilion. This is remarkably sympathetic in style to the E range with a central Serlian window at principal floor flanked by single windows in the end bays, three windows on the upper floor and pediment on the W side. On the rear courtyard side the mid-C18 house was once symmetrical, with its central staircase bay slightly recessed, the Gothick window probably an alteration by Skene.

The INTERIOR was completely replanned in the early C20. The ENTRANCE HALL within the s quadrant opens into a much larger INNER HALL which was formed by opening the southern rooms of the central range into a single unified space. The original entrance hall of *c.* 1795 occupied the centre bay of the E front but in the early C20 this was combined with the adjoining NE apartment to form the present DRAWING ROOM. Within the s range, Kelly's DINING ROOM is distinguished by elegant fluted columns and pilasters at the Serlian window and an Adam-style oval in the centre of its compartmented ceiling. The fireplaces are of different designs, all apparently early C20. In general Kelly's early C20 woodwork closely matches that of the late C18, but the detail of his STAIRS, while of notably fine craftsmanship with scrolled handrails, is more sophisticated Neo-Georgian.

WALLED GARDEN. Rubble-built, of unusual length, perhaps extended. Two-storey pyramid-roofed PAVILION with forestair, late C17 or early C18. The upper storey originally overlooked the garden as at Midmar (q.v.) but has been altered to provide bothy accommodation.

JOHNSHAVEN   K   7060

Recorded *c.* 1620 as 'a little shore for fisher-boats', Johnshaven went on to become one of the most important fishing ports on the E coast. This ended in the mid C18, although manufacturing and a harbour brought renewed prosperity in the C19.

PARISH CHURCH, Castle Street. Simple E.E., built 1859–60 as the United Presbyterian church. The site is compressed and wedged into a slope, hence the unusual two-storey arrangement with hall located in the 'crypt'. Big lancet on the W gable subdivided into five lights. Double-chamfered, gableted entrance in the NW corner. Simple interior as renovated by *W.E. Gauld*, 1906. – Octagonal Gothic PULPIT with tester and high back-board.

DESCRIPTION. The village is curled around a steep coastal brae and has a meandering plan. The focal point remains the HARBOUR, with two stalwart piers of coursed rubble (refurbished in concrete, *c.* 1950). Stilling basin on the W engineered by *J. Willet*, 1884, with a short entrance sliced through its central jetty. Original breakwater to the E, 1871, a long, diagonal arm with canted end forming a triangular reservoir. At its landward end is the former LIFEBOAT STATION, 1891, with Tudor arch and bargeboarded gable. Attached to the l., the former ST DAVID'S CHAPEL, 1851, gutted by fire in 2011 and rebuilt by *A. B. Roger & Young* of Brechin in 2013–14.

From here, New Road goes N to the ANCHOR HOTEL, *c.* 1833 with a pilastered doorpiece in the centre. Opposite is the dull main SQUARE and, parallel to the N, the WAR MEMORIAL by *Alexander Robertson & Son*, 1922–3. Looming above on the N slope is BRAE HOUSE, *c.* 1780, among the oldest houses in the village. The unpromising exterior conceals a fine Georgian staircase with key-blocked wooden balusters and a drawing room chimneypiece carved with garlands and leafy foliage. MAIN STREET then leads W, with the charming HAY COTTAGE near the centre, early C19. Doorcase with fluted pilasters and emphatic pediment. The pantiled building opposite was an early C19 FLAX WAREHOUSE, converted into a FISH-CURING HOUSE during the herring boom.

Perched high on Balandro Loan is SPRINGFIELD, built *c.* 1845 and remodelled *c.* 1890 when it served as the manse. Dormerheads with bold Dutch gables. The very appropriately named SEAVIEW TERRACE then stretches E. Set back near the middle of the street is the former FREE CHURCH MANSE, 1848, still markedly Georgian for such a late date. Bracketed door cornice and piended roof with chimneystacks on the ends. The former CHURCH is next door (now Skerryvore), 1843, its strange triple-gabled form a homage to Canonmills Hall (Edinburgh), where the Free Church movement began. At the end of the street, the attractive former SCHOOL, the far r. pair of buildings *c.* 1850 with good door consoles. School house on the l. dated 1854 on its flank.

BRIDGETON CASTLE, 2 km. WSW, on the A92. Good Baronial mansion, built *c.* 1839.* Semi-elliptical tower advanced

---

* Replacing an earlier house built *c.* 1755 and enlarged *c.* 1808 by Patrick Orr, sheriff clerk of Angus.

off-centre with roll-moulded, segmental entrance. Thick cable moulding around it and the first-floor window, then a square caphouse corbelled out. Two bays to the r. with fish-scaled stair-turret corbelled out in the re-entrant angle. To the l. of the entrance, another quasi-tower with canted bay window and little diagonal square turret.

BROTHERTON HOUSE, 0.9 km. NNE, by the A92. Large L-plan, built *c*. 1952 out of materials from the demolished Station Hotel in Cruden Bay (N). Crowstepped s gable.

DENFINELLA BRIDGE, 2.5 km. WSW, on the A92. Wide, depressed segmental arch, built 1815 next to a cascading waterfall on the Den Finella. s face with original joggled Piranesian masonry. N side extended in concrete and faced with ashlar by *D. J. Bell*, county engineer, 1930–1. – OLD DENFINELLA BRIDGE, 350 m. N for the earlier carriage road. Impressively thick arch springing directly from rocky outcroppings. Datestone of 1760 on the upstream side.

MUIRTON, 2.3 km. NW. Two-storey, five-bay laird's house, late C18, with much-enlarged ground-floor windows. The doorcase has two columns and a corniced lintel; nepus gablet above with later chimneystack.

BROTHERTON CASTLE (now LATHALLAN SCHOOL). *See* p. 634.

JOHNSTON LODGE   K   *7070*
1.1 km. SSE of Laurencekirk

A Regency mansion built *c*. 1805 for James Farquhar, M.P. and Provost of Inverbervie (q.v.). Garden front facing SW, two storeys and seven bays of painted stucco. Full-height, three-bay bow window projecting suavely from the centre. Symmetrical pairs of windows flanking it, long on the ground floor and square on the first. On the wall-head of the l. flank, a delightful sculpture of a female sphinx, showing that the architect – unfortunately his identity remains unknown – knew his Greek sources. The main drive leads up to the r. flank, hence the portico with Greek Doric columns and modillioned cornice. Beyond it, three bays added in 1934, with rounded niche on the far r. and a leaded cupola with weathervane. The rear wall has a re-set dormerhead initialed D.B. and E.D. with the date 1642 – a relic of a tower house which once stood here.

CHALYBEATE MINERAL WELL, 0.25 km. SE. Late C18. Small niche flanked by fluted and panelled pilasters. Original finials now missing. – BEATTIE LODGE, 0.6 km. NNW of the house. So named for Donald Beattie, factor to Lord Gardenstone (founder of Laurencekirk). Harled, of two storeys and six bays, the irregular spacing the result of two campaigns. Original section on the l. built *c*. 1679, the date recorded on a stone inset to the rear. The r. side was added by Lord Gardenstone in 1769 (see the door lintel dated with Roman numerals).

Gardenstone lived here when he visited the parish, as the main house – i.e. the predecessor to the current one – was let out.

KAIR HOUSE
1.9 km. ENE of Fourdoun

A calmly commanding and dignified house, built for George Kinloch after he acquired the estate in 1787. It is decidedly in the Adam tradition, exuding a sense of rectitude, equilibrium and dutiful proportion. Tall, wide central block of two storeys and three bays, all of coursed brown ashlar. Segmental door frame with depressed fanlight; distyle Greek Doric portico in front of it with triglyph architrave and flat-modillioned cornice. Twelve-pane glazing to the l. and r., shorter on the first floor. Large, wide pediment on top, very plain and simple. Prodigiously long chimneystacks on the ends.

Beyond the main block, slightly recessed single bays link up to mirrored, single-storey wings under flat roofs. Their only decoration is a single rectangular window with moulded margin set in a shallow, segmental recess. Cornice and stepped blocking courses above. The flanks each have a pair of tall rectangular windows, the rear another huge pediment over an arched, attenuated stair window.

Inside, a fine Hall with suave elliptical curves and cantilevered staircase, all top-lit by a cupola. Original carpentry with beaded panelling (dado, doors and window shutters) throughout the ground floor. Drawing Room in the l. wing, its marble chimneypiece decorated with lions. Dining Room in the r. with Tudor-headed sideboard recess and Corinthian pilasters to the l. and r. Two more D-ended rooms between them.

Former STABLES and COACHHOUSE, 130 m. NNE. More Neoclassical of the late C18, converted into a house 2003–4. Big pediment echoing the main house, this one with ball finial and oculus.

KEIG

PARISH CHURCH. Tudor Gothic, designed by *John Smith* and built by *William Minto* and *James Daniel* 1834–5. A simple handsome rectangle. Tall entrance gable, facing S, framed by stepped angle buttresses rising into pinnacles; the porch diagonally buttressed and gabled with a splayed four-centred arched doorway. Three-light Perp window at the gallery, timber tracery with small-pane glazing, and quatrefoil panel beneath a diminutive birdcage bellcote with pinnacles and spirelet. Four-bay E flank and plainer two-bay W flank with tall square-headed two-light windows, the original glazing still preserved. N gable identical to S but without the bellcote, doorway blocked during reordering; hammer-dressed pinky-golden granite with grey granite base course throughout. Inside, *Smith*'s original horse-shoe gallery was reduced to a S gallery during remodelling by *A. Marshall Mackenzie* in 1899. Pale oak furnishings including octagonal pedestal PULPIT, Gothic-arcaded COMMUNION TABLE, and PEWS still *in situ*. ORGAN introduced *c.* 1912. – WAR MEMORIAL. N wall. Alabaster tablet of 1919 in C18 style with scroll pediment. The GATEWAY to the churchyard has a delicate wrought-iron overarch of *c.* 1920 supporting a lantern with circular labels commemorating First World War battles. WAR MEMORIAL, a Celtic cross by *Messrs Alex Nicol*, 1921.

The former PARISH MANSE opposite is by *John Smith* 1834, two storeys and three bays in squared rubble. Central doorway with arcaded transom-light and stepped Neo-Tudor hood-mould; chamfered window openings, those at ground floor much taller than first, crowstepped end gables rising into broad coped chimneystacks. At the rear, a half-moon stair and single-storey-and-attic outshot within a small back court.

OLD PARISH CHURCH AND MANSE. *See* Castle Forbes.

BRIDGE OF KEIG, 0.7 km. SE. Designed by *Thomas Telford* and built by *William Minto* in 1817. A very graceful single segmental arch of 31 m. span, carrying the B992 across the Don. The arch-ring is in silver-grey granite, contrasting with the pinky-gold spandrels. Framing the arch, simple pilasters and low parapets splayed at the approaches. Half the cost was defrayed by the government.

RECUMBENT STONE CIRCLE, Old Keig, 1.5 km. W. Stone circle notable for its enormous recumbent stone and flankers. A central ring cairn, sherds of Beaker and Later Bronze Age pottery and fragments of cremated bone were found during excavations by Gordon Childe in the 1930s. (GN)

RECUMBENT STONE CIRCLE, Cothiemuir Wood, 0.6 km. NE. Recent excavations here showed that a low cairn was constructed on a flat hilltop in the third millennium BC. The stone circle was added later, perhaps as a means of closing the site to further use. (GN)

CASTLE FORBES. *See* p. 402.

LICKLEYHEAD CASTLE. *See* p. 650.

PLACE OF TILLIEFOUR. *See* p. 702.

KEITHHALL

8020

A small kirkton – church, manse and school – on the B993.

KEITHHALL & KINKELL PARISH CHURCH. An early example of the church-building programme pursued by Aberdeenshire heritors *c.* 1760–1815. Plans approved by Presbytery in 1768 were built by *William Littlejohn*, wright, with *James Hector*, mason, and *Francis Smith*, slater, in 1772–3. A simple T-plan, similar to St Columba, Pettens (1762, N). It was originally harled with three doorways, that in the long S flank (now blocked) for the minister, those in the end gables for parishioners. The Kintore family aisle projects on the N side. Simple fenestration, a single large window flanking each side of the S doorway, and two smaller windows above to light the pulpit. Steeply pitched roof with dated skewputts and birdcage bellcote over W gable. Bell from Culsalmond Parish Church (q.v.), by *Jan Vanden Ghein* 1611, recast by *John Warner & Sons*, 1879. The interior originally had E and W galleries. It has been remodelled twice, first in 1875 by *James Matthews*, then again in 1907 when the pulpit was moved from S to E (the E-end vestry is of that date) and the ORGAN by *E. H. Lawton* installed, the W gallery being retained. Present PULPIT, COMMUNION TABLE and FONT all mid-C20 in pale oak. Dark-stained BOX PEWS and fragmentary stencilled decoration in the NW corner are of *Matthews*'s time; although he converted the Kintore Aisle to a vestry it was reinstated in 1907. – STAINED GLASS. E window, the Good Shepherd, 1913 by *James Ballantine II.* – In the S wall, Christ performing Communion during the Last Supper by *A. Ballantine & Son*, 1918; and r., continuing the theme of sacrifice, a war memorial window of *c.* 1920: a young soldier in armour with standard and sword, and angels bearing the motto 'Faithful unto Death'.

Former PARISH MANSE, 220 m. NE. Entrance front by *Duncan McMillan*, 1884. Asymmetrical, two-storeyed with broad gabled end bays, doorway set in a small square re-entrant towerlet with pyramidal spirelet. At the rear, the manse designed by *William Littlejohn* in 1768, built *c.* 1772–3 and extended by *Archibald Simpson c.* 1837–40 with further works *c.* 1868–9. The central projecting bay of Littlejohn's manse once accommodated the staircase. – OFFICES. A long single-storey range framed by two-storey end pavilions with piended roofs.

OLD CHURCHYARD, 0.55 km. NW on a rise of ground. Formerly Kirkton of Monkeigie, seemingly a charge of Monymusk (q.v.) dedicated to St Serf. Granted by David Earl of Huntingdon and the Garioch to his Lindores Abbey in 1198 (confirmed 1205). A level platform may represent the church's foundations.

KEITH HALL
1.4 km. WNW

A Scottish Renaissance country house built in 1696–9 for Sir John Keith, Knight Marischal and 1st Earl of Kintore, through whose celebrated wit and courage the Honours of Scotland were saved from Cromwell during the siege of Dunnottar Castle in 1651. Married in 1662 to Margaret, daughter of the 2nd Earl of Haddington who provided a substantial dowry, he purchased the estate in 1663; later he supported the Revolution of 1689 and the

Act of Union, in consequence of which he enjoyed a highly distinguished public career for over fifty years.

Keith Hall is the first major classical building in Aberdeenshire. Its authorship is not known for certain. Its big ogee roofs might seem to suggest the hand of *James Smith* as he had already adopted these at Methven (Perth & Kinross) and probably at Old Tarbat (Highland); he was concurrently using them at Traquair (Borders), Drumlanrig and Durrisdeer Church (both Dumfries & Galloway) and probably at Caroline Park (Edinburgh). Such roofs had however been a feature of Court architecture since the earlier C17, and at Keith Hall the principal-floor entrance characteristic of Smith's later houses is absent. Stylistically it might seem closer to the work of *Alexander Jaffray* but, born in 1677, he would appear too young; and it is possible that the true architects were two relatively unknown masons, *John Reid* and *Alexander Gray*, recorded as being on site in the poll tax book of 1696.

The house incorporates both earlier and later fabric. At the rear of the main block is the Z-plan tower house of Caskieben, formerly the seat of the Johnstouns of that Ilk and probably a work of *Thomas Leiper* dating from the late C16 or early C17. At the time of his marriage in 1729 the 3rd Earl asked *William Adam* to produce designs for rebuilding the tower house and remodelling the remainder in an Early Georgian idiom with Palladian wings, but these were not executed (*Vitruvius Scoticus*, Plates 143–5). After the 5th Earl succeeded in 1778 he engaged *John Paterson* to repair and add to the house *c*. 1782, this was Paterson's first known commission on his own account, predating his management of Robert and James Adam's office in Edinburgh.

John Smith renovated Keith Hall for the 7th Earl in 1821–5, adding a classical rear court. During the early 1850s the 8th Earl engaged first *David Bryce*, who exhibited a scheme for remodelling the house at the Royal Scottish Academy in 1851, then *William Ramage* and finally the *Hays* of Liverpool to work at Keith Hall, but what they did is unclear: the original Neo-Jacobean first-floor oriels on the entrance front and the lower storeys of the canted bay on the E front were added at this time, appearing in a photograph of 1864. From 1897 the 9th Earl commissioned *Sydney Mitchell & Wilson* to further remodel the entrance front and Baronialize the court. In 1984 the house was adapted for multiple occupation by *Kit Martin* with *Douglas Forrest* acting as his on-site architect.

The Scottish Renaissance ENTRANCE FRONT (facing S) is symmetrical and still broadly corresponds in profile with that completed in 1699, although the original compact form was heightened in 1897 to provide a taller principal floor. It is three storeys and nine windows wide, the two bays at either end being carried up into an attic storey to form low square corner towers with ogee-domed roofs flanking a balustraded platform, as in several other Scottish houses built between 1666 and 1700. The entrance is – surprisingly for such a grand classical house of its date – still at ground-floor rather than principal-floor level: its pediment incorporates an eroded sand-stone field-panel carved with the motto 'May Truth and Grace Rest Here in Peace', then at first floor there is a remarkable vertical display of heraldry, itself pedimented, recalling that at Huntly Castle (q.v.) a century earlier: four family coats of arms – top l., Keith's father, the 6th Earl Marischal, and top r., his mother's family, the Earls of Mar; bottom l., Keith's own arms, and bottom r., those of the Earl of Haddington, his wife's father. Beneath these arms are Keith's and his wife's initials, and an earl's coronet and thistles; in the pediment are the Honours of Scotland, a crossed sword and sceptre with the crown above them. The balustraded parapet has finely orna-mented classical urns, all renewed as part of the *Paterson* or *Smith* works; behind this balustrade rise three very tall diag-onally shafted chimneystacks.

All this is more or less original: but the present entrance doorway and flanking two-storey bay windows in grey granite ashlar contrasting against pale golden harl are by *Sydney Mitchell & Wilson* from 1897 onwards. The design of the door-piece is adapted from that at Huntly Castle,* having the same attenuated pilaster detailing and small coats of arms in the entablature, but rises into a broken pediment. Its crispness reveals its true date; so likewise the bay windows, canted at ground floor but corbelling to square at the first, which replaced the 1850s oriels, and the mullions and transoms in the outer ground-floor windows. A stepped string course was inserted across the centre block at second-floor level, and the second-floor windows were re-formed nearer the balustraded parapet. The towers were heightened to provide for larger attic-floor windows, all the stylized window pediments at these upper levels being Sydney Mitchell & Wilson's. At some point the heraldic display appears to have been re-cut.

The relatively short W ELEVATION and longer E ELEVATION were part of the 1696–9 works, and of the same massive scale as the entrance front. The E elevation was originally a simple three-storey-and-attic, four-bay frontage to which a bay window was added at ground and first floors *c.* 1851–5. This bay window was increased in height *c.* 1900, rising into an attic caphouse with steeply raked crowstep gable. The original square attic-floor windows were heightened into pedimented dormerheads, and a small spirelet turret was inserted into the NE re-entrant angle.

On the N side, the TOWER HOUSE of Caskieben is still clearly evident. It was probably built for George Johnstoun (†1593) who had married Christian Forbes, daughter of the 7th Lord Forbes: the celebrated Arthur Johnstoun, 'the Scottish Ovid,' was their son. Caskieben has been a four-storey Z-plan. Its

---

*Of which Francis Troup had helpfully made very precise survey drawings pub-lished in *The Edinburgh Architectural Association Sketchbook* of 1880–3. The original doorpiece at Keith Hall had free-standing Doric columns and a similar broken pediment.

centre block 12.2 m. long E–W by 7.9 m. deep N–S has massively thick walls, but those of its SW corner tower, 10.5 m. by 5.9 m., and the smaller NE tower, 6.5 m. by 5.9 m., are of slighter build. The ground floor is barrel-vaulted; within the NE tower, a broad semicircular stair has led up to the great hall in the centre block at first floor. The upper floors were accessed by stair-turrets rising within both angles on the N side of the house. Overall the plan recalls Arnage (N) before its C19 remodelling, and the stepped profile of alternating square and circular elements seems close in spirit to the stepped S flank of Barra (N). The fenestration has been much altered from the late C17 onwards; one of the dormers is dated 1665, which implies that the 1st Earl made some alterations immediately after he acquired the estate.

The REAR COURT is of several dates. The W range as shown in *James Giles*'s 1851 perspective probably dates from the mid C18 – its ground floor as tall as that of the main block, and its attic floor with small square windows just below the eaves. When *John Smith* remodelled this side of the house in 1821–5, he added parapets to the N range to give it a more classical look, and built the E range entirely anew with an arcaded screen wall and taller central archway.

This court was Baronialized by *Sydney Mitchell & Wilson*. The W range was considerably heightened, its attic floor lit by pedimented dormers, and a two-storey drum tower with a contrastingly slim side turret was added to the SW corner, both tower and turret being crowned with conical roofs on the model of the Castle Fraser forecourt (q.v.). The E range was also rebuilt with steeper roofs and crowstepped gables replacing Smith's screen wall. The N range was removed and the boldly rusticated gateway from Inverugie Castle (N) was inserted and crowned with a bellcote; it dates from 1670. The garden wall coping near here incorporates other fragments from Inverugie, the most remarkable sculpted with a very early horse-drawn carriage.

Keith Hall has now been divided into fourteen apartments but the INTERIORS have been preserved intact. Apart from the first-floor drawing room at the front of the house, which was heightened by *Sydney Mitchell*, it was largely redecorated in the early–mid C19; most of the major apartments were again refitted by *George Bennett Mitchell & Son* for the 10th Earl of Kintore and his new wife, Helena Zimmerman, in 1938–41. Her father was Eugene Zimmerman, an American railroad president several times over and a major shareholder in Standard Oil. She had previously married – and her father had bankrolled, with increasing reluctance – the 9th Duke of Manchester, whom she divorced in 1930; the panelling and perhaps the C18 fireplaces at Keith Hall are said to have been stripped from Tandragee Castle (South Ulster), the Duke's Irish house. The dining room contains a fireplace with a marriage stone overmantel dated 1666 (?) which was brought to Keith Hall from Inverugie. Within the void between the late

C17 entrance front and the earlier tower house of Caskieben is a striking D-plan staircase rising through ground, first and second floors. Its elegant Adam-style iron balusters suggest that it might have been formed by *John Paterson* during the 1780s, although it could equally be by *John Smith c.* 1806–12; its roof-light is *c.* 1900.

The earliest feature of the policies is the flat-topped MOUND (100 m. N of the house) reputedly occupied during the Norman period by the tower or hall of the Garviachs (hence Garioch), although it was perhaps raised by the Leslies who acquired Caskieben *c.* 1224. Roughly circular, it is 43 m. in diameter and would originally have been surrounded by a palisade; its moat is up to 15 m. wide, still as much as 2 m. deep and was probably filled with water from the nearby stream. On its summit, a PICTISH STONE found in the River Don in 1853: 1.5 m. long by 0.6 m. wide, carved on one face with a double-disc and Z-rod, a salmon and a mirror-and-comb, now badly eroded.

Following John Paterson's improvement of the house for the 5th Earl, the present 400-hectare POLICIES were laid out in the Picturesque manner to designs by *Thomas White, Sen., c.* 1794, incorporating elements from the formal layout shown in William Roy's Highland Survey of 1747–55. Further improvements were made for the 8th Earl between 1844 and 1880 and for the 9th Earl between 1895 and 1914, the artificial lake dating from his time, and again more recently since 1984. Parklands extend to the S and E of the house, while the area to the W was laid out as a formal garden at the turn of the C20. ICE HOUSE (280 m. SSE). At the lake's E end, on the far side of the path. Late C18, large cylindrical type, with shallow domed top and oval oculus in granite.

STABLES (200 m. NNW). Probably by *John Smith*, earlier C19. Cool and refined classical frontage with Greek Doric pedimented portico distyle *in antis* built in fine granite ashlar; rubble-built three-bay wings with tall ground-floor doorways and windows and smaller oblong openings at attic level, then projecting pavilions with broad segmentally arched carriage doorways at each far end. Now converted to domestic use.

The plainer HOME FARM and (probably) the John Nash-like octagonal SOUTH LODGE (B993) are by *Smith, c.* 1806–12. The WALLED GARDEN is by *William Ramage*, 1854. Of the same date and by the same architect is the NORTH LODGE, off the B9170 (1.3 km. NNW).

KEMNAY

Standing on the Don's E bank, Kemnay developed from a tiny kirkton when its granite quarry opened in 1830, its growth surging with the arrival of the professional quarry-master John Fyfe in

1858, and the decision by Alexander George Burnett to offer new feus in 1859, a station on the Alford Valley Railway opening in that year. The village continued to develop after the Second World War and, being within commuting distance of Aberdeen, has expanded further as a result of the oil boom.

KEMNAY (EAST) PARISH CHURCH, Fraser Place. By *James Henderson*, 1844, on the site of a church of 1632. Kemnay is one of Henderson's slightly more sophisticated designs, but still plainest rubble-built Gothic. s gable canted out at the centre, with large pointed doorway and single lancet above flanked by windows with timber Y-tracery and diamond-pane glazing, suggesting a nave-and-aisles arrangement; the centre rises almost tower-like into a gablet bellcote and spirelet. The bell by *Andrew Lawson*, 1788, is seemingly the very last to have been cast at the Old Aberdeen foundry. Four-bay flanks and small dormers lighting the gallery in the steeply pitched roof. Both flanks have been altered: on the E side, *James Matthews* added the large square-plan aisle against the two N bays in 1871–2; on the w *Robert Gordon Wilson* erected the NW outshot in 1900. The latter was enlarged into a low vestry in 1907. Large and more sophisticated five-light traceried window in the N gable by *A. Marshall Mackenzie*, 1928, its intersected tracery of Aberdeen Greyfriars type.

The interior, renovated in 2008, retains its furnishings in the ritual area, although the ground-floor pews have gone. Two deep galleries, one at the s end supported by Roman Doric columns, and one in Matthews's side aisle, both with panelled oak fronts. Meeting hall formed beneath the s gallery during the renovation by inserting a simple Gothic glazed screen, also oak. – ORGAN, in the NW outshot, by *E. H. Lawton*, 1907, with improvements by *Rushworth & Dreaper* in 1982. – STAINED GLASS. Excellent five-light N window by *William Wilson* (cf. Kintore), 1958, richly coloured, intricate and intense. The lower tier of figures in the three centre lights represent 'I am the Way, the Truth and the Life' – Christ with the Holy Grail, flanked, l., by 'He that has ears to hear, let him hear' (Christ giving blessing to a man, woman and child) and r., 'Thy faith hath made thee whole'; then, middle tier, l.–r., the Nativity, Good Sower, Baptism in the Jordan, Raising of Lazarus (?) and an angel with a Standard of the Cross; in the smaller intersecting lights, the Evangelists, *Agnus Dei* and Pelican in her piety, with God in Heaven at the apex. Two lancet windows, also presumably by *Wilson*, represent Christ's Ministry and Suffer the Little Children, with delightful characterization of the individual figures. – War memorial window by *John Blyth*, 1972.

In the CHURCHYARD a MORT-HOUSE of 1831. Ice-house-like structure within a mound, its gable front of granite masonry 1 m. thick bound together by iron ties, iron door secured by three locks, vaulted lead-lined interior. – MEMORIALS. Alexander Clarihew (†1904) against w wall. Elaborate Romanesque gravestone. N of the church, a particularly handsome Greek Revival monument consisting of four fluted Doric columns with an entablature rising from a crepidoma; within this shrine, a vase commemorating Joseph Annand and Elizabeth Middleton, both †1940.

ST ANNE (Episcopal), Kendal Road. By *William Gibson Henderson* of Inverurie, 1937–8, seemingly his only known work. Simple W gable front in stugged Kemnay granite, with Art Deco doorway in polished ashlar carved with crucifix in high relief. Near-intact interior with open timber roof, furnishings and brass electrolier, but pews were removed in 2013. – ORGAN signed and dated *Thomas Elliot* of London, 1816, transferred from Castle Fraser (q.v.), repairs in 1938 and by *Harrison & Harrison* 1996. – STAINED GLASS. 'It is I, be not afraid' probably *c.* 1905–10, but adapted and restored by the *Pluscarden Abbey* workshop, 1981.

Former WEST CHURCH, on an elevated situation well above the High Street. Now the CHURCH CENTRE. Former Free Church by *James Ritchie, C.E.*, 1871–3. Five bays with trefoil-headed lights in pairs. SW porch heightened as a clock tower with spire by *Alexander Young* in 1903–4. After conversion to a hall a large extension was built out from the S gable, harled with long-and-short quoins and stepped cusp-headed triple-lights, seemingly those of the original gable reused; roof has matching patterned slates. Built out from the W of this a large glazed extension by *William Lippe Architects*, 2000, with segmentally arched roof for café looking over the town.

JAMES MITCHELL MEMORIAL FOUNTAIN, Grove Road, close to the war memorial. 1936. Larger-than-life statue of James Mitchell, a local carrier (†1857), raised upon an arched classical plinth within a hemicycle enclosure.

BRIDGE OF KEMNAY, crossing the River Don. *c.* 1930. A graceful design in reinforced concrete. Very wide low-rise single segmental span between semicircular abutments faced in granite and forming refuges; the spandrels and parapets have vertically divided panel facings contrasted with horizontal shuttering at the approaches, refined parapet detail with dome-capped die-blocks at the ends. Classical lamp-standards bearing frosted-glass globes.

PRIMARY SCHOOL, Grove Road. To the N is the the original school house and schoolroom in Picturesque cottage style of 1860, L-plan, extended into a Z in 1887. Adjacent is the BOARD SCHOOL. The oldest part visible on the SE side, a tall single storey in grey granite, seems to be by *George Gellie* in 1874 and sets the tone for additions of 1879 and 1894. The long SW side with its stepped triple gables is largely the work of *William Kelly*, 1906.

WAR MEMORIAL, Station Road/Grove Road at the S entrance to town close to the Mitchell fountain. Tall slim slightly tapered shaft of palest Kemnay granite rising from a stepped rock-faced plinth and culminating in a Gothic gablet with Celtic cross over a Scottish saltire in low relief. Unveiled 1922.

KEMNAY HOUSE
0.5 km. s of the village

A long three-storey-and-attic L-plan tower house, altered and extended in the C18 and early C19. The tower house was built in two stages. The Register of the Great Seal records a charter of King James V, dated 1538, granting Kemnay to Archibald Douglas of Glenbervie (*see* p. 620); another charter of the same king four years later refers to '*terras de Kennay cum molendinis*', suggesting that a tower house, presumably the rectangular block at the NW end of the present house, had been built within that time. In 1588 William Douglas of Glenbervie fell heir, through indirect succession, to the Earldom of Angus, and his right to the title was briefly challenged by King James VI. It appears likely that in a bid to assert his worthiness either he or his son William Jun., who succeeded in 1591, decided to extend their house so that it became the wing of a much larger and more handsome one. The long main block and its entrance jamb at right angles which forms the link with the older tower house correspond so closely to the House of Schivas (N, *c.* 1585) and in turn to Tolquhon (N) as to imply very strongly that *Thomas Leiper* was their master mason.

In 1688 Kemnay was purchased by Thomas Burnett, a Writer to the Signet in Edinburgh. His son, also Thomas, who inherited the estate in 1689, was in the service of the Court of Hanover and helped negotiate the Hanoverian Succession before

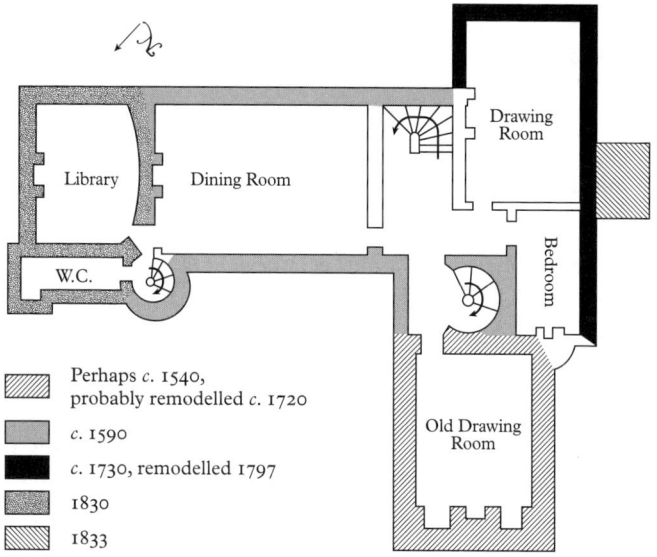

Kemnay House.
Plan

returning to Kemnay in 1713. The younger Thomas had acquired 'a strong liking for the Netherlands'; it was probably he who remodelled the original tower house of *c.* 1540 above its ground-floor level, re-roofing it with a 'Dutch' curvilinear gable. Either he or his son George, who succeeded in 1729, enlarged the windows of Leiper's main block of *c.* 1590 to create brighter and airier apartments.

As part of this substantial programme of works George had built a rather narrow block in plainest vernacular against the rear (w) flank of Leiper's entrance jamb by 1732. This subsequently became the main entrance front, and was raised to its present three-storey height by Alexander, 4th Laird of Kemnay, in 1797. Further works, probably including some redivision and refitting of the internal spaces, were carried out for John, 5th Laird, in 1807–8. For these Elyza Fraser of Castle Fraser (q.v.) recommended an architect who may have been *John Paterson*, although *James Massie* was the actual builder. In 1830 John Burnett commissioned *John Smith* to build a new water tower which was grafted onto the NE end of the main block, and in 1833 a new porch, also by Smith, was added to the w entrance front. This rather *ad hoc* development from Scottish tower house through Dutch classicism and plain Georgian vernacular to 1830s Castellated results in a number of anomalies in the elevations which are part of Kemnay's individual charm.

The TOWER HOUSE's L-plan arrangement comprising a relatively long three-storey main block facing NW over the courtyard and a higher entrance jamb facing NE correspond to Schivas in almost all key respects. At Kemnay, as at Schivas, the entrance is at ground-floor level with a turret corbelled out within the re-entrant angle, and, most distinctively, towards the far end of the main block a four-storey private stair-tourelle breaks up above the wall-head into a conical spirelet. In spite of all the changes made to Kemnay over the intervening centuries – and indeed to Schivas, restored during the mid 1930s with the forecourt which Kemnay has lost* – the basic similarity both of plan form and proportion remains clear. At Kemnay these alterations included not only enlargement of the windows but the formation above the moulded doorway of an oval light with radial glazing bars.

The planning corresponds closely to that of Schivas: vaulted at ground floor, which originally contained the kitchen and cellars; the entrance jamb doorway leading onto the main stair which here rises through first and second floors; the great hall opening off this stair at first floor within the main block, a much tighter service stair rising from the basement at its 'low' end on the s side, and a retiring room for the family beyond the 'high' end; further chambers on second floor which together with the attic were reached by the stair-turret in the re-entrant

*The stub of the forecourt wall can still be seen at the NE corner of the jamb.

angle, those within the main block being also accessed by the private stair-tower on the NW front.

Beyond the entrance jamb, the NW wing appears to constitute the tower house built c. 1540, albeit much remodelled c. 1720. It is relatively short, but its walls rise as high as those of the main block and thus its proportions are strongly vertical. Its ground floor is almost blind, and vaulted internally, but the distinctively tall and rather narrow first- and second-floor windows are characteristic of Aberdeenshire houses of the earlier C18 and were presumably formed when Thomas Burnett, 2nd Laird of Kemnay, reconstructed it with his new 'Dutch' gable.

Grafted onto the opposite far end of the main block is *John Smith*'s three-storey WATER TOWER, dated 1830. Very shallow on plan and ashlar-built with plain wall-head parapets concealing the tank, it incorporates the C16 private stair on the r. and balances it with a square turret on the l.

The vernacular classical ENTRANCE FRONT facing SW is three storeys and five windows wide, but very irregular in appearance. It was probably begun during George Burnett's works of 1732 but has been so much rebuilt that only the small windows at each end of the ground floor appear to be original. It was raised a storey during Alexander Burnett's works in 1797, and perhaps altered during the works of 1807–8, its first and second floors having large windows regularly arranged; its complex history is evident from its piended roof, which covers only three-and-a-half of its five bays. The round-arched porch in granite ashlar is by *Smith* dated 1833.

The SE FRONT is comparatively plain but must once have overlooked the formal gardens. On this side the SW range forms a single-bay projection. Next to it a tall round-headed window lights the stair which *Smith* inserted c. 1830, while at the NE extremity of the original house the roof-line steps up slightly, perhaps a Smith alteration, the twin diagonally shafted chimneystacks rising from the wall-head being his.

INTERIOR. Within the L-plan tower house the ground-floor vaults have survived. Several rooms retain fine C18 timber panelling, notably the old drawing room in the original tower house and the dining room formed within the 1590s great hall. The latter is distinguished by ten grisaille landscapes, the work of *James(?) Norie*. *James Massie* was directly responsible for the plasterwork and fireplaces of 1807–8, which are very modest in character. *Smith*'s work c. 1830 is also modest with simple Neoclassical decoration, but his main stair has fine cast-iron balusters and his library tall and very elegant bookcases.

As befitted a family so closely associated with the new Establishment order, immediately on succeeding in 1729 George Burnett, 3rd Laird of Kemnay, laid out the POLICIES on the most fashionable principles, an extensive collection of horticultural books being acquired for his library. Through the Policies – 'Kind Kemnay's seat, how beautifully placed, / With shady woods and flowery gardens graced' – a beech avenue almost 500 m. long and absolutely straight led up to the house itself, which was surrounded by a 'Wilderness' of trees including firs, larches, ashes, elms, limes, sycamores, yews and chestnuts. The Wilderness was intersected by both long straight avenues and winding paths connecting small clearings which were again encircled by beech trees, the largest being known as the Fairy Ring. There was an artificial lake, with a bridge crossing over to an island, and a Gothick hermitage. The large rubble-built WALLED GARDEN provided a very wide variety of fruit.* From 1756 the gardener was one *Robert Walker*. Trees and plants were sourced not only locally but from London, the Netherlands and later perhaps much further afield, for in 1760 George Burnett engaged *Francis Masson* as an apprentice. He would subsequently enter the King's service as the first collector of plants for the Royal Botanic Gardens at Kew, travelling to southern Africa, the West Indies, Madeira, the Azores and Canaries, Tenerife and Portugal. He was still corresponding with George Burnett's son, Alexander, 4th Laird of Kemnay, some twenty years after he had left.

The ESTATE was similarly a model of its kind. George Burnett was a very early advocate of improvement, clearing and enclosing his home farm, practising crop rotation, growing turnips for cattle and building good stone estate buildings. He planted his tenants' farmyards with ornamental trees and encouraged those who cultivated his land to follow his example. Kemnay's mid-C18 HOME FARM (170 m. NW), built before 1759, comprises coursed rubble steadings. Nearby, the rather finer COACH-HOUSE RANGE is two-storeyed in squared granite with an irregular arrangement of doorways and small windows, and the segmentally arched coach-shed itself at one far end; the four first-floor windows are broadly spaced beneath the eaves of a piended roof. The APPLE HOUSE, a pyramid-roofed pavilion, is slightly later, but before 1790. Also before 1790, and nearer the main house, the OLD LAUNDRY AND BREWHOUSE (100 m. N), long and relatively low two-storey building, five bays broad in squared cherry-cocked granite with a gabled roof, its fenestration symmetrical with two doorways in the intermediate bays. A small crowstep-gabled PUMPING HOUSE in ashlar granite, known as 'the Ram', was built by *Francis Durward*, mason, in 1820.

HOUSE OF AQUHORTHIES, 4 km. N. Built in 1798–9 as a Roman Catholic seminary in succession to Scalan (Moray), it remained in use until St Mary's College, Blairs (q.v.), was opened in 1829. Aquhorthies is attributed to *James Byres* of Tonley (*see* Tough) and, if indeed his, it is his only known work on such a scale. Simple rectangular plan. Long entrance front, three storeys and seven windows wide, in beautiful cherry-cocked granite with

---

*Just within the woods to the s of the walled garden is a finely carved BELLCOTE from a former parish church, dated 1632, framed by colonnettes at the angles, and with hemicycle pediments and finials; the bell is now removed.

central ground-floor doorway, the end bays much more generously spaced; no ornament or enrichment of any kind. Ground-
floor windows have had their sills dropped. Very tall slated piend
roof and piended dormers between gargantuan chimneystacks
which rise from just above the eaves to copings a little above the
roof ridge. Coursed rubble end gables and equally regular rear
elevation, the latter altered in the earlier C20 with a central
window which lights the stair rising continuously from the
ground floor to the wall-head. Interior, doubtless originally very
austere, has been replanned as a country house.*

To the N are the Seminary's MODEL FARM BUILDINGS,
mostly built in squared granite rubble during the early C19 and
still remarkably complete – the COURTYARD STEADING with
long single-storey byre ranges to N and S, and short returns at
the E end, which is open to the central cattle court. At the W
end the THRESHING MILL, two-storeyed within a fall in the
ground, was built in the later C19, certainly after 1869. Near
the mill, a GRANARY, single-storey-and-loft; STABLES, also
single-storey-and-loft with one skewputt carved G.H. for
Bishop George Hay; and two farm-workers' COTTAGES. Both
the courtyard steading (on its S side) and the stables back onto
a large WALLED GARDEN formed in 1811: long parallel walls,
but with irregular ends. A picturesque lake concealed within
the trees is actually the mill dam and lade.

STANDING STONE, Lang Stane o' Craigearn, 1.3 km. SW. A single
large monolith standing on the crest of a small hill. (GN)

FETTERNEAR. *See* p. 490.

MANAR HOUSE. *See* p. 661.

KENNETHMONT   5020

An improvement village on the B9002, once associated with
Leith Hall (q.v.). It was laid out by Alexander Leith-Hay in 1797
to replace two crofter settlements at Earlsfield and Mill of Syde.

Former PARISH CHURCH. Built 1812, its design based on
  Auchindoir (q.v.). Simple Gothick rectangle rubble-built and
  formerly harled with ashlar dressings and margins, gabled roof
  with pronounced skews and stone ridge. Four large Y-traceried
  windows in S flank. E end with pointed doorway and gallery
  window, original basket-weave glazing throughout. W doorway
  concealed by vestry during reordering by *George Bennett
  Mitchell*, 1909–11, in which the interior was gutted, and the
  finialled bellcote transferred from W to E.
Former PARISH MANSE, 0.5 km. ENE. Built 1794. Tall two-
  storey house, three windows wide over a semi-sunk basement,
  with railed flyover stair. Gabled roof with coped stacks and
  old-fashioned moulded skewputts. Large rear wing of same

---

* Professor Peter Davidson thinks it probable that the more widely spaced end bays
originally contained a double-height library and the chapel.

height, possibly 1841 when repairs were carried out. OFFICES. Single-storey L-plan with ball-finialled end gables. Circular HEN HOUSE with conical roof.

OLD PARISH CHURCHYARD, 0.5 km. N. A church, traditionally dedicated to SS Alkmund and Regulus, was granted by David Earl of Huntingdon and the Garioch to his Abbey of Lindores in 1191–5. Standing on a knoll are its foundations, c. 20 m. by 7 m; it was closed c. 1812 when the new church was built (*see* above), the fabric was then being robbed for BURIAL ENCLOSURES. The Leith-Hays' enclosure at the E end is plain Late Georgian Gothic; beyond this the knoll has been truncated by the railway cutting. Some excellent STONES, mid-C17 to mid-C20. One is in the form of a coffin-lid, with three boars' heads couped, saltier, crescent and three étoiles, and the initials of George Gordon and Jane Anderson with date 1648. At the other end a skull-and-crossbones, with part of the arms, three boars' heads and initials of Harry Gordon, dated 1685.

RANNES PUBLIC HALL, on the B9002. By *Thomas G. Archibald* of Huntly, dated 1909. Single-storey single-bay piend-roofed entrance front surmounted by Scots Renaissance commemorative tablet with thistle finial; flanking gallery stair-towers with conical roofs, the whole a conscious reminiscence of Leith Hall's E porch.

ARDMORE DISTILLERY, 1.2 km. E. By *C. C. Doig* for William Teacher & Sons, 1898; it draws water from springs on Knockandy Hill. Coursed granite. The N elevation facing the railway comprises (l.–r.) the MALT BARN, a two-storey triple-gabled frontage, the l. section a later addition. Very deep (thirteen bays) on plan, with cast-iron columns at ground and first floors, steel beams, timber flooring and king-post roof; KILN, square-plan, pyramidal roof and louvred pagoda cupola; then the ENGINE HOUSE, a two-storey, three-bay block, blind at first floor. It contains a single-cylinder horizontal steam engine by *G. Chrystal* of St John's Foundry, Perth, one of the few still *in situ* in a Scottish distillery; MASH ROOM, three-storey gabled frontage, second floor a later addition; and finally the STILL ROOM, long, blind, now dry-dashed. Enlarged from two to four copper stills in 1958, then to eight stills in 1975 following the Allied Brewers' takeover, when on-site malting ceased; until c. 2000 the stills were heated by coal furnaces. CHIMNEYSTACK later C20. Facing the road are BONDED WAREHOUSES, a nineteen-gable frontage, again very deep on plan. Those at the far E end are C20. WORKERS' HOUSES by *Doig*, 1899, predominantly two-storeyed with bargeboarded gablet dormerheads.

STATION (adjacent to the distillery). On the Great North of Scotland Railway's main line, opened 1854. Single-storey, timber-clad, with piended roof and ashlar stacks, to the company's standard design: recessed centre bays for the platform shelter. Closed 1968 but line still in use. Timber SIGNAL BOX and semaphores.

HOWETS OF KENNETHMONT BRIDGE, 3 km. NW. The 'Double Bridge' by *Alexander Gibb*, engineer, 1852–4. It comprises a big semicircular arch carrying the Old Military Road over the Water of Bogie, linked by broad battered buttresses to a semi-elliptical arch over the newly constructed railway.

RECUMBENT STONE CIRCLE, Ardlair, 1 km. SE, with fine views towards Tap o'Noth and Bennachie. The circle consists of a small irregular recumbent stone, two flankers and one other standing stone. Two stones lie a short distance to the E, one of which has the faint markings of a 'Pictish beast', tuning fork and mirror symbols. (GN)

LEITH HALL. *See* p. 641.

WARDHOUSE. *See* p. 761.

KILDRUMMY

4010

A place of habitation from the Stone Age to the C17 which has yielded several important archaeological discoveries. Following the Norman pattern, a sizeable village developed along a hogsback between the old parish church and the motte of a timber castle 650 m. S on the banks of the Don. The village continued to prosper after the foundation of Kildrummy Castle, 2 km. SW, being erected a burgh of barony by 1377, and confirmed as such in 1513, although by then its own castle had decayed. Today only two parish churches and the former manse remain.

PARISH CHURCH. Gothick of 1805–6, probably designed and built by *William Minto*, who had been responsible for the very similar Alford (West) Church (q.v.). Small, almost square on plan, built in cherry-cocked rubble with roughly dressed angle quoins and a tall piended roof. Two big pointed-arch S windows with basket-weave glazing bars but the E and W flanks have only small windows at ground and gallery level off-centre towards the N; on the N side, a wide bowed projection with two doorways opening to the gallery stair. This bow has a central pilaster-buttress rising into a dated, domed and ball-finialled bellcote; bell signed by *John Mowat* of Old Aberdeen, dated 1760. Chaste interior with plain camp ceiling and pan-elled gallery supported on square timber columns extending round the N, E and W sides. Between the S side windows a rostrum PULPIT. – FONT. Medieval stone, roughly carved. COMMUNION TABLES later C19 and 1943, the latter trans-ferred with the LECTERN of the same date from Auchindoir Parish Church (q.v.); very simple PEWS probably *c.* 1845–50. – FIRST WORLD WAR MEMORIAL, in the vestibule. The eleven men killed are remembered by tinted photo-portraits.

The site of the C14 OLD PARISH CHURCH (ST BRIDE) stands on a raised mound immediately to the S. Rectangular on plan, some 23 m. by 7.5 m., only two sides – its N flank and E gable – now remain. A doorway centred in the N wall has subse-quently been heightened as a window, then blocked to accommodate a re-set medieval pointed-arch recess on its inside face. Two moulded corbels (of which one, in red Kildrummy sandstone, has survived) supported a timber canopy over an Easter sepulchre, a rare example of its kind in Scotland, and particularly so in the northern mainland; next to it a small opening, its purpose unclear.

MONUMENTS. In the Easter sepulchre, recumbent stone effigies of a knight and his lady, their hands clasped in prayer, carved in low relief. Around the edge an inscription '*Hic jacet Alexr. de Forbes quondam dns. de Burchis et Mariota sporsa euis 155*' – (Here lies Alexander Forbes sometime laird of Burchis and Mariota his wife). Another upright stone against the back of the recess is dedicated to James Lumsden (†1730) with a winged soul at the top and *memento mori* at the base. Along the N wall, further stones commemorating the Lumsden family, and one in memory of John Reid of New Mill (†1563), an early example of the use of the vernacular and Roman alphabet rather than Latin black-letter script, with three stag's heads and sign of the Resurrection. – Also preserved is the ELPHINSTONE AISLE on the church's s side, 5.25 m. by 5.75 m., which has a steeply pitched slate roof with crowstepped s gable; above the s door an inscription once read 'Yis yle vas built be A.E. [Alexander, 4th Lord Elphinstone] in 1605 yeiris. Lord bliss us.' Above this, a recessed armorial panel recording the aisle's restoration by William, 15th Lord Elphinstone in 1862. Two blocked openings: that on the W flank is partly infilled with a gravestone of 1736; that on the N once opened into the nave. A round-headed stone commemorates the 4th Lord's sons William, Patrick and David shown in low relief with the family arms above. In the floor, a round-headed stone to Louis Elphinstone of Bothkenner (†1616). Two stones to Thomas Esplin (†1636), the Elphinstones' servant for fifty-six years, and his wife, Janet Forbes. On its W side, sunk into the foot of the mound, fine square GATE-PIERS crowned by ball finials and flanked by symmetrical stair-flights.

Former PARISH MANSE, 150 m. E. By *Mackenzie & Matthews*, 1850. Symmetrical Neo-Jacobean front.

43 KILDRUMMY CASTLE, 2.1 km. SW. Although it lies in ruins now, Kildrummy was, for over four centuries, one of Scotland's principal strongholds. Enough remains to give some impression of what this magnificent castle of enclosure must formerly have been, its tall curtain walls surrounding a deep D-plan courtyard entered on the s through a twin-towered gatehouse and with drum towers protruding from its angles. As the strongest link in the chain of fortifications stretching from Brechin to Inverness which were held either by the Crown or by subjects of undoubted loyalty, Kildrummy was probably begun by Bishop Gilbert of Moravia, in whom Alexander II vested civil and military authority in the North to guard the pass at which the ancient roads from the South converged to cross the Mounth into Celtic Moray, then only recently subjugated into a Scottish kingdom

governed on feudal principles. After Gilbert's death in 1245 work presumably continued without any fundamental change of plan by the Mormaers (later Earls) of Mar, who accepted Alexander's Normanizing reforms. Edward I visited Kildrummy during his first invasion of Scotland in 1296, as did William Wallace two years later. Edward returned during his second invasion in 1303, and it was evidently he who built the gatehouse – quite possibly the first the Castle ever had, many decades after construction began – although its forework is later.

By 1305, however, Kildrummy had fallen under control of Robert Bruce as uncle and guardian of Donald, the young Mormaer of Mar, and in 1306 Robert's brother Sir Nigel was besieged by Edward's son and heir, Prince Edward of Caernarvon, assisted by the Earls of Gloucester and Hereford, and with the engineer Thomas de Houghton in their retinue. As recounted in Barbour's *Brus* the Castle finally surrendered as a result not of pressure from without but of treachery within, the great hall being burnt. The w curtain was brought down by the English but soon rebuilt by the Scots, albeit in rough rubble reusing some of the old ashlar blocks; thereafter the Castle was successfully defended by Bruce's sister, Dame Christian, against the Earl of Atholl acting on behalf of Edward Balliol and the pro-English faction in 1335.

Apart from David II's quarrel with the Mormaer Thomas in 1361, Kildrummy remained loyal to the Scottish Royal House. Here Sir Alexander Stewart (a son of the Wolf of Badenoch), who had seized both the Castle and the Mormaer Isabel in 1404, prepared to withstand the onslaught of Donald, Lord of the Isles, before the Battle of Harlaw in 1411, and such was the Castle's strategic importance that in 1435 the Crown took Mar into its own hands and held it despite legal challenges from the heir apparent, Sir Robert Erskine, who stormed it in 1442 but was obliged to give it up. In 1507–8 the Castle and much of the lands passed to Alexander, later 1st Lord Elphinstone. A low point was reached when the Castle was stormed and set on fire by John Strachan of Lynturk in 1530 or 1531, but the Earldom of Mar was restored to the Erskines in 1565, and Kildrummy itself following a further legal dispute in 1626. During the Civil Wars the Roundhead colonel Thomas Morgan took the Castle by siege in just two days in 1654, and part of it was reputedly burned again. 'Bonnie Dundee's' Jacobite soldiers found shelter here in 1690, setting fire to the Castle yet again so that it would not fall into government hands. It was here, too, that John Erskine, 23rd (and 6th) Earl of Mar, put in place the final details of the Jacobite Rising of 1715 which resulted in the Castle's downfall, and his own.

After that the Castle was plundered and partly dismantled. Its chapel was seemingly in use until 1733 and other parts may have remained inhabited until c. 1750; it may also have served as an agricultural steading. The donjon collapsed and the Castle was progressively robbed of its fine masonry until a halt was called in 1809, reflecting an appreciation of its scenic qualities as a

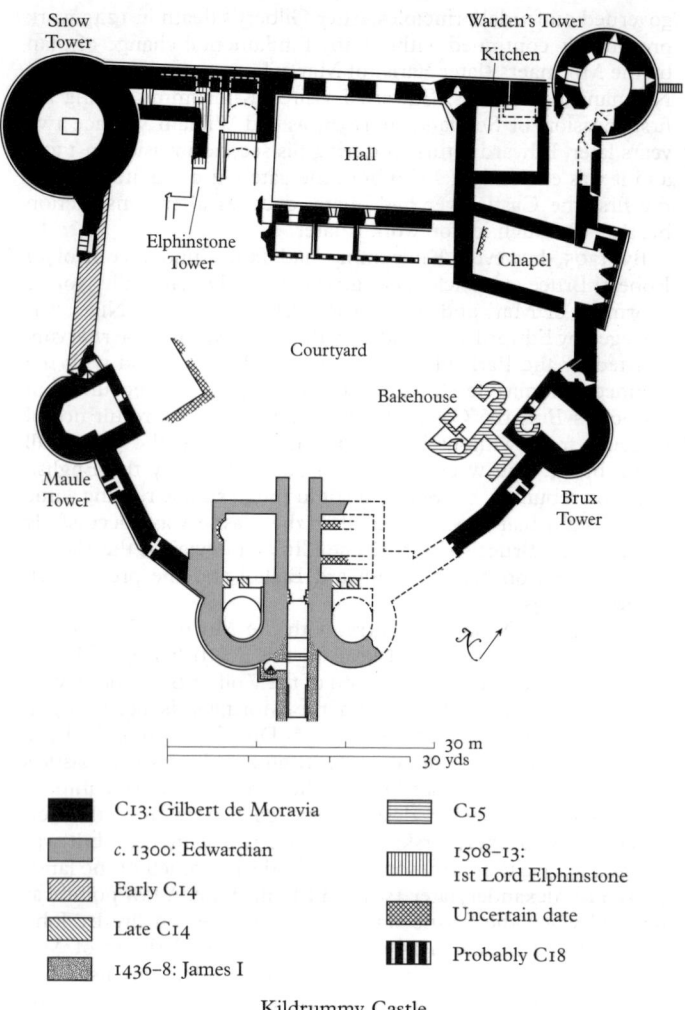

Kildrummy Castle.
Plan

C13: Gilbert de Moravia

C15

c. 1300: Edwardian

1508–13:
1st Lord Elphinstone

Early C14

Uncertain date

Late C14

Probably C18

1436–8: James I

picturesque ruin. In 1898 it was purchased by Col. James Ogston, who initiated a programme of excavation and consolidation. His niece Mrs Yates entrusted it to the Ministry of Works in 1951.

The Castle's SITUATION is a naturally defensive one within fertile and well-watered surroundings. It stands on a promontory – a large, gently inclined terrace of ground, but protected on its N and W sides by very sharp drops to the foot of Back Den some 20 m. below. In Back Den were supplies of the most excellent pale freestone, ideal for building, the likes of which could not be obtained for a considerable distance around. With comparatively few limitations imposed by the site, the basic

PLAN follows the classic symmetrical pattern of C13 military engineering, but – as we shall see – with the most up-to-date and sophisticated characteristics of both French and English origin. It is essentially a pentagon in the form of a D with its curve on the S, very large in Scottish terms at 185 m. broad by 210 m. deep. The gatehouse stands at the narrow S front of the D, two towers at the intermediate angles, then the long wall at the rear, flanked by the largest tower, the donjon, rising from a rocky outcrop on the NW, and the Warden's Tower rising from another on the NE. All the external walls are 2.5 m. thick, except for the donjon's, which were 3.5 m., and pale ashlar of conspicuously high quality was used throughout. Within the courtyard, the Great Hall was also faced in ashlar. It was centred against the N wall, and brightly lit with windows both on the S side overlooking the courtyard and the N side overlooking Back Den. On its W it was linked to a solar which was enlarged, probably by the 1st Lord Elphinstone, into a C16 L-plan tower house, while on the E lay the kitchen. There were once additional lean-to buildings on both the courtyard's E and W sides, while the bakehouse with three ovens near the SE corner was an early addition. But perhaps the most unusual feature of the plan – and part of the original build – is the very large chapel, with exactly correct E–W orientation, its E end protruding through the curtain wall at a slight angle between the Warden's Tower and the intermediate tower on this side.

The GATEHOUSE, probably built by the English c. 1303, has been so much robbed of its stonework that it only rises a few courses above its foundations. It was almost 21 m. broad, its central gateway framed by two round towers each 10 m. in diameter over walls 3 m. thick. They rose from steeply battered bases and were thus quite different from the towers with moulded bases at the four other angles, these being built when the Castle was under Scottish control. The gatehouse towers contained D-plan rooms with two slightly larger square rooms further back behind them; on each side, these front and rear rooms were originally separated by a simple wooden partition with a central column supporting the floor above, but they were subsequently partitioned in stone. The rear room on the W side has a fireplace, the jambs of which once supported a hood. The E tower's floor was paved in herringbone ashlar, now grassed over. The gatehouse's upper floors were accessed by newel stairs between the towers and the adjoining curtain walls; they must have included a room which controlled the gateway's portcullis. Immediately r. of the E tower is a sally-port with splayed and moulded jambs, so that the main gate did not need to be opened for small groups of visitors.

During the C15 when the barbican forework was added, the gatehouse itself was substantially strengthened. Its original gateway would have been almost as wide as the distance between the two towers; the present one, although without a portcullis, is narrower to restrict the opening. The towers themselves were barrel-vaulted and infilled with rubble at ground floor to help them withstand mining and ramming, and the sally-port was blocked up.

Although there is little more than its ground plan to see now, Kildrummy's gatehouse was far stronger than that of any other C13 Scottish castle: indeed, symmetrical gatehouses of this size and strength are English in origin, the only Scottish parallel being the almost intact example at Caerlaverock (Dumfries & Galloway). In his analysis of Kildrummy published in 1928, Dr Douglas Simpson identified the gatehouse's plan as closely related both in design and dimensions to that built by Edward I at Harlech (*see* Gwynedd) in Wales, and on that basis suggested that the military engineer responsible was the Savoyard *Master James of St George*, who was transferred to Scotland in 1299.

The FOREWORK seems from the Exchequer Rolls to have been added during works of *c.* 1436–8, immediately after the Castle's seizure by the Crown. It comprises ashlar-built abutments some 5.5 m. long which together form a transe 2.75 m. wide, so canalizing any attack on the gateway. Within this transe is a pit, 6.5 m. long and 2.5 m. deep, lined with coursed rubble but with ashlar masonry at the ends and drains to keep it clear of water and leaves, which formerly contained a drawbridge balanced on a central axle. A spiral stair in the angle between the l. abutment and the gatehouse's W tower once led up to a room which controlled the drawbridge, its rear end sinking down into the pit as its forward end was raised. The total length of the forework and the entrance passage through the gatehouse was 26.25 m.: it was guarded not only by the drawbridge but by three gateways, the first of which was 8.25 m. in advance of the original gatehouse entrance, and the second in between them; there may even have been another gateway at the passage's N end. This presented a formidable challenge to attackers until the pit was infilled and the courtyard approach cobbled over, probably in the C17.

The two INTERMEDIATE TOWERS at the SW and SE – probably once known as the Brux or Burges and the Maule or Maldis Towers – are each D-plan, three storeys high and 9 m. in diameter. Like the gatehouse towers they contained long D-plan rooms which projected within the courtyard. Their unvaulted ground floors were probably stores as they gave no access to the upper levels, which contained fireplaces; these upper levels were reached by newel stairs in the curtain walls which also provided access to the parapet walks. The doors to the stairs could be barred from within, and thus the intermediate towers conformed to the conventions of medieval castle design in that they were individually defensible even if intruders broke into the courtyard. At some point the E tower's ground floor was converted into an oven. The adjacent BAKEHOUSE with three further ovens is probably C15.

In the courtyard's NW corner the DONJON, known as the 'SNOW TOWER', was much the largest until what was left of it collapsed in 1805. It was completely circular, 15 m. in diameter above its base, and is recorded as having comprised seven vaulted storeys of accommodation, although some of the seven were more probably intermediate timber floors. The entrance was at ground level and there was a gallery with loopholes in the wall thickness at first floor with further mural chambers on the upper storeys. At the crown of each vault there was a circular opening which allowed water to be hoisted up from the well-shaft 1.8 m. square carved out of the rock, presumably at least as far down as the bottom of Back Den. In his analysis, Douglas Simpson noted the Snow Tower's close similarity with the donjon of the Château de Coucy, built *c.* 1220 by Enguerrand le Grand. His daughter Marie married Alexander II in 1239, thus establishing a strong link between Scotland and Coucy which continued throughout the C13.

In the courtyard's NE corner is the WARDEN'S TOWER, circular and much the best preserved, its drum surviving complete outwith the curtain walls, although most of the internal structure is lost. It is 11.5 m. in diameter, and rises four storeys to some 18 m. height. The lowest level, with its own latrine, was probably a prison, its entrance having been secured by two barred doorways closing against the inside; a continuous corbel course implies that the ceiling, unusually for a place of confinement, was of wood, although Simpson suggested a mushroom vault supported on a central pier. As in the two intermediate towers the upper storeys were accessed separately by a turnpike stair. The first-floor room has four large mural chambers narrowing towards loopholes 2 m. in height. The upper rooms comprised the warden's living accommodation, the remains of its fireplaces still surviving. These rooms may originally have had loopholes like the first floor, but if so they were replaced, presumably during the English occupation, by two-light windows similar to those found in Edward I's castles in Wales – each is large enough for an *arblastier*, or bowman, and his *valet* or assistant. The Warden's Tower may have been crowned by a groin-vault; part of its parapet walk and three runnels for drainage survive, although the parapet itself which rose continuously with the wall-head is almost all lost. Presumably for reasons of security, the Warden's Tower evidently had no direct entrance from the courtyard, being reached by a passage running from the Great Hall between the chapel and the kitchen, but it was close to a postern in the N curtain, and must have had access to the room which controlled its portcullis.

The domestic apartments were ranged along the N curtain furthest away from the entrance, but near the donjon. The GREAT HALL, 21.75 m. long by 12 m. deep internally and with walls to the courtyard 1.75 m. thick, had four windows looking out over Back Den and three smaller windows looking into the courtyard. The courtyard's S front originally rose from a bowtell base, with the main doorway at its E corner. This doorway led into a screened-off section at the Hall's 'low' end nearest the kitchen; a turnpike within the NE angle probably accessed a minstrels' gallery and the parapet walk. The windows are set in deep reveals with side benches, that on the N side at the 'high' end where the lord sat having had two lights with a central mullion; traces of a straight stair remain visible high up in this wall, rising towards the W end. The Hall had no fireplace and was presumably heated by central braziers. No evidence survives for the roof, although the Exchequer Rolls of 1436–8 indicate that it was tiled at that time.

A spiral stair in the Hall's SW angle connected to the lord's SOLAR, which was altered, reputedly by Alexander Elphinstone between 1507 and 1513, to form the L-plan ELPHINSTONE TOWER, the older masonry being clearly distinguishable from the new which rises above the N curtain as a crowstepped gable. Barrel-vaults were inserted at ground floor; at first floor a window – part of the original C13 fabric – overlooked the Great Hall so that the lord or his lady could direct their retinue. The KITCHEN itself still preserves remains of its hearth, aumbry, sink and drain in its N wall. At some point the Hall perhaps ceased to be used for its original purpose since additional rooms were built against its S front, obscuring the windows on that side; the window lighting the high end, however, was converted into a fireplace or doorway.

Perhaps reflecting the Castle's establishment by Bishop Gilbert of Moravia, the CHAPEL – 14.25 m. by 5.75 m. internally, raised over an undercroft – was of substantial size and height given the restrictions of the courtyard, so much so that its E gable had to project through the curtain wall between the intermediate tower and Warden's Tower on that side. That it does so at a slight angle, and so achieves exact E–W orientation, was probably to ensure that it was protected by enfilade fire, its triple lancets each 4.5 m. tall and drilled for glazing bars being the most obviously vulnerable feature of the defences. At some point thought was evidently given to extending it into a semicircular apse, its walls widening from 3 m. to 3.5 m. thick, which would have replaced the E gable and been more defensible, but as the surviving foundations have not been bonded into the earlier masonry the intention was clearly never implemented. The lancets are very simply treated but are framed on the gable's inside face by nook-shaft colonnettes with dogtooth around the arches. They appear to be earlier C13, when Bishop Gilbert was still alive. Next to them can be seen remains of an aumbry, and the doorway to a vestry. There was a further smaller lancet, seemingly rebuilt in the C15, in the broken-off gable-head. At some late point in the Castle's history the chapel was deconsecrated, a lean-to structure being built against the inner side of the E gable where the colonnette shafts have been partly cut away to receive a wall-plate. The construction of the roof is unclear.*

Where they survive complete the CURTAIN WALLS are some 10.5 m. high. The wall-head rises flush into plain parapets,

---

*During Simpson's excavation in 1919 several massive roofing slabs of hard schist were found but it is not clear which building they came from.

above which hoardings would presumably have been erected during time of war. In the interests of sanitation all the latrines except that in the ground floor of the Warden's Tower are formed within these walls, rather than in the living accommodation; their shafts run down to openings at the foot of the walls, which are wide but (with one exception, at the SW angle) have central stone impost blocks to prevent anyone from squeezing in or out. Two of these shafts on the S side were kept constantly flushed by the drainage channels in the cobbled courtyard.

The Castle was protected by a DITCH on its S and E sides. It is better preserved on the E where it is 26 m. broad and as much as 6 m. deep, there being traces of an upcast bank on both scarp and counterscarp. The ditch may have been formed before construction of the Castle began if there was still a risk of localized attacks in the earlier C13: this might explain why it does not closely follow the line of the E curtain wall where the postern on that side opened onto an area of ground protected by a chemise partly built in coursed rubble.* On the S side the ditch was partly infilled late in the Castle's history to make access simpler; between the ditch and gatehouse there were further defences, including a clay-bound stone wall some 25 m. long and 2 m. deep. There was probably a small garden on the Castle's W side. The N postern opened into a SUNK PASSAGE, its vault now collapsed; it can still be traced running down Back Den to a cistern tower at the burn, which has been dammed to form a fish pond and pleasaunce.

KILDRUMMY HOUSE (now KILDRUMMY HOUSE HOTEL), 175 m. W of the Castle ruins. A handsome English Neo-Jacobean mansion by *A. Marshall Mackenzie*, completed in 1901 for Col. James Ogston, an Aberdeen soap-manufacturer (cf. Ardoe House, q.v.); it replaced a Tudor cottage transferred to Ardhuncart (*see* below). Kildrummy House is built in ashlar using the same local freestone as the Castle. Raised on a balustraded terrace, its E front is essentially a two-storey-and-attic U-plan, five bays broad with mullioned-and-transomed windows. Its gabled ends have broad canted bays at ground floor and its shallow court is infilled by a single-storey billiard room, the roof of which forms a crenellated terrace for the first-floor apartments. At its N end beyond the balustraded terrace, the principal front has a basement floor, the walls of which are steeply battered: and set well back beyond this is a slightly taller canted entrance tower in the re-entrant angle of the L-plan N front. Stairs lead up to its round-arched main doorway, flanked by Roman Doric columns and crowned by a broken hemicycle pediment containing heraldic arms; the steeply pitched roofs are punctuated by very tall clustered chimneystacks.

---

*But cf. Coull Castle (q.v.) where a similar terrace exists outside the curtain walls. In his first analysis of Kildrummy published in 1920 Simpson suggested that the ditch might be of prehistoric origin but by 1928 he felt that there was not sufficient evidence for such an assertion, which has subsequently been ruled out by Apted.

The perfectly preserved INTERIOR is richly evocative of its period with much use of oak panelling and ceilings, the door-pieces with fluted pilasters and broken pediments, the walls covered in brocade, and the early electric brass switchgear and sockets still in place. On plan the house is almost as deep as it is broad: across the principal front, the library is at the NE corner nearest the entrance tower, the top-lit billiard room is in the centre bays and the Neoclassical drawing room at the SE corner; behind them, a broad hall-corridor heated by a huge fireplace also gives access to the dining room on the S side of the house with its columnar chimneypiece and to the magnificent stairway carved with seated heraldic lions, beasts and Neo-Caroline scroll foliage which leads up to the first floor. A business room immediately behind the entrance tower allowed Ogston to receive visitors without ever troubling the main apartments, and the service court is discreetly located to the rear.

The house faces the Castle (*see* above) across the ravine of the old quarry in which the ROCK GARDENS were formed by a Japanese firm of landscape architects and planted by the nurserymen *Backhouse* of York under the direction of *David Peary* in 1904. To be shown into these magnificent gardens is to leave one's own world behind and descend into an idyll of botanical life obtained from around the globe, reflecting the Backhouses' long-standing interest in alpine species as well as more exotic specimens often collected during missionary work which have prospered in the acidic soil and the peacefulness of their sheltered surroundings. The slopes sink down steeply towards the dark blue ribbon of a stream, and following this like a thread of narrative as it wends its way along the valley basin the ruins of the medieval castle come gradually into sight high up on the far side of the cliffs, at once massively substantial yet also beautifully, intangibly remote. The stream then widens into calm shallow pools and contracts again into tinkling cascades as it passes through carefully orchestrated settings, some with broad open prospects over rolling lawns, others intimate and enclosed, which woven together by the beaten-earth paths flow and merge each one into the next. The climax is the great pointed-arch BRIDGE – by *A. Marshall Mackenzie* 1900, modelled on the Brig o' Balgownie (*see* Aberdeen, p. 196) – which spanning across the ravine the bridge seems in some more than physical sense to hold this magical world together: its single opening perfectly encompasses the views of tall trees and rich garniture of plants which gather around the quietly reflective water's edge on either side. Built of Kildrummy ashlar freestone it carries the driveway towards the house but the sheer height of its stepped parapets and water chutes only serves to reinforce the distance between those who use it as a vantage point and those already exploring within the gardens far beneath.

ARDHUNCART LODGE, 1.2 km. E of the churches, is the Neo-Tudor cottage originally built *c.* 1835 at Kildrummy for Col.

Gordon but re-erected here in 1900 with additions by *A. Marshall Mackenzie* after Col. Ogston built Kildrummy House (*see* above). The original house was a two-storey L-plan, ashlar-built, with upper-floor windows breaking into gableted stone dormers and diagonally shafted clustered chimneystacks. It was reconstructed with a narrow but very deep two-storey addition which contains the four-centred doorway projecting boldly forward from within the angle and an L-plan rear wing. Its long flank elevation is symmetrical with a central gabled bay, but Mackenzie's two-bay veranda on this side has recently been replaced by a conservatory.

MAINS OF BRUX, 1.9 km. ESE. A laird's house of *c.* 1700, reconstructed as a farmhouse in the C19. Within are incorporated fragments from a tower house which stood nearby, including a fireplace lintel with late C17 bolection moulding supported by two late medieval swag-decorated corbels and C16 corbels supporting the chimney-breast.

SOUTERRAIN, 3 km. NNW at Muirs of Kildrummy. This consists of a main passage about 16 m. in length with an entrance to a secondary chamber near the end of the passage. (GN)

KINALDIE HOUSE

8010

3 km. N of Blackburn

Simple classical house, unified in appearance but seemingly built in three stages. The rear wing appears to be the remnant of a house of *c.* 1800. This was single-storey-and-basement, and evidently symmetrical on both flanks, its E-facing end bays canted and those facing W bowed. The whole S end of this house was demolished *c.* 1835 when Kinaldie was rebuilt as a single-storey villa, which survives as the entrance front's ground floor, five bays broad with a Roman Doric pedimented portico and a concealed basement. The first floor was added in the late C19 or earliest C20. Shallow-pitched roof with broad oversailing eaves and two closely spaced chimneystacks clasping a central attic dormer. The ground-floor rooms open off a circular central hall with a saucer dome and oculus; the stairway to the first floor winds around its walls. The plasterwork acknowledges the different construction dates.

KINCARDINE CASTLE *see* FETTERCAIRN

KINCARDINE HOUSE

6000

1 km. ENE of Kincardine O'Neil

The first major commission of the London-based *Niven & Wigglesworth*, entrusted to them by Mary Pickering and built by

John Morgan in 1894–6. Niven had been Aston Webb's draughts-man, while Wigglesworth had worked for Ernest George and for the Vanderbilts' architect George B. Post in New York, and the influence of all these is evident in the design. Tall and very substantial Scots Renaissance château, as scholarly in its architecture as Lorimer but with some very up-to-date London Neo-Baroque details to show that it was a house of its time; it is harled in a pale golden ochre with stone dressings to stand out against its backdrop of densely wooded hillside.

The main entrance is in the SE flank, but the PRINCIPAL FRONT faces SW and comprises a symmetrical three-storey-and-attic, three-bay centre recessed between taller asymmetrical blocks at the ends: that on the l. is the gable of the NW wing and is a slimmer version of the Seton Tower at Fyvie (N); that on the r. is a tall square-plan tower designed to look as if it were the original C15 nucleus but with some Baroque elements and areas of hammer-dressed masonry to leave no doubt that all is new. At principal-floor level the central hall windows open onto a balustraded terrace cantilevered out on enormous moulded brackets in the Bryce manner, here extended across the main (r.) tower with stairs to the formal garden. The hall windows are very tall and linked to those at second floor by apron panels (themselves formerly glazed) to emphasize the design's verticality: at both floors the windows are mullioned and transomed with small-paned metal casements. At attic level the wall-head is of ashlar boldly jettied out on a deep corbel course which zigzags under water cannon and rises into dormers with alternating pediments which continue the verticals of the windows beneath into the steeply pitched roof. The zigzag corbel course continues across the turreted superstructure of the l. gable front where the Seton Tower scheme provides twin bows for the SW end of the drawing room. Within this gable's re-entrant angle is a slim corbelled oriel rising into a pedimented dormer answering those of the central block. To the r. of the centre bays the five-storey main tower contains the front stair hall with its entrance doorway in its SE flank. This stair hall is acknowledged on the principal front by a large lunette window; its astragalled first-, second- and third-floor windows are all later insertions. Its slim circular SW turret rises into a double-height caphouse, while its SE corner is canted in hammer-dressed American brownstone-like masonry as if to suggest a three-tier oriel. At the wall-head moulded corbels support a very deep crenellated ashlar parapet, its large caphouse with crowstepped chimney gables.

On the SE FLANK, the bold Neo-Baroque doorpiece is framed by pairs of stepped and blocked Doric columns supporting a cantilevered segmental pediment and ball-finialled obelisks. The NW and SE flanks are only slightly simpler than the principal front, the Drawing Room on the NW FLANK having the same tall windows and cantilevered terrace as the Hall. At the REAR is the service court, which is embanked into sloping ground and enclosed by two Castle Fraser-inspired wings, low two-storeyed with dormerheaded windows and circular angle towers at the far ends.

The square-plan ENTRANCE STAIR HALL has marble columns with stylized Ionic capitals in plaster and a groin-vaulted ceiling. The stair is also marble, the woodwork oak with coloured-glass windows. Finely detailed doors at the stairhead open into the first-floor GREAT HALL, the most important social space, occupying the central bays of the principal front. This hall, oak-panelled with attached Ionic colonnettes and open screenwork at the central archway to the main stair, has a timber arcaded musicians' gallery at one end and a fireplace (a replacement of the original) at the other, while its ceiling is timber-beamed, all in the Ernest George manner (cf. Poles, Hertfordshire); the light fittings are original but converted from gas to electricity. The MAIN STAIR with a painted ceiling representing the Home Nations – thistle, rose, leek and shamrock – and a splendid iron lantern, and the SERVICE STAIR with laundry lift rising the full height of the house are logically arranged together as the core of the plan. Around them, the handsome classical DINING ROOM which opens off the entrance hall's N side has a mutuled cornice, a coved and painted ceiling, a segmentally arched sideboard recess across its far N end and two doorways to the male domain: the BILLIARD ROOM is behind the stairs and the SMOKING ROOM in the NE wing. The female domain lies furthest from the entrance on the house's NW side – the airy classical DRAWING ROOM with coved and plaster-panelled ceiling, the YOUNG LADIES' ROOM behind it, and the CHAPEL in the N corner lit by five cusp-headed lights with diamond-pane glazing.

The POLICIES lie on a S-facing slope with outlooks across the Dee Valley to Beinn Bhrotain 70 km. away. Their development precedes the current house: a vernacular classical house probably of the early–mid C18 and a Simpsonesque Italianate villa of c. 1830 previously occupied the site. The fields were drained and enclosed and the woodlands planted between c. 1815 and c. 1860, the WALLED GARDEN being laid out within this time. Its arched gateway was formed in 1960, the gates deriving from Carlogie Lodge.

KINCARDINE O'NEIL

5090

Kincardine O'Neil grew up near a ford of the Dee where the Cairn O'Mount road from the Mearns to Strathdon intersected the road running along the N riverbank. The first church was dedicated to St Erchard (or Erchan) and built close to the site of his holy well. As part of the Onele barony the village was granted by Alexander II to Thomas Durward (†1231) who founded a hospital here; its endowments were confirmed *c.* 1250 by his son Alan, who also built a timber footbridge over the river. By 1330 the endowments of the defunct hospital supported a prebend at St Machar's Cathedral in Aberdeen. James IV erected the village into a burgh of barony in 1511, with rights to fairs and markets. In the mid C18 a military road cut across the church-yard's NE boundary; the village's prosperity grew after a new road was formed to Huntly (q.v.) in 1803 and the Potarch Bridge (*see* p. 381) across the Dee was completed 3 km. downstream in 1814.

CHRIST CHURCH (Episcopal), Pitmurchie Road. By *William Hay*, 1865–6. Simple but quite original E.E. Three-bay nave in snecked polychrome rubble with a steeply pitched roof swept low down and extending over a narrower single-bay chancel with plate-traceried E window. Flèche with spirelet and two pretty s dormers. Small priest's N porch; the W porch was added *c.* 1880. Inside, open timber-boarded queenpost roof over the nave, the chancel's roof supported on timber arches. Octagonal PULPIT in pale marble with darker trefoil-headed panels. – ALTAR and ALTAR RAILS, 1894. – Octagonal pedestal FONT in pale marble like the pulpit. – STAINED GLASS. E window: the Nativity, Crucifixion and Last Supper, with *Agnus Dei* and two Apostles in quatrefoils above, 1866. W window. Risen Lord; in l. light an angel, r. the discovery of the empty tomb, by *Heaton, Butler & Bayne*, 1885. Eight other figurative windows, all *c.* 1900.

Former RECTORY, *c.* 1866. Two-storey L-plan, gabled bay projecting on r. Timber porch angled within the re-entrant. Harled with granite margins, lying-pane glazing, decorative bargeboards at gables and dormerhead.

OLD PARISH CHURCH, on the s side of North Deeside Road.* The much-altered shell of the medieval church dedicated to St Erchard with what appear to be the foundations of the C13 HOSPITAL to its E. The church faces the original thoroughfare of the settlement, the 'water lane' leading N–S between the holy well and the old Dee crossing. In 1733 the heather roof of the church burnt off and was replaced with slates. Repairs and alterations are mentioned in 1799 and 1845, but in 1861 the new church was built (*see* below) and the old church's roof removed before division into private burial lairs in 1869.

These C18–C19 interventions are plain to see. Large round-headed doors and windows were inserted in the E and W gables, while two large sash openings were made in the s wall. On the N and s walls are buttresses of dressed ashlar, also from this later phase. The copings and skewputts obviously date from after 1733. Of the medieval fabric there is on the W wall a rubble chamfered plinth and an offset string course halfway up on which two blocked, slender moulded lancets rest. Traces of these are visible in the interior. At the apex a C17 bellcote with ball finials. The s wall has no plinth and a chamfered

*This entry is by Jane Geddes.

lancet at each end. On the E wall, dressed (C18?) ashlar quoins on the SE corner contrast with smaller stones on the NE and both western corners. There are no traces of the hospital's structure above ground level abutting the E wall of the church. Here there is no plinth but the wall is offset halfway up, though without the neat chamfer of the W wall. All surviving features appear to be later insertions. At the upper level are two parallel slots which seem to be the traces of original lancets, like those on the W, whose location is also visible inside. Below them, cutting through the offset are two smaller moulded lancets, possibly reused from the hospital when its walls were taken down. Beside them, re-set in packing and interrupting the offset is a small moulded twin window, suitable to serve as a squint from the hospital looking into the chapel. On the N wall there is one small chamfered lancet at the E end, and a round-topped priest's door with a segmental relieving arch inside. This appears to be a later insertion because the great N portal is blocked with a similar segmental archway.

The finest medieval feature of the church is indeed its N DOORWAY. Of four orders, in which two continuous orders alternate with two others supported by engaged shafts with moulded capitals. More orders and foliage capitals are on the interior. While this could relate to the mid-C14 developments, Richard Fawcett points out that Alan Durward had the ambition and power to create such a sophisticated feature in the C13. If the main entrance for the congregation was through the W wall, elaborated with its plinth, then such a grandiose opening on the N side implies both an important settlement on this side and the entrance for a great patron or cleric.

Former PARISH CHURCH, North Deeside Road, on the opposite side from its predecessor. By *James Matthews*, 1860–1. First Pointed, rectangular plan in coursed rubble (formerly harled) with ashlar dressings. S gable front buttressed with stepped triple lancets which have a single order of shafts; gableted bellcote. Buttressed six-bay flanks with plain single lancets and shouldered doorways nearest S end.

DESCRIPTION. The present village dates from after 1803 when the E–W turnpike road was laid out, creating a charming single street lined on its S side by a slightly irregular row of two-storey houses built in coursed rubble. On the more varied N side towards the far W, the BRETHREN MEETING ROOM, dated 1873; next to it a BLACKSMITH'S, its gable to the road. Near the E end, the former GORDON ARMS, originally built for Francis Gordon of Kincardine, has a log-column porch and extension of 1908 by *George Bennett Mitchell* (of *Davidson & Garden*). Nearby is ST ERCHAN'S WELL, as re-formed to provide watering for horses. Its well-head, dated 1858, is an ashlar box with moulded cornice, low ogee top and iron finial; its water-spout is a cast-iron lion's head. Looking down the street from the E is the former PARISH SCHOOL: mid-C19 master's house with central chimney gablet and what was originally the boys' schoolroom at the rear (partly demolished *c.* 1900 to become a reading room). Behind is the cottage-like GIRLS' SCHOOL in finely crafted granite, its dedication panel (1856) commemorating the Rev. William Morrice.

The village has two TOLL HOUSES of *c.* 1800, one N of the schools with canted end, the other at the far W with a bow.

Former PARISH MANSE, Glebe Park. By *J. & W. Smith*, 1844, in their Tudor English rectory manner.

DESS (or DESSWOOD) HOUSE, 1.9 km. WNW. Scots Baronial by *Thomas Mackenzie* (of *Mackenzie & Matthews*) on an elevated site for the Aberdeen advocate Alexander Davidson, dated 1851. The E half of the main block was demolished in 1956 and the composition is now unbalanced but still handsome. Harled, with granite dressings. Principal elevation facing S is asymmetrical, reducing in height and receding back from r. to l. Tall four-stage entrance tower at SE with rounded angles and a drum turret at one corner rising into a corbelled and crenellated parapet. This steps down into a single three-storey bay with a dormerhead pediment and slim circular angle tower with a bellcast spirelet with fish-scale slates. To the W the elevation steps back again into a two-storey three-bay block with two pedimented dormerheads and a large pepperpot turret corbelled out from its SW angle. Stepped further back beyond the two-storey block, additions by *Walter Ramsay Davidson* for his brother Lt-Col. Duncan Davidson *c.* 1910, these including the still-extant semicircular stair-tower with square caphouse and the arched loggia at the NW. The LODGE is also Scots Baronial, but its style characteristic of *James Matthews c.* 1860.

KINELLAR HOUSE
1 km. W of Blackburn

A vernacular classical country house probably built in the earlier C18, but much altered since. The main block is built along a ridge of ground. Its N elevation is two-storey, and overlooks a small formal courtyard enclosed by two-storey ranges to the E and W. Both the main block and these flanking ranges have gabled roofs and moulded skewputts characteristic of the earlier C18, but the N front's projecting centre rising into an attic gable is absolutely plain without skewputts and would seem to be a later addition. During the later C18 the main block's S elevation was transformed by its remodelling as the principal – and seemingly main entrance – front. Originally rising from lower ground than the courtyard front, the S elevation stood three full storeys in height and was four, perhaps five windows broad. The remodelling sought to create a house of much more sophisticated appearance in which service provision was much better concealed. The ground-floor windows have been partly concealed by banking up earth against them to create a sunk service basement, resulting in longer and

lower, more horizontal proportions and the centre bays have
been built out under a broad chimney gable. A short flight of
railed steps leads to a central transom-lit doorway at principal
floor level, with narrow windows to each side repeated on the
bedroom floor. At the E end of the main block, and slightly set
back, the gable of the E courtyard range appears like a small
hip-roofed pavilion, its single tall window on a mezzanine level
between the present entrance and upper floors of the main
block. At the main block's W end, the house has been extended
by another bay, again set back. The old work is clearly distinguished from the new by the chamfered surrounds of its
windows and the moulded skewputts which find no echo in
the later alterations.

Immediately E of the S front is a GAZEBO in the form of a
two-storey round tower with a conical spirelet. This forms the
outer angle of a second more informal court, entered from the
S, its rear side enclosed by a single-storey range of OFFICES
extending from the house's E wing at its N end. In the later C19
another block of offices was demolished to build the STABLE
COURT, single storey with dormered attic, with the coachhouse
itself slightly projecting under a tall gable.

Inside the main house the finely detailed timber main stair
from principal to upper floor dates from c. 1760 but the tightly
planned semicircular stair rising from the basement storey is a
survival of the house before its remodelling, opposite the original doorway at this level; fabric may also survive of an earlier
house recorded in 1625. The E pavilion contained the kitchen
with an exceptionally large inglenook fireplace, complete with
bread oven and salt-box.

KINGCAUSIE HOUSE   K   *8000*
1.1 km. NNE of Maryculter

Founded in the C15 by Henry Irvine, Kingcausie is one of the
oldest estates on Deeside still inhabited by members of the
same family. Overlooking the Dee across a C17 designed parkland, its ancient sylvan idyll is now ruptured by its close proximity to the Aberdeen bypass. Its current bristling Baronial
appearance was created in 1852–3 by *David Bryce* for John
Irvine Boswell (commemorated by Boswell's Monument, *see*
below), but it incorporates older fabric. Following a fire of
1680, the house was rebuilt by John Irvine, 7th laird, married
to a Forbes heiress, who also 'planted some about it'. It was a
two-storey early classical house, with single-storey wings. This
phase is reflected in the datestone of 1699, now in a garden
wall, the blocked bolection-moulded doorcase on the S façade,
and the Baroque landscape of axial vistas shown on Roy's
survey of 1747–55, with distant entrance gates to the S. Around
1748, following his marriage to Mary Forbes, daughter of the

Earl of Granard, James Irvine deepened the house on the N side to double-pile plan with an additional floor under a piend roof, reorientating it to face N with a five-bay ashlar frontage overlooking the Dee. This house was augmented *c.* 1808 by a single-storey and basement E wing and a charming quadrant plan service court.

In his reconstruction, Bryce retained the 1748 house as the core of his principal front, building out its centre as his characteristic five-light canted bay, corbelled to the square at first-floor level. Its former classical lugged front doorway was moved to a garden entrance. The flanking windows were styled to match by the addition of pedimented dormerheads on the upper floor. Mirror-image tower house wings with angle turrets clasping tall attic gables were added E and W. These projected forward from the 1748 frontage but the first floor cantilevered balconies which were to have tied these new elements together horizontally were never installed. The early C19 E wing was remodelled to match the new work. Whereas on the front there is a clear distinction between the C18 and C19 masonry, the S front shows many phases of alterations.

INTERIOR. The 1748 house determined the plan, with a central entrance hall and stair hall behind it, servants' rooms to l. and library to the r. On the principal floor the drawing room and dining room (which retains C18 panelling), flanked a central bedroom. The family apartments are in Bryce's W wing.

ABERDEEN LODGE, at the entrance on the South Deeside Road, 0.9 km NNE. Early C19. Picturesque single storey with canted angles and a piended platformed roof, its eaves swept over a veranda supported on three sides by Roman Doric columns in timber: in the centre of the front elevation this veranda is slightly projected as a columnar porch. Half-columns frame the entrance doorway, its transom-light and the two flanking casement windows with diamond-pane glazing set into slim ashlar surrounds against a background of harl. Low coped chimneystacks. Handsome ashlar gatepiers with flanking quadrants, good heraldic gates and railings.

BOSWELL'S MONUMENT, Hill of Auchlee, 3.8 km. SW. Dated 1862, erected in memory of John Irvine Boswell of Kingcausie, agricultural improver. A robust round column atop an octagon in fine granite ashlar, with a curious top of ribs remaining from what was a crown spire.

KINKELL

2.7 km. SSE of Inverurie

ST MICHAEL.* Architecturally a largely featureless rectangle in grey rubble. In the C14 it belonged to the Hospitallers of

---

*This entry is by Richard Fawcett.

Torphichen, but in 1420 it was established as a prebend of Aberdeen Cathedral, along with its six dependent chapels. Between *c.* 1516 and 1552 it was the prebendal church of Canon Alexander Galloway, an important churchman and architectural patron in C16 Aberdeenshire, who donated a sacrament house, a Crucifixion panel and a font to his church. Kinkell was united with Keithhall parish in 1754, and in 1771 it was unroofed.

Much of the N wall survives, along with the W wall up to the base of the gable, the return of the E wall and the lower parts of the E and S walls. The only evidence for a window is in the E wall, where the richly moulded N jamb of a large late medieval traceried window remains in place; its lower part has been blocked. The only other opening is a roughly formed entrance towards the E end of the S wall. There was probably much rebuilding when the church served as a burial enclosure. – SACRAMENT HOUSE. A sadly weathered but highly important example of the artistic patronage of Canon Alexander Galloway. The locker forms the shaft of a cruciform arrangement of carved tablets. It is flanked by pinnacles and below it is the relief inscription AN[N]O D[OMI]NI 1524, with MEMORARE above Galloway's arms. Immediately above the locker are traces of a relief carving of angels holding a monstrance, extending out to either side of which are panels with scrolls once inscribed HIC EST [RE?]S[ER]VAT[M] CORPUS DE V[IR]GI[N]E NATUM (here is reserved (?) the body of one born of a virgin). The topmost panel is said to have contained a relief carving of the Crucifixion. – CRUCIFIXION PANEL. To the W of the sacrament house, a stone-framed metal panel replicating a stone panel removed to Aberdeen in 1934. The crucifix is set within an ogee-headed frame, with the Virgin and St Michael (?) on either side of the shaft. Below the Virgin is a priest (Galloway?) at an altar. Galloway's initials are in the spandrel of the ogee head and on the altar, and were carved on the bottom of the stone frame with the date 1525. – GRAVE-SLAB of Gilbert Greenlaw, †1411, almost certainly killed on 24 July at the Battle of Harlaw. An incised figure of Greenlaw, of particular interest for the details of the armour, is flanked by a pair of shields with his arms. The figure is framed by an inscription in the border. The lower third of the slab is lost. The reverse of the slab was later used as a memorial by John Forbes of Ardmurdo †1592, which includes a Greek biblical text.

18

KINMUCK

8010

Former FRIENDS' SETTLEMENT. At the W end of the village. Established by the Quakers in 1662, the oldest and almost certainly the largest such settlement in Scotland, which despite considerable opposition in its earlier years survived until 1940. The MEETING HOUSE is a long single-storey range with its N end gable facing the road, harled in white and piend roofed. At its S end is the caretaker's cottage, and against its rear (E) flank is the taller single-storey-and-attic schoolhouse, both built in 1832 to replace earlier structures. Restored *c.* 1970.

Across the road the GRAVEYARD is like no other in Aberdeenshire: a perfect rubble-walled rectangle, enclosed by trees, and dividing clearly into two halves. The upright stones date from *c.* 1805–1910. Those on the W are all identical in precisely regimented rows, and nearly all commemorate a single person, name, age and date of death only, an expression of equality in the eyes of the Lord. The E half is less organized, though again the stones are of simple character, and as such it provides a curious contrast. Comparatively few families, some of them (Brantingham, Wigham) evidently English, a distinct community like an extended family which lived and died together.

BALBITHAN HOUSE. *See* p. 339.

KINNEFF

An ancient settlement, originally protected by a string of castles set on dramatic cliffside peninsulas.

OLD PARISH CHURCH. Harled Georgian oblong, built 1737–8 by the mason *Alexander Stephen*. Now maintained by a preservation trust. It stands on the foundations of a medieval church dedicated to St Arnty (or Adamnan), and consecrated in 1242 by Bishop David de Bernham of St Andrew's Cathedral (Fife). On the W gable is Stephen's bellcote, 'sufficiently done but not fine', just as the heritors requested. It was restored in 1830. Large alterations in 1873–6 under *J. R. Mackenzie*, who formed a T-plan by adding the N aisle. Porch and stair-tower in the re-entrant angle, the latter with superimposed cusped lancets. The S flank originally had two doors and four arched windows, replaced by Mackenzie's six Y-traceried windows. The airy and light-filled interior is as renovated by him, but retaining the Georgian layout. – GALLERY in the N aisle, reusing the panelling from 1737–8. – Gothic PULPIT, *c.* 1876, in the centre of the long side. – Two fine MONUMENTS are re-set from the medieval church. On the W wall, a MEMORIAL to the Rev. James Grainger †1663, who hid the Regalia of Scotland here when Cromwell's forces besieged Dunnottar Castle (q.v.) in 1651. Latin inscription flanked by nicely unfurled scrolls and engaged columns. Winged soul above; initials on the bottom for Grainger and his wife, Christian Fletcher (Lady Abercrombie). – On the S wall, a mounted SLAB to Robert Graham †1597 of Largie Castle. Perimeter inscription in relief against a dark background, the font so chunky and abstracted that it could easily be mistaken for mid C20.

KINNEFF CASTLE formerly stood 200 m. to the SE, probably built by the de Montfort family in the early C13 and garrisoned and repaired by the English in 1336. Only a few blocks of masonry and turfed footings survive, although in the early C18 its 'high wall' was considered so solid that it 'would last until the end of all time'. The CASTLE OF CADDEN (250 m. ESE of the church) was another promontory fortress, but retains little more than the foundation of a curtain wall, *c.* 2 m. long, and a scarped causeway to the landward side. WHISTLEBERRY CASTLE, a further 500 m. NNE, occupied the most theatrical peninsula of all. Former keep indicated by a small wall fragment at the NE angle, probably early C16. Opposite, in the former SE corner, the possible remains of a newel staircase.

KINTORE

7010

A naturally defensive, fertile situation encircled on its N and E by meanders of the Don, Kintore has been settled since Mesolithic times, the modern town partly occupying the site of the Deers Den Roman camp associated with the Severan invasion of *c.* 200 AD. From the Middle Ages (seemingly the late C12) Kintore was a royal burgh associated with a castle motte, the Thanage of Kintore's *caput* visited by Edward I in 1296, but of this no evidence survives except the name of Castle Hill, a small street opening off The Square. Robert Bruce granted Kintore with its royal forest to Robert Keith, the Great Marischal; local place names suggest that the area had connections with Lindores Abbey. A royal charter of James IV renewed Kintore's privileges in 1506; it was represented in Parliament from 1567 and enrolled in the Convention of Royal Burghs in 1661; the Latin poet Arthur Johnston records that it had a racecourse in the C17. But despite being on the Great North and Donside Roads, from 1805 on the route of Rennie's Aberdeenshire Canal, and from 1854 a junction station on the Great North of Scotland Railway, Kintore was still described by Groome in the late C19 as 'a mere village, consisting of one well-built street with several smaller ones'. Thus indeed the historic core, its heart being the Square. The town grew between the Wars with the Mansefield and Townhead housing estates, but since the oil boom Kintore has witnessed dramatic growth, expanding W towards the A96, its link to Dyce Airport and Aberdeen.

CHURCH AND PUBLIC BUILDINGS

PARISH CHURCH, The Square. It stands on the site of its predecessor, which was perhaps once the chapel of the castle at

Kintore. Neo-Perp of 1819 by *Archibald Simpson*, whose aunt Margaret Dauney was the wife of the minister, the Rev. John Shand.* Simpson's church is closely related in style to his designs for Forgue and Drumoak (qq.v.). Built of roughly squared granite, the tall W gable front is well advanced from the main body of the church to suggest a slim nave with flanking aisles; its diagonal angle buttresses and Tudor bellcote rise into small obelisk pinnacles. Its entrance and three-light gallery window with timber mullions rise into shallow four-centred arches with hoodmoulds. In the flanks of this projecting gable, two slightly smaller pointed doorways; blind pointed window openings in the 'aisles' of the church, and in the N and S flanks, three large windows each of two lights, with slightly simpler tracery than the W front. The chancel is by *William Kelly*, 1914–15, and neatly echoes Simpson's projecting gable, but its E window has a shallow segmental arch, and a small session house is discreetly tucked in against the church on its N side.

The INTERIOR dates from *Kelly*'s reordering, during which Simpson's original curved pew-benches and W gallery focused on an octagonal pedestal pulpit in the E end were removed. Kelly's straight pews and W gallery supported on circular columns are equally simple in character. The other FURNISH-INGS and ORGAN are mid-C20. – CARVED PANEL. C17, from the Harvey family pew in the previous church. – STAINED GLASS. Three-light E window by *William Wilson*, 1956, a Byzantine-like Crucifixion which places particular emphasis on the women who accompanied Christ to the Cross. In the two-light N window, taking as its subject King David, *Wilson*'s figures are perhaps more medieval: an exceptionally intense composition, predominantly deep rich blue with a particularly jewel-like quality, dated 1957. The S window by *Gordon Webster* of 1964, Christ in Majesty receiving the Blessed, is distinctly different in style but nevertheless complementary, the figures again slim and attenuated, and a clean-shaven Christ's sharply angular face primitive and other-worldly, both omniscient and beyond our comprehension. – SACRAMENT HOUSE. Carved stone, much eroded or defaced during the Reformation. It was dated 1528 with initials A.G. (twice) for Canon Alexander Galloway, rector of St Michael, Kinkell (q.v.) to which Kintore's chapel was subordinate. Its detail is very advanced for Scotland at that date. It is 2.17 m. high by 0.95 m. wide and consists of two fields, the upper much taller than the lower, both framed by balusters with foliate decoration. The upper panel represents a monstrance with elaborate tabernacle-work framing a Sacred Heart; it is supported from beneath by two kneeling angels, and rises into a Crucified Christ. The lower field is now empty: it once contained a heraldic or inscription panel.

The WAR MEMORIAL GATEWAY in pale Kemnay granite erected by *Messrs Robertson & Sons* of Aberdeen in 1924 is a

---

*She was perhaps a relative of the architect-builder *William Dauney* (*see* p. 146).

simple slender four-centred arch bearing a crucifix. Immediately within the gateway is a PICTISH SYMBOL STONE displaying a salmon and triple-disc on one face and 'Pictish beast' and crescent and V-rod on the other (GN). Nearby, a large medieval stone FONT. CHURCHYARD (extended 1893) with gravestones from C18 onward, the best John Fowler's (†1748), mounted upright near the gateway.

KINTORE SCHOOL, Castle Walk. Designed and built by *Robertson Eastern* in 2004–6 on the site of its predecessor, it also contains communal facilities including a Library and Sports Pavilion. In a very contemporary style, technical yet warm and approachable in pastel colours, a long single-storey L-plan entrance front with shelter canopy, behind which a court is enclosed by taller two-storey ranges at the rear.

TOWN HOUSE, The Square. A classic of its kind, built at the expense of the Convention of Royal Burghs and the 4th Earl of Kintore. Although seemingly begun in 1737 it was not completed and fitted out until 1748, when *John Rind* is recorded as mason. Two storeys and five bays broad in roughly squared, coursed granite, it has a steep horseshoe stair rising to the first-floor main entrance, a hipped roof with coped end stacks and a low square clock tower rising through the roof and capped by an ogee dome and weathervane. The horseshoe stair, in ashlar with solid parapets, contains a simple doorway beneath its first-floor platt; there are further doors at street level within the outer bays. In the later C18 the Town House was enlarged into an L-plan with a rear wing. As first built it accommodated the council chamber, school, prison and a girnal for grain and meal paid by the Earl of Kintore's tenants; internally it has been much altered but its square-plan council chamber still survives, with door architraves of mid-C19 character. Its clock was donated by George Keith, 9th and last Earl Marischal – by then in the service of Frederick the Great of Prussia – who had inherited the Kintore estates; it was made by *Hugh Gordon* of Aberdeen in 1772 or 1774. Its bell, signed and dated by the Frenchman *Albert Gely* of Aberdeen, 1702, formerly hung in the parish churchyard.

DESCRIPTION

The Town House stands on The Square's W side and the Parish Church on the N. On the S side is the KINTORE ARMS, early C19, its entrance front two storeys and three bays broad in granite ashlar with a gabled roof rising into coped end stacks; its slightly lower two-storey piend-roofed wing was added later. The original doors and windows were replaced in the mid C19 but the former stabling survives at the rear. Completing the group is the former NORTH OF SCOTLAND (now CLYDESDALE) BANK, *c.* 1850, two storeys in granite ashlar with a gabled roof. It is five bays broad, the ground-floor bank offices with a central doorway but the agent's private apartments lit by only three windows at first floor.

Beyond the Bank, NORTHERN ROAD is Kintore's principal shopping thoroughfare, long and straight and lined on its N side with single-storey cottages and two-storey blocks of shops and flats in granite rubble or ashlar. The railway runs behind them and towards the far end stand the former STATION HOTEL by *John Cameron* 1899–1900 and the MASONIC LODGE, dated 1919. On its S side Northern Road is lined with granite-built four-in-a-block council flats and single-storey-and-dormered-attic cottages built during the interwar years. More recently, the excellent DEANS COURT housing development, *c.* 2005, has been built near The Square.

In FOREST ROAD the former PARISH MANSE began as a conventional example of its kind, two storeys and three windows wide, ashlar-built with a gabled roof in 1784. It has been extended, a large wing projecting from the S front in squared rubble being built in 1835–6. Another smaller N wing was added either at that time or by *William Ramage* who carried out repairs, alterations and additions in 1861–2, the house in its final form being a Z-plan.

HALLFOREST CASTLE, 1.5 km. SW. Ruinous, probably early C14, one of the first tower houses in northern Scotland. It bears similarities to the Towers of Drum and Skene (qq.v.), the three together bearing responsibility for guarding the road leading through the Mounth into the Garioch. Hallforest was perhaps built *c.* 1324 when Robert Bruce confirmed Robert Keith, the Great Marischal, in possession of the royal forest of Kintore, and it is presumably '*manerium nostrum foreste de Kyntor*' referred to by David II in a charter of 1361. Hallforest was still grand enough to receive Mary, Queen of Scots in 1562, but from 1639 it was frequently attacked during the Civil Wars, and probably abandoned by the Earls Marischal thereafter.

Hallforest has a simple rectangular plan, 14.5 m. N–S by 9 m. E–W. It still stands four storeys and some 18 m. high, although it must once have risen taller. It is built in pinned rubble, mostly granite, the surviving dressings being paler granite of better quality. The E gable's partial collapse allows the internal structure to be seen all too clearly: the walls are 2 m. thick; two vaults survive, one above the second storey and one above the great hall. Within the lower vault, the timber first floor was supported on rough stone corbels which may still be discerned. It seems likely that, when the tower was first built, there was also a timber floor within the upper vault, for the large openings on the S side would once have been much smaller, similar to those on the W. Above the great hall the walls may have risen into a third vault, although its collapse might have been expected to have more serious consequences for those beneath, suggesting that the roof structure was of timber. There must have been a wall-walk parapet, although all trace of this is lost.

Of the three large openings in the S wall, that nearest the SE corner may have been the main entrance, once accessed by a wooden stair, its height above ground an important feature of defence.* Evidence has been found of a turnpike stair connecting the upper floors in the SE corner. Even in this early tower, certain conventions are already well established. The ground floor has small window loops, and was probably a store. At first floor the windows are larger, but socketed for iron grilles; within the E wall's remains at this level are preserved a kitchen hearth and oven. The great hall at second floor had a fireplace in the W wall, at the 'high' end of the dining table, and furthest away from the stair by which meals were served.

THAINSTONE HOUSE. *See* p. 746.

KIRKSIDE HOUSE   K   7060
1.5 km. SW of St Cyrus

A complex house and a deeply rewarding one. The land of 'Kirksyde' was granted to the Stratons of Lauriston (q.v.) in 1582, and for the next three centuries it served as the base for this 'spur' branch of the family line. In 1619, the estate passed jointly to Arthur Straton, 2nd Laird of Kirkside, and his son Andrew (the 3rd Laird). They built a tower house – or, more likely, a rectangular hall house – of which cellarage and a lintel dated 1675 still survive. The rest of their building was demolished in the mid C18, and a new Georgian house built for Arthur Straton, the 6th Laird. It was completed *c.* 1764, but in less than half a century it became the rear wing for an entirely new house, built *c.* 1805 for the 7th Laird, Joseph Straton. *Robert S. Lorimer* made a fine addition to it in 1907–8 for Colonel George Leith Fraser, and also remodelled the whole ground floor of the interior.

The house now takes the form of a large L-plan with main frontage facing SW. The mid-C18 REAR WING is the best place to start, as it replaced the demolished Jacobean house.† Three storeys of coursed ashlar, now three bays long but originally five, as shown by the blocked windows to the r. of centre. Lugged, moulded doorcase in the middle with pulvinated architrave and cornice. Rough base course to the r. in lighter rubble, very likely *in situ* from the mid–late C17. Above the door, a key-blocked and keystoned window with lintel dated 1764. The l. side of the house is now dominated by an overlarge canted bay added in 1928–9 by *Sir Matthew M. Ochterlony* during his brief association with *William Davidson*. U-plan

---

* David MacGibbon and John Dunbar dissented from this view, holding that the main entrance was in the E gable at second-storey level, and that another doorway was formed or enlarged at ground floor beneath it. These openings have lost their dressings and now form a single wide fissure in the E elevation.

† Garden's map of Kincardineshire (1774) shows only the present rear wing, so no C17 remains were left standing above ground when that house was built. It was divided from the main block after 1979 as a separate house.

FORECOURT in front of the house, the r. side once the stable and coachhouse block, originally single-storeyed but given an upper floor in the late 1920s. The court is entered between good V-channelled GATEPIERS of *c.* 1764, with corniced capitals and modern finials. The originals are in the front garden (*see* below).

The MAIN FAÇADE of the house was built *c.* 1805 over the remains of the C17 cellars. It is of finer, darker ashlar, the original section of two storeys and three bays over a semi-sunk basement. Panelled chimneystacks on the ends. Tall first floor with pilastered Venetian windows set in slightly recessed panels with big voussoirs. Smart doorcase in between them with two Roman Doric columns, alternating glyphs and shields on the architrave, and a dentilled pediment with consoled heraldic shield. Perron staircase curving down with a glazed oculus on the bottom. Advanced off the original l. flank is *Lorimer*'s wing of 1907–8, a single wide bay with a shallow bow rising up the centre and topped by a piended roof. Big tripartite window on the ground floor and a twelve-pane one above to harmonize with the original house. Good, subtle modulation of the curvature to the l. and r.

The whole ground floor of the INTERIOR remains as remodelled by Lorimer. Inside the entrance, a tight, partially cantilevered staircase with Arts and Crafts-style turned wooden balusters. Broad segmental arch leading l. into the DINING ROOM (originally the Drawing Room), with field-panelled dado and a D-ended wall on one side. It is a nice echo to the exterior bow added by Lorimer on the other side of the room. Ribbed ceiling divided into a pattern of square, grid-like panels. Neo-Georgian frieze with urns and palmette tripods, all by Lorimer but looking convincingly C18. Good wooden chimneypiece with paired composite columns, acanthus bases and wavy rinceau on the lintel. Lorimer's DRAWING ROOM lies beyond, with plaster and carpentry work executed by *Nathaniel Grieve* (who did the near-contemporary work for Lorimer at Hill of Tarvit, Fife). Tall, narrow doors flanked by cabinets with canted rear walls. Chimneypiece with Ionic columns and swagged lintel again in Georgian mode; but the metal fire-guard exactly of its date. Vigorous plasterwork on the ceiling, the centre a plain ellipse surrounded by fluttering ribbons. In each of the corners are big rose vines decorated with thorns, crisp leaves, closed buds and open blossoms.

In the CELLAR are the remains of at least three storage compartments from the C17. Thick side walls, just beginning to curve into the springers of what were once segmental barrel-vaults. Over one door, a re-set LINTEL dated 167[5] (r. side renewed) with the initials A.S. and E.M.

WALLED GARDENS. The upper one, added in 1931–2 to plans by *Ochterlony* and *Davidson*, has an iron entrance GATE decorated with squirrels, very Lorimerian.

Former MAIN GATE, 0.5 km. NNW on the A92. Erected *c.* 1820 by General Joseph Straton, the 8th Laird, who acquired the estate in 1816 upon his return from the Battle of Waterloo, to provide access from the new turnpike road to Aberdeen. Square gatepiers with sunken fluted panelling and ogival heraldry niches. Big eagle sculptures on top; pedestrian piers to the l. and r. with acorn finials. Gates with friezes of pierced rosettes.

KIRKTON OF CULSALMOND

Former PARISH CHURCH. Built 1791, closely similar in style to Kirkton of Rayne (q.v.). Closed 1937, now a roofless rectangle. Gables each have a round-headed entrance and gallery window, the old-fashioned skewputts probably reused from the predecessor church of medieval origin; four-bay S flank with round-headed windows, N wall blind with stair to laird's loft. The most remarkable feature is the reused W bellcote, dated 1680. Its uprights are framed by shaft-ringed colonnettes which support a moulded entablature and small pediment with finials and scrolls.

The CHURCHYARD spreads across the site of a circle of twelve standing stones, all lost; no trace either of the medieval church but in the NE corner an early C19 square WATCH HOUSE with pyramidal slate roof, its basement mort-house with heavy iron door. Former PARISH MANSE, N of the church. Vernacular classical two-storey house of c. 1772, substantially enlarged by a piend-roofed wing of similar height built out from the main front c. 1804; then enlarged twice later with non-identical crowstepped wings built against the end gables.

Former FREE CHURCH, SW of the old church on the main road. By *Daniel Macandrew*, 1866–7; it became the parish church in 1937, closed c. 2000, and is now converted to domestic use. First Pointed. Tall T-plan, with entrance tower and spire and crenellated porch in the SW angle between the nave and transept; low flat-roofed vestry at rear. Immediately W, its former MANSE, also by *Macandrew*, 1866–7.

ST THOMAS (Episcopal), Tillymorgan, 3 km. NNE. E.E. Built 1851, perhaps to designs of the *Rev. David Wilson* (later first Dean of Aberdeen & Orkney), who added the chancel in 1855; porch 1905. Derelict but restoration is proposed.

WILLIAMSTON HOUSE, 0.8 km. S. By *Alexander Fraser* of Aberdeen, c. 1825–30, for Charles Fraser Jun., replacing a house described as 'lately built' in 1785. Proto-Italianate in its relaxed proportions and broad-eaved roof, but with a Greek Doric porch and angle pilasters, facing SW with open views towards Suie Hill and Bennachie. Its main block is two-storeyed and five windows wide, white-harled with exposed dressings and margins over a rock-faced semi-sunk basement. Its central bay is slightly projected with tetrastyle porch now glazed in between columns, low piended platformed roof with slim harled gable chimneystacks. The outer windows are very generously spaced, those at ground floor with apron panels. They have been plate-glazed, but the first-floor and basement windows retain their original astragals. The single-storey wings were added c. 1850 and are slightly set back, each with two astragalled ground-floor windows sheltered by console-cornices, broad pedimental gables rising into chimneystacks with paired square shafts. Rear elevation plain, the main block rising from a railed basement area, with round-arched stair window. Well-detailed interior, especially the pilastraded entrance hall with acanthus, floral and lion's-head decoration; inner hall and stair distinguished by good cast-iron balusters.

The HOME FARM STEADING and FARMHOUSE were built for Charles Fraser Sen. in 1798. – POLICIES laid out by Charles Fraser Jun. in the 1830s; extended from c. 1872 by his second son, Edward Fraser, and from 1895 by Edward's niece and her husband, *William Haughton*. Following a period of neglect the grounds were taken in hand by their son *Theodore Haughton* and his wife in the 1930s. They were responsible for the artificial lake, the enclosed gardens incorporating a pre-Christian WELL and the formation of the vista looking towards the Hill of Foudland.

KIRKTON OF DURRIS   K

'Dores', on the S bank of the Dee, was the 'doorway' to the Cryne Corse Pass over the Mounth, a bridge across the river being recorded here in the C13. For these strategic reasons, and as a hunting seat, CASTLE HILL was occupied by Alexander III, and later visited by Edward I in 1296. Standing 7 m. high, and with a summit 41 m. by 30 m., its slopes may have been artificially steepened. The approach was from the W across a broad deep ditch seemingly by a bridge or drawbridge. Castle Hill must have been associated with St Comgall's church first recorded in 1249, which probably stood within the present churchyard. Held by the Frasers from the C13 to the late C17, the Thanedom of Durris was erected into a barony by David II in the mid C14. The barony seat was later transferred inland to Durris Castle (*see* Durris House, below). The present kirkton contains cottages of the C18 (all now altered) and later.

PARISH CHURCH. Originally a simple rectangular preaching-box, built 1822, but substantially heightened c. 1870 with a shallow-pitched roof. The remodelling may have been by *A. Marshall Mackenzie* given the resemblance to Leochel-Cushnie (q.v.). The very tall and broad W entrance porch, again similar to Leochel-Cushnie's, was built by *William D. Ironside* in 1897 following a report by Mackenzie. Four round-arched windows in the nave's s flank. On the s and w the walls are harled; exposed rubble on n, with a single tall window and small outshot, and on the e, where an external stair has been removed. Gableted w bellcote, 1897, the bell a late example by *John Mowat*, 1765. Doorway in porch's s flank with round-arched transom-light, its ashlar surround rising into a Neoclassical pediment. INTERIOR reordered and remodelled following Mackenzie's 1897 report. The w gallery, steeply raked and with an arcaded front, replaced an earlier horseshoe. Octagonal pedestal PULPIT, its sides also arcaded, at the e end. PEWS with trefoil-headed ends. ORGAN by *E.H. Lawton*, 1903. Coloured glass lights. Compartmented, timber-boarded ceiling. Within the porch, the gallery stair with finely twisted cast-iron balusters.

In the CHURCHYARD, the FRASER AISLE probably represents the consolidated remains of the e end of the previous church but the pointed openings date from 1869. The skewputts bear initials S.A.F. (Sir A. Fraser of Durris) and D.V.C. (Dame . . .) another stone being carved with the date 1681. Within is a shallow arched tomb-recess, above which are initials and fraises (strawberry flowers) for Thomas Fraser, 1595. Also preserved, a 1681 datestone and early C19 cast-iron MORT SAFE.

Former PARISH MANSE, 100 m. SSW. Built 1844. Two-storey, three-bay entrance front with unusually broad distyle pedimented portico of slim Doric columns. Ground-floor windows with panelled aprons and console-cornices; first-floor windows break through an eaves course beneath small gablets in the shallow-pitched, oversailing roof. Rear wing in similar style. The office court at the rear perhaps incorporates fabric of the manse of 1773–4.

DURRIS HOUSE, 2.6 km. ENE. Originally an L-plan TOWER HOUSE, its main block orientated E–W with a NE jamb. Although its walls rise only three modest storeys, the main block's lowest level is a double-height vaulted chamber, partly beneath ground. As recently as 2014 this was floored with a timber mezzanine at entrance level. A particularly unusual feature is a long vaulted chamber, completely concealed below ground, which extends from the main block's w end and which was presumably used for storage. The tower house has been remodelled, perhaps after it was burnt by Montrose in 1645. A square tower containing a new turnpike stair was built in the angle, concealing the original doorway. It rises at attic level into a crowstep-gabled caphouse supported on plain corbels. New doorways and windows were formed, and the wall-heads altered with a gabled roof and tall chimneystacks. Inside, the changes are clear to see in the main block's first-floor apartment, where the timber ceiling has been raised slightly above the stone corbels which supported its precedessor, the window reveals being simply detailed with shallow segmental arches.

The very long two-storey EXTENSION projecting from the main block's NW end began as a range linking to a mansion erected for John Innes of Leuchars *c.* 1800 (and remodelled twice by *Archibald Simpson*: in 1824 for Innes and *c.* 1835–8 for the Madras merchant Anthony Mactier). The linking range was reconstructed by *Michael Gilmore* in the 1980s after the mansion had been demolished.

STABLES, 150 m. E. By *Archibald Simpson c.* 1838. Handsome Italianate. Tall single-storey H-plan with slim octagonal doocot tower. Principal (E) front has round-arched central opening with console-keyblock flanked by pairs of anta-pilasters supporting a pedimental gable. Three-bay linking sections, their windows with console-cornices. Boldly projecting single-bay wings, that on the S with two coach-shed arches in its courtyard flank. Golden granite rubble, formerly harled, with ashlar dressings. Shallow-pitched piended roofs, oversailing eaves on timber brackets, low chimneystacks. Tower has round-headed lights and prismatic roof. Flank and rear elevations single storey and loft.

KEITH'S TOWER, 4.4 km. NE, stands on a rise of ground surrounded by pine trees, looking over the S end of Park Bridge crossing the Dee (*see* Drumoak). A slim octagonal Gothick eyecatcher, built by the 4th Duke of Gordon in 1825 to celebrate a legal victory over John Innes of Leuchars, who had leased Durris House (*see* above) from the Gordons in 1795 and made improvements but was ejected by them in 1824. Walls of coursed squared golden granite, four stages with pointed doorway. Blind lancets, smaller lancets and cruciforms in alternate sides; boldly crenellated wall-head parapet some 15 m. above ground. Inside, a turnpike stair, its upper landing removed.

STRATHIEBURN CASTLE, 1.8 km. SE. Self-built by its architect, *Ron Gauld*, 1985. Intriguing T-plan tower house. The different styles on each façade reflect the availability of salvaged stone, the C17 flank using stone from the burnt Georgian wing at Crathes Castle (q.v.) and the Baroque front recycling from Culter paper mills.

KIRKTON OF FETTERESSO

K

A site of great antiquity, occupied in the Iron Age and later by the Picts. Now a small hamlet, first documented in the late C12 and still managing to escape the encroachment of Stonehaven (q.v.).

Former PARISH CHURCH. A chapel was founded here in the C6 by St Ciaran (or Kieran) (*c.* 512–*c.* 544), an Irish monk and missionary to the Picts. A new parish church replaced it in the mid C13, one of the many dedicated by Bishop David de Bernham (St Andrews, Fife) in 1246. It was rectangular and very long, some of the medieval fabric still *in situ*. The present building mostly dates from the C17, when the E end was short-ened by *c.* 4 m., and 1719–20, when the N aisle was added and galleries inserted on the E and W ends. It now stands roofless, abandoned in 1813 for *John Paterson*'s parish church in Stonehaven (q.v.).

Main flank to the S, still very long with some lighter masonry from the C13 (especially in the SW corner). There are nine former openings, eight now blocked. Two straight-headed doorways under shallow relieving arches, both inserted in 1719–20 (only the l. now open). Four large rectangular window frames, the l. pair chamfered (late C17) and the r. pair of the early C18. The two smaller square windows are probably late medieval, as is the door in the centre, low with a thick lintel. The lower section of the E wall is C17 and contains a heraldic plaque for John Mowat †1655 and his wife, Isobel Hervy †1650. Gable above it built in the early C18. The N aisle was added at the same time to form a T-plan, and its N wall (demolished in 1982) formerly had a door frame dated 1720. Beyond it there is an intact DOORWAY from the C13, a pointed arch formed by two large, chamfered voussoirs. More C13 rubble around it. W end again C17 on the bottom with early C18 gable and birdcage bellcote dated 1737.

Inside, a small medieval STOUP next to the main entrance with a round-headed recess. The doorway across from it is trabeated with a reused tomb-slab containing weathered medieval script, including the words 'patr…anno'. – On the E wall, a white marble TOMBSTONE to Robert William Duff †1834, the builder of Fetteresso Castle (*see* below) and family. Suavely consoled sides and acroterial pediment with armorial panel. – On the S wall are two C17 PLAQUES, the l. with a Latin inscription dated 162[1?] and the r. with a stylized cartouche.*

The GRAVEYARD has a good collection of C18 TABLE TOMBS and LEDGER SLABS, some with beautiful calligraphic script. Good mortality emblems as well, some carved by a *Mr Cresswell*, 'a farmer in the parish who could not form a single letter with his pen'.

The S approach to the village passes first through the tall, single-arch RAILWAY BRIDGE (200 m. SSW of the church), built *c.* 1849 for the Aberdeen Railway. Six segmental ribs on the underside and pulvinated string courses above. Just to the E of the burial ground is the combined former SCHOOL and SCHOOL HOUSE of *c.* 1778, two storeys with slate pinnings and modern pantile roofs.

FETTERESSO CASTLE, 1.1 km. W. Ancient seat of the Keiths, Earls Marischal, rebuilt in the C19 and now subdivided into flats. A castle has stood on this spot since the late C12, as

---

*Other fragments, including a plaque from the former pulpit, are now in the new kirk in Stonehaven.

proven by the remains of the former motte (*see* below). William Keith was elevated to the peerage as 1st Earl Marischal in 1457–8 and constructed a new building shortly thereafter. It took the form of a long, rectangular hall house, typical of the late C15, with a similar block to the E forming an L-plan. A charter by Bishop John Lesley refers to 'Fetteresso Palace' in 1578, and it evidently had eight towers. The E arm was burnt by Montrose in 1645 and reconstructed by George Keith, 8th Earl Marischal, in 1670–1. In 1782, the Castle was purchased by Admiral Robert Duff, 2nd Laird of Fetteresso,* who partly rebuilt and greatly extended it. The architect was *John Paterson*, and there were then further improvements under *David Bryce* in 1861–3. The Castle stood roofless and gutted after 1954, but was finally restored in 1993–4 by *Fitzgerald & Associates*. They covered it with stucco-like harling and divided it vertically into separate apartments.

The current appearance is largely as Paterson intended. Large, somewhat sterile, iteration of castellated Georgian, still following the L-plan of its predecessor. The fulcrum is an attenuated octagon, three storeys with a crenellated parapet. Eighteen-pane windows, the middle with lugged hoodmoulds; long, plain walling above and below with bevelled band and string course. The SE corner has an ashlar porch added by Bryce with Tudor-headed entrance, diagonal buttresses and armorial panel. The E arm extends to the r., the first three bays again castellated and with a row of bipartite windows. Taller octagonal tower projecting to the r.; then a crow-stepped gable over big windows with stepped hoodmoulds and a tall chimney-cum-buttress with more crenellations. To the l. of the centre, a single castellated bay and then another tall octagonal tower over a wide, square base with inverted cavettos as broaches. Next two wide sections, each of two bays with tall windows on the ground floor, and separated by another buttress. Two more diagonal buttresses on the far gable. To the rear, the re-entrant angle was filled in by Bryce to accommodate a new staircase and principal entrance, the centre again an octagon and the ends with square towers.[†] The courtyard in front of them is hemmed in by single-storey-and-attic service corridors, also by Bryce. The interior is entirely modern.

S of the castle the terrain declines sharply, the escarpment still following the original MOTTE of the late C12. 150 m. to the SE is a good beehive DOOCOT of the mid–late C16, now in poor condition. Gentle tapering to the upper flight-hole and three encircling rat ledges. There was formerly a LAKE to the S and SW (now drained), still attested by a ruined boathouse

---

* His tombstone is in the former St Ciaran's church (*see* above).
[†]There were originally three doors carved with, respectively, the Marischal arms, the date 1671 and the initials WEM and ACM (for William, 6th Earl Marischal, and his second wife, Anne Douglas).

and a good lenticular-truss FOOTBRIDGE of *c.* 1825.* A large WALLED GARDEN was added 200 m. SSW of the Castle in 1909–10 (surprisingly late), containing a topiary hedge and a re-set stoup from the medieval parish church (*see* above). 125 m. further SE, an ovoid ICE HOUSE of the late C18 with brick top poking out of the turf.

FETTERESSO CEMETERY, 325 m. N. Laid out 1901–2. Handsome, banded gatepiers with ball finials and gates with huge wrought-iron leaves, by *James Milne & Son* of Edinburgh.

CHEYNE, 1.5 km. NNW. Two-storey classical farmhouse, early C19. The centre is narrower with a full-height, projecting bow and lower, semi-conical roof.

KIRKTON OF GLENBERVIE

7080

PARISH CHURCH. By *John Smith*, 1824–6. Gothick, similar to his church at Hatton of Fintray (q.v.). Four-bay rectangular plan, built in ashlar masonry with diagonal buttresses rising into pinnacles, birdcage bellcote with spike finials and spirelet over W gable; bell dated 1789. Doorway at each end with stepped triple lancets and quatrefoil above; the original double-leaf doors at the W end are finely panelled, the E door is mid-C20. The gallery lights' upper sashes rise into basket-weave tracery, the large four-centred windows in the S flank have timber Y-tracery with original glazing. N windows blind. Inside, the original horseshoe gallery supported on clustered colonnettes, its fronts with Gothick panelling. – WAR MEMORIAL. By *A. Marshall Mackenzie*, 1921. Carved in red sandstone, a notably good example. Circular stepped base, pedestal with name plaques and tapered octagonal shaft which rises into a foliate capital supporting four small seated angels kneeling at prayer beneath a Maltese cross.

OLD PARISH CHURCHYARD, 0.25 km. S on a hillock overlooking the confluence of two small burns to the SE. ST MICHAEL'S CHURCH was granted to Brechin Cathedral *c.* 1222 and erected a prebend in 1422. It was partly rebuilt in 1771 and enlarged in 1798 but closed in 1826. Little remains except the DOUGLAS AISLE in red rubble sandstone with dressings which was seemingly reconstructed from the church's presbytery. Part of an arched doorway still survives within its fabric and a round-arched window appears C18. The aisle measures 7.5 m. N–S by 5.4 m. transversely over walls 0.8 m. thick. Inside, the large altar tomb of William Douglas, 9th Earl of Angus, and his countess, Egidia Graham, erected by Egidia on his death in 1591 and displaying their heraldic arms. It supports a mural

*A similar iron bridge was built at Melville Castle (Lothian) in 1817.

monument dated 1680,* with heraldic bearings of the Hassa, Olifant, Melville, Auchinleck and Douglas families, and an inscription in contracted Latin recounting their history from 730 AD. It is set in barley-twist columns with angels trumpeting the Last Judgment over a skeleton above it. Stairs lead into the basement crypt. The PILLAR MONUMENT to the Stuarts of Inchbreck may have been reconstructed from the church's SW angle. Good C17–C19 GRAVESTONES. Two table slabs commemorating Robert Burns's parents and wider family were restored in 1885, 1951 (re-lettered by *Fenton Wyness*) and 1968.

w of the churchyard is the former PARISH MANSE, built *c.* 1725 but 'repaired' three times during the C18, its walls heightened *c.* 1786. Two-storey entrance front facing SW, harled in white with red sandstone dressings. Central gabled porch and canted bay in red sandstone added by *Mr Johnstone* of Auchcairnie (cf. Auchenblae Village Hall) in 1869. The wallhead gable with oval panel and slim chimneystack looks mid-C18. Fine outlook over steeply sloping gardens, U-plan office court.

GLENBERVIE HOUSE, 0.4 km. SE of the church, within the confluence of the Pilkettie Burn and the Bervie Water, and protecting a ford of the Cryne Corse pass. Originally a fortified castle built during the C15 or C16 by either the Melvilles, the Auchinlecks (to whom it passed in 1468), or the Red Douglases (to whom it passed in 1492). It was reconstructed as a country house either after its acquisition by the Burnetts of Leys in 1675 or the Nicolsons of Mergie (q.v.) in 1721, and was further altered for James Badenach in 1854.

The MAIN BLOCK facing E contains the original castle fabric. It is 22 m. long by 9.5 m. deep, the masonry of its front elevation 1.8 m. thick at ground floor; at either end it has round towers 5.5 m. in diameter and of very bold projection. The ground level is divided into four chambers, with a linking corridor at the rear. The largest chamber at the N end is the vaulted kitchen with its hearth in the end gable. The two chambers towards the S end, both vaulted transversely, were once cellars. The central chamber has always contained a stair, which was originally of stone, accessed by the central doorway. The round towers contained vaulted square chambers, with wide-mouthed shot-holes and loopholes with crosslet heads and oilette bases which probably date from the mid–later C16 (cf. Ravenscraig, N) although their dressings have been renewed.

As remodelled from the late C17, the E elevation is symmetrical. Contrasting against the pale harl, the present doorway in its ashlar surround, tall, narrow and round-arched with the Badenach-Nicolson arms flanked by scrolls, dates from *c.* 1680. It appears too large in relation to the height of the ground floor and may have been a courtyard or garden gateway reused. The first and second floors may also date from that time as their

* Not 1630 as given elsewhere.

walls are much thinner than at ground floor and have four large sash-and-case windows at each level. The arrangement of the first-floor apartments internally, with the dining room to the S of the stair and the withdrawing room to the N, may however reflect the original arrangement of great hall and solar. The two towers contain circular rooms. A string course zigzagging across the wall-head announces a parapet rising into round-arched pediments, dating from 1854. The main roof is gabled, with centre and end stacks, and the towers rise into conical roofs, that at the S end having been formed during restoration in 1965 to replace a mid-C19 intervention, a crenellated parapet and small round caphouse which contained a smoking room. The turreted N wing with its balustraded terrace and garden stairs dates from 1854. The interior is mainly of that date with compartmented ceilings but one first-floor room still retains its late C17 panelling. Stair replaced mid C18, very handsome with console bracket tread-ends and slim columnar balusters, blocked at mid-shaft. The walls of its lower flights are panelled, as is the first-floor corridor.

The DESIGNED LANDSCAPE was laid out between *c.* 1750 and 1850, but perhaps incorporates earlier policies shown in Roy's Highland Survey of 1747–55. On the lawn immediately in front of the house stand monkey puzzle, oak, copper beech and larch specimen trees; one of the larches is reputedly among the very oldest in Scotland. Beyond the lawn, separated by a ha-ha, lies the parkland, with the Home Farm – an integral part of the designed landscape – to its N. Between the parkland and Home Farm runs the E drive, lined with beech and syca-more, some over 200 years old, and younger Victorian syca-mores and limes. The landscape's E boundary was planted with coniferous woodland *c.* 1970. A water channel within these woods, surrounded by yews and other ornamental planting, once provided ice for the house. Many of the beeches E of the parkland however date from the earlier C19, with younger naturalized beech and sycamore among them. To the S of the house the woodland garden is old, but that to the N was formed by Patience Badenach-Nicolson in the mid C20.

WALLED GARDEN on sloping ground rising to excellent GLASSHOUSE of *c.* 1850, with canted centre and end bays boldly projecting. SUNDIAL. Octagonal base, fluted baluster shaft and table dial with plate dated 1767.

DOOCOT. Dated 1736. Square-plan, harled in white with red sandstone dressings. Simple doorway, rat course and pyramidal roof with shallow catslide dormer providing an opening for the doos; crowning ball finial.

E GATES. C18. Square, chamfered ashlar. Inner pair with ball finials support carriage gates. Outer pair with ogival heads support smaller side gates. Convex quadrant dwarf-walls and railings with termini. W GATES. Similar to E gates, but all four piers are ball-finialled.

GLENBERVIE MILL, 0.4 km. SW. Earlier C19 in present form. Single-storeyed, mostly rubble-built. Semi-elliptical entrance in centre of s flank with outshot addition to l. Roof piended at E and gabled at w, kiln vent removed. Remains of low-breast paddle wheel in w gable, 3.5 m. in diameter. Re-set over doorway, a 1692 datestone with initials of Robert Burnett and Katherine Douglas.

BRIDGE OF BERVIE, 0.6 km. sw, crossing the Bervie Water within picturesque wooded surroundings. C18. Springing from low cutwater piers, two small segmental arches, rubble-built with dressed voussoirs, one slightly higher than the other as the carriageway rises gently from N to s. A blind round panel within the central spandrel on either side. Low parapets splayed at the ends.

3010   KIRKTON OF GLENBUCHAT

OLD PARISH CHURCH (ST PETER). Much the oldest church to have survived intact in Aberdeenshire, and of exceptional importance in national terms. Standing on a modest eminence, it was first built *c.* 1473 when its parish was separated from Logie of Mar. Of this simple rectangular structure, 17.5 m. long E–w by 8.5 m. broad, the lowest courses survive, squared rubble 0.8 m. thick on all four sides. The existing church dates mainly from reconstruction in 1629, but the large gable windows are late C18, presumably from the further reconstruction *c.* 1792. s flank also rebuilt in the C18. Its unusual arrangement of two deep-set, square-headed doorways, one towards the w for the congregation and one towards the E for the minister, appears to reproduce the original arrangement; the roll-moulded surrounds of the doors and those of two astragalled sash-and-case windows widely spaced between them have been reused. Immediately below the eaves the sw corner has been rounded with a projecting stone ledge, probably for a sundial. The tall gables have ashlar skews and skewputts; the w end gable-head incorporates a triangular stone with raised date and initials M.A.K. for Andrew Kerr, minister 1618–33. It once supported the classical birdcage bellcote in Kildrummy sandstone, stepped at the top and crowned by an urn, which was erected by the architect-builder *William Minto* in 1828 when he replaced the heather-thatched roof with graded Foudland slates. This bellcote, transferred to the E end by the Kildrummy mason *David Wood c.* 1857, contains a bell lettered '*Peter Jansen* Anno 1643 Boni Twn'.

Closed 1932, the church was repaired in 1948 and thoroughly restored in 1964 and 1999–2001. The interior is an almost unique survival in Scottish terms. *Minto* plastered the walls in 1828, and his camp ceiling echoes the form of the roof couples which were originally exposed. Also of 1828 is the LAIRD'S LOFT erected by the carpenter *Ebenezer Ramsay* in Mar Lodge pine with stencilled decoration simulating a fluted frieze over a Vitruvian scroll. Its central panel displays the tinctured Fife coat of arms and its single supporting column has been marbled. The floor is of beaten earth and cobbled, the alleys paved in Correen stone. The PULPIT centred between the S windows and illuminated by skylights was heightened at that time and given a sounding-board with a concave prismatic canopy; in front of it is the PRECENTOR'S BOX with display cards for the psalms and hymns. The simple pine PEWS extend around the church's three other sides, those to the N and the manse pew immediately to the E of the pulpit being of the box-type. The partitions of the N 'pen-fold' pews could be lifted out and their small narrow tables set together once every year for Communion. Neoclassical MEMORIAL TABLETS on the S wall – to the Farquharsons of Badenyon, bronze with black marble or granite surround, c. 1900, and to those lost in the First World War, oak with a gilt Celtic cross and lettering, c. 1920.

Former PARISH MANSE, immediately to S. A composite plain Georgian structure, built c. 1792 but enlarged to T-plan by *Minto* 1828 and reconstructed by *Alexander Brown* (of *Brown & Watt*) in 1903–5.

Former FREE CHURCH, Belnacraig, 1.2 km. N. By *William Henderson*, opened 1865. Simple First Pointed. The interior originally accommodated a school which could be enclosed from the pulpit area by a movable wooden partition.

MILL OF GLENBUCHAT, 1.6 km. NNW. C18, altered 1829, built for grinding oats. Single storey and attic stepped into a sloping site. An early example with an integrated drying kiln which here stands slightly taller since it rises from the higher ground nearest the road. The kiln 'funnel' was of clay-lined timber, and its roof was once crowned by a timber ventilator.

GLENBUCHAT CASTLE
2.1 km. E

Situated within the confluence of the Buchat Water and the Don, one of the finest tower houses on a stepped Z-plan. It was built to replace an earlier castle at Badenyon by John Gordon of Cairnbarrow on the occasion of his marriage to his second wife, Helen Carnegie, in 1590. Helen was the daughter of Sir Robert Carnegie of Kinnaird, who had served as Ambassador-extraordinary to the court of Henri II. Similarities in plan with Hatton Castle (Angus) suggest that Glenbuchat's master mason came from there, and knew something of work on the Continent. Although roofless and altered internally, Glenbuchat's shell survives almost intact.

Built in pinned field rubble, Glenbuchat was originally harled with dressings in Kildrummy freestone, some still displaying their masons' marks. It comprises a rectangular main block approximately 14 m. long E–W and 8 m. deep, with two towers which are almost square stepped out on each side from diagonally opposite angles: the SW is the entrance jamb, 6.6 m. long by 6.9 m. deep, and the NE the private apartments, slightly larger at 6.7 m. by 7.3 m. As first built the accommodation was laid out over ground, first and second floors, the attic level having pedimented dormerheads. Two long slim turnpike stairs rise from first floor within the angles formed by the Z-plan on the N side of the house: these rest on *trompe* arches, a distinctly French motif absent from Hatton, where the stairs rise from ground level. On the opposite side, the SW entrance jamb has two turrets, one circular and one square – this accommodated the castle bell – while there is another square turret at the main block's SE angle. These turrets, together with a further circular turret at the NE and the tall coped chimneystacks at the crowstepped gables, must once have constituted an impressive skyline.

The sole entrance is at ground floor in the E flank of the SW tower, close into the angle with the main block. It has a roll-moulded architrave, the inscription above which, although much eroded, was fortunately recorded by Alexander Laing:

IHONE GORDONE HELEN CARNEGE 1590
NOTHING ON EARTH REMANIS BOT FAME

Immediately behind its stout wooden door was an inner iron yett of which only the hinge-pins survive. The entrance was protected by shot-holes in the main block and the tower at ground floor, and the turrets overlooking it from above. The ground floor is almost blind, while the larger windows above were once barred with iron grilles; these were modified early in the C18 and the large mullioned-and-transomed second-floor window at the W gable is also an insertion of that date as will be seen below.

Internally the main block's ground floor is vaulted and has the customary arrangement of a passage leading to a cellar and then to the kitchen. The kitchen has an arched hearth occupying almost the whole width of the E gable; this has small cupboards within its cheeks to keep salt dry. There is a sink with a slop drain on the kitchen's N side. The SW entrance jamb has always contained the main stair up to first floor, but the original wheel stair has been replaced by a much tighter one to create space for an L-shaped guardroom, and at first floor the tighter arrangement made room for a small bedchamber with a recess for a heather crib.

As originally built the main block contained the hall, occupying the whole of its first-floor level, with a large fireplace near the centre of its long S flank. The 'high' end of the hall was at the E nearest Gordon's private chamber in the NE tower, which had its own fireplace, press and privy. Food and drink were brought in at the hall's 'low' end either by the main stair or by a small turnpike within the cellar's NW angle.

Access to the upper floors was by the turret stairs on the N side of the house, both of which had recesses to allow people to pass. The second floor was probably Helen Gordon's domain, the main block originally comprising a single large apartment which corresponded to the great hall beneath, while the low attic floor in the roof-space probably consisted of smaller rooms. Two carved stone dormerheads have been re-set into the walls, one displaying Helen's arms and initials: a shield charged with an eagle displayed, bearing on its breast an antique covered cup.

At some point, perhaps shortly after 1701, when Glenbuchat was purchased by the Gordons of Knockespock (q.v.), the internal accommodation was drastically rearranged both horizontally and vertically to meet changing social patterns. In the main block, the ground-floor cellar was divided N–S and partly infilled to provide support from beneath for a masonry wall with fireplaces which divided the first-floor hall into two smaller, more intimate rooms: a dining room nearest the main stair in the sw tower, and a drawing room nearest the private apartments in the NE tower. This wall contains the enormous lintel of the original fireplace on the s side, the wall-head chimneystack of which was taken down. The first-floor ceiling was lowered to allow the second floor to become a full-height storey beneath the eaves, and this was divided into four bedchambers by further timber partitions running E–W; the w bedchamber was of considerable height with a tall two-light window in the gable. Within the gutted structure the evidence of these alterations remains visible not just in this window but in the positions of the joist holes, and in the blocking-up of former windows, fireplaces and doorways to the turret stairs, and in the absence of dormers.

By the time that the Gordons sold the estate to Lord Braco in 1738 the castle had been let to a tenant farmer and had begun to deteriorate. Of the 'gate' – presumably the forecourt gateway – mentioned by Alexander Laing in 1828 with its square granite panel bearing the Monro motto 'Dreid God' nothing remains. James Giles's 1840 watercolour of the castle shows only the main block's roof still surviving, and when Robert Billings drew it five years later that too had gone. The 6th Earl Fife sold Glenbuchat to Henry Curtis Burra in 1883. He instructed restoration proposals from *Reginald Blomfield* in 1886 but these were not carried out. Repairs were put in hand for James Barclay M.P. in the early c20, and the castle was taken into Ministry of Works care in 1946.

At least part of the formal layout which surrounded the castle still survives in its rubble-walled FORECOURT to the s and large walled GARDEN to the E. The ball-finialled gatepiers of the latter are probably *c.* 1826 and the plan of the garden itself may have been modified when it was adopted by Castle Lodge (*see* below).

CASTLE LODGE, 70 m. s. Extended from a modest cottage for John Grassick, a tenant farmer, in 1826. White-harled. Principal (s) front is three bays, symmetrical, with boldly projecting semicircular bows. Roof with oversailing eaves and tall square clustered chimneystacks. Altered for James Barclay after he purchased Glenbuchat in 1901, the designs by *Jenkins & Marr c.* 1903, with further work by *William Kelly* later. Central doorway recent.

8010

KIRKTON OF KINELLAR

PARISH CHURCH. Built 1800–1; disused; conversion for residential use is planned in 2013. A rectangular plan in harled rubble. N gable with a ball-finialled birdcage bellcote. Two tall round-arched windows with original glazing in centre of W flank, and smaller oblongs in the outer bays at ground floor beneath the gallery. The bell is one of the finest in Aberdeenshire. Its beautifully lettered inscription with the arms of Mechelen in Flanders records that it was cast by *Peter Vanden Ghein III* in 1612; above the inscription a delicate ornamental band, and underneath three angels supporting plaques which hang from strings from their mouths. The church's N porch was added by *Jenkins & Marr* in 1900–1, and the S vestry is perhaps of the same date. Unaltered interior with box pews and U-plan gallery supported on slender Doric columns facing the pulpit in the W wall. The church stands on the rising ground occupied by its predecessor, reputedly pre-Reformation, dedicated to St Triduana; the CHURCHYARD contains a few lying stones, one with Death standing on an orb with scythe and hourglass in outstretched arms. In the S wall, three large stones probably from a stone circle which stood nearby.

Former PARISH MANSE, 120 m. WSW. Dated 1778. Two storeys and three bays broad over a semi-sunk basement, much altered. The original entrance front was on the E side. In 1903 or possibly earlier a wing was added to the W side which then became the new entrance front. This wing was demolished in the mid C20 and a neat porch built beneath the mezzanine stair window. Long two-storey extension built against the N gable in 1978. The manse stands on the W side of a large walled garden. On either side above a round-arched side gate, carved stones seemingly from the bellcote of St Triduana, one dated 1615 and the other perhaps with minister's or heritor's initials (M.I.W.?). OFFICES probably by *George Jaffray*, 1800–2.

8090

KIRKTON OF MARYCULTER

PARISH CHURCH. Begun in 1786–7 (the dates cast on the old bell) as a rectangular preaching-box in coursed granite rubble with a transom-lit doorway at each end and arched windows. Birdcage bellcote over W gable. The church was much altered in 1878 by *James Garvie & Sons*, the date of the timber Y-tracery, but the cruciform plan dates from 1882–3 when the S organ-chamber, with Lombardic tracery, and the N hall were added. Inside, the nave's canted timber-boarded ceiling of 1878 is supported on arched trusses in dark wood, springing from corbels. Some original BOX PEWS including one with balustrade top. Otherwise mostly reseated in 1878. N, E and W gallery on square columns. The organ chamber arch has round columns of richly Greek detail. Splendid architectonic furnishings in the ritual area: octagonal PULPIT of 1886 and COMMUNION TABLE of 1908 on columns with Neo-Byzantine capitals; it cleverly incorporates the FONT basin. – ORGAN with decorated pipes by *Wadsworth & Bro.*, 1883. – STAINED GLASS. Organ chamber. Figures of the Evangelists and SS Peter, Paul, James and Jude by *James Ballantine & Son*, 1887. – MEMORIAL. An alabaster tablet with glass mosaic centre showing Our Lord enthroned. By *Peter Macgregor Chalmers*, 1901, in memory of the Rev. George Duncan, who carried out the improvements.

– WAR MEMORIAL. Kemnay granite Celtic cross with strapwork, 1920 by *Rust & Alexander*.

ST MARY (R.C.). *See* BLAIRS, ST MARY'S COLLEGE.

ST MARY'S PARISH CHURCHYARD, 1.5 km. WNW. The Culter lands on the Dee's S bank were granted by David I to the Knights Templar in the late C12, and a preceptory was established by Walter Bisset *c.* 1225. The CHURCH dedicated to the Templars' patron, St Mary – hence Maryculter – of which little more than foundations remain, was built in 1287 and abandoned in 1782. It was rectangular, 23 m. by 6.6 m. over rubble walls 0.7 m. thick, now standing at their highest at the chancel end. Some carved fragments of Gothic doors and windows suggest a resemblance to the Chapel of the Blessed Virgin Mary at Cowie (pp. 731–2); the piscina in the S wall comprises a delicately fluted bowl and supporting column.* The high rubble WALLS enclosing the churchyard are mid C19. A simple gateway has a handsome tablet commemorating the Templars, erected in 1925. Some good STONES. Lying slab I.M. MS. 1719 with a finely carved soul, *memento mori* and symbols of immortality; upright slab to Alexander E—k and his wife, carved with a crown and hammer, erected in 1777.

Former PARISH MANSE. Designed by *William Smith* in 1867, built 1868–9. Two storeys, three windows wide with its l. bay projecting under a gable, and central single-storey porch in the angle. Coursed squared grey granite rubble walls with golden ashlar dressings. Tripartite windows at ground floor. Double-pile plan. Offices 'lately rebuilt' in 1833.

---

*A slab referred to in some old sources as carved with effigies of a knight and his lady, believed to represent Gilbert Menzies who feued Blairs from 1535, together with his wife, Marjory, was transferred to St Nicholas's West Kirk in Aberdeen *c.* 1890.

MARYCULTER HOUSE, 1.5 km. NW on the E bank of the Dee. An early vernacular country house, its main block dated 1717(?) at its skewputts. Two-storey three-bay entrance front raised over a semi-sunk basement. Relatively narrow but boldly projecting gabled centre contains the doorway approached by railed stairs. The doorway has been widened, the stair is modern and the fenestration has been significantly altered, but both the projecting bay itself and the entrance raised above ground level are unusually sophisticated features for North-East Scotland in the early C18; they have at least partly been determined by the fact that the basement is vaulted internally. The builders' initials W.M. M. (Menzies) are carved into the attic window's lintel. Two-storey reversed L-plan wing extending forward on the l. side, with a three-windows-wide bow at the angle, c. 1830 for John Gordon of Fyvie. Additional outbuildings at rear. Substantial modern extensions.

In Templars' Park, NE of Maryculter House is the OLD PARISH MANSE, probably the former seat of the Maryculter estate built c. 1670–90, which was given over as a manse in 1717. Two storeys in harled rubble; gabled roof with pronounced skews, moulded skewputts and coped end stacks. The original entrance front was presumably in the SW flank, with small windows in the end bays only at ground floor for security, but five windows evenly spaced at first floor (cf. Birkenbog, N, 1693); the larger windows at ground floor – one of which was originally the doorway – and the clumsy outshot are additions. The N elevation also has small windows, perhaps a necessity to admit sufficient light; one in the centre bay at first floor may have been blocked up to support a wall-head bellcote. Repaired by *Fenton Wyness*, 1936.

BLAIRS. *See* p. 384.

KIRKTON OF PREMNAY

A tiny settlement within the confluence of the Gadie and Foreside Burns.

Former PARISH CHURCH. Opened 1792. Simple four-bay rectangular plan in squared reddish-gold Bennachie granite, with a ball-finialled birdcage bellcote over its W gable. Its steeply pitched roof with moulded skewputts allowed just enough height for the insertion of a W gallery in 1828. W porch and polygonal E vestry by *William Henderson & Son*, 1900, concealing the original doors. Now converted to domestic use.

Across the road, the GRAVEYARD was the site of St Caran's church, granted to Lindores Abbey c. 1196. Remains of its bellcote are incorporated into the boundary wall W of the gate.

KIRKTON OF RAYNE   6030

PARISH CHURCH. Built 1789. A four-bay preaching-box with round-headed doorway and windows, built in coursed, squared granite which has been harled. w door with fanlight deeply recessed in its arch and gallery window above; dated skewputts. During reordering by *George Bennett Mitchell* in 1930 the E doorway was blocked and the E window lengthened. Finely detailed bellcote from previous church, similar to Culsalmond's (q.v.) but rather oddly perched on balusters. It has moulded colonnettes, gablets and finials, initials M.W.A. (Minister Walter Abercrombie) and date 1619. Two substantial N outshots: one the laird's aisle, which stood against the previous church, its loft approached by crude steps over a burial vault – note the skulls at the skewputts – and entrance lintel incised 'Alexander Leith of Freefield [*see* below] 1754'; the other a C19 vestry. The church is now entered through the vestry doorway at the E end. w gallery of 1789 with prayer room recently formed beneath it. – PULPIT. Platform-type of *c.* 1870 but the Gothic panelling is probably an embellishment by *Mitchell*. – ORGAN by *E. H. Lawton* behind it. Simple Gothic PEWS probably *c.* 1870 but two PANELS seem to be from family pews, one with initials I.L.H. – John Leith of Harthill (q.v.), with arms and motto 'Trewe to the End', the other to Beatrix Fraser with her arms and date 1602, suggesting the year of their marriage. STAINED GLASS. E window. The Good Shepherd, 1930s. – MONUMENTS. Against the church's s wall, a Gothic memorial to the Leslies of Warthill (*see* below) and Folla, their coat of arms in a fini-alled gablet, and beneath a slab in memory of Patrick, Walter and George Leslie, pioneers of sheep-farming in Queensland. – In the sw corner, a large simple classical monument to the Rev. Dr Davidson, †1819, three bays articulated by four Greek Doric antae without an entablature to support the pediment.

Former PARISH MANSE, next to the church. Irregular two-storey U-plan, facing s to the garden. The oldest part, represented by the longer, taller roof ridge within the central range, was built in 1750 by *William Milne*, mason for the Rev. John Marr; the skewputts on the rear elevation, dated 1627, were reused. Additional offices *c.* 1771 and 1826, the latter date visible in the E wing's gable; the w wing acquired its present piend-roofed appearance in 1875–8 from *William Low Henderson*.

FREEFIELD HOUSE, 2.5 km. NW. Built for the Leiths of Freefield. A Palladian villa reinterpreted for North-East Scotland, its fine approach is a tree-lined avenue running dead straight for over 1 km. Main block and its advanced pavilions, symmetrically composed, are mid-C18, with linking quadrants added in the late C18 or early C19, all built in rubble and formerly harled. The main block's entrance front, facing SSW, is three-storey, three bays broadly spaced, its slightly projected centre rising above the wall-head into a shallow-pitched gable with urn finials, moulded skews and a tall ashlar chimneystack; the second-floor windows in the flanking bays break up into mid-C19 gableted stone dormerheads. Very tall gabled roof with stone ridge and end stacks. The doorpiece, channelled and round-arched set in Ionic columns, and the projecting tripartite windows at ground floor on either side are additions by *Matthews & Mackenzie* 1885–7. Pavilions low two-storeyed with tall piended roofs, each with a central stack. The main block's original doorway in blocked rustication has been re-set at the centre of the l. quadrant. Interior remodelled by Matthews & Mackenzie with smart panelled stair hall.

WARTHILL HOUSE, 1.75 km. NE. The Leslies can trace their association with Warthill back through the generations to John Cruikshank, a crusader granted the estate by William the Lion in the late C12. An early C17 tower house was blown up after the 'Forty-five and replaced by a modest classical house which was transformed into a Scottish Baronial house by *Mackenzie & Matthews c.* 1851. In 1971 its principal E elevation was demolished, its site now occupied by a walled garden.

In the centre of the S elevation is the house of *c.* 1750. It is two storeys and three bays broad with astragalled sash-and-case windows and chamfered sandstone dressings, but was remodelled *c.* 1851 with an ashlar wall-head supported on corbels and punctuated by pedimented stone dormers. The doorway is earlier C20, with C17 heraldic panels flanking it on each side. One of the dormers is dated 1801, but this relates to an event in Leslie family history rather than any rebuilding. Also of 1851 are the small spirelet turrets at its l. angle and at the crowstepped gable front which projects forward on the r., its canted bay rising through ground and first floors: this is a remnant of the lost E wing, perhaps incorporating older masonry, and beyond it on the r. at the SE angle is a much remodelled fragment of the C17 tower house with a small square angle turret still surviving from the demolished E range. On the far l. of the S front, and slightly set back from the Georgian house, is the gable of the low two-storey early C19 W range, again remodelled with crowstepped gables and a circular angle tower by Mackenzie & Matthews. At the W elevation, the twin crowstepped end gables of the N and S ranges are the dominant elements, the lower two-storey block between them sheltering the present main entrance. Its low-pitched roof and its doorpiece and lying-pane windows are of the 1840s.

The N WING is plain earlier C19, with relatively few windows, but gains in stature from being set back in a railed forecourt with ashlar gatepiers. This forecourt is enclosed on the W by a single-storey gabled outshot, again *c.* 1840, and balanced on the E by a cut-down remnant of the E front which includes its service archway with bellcote. This archway links to another single-storey-and-attic block, probably part of further works by *James Matthews* of 1862. Behind it is a second small court, with pretty drum tower corbelled at the top into a ball-finialled spirelet, this too the work of Matthews.

KIRKTON OF SKENE

Until recently, a tiny village – a single row of cottages, with church and manse nearby, bordered by the Easter Skene and Kirkton House estates. Significant development from *c.* 1975 towards the N.

PARISH CHURCH. Built 1801. The first Post-Reformation Gothic church in rural Aberdeenshire, reflecting the antiquarian interests of the Skene family; it is nevertheless conspicuously simple, rational and economical. A tall harled rectangle with a piended roof, orientated E–W, it has very large pointed windows in slim ashlar margins on all four sides, those on the S, W and N retaining their original glazing with basket-weave tracery. The centre bays of the four-bay S flank rise into a shallow-pitched gable – its quatrefoil and bellcote are additions by *John Smith*, 1840 (the bell is by *John Mowat* of Old Aberdeen, 1735). E and W gables have two windows flanking a relatively small central doorway with gallery roundel above, the W doorway still with basket-weave transom-light, the E doorway blocked during reordering by *George Bennett Mitchell*, 1931–2. Two windows on N side, plain session house added 1884. Classical interior. The pulpit was originally centred on the S side facing a U-plan gallery on Roman Doric columns. In Mitchell's reordering the pulpit was transferred to the E, with a single gallery reusing the Doric columns and panelled front on the W. The PULPIT itself is of 1924, with engaging carved roundel representing St Bride and a cow, finely lettered inscription and low-relief panels with floriate decoration; *Mitchell's* COMMUNION TABLE and CHAIR of 1932 are similar in style. – PEWS. From the Free Church at Kintore (dem.), installed 1932. – STAINED GLASS. E windows, large and richly coloured designs of saints signed by *John Blyth* (designer) and *William Blair* (maker), dated 1977–8. Roundel representing a Sower, presumably by the same artists. – SECOND WORLD WAR MEMORIAL. Carved oak panel designed by *T. B. Huxley-Jones* of Gray's School of Art, Aberdeen.

The previous St Bride's church, a pendicle of Kinkell (q.v.), stood on the site of the Skenes' burial enclosure in the churchyard. Near the present church door two rough basins, perhaps the medieval FONT and PISCINA. Also a MORT SAFE *c.* 1829. – MONUMENT. Scholarly Late Scots Gothic cusped arch recess and tomb-chest in pink granite for William McCombie of Easter Skene (*see* below) and Lynturk (q.v.), 1890, with his and his wife's arms, based on the Tolquhon Monument, Tarves (N).

Former PARISH MANSE, 0.45 km. N. By *John Smith*, 1840. Scots Neo-Jacobean. Two-storey three-bay entrance front with centre slightly projected under a crowstepped gablet. Cavetto-splayed doorway with hoodmould, tall ground-floor windows and lower first-floor windows set in dressed granite surrounds

against the harl. Earlier manse of 1779 incorporated as a parallel rear wing. Pedestal SUNDIAL unusually fine in design and
carving, inscribed 'Manse of Skene 1810', with four concentric
dials, giving time in Rome, Montreal, Jerusalem and Peking.

Former FREE CHURCH, Lochside, 0.85 km. W. Built c. 1844,
perhaps by *James Henderson*. First Pointed. A low wide-span
church in squared granite rubble, the proportions of its gable
front masked by canted aisle-fronts on the model of the Triple
Kirks, Aberdeen. Three stepped lancets and token angle buttresses rising into pinnacles, originally with a belfry. A tower
and spire were added to the r. aisle front by *Daniel Macandrew*
in 1857 but burnt in 1927 and reduced to a stump when the
church was altered for commercial use in 1946.

Former PROCTOR'S ORPHANAGE, 0.6 km. E. By *George Marr*
(of *Jenkins & Marr*), dated 1891. Single-storey three-bay front
with projecting centre, tall stone dormers set into steeply
piended roof. Simple robust Northern Renaissance detailing,
central dormer pedimented with flanking scrolls.

EAST LOCHSIDE FARMHOUSE, 0.9 km. W. By *William Kelly*,
with *David Morris*, the Dunecht estate factor, 1931. Very neat
crowstepped Arts and Crafts Scots vernacular. Single-storey-
and-attic three-bay house in granite rubble, outer bays rising
into broad dormer gablets. Above the moulded central entrance,
the interlocking Cowdray Cs and Viscount's coronet; beneath
the windows, sculpted heads of Cowdray griffins. Adjacent
STEADING by the same architects, 1927.

EASTER SKENE HOUSE, 0.55 km. NW. On the banks of Loch
Skene and overlooking the Grampians, by *John Smith* 1832 for
the cattle-breeder William McCombie. Neo-Tudor. Two-storey
four-bay asymmetric entrance front facing SW with broad gable
at its l. end, the central entrance bay boldly canted out and the
two r. bays with first-floor windows breaking up into dormer
gablets. Round-arched fanlit entrance door, lying-pane glazing
with timber mullions and transoms; ground-floor canted bay
windows in the l. gable bay and in the SE flank elevation identify the principal apartments. Roof-line punctuated by tall
diagonally shafted chimneystacks. Very deep flanks, the SE
semi-symmetrical with gables at each end, but set into the re-
entrant angle of that on the r. a slim circular tower with bellcast
slated spirelet.

KIRKVILLE (KIRKTON) HOUSE, 0.45 km. SSE. Now a nursing
home. Built 1823–7 by *John Smith*, 1823–7, for James Knowles,
woollen manufacturer and art collector; extended by *J. & W.
Smith* in 1848 for Capt. Thomas Shepherd of the East India
Company. Picturesque Greek Revival villa, single-storeyed
with tetrastyle Doric portico in timber, rock-faced basement.
S elevation with central canted bay, W with twin bows; low-
pitched broad-eaved roof. The NORTH LODGE was remodelled with a gable inglenook by *William Kelly* (with *David
Morris*, cf. East Lochside, above) after Viscount Cowdray
bought the estate in 1924.

NETHER TERRYVALE FARMHOUSE, 2.5 km. NW. C18, much altered. Two carved figures on the roof look *c.* 1600: a full-length but headless woman, and a half-length man with a prob-ably a shot-putter; crude, but very jovial, reputedly from House of Fornet (dem.). An interesting comparison with the more refined figures at Craig Castle (q.v.) and Fyvie Castle (N).

AUCHINCLECH, 2.25 km. NE. The single-storey mansion of a small estate, remodelled *c.* 1835. Entrance front of that date: three gabled bays, a narrow projecting central entrance flanked by much broader ends. Deeply recessed round-headed doorway, eight-panelled door transom-lit; tall but relatively narrow windows in the end bays (two on the l., one on the r.) with large diamond-pane glazing; all three gables rise into chimneystacks, that at the centre with a decorative can. Extending across the rear, the C18 cottage onto which the new entrance front was grafted. Square-plan courtyard STEADING has symmetrical battlemented coachhouse with low tower adjoining the SE corner.

Former BRIDGEND SMITHY, 4 km. NE. Early C19 and surpris-ingly formal. Single-storey three-bay blacksmith's cottage, flanked by slightly lower projecting wings, one (N) the byre and the other (S) the smithy, with the position of the forge still identified by its tall chimneystack. All in golden granite, fore-court enclosed by railings.

SKENE HOUSE. *See* p. 714.

KIRKTONHILL HOUSE *see* MARYKIRK

KNOCK CASTLE *see* GLENMUICK

KNOCKESPOCK HOUSE   *5020*
2 km. S of Clatt

A complex Scots vernacular house built for the Gordons of Knockespock and recently restored and rationalized. Originally a seat of the Bishops of Aberdeen, a tower house was seemingly built in the C16 or C17 (perhaps 1654), of which two drum towers, very closely spaced, survive, forming the core of the present structure. A plain vernacular house was built immedi-ately E of these towers in the later C18, and is shown with them in a survey plan dated 1794. Two further blocks were built in the earlier C19; that to the N of the towers is probably *c.* 1810–20, that on the W forms a large rear wing. Between the drum towers a simple square belvedere tower may also be of this time, or *c.* 1838, when a single bay seems to have been formed in the angle between the E block and the S drum. Proposals by *Mackenzie & Matthews*, dated 1849, to transform the house for Sir Henry Gordon with a Baronial addition clearly inspired by the Seton Tower of Fyvie Castle (N) against the E front were not èxecuted. Further proposals for what was effectively a new house on the W in a C17 Scots style, probably by *Jenkins & Marr*, were built *c.* 1889 for Harry Fellowes Gordon but demolished in the later C20.

All these changes have been unified by consistently harled wall surfaces. The ENTRANCE (E) FRONT is vernacular classical – almost square in proportion – two storeys and three bays broad over a semi-sunk basement, with a railed forestair leading up to a transom-lit doorway; the windows are evenly spaced but arranged slightly off-centre to the r. within the wall-plane. The dressings are pinky-gold sandstone; the gabled roof has moulded skewputts and coped chimneystacks. The N BLOCK is the same eaves height as the E block but its doorway is at ground level and its three-storey three-bay frontage is again arranged slightly off-centre; its dressings are in granite and the roof is piended. The W BLOCK is also early C19, but significantly altered, having been largely concealed by the former late C19 addition on its S side. It is now two storeys and three bays broad with a very tall wall-head, and canted dormers in its gabled roof, shallow-pitched on account of the depth of its plan. The two DRUM TOWERS at the core of the structure stand remarkably close together and appear to have been conjoined like a figure-of-eight before a narrow corridor was forced between them. Protected by ground-floor shot-holes, their conical roofs rise into carved finials. The square belvedere breaking up between them is in a simple castellated style with corbelled and crenellated parapet. Internally the plan is complex with many recent changes.

The small formal GARDEN fronting the W wing is late C20, standing on the site of the 1886 addition. The POLICIES contain three artificial lakes – one immediately N of the house, with an island reached by a small bridge, and two conjoined by a canal near the Suie road, the larger again with an island and boathouse.

TOWER LODGE, 1.6 km. NE. Mid-C19, perhaps by *Thomas Mackenzie*. A very remarkable composition. A relatively low circular base supports an outsized crowstep-gabled caphouse which contains both upper storey and attic, the stair incorporated within a slim round tower immediately to one side. The single-storey buildings in front are additions by *James Masson* and *Robert Crabbe*, who restored the lodge in 1992.

LATHALLAN SCHOOL
900 m. NE of Johnshaven

Originally BROTHERTON CASTLE. The estate was purchased *c.* 1570 by James Scott of Logie (Angus), whose large tower house was augmented several times and remained the Scott residence until the mid C19. It was demolished and the present mansion built in 1866–8 by *Matthews & Lawrie* for Hercules James Scott and his wife, Anna Moon. Lathallan School moved here in 1949 after the original Lathallan House (near Largoward, Fife) was gutted by fire.

The style is large, competent Baronial, but in a restrained idiom – none of the usual gymnastics, no epic struggle to cram in every last motif. Entrance front to the NW, three storeys with a tower slightly advanced off-centre. Chamfered angles, corbelled parapet and then a canted oriel; crowstepped caphouse corbelled out above. Porte cochère in front of it with dummy tourelles, rope moulding and round arches with dogtooth. To the l., a square tower sweeping up an additional two storeys with crenellated parapet and stair-turret. Two more bays to either side with triangular dormerheads. Tourelle in the far l. angle and a diagonal squared-off window on the r. Beyond it, the lower service wing in a similar style.

Towards the sea, the garden frontage cuts an impressive but self-controlled figure, seven bays with balustraded drum tower in the l. angle. Below it, stairs lead down to the WALLED GARDEN, laid out in the mid C18 by the Scotts but retained for the new mansion. Balustraded terraces and two small pavilions on the NE side, the lower with an ogival roof.

The INTERIOR of the house is well preserved, surprisingly so given its long use as a school. Top-lit rectangular stair hall rising up full height, the wooden balusters carved with thick barley-twist. The original drawing room, dining room and morning room (now headmaster's office) have elaborate geometric ceilings with foliate accents, the colour restored in 2013–14. Good original overdoors, valences and chandeliers.

LAURENCEKIRK   K   7070

Site of an ancient kirkton, originally known as Conveth and first documented in the late C12. It was, however, certainly much older, as C13 chroniclers refer to the 'ancient' church of St Laurence and the annual celebrations of his martyrdom. In 1765, Lord Gardenstone of Thornton Castle (q.v.) began laying out a modern village to the SW on a grid plan, and Laurencekirk was made a burgh of barony in 1779. The two main industries of the village were box-making and linen-weaving, and population growth continued through the mid C19. It now stands at about 1,800.

CHURCHES

Former FREE CHURCH, High Street. Now the Masonic Hall. Simple E.E., 1857–8. Advanced centre with double-chamfered entrance swept up into a short clock tower. Broached octagonal stone spire above it. Hall to the rear by *D. Wishart Galloway*, 1898–9.

PARISH CHURCH, off High Street. Site of the medieval church, which was dedicated by Bishop David Benham in 1244. The houses of the original kirkton were once huddled around it. Present church by *James Duirs*, 1804, the usual Georgian rectangle of rubble.* Major renovation by *Matthews & Mackenzie* in 1894–6, including a new N aisle, SW porch and three windows with intersecting tracery. They also extended the building 5.2 m. to the W and added the tall, bland bell-turret with its broached spirelet.

Good interior as recast and renovated in the late C19. A-frame timber roof with pendant finials carried on quadrant braces. N aisle delimited by pointed wooden arcades carried on cast-iron columns. Spandrels pierced with graduated lancets. – L-plan GALLERY on the N and W. – Semi-hexagonal PULPIT by *A. Dunbar*, 1896, with linenfold panelling. Elaborately scrolled GASOLIERS on the back-board. – STAINED GLASS. Garden of Gethsemane by *Ballantine & Gardiner*, 1895 (upper E wall). – Two windows below by *Oscar Paterson*: David gathering stones and the Women at the Sepulchre (1922); Meeting at Emmaus (1928) – S wall with Virgin and Child flanked by Charity and Faith, also 1928 by Paterson.

Former MANSE to the NW, now a nursing home. Two-storey, four-bay main block, 1805. Rear additions by *William Fettis*, 1873.

ST LAURENCE (Episcopal), High Street. By *Alexander Ross*, 1871–2, replacing a church on the same site (designed by *John Gibson* of Montrose, 1791–3). E.E. rectangle covered by a long, steep roof. Main W gable with two skinny lancets and quatrefoil set in a spherical triangle. Gabled porch projecting SW and a vestry to the NE. More little lancets on the flanks. The interior is pleasant and a good example of Ross's 'Episcopal' style. Wooden A-frame roof carried on tall pointed arches formed of curved braces. Chancel arch also wood, carved with quatrefoils and set on chamfered stone piers. – Carved oak REREDOS by *Jones & Willis*, 1886, incorporating a PAINTING of the Presentation of the Virgin in the style of Poussin, donated in the early C19. Flanking it are individual figures of SS Andrew, Laurence, Ternan, Palladius, David and Drostan. – PISCINA to the r. and AUMBRY to the l. – ORGAN by *Wadsworth & Bro.*, 1909. Rectangular case. – STAINED GLASS. Mostly by *John Hardman & Co.*, the three chancel windows from 1872. Cross and foliage (E sexfoil); Maries at the empty tomb (N); Annunciation and Visitation (S). – In the nave lancets, Christ, James, Paul and Simeon (S side); Good Shepherd, Charity, Angel and infant, Andrew (N side). Variously dated 1872 to 1921. – In the W windows, an angel over verses of the Requiem and Resurrection.

---

*The medieval church had already been rebuilt twice, in 1626 and again in 1754.

PUBLIC BUILDINGS

DICKSON MEMORIAL HALL, Station Road. By *William Kelly* of *W. & J. Smith & Kelly*, 1899–1901, and easily mistaken for a church. Gothic style, in rock-faced masonry with pairs of cusped lancets. Stylized diaper over the porch entrance; octagonal timber flèche on the roof. The gables have Dec windows (three-light to the N, oculus to the S). Fine interior with A-frame timber roof carried on semicircular braces with kingpost trusses above. The false hammerbeams are, charmingly, carved with alternating angels and grills (the instrument of Laurence's martyrdom). Pair of arcades leading to the original kitchen; Art Deco glass panels in the lobby.

LIBRARY, Johnston Street. Built as the Episcopal school, 1858. Off-centre porch with pointed quatrefoil and a little gableted bellcote. Groups of cusped lancets.

MEARNS ACADEMY COMMUNITY CAMPUS, Aberdeen Road. By *Halliday Fraser Munro*, 2012–14. Long two-storey blocks with rectangular windows. Vertical weatherboarding on the right angles and curved entrances.

MEARNS COMMUNITY CENTRE, High Street. *See* Description.

RAILWAY STATION, off Station Road. Opened 1849 for the Aberdeen Railway; rebuilt by the Caledonian Railway, 1909–10. Closed in 1967 and reopened after restoration in 2009. Four bays, the ends crowstepped and set on rock-faced base courses. Good iron-and-glass platform shelter between them.

ST LAURENCE HALL, Conveth Place. *See* Description.

WAR MEMORIAL, off Garvock Road. By *Garden & Co.*, 1922. Very tall, rough-hewn obelisk with crenellated top. Over the inscriptions, a laurel swag set in strapwork with lion rampant above. Long swords carved on the sides.

DESCRIPTION

The green space of KINNEAR SQUARE sits at the S end of the burgh, originally gifted by Lord Gardenstone for the purposes of a weekly market. The dimensions are pleasantly large and broad, but as so often in Scotland it is surrounded by excessively squat buildings. In the NW corner is the late C19 WESTERN INN, Baronial, with crowstepped gables and canted oriels on striated bases. Faux tourelles are corbelled out on the r. flank. Across the street is the former DRILL HALL by *Walker & Duncan*, 1911. HIGH STREET then leads straight on, lined with single-storey cottages of the late C18 and early–mid C19. Its length – and, more importantly, its narrowness – were dictated by the very long feus that were required for the weavers to produce their linen. Just past Blackiemuir Avenue is the MEARNS COMMUNITY CENTRE, its r. section built as an Infants' School, late C19. Across the street is a pair of early C19 GATEPIERS with alternating vermiculation and studded ball finials. The path between them leads to GARVOCKLEA HOUSE, a shooting lodge built *c.* 1820 and originally named The Villa, as it was the only such building in the burgh. Advanced three-bay section with bowed centre and two Venetian windows. Roman Doric portico to the l.; fanciful parapet with wavy crenellations. The adjoining bays have good anthemion and palmette railings.

At the other end of High Street, slightly less than 1 km. NE, is the former NORTH OF SCOTLAND BANK (No. 24), 1872 by *James Matthews*. More Baronial with crowsteps, triangular dormerheads and a tourelle over a rounded angle. Across sits the severely classical ROYAL BANK OF SCOTLAND, c. 1840. Ground floor of channelled, streamlined ashlar. Wide, canted angle in the centre topped by a strange, very large Dutch gable with anthemion.

Across Alma Place is a combined shop and tenement, early C19, with bowed angle under scrolls. Quoins of polished red sandstone. CONVETH PLACE lies diagonally opposite, its S end anchored by the ROYAL HOTEL, established on this site by at least the late C18, but in its present form of 1894, multi-gabled and with channel-pilastered entrance. Beyond it on the l. is ST LAURENCE HALL, big Scots Renaissance of 1866 by *William Fettis*. Crowstepped gable and an advanced, square tower with pyramidal roof. At the end of Conveth Place, the former ABERDEEN TOWN & COUNTY BANK, 1854. T-plan, the centre with chamfered angles corbelled into a gable via massive ogival stops. Station Road then leads on to the Dickson Memorial Hall (*see* Public Buildings, above) with, just before it, the drive to FROGFIELD – the only other real villa in the burgh. Two storeys and three bays, dated 1832 in the blind lunette on the r. flank. Central portico with two Roman Doric columns. Rear wing added c. 1850 with rectangular Neo-Perp window and a canted, crenellated bay.

MAINS OF HAULKERTON, 1.3 km. NNW. On a farm building are two re-set stones from the destroyed Castle of Haulkerton, founded in the late C15 and expanded in the mid C17 by Sir Alexander Falconer.* One is a corbel of a woman pulling back her head-dress and revealing wild almond eyes. It formerly had the full date of 1556. Also a plaque initialled A.F. and inscribed 'ANNO 1648'.

BEATTIE LODGE. *See* p. 571.
JOHNSTON LODGE. *See* p. 571.

LAURISTON CASTLE   K
2.1 km. NE of St Cyrus

Now an eclectic and disparate conglomeration of buildings, but originally one of the premier strongholds on the E coast. The name derives from a vanished chapel dedicated to St Laurence,

---

*Dem. c. 1790 and most of the stone later used to build the Parish Church (*see* above).

first documented in 1243. Sir Richard Straton acquired the land
c. 1260 and soon built a polygonal castle of enceinte. It was re-
fortified by Edward III in 1336. In the late C16, Lauriston was
extended into an L-plan tower house, and this remained the
Stratons' power base until they sold the estate in 1695. In the
late C18, the castle was subsumed within a new mansion for John
Brand, newly rich off slaves and tobacco. The house had datestones of 1765 and 1789, the latter now re-set inside near the
entrance. Its architect remains unknown: probably for the best,
as the style was Neo-Palladian at its most unimaginative.
Alexander Porteous added another extension after acquiring
the estate in 1849. Dereliction followed throughout the C20 and
part of the tower came crashing down into the gorge below;
the Georgian mansion was demolished in the 1970s. Excellent
restoration took place after 1986, with new buildings inserted by
Ian Begg Architects to occupy the space left by the old Georgian
block.

Begg's work is now the pivot of the building and was completed
in 1994. His style is sensitive but self-assured C17, all harled in
off-yellow. Great Hall on the r., two storeys with gabled roof
and a tall, thick drum tower under conical roof. Tourelle in the
l. angle. Beyond, a trabeated gate leading to a round tower
corbelled into a square caphouse. It has flight-holes on its l.
flank, fully enacting the illusion that it is an ancient doocot.
Porteous's EXTENSION lies somewhat incongruously to the
NE, a plain two storeys and six bays enlivened by balustraded
parapet with urn finials. It is of two different builds, the ashlar
on the l. side more highly finished.

The remains of the TOWER HOUSE rise up like a totem to
the SW. Only the lower three storeys are original, the upper
three added in bland 'Baronial *campanile*' style in the mid–late
C19. From the gorge, the base of the tower is, unbelievably,
cantilevered out on a segmental arch, appearing to hover
directly over the deepest ravine. Original tall corbelled parapet
above with open round corners. From the courtyard, the basement of the tower is slightly sunken and the first floor carried
on corbels. Above to the l. is the side door that formerly led
out to the wall-walk. The kitchen lay below it: *see* the late
medieval aumbry and slop drain.

Tall WALLS beyond form a large irregular COURTYARD, very
likely the same footprint as the C13 enceinte. Parts of the N
and W walls are certainly of that date, but all now topped by
Victorian crenellations.

Massive WALLED GARDEN to the NNE, rebuilt in the mid
C19. – Surrounding it and the Castle is a designed LAND-
SCAPE, laid out in the mid–late C18 and of very high quality,
although now overgrown. Picturesque footbridges, little
stepped terraces and meandering waterfalls. – SW of the
Castle, a substantial one-arch VIADUCT over Lauriston Burn,
first documented *c.* 1792 and thus part of John Brand's
improvements.

LEARNEY HOUSE

3 km. NNE of Torphins

A country house, begun 1747 or shortly afterwards for William Brebner, who had married Jane Buchan of Auchmacoy in 1743 and acquired the Learney estate about that time. Substantially reconstructed for William Innes and Jean Brebner by *John Smith* 1838–40 after a fire; further alterations were carried out for them in 1847, probably by John Smith with his son *William*, and in 1868 by *J. R. Mackenzie*'s assistant *Robert Ewan*, all in a low-key Scots Baronial manner.

The open courtyard plan, facing N, derives from the original house, which comprised a two-storey main block with its basement almost completely concealed on the entrance front, and flanking wings to each side. This original house is represented now by the CENTRAL RANGE, two storeys and five windows wide, its ground floor much taller than the first, built in squared granite with a projecting central bay carried above the wallhead into a tall crowstepped gable. This gable is part of the 1838–40 works, as is the round-arched doorway with a hoodmould stepping over an armorial. Flanking the central block, the two wings present a semi-symmetrical appearance. The two-storey-and-attic E WING is two bays long, with field-panels between the ground- and first-floor windows and stone attic dormers rising into pedimental gablets; in the angle formed with the central block, a splayed and crowstep-gabled bay contains a secondary luggage entrance, the large first-floor window above being corbelled out. The W WING was heightened to two storeys in 1868, its N end with rounded angles corbelled to the square a little above first floor.

During the 1838–40 works *John Smith* completely rebuilt the central block's S front, here rising three storeys since the basement was largely exposed on this side. In 1847 however this was largely concealed by a parallel S RANGE, three storeys and five windows wide, the three l. bays' second-floor windows breaking up under dormer gablets, and the two r. bays slightly projected as a broad crowstepped gable. On the W FRONT the central block's gable has a tripartite doorway opening onto a broad garden stair and is flanked on the l. by a drum tower crowned by a conical spire and on the r. by the S range's gable slightly stepped back. The E FRONT is plain.

STABLES, 80 m. E. Classical S front by *John Smith*, c. 1838–40. Tall pedimented central bay with segment-headed carriage arch and two first-floor windows, flanked by banded pilasters. Lower three-bay flanking ranges, ground floor much taller than first, with transom-lit doorways. End pavilions with segmental arches and blind first-floor panels.

POTTING SHED, 90 m. ESE. Picturesque, like a *cottage orné*, probably by *J. & W. Smith* c. 1847. Low granite ground floor lit by two small windows supports much taller timber-fronted first floor with tripartite lights corbelled out above. Steeply raked gable with finely carved bargeboards, pair of diagonally shafted chimneystacks to one side.

'DONKEY HOUSE', 190 m. SW. C17 or early C18. Former gazebo. Two-storey square-plan, coursed granite with bellcast pyramidal roof.

LEITH HALL
0.8 km. N of Kennethmont

5030

Few country houses have such a complex history as Leith Hall, and its development to some extent remains uncertain. The estate was seemingly purchased in the earlier C17 by John Leith and his wife, Marjorie Forbes. Tradition holds that 'Peill Castle' – perhaps simply a pele tower – existed then, but that their eldest son James began a new country house c. 1649. This stands on the N side of the present house, which is essentially a square quadrangle with an unusually small courtyard and which developed around an old barmkin. It had a W forecourt with corner pavilions until the mid C18.*

Whether the present E and S ranges incorporate any fabric of C17 'laigh biggings' is unclear; the original stables were on the S on a set-back building line. These ranges were built up only gradually. John Leith III (James's great-grandson) was apparently responsible, shortly after he inherited the estate in 1753, for raising the E range to two storeys, and for reconstructing the S range as kitchen quarters. Although both ranges were subsequently remodelled, their modest scale at that time is preserved in the symmetrical two-bay piend-roofed pavilions of that date at all four corners of the quadrangle. In 1789 John's son Alexander inherited Rannes in Banffshire from his maternal great-uncle, the Jacobite Andrew Hay, and then a Tobago plantation from his cousin Elizabeth Leith, the latter being sold for the colossal sum of £29,000. This double windfall allowed Alexander, having taken the name Leith-Hay, to substantially remodel Leith Hall. First the S range was increased to its present three storeys, work being completed in 1797; then the E range was radically rebuilt to three storeys only a few years later, the original N range being relegated to service quarters. The W range, originally no more than a screen wall with a central gateway, was seemingly deepened to provide service accommodation, and was given a crenellated parapet. It assumed its final form in 1868 when Alexander's grandson, also Alexander, reconstructed it with a very tall first floor to provide what is now the music room. His nephew Charles Leith-Hay added the present E porch and small drum towers on

---

*The S side of the forecourt has been excavated and the footings of its S pavilion found.

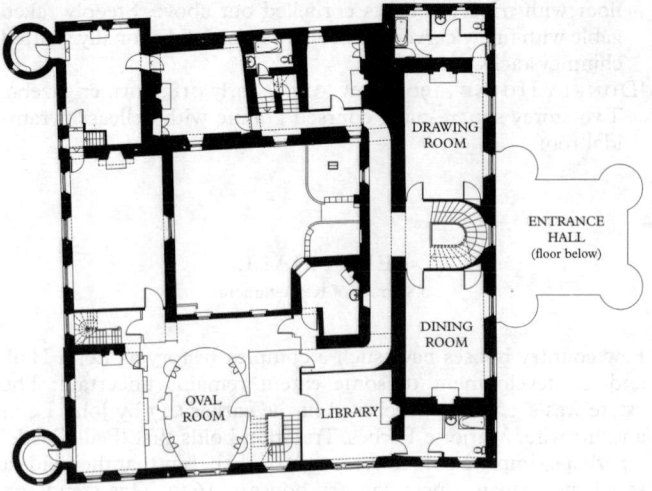

Leith Hall.
First-floor plan

the w c. 1900–6, probably with *Thomas Archibald* of Huntly as his architect (cf. Rannes Public Hall at Kennethmont).

As a result of Leith Hall's protracted development, its four main elevations are each quite different in their architecture, but its compact form, consistent scale, uniform harling and early C20 attempts to complement what existed before result in a house which is both unified and picturesquely varied in design.

55   The N RANGE remodelled by James Leith in the later C17 is four-storeyed with dormerheads rising into a tall gabled roof. It was seemingly always a simple narrow rectangle, all four corners having small round turrets corbelled out from the angles and crowned by conical spirelets. Its entrance front was on the s side. The central doorway has dressed sandstone jambs but its lintel is concealed under harling; small oblong windows above it light the scale-and-platt stairway within. The ground floor which contained the services is lit only by slit-windows, imply-ing that defence was still a consideration, the kitchen hearth being at the E end; on the upper levels the windows lighting the rooms in the outer bays are surprisingly close to the ends, those on the third floor having risen through the wall-head into gabled stone dormers which seemingly survived into the mid-C19 or later. On the N elevation the outer windows are comparatively near the central stair; the finialled third-floor dormers are later, c. 1898 or after.

On plan the house is somewhat unusual for its date in having no entrance jamb and in being a parallelogram rather than rectangular, a characteristic of earlier tower houses such as

Pitsligo (N), but there is nothing to indicate it being of more than one build. The scale-and-platt stair within is a parallelogram on a different alignment from the gables, orientated NNW and SSE and dividing the upper floors into an irregularly shaped room on either side at each level. Although less elaborate it has parallels with the near-contemporary scale-and-platt stair at Glenkindie (q.v.), the family seat of James Leith's wife, Margaret Strachan. At third floor the stair's side walls incorporate fireplaces and flues breaking through the roof into the two central chimneystacks.

The E RANGE, completed *c.* 1800–5, acknowledges its building history less obviously, the original small-scale build being evident only at ground floor. Plain vernacular classical, it is three-storeyed and five windows wide with central staircase windows at intermediate levels, a dentilled cornice, piended roof and very tall ashlar chimneystacks rising from the end gables. Its large single-storey porch of *c.* 1900–6 replaced a much shallower predecessor in the same idiom. Drum towers with conical spirelets flank the studded timber doors, and above a rope moulding the Leith arms with supporters – two bearded male nudes with clubs – are framed by elaborate scrolls with thistle and rose in the spandrels; smaller quarter-drums fill the angles with the main frontage. In the drum to the r. of the entrance a sculpted panel represents the portrait-head of a Renaissance gentleman.* The porch's design, and that of its predecessor, recalls that at Fyvie (N) as first built. The very tall first-floor windows light two principal apartments – the Dining and Drawing Rooms – and the second-floor windows rise right up to the eaves. At each end, the low two-storey corner pavilions have been inset with wide-mouthed shot-holes. The NE pavilion incorporates windows of C16 date, which have been reused.

The S RANGE, which assumed its final form in 1797, is again of three storeys but only three bays. It has single windows in the centre lighting the S stair and tripartite windows in blocky surrounds at the ends, those at first floor (the Library and Oval Room) being Serlians with simple flush pediments. At second floor small turrets with conical spirelets convincingly echo those at the N block but they are actually dummies containing no rooms inside, designed to make the house symmetrical as seen from the W. At the gabled roof the attics are lit by a pair of plain stone dormers, antique-looking but earlier C20.

The W RANGE is different again, raised to its present form in 1868 and closing the court, hitherto open on this side at its upper levels. The architects were perhaps *A. & W. Reid & Melven*, who carried out further work at Leith Hall in 1875. Its central segment-headed gateway leading into the courtyard is framed by simple attached columns which support a

---

*This may be James Leith himself, perhaps re-set from the walled garden; or it may simply be an item of random architectural salvage, collected and built in by Charles Leith-Hay.

contrastingly elaborate curvilinear tympanum sculpted with the Leith arms and supporters, the gate itself being a simple wrought-iron grid. The tall first-floor windows reflect the height of the Music Room, while above a very slim moulded gutter-cornice the second-floor windows break through the wall-head as scrolled and finialled dormer gablets. Re-set into the wall above the gateway are two old stones, a wasted shield-panel and further up a dormer gablet displaying a thistle, rose and harp. The roof is of shallower pitch than the others, its crowstepped gables having ball finials and coped chimney-heads. At the outer corners of the piend-roofed pavilions, two-storey drum towers with conical roofs were added c. 1900–6, their forms echoing the turrets of the N and S ranges; that on the S side has a re-set square panel, again carved with thistles.

The COURTYARD ELEVATIONS are irregular, most of the windows being of good size to maximize lighting of the rooms within. The E range has been deepened on this side by a two-storey extension, seemingly in existence by c. 1840. Porches give service access to the house in the NE, SE and SW corners; in the NW corner a panel displaying the arms and initials of Alexander Sebastian Leith-Hay and his wife, Christina Grace Agnes Hamilton, is dated 1868.

INTERIOR. The entrance area was once much more elaborate than it is now. Motivated by his cousin Alexander Forbes-Leith's lavish refitting of Fyvie (N), Charles Leith-Hay had been buying antique woodwork for some years before he inherited in 1900. His new ENTRANCE HALL still has its recycled panelled ceiling on reeded cross-beams; the round-headed niches with alabaster vases are a survival from the previous entrance hall. Similarly enriched with antique oak was the INNER HALL in the NE corner of the E block, but most of this was stripped out as an aberration of good taste c. 1970. The later C17 oak chimneypiece of the inner hall, Continental Baroque with caryatid figures and an armorial panel, was reinstated in 2014. The screen of plain Doric columns at the S end of the inner hall dates from the redecoration of c. 1970, a guess at what might have been there before Charles Leith-Hay installed slim Baroque columns adapted from antique bed-posts. Beyond the inner hall Leith-Hay made fewer changes, the interiors of the E and S ranges being still essentially mid-Georgian. The tightly planned but graceful E STAIR is very simple with plain cast-iron balusters; at FIRST FLOOR it has Adamish plasterwork by good provincial craftsmen. Their hand is also to be seen in the principal apartments, which have shallow moulded friezes and cornices and Adam School wood-and-gesso fireplace surrounds with cast-iron registers by the *Carron Iron Co.* The DINING ROOM seems originally to have been to the N of the stair and the DRAWING ROOM to the S but at some point their rôles were reversed; both have panelled dadoes. All four pavilions have more modestly scaled rooms, that on the SE – bypassed by a vaulted corridor – having a coved ceiling. In the s range is the present LIBRARY with a large Serlian window, its chimneypiece recently reinstated; it was originally a bedroom with *en suite* bathroom and dressing room. Across the landing of the central s STAIRCASE, also recently reinstated after the removal of a lift, is the original library, the OVAL ROOM, which has an Adam School ceiling of uncertain date. It now has four round-arched china niches, but until *c.* 1960 there were bookcases with brass trellis-work doors, still extant and awaiting reinstatement.

The DESIGNED LANDSCAPE extends over almost 150 hectares, sheltered by Knockandy Hill to the N and enclosed by the B9002 to the E, s and w, with the Correen Hills and the Grampians beyond. William Roy's Highland Survey of 1747–55 shows the original N block of Leith Hall enclosed by a rectangle of trees and another rectangle (perhaps Craigfall Wood) lying to the NE.

The policies originate from the mid 1750s when the house was remodelled by John Leith III. A survey of 1758 shows the tree-lined W DRIVE and the N–S DRIVE which, crossing it at right angles, links the stables to St Alkmund's Churchyard (*see* Kennethmont). The STABLES (180 m. N) dated I.L. 1754 are a half-circle on plan, harled single-storey-and-loft with three segment-headed key-blocked doorways arranged not quite symmetrically and a tall piended roof. The 1758 proposals suggest that the stables were intended to be balanced by another half-circle, so creating a complete circle bisected by a central driveway: this however was not built, probably because of John Leith III's unexpected death and subsequent financial collapse of the estate. Lying immediately to the SW, what is now known as the EAST GARDEN also dates from this period, the present walled garden to its w not being formed until much later (*see* below). The house must once have had walled gardens close to it but these had been completely removed by the mid C18 to create an up-to-date formal landscape.

In 1797 *George Brown* produced a plan proposing that the mid-C18 formal layout should be transformed into open PARK-LAND. In the event this parkland was extended only as far westwards as the N–S drive; to the E it was planted with clumps of sycamore and beech, and SHELTER BELTS were created following the landscape contours. The N and E shelter belts have been commercially replanted with Scots pine and spruce, but those to the s and w still incorporate some C18 planting. Further afield the surrounding farmlands were cleared, drained and enclosed, and a new village established at Kennethmont (q.v.), the parish church being demolished after a replacement was built in the new village in 1812. Also of this period is the HOME FARM STEADING (630 m. NE), a plain quadrangular courtyard built in rubble, its long principal front single-storey-and-loft with a three-stage entrance tower lit by a Gothic first-floor window rising above a square clock face into a crenellated parapet. It is doubtful whether Brown's walled garden (N of the present one) was ever built, and his intention of clearing the East Garden was not carried out. His E DRIVE was eventually formed *c.* 1834, prompted by a new turnpike, and the UPPER or EAST POND (0.6 km. SE) is in a different situation from that proposed. The egg-shaped ICE HOUSE (280 m. SSE) first appears in a survey of 1847.

The Great North of Scotland Railway's route through the policies was built in 1852–4. A handsome BRIDGE (0.5 km. SE) designed by *Alexander Gibb* (of *Alexander McKinnon & Co.*, Aberdeen) or perhaps by his brother-in-law, *William Smith*, carries the E drive over the track on a semi-elliptical skew arch beautifully executed in granite ashlar; its parapets are balustraded at the centre and slightly splayed towards the ends. The railway was subsequently hidden by planting, the views to the S being lost for ever. The WEST LODGE (420 m. W, on the B9002) and GARDENER'S COTTAGE (360 m. NW) were both built in the later C19, as was the EAST LODGE (1 km. SE, on the B9002).

The GATES themselves however are early C20, designed by *Charles Leith-Hay*, who was responsible for further developments in the policies *c.* 1900–6, these again coinciding with alterations to the house. It was he who designed the WEST or WALLED GARDEN (200 m. NW) which, on ground rising gently to the N, is divided N–S into two sections. It is entered from the W drive through square gatepiers on which sit two savage feline beasties. A pathway leads to the W section's central focus, a rockery which has been restored in 2015 to the form which Leith-Hay created in the 1920s.* Leith-Hay's CHINESE MOON-GATE – a circular gateway opening of 1900, approached by stairs with two fine vases – survives in the N wall. His wrought-iron gates were made by *Mackenzie*, a local blacksmith. Nearby, the LOWER or WEST POND (0.3 km. SE) was excavated by hand and planted under his supervision, its BOATHOUSE of distinctly rustic character. Two BRIDGES on the E drive are again his work, their circular termini with conical caps echoing the drum towers and turrets of the house itself.

In niches either side of the entrance to the WEST WALLED GARDEN are two notable PICTISH STONES, recovered from elsewhere on the Leith-Hay estates. The WOLF STONE was found at Newbigging Farm, Leslie *c.* 1841, and built into a dyke where part of it was broken off; it was retrieved *c.* 1860. It is carved with decorated rectangles and a mirror-and-comb (possibly C6), but takes its name from a very fine naturalistic representation of a wolf (probably late C7–early C8), a creature featured only rarely in Pictish art. The SALMON or PERCYLIEU STONE was found complete within a 'paved structure' at Hillhead of Clatt before 1840, but had been trimmed for construction purposes by 1844. Two fins are just visible at the top,

*See *Country Life*, 12 March 1938.

probably late C7; the main feature however is a decorated arc or horseshoe. The niches were formed *c.* 1914–20.

LEOCHEL-CUSHNIE

PARISH CHURCH. Originally built 1797–8 but substantially remodelled by *A. Marshall Mackenzie* (of *Matthews & Mackenzie*) in 1878–9. Very plain. Tall broad W gable harled in gold with granite quoins and margins, its gableted bellcote added by Mackenzie, who also built the double-height granite ashlar porch. It contains a stair lit by a two-light window with roundel plate tracery. The church's four-bay N and S sides are lit by round-arched windows with simple Y-tracery: the taller windows rising into gables over the W bay are Mackenzie alterations to improve the lighting of his gallery. E gable wheel window, small vestry on N. Bell from St Marnoch's church, Kirkton of Leochel, by *John Mowat* of Old Aberdeen, 1754. Interior reordered by *Mackenzie*. Gallery at W end, platform PULPIT at E with canted front, twisted baluster railings and low back-board.

Former PARISH MANSE. Built 1797–8. Two-storeyed, three windows wide. Harled, gabled roof with moulded skewputts, stone ridge and simply coped end stacks. Porch with overhanging eaves and windows with slim margin-panes added *c.* 1870. Piend-roofed rear wing forming L-plan and well-preserved STEADING complete with threshing machine.

At KIRKTON OF CUSHNIE, 2.1 km. W, the ruins of ST BRIDE'S CHURCH. Rectangular plan, rubble-built, 20 m. by 6 m. Apparently medieval but dressed quoins show it was heightened, probably in 1637, a date once recorded on a skewputt. Only its E gable with small transomed window survives to full height. The chamfered doorway was at the W end of the S flank.

At KIRKTON OF LEOCHEL, 2.5 km. ESE, ST MARNOCH'S CHURCH. C17, 'in bad repair' by the late C18. Only the W gable with its tall transomed window and ball-finialled birdcage bellcote survives to full height. Simple N aisle with stairs to subterranean burial vault. Some good stones, two carved with jolly reapers; table tombs and railed enclosures.

OLD HOUSE OF CUSHNIE (Cushnie Lodge), 0.75 km. NW of the Parish Church. Vernacular house for Alexander Lumsden and Elizabeth Leith, 1707, much remodelled. Entrance front facing SE is two storeys and five windows wide with central crowstepped attic gable which has lost its chimneyhead. The two l. windows are restorations replacing C19 tripartites but their proportions do not match the originals. Rear wing forms a T-plan, with the quartered arms of Lumsden and Leith re-set over the back door. Harled with margins, previously harl-pointed.

OLD MAINS OF CUSHNIE, 0.2 km. W of the Old House. Perhaps late C17, much modified. Low two-storey steading, with gablet dormerheads, built in field rubble; side wing later. In one end a preserved dormer gablet bearing the Lumsden arms.

MAINS OF HALLHEAD, 1.75 km. s of the Parish Church. The transition point between small tower house and country house. Built by a descendant of the Gordons of Ruthven (q.v.), its date (on the door jambs, now illegible) variously given as 1668, 1686 or 1688. T-plan entrance front, the two-storey three-bay main block with a central three-storey entrance jamb projecting to the E. The jamb has a roll-moulded doorway in its s flank and contains the main stair to first floor. A small turret corbelled in the re-entrant angle contains stairs to the attic and garret within the steeply pitched roofs. Single windows on each floor to l. and r. Plain rear elevation with only two windows of different sizes on each floor. The build is simple and somewhat rugged, harled with long and thin rough quoins, and crowstepped gables with coped chimneystacks. Some windows slightly enlarged and blocky over-scaled crowstepped dormers added during conversion as a farmhouse in 1866, but smaller chamfered lights still survive particularly at the jamb, gables and rear elevation. As illustrated by David MacGibbon, Hallhead was flanked by forecourt wings to N and s, both since lost. The carriage-shed arch with datestone I.G. M.R. 1703 and shot-hole survives but has been repositioned as part of the present steading, probably in the 1890s.

CRAIGIEVAR CASTLE. *See* p. 431.

LESLIE

A kirkton; a 'kirk of Lesselyn' is first recorded in 1257. Created a burgh of barony in 1649.

PARISH CHURCH. Designed by two Aberdeen master masons, *William Littlejohn* and *Peter Nicol*, and built by *John Watt*, mason in Huntly, with *Alexander Pittendrich*, carpenter, Kirkhill of Kennethmont. Opened in 1815, but very similar in spirit to Keithhall Church (q.v.) of 1772. Rectangular on plan: each gable originally had a doorway and square gallery window. w end with a finely carved bellcote initialled I.F.L. for John Forbes of Leslie and M.J.D. for James Douglas the minister, dated 1635 (bell by *Michael Burgerhuys*, 1642). Smaller windows were formed each side of the w doorway probably when the E door was blocked during the church's reordering by *A. Marshall Mackenzie* in 1897. Long s flank with only two square-headed windows, N flank blind.

Former PARISH MANSE, 50 m. SSE. Built 1794–5. Two storeys, three bays broadly spaced over a semi-sunk basement, doorway approached by a railed flyover stair; ground-floor windows enlarged as tripartites 1878–9. Harled rubble, slim ashlar dressings; projecting rear stair bay extended as back wing, seemingly before 1879.

Former DUNCANSTONE CONGREGATIONAL CHURCH, 2.8 km. NW. Dated 1820. W gable has pointed-arch doorway and tiny bellcote with cruciform finial, E gable with twin lancets and date of alterations in 1871, three-bay flanks; diamond-pane glazing throughout.

Former LESLIE & PREMNAY FREE CHURCH, 1.2 km. E. Simple Gothic gable front with slightly projected centre rising into a bellcote, rebuilt 1876, much altered in conversion to domestic use. It replaced a church by *James Henderson* of 1844; his small MANSE (1845) survives.

LESLIE CASTLE
0.25 km. NE of the church

Almost the last tower house to be built in Aberdeenshire, begun in 1661 for William Forbes, into whose family the Barony of Leslie had come by marriage; one of its dormers is dated 1664. It is unusually sophisticated both in its external form and in its internal plan and construction.

Leslie Castle is a stepped L-plan. It differs from most other L-plan towers in not having different floor levels in its jamb, being four storeys throughout with gables of the same 4 m. width on the W and S, and a stairwell 2 m. square in the re-entrant angle. The N elevation is 8.8 m. long, and the E elevation 7.5 m. The ground floor is still almost solid with only slit-windows and wide-mouthed shot-holes, but the first-floor principal apartments have large windows which were formerly barred, those at second floor being slightly smaller and those at third floor smaller again, breaking up through the wall-head beneath pedimental dormer gablets. Small pepperpot turrets with tall fish-scale-slated spirelets frame the twin attic windows of the gables. The tall stair-tower is entered through a moulded doorway on its S side and rises through six storeys into a solid parapet and spirelet turret stair at its NE angle. Above the doorway is the motto *Haec corp sydera mentem* ('Here the body, in the stars the mind') while the Forbes arms appear in several places; very slim splayed windows are inserted in the angle between the stair-tower and W wing. The late date is particularly evident in the straight rather than crowstepped gables and the diagonally shafted chimneystacks, a motif of English origin. Its construction is in harled rubble, with ashlar dressings in the distinctive reddish-gold granite found near Bennachie.

The PLAN AND CONSTRUCTION are very unusual since the scale-and-platt stair does not intrude on the accommodation within the wings as in a conventional L-plan, but rises in its tower to third-floor level with small turnpike stairs to the upper rooms and parapet. Very remarkably, the stair seemingly contained a fireplace in the base of its hollow newel to mitigate

the draught of its doorway and ensure that heat rose throughout the house. The ground floor is vaulted in four compartments with a service corridor behind the stair, the kitchen
occupying the NE compartment being well equipped with
water trough, sink and drain. The first floor contains a sequence
of three principal apartments: the hall in the W wing, with its
fireplace at the W gable furthest away from the stairs; a smaller
drawing room almost square on plan within the angle, and like
the hall linked by a stair direct to the wine cellar; then in the
SE wing the laird's chamber, slightly smaller again, with a
vaulted safe in its SE corner. Both the hall and the laird's
chamber could be reached directly off the main stair.

The castle, its western outer court and the eastern garden
were formerly enclosed by a much earlier moat, 68 m. E–W by
60 m. N–S. This had an oblong gatehouse and drawbridge
dated 1663 on the W side, still fairly complete when James Giles
drew it in 1840. Notwithstanding its sophisticated planning,
the castle had by then been stripped to a shell and the top of
its stair-tower lost. Its RESTORATION was undertaken between
1979 and 1989 by *David Leslie* and his wife *Leslie Leslie*, who
personally engaged in the work with the assistance of the
master mason *Slessor Troup*. Their plain parapet is conjectural
– the original having perhaps been balustraded as at Craigievar
(q.v.) and Innes House (Moray).

LESMOIR see RHYNIE

6020

LICKLEYHEAD CASTLE
5 km. NNE of Keig

A tower house begun in the 1560s for a Forbes of Monymusk
(q.v.), and remodelled in 1629; the distinctive Scots Renaissance
treatment of its upperworks, particularly on the longer N and W
flanks, suggests the hand of the *Bell* family of master masons. Its
development has been the subject of speculation. Ian Shepherd
ascribed the basic L-plan structure to the later C16, but Harry
Gordon Slade, in one of his earliest writings, concluded that the
main block had been a rectangular tower house of *c.* 1560 with
its doorway at first floor, and that the SW entrance jamb was part
of the 1629 works, on the grounds that the SE turnpike stair did
not rise from ground floor. However *c.* 1560 seems improbably
late for a rectangular tower such as he envisaged, and the resemblance to Balfluig (q.v.), also built for a Forbes of Monymusk,
appears too close to be discounted, notwithstanding that
Lickleyhead has square rather than rounded angles and a more
advanced stair arrangement. It has also been suggested that as
remodelled in 1629 Lickleyhead may have been a U-plan, its SE
jamb being lost when the SE wing was added in the mid C18, but
of that there is no visible evidence.

The ENTRANCE FRONT comprises the main block, 10.5 m. by 7.5 m., which is three storeys with dormerheads in its tall slated roof, and the SW entrance jamb, 5.2 m. square, which is significantly taller at four storeys and attic, its crowstepped gable very austere in appearance with small windows on its r. side only. Both the main block and jamb, however, share the same roof-ridge height. Within the main block, a single large first-floor window lights the hall; above it, a smaller second-floor window breaks through the wall-head as a gableted dormer with scrolls and thistle finials. Above the jamb's boldly moulded doorway within the re-entrant is an empty field-panel, once distinguished by heraldic sculpture, with initials V.F. M.S. for William Forbes and Margaret Skene, and date 1629. The mid-C18 WING, of two modest storeys, is however 16 m. long and a generously spaced four windows wide; its extension to T-plan on the E side c. 1825 to provide a new kitchen is similar in style, and results in a second L-plan frontage, a much lower echo of the old tower house.

The N and W ELEVATIONS are richer. On the N the main block has two windows lighting the hall as at Balfluig and two second-floor dormers, one with gablet and one with hemicycle pediment. These are flanked by two-storey angle turrets lit by small square windows at second floor and oval windows at attic level beneath fish-scale-slated spirelets: intended as closets, their 'shot-hole' openings are really for ventilation. Corbelled out within the re-entrant angle formed between main block and jamb on this side, a stair-turret rises from first-floor level; the way it is curtailed just beneath the roof ridge clearly implies that its caphouse has been cut down, perhaps during the C18 alterations. Two-storey turrets, usually reserved for the very grandest houses, are a particular Bell motif: Lickleyhead's oval windows are also found at Castle Fraser (q.v.), and indeed at Glamis in Angus.

On PLAN the main block has walls 1 m. thick, but the jamb's are much thinner on its S and E sides. The main block's ground floor is vaulted with two cellars; it has a corridor on the S and a service stair in the western cellar's N wall. There is no kitchen hearth although the very thick E wall may have accommodated one. The three-quarter-turn wheel stair in the jamb is skilfully planned to admit of two small chambers as well as the turnpike stair to the upper floors at the first-floor platt. It opens into the 'low' end of the hall, the fireplace being at the 'high' end in the E gable, where there is a private turnpike to the eastern second- and third-floor apartments.

During Duff ownership in the earlier C18 the first and second floors were refitted, the hall being partitioned at its W end. The present 'Great Chamber' still retains its three-tier bolection-moulded wood panelling from that time, carefully restored in the early 1920s. More survives at second floor, but there the original single large bedchamber was divided into two rooms in the C19. Some of the SE wing's mid-C18 fielded panelling survives at first floor, but that part of the house was partly replanned in the C19 and C20 to provide the present drawing and dining rooms. Lickleyhead was 'inhabited, but much dilapidated' in 1842. It was restored *c.* 1876.

5010

LITTLEWOOD PARK

5 km. WSW of Tullynessle

By *George Bennett Mitchell*, 1930–2. A late Scots Renaissance country house built for Alan McLean M.P. after he purchased the estate from the Forbes family; it occupies the footprint of an Old English predecessor of the mid C19, reusing some of its fabric particularly at the E end. Asymmetric N ELEVATION is two storeys, its three broad bays breaking into crowstepped attic gables with coped chimneystacks; the centre and W bays are paired together with the E bay standing slightly separate. The house rises from a sunk basement area enclosed by a low stone parapet, its round-arched doorway being in a crenellated porch with bartizans; a small round turret with spirelet is corbelled out from the NW angle. Irregular fenestration, with astragalled sash-and-case windows, some mullioned and transomed. S ELEVATION overlooking the gardens stands rather taller, the basement fully exposed by the falling ground on this side. Broad crowstepped gables at each far end, that to the W with a two-storey SW turret; the E gable is slightly advanced, with a single-storey turret on the W and a large conical-roofed drum tower at the SE angle. The three intermediate bays have stone attic dormers with carved thistle finials. Fenestration more regular than N side, and detail simpler. E ELEVATION with crowstepped porch dated 1931 and large mullioned-and-transomed window, the latter reused from the previous house; W ELEVATION similar in style to S front. Pale golden harl with ashlar dressings throughout.

The plan of the interior is arranged round an axial corridor at each level, with the more important rooms on the S and the main and servants' stairs on the N. At ground floor the E porch opens into an outer hall panelled in oak, the corridor beyond linking together the principal apartments: the inner hall which is again oak-panelled with a recess in the SE drum tower and a stone fireplace with a deep hood; the drawing room with painted panelled walls and low-relief ceiling plasterwork in C17 style; and the dining room, its compartmented ceiling with egg-and-dart mouldings. The main stair, also in oak, has twisted balusters and ball finials over the newel posts. A similarly high finish prevails in the first-floor bedrooms. The kitchen and small servants' hall are in the basement, the games room having a red-brick fireplace with round-arched opening. All the fittings, from the iron door furniture to the former gun room's lockers, are notably well crafted.

WATER GARDEN. Laid out by *Gavin Jones Nurseries*, *c.* 1939. – EAST LODGE, 1 km. SSE (A944). Scots Renaissance, 1925.

LOGIE COLDSTONE

4000

Logie Coldstone parish was formed in 1618 when Logie-Mar was annexed to Coldstone, but the village was not founded until 1780 when a new church was built roughly midway between its two predecessors.

Former PARISH CHURCH. Now converted for domestic use. Begun as a simple rectangle in 1780–1, reconstructed and heightened with a new NW tower, porch and vestry in 1875–7 by *William Duguid & Sons*, builders of Ballater, whose plans were revised by *Alexander Ogilvy*. It is nevertheless of consistent appearance in squared golden rubble. Crowstepped end gables, the original W entrance now within a porch; the E entrance survives, with a round-arched gallery window over. S flank almost entirely rebuilt in the 1870s with four taller round-arched windows, Lombardic tracery. Square NW tower of four stages with bellcast pyramidal spire, slated with gableted lucarnes. It is Rhenish rather than Scottish and secular rather than ecclesiastical in character.

COLDSTONE CHURCHYARD, 1.3 km. N. A prebend of Aberdeen, the church (removed in the late C17) was dedicated to St Neachtan or St Walloch. Near the gate a tall Celtic CROSS on plinth and pedestal to Col. Sir John Farquharson of Corrachree (Tarland, q.v.), R.E. (†1905). He was director of the Ordnance Survey 1894–9.

Former COLDSTONE PARISH MANSE, 150 m. SW of Coldstone Churchyard. Built 1803. Two-storey three bays broadly spaced, harled with gabled roof and coped ashlar chimneystacks. Gableted porch with elegant transom-light added 1826. Predecessor manse of 1783 and further addition of 1826 at rear. Inside a handsome stair with cast-iron balusters. OFFICES. Begun 1793–4, extended into an irregular E-plan. WALLED GARDEN approximately semicircular.

LOGIE CHURCHYARD, Galton, 2 km. S. Site of St Walloch's church (closed *c.* 1780), of which no clear trace remains. ST WOLOCH'S STONE, an upright granite slab 1.6 m. high, displays no obvious markings but indicates a site of great antiquity.

BLELACK HOUSE, 1 km. SSE. Dated 1881 and 1892, presumably built for William Coltman, son of the judge Sir Thomas Coltman, who bought the estate in 1865. A very upright shooting lodge, rubble-built and rather severe. Tall three-storey three-bay front, with gabled and dormered attic. Double-pile plan, the S range longer than the N, with a square tower rising into a pyramid spirelet recessed in the angle between them. The lower E wing is perhaps a remnant of the house burnt in 1850.

HOPEWELL LODGE, 2.3 km. NE. Built for Dr Andrew Robertson, Commissioner to Queen Victoria and the Prince of Wales on the Balmoral and Abergeldie estates (qq.v.). A Picturesque villa of *c.* 1870, standing on a terrace looking over a steeply sloping landscape. Entrance (S) front two storeys and four bays with near-symmetrical gable fronts at either end, that on the l. projecting with a timber porch in the angle. Canted ground-floor bay window on W, shallow rectangular bay on E, Tudor hoodmoulds over first-floor windows. Grey granite, with pink granite quoins and chamfered window surrounds, shouldered at lintels; steeply pitched roofs with timber bracketed eaves and tall single diagonal chimneystacks, clustered stacks rising from behind the roof ridge. Complex double-pile plan, the N front overlooking a courtyard. Opposite, the STEADING, now in domestic use. Asymmetric single storey in coursed squared masonry with two gabled bays slightly projecting: the one which contained the gig house is crowned with a bellcote. In the WALLED GARDEN, an octagonal SUMMERHOUSE with swept prismatic roof.

MELGUM LODGE, 3.5 km. ENE. By *George Bennett Mitchell c.* 1910. A large two-storey villa with a jettied half-timbered superstructure, its low gables Continental rather than English in character. Entrance front facing W, central tripartite doorway in oak with small-paned leaded glass sheltered under the deep canopy on elaborate metal brackets. Canted four-light bay window on l. in ashlar contrasting against white harl. N and S elevations taller, again with low-pitched gables: S side has a porch overlooking the steeply falling garden. Long and slightly lower two-storey service wing in same idiom projecting from the E.

TILLYPRONIE HOUSE. *See* p. 750.

LOGIE DURNO *see* PITCAPLE

7020

LOGIE HOUSE
1.7 km. WNW of Pitcaple

A vernacular house built for James Elphinstone *c.* 1677–80 which has been enclosed on three sides by a later classical house progressively built around it during the mid and late C18: the original entrance front, facing E, now overlooks an open court with an arched gateway. The vernacular house is of particular interest since it incorporates some features of both the tower house tradition and the early classical tradition. The entrance front would once seem to have resembled that of Kinnaber

House in Angus: a tall three-storey main block with regular fenestration four – probably originally five – windows wide, and a plain wall-head and gabled roof with end stacks, the original stair (since gutted out) having been a turnpike within the drum tower which stands at the r.-hand (NE) angle. It is however possible that before the main block was extended to the S in the mid-C18, there was a matching SE tower resulting in a symmetrical frontage. Although of the same height as the main block, the mid-C18 extension comprises only two much taller storeys with a three-windows-wide bow as its S gable overlooking the Don. The long two-storey COURTYARD wings projecting on each side are of different dates, entered through a GATEWAY with a round-headed opening at the far E end. The N WING, hinged to the round tower, is of c. 1740. The much-modified S WING which projects from the extended main block is c. 1760. Until the late C18, however, the entrance front remained that of the original house, on the E side within its forecourt.

The present main entrance front, the W ELEVATION, is classical, two storeys and three bays broadly spaced. Its pedimented centre projects slightly and rises higher into the piended roof with twin central stacks. It is however of more than one build, with differences in the roofs, the masonry and formerly the plasterwork suggesting that the S bay was built first and the centre and N bays very shortly after: until 1975 the S bay had a separate pavilion roof. Perhaps because of this two-stage build, reflecting the original E–W orientation of the S bay, or perhaps simply reflecting the development of house-planning in the later C18, the W range is notably deep on plan, much more so than the house of 1680. There are single-storey canted bays with semi-prismatic roofs at both end gables. A crenellated Victorian battlemented porch encloses the original doorway and some alterations were made in the courtyard at the same date. These alterations were reversed after fire damage in 1975, when several of the upper floors collapsed and the fine plaster ceilings in the dining and drawing rooms were lost. Although the N wing was very quickly returned to habitable condition, the remainder of the house was only restored by *Tansy Grigor-Taylor* in the early C21. Five ARMORIAL PANELS have been re-set, three above the gateway arch, one into a porch on the house's N side, and one inside. Among these one has a chevron and bishop's mitre between three boar's heads for Elphinstone, and a chevron and crescent (or hunting horn?) between three crane's heads for Denholm; another has three hunting horns for Dalrymple Horn Elphinstone; and a third has a saltire surmounted by lozenges, flanked by initials M.

In the grounds are three PICTISH SYMBOL STONES, found on the Moor of Carden. The largest is carved with a crescent and V-rod and double-disc and Z-rod, both of which have been imposed on a double-disc carved at an earlier date. Above these is a circular ogham inscription. Another stone has a double-disc and crescent and V-rod and the third a crescent and V-rod and a 'Pictish beast'. (GN)

LUMPHANAN

Llan-Finnan – Finan's Church – began as a kirkton on the Cairn O'Mount Road, now A980. The Peel Bog of Lumphanan and the church (*see* below) lying to the w were cut off when the Deeside Railway's Aboyne extension opened a station in 1859. This spurred growth of a separate village and led to the forma-tion of STATION SQUARE. The STATION HOTEL is a simple two-storey three-bay frontage, white-harled with ashlar gable stacks and a bay window in one flank. Next to it the OLD POST OFFICE, also two-storeyed but arcaded at ground floor. Both were designed in 1860 by *John Stuart* of Muchalls. The former ABERDEEN TOWN & COUNTY BANK is by *William Smith* c. 1867, like a single-storey basement and attic villa with a distyle Doric portico and flanking canted bays. On the Cairn O'Mount Road, the PARISH HALL is by the local builder *George Spark*, 1897–8; the SCHOOL nearby, c. 1960, reflects Lumphanan's growth with COUNCIL HOUSING to the E and w, and its exten-sion c. 2000 further residential development to the s.

Former PARISH CHURCH, 0.7 km. sw. On a knoll overlooking the Lumphanan Burn, reputedly occupying the site of an earlier church first recorded in 1238. Built in 1762, it was reordered internally in 1795, then 'repaired and enlarged' by *James Matthews* in 1851. Simple rectangular plan in coursed squared rubble, formerly harled. s flank with four tall narrow windows in chamfered surrounds. End gables each with narrow chamfered doorway and gallery window. Three N windows, all with diamond-pane glazing and timber tracery with cusped heads, clearly part of Matthews's remodelling. The moulded skewputts are also his, as is the simple Baroque bellcote over the w end with its segmental key-blocked opening, hemicycle pediments and spiked ball finials.

Former PARISH MANSE. Essentially mid-C19 in character but the central block was built in 1782, originally three storeys facing s, but afterwards reduced to two, with a taller first floor. Two gable-fronted s wings were added in 1828–9 by *John Smith*, but only the sw wing survives. NE wing of 1869 by *George Spark*, plans revised by *James Thomson* of Crathes. OFFICES of same date, the taller two-storey block at the s end having originally been a watch house.

Former STOTHERT MEMORIAL CHURCH, Glen Road, on a prominent rise of ground looking s over the village. Designed by *William Henderson & Son*, 1869–70, it replaced a Free Church (1844) which stood 300 m. E. Predominantly First Pointed, some elements perhaps reused from the previous church. Entrance tower in granite ashlar with pointed doorway and hoodmould, large window with archaic timber tracery, clock dial in lozenge panel and angle buttresses progressively intaken, rising into a broached ashlar spire with lucarnes on alternate sides. Behind it a harled gable, again with ashlar diagonal buttresses, and lit by lancets. Plain flanks each with four closely spaced lancets, perp window in the chancel. Spacious interior with open kingpost roof supported on corbels, s gallery and chancel arch framed by slim clustered colonnettes. Leaded diamond-pane windows with slim margins and original furnishings still in place. – Classical wall tablets to the Rev. Thomas Stothert (†1893) and his wife, Helen Lundin Brown (†1880) by *Macdonald & Co.*

MANSE, 50 m. E, also by the *Hendersons*. Two-storey harled L-plan frontage of 1867–9; its projecting gable on the l. has a canted bay in timber.

PEEL BOG OF LUMPHANAN, 1 km. SW. Probably C13, raised by the de Lundins (Durwards) to defend a strategic route into Moray. In excellent condition, it comprises a natural mound formed into a motte 45.7 m. in length NE–SW and 36.6 m. in breadth NW–SE, its summit once defended by a turf rampart or timber palisade. The motte rises 9 m. above an encompassing ditch, *c.* 15 m. wide, which was flooded from the Lumphanan Burn as a 'bog' or moat. This moat was retained around its outer circumference by an earthen bank 3 m. high and 2.5 m. wide across its top, with seemingly another shallower ditch (itself 3 m. wide) running around outside this. Entrance was apparently by a cobbled causeway on the NE, although the defences are also breached on the W; remains of what was believed to be the moat's sluice system and the position of the drawbridge were exposed during the Great Flood of 1829. Edward I reputedly received the submission here of Sir John de Malvill of Raith in 1296; afterwards Robert Bruce granted it to Duncan, Earl of Fife but by *c.* 1330 when it passed to the Garviachs of Caskieben (*see* Keith Hall) it had evidently declined in importance or been abandoned. It was reoccupied when Thomas Charteris of Kinfauns built a MANOR HOUSE after he was granted the lands of Ha'ton Peill, Pitmurchie and Craiganmore in 1487: its footings show that it was rectangular, *c.* 15 m. by 3.5 m. internally. It was demolished in 1768, its stones reused by a 'zealous agriculturalist' to build a dyke around the summit and local houses.

AUCHLOSSAN HOUSE, 2.6 km. SSW. Early vernacular classical, *c.* 1700 for the Rosses of Auchlossan, a member of the first generation of country houses in North-East Scotland. Entrance front facing S, two storeys, five bays very broadly spaced, central doorway (now within a sun-lounge) and large square field-panel which once contained heraldic arms above. Small round shot-holes at ground floor and first floor. Astragalled sash-and-case windows set in slim chamfered granite surrounds against a background of harl. Gabled roof with stone ridge, pronounced skews rise into coped ashlar chimneystacks.

Interior remodelled *c.* 1790–1800, but one fine bolection-moulded fireplace survives.

CAMPHILL HOUSE, 3.5 km. NNW. Two-storey front, three windows wide in pink ashlar granite with gabled roof and coped stacks, dated 1827 at its skews, similar in character to the manse (*see* above). Recessed timber tripartite doorpiece, ground-floor canted bays and canted attic dormers later. Asymmetric single-storey-and-attic wings, that on the r. added recently. Inside, the dining room contains three murals by *George Melvin Rennie*, dated 1914.

CORSE CASTLE, 4.5 km. NW. A ruinous small tower house built for William Forbes and his wife, Elizabeth Strachan of Thornton, in 1581. Constructed mostly in granite field rubble, it represents an interesting variation on the standard Z-plan. It comprised a three-storey main block approximately 11 m. long by 6.3 m. broad, orientated N–S, and a four-storey-and-attic SE entrance jamb 4.8 m. by 5.7 m., resulting in re-entrant flanks and end gables which are of near-equal length and breadth. At the main block's NW angle there was a second jamb, a drum tower 4 m. in diameter. A slimmer drum tower protruding from the centre of the S front is 3.4 m. in diameter and contains a turnpike stair. This unusual feature appears to be a result of Corse's modest dimensions; it is unlikely to have been an alteration.

Since the round NW drum tower has collapsed, and the partition walls have been gutted, the internal arrangements are not entirely clear. Within the main block the ground floor contained two apartments, a cellar to the S and a kitchen to the N with a deep hearth recess in its end gable. The first-floor hall was lit by three windows, one facing E, one S and another smaller one in the partly collapsed W flank. It had a modest fireplace in its E wall near the jamb, the flue of which is visible externally, being corbelled from the re-entrant angle as a chimney-breast. The jamb itself must once have contained the principal stair leading from the entrance to the hall; there appears to have been a small service room on its upper landing, on the jamb's N side. The jamb's ground floor is 1 m. lower on its S side to form a pit or guardroom beneath the stair's upper flight. The upper storeys were reached by the turnpike stair on the S flank. This rose from ground level, its first flight providing a service stair from the cellar to the hall. Thinner walls at second and third floor allowed the private accommodation on these upper levels to be much more generous, with fireplaces and window recesses still evident in the E gable; the third floor probably comprised part of Elizabeth Strachan's apartment.

Although of modest size Corse's remarkable plan form must have resulted in a notably picturesque skyline, enhanced by the angle turrets of its jamb and gables at different heights rising into broad coped chimneystacks. The initials of Forbes and his wife together with the date are carved in raised letters and numerals over the doorway, and above this are two empty field-panels, the upper one of which has an ogival top. The castle has two unusual features: a high-level wide-mouthed shot-hole covering the entrance from the service room, and, further up the jamb, two small lozenge openings at the Forbes's private chambers.

CORSE HOUSE, 4.8 km. NW. By *Alexander Ellis* for James Ochoncar Forbes of Craigievar (q.v.), 1863. An Italianate villa, essentially a two-storey T-plan comprising an E entrance front and a long block facing S which contains the principal apartments. The entrance front is asymmetrical, its slim central tower of four stages flanked on the l. by the broad end gable of the S front with a porch in the re-entrant angle, and two bays on the r. with a chimney-breast rising between them into a tall stack. The S front has a slightly recessed centre, the five round-headed arches of its central canted bay at ground floor echoed in the single windows of the broad end bays. White-harled with sparing grey granite details, low-pitched slate roofs with oversailing bracketed eaves. The interior is grander: the galleried hall is distinguished by Corinthian columns and the principal apartments all have fine plasterwork. The POLICIES including the walled garden a little W of the house were originally laid out by *James Giles*; the main outlook was once to a lake which has been drained.

FINDRACK HOUSE, 2.5 km. E. Begun as an C18 (?) farmhouse, extended into a small two-storey country house as a result of additions by *William Smith* after 1862, *c.* 1910 and again more recently. Entrance front facing E comprises (l.–r.) the gable of Smith's garden front, its SE corner restyled with a first-floor oculus *c.* 1910; the entrance tower, circular with a segmentally canopied Baroque doorpiece and ball-finialled conical roof; three bays with dormerheads over the first-floor windows, Smith perhaps remodelling earlier work; and the plain gable of the original small-windowed farmhouse. On the garden side *William Cowie* opened up a two-storey glass bay, in the 1980s.

GLENMILLAN HOUSE, 1.3 km. NE. Baronial by *James Matthews*, 1872, incorporating an earlier vernacular classical house. Matthews's principal front facing W is a two-storey L-plan with a three-storey drum tower in the re-entrant angle, the remodelled older house being on the r., and all harled with ashlar dressings. The drum tower has a transom-lit doorway, the field-panel carved with monogrammed initials and date. It is crowned by a corbel course and balustraded parapet accessed by a spirelet stair-turret in the angle with the old house. Matthews's NW wing is bigger in scale, its canted gable front having a large two-storey canted bay. The single exposed bay of the old house has an armorial panel between its ground- and first-floor windows, the latter with a Matthews pedimental dormerhead. Inside, C18 marble fireplaces in the old house; stained glass window on the stair commemorating Dr James Mackie. STABLES incorporate a tympanum dated 1688.

LUMSDEN

A late example of an improvement village, established *c.* 1825–30 by Henry Leith Lumsden of Clova (q.v.). It lies along a moorland ridge, sheltered by the Buck of Cabrach, with a single Main Street running 500 m. N–S, which skirts a Market Square on its E, a plan recalling Rhynie (q.v.). The village attracted 250 souls 'from all parts of the country' within a few years and by 1860, when a parish school was opened in the village, the population had stabilized at about 500.

AUCHINDOIR PARISH CHURCH, The Square. The former United Presbyterian Church by *R. Duncan* of Huntly, 1889–90. Robust W entrance front in hammer-dressed red sandstone with ashlar dressings, rising into a big curvilinear gable with scrolls and bellcote. Fractionally projected centre with polygonal entrance porch and trefoil roundel lighting the gallery. Simple but atmospheric interior. Stained pine woodwork including the canted timber-boarded ceiling and Duncan's high-backed PULPIT, CHOIR STALLS and PEWS remain in place.

LUTHERMUIR

Humble L-plan village developed by crofters in the early C19.

PARISH CHURCH, Church Road. Originally a Secessionist chapel built *c.* 1773. Near-square plan, the original low thatched roof removed in 1822 and the gables raised to present height. One lancet on each flank, given their present heads in 1888. Open bellcote with ogee top. Brick session house, late C19. Interior as restored in 1876, including the ceiling with trilobe vents. Very high GALLERY on the W. – Semi-hexagonal PULPIT with linenfold panelling and key-blocked, barley-twist balusters. – STAINED GLASS. Descending dove, *c.* 1911 (E oculus).
    MUIRTON HOUSE, 140 m. ESE. Formerly the manse. Harled original block by *David Reid*, 1847.
Former BEREAN CHAPEL, Sauchieburn, 1.5 km. NE. Large, simple rectangle with crumbling harling. It is the essence of simplicity, built 1773 for a Protestant sect which professed to base its beliefs on Scripture alone. E and W gables with just a rectangular doorway and a window to light the gallery. – TABLET on the W commemorating James Macrae, the first minister. – Former MANSE adjacent, mid-C19.
CALDHAME, 1.3 km. E, on the B974. On the wall of the steading are three re-set DORMERHEADS from a tower house built for the Barclay family in the mid-late C17. The l. has a coat of arms flanked by the initials A.B. and I.S. In the middle is the Barclay heraldic shield, formerly dated 1671. – BRIDGE,

200 m. SE. Three low segmental arches over the Luther Water, first built 1744 and reconstructed in 1783. Sculpted plaque on the S face with dated sill and lintel. Triangular cutwaters.

HATTON MAINS HOUSE, 2.4 km. ESE. Good, straightforward example of an early–mid-C18 laird's house. Two-storey U-plan, the original datestone of 1746 now covered by dingy brown harling. Square front porch added *c.* 1830. Good fielded wall panelling in the ground-floor study, dated 1742 with initials R.M. and P.M. for the Montgomery family, who owned it until *c.* 1920. – DOOCOT, 440 m. SSW. Steep crowstepped lectern, also mid C18, now roofless and in poor condition. Two chambers with nesting boxes separated by an internal wall.

MARYKIRK WAR MEMORIAL, 1.8 km. ESE, Crosspoles. 1921. Tall, flat slab of rough-hewn granite panels. Encircled cross at the top surrounded by Celtic knot work.

INGLISMALDIE CASTLE. *See* p. 546.

LYNTURK

6010

Former UNITED PRESBYTERIAN CHURCH. Built in 1865–6 but in the 'Heritors' Gothic' of thirty years earlier, similar to churches by *William Clarke* of Strichen (N). Entrance W gable with pointed doorway and slim flanking lancets, gallery window with timber Y-tracery; deep skewputts and a small pointed-arch birdcage bellcote with spike finial. Three-bay flanks also with Y-tracery, original small-paned glazing throughout. Small wheel window at E end above large rear outshot. Former MANSE, 1866. Neat two storeys, three windws wide, first-floor windows and canted dormers in gabled roof with astragalled sashes.

CASTLEKNOWE OF LYNTURK, 2.7 km. E. Early C19 farmhouse, probably for Peter McCombie, who bought the estate in 1816. Two storeys, three bays with small windows widely spaced, mid-C19 lying-pane glazing. Gabled roof with stone ridge and coped stacks. Stands on the site of a castle reputedly built by John Strachan in 1514, its ruins still surviving in 1792. Part of the defensive ditch remains, a plastered wall recess behind the house, and a gunloop re-set into the steading which, like the ruined SECESSION CHURCH of 1762 nearby, incorporates ancient masonry.

MANAR HOUSE

7020

4 km. N of Kemnay

Built by *John Smith* for a branch of the Gordons, dated 1811, similar in character to another Gordon house, Cortes (N,

1810), perhaps also his work.* A refined classical country house standing on the Hill of Manar's SE slopes, overlooking the Don valley. Two-storey entrance front, five bays broadly spaced, the central one minimally advanced with a generously proportioned distyle Greek Doric portico framing a tripartite doorway. The double-leaf doors are finely carved and the transom-light consists of interlocking circles. The tall ground-floor windows have been plate-glazed but the first floor retains its original astragals. Slim cornice and shallow blocking course over the centre bay, the gabled roof's long lines unbroken by its twin chimneystacks which are set back and very inconspicuous. The deep NE flank contains the principal apartments with a two-storey bow on the r. and slightly projecting bay (added later) on the l.

63   HOME FARM STEADING, 550 m. ENE, c. 1800–5. Single storey and attic with two-storey central bay containing a segment-headed pend and first-floor oculus rising into a curvilinear gable and bellcote in front of a low pyramid roof. Cream-harled with granite margins, the attic-floor windows in the wings now rise through the eaves as piend-roofed dormers. Square courtyard plan, with cartshed arcade in one flank, now converted to domestic use.

DOOCOT. C18. Circular, with high rat course and landing ledge. Conical roof with cupola.

EAST LODGE, 950 m. E. Built c. 1800. Ink-bottle type, circular with chimney poking up from the centre of its tall roof.

0090

MAR LODGE

5.75 km. WSW of Braemar

As illustrated in the late C18, the original Mar Lodge, known as Dalmore House, was built by William Duff, Lord Braco, 1st Earl Fife (1696–1763). He acquired the estate in the 1720s after it was forfeited by the 23rd (and 6th) Earl of Mar. It was a plain three-bay, two-storey gable-ended house, flanked by bow-fronted pavilion blocks on either side. It was a hunting seat for the Earls Fife. The Great Flood of 1829 caused severe damage to the structure, leading the Earl to migrate up the hill to the S to Corriemulzie (*see* below). Upon his marriage to Louise, granddaughter to Queen Victoria and later Princess Royal, the 6th Earl Fife was raised to the Dukedom in 1889. Thus, when Corriemulzie burnt down in 1895, the Duke rebuilt on a royal scale, near the site of Old Mar Lodge, down on the plain. The architect *A. Marshall Mackenzie* was recommended by Queen Victoria on account of his success at Crathie Parish Church, 1893–5 (q.v.).

p. 663

The result is an incongruous but pleasing surprise. The splayed U-plan house with half-timbered gables, mullion windows,

*The name derives from the Manner Estate in Ceylon (Sri Lanka).

Mar Lodge.
Engraving by C. Cordiner and P. Mazell, 1795

orange roof tiles and lofty chimneys looks like an enormous
Home Counties mock-Tudor villa. Apart from the rugged use
of pink rock-faced granite and the continuous tree-trunk
veranda (now removed) it scarcely speaks to its dramatic
setting from a distance. Close up, however, the detail is crisp
and uncluttered. The regular Aberdeen bond is only interrupted by a discreet winding string course, and a band of
darker pink granite halfway up the walls. What appears to be
white pebbledash between the half-timbering is an attractive
application of quartz mosaic. All principal rooms face outwards while a corridor down the spine of the building separates
the service wings and courtyard to the rear.

During restorations in 1991, when all the original furniture
had been removed from the house, the entire interior of the
central block was destroyed by fire. Insurance regulations
required an exact replica to be recreated, so the panelled
entrance hall, balustered staircase and stag-filled reception
rooms can still be enjoyed. However, the rest of the hunting
lodge was relatively plain and responded easily to conversion
to holiday apartments. The entire estate was acquired by the
National Trust for Scotland in 1995.

The BALLROOM, W of the Lodge, was originally erected for the
previous Mar Lodge at Corriemulzie but moved here in 1898.
It is a white weatherboarded shed covered in lattice trellis
painted the estate livery of dark red. Cast-iron gablets in the
roof provide ventilation. The interior is tongue-and-groove
panelled with an open timber-framed roof supporting over
2,000 stags' skulls and antlers, some of them trophies over 200
years old. An eerie sight. The STABLES are a fine clean design,
modestly reflecting the gables of the main house.

ST NINIAN'S CHAPEL (Episcopal), in the garden beside the house. 1898, by *A. Marshall Mackenzie*. Built as a private estate chapel for the Duke of Fife. Three-bay rectangular box with stone porch on SW end, Neo-Romanesque style. Exposed rough-cut granite externally and internally. Exposed hammerbeam roof. Although the architecture is plain, the chapel has an intense Anglo-Catholic feel, with painted panels of Stations of the Cross between the windows, and gilded reredos (possibly by *Kempe*) behind the brightly embroidered altar frontal. Under the granite steps to the altar is the burial vault for the Duke of Fife and his family, plainly designed by *William Kelly*, 1912. – STAINED GLASS. In this intimate space, the seven small windows produced by *Kempe & Co.*, 1912 (designed by *John William Lisle*), create an intense effect. E window, Resurrection; W window, Michael and the dragon; nave windows, angels with musical instruments.

DAIRY AND KEEPER'S COTTAGE, 1.4 km. ESE at Corriemulzie. All that remains of the buildings associated with the mansion built by Earl Fife after 1829 and destroyed in the fire of 1895. It was a holiday confection in woodland style, 'a rambling structure, between a Swiss chalet and an Indian bungalow': the wooden building was covered in a lattice trellis, verandas, balustrades and balconies made of tree trunks, and bargeboards framed with antlers. The weatherboarded dairy is octagonal with Gothic arched door and windows, and a bellcast octagonal roof supported by a rustic veranda. Inside, flagstone floor and slate work benches. The cottage preserves the lattice theme on two walls.

VICTORIA BRIDGE, 0.65 km. SE of the house, for the entrance drive across the Dee. Erected 1905, a lattice-girder frame with horseshoe arch over entrance but handrail from the bridge of 1848. GATE LODGE, originally a compact box with elliptical recesses framing the windows and doors, all in crisp ashlar, and with a lower roof-line. The overdeveloped stubby Ionic portico with pink granite monolith columns was a slightly later addition, resting upon the entrance steps. First mentioned in 1823 but possibly erected soon after the Earl Fife purchased the estate in 1785 and built the first bridge in 1788. Vastly ambitious for a tiny house, but an imposing foretaste to the C18 Mar Lodge across the bridge.

LINN OF DEE BRIDGE, 3.5 km. W along the Dee. 1857, by *A. & W. Reid*. Sited over a most dramatic cleft in the rock with surging water, the pink granite bridge has a single Gothic arch and crenellated parapet. An unusual style for the Dee bridges, this example is nicely detailed with mouldings.

MARYKIRK

Originally a thanedom known as Aberluthnot, and still a good example of a kirkton. The name was officially changed by Queen

Mary shortly before the Reformation. Although it was elevated to a burgh of barony in 1543, Marykirk seems never to have exercised any of its municipal privileges.

ABERLUTHNOT PARISH CHURCH. Simple, good preaching-box of pinned rubble, built 1806 to replace the medieval church (*see* below). Three lancets on the W flank (to the road), the ends with raised sills to accommodate doors. Y-tracery with lattice-pane glazing added during renovations by *Matthews & Mackenzie*, 1893–4. Theirs also the four Gothick windows on the E flank, the gableted S bellcote and the recast interior. Broad coomb ceiling carried on paired open arches resting on rafters. Baluster-like struts flanking them. – Blocked GALLERY on the S. – Wooden BACK-BOARD with brattishing. – Richly E.E. wooden FONT with shafts and stiff-leaf.

OLD BURIAL GROUND, S of the church. Site of the medieval parish church, founded in the late C12 and consecrated by Bishop David Benham in 1242. A late C18 description records that it had a fine oak roof carved with cross, crown, St Peter's keys and heraldry for Bishops Dunbar and Elphinstone.

The former SOUTH AISLE is still *in situ* and now sits free-standing. It was built in the early C16 for the Strachan, Forbes and Foulerton families, all of whom had connections to Thornton Castle (q.v.) – hence its usual name, the Thornton Aisle. Broad, roll-moulded arch originally leading into the church, now blocked. Gable with mega-crowsteps added in the early C19. Plain W flank with blocked door and lintel dated 1615 with the initials A.S. S gable with a blocked door under a chamfered window. – Excellent MONUMENTS inside. On the r., a large WALL MEMORIAL to Elizabeth Forbes, Lady Thornton, †1661 and her husband, Sir James Strachan †*c.* 1715. It is proficiently classical and very well carved – a sign of just how cosmopolitan both the sculptors and the patrons of North Scotland could be. Engaged Corinthian columns with curling trails of foliage; inscription in the middle with angel's head, fruit and unfurling scrolls. Ogival pediment with helm, and then vermiculation with two figures holding scrolls and long candles, the l. now missing. Ogee-headed PISCINA on the opposite wall.

Diagonally opposite to the aisle is the BARCLAY VAULT, originally attached to the NE corner of the parish church. It is partially subterranean with rocky walls and turfed roof. SE skewputt dated 1653 with the initials I.B. – originally on the parish church and transferred here when the church was dem. *c.* 1806.

Former FREE CHURCH, Crosspoles, 2.6 km. NNW. Lanceted box of 1846; closed *c.* 1933 and now a house. Pyramidal bellcote on the W gable and an obelisk finial on the E. – Former MANSE to the NE, 1849 by the mason *James Orkney* and much reconstructed by *William Orkney* in 1895. Veranda with perforated brackets and fish-scale slates.

WAR MEMORIAL. *See* Luthermuir, p. 661.

The main road is pleasant and lined with C18 and C19 buildings. At the S end is NORTH ESK HOUSE, formerly the Manse, built 1732 but owing its current appearance to a major renovation in 1838. Two storeys and three bays, the central door with primitive pilasters and a keystoned, semicircular fanlight. The Parish Church and Old Burial Ground follow (*see* above). Next, the GATE to the former Kirktonhill House (*see* below), mid-C19 and of good ashlar. Two mirrored screen walls with slightly recessed arch openings – the inner ones for pedestrians, the outer ones glazed for the lodges behind. Gatepier pilasters panelled with blind lancets. Just beyond is the MARYKIRK HOTEL, its two-storey, three-bay core built in the late C18. In its forecourt are the remains of the MARKET CROSS, sculpted *c.* 1543 and moved here from the Burial Ground in 1857. Square shaft with stopped chamfers, *c.* 1.1 m. high and crudely broken off. Large, blocky plinth.

Further up on the r. is ADAMS COTTAGE, late C18, harled with margins painted black. Roll-moulded door frame, the lintel topped by carved Masonic symbols including T-square and compass. Opposite is a cast-iron LAMP memorializing John Carnegie †1897, a native of the village. Cross-bar over little brackets; lantern with mini-brattishing and a pierced crown finial.

BALMANNO HOUSE, 1 km. NNE. A confident and patrician house, built *c.* 1790 for the Cruickshank brothers from profits made in the West Indies. Two storeys and five bays of good coursed rubble. Grand central doorcase with lugged architrave, keystone and modillioned cornice. Three canted dormers originally added in the late C19. – Serene WALLED GARDEN to the rear. – Former COACHHOUSE in the NW corner with big round arch.

DUNTHILL HOUSE, 1.9 km. N. Former L-plan school house, built *c.* 1833. Three harled bays facing SW. Attached to the r. is the two-bay former school, originally single-storeyed and given an upper floor *c.* 2000 after a fire.

FOREBANK HOUSE, 1.7 km. SE. Built as the dower house to Inglismaldie Castle (q.v.), hence its very fine design and execution. Two storeys and five bays over a raised basement, dated 1757 on its SW skewputt. Smart ashlar doorcase with lugged margin, pulvinated architrave and cornice. Radial fanlight. The spacing between the outer pairs of windows is gently and subtly elongated. The flanks are wide and harled, the W one with a large, elliptical bullseye on the first floor and two smaller oculi in the gable. They ensured a theatrical approach as one came down the main drive. – Ball-finialled GATEPIERS framing the front garden, late C18.

Former KIRKTONHILL HOUSE, 700 m. NE. Large, austere house built 1795 for the Taylors of Montrose and dem. *c.* 1965. The rear wings – originally the servants' block and nursery – once formed a U-plan but now sit detached as two separate houses. – Huge WALLED GARDEN to the NNW, mostly of whitewashed brick. – KIRKTONHILL TOWER, 1.7 km. NE.

Marykirk Bridge.
Engraving by J. Steedman and R. Scott, 1817

Large stone folly built *c.* 1830 and restored *c.* 2008. Octagonal ground stage with dummy cruciform arrowslits. Two narrower circular stages above, all crenellated.

MARYKIRK BRIDGE, 0.6 km. s on the A937. Four broad segmental arches by *Robert Stevenson*, 1811–14, over the North Esk. Alternately raised voussoirs under hoodmoulds, blind oculi in the spandrels. Rounded cutwaters with good channelled masonry. – Fine TOLL HOUSE on the s shore, 1813–14 by *David Logan* (Stevenson's assistant). Three bays of fine coursed ashlar, the centre and flanks bowed under a sharp cornice and semi-conical piended roofs.

NORTH ESK VIADUCT, 370 m. E. Thirteen spans, built *c.* 1849 for the Aberdeen Railway. The supports were originally wooden arches, replaced with steel trusses *c.* 1880, likely by *A. & W. Smith* of Glasgow.

BALMAKEWAN HOUSE. *See* p. 350.

105

MENZIES HOUSE *see* BLAIRS   K

MERGIE HOUSE   K   *7080*
1.9 km. w of Rickarton

A T-plan house, characteristic of the mid–later C17; its jamb was enlarged with Gothick windows *c.* 1800. Built in harled rubble with tooled dressings, the three-storey main block is orientated N–S, with the jamb which contains the main entrance and stair on the E front slightly to the s of centre; a small turret is formed at second floor within the N re-entrant. The w front also has a doorway off-centre to the s, and corbelled out above this a small stair-turret rises through the first and second floors into an ovoid conical spirelet. The ground-floor windows are relatively small; those at first floor express the principal apartments and those at second floor rise through the eaves into piended dormers. The tall gabled roof contains an attic lit by skylights and has three chimneystacks, two at the ends and one rising from an internal gable. The ground floor, which has a timber-beamed ceiling rather than vaulting, contains the services, the kitchen with a large segmentally arched hearth. The first floor contains the principal apartments, which judging by the internal gable and the windows originally consisted of just two apartments, a hall (N) and private apartment (S), the latter giving access to the turret stair and the bedrooms above. The present division into three apartments can be dated to the C18 by their fine timber panelling with bolection-moulded fireplaces and simple but elegant door-surrounds and cornices. The Victorian fireplace at second floor is reputedly from Fetteresso Castle (q.v.).

Mergie stands on or near the site of a fortalice recorded in 1590 and may even incorporate some of its fabric; a mound to the W of the house has the appearance of a medieval MOTTE. TERRACED GARDENS with pavilions at either end, both ruinous, but one of particular distinction, two storeys with a fireplace.

<small>6000</small>

MIDMAR

PARISH CHURCH. Designed by *John Midleton* of Shiels (*see* Sauchen), architect, 1786; built 1787. Rectangular plan. Rubble W gable reconstructed *c.* 1885 with entrance porch, three gallery lancets with small-paned glazing and quatrefoil roundel above. Birdcage bellcote with spike and ball finials contains bell by *Peter Jansen*, 1642, brought from St Mary, Kinnernie (*see* below). It is cast with a bowl of fruit flanked by two angels with cornucopiae in their hands. S flank in cherry-cocked ashlar has five round-arched windows, their timber Y-tracery of *c.* 1885. N flank has single window at W and later organ chamber at E. E gable with single round-arched window and vestry outshot slightly off-centre to r. Interior with coved ceiling predominantly *c.* 1885. W gallery (now enclosed) with herringbone front supported on two cast-iron columns. E-end PULPIT with tall gabled back. Gothic COMMUNION TABLE, buttressed with pierced front, carved with Holy Monogram, cruciform and foliate decoration. Finely moulded pedestal FONT. Simple PEWS still with paraffin lamp standards. ORGAN within NE chamber 1914. WALL TABLETS in marble, timber and champlevé enamel.

The graveyard has been formed around the site of a RECUMBENT STONE CIRCLE. It consists of a large recumbent stone with shaped flankers and five other standing stones graded in height towards the SW. (GN)

ST NIDIAN, 0.7 km. SSE. Probably of C12–C13 origin, on raised ground facing the Motte of Cunningar 150 m. NW (*see* below); a medieval village formerly occupied the ridge between them, protected by a burn on either side. Long narrow plan, remodelled in 1677. Roofless but substantially intact, the shell is rubble-built with massive rough quoins and steeply pitched gables. Long S flank, its windows blocked and doorways formed for burial enclosures; its raised centre marks the former position of the pulpit, transferred here during internal reordering *c.* 1730. W gable once crowned by a bellcote, E gable has large two-light window mullioned and transomed in stone. Moulded skewputts. In the graveyard, immediately S of the church, the grave-slab of master mason George Bell (†1575), now much overgrown.

Former WEST CHURCH, 3.6 km. WNW. Disused. Built for an Associate Burgher congregation in 1832. Small coursed rubble rectangle. Tall walls, with three round-arched windows in S flank. Slim refined bellcote, 1858, originally rose over W gable. Reorientated 1898–9, porch formed at E gable and vestry at W by *Davidson & Alexander*, masons in Cluny, and *Robert Elrick*, wright in Shiels.

MOTTE OF CUNNINGAR, 150 m. NW of St Nidian, and probably associated with it as part of a C12–C13 settlement. A grass-covered sandy mound, *c.* 24 m. NW–SE by 22 m. transversely, and 7 m. high, its summit badly affected by quarrying. Remnants of a ditch on its NW and SE sides.

Former PARISH MANSE, 250 m. NW of the Motte. A two-storey three-bay manse of *c.* 1824, its porch with round-arched doorway added 1840, probably by *John Smith*, and a broad gabled bay at the r. end by *James Matthews* in 1861, resulting in the present L-plan.

SUNHONEY FARMHOUSE, 2.1 km. SE. *c.* 1800. Two-storey entrance front three bays broadly spaced in coursed squared rubble. First-floor windows retain mid-C19 lying-pane glazing. Gabled roof with coped end stacks. Just N is a large RECUMBENT STONE CIRCLE, *c.* 27 m. in diameter with eleven standing stones and a recumbent. Traces of a cremation pyre and deposits of burnt bone have been found within a central cairn which survives as a low platform in the centre of the circle. The recumbent (which has fallen on its side) has many cup marks on its upper surface. (GN)

OLD KINNERNIE, 4 km. NE. Foundations of ST MARY'S CHURCH granted to Arbroath Abbey by Thomas de Lundin in the early C13. Rectangular, 20.5 m. by 6 m., reduced to foundations either when Kinnernie was united with Midmar in 1740 or when Midmar Parish Church (*see* above) was built in 1788. Two mort safes.

MIDMAR CASTLE

1.3 km. SSE

A Z-plan tower house, once known as Ballogie, perhaps the work of the *Leiper family* remodelled by the *Bell family*. Its origins are unclear, but comparison with other Z-plans suggests that it was begun *c.* 1560–70. The antiquarian James Skene of Rubislaw who discovered the grave-slab of *George Bell* (†1575, 'deceisit in Balogy') in St Nidian's churchyard nearby suggested that he had been responsible, citing the obvious resemblance to Castle Fraser (q.v.) in the lively treatment of the upperworks characteristic of that family of master masons. However Harry Gordon Slade has demonstrated that the tower house at Midmar, like Castle Fraser, was built in at least two phases: the basic Z-plan for Alexander Gordon, 4th Laird of Abergeldie, was perhaps the work of *Thomas Leiper* or *James Leiper*, being similar on plan to the Old House of Carnousie (N, *c.* 1577); it may or may not pre-date the plundering and brief forfeiture of Alexander's lands after the Battle of Corrichie in 1562. It was 'burned and destroyed' after his son Alexander's involvement in the Catholic earls' rebellion in 1594, and probably rebuilt *c.* 1600 for William, 5th Laird of Abergeldie. Some details suggest the involvement of the unidentified mason responsible for Birse, Westhall, Knock and Allardice (qq.v.), but the distinctive upperworks are perhaps by *I. Bell*, who was subsequently to remodel Castle Fraser in 1617–18. The original forecourt has been replaced by two parallel wings. The long W wing may be late C17; the E wing is a shorter L-plan, probably built for Capt. Alexander Grant between 1727 and 1732.

The Z-plan TOWER HOUSE comprises a four-storey main block 10 m. square with an attic and garret concealed in its roof; a NW jamb, four storeys and gabled attic, which is 6.5 m. square; and a six-storey SE drum tower 8.5 m. in basal diameter. The walls are harled rubble, with pink granite dressings: both the main block and the NW jamb are unusual in that their exposed angles are widely splayed rather than rounded. The doorway at ground floor within the NW jamb's E flank is segment-headed with a heavy roll moulding, which implies that it was formed during the works of *c.* 1600, but in the position of its predecessor since the wide-mouthed shot-hole protecting it in the main block's flank is of *c.* 1560–70. There is a further pistol-hole immediately next to the doorway. Directly above the doorway, a turnpike stair-tourelle corbelled out in the angle rises above the eaves into a conical spirelet. The NW jamb has attic pepperpots with spirelets echoing that of the stair; those on the N side constrict its gable to a small crowstepped chimney gablet. The main block's third floor is boldly projected on fretted label key-pattern mouldings, similar to those of the Birse–Westhall group; its square NE corner turret has very slim angle shafts with Ionic capitals and a pedimented cartouche, its gablet crowned by finials. The main block's roof has crowstepped end gables rising into coped chimneystacks and its attic was once lit by a large attic dormer. On the rear (S) elevation, a second turnpike stair-tourelle rises from ground level within the re-entrant angle of the main block and the drum tower, culminating in an ogee domelet just above its crenellated parapet. A *trompe* arch, finely moulded, links the drum tower to the

Midmar Castle.
Engraving by R.W. Billings, 1852

tourelle, a feature repeated at the main block's E end gable; these must date from the works of *c.* 1600. At the SW angle, the main block is again jettied out at third floor with a square gablet turret, its corbelling following the same pattern as on the N front; the W elevation is simpler, with corbelling only at its angle turrets.

Two WINGS occupy the site of the original entrance fore-court. The W wing extending from the NW jamb possibly dates from the late C17. It is two storeys and seven bays broad, its ground floor barrel-vaulted with a narrow pend entered through a moulded archway, and its upper-floor windows rising into dormer gablets. The E wing, probably built between 1727 and 1732, is an L-plan extending from the angle between the main block and the drum tower. It is again two-storeyed but taller, without dormers. Its garage extension, with three segment-headed arches like those of old cartsheds and a correspondingly steep roof, was built *c.* 1980. The C17–C18 wings are plainly treated, but both have coped stacks like the tower house's. The raised terrace formed between the E wing and the NW jamb is also early C18, with bolection-coped parapets and big ball finials at the head of the stairs.

PLAN AND INTERIOR. Examination of the doorway confirms its alteration *c.* 1600. Originally a timber door was secured by a wooden bar which still survives, but subsequently the entrance was protected by an iron yett mounted on the same iron hinge-pins as the door itself. The NW jamb contains a vaulted staircase with handsome scale-and-platt stair rising in four flights to first floor, and with a guardroom beneath (cf. Carnousie). The guardroom has two loopholes, one original, one modern. The main block's ground floor is vaulted and contained the original kitchen, entered from the E end of a passage running down the N side; the hearth was in the W gable and there is a water intake beneath one of the two S-side windows. The drum tower contains a vaulted cellar. The arrangement of the SE stair-tourelle with two adjacent entrances, one from the diagonal lobby linking the kitchen and larder, implies alteration. It has two shot-holes, one blocked, perhaps always for decoration.

At first floor the hall occupies the whole of the main block. It is accessed by the scale-and-platt stair at its 'low' W end and by the private SE stair at its 'high' end. The hall was originally lit by one N and one S window, both secured by iron grilles, and when the W window was formed or enlarged in the C18 it cut through the original kitchen flue. The plaster ceiling with its central oval and heavy cornice is also C18. The E-end fireplace is plain: its jambs of *c.* 1600 may be those preserved within the garden summerhouse. Beyond a diagonal lobby, the SE drum tower contains the Gordons' private chamber, an irregular pentagon, again with C18 woodwork. A small vaulted room entered off the scale-and-platt stair's first-floor landing in the NW jamb, with a gunloop in its W wall, may have been a strongroom for charters.

The arrangement of the upper floors implies a social division. The rooms in the NW jamb were accessed by the NW turnpike stair and kept quite separate from the rooms in the main block and the drum, which were accessed by the private SE stair; the doorways now linking them at second and fourth floors are alterations. The main block's second-floor room – the 'Great Chamber' – is the most elaborately panelled; its doorway off the SE stair has a moulded architrave with heavy entablature and pulvinated frieze. It is framed by fluted pilasters, their capitals breaking forward from the timber ceiling cornice. The bolection-moulded fireplace is of similar pattern, its overmantel again framed by pilasters. The main block's third-floor room also retains most of its panelling. Its doorway is set in a lugged surround with an entablature; the fireplace

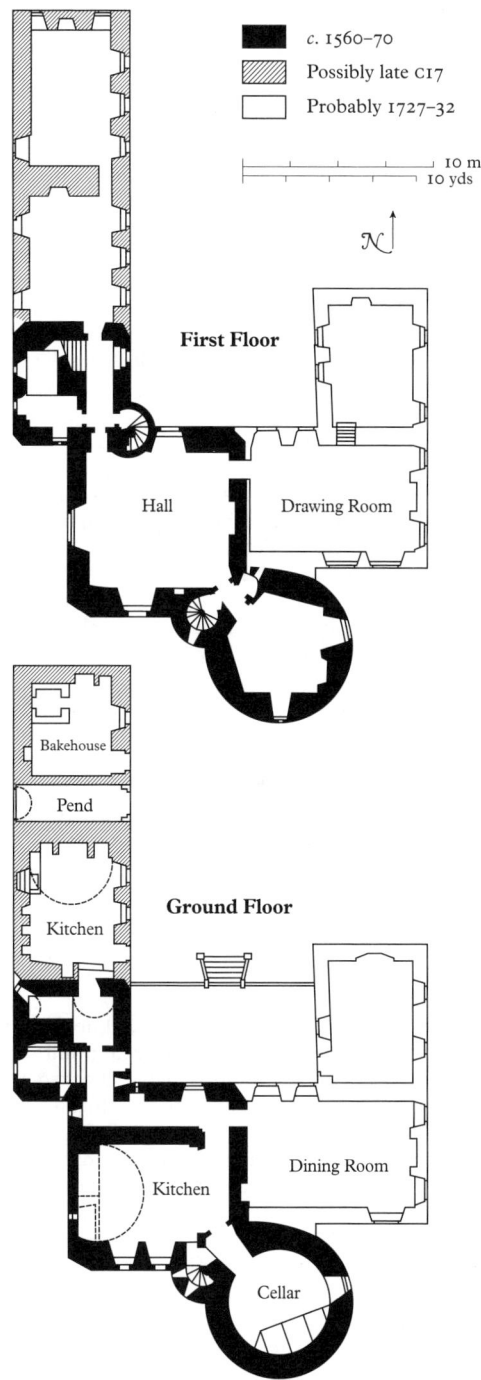

c. 1560–70

Possibly late C17

Probably 1727–32

10 m
10 yds

N

First Floor

Hall

Drawing Room

Bakehouse

Pend

Kitchen

Ground Floor

Kitchen

Dining Room

Cellar

Midmar Castle.
Plan of ground and first floors

is similar to that below, but without pilasters. There are three closets, two of them within the square angle turrets. Within the jamb 'Queen Mary's Chamber' has a moulded fireplace. Its ceiling is low and of timber, supported on square joists. The attic room within the main block provided a gallery, once lit by two large dormers as well as the windows in the end gables. It was not open to the roof (as was latterly the case), having had a garret for servants or storage.

The W wing's vaulted ground floor contained a new kitchen with a hearth and a bakehouse with an oven; they are separated by a pend with a suite of two good rooms above accessed from the main stair. The E wing contained services and a dining room at ground floor, its fenestration possibly altered: the dining room's plain bolection-moulded fireplace is *c.* 1730 although the mantelshelf is later. The woodwork and plaster ceiling and cornice are elegant late C18 or early C19, the windows in semi-elliptically arched recesses. The first floor contained a panelled drawing room, again with bolection-moulded fireplace, and a private chamber, both altered during the C19. The attic contained box beds for maids.

SUNDIAL, immediately S. Perhaps early C18. Hollow dial-type with ball-finial on square baluster.

WALLED GARDEN, against the E wing. C16–C17, large irregular pentagon with rubble walls containing beeboles with broken pediments and ball-finialled tops. SUMMERHOUSE in NE corner.

BARNYARDS OF MIDMAR, 250 m. NW. Probably *c.* 1796. Gothick home farm steading and stables, quadrangular courtyard plan. E front with central round-headed archway framed by slim towers with shallow niches and roundels. Three-bay linking sections with lancets. Big drum towers at the corners, l. single-storeyed, r. two-storeyed. Crenellated parapets.

4000

MIGVIE

Former PARISH CHURCH. Built *c.* 1787, almost cottage-like in its simplicity and scale. Coursed squared granite rubble. Two windows in S flank and one in W gable checked for shutters, doorway in E end, gabled roof, no specifically ecclesiastical features. Repaired and converted for Philip Astor in 2001 as a place for small concerts and peaceful contemplation, with local artists' works in various media; DOORS carved in Pictish style by *Gavin Smith* of Corgarff. – (STAINED GLASS. Three windows designed by *Peter Goodfellow* and made by *Jennifer-Jane Bayliss*, 2001, on the theme of Christianity coming to Scotland, with figures derived from Pictish carvings.)

On sloping ground the rubble-walled CHURCHYARD formerly contained St Finan's church, its site discernible in raised ground immediately in front of its successor; it was dedicated to St Andrew's Priory in the late C12. It was presumably associated with Migvie Castle (first mentioned 1268), of which only scant ruins remain but which was once the *capital messuage* of the Lordship of Cromar.* C18–C19 stones including lying slabs, some carving similar to that at Tarland and Coull (qq.v.). Square gatepiers with cast-iron spoked-wheel gates.

PICTISH SYMBOL STONE with elaborately carved interlaced cross. The cross frames four additional images, one in each quadrant. These are a horseman, a pair of shears, a double-disc and Z-rod and a horseshoe. On the reverse there is another horseman; both these equestrian figures were re-carved in the mid C19. A smaller CROSS-INCISED STONE is now built into the church walls. (GN)

MONBODDO HOUSE
1.9 km. ESE of Auchenblae

K   7070

The land was acquired by Robert Irvine and his wife, Elizabeth Douglas, in 1630.† They built a tower house on the foundations of a 'keep long occupied by the Strachans'. A new wing was added in the C18 and then a huge Baronial extension by *Matthews & Mackenzie* in 1866–7. Restoration in 1977–9 by *Alistair McAlpine* and *Christopher Davey* included the demolition of all the later accretions and the return of the building to its original T-plan.

Original block running E–W, the flat N side of three storeys and five bays. Tourelle projecting from either end on good chequered corbel courses. Conical roofs and the two dormerheads in between by *Matthews & Mackenzie*; theirs also the short lower wing to the l. Crowsteps on the w gable reinstated in the late 1970s. Below them, a plaque dated 1635 with initials for Irvine and his wife. The jamb projecting to the S all dates from 1977–9 but nicely echoes the original C17 plan. In the E re-entrant angle, a good original doorpiece with bolection moulding and a re-set dormerhead dated 1635 with Irvine's monogram.

The interior is mostly modern, but retains a large arched fireplace on the ground floor and turnpike stairs with good ogee mouldings on the undersides of the treads. – Long former STABLE BLOCK directly to the E, originally built in the mid C18. Much restored and turned into three houses during the C20 renovation.

---

*See Dr W. Douglas Simpson, 'The Early Castles of Mar', *Proceedings of the Society of Antiquaries of Scotland* 53 (1928–9), pp. 102–38; also his *Earldom of Mar* (1949).
† *See* also their tomb-chest in Auchenblae Parish Church.

MONTGARRIE

Chiefly notable for its MEAL MILL, of exceptional size for North-East Scotland, probably built 1882 and still in use. Tall four storeys and attic, six bays broad, rubble-built and reinforced by iron ties; the kiln occupies the two N-end bays, its octagonal ventilator rising high above the gabled roof. On the mill's E flank near the S end, the ten-spoke overshot wheel in cast iron and timber is over 7 m. in diameter, with maker's plate of *James Abernethy & Co.* 1882; it has a 4.5 m. sprocket wheel inside. Its reinforced concrete lade of 1947 is supplied with water from the Esset Burn. The mill's W flank is largely obscured by additions in corrugated iron. The wheel once powered five pairs of millstones arranged in-line through its chain-drive and big cast-iron gearbox.

MONYMUSK

Originally a Culdee settlement, but by 1245 the site of an Augustinian priory. Centuries later Monymusk became Aberdeenshire's first improvement village, its Square laid out as a cattle pend for Banffshire drovers by Sir Archibald Grant in 1716. He established a grain mill and lint mill nearby in 1748–9, and a stone-polishing mill before his death in 1778.

CHURCHES AND PUBLIC BUILDINGS

MONYMUSK PRIORY AND PARISH CHURCH.* The priory and parish of Monymusk evidently shared use of the church, despite no clear institutional link existing between them. There were grants to Céli Dé (Culdees) here in the C12, a community transformed into an Augustinian priory dedicated to the Virgin by no later than 1245. The parish belonged to the Bishop of St Andrews, though by 1437 he had agreed to the first teinds being annexed to Aberdeen Cathedral, and in 1445 they formed a prebend of that Cathedral. In the mid C16 the priory is repeatedly referred to as ruinous, though in 1550 there was still a community of a prior and four canons. After passing through various hands, with proposals that its buildings should be adapted as a school in 1574, in 1617 the priory was granted to the Bishops of Dunblane. Of the PRIORY BUILDINGS, remains of a large structure were said in 1722 to be *c.* 20 m. NE of church, but excavation in 1981 failed to locate it.

The CHURCH, with walls of pink rubble, was presumably built to its present basic form around the second quarter of the C12; it has a three-compartment plan, consisting of rectangular chancel of uncertain initial length, a wider rectangular

*This entry is by Richard Fawcett.

nave and a square w tower. Following the Reformation the church was adapted for reformed worship, with the pulpit set against the s wall. In major changes of 1822 a rectangular N aisle was added, the tower was lowered and a spire constructed (removed 1891), and the nave roof was replaced at a lower level. At some stage the E part of the chancel was unroofed and adapted as a burial enclosure for the Grants of Monymusk; in the mid C19 it was said that the w part of the chancel remained in use, housing seats for forty people, though that part was later adapted as a vestry and coal store. In 1929–32 a major restoration and reordering by *A. Marshall Mackenzie* reorientated the interior towards a sanctuary in the w part of the chancel, and the N aisle was walled off as a vestry and organ chamber.

The EXTERIOR now shows few features of C12 origin. It is unclear if the E limb (16.1 m. by 6.4 m.) represents the extent of the medieval CHANCEL. Its E part (11 m.) is a burial enclosure, the walls of which have clearly been extensively rebuilt, with a simple N doorway. In its S wall is a blocked window with ogee mouldings, probably later C16. Nevertheless, a church which served both a parish and a religious community would have required a chancel of greater than parochial length, and what is now seen may perpetuate the original plan. The part of the E limb restored as the sanctuary in 1929–32 is lit by a round-arched window in the s wall and another in the E wall. The NAVE s wall has a symmetrical arrangement of windows dating from 1822: two large round-arched windows towards the centre flank the site of the early C19 pulpit; two tiers of windows E and W, the upper windows for the gallery having semicircular arches and the lower ones segmental heads. Between the central windows are traces of a doorway cut in 1685–6, when the interior was also re-seated, to provide access to the pulpit, and of an adjacent rectangular window. The N aisle of 1822 has an upper round-headed window and a lower rectangular window. E and W of the aisle there were forestairs to the E, N and W galleries, but only that to the W survived the changes of 1929–32, with doors into the upper floor of the aisle and the W gallery. The round-arched door with a simple hoodmould in the w face of the TOWER is the only externally visible medieval feature. At the upper levels of the tower are various rectangular openings (some blocked), those at the top stage on the N, E and s sides being of two lights. On the W side a clock face (dated 2000). The tower was lowered by 4.25 m. in the alterations of 1822 and following the removal of the spire in 1891 was given its its crenellated parapet of rock-faced granite.

The appearance of the INTERIOR is largely of 1929–32; no more than the remodelled panelled-front W gallery survives from 1822, when pews and galleries were directed symmetrically towards a pulpit at the centre of the s wall. The only identifiably medieval features are the C12 chancel and tower arches, and an inserted barrel-vault over the lowest storey of

13

the tower porch. The tower arch is of two rectangular orders towards the nave, with chamfered imposts at arch-springing level of the inner order. The chancel arch is the outstanding feature of the church. It is of two orders: in the jambs it has a substantial half-shaft to the leading face, flanked on each side by set-back three-quarter shafts; in the arch there is a rectangular soffit order, while the outer order has three-quarter angle rolls combined with hollow chamfers to the faces. A scalloped cap supports the inner order on each side (that on the N renewed in cement) and there are cushion caps to the outer order. Both chancel and nave have pine ribbed ceilings of double-pitched profile.

FURNISHINGS. COMMUNION TABLE and CHAIR with Gothic arcading, chair with pinnacle terminals, both *c.* 1921. – CHAIR. Jacobethan with sacred monogram, 1892. – STAINED GLASS. E window. A Culdee priest preaching, by *Alexander Strachan*, 1929. – W window. Virgin and Child, by *Gordon Webster*, 1963. – CROSS-SLAB. Within the SE corner of the church tower. Granite, roughly shaped. Possibly C8 or C9. The equal-arm incised cross-head has spiral work in a central boss, and plait decoration on the arms, with further plait work on a narrow shaft below the lower arm. The cross rises from a stepped base decorated with leaf patterns and with spiral terminals. Below the cross is a disc and double-ring symbol, the disc decorated with a rosette. First recorded in a field one mile E of Monymusk House, subsequently at Monymusk House. Also within the tower are two small roughly shaped CROSS-INCISED STONES, one with a swastika-shaped cross, the other a simple cross in circle. – MEMORIALS. S of chancel arch, arched tablet to John Forbes of Abersnithack and members of his family, †1583 and †1590, with a final date uncut. – Several memorials to members of the Grant family, including: N of chancel arch, oval marble tablet to Archibald Grant, lost on the Indiaman Abergavenny, 1805; S nave wall, Commander Arthur Grant 'killed by a fall from his horse' 1850, scroll against an anchor, a cannon, a flag and a book. – BELL. By *John Mowat* of Old Aberdeen, 1748.

Former PARISH MANSE. Within its own grounds E of the Square. Designed by *William Ramage*, 1859. Two storeys, three bays. Refined door architrave with slim consoles supporting a plain cornice. Harled with slim granite dressings, margins and eaves course. Ground-floor windows astragalled with timber mullions and sidelights, first floor now plate-glazed. Shallow-pitched gabled roof with end stacks and canted dormers.

SCHOOL, 150 m. N of The Square. By *William Gauld*, dated 1907. Tall single-storey three-bay asymmetric front. Slightly projecting l. gabled bay with piends at the angles. Centre bay rises into a piend-roofed dormerhead. The r. bay rises into a gablet. Construction in robust pinned rubble. Large paired and triple-light windows with astragals in their upper sashes. Well-detailed timber doors, cast-iron drinking fountains and outbuildings. Extensions mid C20.

DESCRIPTION. Monymusk village owes its unique character to the exceptional standard to which it was rebuilt for Robert Grant *c.* 1825–40 and then remodelled for Sir Arthur Grant *c.* 1886–1902. Sir Arthur had spent £60,000 improving the village and its surrounding farms by 1911. The approach to the church is between the oldest houses in The Square: two plain classical blocks, probably designed by *John Smith c.* 1826 but reusing older materials. Each is two storeys and four bays broad, harled with gabled roofs and low coped chimneystacks. Directly opposite on The Square's w side stands the GRANT ARMS HOTEL, again earlier C19. This is also two-storey plain classic but built in granite ashlar, three windows wide with a pedimented doorway. It has a large rear wing and later C19 stable offices within its back court. At either end of The Square's w side are two Neoclassical pavilions of *c.* 1830–40, single-storey and attic with boldly stepped parapets masking their roofs: one has probably been the POST OFFICE from the beginning, the other a coachhouse with a segmental arch. The single-storey COTTAGES are modestly scaled by comparison, but remarkable in that almost all are constructed of fine granite ashlar. Although built for Robert Grant, their present English Picturesque appearance with timber canopies over their doorways, diamond-pane casements, bargeboarded dormers and overhanging eaves dates from the later C19 when they were progressively remodelled for Sir Arthur Grant by *John Birch*, author of *Picturesque Lodges* (1879): each group is different.[*] In the centre of the green is the WAR MEMORIAL, a Neoclassical cenotaph in Kemnay granite erected by *Bower & Florence*, 1921.

Just s of The Square stands the ARTS CENTRE, originally a stone-polishing mill, converted to a chapel in 1801 and substantially rebuilt in 1834 as an Episcopal church. Its simple rectangular nave in squared rubble is orientated N–S. It has a crowstep-gabled porch in the centre of the E flank between two round-arched windows with original glazing. Organ chamber towards s end. Chancel enlarged 1908. W of The Square, the mid-C19 former LIBRARY, a single-storey-and-attic gable front built of boulder rubble with the librarian's cottage next to it, and the remains of a distillery in its garden. GLOIE'S FARMSTEADING was originally built for Sir Archibald Grant as a lint mill by *James Fordyce* of Arbroath in 1748–9 and reconstructed for Sir Arthur Grant in 1899; further W the GRAIN MILL dated 1749 is perhaps also by *Fordyce*. Immediately N of The Square is a GIG HOUSE or HEARSE HOUSE, single storey and loft with twin segmental arches, early C19. E of The Square, behind Nos. 8–10, the single-storey school by *John Smith* 1826, converted to a PUBLIC HALL in the C20.

SIR ARTHUR GRANT CENTRE, 1.5 km. NNE. Formerly Sir Arthur Grant's School, built 1890. Monymusk Picturesque,

[*]Other examples of Sir Arthur's rebuilding in this style are at Woodhead (1889) and Mosside (1891).

presumably by *John Birch*. Villa-like single storey in pink granite rubble with very tall gabled roof, small gabled porch at one corner. Paired and triple-light windows, chimney-breasts with immensely tall stacks breaking through the overhanging eaves. Single-storey-and-attic master's house entered from rear.

BRAEHEAD FARM, 2.4 km. N. Late Improvement Era, *c.* 1830. Simple classical style. Single-storey entrance front three bays broad raised over semi-sunk basement, harled with granite dressings and rudimentary bracket cornices. Canted dormers in gabled roof. Large U-plan steading. Later outbuilding in Monymusk Picturesque. Derelict in 2014.

NETHER MAINS FARM, 2 km. ESE. Early Improvement Era. Built *c.* 1740, with late C18 alterations and a non-matching addition of 1894. Original two-storey, three-bay farmhouse harled with relatively small windows broadly spaced. Gabled roof with simple skew details, stone ridge and end stacks. Later glazed porch. Extensive steading. Derelict in 2014.

RAMSTONE, 2.5 km. N, is a hamlet on the Don with former corn mill and sawmill built by the Monymusk estate in the mid C19. A quarry was opened in the late C19. The CORN MILL preserves a timber-framed wheel *c.* 4.5 m. in diameter within a masonry lade. Three houses all in Monymusk Picturesque, presumably by *Birch*.

HOUSE OF MONYMUSK*
0.5 km. ENE

The House of Monymusk has its origins in the tower house built by Duncan Forbes shortly after he received the lands of Monymusk Priory in 1549. Forbes was a wealthy lawyer, businessman and political figure who as 'tutor' or guardian controlled the assets both of his nephew William, 4th Laird of Corsindae (q.v.) and his kinsman William, 7th Laird of Tolquhon (N). During the later C16 or early C17 wings were added to the tower house. In 1713 Sir William Forbes of Pitsligo sold Monymusk to Sir Francis Grant, Lord Cullen, who three years later entrusted it to Archibald, his twenty-year-old son. In 1719 Archibald asked the Quaker architect *Alexander Jaffray* of Kingswells to suggest alternative proposals for a new house or for the enlargement of the old one. Jaffray produced designs for a classical house, two storeys and basement, three windows wide with a central attic pediment, but this was probably too modest for the ambitious young man, who was elected Aberdeenshire's M.P. in 1722 and who by the time he inherited his father's fortune in 1726 was smitten by the first agricultural improvements and diversification into industry which he had witnessed in England. Jaffray's proposals for the existing house – in which a suite of principal apartments extended across first floor from one wing to the other – were not pursued either, although they may have influenced

*This account is deeply indebted to research by Lorraine Hesketh-Campbell.

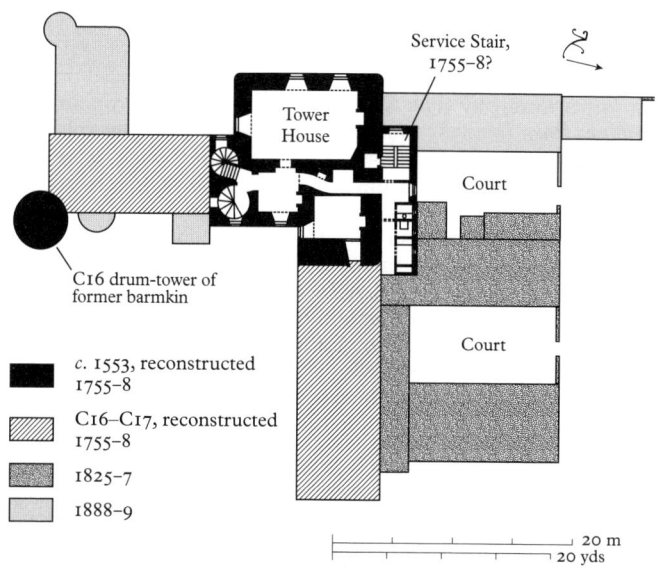

Service Stair,
1755–8?

Tower
House

Court

Court

C16 drum-tower of
former barmkin

c. 1553, reconstructed
1755–8

C16–C17, reconstructed
1755–8

1825–7

1888–9

20 m
20 yds

Monymusk House.
Block plan

the reconstruction which took place some thirty-five years later. For the moment Grant decided to improve the policies, and the lesser buildings of the tower house barmkin were demolished to open up views to the surrounding landscape.

During the 1720s Grant invested heavily in various financial enterprises. He probably lost out as a result of the difficulties faced by the York Buildings Company, which purchased forfeit Jacobite estates after the 1715 Rising. He was much more severely embarrassed, however, by the fraudulent activities of the Charitable Corporation, avoiding bankruptcy only through the assistance of friends. He was obliged to give up his Parliamentary seat and returned to Aberdeenshire in 1734 in much reduced circumstances, but determined to redress his situation through zealous pursuit of agricultural improvement, industry and better conditions for his tenants. The family's position eased gradually, his son Archie joining the East India Company and he himself marrying Elizabeth Clark, a wealthy heiress, in 1751.

This enabled reconsideration of Jaffray's proposals when the roofs were found to be in parlous condition in 1754, but on this occasion Grant consulted the Edinburgh mason *James Wyllie* (then building James Gibbs's West St Nicholas, Aberdeen) and the Edinburgh wright *Michael Naismith*. They produced a scheme for radically reconstructing the House of Monymusk with a new entrance in its s wing and a railed forecourt on the site of the original barmkin. The work was contracted for by the Aberdeen mason and plasterer *John Murdo* under Grant's supervision in

1755–8. The reconstructed house still survives much as they knew it, but their forecourt has gone and service courts concealed at the rear have been added. These later works were carried out for Sir James Grant by *John Smith* in 1825–7. Further proposals by *William Burn* in 1838, which would have substantially enlarged the house with a new Scots Jacobean entrance wing, were not implemented. Since then the only significant alterations to the entrance front have been a new porch, bow window and oriel by *Jenkins & Marr*; they also added a billiards and drawing room wing to the rear (sw) of the house for Sir Arthur Henry Grant, all in 1888–9. Inside, *John More Dick Peddie* (of *Kinnear & Peddie*) had overseen a partial restoration of the Great Hall's murals for Sir Francis Grant in 1886; the Edinburgh furniture manufacturers and decorators *John Taylor & Son* carried out some work about this time, notably in the entrance hall. The Great Hall was further restored for Sir Arthur Lindsay Grant in 1937 and Sir Francis Cullen Grant in 1964.

On plan the first three storeys constituting the original tower house bear close relationship to that at Crathes (q.v.): indeed it seems likely that the Crathes mason also worked at Monymusk. The footprint is almost exactly 13 m. square but with two shallow jambs, one protruding modestly from the northern half of the E front, and the other from the eastern half of the s front. In fact, as at Crathes, the familiar L-plan arrangement of principal apartments at first floor appears clearly evident: the great hall, orientated N–S, occupies the whole w half of the house, and a private chamber the NE corner. But at Monymusk – as at Crathes – neither the stair rising from ground floor to first nor that rising from first to second is allowed to intrude on the living accommodation: rather, by infilling the SE corner of the L-plan to create a square, space is provided for turnpikes of substantial size without any intrusion or disruption of the floor levels. That Monymusk's dimensions are slightly larger than Crathes' allows the small rooms within the infill block next to the turnpikes to be of a more useful size. The development of the Monymusk plan over Crathes is particularly notable in its defensive capabilities. At Monymusk the entrance is at ground floor within the shallow s flank of the E jamb. It is clearly overlooked from the E flank and allows attackers no place to hide; and in the event of a break-in, instead of finding themselves at the foot of the main stair as in a conventional L-plan or indeed as at Crathes, assailants would have to fight their way firstly through the guardroom which originally occupied this NE corner of the house, then along the corridor running down the E side past the ground-floor kitchen and cellar before reaching the turnpike stair from ground floor to first within the s jamb, all the while having to orientate themselves within a plan form unlike any other. Further confusion is quite intentionally caused by the turnpike stairs from first to second floor being accommodated in a separate (if adjacent) stairwell, in itself a neat social distinction for more peaceable visitors of the privacy of the upper storeys. The second jamb creating additional angles in the plan forms a further defensive feature: and in comparison with the stair-jamb at Crathes its walls are much thicker and stronger. Until the alterations of the 1750s there was also a private stair on the house's N side.

A sketch by Jaffray records the appearance of the house in 1719. The tower house occupied the NW angle of a walled barmkin approximately 30.5 m. (exactly 100 feet) square. This had habitable circular towers two storeys and attic high with tall conical roofs at its SW and SE angles. Its arched main gate was between them on the S. In the late C16 or early C17 the tower house was augmented by wings to the S and E. Originally they were both two-storey and evidently contained services at ground floor and galleries at first, as at the Forbes' Pitsligo Castle (N), the upper windows rising into dormerheads.

EXTERIOR. The Early Georgian vernacular character of the house is largely due to *Wyllie*, *Naismith* and *Murdo*'s radical remodelling of the old Forbes castle as an up-to-date if rather unconventional country house. It was they who raised the tower house from three to five storeys to provide two floors of additional bedchambers on the E and a double-height library on the W: as a result, the tower stands taller than it did when truly defensive.

Wyllie, Naismith and Murdo also transferred the main entrance to the S wing, where their Doric porch has since been replaced. They regularized the tower house's fenestration, two windows at each level within the main block's E courtyard front and one within the jamb's S flank, their third- and fourth-floor windows having chamfered surrounds. In this heightened form the tower house's wall-heads are plain except for an eaves course. The gables are shallow-pitched, and the platformed roof-lines are punctuated by sturdy coped chimneystacks to accommodate the numerous fireplaces and flues. The attics are lit by twin oculi in the gables and above the small turnpike in the S gable is a small square belvedere, formerly with a balustrade. The retention of details such as the second-floor segmental hoodmoulds with dripstone heads, the former parapet brackets immediately above and the turret corbel tables probably owes less to economy than a desire to emphasize that Monymusk House had indeed been a tower house – and that the Grants were an old family, even if they had purchased Monymusk itself only recently.

Wyllie, Naismith and Murdo's scheme also reconstructed the C16–C17 wings, repeating the twin attic oculi of the tower house in their gables as a unifying feature. The E WING was heightened to two full storeys, but its earlier origin remained evident in the irregularities of its six-windows-long elevation. The S WING's rebuilding was more ambitious, three storeys high with its eaves cornice aligned with the corbel table of the tower house as a long unifying horizontal. It is four bays broad, its windows grouped as two pairs, and at its SE angle it incorporates the heightened C16 drum tower of the former barmkin. The drum's early date is evident in the marked batter of its build and at the original stair-turret now embedded within the re-entrant angle on the N. The flues on its S face have a triple-shafted chimneyhead, a feature also found at Culter (*see* p. 287) and Keith Hall (q.v.), both of *c.* 1700, and may pre-date the 1750s works. In Wyllie, Naismith and Murdo's remodelling this SW tower was answered by the retained SE tower as part of their railed clairvoie forecourt which had Baroque gateways to the S and E opening onto the axial routes of Jaffray's designed landscape. These are recorded in Hugh Irvine's painting of 1811 but regrettably they were removed by *John Smith* in 1825–7.

As they exist now Wyllie, Naismith and Murdo's elevations have a few Late Victorian additions by *Jenkins & Marr*: a mullioned-and-transomed first-floor oriel at the E wing's E end to light Sir Arthur's principal bedroom and a conical-roofed ground-floor bow window near the S end of the S wing. Jenkins & Marr also enclosed the open porch as a solid structure, but still with Doric columns at its angles.

On the REAR (W) ELEVATION the tower house is of four storeys rather than five, the library inside being double-height. The ground-, first- and second-floor windows are not quite regular in arrangement. As Douglas Simpson observed, this original part of the elevation is reminiscent of the back wall of Balfluig (q.v.) although rather larger; likewise similar is the W half of the S gable which relates to the stair jamb in much the same way, with a corbelled splay in the re-entrant angle. These features confirm that the C16 tower house had no parapets on this side and that the corbelling at the angles carried Balfluig-type turrets as in Jaffray's sketch. The back of the S wing had regular fenestration but its S end is now obscured by *Jenkins & Marr's* SW ADDITION of 1888–9 which provided a ground-floor billiard room and a greatly enlarged drawing room. Incorporated in its masonry is a cruciform loophole with an oilette, probably a surviving detail from the old barmkin.

INTERIOR. Within the S wing, the ENTRANCE HALL was refitted in the 1880s by *John Taylor & Sons*, its chimneypiece hood and mantelshelf borne aloft by Grant supporters. On the N side, the main turnpike stair rises to the GREAT HALL at first floor within the tower house. Its decorative scheme is a familiar Renaissance mix of biblical, classical and heraldic motifs balancing the moralistic and profane, but most of that above the fireplace is reproduction of 1964. The largest panel, somewhat off-centre, features an escutcheon displaying the lion rampant with helm and seated lion front-face above, and two rampant unicorns as supporters with Scottish saltire and lion rampant standards. To the l., the arms of Mary of Lorraine and Margaret Tudor, one above the other, are flanked by representations of Adam, still in his innocence, standing on a column. To the r., Darnley's and Anne of Denmark's arms are flanked by Eve, looking suspiciously like Botticelli's Venus. She too stands on a column, writhing seductively as she caresses the serpent which enfolds her, while beneath treacherous apples wrap up the column shafts like creepers. To either side of the fireplace, and in the room's r. corner, are the arms of Dame Margaret Douglas, wife of William Forbes, and charming heraldic bears. Elsewhere in the Great Hall the surviving decoration appears more original (richly painted tempera on plaster) although some may have been touched up during *Peddie*'s partial renovation of 1886. In one window, a clever Renaissance deceit: Hector and Achilles – looking like cultured Scottish noblemen – are painted one on each reveal conversing in a tent during a truce in the Trojan War, while above hangers-on lift up *trompe l'œil* flaps to eavesdrop, the tent's main opening being the window glass itself which is closed by the curtain. The timber ceiling beams are painted with crouching and prancing animals, zigzags and vine scrolls in light colours against a dark background. Just l. of the fireplace, an aumbry rises into an ogee-arched hoodmould with scrolled finial. The tympanum within it has a banner carved with a hand pointing to the motto LATYAMSAY in C16 relief lettering. To the r. of the chimneypiece in the NE corner another C16 survival, the corbelling of the lost N turnpike.

In Archibald Grant's remodelling the Great Hall was panelled, with a chimneypiece provided by *John* and *James Adam* to the latter's design, but these features were removed in 1937. In Sir Archibald's LIBRARY however the panelling survives; the ceiling has a deep classical frieze with mutuled cornice, and a central plaster oval of fruit and flowers. This appears to be the work of *Murdo* and is still surprisingly Carolean in character, perhaps from late C17 moulds. The chimneypiece was made by *William Lunan* to *John Adam*'s design. The SMALL DRAWING ROOM's panelling is of the same period, but its moulded cornice is simpler. *Jenkins & Marr*'s bicameral DRAWING ROOM, partly formed within the S wing and partly in their addition of 1888–9, has coved ceilings.

Monymusk House stands on the Don's S bank, its DESIGNED LANDSCAPE of 202 hectares lying in a shallow bowl of ground; Pitfichie Hill and Millstone Hill rise on either side of the river to the NW with Cairn William and Bennachie beyond. *Alexander Jaffray* laid out formal POLICIES with axial routes extending S, E and W from the house *c.* 1720; many of the S avenue's beeches are probably original. Then *c.* 1730 he formed a delightful 'PARADISE' in the Don Valley 3 km. NNW, which appears in William Roy's Military Survey of 1747–55. Its beech tree ring and quadrants of yews survive but during the mid C19 the surroundings were planted with wellingtonia, hemlock and Douglas fir and today Paradise Wood contains 180 species of vascular plants.

Jaffray's vision remained intact when surveyed by *Robert Robinson* in 1762, but *George Brown*'s survey of 1774 shows his formal policies being softened by the fashion for the Picturesque. The wider surroundings reflect Sir Archibald Grant's efforts to drain and enclose his farmland. Before his death in 1778 he reputedly planted over 48 million trees around the house and on the steeper hill-slopes: the Kirktown, Glashie, Moor of Mains and Gallowhill Woods were all probably begun by him and Pitfichie Wood substantially extended. Further enlarged during the mid C19, they consist of broad-leaf varieties chiefly oak, ash, birch and gean with some fir trees.

The HOME FARM (250 m. SSE) is of various dates between the early–mid C18 and the mid C19. Its principal frontage, facing N, is exceptionally long: towards the W, between two projecting wings, is a pedimented two-bay centre with segmental cartshed arches, probably by *John Smith c.* 1825. The WALLED GARDEN – a parallelogram on plan – which lies immediately S belongs to the earlier period. The S avenue's GATEPIERS are of two different dates. The inner pair have been reused from the fore-court of *c.* 1754–5: they were transferred here *c.* 1825. Magnificently Baroque, square-plan in banded ashlar with urn finials, they are set on the diagonal. The outer piers supporting the side gates are C19 and the gates themselves mid-C20.

PITFICHIE CASTLE. *See* p. 700.

MUCHALLS

Small improvement village, originally named Stranathro and built during the C19.

ST TERNAN (Episcopal), 900 m. NW across the A90. Built in three campaigns, and the successor to the Episcopal chapels at Muchalls Castle (*see* below) and Elsick House (*see* p. 481). Harled and crowstepped nave, the three E bays built in 1831. Tudor-headed windows subdivided into three. The narrower chancel was added in 1865 by *Alexander Ellis*, of rubble with a polygonal end. Lancet windows and an oculus in the E face. In 1870, *Ellis & Wilson* added the crowstepped porch, W bay and W gable with its triple lancets and gableted bellcote.

Inside, the semicircular, chamfered chancel arch has cone corbels with acanthus capitals. – Tiled REREDOS behind the altar, quite precocious for 1865. – Wooden STALLS in the chancel with fleur-de-lys bench-ends. – C17 wooden CHAIR, made for the chapel in the Castle (*see* below). – ORGAN by *Wadsworth* of Manchester, 1882. Good stencilled pipes with blue and gold. – STAINED GLASS. Good Shepherd, *c.* 1867 (E window).

VIADUCT, 1 km. SSW. Four-span bridge with rectangular piers, built *c.* 1849 for the Aberdeen Railway. Original wooden trusses replaced in 1886 with plate girders and lattice pylons by *A. & W. Smith* of Glasgow.

MUCHALLS CASTLE
1.2 km. WSW

A very rewarding building, little altered from the C17 and retaining exceptionally fine plasterwork. The lands of Muchalls originally formed part of the Barony of Cowie (Stonehaven), given by Robert the Bruce to Sir Alexander Fraser, his Lord Chamberlain. Fraser built a castle here by *c.* 1320, of which there are still traces inside.* The estate passed to the Hays of Errol in the C15 and in 1606 Francis, the 9th Earl, sold it to Alexander Burnett of Leys. It was he who began the present building in 1619, although little progress can have been made as he died the same year. Alexander had just completed Crathes Castle (q.v.), so Muchalls was probably intended as a dower house – or else as a home for one of his fourteen children. Sir Thomas, Alexander's son (and the 1st Baronet), completed the building in 1627, a feat which is recorded over the main entrance. Muchalls remains nearly as he left it: the castle has stayed blessedly free of both Georgian additions and the near-inevitable Baronialization in the C19.

Sir Thomas died in 1653 and in 1705 the estate was sold to Thomas Fullerton. In 1885 it was taken over as a summer house by J.P.B. Robertson, Lord Justice General of Scotland. At the start of the C20 it was acquired by the Aberdeen Endowments Trust and subsequently restored.

The EXTERIOR is approached by an intact BARMKIN enclosing a FORECOURT, one of the few remaining examples to have survived in Scotland. Four open tourelles lining a parapet (formerly with a wooden cat-walk, now much altered). Main entrance via a segmental arch with thick roll moulding. Triple shot-holes to the l. and r., the middle one lozenge-shaped and the outer ones round. Above it, a worn TABLET carved with the inscription:

This work begun on the East & North be A^r Burnet of Leyis, 1619: Ended be S[i]r Thomas Burnet of Leyis his sonne, 1627

The Castle itself is large, harled and solidly unassuming. It takes the form of a large L-plan, with wings on the N and E sides and a stair-tower protruding from the SE corner, just returning around the S side of the courtyard. As with the entrance, the walls employ C17 defensive features quite sparingly, and mostly for decorative effect. So Muchalls is a hybrid tower house, already resembling a small but recognizably 'modern' country house. The ancient vocabulary has been transformed into something built for cosmopolitan luxury and contemporary living. The NW gable is tall and narrowly crowstepped, with two tourelles corbelled out below to the l. and r. Each has a conical roof and a pair of small shot-holes. SW gable (for the short stair jamb, inside the courtyard) also

---

*Fraser's castle is shown on Pont's map of *c.* 1590 and was declared 'a very fine palace' in 1609.

Muchalls Castle.
Engraving by R. W. Billings, 1852

crowstepped, its top floor slightly jettied on two rows of thick
tripartite corbels. Original entrance in the s re-entrant angle
with rectangular, bolection-moulded doorpiece. Plaque above
it with the Burnet coat of arms; original iron grill over the
window to the r. On the wall-head above it, a triangular dormerhead with consoled sides. On the E face (towards the courtyard), a large PLAQUE of the royal coat of arms with worn date
of 1629. Shallow stair-turret sunk in the N re-entrant angle and
a lower staircase wrapped around it from the late C19. Plain N
flank beyond with rectangular windows. Three big chimneys
protruding from the gabled roof, which was never slated and
is still covered with its original stone slabs (again a rare survival, cf. Coxton Tower in Moray). Outside the courtyard, the
long E front has crowstepped gables with a tourelle in each far
angle. Enlarged rectangular windows in between and a canted
oriel. Off to the NE is a SERVICE BLOCK added by *Walker &
Duncan* in 1898–9, itself a smaller L-plan with stair drum tower
under conical roof. It partially clasps the N arm of the Castle,
which is tall and sheer with three crowstepped dormerheads.

The relatively subdued outside gives little indication of the
glories of the INTERIOR. Six former CELLAR CHAMBERS on
the ground floor, each covered – quite unexpectedly – with a
groin-vault rather than the usual barrels. Former KITCHEN in
the NE corner (now a dining room) with a massive fireplace
arch. The massively thick wall behind it incorporates a narrow
spiral staircase that now leads nowhere, almost certainly a
reused section of the C14 castle that became obsolete in the
early C17. In the N wing, a groin-vault is truncated by a wall

that can only have been inserted by Burnett's masons and so another relic of Fraser's castle.

The GREAT HALL spans the whole first floor of the E wing and features some of the finest PLASTERWORK in Scotland, much of it still with original tinctures. It is dated 1624. Moulded ribs enriched with foliage and fruit creating square and quatre-foiled patterns. Good pendant bosses arranged in three rows, those in the middle designed for hanging lights. The ends of the centre are vigorously ball-like and reeded, the middle a tour de force with eagles, lions, angels, men's faces and two monkeys flanking the light hook. Framed by the ribs are coats of arms of Burnett's political allies (e.g. Hamilton, Dunfermline, Lauderdale) and, flanking the big central boss, those of Sir Thomas himself and his parents. Interspersed with these are also medallion heads of 'Worthies' (e.g. Alexander the Great, David, Joshua and Hector), prominent advertisements of Renaissance erudition. More heraldry for Arbuthnot, Hamilton, Gordon and Forbes in the upper window embrasures. Many of the details of the Muchalls ceiling are identical to those in the Great Hall at Glamis (Angus), completed in 1621 and Craigievar (q.v.), completed in 1625 and no doubt cast from the same moulds. The medallions of Worthies are adapted from a set of engravings published in Amsterdam by Nicolas de Bruyn (*Heads of Worthys*) in 1594 and were a popular subject in much early C17 Scottish plasterwork. Below the ceiling is a fine frieze with geometric patterns and more flowers and fruit. Against the N wall, a pilastered chimneypiece with wonderfully bombastic overmantel featuring the Royal Arms, painted and gilt and again dated 1624. The unicorn holds the banner of St Andrew, as at Craigievar. To the l. and r. are pairs of gloriously primitive Atlantes and caryatids, their arms linked and fingers stretched in the air as if enacting an Egyptian ritual. They stand on baluster-like pedestals, and the flanking oak doors are original.

In the N wing, the former WITHDRAWING ROOM (now the Dining Room) and the former SOLAR (now the Study) both retain more excellent plasterwork, again dated 1624. No pendants here, but more medallions from the series of Worthies including Tarquin, Lucretia and Justinian. More Burnett arms in the overmantels, as well as monograms for Alexander and his wife, Katharine Gordon, and Sir Thomas and his wife, Jean Moncrieff.

Just off the S side of the Castle, swollen turf shows the location of the CHAPEL commissioned by Sir Thomas in 1621 and completed in 1624. It was burned down by Cumberland's army in 1746, but a small vaulted compartment (almost certainly a crypt) is intact below the surface.* – Stretching E of the house are the remains of an extensive DESIGNED LANDSCAPE, probably laid out in the reign of Charles II and meant to be admired from the Great Hall. – Just W of the Castle (on the drive) is a

*The only surviving furnishing is the wooden chair, now in St Ternan (*see* above).

SERVICE FORECOURT by *Walker & Duncan*, 1894–6. COACH-
HOUSE and STABLE BLOCK on the N with two segmental cart
bays and ridge-tiled roof. It has a little Scots Renaissance
cupola and a pair of tall catslide dormers. Across from it, a
crowstepped, L-plan GARDENER'S COTTAGE. – Just E is the
original early C17 DOOCOT, also built by Sir Thomas Burnett
and remodelled in the late C19, when the vaulted basement
was used as a garden pavilion. Small, harled square with steep
gabled roof and chamfered rectangular entrance. Much taller
on the W, as it is set into a hillside.

NETHERLEY HOUSE   K

2.5 km. WNW of Cookney

An austerely elegant mansion, built *c.* 1750 by Alexander Silver,
who died here after amassing a fortune from sugar and tea plantations in Jamaica. The house is now split into three separate
dwellings and hemmed in by bland modern housing.

Two-storey, three-bay main block facing NE, the centre bay minimally advanced and swept past the wall-head into a bellcast
segmental gable with chimneystack and attic window. Long
first-floor windows surrounded by good cherry-cocking; low,
advanced entrance of ashlar with shallow Roman Doric portico.
Two-storey wings projecting forward to the l. and r., originally
forming a U-plan. The r. was extended in the early C19 by
Alexander's son, George, with double-piended roofs and a
two-storey bow window facing W.
　　The stair hall was once very fine, originally soaring up two
storeys but regrettably divided horizontally in the conversion.
Good Adam-style plaster ceiling still *in situ* here and in the
ante-room. Former chapel in the W section with Gothic glazing;
dining room in the E wing with a coffered, gilded cupola.

NEWMACHAR

A small village on the A947, formerly known as Summerhill,
which has grown substantially as a result of the oil boom.

PARISH CHURCH, School Road. As first built in 1791 a simple
rectangular plan in coursed squared golden granite, four
round-arched windows with astragalled sash-and-case windows
in its long S flank, and doorways in the W and possibly E gables.
The ball-finialled birdcage bellcote over the W end contains a
bell by *Michael Burgerhuys*, 1635. In 1913 the church was reordered by *John Robertson* of Inverness, who enlarged it substantially to the E with a single entrance nearest School Road and

transferred the pulpit area from the centre of the s flank to the w. He built two gabled bays flanking his new doorway, that to the SE containing a stair and that to the NE slightly bowed containing an organ with a half-hexagonal vestry on its N flank. In 2007 *Ken Mathieson* of Bucksburn filled the space between these gables to produce the present frontage with its central fanlit doorway. The very shallow W chancel with cinquefoil roundel is *Robertson*'s, as are the four N-side windows which though similar in size to the s side's have two-light tracery. The interior is all *Robertson*'s, his division of it into bays by the insertion of clustered timber wall-shafts bearing semi-elliptical arches recalling his work at Glass Parish Church (q.v.), and his wooden groin-vaulting over the windows that at Holyrood Chapel, Newburgh (1906–9, N). His deep E-end gallery has an arcaded front. – FURNISHINGS. 1913. – STAINED GLASS window by *Douglas Strachan*, 1915, represents the Virgin Mary, St Machar and William the Lion granting a charter to Bishop Matthew.

In the CHURCHYARD the RAMSAY ENCLOSURE is plain ashlar, its gate removed. Earliest grave is that of Robert Gordon (1580–1661), historian, cartographer, musicologist and mediator.

Nos. 11–39 STATION ROAD. Environmentally friendly accommodation for *Grampian Housing*, in architectural terms easily the best post-war development in Newmachar. Single storey and attic beneath big monopitch roofs. Ground floor in light-coloured timber-boarding; windows shaded by canopies stained in a darker colour at the upper floor.

Former PARISH MANSE, 0.5 km. W off Corseduick Road. Built 1781. Principal front facing SSW over its walled garden is two storeys and three windows wide, raised slightly over a basement. Central transom-lit doorway flanked by ground-floor canted bays added either in 1840 or more probably by *James Matthews* in 1877. Gabled roof with end stacks and later box dormers. Rear elevation flanked by long low steadings on each side creating a handsome court. To the NW of the manse, an associated threshing mill (horse-driven), now a house.

Former FREE CHURCH MANSE. By *James Henderson*, 1843. A classic Aberdeen villa type. Single-storeyed with three bays raised over a tall basement plinth, harled with ashlar dressings. Stairs with ashlar parapets rising to the central doorway, its deep plate-glazed transom-light sheltered by a block pediment supported on consoles. Large main floor windows with apron panels resting on ashlar belt-course. Original broad-eaved canted attic dormers in shallow roof reflecting a notably deep plan; coped chimneystacks.

Former DISTRICT ASYLUM FOR ABERDEEN, Kingseat, 1.6 km. ESE. With Bangour (*see The Buildings of Scotland: Lothian*), the first Scottish mental hospital arranged on the 'colony plan' inspired by Alt Scherbitz, Germany, its wards mostly in individual villa-blocks set in picturesque grounds rather than a single large building with surrounding wall. The layout was nevertheless symmetrical, reflecting similar provision for males and females. The estate was purchased by Aberdeen District Lunacy Board in 1899. The original buildings were designed by *A. Marshall Mackenzie* in plain Scots vernacular and Old English styles, all pink pinned granite with Welsh slate roofs. Additions by *Gall & Hay* 1926. Converted for residential use since 2008.

DISBLAIR HOUSE, 2.4 km. W. For the Rev. Dr Morrison, *c.* 1830. Rustic Italianate version of a classic Aberdeen villa type. Single-storey three-bay entrance front with segment-headed doorway and windows at main floor raised over a semi-sunk basement with thermals. Heraldic panel re-set. Piended roof with oversailing eaves on shapely timber brackets, coped end stacks. The lower pavilion wings slightly recessed with blind round-arched openings extend back into a U-plan. Interior gutted by fire, but renovated, the Alexander Thomson-school woodwork having been imported. Nearby, tall rectangular DOOCOT, rubble-built with rat course, saddleback slate roof.

PARKHILL ESTATE, 4.9 km. S at the edge of Aberdeen. Mid-C18 mansion demolished *c.* 1960, but the policies remain well wooded with a lake. WEST LODGE on the A974 just N of the Don. Single-storey three bays fronted by a miniature Doric colonnade supporting the bracketed eaves of a low piended roof, with a central chimneystack rising into a pair of very short diagonally shafted chimneystacks. Within the colonnade, a pointed-arch doorway and two round-headed windows. BEECH COTTAGE. Pretty single-storey villa with canted dormers set into tall roof, external window shutters.

GOVAL BRIDGE, 4.6 km. S, carrying the A947 over the Goval Burn. *c.* 1800, widened *c.* 1880. A segmental arch with hump-backed parapets supported on corbels. It is framed by pilasters which rise into panels with blind quatrefoils and arrow loops.

DYCE & WATERTON PUMPING STATION, 4.6 km. S, near Goval Bridge. Dated 1898. Early example of mass-concrete construction, disguised as a two-storey farmhouse. Against the rear, on higher ground, tall twin arches feed an embanked lade leading to Overton and Kirkhill reservoirs.

ELRICK HOUSE. *See* p. 480.

6020

NEWTON HOUSE
1.8 km. NW of Old Rayne

Late C17 or early C18, perhaps 1692. Unusually large and up-to-date for a North-East country house of that time, although comparable examples exist in Central and Southern Scotland, suggesting that its mason may have come from there. The house was probably once entered through its courtyard on the N side. It was re-ordered in 1778 with the entrance transferred to the S front, the service court thereafter being relatively concealed. Further alterations were made in the C19.

The MAIN BLOCK which is harled with pale grey granite dressings and margins rises through three full storeys with a basement on its S side formed in a fall of the ground. Originally both sides seem to have been expressed by four windows on each floor, broadly spaced though with the inner pair relatively close together. All three storeys, and the basement, are of substantial height; but immediately above the lintels of the second floor windows, an eaves-course announces a steeply pitched hipped and bellcast roof containing substantial attic accommodation and with two low chimneystacks straddling its ridge: this hipped roof is in itself an unusual feature for its date, gabled roofs being more common until the later C18. The main entrance formed between the centre pair of windows at ground floor during the reordering of 1778 is approached by a railed stair flying over the basement area; the land may have been raised on this side so that the basement storey, while forming a suitable plinth, was partly concealed. The transom-lit entrance itself is sheltered by an open pediment of deep projection supported on console brackets; it is dated with the initials of the owners A.D. I.D. On plan the house is deep single-pile; shallow bows were added to the end gables in the early C19. The N front of the main block has been much altered, with a canted bay being formed in its centre to accommodate the present internal stair. The COURTYARD's pavilion wings which project from the outer bays at ground floor may have been altered as part of the early C19 works, but their hipped bellcast roofs, echoing that of the main block, look early. They extend into lower ranges, the courtyard being entered on the N side through a segmentally arched screen wall with initials A.G. and date 1883 or 1893 on its inside face. A pineapple finial – a symbol of hospitality – hints at the courtyard's former status as the original approach to the house. INTERIOR generally simple, the stair approached from the entrance hall through a triple archway. Entrance hall's dado panelling is good modern work, but the finely reeded doorcases between the principal apartment and the later pavilion on the W side date from the time of the early C19 alterations, as does their still-crisp plasterwork; the corresponding rooms on the E side are plainer.

HOME FARM STEADING, 150 m. NNW. By *John Smith*, 1831. Rectangular courtyard plan. Principal elevation single-storey-and-loft, its pedimented centre slightly projected with twin segmental archways, and four-bay flanking ranges resulting in an impressive ten-bay front, ashlar-faced and deeply shadowed by its broad-eaved roof.

The POLICIES with outlooks S to Bennachie were probably laid out in the late C18 and evidently much improved *c.* 1846 when Alexander Gordon formed the WALLED GARDEN 300 m. E of the house, square-plan and divided into four compartments.

The stone FOUNTAIN purchased by Gordon in Italy in 1846 was formerly adorned by lions.

The 'NEWTON STONE' in blue gneiss, 2.03 m. high, formerly stood at Shevack toll. Six lines of Old Roman Cursive (or another ancient language of the Mediterranean littoral) near its top and an ogham inscription down the l.-hand angle and lower front (are they genuine?). The SYMBOL STONE, 2.06 m. high in blue-grey gneiss displays double-disc and serpent crossed by Z-rod. It reputedly came from somewhere between Newton and Rothney.

MAUSOLEUM, 0.8 km. SSE on the bank of the River Urie. It has the name of Alexander Gordon over the doorway and the date 1809.

6020

OLD RAYNE

This fertile location by the River Urie has evidently been import-ant since medieval times. Rayne was the seat of the Archdeacon of St Machar's Cathedral, a post held in the C14 by John Barbour, author of *The Brus*, whose earthwork castle stood on the site now occupied by the school. From 1493 Rayne was a burgh of barony under the Bishop's superiority, its status reaffirmed in the late C17 under the superiority of John Horn of Westhall (q.v.). Presumably from Horn's time dates the MARKET CROSS in the centre of the village, a slim rectangular shaft of hewn granite, stop-chamfered at its edges, with moulded cornice, pyramidal top and ball finial supporting a saltire weathervane. The two-storey HEADHOUSE immediately S, with external stair to first floor, may have been the tolbooth.

PLOUGHMAN'S HALL, 1 km. N. Headquarters of the Ploughman Society, established 1819; the hall is dated 1820. Two storeys in roughly squared, coursed and pinned masonry, and a gabled roof with end stacks. Principal front facing S is four windows broad, widely spaced, with twin central doorways. Above, in the centre, a round-arched recess incorporates the datestone, a representation of a plough, with inscription 'Ploughman Soc^{ys} Hall' and re-set armorial panel dated 1778 with quartered arms and initials of Alexander Leith of Freefield (q.v.) and his two wives, Jane Garden of Troup and Martha Ross of Arnage (N). The Leiths perhaps gave the site and their tenants once paid their rents here and received a glass of porter. Originally the only stair was that on the l. end gable; inside an ante-room led to the first-floor meeting hall. Restored in the late 1980s by *Douglas Forrest* for residential use but preserving the large room on the upper floor. The gatepiers are from Keith Hall (q.v.).

BONNYTON MILL, 1.3 km. NE. The mill has two storeys and a loft, scarped into a sharp fall in the ground, so allowing grain to be delivered directly into the loft. It has retained its mill-stones, oat-bruiser, pearl-barley machine and drying kiln.

Remains also of a timber and iron mid-breast paddle wheel (3.2 m. diameter), made by the *Grandholm Foundry c.* 1835.
NEWTON HOUSE. *See* p. 692.

OYNE

Really several small settlements – including Oyne, Old Westhall and Kirkton of Oyne – strung out along the B9002.

Former FREE CHURCH, Old Westhall. By *George Gilchrist*, mason, and *Peter Anderson*, carpenter, 1848. Gothic gable front with pinnacled buttresses suggesting nave and aisles. Pointed doorway and gallery window with lancets to each side and a gableted bellcote, all in local red sandstone. Harled three-bay flanks. Later C19 hall and vestry at rear. Now residential. – Former MANSE, 60 m. SW, also by *Gilchrist* and *Anderson*, 1848 9. Two storeys, three bays. Console-cornice over central doorway, cream-harled, slim granite margins and gabled roof with end stacks.

Former ST NINIAN'S PARISH CHURCH, Hart Hill. By *William Sangster*, square-wright, 1807–8. Burnt out in the late C20. Very simple three-bay rectangle in roughly coursed red granite, but one of the earliest Gothic churches in Aberdeenshire. Its relatively short length called for a layout which did not become common until a decade later: a single entrance in the W gable and a single gallery facing the pulpit at the E. Another pioneering feature was the E end's stepped triple lights, their heads still visible above a later slapping. Birdcage bellcote over E gable.

Some 175 m. SW is ST NINIAN'S CHURCHYARD, perhaps the site of the church recorded in 1256. The former PARISH MANSE, 50 m. ESE of the churchyard, was built in 1796 and extended *c.* 1839–42. A two-storey five-bay frontage raised over a semi-sunk basement with its broad far l. gabled bay projecting, and a stair to the doorway close into the angle on the main front. The doorway is distinguished by a pediment on console-brackets and the gabled bay has a bay window rising through ground and first floors with windows only in its centre face. White-harled, with granite dressings. The three r. bays represent the original manse.

HILL-FORT, Mither Tap o' Bennachie, 3.5 km. S. A prominent landmark across large areas of Aberdeenshire. Two massive stone-defined ramparts enclose a granite tor. The outer rampart is around 7 m. thick and entry is given through a curving entrance passage. The inner wall is on a steeper slope, set close to the edges of the tor. Traces of buildings can be seen within the inner and outer ramparts. Recent radiocarbon dates from the interior suggest occupation in the early medieval period *c.* 300–700 AD. (GN)

HARTHILL CASTLE. *See* p. 517.
WESTHALL. *See* p. 762.

HARTHILL CASTLE. *See* p. 517.
WESTHALL. *See* p. 762.

7090

PARK HOUSE
1.75 km. SW of Drumoak

William Moir, son of the owner of Denmore, near Bridge of Don, acquired the estate in 1821 and immediately engaged *Archibald Simpson* to replace the existing residence. Completed in 1822 it is Simpson at his most Grecian, a temple villa in Arcadia.

65   The house is stuccoed in imitation of ashlar. The centre of the principal (SE) front is single-storeyed, seven bays wide with a parapet but with projecting two-storey outer bays under piend roofs. Tetrastyle Greek Doric portico in the centre with low pediment and a frieze of laurel wreaths, continued on the three bays l. and r. Windows recessed from the wall-plane, without mouldings. The flanks of the house are of three bays, the E flank slightly altered by insertion of a large door in the centre and the W flank with a conservatory (early C21). The back of the house is mostly harled, with granite dressings, and given the steep rise in the wooded ground immediately behind was evidently not intended to be seen. The penultimate bays l. and r. project in two depths for the service wings (originally for kitchen etc. E and coachhouse and stables W).

Inside, a double-pile plan bisected by an E–W corridor. Behind the portico is the top-lit entrance VESTIBULE, with refined coffered dome ceiling, oval on shallow pendentives. Mahogany doors. A Doric screen separates this from the central corridor. The principal rooms E and W are also very restrained, almost Soanean in their control. Both have coved ceilings above a cornice. The DRAWING ROOMS (W) are in two parts, the first drawing room with plain unmoulded alcoves in the wall and one with a segmental head framing the entrance to the smaller drawing room. This has curved ends, a flat ceiling and connects N to the former LIBRARY, an octagon. The DINING ROOM E of the entrance is essentially the same as the larger drawing room, with segmental-headed buffet recess. The grey marble chimneypiece here is original (that in the larger drawing room in Adam's style is imported). In the centre of the N front is the former BILLIARD ROOM. The staircases are to E and W, the principal stair opening N from the corridor and cantilevered around a semicircle with beautiful cast-iron stick balusters with honeysuckle leaves in teardrop-shaped openings. Top-lit at first floor. The motifs at this level and in the bedrooms in the E and W ranges are as understated as those below. The house was restored in 1996 as a fishing lodge, the former stable wing now converted to a billiard room etc.

PHESDO HOUSE   K   6070
3.3 km. NE of Fettercairn

Regally calm and poised, and certainly among the finest Regency houses in North Scotland. Phesdo was built 1814–15 for Alexander Crombie (†1832), an advocate in Aberdeen who purchased the estate *c.* 1805. He found nothing but 'crude, ancient fabric' and commissioned *John Smith* to provide him with a proper house outside the 'commotion and anarchy' of city life. Smith's prolific output can sometimes lead to weariness, but here he is at the height of his powers, showing how much can be achieved through nothing more than high-quality materials and skilful proportion. Smith's mastery is all the more striking as Phesdo is an early work, made two years after he laid out the W end of Union Street in Aberdeen (*see* p. 169), and before *Archibald Simpson* had done so much to popularize the Greek Revival style.

The main façade is to the S, of two storeys and five bays, minimalist and pleasing in equal measure. The stone is gleaming, silvery granite, pristinely dressed and coursed and transported here at great expense. Minimally advanced centre delineated by giant pilasters. Tetrastyle portico in front of it with Greek Doric columns, triglyph architrave and guttae cornice. Symmetrical pairs of windows to the l. and r., those on the ground floor longer with bracketed cornices on top. Angle pilasters beyond them; panel of overlapping discs in the centre of the wall-head providing the only other ornament. The flanks are of three bays and similarly treated, the r. one with the central windows blind. Rear wings then extend to form a U-plan, the l. one of granite (with veranda) and the r. one a rather jarring contrast of dark-brown rubble.

The interior is very fine and unleashes the full Grecian ornament that was only hinted at outside. Wooden doors with acanthus leading into square entrance hall with Empire garland frieze. Coffered ceiling with central rose set in a rectangular panel. A distyle screen with fluted Ionic columns gives way to the STAIR HALL, rising up full height to a ceiling with another good rose. Cantilevered staircase with spiralled newels and pierced, rectangular balusters. Greek key frieze wrapping around the first floor. DRAWING ROOM to the l. of the entrance with foliate frieze and white marble chimneypiece. Long acanthus leaves with scrolled ends. Consoled double doors (the r. one blind) lead to the original DINING ROOM on the other side. Rinceau frieze and bracketed cornice. Another distyle screen (for the sideboard), this one with unfluted Corinthian columns. To the r. of the entrance is the STUDY, nicely designed as a tight ellipse. Frieze with anthemion and grey marble chimneypiece with shell ornament. The former MORNING ROOM (now Dining Room) lies beyond, similarly treated with chimneypiece in a D-ended wall and a door to the l. and r.

Former STABLES, 190 m. NNE. Symmetrical five bays, *c.* 1815 and also by *Smith*. Minimally advanced centre with elliptical arch, corniced window and pediment with blind oculus. – Square DOOCOT (220 m. NNW of the house), tall and compact with pyramidal roof. Vent lintel dated 1838. Truncated alighting ledge with five flight-holes. – WALLED GARDEN. Designed as a huge ellipse and surely also by *Smith*. It is an unusual and wonderful shape for a walled garden, and a fine echo of the curved geometry inside the main house.

PITCAPLE

A small village on the A96. No churches.

PITCAPLE CASTLE, 0.9 km. NE. A Z-plan tower house. The centre block reputedly dates from *c.* 1470, the Leslies having been granted their lands in 1457; the two drum towers at diagonally opposite corners were added in the mid C16. In 1830 this tower house was incorporated into the E side of a larger two-storey house built for Hugh Lumsden by *William Burn*, which was further extended in 1870 by *Duncan McMillan*.

The TOWER HOUSE's four-storey central block, orientated N–S, rises into a crowstep-gabled roof; the drum towers at the NE and SW angles rise through five storeys, the NE being much the larger of the two. The drum towers break up into shapely spired roofs with a marked bellcast, but these are Burn replacements of much lower originals. The NW and SE angles have turrets corbelled out from third floor, and within the re-entrant angles formed between the main block and the drum towers there are further small stair-turrets corbelled out at a slightly higher level. All of these have spirelet roofs, resulting in a very picturesque roof-line.

The main block of *c.* 1470 is 15 m. long by 8.8 m. deep. Its walls rise with a slight batter and it has rounded angles. Inside at ground-floor level, a corridor running along the W side gives access to three vaulted chambers, the largest being the kitchen with its hearth in the N gable. The first floor comprised the hall; originally the entrance was perhaps at this level, accessed by an external wooden stair. The wall-head was probably once crenellated with an attic caphouse. At some point a now-blocked doorway was formed in the centre of the W wall at ground floor, and protected from above by a machicolated chamber which still survives.

The addition of the two big drum towers in the mid C16 allowed for much more sophisticated planning. The SW tower, 3.5 m. in diameter, provided a new turnpike stair, although the doorway at its foot is not original, and the larger NE tower of 5.2 m. diameter provided bedchambers. The upper floors of the original tower house were divided by a masonry cross wall into two apartments in the late C17 or early C18, and these, together with the smaller rooms in the NE tower, provided the familiar arrangement of hall, outer chamber and inner chamber which became fashionable at this time, the first-floor hall having a service stair from the S cellar. At ground, first and second floors the rooms in the NE tower are square and vaulted, at third floor the room is octagonal and at attic level – accessed by a separate stair – it is circular.

A drawing by the antiquarian James Skene of Rubislaw in 1827 shows the forecourt still surviving but it is absent from Hullmandel's lithograph. Skene's drawing shows the forecourt with a gateway in its S wall near the E angle. This gateway comprised a round-headed arch with a guardhouse entered through the reveals on each side and an armorial above. It was once enclosed by a moat flooded by a burn on its N side.

Given the requirement that they should provide more generous accommodation, William Burn's ADDITIONS of 1830 were as sympathetic to the old tower house as they could be at that date, harled and lower in height – consistently two-storeyed – with a new entrance, canted bays, crowstepped gables, tourelles and slim dummy turrets with conical spirelets. The glazing was originally lying-pane throughout. The same style was adopted in *McMillan*'s enlargement and lower N service wing in 1870, but his windows were plate glass and his NE turret more generously proportioned.

Inside, Burn's principal apartments form the right-angled suite characteristic of his smaller houses, all quite simple with Greek chimneypieces. The original rather narrow hall-corridor was greatly aggrandized by McMillan, who rebuilt the STAIR HALL, an impressive space entered through a screen of composite columns and pilasters with red granite shafts. The balustraded stair rises to a first-floor landing where fluted Ionic columns support a compartmented ceiling with stencil decoration.

Former FREE CHURCH MANSE, S of the A96 on the road to Chapel of Garioch. Built 1853, its church now demolished. Cottage style, symmetrical two-storey front with central entrance flanked by slightly projecting gabled end bays, all harled in white with grey granite dressings and lying-pane glazing. Doorpiece framed by slim timber pilasters, simple granite console-cornice with shallow block pediment, narrow sidelights. Paired first-floor windows above rise into a dormer. All three gables have quatrefoil roundels.

PITBEE FARMHOUSE, 0.35 km. W of the Free Church manse. A farm of the early C19 Improvement Era. The entrance front is two storeys and three bays, harled with gabled roof and ashlar end stacks. Mid-C19 single-storey wing on r. flank. Small windows in l. gable, one for paying farm workers. Steadings now domestic.

BRIDGE OF PITCAPLE carries a minor road over the River Urie. *c.* 1800. A single segmental span with dressed granite voussoirs and rubble spandrels rising from cutwater abutments. Low slightly hump-backed parapets secured by iron pins and splayed towards coped termini.

LOGIE DURNO CHURCHYARD, 2 km. NW. Dedicated to St Mary, the church belonged to Lindores Abbey and fell into disuse after Logie Durno was united with Chapel of Garioch in the early C17; ruinous by 1840, only its overgrown footings remain. It was *c.* 21 m. long by 8 m. wide, possibly with an apse-ended chancel. The DALRYMPLE HORN ELPHINSTONE BURIAL ENCLOSURE was built shortly after 1798. Gothick with some classical details; heavily moulded pointed-arch entrance with moulded blind lancets flanking it and plain pilasters supporting a convex gable with armorial panel.

LOGIE HOUSE. *See* p. 654.

6010

PITFICHIE CASTLE

1.6 km. NNW of Monymusk

A tower house probably built in the later C16 by the Hurrie family, who had seemingly held Pitfichie since the late C14. Sold to John Cheyne of Fortrie in 1597, Pitfichie passed *c.* 1650 to the Forbes of Monymusk (q.v.). It became their chief seat after they sold Monymusk to the Grants in 1713 and it was repaired in 1736. Eventually *c.* 1770 the Forbes sold Pitfichie to the Grants as well, and in the 1796 edition of *Don: A Poem* it is described as unroofed. In such condition it was recorded by Dr Douglas Simpson in 1920; in 1936 its S and E walls collapsed and only Simpson's intervention prevented it from being demolished altogether. Fortunately it was purchased by Colin Wood in 1978. He engaged the architect *Bill Cowie* and master mason *Slessor Troup* to restore it with the assistance of *Alec Killoh* and *Les Henderson*, work being completed in 1996.

Built in harled rubble, the main block is 11 m. long E–W by 8.5 m. deep. It rises three storeys, its ground floor being vaulted internally with only slit-lights although its first- and second-floor windows are rather larger. Its steeply pitched roof with crowstepped gables contains an attic and garret, and at its SE angle it has a very large four-storey drum tower 7 m. in diameter rising into a conical roof. Certain aspects of its planning which bear on its defensive qualities are unusually interesting, revealing evidence of modification during construction. The stair is a turnpike 1.2 m. in diameter formed within the junction of the drum tower and the E end gable. It has been so skilfully planned so that at its base it is completely concealed within the thickness of the walls; only at some height above ground, where it is less vulnerable to attackers, is its NE quadrant corbelled out to form a turret rising into a caphouse just below the main roof-lines. This caphouse is answered by a square attic turret at the SW angle.

The entrance arrangements reveal the same concern for security. Originally the master mason intended the doorway to be within the main block, immediately w of its present position, its rere-arch still visible internally: only during construction did the client realize this would give attackers direct access onto the stair. In moving the doorway into the drum tower the mason was obliged to form a corridor which inconveniently cut across the guardroom and reduced the kitchen in size.

In other respects the planning is conventional. At ground floor the main block contains a kitchen with hearth and oven in the N wall, a serving hatch onto the stair, and a large cellar adjacent. At first floor the hall in the main block is lit by two windows facing s and one facing E, with its fireplace in the w wall. The laird's private chamber is square within the circular tower, resulting in wall-segments deep enough to provide a bed recess and garderobe. Its windows again face s and E. The barmkin was on the w side, entered through a roll-moulded gateway with a caphouse above.

PITTODRIE HOUSE

6020

2.1 km. w of Chapel of Garioch

A complex house of several dates. The entrance front at the E end is Neo-Jacobean by *Archibald Simpson* for Col. Knight Erskine, 1841. Behind it lies a stepped L-plan tower house chiefly of the early–mid C17, partly concealed on the s side by a single-storey billiard room of the later C20; still further back on the sw, a small two-storey block of *c.* 1860, and then at the w end a very large three-storey T-plan extension, the entrance front on that side in the style of the mid C17 but actually by *Michael Rasmussen c.* 1990, built when the house was converted into a hotel.

Simpson's Neo-Jacobean E ENTRANCE FRONT comprises a big three-storey tower with a shallow entrance porch, balanced by a broader two-storey block with a gabled roof to its l.; both are harled in an ochre colour with golden sandstone dressings and margins, the larger windows having timber mullions and transoms with lying-pane glazing. The tower is large and square on plan. Its porch has a round-arched doorway and a plain parapet which rises at its centre to incorporate a heraldic panel reused from Balhargardy, dated 1605. Three relatively tall narrow windows at first and second floor are linked together by stepped hoodmoulds; an arcaded parapet crowns the wall-head, the die-blocks concealing chimney flues. The lower two-storey block has a shallow canted bay with tall tripartite windows. The E part of the s ELEVATION is also Simpson's work, the gable of his entrance front being balanced by a circular ogee-domed angle tower. The elegantly arcaded four-light window is his but the canted bay at the gable is a 1926 addition.

To the w, and at the centre of the house as enlarged in 1990, is the original stepped L-plan TOWER HOUSE. It comprises a three-storey-and-attic main block running N–S with its gable on the present S front and a taller four-storey jamb running w–E with its E gable embedded in the back of Simpson's entrance front. Within its SE re-entrant angle is a small rectangular outshot with a catslide roof containing a turnpike stair, and on its N side at the junction of the main block with the jamb is a smaller circular turnpike stair with a conical roof. Against the the N side of the jamb itself stands a lower parallel three-storey block of *c*. 1675–80, its gable and square-plan pyramid-roofed NE tower visible on the E entrance front although rather stepped back. Immediately to the SE is a detached piend-roofed two-storey pavilion of the early–mid C18 which may relate to an uncompleted scheme for a symmetrical N forecourt. As it exists now the tower house has relatively low-pitched roofs with straight skews, skewputts and big coped chimneystacks which are clearly mid-C18. It is not vaulted, even at the ground floor. This suggests a date in the early–mid C17 but Dr Douglas Simpson believed that the main turnpike stair in the S re-entrant angle was *c*. 1490, which would seem to indicate that the jamb was reconstituted from previous tower house fabric.

The single-storey BILLIARD ROOM which lies between the original house and Simpson's E entrance front is later C20. The TWO-STOREY BLOCK which lies to the w of the tower house's S gable is *c*. 1860, very simple two windows wide, those at first floor breaking up into gablet dormerheads.

In the HOTEL EXTENSION of *c*. 1990 the long frontage facing S is comparatively plain, with French windows at ground floor. Drum towers of good profile fill its N and S re-entrant angles. Rasmussen's w entrance front is an engaging reiteration of mid-C17 style. Three storeys and five bays broad, near-symmetrical with a central pend-like round-arched doorway and astragalled sash-and-case windows, the ground floor appears relatively tall as if it had vaults, the first-floor windows are rather smaller, while those at second floor break up into dormer gablets.

PLACE OF TILLIEFOUR
4.7 km. E of Keig

(Originally a Z-plan tower house built in 1626–7 for the Leslies of Wardhouse on the banks of the Don, possibly by *James Leiper*. It fell into ruin and was reconstructed and much extended in a Scots Renaissance vernacular idiom in 1885–6 for Francis Robert Gregson, who had married Mary Grant of nearby Monymusk (q.v.). Their architect was *Hew Montgomerie Wardrop* of *Wardrop, Anderson & Browne*, and the clerk-of-works a young *Robert S.*

Lorimer, on whom Tilliefour would exert an important influence. Further alterations, especially to the interior, were carried out by *Sydney Mitchell & Wilson* in 1897; the house was refurbished by *Leslie Hunter* in 1993–2003.

The Z-PLAN TOWER HOUSE standing at the S end of the present structure was a very simple example of a group seemingly associated with the *Leiper* family of master masons, which includes nearby Harthill (q.v.) and the Old House of Carnousie (N). Tilliefour's main block is 10.7 m. long E–W by 7.6 m. deep, rather smaller than Harthill or Carnousie; the entrance jamb at its SE corner is however almost identical in size to those of the two larger houses, 4.9 m. across the entrance front by 6.7 m. deep, reflecting the fact that its main stair up to the first-floor hall could not be miniaturized. The NW jamb is square rather than round as in the larger houses, and would have contained private family rooms, square-plans being very much a *Leiper* motif. Two turnpike stairs are neatly incorporated into the plan, one in the NE corner of the main block rising from the ground-floor services to the 'low' end of the great hall, and one at the SE corner in the angle between the main block and the entrance jamb rising to the attic floors as at Harthill. James Giles's view of the house in ruins indicates that it never rose any higher: it may have been an extended version of the two-storey-and-attic concept seen at Avochie (q.v.), but its relatively large footprint suggests that Tilliefour was originally intended to rise to three storeys and attic, circumstances forcing a change of plan when the house was half-built.

Wardrop's drastic RECONSTRUCTION of the ruined Z-plan house was dictated by a desire for the comfort of horizontal living and an *avant-garde* image of Arts and Crafts sophistication just before MacGibbon and Ross made the simple virtues of early Scottish houses more widely appreciated and understood. The astragalled windows formed or enlarged during the remodelling are all of good size and semi-regular in arrangement: many are set in deep ashlar surrounds in contrast to the rubble masonry, which was left exposed without harling to retain the evidence of its age. At first floor the windows in both the main block and the NW jamb are mullioned and transomed, rising through the eaves as dormers; the tall slated roofs have crowstepped gables and stumpy coped chimneystacks. The 1626 datestone has been re-cut.

Wardrop's substantial ADDITION comprises a single very long wing extending N for some 36 m. from the tower house's NW jamb – and thus almost trebling it in size – but stepped back midway along its length to form two distinct ranges, the elevations of which are further modelled for picturesque effect. The W elevation is reminiscent of such low-rise C17 houses as Fountainhall (*see* Lothian) but it is almost like a vernacular streetscape – small ground-floor windows set in Arts and Crafts rubble work, and part of the first floor corbelled out slightly, its windows breaking through eaves at different heights into dormers with stone gablets, some of them finely carved. Castellated iron rainwater goods are a delightful touch, dated lest anyone should think they are original. The E elevation is plainer, an extended composition of crowstepped gables on different planes.

As reconstructed by Wardrop, the tower house contained the only public apartments, the former hall and two rooms in the NW jamb. His addition consisted of ground-floor services, with a double-height kitchen on the E side, and ten family and two maidservants' bedrooms at first floor. Several fireplaces are based on C17 Scots examples.

The COURTYARD GARDEN was formally laid out by *Gertrude Jekyll*, *c.* 1900, in four compartments with a SUNDIAL at its centre. Rising from a deep moulded base, a tapered shaft with carved decoration supports a facet-headed dial with hollows in all twenty-four faces and a crowning ball finial: its similarity to that at Ellon Castle (N) implies an early C18 date. The segmental archway leading into the courtyard has fine wrought-iron gates. The STABLE BLOCK (50 m. E) is Z-plan single-storey-and-attic with a tourelle at one corner, similar in style to the main house.)

PORT ELPHINSTONE *see* INVERURIE

9090 ## PORTLETHEN K

A former fishing village on the coast, but since the oil boom of the 1970s a much larger secondary settlement with numerous industrial parks has grown up inland between the railway and the A90.

PARISH CHURCH, Bruntland Road, 0.9 km. WNW of the old village. Built *c.* 1840. Meagre Gothic box with bellcote.

6090 ## RAEMOIR HOUSE K
3.5 km. N of Banchory

An attractive house of more than one phase, rather oddly composed. The earliest part must be that which stands in the middle of the S front and appears to be a five-bay house of before 1808 when it was called 'a plain modern house' in Robertson's *General View of Kincardineshire*. Two full storeys above a basement with an attic floor in a mansard. To this *John Smith* added the two-storey W wing in 1817, a neat composition of three bays with the middle only slightly projecting under a pediment that is raised above the eaves cornice. The width of its garden front is devoted to an elegant full-height bow. Ashlar walls above heavy rustication. The client was William Innes, a member of the East India Company, and *John & William Smith* returned to make additions for him in 1844, which must include the pedimented entrance porch at the l. of the W front (it bears both dates) which has a mid-C19 ceiling inside of ribbed patterns. Considerable changes were made for the Cowdrays of Dunecht by *William Kelly* of *Kelly & Nicol* in 1927, principally the addition of the E wing with its crowstep gable.

In the W wing the former DRAWING ROOM (now dining room) occupies nearly the whole of the W front extending into the S bow and with a corresponding apsidal N end. Excellent mahogany doors and good Regency joinery and plasterwork. The other principal room is the 1920s DINING ROOM (now drawing room), darkly panelled from floor to ceiling.

THE HA' HOOSE to the N is the house built for the Hogg family, whose arms are above the door with the initials RH, probably for Robert Hogg, proprietor in 1745. The house itself is probably *c.* 1715, of red granite quarried nearby at Hill of Fare. Unusual front of five bays with the outer bays projecting as wings under piended roofs; above the unmoulded central door, two oval windows, one horizontal, the other vertical with pretty weaving patterns in the glazing. All this is very similar to the original appearance of Kingswells House, Aberdeen (p. 282) by *Alexander Jaffray*, but may date from the restoration by *Kelly*. Rear stair-tower.

RHYNIE

4020

A place of strategic importance since earliest times, being at the juncture of two valleys forming an ancient route into Moray. The present village sheltered in the lee of Taip a Nochd ('the Hill of Observation,' 563 m.) was established by Alexander, 4th Duke of Gordon, during the improvement era *c.* 1795. Within an area of limited communications, Rhynie remained important throughout the mid C19 by virtue of its cattle markets, the village being built up with simple cottages, but after the agricultural recession of the 1870s its population went into prolonged decline.

Former CONGREGATIONAL CHURCH, Main Street. Opened 1829. Simple Gothic preaching-box. S flank in ashlar granite, originally three bays broad, very neatly rebuilt as four bays after *c.* 1970. Y-traceried windows. Entrance porch and school at E end added *c.* 1870. Presently derelict. Its 1840s manse stands directly opposite.

Former FREE CHURCH, set back from The Square and concealed by its manse, a two-storey house of the earlier C19. A simple Gothic granite preaching-box, built by *Ingram & Green*, masons, with *Souter*, carpenter, 1851. Became a church hall in 1931, now derelict.

NOTH PARISH CHURCH. Begun as a simple Gothic preaching-box in 1823, its four-bay S flank facing The Square; almost doubled in size by the addition of a N transeptal aisle in 1838; it achieved its present form when the aisle was lengthened, a small porch was added to the W gable, the walls were heightened and a tall slim entrance tower and spire 26.5 m. high was added to the SE corner, all by *R. Duncan* of Huntly in 1889. The original church is in coursed squared masonry with polished ashlar dressings and timber Y-tracery, that of the original windows in the centre bays rather richer with coloured glass margins; the slightly smaller outer windows date from reorientation of the church interior in 1889. Steeply pitched roof with trefoil dormer ventilators. The rock-faced SE tower is of four stages, square-plan at ground level, broaching to octagonal with its internal stair lit by very tall narrow lancets; above clock dials in alternate sides, it is slightly intaken beneath its louvred belfry, the fish-scale slated spire with lucarnes rising into a delicate cast-iron finial. Despite its two-phase construction, the aisle is neatly unified with the original church, being built of the same coursed rubble with Y-traceried windows. Interior totally remodelled by *Duncan*, with canted timber-boarded ceilings supported on trusses, and a single deep gallery within his enlarged aisle; most of his PEWS survive but the ORGAN – its case perhaps also his work – dates from ten years later, the instrument itself the earliest-known example by *E. H. Lawton*, with the PULPIT in front of it approached by a side stair above the console. A roughly hewn FONT is reputedly C12.

ST LUAG'S CHURCHYARD, Manse Road. An early site on the banks of the Bogie. St Luag's church was perhaps built when Rhynie and Essie parishes were united *c.* 1612; it was demolished when the new church (*see* above) was built in 1823. Its *Michael Burgerhuys* bell, preserved at the village school, is dated 1620. Rebuilt against the churchyard's W wall (at the S end), a TOMB-RECESS – a roll-moulded, pointed arch containing heraldic arms of Alexander Gordon of Muirack (†1668) with Holy Monogram and *memento mori*; next to it a stone SARCOPHAGUS, some 2 m. in length.

9   Just W of the churchyard, on a prominent rise, is the 'CRAW STANE', a block of grey granite with a salmon and 'Pictish beast' carved on one side. Further PICTISH SYMBOL STONES can be found in a shelter built near the churchyard by the Bogie Water. These are part of a group of eight stones known from Rhynie including the 'Rhynie Man' (*see* Woodhill House, Aberdeen, p. 244). (GN)

ST MARY (Episcopal), 0.4 km. E. Built 1859 for Eliza Foulerton-Grant of Druminnor (q.v.). E.E., small rectangular plan in snecked granite masonry with steeply pitched roof crowned by simple bellcote. Entrance W gable with chamfered depressed-arch doorway and small roundel. Lancets in flanks, small vestry with shouldered doorway on S. E gable with stepped triple lancet and cruciform finial. – STAINED GLASS. E window, Our Lord blessing little children, 1882. – N window (Sir Henry Percy Gordon memorial) by *J. Powell & Sons*, 1883.

Former NICOLL HOSPITAL, Manse Road. Named after Dr Patrick Nicoll, a native of Rhynie who provided much of the funding, and built to designs of *T. Scott Sutherland & Taylor*, 1929–31. Villa-like Neo-Georgian. Closed 1961.

DESCRIPTION. Rhynie village began in the 1790s as a single MAIN STREET extending along a ridge of ground: the only building surviving from that time is near its N end, a two-storey block in dark squared granite with a pend arch. At its S end Main Street extends into THE SQUARE, with a number of simple early–mid-C19 houses built from local granite. The Square itself first took shape when Rhynie's new parish church, on the opposite far side, was begun in 1823 (*see* above). On The Square's W side stands the former North of Scotland Bank, mid-C19 but still in the Georgian idiom. The Square was laid out as a formal park for Queen Victoria's Diamond Jubilee in 1897. At its centre, the WAR MEMORIAL, a young infantryman carved in granite, standing on a plinth, by *D. Morren & Co.* of Aberdeen, 1920; it was the first sculpted by *Robert Warrack Morrison*, 'the king of the granite carvers'.

In RICHMOND TERRACE, some good early COUNCIL HOUSING seemingly by *Tawse & Allan*, 1934.

LESMOIR CASTLE, 3 km. WNW. *Lios mor*, 'a big fortified enclosure', guarding the ancient route from Rhynie into the Cabrach and ultimately to Moray. Enclosed by three small burns, it comprises a circular motte roughly 34 m. in diameter and a long triangular bailey 42.5 m. by 52.5 m. with a dry-built revetment of stone boulders. With the church (dem.) at nearby Essie it was once the focal point of a manor probably founded by the Fernyndrachts (Frendraughts) or the Aberkourdours, to whom the lands passed *c.* 1256–80. A stone castle is traditionally said to have been built here in 1508, the motte being seemingly truncated at that time. Lesmoir was granted by George Gordon, 4th Earl of Huntly, to his close kinsman James Gordon before 1537, and 'a place and house' are recorded in a confirmation charter of 1544; in the 1590s Alexander Gordon, 3rd Laird of Lesmoir, 'repaired and builded . . . more sumptuouslie by farr than it was befor', evidently as a tower with outbuildings enclosed by a walled court. The description *c.* 1725 of 'a pretty house with seven clusters of chimneys' suggested to Douglas Simpson that it was rebuilt in a style akin to Leslie Castle (q.v.). The fortunes of the Lesmoir Gordons having collapsed in the early C18, their castle was gradually dismantled by John Grant of Rothmaise from 1759, although remains of a 'tower and fortalice' still survived twenty years later.

HENGE, Wormy Hillock, 5.5 km. NW. A Neolithic henge monument, consisting of an external bank and internal ditch enclosing a central area around 45 m. in diameter. These sites are thought to have been used for ceremonial gatherings in the Later Neolithic or Early Bronze Age (*c.* 2500–2000 BC). (GN)

7   HILL-FORT, Tap o'Noth, 2.5 km. NW, overlooking the village. An extremely impressive vitrified hill-fort situated some 563 m. above sea level, the second highest in Scotland. On the summit, the oblong vitrified fort encloses an area around 85 m. by 30 m. and includes a rock-cut well and possible traces of a round-house. The stone wall that defines the oblong enclosure is more than 6 m. in width and 3 m. high and is heavily vitrified, the stones fused together through intense burning. A second and much larger circumference of walling lies further down the hill enclosing its lower flanks. Between these two ramparts more than 100 house-platforms have been recorded. (GN)

HOUSE OF DRUMINNOR. *See* p. 521.

8080   RICKARTON   K

Roadside hamlet with a converted parish church (now the AULD KIRK), 1870–1 in harled, E.E. style. Gableted bellcote.

RICKARTON HOUSE, 2.4 km. ESE. Pleasant villa set amid ancient, romantic woodland. The gable-ended core in the centre was built *c.* 1804 for Col. William Rickart Hepburn, nobleman and politician. Large, wider refronting to the E (now the main façade) by *John Smith*, 1829–32. Two storeys and five bays with minimally advanced centre; precociously long glazing on the ground floor.

Smith's entrance PORTICO was removed in 1975 and now sits detached, folly-like, to the SE.

COWTON BRIDGE, 1.3 km. ENE, in a hairpin curve of the A957 (Slug Road). Tall, stilted segmental arch over the Cowton Burn, early C19.

LANG STANE, Auquhollie, 2 km. NNE. Tall Pictish stone (*c.* 2.4 m. high), the only survivor of a stone circle that was removed in the early C19. The NE face has a double-disc with cross-bar and rectangle with circular corners (all very weathered). In the SE angle, a well-preserved Ogham inscription reading 'VUO NO N (I) TEDOV'.

8070   ROADSIDE OF KINNEFF   K

Bland collection of buildings along the A92.

Former KINNEFF & CATTERLINE PARISH CHURCH (now the Bell Hoose). Built as the Free Church by *William & James Henderson*, 1843; renovated by *Hutcheson & Henderson* in 1888–9 and converted into a house by *Inspired Design & Development Ltd*, 2011–12. Romanesque E gable with shafted windows and porch. Scallop capitals, thin roll mouldings and

gableted bellcote. – Celtic cross MEMORIAL in front, *c.* 1933.
– Former MANSE (now Rostov) to the N, also 1843. Piended
main block, the r. rear wing original but widened in the late
C19.

FAWSYDE HOUSE, 700 m. N of the church. A harled, freely
Picturesque country villa by *J. R. Mackenzie*, 1865–7, built on
an H-plan. Ends advanced and gabled with canted bay windows
on the ground floor (central lights four-centered) and Venetian
ones above. Veranda between the wings with square wooden
posts on good stone balustrade and small gable with a spike.
Three dormers with Tudor-Gothic and Lombardic glazing.
The house was originally a riot of decoration (including bargeboarding and window guards), but only the fleur-de-lys cresting remains.

Up the ridge to the N, a FOLLY of an Elizabethan prospect
tower, late C19 and now in poor condition. Mightily corbelled
parapet and octagonal stair turret clasping the NW corner.

LARGIE, 950 m. WSW of the church, off the A92. On the NW
gable of a farm building, a re-set dormerhead from the
destroyed Largie Castle, dated 1611 with initials for James
Arbuthnott.

RUTHVEN

A small village on the Cairnie Burn, once a parish centre, with
medieval church, corn mill and school.

PARISH CHURCH (St Carol or St Cyril). Ruinous. A medieval
gable of substantial height, built in rough rubble, with a broad
central buttress bearing a C17 bellcote that still contains its
bell, dated 1643. The inscription from Luke 11:17, *Omne
regnum in seipsum divisum desolabitur* ('every kingdom divided
against itself shall be laid waste') was particularly apt during
the Civil Wars. N wall forms part of the present churchyard
boundary, with an arched recess containing a recumbent
EFFIGY thought to represent the C16 Sir Thomas Gordon of
Daugh dressed in full armour; it was restored in the C19.
Ruthven merged with Cairnie (q.v.) in 1618, but services were
conducted here until *c.* 1721. The CHURCHYARD on rising
ground above the Cairnie Burn suggests a site of considerable
antiquity.

AUCHANACHIE CASTLE, 0.8 km. W. Formerly held by a branch
of the Gordons, dated 1594, and much the earliest departure
from the conventional tower house format in Aberdeenshire.
Here the tower element is relatively small, three storeys and
square on plan. Most of the accommodation is in the relatively
long two-storey 'laigh bigging' which contains the main
entrance in the centre of its E front, a massive chimney-breast
rising from the immediate l. with three set-offs and a battered

stack. The tower is hinged to the laigh bigging at its NW corner, so forming an offset L-plan, there being a turnpike stair in the angle between them. Crowstepped gables. Over the doorway the inscription 'From Our Enemies Defend Us O Christ', perhaps surprising in a house which, though composed of simple rugged masses, is domestic in scale and character, cream-harled with small windows now fitted with sashes and cases. Inside the rooms are small and cosy; the tower is vaulted at ground floor with carved stone bosses displaying the arms of Gordon, Fraser and Campbell, and the first-floor hall is also vaulted. Auchanachie was repaired *c.* 1870 when the two-storey wing was deepened at the rear and restored by *Acanthus Architects Douglas Forrest* in 2004. Within the setting of a beautiful orchard, the house opens directly into a large walled garden; the DOOCOT, circular with a conical roof, is probably C18.

DEVERON VIADUCT, 3 km. ESE. Erected 1894 by *Patrick M. Barnett*, Chief Engineer of the Great North of Scotland Railway, for its double-track main line from Aberdeen to Keith (Moray). Impressive Whipple–Murray steel lattice truss spanning low across the Deveron for 60 m. between carved abutments in cyclopean granite.

ST CYRUS   K

The finest coastal village in Kincardineshire. The base of the cliffside was the site of the early Christian community of Ecclesgreig, probably founded by Grig (Pictish ruler and 'liberator of the Scottish church') in the late C9. He was also known as Ciric or Ciricus, hence the name St Cyrus.

PARISH CHURCH, Beach Road. 1852–4 by *David Mitchell* of Montrose (cf. Ecclesgreig House, q.v.), its spire a prominent landmark and serving as the 'ecclesiastical lighthouse' of Montrose Bay. Big triple-lanceted box, the buttresses topped by crenellations. Advanced on the N side is a square four-stage tower with octagonal angle buttresses, long lancet window, round clock faces and paired, louvred lancets for the belfry. Spire and weathervane on top. Entrance in the S gable under Y-glazed window.

Interior as renovated by *A. Marshall Mackenzie & Son* in 1901–5. Flat, panelled ceiling with blue squares and crossed crocket fleurons in the angles. Dado rail with thick quatrefoils. – ORGAN by *Eustace Ingram*, 1902. Big rectangular case against the N wall. – STAINED GLASS. Two colourful lancets of 1952–3 (N wall). Moses, Abraham and Isaac over the parable of the Sower. Christ and Paul over 'Suffer the little children'.

In the rear GRAVEYARD, the former S AISLE of the old parish church of Ecclesgreig, built in 1632 by Sir Alexander Straton of Lauriston (q.v.) and replacing the medieval parish church in the old burial ground.* Roofless rectangle (*c.* 7 m. by 5.7 m.), the N side with a partially blocked round arch that once led into the main church. The W cornice fragment is monogrammed I.S and E.O.

Former UNITED FREE CHURCH, corner of A92 and Station Road. Quite large, lancet-windowed box by *John Robertson*, 1904 (converted into a house *c.* 2009).† Square, three-stage tower at the SW corner with pointed entrance, triple louvred lancets, crenellated parapet and crocketed pinnacles. Little transept-like outshots to the E.

OLD BURIAL GROUND, 1.2 km. SSW. A magical setting, nestled between high, rocky cliffs and the sea. The church of Ecclesgreig is first documented *c.* 1175 but must have been founded by Grig (St Cyrus) in the late C9 as it appears to have been used for his burial. The church was rebuilt in 1242 and dedicated by Bishop David de Bernham of St Andrews; no trace now above ground.

Good collection of MEMORIALS. – Near the centre, the BURIAL AISLE for the Grahams of Morphie Castle, which stood 3.7 km. WNW (foundations removed *c.* 1858). The aisle was mostly rebuilt in the mid C19. Crowstepped W gable with good heraldic PLAQUE over the door. E gable collapsed inside. – To the W, a railed BURIAL ENCLOSURE with partially shattered SARCOPHAGUS to Arthur Straton †1646 and his wife, Margaret Leonis. Sides carved with skull, angel, phoenix and mortality emblems. – To the W, a free-standing PLAQUE for Alexander Webster †1759 and family. Primitive fluted pilasters flanking a depiction of him setting a patient's broken arm (on the r.) while three people look on. Ball-finialled triangular pediment with hourglass and 'As runs the glass, man's life doth pas. Memento mori'.

Roofless BURIAL AISLE to the E built in 1673 by David Campbell, minister of Ecclesgreig, for his wife, Margaret Carnegie, family and three friends. W lintel with long Latin inscription in capital letters. – In the SE corner, an early C19 MORT-HOUSE with square chimney.

KIRKTON HOUSE, 270 m. WSW of the parish church. Formerly the manse. Original main block facing SW, 1796–7 by the mason *James Dewar*. The outer first-floor windows are large and the central one very small. Angle-pilastered porch added *c.* 1830; advanced r. wing by *James Maclaren* of Dundee, 1871–2. – Converted old OFFICES behind, 1785–6. – Partial WALLED GARDEN, early C19, with corniced gatepiers at the entrance.

PRIMARY SCHOOL, SW of the parish church. By *William Fettis*, 1866–8. Large, Gothic, the main entrance under a gabled

---

*The C17 church was replaced with one by *John Gibson*, 1785–7, dem. when the current church was built.
†It replaced the original Free Church of 1843–4 on the same site.

bellcote; quadruple lancets to the l. with foliate capitals and mask corbels. Diagonally opposite, Beach Road leads down to the former SCHOOL HOUSE, *c.* 1781, two storeys and three bays, unharled.

PUBLIC HALL (AND LIBRARY), on the A92. 1911–12 by *David Wishart Galloway*, crowstepped Scots Renaissance on an L-plan. Entrance splayed across the inner angle, flanked by covered seats, a typical motif of Arts and Crafts architects. Plaque in the re-entrant angle ornamented with fleuron and a cherub's head.

KAIM OF MATHERS, 1.3 km. E. Small remains of a castle, built *c.* 1420 and perched precariously – almost impossibly – over the sea. After boiling the Sheriff of Kincardine alive and sipping his entrail-laden broth, David de Berkeley was ordered by King James I to live 'neither on land nor water'. And so he did. Ruined N and E walls of a square tower, *c.* 4.5 m. high and 0.6 m. thick. Two rows of crenellated battlements originally lined the isthmus back to the mainland (now mostly eroded).

LOWER NORTH WATER BRIDGE, 3.7 km. SW, on the A92. Good Georgian engineering of 1770–5, recorded on the S approach as a joint effort by *John Smeaton, John Adam* and *Andrew Barrie* of Montrose. Barrie was actually the one responsible, having modified one of Smeaton's designs for an earlier bridge.* Seven segmental arches over the River North Esk, the central one keystoned; towards the Angus side the middle is flanked by key-blocked oculi. Triangular cutwaters. Extending to the NW, a long, rather turgid rubble span accommodating a flood arch.

Disused VIADUCT to the NE, 1861–5 for the Montrose & Bervie Railway (opened in 1865 and closed to passengers in 1951) by *Blyth & Blyth*, engineers. Twelve segmental arches carried on tall, rock-faced piers. The central five are wider and have rounded cutwaters.

ROCK HALL, 1.6 km. E. Whitewashed former fishing station, dated 1835 on its NE door lintel. Former ice house underneath with datestone of 1842 and two inner chambers.

Former WOODSTON FISHING STATION, 700 m. E. Established *c.* 1826 by Joseph Johnston & Sons, Ltd to supply fish to Edinburgh and London. Low, rectangular former skipper's quarters and bothy. – Good ICE HOUSE submerged to the E, probably late C18. Two chambers (vestibule and main store-room) covered by stilted barrel-vaults. Square ice chute.

STONE OF MORPHIE, 3.9 km. SW. Uninscribed standing stone of *c.* 3.5 m., its rugged grandeur holding court amidst modern farm buildings. Several scooped-out cup marks on the S face.

---

*Adam only offered advice to the trustees and drafted the contract; ironically, his name on the S dedication tablet is spelt incorrectly. *Andrew Barrie* (of Montrose) and *Patrick Brown* (Drybugh) are recorded as 'masons' but served as joint contractors.

SAUCHEN

A Free Church kirkton, established immediately after the Disruption.

Former FREE CHURCH. By *Robert Gordon Wilson* (of *Wilsons & Walker*), 1914, a reconstruction of *James Henderson*'s church of 1843–4. Simple S gable front with round-arched doorway and windows flanked by aisles which contained the gallery stairs, all in roughly squared granite rubble with ashlar dressings and a gableted bellcote over the apex. The former MANSE, 1843–4, is presumably by *Henderson*. Handsome two storeys, its entrance front with a broad gabled bay slightly projecting to the r. of the central porch. Segment-headed windows at ground floor and round-arched windows at first, harled with ashlar dressings. Offices by *William Henry* of Echt (q.v.), 1864–5. Former SCHOOL, Tudor Gothic by *Henderson*, 1844, with addition 1875.

Former MIDMAR UNITED PRESBYTERIAN CHURCH, 1 km. ESE, on the A944. By *W.B. Coutts*, 1877. First Pointed, simple rectangular plan. Liturgical W gable front divided by buttresses to suggest a tall slim nave and aisles, built in rough granite ashlar with polished dressings. Pinned rubble four-bay flanks with small gabled entrance porch, steep roof. Converted to warehouse, large opening in W gable beneath twin lancet gallery windows. MANSE by *James Henderson*, 1840–1, concurrent with the predecessor church.

LINTON HOUSE, 1 km. SSE. An Italianate villa by *Archibald Simpson*, probably 1835. It is ingeniously composed: its U-plan main block on the N interlocks with a lower U-plan service block on the S, the openings between them forming a top-lit central hall and an integrated service court around which all the accommodation is arranged. Entrance front of the main block faces E, two storeys, three bays broad, with its centre projecting as a round-arched open porch with a pedimental gable. Its ground-floor windows are much taller than first, with console-cornices above their lintels. Slightly set back, the service wing faces S, its three central bays recessed between pedimented gable bays. Harled with ashlar dressings, lying-pane glazing, shallow-pitched roofs with broad eaves and tall chimneystacks. Refined classical interior. Cubical vestibule leads into central top-lit stair hall, its cantilevered scale-and-platt stair with elaborate cast-iron balusters. Principal apartments to N and W, dining room lit by a canted bay.

MAINS OF SHIELS, 4.5 km. WSW. Vernacular classical house, dated 1742, possibly the home of John Midleton of Shiels, architect, in the 1780s. Entrance front facing SE, two storeys and five bays, built in fine ashlar. Central transom-lit doorway, all openings chamfered, first floor taller than ground floor with the windows now plate-glazed. Gabled roof with slightly bell-cast skews and moulded skewputts (dated), coped end stacks

and stone roof ridge. Single-storey NE wing on r. forms an open
forecourt. Inside, the main block's stair accommodated within
a bay projecting from the rear rises in granite to mezzanine
level and in wood thereafter. First-floor rooms panelled. Wing
contains a large arched kitchen hearth with ingle-seats.

CASTLE FRASER. *See* p. 405.
CORSINDAE HOUSE. *See* p. 424.
TILLYCAIRN CASTLE. *See* p. 749.

SKELLATER HOUSE

4.5 km. SW of Strathdon

3010

Symmetrical vernacular house of 1727 for Lachlan Forbes, very
similar to nearby Edinglassie (q.v.). Two-storey entrance front,
five windows wide, its projecting end bays rising with a very
slight batter into gables with ball finials. Built in pinned
boulder rubble, harled in pale grey, only its simply moulded
door surround is left exposed as if to emphasize its distinctly
rugged character. Above the doorway, an elliptical window and
heraldic panel, dated 1770: the inscription *Solus inter Plures*
('Alone among Many') is probably a reference to the Forbes
of Skellater's Catholicism and Jacobitism when most of the
clan were Protestant and Hanoverian. Astragalled sash-and-
case windows, gabled roof with coped chimneystacks. Three
stone dormers are neat additions of 1857, their moulded
skewputts echoing those of the earlier fabric; the slits in the
gables and small square windows in the flanks are original.
Used as a hay store from *c.* 1900, renovated 1975–6 by *Alastair
Harper* who gutted what remained of the interior, including
the stair which was accommodated in a gabled bay projecting
at the back. Rear extensions 1857 and 2004–5, the latter a
glazed kitchen wing by *Michael Rasmussen* of Aboyne; interior
refurbished at that time by *Mikhail Pietranek* of Ballater.
The adjacent single-storey COTTAGE had been the kitchen
with an unusually large hearth, one of several examples in
Strathdon.

SKENE HOUSE

4 km. WNW of Kirkton of Skene

7000

A large and powerfully composed Scots Baronial country house
reconstructed in 1847–50 for the antiquarian James Duff, 4th
Earl Fife, as a suitable home for himself and his heir, also James,
who had recently married Lady Agnes Hay, daughter of the 17th
Earl of Erroll and a granddaughter of William IV. The designs
were prepared by *Archibald Simpson* with his assistant *William
Ramage*, who oversaw work to completion after Simpson's death.

Most of the house is, however, substantially older. As shown in James Giles's watercolour just before its remodelling it presented an ENTRANCE FRONT (facing NE) which was essentially a U-plan – the tall central block, four-storey-and-attic, was built by Jean Burnet after the death of her husband John Skene in 1680, with its NW wing formed by remodelling the original C14 tower house. The broader SE wing was built to balance it by George Skene *c.* 1745, the designs perhaps the work of *William* or *John Adam*. Corbelled turrets in the internal angles contained spiral stairs to the upper floors, that on the N commencing at first floor and that on the S at second. The court was entered on the NE by a fine classical gateway (dated 1696) of which more below.

Simpson and *Ramage* transformed this house by extending its SE wing forward to the NE, and its NW wing rearward to the SW, effectively converting the U-plan into the present reversed H-plan. They enclosed the court with a new crowstepped gatehouse framed between slim tourelles, their spirelet roofs echoing those of the earlier stair-turrets – the coat of arms and supporters over the round-arched doorway, carved by *George Russell* of Aberdeen, are those of Clan Skene – and within the court they built an entrance hall and stair hall. They enlivened the wall-heads with small dormers rising into gablets, increased the height of the N stair-turret (but not the S), carrying it high above the main roof ridge before crowning it with a conical spirelet; this they balanced with a slim square-plan tower with an ogee dome rising from the SE wing's inner flank. These upward thrusts were complemented by the tall chimneystacks clustered over Simpson and Ramage's NE extension of the SE wing and by the chimney-breast added to the gable of the NW wing which rises into three stumpy stacks playfully suggesting crenellation, a feature re-erected from the late C17 work. This has dummy slit-windows, a feature repeated in the gatehouse tourelles and forecourt wall where a string course is stepped over their heads as hoodmoulds. To the NW of the house Simpson and Ramage extended this forecourt wall to the same design to screen their new SERVICE COURT, balancing the asymmetrical verticals of the gable fronts of the house with a long low interlocking horizontal, interrupted by the re-erected gateway of 1696 which has fluted pilasters and moulded capitals and bases. Its ogee-domed bellcote bears two dates, 1835 on the front and 1784 on the rear. At the far N end of the service court a two-storey corner tower set on the diagonal with an ogee dome answers that added to the SE wing.

The SW GARDEN ELEVATION was less thoroughly Baronialized in the 1847–50 works. It is simpler and more relaxed, its interest deriving chiefly from its massing. The three-storey-and-attic gable of the SE wing on the r. retained its arched and key-blocked windows of 1745, but was enriched by the addition of spirelet angle turrets and a lion finial presumably sculpted by *George Russell*; at the central block a C18 bow was remodelled as an oriel and at the re-entrant angle a

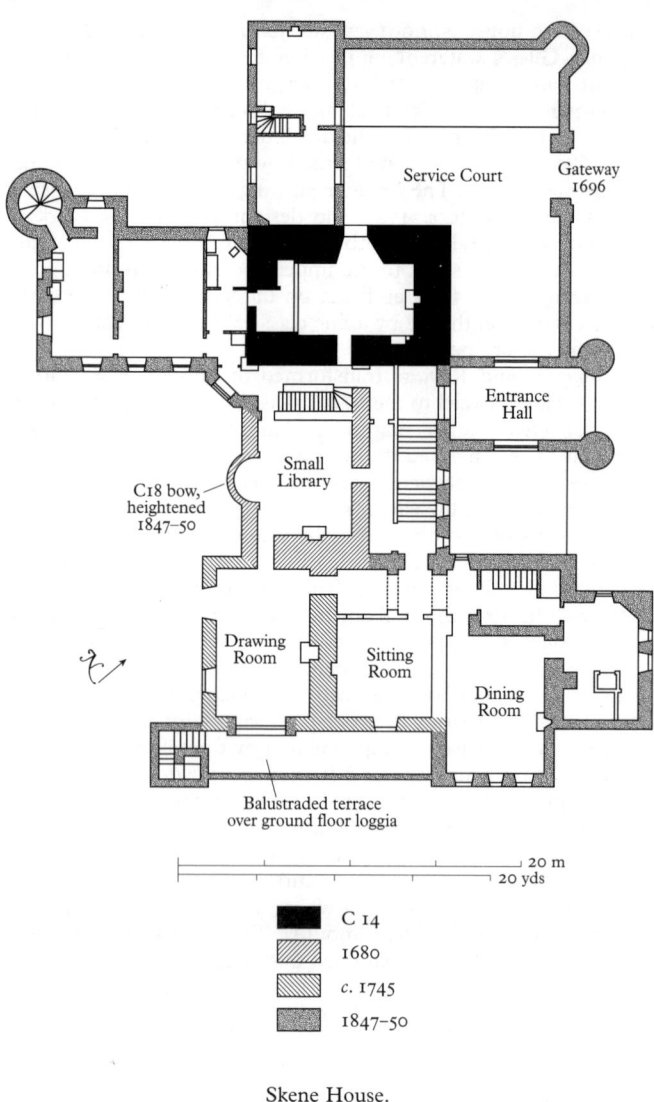

Service Court

Gateway
1696

Entrance
Hall

C18 bow,
heightened
1847–50

Small
Library

Drawing
Room

Sitting
Room

Dining
Room

Balustraded terrace
over ground floor loggia

⌐————————————————⌐ 20 m
⌐————————————————⌐ 20 yds

■ C 14

▨ 1680

▨ c. 1745

▨ 1847–50

Skene House.
Plan

canted bay was inserted, both of these being provided to
command a view of the terraces. At their new s w wing Simpson
and Ramage provided a very unusual rectangular oriel looking
over the terraces to the s e, a tall and elegant Wardian case-type
design on a cantilevered timber base. By way of contrast, the
s w tourelle has slim lights with diamond-pane glazing – that
at ground floor a double-keyhole 'gunloop' – square heraldic
panels (one dated 1603) and a conical spirelet which rises into
an earl's coronet.

The SE GARDEN ELEVATION is likewise relatively plain but very dignified with a six-bay loggia of semi-elliptical arches, the substructure of a generously proportioned balustraded terrace running in front of the principal apartments; its blind end bay encloses the stair to the gardens. This is by Simpson and Ramage, who also added the gabled bay projection to its r. This gabled bay enlarged the dining room; it has a tall tripartite window surmounted by a Neo-Jacobean heraldic cartouche, the remainder of the elevation being still mainly that of 1745. The NW SIDE is the service court, with a small two-storey outshot between the former C14 tower house and the courtyard wall.

The INTERIORS are of astonishing splendour for a family whose fortunes were supposedly in decline. They include, within *Simpson* and *Ramage*'s gatehouse, the ENTRANCE HALL finished in scagliola, with ten-panelled doors and three fine plaster-casts: one represents the founder of the Skene family saving an C11 Scots king from a wolf; another represents Adam Skene's death at the Battle of Harlaw in 1411; while that over the inner doorway represents in heraldic terms the marriage of the 4th Earl to his late wife, who had died in 1805. Opening off the hall at right angles is the GREAT STAIR – in pine grained to look like oak – which *Simpson* and *Ramage* formed in front of the 1680 central block during their remodelling of 1847–50: the stair rail with Jacobean strapwork rises between Doric arcades which frame its windows on one side and the first-floor landing on the other. The great stair's ceiling is coved and compartmented, its panels with richly painted heraldic decoration, and on the landing is a carved stone panel displaying the arms of Alexander, 16th Laird of Skene, and his wife, Giles Aedie, dated 1692.

Within the SE wing the exceptionally fine decoration of the three principal apartments was instructed and supervised by *Lady Agnes Duff*, scarcely twenty years old, who would later enrich several other Duff Houses: here she may have been guided by her husband's uncle, *James Duff*, the 4th Earl Fife, who had been elected Vice-President of the Society of Antiquaries of Scotland in 1838. Detailed accounts survive in the Montcoffer Papers for the furniture, fabric and trimmings provided by *Charles Hindley & Sons* of London in 1849, and other items provided by *James Allan & Co.*, the cabinet-makers. The complexity of the heraldic displays has led to the suggestion that they took advice from their neighbour George Burnett of Kemnay (q.v.), an early heraldic scholar and later Lord Lyon King of Arms. A *Mr Begg* of Elgin was responsible for the painting and decorative work, but he may have been carrying out a scheme devised by *David Ramsay Hay*, whose firm undertook the carving and gilding. Hay was the leading Edinburgh decorator and a natural choice for the 4th Earl, having carried out work for Sir Walter Scott at Abbotsford (*see The Buildings of Scotland: Borders*) in 1824.

In the DINING ROOM, the ceiling supported by bold console scrolls displays the complete heraldic achievement of the Clan Skene with coronets along the coving; from this ceiling is suspended a magnificent early electrolier, the fireplace is granite and even the delicately carved C19 window pelmet has survived. The small square SITTING ROOM is pilastered at one end only; it too retains its C19 wallpaper and a window pelmet carved with faces which appear to be portraits, presumably of the Fifes. Then in the DRAWING ROOM the walls are divided into shouldered panels with exceptionally rich and bold C19 wallpaper; there is a Louis XIV chimneypiece with a magnificent overmantel mirror, and a full-length pier glass and pier table between the windows on the SW side; the pelmets are in the Rococo style, and the ceiling decoration stencilled. Within the house's central block is the cubical SMALL LIBRARY, its shelves rising almost to ceiling height with the upper shelves accessed from a narrow mezzanine gallery with a precariously low guard rail. Its C18 bow window, heightened in 1847–50, is framed by Composite square columns. The doors' heraldic lozenge panels are in a different hand from the heraldic display in the Dining Room.

Then in the N wing is the old TOWER HOUSE, now of four storeys: it was one of three tower houses – with Drum and Hallforest (qq.v.) – built to guard the route over the Mounth and into the Garioch, seemingly after 1317 but before the end of the century. The original rectangular structure, 12 m. by 8 m., comprised three superimposed vaults within walls some 2 m. thick: it was strong enough to remain standing after Jean Burnett removed most of the vaulting during the 1680 renovation. Some of her interior work survives.

A fine oak CANTILEVER STAIR leads up to the original first-floor drawing room and then at second floor to the MAIN LIBRARY – large enough, the *New Statistical Account* tells us, to accommodate 6,000 books, collected by the Skenes since the C17 – as well as the two PRINCIPAL BEDROOMS and the NURSERY. An interesting feature of *Simpson* and *Ramage*'s SW extension is that some of its sash-and-case windows are positioned midway between the first and second floors, the upper sash actually rising from the second floor's floor level.

On the GROUND FLOOR the services have largely survived intact, some of the rooms (e.g. the butler's pantry) being finished to a high standard as they were once public rooms in the pre-1850 house; the servants' hall looks S through the S wing's arcade. On the N side within the service court the garage was formed during the mid C20 after fire destroyed the BILLIARD ROOM.

On the FORMAL TERRACES, laid out by *David Steele* in 1849, stands a fine collection of works of sculpture. There are three identical fountains: each has a round basin in the centre of which three dolphins rear up their intertwined tails to support a large conch with a cherub holding a cornucopia which gushes forth water, while close by a disconsolate heron stoops down unblinkingly in an endless search for its supper. These were supplied by *Austin & Seeley* of London, as were two wild boar; there is also a young huntsman with his club and a hound, and numerous classical urns for flowers, one complete with a flourish of stone roses. One pair is particularly notable, their urns supported by caryatids of late C18 pattern. The fine table SUNDIAL was carved by *J. Williamson* of Aberdeen in 1736.

On a modest eminence, approached by stairs, the remains of a GAME LARDER – a battered octagonal base in cyclopean granite which once supported a vertically boarded timber upper stage and tent-like roof swept up into a finial; it contained a fountain to keep it cool. Near the house on its N side is a large rectangular WALLED GARDEN of C18 and C19 date, part stone, part brick with a fine iron gate and gazebos at its SE and SW corners.

The PARK was planted in 1788 with 38,200 saplings provided by the nurseryman *John Adam*. It is enclosed by shelter belts, the magnificent approach drive wending its way through Balmuir Woods. Within Skene Woods the MAUSOLEUM is an ice-house-like structure with rubble entrance gable initialled and dated G(eorge) S(kene) 1769: sixteen coffin recesses, never used. A pair of columns once stood at its entrance.

STABLES (250 m. ENE). By *Archibald Simpson* or *William Ramage*, c. 1860. Robustly handsome Baronial, built in granite. Long shallow U-plan, with three-storey clock tower rising into corner turrets, battlemented parapet and crowstep-gabled attic caphouse. Wings two-storeyed with tall ground floor and the upper floor's low oblong windows breaking into dormerheads; spired tourelles at far outer corners. Residential conversion 1984.

STONEHAVEN 8080

INTRODUCTION

Stonehaven lies on the wide sweep of Stonehaven Bay. Just S of the Highland Fault, it contrasts with nearby granite Aberdeen because it is predominantly built of warm red-brown sandstone, a factor which allows for both increased carved decoration and more rapid weathering. At the S end, a cove between the rocky promontory of Bellman's Head and the cliffs of Downie Point makes a natural haven, although it required extensive engineering

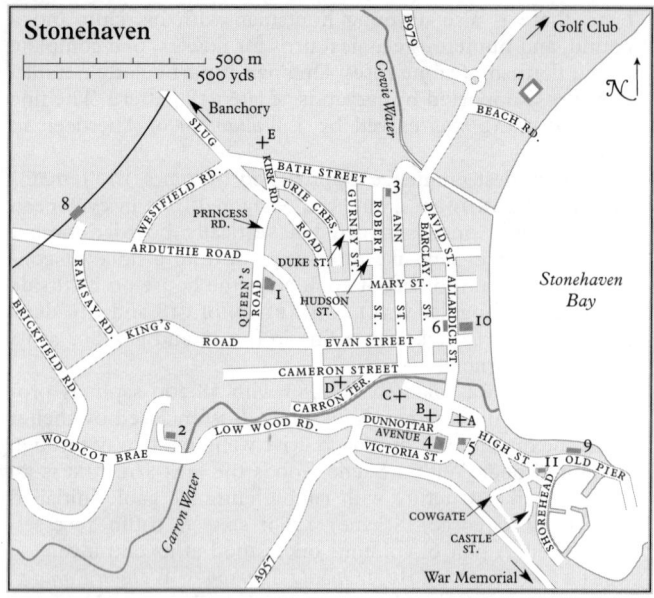

A	Immaculate Conception (R.C.)	1	Arduthie School
B	St Bridget	2	Combination Poorhouse
C	St James (Episcopal)	3	Community Centre
D	South Parish Church	4	County Buildings
E	Stonehaven Fetteresso Church	5	Dunnottar Primary School
		6	Market Buildings
		7	Open Air Swimming Pool
		8	Railway Station
		9	Tolbooth
		10	Town Hall
		11	Town House

works to turn it into a safe harbour. The town has two distinct parts, an unplanned Old Town in the parish of Dunnottar, and a planned New Town in the neighbouring parish of Fetteresso. The Old Town – 'a straggling and irregularly built place' (John Wood, 1828) – grew up around the harbour. In 1587, reputedly, it was made a burgh of barony under the superiority of the Earl Marischal, and it became the county town of Kincardineshire *c.* 1600. The Carron Water enters the sea just N of it, and was formerly joined there by a second river, the Cowie. In the C20, however, the final stretch of the Cowie was redirected from its old course, which ran parallel with the beach, and it now joins the sea 500 m. further N.

Robert Barclay of Urie (1732–97) established the New Town immediately N of the old one, on the Links of Arduthie between the Carron and the Cowie. He acquired the land *c.* 1759, laying it out on a regular grid plan, with broad streets (named after members of his family) and a large central market square. A bridge over the Carron, connecting new and old, was built in 1781, and by *c.* 1790 the square was partly feued and built up. By 1823, when John Wood made a survey, Allardice Street and Barclay Street were largely complete, and houses had spread along Evan Street and Cameron Street. The railway arrived from the s in 1849, reaching Aberdeen the following year. Until the late C19, New Stonehaven was administratively separate from the old burgh. It had its own Town Council, set up in 1856, and it was not until 1889 that a board of Police Commissioners was appointed as a single authority to govern both New and Old Towns.

Stonehaven's role as a regional centre is reflected in the dignified County Buildings and a handful of banks. Apart from the harbour, where the herring fishery peaked in the 1880s, there is now little evidence of C19 industry. The trade which has shaped the town more than any other is tourism. In the second half of the C19, and especially in the 1890s, bracing air, attractive scenery and sea bathing made Stonehaven a popular resort, to which city-dwellers from England as well as Scotland decamped for the summer. Villas colonized the higher ground towards the railway station, mostly servicing the holiday trade. Even some of the grandest, though built and occupied by local worthies, were rented out during the summer season. Aberdeen architects were regularly employed, especially *D. & J. R. McMillan*, but the locals *George Gregory* and *John Ellis* were kept busy too. Recreation grounds were laid out in 1885, a golf course in 1888 and a promenade along the beach in 1895. In August 1899, a census of summer visitors counted 1,600 of them – this at a time when the burgh's permanent population was about 4,500. Meanwhile, the lack of houses for working people was repeatedly criticized. The first council housing appeared in Fetteresso Terrace after 1919, and in the 1930s a large scheme was begun in Brickfield Road. Dilapidated housing in the heart of the Old Town was comprehensively – and sensitively – rebuilt in the 1940s. Since the start of the Aberdeen oil boom in the 1970s, Stonehaven has acquired much peripheral housing for commuters, while the A90 bypass has relieved the centre of heavy traffic.

CHURCHES

IMMACULATE CONCEPTION (R.C.), Arbuthnott Place. By *J. R. Mackenzie* (of Aberdeen), completed 1877. Diminutive but delightfully ornate Gothic church, standing alone in its neat garden enclosure and looking almost toy-like. Aisleless nave, extremely shallow transepts and apsidal chancel with sacristy on one side and slender tower and spire on the other. Windows mostly lancets with cusped heads. w door flanked by triplets of tiny lancets behind detached arcades, below a gable window of geometric tracery. The tower starts square, becoming octagonal, with an open stage carrying the spire and a surrounding cluster of pinnacles. Inside, transepts and nave are divided by pairs of arches, each springing from a single column. Open timber roof on corbels. – STATIONS OF THE CROSS. Paintings by *F. Walterson*, 1954, mildly expressionist. – STAINED GLASS. Transept windows by *Edinburgh Stained Glass House*, 2003 and 2004; W window, St Margaret of Scotland surrounded by angel heads in roundels, probably late C19, in a style reminiscent of Daniel Cottier.

ST BRIDGET, Dunnottar Avenue. 1886, by *G. P. K. Young* of Perth. Built as a mission of Dunnottar Parish Church to serve the Old Town; converted to a multi-functional church hall, 1970. Single vessel, with big slated roof and low, buttressed sides. Square window openings, with cusped timber frames. Porch at S end. At the apex of the gable, a portion of the roof projects on brackets as a bell-housing. Square flèche in centre of ridge. Interior modernized.

34   ST JAMES (Episcopal), Arbuthnott Street. By *Robert Rowand Anderson*, 1875–7; additions by *Arthur Clyne*, 1885 and 1906. The most important ecclesiastical building in Stonehaven, more than a match for the Parish Church, and a testament to the strength and tenacity of Episcopacy in this area. It replaced an C18 chapel in the High Street. Anderson's five-bay nave with lean-to aisles and clearstorey is Transitional Romanesque in snecked sandstone rubble, the overall impression one of rugged solidity. W front with pointed blind arcading flanking a single round-arched window, with a pointed oval in the gable above; down the sides, heavy string courses provide the only ornament, stepping up and over the windows. Anderson intended an apse with ambulatory, but the church opened in 1877 with a temporary E wall. When Clyne finished the E end, eight years later, he provided a round apse with pointed lancets but no ambulatory, plus a N transept for an organ chamber. On the S, he added an elaborate polygonal vestry with a pyramid roof – like a chapter house – and a slender square tower with round, conical-roofed top. There are intriguing, complicated shapes where the angles of the vestry meet the body of the church, and Anderson's string courses are echoed, but with a knowing trickiness. Clyne returned in 1906 to add the lean-to porch and octagonal baptistery in the centre of the W front. All his additions, especially the unusually positioned baptistery, add interest and complexity, but without undermining Anderson's seriousness.

Inside, the nave arcades are relatively low: cylindrical piers with massive bases and cushion capitals carry the round, chamfered arches. The capitals are roughly finished, and the angles of the bases – like blocked-out leaf ornaments – have the same rough-hewn quality. Mighty chancel arch with clustered shafts. As on the exterior, string courses meander round the clearstorey windows. Nave roof with arch-braced trusses, ceiled at the level of the collar-beams; coved timber ceiling to chancel. The baptistery, disappointingly, has only a flat plaster ceiling. – FURNISHINGS. Impressive REREDOS designed by *S. Gambier Parry* and carved by *Earp, Son & Hobbs*, 1886.

Alabaster figures of Christ and SS Andrew, Peter, James and John under elaborately crocketed canopies of Corsham stone. Of the same date, the PULPIT, designed by Clyne and carved by *James Bremner* of Broughty Ferry. Octagonal, of Caen stone, with vivid heads in high relief of St Ninian, David, King of Scotland, and three Scottish ecclesiastics. At w end of the nave, octagonal, white marble FONT, perhaps early C19, from St John's Chapel, Golden Square, Aberdeen (dem.); in the baptistery, and forming its focal point, a more splendid font carved from a single block of brown alabaster with panels of Celtic interlace. – STAINED GLASS. w windows, s aisle, Raising of Jairus's daughter, 1877, and N aisle, Adoration of the Magi, 1880, both designed by *Anderson*. Three chancel windows with scenes of the Passion: Crucifixion, 1886, flanked by Christ carrying the Cross and the Deposition, 1892, all *Clayton & Bell*. Window above w door, Baptism of Christ, 1939, by *Douglas Strachan*. Below the biblical scene, a representation of the baptisms performed by Episcopal clergy while imprisoned in the Stonehaven Tolbooth, against a dramatic background of cliffs, beach and sea. In the baptistery, five lancets with single figures by *J. N. Comper*: St Nathalan, David, King of Scotland, a youthful John the Baptist, St Francesca (dated 1929) and St Kieran (1930). – MEMORIAL TABLET on s wall of chancel to Sir Robert William Duff of Fetteresso Castle, †1895 while Governor of New South Wales. The architectural frame is modelled on part of Government House, Sydney and the tablet was designed by *H. C. Kent* of Sydney, and carved there, a gift to Duff's widow from the ladies of the colony.

SOUTH PARISH CHURCH, Cameron Street. By *James Souttar*, 1868. Built as a Free Church, replacing one of 1843–4 by *James Henderson* on the same site. Gothic, cruciform, with a single large window of flowing Dec tracery to the street. Entrance in pyramid-roofed tower, r., filling the angle between nave and transept. The tower was part of the original design but only added in 1896 by *George Coutts*, to give access to a new nave gallery. Interior with panelled, stencilled ceiling. Stained glass window above organ: Christ blessing the little children, 1896, given by William Mowat, proprietor of the Carron Tan Works.

STONEHAVEN FETTERESSO CHURCH, Bath Street. By *John Paterson*, 1810–12; altered 1876–8, 'from the designs' of *James Garvie & Sons*, builders, of Aberdeen. It replaced the parish church founded in the C13 at Kirkton of Fetteresso (*see* p. 616), 2 km. sw, which had become dilapidated. Though closer to the New Town, the new site was still well outside the built-up area, and remained so until after the coming of the railway. A striking Late Georgian Gothic building – drydashed, with stone details, and battlemented throughout – it recalls Paterson's 1808 rebuilding of Fetteresso Castle (*see* p. 617). The convex entrance front follows the curve of the U-plan auditorium, so that it resembles a bastion. Octagonal stair-turrets at each side, and a square, diagonally buttressed tower over the central entrance, crowned with heavy corner tourelles with pointed tops. Simple pointed lancets (with Y-tracery added 1876–8, although seemingly intended by Paterson).

Inside, gallery on cast-iron columns, with a further tier of columns supporting the flat ceiling. The columns belong to the 1876–8 alterations, along with the pulpit and organ recess above, all in pitch pine like the new gallery front. The church was given new pews at the same time, but these only survive in the gallery. Chair incorporating a CARVED PANEL from the old church, dated 1682. – STAINED GLASS. Two two-light windows on E side. The Good Shepherd and Faith, Hope and Love, 1902, by *Kemp, Benson & Co.* of Glasgow; and St Clare with spinning wheel and St Francis preaching to the birds, an excellent work of 1990 by *Crear McCartney*. – MONUMENTS. In the porch, presumably brought from the old church: John Lumsden of Blairmormouth †1799, a chaste white and grey marble tablet; and Capt. William Gavin †1792, marble inscription in a sandstone frame with urn and oak garlands above. – BELL. From the old church, dated 1736, by *Richard Phelps* of Whitechapel. Also in the porch, a rough, horizontal slab of stone with a shallow rounded hollow. Traditionally identified as an ancient font, but more probably a cresset stone, where wicks floating in oil provided more economical illumination than candles. – HALL and OFFICES, 1970, set back on W side.

PUBLIC BUILDINGS

ARDUTHIE SCHOOL (originally Mackie Academy), Arduthie Road. Central block 1893 by *D. & J. R. McMillan*, wings added 1903 by *Kelly & Nicol*. Reconstructed and extended by D. & J.R. McMillan after a fire in 1929. Centre plainest classical, simplified post-fire, but wings more elaborate: round-headed windows on the ground floor, forming an arcade; square-headed windows above, grouped together with pilasters between. Pedimented entrances, recessed between wings and centre. Assorted buildings at rear, one dated 1931 on a Dutch gable facing Queen's Road. – School WAR MEMORIAL on axis, facing Arduthie Road. A low, three-sided, stone enclosure, incorporating a bench and inscribed bronze panels, by *John Ellis*, 1921.

Former COMBINATION POORHOUSE, Woodcot Brae. *William Henderson*, 1865–6. Classical. Two-storey front range with rear wing at right angles and single-storey range behind, parallel to the front, making an H. Central pediment above radically simplified entablature and pilasters – just flat strips, without capitals or bases. A plain building, but good proportions make it dignified rather than grim. Converted to flats, 2000.

COMMUNITY CENTRE (former Stonehaven Public School), corner of Ann Street and Bath Street. 1876, by *J. R. Mackenzie*. Gabled end bays with three smaller gables between, all with ball finials. Mostly square-headed windows, grouped together under pointed arches. Contemporaries called it 'Elizabethan'.

COUNTY BUILDINGS, Dunnottar Avenue. Administrative buildings for Kincardineshire, including a jail, were erected on this
site in 1767, and altered in 1822 by *John Smith*. What first meets
the eye today, however, is the front block of 1863–5 by *James
Campbell Walker*. Broad, of two storeys, with slightly advancing
outer bays. Ground floor with channelled rustication and
round-arched windows. Centre emphasized by single-storey
porch and a pair of close-set chimneystacks, breaking the balustraded roof-line. It closes the view down Allardice Street and
makes a very effective s termination to the town centre. From
the back, a higher central block with round-arched windows is
visible – apparently the C18 building altered by Smith. The E
wing containing the police station is late C20, rusticated to
match Walker's front; the rest of the building closed in 2014.

DUNNOTTAR PRIMARY SCHOOL, High Street. By *George
Gregory*, 1889. A big, plain Board School, relieved by bits of
strapwork over the windows. It looms over the former County
Buildings next door.

MARKET BUILDINGS, Market Square and Allardice Street.   97
1826, by *Alexander Fraser*. The architectural centrepiece of the
New Town. A long, two-storey, classical building in pink
granite ashlar, symmetrical about a clock tower and spire. The
short ends have open arcades on the ground floor, the long
sides round-arched doors and segment-headed shop windows.
The upper floor is reached by an entrance in the tower. This
starts with a square, pedimented stage, becomes octagonal
above, then round with pilasters, then octagonal again for the
clock. The spire was included in the original design but only
carried out in 1857–8, almost the first act of the newly constituted Town Council, who raised the money by subscription. It
is of timber, with eight cast-iron Doric columns and four pediments round the base. The Council sought the services of
William Smith of Aberdeen, but he declined when it was
decided not to build in stone, and the job was supervised
instead by *Mr Davidson*, Inspector of Works for the contemporary rebuilding of Ury House (q.v.). The tower is on the
Allardice Street side; the much more prominent elevation to
the Market Square is sadly only the back. FOUNTAIN, N of the
Market Buildings, 1897. Pink and grey polished granite. Round
basin supporting a short, square spire on four stubby columns.

OPEN AIR SWIMMING POOL, Beach Road. *R. Gall* of *Gregory
& Gall*, 1934. This was the climax of Stonehaven's provision
for holiday-makers. Enclosed by buttressed walls on three
sides; the fourth, with classical centrepiece, contains the
entrance and changing rooms and has a Doric colonnade
overlooking the pool itself. Red pantiles and white render hint
at Mediterranean warmth, but are equally suited to an E coast
fishing village.

STATION, *c.* 1849. Italianate, asymmetrical, with deep eaves and
paired, round-arched windows. In 1850 and 1851, Queen
Victoria and Prince Albert stopped here on their way to and
from Balmoral, and briefly the little building was 'converted

into a miniature palace' to receive them. NE addition and other improvements, 1899–1900, including the cast-iron-framed platform roof with heavy scrollwork in the spandrels. Restored 2000, and altered to provide disabled access. The timber former GOODS SHED, opposite, appears to have been in existence since the 1860s at least. 600 m. NE, the GLENURY VIADUCT carries the line over the valley of the Cowie Water. Ten sandstone piers, narrowing in stages as they rise. Original timber arches replaced with wrought-iron plate girders, *c*. 1884. Tops of piers strengthened with concrete, late C20.

82 TOLBOOTH, Old Pier. Stonehaven's earliest surviving building. L-plan. The longer wing, overlooking the harbour, is believed to have been built as a storehouse by the Earl Marischal towards the end of the C16; it probably became the Tolbooth *c*. 1600, when Stonehaven succeeded Kincardine as the county town. The shorter wing may be C17. Random sandstone rubble, much weathered, with crowstepped gables and irregular openings, some blocked. A large, first-floor loading door has become a picture window. External stairs to first floor at W end. Reopened after restoration, 1963, with museum on ground floor and restaurant above (*Leslie Grahame-Thomson* exhibited a scheme for this in 1951).

TOWN HALL, Allardice Street. By *Matthews & Lawrie* of Inverness, dated 1878. Six-bay palazzo of grey-pink sandstone, with orange sandstone dressings. Windows segment-headed on ground floor, round-headed above. Parapet with urns. The front block contained ground-floor news room and billiard room, with meeting room and supper room above. The public hall is behind.

TOWN HOUSE, High Street. Built 1789–90 by *James Rhind*, mason, of Aberdeen. Just a square tower of four stages, quite plain apart from its chamfered quoins, with a window to each stage on the two principal fronts. These parts are ashlar, the rear rubble. Short, lead-covered, bellcast spire on octagonal timber belfry, surrounded by timber balustrade. A pedimented projection above the wall-head, dated 1896, contains a clock. In front, the MERCAT CROSS (not visible owing to building works, 2014). C17 shaft, head restored 1887.

WAR MEMORIAL, Black Hill (750 m. SSE along cliff path). *John Ellis*, 1921–3. There can be few war memorials so magnificently sited. The rocky coast lies just below, with the sweep of Stonehaven Bay to the N and Dunnottar Castle to the S. Prominent on the skyline from far away, Ellis's design responds to its dramatic setting by echoing classical cliff-top temples such as Sounion and Assos. Octagonal colonnade, raised on a stylobate of rough-hewn stones. The columns are primitive Doric, unfluted and roughly dressed, and parts of the entablature are deliberately omitted (whether to suggest ruin or incompleteness is unclear). Names of battles are inscribed on each face. Broad steps flanked by heaps of tumbled stones lead to a square granite monolith within the colonnade, bearing the names of the dead.

DESCRIPTION

1. Old Town

The HARBOUR is the focus, enclosed on the N and NE by the   5
sandstone OLD PIER. A pier on this site was in existence in
the mid C18, and harbour-works of some kind are recorded in
the early C17, though precise details are lacking. An improvement scheme by *Robert Stevenson* was implemented in 1826,
when the SOUTH PIER was constructed and a mass of rock at
the harbour entrance was blasted out. In 1837–8, two JETTIES
were built, one extending W from the point of the South Pier,
the other extending E from the shore in line with it, the narrow
gap between them giving access to a safe inner harbour. *John
Gibb* of Aberdeen was consultant, and the work was supervised
by *John Forbes*. In the first decade of the C20, *James Barron* of
Aberdeen built the concrete BREAKWATER, E of the Old Pier,
providing additional protection. Today, the harbour is largely
given over to recreational use.

On the quayside opposite the Tolbooth (*see* Public Buildings)
is a SUNDIAL dated 1710, and at the landward end of the Old
Pier, DUTHIE'S WELL, a plain, square, ashlar structure with
cornice, early C19. From here, the SHOREHEAD leads S, with
varied houses and commercial buildings overlooking the water,
still attractive despite unsympathetic late C20 changes. No. 7,
a three-bay house, looks basically C18, with chamfered quoins
at the angles and round the door. The neighbouring MARINE
HOTEL, 1884, looms higher. Vaguely Gothic gabled dormers,
and what may be genuine C17 carvings along the ground floor:
a series of damaged stone heads, mostly animals, said to come
from Dunnottar Castle. The developer was Baillie James
Knowles, a fish-curer. The height of the hotel matches the
adjoining harled GRANARY, a four-storey warehouse of uncertain date, but definitely earlier than the hotel. Converted to
residential use, 1970s, with new domestic windows at the front,
but the original small openings remain at the rear. Further S,
the Aberdeen and Stonehaven Yacht Club occupies another
former warehouse. The harled late C17 house next door, No.
19, has chamfered ashlar margins to the windows, and its gable
faces the sea. In the network of lanes behind these waterfront
buildings, only fragments of the pre-C20 Old Town survive,
including some simple cottages in Castle Street (leading to the
coastal path to Dunnottar Castle).

Back at Duthie's Well, the HIGH STREET leads W to form
the Old Town's backbone. Its early buildings – picturesque but
insanitary – were mostly replaced from the 1890s onwards. A
comprehensive redevelopment scheme by *J. A. W. Grant* of
Edinburgh was begun in 1939, and work proceeded during
the Second World War. The S side, from the Shorehead to The
Cross, is presumably Grant's, along with similar houses on the
N side, and also S of the High Street in KING STREET, ALBERT
LANE and THE CROSS. It is a notably sensitive exercise. Two-
storey houses of squared rubble with cast-stone dressings,

breaking forward here and there to avoid monotony. A turret at the corner of Shorehead has a Lorimer-ish dome. Crowstepped gables, bolection-moulded doorways, and arched openings leading to back greens re-create not just the traditional style of the buildings they replaced, but also their tight-knit character (contrast this with the slightly earlier, detached, flatted blocks on the s side of King Street, apparently by *D. & J. R. McMillan*, with suburban front gardens).

KEITH'S PLACE, branching NE from the E end of the High Street, has more of Grant's houses. It leads to RIVENDELL, a C17 house with imaginative C21 additions. The old part is a simple rubble oblong with crowstepped s gable (skewputt carved with human head); the main E front has a baffling variety of openings, some bolection-moulded, others chamfered, the lowest with sills at pavement level. The addition – *c.* 2000, by *Grampian Design Associates* – is enclosed at ground-floor level by a massive curved rubble wall (part of the town's flood defences, in existence by the 1860s). The first floor is a railed viewing platform supporting a lozenge-shaped sun-room with a jaunty folded roof, like the wheel house of a boat.

Back in the High Street, at the SE corner of The Cross stands the Town House (*see* Public Buildings), clamped into Grant's housing scheme and forming its hinge. Continuing W, No. 51, s side, is a four-bay C17 house of some grandeur, now part of a terrace with adjoining C20 council housing. Corbelled turret, cut off by the slope of the roof. The moulded door surround has weathered carvings, including a just-recognizable human figure. Opposite, preserved in the harling of Nos. 58–60, is the outline of the blocked Water Yett. This gateway gave access to the river mouth and beach, and once formed the Old Town's principal entrance from the N. It seems to have been an open lane until at least the 1860s, only later becoming a covered passage when the first floor of the house on the r. was extended over it. Further W, back on the s side, the former EPISCOPAL SCHOOLS (now Sea Cadet headquarters), 1851, but with a tall, Gothic front block added in 1897 by *J. A. Souttar*. Returning to the N side, Nos. 28–32 are CHRISTIAN'S HOUSE. 1712, but heavily restored. Five bays, the doorway prettily framed by C19 cast-iron columns supporting an arch and lamp. For Dunnottar Public School and the former County Buildings, *see* Public Buildings. (Behind the County Buildings, built into the wall of a lane running s from the E end of Victoria Street, two C17 TOMBSTONES, discovered nearby on the site of a former burial ground.)

In front of the County Buildings, turn N into Bridgefield. On the r., RICKARTON COTTAGES, a terrace of five alms-houses, were built at the same time as the Immaculate Conception R.C. church (*see* Churches) to the E, and designed by the same architect, *J. R. Mackenzie*. The larger middle house breaks forward, with gable and veranda. Church and cottages were the gift of Mrs Hepburn of Rickarton in memory of her husband: a granite tablet on the middle house records his

death in 1873. Turn l. into Bridgefield Terrace. The former
MILL INN at the end was a coaching inn for travellers on
the Edinburgh to Aberdeen turnpike road. Plain, seven-bay
Georgian front, the long Doric portico a modern replacement
for one shown in a print of 1840. (Another relic of turnpike
days is the single-storey early C19 INVERCARRON TOLL
HOUSE, 300 m. SW on the A957.) Before this, on the N side
of Bridgefield Terrace, and turning the corner into Bridgefield,
five red brick houses by *George Gregory*, 1903, with a touch of
Norman Shaw about their bay windows with swept, lead-
covered roofs. They would pass unnoticed in an English
suburb, but here their alien materials stand out. Just N of these,
ARBUTHNOTT STREET leads W from Bridgefield to St James's
church. Straight and regular: old Stonehaven no doubt taking
a leaf out of the New Town's book. No. 1 is a three-storey,
three-bay Late Georgian house, with pretty segmental iron
balconies to the outer top-floor windows. No. 8, next to the
church, was built by the stonecutter *Robert Taylor* for himself
in 1890. The grotesque heads on the skewputts must be his
own work. Back at Bridgefield, ARBUTHNOTT PLACE leads E,
where another substantial Late Georgian residence, BOWMONT
HOUSE, faces the R.C. church.

2. New Town

The starting point is the road bridge over the Carron Water, a
1973 replacement for the original, built by Robert Barclay of
Urie, 1781. A stone embedded in the building at the SW corner
reproduces the inscription from the bridge's central arch, with
significant dates from the history of the Barclay family.
ALLARDICE STREET leads N, the main commercial thoroughfare. Early houses here were rebuilt from the later C19 onwards,
resulting in a flurry of architectural display opposite the Market
Buildings (*see* Public Buildings). On the NE corner of Market
Lane, the former CROWN HOTEL was extended by *D. & J. R.
McMillan*, 1898–9, and has ogee-gabled dormers and a little
corner turret. After this, the Town Hall (*see* Public Buildings).
No. 44 is the ROYAL HOTEL, 1903 by *John Ellis*. Two mullioned-and-transomed bay windows rise through first and
second floors, finishing with a pair of gabled timber dormers.
Not much of interest after this. BRUCE COURT, on the E side,
is Postmodern sheltered housing, 1988, reached by a pend with
columns.

Allardice Street becomes DAVID STREET and veers NW to
be joined by Barclay Street. More sheltered housing on the r.
here, set back from David Street and overlooking the Cowie
Water: HANOVER COURT, *c.* 1981, by *GRM Kennedy &
Partners*. Rendered blocks, some with monopitch roofs, grouped
round an open space. David Street ends at the COWIE BRIDGE.
James Fraser, mason, contracted to rebuild it in 1826, replacing
a predecessor of 1732 by *William Adam*. Three segmental

arches with triangular cutwaters. Evidently widened, but with Fraser's original facings reused. On the W side of David Street, just before the bridge, two substantial Late Georgian dwellings. Elevated BELMONT HOUSE (actually in Belmont Brae) is stone, of three bays, and was in existence by 1823. More impressive is harled INVERCOWIE HOUSE, 100 m. S, just in Barclay Street. Two storeys plus attics, raised above a basement. The outer bays have shallow bow windows from basement to eaves. The grandest residence in Stonehaven in the early C19, it was almost certainly the 'large new house at the entrance to the town, the property of Mr Richardson', offered for sale in 1806. Its once extensive grounds had already been built on before it was converted to flats in the 1970s.

From here we return S to the Market Square by Barclay Street, lined with one- and two-storey houses. Nothing of note on the N side of the Square, except the Italianate former BANK OF SCOTLAND (now Royal British Legion) at the W end. 1862 by *Peddie & Kinnear* (their monogram is on one of the quoins). Although part of the terrace, it is set back behind a railed area. Two-light windows divided by column mullions with foliate capitals. Continuing down the Square's W side, Nos. 12–16 on the corner of Evan Street, 1820s or 30s, are the grandest of Stonehaven's early commercial premises. Originally three shops, now one, with continuous shop front and other alterations of 1913 by *John Ellis*. Three storeys high, in grey granite, they look as if they had strayed here from the centre of Aberdeen. Blind Venetian window in Evan Street gable (a feature of several corner buildings in the New Town). First floor mangled by turning six original windows into three enormous glazed openings, but with attractive early C20 signage above.

Turning W into EVAN STREET leads to two sober Italian Renaissance commercial buildings on the N side. First, the CLYDESDALE BANK (originally North of Scotland Bank), by *James Matthews*, 1875. Five-bay palazzo with consoled cornice, entered via a Doric porch in the shorter side facing Ann Street. (Single-storey solicitors' offices at No. 20 Ann Street form an attached pavilion, 1901, by *George Gregory*.) Next door at the corner of Robert Street, KINNEAR HOUSE, by *William Smith*, 1854. Now flats, but originally the Aberdeen Town & County Bank. Windows grouped 1–3–1, with a heavy first-floor balcony on brackets in front of the middle three.

Opposite this dignified Victorian pair, something much less solemn. Nos. 26–32 Evan Street were built in two phases for the Northern Co-operative Co. Ltd. First came the higher corner block by *D. & J. R. McMillan*, 1915, in rough grey granite with battlements and crowstepped gables. Then, in 1936, *Tawse & Allan* added three single-storey shops to the W end. These have sleek Art Deco fronts in smooth grey granite, and the same treatment is wrapped around the ground floor of the earlier block. The larger shop windows at each end have outsize keystones with stepped profiles, and the bronze-framed

Art Deco glazing incorporates small coloured motifs indicating the type of shop – a bull's head for the butcher, wheat sheaf for the baker, etc. Turning s down Ann Street and r. into Cameron Street reveals that the shops have an even more elegant face to the rear, the CARRON RESTAURANT. Only one storey, set back behind a garden, but raised high on a stepped terrace giving views over the Carron Water. Fully glazed front with central bow. Loggia right across, also bowed, with square piers. Materials are brick and white-painted render. Carefully restored 1999–2000, including the interior with its smoothly wood-panelled walls. Opposite, the WHITE BRIDGE, 1879, a pretty segmental-arched iron footbridge over the Carron, leading to St James's church. Made by *Blaikie Bros* of Aberdeen with *G. S. Hird* as engineer, as the inscription proudly proclaims. The lacy quatrefoil balustrades are a richer variation on the same manufacturers' Garbh Allt bridge of the previous year (*see* Crathie p. 445). Finally, Nos. 26 and 28 Cameron Street, w of the restaurant and on the same side, are later commercial interlopers in this early residential street. Built for the Savings Bank, 1892, by *George Gregory*. Classical. Arcaded round-arched windows on the ground floor, square-headed windows and pilasters on the floor above.

3. Cowie

Historically a separate burgh, Cowie is now essentially the n end of Stonehaven. The few interesting buildings are fairly widely scattered. Just e of the B979, 50 m. n of Cowie Bridge, a pretty timber PAVILION overlooking the tennis courts, 1909, by *George Gregory*. This and the surrounding recreation grounds reflect Stonehaven's growth as a holiday resort around 1900 (for the open air swimming pool, 250 m. NE on the seafront, *see* Public Buildings). On the opposite side of the main road, 150 m. NW, COWIE MILL. A meal mill here was described in 1797 as lately erected; it was enlarged in the C19, remodelled in 1920 by *Duncan Thompson & Son*, and converted to housing in 1993–4. The oldest part appears to be w of the cart entrance. The pyramid-roofed kiln is prominent; mill lade and wheel no longer exist.

Following the old main road NE, parallel with the sea, leads past COWIE HOUSE, l., set among woods. Described *c.* 1808 as 'a modern mansion of no great extent', it was enlarged by *William Henderson*, *c.* 1851, forming an irregular group round a court. (On the cliff path, 200 m. SE, remains of a GUN BATTERY, second half of C19, built by the Stonehaven Artillery Volunteers. Low stone walls with embrasures.) 500 m. after Cowie House is the GOLF CLUBHOUSE. First phase by *George Coutts*, 1897, altered and extended w by *George Gregory*, 1909. Timber, with veranda and polygonal corner bay. A late C20 addition disfigures the front. Finally, 100 m. s of the Golf Clubhouse, the ruined CHAPEL OF THE BLESSED VIRGIN

MARY AND ST NATHALAN. Dedicated by the Bishop of St Andrews, 1276. A simple C13 rectangle, lengthened at the w end. The E wall survives to its full height, with three stepped lancets. Moulded s doorway, aumbry in n wall. Built against the w end, a semi-subterranean MORT-HOUSE, c. 1830. The vaulted roof is grassed over, leaving only the segmental gable visible.

VILLAS

Stonehaven already had a sprinkling of larger detached houses on the fringes of the grid plan before the mid C19. In the 1890s, the town experienced a surge in villa-building, for residents but more especially for summer visitors. These are in the higher streets, the larger and later ones generally closer to the railway station. The following route is about 2.5 km. long and takes in most of them; for the highlights, it is enough to visit Arduthie Road and the area round Bath Street.

Starting from the N end of the White Bridge, follow the Carron Water w along CARRON TERRACE. One- and two-storey-plus-attic houses, beginning with a couple of late C18 examples at Nos. 1 and 2. Nos. 7 and 8 are a mid-C19 pair, with boldly consoled cornices to the doors and windows. Turn r. into Arduthie Street, then l. into CAMERON STREET. The w end has a cluster of early detached villas. No. 48, opposite the South Church, is KEITH LODGE. Large, and set well back from the street, it was in existence by 1823, but the canted bay windows are Victorian. Recently bookended with insensitive additions as part of a flat conversion, with much glazing and timber cladding. No. 74, SOUTH CHURCH MANSE, is 1844 and attributed to *James Henderson*, architect of the original church. No. 82, ROSEBANK COTTAGE, is 1836 and possibly by *John Smith* of Aberdeen. Originally a single-storey three-bay house, harled, with stone margins and simple console-cornices over the windows. It was raised a storey by *William Campbell Davidson* in the early C20. Finally, the best of this early group is No. 85, CARRONBANK HOUSE, beautifully set in spacious grounds above the river. Again perhaps by *Smith*, 1835–6, and with similar details to Rosebank Cottage, but square, and with a SE bow window for the view.

Return to Rosebank Cottage and turn l. up the steep footpath beside it. At the top, turn l. into Evan Street, which straight away becomes KING'S ROAD. Among trees on the s side is LANGDON, 1891, possibly by *Ellis & Wilson* of Aberdeen. A square, classical house, with ball finials on the parapet. More prominent is the silver granite CLAREMONT, on the N side at the corner of Queen's Road. 1901 by *John Ellis*, for the solicitor D. C. Booth. A polygonal bay window marks the corner, merging with a battered rock-faced chimneystack. (Immediately NW of these affluent dwellings, early C20 council housing begins. Following King's Road uphill to its end leads to

BRICKFIELD ROAD, where the Council started building in 1935, with *Gregory & Gall* as architects.)

From Claremont, Queen's Road leads NE past Arduthie School (*see* Public Buildings) to ARDUTHIE ROAD. This is the main route between the centre and the station, and a key location for villas. Later ones, further up the hill, are mostly decent but unexceptional semis and three-bay detacheds. In a different class is EDENHOLME, N side, 100 m. uphill from Queen's Road. 1901, by *A. H. L. McKinnon* for an Aberdeen doctor. A large house in generous grounds, with lower wings r. and l. Tall chimneys, bellcast roof and a polygonal bay to one side. Scrolled pediment over entrance. Back down the hill, just after the school is CARLTON HOUSE (described as 'recent' in 1889; dripmoulds over the windows, and a square, pyramid-roofed tower with iron cresting) followed by the more imposing VIEWMOUNT, 1881, perched on an eminence. Viewmount was built for William Mowat of the Carron Tan Works, a leading citizen. Two storeys, with double-height bay window, armorial carving over the arched entrance, and other Gothic touches. *George Coutts* enlarged it in 1903, adding a full-height extension, l., and single-storey bay window, r. Use as Council offices since the 1920s has resulted in large C20 additions to both Viewmount and Carlton House (a 1988 NUCLEAR BUNKER in the grounds of Viewmount is an evocative legacy of the Cold War). Earlier houses on the opposite side of Arduthie Road are single-storeyed, set back behind large gardens.

Continue down Arduthie Road to the junction with Evan Street. On the NW corner, EWEN BURN, an unusual house of 1912 by *George Gregory*, with gables to both streets, patterned glazing bars and a veranda. Turn l. here, and l. again into SLUG ROAD. This important thoroughfare, which goes all the way to Banchory, begins in an unassuming way but becomes more interesting. On the W side, at the top of a steep bank, Nos. 8 and 10 are an attractive semi-detached pair of 1913 by *D. & J. R. McMillan*. Triangular dormers, and deep eaves making verandas front and back. URIE CRESCENT, overlooking Slug Road from higher ground, NE, has close-set villas of the 1890s. On the NE side of Slug Road itself, the much grander ARDLUI, by *J. R. McMillan*, 1897, and CARDOWAN, by *J. A. Souttar*, 1900. Further along on the same side, but with its entrance in Kirk Road, is THE GABLES. Prominently dated 1905, it was designed by *Kelly & Nicol* for the rector of the Mackie Academy (now Arduthie School), where the same architects had recently made major additions. On an important corner site, where Westfield Road branches W from Slug Road towards the station, stands THE HEUGH, a substantial Baronial mansion of 1897 in silver Kemnay granite. *James Souttar* designed it for his son-in-law, Sydney Herbert, a Surrey stockbroker. The usual ingredients: battlemented porte cochère, square tower with crowstepped gable, conical-roofed stair-turrets.

From The Heugh, BATH STREET leads E, the high point of Stonehaven villadom. Immediately W of Stonehaven Fetteresso Church (*see* Churches) is MAXIEBURN, 1897, by *James Souttar*, possibly with his son, J.A. Souttar. Stone below, half-timbering above, with deep eaves and a timber veranda and balcony. ARDGOUR, opposite, but entered from Kirk Road, is now a private house but was originally the parish school. By *James Henderson*, *c.* 1845. The master's house with gabled dormers and porch faces S, with attached schoolrooms at each end and a taller one at the back, extending to Bath Street. On the E side of the church, No. 20, THE LILIES, 1897, for the Burgh Treasurer, A. Thomson Wood. *George Gregory* was both architect and builder of this unusual and ambitious house. Queen Anne style but of an individual stamp. Pink stone, two storeys, one in the huge, red tiled mansard roof. Small-paned windows, including long sashes with semicircular timber pediments in the mansard. Off-centre entrance framed by a pair of Dutch gables, each with a two-storey polygonal bay window. The lower bays, which have a larger radius, are linked to the upper ones by ogival, lead-covered roofs, and the upper ones have complicated leaded roofs of their own. Venetian window, l., lighting what was probably Wood's office, with separate side entrance.

Next door is TUDOR LODGE, dated 1909. Formerly attributed to William Kelly, but more probably designed by *George Coutts*, for the Bank of Scotland's local agent. 'Old English' in the manner of Norman Shaw, with a central Gothic doorway, mullioned-and-transomed windows, and three half-timbered gables. Opposite is FETTERESSO LODGE, 1898, by *J. & J.A. Souttar*. The flanking bay windows are ordinary enough, but the striking entrance is a sharply pointed Gothic arch, springing from low down, with a bullseye window each side. Back on the N side, No. 6, BATH LODGE, is the only pre-Victorian house in the street, a Late Georgian three-bay villa, in existence by 1823. NE of it, reached from a lane off Baird Street, THE HERMITAGE, 1908, by *D. & J.R. McMillan*. A harled Arts and Crafts house with stone quoins, now painted. Entrance set diagonally in the angle between two wings, with a little canted bay window nestling on top and a triangular oriel in the gable above. Almost a repeat of the same architects' No. 2 Devanha Gardens West, Aberdeen (*see* p. 251). Just E of Bath Lodge, GURNEY STREET leads S. It was begun and largely completed during the 1890s, at the height of the villa boom. No. 39 on the E side is the Baronial KENSIT, 1903, by *W.E. Gauld*. Tall and rather narrow, with a single column of bay windows from top to bottom, like a vertical slice from a row of tenement flats. Finally, turn E into Duke Street to reach the rear of CLASHFARQUHAR HOUSE at No. 23 Robert Street. 1902–3, by *A. Marshall Mackenzie*. Built as the Stonehaven Bay Hotel by a business consortium, squarely in the residential part of town (though many of its villa neighbours catered for summer visitors too). Splendidly sited, and visible from all over

Stonehaven, but disappointingly dull. The front faces the sea: five storeys, with three big, bargeboarded gables, and canted bay windows on the lower floors.

STRACHAN   K   6090

A small kirkton on the Water of Feugh's N bank close to its confluence with the Water of Dye; it lines the B976 near its junction with the B974.

Former STRACHAN PARISH CHURCH. 1865–6 by *James Matthews*; the gift of Lady Catherine Gladstone. Simple First Pointed, rectangular plan, built in coursed golden granite with ashlar dressings. S gable with stepped triple lancets under hoodmould, diamond-pane glazing. Diagonal buttresses progressively intaken, gabled bellcote with a delicate iron crucifix finial. Five-bay flanks with lancets, SE porch with pointed doorway, small session house at NW. In a dwarf-wall, a commemorative panel for William Burnett Ramsay †1866 (*see* Banchory Lodge, Banchory).
    The CHURCHYARD is the site of a church belonging to the Archdiocese of Brechin, dedicated to the Virgin in 1242. No trace remains of this nor its successor built in 1790. Near the NE corner, a winged cherub kneeling on a cushion prays for Mary Rattray Reid (†1892) and James Cargill; close by a tablet carved with bas-relief falcon and initials of James Toner Hay and Maria Douglas Hay (†1924 and 1939).
    Former PARISH MANSE. A reused skewput dated 1630 indicates an ancient site, but another, dated 1777, relates to the present building. The S elevation comprises the original two-storey three-bay manse in coursed squared granite rubble to the E, with a gabled roof and moulded skewputts, and later W wing of 1828 with a piended roof at the SW angle. Entrance porch concealing the original doorway perhaps by *William Smith*, who built a rear bedroom wing within the angle in 1877.
Former FREE CHURCH, 150 m. W of the Parish Church. Simplest Gothic, built 1843, with gabled centre to the street. W bellcote.
SCHOOL, W of the church. By *William Smith* (of *J. & W. Smith*), 1876–7. Tudor Gothic. Single-storey L-plan built in rubble with ashlar dressings. Porch in the angle. Tall wall-head chimneystacks.
LARACHMHOR, just W of the village on the B976. The architect *William Smith*'s weekend home, built 1859. Two storeys, three windows wide, its central entrance flanked by ground-floor canted bays and the first floor rising into gabled dormerheads. Harled, with granite dressings and margins.
LIMEKILN, Knockhill, 3 km. ESE. Perhaps early C19. A small drum in boulder rubble with battered sides, single fire-hole. Built into a hill-slope, loaded from the top.

BRIDGE OF DYE, 6.7 km. SSW, formerly carrying the B974 – the Cairn o'Mount road – across the Water of Dye, now bypassed. Built *c.* 1680, this is the second oldest bridge on Deeside. Deeply impressive. A single semicircular span of 13 m., rubble-built with dressed voussoirs and slightly hump-backed parapets, triangular retreats at the S end. The intrados is strengthened by two stone ribs similar to those of Bridge of Dee, Aberdeen (q.v.).

BRIDGE OF BOGENDREEP, 2 km. SW over the Water of Dye, now bypassed. Late C18. Segmental span, rubble-built with dressed voussoirs, low parapets widening at the approaches.

8020

STRALOCH HOUSE

2.5 km. S of Whiterashes

Late vernacular classical house built by the Ramsays of Barra *c.* 1790, with Aberdeen School details, alterations in the C19 and early C20.

The MAIN BLOCK's entrance front facing S is symmetrical, two storeys and five windows wide over a slightly raised basement, its broad centre bay fractionally advanced. Deeply splayed doorway set within lugged architrave and shallow cornice, finely detailed timber transom-light, the approach steps with ornate iron railings. Ground-floor windows in moulded lugged architraves, with cast-iron basket-weave balconies, first-floor windows in more simply detailed ashlar surrounds. Harled masonry with long-and-short quoins, discreet eaves course just beneath the wall-head parapet, the central bay rising into a low pediment with oval oculus. Curvilinear twin end gables with panelled chimneystacks acknowledge a double-pile plan, the roof inset with catslide dormers of *c.* 1900.

On each side, WINGS extend back from the main block to enclose a service court on the N. These comprise single-storey links to two-storey three-bay blocks with curvilinear end gables and panelled stacks, echoing those of the main block's. By 1865 the main block had been linked to the wings by neat quadrants, that on the W side still surviving: the oriel in the main block's W gable is about that date. In the early C20 the angle between the main block and E wing was infilled by a larger single-storey piend-roofed link with a rectangular tripartite bay on its S front.

The REAR ELEVATION is simple, the main block asymmetric with the second bay from the W projecting; a central round-arched window at mezzanine level lights the main stair; good simple transom-lights in both the main block and the W wing. Entrance hall with a distyle *in antis* columnar screen opening into a square stair hall, plain late C18 with dining room on l. and drawing room on r.

STABLE BLOCK, 200 m. W, dated 1872, converted to domestic use by *Tansy Grigor-Taylor Associates*. Symmetrical entrance front, tall single storey and attic, with gabled end bays slightly advanced. Central range in red hammer-dressed masonry with grey granite dressings, simple square-headed doorway and windows and twin gableted stone dormers breaking through the wall-head; long roof crowned by a slim clock tower with bellcote and spirelet. End gables seemingly earlier, in contrasting pale harl with smooth ashlar dressings, each lit by two ground-floor pointed-arch windows and a single pointed window above. Four roundels display the date, initials of John Ramsay of Barra, and family motifs.

ST MARY'S CHAPEL (Episcopal), 170 m. E. Built 1905. Simplest Gothic. – DAIRY AND GAME LARDER, 50 m. W. Octagonal, brick-built, surrounded by an iron-columned veranda. – NORTH LODGE, 450 m. NE. Tudor, early C19.

STRATHDON

3010

Strathdon is a kirkton on the S side of the River Don, close to its confluence with the Nochty Water where it is crossed by the A944. On the other side of the water is the small village of BELLABEG.

STRATHDON PARISH CHURCH. Very ambitious for such a remote rural parish, designed by *James Matthews* (of *Mackenzie & Matthews*) when George Gilbert Scott's office was still fresh in his memory. Largely paid for by Sir Charles Forbes of Newe (*see* below), opened 1852 but completed 1853. Handsome Early Dec, cruciform with short transepts, built in roughly squared rubble with extensive use of pale gold dressings, its square tower within the NE angle rising into a broached spire. Four-bay nave with stepped buttresses, each bay being lit by a two-light window with circled tracery. At the W end, a pointed doorway framed by shafts with moulded capitals and oversailing hoodmould; three-light window with quatrefoil and trefoil tracery; small fleur-de-lys finial over gable apex. Similar windows light the transepts and E end (which has a Celtic cross finial), all with diamond-pane glazing. Stair-turrets at the nave's NW corner and SW angle of the S transept rise into prismatic roofs. Tower of three stages with angle buttresses: its first stage the doorway like that at the W end, second stage tall lancets, third stage the belfry with louvred two-light openings, then above the trefoiled corbel table the broached stone spire with finialled clock-dial gables at its base (no clock mechanism was ever fitted) and slim lucarnes.

Aisleless INTERIOR, wide-span hammerbeam roof; W, N and S galleries accessed from stairs in the tower and angle turrets, arcaded fronts over cast-iron columns. A plain double-

33

chamfered arch opens into the chancel, its floor raised and walls panelled in 1936. At the same date Matthews's Gothic PULPIT was moved to its present position on the arch's s side and the present COMMUNION TABLE introduced. FONT, tall and vase-like in black marble, gifted 1932. Preserved in the chancel are five heraldic PANELS in pitch pine, reputedly from the Auchernach family pew. The monogrammed initials are those of the Elphinstone of Bellabeg and Forbes of Skellater families; they are dated 1597, 1636 and 1686, but all look late C17. Fine WALL MONUMENTS, all in white marble, notably the Rev. George Forbes (†1799), crowned by a hemicycle pediment with a funereal vase in low relief; Lt-Gen. Nathaniel Forbes (†1851), crowned by a display of militaria; and Sir Charles Forbes (†1877), a Gothic tablet. In the chancel, a heraldic lying slab commemorating William Forbes of Newe (†1698). In the narthex, a wall monument to the Andersons of Candacraig, dated 1757, with fluted pilasters and an armorial overarch.

A kirk is shown in the CHURCHYARD in *Blaeu's Atlas* of 1654; its replacement of 1662 was rebuilt *c.* 1757 with further alterations 1808–9. At the churchyard's w end, Matthews's cast-iron GATES hang from square gatepiers with low pyramidal copings; at its E end, two pairs of timber GATES with open Gothic arcading and square piers also with pyramidal copes, 1928. FORBES-MITCHELL MAUSOLEUM. Perhaps by *Archibald Simpson c.* 1829. An impressive Egyptic edifice of two diminishing square stages in ashlar masonry, gently tapering towards boldly fluted cavetto cornices and a low stepped roof. Lower stage, with simple blocked entrance architrave on its E side, is stepped in at its angles to form a Greek-cross plan with short arms; the upper stage has blind openings on all four sides (those on the E and W inset with inscription panels) and its angles are roll-moulded. FORBES OF BLELACK AND INVERERNAN ENCLOSURE, 1835. Neo-Greek, rectangular. Architraved entrance rising into low block pediment with hemicycle acroteria at the angles, cast-iron lattice gate, block-pedimented inscription panel within. Two WALL MONU-MENTS, set into the church's s side: one to Donald McSween (†1730), Minister at Strathdon, with a finely carved winged soul, the other to Robert Farquharson (†177–) and Isabel Anderson, the inscription framed by primitive but handsome pilasters, bearing an armorial. LYING SLABS with grim reapers standing on orbs, arms outstretched with hourglasses and scythes, and TABLE TOMBS dated as late as 1867.

The former PARISH MANSE beside the church is of 1831–3 by *W. Clark*, architect and builder, for the minister who had married Sir Charles Forbes of Newe's daughter. Incorporated at the rear is the previous manse of 1791–2, hence the double-pile plan. Clark's entrance front, harled with margins, is two storeys and three windows wide, with round-arched central doorway and advanced rectangular bays which now rise above the eaves into gables. Originally it had parapets and its windows were mullioned and transomed. The previous manse is two-storeyed and had a front five windows wide.

DOUNE OF INVERNOCHTY, 0.4 km. WNW of the church, within the confluence of the Nochty and Bardoch Waters with the River Don. One of the largest mottes in Scotland, only Duffus Castle (Moray) and the Mote of Urr (Dumfries & Galloway) being comparable in size. Probably late C12, this was the *capital messuage* of Strathdon until it was superseded by Kildrummy Castle (q.v.) during the C13. An oval on plan, roughly 80 m. long WNW by ESE and 40 m. broad, its slopes rise at an angle of 50 degrees for a height of 12 m. above the broad ditch which surrounds it. At some early date a stone wall was built around its summit, 180 m. in overall length. The entrance was apparently at the ESE where the walls were over 2 m. thick. Foundations of two stone buildings were discovered: one near the entrance 9.5 m. by 7.3 m., with a doorway in its E end; the other apparently a CHAPEL within the N half of the enclosure, 29 m. by 10 m. NE by SW, a stoup (probably a piscina) being found nearby. The DITCH varies in breadth from 6.5 m. to 10 m.; it could be flooded as a moat, and remained so until 1823. The arrangements were very sophisticated: a reservoir on the Doune's W side fed by the Bardoch Burn supplied water to the ditch at its N end, and it could be released from the S through sluices. The ditch's counterscarp was seemingly protected by a wooden palisade. A crescent-shaped BERM embracing the outside of the ditch on the W probably acted as a bailey, there being evidence of stone structures on its platform.

BELLABEG HOUSE, 0.25 km. N. Built 1765 but in the style of *c.* 1730, reflecting the survival of older traditions in this remote part of the country; Inverernan (1764, q.v.) was originally so similar as to clearly imply that both were built by the same master mason. Vernacular classical entrance front (facing S) two storeys and five bays in silver and tawny granite, coursed and cherry-cocked, rising above the wall-head into a hemicycle chimney gable with moulded tabling and club skewputts: the chimneystack is now capped by a ball finial. Doorway framed by slim inset timber pilasters with simple transom-light; above it a small armorial commemorating the marriage of John Forbes to Christian Shepherd. Astragalled sash-and-case windows, the gable's small round-headed light key-blocked. Gabled roof with stone ridge and skews rising into tall coped chimneystacks. Rear (N) elevation harled, near-blind, with a gabled staircase outshot resulting in a T-plan.

The INTERIOR is unusually well preserved with relatively small rooms, perhaps reflecting the short timbers available this far inland, and very compactly planned. The main entrance opens directly onto the stair, which rises to the attic floor. Its simply turned balusters, the treads' decorated ends and the handrail elegantly scrolled at its foot are characteristic of the woodwork throughout the house, modest but finely executed.

The ground-floor door architraves are lugged in characteristic CI8 fashion; the rooms here, originally partitioned into front and back, were apparently bedchambers, the principal apartments being on the slightly taller first floor.

The harled single-storey W RANGE is contemporary, standing at right angles to the main house, but was only linked to it *c*. 1920; together they form the sheltered forecourt characteristic of Aberdeenshire houses of the earlier CI8. This W range contains a very large round-arched and voussoired inglenook kitchen hearth with two salt-boxes. To the rear of this wing, and partly abutting the main house's W end though invisible from the entrance front, is a modern EXTENSION of *c*. 2010, a single-storey T-plan with its W-facing gable lit by a glazed tripartite doorway in the form of a large Serlian window. Built in mixed granites like the main house, but roughly squared and pinned, it was designed by *Kenneth Lawson* and built by *Alan Grant* of Alford.

COLQUHONNIE CASTLE, 0.9 km. ESE. A much-reduced mid-CI6 L-plan tower house, presumably built for the Elphinstones, who were granted the estate in 1507; the masons may have been the *Conns* of Auchry as it conforms to the basic plan-type with which they are associated (cf. Craig (q.v.); Delgatie, Gight and Towie Barclay (N)). It was still listed as a gentleman's seat in 1724 and its moat remained in existence in 1866.

It comprised a main block orientated N–S, 12.5 m. by 8 m., with a NE jamb almost square at 6.3 m. by 6.6 m. Its doorway is in the jamb's S face, close into the re-entrant angle, and protected by a wide-mouthed shot-hole in the main block. Built in pinned field rubble, its walls are 1.4 m. thick; most of its dressings have been ripped out.

Of the main block only the ground floor survives but the jamb is fairly complete up to second-floor level. The ground floor is vaulted throughout and its plan is a variation on the usual Conn-school plan-types, the entrance vestibule entering directly into the stair, well protected by a large guardroom in the jamb. On the W the vestibule opens into the main block, which comprises the kitchen on the N and the cellar on the S, the latter with a small room, perhaps a prison, on its E side. The kitchen has its hearth in the N wall and a slop chute in the W wall. The tightly planned turnpike stair approx. 2.5 m. in diameter is within the N jamb near the junction with the main block; at first floor the hall has completely gone but the vaulted solar survives substantially intact with a fireplace in its E wall and mural recesses.

POLDHULLIE BRIDGE, 0.75 km. WSW of the parish church, within a gorge of the Don. Built for John Forbes of Inverernan in 1715. Big semicircular arch of over 21 m. span with dressed voussoirs springing from coursed foundations on the riverbanks. Slightly hump-backed with coped parapets increasing in height towards the centre. Long curved W approach, splayed at E. Reputedly one of only two bridges on the river to survive the Great Flood of 1829.

TOLL HOUSE, 1 km. SW on the A944. *c.* 1800. Single storey with bowed centre bay, harled, piended roof. Similar to Glenkindie toll house (now West Lodge, q.v.).

At FORBESTOWN, 0.65 km. E, the former GIRLS' SCHOOL. Perhaps 1838. Gable-fronted, with single-storey teacher's house adjoining at right angles. Within the gable, tall paired depressed-arch windows with timber mullions and transoms, roundel above; two similar three-light windows in the flank.

MILL OF NEWE, 1.7 km. ESE. C18 and later. Large L-plan. Main block tall two-storey-and-loft, its S flank with a fractionally projecting gable at the E end. Kiln slightly lower two storeys projecting from the N flank at the W end, with kiln ventilator over its roof. Picturesque MILLER'S HOUSE. Ground-floor doorway and windows with stepped hoodmoulds, first floor rising into dormer gablets with decorative bargeboards and spike finials.

BRIDGE OF NEWE, 2 km. E of the church, carrying the A944 across the Don. Built in 1858–9 when Sir Charles Forbes re-routed the road to allow for the enlargement of the Castle Newe policies.* It was designed by *John Willet*, the ironwork contractors were *James Abernethy & Co.* of Aberdeen, with *John Fyfe & Co.* responsible for the masonry. The cast-iron segmental span (over 21 m.), with railed interlace parapets displaying the arms of Newe, is supported at each end by a 7.5 m. flood arch in bull-faced masonry. In 1992–3 the bridge was rebuilt by *Alan Silver* of Grampian Regional Council as a precaution against heavier loads. The two inside arches which supported the underside of the central span's road-deck on transverse brick jack-arch vaults were replaced by three new steel arches supporting a reinforced concrete superstructure, but the outer two arches were retained (although no longer load-bearing) in an attempt to maintain the bridge's appearance. DESKRY BRIDGE, 3 km. E, and BRIDGE OF BUCHAAM, 3.5 km. E, also by *Willet* 1858.

AUCHERNACH. *See* p. 333.
CANDACRAIG HOUSE. *See* p. 400.
EDINGLASSIE HOUSE. *See* p. 479.
INVERERNAN HOUSE. *See* p. 558.
SKELLATER HOUSE. *See* p. 714.

TARLAND

Erected a burgh of barony for the Irvines of Drum (q.v.) in 1683.

OLD PARISH CHURCH. Dated 1762. Simple rectangular plan with round-arched and key-blocked windows, reduced to a

---

* Castle Newe was designed by *Archibald Simpson* in a Jacobean style to complement an existing tower house; its construction began in 1831. It was demolished in 1927. The present house is by *Oliver Humphries*, 1992.

shell. W gable has blocked doorway with lintel inscribed 'MR TM' for Master Thomas Mitchell, the minister; gallery window above, moulded skewputts and finialled birdcage bellcote perhaps from still older church. Six-bay S flank, the second opening from the l. with a transom-light having been a doorway. Single window in E gable, N flank blind.

CHURCHYARD. Of the C18 stones, the best are arranged together in the SE corner, several carved with winged souls. Their similarity to stones in Migvie and Coull churchyards (qq.v.) suggest the same mason. In the W wall a Gothic triptych monument to Dr Andrew Robertson of Hopewell (†1881) and family; *see* Logie Coldstone. Piend-roofed pavilion at NW corner.

PARISH CHURCH (St Moluag), Cromar Drive at the NE edge of the village. Designed by *William Smith* 1869, probably with his son *John*, and completed by the *Aberdeen Operative Masons Building Co.* in 1870. Gothic, notably ambitious for a country parish and greatly enhanced by its densely wooded setting. Entrance S front in golden granite ashlar comprises a tall asymmetric gable curtailed on its r. side by a short bay linking to a four-stage tower with louvred belfry openings, its banded and broached stone spire added in 1889–90; this is answered by a gabled bellcote on the l., supported on an elaborate composition of buttresses. Within the gable a triple arcade with doorways in the outer openings, a set-off and large mincer-plate gallery window with a hoodmould and polychrome voussoirs. Six-bay nave built in coursed squared rubble. Triple light in the N gable above a vestry annexe. Simple but intact INTERIOR with open ceiling supported on arched trusses. Gallery at S end supported on cast-iron columns, now enclosed beneath. – STAINED GLASS. N lancets, to Lt-Col. John Farquharson †1871. Patterns except the central figure of Christ in the Garden. – S window, the Adoration, by *Douglas Strachan* c. 1911; Christ in Majesty in the centre orbited by angels in roundels.

DESCRIPTION. Standing on elevated ground, the Old Parish Church (*see* above) overlooks the long narrow SQUARE from its E end, but the village was rebuilt from 1799 when nineteen-year leases were offered to encourage the construction of better houses. Of about that date the ABERDEEN ARMS stands nearest the church at The Square's NE corner, its two-storey three-bay frontage in squared granite with club skewputts. Much of its custom would have approached *via* BRIDGE STREET which, crossing the Tarland Burn over an arch dated 1824 at its parapets, skirts The Square directly beneath the church on the E side. Today's Tarland is predominantly plain mid-Victorian to Edwardian. In Bridge Street, one of two former banks and next to it a reading room; The Square is lined with single-storey cottages in granite rubble and two-storey buildings in granite ashlar with simple gabled dormers, the COMMERCIAL HOTEL in the NW corner catching custom from Melgum Road. On the S once stood the Cromar Hall, similar to that at Mintlaw (N); it was replaced by the MACROBERT MEMORIAL HALL of 1951–3. At The Square's w end, the WAR MEMORIAL, a young soldier standing with his rifle reversed, carved by *Robert Warrack Morrison* in 1920.

Further w in Duncan Road, the 'OLD MILL' is early C19, L-plan single-storey-and-loft in yellow sandstone with a kiln ventilator. E of The Square in Balmuir Wood, a former bank has been remodelled by *Michael Rasmussen Architects* as BALMUIR, with round towers rising into conical roofs, a sculpted doorpiece, crowstepped gables and coped chimney-stacks all trying their hardest to suggest a C16 tower house.

Former PARISH MANSE, SE of the old parish church. By *William Smith* (of *J. & W. Smith*), 1846, its design following their earlier manse at Kincardine O'Neil (q.v.). Plain Tudor with tall square-shafted chimneystacks in Smith's English rectory manner.

CORRACHREE HOUSE, 1.7 km. W. By *James Henderson* for Major John Farquharson of the East India Company, 1842. Plain classical, two-storey front, three windows broadly spaced, with very tall ground-floor windows rising from a deep belt course. Slightly projected centre in granite ashlar contrasting with the pink harl of the flanking bays rises into a pedimented wall-head gable: the single-storey portico with paired Roman Doric columns supporting a timber entablature with triglyphs and balustrade is an addition, but remarkably pure classicism for *c.* 1880. Deep end gables with two windows on each floor, shallow-pitched roof with ashlar end stacks.

DOUNESIDE HOUSE, 1.6 km. N. A white-harled Scots Revival villa, reconstructed from a late C19 farmhouse in three stages *c.* 1907–*c.* 1917. The client was Sir Alexander MacRobert, 1st Baronet of Cawnpore and Cromar, who had made his fortune in the textile and tanning industries; the architect for at least part of the works was *Clement George*, who had left the Mackenzies in 1906 to establish a practice with George Sutherland. The farmhouse was originally single-storeyed with a central doorway flanked by paired windows on each side, but was raised to two storeys with a square-plan crenellated entrance tower dated 1907. Log-columned verandas were built across the main front to link with crowstep-gabled wings with canted bays, that on the l. two-storeyed with a round tower rising into a conical spirelet at its outer corner, that on the r. single-storey only. At the outer bays, the first-floor windows rise into finialled hemicycle pediments. Inside, a panelled lobby leads to a finely carved central staircase. Drawing room in a simple Adam style. Dining room early C20 Neoclassical with fluted pilasters and compartmented ceiling.

The POLICIES are the work of MacRobert's second wife, *Rachel MacRobert*, a daughter of William and Fanny Workman, Himalayan explorers and authors, and herself a botanist and one of the first three women fellows of the London Geological Society. She laid out the lawn surrounded by trees and shrubs from overseas, and within a nearby gully formed the ROCK

GARDEN with the aid of two plantsmen from *Backhouse* of York (cf. Kildrummy House): 'Our little glen became transformed with miniature rock cliffs, waterfalls, two lakes, bridges and rocky eminences planted with rare miniature trees and plants of every sort.' Between 1934 and 1940 she was assisted by *William Heughan*, with whom she transformed the WALLED GARDEN into a terraced rose garden.

TILLYCHARDOCH FARMHOUSE, 2.2 km. ENE. Later C18. Two-storey three bays broadly spaced. Harled with dressings, gabled roof with club skewputts and end stacks.

CROSSFOLD FARM 'BOTHY', 2.3 km. SSE. Early–mid-C19. A very unusual farm building, reputedly built by the *George family* of masons who farmed at Wester Coull. A small two-storey drum tower with a conical roof and single-storey side wing, both built in rubble and formerly harled. The tower's upper storey is approached by its own forestair; it has a fire-place, but was not big enough to sleep in.

RECUMBENT STONE CIRCLE, Tomnaverie, on the crest of a hill 1 km. SE of the village. This site was once threatened by a quarry but has now been thoroughly excavated and recon-structed. The earliest feature was a cremation pyre which was then covered by a circular cairn which was in turn enclosed by a recumbent stone circle. The monument has been dated to the second half of the third millennium BC. The recumbent and flankers frame the distant mountain of Lochnagar. (GN)

SOUTERRAIN, Culsh, 2 km. NNE. Late Bronze Age or early Iron Age, this consists of a curved underground passage cut into the bedrock made of drystone walling with a stone slab roof. The entrance is at the S end, from which the passage curves towards the NE, measuring 10.4 m. in length, up to 1.75 m. wide and up to 1.7 m. high. (GN)

ALASTREAN HOUSE. *See* p. 313.

TERPERSIE CASTLE

1.2 km. WNW of Tullynessle

Within a valley of the Correen hills, built for William Gordon, fourth son of James Gordon of Lesmoir, and his wife, Margaret Ogilvie, who acquired the estate from the Bishop of Aberdeen in 1556. A Z-plan tower house of three storeys – one of several built N of the Mounth from the mid C16 – but unusually small and particularly distinctive in that it has two circular jambs. Although by no means the earliest Z-plan, it is seemingly the first in Scotland to be dated, 1561.

According to the Balbithan Manuscript, Terpersie was once surrounded by a moat flooded from the Esset Burn. It was burnt during the Civil Wars in 1645, the sandstone dressings of its SW tower, in particular, bearing signs of intense heat damage, but was afterwards restored. In the earlier C17 a relatively large

rectangular wing was added at right angles on its E flank, concealing its original entrances and providing a new turnpike stair, the
original intramural flight being blocked up. Terpersie remained
with William Gordon's descendants until after the 1745 rising,
and was still inhabited by a tenant-farmer in the late C19, but by
1907 it was a roofless ruin. The C17 wing had almost completely
collapsed by the 1960s. Its remains were removed and the original
entrance front rebuilt when Terpersie was restored by Captain
Lachlan Rhodes in 1983–9 with *Bill Cowie* as his architect, *Alistair
Urquhart* as master mason and *Major Michael Taitt* as general
contractor. While the works were in progress they discovered a
fireplace from the demolished Castle of Lesmoir – from which
house the Gordons of Terpersie were descended – incorporated
into a derelict steading. That fireplace now occupies the position
of the original one in the hall's E wall.

The main block is 8.5 m. long N–S by 5.4 m. deep, the jambs at
its NE and SW angles each 5.1 m. in diameter. Construction is
in field rubble with small loose pinnings and roughly dressed
quoins, all harled over, and the dressings in red sandstone or
andalusite mica-schist. The ground-floor doorway is near the
S end of the main block's E flank: it was formerly protected by
an iron yett secured by a drawbar. The ground floor is otherwise almost blind with narrow slit-windows, but formerly had
two circular shot-holes on the W and a smaller one in the N
gable; and at second floor the main block has catslide dormerheads, a big wall-head stack on the E and crowstepped gables
with cavetto skewputts. The circular jambs rise slightly above
the main block's wall-heads into conical roofs and both have
big wall-head stacks. Within the S re-entrant angle there is a
stair-turret on four tiers of corbels, the lowest carved with the
letter G; near to it is a loop carved with a boar's head – a
symbol of the Gordons – and the date.

The plan is somewhat unusual. At ground floor the walls of
the main block are a relatively modest 0.9 m. thick but formerly carried a vault, the present ceiling being the first-floor
joists. There is no trace of a hearth: the kitchen must have
been in an outbuilding. The entrance to the stair, a straight
flight in the thickness of the S gable, is at the SW corner of the
ground floor, opposite the doorway. The stair is lit by loopholes, that at the head of the stair once having an inbuilt stone
sink, the projecting stone drain of which can still be seen.
Whether this was the original main stair, or whether it was a
service stair with the original main door at first floor over the
existing one, is now difficult to determine.

The hall has two fireplaces: the original one was in the E
wall towards its N end, but was subsequently removed and
replaced by another smaller fireplace in the N wall. The position of these two fireplaces implies that the NE jamb contained
William Gordon's chamber with two windows, a fireplace,
garderobe and aumbry; there was a second bedchamber in the
SW jamb with a single window, fireplace, garderobe and two

shot-holes, both rooms being irregular hexagons internally. A turnpike stair-turret between the sw jamb and the main block's s flank rose to the second floor, which was similarly arranged.

TERTOWIE HOUSE
3 km. s of Blackburn

A Scots Baronial country house for Colonel Ross King by *James Matthews*, 1867, which reputedly incorporates earlier fabric; large wing for Lieutenant-Colonel James King added by *William Kelly*, 1905. Proposals for a central tower were abandoned at the onset of the First World War. The house later became a school, was burnt in 2011 and is now a shell, but reconstruction is in prospect.

Matthews's house presents a stepped entrance frontage. On the l., a three-storey bay with a second-floor turret rises into a crowstepped chimney gable; the centre and r. bays are two-storeyed with attic dormers slightly set back, and a single-storey porch and bipartite bay fill the angle at ground floor. The moulded doorway is segment-headed; the upper floor windows had astragalled sashes and cases and probably represented the earlier house. Within the tall l. bay a square panel with King's initials. A short two-storey link with paired segmental carriage arches connects Matthews's house with *Kelly*'s wing, a tall single storey with attic dormers over a rock-faced basement built into rising ground. An angle turret and a round tower at the far end answer Matthews's work. Simple three-windows-wide garden front, its l. bay gabled. Good planting close to the house with a small stone bridge crossing a burn. A STANDING STONE commemorates Queen Victoria's golden jubilee in 1887.

Below the house is a NUCLEAR BUNKER of 1962, originally for the North East Sector Civil Defence Group but refurbished in 1987 as the Grampian Regional Council Emergency Centre. Closed 1988, now gutted. It contained a decontamination area, generators, tank room, kitchen, store, canteen and rest room, rooms for scientific advisors, operations, communications and dormitory.

MAINS OF TERTOWIE, 0.5 km. WNW. Crowstepped steading by *J. & W. Smith*, 1851.

THAINSTONE HOUSE
3 km. NW of Kintore

A classical Italianate country house by *Archibald Simpson*, 1835–6, for Duncan Forbes-Mitchell. Its two-storey frontages conceal a house of C18 origin on its N side which was plundered and burnt by the Jacobites in 1745 and rebuilt as the seat of Sir Andrew Mitchell F.R.S., M.P. for the Elgin Burghs and British envoy to the Prussian Court during the Seven Years War. He was at various times a protégé of the Duke of Newcastle, an enduring friend of Montesquieu and a close confidant of Frederick the Great. Thainstone is now a hotel, much extended by *William Lippe* in 1992.

The tall and handsome porte cochère – square on plan, round-arched, with a pediment – which dominates the centre of the E flank is *Simpson*'s work, as is the broad six-bay frontage which faces S over the lawn, the tall windows of the first-floor principal apartments raised over the ground-floor services, and, on the W side, the small square tower with a very low pyramidal roof. Simpson's house is faced in sandy golden harl (almost an echo of Italian stucco) with grey granite ashlar dressings and shallow-pitched roofs with boldly oversailing bracketed eaves. Its tall individual chimneystacks in the form of Doric columns, clustered together in two groups of four, are almost like closely spaced colonnades. The steeper roof seen rising behind them is that of the older house of the C18, its end gable remodelled as part of Simpson's entrance front to the r. of his portico with its wall-head curving up into a single broad stack. *William Lippe*'s additions, respectfully stepped back from Simpson's garden front although they extend it substantially, borrow his two-storey Italianate style and even add a second tower, their grey harl a discreet acknowledgement that they are later work.

Simpson's porte cochère opens directly into an impressive segmentally vaulted and top-lit stairway formed in the centre of the house between his S-side principal apartments and the old house on the N side. The walls of this stair are distinguished by fine plaster reliefs, and it reaches the *piano nobile* through a distyle *in antis* screen of fluted and marbled Ionic columns. Two principal apartments call for special note, one with a fine compartmented ceiling and the other with a segmental vault. The C18 house retains its winding service stair.

EAST LODGE, 700 m. E, on the far side of roundabout on the A96. By *Simpson*, Italianate to match the house, with a squat cubical tower. Much extended in the same idiom with single-storey bays in the mid C20.

THORNTON CASTLE K *6070*
2.9 km. WNW of Laurencekirk

Sir James Strachan obtained the estate (and became the 4th Laird of Thornton) by marrying Agnete, heiress of the barony, in 1348. The couple built a fortalice on this site, probably quadrangular in plan and surrounding a central forecourt. The building as it stands now is essentially a large rectangle, comparatively small but with excellent, well-preserved work of the C16. The last of the Strachan lairds, Sir James (3rd Bt.) became a minister in Keith (Moray) and was deposed for nonconformity in 1690. The estate then passed to the Fullertons, to Lord Gardenstone (founder of the new Laurencekirk, q.v.), the Crombies (who made additions in the mid C18) and finally back to its original family in 1893. Sir Thomas Thornton then carried out improvements and renovated the interior.

The N elevation is the principal one, now 'book-ended' by two late medieval structures that rise up like sentinels. On the r. is a mighty L-plan tower house, dated 1531 on a renewed panel but likely incorporating earlier material. Two-bay front, projecting backwards as a thick rectangle. Four storeys topped by a crenellated parapet carried on rows of multi-lobed corbels, their spacing creating a lively staccato rhythm. Open tourelles in the corners, and a rounded projection on the E side to allow passage around a chimneystack. The wall-walk surrounds a large crow-stepped garret, its masonry much renewed in the C19 and given a coped chimneystack. Smaller caphouse to the rear over the jamb; good weathervane on top of it inscribed with the date 1680.

On the opposite side is a thick, round tower of four storeys ending in another crenellated parapet (also renewed). The base course consists of thick, ragged whinstone blocks, almost certainly incorporated from the fortalice of the mid C14. They appear not to have been re-set, so the original Thornton complex probably featured four round towers in the angles. In the re-entrant angle, a fine heraldic plaque carved with the Thornton arms and motto, 'Constant[e] et fidele' ('Constant and faithful'). Running between the two latter buildings is a long, lower link of two storeys, dated 1662 on a window lintel over the present entrance but almost certainly incorporating work of the late C16. Below the date, a stone achievement added by Sir Alexander Strachan soon after 1625 when he was appointed one of the three original baronets of Nova Scotia. The crenellated parapet was added in 1822 for the Crombies of Phesdo House (q.v.), along with a new rear wing facing the garden with a square tower.

The INTERIOR retains few early features beyond the barrel-vaulted cellar of the N wing, including a colossal hearth and arch for a fireplace. This could indicate that the first storey of the link served as a great hall after the Reformation. The current entrance hall was built 1894–5 and replaces the original drum tower in the re-entrant angle with fine Victorian bravado. Broad imperial staircase with good carpentry, the balusters moulded in Neo-Jacobean style. Stained glass windows on the half-landing of the Three Graces. Billiard room further to the l., top-lit by good glazed and piended lantern. Behind Victorian panelling in the original great hall is a wall painting of Dame Elizabeth Forbes (d. 1661), whose tomb is in the Thornton Aisle at Marykirk (q.v.).

TILLYCAIRN CASTLE

3.5 km. w of Sauchen

A small L-plan tower house with an interesting building history. Begun by William Forbes (afterwards the 7th Lord Forbes) *c.* 1538, and continued by Matthew Lumsden after his marriage to Forbes's half-sister Annabel in 1540. It was nominally completed in 1546, then altered later. Work may have been in progress when Matthew Lumsden died in 1580. The relatively rich treatment of the upperworks has led to speculation that the *Bell family* was responsible for them, although they were never finished as intended, perhaps curtailed by Matthew's son John. Their date remains unclear, and they may have been modified as late as *c.* 1700, by which date Tillycairn was back in the hands of the Forbes family. It then passed to the Gordons of Cluny (q.v.) and was a ruin by 1722, apparently as the result of fire. It was restored by *Ian Begg* for David Lumsden of Cushnie (Leochel-Cushnie, q.v.) in 1980–1.

Tillycairn's main block, orientated N–S, is 10.7 m. long by 8.8 m. deep, and its NE jamb is 5.4 m. by 4.9 m. Such dimensions result in arms of almost equal length, and its relatively modest size makes its four-storey height seem all the more impressive. Within the angle a quarter-round stair-tower rises up to a boldly detailed wall-head corbel course and then into an ashlar-faced attic-storey caphouse, while corbelled turrets crowned by conical spirelets flank big coped chimneystacks over the end gables. The caphouse was clearly intended to open onto wall-walks supported by the corbel course, which, if the upperworks had been completed, would have resulted in much taller two-storey turrets as at Craigievar (q.v.). Such turrets – and the bold detailing of the corbel course – are very much a *Bell* motif, as can be seen in the tower house of Castle Fraser (q.v.) only 6 km. away. The original – or intended – appearance of the caphouse is not known, its present monopitch ('bucket') roof a traditional solution arrived at during the 1980s restoration in the absence of any firmer evidence.

As the L-plan entrance frontage faces E there must once have been a forecourt or a barmkin on that side but no trace of it remains. The segment-headed doorway is set in the main block at ground level immediately to the l. of the stair-tower and protected by a wide-mouthed shot-hole. The corners of the walls are rounded, confirming a date sometime before 1570, and at ground floor they are almost blind, having only decorative crosslet gunloops with oilettes, a distinctly North-East feature. The large windows at first and second floor – at the same height in the main block as in the jamb – are set in dressed ashlar surrounds, and were formerly barred; the lower third floor is lit by small square windows beneath the corbel course, and the stair is lit by narrow slits. The attic caphouse and turrets also have small windows, the latter with ventilation holes (perhaps they were closets) and shot-holes in their corbel courses.

There are three field-panels for heraldic arms between the first- and second-floor levels, that in the stair-tower with an ogival top now empty, but those in the flanking elevations with new arms inserted by David Lumsden, one commemorating the castle's construction by Matthew Lumsden and his wife Annabel Forbes *c.* 1546, and the other his own restoration in 1980–1.

INTERIOR. The walls are as much as 1.4 m. thick with deep hearths, recesses and (at the upper levels) wall chambers. At ground floor the entrance opens into a vaulted dog-leg corridor which gives access to the turnpike stair – completely renewed in 1980–1 – to a vaulted kitchen and cellar in the main block, and another vaulted cellar in the jamb. The kitchen has a large segmentally arched hearth (but with no side oven) and a sink which discharges through a chute on the N side; the cellar in the main block has a service stair which rises in the SE corner to the lower end of the hall at first floor, although food seems to have been taken up the main stair as a serving hatch opens directly onto it from the kitchen. The cellar in the jamb has a deep recess.

At first floor the hall occupies the whole of the main block, and is lit by two windows on the W flank and one on the S: it has what appears to be a small cupboard (rebuilt as a buffet) and a laver for rinsing at this 'low' end, while at the 'high' (N) end is a large fireplace with a small recess in one side, probably for keeping salt dry. Its timber ceiling is carried on joists, but the private room in the jamb is vaulted, with a double safe in one corner.

There would seem to have been three chambers at second floor, two in the main block and one in the jamb; the S chamber and jamb chamber both have bed recesses – these perhaps formed the Lumsdens' private apartments – and all three have closets. The much lower third floor contained a gallery or dormitory in the main block with a fireplace in the N wall, and another chamber in the jamb, the stair continuing up to the attic and the intended parapet walks.

TILLYPRONIE HOUSE

3.6 km. N of Logie Coldstone

Built for Sir James Clark, Physician to the Queen, *c.* 1867–8, seemingly to designs by his diplomat son *John Forbes Clark* working with *Alexander Ogilvy*. Baronial, but with some Tudor and Northern European features, built in local granite rubble with Kildrummy sandstone dressings. The entrance (W) front is two storeys and five bays broad, asymmetrical with a low central tower rising into a piended roof. Shallow gabled entrance porch. The centre bay on the l. rises into a gablet, the r. bay into a pyramidal roof carried on chamfers at the corners – a motif repeated on the s front with its projecting wings. Some windows mullioned and transomed, the principal apartments lit by casements with leaded lights. The broad two-storey canted bay window to the l. of the entrance front and the long, low service wing were added by the shipowner Sir Thomas Royden, 2nd Bart, *c.* 1928, three years after he bought the estate. A door lintel from the previous house, with initials A.G. (Gordon) B.S. 1706, was re-laid by Queen Victoria in March 1867, with her monogram above. The original internal woodwork was carried out by *William Pittendreigh*, but the oak panelling in the hall has been transposed from Deene Park (Northamptonshire), and that in the inner hall was salvaged from Carden Hall (Cheshire) after it was burnt out in 1912; the oak staircase and all the oak doors – including the front door – came from Widnes House (Lancashire), being installed at Tillypronie by *Messrs Wynne & Sons*.

On the terrace on the s side of the house, a small GAZEBO may have been where John Brown, Queen Victoria's personal servant, took his meals when she visited Tillypronie, as tradition relates apart from other household staff. The POLICIES occupy the s-facing slope of Baderonach Hill, an exposed situation but with fine prospects over the Howe of Cromar, taking in the Hill of Morven, Clachnaben and Lochs Kinord and Davan. Their development was begun by Sir John Clark from the late 1860s. The PLEASURE GROUNDS in their current form were begun by Sir Thomas Royden in the decade after he bought Tillypronie in 1925. Designs were commissioned from *George Dillistone*, garden architect of Tunbridge Wells, in 1926 but not carried out; instead Sir Thomas laid out the TERRACES over former parkland immediately to the s of the house and created an informal WATER GARDEN beyond which the policies extend to a lochan and an earlier woodland established by Clark *c.* 1910. The ARBORETUM and much of the magnificent planting reflects the efforts of the Astor family from 1951, their four-hectare pinetum with its 300 named varieties of pine being established in 1958, and the terraces laid out on formal principles; the water garden was improved with advice from *Vernon Russell-Smith* in 1983.

COTTAGE ORNÉ, 1.7 km. WNW, off the A97. Earlier C19. Single storey, three bays in squared red granite with a jerkin-head roof.

TILQUHILLIE CASTLE

3 km. SE of Banchory

The date given for the castle by MacGibbon & Ross is 1576, said to have been built for John Douglas, whose family seem to have held land at Tilquhillie from at least the late C15, when David Douglas married Janet Ogstoun of Fettercairn. His descendants abandoned Tilquhillie in the late C18 for Invery House (q.v.) and the castle was reduced to the status of a farmhouse. Unoccupied by the mid C20 it was returned to residential use by a careful restoration from 1985 by *John* and *Kay Coyne* with *France Smoor* as their architect and *Slesser Troup* as their mason.

Tilquhillie is a Z-plan with the central tower between jambs at the NE and SW angles but the three elements are surprisingly equal in scale and appearance so that the hall range does not obviously dominate. The walls are harled and relentlessly plain with chimneys on the gable-ends, small windows and shot-holes (many reopened in the restoration), and rounded corners that are only corbelled out close to the very top to support the crowstepped gables of the roofs. Spanning the angle between the main range and the SW tower is a flat section containing the entrance. Carved heraldic panel over of the Douglas arms. The yett with its iron bar is the original reinstated, having been discarded into an outbuilding. Pressed into the angle between the main range and the NE tower is a stair-turret, corbelled in steps to a quarter circle.

Inside a vaulted ground floor for kitchen and cellars, one with a stair rising to the hall above. Unlike most stairs of this type it is not completely contained in the wall, but rises into a projecting chamber at hall level. The principal stair flies straight from the entrance to first floor and the upper floors are reached by the newel stairs over the entrance and in the angle with the NE tower. At each floor the jambs contain very similar chambers. The first floor chamber of the NE tower is entered directly from the hall, the remaining chambers in the tower being accessed from the newel stair. The chambers in the SE tower feed off the straight stair and main newel stair as do the upper chambers of the central block. The interiors were completely restored after 1985, with original door openings, corbels and squinches reinstated. The oak beams and roof members are original and there are two original floors. In the adjoining Laird's room a fireplace with roll-moulded surround (possibly rather similar to one in the Business Room at Drum Castle).

6000   TORPHINS

A village on the S-facing slope of the Beltie valley, at the cross-roads of the A980 and B993, largely developed after the Deeside Railway opened its station in 1855.

MID-DEESIDE CHURCH, St Marnan Road. Designed by *J. R. Mackenzie* and built by *Wilson & Johnston* of Banchory *c.* 1874–6, reordered with a new entrance porch built against the former apse *c.* 1915. Mackenzie's church comprised the low nave in coursed whinstone rubble, with the original entrance (now blocked) centred in the s flank, a small rubble tower with a Germanic piended roof r. of centre against the N flank, and a canted apse facing E nearest the road. The porch is built in ashlar granite and timber and both it and the windows of the former apse break up into steeply raked gablets, their barge-boards with scissor-braces, although the main roof is shallow-pitched; the apse is supported by angle buttresses, one doubling as the chimneystack for the boiler room in the porch's base-ment. Lattice glazing contributes a jewel-like quality. The two-stage rectangular tower has louvred pointed belfry openings, tall swept piended roof with patterned slates and oversailing eaves on simple brackets. Small ventilator on nave roof; deli-cate metal finials.

Former UNITED FREE CHURCH, Craigour Road. 1901–5, by *George Watt* (of *Brown & Watt*). Gabled N front with stepped triple lancets, the skews stepped out at the ends. Square NW tower-porch, the paired openings at its set-back top stage clasped by vestigial buttresses, stepped parapet and tiled spire-let. Canted apse at s end, basement hall in the fall of the ground. Wagon ceiling inside on sculptured corbels.

LEARNEY HALL, Beltie Road. By *George Marr* (of *Jenkins & Marr*), 1899. Scots Renaissance, in robust granite ashlar. Tall crowstepped gable front with three banded ground-floor windows and a large triple-light mullioned-and-transomed window in stone. Square tower on l. with round-arched doorway in flank, clock stage and crenellated parapet.

Former MEMORIAL HOSPITAL, St Marnan's Road. Built *c.* 1920, extended by *George Bennett Mitchell & Son c.* 1935. Pleasant single-storey building, half-timbered with a veranda.

DESCRIPTION. The Deeside Railway resulted in Torphins' devel-opment during the later C19 as a commuter village with pros-perous villas, many by the builder *John Morgan*. His own house WOODCOTE (No. 20 William Street) was built in 1890 as a Canadian-inspired Arts and Crafts bungalow. Principal (s) front single-storeyed with five bays in reddish-brown brick and half-timber. Its three bays to the r. rise into a gambrel roof, originally red tile, later green slate, their central canted bay having a braced gable with apex doocot. A lower roof over the two l. bays, one canted and rising into a gable, and a later bow at the far l. corner. Fine interior with good woodwork, fireplaces and coloured glass roundels. Woodcote inspired Morgan's architect brother-in-law *Alexander Ellis* to build THE FIRS, No. 70 Beltie Road, as his holiday home *c.* 1895. Its ground floor is brick, but its jettied-out first floor is half-timbered, its mullioned windows with unusual Japanese-inspired glazing patterns. Gambrel roof rising into red tiled dormer and a prospect tower. Smaller pyramid roof over the entrance bay at one corner, elegant metalwork details, good interior.

To the S, COUNCIL HOUSING begun by *A. H. L. Mackinnon* *c.* 1935 was continued after the Second World War. Near the crossroads, the LEARNEY ARMS HOTEL by *Jenkins & Marr*, 1898–9. Built in granite ashlar, its two-storey three-bay centre with cast-iron veranda at ground floor and dormers in the roof is flanked l. by a single-bay tower with a bellcast pyramidal spirelet and r. by two bays rising into a crowstepped attic gable. Behind it is the original inn of *c.* 1835, a low two-storey irregular L-plan, its broad canted entrance porch with first-floor armorial in the angle and a picturesquely varied roof-line.

CRAIGMYLE, 1.6 km. ESE. Originally a tall, compact house of 1676, with central Dutch wall-head gable, rather like Frendraught (q.v.), built for a branch of the Burnett family from Crathes. Extended in 1902 by *Robert S. Lorimer*, but demolished and replaced by a bungalow in 1960. Stones of the main house lie beneath the rockery while a fine carved stone doorway and three arches by Lorimer are incorporated in the bungalow. WEST LODGE, 0.85 km. WNW of the house, also by Lorimer. Two storeys, tall Dutch gables, harled with ashlar granite dressings. Semicircular staircase bay in coursed rubble against one flank, tall chimneystack rising from the other. Similar to his lodge at Pitkerro (Dundee & Angus). Faceted gatepiers of broken pediment type, cast- and wrought-iron gates. Also perhaps by Lorimer is CRAIGMYLE MAINS FARMHOUSE, 0.25 km. N on the same road. It is dated 1905. Single-storey and attic L-plan front, the broad l. bay projecting. Ground floor in pinned pink granite, the big attic gables harled in white with bargeboards and half-timbering. Small glazed wooden porch with gablet in the angle. Astragalled casement windows.

MILL OF LEARNEY, 1.5 km. NNE. Early–mid-C19. Two storeys, originally four bays in coursed squared masonry, reconstructed as five bays in the later C20. Aberdeenshire kiln ventilator repositioned near-centrally over gabled roof. Cast-iron eight-spoke overshot wheel (4.4 m. diameter) at one end. Now residential. Detached granary.

LEARNEY HOUSE. *See* p. 640.

TOUGH

A small kirkton.

PARISH CHURCH. By *John Smith*, 1837–8. One of the several tall and simple yet sophisticated rural churches built by Smith at this time. Its N gable front has its centre slightly projected to suggest a nave-and-aisles arrangement. Splayed central doorway with hoodmould: above it tall triple lights under raking parapets with blocky skew-ends, an arched birdcage bellcote with simple capitals and a ball-finialled spirelet surrounded by smaller obelisks. Four-bay E flank with very large two-light mullioned-and-transomed windows with small-pane glazing; on the W side the outer bays are blind to conceal the gallery stairs; S gable has gallery triple lights answering those on the N. The vestry outshot was added by *Jenkins & Marr* in 1892 in a complementary style. Substantially unaltered INTERIOR, its deep horseshoe gallery with an arcaded front enclosing the pulpit in the centre of the E side. The PULPIT is original with a tall traceried back rising into a broken hemicycle pediment; its stair and the elders' enclosure are *c*. 1870, but the COMMUNION TABLE and FONT are mid-C20; the PEWS are still *Smith*'s. Several Neoclassical WALL MONUMENTS, the most important beneath the gallery in the W wall, a recess with finely carved funereal urn and two oval bas reliefs: one a conventional pose of mourning, and one an C18 double portrait presumably of William Byres of Tonley and his wife.

The site of the OLD CHURCHYARD is memorable: steeply sloping and enclosed by low stone walls above a bend in the Burn of Lyne. The earliest gravestone (in the N wall) is of 1732 although the predecessor church of 1731–3 has left no visible trace. MORT SAFE preserved near the church door. NEW CHURCHYARD to the N formed in 1908. – WAR MEMORIAL. A very young Highland soldier leaning on a reversed rifle in sad contemplation, by *Messrs Stewart & Co.* of Aberdeen, 1921.

The former MANSE, 120 m. NE, was built by *John Smith* in 1835 in his Neo-Tudor English rectory manner, but its porch is round-arched to match the church. Internally the stair has a good Neo-Tudor ceiling. Offices to the rear by *Alexander Adam*, 1863.

KIRKTON COTTAGE, 40 m. SSE. Former girls' school, *c*. 1800. Single storey, with rustic gabled porch flanked by tripartite windows on each side. Coursed local red and blue granite with coped end stacks.

TILLYFOUR FARMHOUSE, 3.3 km. SW. A two-storey three-bay farmhouse of *c*. 1800, with slightly taller, broader gabled end bays added *c*. 1840. Once the seat of William McCombie, the originator of Aberdeen Angus cattle, who was visited by Queen Victoria in 1866.

TONLEY HOUSE, 650 m. NW. Ruinous seat of the Byres family of whom the Roman antiquary and architect James Byres (†1817) was the most distinguished member. In its final Baronial form, the work of *Matthews & Mackenzie*, *c*. 1891, recast from an earlier plain classical house by *John Smith* 1829 which incorporated still older fabric. – The WALLED GARDEN lies 1 km. S at Tillymair. James Byres selected the site, a dell of the Lyne Burn close to Kirkton of Tough in the late C18. It is protected by a wall on its N side only: built in pale granite, roughly coursed and squared, and of substantial 2.7 m. height to its grassy coping, the manner in which it wends its way through the gently undulating countryside until it disappears out of sight suggests that it continues without end; a single

broad segmental gateway somewhere about its centre rein-
forces the impression of an ancient line of defence protecting
a civilized idyll from the outside world. It was a novel experiment in the Picturesque, perhaps inspired by Italy where Byres
spent much of his life. Its layout on such steeply sloping ground
is exceptional, as for its time was the use of water at its foot:
Byres formed a lake flooded by the Lyne Burn with three or
four small islets: 'the proprietor intends to put a boat upon it,
so as to occasionally afford a pleasing source of amusement,
and a healthy exercise'. Some trees are as old as the garden,
although few if any specimen trees survive; Byres planted the
garden and two other dells on his estate with fir, larch, birch
and oak. The garden was maintained until 1953, and is now
being restored to something near to its original condition. In
its SE corner, the GARDENER'S COTTAGE, itself an eyecatcher,
with a bowed frontage and a big circular chimneystack like a
contemporary toll house, looks out across the prospect; from
a distance its modest scale makes the dell seem like a deep
ravine.

WHITEHOUSE, 2 km. NE. Built as a large Baronial villa by
A. Marshall Mackenzie for George Leslie Farquharson *c.* 1898,
substantially reconstructed by *George Bennett Mitchell c.* 1937
after a fire. The main block's entrance front facing W comprises
two gables with bay windows at ground floor flanking a round-
arched porch, and a fourth bay set back on the r. A single-
storey wing extends from the main block to the N and two
further wings, each single storey with dormered attic extend
to the E. Coat of arms in the main block's N flank. The family
accommodation is concentrated within the main block around
the central stair hall, the drawing room and morning room on
the S and the dining room with Tudor fireplace on the N; the
male domain comprising business and billiard rooms occupies
the E wing with its own porch at the rear, while the services
are accommodated at ground floor within the two N wings
which enclose a discreet service court. STABLES by *Jenkins &
Marr c.* 1897–1901.

4010

TOWIE

A small kirkton on a loop of the Don. An L-plan tower house
was built by the Forbes of Brux after 1618. Ruinous when
depicted by James Giles in 1841, it was demolished in 1968.

PARISH CHURCH. Plans for the church were prepared in 1802–4
by *William Wilson*, mason, and *Matthew Daniel*, wright. Simple
four-bay rectangular plan, harled rubble with slim dressed
margins, round-arched openings with original glazing throughout. Doorway and gallery window in each gable, the W end

crowned by a ball-finialled birdcage bellcote incised with the date; the bell itself by *Thomas Lester* of Whitechapel with inscription 'Mr James Lumsden of Corachrie / Minnister att / Towie 1743'. N flank near-blind with later lean-to boiler house. Simple interior with plain camp ceiling, re-floored and re-seated *c.* 1894 by *Ross* of Mill of Glenkindie. The panelled horseshoe gallery supported on square timber columns is original and partly obscures the outer S flank windows; since 1963 part of it has been partitioned off as a meeting room. The PULPIT is original and still centred against the S wall, but the daïs beneath it has been reduced in height so that its back and octagonal ogee-domed sounding-board now seem exceptionally tall.

The CHURCHYARD is supposed to date from 1662, the previous church having been at Nether Towie, but it has a medieval grave-slab with a calvary cross and chalice; C18 recumbent stones, early C19 table tombs, a built-up burial enclosure and an upturned mort safe.

Bounding the churchyard's S edge is the former PARISH SCHOOL of 1811. A rare survival of its kind for that date. Two-storeyed, with three asymmetrically arranged windows and doorway off-centre; harled with slim margins and gabled roof with sturdy end stacks, small square attic lights at both gables. Low single-storey W outshot with splayed angle and prismatic roof. Single-storey classroom to E by *James Henderson c.* 1871–2, its windows breaking up into piended dormerheads.

NW is the former PARISH MANSE of 1819–20,* secluded in its gardens overlooking the Don. Neatly proportioned, two-storey three-bay symmetrical front, harled with slim ashlar dressings and margins, sunk service basement and gabled roof with end stacks; railed forestair leading to the elegant transom-lit door. – OFFICES. Single-storey U-plan, also 1820.

KINBATTOCH FARMHOUSE, 1.5 km. SW. Simple and solid Improvement Era of the earliest C19 and relatively unaltered. The farmhouse is two-storeyed, three bays broadly spaced with small attic lights at the gables and big end stacks. The courtyard STEADING is now roofed over. Entrance front single-storeyed in squared red rubble, the projecting centre containing three segment-headed cartshed arches and crowned by a tall and wide pedimental gable with round-arched attic light and small doocot openings.

430 m. S is the site of a medieval FORTIFIED FARMSTEAD, a raised quadrilateral area of ground, approximately 14 m. by 21 m., enclosed by two banks with a ditch between them. The outer bank was about 10 m. thick, the ditch (possibly flooded) 15 m. broad and the inner bank 6 m. thick, although their profiles have suffered as a result of the plough.

---

* The surviving datestone of 1778 relates to the repair of the previous manse at that time.

TULLICH

ST NATHALAN. Excavations in 2013 confirm C7 occupation of this site, founded by Nathalan (†679). The church lies across a geological fault visible on the hillside to the N and expressed by the springs at Pannanich Wells (*see* below) to the S. With the largest number of early Christian monuments in Deeside, its strategic importance relates to the routes of missionaries from the West, across the Pass of Glenshee. It was given to the Knights Templars in the C13 and transferred to the Knights Hospitallers in 1312. In 1510, the sick were still coming to Tullich church for a cure. In 1798, the three parish churches of Glenmuick, Glentullich and Glengairn were replaced by a new church in Ballater (q.v.), leaving Tullich abandoned as a burial lair. The distinctive circular churchyard contains a much altered and ruined medieval box church of indeterminate date whose N doorway has early C15 mouldings. – FONT. A primordial boulder 117 cm. in diameter, with rough-hewn bowl and drain hole, possibly C8–C9. Largest of the boulder fonts of Deeside (cf. Lumphanan and Braemar, qq.v.). – PICTISH SYMBOL STONE AND CROSS-SLABS. Found in the churchyard and built into the church. The symbols are double-disc and Z-rod, Pictish beast and mirror. The sixteen cross-slabs are slight variations on plain incised crosses, testimony to a thriving religious community for the conversion of Deeside in the C8–C9.

TULLICH LODGE, 0.8 km. W. Built in 1897 by *A. Marshall Mackenzie* as a hunting lodge for Aberdeen advocate William Reid; the tower was added *c.* 1910 by *E. Vincent Harris*. The W elevation, with its four-storey crenellated tower swelling at the upper level, bay windows and expansive crowstepped gable is a commanding presence over the Plain of Ballater. The entrance elevation, in the re-entrant angle of the Z-plan, has a generous deep-set doorway and oriel turret, all in finely dressed granite. Thistle-sprigged cast-iron gutter hoppers. Inside, high-quality timber panelling, plasterwork and chimneypieces.

PANNANICH HOTEL, 0.9km. SSE, across the River Dee. Built by Francis Farquharson of Monaltrie (Ballater) in the late C18 to serve visitors taking the health-giving waters from the adjacent well, which were discovered in the mid C18. In the C18 they were described as including public and private baths, an octagon 'for the better sort to retire to' and several houses for sheltering the poor. What survives is a pair of distinctive shallow, parallel ranges, clinging to the steep, soggy hillside. The road elevation is nine bays long, two storeys high with a canted central bay. Owing to the angle of the hill, the front wall-head is much lower than the rear. The S range was originally five bays long, with a lower E addition. PANNANICH WELLS are marked by a rough pyramidal well-head with stone seating, and a simple triangular pediment, above covered basins. The water is now bottled by the Deeside Spring Water Co.

TULLYNESSLE

TULLYNESSLE & FORBES PARISH CHURCH. By *William Smith*, 1876. A simple example of the larger First Pointed-style churches designed by the Smiths for agricultural parishes about this time, similar to Belhelvie (N). Built in local Syllavethy granite ashlar, elegant yet robust. The broad w entrance front rising into a steeply pitched gable is framed by intaken buttresses to suggest a nave-and-aisles arrangement internally. Paired pointed-arch doorways with double-leaf doors hung on decorative iron hinges, stepped triple lancets with hoodmoulds above lighting the gallery and quatrefoil ventilator just beneath the apex. The N (l.) bay extends into a simple wall which has been carried up into a bellcote supported on moulded corbels as a two-dimensional tower (cf. Tarland); the bellcote now reduced to a gablet. To the r. a slightly recessed transeptal stair bay with a two-light plate-traceried window. Six-bay flanks with pointed lights; the E end has two-shouldered doorways and a large cinquefoil mincer-plate roundel with the gable concealing the low boiler-room chimneystack. Interior altered between 1928 and 1940, when a new pulpit was erected and the vestry formed; new communion chairs *c*. 1950. – FONT. In the form of a kneeling angel. It came from the mausoleum of Whitehaugh House (q.v.). In the CHURCHYARD, a few lying slabs, and a BELLCOTE dated 1604 with pediments and finials.

Former PARISH MANSE. Built 1803. Simple vernacular classical. Two-storey entrance front three bays broad, raised over a semi-sunk basement; railed forestair to main entrance with elegant fanlight. Coursed squared cherry-cocked rubble with slightly paler dressings; gabled roof with coped end stacks, later canted dormers. Lower two-storey rear wing forming an L-plan before 1838.

FORBES PARISH CHURCH, 4.7 km. SW, lying S of the A944 within a loop of the Don. A church dedicated to the Nine Maidens of St Donald was erected into a prebend of Aberdeen by Bishop Henry le Chen in 1325. The present church appears C17. Closed after 1808 when Tullynessle and Forbes were united, it is now gutted and roofless. Rectangular plan with low walls but relatively tall crowstepped end gables, it is 11.8 m. long E–W by 4.6 m. deep; the walls themselves are 0.8 m. thick. The w gable has a window and was once crowned by a finial. In the S flank the chamfered doorway is towards the w, with two windows checked for glazing. The E gable has a blocked doorway and window above which was formerly another door giving entry to the gallery by means of a timber stair. The skewputts

have cavetto mouldings and some of the w gable crowsteps on
the s side are incised with small crosses. Inside, towards the
blind N wall's E end, a burial recess and next to it a small
aumbry. Octagonal CHURCHYARD with lying slabs of *c*. 1800.
LITTLEWOOD PARK. *See* p. 652.
TERPERSIE CASTLE. *See* p. 744.

URY HOUSE   K
1.7 km. NW of Stonehaven

Now a roofless shell, hulkingly large and hyperbolically Neo-
Elizabethan in style. The Hays of Errol acquired the land from
the Frasers of Cowie *c*. 1413, and an L-plan tower house was
built at the end of the C17. The estate was taken over by the
Barclay family (later developers of the New Town in
Stonehaven) in 1647, and in 1778–9 *James Playfair* submitted
plans to remodel the tower house in either the Gothic or castellated styles. But nothing was ever done.

The Baird family bought Ury in 1854, when the ancestral
home was swept away and all caution thrown to the wind. In
the MAIN BLOCK, by *John Baird* ('*Primus*'), 1855, everything
is pushed to the limits: huge mullioned-and-transomed windows,
central tower with canted oriel and panelled parapet, and an
absurdly oversized porte cochère with four-centred arches and
ogee-capped pinnacles. To the rear, a full-height, triple-decker
bay window and stone terrace for admiring the view. Attached
is a huge EAST WING by *Alexander Ross*, 1882–4, in similar but
slightly restrained style. It was commissioned by Sir Alexander
Baird, Lord Lieutenant of Kincardineshire from 1889 to 1918.

The house has stood abandoned and gutted since 1945, but
the POLICIES have some good buildings, again by Baird and
c. 1855. – Single-girder iron BRIDGE just ENE of the house,
over the Ury Burn. Lattice parapets. – Former COACHHOUSE,
250 m. NNW of the house. Five-bay s front, the centre tall with
jinked gable and octagonal buttresses (ogival domelets now
missing). Tudor-headed cart arch converted to a door *c*. 1980.
– COACHMAN'S COTTAGE across the drive, *c*. 1895. – Big
WALLED GARDEN to the W with tall, coped brick walls. Boiler
house and chimney cans to the N. – 230 m. SW of the garden,
a fine VIADUCT over the Cowie Water, necessary for bringing
in the massive amounts of material for the new house. Three
arches with rock-faced detailing; polygonal pier ends extended
into pilasters. – Just off to the N, the humble, single-arch
BRIDGE, built 1821, that it superseded. – SOUTH LODGE on
Slug Road, 1857, by *John Baird*. Single-storey Tudor with
chimneystacks and gables with ball-and-spike finials.

HOUFF MAUSOLEUM, 1.3 km. NNW of the house. Harled oblong
with quasi-Dutch gables and thick mullions of Y-tracery. Built
1741 and remodelled in the mid–late C19.

WARDHOUSE

3 km. NE of Kennethmont

A Palladian mansion, built by a branch of the Gordon family, and bearing marked resemblance to the Earl of Aberdeen's much larger Haddo (N); it may be by *John Adam* or (more probably) *John Douglas*. An inscription records that it was built in two stages, the first for Arthur Gordon in 1757 and the second later in the C18 probably for Charles Edward Gordon although the date is now illegible.

Facing S, Wardhouse's entrance front is symmetrical, its tall main block linked by quadrants to pavilions. The three-storey main block comprises a broad projecting centre rising into a pediment, with two lower flanking bays on either side. It seems likely that the original intention was to form a grand external stairway leading to the tall first-floor Serlian opening which is boldly treated in the Gibbsian manner. In the event a simple doorway was formed in the low ground floor, the services at this level being lit by small square windows. A band course defines first-floor level, and above the Serlian there is an oval niche between the two small windows at second floor; the pediment is inset with an attic oculus and is flanked by tall slim panelled chimneystacks which once rose from a piended roof. In contrast to the predominantly dark grey granite ashlar used for the centre, the flanking bays are in golden granite rubble coursed and squared, with dark grey window surrounds, angle quoins and eaves cornice. The concave quadrants are single-storey, each with a centre door and two windows. They link to very broad two-storey two-bay end pavilions again in coursed squared rubble with ashlar dressings and central chimneystacks; that on the E has been considerably extended. On the N the central block has a tall semi-hexagonal bay but is otherwise plain, as are the E and W elevations.

Although the Wardhouse Gordons had established themselves in Spain, the estate thrived until the fall of the Spanish monarchy left Rafael Carlos Gordon comparatively destitute in 1931. Wardhouse was requisitioned during the Second World War; in 1952 the estate was sold and the house gutted. Little of the interior now survives, the central timber stair enclosed within the half-hexagonal bay on the N having been completely lost. Reconstruction by *Acanthus Architects Douglas Forrest* is expected to begin in 2015.

HOME FARM AND STABLES, 0.35 km. E. Perhaps by *Archibald Simpson*, reputedly for Pedro Carlos Gordon in 1842. Classical Italianate quadrangular courtyard. Impressive pedimented semi-elliptical archway at the centre of the long single-storey S front; tall single-storey four-bay links to two-storey two-bay end pavilions expressing the gables of the E and W ranges.

BRIDGE (0.8 km. SSE) carrying the drive across the railway, by *Alexander Gibb*, engineer, 1852–4. Ashlar-built, a semi-elliptical key-blocked arch framed by boldly rusticated pilasters.

HOWETS OF KENNETHMONT BRIDGE. 'The Double Bridge',
by *Alexander Gibb* 1852–4. A remarkable structure replacing
the still-surviving C18 bridge when the railway was built. It
comprises a big semicircular arch over the Water of Bogie
linked by broad battered buttresses to a semi-elliptical arch
over the railway, all with a levelled roadway enclosed by plain
parapets.

WESTHALL
0.9 km. N of Oyne

A U-plan tower house built shortly after 1590 when James VI
granted Westhall to Alexander Abercromby of Pitmedden. Its
rear wing probably dates between 1710 and 1743, although the
service court is 1838, almost certainly by *John Smith*, reusing the
original gateway of the vanished forecourt. From the same period
dates the first two-storey extension of the tower house to the E,
further extended by *A. & W. Reid* in 1863 to create the present
entrance front.

The TOWER HOUSE is closely related to Birse (q.v.). The main
block is three-storeyed, orientated E–W, and approximately
9 m. in length, although it is slightly shallower at only 5 m. deep.
At its SE angle it has an elliptical drum tower containing the
turnpike stair, 4.5 m. in diameter across its major axis, with a
shallow conical roof. Unlike Birse however it has a second
jamb 4.3 m. broad by 5 m. deep, which, rising from a crudely
battered base, is hinged to the main block's SW angle in a
manner characteristic of the later C16 so that all four of its sides
provide fields of fire. This jamb may be a very early addition,
but is more probably original, for its deep wall-head parapet
with rounded bartizans and the drum turret which rises from
first floor within the SE angle are both supported on the same
very distinctive key-pattern corbel courses found at Birse,
Knock and Allardice (qq.v.). The turret corbelling is supported
on a *trompe* arch, as at Glenbuchat (q.v.); the parapet is itself
unusual for so late a date although it finds a parallel in the
early C17 upperworks at Udny (N). Several Z-plan tower
houses with one round and one rectangular jamb exist in
North-East Scotland, but Westhall's U-plan arrangement of
these features is unique, and still more remarkable in that the
elliptical jamb's turnpike stair rises through all three floors.

The ground floor contained two vaulted cellars and presumably the kitchen in the SW jamb, there being a hearth in its N
wall. The hall was at first floor, its 'high' end at the W, furthest
from the main stair but adjacent to the SW jamb which would
have contained Abercromby's apartment. It was linked by the
turret stair to the second floor, perhaps providing a similar
arrangement of hall and private chamber for his wife, and

family rooms in the attic. The position of the entrance is unclear but was probably within the main block at ground floor close to the elliptical tower, as at Birse. The ground floor is lit only by slit-lights for reasons of defence, but the larger first- and second-floor windows are later, probably sometime after Westhall was acquired by the Rev. John Horn in 1681.

The E WING which, with the tower house, forms the present entrance front is a succession of two-storey gabled bays of varying width and projection, essentially plain Neo-Jacobean. Its first three bays were added for the Dalrymple Hornes in 1838, possibly by *John Smith*, the l. bay being a remodelling of the late C17 wing shown in Hulmandell's drawing, hence the inconsistency in floor levels. The windows here have distinctive lying-pane glazing. The second bay's crenellated porch dates from 1863 when the fourth bay was added for Robert Leith of Freefield (q.v.) by *A. & W. Reid*, bigger in scale with a plate-glass canted bay. On the tower house's rear side, a two-storey N WING orientated N–S was probably built for John Horn, advocate in Edinburgh, between 1710 and 1743. Small single-storey PAVILIONS with crowstepped gables, similar to those at Castle Fraser (q.v.), were added to its w side in 1838 to create a small service court. Its entrance arch is almost certainly that of the old forecourt reused. How much of the FORECOURT survived at that time is unclear but the archway stood adjacent to the tower house's SW jamb in Hulmandell's view. Further to the S the footings of a forecourt drum tower survive in embanked ground.

The E wing's INTERIOR was remodelled in 1863. Most of the detail is simple but the main stair has very ornate cast-iron balusters and two of the principal apartments have rich plaster cornices.

WESTHILL   *8000*

Westhill is a town laid out on Garden City principles. Although it has grown as a result of its proximity to Aberdeen, its development coinciding with the discovery of oil in 1969, the first development proposals were submitted in 1963. It was the brainchild of Ronald Fraser Dean, factor of the Westhill Estate. Westhill Developments (Aberdeen) engaged as architects *Thomas Cordiner, Cunningham & Partners*, through whom *Prof. Tom Findlay Lyon* drew up the plan for the site, a s-facing slope traversed E–W by the A944 from Aberdeen to Alford (q.v.) and, further uphill, by Old Skene Road.

Following Lyon's plan, OLD SKENE ROAD was realigned in 1973, with HAY'S WAY laid out roughly parallel on higher ground. Both were linked to the A944 by WESTHILL DRIVE, BROADSTRAIK ROAD and WELLGROVE ROAD, so forming

an irregular grid. Side streets were developed with clusters of
houses similar in style but adopting as many different designs
as possible, Cordiner Cunningham appointing *Liam Findlay* as
project architect. To the N, a GOLF COURSE laid out by *Charles
Lawrie* (of *Cotton, Pennink, Lawrie & Partners*) opened in 1976.
To the S, the Arnhall Moss was preserved as a natural habitat
and next to it a public park, DENMAN GARDENS, was laid out
by *Philippa Rakusen* and opened in 1979, its name honouring
Sidney Denman of the *Ashdale Land & Property Co.*, which
oversaw development. The INDUSTRIAL ESTATE on the town's
S edge was screened from the residential area by a boundary
of trees.

The first house, No. 4 Arnhall Drive, was occupied in October
1968. Several developers were subsequently involved, among
them the *Scottish Special Housing Association* (1975–7) and
Stewart Milne Construction. The first phase of the SHOPPING
CENTRE near Westhill Drive opened in 1979–80. Nearby is
TRINITY CHURCH (multi-denominational, 1981) and opposite this the LIBRARY (1983, extended 2011). The ASHDALE
HALL dates from 1993, as does the SWIMMING POOL next
to Westhill Academy in Hay's Way.

Westhill swallowed two historic settlements. Old Westhill –
BLACKHILLS – contained a plain lancet Congregational
church (1872), hall (1903), cottagey manse (1868) and two
schools: the long and low subscription school (now Prospect
Cottage, 1834) and the Board School by *William Henderson &
Son* (1878). ELRICK possesses the town's best building in
architectural terms, the delightful BROADSTRAIK INN on the
A944. Built in 1905, it is symmetrical English Arts and Crafts
with canted bays and a tall Germanic roof with two tiers of
dormers, built in 1905.

5010

WHITEHAUGH HOUSE

2.4 km. NE of Alford

Built for John Forbes-Leith, a classical house dated 1745 – and
very sophisticated for that time – with alterations and additions
for Lt-Col. James Forbes-Leith by *John Smith* dated 1838.
Facing S, the entrance front of the C18 house is grey granite
ashlar with yellow sandstone dressings for contrast. Two
storeys over a raised basement, and seven windows wide, its
centre three bays are slightly advanced and rise into a pediment
with an attic window. A cornice and shallow parapet run right
round the building, partly screening its piended platform roof,
which is punctuated by tall symmetrical chimneystacks at both
gables and platform. Smith's additions are also in grey granite
ashlar, but his classicism, while complementary to the original
house, is clearly later. He built out the centre bays slightly
further at basement and ground floor and added the tetrastyle

Roman Doric portico crowned by a balustrade and approached by a broad flight of stairs; this shelters a transom-lit doorway with eight-panelled double-leaf doors and niches. The triple-light windows in the flanking bays at ground floor are late C19. Smith was also responsible for the single-storey-and-basement wings which flank the full depth of the house. On the entrance front these are single-bay, their basements blind with moulded panels, but at principal-floor level the windows are set within anta-pilasters which support entablatures and pediments. Plain three-bay flank elevations to the E and W. Smith deepened the centre bays of the main block over a flat-roofed, single-storey rear wing with proto-Doric (abacus only) columns. Interior remodelled by *Smith*, his entrance hall staircase with Roman Doric columns and Ionic columnar screens to either side.

WALLED GARDEN, 100 m. N. Perhaps by *Smith c.* 1838. Roughly square, but with very rounded corners. Two-storey octagonal gazebo on N side with prismatic roof and datestones built into rear face.

MAUSOLEUM CHAPEL, Temple Glen, in woodland, 1 km. WNW. Built *c.* 1842, following the death of Lt-Col. Forbes-Leith, perhaps by *Smith*. Severely derelict and overgrown. Square-plan in rock-faced granite with smooth ashlar dressings. Twin-arched bellcote over shallow-raked W gable with three small round-arched lights and flamboyant five-light E window which looks later C19. Urns at the corners now fallen. Barrel-vaulted internally. Grave-slabs from 1588. The monument to Alexander Leith and Bessie Gray was originally erected in Keig Old Parish Church in 1655. Font transferred to Tullynessle Church (q.v.).

WHITERASHES

ALL SAINTS (Episcopal). Built as a school to designs by *James Matthews*, 1858, the gift of John Ramsay of Barra and Straloch (q.v.). Dedicated as a chapel in 1885. A low four-bay nave with paired lights in square-headed openings but no buttresses; the very steeply pitched roof with blocky skewputts is swept over a side-aisle and vestry on the N. Slightly lower and narrower chancel with three-light E window. The Gothic windows, small bellcote and W porch were added by *J. Ninian Comper* (of *Bucknall & Comper*), 1898–1900.

Interior simple with exposed roof-beams, two-bay timber arcade to aisle and pointed chancel arch. – PULPIT. Carved with low-relief panels by *Ernest Gregory*, 1904. – FONT. By Matthews, sculpted by *Thomas Goodwillie*, 1881. – REREDOS, LECTERN and STALLS by *Comper*, 1899. – LITANY DESK. Panels carved by *Sir Harry Lumsden*, 1900. – STAINED GLASS by *Comper*. Chancel, 1898; nave S windows, 1905–10, and nave N window, 1919.

STRALOCH HOUSE. *See* p. 736.

GLOSSARY

Numbers and letters refer to the illustrations (by John Sambrook)
on pp. 778-785

ABACUS: flat slab forming the top of a capital (3a).

ACANTHUS: classical formalized leaf ornament (3b).

ACCUMULATOR TOWER: *see* Hydraulic power.

ACHIEVEMENT: a complete display of armorial bearings (i.e. coat of arms, crest, supporters and motto).

ACROTERION: plinth for a statue or ornament on the apex or ends of a pediment; more usually, both the plinth and what stands on it (4a).

ADDORSED: descriptive of two figures placed back to back.

AEDICULE (*lit.* little building): architectural surround, consisting usually of two columns or pilasters supporting a pediment.

AFFRONTED: descriptive of two figures placed face to face.

AGGREGATE: *see* Concrete, Harling.

AISLE: subsidiary space alongside the body of a building, separated from it by columns, piers or posts. Also (Scots) projecting wing of a church, often for special use, e.g. by a guild or by a landed family whose burial place it may contain.

AMBULATORY (*lit.* walkway): aisle around the sanctuary (q.v.).

ANGLE ROLL: roll moulding in the angle between two planes (1a).

ANSE DE PANIER: *see* Arch.

ANTAE: simplified pilasters (4a), usually applied to the ends of the enclosing walls of a portico (q.v.) *in antis*.

ANTEFIXAE: ornaments projecting at regular intervals above a Greek cornice, originally to conceal the ends of roof tiles (4a).

ANTHEMION: classical ornament like a honeysuckle flower (4b).

APRON: panel below a window or wall monument or tablet.

APSE: semicircular or polygonal end of an apartment, especially of a chancel or chapel. In classical architecture sometimes called an *exedra*.

ARABESQUE: non-figurative surface decoration consisting of flowing lines, foliage scrolls etc., based on geometrical patterns. Cf. Grotesque.

ARCADE: series of arches supported by piers or columns. *Blind arcade* or *arcading*: the same applied to the wall surface. *Wall arcade*: in medieval churches, a blind arcade forming a dado below windows. Also a covered shopping street.

ARCH: Shapes *see* 5c. *Basket arch* or *anse de panier* (basket handle): three-centred and depressed, or with a flat centre. *Nodding*: ogee arch curving forward from the wall face. *Parabolic*: shaped like a chain suspended from two level points, but inverted.
Special purposes. *Chancel*: dividing chancel from nave or crossing. *Crossing*: spanning piers at a crossing (q.v.). *Relieving* or *discharging*: incorporated in a wall to relieve superimposed weight (5c). *Skew*: spanning responds not diametrically opposed. *Strainer*: inserted in an opening to resist inward pressure. *Transverse*: spanning a main axis (e.g. of a vaulted space). *See also* Jack arch, Overarch, Triumphal arch.

ARCHITRAVE: formalized lintel, the lowest member of the classical entablature (3a). Also the moulded frame of a door or window (often borrowing the profile of a classical architrave). For *lugged* and *shouldered* architraves *see* 4b.

ARCUATED: dependent structurally on the arch principle. Cf. Trabeated.

ARK: chest or cupboard housing the tables of Jewish law in a synagogue.

ARRIS: sharp edge where two surfaces meet at an angle (3a).

ASHLAR: masonry of large blocks wrought to even faces and square edges (6d). *Broached ashlar* (Scots): scored with parallel lines made by a narrow-pointed chisel (broach). *Droved ashlar*: similar but with lines made by a broad chisel.

ASTRAGAL: classical moulding of semicircular section (3f). Also (Scots) glazing-bar between window panes.

ASTYLAR: with no columns or similar vertical features.

ATLANTES: *see* Caryatids.

ATRIUM (plural: atria): inner court of a Roman or C20 house; in a multi-storey building, a toplit covered court rising through all storeys. Also an open court in front of a church.

ATTACHED COLUMN: *see* Engaged column.

ATTIC: small top storey within a roof. Also the storey above the main entablature of a classical façade.

AUMBRY: recess or cupboard, especially one in a church, to hold sacred vessels used for the Mass.

BAILEY: *see* Motte-and-bailey.

BALANCE BEAM: *see* Canals.

BALDACCHINO: freestanding canopy, originally fabric, over an altar. Cf. Ciborium.

BALLFLOWER: globular flower of three petals enclosing a ball (1a). Typical of the Decorated style.

BALUSTER: pillar or pedestal of bellied form. *Balusters*: vertical supports of this or any other form, for a handrail or coping, the whole being called a *balustrade* (6c). *Blind balustrade*: the same applied to the wall surface.

BARBICAN: outwork defending the entrance to a castle.

BARGEBOARDS (corruption of 'vergeboards'): boards, often carved or fretted, fixed beneath the eaves of a gable to cover and protect the rafters.

BARMKIN (Scots): wall enclosing courtyard attached to a tower house.

BARONY: *see* Burgh.

BAROQUE: style originating in Rome *c.*1600 and current in England *c.*1680–1720, characterized by dramatic massing and silhouette and the use of the giant order.

BARROW: burial mound.

BARTIZAN: corbelled turret, square or round, frequently at an angle (8a).

BASCULE: hinged part of a lifting (or bascule) bridge.

BASE: moulded foot of a column or pilaster. For *Attic* base *see* 3b. For *Elided* base *see* Elided.

BASEMENT: lowest, subordinate storey; hence the lowest part of a classical elevation, below the piano nobile (q.v.).

BASILICA: a Roman public hall; hence an aisled building with a clerestory.

BASTION: one of a series of defensive semicircular or polygonal projections from the main wall of a fortress or city.

BATTER: intentional inward inclination of a wall face.

BATTLEMENT: defensive parapet, composed of *merlons* (solid) and *crenelles* (embrasures) through which archers could shoot (8a); sometimes called *crenellation*. Also used decoratively.

BAY: division of an elevation or interior space as defined by regular vertical features such as arches, columns, windows etc.

BAY LEAF: classical ornament of overlapping bay leaves (3f).

BAY WINDOW: window of one or more storeys projecting from the face of a building. *Canted*: with a straight front and angled sides. *Bow window*: curved. *Oriel*: rests on corbels or brackets and starts above ground level; also the bay window at the dais end of a medieval great hall.

BEAD-AND-REEL: *see* Enrichments.

BEAKHEAD: Norman ornament with a row of beaked bird or beast heads usually biting into a roll moulding (1a).

BEE-BOLL: wall recess to contain a beehive.

BELFRY: chamber or stage in a tower where bells are hung. Also belltower in a general sense.

BELL CAPITAL: *see* 1b.

BELLCAST: *see* Roof.

BELLCOTE: bell-turret set on a roof or gable. *Birdcage bellcote*: framed structure, usually of stone.

BERM: level area separating a ditch from a bank on a hillfort or barrow.

BILLET: Norman ornament of small half-cylindrical or rectangular blocks (1a).

BIVALLATE: of a hillfort: defended by two concentric banks and ditches.

BLIND: *see* Arcade, Baluster, Portico.

BLOCK CAPITAL: *see* 1a.

BLOCKED: columns etc. interrupted by regular projecting blocks (*blocking*), as on a Gibbs surround (4b).

BLOCKING COURSE: course of stones, or equivalent, on top of a cornice and crowning the wall.

BÖD: *see* Bü.

BOLECTION MOULDING: covering the joint between two different planes (6b).

BOND: the pattern of long sides (*stretchers*) and short ends (*headers*) produced on the face of a wall by laying bricks in a particular way (6e).

BOSS: knob or projection, e.g. at the intersection of ribs in a vault (2c).

BOW WINDOW: *see* Bay window.

BOX FRAME: timber-framed construction in which vertical and horizontal wall members support the roof. Also concrete construction where the loads are taken on cross walls; also called *cross-wall construction*.

BRACE: subsidiary member of a structural frame, curved or straight. *Bracing* is often arranged decoratively, e.g. quatrefoil, herringbone. *See also* Roofs.

BRATTISHING: ornamental crest, usually formed of leaves, Tudor flowers or miniature battlements.

BRESSUMER (*lit.* breast-beam): big horizontal beam supporting the wall above, especially in a jettied building.

BRETASCHE (*lit.* battlement): defensive wooden gallery on a wall.

BRICK: *see* Bond, Cogging, Engineering, Gauged, Tumbling.

BRIDGE: *Bowstring*: with arches rising above the roadway which is suspended from them. *Clapper*: one long stone forms the roadway. *Roving*: see Canal. *Suspension*: roadway suspended from cables or chains slung between towers or pylons. *Stay-suspension* or *stay-cantilever*: supported by diagonal stays from towers or pylons. *See also* Bascule.

BRISES-SOLEIL: projecting fins or canopies which deflect direct sunlight from windows.

BROACH: *see* Spire and 1c.

BROCH (Scots): circular tower-like structure, open in the middle, the double wall of dry-stone masonry linked by slabs forming internal galleries at varying levels; found in W and N Scotland and mostly dating from between 100 B.C. and A.D. 100.

BÜ or BÖD (Scots, esp. Shetland; *lit.* booth): combined house and store.

BUCRANIUM: ox skull used decoratively in classical friezes.

BULLSEYE WINDOW: small oval window, set horizontally (cf. Oculus). Also called *oeil de boeuf*.

BURGH: formally constituted town with trading privileges. *Royal Burghs*: monopolized foreign trade till the C17 and paid duty to the Crown. *Burghs of Barony*: founded by secular or ecclesiastical barons to whom they paid duty on their local trade. *Police Burghs*: instituted after 1850 for the administration of new centres of population and abolished in 1975. They controlled planning, building etc.

BUT-AND-BEN (Scots, *lit.* outer and inner rooms): two-room cottage.

BUTTRESS: vertical member projecting from a wall to stabilize it or to resist the lateral thrust of an arch, roof or vault (1c, 2c). A *flying buttress* transmits the thrust to a heavy abutment by means of an arch or half-arch (1c).

CABLE or ROPE MOULDING: originally Norman, like twisted strands of a rope.

CAMES: *see* Quarries.

CAMPANILE: freestanding belltower.

CANALS: *Flash lock*: removable weir or similar device through which boats pass on a flush of water. Predecessor of the *pound lock*: chamber with gates at each end allowing boats to float from one level to another. *Tidal gates*: single pair of lock gates allowing vessels to pass when the tide makes a level. *Balance beam*: beam projecting horizontally for opening and closing lock gates. *Roving bridge*: carrying a towing path from one bank to the other.

CANDLE-SNUFFER ROOF: conical roof of a turret (8a).

CANNON SPOUT: *see* 8a.

CANTILEVER: horizontal projection (e.g. step, canopy) supported by a downward force behind the fulcrum.

CAPHOUSE (Scots): small chamber at the head of a turnpike stair, opening onto the parapet walk (8a). Also a chamber rising from within the parapet walk.

CAPITAL: head or crowning feature of a column or pilaster; for classical types *see* 3a; for medieval types *see* 1b.

CARREL: compartment designed for individual work or study, e.g. in a library.

CARTOUCHE: classical tablet with ornate frame (4b).

CARYATIDS: female figures supporting an entablature; their male counterparts are *Atlantes* (*lit.* Atlas figures).

CASEMATE: vaulted chamber, with embrasures for defence, within a castle wall or projecting from it.

CASEMENT: side-hinged window. Also a concave Gothic moulding framing a window.

CASTELLATED: with battlements (q.v.).

CAST IRON: iron containing at least 2.2 per cent of carbon, strong in compression but brittle in tension; cast in a mould to required shape, e.g. for columns or repetitive ornaments. *Wrought iron* is a purer form of iron, with no more than 0.3 per cent of carbon, ductile and strong in tension, forged and rolled into e.g. bars, joists, boiler plates; *mild steel* is its modern equivalent, similar but stronger.

CATSLIDE: *see* 7.

CAVETTO: concave classical moulding of quarter-round section (3f).

CELURE or CEILURE: enriched area of roof above rood or altar.

CEMENT: *see* Concrete.

CENOTAPH (*lit.* empty tomb): funerary monument which is not a burying place.

CENTRING: wooden support for the building of an arch or vault, removed after completion.

CHAMBERED TOMB: Neolithic burial mound with a stone-built chamber and entrance passage covered by an earthen barrow or stone cairn.

CHAMFER (*lit.* corner-break): surface formed by cutting off a square edge or corner. For types of chamfers and *chamfer stops see* 6a. *See also* Double chamfer.

CHANCEL: E end of the church containing the sanctuary; often used to include the choir.

CHANTRY CHAPEL: often attached to or within a church, endowed for the celebration of Masses principally for the soul of the founder.

CHECK (Scots): rebate.

CHERRY-CAULKING or CHERRY-COCKING (Scots): decorative masonry technique using lines of tiny stones (*pins* or *pinning*) in the mortar joints.

CHEVET (*lit.* head): French term for chancel with ambulatory and radiating chapels.

CHEVRON: V-shape used in series or double series (later) on a Norman moulding (1a). Also (especially when on a single plane) called *zigzag*.

CHOIR: the part of a church E of the nave, intended for the stalls of choir monks, choristers and clergy.

CIBORIUM: a fixed canopy over an altar, usually vaulted and supported on four columns; cf. Baldacchino.

CINQUEFOIL: *see* Foil.

CIST: stone-lined or slab-built grave.

CLACHAN (Scots): a hamlet or small village; also, a village inn.

CLADDING: external covering or skin applied to a structure, especially a framed one.

CLEARSTOREY: uppermost storey of the nave of a church, pierced by windows. Also high-level windows in secular buildings.

CLOSE (Scots): courtyard or passage giving access to a number of buildings.

CLOSER: a brick cut to complete a bond (6e).

CLUSTER BLOCK: *see* Multi-storey.

COADE STONE: ceramic artificial stone made in Lambeth 1769–*c*.1840 by Eleanor Coade (†1821) and her associates.

COB: walling material of clay mixed with straw.

COFFERING: arrangement of sunken panels (coffers), square or polygonal, decorating a ceiling, vault or arch.

COGGING: a decorative course of bricks laid diagonally (6e). Cf. Dentilation.

COLLAR: see Roofs and 7.

COLLEGIATE CHURCH: endowed for the support of a college of priests, especially for the saying of masses for the soul(s) of the founder(s).

COLONNADE: range of columns supporting an entablature. Cf. Arcade.

COLONNETTE: small column or shaft.

COLOSSAL ORDER: see Giant order.

COLUMBARIUM: shelved, niched structure to house multiple burials.

COLUMN: a classical, upright structural member of round section with a shaft, a capital and usually a base (3a, 4a).

COLUMN FIGURE: carved figure attached to a medieval column or shaft, usually flanking a doorway.

COMMENDATOR: receives the revenues of an abbey *in commendam* ('in trust') when the position of abbot is vacant.

COMMUNION TABLE: table used in Protestant churches for the celebration of Holy Communion.

COMPOSITE: see Orders.

COMPOUND PIER: grouped shafts (q.v.), or a solid core surrounded by shafts.

CONCRETE: composition of *cement* (calcined lime and clay), *aggregate* (small stones or rock chippings), sand and water. It can be poured into *formwork* or *shuttering* (temporary frame of timber or metal) on site (*in-situ* concrete), or *pre-cast* as components before construction. *Reinforced*: incorporating steel rods to take the tensile force. *Prestressed*: with tensioned steel rods. Finishes include the impression of boards left by formwork (*board-marked* or *shuttered*), and texturing with steel brushes (*brushed*) or hammers (*hammer-dressed*). See also Shell.

CONDUCTOR (Scots): down-pipe for rainwater; see also Rhone.

CONSOLE: bracket of curved outline (4b).

COPING: protective course of masonry or brickwork capping a wall (6d).

COOMB or COMB CEILING (Scots): with sloping sides corresponding to the roof pitch up to a flat centre.

CORBEL: projecting block supporting something above. *Corbel course:* continuous course of projecting stones or bricks fulfilling the same function. *Corbel table*: series of corbels to carry a parapet or a wall-plate or wall-post (7). *Corbelling*: brick or masonry courses built out beyond one another to support a chimneystack, window etc. For *continuous* and *chequer-set* corbelling see 8a.

CORINTHIAN: see Orders and 3d.

CORNICE: flat-topped ledge with moulded underside, projecting along the top of a building or feature, especially as the highest member of the classical entablature (3a). Also the decorative moulding in the angle between wall and ceiling.

CORPS-DE-LOGIS: the main building(s) as distinct from the wings or pavilions.

COTTAGE ORNÉ: an artfully rustic small house associated with the Picturesque movement.

COUNTERSCARP BANK: low bank on the downhill or outer side of a hillfort ditch.

COUR D'HONNEUR: formal entrance court before a house in the French manner, usually with flanking wings and a screen wall or gates.

COURSE: continuous layer of stones etc. in a wall (6e).

COVE: a broad concave moulding, e.g. to mask the eaves of a roof. *Coved ceiling*: with a pronounced cove joining the walls to a flat central panel smaller than the whole area of the ceiling.

CRADLE ROOF: see Wagon roof.

CREDENCE: shelved niche or table, usually beside a piscina (q.v.), for the sacramental elements and vessels.

CRENELLATION: parapet with crenelles (see Battlement).

CRINKLE-CRANKLE WALL: garden wall undulating in a series of serpentine curves.

CROCKETS: leafy hooks. *Crocketing* decorates the edges of Gothic features, such as pinnacles, canopies etc. *Crocket capital*: see 1b.

CROSSING: central space at the junction of the nave, chancel and transepts. *Crossing tower*: above a crossing.

CROSS-WINDOW: with one mullion and one transom (qq.v.).

CROWN-POST: *see* Roofs and 7.

CROWSTEPS: squared stones set like steps, especially on a crowstepped gable (7, 8a).

CRUCKS (*lit.* crooked): pairs of inclined timbers (*blades*), usually curved, set at bay-lengths; they support the roof timbers and, in timber buildings, also support the walls. *Base*: blades rise from ground level to a tie-or collarbeam which supports the roof timbers. *Full*: blades rise from ground level to the apex of the roof, serving as the main members of a roof truss. *Jointed:* blades formed from more than one timber; the lower member may act as a wall-post; it is usually elbowed at wall-plate level and jointed just above. *Middle*: blades rise from halfway up the walls to a tie-or collar-beam. *Raised*: blades rise from halfway up the walls to the apex. *Upper*: blades supported on a tie-beam and rising to the apex.

CRYPT: underground or half-underground area, usually below the E end of a church. *Ring crypt*: corridor crypt surrounding the apse of an early medieval church, often associated with chambers for relics. Cf. Undercroft.

CUPOLA (*lit.* dome): especially a small dome on a circular or polygonal base crowning a larger dome, roof or turret. Also (Scots) small dome or skylight as an internal feature, especially over a stairwell.

CURSUS: a long avenue defined by two parallel earthen banks with ditches outside.

CURTAIN WALL: a connecting wall between the towers of a castle. Also a non-load-bearing external wall applied to a C20 framed structure.

CUSP: *see* Tracery and 2b.

CYCLOPEAN MASONRY: large irregular polygonal stones, smooth and finely jointed.

CYMA RECTA and CYMA REVERSA: classical mouldings with double curves (3f). Cf. Ogee.

DADO: the finishing (often with panelling) of the lower part of a wall in a classical interior; in origin a formalized continuous pedestal. *Dado rail*: the moulding along the top of the dado.

DAGGER: *see* Tracery and 2b.

DEC (DECORATED): English Gothic architecture *c.* 1290 to *c.* 1350. The name is derived from the type of window tracery (q.v.) used during the period.

DEMI- or HALF-COLUMNS: engaged columns (q.v.) half of whose circumference projects from the wall.

DENTIL: small square block used in series in classical cornices (3c). *Dentilation* is produced by the projection of alternating headers along cornices or stringcourses.

DIAPER: repetitive surface decoration of lozenges or squares flat or in relief. Achieved in brickwork with bricks of two colours.

DIOCLETIAN or THERMAL WINDOW: semicircular with two mullions, as used in the Baths of Diocletian, Rome (4b).

DISTYLE: having two columns (4a).

DOGTOOTH: E.E. ornament, consisting of a series of small pyramids formed by four stylized canine teeth meeting at a point (1a).

DOOCOT (Scots): dovecot. When freestanding, usually *Lectern* (rectangular with single-pitch roof) or *Beehive* (circular, diminishing towards the top).

DORIC: *see* Orders and 3a, 3b.

DORMER: window projecting from the slope of a roof (7). *Dormer head*: gable above a dormer, often formed as a pediment (8a).

DOUBLE CHAMFER: a chamfer applied to each of two recessed arches (1a).

DOUBLE PILE: *see* Pile.

DRAGON BEAM: *see* Jetty.

DRESSINGS: the stone or brickwork worked to a finished face about an angle, opening or other feature.

DRIPSTONE: moulded stone projecting from a wall to protect the lower parts from water. Cf. Hoodmould, Weathering.

DRUM: circular or polygonal stage supporting a dome or cupola. Also one of the stones forming the shaft of a column (3a).

DRY-STONE: stone construction without mortar.

DUN (Scots): small stone-walled fort.

DUTCH or FLEMISH GABLE: *see* 7.

EASTER SEPULCHRE: tomb-chest, usually within or against the N wall of a chancel, used in Holy Week ceremonies for reservation (entombment) of the sacrament after the mass of Maundy Thursday.

EAVES: overhanging edge of a roof; hence *eaves cornice* in this position.

ECHINUS: ovolo moulding (q.v.) below the abacus of a Greek Doric capital (3a).

EDGE RAIL: *see* Railways.

EDGE-ROLL: moulding of semicircular section or more at the edge of an opening.

E.E. (EARLY ENGLISH): English Gothic architecture *c.* 1190–1250.

EGG-AND-DART: *see* Enrichments and 3f.

ELEVATION: any face of a building or side of a room. In a drawing, the same or any part of it, represented in two dimensions.

ELIDED: used to describe a compound feature, e.g. an entablature, with some parts omitted. Also, parts of, e.g., a base or capital, combined to form a larger one.

EMBATTLED: with battlements.

EMBRASURE: splayed opening in a wall or battlement (q.v.).

ENCAUSTIC TILES: earthenware tiles fired with a pattern and glaze.

EN DELIT: stone laid against the bed.

ENFILADE: reception rooms in a formal series, usually with all doorways on axis.

ENGAGED or ATTACHED COLUMN: one that partly merges into a wall or pier.

ENGINEERING BRICKS: dense bricks, originally used mostly for railway viaducts etc.

ENRICHMENTS: the carved decoration of certain classical mouldings, e.g. the ovolo with *egg-and-dart*, the cyma reversa with *waterleaf*, the astragal with *bead-and-reel* (3f).

ENTABLATURE: in classical architecture, collective name for the three horizontal members (architrave, frieze and cornice) carried by a wall or a column (3a).

ENTASIS: very slight convex deviation from a straight line, used to prevent an optical illusion of concavity.

ENTRESOL: mezzanine floor subdividing what is constructionally a single storey, e.g. a vault.

EPITAPH: inscription on a tomb or monument.

EXEDRA: *see* Apse.

EXTRADOS: outer curved face of an arch or vault.

EYECATCHER: decorative building terminating a vista.

FASCIA: plain horizontal band, e.g. in an architrave (3c, 3d) or on a shopfront.

FENESTRATION: the arrangement of windows in a façade.

FERETORY: site of the chief shrine of a church, behind the high altar.

FESTOON: ornamental garland, suspended from both ends. Cf. Swag.

FEU (Scots): land granted, e.g. by sale, by the *feudal superior* to the *vassal* or *feuar*, on conditions that usually include the annual payment of a fixed sum of *feu duty*. Any subsequent proprietor of the land becomes the feuar and is subject to the same obligations.

FIBREGLASS (or glass-reinforced polyester (GRP)): synthetic resin reinforced with glass fibre. GRC: glass-reinforced concrete.

FIELD: *see* Panelling and 6b.

FILLET: a narrow flat band running down a medieval shaft or along a roll moulding (1a). It separates larger curved mouldings in classical cornices, fluting or bases (3c).

FLAMBOYANT: the latest phase of French Gothic architecture, with flowing tracery.

FLASH LOCK: *see* Canals.

FLATTED: divided into apartments. Also with a colloquial (Scots) meaning: 'He stays on the first flat' means that he lives on the first floor.

FLÈCHE or SPIRELET (*lit.* arrow): slender spire on the centre of a roof.

FLEURON: medieval carved flower or leaf, often rectilinear (1a).

FLUSHWORK: knapped flint used with dressed stone to form patterns.

FLUTING: series of concave grooves (flutes), their common edges sharp (arris) or blunt (fillet) (3).

FOIL (*lit.* leaf): lobe formed by the cusping of a circular or other shape in tracery (2b). *Trefoil* (three), *quatrefoil* (four), *cinquefoil* (five) and *multifoil* express the number of lobes in a shape.

FOLIATE: decorated with leaves.

FORE-BUILDING: structure protecting an entrance.

FORESTAIR: external stair, usually unenclosed.

FORMWORK: *see* Concrete.

FRAMED BUILDING: where the structure is carried by a framework - e.g. of steel, reinforced concrete, timber - instead of by load-bearing walls.

FREESTONE: stone that is cut, or can be cut, in all directions.

FRESCO: *al fresco*: painting on wet plaster. *Fresco secco*: painting on dry plaster.

FRIEZE: the middle member of the classical entablature, sometimes ornamented (3a). *Pulvinated frieze* (*lit.* cushioned): of bold convex profile (3c). Also a horizontal band of ornament.

FRONTISPIECE: in C16 and C17 buildings the central feature of doorway and windows above linked in one composition.

GABLE: peaked external wall at end of double-pitch roof. For types *see* 7. Also (Scots): whole end wall of whatever shape. *Pedimental gable*: treated like a pediment.

GADROONING: classical ribbed ornament like inverted fluting that flows into a lobed edge.

GAIT or GATE (Scots): street, usually with a prefix indicating use, direction or destination.

GALILEE: chapel or vestibule usually at the W end of a church enclosing the main portal(s).

GALLERY: a long room or passage; an upper storey above the aisle of a church, looking through arches to the nave; a balcony or mezzanine overlooking the main interior space of a building; or an external walkway.

GALLETING: small stones set in a mortar course.

GAMBREL ROOF: *see* 7.

GARDEROBE: medieval privy.

GARGOYLE: projecting water spout, often carved into human or animal shape. For cannon spout *see* 8.

GAUGED or RUBBED BRICKWORK: soft brick sawn roughly, then rubbed to a precise (gauged) surface. Mostly used for door or window openings (5c).

GAZEBO (jocular Latin, 'I shall gaze'): ornamental lookout tower or raised summer house.

GEOMETRIC: English Gothic architecture *c*. 1250–1310. *See also* Tracery. For another meaning, *see* Stairs.

GIANT or COLOSSAL ORDER: classical order (q.v.) whose height is that of two or more storeys of the building to which it is applied.

GIBBS SURROUND: C18 treatment of an opening (4b), seen particularly in the work of James Gibbs (1682–1754).

GIRDER: a large beam. *Box*: of hollow-box section. *Bowed*: with its top rising in a curve. *Plate*: of I-section, made from iron or steel plates. *Lattice*: with braced framework.

GLACIS: artificial slope extending out and downwards from the parapet of a fort.

GLAZING-BARS: wooden or sometimes metal bars separating and supporting window panes.

GLAZING GROOVE: groove in a window surround into which the glass is fitted.

GNOMON: vane or indicator casting a shadow onto a sundial.

GRAFFITI: *see* Sgraffito.

GRANGE: farm owned and run by a religious order.

GRC: *see* Fibreglass.

GRISAILLE: monochrome painting on walls or glass.

GROIN: sharp edge at the meeting of two cells of a cross-vault; *see* Vault and 2b.

GROTESQUE (*lit.* grotto-esque): wall decoration adopted from Roman examples in the Renaissance. Its foliage scrolls incorporate figurative elements. Cf. Arabesque.

GROTTO: artificial cavern.

GRP: *see* Fibreglass.

GUILLOCHE: classical ornament of interlaced bands (4b).

GUNLOOP: opening for a firearm (8a).

GUSHET (Scots): a triangular or wedge-shaped piece of land or the corner building on such a site.

GUTTAE: stylized drops (3b).

HALF-TIMBERING: archaic term for timber-framing (q.v.). Sometimes used for non-structural decorative timberwork.

HALL CHURCH: medieval church with nave and aisles of approximately equal height. Also (Scots C20) building for use as both hall and church, the double function usually intended to be temporary until a separate church is built.

HAMMERBEAM: see Roofs and 7.

HARLING (Scots, *lit.* hurling): wet dash, i.e. a form of roughcasting in which the mixture of aggregate and binding material (e.g. lime) is dashed onto a wall.

HEADER: see Bond and 6e.

HEADSTOP: stop (q.v.) carved with a head (5b).

HELM ROOF: *see* 1c.

HENGE: ritual earthwork with a surrounding ditch and outer bank.

HERM (*lit.* the god Hermes): male head or bust on a pedestal.

HERRINGBONE WORK: see 6e (for brick bond). Cf. Pitched masonry.

HEXASTYLE: see Portico.

HILLFORT: Iron Age earthwork enclosed by a ditch and bank system.

HIPPED ROOF: see 7.

HOODMOULD: projecting moulding above an arch or lintel to throw off water (2b, 5b). When horizontal often called a *label*. For label stop *see* Stop.

HORIZONTAL GLAZING: with panes of horizontal proportions.

HORSEMILL: circular or polygonal farm building with a central shaft turned by a horse to drive agricultural machinery.

HUNGRY-JOINTED: *see* Pointing.

HUSK GARLAND: festoon of stylized nutshells (4b).

HYDRAULIC POWER: use of water under high pressure to work machinery. *Accumulator tower*: houses a hydraulic accumulator which accommodates fluctuations in the flow through hydraulic mains.

HYPOCAUST (*lit.* underburning): Roman underfloor heating system.

IMPOST: horizontal moulding at the springing of an arch (5c).

IMPOST BLOCK: block between abacus and capital (1b).

IN ANTIS: *see* Antae, Portico and 4a.

INDENT: shape chiselled out of a stone to receive a brass. Also, in restoration, new stone inserted as a patch.

INDUSTRIALIZED or SYSTEM BUILDING: system of manufactured units assembled on site.

INGLENOOK (*lit.* fire-corner): recess for a hearth with provision for seating.

INGO (Scots): the reveal of a door or window opening where the stone is at right angles to the wall.

INTERCOLUMNATION: interval between columns.

INTERLACE: decoration in relief simulating woven or entwined stems or bands.

INTRADOS: see Soffit.

IONIC: *see* Orders and 3c.

JACK ARCH: shallow segmental vault springing from beams, used for fireproof floors, bridge decks etc.

JAMB (*lit.* leg): one of the vertical sides of an opening. Also (Scots) wing or extension adjoining one side of a rectangular plan making it into an L-, T- or Z-plan.

JETTY: the projection of an upper storey beyond the storey below. In a stone building this is achieved by corbelling. In a timber-framed building it is made by the beams and joists of the lower storey oversailing the wall; on their outer ends is placed the sill of the walling for the storey above.

JOGGLE: the joining of two stones to prevent them slipping by a notch in one and a projection in the other.

KEEL MOULDING: moulding used from the late C12, in section like the keel of a ship (1a).

KEEP: principal tower of a castle.

KENTISH CUSP: see Tracery.

KEY PATTERN: see 4b.

KEYSTONE: central stone in an arch or vault (4b, 5c).

KINGPOST: see Roofs and 7.

KNEELER: horizontal projecting stone at the base of each side of a gable to support the inclined coping stones (7).

LABEL: see Hoodmould and 5b.

LABEL STOP: see Stop and 5b.

LACED BRICKWORK: vertical strips of brickwork, often in a contrasting colour, linking openings on different floors.

LACING COURSE: horizontal reinforcement in timber or brick to walls of flint, cobble etc.

LADE (Scots): channel formed to bring water to a mill; mill-race.

LADY CHAPEL: dedicated to the Virgin Mary (Our Lady).

LAIGH or LAICH (Scots): low.

LAIR (Scots): a burial space reserved in a graveyard.

LAIRD (Scots): landowner.

LANCET: slender single-light, pointed-arched window (2a).

LANTERN: circular or polygonal windowed turret crowning a roof or a dome. Also the windowed stage of a crossing tower lighting the church interior.

LANTERN CROSS: churchyard cross with lantern-shaped top.

LAVATORIUM: in a religious house, a washing place adjacent to the refectory.

LEAN-TO: see Roofs.

LESENE (lit. a mean thing): pilaster without base or capital. Also called pilaster strip.

LIERNE: see Vault and 2c.

LIGHT: compartment of a window defined by the mullions.

LINENFOLD: Tudor panelling carved with simulations of folded linen.

LINTEL: horizontal beam or stone bridging an opening.

LOFT: gallery in a church. Organ loft: in which the organ, or sometimes only the console (keyboard), is placed. Laird's loft, Trades loft etc. (Scots): reserved for an individual or special group. See also Rood (loft).

LOGGIA: gallery, usually arcaded or colonnaded along one side; sometimes freestanding.

LONG-AND-SHORT WORK: quoins consisting of stones placed with the long side alternately upright and horizontal, especially in Saxon building.

LOUVRE: roof opening, often protected by a raised timber structure, to allow the smoke from a central hearth to escape. Louvres: overlapping boards to allow ventilation but keep the rain out.

LOWSIDE WINDOW: set lower than the others in a chancel side wall, usually towards its w end.

L-PLAN: see Tower house and 8b.

LUCARNE (lit. dormer): small gabled opening in a roof or spire.

LUCKENBOOTH (Scots): lock-up booth or shop.

LUGGED ARCHITRAVE: see 4b.

LUNETTE: semicircular window or blind panel.

LYCHGATE (lit. corpse-gate): roofed gateway entrance to a churchyard for the reception of a coffin.

LYNCHET: long terraced strip of soil on the downward side of prehistoric and medieval fields, accumulated because of continual ploughing along the contours.

MACHICOLATIONS (lit. mashing devices): series of openings between the corbels that support a projecting parapet through which missiles can be dropped (8a). Used decoratively in post-medieval buildings.

MAINS (Scots): home farm on an estate.

MANOMETER or STANDPIPE TOWER: containing a column of water to regulate pressure in water mains.

MANSARD: see 7.

MANSE: house of a minister of religion, especially in Scotland.

MARGINS (Scots): dressed stones at the edges of an opening. 'Back-set margins' (RCAHMS) are actually set forward from a rubble wall to act as a stop for harling (q.v.). Also called rybats.

MARRIAGE LINTEL (Scots): door or window lintel carved with the initials of the owner and his wife and the date of building work, only coincidentally of their marriage.

MATHEMATICAL TILES: facing tiles with the appearance of brick, most often applied to timber-framed walls.

MAUSOLEUM: monumental building or chamber usually intended for the burial of members of one family.

MEGALITHIC: the use of large stones, singly or together.

MEGALITHIC TOMB: massive stonebuilt Neolithic burial chamber covered by an earth or stone mound.

MERCAT (Scots): market. The Mercat Cross of a Scottish burgh was the focus of market activity and local ceremonial. Most examples are post-Reformation with heraldic or other finials (not crosses).

MERLON: *see* Battlement.

MESOLITHIC: Middle Stone Age, in Britain *c.* 5000 to *c.* 3500 B.C.

METOPES: spaces between the triglyphs in a Doric frieze (3b).

MEZZANINE: low storey between two higher ones or within the height of a high one, not extending over its whole area.

MILD STEEL: *see* Cast iron.

MISERICORD (*lit.* mercy): shelf on a carved bracket placed on the underside of a hinged choir stall seat to support an occupant when standing.

MIXER-COURTS: forecourts to groups of houses shared by vehicles and pedestrians.

MODILLIONS: small consoles (q.v.) along the underside of a Corinthian or Composite cornice (3d). Often used along an eaves cornice.

MODULE: a predetermined standard size for co-ordinating the dimensions of components of a building.

MORT-SAFE (Scots): device to secure corpse(s): either an iron frame over a grave or a building where bodies were kept during decomposition.

MOTTE-AND-BAILEY: C11 and C12 type of castle consisting of an earthen mound (motte) topped by a wooden tower within or adjoining a bailey, an enclosure defended by a ditch and palisade, and also, sometimes, by an inner bank.

MOUCHETTE: *see* Tracery and 2b.

MOULDING: shaped ornamental strip of continuous section; *see* Cavetto, Cyma, Ovolo, Roll.

MULLION: vertical member between window lights (2b).

MULTI-STOREY: five or more storeys. Multi-storey flats may form a *cluster block*, with individual blocks of flats grouped round a service core; a *point block*, with flats fanning out from a service core; or a *slab block*, with flats approached by corridors or galleries from service cores at intervals or towers at the ends (plan also used for offices, hotels etc.). *Tower block* is a generic term for a high multi-storey building.

MULTIVALLATE: of a hillfort: defended by three or more concentric banks and ditches.

MUNTIN: *see* Panelling and 6b.

MUTULE: square block under the corona of a Doric cornice.

NAILHEAD: E.E. ornament consisting of small pyramids regularly repeated (1a).

NARTHEX: enclosed vestibule or covered porch at the main entrance to a church.

NAVE: the body of a church W of the crossing or chancel, often flanked by aisles (q.v.).

NEOLITHIC: New Stone Age in Britain, *c.* 3500 B.C. until the Bronze Age.

NEWEL: central or corner post of a staircase (6c). For Newel stair *see* Stairs.

NIGHT STAIR: stair by which religious entered the transept of their church from their dormitory to celebrate night offices.

NOGGING: *see* Timber-framing.

NOOK-SHAFT: shaft set in the angle of a wall or opening (1a).

NORMAN: *see* Romanesque.

NOSING: projection of the tread of a step (6c). *Bottle nosing*: half round in section.

NUTMEG: medieval ornament with a chain of tiny triangles placed obliquely.

OCULUS: circular opening.

OEIL DE BOEUF: *see* Bullseye window.

OGEE: double curve, bending first one way and then the other, as in an *ogee* or *ogival arch* (5c). Cf. Cyma recta and Cyma reversa.

OPUS SECTILE: decorative mosaic-like facing.

OPUS SIGNINUM: composition flooring of Roman origin.

ORATORY: a private chapel in a church or a house. Also a church of the Oratorian Order.

ORDER: one of a series of recessed arches and jambs forming a splayed medieval opening, e.g. a doorway or arcade arch (1a).

ORDERS: the formalized versions of the post-and-lintel system in classical architecture. The main orders are *Doric*, *Ionic* and *Corinthian*. They are Greek in origin

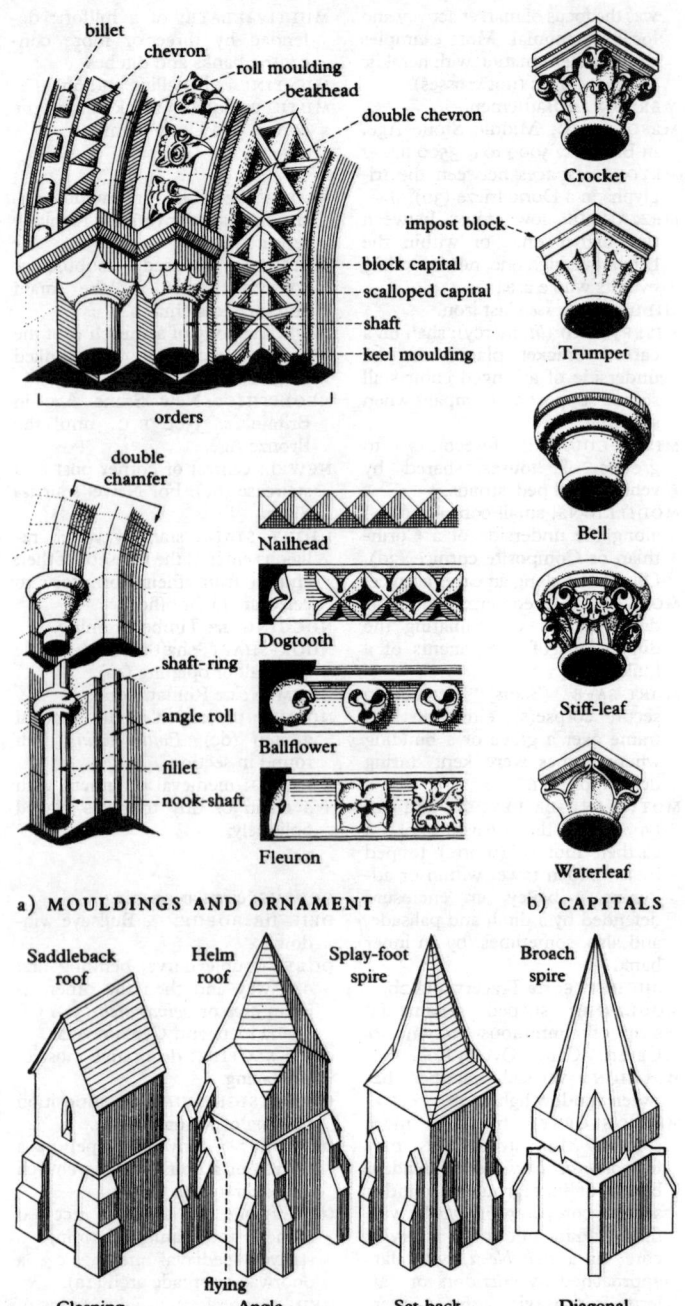

a) MOULDINGS AND ORNAMENT

b) CAPITALS

c) BUTTRESSES, ROOFS AND SPIRES

FIGURE 1: MEDIEVAL

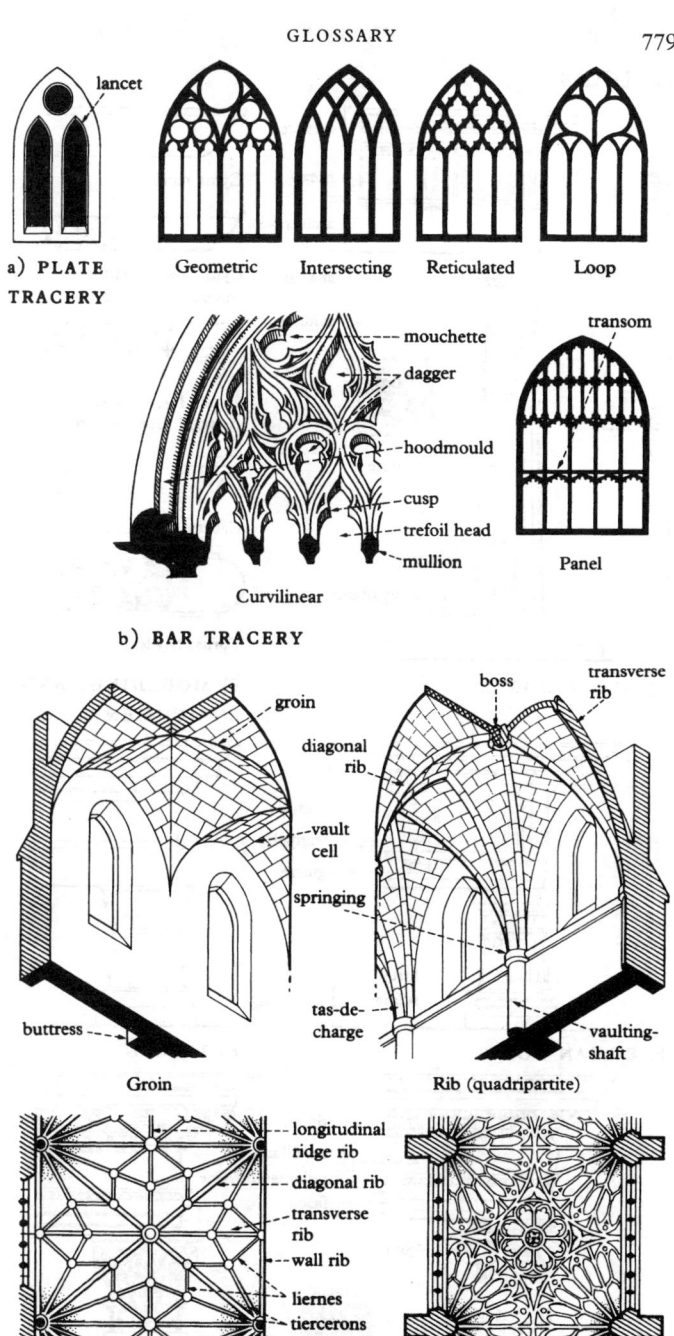

a) PLATE TRACERY

Geometric   Intersecting   Reticulated   Loop

lancet

mouchette

dagger

hoodmould

cusp

trefoil head

mullion

Curvilinear

transom

Panel

b) BAR TRACERY

groin

boss

transverse rib

diagonal rib

vault cell

springing

tas-de-charge

vaulting-shaft

buttress

Groin

Rib (quadripartite)

longitudinal ridge rib

diagonal rib

transverse rib

wall rib

liernes

tiercerons

Lierne

Fan

c) VAULTS

FIGURE 2: MEDIEVAL

ORDERS

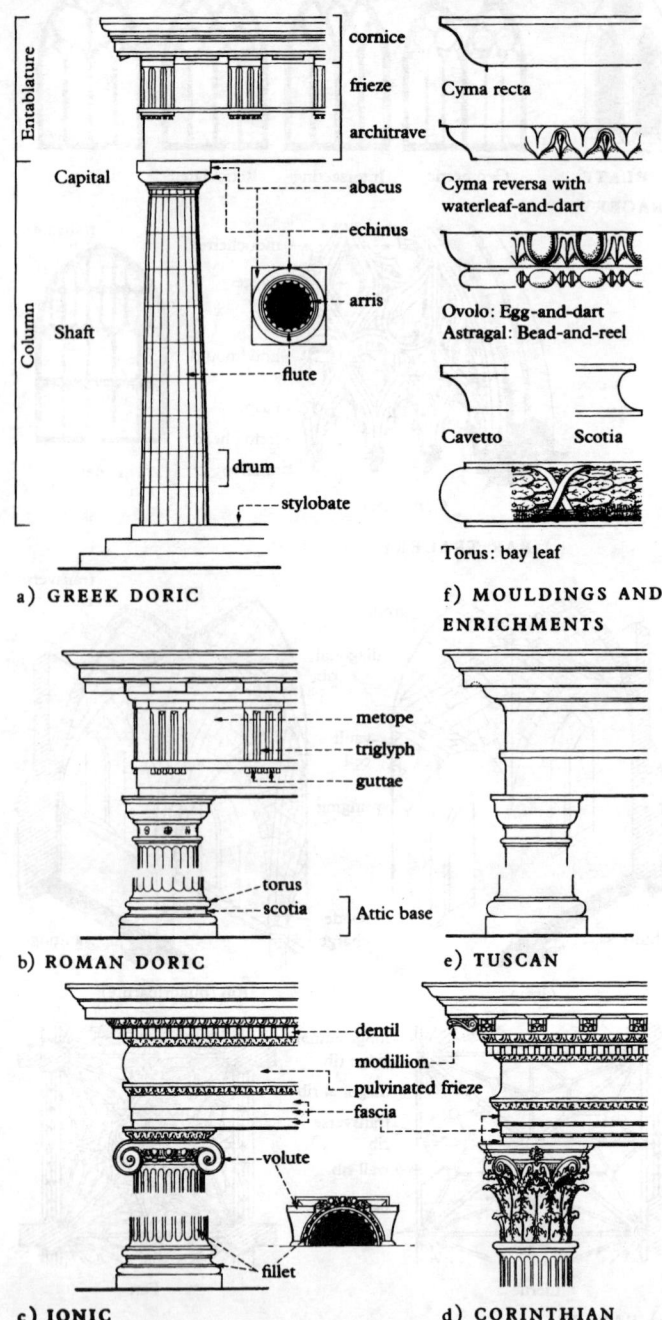

a) GREEK DORIC

b) ROMAN DORIC

c) IONIC

d) CORINTHIAN

e) TUSCAN

f) MOULDINGS AND ENRICHMENTS

Cyma recta

Cyma reversa with waterleaf-and-dart

Ovolo: Egg-and-dart
Astragal: Bead-and-reel

Cavetto　　Scotia

Torus: bay leaf

FIGURE 3: CLASSICAL

a) **PORTICO**

Distyle in antis Prostyle

Anthemion & Palmette Guilloche Key pattern

Rinceau Husk garland Vitruvian scroll

Console Diocletian window Acanthus

Broken pediment Lugged architrave

Segmental pediment Shouldered architrave

Venetian window

Open pediment Swan-neck pediment Gibbs surround

b) **ORNAMENTS AND FEATURES**

FIGURE 4: CLASSICAL

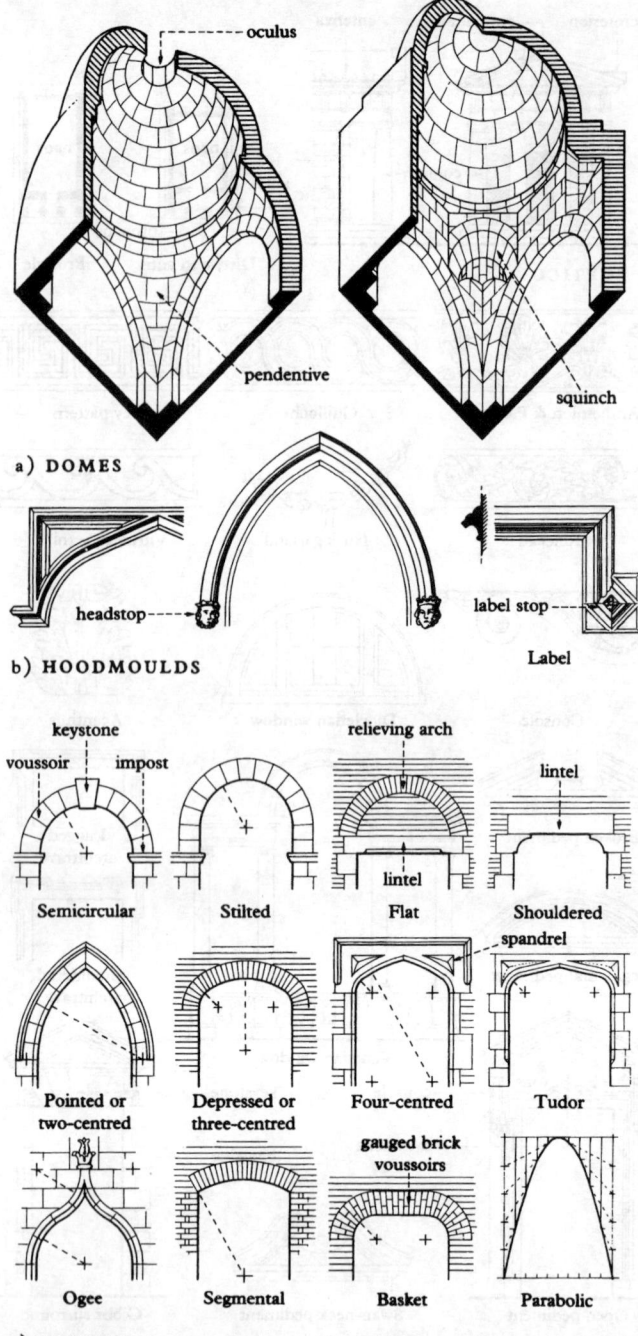

a) DOMES

b) HOODMOULDS

c) ARCHES

FIGURE 5: CONSTRUCTION

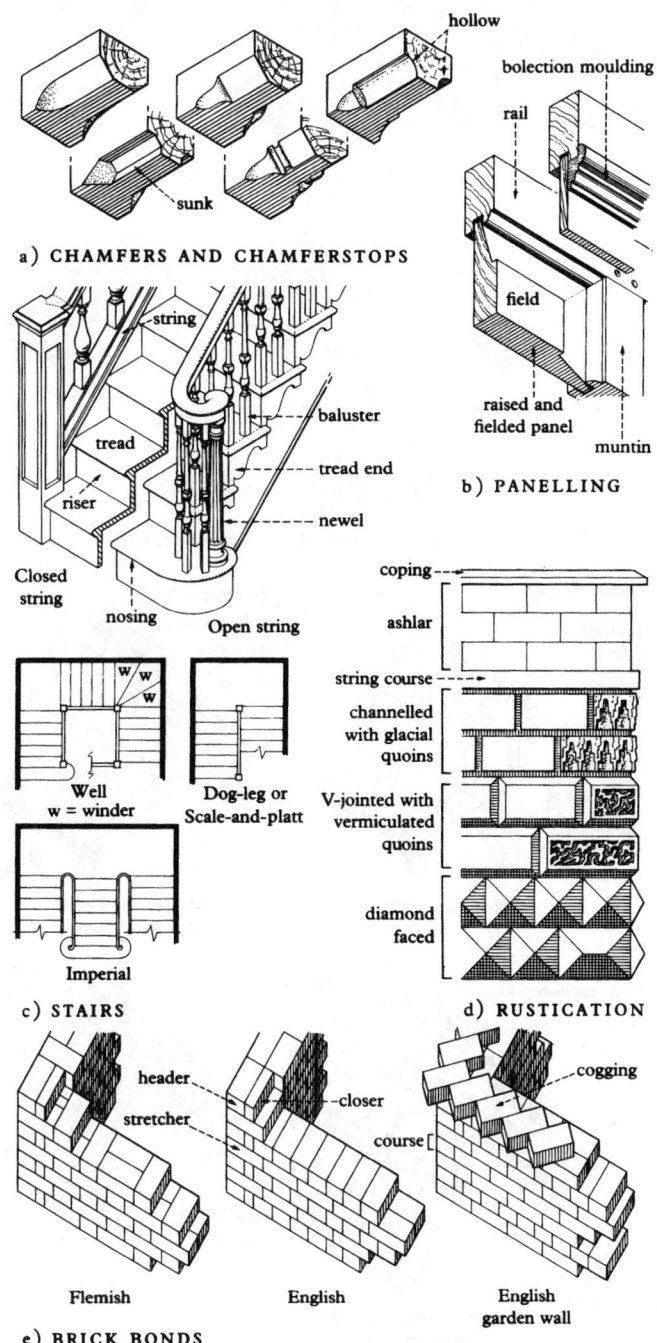

a) CHAMFERS AND CHAMFERSTOPS

hollow
bolection moulding
rail
field
raised and
fielded panel
muntin

b) PANELLING

string
baluster
tread
tread end
riser
newel
Closed
string
nosing
Open string

Well
w = winder
Dog-leg or
Scale-and-platt

Imperial

c) STAIRS

coping
ashlar
string course
channelled
with glacial
quoins
V-jointed with
vermiculated
quoins
diamond
faced

d) RUSTICATION

header
stretcher
closer
cogging
course

Flemish
English
English
garden wall

e) BRICK BONDS

FIGURE 6: CONSTRUCTION

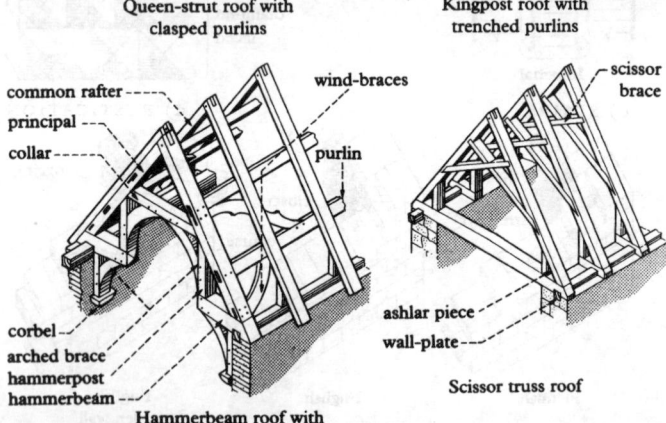

FIGURE 7: ROOFS AND GABLES

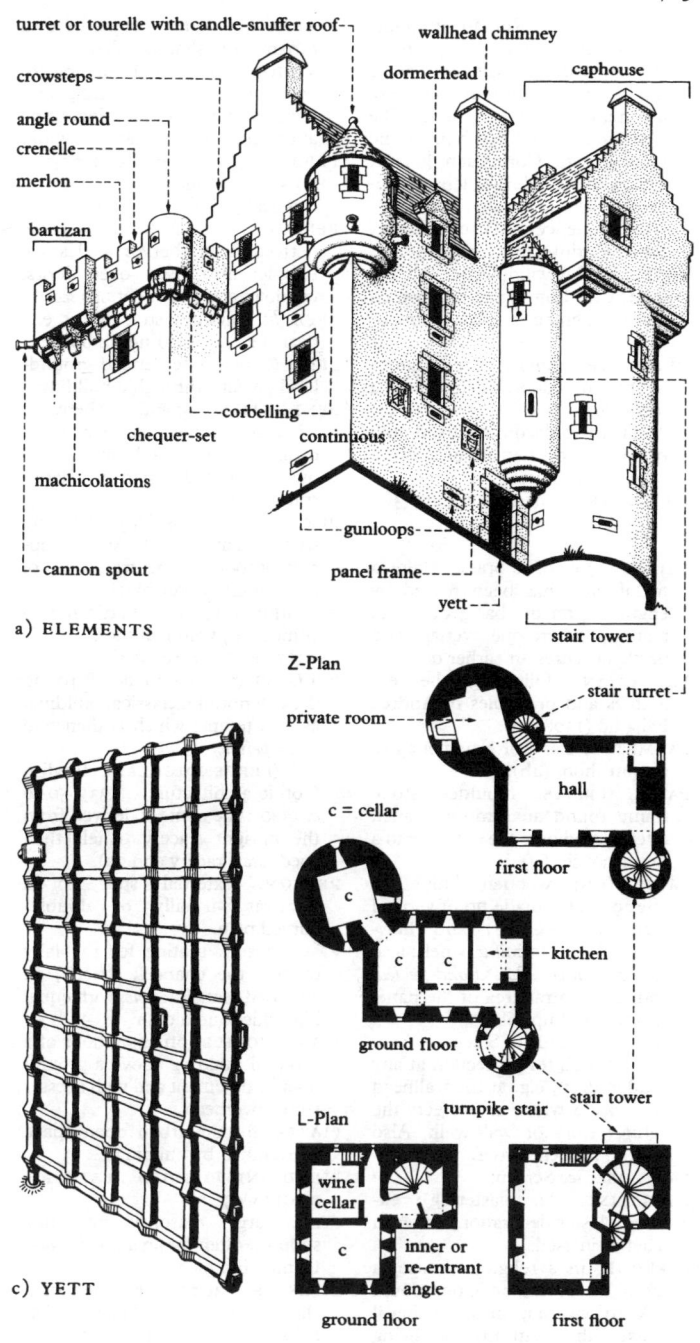

turret or tourelle with candle-snuffer roof
wallhead chimney
dormerhead
caphouse
crowsteps
angle round
crenelle
merlon
bartizan
corbelling
chequer-set
continuous
machicolations
cannon spout
gunloops
panel frame
yett
stair tower

a) ELEMENTS

Z-Plan
stair turret
private room
hall
first floor

c = cellar
c
c c
kitchen
ground floor
turnpike stair
stair tower

L-Plan
wine cellar
c
inner or re-entrant angle
ground floor
first floor

c) YETT

b) FORMS

FIGURE 8: THE TOWER HOUSE

but occur in Roman versions. *Tuscan* is a simple version of Roman Doric. Though each order has its own conventions (3), there are many minor variations. The *Composite* capital combines Ionic volutes with Corinthian foliage. *Superimposed orders*: orders on successive levels, usually in the upward sequence of Tuscan, Doric, Ionic, Corinthian, Composite.

ORIEL: *see* Bay window.

OVERARCH: framing a wall which has an opening, e.g. a window or door.

OVERDOOR: painting or relief above an internal door. Also called a *sopraporta*.

OVERTHROW: decorative fixed arch between two gatepiers or above a wrought-iron gate.

OVOLO: wide convex moulding (3f).

PALIMPSEST: of a brass: where a metal plate has been reused by engraving on the back; of a wall painting: where one overlaps and partly obscures an earlier one.

PALLADIAN: following the examples and principles of Andrea Palladio (1508–80).

PALMETTE: classical ornament like a palm shoot (4b).

PANEL FRAME: moulded stone frame round an armorial panel, often placed over the entrance to a tower house (8a).

PANELLING: wooden lining to interior walls, made up of vertical members (*muntins*) and horizontals (*rails*) framing panels: also called *wainscot*. *Raised-and-fielded*: with the central area of the panel (*field*) raised up (6b).

PANTILE: roof tile of S section.

PARAPET: wall for protection at any sudden drop, e.g. at the wallhead of a castle where it protects the *parapet walk* or wall-walk. Also used to conceal a roof.

PARCLOSE: *see* Screen.

PARGETING (*lit.* plastering): exterior plaster decoration, either in relief or incised.

PARLOUR: in a religious house, a room where the religious could talk to visitors; in a medieval house, the semi-private living room below the solar (q.v.).

PARTERRE: level space in a garden laid out with low, formal beds.

PATERA (*lit.* plate): round or oval ornament in shallow relief.

PAVILION: ornamental building for occasional use; or projecting subdivision of a larger building, often at an angle or terminating a wing.

PEBBLEDASHING: *see* Rendering.

PEDESTAL: a tall block carrying a classical order, statue, vase etc.

PEDIMENT: a formalized gable derived from that of a classical temple; also used over doors, windows etc. For variations *see* 4b.

PEEL (*lit.* palisade): stone tower, e.g. near the Scottish-English border.

PEND (Scots): open-ended ground-level passage through a building.

PENDENTIVE: spandrel between adjacent arches, supporting a drum, dome or vault and consequently formed as part of a hemisphere (5a).

PENTHOUSE: subsidiary structure with a lean-to roof. Also a separately roofed structure on top of a C20 multi-storey block.

PEPPERPOT TURRET: bartizan with conical or pyramidal roof.

PERIPTERAL: *see* Peristyle.

PERISTYLE: a colonnade all round the exterior of a classical building, as in a temple which is then said to be *peripteral*.

PERP (PERPENDICULAR): English Gothic architecture *c.* 1335–50 to *c.* 1530. The name is derived from the upright tracery panels then used (*see* Tracery and 2a).

PERRON: external stair to a doorway, usually of double-curved plan.

PEW: loosely, seating for the laity outside the chancel; strictly, an enclosed seat. *Box pew*: with equal high sides and a door.

PIANO NOBILE: principal floor of a classical building above a ground floor or basement and with a lesser storey overhead.

PIAZZA: formal urban open space surrounded by buildings.

PIEND AND PIENDED PLATFORM ROOF: *see* 7.

PIER: large masonry or brick support, often for an arch. *See also* Compound pier.

PILASTER: flat representation of a classical column in shallow relief. *Pilastrade*: series of pilasters, equivalent to a colonnade.

PILE: row of rooms. *Double pile*: two rows thick.

PILLAR: freestanding upright member of any section, not conforming to one of the orders (q.v.).

PILLAR PISCINA: *see* Piscina.

PILOTIS: C20 French term for pillars or stilts that support a building above an open ground floor.

PINS OR PINNINGS (Scots): *see* Cherry-caulking.

PISCINA: basin for washing Mass vessels, provided with a drain; set in or against wall to S of an altar or freestanding (*pillar piscina*).

PITCHED MASONRY: laid on the diagonal, often alternately with opposing courses (*pitched and counterpitched* or herringbone).

PIT PRISON: sunk chamber with access from above through a hatch.

PLATE RAIL: *see* Railways.

PLATEWAY: *see* Railways.

PLATT (Scots): platform, doorstep or landing. *Scale-and-platt stair*: *see* Stairs and 6c.

PLEASANCE (Scots): close or walled garden.

PLINTH: projecting courses at the foot of a wall or column, generally chamfered or moulded at the top.

PODIUM: a continuous raised platform supporting a building; or a large block of two or three storeys beneath a multi-storey block of smaller area.

POINT BLOCK: *see* Multi-storey.

POINTING: exposed mortar jointing of masonry or brickwork. Types include *flush*, *recessed* and *tuck* (with a narrow channel filled with finer, whiter mortar). *Bag-rubbed*: flush at the edges and gently recessed in the middle. *Ribbon*: joints formed with a trowel so that they stand out. *Hungry-jointed*: either with no pointing or deeply recessed to show the outline of each stone.

POPPYHEAD: carved ornament of leaves and flowers as a finial for a bench end or stall.

PORTAL FRAME: C20 frame comprising two uprights rigidly connected to a beam or pair of rafters.

PORTCULLIS: gate constructed to rise and fall in vertical gooves at the entry to a castle.

PORTE COCHÈRE: porch large enough to admit wheeled vehicles.

PORTICO: a porch with the roof and frequently a pediment supported by a row of columns (4a). A portico *in antis* has columns on the same plane as the front of the building. A *prostyle* porch has columns standing free. Porticoes are described by the number of front columns, e.g. tetrastyle (four), hexastyle (six). The space within the temple is the *naos*, that within the portico the *pronaos*. *Blind portico*: the front features of a portico applied to a wall.

PORTICUS (plural: porticūs): subsidiary cell opening from the main body of a pre-Conquest church.

POST: upright support in a structure.

POSTERN: small gateway at the back of a building or to the side of a larger entrance door or gate.

POTENCE (Scots): rotating ladder for access to doocot nesting boxes.

POUND LOCK: *see* Canals.

PREDELLA: in an altarpiece, the horizontal strip below the main representation, often used for subsidiary representations.

PRESBYTERY: the part of a church lying E of the choir where the main altar is placed. Also a priest's residence.

PRESS (Scots): cupboard.

PRINCIPAL: *see* Roofs and 7.

PRONAOS: *see* Portico and 4a.

PROSTYLE: *see* Portico and 4a.

PULPIT: raised and enclosed platform for the preaching of sermons. *Three-decker*: with reading desk below and clerk's desk below that. *Two-decker*: as above, minus the clerk's desk.

PULPITUM: stone screen in a major church dividing choir from nave.

PULVINATED: *see* Frieze and 3c.

PURLIN: *see* Roofs and 7.

PUTHOLES or PUTLOG HOLES: in wall to receive putlogs, the horizontal timbers which support scaffolding boards; not always filled after construction is complete.

PUTTO (plural: putti): small naked boy.

QUARRIES: square (or diamond) panes of glass supported by lead strips (*cames*); square floor-slabs or tiles.

QUATREFOIL: *see* Foil.

QUEEN-STRUT: *see* Roofs and 7.

QUILLONS: the arms forming the cross-guard of a sword.

QUIRK: sharp groove to one side of a convex medieval moulding.

QUOINS: dressed stones at the angles of a building (6d).

RADBURN SYSTEM: pedestrian and vehicle segregation in residential developments, based on that used at Radburn, New Jersey, U.S.A., by Wright and Stein, 1928–30.

RADIATING CHAPELS: projecting radially from an ambulatory or an apse (*see* Chevet).

RAFTER: *see* Roofs and 7.

RAGGLE: groove cut in masonry, especially to receive the edge of a roof-covering.

RAIL: *see* Panelling and 6b.

RAILWAYS: *Edge rail*: on which flanged wheels can run. *Plate rail*: L-section rail for plain unflanged wheels. *Plateway*: early railway using plate rails.

RAISED AND FIELDED: *see* Panelling and 6b.

RAKE: slope or pitch.

RAMPART: defensive outer wall of stone or earth. *Rampart walk*: path along the inner face.

RATCOURSE: projecting string-course on a doocot to deter rats from climbing to the flight holes.

REBATE: rectangular section cut out of a masonry edge to receive a shutter, door, window etc.

REBUS: a heraldic pun, e.g. a fiery cock for Cockburn.

REEDING: series of convex mouldings, the reverse of fluting (q.v.). Cf. Gadrooning.

RENDERING: the covering of outside walls with a uniform surface or skin for protection from the weather. *Lime-washing*: thin layer of lime plaster. *Pebble-dashing*: where aggregate is thrown at the wet plastered wall for a textured effect. *Roughcast*: plaster mixed with a coarse aggregate such as gravel. *Stucco*: fine lime plaster worked to a smooth surface. *Cement rendering*: a cheaper substitute for stucco, usually with a grainy texture.

REPOUSSÉ: relief designs in metalwork, formed by beating it from the back.

REREDORTER (*lit.* behind the dormitory): latrines in a medieval religious house.

REREDOS: painted and/or sculptured screen behind and above an altar. Cf. Retable.

RESPOND: half-pier or half-column bonded into a wall and carrying one end of an arch. It usually terminates an arcade.

RETABLE: painted or carved panel standing on or at the back of an altar, usually attached to it.

RETROCHOIR: in a major church, the area between the high altar and E chapel.

REVEAL: the plane of a jamb, between the wall and the frame of a door or window.

RHONE (Scots): gutter along the eaves for rainwater: *see also* Conductor.

RIB-VAULT: *see* Vault and 2c.

RIG (Scots): a strip of ploughed land raised in the middle and sloped to a furrow on each side; early cultivation method (runrig) usually surrounded by untilled grazing land.

RINCEAU: classical ornament of leafy scrolls (4b).

RISER: vertical face of a step (6c).

ROCK-FACED: masonry cleft to produce a rugged appearance.

ROCOCO: style current between *c.* 1720 and *c.* 1760, characterized by a serpentine line and playful, scrolled decoration.

ROLL MOULDING: medieval moulding of part-circular section (1a).

ROMANESQUE: style current in the C11 and C12. In England often called Norman. *See also* Saxo-Norman.

ROOD: crucifix flanked by representations of the Virgin and St John, usually over the entry into the chancel, painted on the wall, on a beam (*rood beam*) or on top of a *rood screen* or pulpitum (q.v.) which often had a walkway (*rood loft*) along the top, reached by a *rood stair* in the side wall. *Hanging rood*: cross or crucifix suspended from roof.

ROOFS: For the main external shapes (hipped, gambrel etc.) *see* 7. *Helm* and *Saddleback*: *see* 1C. *Lean-to*: single sloping roof built against a vertical wall; also applied to the part of the building beneath. *Bellcast*: sloping roof slightly swept out over the eaves. Construction. *See* 7. *Single-framed* roof: with no main trusses. The rafters may be fixed to the wall-plate or ridge, or longitudinal timbers may be absent altogether.

Double-framed roof: with longitudinal members, such as purlins, and usually divided into bays by principals and principal rafters. Other types are named after their main structural components, e.g. *hammerbeam*, *crown-post* (*see* Elements below and 7).

Elements. *See* 7.

Ashlar piece: a short vertical timber connecting a inner wall-plate or timber pad to a rafter.

Braces: subsidiary timbers set diagonally to strengthen the frame. *Arched braces*: curved pair forming an arch, connecting wall or post below with a tie- or collar-beam above. *Passing braces*: long straight braces passing across other members of the truss. *Scissor braces*: pair crossing diagonally between pairs of rafters or principals. *Wind-braces*: short, usually curved braces connecting side purlins with principals; sometimes decorated with cusping.

Collar or *collar-beam*: horizontal transverse timber connecting a pair of rafter or cruck blades (q.v.), set between apex and the wall-plate.

Crown-post: a vertical timber set centrally on a tie-beam and supporting a collar purlin braced to it longitudinally. In an open truss lateral braces may rise to the collar-beam; in a closed truss they may descend to the tie-beam.

Hammerbeams: horizontal brackets projecting at wall-plate level like an interrupted tie-beam; the inner ends carry *hammerposts*, vertical timbers which support a purlin and are braced to a collar-beam above.

Kingpost: vertical timber set centrally on a tie-or collar-beam, rising to the apex of the roof to support a ridge piece (cf. Strut).

Plate: longitudinal timber set square to the ground. *Wall-plate*: along the top of a wall to receive the ends of rafters; cf. Purlin.

Principals: pair of inclined lateral timbers of a truss. Usually they support side purlins and mark the main bay divisions.

Purlin: horizontal longitudinal timber. *Collar purlin* or *crown plate*: central timber which carries collar-beams and is supported by crown-posts. *Side purlins*: pairs of timbers placed some way up the slope of the roof, which carry common rafters. *Butt* or *tenoned purlins* are tenoned into either side of the principals. *Through purlins* pass through or past the principal; they include *clasped purlins*, which rest on queenposts or are carried in the angle between principals and collar, and *trenched purlins* trenched into the backs of principals.

Queen-strut: paired vertical, or near-vertical, timbers placed symmetrically on a tie-beam to support side purlins.

Rafters: inclined lateral timbers supporting the roof covering. *Common rafters*: regularly spaced uniform rafters placed along the length of a roof or between principals. *Principal rafters*: rafters which also act as principals.

Ridge, ridge piece: horizontal longitudinal timber at the apex supporting the ends of the rafters.

Sprocket: short timber placed on the back and at the foot of a rafter to form projecting eaves.

Strut: vertical or oblique timber between two members of a truss, not directly supporting longitudinal timbers.

Tie-beam: main horizontal transverse timber which carries the feet of the principals at wall level.

Truss: rigid framework of timbers at bay intervals, carrying the longitudinal roof timbers which support the common rafters. *Closed truss*: with the spaces between the timbers filled, to form an internal partition.

See also Cruck, Wagon roof.

ROPE MOULDING: *see* Cable moulding.

ROSE WINDOW: circular window with tracery radiating from the centre. Cf. Wheel window.

ROTUNDA: building or room circular in plan.

ROUGHCAST: *see* Rendering.

ROUND (Scots): bartizan, usually roofless.

ROVING BRIDGE: *see* Canals.

RUBBED BRICKWORK: *see* Gauged brickwork.

RUBBLE: masonry whose stones are wholly or partly in a rough state. *Coursed*: coursed stones with rough faces. *Random*: uncoursed stones in a random pattern. *Snecked*: with courses broken by smaller stones (snecks).

RUSTICATION: *see* 6d. Exaggerated treatment of masonry to give an effect of strength. The joints are usually recessed by V-section chamfering or square-section channelling (*channelled rustication*). *Banded rustication* has only the horizontal joints emphasized. The faces may be flat, but can be *diamond-faced*, like shallow pyramids, *vermiculated*, with a stylized texture like worm-casts, and *glacial* (frost-work), like icicles or stalactites.

RYBATS (Scots): *see* Margins.

SACRAMENT HOUSE: safe cupboard in a side wall of the chancel of a church and not directly associated with an altar, for reservation of the sacrament.

SACRISTY: room in a church for sacred vessels and vestments.

SADDLEBACK ROOF: *see* IC.

SALTIRE CROSS: with diagonal limbs.

SANCTUARY: part of church at E end containing high altar. Cf. Presbytery.

SANGHA: residence of Buddhist monks or nuns.

SARCOPHAGUS: coffin of stone or other durable material.

SARKING (Scots): boards laid on the rafters to support the roof covering.

SAXO-NORMAN: transitional Romanesque style combining Anglo-Saxon and Norman features, current c. 1060–1100.

SCAGLIOLA: composition imitating marble.

SCALE-AND-PLATT (*lit.* stair and landing): *see* Stair and 6c.

SCALLOPED CAPITAL: *see* IA.

SCARCEMENT: extra thickness of the lower part of a wall, e.g. to carry a floor.

SCARP: artificial cutting away of the ground to form a steep slope.

SCOTIA: a hollow classical moulding, especially between tori (q.v.) on a column base (3b, 3f).

SCREEN: in a medieval church, usually at the entry to the chancel; *see* Rood (screen) and Pulpitum. A *parclose screen* separates a chapel from the rest of the church.

SCREENS or SCREENS PASSAGE: screened-off entrance passage between great hall and service rooms or between the hall of a tower house and the stair.

SCRIBE (Scots): to cut and mark timber against an irregular stone or plaster surface.

SCUNTION (Scots): reveal.

SECTION: two-dimensional representation of a building, moulding etc., revealed by cutting across it.

SEDILIA (singular: sedile): seats for clergy (usually for a priest, deacon and sub-deacon) on the S side of the chancel.

SEPTUM: dwarf wall between the nave and choir.

SESSION HOUSE (Scots): a room or separate building for meetings of the minister and elders who form a kirk session. Also a shelter by the church or churchyard entrance for an elder collecting for poor relief, built at expense of kirk session.

SET-OFF: *see* Weathering.

SGRAFFITO: decoration scratched, often in plaster, to reveal a pattern in another colour beneath. *Graffiti*: scratched drawing or writing.

SHAFT: vertical member of round or polygonal section (1a, 3a). *Shaft-ring*: at the junction of shafts set *en délit* (q.v.) or attached to a pier or wall (1a).

SHEILA-NA-GIG: female fertility figure, usually with legs apart.

SHELL: thin, self-supporting roofing membrane of timber or concrete.

SHEUGH (Scots): a trench or open drain; a street gutter.

SHOULDERED ARCH: *see* 5a.

SHOULDERED ARCHITRAVE: *see* 4b.

SHUTTERING: *see* Concrete.

SILL: horizontal member at the bottom of a window-or door-frame; or at the base of a timber-framed wall into which posts and studs are tenoned.

SKEW (Scots): sloping or shaped stones finishing a gable upstanding from the roof. *Skewputt*: bracket at the bottom end of a skew. *See* 7.

SLAB BLOCK: *see* Multi-storey.

SLATE-HANGING: covering of overlapping slates on a wall. *Tile-hanging* is similar.

SLYPE: covered way or passage leading E from the cloisters between transept and chapter house.

SNECKED: *see* Rubble.

SOFFIT (*lit.* ceiling): underside of an arch (also called *intrados*), lintel etc. *Soffit roll*: medieval roll moulding on a soffit.

SOLAR: private upper chamber in a medieval house, accessible from the high end of the great hall.

SOPRAPORTA: *see* Overdoor.

SOUNDING-BOARD: *see* Tester.

SOUTERRAIN: underground stone-lined passage and chamber.

SPANDRELS: roughly triangular spaces between an arch and its containing rectangle, or between adjacent arches (5c). Also non-structural panels under the windows in a curtain-walled building.

SPERE: a fixed structure screening the lower end of the great hall from the screens passage. *Spere-truss*: roof truss incorporated in the spere.

SPIRE: tall pyramidal or conical feature crowning a tower or turret. *Broach*: starting from a square base, then carried into an octagonal section by means of triangular faces; *splayed-foot*: a variation of the broach form, found principally in the south-east of England, in which the four cardinal faces are splayed out near their base, to cover the corners, while oblique (or intermediate) faces taper away to a point (1c). *Needle spire*: thin spire rising from the centre of a tower roof, well inside the parapet: when of timber and lead often called a *spike*.

SPIRELET: *see* Flèche.

SPLAY: of an opening when it is wider on one face of a wall than the other.

SPRING OR SPRINGING: level at which an arch or vault rises from its supports. *Springers*: the first stones of an arch or vaulting-rib above the spring (2c).

SQUINCH: arch or series of arches thrown across an interior angle of a square or rectangular structure to support a circular or polygonal superstructure, especially a dome or spire (5a).

SQUINT: an aperture in a wall or through a pier, usually to allow a view of an altar.

STAIRS: *see* 6c. *Dog-leg stair* or (Scots) *Scale-and-platt stair*: parallel flights rising alternately in opposite directions, without an open well. *Flying stair*: cantilevered from the walls of a stairwell, without newels; sometimes called a *geometric* stair when the inner edge describes a curve. *Turnpike* or *newel stair*: ascending round a central supporting newel (8b); also called a *spiral stair* or *vice* when in a circular shaft, a *winder* when in a rectangular compartment. (Winder also applies to the steps on the turn.) *Well stair*: with flights round a square open well framed by newel posts. *See also* Perron.

STAIR TOWER: full-height projection from a main block (especially of a tower house) containing the principal stair from the ground floor (8a).

STAIR TURRET: turret corbelled out from above ground level and containing a stair from one of the upper floors of a building, especially a tower house (8a).

STALL: fixed seat in the choir or chancel for the clergy or choir (cf. Pew). Usually with arm rests, and often framed together.

STANCHION: upright structural member, of iron, steel or reinforced concrete.

STANDPIPE TOWER: *see* Manometer.

STEADING (Scots): farm building or buildings; generally used for the principal group of buildings on a farm.

STEAM ENGINES: *Atmospheric*: worked by the vacuum created when low-pressure steam is condensed in the cylinder, as developed by Thomas Newcomen. *Beam engine*: with a large pivoted beam moved in an oscillating fashion by the piston. It may drive a flywheel or be *non-rotative*. *Watt* and *Cornish*: single-cylinder; *compound*: two cylinders; *triple expansion*: three cylinders.

STEEPLE: tower together with a spire, lantern or belfry.

STIFFLEAF: type of E.E. foliage decoration. *Stiffleaf capital*: *see* 1b.

STOP: plain or decorated terminal to mouldings or chamfers, or at the end of hoodmoulds and labels (*label stop*), or stringcourses (5b, 6a); *see also* Headstop.

STOUP: vessel for holy water, usually near a door.

STRAINER: *see* Arch.

STRAPWORK: decoration like inter-laced leather straps, late C16 and C17 in origin.

STRETCHER: *see* Bond and 6e.

STRING: *see* 6c. Sloping member holding the ends of the treads and risers of a staircase. *Closed string*: a broad string covering the ends of the treads and risers. *Open string*: cut into the shape of the treads and risers.

STRINGCOURSE: horizontal course or moulding projecting from the surface of a wall (6d).

STUCCO: decorative plasterwork. *See also* Rendering.

STUDS: subsidiary vertical timbers of a timber-framed wall or par-tition.

STUGGED (Scots): of masonry hacked or picked as a key for ren-dering; used as a surface finish in the C19.

STUPA: Buddhist shrine, circular in plan.

STYLOBATE: top of the solid plat-form on which a colonnade stands (3a).

SUSPENSION BRIDGE: *see* Bridge.

SWAG: like a festoon (q.v.), but rep-resenting cloth.

SYSTEM BUILDING: *see* Industri-alized building.

TABERNACLE: safe cupboard above an altar to contain the reserved sacrament or a relic; or architec-tural frame for an image or statue.

TABLE STONE or TABLE TOMB: memorial slab raised on free-standing legs.

TAS-DE-CHARGE: the lower courses of a vault or arch which are laid horizontally (2c).

TENEMENT: holding of land, but also applied to a purpose-built flatted block.

TERM: pedestal or pilaster tapering downward, usually with the upper part of a human figure growing out of it.

TERRACOTTA: moulded and fired clay ornament or cladding.

TERREPLEIN: in a fort the level sur-face of a rampart behind a parapet for mounting guns.

TESSELLATED PAVEMENT: mosaic flooring, particularly Roman, made of *tesserae*, i.e. cubes of glass, stone or brick.

TESTER: flat canopy over a tomb or pulpit, where it is also called a *sounding-board*.

TESTER TOMB: tomb-chest with effigies beneath a tester, either freestanding (tester with four or more columns), or attached to a wall (*half-tester*) with columns on one side only.

TETRASTYLE: *see* Portico.

THERMAL WINDOW: *see* Diocletian window.

THREE-DECKER PULPIT: *see* Pulpit.

TIDAL GATES: *see* Canals.

TIE-BEAM: *see* Roofs and 7.

TIERCERON: *see* Vault and 2c.

TIFTING (Scots): mortar bed for verge slates laid over gable skew.

TILE-HANGING: *see* Slate-hanging.

TIMBER-FRAMING: method of con-struction where the structural frame is built of interlocking timbers. The spaces are filled with non-structural material, e.g. *infill* of wattle and daub, lath and plaster, brickwork (known as *nogging*) etc., and may be covered by plaster, weatherboarding (q.v.) or tiles.

TOLBOOTH (Scots; *lit.* tax booth): burgh council building containing council chamber and prison.

TOMB-CHEST: chest-shaped tomb, usually of stone. Cf. Table tomb, Tester tomb.

TORUS (plural: tori): large convex moulding, usually used on a column base (3b, 3f).

TOUCH: soft black marble quarried near Tournai.

TOURELLE: turret corbelled out from the wall (8a).

TOWER BLOCK: *see* Multi-storey.

TOWER HOUSE (Scots): for elements and forms *see* 8a, 8b. Compact fortified house with the main hall raised above the ground and at least one more storey above it. A medieval Scots type continuing well into the C17 in its modified forms: *L-plan* with a jamb at one corner; *Z-plan* with a jamb at each diagonally opposite corner.

TRABEATED: dependent structurally on the use of the post and lintel. Cf. Arcuated.

TRACERY: openwork pattern of masonry or timber in the upper part of an opening. *Blind* tracery is tracery applied to a solid wall. *Plate tracery*, introduced *c.* 1200, is the earliest form, in which shapes are cut through solid masonry (2a).

Bar tracery was introduced into England *c.* 1250. The pattern is formed by intersecting moulded ribwork continued from the mullions. It was especially elaborate during the Decorated period (q.v.). Tracery shapes can include circles, *daggers* (elongated ogee-ended lozenges), *mouchettes* (like daggers but with curved sides) and upright rectangular *panels*. They often have *cusps*, projecting points defining lobes or *foils* (q.v.) within the main shape: *Kentish* or *split-cusps* are forked.

Types of bar tracery (*see* 2b) include *geometric(al)*: *c.* 1250–1310, chiefly circles, often foiled; *Y-tracery*: *c.* 1300, with mullions branching into a Y-shape; *intersecting*: *c.* 1300, formed by interlocking mullions; *reticulated*: early C14, net-like pattern of ogee-ended lozenges; *curvilinear*: C14, with uninterrupted flowing curves; *loop*: *c.* 1500–45, with large uncusped loop-like forms; *panel*: Perp, with straight-sided panels, often cusped at the top and bottom.

TRANSE (Scots): passage.

TRANSEPT: transverse portion of a cruciform church.

TRANSITIONAL: generally used for the phase between Romanesque and Early English (*c.* 1175–*c.* 1200).

TRANSOM: horizontal member separating window lights (2b).

TREAD: horizontal part of a step. The *tread end* may be carved on a staircase (6c).

TREFOIL: *see* Foil.

TRIFORIUM: middle storey of a church treated as an arcaded wall passage or blind arcade, its height corresponding to that of the aisle roof.

TRIGLYPHS (*lit.* three-grooved tablets): stylized beam-ends in the Doric frieze, with metopes between (3b).

TRIUMPHAL ARCH: influential type of Imperial Roman monument.

TROPHY: sculptured or painted group of arms or armour.

TRUMEAU: central stone mullion supporting the tympanum of a wide doorway. *Trumeau figure*: carved figure attached to it (cf. Column figure).

TRUMPET CAPITAL: *see* 1b.

TRUSS: braced framework, spanning between supports. *See also* Roofs.

TUMBLING or TUMBLING-IN: courses of brickwork laid at right angles to a slope, e.g. of a gable, forming triangles by tapering into horizontal courses.

TURNPIKE: *see* Stairs.

TUSCAN: *see* Orders and 3e.

TUSKING STONES (Scots): projecting end stones for bonding with an adjoining wall.

TWO-DECKER PULPIT: *see* Pulpit.

TYMPANUM: the surface between a lintel and the arch above it or within a pediment (4a).

UNDERCROFT: usually describes the vaulted room(s) beneath the main room(s) of a medieval house. Cf. Crypt.

UNIVALLATE: of a hillfort: defended by a single bank and ditch.

VAULT: arched stone roof (sometimes imitated in timber or plaster). For types *see* 2c.

Tunnel or *barrel vault*: continuous semicircular or pointed arch, often of rubble masonry.

Groin vault: tunnel vaults intersecting at right angles. *Groins* are the curved lines of the intersections.

Rib vault: masonry framework of intersecting arches (ribs) supporting *vault cells*, used in Gothic architecture. *Wall rib* or *wall arch*: between wall and vault cell. *Transverse rib*: spans between two walls to divide a vault into bays. *Quadripartite* rib vault: each bay has two pairs of diagonal ribs dividing the vault into four triangular cells. *Sexpartite* rib vault: most often used over paired bays, has an extra pair of ribs springing from between the bays. More elaborate vaults may include *ridge-ribs* along the crown of a vault or bisecting the bays; *tiercerons*: extra decorative ribs springing from the corners of a bay; and *liernes*: short decorative ribs in the crown of a vault, not linked to any springing point. A *stellar* or *star* vault has liernes in star formation.

Fan vault: form of barrel vault used in the Perp period, made up of halved concave masonry cones decorated with blind tracery.

VAULTING-SHAFT: shaft leading up to the spring or springing (q.v.) of a vault (2c).

VENETIAN or SERLIAN WINDOW: derived from Serlio (4b). The motif is used for other openings.

VERMICULATION: see Rustication and 6d.

VESICA: oval with pointed ends.

VICE: see Stair.

VILLA: originally a Roman country house or farm. The term was revived in England in the C18 under the influence of Palladio and used especially for smaller, compact country houses. In the later C19 it was debased to describe any suburban house.

VITRIFIED: bricks or tiles fired to a darkened glassy surface. *Vitrified fort*: built of timber-laced masonry, the timber having later been set on fire with consequent vitrification of the stonework.

VITRUVIAN SCROLL: classical running ornament of curly waves (4b).

VOLUTES: spiral scrolls. They occur on Ionic capitals (3c). *Angle volute*: pair of volutes, turned outwards to meet at the corner of a capital.

VOUSSOIRS: wedge-shaped stones forming an arch (5c).

WAGON ROOF: with the appearance of the inside of a wagon tilt; often ceiled. Also called *cradle roof*.

WAINSCOT: see Panelling.

WALLED GARDEN: in C18 and C19 Scotland, combined vegetable and flower garden, sometimes well away from the house.

WALLHEAD: straight top of a wall. *Wallhead chimney*: chimney rising from a wallhead (8a). *Wallhead gable*: gable rising from a wallhead.

WALL MONUMENT: attached to the wall and often standing on the floor. *Wall tablets* are smaller with the inscription as the major element.

WALL-PLATE: see Roofs and 7.

WALL-WALK: see Parapet.

WARMING ROOM: room in a religious house where a fire burned for comfort.

WATERHOLDING BASE: early Gothic base with upper and lower mouldings separated by a deep hollow.

WATERLEAF: see Enrichments and 3f.

WATERLEAF CAPITAL: Late Romanesque and Transitional type of capital (1b).

WATER WHEELS: described by the way water is fed on to the wheel. *Breastshot*: mid-height, falling and passing beneath. *Overshot*: over the top. *Pitchback*: on the top but falling backwards. *Undershot*: turned by the momentum of the water passing beneath. In a *water turbine*, water is fed under pressure through a vaned wheel within a casing.

WEALDEN HOUSE: type of medieval timber-framed house with a central open hall flanked by bays of two storeys, roofed in line; the end bays are jettied to the front, but the eaves are continuous.

WEATHERBOARDING: wall cladding of overlapping horizontal boards.

WEATHERING: or SET-OFF: inclined, projecting surface to keep water away from the wall below.

WEEPERS: figures in niches along the sides of some medieval tombs. Also called *mourners*.

WHEEL HOUSE: Late Iron Age circular stone dwelling; inside, partition walls radiating from the central hearth like wheel spokes.

WHEEL WINDOW: circular, with radiating shafts like spokes. Cf. Rose window.

WROUGHT IRON: see Cast iron.

WYND (Scots): subsidiary street or lane, often running into a main street or gait (q.v.).

YETT (Scots, *lit.* gate): hinged openwork gate at a main doorway, made of iron bars alternately penetrating and penetrated (8c).

Z-PLAN: see Tower house and 8b.

INDEX OF ARCHITECTS AND ARTISTS

Entries for partnerships and group practices are listed after entries for a single name.

INDEX TO ABERDEEN

Principal references are in **bold** type; demolished buildings are shown in *italic*.

Buildings whose title begins with a person's name are indexed under the first word, not the person's surname; thus Robert Gordon University is indexed under 'Robert' and John Lewis is under 'John', not 'Lewis'.

Principal references are in **bold** type; demolished buildings are shown in *italic*.

Buildings in Aberdeen are indexed separately above.

(K) = Kincardineshire (*see* p. xvii)